ENCYCLOPEDIA OF NORTH AMERICAN IMMIGRATION

JOHN POWELL

Facts On File, Inc.

Encyclopedia of North American Immigration

Copyright © 2005 by John Powell
Maps and graphs copyright © 2005 by Facts On File

Facts On File, Inc.
132 West 31st Street
New York NY 10001

Library of Congress Cataloging-in-Publication Data

Powell, John, 1954–
Encyclopedia of North American immigration / John Powell.
p. cm.
Includes bibliographical references and index.
ISBN 0-8160-4658-1
1. United States—Emigration and immigration—Encyclopedias. I. Title.
JV6465.P68 2005
304.8′7′003—dc22   2004007361

Facts On File books are available at special discounts when purchased in bulk
quantities for businesses, associations, institutions, or sales promotions.
Please call our Special Sales Department in New York at
(212) 967-8800 or (800) 322-8755.

You can find Facts On File on the World Wide Web at
http://www.factsonfile.com

Text design by Erika K. Arroyo
Cover design by Cathy Rincon
Maps and graphs by Jeremy Eagle and Dale Williams

Printed in the United States of America

VB Hermitage 10 9 8 7 6 5 4 3 2 1

This book is printed on acid-free paper

To the Martel Clan

Contents

List of Entries

Acknowledgments

From an early age I was inspired by the Martel clan, hardworking German farmers who immigrated first to Russia, then to the prairies of South Dakota in the 1870s. The immigration story needs to be known, and I am grateful to the editors and staff at Facts On File who have helped me tell it. I also wish to thank Eric Mattingly and Grady Powell for their assistance in preparing the manuscript.

Author's Preface

Good reference books on immigration are plentiful today, for the subject has been in vogue for two decades. Still, there is room for a well-organized, easy-to-use volume devoted to the historical context of immigration to English- and French-speaking regions of North America during the past 500 years (Mexico and Central America are not covered). Many reference books deal exclusively with the individuals and circumstances related to a single ethnic group. Others cover the whole range of immigration topics, most in lengthy articles with particular ethnic groups or conceptual topics as their organizational focus. Some deal primarily with the process of acculturation after immigration, while others seek to demonstrate the vitality of culture groups through organization and identification with the values of the "old" countries. Almost all have a heavy sociological bent and were written within the pre–September 11, 2001, framework of cold war and labor migration themes. Most pay little attention to the Canadian experience, which is an important component in understanding the overall process of migration to North America. In considering British immigration in the colonial period—by far the largest early element—there was no clear legal demarcation between "Canadian" and "American" colonies. British policy making often incorporated considerations regarding both areas. Even after the American Revolution, the close geographical and cultural relationship between the Canadian colonies and the United States continued to influence immigration patterns in each region. Immigrants frequently first went to Canada with the intention of continuing on to the United States. It was not unusual for dissatisfied immigrants, particularly in agricultural areas, to cross the border in either direction. Finally, when restrictive legislation was passed in the United States, Canada was frequently a second choice. In *Encyclopedia of North American Immigration,* I hope to address some of these needs by providing a convenient one-volume reference full of straightforward and concise information on people, groups, policies, and events that defined the world's greatest migration of peoples to a continent and shaped their reception in North America. Each of the more than 300 articles includes an extensive and up-to-date bibliography that will facilitate further research. Finally, information on ethnic groups is based on the most recent census figures (U.S. Census 2000; Canadian Census 2001) and a variety of U.S. and Canadian governmental sources.

General Historiography

The transformation of the culture of the North American continent since the 15th century is one of the great historical events of the past 500 years. For good or ill, it has shaped the destinies of millions of people of all ethnic groups, transformed the nature of international politics, and altered the concept of personal possibilities in every country. The magnitude and diversity of the migration to North America has made analysis of the process as a whole difficult. While there are excellent studies of particular peoples, specific locales, and isolated time periods, no one has yet encompassed this great movement of peoples in a single conceptual framework. The most important reason for the difficulty is that the peopling of North America was not a single movement but hundreds of separate movements, each with its own story, foundations, rationale, and outcome. Some immigrants, including slaves and convicts, were forced to resettle; others were free to make the choice; still others were living in such desperate conditions that the choice was only nominally free. Of those who came freely, some longed for nothing more than the ability to feed and clothe their families, while others were lured from their families and familiar surroundings by the hope of wealth. Some came with charters from kings; others fled from those same monarchs. Some immigrants had ideological purposes, while others were wanderers, merely wanting to get away from a deadening social order. Even when studying the movement of a specific ethnic group, one is constantly reminded that motivations varied from year to year and from one village to the next. It may truly be said that every immigrant story is unique.

Nature of the *Encyclopedia of North American Immigration*

I have undertaken this work with the following goals in mind:

1. To focus attention on the historical factors that made immigration necessary, desirable, or possible. With cultural studies today infused with presentism, and with an eye toward specific political agendas regarding ethnicity, I have chosen to emphasize historical factors.

2. To examine immigration factors and results for both Canada and the United States. There are many reasons why scholars focus on a particular country in the course of their research. Canada and the United States are both sovereign states, each exercising the prerogatives of an independent immigration policy. On the other hand, both regions were part of the same British empire for almost 200 years prior to 1776; immigrants to Canada frequently continued on to the United States; and since 2001, the two countries have worked closely to develop an integrated approach to common immigration problems.

3. To provide data from the most recent census undertaken in each country, as well as up-to-date figures regarding immigration. In most articles, I have employed figures drawn from the United States census of 2000 and the Canada census of 2001.

4. To provide extensive and up-to-date further reading lists with all entries, enabling users to quickly locate the most detailed and recent studies related to their areas of interest.

    The goal of each entry's further reading list is to provide readers readily accessible research materials, preferably in English. The study of immigration, however, presents some unique challenges. The great period of global migration that began in the 1820s has involved the movement of hundreds of ethnic groups from their homelands to

North America. Some of the smaller groups, or those arriving recently, have as yet received relatively little attention from English-speaking scholars. It is natural, too, that men and women would write the histories of their migration in their own languages. Canada itself, one of two focal points in this study, has large numbers of Anglophone and Francophone citizens, and English and French are both official languages of the country. Research on Canadian immigration topics often has been published in both English and French but usually not in both. As a result of these considerations, important non-English publications are sometimes included in the further reading lists and bibliography.

5. To provide a thorough system of indexing and cross-referencing in order to provide maximum ease of access to specific historical and bibliographic information. Terms set in SMALL CAPITAL letters indicate another entry in the book.

A Note on Immigration Statistics

Quantifying immigration, tracing immigrants, and assessing their impact in North America has always been a difficult task. Prior to 1850, it was scarcely attempted, but since that time the process has become more complex, varied, and thorough. For the period following World War II, numbers and assessments provided by the U.S. Immigration and Naturalization Service (INS) and since spring 2003 by the Office of Immigration Statistics, the Canadian Department of Manpower and Immigration (DMI), Statistics Canada, and the U.S. Census Bureau do provide a reasonably accurate picture of the broad landscape of immigration and of its relation to the ethnic composition of American and Canadian societies. One should not seek for more precision than the numbers will bear, however. Anytime one reads that "125,000" Cubans immigrated to the United States in 1981, or "40,000" Hungarians to Canada in 1956–57, for example, the statement should be read as an approximation; and the farther back in time, generally speaking, the less precise the number. It is possible to cite exact numbers as they are reported by official agencies, but the official reports themselves clearly acknowledge the limitations of their own data. In the INS table "Immigration by Region and Selected Country of Last Residence for Fiscal Years 1820–2002," for instance, there are 25 qualifications indicated in footnotes, in addition to a general note on data limitations. Thus, in using this work, one should bear in mind the variety of reasons that numbers should be used with caution:

1. Official records often were not kept in the 18th and 19th centuries, and when they were kept, they recorded kinds of information according to the perceived needs of the day. The earliest immigration records were simply ship manifests, varying widely in terms of information. The British government, for instance, theoretically registered the name, age, and occupation of all emigrants from December 1773 to March 1776. Newspaper accounts and individual ship registers, however, suggest a 15–30 percent underregistration. In the United States, information from 1820 to 1867 represented alien passengers arriving at seaports; thereafter, official numbers sometimes represented all arrivals, sometimes only those admitted for permanent residence. There was no attempt to fully document land arrivals until 1908. Even when related information is available, it often is not comparable. Prior to 1906, for instance, data was collected on the country from which the

alien emigrated; from 1906 to 1979 and 1984 to 1998, the country of last permanent residence; and from 1980 to 1983, country of birth.

2. Changing geopolitical boundaries undermine precise counting of certain ethnic groups. Polish immigrants, for instance, were included in numbers for Germany, Austria-Hungary, and Russia or the Soviet Union between 1899 and 1919. Data for the Austro-Hungarian Empire, composed of more than a dozen ethnic groups, was not recorded until 1861, and thereafter the various ethnic groups were not delineated. Thus, it is impossible to know with any precision how many Czechs or Hungarians entered the United States or Canada. Prior to 1934, Filipinos were considered U.S. nationals and thus not subject to either immigration restrictions or registration that would enable exact numbers to be determined. Immigrants from British India in the 19th and early 20th centuries were often classed as "Hindus," though most were in fact Muslims. In Canada, immigrants from modern India, Pakistan, Bangladesh, and Sri Lanka were frequently referred to as "East Indians," along with immigrants of Indian descent from Fiji, the West Indies, Uganda, South Africa, and Mauritius.

3. The nature of immigration varies widely, thus making it impossible to create a single category for accurately comparing either numbers or the immigrant experience. In some cases, culture groups seem to be the relevant category; in other cases, country of origin. Jews, for instance, were usually counted as immigrants from their country of birth or of last residence, along with non-Jewish immigrants from the same country. Any estimates involved in sorting the subgroups from the total—Russian Jews from other Russian immigrants, for instance—must take into account further differences among those who actually practiced Judaism, nonobservant Jews, and radicalized Jews who specifically rejected religion as a basis for social organization. In some cases, the cohesion of an immigrant group such as the Doukhobors or the Mennonites proved more powerful than cultural ties to their home countries, thus leading to a virtually clean break with the source country. On the other hand, immigrants from Mexico, Cuba, the Philippines, India, Pakistan, and Bangladesh frequently immigrate in order to maintain economically their families at home, remitting billions of American and Canadian dollars to their source countries each year.

4. Illegal immigration has always been present and officially uncounted. In most cases, this does not greatly alter the overall immigration numbers or affect the general government response. In some cases, however, such as illegal immigration of Mexicans into the United States, the flow becomes so great as to require separate study based on unofficial sources, projections, and secondary figures related to provision of government services. In monitoring the U.S.-Mexican border, officials have apprehended aliens from 63 different countries.

5. Multiple agencies are responsible for varying aspects of the immigration process, and their numbers are often at odds. Sometimes these differences are reconciled in the course of future reporting, but not always. For instance, in the United States, newly arriving aliens are granted visas by the U.S. Department of State, while aliens already temporarily in the United States and eligible to become adjusted to legal permanent resident status are granted immigrant status by the U.S. Citizenship and Immigration Services (USCIS), a bureau of the U.S. Department of Homeland Security. There have been a variety of

methods for determining the date by which an alien is determined to have "immigrated" to the United States, depending on the original status as permanent resident alien, refugee, asylee, parolee, or other. Methods include date of approval, most recent date of data entry, or the application of a specific formula to a specific circumstance.

6. The U.S. and Canadian censuses, upon which much of the national ethnic profiles are based, are compiled using unscientific methods of self-identification. As a result, one person might identify him- or herself as a part of every ethnic group in his or her ancestry, and another might only select a predominant ancestry group for identification. Respondents may even report family traditions or hearsay, without actual knowledge of ancestry. Thus, for some groups such as Germans and Poles, numbers may be overreported in the sense that there is no strong sense of ethnic identity for most of those reporting. In the case of nationals from many Central and South American countries, numbers are underreported, as a large percentage of their populations are unauthorized and therefore subject to official proceedings should their ethnic origin become known. Also, ethnic identification is confused across time by marriages between members of different ethnic groups and the variation of group cohesion from one ethnic group to another. This led Census Canada to reinstate in 2001 a question on "birthplace of parents," in order to more accurately trace developments in the second-generation community.

7. Some migrants may reside permanently in a country without being required to adjust to permanent resident status and thus are not officially counted as immigrants. Parolees, refugees, and asylees generally fall into this category. These numbers are generally small but can fluctuate dramatically in times of international crisis or war.

In most cases, the figures available are sufficient for establishing the scope of immigration and for pointing toward specific areas requiring more detailed study. The implications of introducing a new people to a prairie, village, town, or country have been dramatic throughout North America. Immigration has changed the way North Americans think and do business, the way they entertain and interact with the world. Immigration changed the immigrants too and the countries they came from, as thousands of separated kinsfolk eloquently testified in letters, diaries, and articles. Though the number of immigrants who touched the shores of the United States and Canada will never be known precisely, the impact of their presence is clear. In the end, the people matter more than the statistics anyway.

A to Z
Entries

Acadia

Acadia is the region of North America bounded by the St. Lawrence Seaway on the north, the Gulf of St. Lawrence on the east, and the Atlantic Ocean on the south. It includes the present-day Canadian provinces of NEW BRUNSWICK, NOVA SCOTIA, Prince Edward Island, and parts of the province of QUEBEC and the U.S. state of Maine. It was first colonized in 1604, when SAMUEL DE CHAMPLAIN and Pierre du Gua, sieur de Monts, established a settlement on St. Croix Island in the Bay of Fundy. After a disastrous winter that killed half the settlers, the colony was moved across the bay to Port Royal, though this too was abandoned when Champlain and de Monts lost their fur-trading monopoly. French settlers returned in 1610, but Port Royal was destroyed by an English force from Virginia in 1613. King James I of England (r. 1603–25) granted the region to Sir William Alexander, who named it Nova Scotia, Latin for "New Scotland." In 1632, it was returned to France.

With the rapid influx of British settlers into New England during the 1630s, the French government hoped to establish firm control of Acadia. In 1632, Governor Isaac de Razilly took control of Port Royal, imported "300 gentlemen of quality," and moved the capital to Le Heve on the Atlantic seaboard. Territorial disputes among the great fur merchants and frequent warfare between Britain and France nevertheless inhibited development of the region. The limited flow of immigrants, chiefly from the French region of Poitou, came to a standstill between 1654 and 1667, when the region was under British control. In 1686,

French intendant Jacques de Meulles counted only 885 colonists in the entire region, most living along the Bay of Fundy. Meulles reported that "receiving no help from France," many Acadians were following their commercial interests and immigrating to Boston. As a result, the Acadian population remained small and isolated. The farmers, hunters, and fishermen of Acadia became known for their self-reliance and were immortalized in Henry Wadsworth Longfellow's epic poem *Evangeline*.

Throughout the 18th century, control of Acadia was disputed by France and Britain. The Treaty of Utrecht (1713), ending Queen Anne's War (1702–13, the American phase of the War of the Spanish Succession in Europe), ceded Acadia to Britain, though only Nova Scotia was clearly turned over. In 1730, it was agreed that Acadians could swear loyalty to the British Crown without being required to bear arms against France or its Indian allies. British settlers established Halifax, Nova Scotia (1749), and encouraged settlement by French, German, and Swiss Protestants during the 1750s. Despite their traditional commercial contacts with the British, most Acadians remained loyal to France and sometimes encouraged American Indian attacks on British settlements. During the French and Indian War (1754–63, which corresponds to the European SEVEN YEARS' WAR), the British deported some 6,000 Acadians who refused to swear loyalty to George II (r. 1727–60), an event that came to be known as Le Grand Dérangement (The Great Disturbance). When the principal French fortress of Louisbourg fell to the British in 1758, the fate of Acadia and Canada was sealed. The formal signing of the Capitulation of Montreal in 1760 led many French inhabitants to return to Europe and some 4,000 to migrate to LOUISIANA, which remained in French hands. Only about 1,000 French settlers remained in Acadia. In their place came hundreds of New Englanders in the 1760s and, during and after the American Revolution (1775–83; see AMERICAN REVOLUTION AND IMMIGRATION), thousands of United Empire Loyalists who had refused to take up arms against the British Crown.

Further Reading

Arsenault, Bona. *History of the Acadians.* Montreal: Lemeac, 1978.

Brasseaux, C. A. *The Founding of New Acadia: The Beginnings of Acadian Life in Louisiana, 1765–1803.* Baton Rouge: Louisiana State University Press, 1987.

Clark, Andrew Hill. *Acadia: The Geography of Early Nova Scotia to 1760.* Madison: University of Wisconsin Press, 1968.

Daigle, Jean, ed. *Acadia of the Maritimes: Thematic Studies from the Beginning to the Present.* Moncton, Canada: Centre d'études acadiennes, 1995.

LeBlanc, Dudley J. *The Acadian Miracle.* Lafayette, La.: Evangeline Publishing, 1966.

Shriver, Edward, ed. *The French in New England, Acadia and Quebec.* Orono: New England–Atlantic Provinces–Quebec Center at the University of Maine Orono, 1975.

Trigger, Bruce G. *Natives and Newcomers: Canada's "Heroic Age" Reconsidered.* Kingston, Canada: McGill–Queen's University Press, 1985.

Trudel, Marcel. *The Beginnings of New France, 1524–1663.* Toronto: McClelland and Stewart, 1972.

Vachon, André. *Dreams of Empire: Canada before 1700.* Ottawa: Public Archives of Canada, 1982.

Addams, Jane (1860–1935) *social reformer*

One of the most influential advocates of social justice for immigrants, minorities, and the poor, Jane Addams attempted to reconcile human needs to the demands of modern industrial urban life. She is best known for founding the CHICAGO settlement known as Hull-House and was the first woman to be awarded the Nobel Peace Prize (1931).

Addams was born in the small town of Cedarville in northern Illinois, the daughter of state senator John Huy Addams. Well educated but sickly, she spent a total of three years in Europe between 1883 and 1888. While in London, she visited Toynbee Hall, an East End settlement house for aiding the cultural development of the poor. In September 1889, she and college friend Ellen Gates Starr opened the old Hull mansion as a settlement house for mainly middle-class women who wished to participate in the life of a poor West Side Chicago neighborhood. At first, the activities of Hull-House were primarily social, providing education and cultural opportunities and a day nursery for working women.

Jane Addams, progressive reformer and founder of Hull-House, did much to ameliorate the plight of new immigrants between 1889 and her death in 1935. *(Library of Congress, Prints & Photographs Division [LC-USZ62-95722])*

As immigrants from Greece, Italy, Russia, and Austria-Hungary increasingly displaced older immigrant groups from Britain and Germany, local conditions worsened, and there was greater hostility toward the "new immigrants." Through research and close involvement with the people of the neighborhood, Addams determined that the industrial system, rather than individual weaknesses, was principally to blame for the plight of the urban poor. As many critics condemned the newer immigrants on ethnic grounds, she argued that they would be naturally assimilated in the second generation. In 1908, workers at Hull-House established the Immigrants' Protective League, which assisted newly arrived immigrants with a special mission of helping young women avoid prostitution and other forms of exploitation.

Addams was one of the foremost advocates of progressive reform, calling for legal protection for immigrants, compulsory education, federal support for vocational education, and restrictive child-labor legislation. As a committed suffragist, she actively supported Theodore Roosevelt's Progressive Party candidacy for president in 1912. Addams opposed U.S. entry into World War I, but in 1918, she worked for humanitarian reasons in the Department of Food Administration. Throughout the 1920s, she supported international peace initiatives such as the League of Nations and worked tirelessly on behalf of women and the poor, serving as president of the Women's International League for Peace and Freedom (1919–35). Her most important written works include *Democracy and Social Ethics* (1902), *The Spirit of Youth and the City Streets* (1909), and *Twenty Years at Hull-House* (1910).

Further Reading

Addams, Jane. *Twenty Years at Hull-House: With Autobiographical Notes.* 1910. Reprint, New York: Signet, 1999.

Davis, Allen F. *American Heroine: The Life and Legend of Jane Addams.* New York: Oxford University Press, 1973.

Diliberto, Gioia. *A Useful Woman: The Early Life of Jane Addams.* New York: Scribners, 1999.

Levine, Daniel. *Jane Addams and the Liberal Tradition.* Madison: State Historical Society of Wisconsin, 1971.

Lissak, Shpak Rivka. *Pluralism and Progressives: Hull House and the New Immigrants, 1890–1919.* Chicago: University of Chicago Press, 1989.

Stebner, Eleanor J. *The Women of Hull-House: A Study in Spirituality, Vocation, and Friendship.* New York: State University of New York Press, 1997.

Afghan immigration

Almost all Afghans in North America are refugees or asylees relocated to the United States and Canada in the wake of the Soviet invasion of Afghanistan (1979), often after having spent time in refugee camps in Pakistan. According to the U.S. census of 2000 and the Canadian census of 2001, 53,709 Americans and 25,230 Canadians claimed Afghan descent, though the actual numbers are probably considerably higher. Although widely dispersed initially, most Afghans eventually congregated in San Francisco, New York, and Washington, D.C., in the United States and in Toronto and Vancouver in Canada. It is estimated that about 60 percent of Afghan Americans live in the San Francisco Bay area.

Afghanistan occupies 249,700 square miles of southwest Asia between 29 and 38 degrees north latitude. The country is bordered by Turkmenistan, Tajikistan, Uzbekistan, and China to the north, Pakistan to the east and the south, and Iran to the west. The land is covered in high mountains and deserts with patches of fertile lands along river valleys. In 2002, the population was estimated at 26,813,057. The Pashtun ethnic group composed 38 percent of the population; the Tajik, 25 percent; the Hazara, 19 percent; and the Uzbek, 6 percent. Afghanistan is an Islamic state in which the majority of the people are Sunni Muslims; 15 percent are Shia Muslims. Afghanistan has long been a crossroads for imperial invasions across Asia. Until the 18th century, local nobles or foreign empires ruled the country. In 1973, a republic was proclaimed by a military coup. Following a 1978 coup of leftist forces, the Soviet Union moved thousands of troops into Afghanistan in 1979 in support of a new government. A war ensued until 1989, when the Soviet Union withdrew its troops in accordance with a United Nations (UN) agreement. Afghan rebels finally deposed the pro-Soviet government in 1992, ending a war that had killed more than 2 million and caused more than 6 million to flee the country. Fighting continued, however, as a radical Islamic fundamentalist division known as the Taliban gained increasing control of the country. In 1996, it captured the capital city of Kabul, executed the former president, and began to impose a strict religious regime in which women were highly restricted. By 1998, the Taliban held most of the country but had come under increasing criticism from world powers. The United States attacked terrorist training camps of al-Qaeda leader Osama bin Laden with cruise missiles in 1998 and demanded that he be handed over. In 1999, when the United States's demands were not met, UN sanctions against Afghanistan went into effect. A UN ban on military aid followed in 2001. Following the September 11, 2001, terrorist attacks on the World Trade Center in New York City and the Pentagon in Washington, the Taliban again refused to hand over bin Laden, who had masterminded the attack. Military strikes against Afghanistan began shortly thereafter under a newly stated U.S. policy that those who harbored terrorists would also be treated as terrorists. Thousands of Afghan refugees fled to Pakistan where they received substantial aid from the United States.

Early records are virtually nonexistent, but the 200 Pashtuns who immigrated to the United States in 1920 are believed to have been the first Afghan immigrants. Immigration remained small, however, until the Soviet-inspired coup of 1978 and was limited almost entirely to the well-educated and the upper classes. Prior to 1978, only about 2,500 Afghans lived in the United States. Between 1980 and 1996, more than 32,000 were admitted as refugees, along with 40,000 under regular immigrant visas, most as part of the family reunification program. Immigration declined dramatically as the Taliban extended its influence in the mid-1990s, but it began to revive following the United States invasion of 2001. Between 1992 and 2002, 17,501 Afghans immigrated to the United States.

Prior to 1978, only about 1,000 Afghans lived in Canada. Because Canada did not create a special category to allow more Afghan refugees to enter the country, during the 1980s, Afghan immigration remained small, leading to complaints by some of anti-Muslim bias. Of the 21,710 Afghans in Canada in 2001, about 10,000 came between

1981 and 1995; more than 11,000 arrived between 1996 and 2001.

In both the United States and Canada, Afghans have tended to divide into subcommunities based on tribal affiliation, religious sect (Sunni or Shiite), or language. Also, they have preferred creating their own businesses to wage labor. It is still too early to evaluate the nature of their integration into North American society.

Further Reading

Anderson, E. W., and N. H. Dupree. *The Cultural Basis of Afghan Nationalism.* New York: Pinter Publishers, 1990.

Gaither, Chris. "Joy Is Muted in California's Little Kabul." *New York Times,* November 15, 2001, p. B5.

Goodson, Larry. *Afghanistan's Endless War: State Failure, Regional Politics, and the Rise of the Taliban.* Seattle: University of Washington Press, 2001.

Omidian, P. A. *Aging and Family in an Afghan Refugee Community.* New York: Garland, 1996.

Rais, R. B. *War without Winners: Afghanistan's Uncertain Transition after the Cold War.* New York: Oxford University Press, 1994.

Rogers, David. "Afghan Refugees' Return Is Taxing Relief Resources." *Wall Street Journal* April 19, 2002, p. A5.

Thomas, J. "The Canadian Response to Afghanistan." *Refuge* 9 (October 1989): 4–7.

African forced migration

Throughout most of America's history, Americans of African descent were its largest minority group. In July 2001, they were overtaken by Hispanics (see HISPANIC AND RELATED TERMS) but still made up 12.7 percent of the U.S. population (36.1 million/284.8 million). Most African Americans are descended from slaves forcibly brought by Europeans to the United States and the Caribbean during the 18th and early 19th centuries.

The continent of Africa was the native home to dark-skinned peoples who came to be called Negroes (blacks) by Europeans. Between the 16th and 19th centuries, about 11 million Africans were forced into slavery and brought to the Americas. Some 600,000 of these were brought to lands now comprising the United States and Canada. Their most frequent destinations included Virginia, Maryland, and the Carolinas, where by the 1770s, blacks constituted more than 40 percent of the population.

Most black Africans lived south of the vast Sahara desert, which minimized contact between them and Europeans until the 15th century, when Italian and Portuguese merchants began to cross the Sahara, and Portuguese mariners, to sail down the western coast. In 1497, Bartolomeu Dias reached the Cape of Good Hope at the southernmost tip of Africa, and in the following year Vasco da Gama reached the east coast port of Malindi on his voyage to India. The Portuguese expanded their coastal holdings, particularly in the areas of modern Angola and Mozam-

bique, where they established plantations and began to force native peoples into slavery. When the Portuguese arrived in Africa, there were few large political states. Constant warring among hundreds of native ethnic groups provided a steady supply of war captives for purchase. With the decimation of Native American populations in Spanish territories and the advent of British, French, and Dutch colonialism, demand for slaves increased dramatically during the 17th and 18th centuries. Sometimes they were captured by European slavers, but most often African middlemen secured captives to be sold on the coast to wealthy European slave merchants.

Although the earliest slaves were taken from the coastal regions of Senegambia, Sierra Leone, the Gold Coast, the Bight of Benin, the Bight of Biafra, Angola, and Mozambique, by the 17th century most were being brought from interior regions, further diversifying the ethnic background of Africans brought to the Americas. Once at the coast, captives usually would be held in European forts or slaving depots until their sale could be arranged with merchants bringing a variety of manufactured items from Europe or America, including textiles, metalware, alcohol, firearms and gunpowder, and tobacco. Africa thus became part of the infamous triangular trade: New England merchants would exchange simple manufactured goods on the western coast of Africa for slaves, who would in turn be shipped to the West Indies where they were traded for rum and molasses.

Once a merchant had secured a full cargo, Africans were inhumanely packed into European ships for the Middle Passage, a voyage of anywhere from five to 12 weeks from West Africa to the Americas. Some slavers were loose packers, which reduced disease, while others were tight packers who expected a certain percentage of deaths and tried to maximize profits by shipping as many slaves as space would allow. It is estimated that 15 to 20 percent died en route during the 16th and 17th centuries, and 5 to 10 percent during the 18th and 19th centuries. African men, who were most highly valued, were usually separated from women and children during the passage. The holds of the ships rarely allowed Africans to stand, and they were often unable to clean themselves throughout the voyage. Upon arrival in the Americas, slavers would advertise the auction of their cargo, often describing particular skills and allowing Africans to be inspected before sale. It was common for slaves to be sold more than once, and many came to North America after initial sales in the West Indies.

The first Africans were brought to British North America in 1619 to Jamestown, VIRGINIA, probably as servants. Their numbers remained small throughout the 17th century, and SLAVERY was not officially sanctioned until the 1660s, when slave codes began to be enacted. This enabled a small number of African Americans to maintain their freedom and even to become landholders, though this practice was not common. By that time, passage of the NAVIGATION ACTS, lower tobacco prices, and the difficulty in obtaining indentured servants had led to a dramatic rise in the demand for slaves. Although only 600,000 slaves were brought into the region, as a result of the natural increase that prevailed after 1700, the number of African Americans in the United States rose to 4 million by 1860.

The first Africans to arrive in New France were brought in 1628. Although the lack of an extensive plantation economy kept their numbers small, they were readily available from Caribbean plantations and French LOUISIANA. Slaves were never widely used in northern colonies in either British or French territories, where most were employed as domestic servants. Around 1760, the slave population in Canada was about 1,200, and in New England around 2,000.

The massive forced migration of Africans to North America created a unique African-American culture based on a common African heritage, the experience of slavery, and the teachings of Christianity. As a result of the patterns of the slave trade, it was impossible for most slaves to identify the exact tribe or ethnic group from which they came. African music and folktales continued to be told and were adapted to changing circumstances. Although African religious practices were occasionally maintained, most often the slaves' belief in spirits was combined with Christian teaching and the slave experience to produce a faith emphasizing the Old Testament themes of salvation from bondage and God's protection of a chosen people. The majority of slaves labored on plantations in a community of 20 or more slaves, subject to beatings, rape, and even death, without the protection of the law and usually denied any access to education. Despite the fact that slaves were not allowed to marry, the family was the principal bulwark against life's harshness, and marriage and family bonds usually remained strong. Strong ties of kinship extended across several generations and even to the plantation community at large.

The 500,000 free African Americans in 1860 were so generally discriminated against that they have been referred to as "slaves without masters," but their liberty and greater access to learning enabled them to openly join the abolitionist movement, which expanded rapidly after 1830, and to bring greater knowledge of world events and technological developments to the African-American community after the Civil War. Some, like the former slave Frederick Douglass, inspired reformers and other members of the white middle class to abandon racial prejudice, though this was uncommon even among abolitionists.

The first large-scale migration of free African Americans included some 3,000 black Loyalists who fled New York for NOVA SCOTIA at the end of the American Revolution in 1783, most settling in Birchtown and Shelburne (see AMERICAN REVOLUTION AND IMMIGRATION). Toward the end of the war, slaves were promised freedom in return for claiming protection behind British lines. Facing racism and difficult farming conditions, in 1792 nearly 1,200 returned to Sierra Leone in Africa.

African-American farmworkers in the 1930s board a truck near Homestead, Florida. The enslavement of millions of Africans between the 1660s and the 1860s led to the creation of a highly segregated society in the United States, still persistent at the start of the 21st century. *(Library of Congress, Prints & Photographs Division [LC-USF33-030490-M2])*

In response to the Enlightenment ideals of natural rights and political liberty and the evangelical concern for humanitarianism and Christian justice, between 1777 and 1804 the northern states gradually abolished slavery. The slave trade was banned by Britain in 1807, and slavery abolished throughout the empire in 1833. The slave trade was prohibited in the United States in 1808, but the invention of the cotton gin in 1793 and the rise of the short-staple cotton industry reinvigorated Southern reliance on slave labor at the same time that the antislavery movement was growing in strength. It is estimated that after the abolition of the slave trade, more than 500,000 slaves were sold from farms and plantations in Virginia, Maryland, Kentucky, and other states to the cotton plantations of the Deep South, with little regard for the preservation of slave families. As a result, when President Abraham Lincoln freed slaves under Southern control in 1863 and slavery was abolished in 1865, many African Americans not only came from a legacy of forced enslavement but had also been uprooted themselves.

See also RACIAL AND ETHNIC CATEGORIES; RACISM.

Further Reading
Alexander, Ken, and Avis Glaze. *The African-Canadian Experience.* Toronto: Umbrella Press, 1996.
Berlin, Ira. *Many Thousands Gone: The First Two Centuries of Slavery in North America.* Cambridge, Mass.: Belknap Press, 1998.
———. *Slaves without Masters: The Free Negro in the Antebellum South.* New York: Pantheon, 1974.
Conniff, Michael L., and Thomas J. Davis. *Africans in the Americas: A History of the Black Diaspora.* New York: St. Martin's Press, 1994.
Coughty, Jay A. *The Notorious Triangle: Rhode Island and the African Slave Trade, 1700–1807.* Philadelphia: Temple University Press, 1981.
Curtin, Philip D. *The Atlantic Slave Trade: A Census.* Madison: University of Wisconsin Press, 1969.
Eltis, David. *The Rise of African Slavery in the Americas.* New York: Cambridge University Press, 2000.
Greene, Lorenzo J. *The Negro in Colonial New England.* New York: Columbia University Press, 1942.
Klein, Herbert S. *The Atlantic Slave Trade.* New York: Cambridge University Press, 1999.
Litwack, Leon. *North of Slavery: The Negro in the Free States, 1790–1860.* Chicago: University of Chicago Press, 1961.
Nash, Gary B. *Forging Freedom: The Formation of Philadelphia's Black Community, 1720–1840.* Cambridge, Mass.: Harvard University Press, 1988.
Walker, James W. St. G. *The Black Loyalists: The Search for a Promised Land in Nova Scotia and Sierra Leone, 1783–1870.* New York: Africana Publishing Company/Dalhousie University Press, 1976.
Winks, Robin W. *The Blacks in Canada.* Montreal: McGill–Queen's University Press, 1971.

agriculture and immigration See LABOR ORGANIZATION AND IMMIGRATION.

Aheong, Samuel P. (Siu Pheoung, S. P. Ahiona)
(1835–1871) *missionary*
Samuel P. Aheong became one of the most influential Christian missionaries in Hawaii, encouraging the local Christian community to embrace newly arriving Chinese immigrants.

Aheong was born in Kwangtung (Guandong) Province, China, the son of a school superintendent. Separated from his family during the Taiping Rebellion, in 1854 he joined a work crew headed for the sugar plantations of Hawaii. During his five years of contracted service, he learned English and converted to Christianity. Already a master of a dozen Chinese dialects, he soon became conversant in English, Hawaiian, and Japanese, and became a successful

merchant in Lahaina. Aheong's zeal for sharing the Christian gospel with his fellow countrymen led to his commissioning as an evangelist by the Hawaiian Evangelical Association in 1868 and the integration of many Christian churches throughout the Hawaiian Islands. In 1870, he returned to China to evangelize his native land and died there the following year.

Further Reading
Char, Tin-Yuke. *The Bamboo Path: Life and Writings of a Chinese in Hawaii.* Honolulu: Hawaii's Chinese History Center, 1977.
———. *The Chinese in Hawaii.* Peiping: n.p., 1930.
———. "S. P. Aheong, Hawaii's First Chinese Christian Evangelist." *Hawaiian Journal of History* 11 (1977): 69–76.

Albanian immigration
Albanians began immigrating to North America in significant numbers around 1900, though thousands returned to their homeland after World War I (1914–18). Yugoslav attempts to purge the Kosovo Province of ethnic Albanians in 1999 created a new wave of immigration. In the U.S. census of 2000 and the Canadian census of 2001, 113,661 Americans and fewer than 15,000 Canadians claimed Albanian descent. The greater Boston area has been from the first the center of Albanian-American culture, with other significant concentrations in New York City; Jamestown and Rochester in New York State; Chicago, Illinois; and Detroit, Michigan. Metropolitan Toronto is the center of Canadian settlement, especially the Mississauga area.

Albania occupies 10,600 square miles of the western Balkan Peninsula in southeastern Europe. It lies along the Adriatic Sea between 41 and 43 degrees north latitude and is bordered by Greece on the south, Serbia and Montenegro on the north, and Macedonia on the east. The land is dominated by rugged hills and mountains, with a narrow coastal plain. In 2002, the population was estimated at 3,510,484. Albanians are religiously divided, with some 70 percent Muslim, 20 percent Albanian Orthodox, and 10 percent Roman Catholic. The two major ethnic groups are the Gegs, inhabiting the most isolated northern portions of the region, and the Tosks, occupying the more accessible southern area. These and smaller related groups have throughout most of their history been subjects of Rome, the Byzantine Empire, the Goths, Bulgarians, Slavs, Normans, and Serbs. When Albania was conquered by the Ottoman Turks in the late 15th century, the majority of Albanians converted to Islam, though Orthodox and Roman Catholic minorities remained strong. Albania gained its independence in 1913, though large numbers of Albanians remained within the neighboring country of Serbia (later Yugoslavia), with most concentrated in the Serbian province of Kosovo.

The earliest Albanian immigrant to the United States came in the mid-1870s, though there were only about 40 by the turn of the century. The first substantial wave of immigrants were largely young Orthodox Tosk laborers, escaping civil war (1904–14) and seeking ways to support their families, who remained in Europe. As with many eastern European groups, most early immigrants were young men who hoped to earn money before returning home. Of the 30,000 Albanians in the United States in 1919, only 1,000 were women. As many as 10,000 Albanians are estimated to have returned to their homeland shortly after World War I. Between World War I and World War II (1939–45), a new wave of Tosks arrived in the United States, with most intending to settle.

Immediately after World War II, the majority of Albanians coming to North America were escaping the rigidly orthodox rule of the marxist government. Most settled in urban areas. Between 1946 and 1992, Albania was ruled by a Communist government that discouraged emigration. During the 1960s and 1970s, it was closely associated with Chinese, rather than Russian, communism but became largely independent of all communist nations in 1978, remaining one of the poorest of all European countries. The longtime ruler of Albania, Enver Hoxha, died in 1985, and the country began to liberalize. Reforms included allowances for foreign travel and increased communication with other countries. As the Communist regime teetered on the brink of extinction in 1990, thousands of dissidents immigrated to Italy, Poland, Hungary, Czechoslovakia, France, and Germany. With the fall of the government in early 1992, a massive migration was unleashed, estimated at 500,000 (1990–96). Most settled in Greece (300,000) or Italy (150,000), but a significant number immigrated to the Western Hemisphere. Between 1990 and 1995, about 7,000 Albanians, including many professionals, emigrated.

Tracing early Albanian immigration to Canada is difficult, as prior to 1981, Albanians were classified either as "Other" or "Balkans." The earliest immigrants probably came in the 1890s, though they may have numbered 100 or fewer. As in the United States, most returned to Europe after 1914. Immigration remained small throughout the communist years, though some ethnic Albanians from Kosovo and Macedonia managed to leave Yugoslavia. Of Canada's 5,280 Albanian immigrants in 2001, fewer than 400 arrived prior to 1990.

An economic crisis in 1996 led the country into violent rebellion and political disarray, which were eventually stabilized by United Nations troops. By 1998, widespread killing of Albanian-speaking Muslims in the Yugoslav province of Kosovo led to a massive international crisis, with more than 1 million Kosovars left homeless, displaced, or in refugee camps outside the country. In May 1999, Canada accepted some 7,500 ethnic Albanians from Kosovo, though eventually almost 2,000 chose to return to their homeland (redefined as an autonomous region in Serbia and Montenegro) after the fall of president Slobodan Milošević. After

housing some refugees in primitive conditions at Guantánamo Bay, Cuba, the U.S. government in April 1999 agreed to provide 20,000 annual refugee visas, with preference given to those with family connections in the United States and others who were particularly vulnerable to persecution. Between 1996 and 2002, annual immigration averaged more than 4,100. As a result, the number of Albanians in the United States more than doubled between 1990 (47,710) and 2000 (113,661).

Further Reading

Demo, Constantine A. *The Albanians in America: The First Arrivals.* Boston: Society of Fatbardhesia of Katundi, 1960.

Federal Writers Research Project. *The Albanian Struggle in the Old World and the New.* Boston: The Writer, 1939.

Jacques, Edwin E. *The Albanians: An Ethnic History from Prehistoric Times to the Present.* Jefferson, N.C., and London: McFarland, 1995.

Kule, Dhori. *The Causes and Consequences of Albanian Emigration during Transition: Evidence from Micro-Data.* London: European Bank for Reconstruction and Development, 2000.

Nagi, D. *The Albanian American Odyssey.* New York: AMS Press, 1989.

Pearl, Daniel. "Albanian Refugees from Kosovo Opt Not to Fill Open Slots to U.S." *Wall Street Journal,* June 28, 1999, p. A18.

Puskas, Julianna. *Overseas Migration from East-Central and Southeastern Europe, 1880–1940.* Budapest: Hungarian Academy of Sciences, 1990.

Trix, Francis. *Albanians in Michigan.* Ann Arbor: University of Michigan Press, 2001.

Vickers, Miranda. *Between Serb and Albanian: A History of Kosovo.* New York: Columbia University Press, 1998.

Westen, Henry. *The Albanians in Canada.* privately published, n.d.

alien   See ILLEGAL ALIENS.

Alien and Sedition Acts (United States) (1798)

The Alien and Sedition Acts is the collective name given to four laws enacted by the U.S. Congress in the midst of its undeclared naval war with France known as the Quasi War (1798–1800). The laws were ostensibly a reaction to French diplomacy and depredations on the high seas but were mainly aimed at undermining the growing strength of Thomas Jefferson's Republican Party. With Irish, French, and other newly arrived immigrants strongly supporting the Republican Party, Federalists were intent on neutralizing the potential political value of "new" Americans.

The Naturalization Law extended the residency qualification for full citizenship—and thus the right to vote—from five to 14 years. The Alien Enemies Law gave the president wartime powers to deport citizens of countries with whom the United States was at war, and the Alien Law empowered the executive to expel any foreigner "suspected" of treasonous activity, though its tenure was limited to two years. The Sedition Law proscribed criticism of the government, directly threatening First Amendment guarantees regarding freedom of speech and freedom of the press. The alien laws were not used by Federalist president John Adams, but a number of prominent Jeffersonian journalists were prosecuted for sedition. The main result of the Alien and Sedition Acts was to unify the Republican Party. After Jefferson's election as president in 1800, the Naturalization Law was repealed, and the others measures were allowed to expire (1800–1801). A new NATURALIZATION ACT was passed in 1802.

See also NATURALIZATION ACTS.

Further Reading

Hutchinson, E. P. *Legislative History of American Immigration Policy, 1798–1965.* Philadelphia: University of Pennsylvania Press, 1981.
Levy, Leonard W. *Legacy of Suppression: Freedom of Speech and Press in Early American History.* Cambridge, Mass.: Belknap Press of Harvard University Press, 1960.
Miller, John C. *Crisis in Freedom: The Alien and Sedition Acts.* Boston: Little Brown, 1951.
Smith, James Morton. *Freedom Fetters: The Alien and Sedition Laws and American Civil Liberties.* Ithaca, N.Y.: Cornell University Press, 1956.

Alien Contract Labor Act (Foran Act)
(United States) (1885)

Reflecting a growing concern about the effects of organized labor, Congress enacted the Alien Contract Labor Act, also known as the Foran Act, on February 26, 1885. It was the first of a series of measures designed to undermine the practice of importing contract labor.

Although concern about the negative impact of contract labor had become prevalent as early as 1868, it gained new force during debate surrounding the CHINESE EXCLUSION ACT (1882). In 1883 and 1884, Congress received more than 50 anticontract petitions from citizens in 13 states, as well as from state legislatures and labor organizations. The result was the Alien Contract Labor Act of February 26, 1885. Its major provisions included

1. Prohibition of transportation or assistance to aliens by "any person, company, partnership, or corporation. . . . under contract or agreement . . . to perform labor or services of any kind"
2. Voiding of any employment contracts agreed to prior to immigration
3. Fines of $1,000 levied on employers for each laborer contracted
4. Fines of $500 levied on ship captains for each contract laborer transported, and imprisonment for up to six months

Exempted from the provisions were aliens and their employees temporarily residing in the United States; desirable skilled laborers engaged in "any new industry" not yet "established in the United States"; and "professional actors, artists, lecturers, or singers," personal or domestic servants, ministers of "any recognized religious denomination," professionals, and "professors for colleges and seminaries." The most commonly utilized loophole was an explicit declaration that nothing in the act should "be construed as prohibiting any individual from assisting any member of his family to migrate from any foreign country to the United States, for the purpose of settlement here."

Further Reading

Daniels, Roger. *Guarding the Golden Door: American Immigration Policy and Immigrants since 1882.* New York: Hill and Wang, 2004.
Hutchinson, E. P. *Legislative History of American Immigration Policy, 1798–1965.* Philadelphia: University of Pennsylvania Press, 1981.
LeMay, Michael C. *From Open Door to Dutch Door: An Analysis of U.S. Immigration Policy since 1820.* New York: Praeger, 1987.

Alien Labor Act (Canada) (1897)

Designed to support the Canadian policy of preferring agriculturalists to all other immigrants, this measure made it illegal to contract and import foreign laborers. The act was a response principally to the highly organized and rapid influx of Italian, Polish, Ukrainian, Russian, and Bulgarian laborers in the late 19th century. Although labor unions bitterly complained that the measures were routinely flouted, the government took no effective steps to enforce the act beyond applying more rigorous medical tests to Japanese immigrants from Hawaii. Although Minister of the Interior Clifford Sifton preferred agriculturalists seeking homesteading funds over contract laborers, the Canadian government generally deferred to industry's need for additional laborers. In 1900, the measure was amended to prohibit advertisement for laborers in U.S. newspapers and to prohibit entry of non-American workers by way of the United States. Provisions of the measure were applied selectively after the VANCOUVER RIOT of 1907 in order to keep Japanese and Chinese laborers from entering from Hawaii. In order to further limit the influence of labor unions and to allow U.S. laborers to relieve labor shortages in Canada, the government suspended the Alien Labor Act in 1916.

Further Reading

Craven, Paul. *"An Impartial Umpire": Industrial Relations and the Canadian State, 1900–1911.* Toronto: University of Toronto Press, 1980.
Imai, Shin. "Canadian Immigration Law and Policy: 1867–1935." LLM thesis. Toronto: York University, 1983.

Kelley, Ninette, and Michael Trebilcock. *The Making of the Mosaic: A History of Canadian Immigration Policy.* Toronto: University of Toronto Press, 1998.

Timlin, Mabel. "Canada's Immigration Policy, 1896–1910." *Canadian Journal of Economics and Political Science* 26 (1960): 517–532.

Alien Land Act (United States) (1913)

Passed by the California legislature in 1913, the Alien Land Act prohibited noncitizens from owning land in California. Californians had for 20 years been campaigning against Chinese and Japanese immigrants, who they feared were overrunning their state and threatening their traditional culture. An increasing number of Indian immigrants after the turn of the century (see INDIAN IMMIGRATION) led to a variety of discriminatory measures, including the Alien Land Act. The measure was challenged by Takao Ozawa, who first immigrated to the United States from Japan in 1894, but the U.S. Supreme Court ruled in *OZAWA V. UNITED STATES* that by race he was excluded from U.S. citizenship.

Further Reading

Curran, Thomas J. *Xenophobia and Immigration, 1820–1930.* Boston: Twayne, 1975.

Takaki, Ronald. *Strangers from a Different Shore: A History of Asian Americans.* Boston: Little, Brown, 1989.

Amalgamated Clothing Workers of America

See INTERNATIONAL LADIES' GARMENT WORKERS' UNION.

American Federation of Labor and Congress of Industrial Organizations (AFL-CIO)

The AFL-CIO is the largest labor organization in the United States, comprising some 66 self-governing national and international labor unions with a total membership of 13 million workers (2002). The quadrennial AFL-CIO convention is the supreme governing body, electing the executive council, which determines policy. There are some 60,000 affiliated local unions. Throughout most of its history, the AFL-CIO opposed immigration, though its policy began to change in the 1990s.

The American Federation of Labor (AFL) was one of the earliest labor organizations in the United States, founded in 1881 as the Federation of Organized Trades and Labor Unions of the United States and Canada. It encouraged the organization of workers into craft unions, which would then cooperate in labor bargaining. Under the energetic leadership of Samuel Gompers, an English Jewish immigrant, the AFL gained strength as it won the support of skilled workers, both native and foreign born. The official policy of the AFL was to represent all American workers, without reference to race, ethnicity, or gender. In practice, however, Japanese and Chinese workers were excluded, and after 1895, many affiliated unions began banning African-American workers. Despite the egalitarian language of the AFL and its affiliated unions, in practice they represented the skilled workers of America, most of whom were either native born or first- or second-generation immigrants from northern and western Europe. By the turn of the 20th century, the AFL was staunchly defending the prerogatives of skilled workers against threats from the "new immigration." In 1896, the organization first established a committee on immigration and in the following year passed a resolution calling on the government to require a literacy test as the best means of keeping out unskilled laborers. The AFL also continued to oppose Chinese and Japanese immigration and supported the Immigration Act of 1917, which required a literacy test and which barred virtually all Asian immigration.

In 1935, the AFL broke with tradition by encouraging the organization of unskilled workers, particularly those in mass-production industries. Disagreements in the leadership led to the breakaway Congress of Industrial Organizations (CIO) in 1938. The two organizations merged in 1955 to form the AFL-CIO. Two years later, the Teamster's Union, the largest union in the United States, was expelled from the AFL-CIO for unethical practices. In 1963, the AFL-CIO passed a resolution supporting "an intelligent and balanced immigration policy" based on "practical considerations of desired skills." The organization applauded the IMMIGRATION REFORM AND CONTROL ACT (IRCA) of 1986, particularly for its tough sanctions on employers of illegal immigrants. As labor membership continued to decline, the organization moved further toward support of immigration, in 1993 explicitly stating that immigrants were not the cause of labor's problems and encouraging local affiliates to pay special attention to the needs of legal immigrant workers. In February 2000, the AFL-CIO made the historic decision to reverse its position and to support future immigration. The Executive Council emphasized three areas: elimination of the "I-9" sanctions process, tougher penalties for employers who take advantage of undocumented workers, and a new amnesty program for undocumented workers. On July 25, 2000, AFL-CIO president John J. Sweeney openly endorsed the Restoration of Fairness in Immigration Act, formally introduced in March 2002, which expanded amnesty provisions for long-term workers who entered the country illegally. It is unclear how vigorously this policy will be pursued, and if it will be adopted generally by organized labor, particularly in the wake of the terrorist attacks of September 11, 2001.

See also LABOR ORGANIZATION AND IMMIGRATION.

Further Reading

AFL-CIO Executive Council Actions. New Orleans, February 16, 2000, pp. 1–4.

Briggs, Vernon M., Jr. *Immigration and American Unionism*. Ithaca, N.Y.: Cornell University Press, 2001.

Brundage, Thomas. *The Making of Western Labor Radicalism: Denver's Organized Workers, 1878–1905*. Urbana: University of Illinois Press, 1994.

Buhle, Paul. *Taking Care of Business: Samuel Gompers, George Meany, Lane Kirkland, and the Tragedy of American Labor*. New York: Monthly Review Press, 1999.

Dubofsky, Melvin. *Industrialism and the American Worker*. Arlington Heights, Ill.: Harlan Davidson, 1985.

Galenson, Walter. *The CIO Challenge to the AFL*. Cambridge, Mass.: Harvard University Press, 1960.

Goldfield, Michael. *The Decline of Organized Labor in the United States*. Chicago: University of Chicago Press, 1987.

Greene, Julie. *Pure and Simple Politics: The American Federation of Labor and Political Activism, 1881–1917*. Cambridge: Cambridge University Press, 1998.

Kaufmann, S. B. *Samuel Gompers and the Origins of the American Federation of Labor*. Westport, Conn.: Greenwood Press, 1973.

Livesay, Harold C. *Samuel Gompers and Organized Labor in America*. Boston: Little, Brown, 1978.

Milkman, Ruth, ed. *Organizing Immigrants: The Challenge for Unions in Contemporary California*. Ithaca, N.Y.: Cornell University Press, 2000.

Montgomery, David. *The Fall of the House of Labor: The Workplace, the State, and American Labor Activism, 1865–1925*. New York: Cambridge University Press, 1987.

Sweeney, John J. "Statement on the Restoration of Fairness in Immigration Act of 2000." July 25, 2000. AFL-CIO Web site. Available online. URL: http://www.aflcio.org/publ/press2000/pr0725.htm. Accessed July 9, 2002.

American immigration to Canada

American immigration to Canada has always been a relatively easy process, fostered by a long shared border, similar cultural values, and a common language. According to the 2001 Canadian census, 250,010 Canadians claim American descent, though the number clearly underrepresents those whose families once inhabited the United States.

Prior to the AMERICAN REVOLUTION (1775–83), migration to Canada was small and usually associated with the imperial rivalry between Great Britain and France. New Englanders carried on a lively trade with maritime territories and on several occasions attacked French interests in ACADIA. Between 1755 and 1760, 10,000 French Acadians were driven out of the region. Beginning in 1758, the government of Nova Scotia began advertising throughout its colonial territories in North America encouraging settlers to take up land claims in Acadia. With the promise of free land, transportation, and other forms of assistance, 7,000 New Englanders migrated to Nova Scotia between 1760 and 1766 and by the time of the American Revolution made up more than 50 percent of the population.

Britain's loss of the thirteen colonies led to the first great American migration of 40,000 to 50,000 United Empire Loyalists, families who had refused to take up arms against the British Crown and were thus resettled at government expense, most with grants of land in NOVA SCOTIA, NEW BRUNSWICK, and western QUEBEC. In a separate influx, thousands of American farmers migrated to Upper Canada (Ontario) in search of cheap land after 1783. By the outbreak of the War of 1812 (1812–15), when borders were once again closed, they composed more than half the population there. After the war, the British government discouraged emigration from the United States, restricting the sale of Crown lands and more actively seeking British and European settlers. While Britain feared U.S. expansionist tendencies, Canada's acceptance of up to 30,000 freed and escaped slaves prior to the Civil War (1861–65) further heightened tensions between the two countries. The discovery of gold along the Fraser River of British Columbia nevertheless attracted several thousand emigrants from California after 1857, though few of these remained there for long.

As tensions began to subside in the wake of Canadian confederation (1867), immigrants dissatisfied with conditions in the United States sometimes continued on to Canada, though for 30 years more people left Canada than arrived as immigrants, most lured away by economic prospects in the rapidly industrializing United States. Under Minister of the Interior CLIFFORD SIFTON, however, the Canadian government began to actively recruit agriculturalists, offering free prairie lands. In 1896, when Sifton took office, about 17,000 immigrants arrived annually; by his retirement in 1905, annual immigration was up to 146,000. American immigrants, because of their cultural affinity and capital, were highly sought and were second only to British immigrants in number. Few records were kept of migrations between the United States and Canada prior to the census of 1911, so exact numbers are uncertain. Between 1910 and 1914, however, almost 1 million Americans—most from German, Scandinavian, Icelandic, and Hungarian immigrant families—went north. Though some Canadians complained of the profits reaped by American land companies who speculated in western land settlement, the Canadian government continued to encourage emigration from the United States.

Throughout most of the 20th century, Americans continued to be welcomed into Canada, though overall numbers remained relatively small. After World War II, numbers gradually increased, averaging more than 12,000 annually between 1946 and 1970. After the immigration regulations of 1967 and final passage of Canada's 1976 IMMIGRATION ACT, which formally abandoned race as the determining factor in immigration, the percentage and number of U.S. immigrants declined significantly. Undocumented immigration nevertheless spiked during the late 1960s, as thousands of young Americans fled to Canada in order to avoid conscription and possible service in Vietnam. After some confusion, the Canadian government clarified its policy in 1969, determining that military status would have no bearing on admission to the country. It has been estimated that some 50,000 American "draft dodgers" took refuge in Canada, though only about 100 applied for landed immigrant status. Most eventually returned to the United States. Between 1967 and 1971, the United States rose from third to first source country for immigrants to Canada, with annual immigration of more than 22,000. Between 1994 and 2002, it fluctuated between sixth and ninth, averaging 5,500 immigrants annually.

See also CANADA—IMMIGRATION SURVEY AND POLICY OVERVIEW.

Further Reading

Brown, Wallace. *The King's Friends: The Composition and Motives of the American Loyalist Claimants.* Providence, R.I.: Brown University Press, 1965.

Careless, J. M. S., ed. *Colonists and Canadiens, 1760–1867.* Toronto: Macmillan of Canada, 1971.

Ells, Margaret. "Settling the Loyalists in Nova Scotia." *Canadian Historical Association Report for 1934* (1934), pp. 105–109.

Hansen, M. L., and J. B. Brebner. *The Mingling of the Canadian and American People.* 1940. Reprint, New York: Arno Press, 1970.

Long, John F., and Edward T. Pryor, et al. *Migration between the United States and Canada.* Washington, D.C.: Current Population Reports/Statistics Canada, February 1990.

Moore, Christopher. *The Loyalists: Revolution, Exile, Settlement.* Toronto: Macmillan of Canada, 1984.

Troper, Harold. "Official Canadian Government Encouragement of American Immigration, 1896–1911." Ph.D. diss., University of Toronto, 1971.

Ward, W. Peter. *White Canada Forever.* Montreal: McGill–Queen's University Press, 1978.

Wilson, Bruce. *Colonial Identities: Canada from 1760–1815.* Ottawa: National Archives of Canada, 1988.

American Protective Association

The American Protective Association (APA) was a secret, anti-Catholic organization founded by Henry F. Bowers in Clinton, Iowa, in 1887. It reached a peak membership of perhaps 500,000 immediately following the economic depression of 1893, before rapidly diminishing by the end of the century.

Following the Civil War (1861–65), many Anglo-Americans were concerned with the growing Roman Catholic influence in education, politics, and labor organization. In addition to millions of Irish and German Catholics who had been entering the country since the 1830s, after 1880 their numbers were enhanced by the admission of hundred of thousands of Catholic Italians and Poles. Bowers suspected Catholic conspiracies against public education and political campaigns in his hometown of Baltimore, Maryland. Founding the APA, he required members to swear that they would never vote for a Catholic political candidate, would never deprive a Protestant of a job by hiring a Catholic, and would never walk with Catholics in a picket line. With the onset of depression in 1893, Protestant workers in the Midwest and Rocky Mountain states were quick to blame immigrants for their plight. With the Democratic Party heavily reliant on Irish Americans, especially in major urban centers, those most concerned often turned to private lobbies such as the APA, though they usually voted Republican. Although anti-Catholic sentiment was heavily influenced by fears of economic competition, the movement also contained an undercurrent of ethnocentrism aimed at non-Protestant European immigrants. Hostile toward many immigrant groups, the APA nevertheless enjoyed enthusiastic support from many Protestant immigrants from northern Ireland (Ulster), Scandinavia, and Canada, leading the organization to focus on anti-Catholic policies, including the repeal of Catholic Church exemptions from taxation. As German and Irish Catholics became more prominent in national life in the late 1890s, it became political suicide for a national candidate to openly espouse an anti-Catholic policy, thus leading to the decline of such openly hostile societies.

See also NATIVISM.

Further Reading

Higham, John. *Strangers in the Land: Patterns of American Nativism, 1860–1925.* New Brunswick, N.J.: Rutgers University Press, 1988.

Kinzer, Donald L. *An Episode in Anti-Catholicism: The American Protective Association.* Seattle: University of Washington Press, 1964.

American Revolution and immigration

When tensions arising from the financial strain of the SEVEN YEARS' WAR (1756–63) erupted into war between Britain and 13 of its American colonies in 1775, colonists were forced to take sides. In 1763, most had considered themselves loyal subjects of the British Crown, but a series of measures enacted by the government in London over the next 12 years had slowly turned most Americans against the arbitrary rule of King George III (r. 1760–1820). The Proclamation of 1763, limiting westward expansion; the Sugar Act (1764), Stamp Act (1765), Townshend duties (1767), and Tea Act (1773), aimed at raising revenue in the American colonies, despite their lack of representation in the British parliament; and the Coercive (Intolerable) Acts (1774), QUEBEC ACT (1774), and Prohibitory Act (1775), designed to enforce royal authority gradually eroded American support for the British monarch.

By 1775 only about one in five Americans declared themselves loyal to the British Crown. As the American

Revolution progressed and the rebels gained the upper hand, particularly in the southern colonies, these Loyalists congregated in ports controlled by the British navy. Following the peace settlement in the Treaty of Paris (1783), between 40,000 and 50,000 Loyalists were resettled in Britain's northern colonies. About 15,000 went to both NOVA SCOTIA and NEW BRUNSWICK, about 10,000 to QUEBEC. Included among the Loyalist settlers were 3,000 blacks who had been granted freedom in return for military service. The rapid influx of Loyalists into largely French-speaking Quebec led directly to a reevaluation of British governance in its remaining colonies. Settlers, many of whom had served in the British military, were dissatisfied with the French institutions they found there. As a result, Quebec was divided into the provinces of Lower Canada (modern Quebec) and Upper Canada (modern Ontario), a division made permanent by the Constitutional Act of 1791. Loyalists were encouraged to move to Upper Canada, where they were allowed to establish traditional British laws, customs, and institutions.

Further Reading

Alexander, Ken, and Avis Glaze. *Towards Freedom: The African-Canadian Experience.* Toronto: Umbrella Press, 1996.
Brown, Wallace. *The King's Friends: The Composition and Motives of the American Loyalist Claimants.* Providence, R.I.: Brown University Press, 1965.
Careless, J. M. S., ed. *Colonists and Canadiens, 1760–1867.* Toronto: Macmillan of Canada, 1971.
Conway, Stephen. *The British Isles and the War of American Independence.* New York: Oxford University Press, 2000.
Fischer, David. *Albion's Seed: Four British Folkways in America.* New York: Oxford University Press, 1989.
Fleming, Thomas. *Liberty! The American Revolution.* New York: Viking, 1997.
Fryer, Mary Beacock. *King's Men: The Soldier Founders of Ontario.* Toronto: Dundurn Press, 1980.
Moore, Christopher. *The Loyalists: Revolution, Exile, Settlement.* Toronto: Macmillan of Canada, 1984.
Walker, James W. St. G. *The Black Loyalists: The Search for a Promised Land in Nova Scotia and Sierra Leone, 1783–1870.* New York: Africana Publishing Company/Dalhousie University Press, 1976.
Wilson, Bruce. *Colonial Identities: Canada from 1760–1815.* Ottawa: National Archives of Canada, 1988.

Amish immigration

The Amish are one of the few immigrant peoples to maintain their distinctive identity over more than three or four generations after migration to North America. Their identity is based largely on two factors: the Anabaptist religious beliefs that led to persecution in their German and Swiss homelands and a simple, agricultural lifestyle that rejects most modern technological innovations. There are more than 150,000 practicing Amish in North America living in 22 U.S. states and in Ontario, Canada. About three-quarters of them live in Pennsylvania, Ohio, and Indiana, but there are also large settlements in New York and Ontario. As farmland became scarce in southeastern Pennsylvania and other traditional areas of Amish settlement, new communities were established in rural areas of other states.

The Amish were followers of Jacob Amman, an Anabaptist Mennonite who in the 1690s introduced ritual foot washing and the shunning of those who failed to adhere to the rules of the community. These practices distinguished his followers from other Protestant groups that also believed in adult baptism, separation of church and state, pacifism, non-swearing of oaths, and communal accountability. The Amish, like all Anabaptist groups, were persecuted in an age when state religions were the rule and military service was expected. They were often forbidden to own land and encouraged to emigrate. During the 18th century, about 500 Amish immigrated to Pennsylvania from Switzerland and the Palatinate region of southwestern Germany. The first families arrived in 1727, with the majority following between 1737 and 1754. All remained in Pennsylvania. The greatest period of immigration was between 1804 and 1860, when 3,000 Amish emigrated from Alsace, Lorraine, Montbeliard, Bavaria, Hesse, Waldeck, and the Palatinate. Many settled in Pennsylvania, but 15 additional settlements were founded throughout the United States.

As good land became more expensive in the United States, a few Amish families purchased land in Canada, mainly in Waterloo County, Ontario. Christian Nafziger obtained permission from the government to settle in Wilmot Township, just west of an already-established Mennonite settlement (see MENNONITE IMMIGRATION). Between 1825 and 1850, some 1,000 Amish were living in the province, with most coming directly from France and Germany. Though few Amish came to the United States after the Civil War (1861–65) and many became acculturated, a high fertility rate led to a small but steady growth of the Amish community in the United States and Canada. In 1900, there were only 5,000 Amish; by 1980, their number had risen to about 80,000.

Further Reading

Gingerich, Orland. *The Amish of Canada.* Scottdale, Pa.: Herald Press, 2001.
Hostetler, John A. *Amish Society.* 4th ed. Baltimore: Johns Hopkins University, 1993.
Kraybill, Donald B., and Carl F. Bowman. *On the Backroad to Heaven: Older Order Hutterites, Mennonites, Amish, and Brethren.* Baltimore: Johns Hopkins University Press, 2001.
Luthy, David. *The Amish in America: Settlements That Failed, 1840–1960.* Aylmer, Canada: Pathway Publishers, 1986.
Nolt, S. M. *A History of the Amish.* Intercourse, Pa.: Good Books, 1992.
Schlabach, Theron F. *Peace, Faith, Nation: Mennonites and Amish in Nineteenth-Century America.* Scottdale, Pa.: Herald Press, 1989.

Yoder, Paton. *Tradition & Transition: Amish Mennonites and Old Order Amish, 1800–1900.* Scottdale, Pa.: Herald Press, 1991.

Angel Island

Angel Island, sometimes called "the Ellis Island of the West," was the site of the Immigration Detention Center in San Francisco Bay, about two miles east of Sausalito. During its 30-year history (1910–40), as many as 1 million immigrants passed through the facilities—both departing and arriving—including Russians, Japanese, Indians, Koreans, Australians, Filipinos, New Zealanders, Mexicans, and citizens of various South American countries. Almost 60 percent of these immigrants were, however, Chinese. The immigration center, located on the largest of the bay's islands, was built to enforce anti-Chinese legislation, rather than to aid potential immigrants. Whereas the rejection rate at Ellis Island was about 1 percent, it was about 18 percent on Angel Island, reflecting the clear anti-Chinese bias that led to its establishment.

The CHINESE EXCLUSION ACT (1882), the first ethnic restriction on immigration to the United States, prohibited the entry of Chinese laborers to the United States. Its provisions did not touch the 150,000 laborers already in the country before the measure took effect, and who could legally come and go. Those who had earned citizenship were allowed to travel to China to marry or to spend time with their wives, who, as aliens, were ineligible for entry to the United States. On the other hand, their children were eligible for entry. The "paper sons" who entered the United States with returning Chinese Americans often were not sons at all, but the children of neighbors or of friends in China seeking opportunities in the United States. Chinese officials, merchants, tourists, and students also were allowed to travel freely. Until 1924, merchants were allowed to bring partners and wives. Many of the "partners" in fact had no legitimate role in the businesses they claimed to be associated with, using the lax enforcement of the law as a loophole for getting ineligible Chinese into the country. Although all aspects of exemption to the exclusion were brought before the courts, it was consistently determined that in the absence of credible evidence that a professed merchant was not who he claimed, he was allowed to enter under the provisions of the Sino-American (Angell) Treaty of 1881. As a result, thousands of Chinese entered the country fraudulently as sons or partners of Chinese Americans already in

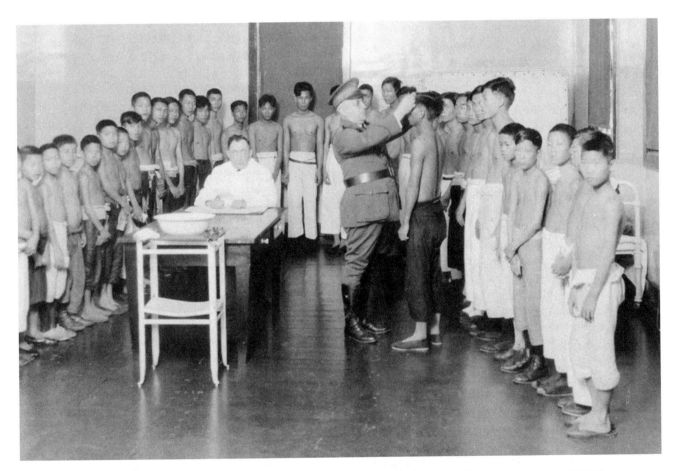

Medical inspection was required of Asian immigrants at the Angel Island depot, California. Sixty percent of the 100,000 immigrants who passed through Angel Island were Chinese. *(National Archives #090-G-125-45)*

the country. Although most of the methods of gaining illegal entry were well known, fraud was difficult to prove. In the absence of regular immigration officials—the government had no official immigration bureaucracy before 1892—most screening fell to the understaffed customs officials who were aware of the fraudulent methods used to skirt the Chinese Exclusion Act and thus came to presume that the Chinese were inveterate liars and likely criminals. With the destruction of most immigration records during the earthquake and resulting fires in San Francisco in 1906, evading detection became even easier.

With increasing government regulations, it became impossible to effectively screen immigrants in the two-story shed at the Pacific Mail Steamship Company wharf in San Francisco. The Bureau of Immigration (see IMMIGRATION AND NATURALIZATION SERVICE) followed the example of New York City's founding of an immigrant station on ELLIS ISLAND, separated from the city itself. Established in 1910, the Angel Island detention center on San Francisco's old quarantine island included barracks, a hospital, and various administrative buildings. Here, immigrants could be isolated, both to protect the population from communicable diseases and to provide time for examination of possible fraudulent entry claims.

Upon arrival in San Francisco, Europeans and first- and second-class travelers were usually processed on board and allowed to disembark directly to the city. All others were ferried to Angel Island where the men and women were separated before undergoing stringent medical tests, performed with little regard for the dignity of the immigrant, looking particularly for parasitic infections. Afterward, prospective immigrants were housed in crowded barracks, sleeping in three-high bunk beds, awaiting interrogation. The grueling interviews, held before the Board of Special Inquiry, which included two immigrant inspectors, a stenographer, and a translator, covered every detail of the background and lives of proposed entrants. Any deviation from details offered by family members resulted in rejection and deportation. And if a successful entrant ever left the country, the transcript of his or her interrogation was on record for use when he or she returned. The whole process could take weeks, as family members on the mainland had to be contacted for corroborating evidence. In the case of deportation proceedings and their appeals, an immigrant might spend months or more than a year on Angel Island. Although this process applied to all steerage-class passengers, most had fewer obstacles to surmount than the Chinese did. The Japanese, for instance, as a result of the GENTLEMEN'S AGREEMENT (1907), often had documents prepared by the Japanese government that shortened the process.

While incarcerated for weeks or months in crowded, filthy conditions and eating wretched food, many Chinese immigrants despaired and longed for their homeland. Their relatives and community officials began to complain of safety and health concerns. One of hundreds of poems, either written on or carved into the wall of the buildings, expressed the helpless feeling of the unknown author's situation:

> *Imprisoned in the wooden building day after day,*
> *My freedom is withheld; how can I bear to talk about it?*
> *I look to see who is happy but they only sit quietly.*
> *I am anxious and depressed and cannot fall asleep.*
> *The Days are long and bottle constantly empty;*
> *My sad mood even so is not dispelled.*
> *Nights are long and the pillow cold; who can pity my loneliness?*
> *After experiencing such loneliness and sorrow,*
> *Why not just return home and learn to plow the fields?**

It was a fire, however, rather than government action, that finally shut down the Angel Island facility. The administration building burned to the ground in April 1940, and by the end of the year, all detainees had been moved to the mainland. Three years later in the midst of World War II, the Chinese Exclusion Act was repealed, thus allowing Chinese immigrants to become naturalized citizens.

The old site of the detention center was briefly used as a prisoner-of-war processing center during World War II, before falling into decay. In 1963, it was incorporated into the Angel Island State Park, and 13 years later, the California state legislature appropriated $250,000 to restore the barracks, which were opened to the public as a museum in 1983. Also in that year, the Angel Island Immigration Station Foundation was created to partner with the California State Parks and the National Park Service to continue programs of restoration and education. In 1997, the site was declared a National Historic Landmark.

Further Reading

Chen, Helen. "Chinese Immigration into the United States: An Analysis of Changes in Immigration Policies." Ph.D. diss., Brandeis University, 1980.

Daniels, Roger. "No Lamps Were Lit for Them: Angel Island and the Historiography of Asian American Immigration." *Journal of American Ethnic History* 17 (Fall 1997): 3–18.

Lai, Him Mark. *Becoming Chinese American: A History of Communities and Institutions.* Walnut Creek, Calif.: AltaMira Press, 2004.

Lai, Him Mark, Genny Lim, and Judy Yung, eds. *Island: Poetry and History of Chinese Immigrants on Angel Island, 1910–1940.* Seattle: University of Washington, 1991.

Lee, Erika. *At America's Gates: Chinese Immigration During the Exclusion Era, 1882–1943.* Chapel Hill: University of North Carolina Press, 2003.

*From Him Mark Lai, Genny Lim, and Judy Yung, eds. *Island: Poetry and History of Chinese Immigrants on Angel Island, 1910–1940* (Seattle: University of Washington, 1991), p. 68.

McGinty, Brian. "Angel Island: The Door Half Closed." *American History Illustrated* (September–October 1990): 50–51, 71.

Naka, Mary. "Angel Island Immigration Station." *Survey of Race Relations (1922).* Stanford, Calif.: Stanford University, Hoover Institution Archives, 1922.

Stolarik, M. Mark, ed. *Forgotten Doors: The Other Ports of Entry into the United States.* Philadelphia: Balch Institute Press, 1988.

Takaki, Ronald. *Strangers from a Different Shore: A History of Asian Americans.* New York: Penguin Books, 1989.

Wong, Esther. "The History and Problem of Angel Island." *Survey of Race Relations (March, 1924).* Stanford, Calif.: Stanford University, Hoover Institution Archives.

Anti-Defamation League

The Anti-Defamation League (ADL), a branch of the Jewish service organization B'NAI B'RITH, is committed to fighting racial prejudice and bigotry. Through an extensive program of publication, public speaking, and lobbying, it has developed considerable political influence. Concerned especially with First Amendment issues, the ADL has been especially active in monitoring the activities of hate groups and militias.

A series of pogroms in Russia (1903–06) led Americanized German Jews to form the American Jewish Committee (1906), dedicated to protecting Jewish civil rights around the world. The concept was directly tested in the United States itself in 1913 when Leo Frank, a Jewish factory superintendent, was convicted of an Atlanta, Georgia, murder, kidnapped from prison, and lynched. He was later exonerated of the crime. Within a month, midwestern Jews founded the ADL in order to counter racially based claims emanating from the controversy. The ADL played an especially large cultural role from the time of its founding until the end of World War II, a period when overt anti-Semitism was common in the United States.

Further Reading

Dinnerstein, Leonard. *Antisemitism in America.* New York: Oxford University Press, 1994.

Sorin, Gerald. *A Time for Building: The Third Migration, 1880–1920.* Baltimore: Johns Hopkins University Press, 1992.

Soyer, Daniel. *Jewish Immigrant Associations and American Identity in New York, 1880–1939.* Cambridge, Mass.: Harvard University Press, 1997.

Antin, Mary (1881–1949) *author*

Mary Antin was a powerful voice for immigrant assimilation in America and one of the foremost champions of an open immigration policy in the early 20th century.

Born in Polotsk, Russia, she, her mother and her siblings joined her father, who had emigrated in 1891, in Massachusetts in 1894. Her first book, *From Plotzk to Boston* (1899), was written in Yiddish. She became nationally famous with her autobiographical *The Promised Land* (1912), which had been serialized in the *Atlantic Monthly*. Following the success of *The Promised Land,* she lectured widely and frequently spoke on behalf of Theodore Roosevelt and the Progressive Party. Antin's ardent support for immigrant conformity to Anglo societal norms made her popular with mainstream audiences and led to widespread use of her works in public schools.

Further Reading

Guttmann, Allen. *The Jewish Writer in America: Assimilation and the Crisis of Identity.* New York: Oxford University Press, 1971.

Proefriedt, William A. "The Education of Mary Antin." *Journal of Ethnic Studies* 17 (1990): 81–100.

Tuerk, Richard. "At Home in the Land of Columbus: Americanization in European-American Immigrant Autobiography." In *Multicultural Autobiography: American Lives.* Ed. James Robert Payne. Knoxville: University of Tennessee Press, 1992.

Arab immigration

The majority of Arabs in North America are the largely assimilated descendants of Christians who emigrated from the Syrian and Lebanese areas of the Ottoman Empire between 1875 and 1920. A second wave of immigration after 1940 was more diverse and more heavily Muslim, including substantial numbers from Egypt, Iraq, Jordan, Lebanon, Morocco, Palestine, Syria, and Yemen. In the U.S. census of 2000 and the Canadian census of 2001 1,202,871 Americans and 334,805 Canadians claimed Arab ancestry or descent from peoples of predominantly Arab countries. Some analysts estimate the U.S. figure at closer to 3 million. As late as 1980, about 90 percent were Christians, though the majority of immigrants since 1940 have been Muslims. The greatest concentration of Arabs in the United States is in the greater Detroit, Michigan, area, particularly Dearborn, with a population estimated at more than 200,000. Los Angeles County, California; Brooklyn, New York; and Cook County, Illinois, also have large Arab populations. Montreal, Quebec, has by far the largest Arab population in Canada.

Arab is a general ethnic term to designate the peoples who originated in the Arabian Peninsula. In modern times, it more generally applies to those who speak Arabic and embrace Arab culture. Arabs form the majority populations in Saudi Arabia, Kuwait, Yemen, Oman, the United Arab Emirates, Qatar, Bahrain, Iraq, Syria, Lebanon, Jordan, Egypt, Libya, Tunisia, Algeria, and Morocco. Sudan is about 50 percent Arab. Some Arabs migrated northward into the Tigris and Euphrates river valleys about 5,000 years ago, mixing with various Persian and Indo-European peoples to form a common Mesopotamian culture. Arab culture was widely spread only with the advent of the expansionistic Islamic faith. In the 120 years following the Prophet

Muhammad's death in 632, Arab leaders conquered the entire region stretching from modern Pakistan to Spain. This resulted in the spread of both Islam and the broader Arab culture. In some regions, Islam was embraced within the context of deeply rooted, non-Arabic culture patterns. This was the case most notably in Pakistan, Afghanistan, Iran (ancient Persia), and Turkey. From the late 16th century, most Arab lands were controlled or influenced by the Turkish Ottoman Empire. Though Turkish influence waned in the 18th and 19th centuries, leading to greater European influence in northern Africa and the coastal regions of southwest Asia, the Ottoman Empire continued to control Kuwait, Iraq, Syria, Lebanon, Palestine, Jordan, and much of the Arabian Peninsula until the end of World War I (1918).

The term *Arab* has been used in so many different ways that exact immigration figures are difficult to arrive at. When the number of people arriving in North America from the region of North Africa/Southwest Asia was small, immigrants from the Ottoman Empire were usually classified in the category "Turkey in Asia," whether Arab, Turk, or Armenian. By 1899, U.S. immigration records began to make some distinctions, and by 1920, the category "Syrian" was introduced into the census, though religious distinctions still were not noticed. Throughout the 20th century, there was little consistency in designation, principally because overall numbers remained small. As a result, Arabs might variously have been listed according to country, as "other Asian" or "other African," or as nationals of their last country of residence.

The first major movement of Arabs to North America came from Lebanon in the late 19th century. At the time, Lebanon was considered a region within the larger area of Syria, so the term *Syrian* was most often used. As "Syrian" Christians living in an Islamic empire, Lebanese Arabs were subject to persecution, though in good times they were afforded considerable autonomy. During periods of drought or economic decline, however, they frequently chose to emigrate. Between 1900 and 1914, about 6,000 immigrated to the United States annually. Often within one or two generations these Lebanese immigrants had moved into the middle class and largely assimilated themselves to American life. Although Syrians began migrating to Canada about the same time, their numbers were much smaller. As late as 1961, the population was less than 20,000. Though mostly Christians, they were divided into several branches, including Maronites, Eastern Orthodox, and Melkites. The next wave of Arabs to immigrate to North America, most in the wake of the Arab-Israeli War of 1967, were overwhelmingly Muslim and had little in common with those who had arrived early in the century.

See also EGYPTIAN IMMIGRATION; IRAQI IMMIGRATION; LEBANESE IMMIGRATION; MOROCCAN IMMIGRATION; PALESTINIAN IMMIGRATION; SYRIAN IMMIGRATION.

Further Reading

Booshada, Elizabeth. *Arab-American Faces and Voices: The Origins of an Immigrant Community.* Austin: University of Texas Press, 2003.

Elkholy, Abdo. *The Arab Moslems in the United States: Religion and Assimilation.* New Haven, Conn.: College and University Press, 1966.

Kashmeri, Zuhair. *The Gulf Within: Canadian Arabs, Racism, and the Gulf War.* Toronto: J. Lorimer, 1991.

Koszegi, Michael A., and J. Gordon Melton, eds. *Islam in North America: A Sourcebook.* New York: Garland Publishing, 1992.

McCarus, Ernest, ed. *The Development of Arab-American Identity.* Ann Arbor: University of Michigan Press, 1994.

Naff, Alixa. *Becoming American: The Early Arab American Experience.* Carbondale: Southern Illinois University Press, 1985.

Orfalea, Gregory. *Before the Flames: A Quest for the History of Arab Americans.* Austin: University of Texas Press, 1988.

Suleiman, Michael W., ed. *Arabs in America: Building a New Future.* Philadelphia: Temple University Press, 2000.

Zogby, John. *Arab America Today: A Demographic Profile of Arab Americans.* Washington, D.C.: Arab American Institute, 1990.

Argentinean immigration

Argentineans first arrived in the United States and Canada in significant numbers during the 1960s, primarily seeking economic opportunities. In the 2000 U.S. census, 100,864 Americans claimed Argentinean descent, compared to 9,095 Canadians in their 2001 census. Most Argentinean immigrants, many of Italian origin, settled in large metropolitan areas, with New York and Los Angeles being most popular. More than half of Argentinean Canadians live in Ontario, with most having settled in Toronto.

Argentina occupies 1,055,400 square miles of southern South America between 21 and 55 degrees south latitude. Bolivia and Paraguay lie to the north and Brazil, Uruguay, and the Atlantic Ocean to the east. The Andes Mountains stretch north to south along Argentina's western border with Chile. East of the mountains lie heavily wooded areas known in the north as the Gran Chaco. The Pampas, an area of extensive grassy plains, cover the central region of the country. In 2002, the population was estimated at 37,384,816, with more than 12 million in the urban vicinity of Buenos Aires. The majority practice Roman Catholicism. Beginning in the early 16th century, Spanish colonists migrated to Argentina, driving out the indigenous population. In 1816, colonists gained independence, and by the late 19th century Argentina was competing with the United States, Canada, and Australia for European immigrants. By 1914, 43 percent of Argentina's population was foreign born, with most coming from Spain, Italy, and Germany.

Military coups slowed modernization from 1930 until 1946 when General Juan Perón was elected president. Perón ruled until 1955, when he was exiled by a military coup. Military and civilian governments followed until Perón's reelection in 1973. In 1976, a military coup ousted Perón's wife, Isabel, who had assumed the presidency following her husband's death in 1974. During the Dirty War (1976–83), approximately 30,000 opponents of the right-wing regimes that succeeded Perón were tortured and killed, leading to increased international interest in Argentine refugees. In 1978, the United States launched the Hemispheric 500 Program, providing parole for several thousand Chilean and Argentinean political prisoners. In the following year, Canada created a new refugee category for Latin American Political Prisoners and Oppressed Persons. In both cases, the standards for entry were higher than for refugees from Southeast Asia and Eastern Europe, where applicants were fleeing from communist regimes, leading critics to argue that immigration policy was being driven by COLD WAR concerns.

As the military's hold on power weakened, Argentina invaded the British-held Falkland Islands in April 1982 but surrendered them less than three months later. The national economy thereafter faced prolonged recession, leading many professionals to continue to seek employment in the United States and Canada. Argentines are economically better off than most Hispanic immigrant groups and less likely to live in communities defined by ethnicity.

Prior to 1960, the U.S. Census Bureau did not separate Hispanic nationalities, so it is difficult to determine exactly how many Argentineans had entered the United States before that time. By the 1970 census, however, there were 44,803 living in the United States, most of whom were well-educated professionals. A second wave of immigration began in the mid-1970s, with refugees fleeing the Dirty War of the right-wing military regime. By 1990, almost 80 percent of Argentinean Americans had been born abroad. Between 1992 and 2002, Argentinean immigration averaged about 2,500 annually.

A very limited Argentinean immigration to Canada began early in the 20th century, the most notable being a small community of about 300 Welsh Argentines who relocated to Saskatchewan. Between passage of the IMMIGRATION ACT of 1952 and the early 1970s, Argentinean immigration averaged several hundred per year, driven both by Argentina's economic decline and by Canada's new provisions for highly trained immigrants. Between 1973 and 1983, rapid inflation and government oppression during the Dirty War led an average of more than 1,000 Argentineans to relocate to Canada. Of 13,830 Argentinean immigrants in Canada in 2001, 3,180 arrived between 1971 and 1980, 2,790 between 1981 and 1990, and 4,200 between 1991 and 2001.

Further Reading

Barón, A., M. del Carril, and A. Gómez. *Why They Left: Testimonies from Argentines Abroad.* Buenos Aires: EMECE, 1995.
Lattes, Alfredo E., and Enrique Oteiza, eds. *The Dynamics of Argentine Migration, 1955–1984: Democracy and the Return of Expatriates.* Trans. David Lehmann and Alison Roberts. Geneva: United Nations and Research Institute for Social Development, 1987.
Marshall, A. *The Argentine Migration.* Buenos Aires: Flasco, 1985.
Pinal, Jorge del, and Audrey Singer. "Generations of Diversity: Latinos in the United States." *Population Reference Bureau Bulletin* 52, no. 3 (1997): 1–44.
Rockett, Ian R. H. "Immigration Legislation and the Flow of Specialized Human Capital from South America to the United States." *International Migration Review* 10 (1976): 47–61.

Armenian immigration

Armenians first migrated to North America in large numbers following the massacres of 1894–95 at the hands of the Ottoman Empire. An attempted genocide during World War I (1914–18) led to another influx. Finally, the rise of Arab nationalism during the 1950s led to the emigration of tens of thousands of Armenians from Islamic countries throughout the Middle East. In the U.S. census of 2000 and the Canadian census of 2001, 385,488 Americans claimed Armenian descent, while 40,505 did so in Canada. The early centers of Armenian settlement in the United States were New York City, Boston, and Fresno, California. Since 1970, the majority of Armenians settled in the Los Angeles area, making it the largest Armenian city outside their homeland, with a population of more than 200,000. Brantford, Ontario, was the largest Canadian settlement of Armenians prior to World War II (1939–45), though by 2000, almost half lived in Montreal and about one-third in Toronto.

The modern state of Armenia that emerged from the breakup of the Soviet Union in 1991 occupies 11,500 square miles of Southwest Asia between 38 and 42 degrees north latitude. The ancient kingdom was almost 10 times larger. Georgia lies to the north of modern Armenia; Azerbaijan, to the east; Iran, to the south; and Turkey, to the west. The land is mostly mountainous. In 2002, the population was estimated at 3,336,100, with over a third in the urban area of the capital city Yerevan. Ninety-three percent of the population is ethnically Armenian. Minority ethnic groups include Azeri, Russian, and Kurd. Armenian Orthodox is the principal religion of the country.

Armenians are an ancient people who have inhabited the Caucasus mountain area and eastern Anatolia (modern Turkey) for more than 2,500 years. Although various Armenian states exercised sovereignty in the ancient and medieval periods, the region was most often dominated by more powerful neighbors, including Persia, Rome, the Seljuk Turks, and the Ottoman Turks. As Christians, Armenians were subject to frequent persecution at the hands of Islamic governments. In the 1890s, an Ottoman attempt to rid the empire of this troublesome minority led to the murder of several hundred thousand Armenians and an international call for reforms. After Ottoman defeat in World War I, Armenia briefly declared a republic (1918). Fearing Turkish aggression, the country accepted the protection of the Soviets in 1920 and in 1922 joined with Georgia and Azerbaijan to form the Transcaucasian Soviet Federated Socialist Republic within the Union of Soviet Socialist Republics (USSR). In 1936, Armenia became an independent constituent republic of the USSR. In 1988, nearly 55,000 Armenians were killed in an earthquake that destroyed several cities. Since independence, in 1991, fighting between Armenia and largely Muslim Azerbaijan over the Armenian enclave of Nagorno-Karabakh has kept political tensions high in the country.

Despite the fact that an Armenian farmer immigrated to Virginia as early as 1618, it is estimated that there were fewer than 70 Armenians in the United States prior to 1870. The first great migration came in the wake of the massacres of 1894–95. During the remainder of that decade, perhaps 100,000 Armenians immigrated to the United States. After the Turkish government killed more than a million Armenians during World War I, another 30,000 escaped to America before the restrictive JOHNSON-REED ACT (1924) effectively closed the door, reducing the annual quota to 150. Following World War II, the DISPLACED PERSONS ACT (1948) enabled some 4,500 Armenians to come to the United States outside the quota. Finally, tens of thousands of Armenians who had been driven by Turkey into Iran, Iraq, Lebanon, Egypt, Palestine, and Syria following World War II immigrated during the 1950s. It is difficult to determine with precision the number of Armenians who have come to North America, because they emigrated from many Middle Eastern countries and often were counted on the basis of their immediately previous country of residence. Between 1960 and 1984, about 30,000 Armenians fled the USSR, most settling in the greater Los Angeles area. As Soviet control of its republics began to weaken in the late 1980s, thousands more immigrated to the United States. It has been estimated that more than 60,000 came during the 1980s. Following the initial turmoil surrounding Armenian independence in 1991, numbers gradually declined. Between 1994 and 2002, Armenian immigration to the United States averaged about 2,000 annually. This figure does not include Armenians from Turkey or Iran.

During the 1890s, a small number of Armenians settled on the western prairies of Canada, but a substantial community failed to develop. Around the turn of the century, a larger contingent of mainly entrepreneurs and factory workers settled in southern Ontario. By 1914 there were about 2,000 Armenians in Canada. Restrictions classifying Armenians as "Asiatics" effectively stopped immigration until the 1950s, though about 1,300 were admitted as refugees during the 1920s. Many were orphans sponsored by religious or charitable organizations. With the IMMIGRATION ACT of 1952, Armenians were no longer classified as Asiatics and thus found immigration easier. The Canadian Armenian Congress sponsored hundreds of Armenian immigrants in the 1950s and 1960s, with most settling near their headquarters in Montreal. Only about 4 percent of Armenian Canadians immigrated after 1961, with 1,130 coming between 1991 and 2001.

Further Reading

Armenians in America—Celebrating the First Century on the Occasion of the National Tribute for Governor George Deukmejian, October 10, 1987. Washington, D.C.: Armenian Assembly of America, 1987.

Avakian, A. S. *The Armenians in America*. Minneapolis, Minn.: Lerner, 1977.

Bakalian, Anny. *Armenian-Americans: From Being to Feeling Armenian*. New Brunswick, N.J.: Transaction, 1993.

Bournoutian, A. G. *A History of the Armenian People*. 2 vols. Costa Mesa, Calif.: Mazda, 1993–94.

Chichekian, Garo. *The Armenian Community of Quebec*. Montreal: G. Chichekian, 1989.

Deranian, Hagop Martin. *Worcester Is America: The Story of Worcester's Armenians, the Early Years*. Worcester, Mass.: Bennate Publications, 1998.

Kulhanjian, Gary A. *The Historical and Sociological Aspects of Armenian Immigration to the United States, 1890–1930*. San Francisco: R. and E. Research Associates, 1975.

Malcolm, M. Vartan. *Armenians in America*. Boston and Chicago: Pilgrim's Press, 1919.

Mirak, Robert. *Torn between Two Lands: Armenians in America 1890 to World War I*. Cambridge, Mass.: Harvard University Press, 1983.

Takooshian, Harold. "Armenian Immigration to the United States Today from the Middle East." *Journal of Armenian Studies* 3 (1987): 133–155.

Tashijian, James H. *The Armenians of the United States and Canada: A Brief Study*. Boston: Armenian Youth Federation, 1970.

Vassilian, Hamo B., ed. *Armenian American Almanac*. 3d ed. Glendale, Calif.: Armenian Reference Books, 1995.

Waldstreicher, D. *The Armenian Americans*. New York: Chelsea House, 1989.

Wertsman, Vladimir. *The Armenians in America, 1616–1976: A Chronology and Fact Book*. Dobbs Ferry, N.Y.: Oceana Publications, 1978.

Australian immigration

As a traditional country of reception for immigrants, large numbers of Australians never immigrated to North America. In the U.S. census of 2000 and the Canadian census of 2001, 78,673 Americans claimed Australian descent, compared to 25,415 Canadians. Unofficial estimates place the number much higher. As many of these immigrants had either previously immigrated to Australia from somewhere else or were the descendants of immigrants, it is suspected that census data often reflects country of earliest ancestry rather than country of last residence. Australians are spread throughout the United States, with the largest concentration in southern California. They blend easily into mainstream

American and Canadian cultures and do not readily join ethnic groups.

Australia, the only country occupying an entire continent, covers 2,966,150 square miles, almost as large as the lower 48 states of the United States. Like the North American continent, Australia was lightly populated by native peoples, the Aborigines, when Europeans arrived in the late 18th century. Unlike the United States and Canada, its great distance from Europe and restrictive immigration policies limited population growth. In 2002, Australia's population was just under 20 million, with 92 percent being of European descent, 6.4 percent of Asian descent, and 1.5 percent of Aboriginal descent.

The Dutch explored Australia in the early 17th century but did not colonize it. Captain James Cook's explorations between 1769 and 1777 led to an English settlement in New South Wales, dominated by convicts, soldiers, and officials. After the American Revolution, with the thirteen colonies no longer available for convict transportation, the British government began to exile convicts to Australia, a policy that led to the forced immigration of 160,000 men, women, and children between 1788 and 1868. By 1830, Great Britain claimed the entire island. In 1901, Australia became a commonwealth and immediately barred almost all "coloreds" from entry. Australia became fully independent of Great Britain in 1937. Since 1973, Australia's immigration policy has been nonracial. About one-third of immigrants in 2000 were Asian.

Australians usually immigrated to North America in pursuit of economic opportunity, beginning with more than 1,000 during the first years after the CALIFORNIA GOLD RUSH (1848). In 1851, however, most returned when gold was discovered in western Australia. During the 19th century, immigration to the United States averaged less than 1,000 per year. World War II (1939–45) led to a significant rise in immigration, boosted by 15,000 Australian war brides returning with American soldiers who had been stationed there. Between 1960 and 2000, Australian immigration rose as economic conditions at home worsened and fell as they improved, with the annual average at about 4,000. Throughout the 19th and early 20th centuries, there was little immigration from Australia to Canada, in part because of unwritten agreements to avoid competition for immigrants. Data for Australian immigration to Canada are unreliable, but there were only 2,800 Australian-born Canadians in 1941. Immigration began to grow during the 1950s, as working conditions for nurses, academics, and other professionals were similar in both countries, but pay was generally better in Canada. It peaked in 1967, with almost 5,000 Australians entering. As was true throughout the 20th century, however, many came for education or temporary jobs and frequently returned to their homeland. As a result of the 1976 IMMIGRATION ACT, which made it more difficult to be admitted for work if Canadians could be found to do the job, immigration dropped significantly. Of the 16,030 Australian Canadians in 2001, about 6,400 came after 1980.

Further Reading

Bateson, Charles. *Gold Fleet for California: Forty-Niners from Australia and New Zealand.* East Lansing: Michigan State University Press, 1963.

Cuddy, Dennis Laurence. "Australian Immigration to the United States: From Under the Southern Cross to 'The Great Experiment.'" In *Contemporary American Immigration: Interpretive Essays.* Ed. Dennis Laurence Cuddy. Boston: G. K. Hall, 1982.

Moore, J. H., ed. *Australians in America, 1876–1976.* Brisbane, Australia: University of Queensland Press, 1977.

Austrian immigration

In the U.S. census of 2000 and the Canadian census of 2001, 735,128 Americans and 147,585 Canadians claimed Austrian ancestry. Because German speakers were divided among several states during the great European age of immigration (1820–1920), yet almost always embarked for the New World from German ports, it is difficult to determine exactly how many immigrants came from various states of the old German Confederation (to the 1860s); from the German Empire (from 1870); or from Austria and the Sudeten regions of the Austro-Hungarian Empire. Between 1861 and 1910, the U.S. Bureau of Immigration drew no distinctions among more than a dozen ethnic groups emigrating from the empire (see AUSTRO-HUNGARIAN IMMIGRATION). After 1919, Austrian immigration corresponds to the successor state of Austria, one of six created from the breakup of the Austro-Hungarian Empire following World War I. Austrian immigrants, many of whom were Jewish, tended to settle in New York, Chicago, and other large cities during the 19th and early 20th centuries. New York City remains the center of Austrian settlement in the United States, though there are growing concentrations in California and Florida. Although Austrians tended to settle on the Canadian prairies during the first half of the 20th century, by the end of the century, the greatest concentration was in Toronto, with significant pockets of settlement in other cities of Ontario. In both the United States and Canada, Austrians assimilated rapidly and were not inclined to join purely Austrian groups.

Austria is a mountainous, landlocked country of 31,900 square miles, lying between 46 and 49 degrees north latitude. It is surrounded by Switzerland and Liechtenstein on the west; Germany and the Czech Republic on the north, Slovakia and Hungary on the east, and Italy and Slovenia on the south. Its population of 8,150,835 is 99 percent ethnic German, 78 percent of whom are Roman Catholic. From the Middle Ages, Austria formed the core of a large multiethnic empire that was finally broken apart following defeat in World War I.

After the war, the economic situation was unsettled in the old German-speaking center of the empire, leading 18,000 Austrians to immigrate to the United States between 1919 and 1924. With the imposition of restrictive quotas in the JOHNSON-REED ACT (1924), Austrian immigration was first limited to 785 per year, though it was revised upward to 1,413 in 1929. Eventually another 16,000 immigrated between 1924 and 1937. As a result of American restrictions, Austrian immigration to Canada, Argentina, and Brazil increased, with more than 5,000 settling in Canada during the interwar years. With mounting pressure on European Jews in the 1930s, Jewish Austrians of means increasingly sought opportunities to leave. President Franklin Roosevelt relaxed restrictions on refugee immigrants in 1937, leading to an increase in visas. Between the incorporation of Austria into the German Reich in 1938 and the entry of the United States into World War II in 1941, 29,000 Austrian Jews entered the United States, most of whom were well educated, and many of whom were internationally renowned in their various fields of study (see WORLD WAR II AND IMMIGRATION). In the first two decades following World War II, more than 100,000 Austrians immigrated to the United States, the numbers boosted by the allocation of nonquota visas for refugees and their families during the 1950s. Immigration declined and return migration quickened, however, as Austria established a strong economy and effective social service system by the mid-1960s. Between 1992 and 2002, average annual immigration was just under 500.

Most immigrants from the Austro-Hungarian Empire to Canada were not from the present-day country of Austria. Of perhaps 200,000 immigrants prior to World War I, most were Slavic; probably fewer than 10,000 were German speakers from the modern region of Austria. A large number came from the province of Burgenland. Prior to World War I, most of these settled on the prairies of Saskatchewan, where they were joined by small numbers of Burgenlanders from the United States. Following World War I, they were designated "nonpreferred" because of their association with the defeated Central Powers. As a result, during the 1920s and 1930s, about 5,000 Austrians immigrated to Canada, with most settling in the western provinces, around 70 percent in Manitoba alone. After World War II, Austria faced a long and difficult rebuilding process that prompted many Austrians to immigrate to Canada, with the majority settling in Ontario. Of the 22,130 Austrian immigrants in Canada in 2001, about 62 percent (13,645) arrived prior to 1961.

Further Reading

Engelmann, Frederick, Manfred Prokop, and Franz Szabo, eds. *A History of the Austrian Migration to Canada.* Ottawa: Carleton University Press, 1996.

Goldner, Franz. *Austrian Emigration, 1938–1945.* Trans. Edith Simons. New York: F. Ungar, 1979.

Pick, Hella. *Guilty Victim: Austria from the Holocaust to Haider.* New York: I. B. Tauris, 2000.

Schlag, Wilhelm. "A Survey of Austrian Emigration to the United States." In *Österreich und die angelsächsische Welt.* Ed. Otto von Hietsch. Vienna, Austria, and Stuttgart, Germany: W. Braumüller, 1961.

Spaulding, E. Wilder. *The Quiet Invaders: The Story of the Austrian Impact upon America.* Vienna: Österreichischer Bundesverlag, 1968.

Stadler, F., and P. Weibl, eds. *Cultural Exodus from Austria.* 2d rev. ed. Vienna: Springer Verlag, 1995.

Szabo, F., F. Engelmann, and M. Prokop, eds. *Austrian Immigration to Canada: Selected Essays.* Ottawa: Carleton University Press, 1996.

Austro-Hungarian immigration

Austria-Hungary was a large, landlocked dynastic state situated in central and southeastern Europe; it was partitioned following World War I (1914–1918). In the great wave of European migration between 1880 and 1919, Italy and Austria-Hungary each sent more than 4 million immigrants to the United States, totaling more than one-third of the 24 million total immigrants from that period. Migration to Canada was severely restricted by German travel requirements—from whose ports almost all Austrians traveled—which made migration to the United States vastly easier. Some 200,000 Austro-Hungarians nevertheless eventually made their way to Canada between 1880 and 1914, with the vast majority being Slavs.

Austria-Hungary was a vast, multinational empire that lagged far behind western European countries in both economic development and individual freedom, thus providing impetus for the empire's Poles, Czechs, Jews, Magyars (Hungarians), Slovenes, Croatians, Slovaks, Romanians, Ruthenians, Gypsies, and Serbs to seek new opportunities in North America. The exact number of immigrants from the Austro-Hungarian Empire cannot be determined, nor can the numbers within particular ethnic groups. Not only were official records not kept in Austria-Hungary during most of the period, the nomenclature used to classify immigrants frequently changed. Also, members of various central and eastern European ethnic groups arriving in the United States or Canada were often mistaken for one another.

In the 18th century, what would become Austria-Hungary was usually referred to by its dynastic name, the Habsburg Empire, and increasingly in the 19th century as the Austrian Empire. Thus, all subjects of the Habsburg crown were properly referred to as "Austrians." With the rise in nationalistic sentiment from the early 19th century, more Austrians began to identify themselves according to their native culture and language. This growing sense of nationalism led to a number of revolutions in 1848 and eventually in 1867 to the creation of a new federal system of government in which Hungarian Austrians were given legislative equality with German Austrians. Both partners discriminated against other ethnic groups, particularly the Slavs.

Galician immigrants from the Austro-Hungarian Empire at immigration sheds in Quebec province: Peasant families such as this were considered ideal immigrants by the Canadian government during the early 20th century. Galicia was a former Austrian Crown territory, now divided between Ukraine and Poland. *(John Woodruff/National Archives of Canada/C-4745)*

Only a handful of Austrians immigrated to North America prior to the mid-19th century. When the Catholic bishop-prince of Salzburg exiled 30,000 Protestants from his lands in 1728, several hundred settled in Georgia. A few radical reformers fleeing the failed revolutions of 1848 settled in the United States as political refugees. Most were middle class and reasonably well educated and tended to cluster in New York City and St. Louis, Missouri, where there were already large German-speaking settlements. Although the official estimate that fewer than 1,000 Austrians were in America in 1850 is almost certainly wrong, it does suggest the limited migration that had taken place by that time.

By the 1870s, however, several factors led to a rapid increase in immigration. The emancipation of the peasantry beginning in 1848 led to the creation of a market economy and the potential for wage earnings and individual choices about migration. Overpopulation also contributed to the rapid increase in immigration. With a rapidly growing population, laws and inheritance patterns reduced the majority of farms to tiny plots that could barely support a family. As more agricultural workers were uprooted from the land, it became more common for them to try their hand in North America when prospects in Austrian cities failed. Finally, a heightened sense of nationalism encouraged Austro-Hungarian minorities to escape the discriminatory policies of the Austrians and Hungarians.

From 1870 to 1910, immigration increased dramatically each decade, despite restrictions on immigration propaganda. Many ethnic groups, including Poles, had high rates of return migration, suggesting immigration as a temporary economic expedient. On the other hand, German Austrians, Jews, and Czechs tended to immigrate as families and to establish permanent residence. With the United States and Austria-Hungary on opposite sides during World War I (1914–18), immigration virtually ceased. More than 100,000 Canadians of Austro-Hungarian origin were declared enemy aliens. At the end of the war, the anachronistic, multiethnic Austro-Hungarian Empire was dismembered and replaced by the successor states of Austria, Hungary, Poland, Czechoslovakia, Romania, and Yugoslavia.

See also AUSTRIAN IMMIGRATION; CROATIAN IMMIGRATION; CZECH IMMIGRATION; HUNGARIAN IMMIGRATION; JEWISH IMMIGRATION; POLISH IMMIGRATION; ROMANIAN IMMIGRATION; SERBIAN IMMIGRATION; SLOVAKIAN IMMIGRATION; SLOVENIAN IMMIGRATION.

Further Reading

Alexander, J. G. *The Immigrant Church and Community: Pittsburgh's Slovak Catholics and Lutherans, 1880–1915*. Pittsburgh, Pa.: University of Pittsburgh Press, 1987.

Avery, Donald. *Reluctant Host: Canada's Response to Immigrant Workers, 1896–1994*. Toronto: McClelland and Stewart, 1995.

Chmelar, John. "The Austrian Emigration, 1900–1914." *Perspectives in American History* 7 (1973): 275–378.

Frajlic, Frances. "Croatian Migration to and from the United States between 1900 and 1914." Ph.D. diss., New York University, 1975.

Greene, Victor. *For God and Country: The Rise of Polish and Lithuanian Ethnic Consciousness in America, 1860–1910*. Madison: State Historical Society of Wisconsin, 1975.

Habenicht, Jan. *History of Czechs in America*. 1910. Reprint, St. Paul: Geck and Slovak Genealogical Society of Minnesota, 1996.

Hoerder, Dirk, and I. Blank, eds. *Roots of the Transplanted*. New York: Columbia University Press, 1994.

Horvath, T., and G. Neyer, eds. *Auswanderung aus Österreich*. Vienna: Bohlau Verlag, 1996.

Korytova-Magstadt, Stepanka. *To Reap a Bountiful Harvest: Czech Immigration beyond the Mississippi, 1850–1900*. Iowa City, Iowa: Rudi Publishing, 1993.

Laska, V., ed. *The Czechs in America, 1633–1977: A Chronology and Fact Book*. Dobbs Ferry, N.Y.: Oceana Publications, 1978.

Lengyel, Emil. *Americans from Hungary*. Philadelphia: J. B. Lippincott, 1948.

Okey, Robin. *The Habsburg Monarchy: From Enlightenment to Eclipse*. New York: St. Martin's Press, 2000.

Prisland, M. *From Slovenia to America*. Chicago: Slovenian Women's Union of America, 1968.

Puskas, Julianna. *From Hungary to the United States (1880–1914)*. Budapest: Akademiai Kiado, 1982.

Rasporich, Anthony W. *For a Better Life: A History of the Croatians in Canada*. Toronto: McClelland and Stewart, 1982.

Schlag, William. "A Survey of Austrian Emigration to the United States." In *Österreich und die angelsächsische Welt*. Ed. Otto von Hietsch. Vienna, Austria, and Stuttgart, Germany: W. Braumüller, 1961.

Spaulding, E. Wilder. *The Quiet Invaders: The Story of the Austrian Impact upon America*. Vienna: Österreichischer Bundesverlag, 1968.

Stolarik, M. Mark. *Immigration and Urbanization: The Slovak Experience, 1870–1918*. Minneapolis, Minn.: AMS Press, 1974.

Szabo, F., F. Engelmann, and M. Prokop, eds. *Austrian Immigration to Canada*. Ottawa: Carleton University Press, 1996.

Széplaki, Joseph, ed. *The Hungarians in America, 1583–1974: A Chronology and Fact Book*. Dobbs Ferry, N.Y.: Oceana Publications, 1975.

Taylor, A. J. P. *The Habsburg Monarchy, 1809–1918: A History of the Austrian Empire and Austria-Hungary*. London: H. Hamilton, 1941.

B

Baltimore, Lord   See MARYLAND COLONY.

Baltimore, Maryland

The city of Baltimore's population has been in decline throughout much of the 20th century. While the suburban county population continues to grow with the development of the Baltimore–Washington, D.C., corridor, the city population in 2001 was 635,210, down 11.5 percent from 1990.

Baltimore became an important port of entry for immigrants during the 1820s. As the eastern terminus of the National (Cumberland) Road that ran across the Appalachian Mountains, it was a natural starting point for recently arrived immigrants seeking land in the interior of the country. Like most Atlantic seaboard cities, Baltimore received significant numbers of French exiles during the French Revolution and the early part of the ensuing revolutionary wars (1789–95). By 1860, more than one-third of the population was foreign born, including large German and Irish communities. During the great wave of new immigration between 1880 and 1920, Baltimore, and most eastern seaboard ports, received immigrants from dozens of countries, with Italian and Greek communities becoming especially prominent. Baltimore was not a popular immigrant destination after 1920.

See also MARYLAND COLONY.

Further Reading

Fein, Isaac. *The Making of an American Jewish Community: The History of Baltimore Jewry from 1773–1920.* Philadelphia: Jewish Publication Society of America, 1971.

Olesker, Michael. *Journeys to the Heart of Baltimore.* Baltimore: Johns Hopkins University Press, 2001.

Olson, Sherry H. *Baltimore: The Building of an American City.* Rev. ed. Baltimore: Johns Hopkins University Press, 1997.

Sandler, Gilbert. *Jewish Baltimore: A Family Album.* Baltimore: Johns Hopkins University Press, 2000.

Stolarik, M. Mark, ed. *Forgotten Doors: The Other Ports of Entry to the United States.* Philadelphia: Balch Institute Press, 1988.

Bangladeshi immigration

In the U.S. census of 2000 and the Canadian census of 2001, 57,412 Americans and 13,080 Canadians claimed Bangladeshi descent, though the numbers are speculative. Between 1981 and 1998, legal immigrants from Bangladesh to the United States numbered 68,000, but it was generally conceded that the actual number was twice as great. Most Bangladeshis (sometimes referred to as Bengalis or Bangalis) came as students, though many were secondary migrants from Saudi Arabia, Oman, Dubai, and Kuwait. They were concentrated in large urban areas, particularly New York City, Los Angeles, Atlanta, Georgia, and Miami, Florida. Almost 90 percent of Bangladeshi Canadians live in urban centers throughout Ontario and Quebec.

Bangladesh occupies 51,600 square miles of South Asia between 21 and 27 degrees north latitude and is almost entirely surrounded by India, to the north, east, and west. The Bay of Bengal lies to the south and Myanmar to the southeast. The land is mostly flat and lies in a wet tropical climate zone dominated by the Ganges and Brahmaputra Rivers. In 2002, the population was estimated at 131,269,860, with more than 12 million in the urban area of Dhaka. Ninety-eight percent of the population is Bengali, while the remainder is Bihari or tribal. Islam is the predominant religion and is practiced by 88 percent of the population; 11 percent are Hindus. Hindus occupied Bangladesh until the 12th century when Muslims invaded. Britain gained control of the region in the 18th century and in 1905 partitioned the region into Muslim and Hindu areas, presaging the eventual partition of India in 1947 along religious lines and dividing the Bengali people. At the time of partition, East Bengal was joined with the Muslim areas of western India, more than 1,000 miles away, to became a province of the new state of Pakistan. In 1971, civil war broke out between Pakistan and troops in the east. Pakistan surrendered after India joined the war in which 1 million died and 10 million refugees fled to India. Bangladesh's independence was declared in December 1971. During the 1970s much of the economy was nationalized as the country came under the influence of India and the Soviet Union. Following several military coups, Bangladesh was declared an Islamic republic in 1988. Three years later a parliamentary democracy was declared. Bangladesh, one of the poorest countries in the world, has been subject to many natural disasters, including a 1991 cyclone that killed more than 131,000 people. Cyclones and floods regularly displace millions in a land of high population density and low-lying land.

Bengali immigrants began arriving in the United States as early as 1887, though their numbers remained small due to discriminatory legislation. Some were Hindu and Muslim activists who fled following the British partition of the region into Hindu and Muslim zones in 1905. Almost all early immigrants were single men, many of whom married Mexican or mixed-race women. During the first wave of immigration following independence in 1971, most immigrants were well-educated professionals, fleeing the political turmoil of their country and frequently granted refugee status. As late as 1980, there were still fewer than 5,000 foreign-born Bangladeshis in the United States, though their numbers steadily increased through the end of the century. During the 1990s, the minority Chittagong Hills people were more frequent immigrants, escaping political repression in Bangladesh. Between 1992 and 2002, almost 70,000 Bangladeshis were admitted to the United States.

Throughout the 19th century many educated Bengalis became part of the British colonial establishment, playing a large role in the nationalist movement and occasionally immigrating to various parts of the empire, including Canada, though their numbers were very small. In the first decade of uncertainty following independence, fewer than 1,000 Bangladeshis immigrated to Canada, joining perhaps twice that number from the Indian state of Bengal. The number of immigrants began to rise gradually during the 1970s, then more significantly after the mid-1980s, as earlier immigrants began to sponsor their family member. Of 21,595 Bangladeshis in Canada in 2001, more than 81 percent entered the country between 1991 and 2001.

See also INDIAN IMMIGRATION; PAKISTANI IMMIGRATION; SOUTH ASIAN IMMIGRATION.

Further Reading

Baxter, Craig. *Bangladesh: From a Nation to a State.* Boulder, Colo.: Westview Press, 1997.

Buchignani, Norman, and Doreen M. Indra, with Ram Srivastava. *Continuous Journey: A Social History of South Asians in Canada.* Toronto: McClelland and Stewart, 1985.

Hossain, Mokerrom. "South Asians in Southern California: A Sociological Study of Immigrants from India, Pakistan and Bangladesh." *South Asia Bulletin* 2, no. 1 (Spring 1982): 74–83.

Jensen, Joan M. *Passage from India: Asian Indian Immigrants in North America.* New Haven, Conn.: Yale University Press, 1988.

Johnston, Hugh. *The East Indians in Canada.* Ottawa: Canadian Historical Association, 1984.

Leonard, Karen Isaksen. *South Asian Americans.* Westport, Conn.: Greenwood Press, 1997.

Novak, J. J. *Bangladesh: Reflections on the Water.* Bloomington: Indiana University Press, 1993.

Petivich, Carla. *The Expanding Landscape: South Asians in the Diaspora.* Chicago: Manohar, 1999.

Rahim, Aminur. "After the Last Journey: Some Reflections on Bangladeshi Community Life in Ontario." *Polyphony* 12, nos. 1–2 (1990): 8–11.

Sisson, R., and L. E. Rose. *War and Secession: Pakistan, India, and the Creation of Bangladesh.* Berkeley: University of California Press, 1990.

Tinker, Hugh. *The Banyan Tree: Overseas Emigrants from India, Pakistan, and Bangladesh.* New York: Oxford University Press, 1977.

Van der Veer, Peter, ed. *Nation and Migration: The Politics of Space in the South Asian Diaspora.* Philadelphia: University of Pennsylvania Press, 1995.

Barbadian immigration

As the most densely populated island nation in the Caribbean Sea, Barbados has long experienced strong demographic pressures resulting in emigration. At first, Barbadians focused on labor opportunities in the Caribbean basin; however, after World War II (1939–45), Barbadians increasingly sought access to the United States, Canada, and Great Britain. In the U.S. census of 2000 and the Canadian census of 2001, 54,509 Americans and 23,725 Canadians claimed Barbadian descent. The largest concentration in the United

States by far is in New York City; in Canada, it is in Toronto and to a lesser extent Montreal.

Barbados is an Atlantic island occupying 170 square miles of the eastern West Indies near 13 degrees north latitude. St. Lucia and St. Vincent are the nearest islands and lie to the west. The island of Barbados is somewhat mountainous and is surrounded by coral reefs. In 2002, the population of Barbados was estimated at 275,330 and was principally black. Two-thirds of the population were Protestant Christians, while a small percentage practiced Roman Catholicism. British colonists first settled Barbados in 1627, establishing plantations to take advantage of the lucrative sugar trade. The island became one of the main importers of African slaves. During the 17th and 18th centuries, planters sometimes invested their plantation wealth in the American colonies, particularly the Carolinas. Black emigration came after emancipation in 1838, though the numbers remained small until the 20th century. Barbados began to move toward independence in the 1950s and in 1958 joined nine other Caribbean dependencies to form the Federation of the West Indies within the British Commonwealth. The federation dissolved in 1962, and Barbados became fully independent in 1966.

Early immigration figures for Barbados are only estimates. Prior to the 1960s, both the United States and Canada categorized all immigrants from Caribbean basin dependencies and countries, as "West Indians." Due to the shifting political status of territories within the region during the period of decolonization (1958–83) and special international circumstances in some areas, the concept of what it meant to be West Indian shifted across time, thus making it impossible to say with certainty how many immigrants came from Barbados. Also, migration from island to island within the Caribbean was common, making statistics after the 1960s less than reliable (see WEST INDIAN IMMIGRATION).

Black Barbadians had been migrating as workers to Guyana, Panama, and Trinidad from the 1860s, but it was not until the turn of the 20th century that they came to the United States in significant numbers. Between 1900 and 1924, about 100,000 West Indians, including significant numbers of Barbadians, immigrated to the United States, many of them from the middle classes. The restrictive JOHNSON-REED ACT (1924) and economic depression in the 1930s virtually halted Barbadian immigration. Barbadian workers were among 41,000 West Indians recruited for war work after 1941, but isolationist policies of the 1950s kept immigration low until passage of the Immigration Act of 1965. It is estimated that more than 50 percent of Barbadian immigrants prior to 1965 were skilled or white-collar workers. The MCCARRAN-WALTER IMMIGRATION AND NATURALIZATION ACT of 1952 established an annual quota of only 800 for all British territories in the West Indies, including Barbados. When Barbados gained full independence from Britain in 1966, in a new wave of immigration that was dominated by workers, Barbadian immigrants continued to head to the northeast, with 73 percent of them living in Brooklyn, New York, by 1970. Though overall numbers of immigrants remained relatively small, averaging less than 2,000 per year since 1965, Barbadians were generally better educated than most Caribbean immigrants and thus fared better economically and exercised a disproportionate share of leadership. By 1990, the total number of Barbadian Americans was 33,178, with almost three-quarters of them being foreign born. Between 1992 and 2002, an average of about 800 Barbadians immigrated to the United States each year.

Restrictive elements of the IMMIGRATION ACT of 1952 in Canada excluded most black immigration, though a special program was instituted in 1955 to encourage the immigration of Barbadian and Jamaican domestic workers "of exceptional merit." Single women with no dependents, healthy, and having had at least an eighth-grade education qualified for landed immigrant status in return for a one-year commitment to domestic service. This program, continued until 1967 when the nonracial point system was introduced for determining immigrant qualifications, brought perhaps 1,000 Barbadian women to Canada.

Caribbean immigration to Canada peaked between 1973 and 1978, when West Indians composed more than 10 percent of all immigrants to Canada. A substantial number of these were Barbadians, almost all coming for economic opportunities. The proportion can be inferred from the number of immigrants living in Canada in 2001. Among almost 300,000 West Indian immigrants, Barbados had the fourth-highest number (14,650), behind Jamaica (120,210), Trinidad and Tobago (65,145), and Haiti (52,625). Of those, more than 63 percent (more than 9,000) arrived during the 1960s and 1970s; fewer than 2,000 arrived between 1991 and 2001. The proportion of women to men remains high, primarily because of the domestic workers' program of the 1950s and 1960s. There is an additional but undetermined number of Barbadians (perhaps a thousand or more) who came as part of the "double lap" migration, immigrating first from Barbados to Great Britain and then to Canada. A growing racism in Britain is often cited by "double lap" migrants as their cause for leaving.

See also IMMIGRATION REGULATIONS.

Further Reading

Beckles, Hilary McDonald. *A History of Barbados: From Amerindian Settlement to Nation-State.* Cambridge: Cambridge University Press, 1990.

Bristow, Peggy, et al., eds. *"We're Rooted Here and They Can't Pull Us Up": Essays in African Canadian Women's History.* Toronto: University of Toronto Press, 1994.

Calliste, Agnes. "Canada's Immigration Policy and Domestics from the Caribbean: The Second Domestic Scheme." In *Race, Class,*

Gender: Bonds and Barriers. Socialist Studies: A Canadian Annual, vol. 5. Ed. Jesse Vorst. Toronto: Between the Lines, 1989.

———. "Women of 'Exceptional Merit': Immigration of Caribbean Nurses to Canada." *Canadian Journal of Women and the Law* 6 (1993): 85–99.

Gmelch, G. *Double Passage: The Lives of Caribbean Migrants Abroad and Back Home.* Ann Arbor: University of Michigan Press, 1992.

Howe, G., and Don D. Marshall, eds. *The Empowering Impulse: The Nationalist Tradition of Barbados.* Kingston, Jamaica: Canoe Press, 2001.

Kasinitz, Philip. *Caribbean New York: Black Immigrants and the Politics of Race.* Ithaca, N.Y.: Cornell University Press, 1992.

Kent, David L. *Barbados and America.* Arlington, Va.: C. M. Kent, 1980.

LaBrucherie, Roger A. *A Barbados Journey.* Pine Valley, Calif.: Imagenes Press, 1985.

Levine, Barry, ed. *The Caribbean Exodus.* New York: Praeger, 1987.

Owens-Watkins, Irma. *Blood Relations.* Bloomington: University of Indiana Press, 1996.

Palmer, R. W. *Pilgrims from the Sun: West Indian Migration to America.* New York: Twayne, 1995.

Richardson, Bonham. *Caribbean Migration.* Knoxville: University of Tennessee Press, 1983.

Tennyson, Brian Douglas. *Canada and the Commonwealth Caribbean.* Lanham, Md.: University Press of America, 1988.

Walker, James W. St. G. *The West Indians in Canada.* Ottawa: Canadian Historical Association, 1984.

Westmoreland, Guy T., Jr. *West Indian Americans.* Westport, Conn.: Greenwood Press, 2001.

Winks, Robin. *Canadian-West Indian Union: A Forty-Year Minuet.* London: Athlone Press, 1968.

Barnardo, Thomas John (1845–1905) *social reformer*

Thomas John Barnardo was best known for his philanthropic work among London's destitute children. As a result of his efforts, some 20,000 HOME CHILDREN were dispatched to Canada as agricultural and domestic apprentices in order to remove them from the evils of urban London.

Barnardo was born in Dublin, Ireland. After converting to evangelical Christianity (1862), he preached in Dublin's slums. In 1866, he traveled to London to study medicine, with a view toward joining the China Inland Mission. While still in school, he was drawn to the plight of

Immigrant children from Dr. Thomas John Barnardo's homes at Landing Stage, St. John, New Brunswick, ca. 1905. Barnardo's homes for destitute children eventually brought more than 30,000 British children to Canada as apprentices between the 1880s and the 1930s. *(National Archives of Canada/PA-41785)*

London waifs and in 1867 founded the East End Juvenile Mission in Stepney. A powerful speaker, Barnardo addressed the Missionary Conference in 1867 and soon enlisted the seventh Earl of Shaftesbury and banker Robert Barclay to help establish the first of his homes for destitute children (1868), soon known as "Dr. Barnardo's homes." Barnardo abandoned his medical studies after 1870 in order to devote himself full time to the cause of homeless children. With a charter stating that "no destitute child" would ever be refused admission, by 1878 he had established 50 homes in the capital. He also was an active supporter of legislation promoting the welfare of children.

As early as 1872, Barnardo was sending destitute children to Canada through an emigration network run by a Quaker activist, Annie Macpherson. By 1881, he became convinced that emigration offered the best hope for most of London's poor children. After visiting Canada and speaking with government officials, he established homes there and arranged to apprentice thousands of slum children in rural Canadian areas. At the time of his death, more than 12,000 children were either resident in his homes or boarded out to others. It is estimated that Barnardo's homes were responsible for sending some 30,000 children to Canada. They continued to be sent to Canada until 1939, as well as to Australia into the 1960s.

Further Reading
Barnardo, Syrie Louise Elmsie. *Memoirs of the Late Dr. Barnardo.* London: Hodder and Stoughton, 1907.
Rose, June. *For the Sake of the Children: Inside Dr. Barnardo's, 120 Years of Caring for Children.* London: Hodder and Stoughton, 1987.
Williams, Arthur E. *The Adventures of Dr. Barnardo.* 3d ed. London: Allen, 1966.
Wymer, Norman. *Dr. Barnardo.* London: Oxford University Press, 1954.

Barr colony
The Barr colony was the attempt of two Anglican clergymen to establish a British colony in 1903 in remote Saskatchewan, almost 200 miles northwest of Saskatoon. Although few of the 2,000 original settlers had any agricultural experience and the administration of the colony was a disaster, the coming of the railway in 1905 guaranteed its existence.

Reverend Isaac Barr had hoped to join forces with the British colonial administrator Cecil Rhodes in extending the British Empire into western Canada (see CANADA—IMMIGRATION SURVEY AND POLICY OVERVIEW). With Rhodes's death in 1902, Barr joined Reverend George Lloyd in his plan for settling unemployed British workers and soldiers demobilized following the Boer War (1899–1902). Barr negotiated with the Canadian government to reserve a block of land for his settlers and arranged for them to be transported on the SS *Lake Manitoba,* equipped to handle less than one-third the total number of immigrants. After numerous organizational disasters, the colonists deposed Barr and elected Lloyd leader. In 1905, Saskatchewan was organized as a province of the Dominion of Canada.

Further Reading
Macdonald, Norman. *Canada: Immigration and Colonization, 1841–1903.* Toronto: Macmillan of Canada, 1966.
Timlin, Mabel. "Canada's Immigration Policy, 1896–1910." *Canadian Journal of Economics and Political Science* 26 (1960): 517–532.

Basque immigration
The Basques make up a very small proportion of European immigration to North America. In the U.S. census of 2000 and the Canadian census of 2001, 57,793 Americans and 2,715 Canadians claimed Basque descent, though the numbers probably underrepresent the actual figure. Until 1980, Basque Americans were included by the U.S. Immigration and Naturalization Service in aggregate figures for Spain and France. The majority of Basque Americans live in California. Canadian Basques are spread throughout the country. Though they traditionally worked the eastern fisheries and settled in Quebec, there is a substantial and growing community in Ontario, as well as other settlement in Newfoundland, Nova Scotia, and British Columbia.

The Basque homeland is a historic region in the western Pyrenees Mountains, extending from southwestern France to northern Spain and the Bay of Biscay. Almost 90 percent of the region is in Spain, and all but about 200,000 of almost 3 million inhabitants are on the Spanish side of the line. The Basques are racially and linguistically unlike either the French or the Spanish, and the origins of their non-Indo-European language remain a mystery. The Kingdom of Navarre was largely a Basque state and managed to maintain its independence until the 16th century, when it came under the formal control of its two large neighbors. In 1512, Spain and France signed a treaty dividing their territory. Because the Basques had resisted the Moorish invasion of the Iberian Peninsula, they were granted significant privileges that enabled them to hold important government and church positions in the Spanish colonial bureaucracy. In 1980, Spain constituted the provinces of Álava, Guipúzcoa, and Vizcaya as an autonomous community known as the Basque Country. Radical factions among the Basques were dissatisfied and began a terrorist campaign to gain complete independence.

Basques have had a tendency to migrate throughout their history, in part because of a strong seafaring tradition. They made up the largest ethnic contingent in Christopher Columbus's voyages to the New World and served routinely on crews exploring the coasts of the Americas. They also played major roles in the Spanish exploration, settlement, and governance of the Americas between the 16th and 18th centuries. The upheavals of the French Revolution and ensuing revolutionary wars (1789–1815) and Basque support for the defeated pretender to the Spanish throne, Don Carlos, led thousands more to emigrate in the 19th century; most went to South America and Mexico. Whereas the earlier Basques had generally been of aristocratic background, most of the second wave were of modest circumstances.

Basque immigration to the United States began in earnest during the California gold rush (1848), when South American Basques tried their hand in the goldfields. Most eventually went back to the sheep grazing that they had transported from the Old World to South America. By the 1870s, Basque shepherds were in every western U.S. state. Given that few Basques learned English and that most were isolated by their seminomadic work, they were often derided and exercised little political clout. They nevertheless continued to recruit family members from Europe until restrictive immigration legislation was passed in the 1920s. As a result of the Taylor Grazing Act (1934), free access to public lands was ended and with it much of the viability of Basque shepherding that depended upon the free movement of sheep from mountain pastures to valley grazing. Under the JOHNSON-REED ACT (1924), Spain's entire annual quota was reduced to only 121 immigrants, virtually ending Basque immigration. As a result of the economic dislocations of World War II (1939–45), Basque shepherds were in much demand. Under pressure from groups like the Western Range Association, special legislation was passed to exempt them from the Spanish quota, enabling more than 5,000 to come between 1957 and 1970, though many of them were required to return to Europe after three years. As the Basque economy improved in the 1970s, immigration to the Americas was not viewed as an attractive option. By the mid-1990s, the number of Basque-American shepherds had dropped from 1,500 to a few dozen. While Los Angeles was the early center of Basque settlement in the United States, by the mid-20th century Basques had spread widely throughout the grazing lands of the West. Those settling in California, Arizona, New Mexico, Colorado, Wyoming, Montana, and central Nevada tended to be from Navarra and France; those in northern Nevada, Idaho, and Oregon, principally from the Vizcaya province of Spain.

Basques were regularly fishing in Canadian waters by the early 16th century. Although hundreds of Basques worked the banks and made use of Canadian shores, there appears to have been no permanent settlements until the 1660s, when the French government founded Plaisance in Newfoundland. Inhabited mainly by Basque fishermen, the colony was handed over to the British by the Treaty of Utrecht in 1713, when most of the inhabitants moved to Île Royale (Cape Breton). Although their numbers remained small, they often came from prominent families and served

in responsible positions of government. Between 1718 and 1758, for instance, the king's commander of the Labrador coast was a Basque Canadian. Most Basques in Canada remained itinerants, however, with permanent residents of NEW FRANCE seldom numbering more than 120. Although a handful of French Basques continued to settle the Magdalen Islands and along the St. Lawrence Seaway, their numbers remained very small until early in the 20th century. In 1907, about 3,000 Basque fishermen migrated from Saint-Pierre and Miquelon to Montreal, hoping to improve their economic condition, though most eventually returned to their homeland.

Further Reading

Bélanger, René. *Les Basques dans l'estuaire du Saint-Laurent.* Montreal: Presses de l'Université du Quebec, 1971.

Clark, Robert. *The Basques: The Franco Years and Beyond.* Reno: University of Nevada Press, 1980.

Decroos, J. F. *The Long Journey: Social Integration and Ethnicity Maintenance among Urban Basques in the San Francisco Bay Region.* Reno: Basque Studies Program, University of Nevada, 1983.

Douglass, William. "The Vanishing Basque Sheepherder." *American West* 17 (1980): 30–31, 59–61.

Douglass, William, and John Bilbao. *Amerikanuak: Basques in the New World.* Reno: University of Nevada Press, 1975.

Etulain, Richard W., ed. *Portraits of Basques in the New World.* Reno: University of Nevada Press, 1999.

Irigaray, Louis, and Theodore Taylor. *A Shepherd Watches, a Shepherd Sings: Growing Up a Basque Shepherd in California's San Joaquin Valley.* Garden City, N.Y.: Doubleday and Company, 1977.

Laxalt, Robert. *Sweet Promised Land.* New York: Harper and Row, 1957.

McCall, G. E. *Basque-Americans and a Sequential Theory of Migration and Adaptation.* San Francisco: R. and E. Research Associates, 1973.

Belarusan immigration   See RUSSIAN IMMIGRATION.

Belgian immigration

Belgians were among the earliest settlers in colonial North America, although they immigrated in significant numbers only between 1820 and 1920. In the U.S. census of 2000 and the Canadian census of 2001, 360,642 Americans and 129,780 Canadians claimed Belgian descent. Because Belgians assimilated more quickly than many immigrant groups, there are few distinct Belgian communities in North America. In the United States, the greatest concentrations are in Michigan and Wisconsin. In Canada, Belgians are widely dispersed throughout the country, with Ontario having the largest provincial population and Montreal having the largest urban population.

Belgium occupies 11,700 square miles of western Europe between 49 and 52 degrees north latitude. A coastline on the North Sea forms its northern border along with the Netherlands. Germany and Luxembourg lie to the east and France to the west. The land is mostly flat. In 2002, the population of Belgium was estimated at 10,258,762, three-quarters of which practice Roman Catholicism. The remaining quarter is Protestant. Dutch-speaking Flemings make up 55 percent of the population and inhabit the north. The other major ethnic group is the French-speaking Walloons, who make up another third of the population and inhabit the southern regions. Ethnic tension continues to cause political conflict and led the parliament to federalize the government in 1993.

Belgium was first settled by Celts and then frequently conquered, beginning with the Romans under Julius Caesar. Thereafter the Franks, Burgundy, Spain, Austria, and France controlled the region until Belgium was made part of the Netherlands in 1815. In 1624, Walloon Protestants migrated to New Holland (later NEW YORK) seeking greater religious freedom, though these early colonial migrants were few. A few Belgian artisans also settled in NEW FRANCE after 1663. Belgium gained independence in 1830, when its territorial integrity was guaranteed by the major powers. Economic opportunity, however, far outweighed religious or political factors in the choice of poor Belgian farmers to emigrate. With Belgium rapidly growing and in the vanguard of the European Industrial Revolution, farmers were rapidly displaced and after 1840 were encouraged by their governments to emigrate, though more than 80 percent chose to stay in Europe prior to the 1880s. About 63,000 Belgians came to the United States before 1900 and another 75,000 between 1900 and 1920. As many as 18,000 Walloons may first have migrated to Canada before crossing over into the United States. Prior to 1910, there were fewer than 10,000 Belgians in Canada, but another 20,000 arrived before 1930, with most settling in Manitoba and the prairie provinces. In the Canadian IMMIGRATION ACT of 1869, Belgians were listed as a "preferred" group, and their farmers remained in high demand. After 1930, immigrants were more frequently artisans, skilled workers, or professionals. Though many Belgians in both the United States and Canada assimilated quickly—the Flemings with the Dutch, and the Walloons with the French and French-Canadians—a Walloon-speaking enclave remained into the 21st century in the Door Peninsula of northeastern Wisconsin. By 1860, Belgians owned 80 percent of a three-county area northeast of Green Bay.

As a result of German invasions in 1914 and 1940, small numbers of Belgians were admitted to the United States and Canada as refugees during both World War I and World War II. The disruptions of World War II led large numbers of Belgians to seek economic opportunity in North America. Between 1945 and 1975, almost 40,000 immigrated to Canada and a similar number to the United States. From the 1980s, numbers were small, generally well below quotas, and most often represent well-educated professionals seeking career opportunities. Between 1992 and 2002, Belgian immigration to the United States averaged annually a little more than 600. Of 19,765 Belgian Canadians identified in the 2001 census, almost half immigrated prior to 1961, and only 2,185 between 1991 and 2001.

Further Reading

Amato, Joseph. *Servants of the Land: God, Family and Farm: The Trinity of Belgian Economic Folkways in Southwestern Minnesota.* Marshall, Minn.: Crossings Press, 1990.

Bayer, Henry G. *The Belgians: First Settlers in New York.* New York: Devin-Adair Co., 1925.

Holand, H. *Wisconsin's Belgian Community.* Sturgeon Bay, Wis.: Door County Historical Society, 1933.

Jaenen, Cornelius J. *The Belgians in Canada.* Ottawa: Canadian Historical Association, 1991.

Kurgan, Ginetterand E. Spelkens. *Two Studies on Emigration through Antwerp to the New World.* Brussels, Belgium: Center for American Studies, 1976.

Laatsch, W. G., and C. Calkins. "Belgians in Wisconsin." In *To Build a New Land: Ethnic Landscapes in North America.* Ed. A. G. Noble. Baltimore: Johns Hopkins University Press, 1992.

Lucas, Henry. *Netherlanders in America.* Ann Arbor: University of Michigan Press, 1955.

Magee, Joan. *The Belgians in Ontario: A History.* Toronto: Dundurn, 1987.

Sabbe, Philemon D., and Leon Buyse. *Belgians in America.* Thielt, Belgium: Lannoo, 1960.

Wilson, Keith, and James B. Wyndels. *The Belgians in Manitoba.* Winnipeg: Peguis, 1976.

Bill C-55 (Canada) (1989)

With the Canadian Supreme Court's decision in *SINGH V. MINISTER OF EMPLOYMENT AND IMMIGRATION* (1985) that oral hearings were required in every case for the determination of refugee status, there was an immediate need to restructure the hearing process. The first Bill C-55 (1986), proposed as an amendment to the IMMIGRATION ACT of 1976, dramatically increased the maximum number of potential refugee-claim adjudicators. The maximum number of members of the Immigration Appeal Board (IAB) was raised from 18 to 50, and of vice-chairs from five to 13. The new administrative machinery was nevertheless unable to meet the backlog of hearings, which extended to more than three years. At the same time, many immigrants claimed refugee status in the hope that the backlog of cases might lead to grants of amnesty. There were concerns on both sides of the political spectrum, leading to a bitter and protracted debate over Canada's immigration policy. On the Right, there was widespread concern over unregulated immigration and abuse of the system; on the Left, over human rights and procedural fairness.

While the backlog of hearings mounted, there were two celebrated cases, one in which ships carrying undocumented

Tamils (1986) and Sikhs (1987) landed on Canadian shores and another concerning an influx of refugee claimants from Portugal and Turkey. A second Bill C-55 (the Refugee Reform Bill, introduced 1987) restructured the process for determining refugee status, replacing the IAB with the Immigration and Refugee Board (IRB), which had two divisions, the Immigration Appeals Division (IAD) and the Convention Refugee Determination Division (CRDD). It also provided for a two-stage hearing process. In the first stage, which sought to eliminate patently unfounded claims, a preliminary joint inquiry by an independent adjudicator and a CRDD member would first determine a claimant's admissibility. The second stage of the process involved a full hearing before two members of the CRDD. The companion Bill C-84 (introduced 1987) increased penalties for smuggling refugees, levied heavy fines for transporting undocumented aliens, and extended government powers of search, detention, and deportation. Both measures were widely opposed by liberals and more than 100 organizations, including the Canadian Civil Liberties Association, the Inter-Church Committee on Refugees, and the Canadian Bar Association. The major criticisms were that no hearing was guaranteed before the IRB at the first stage of eligibility screening and that provisions for a "safe country" while awaiting the results of the hearing were not adequate. Both measures were passed in 1988 and became effective in 1989.

Further Reading
Creese, Gillian. "The Politics of Refuges in Canada." In *Deconstructing a Nation*. Ed. Vic Satzewich. Halifax, Canada: Fernwood, 1992.

Dirks, Gerald E. *Controversy and Complexity: Canadian Immigration Policy during the 1980s.* Montreal and Kingston, Canada: McGill–Queen's University Press, 1995.

Glenn, H. Patrick. *Refugee Claims, the Canadian State and North American Regionalism in Hemispheric Integration, Migration and Human Rights.* Toronto: York University Centre for Refugee Studies, 1994.

Kelley, Ninette, and Michael Trebilcock. *The Making of the Mosaic: A History of Canadian Immigration Policy.* Toronto: University of Toronto Press, 1998.

Plaut, W. G. *Refugee Determination in Canada.* Ottawa: Minister of Supply and Services, 1985.

Bill C-86 (Canada) (1992)

One of the earliest measures designed to deal with the threat of terrorism, Bill C-86 was introduced in the House of Commons on June 16, 1992, as an alteration to the IMMIGRATION ACT of 1976. The Conservative government argued that in the post–COLD WAR era, there were few refugees from communist regimes, for whom the refugee provisions were principally designed, but many potential immigrants with ties to globalized crime syndicates and terrorist organizations. The measure gave the government

greater powers to exclude persons suspected of ties to criminal or terrorist organizations, and gave medical examiners more authority in screening those deemed medically inadmissible. It also provided for fingerprinting and videotaping of refugee hearings. In streamlining the refugee determination process, the two-stage hearing of BILL C-55 was replaced by a single hearing, with a senior immigration officer given authority to make a determination regarding refugee status. The most controversial aspect of the bill prohibited admission from a "safe" third country prepared to grant refugee status. Many groups, including B'NAI B'RITH and the Canadian Ethnocultural Council objected, fearing that political rather than humanitarian standards would be applied in determining how safe a refugee would be in another country. The government defended the provision as an encouragement to other countries to aid in the protection of refugees. Although opposition by humanitarian, religious, legal, and ethnic organizations led to a modification of some of the more stringent provisions, the bill was largely implemented as designed.

Further Reading
Badets, Jane, and Tina Chui. *Canada's Changing Immigrant Population.* Ottawa: Statistics Canada, 1994.

Kelley, Ninette, and Michael Trebilcock. *The Making of the Mosaic: A History of Canadian Immigration Policy.* Toronto: University of Toronto Press, 1998.

Stoffman, Daniel. *Toward a More Realistic Immigration Policy for Canada.* Toronto: C. D. Howe Institute, 1993.

Swan, Neil, et al. *The Economic and Social Impacts of Immigration.* Ottawa: Economic Council of Canada, 1991.

B'nai B'rith (Children of the Covenant)

B'nai B'rith is the largest Jewish service organization in the world, with 500,000 members in some 58 countries. It has traditionally promoted greater understanding of Jewish culture, a heightened sense of Jewish identity, and protection of human rights generally. Its major component organizations include the Hillel Foundation for college students, the ANTI-DEFAMATION LEAGUE (ADL), and B'nai B'rith Women.

The organization was founded by 12 German Jewish Americans in New York City in 1843 in order to protect Jewish rights around the world and to serve the greater needs of humanity. It became active in Canada in 1875. During the 19th century, members spoke out against the threatened expulsion of Jews from several states during the Civil War, raised money for cholera victims in Palestine, and raised awareness of the persecution of Jews in Romania and Russia. In the 20th century, the organization became more directly involved in public policy, especially through the activities of the ADL. B'nai B'rith regularly monitors the activities of the United Nations and the European Union

The newspaper *Social Justice*, founded by Father Charles Coughlin, railed against the "British-Jewish-Roosevelt conspiracy." His strongly anti-Semitic message earned him 30 million radio listeners in the mid-1930s, the largest radio audience in the world, and pointed to the need for organizations like B'nai B'rith. *(Photo by Dorothea Lange, 1939/Library of Congress, Prints & Photographs Division [LC-USF34-019817-E])*

was managed by the IMMIGRATION AND NATURALIZATION SERVICE (INS). The Border Patrol was established in 1924 primarily to control the entry of undocumented (illegal) aliens. The immediate impetus for its establishment was the dramatic influx of Mexicans, estimated at some 700,000, due to the Mexican Revolution (1910–17). Whereas almost all Mexican migrant labor had been temporary before, the revolution permanently displaced thousands who were prepared to stay in the United States. Although the 2,000-mile U.S.-Mexico border was the focal point of Border Patrol activity throughout much of the 20th century, the agency was responsible for approximately 250 ports of entry and more than 8,000 miles of land and sea borders. From the 1960s, it played an increasingly prominent role in the interception of Caribbean and Central American immigrants along the Gulf and Florida coasts. As the issue of illegal immigration became more highly politicized in the 1990s, the size and budget of the agency doubled, most directly through the ILLEGAL IMMIGRATION REFORM AND IMMIGRANT RESPONSIBILITY ACT (1996). With increased budgets came more sophisticated technologies, including ground sensors and infrared tracking equipment, as well as stronger permanent fences along areas of high crossing. In the 1990s, the Border Patrol made about 1.5 million arrests annually. Increased border patrols had little effect on the numbers of illegal immigrants, however, as they simply turned to more remote crossing points or paid higher prices to smugglers for riskier enterprises. In the wake of the SEPTEMBER 11, 2001, terrorist attacks, Border Patrol duties along the U.S.-Canadian border were greatly enhanced, with additional agents and funding allotted under the USA PATRIOT ACT (2001).

See also BRACERO PROGRAM; MEXICAN IMMIGRATION.

and has played a significant role in bringing Nazi war criminals to justice. The organization also funds a wide variety of humanitarian projects, include disaster relief, feeding of the hungry, and literacy programs. B'nai B'rith furthers its agenda through an extensive program of speaking and publication, including the *International Jewish Monthly*.

Further Reading
Cohen, Naomi Werner. *Encounter with Emancipation: The German Jews in the United States, 1830–1914*. Philadelphia: Jewish Publication Society of America, 1984.
Grusd, Edward E. *B'nai B'rith: The Story of a Covenant*. New York: Appleton-Century, 1966.
Moore, Deborah Dash. *B'nai B'rith and the Challenge of Ethnic Leadership*. Albany: State University of New York Press, 1981.
This is B'nai B'rith. Rev. ed. Washington, D.C.: B'nai B'rith International, 1979.

Border Patrol, U.S.

The U.S. Border Patrol is the uniformed enforcement arm of the U.S. Customs and Border Protection agency of the U.S. CITIZENSHIP AND IMMIGRATION SERVICES, in the DEPARTMENT OF HOMELAND SECURITY. Prior to 2003, it

Further Reading
Calavita, Kitty. *Inside the State: the Bracero Program, Immigration, and the I.N.S.* New York: Routledge, 1992.
Dunn, Timothy J. *The Militarization of the U.S.-Mexico Border, 1978–1992: Low-Intensity Conflict Doctrine Comes Home*. Austin: Center for Mexican-American Studies, University of Texas at Austin, 1996.
Jacobson, David. *The Immigration Reader*. Malden, Mass.: Blackwell, 1998.
Mitchell, Christopher, ed. *Western Hemisphere Immigration and United States Foreign Policy*. University Park: Pennsylvania State University Press, 1992.
Perkins, Clifford Alan, and C. L. Sonnichsen. *Border Patrol: With the U.S. Immigration Service on the Mexican Boundary, 1910–54*. El Paso: Texas Western Press, 1978.

Bosnian immigration

Bosnians began to immigrate to North America around 1900, though their numbers remained small until the breakup of Yugoslavia and the resultant civil war in the early 1990s produced a flood of refugees. In the U.S. 2000 census, of the 328,547 Americans who claimed Yugoslav descent, about 100,000 were Bosniaks (Bosnians of Muslim descent). In the 2001 Canadian census, 25,665 people claimed Bosnian descent. In both countries, the vast majority of Bosnians were refugees. The earliest Bosnian immigrants settled in Chicago, Detroit, and other industrial cities of the North. In 2000, more than 75 percent lived in Chicago, Milwaukee, and Gary, Indiana. The rapid influx of refugees after 1992 led to Bosnian settlements in New York City; St. Louis, Missouri; St. Petersburg, Florida; Chicago; Cleveland, Ohio; and Salt Lake City, Utah. Bosnian Canadians have gravitated toward Toronto and southern Ontario, mainly because of developing economic opportunities there.

The modern country of Bosnia and Herzegovina occupies 19,700 square miles of the western Balkan Peninsula along the Adriatic Sea between 42 and 45 degrees north latitude. Serbia and Montenegro lies to the east and the south, Croatia to the north and west. The land is mountainous with areas of dense forest. In 2002, the population was estimated at 3,922,205. The people are ethnically divided between Bosniaks, who make up 44 percent of the population; Serbs, 31 percent; and Croats, 17 percent. The population is similarly divided along religious lines: 43 percent Muslim, 31 percent Orthodox, and 18 percent Catholic. All groups speak similar Serbo-Croat languages. Throughout history, Bosnia and Herzegovina have been ruled both as independent provinces under larger nations and as a joint province. Bosnia was first ruled by Croatia in the 10th century, before control passed to Hungary for 200 years. The region came under Turkish rule (Ottoman Empire) from 1463 until 1878, during which time large portions of the population were converted to Islam. As the border regions of the Ottoman Empire became embroiled in international conflict during the 19th century, Catholics from Bosnia generally adopted a Croatian identity and Orthodox Christians a Serbian one, leaving Muslims as the only remaining "Bosnians." When Austria-Hungary took control of the region in 1878, Bosnia was united with Herzegovina into a single province. In 1918, Bosnia became a province of Yugoslavia until 1946 when it was again united with Herzegovina as a joint republic under the new Communist government of Josip Broz, Marshal Tito. Yugoslavia struggled economically in the 1980s, leading to increased tensions between the country's various ethnic groups and a declaration of Bosnia and Herzegovina's independence in 1991. The following year the question of independence was decided by a referendum that flung the country into a three-way ethnic civil war. Bosnian Serbs purged Bosnian Muslims from their territory, laid siege to the capital of Sarajevo, and embarked on a campaign of "ethnic cleansing." In 1994, Muslims and Croats joined in a confederation to fight the Bosnian Serbs who had taken control of most of the country. In 1995, with the help of North Atlantic Treaty Organization (NATO) air strikes, the Muslim-Croat confederation regained all but a quarter of the land. NATO stabilization forces continued into 2004 to occupy the country, which was governed as a republic under a rotating executive.

It is difficult to arrive at precise figures for Bosnian immigration. Prior to the 1990s, *Bosnian* in Yugoslavia was equated with *Muslim,* and religious categories were not used for enumeration of immigrants. Bosnians ordinarily identified themselves in political terms as Turks or Austro-Hungarians prior to World War I, or as Serbs, Croatians, or Yugoslavs after World War I. Only with the growing sense of nationalism in the wake of independence did the term *Bosnian* (meaning "from Bosnia") become widely used and finally incorporated into the record keeping of the United States and Canada.

The first Bosnian settlers to enter the United States in significant numbers were peasant farmers from the poorest areas of Herzegovina. Most settled in Chicago and other midwestern cities after 1880, where they worked on the new subway system and in other construction projects. A second group of Bosnians, implicated by their association with Serbian monarchists or the fascist Croatian Ustasha regime, immigrated to the United States in the wake of the 1946 Communist takeover of Yugoslavia. They tended to be well educated and broadly representative of the diverse Muslim society of Bosnia. The largest group of immigrants came in the wake of the 1992 war with Serbia, in which 2 million Bosnians, mostly Bosniaks, were made refugees. From only 15 immigrants in 1992, Bosnian immigration jumped dramatically as the fighting wound down, with almost 90,000 being admitted to the United States by 2002.

The first influx of Bosnians into Canada was after World War II, fleeing from the Communist regime. Although most were Muslims, they largely considered themselves Croatians of Muslim faith. By the late 1980s, there were about 1,500 Bosnian Muslims in Canada, the majority having come into the country after the mid-1960s, when Yugoslavia relaxed its emigration policies. In the wake of the "ethnic cleansing" between 1992 and 1995, thousands of refugees were admitted to Canada. Of the 25,665 Bosnian immigrants in 2001, 88 percent (22,630) arrived between 1991 and 2001.

See also AUSTRO-HUNGARIAN IMMIGRATION; CROATIAN IMMIGRATION; SERBIAN IMMIGRATION; YUGOSLAV IMMIGRATION.

Further Reading

Friedman, F. *The Bosnian Muslims: Denial of a Nation.* Boulder, Colo.: Westview Press, 1996.
"Hope for Bosnian Refugees." *New York Times,* March 10, 2000, p. A7.

Malcolm, Noel. *Bosnia: A Short History.* New York: New York University Press, 1996.
Mertus, Julie, and Jasmina Tesanovic. *The Suitcase: Refugee Voices from Bosnia and Croatia, with Contributions from over Seventy-five Refugees and Displaced People.* Berkeley: University of California Press, 1997.
Silber, Laura, and Allan Little. *Yugoslavia: Death of a Nation.* New York: Penguin, 1995.

Boston, Massachusetts

The capital of Massachusetts since colonial times, Boston has also been an important immigrant city since its founding in 1630. Although settled by Puritans, many non-Puritans chose to settle in Boston. By the early 18th century it had become a diverse commercial, fishing, and shipbuilding center in British North America. Bostonians were among the most prominent leaders of the patriot movement of the 1760s and 1770s that led to the AMERICAN REVOLUTION and the independence of the United States of America. As a thriving port of the rapidly developing new republic, Boston's population included a large number of foreign merchants and mariners, but at the turn of the 19th century, its permanent population was decidedly Anglo-Saxon. The character of the city was greatly transformed after 1830 by the influx of Irish settlers escaping economic hardship and, after 1847, the devastating effects of the potato famine. The port of Boston, which had not been a major receiving area for immigrants prior to 1847, took in 20,000 Irish immigrants annually between 1847 and 1854. By 1860, more than one-third of the population of 136,181 was foreign born, and nearly three-quarters of these were Irish. After 1880, Boston was second only to New York in number of immigrants received. It reached its peak in 1907, taking in 70,164.

Throughout the 19th century, immigrants provided the backbone for the industrial development of Boston. Before World War I (1914–18), Boston became the center of American settlement for the Irish and Albanians, with substantial communities of Armenians, Greeks, and Italians. The high percentage of immigrants led to widespread NATIVISM and discrimination. Many immigrants nevertheless improved their positions, in part because of their dominance in the hierarchy of the Catholic Church. By the 1870s, the police and fire departments were dominated by the Irish, and by the 1880s, one in four teachers was Irish. By the early 20th century, second- and third-generation Irish were moving into positions of prominence in business, public services, and politics and by the 1940s, had moved into the economic and political mainstream. After World War II (1939–45), Barbadians, Brazilians, Haitians, Hasidic Jews, Soviet Jews, Hondurans, Latvians, Lithuanians, and Panamanians established substantial communities in Boston.

Further Reading
Handlin, Oscar. *Boston's Immigrants: A Study in Acculturation.* Rev. ed. New York: Atheneum, 1968.
Levitt, Peggy. "Transnationalizing Community Development: The Case of Migration between Boston and the Dominican Republic." *Non-Profit and Voluntary Sector Quarterly* 26 (1997): 509–526.
O'Connor, Thomas H. *The Boston Irish: A Political History.* Boston: Northeastern University Press, 1995.
Stolarik, M. Mark, ed. *Forgotten Doors: The Other Ports of Entry to the United States.* Philadelphia: Balch Institute Press, 1988.
Thernstrom, Stephen. *The Other Bostonians: Poverty and Progress in the American Metropolis, 1880–1970.* Cambridge, Mass.: Harvard University Press, 1973.
———*Poverty and Progress: Social Mobility in a Nineteenth-Century American City.* Cambridge, Mass.: Harvard University Press, 1964.

Bracero Program

Bracero, the Spanish word for "manual laborer," is the name given to "temporary" Mexican laborers who entered the United States under congressional exemptions from otherwise restrictive immigration legislation. More specifically, the Bracero Program was the informal name given to the Emergency Farm Labor Program initiated in 1942 and extended until 1964 that enabled Mexican farmworkers to legally enter the United States with certain protections in order to ensure the availability of low-cost agricultural labor. At the same time that the Mexican government selected the allotted quota of workers for the Bracero Program—averaging almost 300,000 annually during the 1950s—a similar number were entering illegally and became commonly known as "wetbacks" (many having waded across the Rio Grande). Together, the legal and illegal immigrants of this period made Mexico the predominant country sending immigrants to the United States.

Mexican laborers first came to the United States in significant numbers in the first decade of the 20th century, replacing the excluded Chinese and Japanese laborers. Wartime demands for labor during World War I (1914–18) coupled with the labor needs of southwestern agriculturalists, encouraged the U.S. Congress to exempt Mexicans as temporary workers from otherwise restrictive immigrant legislation. As a result, almost 80,000 Mexicans were admitted between the creation of a "temporary" farmworkers' program in 1917 and its termination in 1922. Fewer than half of the workers returned to Mexico. Linking with networks that organized and transported the Mexican laborers, workers continued to enter the United States throughout the 1920s, with 459,000 officially recorded. Although there were no official limits on immigration from the Western Hemisphere, many Mexicans chose to bypass the official process, which since 1917 had included a literacy test; the actual number of Mexican immigrants was therefore much higher.

Most of these Mexicans worked in agriculture in either Texas or California, but their numbers were also significant in Kansas and Colorado, and migrants began to take more industrial jobs in the upper Midwest and Great Lakes region, leading to a general dispersal throughout the country. Between 1900 and the onset of the Great Depression in 1930, the number of foreign-born Mexicans in the United States rose from 100,000 to 639,000. With so many American citizens out of work, more than 500,000 Mexicans were repatriated during the 1930s. When the United States entered World War II in December 1941, the need for labor was urgent, leading to passage of the Emergency Farm Labor Program in August 1942. The Bracero Program, as it was commonly called, emerged from an agreement between the U.S. and Mexican governments with five major provisions:

1. Mexicans would not engage in military service
2. Mexicans would not suffer discrimination
3. Workers would be provided wages, transportation, living expenses, and repatriation in keeping with Mexican labor laws
4. Workers would not be eligible for jobs that would displace Americans
5. Workers would be eligible only for agricultural jobs and would be subject to deportation if they worked in any other industry

Despite wages of only 20¢ to 50¢ per day and deplorable living conditions in many areas, braceros both legal and illegal continued to come, finding the wages sufficient to enable them to send money home to their families.

The original Bracero Program ended in 1947 but was extended in various ways until 1964. During the 22 years of its existence, almost 5 million braceros worked in the United States, contributing substantially to the agricultural development of the United States and remitting more than $200 million to relatives in Mexico. The growth of liberal political power in the United States, increased mechaniza-

Company housing for Mexican migrant laborers, Corcoran, California, San Joaquin Valley, 1940 *(National Archives #NWDNS-83-G-4147b)*

tion in agriculture, and a rising demand for labor in Mexico all contributed to the ending of the program in 1964.

Further Reading

Briggs, Vernon M., Jr. "Foreign Labor Programs as an Alternative to Illegal Immigration: A Dissenting View." In *The Border That Joins: Mexican Migrants and U.S. Responsibility.* Ed. Peter G. Brown and Henry Shue. Totowa, N.J.: Rowman and Littlefield, 1983.

Calavita, Kitty. *Inside the State: The Bracero Program, Immigration, and the I.N.S.* New York: Routledge, 1992.

Driscoll, Barbara A. *The Tracks North: The Railroad Bracero Program of World War II.* Austin: University of Texas Press, 1999.

Galarza, Ernest. *Merchants of Labor: The Mexican Bracero History.* Santa Barbara, Calif.: McNally and Loftin, 1964.

Gamboa, Erasmo. *Mexican Labor and World War II: Braceros in the Pacific Northwest, 1942–1947.* Austin: University of Texas Press, 1990.

Rasmussen, Wayne D. *A History of the Emergency Farm Labor Supply Program, 1943–1945.* Washington, D.C.: GPO, 1951.

Bradford, William (1590–1656) *religious leader and colonizer*

One of the chief architects of the Pilgrim migration from Holland to Plymouth in 1620 (see PILGRIMS AND PURITANS; MASSACHUSETTS COLONY), William Bradford served as Plymouth Colony's governor between 1622 and 1656 (excepting 1633–34, 1636, 1638, and 1644). His wise leadership inspired confidence and helped ensure the survival of England's second colony in America.

Bradford was born in Austerfield, Yorkshire, into a yeoman farming family. He joined a separatist congregation as a young man and in 1608 followed John Robinson to Leyden, Holland, to avoid religious persecution by King James I. Though granted complete freedom of conscience there, the separatists feared that their families were losing their English identity and began searching for a new home. In 1617, Bradford served on a committee to arrange migration to America and in 1620 was one of 102 Pilgrims to set sail for the New World aboard the *Mayflower,* an expedition funded by an English joint-stock company with only nominal interest in the Pilgrims' religious cause. Bound with a royal patent to settle in Virginia, the Pilgrims had no legal standing in New England, where they landed as the result of a navigational error. This led Bradford and the other men in the group to sign the Mayflower Compact (November 11), establishing "a civil body politick" to protect the colony from anarchy.

After the 1621 death of John Carver, the colony's first governor, Bradford was elected to the position. As leader of a small band of poor settlers, he faced many difficulties. In 1623, he abandoned Pilgrim communalism as detrimental to initiative; in 1636, he encouraged the codification of local laws and a basic statement of rights. Bradford led the Pilgrims to honor their financial commitments, though it took more than 20 years to repay their English investors. Much of Plymouth's success owed to Bradford's religious tolerance and good relations with the native peoples of the region. His historical masterpiece, *Of Plimmoth Plantation,* is one of the most vivid accounts of early settlement in America. It was written between 1630 and 1650, but not published in full until 1856.

Further Reading

Bradford, William. *Of Plimmoth Plantation.* Ed. Charles P. Deane. Boston: Massachusetts Historical Society, 1856.

Langdon, George D. *Pilgrim Colony: A History of New Plymouth, 1620–1691.* New Haven, Conn.: Yale University Press, 1966.

Smith, Bradford. *Bradford of Plymouth.* Philadelphia: J. B. Lippincott, 1951.

Brazilian immigration

Throughout the 19th and early 20th centuries, few Brazilians immigrated to North America, as their country was actively promoting immigration to Brazil to develop the untapped resources of the country. As late as 1960, only 27,885 Americans claimed Brazilian descent. By 2000, however, the number had risen to 181,076. In 2001, 9,710 Canadians claimed Brazilian descent. Most observers place the actual figures in both countries at almost twice that number as a result of illegal immigration. New York City has the largest Brazilian population in North America, with the greatest concentration in Queens. Most Canadian Brazilians live in Toronto and southern Ontario.

Brazil occupies 3,261,200 square miles of the eastern half of South America between 5 degrees north latitude and 33 degrees south latitude. French Guiana, Suriname, Guyana, and Venezuela lie to the north; the Atlantic Ocean, to the east; Uruguay, to the south; and Colombia, Peru, Bolivia, and Paraguay to the west. The Amazon River basin is located in the northern part of the country and is densely covered in tropical forests. In the northeast, flat arable land provides a home for the majority of the estimated 174,468,575 people who live in Brazil. Over 10 million people live in both São Paulo and Rio de Janeiro. Over half the population, about 55 percent, is descended from Portuguese, German, Italian, and Spanish immigrants. About 6 percent is black, and 38 percent is of mixed black and white ancestry. Most Brazilian immigrants to North America have been of European descent, often representing the well educated seeking economic opportunities in a time of domestic economic stress. Roman Catholicism is practiced by approximately 70 percent of the population.

The Atlantic seaboard of Brazil was colonized by Portugal in the 16th century. Settlers brought African slaves into the country until 1888 when slavery was abolished. Brazil declared its independence from Portugal in 1822 and was ruled by an emperor until 1889, when a republic was proclaimed. Beginning in 1930, Brazil was ruled by military leaders, excepting a 19-year span of democratic regime from 1945 to 1964. Democracy was returned to Brazil in the presidential elections of 1985.

Immigration figures are unreliable. Prior to 1960 in the United States and 1962 in Canada, Brazilians were counted collectively as "South Americans" or in some other general category, making it impossible to distinguish exact numbers for particular countries. It has been estimated that about 50,000 Brazilians legally entered the United States prior to 1986, and about 15,000 entered Canada.

Throughout the 20th century Brazil's economy grew to become one of the largest in the world, substantially based on development of resources in the vast Amazonian rain forest. Most of the early immigration to Canada was in some way related to the close economic ties between large Canadian corporations and the developing Brazilian economy. Companies including Brascan, Alcan Aluminum, and Massey-Ferguson invested billions of dollars in Brazil in the four decades following World War II (1939–45), and Brazil remained Canada's third leading target country for investment, behind only the United States and Great Britain. By 1951, Canada was the second leading investor in Brazil, behind only the United States. When the economic boom collapsed in 1981, Canadian companies began to pull out of the country. By 1986, their share of foreign holdings there had dropped from 30 percent to 5 percent.

In the midst of considerable wealth, much of Brazil remained in poverty, even before the economic collapse of the 1980s. The return of a democratic government in 1985 made emigration easier, leading as many as 1.4 million Brazilians to leave the country between 1986 and 1990. Whereas many Brazilian immigrants prior to the mid-1980s were from the professional or upper classes, most after 1986 were small entrepreneurs or workers, seeking fresh economic opportunities. Given the continued weakness of the economy into the 21st century, many observers believe that Brazilian immigration to North America will continue to grow significantly. Some have estimated that in 2000 there were as many as 350,000 Brazilians in the United States, half of them illegally. The official government estimate of the unauthorized Brazilian resident population in 2000 was 77,000, up from 20,000 in 1990 and almost certainly significantly lower than the actual number. Between 1992 and 2002, more than 63,000 Brazilians entered the United States legally. Of Canada's 11,700 Brazilian immigrants in 2001, more than half (5,995) entered the country between 1991 and 2001. Brazilian immigration to both the United States and Canada grew from the late 1990s onward.

Further Reading
Burns, E. Bradford. *A History of Brazil.* 3d ed. New York: Columbia University Press, 1993.
Canak, W. L., ed. *Lost Promises: Debt, Austerity, and Development in Latin America.* Boulder, Colo.: Westview Press, 1989.
DaMatta, Roberto. *Carnavals, Rogues, and Heroes: An Interpretation of the Brazilian Dilemma.* Trans. John Drury. Notre Dame, Ind.: University of Notre Dame Press, 1991.
Goza, Franklin. "Brazilian Immigration to North America." *International Migration Review* 28 (Spring 1994): 136–152.
McDowall, Duncan. *The Light: Brazilian Traction, Light and Power Company Limited, 1899–1945.* Toronto: University of Toronto Press, 1988.
Margolis, Maxine L. *Little Brazil: An Ethnography of Brazilian Immigrants in New York City.* Princeton, N.J.: Princeton University Press, 1994.
———. "Transnationalism and Popular Culture: The Case of Brazilian Immigrants in the United States." *Journal of Popular Culture* 29 (1995): 29–41.

Britannia colony   See BARR COLONY.

British immigration

In the U.S. census of 2000, more than 67 million Americans claimed British descent (English, Irish, Scots, Scots-Irish, Welsh), while in the Canadian census of 2001, almost 10 million reported British ancestry. From the time of the first permanent British presence in the New World at Jamestown, Virginia, in 1607, until 1900, British immigrants outnumbered all others in the United States and Canada. And though the French took the lead in settling ACADIA and QUEBEC, the transfer of NEW FRANCE to Britain at the conclusion of the SEVEN YEARS' WAR in 1763 spelled the end of significant French immigration. Between 1783 and 1812, the lands of modern Canada were flooded with Loyalists and land seekers from the newly formed United States of America. Economic distress and famine in Ireland led to the emigration of some 5 million Irish between 1830 and 1860, most choosing to go to the United States or Canada. By the time Canada took its first post-confederation census in 1871, 26 percent of Canadians were of Scottish descent; 24 percent, Irish; and 20 percent, English. By the time other immigrant groups overtook the British in numbers immigrating to the United States, around the turn of the 20th century, the British culture pattern had been firmly established as the American model. In Canada, the early French enclave of Quebec became increasingly isolated as British customs and institutions took root throughout the remainder of Canada.

British is an imprecise but useful term to describe four major ethnic groups that inhabited the two largest of the British Isles, Britain and Ireland. In ancient times, the islands were inhabited by Celtic peoples, who were the ancestors of the Scots, Welsh, and Irish. After 500 years of Roman rule, in the fifth century, Britain was overrun by the Nordic Angles, Saxons, and Jutes, who formed the basis of the modern English peoples. In the medieval period, the islands were ruled by various Irish, English, Welsh, Scottish, and Danish (Viking) kings. During the 11th century, French-speaking Normans conquered England but were gradually absorbed into the old Anglo-Saxon traditions of the country and by the 15th century had become fully English in culture. Between the 9th and 14th centuries, English kings consolidated control over the Danes and Welsh, gained considerable influence over the Scottish monarchy, and made inroads into eastern Ireland. During the 17th century, England expanded into the New World, establishing colonies along the Atlantic seaboard of North America and throughout the Caribbean, as well as in the Indian Ocean. England also finally brought northeastern Ireland (ULSTER) under its control, formally annexing the region in 1641. As early as the 16th century, the English government began parceling out confiscated Irish lands to caretakers willing to undertake the settlement of loyal English or Scottish farmers, though their numbers remained small until the 17th century. Between 1605 and 1697, it is estimated that up to 200,000 Scots and 10,000 English resettled in Ireland. Most settlers in the early stages were poverty-stricken Lowland Scots. From the 1640s, however, an increasing number were Highland Scots.

In 1603, the Scottish and English crowns were joined under James VI of Scotland (James I of England), and by 1707, Scotland and England agreed to The Act of Union, creating a new state named Great Britain. After the disastrous loss of the thirteen colonies during the AMERICAN REVOLUTION (1775–83) and a brief period of Irish legislative independence from 1782, Ireland's parliament was abolished, in 1801 and the country was administratively united with Great Britain, forming the United Kingdom of Great Britain and Ireland. Between the late 18th and the mid-19th centuries, Britain was the leading industrial and economic power in the world, which in part led to the creation of the largest colonial empire on earth. At the start of the 20th century, Great Britain ruled Ireland, Canada, South Africa, Australia and New Zealand, much of tropical Africa, India, and island and coastal regions throughout the Atlantic and Pacific Oceans and the Caribbean and Mediterranean Seas. As a result of the Anglo-Irish War (1919–21), the Irish Free State was created in southern Ireland, nominally under British direction but gradually emerging as a fully independent nation, the Republic of Eire, by 1937. The devastation of two world wars led to a relative economic decline during the 20th century and a gradual dismemberment of the empire between the 1940s and the 1960s. The United Kingdom, or UK—often referred to simply as Britain or Great Britain—joined the European Community in 1973. The weak economy of the 1970s gave way to a booming growth in the 1980s under Prime Minister Margaret Thatcher.

There was no typical British immigrant to North America. Immigrants were English, Welsh, Scots, Scots-Irish, and Irish. Some came as proprietors or representatives of the government, some as soldiers, some as seekers of religious freedom, some as indentured servants (see INDENTURED SERVITUDE), and some as paupers. Most came to better their economic circumstances in some way, driven by overcrowding and poor economic conditions in Britain. The British came in four waves, each prompted by a peculiar set of circumstances. After unsuccessfully seeking reforms in the Church of England, about 21,000 Puritans migrated to Massachusetts, mainly from East Anglia, during the 1630s. During the mid-17th century, about 45,000 Royalists, including a large number of indentured servants, emigrated from southern England to Virginia. During the late 17th and early 18th centuries, about 23,000 settlers, many of them Quakers, emigrated from Wales and the Midlands to the Delaware Valley. Finally, in the largest migration, during the 18th century, about 250,000 north Britons and Scots-Irish immigrated, more than 100,000 of them from Ireland, many settling along the Appalachians.

It is estimated that more than 300,000 Britons immigrated to America between 1607 and 1776, and a large natural increase led to a white population of some 2 million by the time of the American Revolution, half of them English and most of the remainder Scots, Scots-Irish, or Welsh. Neither the French before 1763 nor the British in the following two decades had much success in attracting settlers to the Canadian colonies. The population of the entire Canadian region at the end of the American Revolution was about 140,000, most of whom were French and accounted for by a high rate of natural increase. But Britain's loss of the American colonies led to a dramatic demographic shift in its remaining North American colonies. Before the end of the 1780s, 40,000–50,000 Loyalists left the new republic for NOVA SCOTIA, NEW BRUNSWICK, and Quebec. In addition, another several thousand Americans seeking better farmlands moved to western Quebec. As a result of this great influx of largely English-speaking settlers, in 1791, Quebec was divided into Upper Canada (Ontario) and Lower Canada (Quebec), roughly along British and French lines of culture.

The French Revolution, French Revolutionary Wars, and Napoleonic Wars (1789–1815) led to a lull in immigration, but economic recession in England and Ireland led to a steady immigration from the 1820s, culminating in the mass migration of the 1840s and 1850s in the wake of a potato famine in Ireland. Between 1791 and 1871, the population of British North America jumped from 250,000 to more than 3 million, more than one-quarter of it Irish. By 1851, the largely British population of Upper Canada finally surpassed that of Lower Canada, and 10 years later, the

French-Canadian population of Lower Canada dipped below 80 percent.

Despite the vast influx of immigrants, emigration from Canada to the United States was a routine feature throughout the 19th century. Agricultural crises, rebellions, and the difficulty of obtaining good farmland led more than 300,000 people to migrate south of the border. The outmigration became even more pronounced after 1865. Despite government policies actively encouraging British immigration, until the turn of the 20th century, more emigrants left Canada than those who entered, and a large number of these emigrants were British. Beginning in 1880, control of immigration fell under the auspices of the Canadian high commissioner, who began to promote immigration more aggressively, sending out immigration agents, who arranged lectures and organized fairs, and advertising throughout Britain. Though less successful than hoped, the program did lead to some 600,000 British immigrants between 1867 and 1890. They continued to come in large numbers after 1890, more than 1 million between 1900 and 1914 alone. The percentage of British immigration declined to 38 percent by 1914, as larger numbers of southern and eastern Europeans chose to settle in Canada, but British immigration continued to be the largest of any country. Between 1946 and 1970, 923,930 Britons settled in Canada and another 311,911 Americans, many of British descent. After 1970, numbers declined each decade as non-European immigration took off. Between 1996 and 2000, immigration from the United Kingdom ranked 10th as a source country for immigration to Canada, averaging about 4,600 immigrants per year, about 2.2 percent of the total, although immigration dropped steadily from the 1950s. Of almost 632,000 immigrants from the United Kingdom and Ireland (Eire) in Canada in 2001, 62 percent (392,700) had entered the country before 1971.

Following the American Civil War (1861–65), the United States received a steady stream of British immigrants from both Europe and Canada. Though they constituted the largest national immigrant group by decade until 1900, their numbers peaked in three periods: from the mid-1840s to the mid-1850s, from 1863 to 1873, and from 1879 to 1890. Many were escaping famine in Ireland and economic hardship elsewhere, but the rapidly industrializing United States also lured large numbers of skilled workers, machinists, and miners to help drive industrial development. In 1860, more than half of America's foreign-born population was British. By the turn of the 20th century, British immigration to the United States was declining, as an increasing percentage of British immigrants chose to go to Canada, Australia, or New Zealand. Inexpensive land had become difficult to find and the specialized skills of British workers were less needed as industry became more mechanized. This, in conjunction with Britain's passage of the Empire Reset-

tlement Act (1922), which assisted migration within the empire, played a major role in the decline. After World War II (1939–45), British immigration to the United States rebounded, aided initially by wartime evacuations and the entry of 40,000 British war brides, and then by a burgeoning economy. Between 1950 and 1980, about 600,000 British and Irish citizens immigrated to the Unites States; about 310,000 immigrated between 1981 and 2002. Average annual immigration to the United States from the United Kingdom and Ireland (Eire) between 1992 and 2002 was almost 20,000. California became home to more British immigrants in the 1980s and 1990s than any other state, in part because of the movie, music, and computer industries centered there.

See also AMERICAN REVOLUTION AND IMMIGRATION; CANADA—IMMIGRATION SURVEY AND POLICY OVERVIEW; IRISH IMMIGRATION; SCOTTISH IMMIGRATION; UNITED STATES—IMMIGRATION SURVEY AND POLICY OVERVIEW.

Further Reading
Bailyn, Bernard. *The Peopling of British North America: An Introduction.* New York: Alfred A. Knopf, 1986.
———. *Voyagers to the West.* New York: Knopf, 1986.
Baseler, Marilyn C. *"Asylum for Mankind": America, 1607–1800.* Ithaca, N.Y.: Cornell University Press, 1998.
Berthoff, Rowland Tappan. *British Immigrants in Industrial America: 1790–1950.* Cambridge, Mass.: Harvard University Press, 1953.
Bumsted, J. M. *The People's Clearance: Highland Emigration to British North America, 1770–1815.* Edinburgh, Scotland: Edinburgh University Press, 1982.
Cressy, David. *Coming Over: Migration and Communication between England and New England in the Seventeenth Century.* Cambridge: Cambridge University Press, 1987.
Dickson, R. J. *Ulster Immigration to the United States.* London: Routledge, 1966.
Donaldson, Gordon. *The Scots Overseas.* London: R. Hale, 1966.
Erikson, Charlotte. *The Invisible Immigrants: The Adaptation of English and Scottish Immigrants in Nineteenth-Century America.* Miami, Fla.: University of Miami Press, 1972.
Erikson, Charlotte. *Leaving England: Essays on British Emigration in the Nineteenth Century.* Ithaca, N.Y.: Cornell University Press, 1994.
Fischer, David Hackett. *Albion's Seed: Four British Folkways in America.* New York: Oxford University Press, 1989.
Graham, Ian C. C. *Colonists from Scotland: Emigration to North America, 1707–1783.* Ithaca, N.Y.: Cornell University Press, 1956.
Griffin, Patrick. *The People with No Name: Ireland's Ulster Scots, America's Scots Irish, and the Creation of a British Atlantic World, 1689–1764.* Princeton, N.J.: Princeton University Press, 2001.
Johnson, Stanley. *A History of Emigration from the United Kingdom to North America, 1763–1912.* London: Routledge and Sons, 1913.
Leyburn, James G. *The Scotch-Irish: A Social History.* Chapel Hill: University of North Carolina Press, 1962.
Lines, Kenneth. *British and Canadian Immigration to the United States since 1920.* San Francisco: R. and E. Research Associates, 1978.

Lines, Kenneth. "Britons Abroad." *Economist* 325, no. 7791 (1993): 86–88.

Reid, W. Stanford. *The Scottish Tradition in Canada*. Toronto: McClelland and Stewart, 1976.

Shepperson, David. *British Emigration to North America: Projects and Opinions in the Early Victorian Period*. Oxford: Blackwell, 1957.

Van Vugt, William E. *Britain to America: The Mid-Nineteenth Century Immigrants to the United States*. Champaign, Ill.: University of Illinois Press, 1999.

Wilson, David A. *United Irishmen, United States: Immigrant Radicals in the Early Republic*. Ithaca, N.Y.: Cornell University Press, 1998.

Woods, Lawrence M. *British Gentlemen in the Wild West: The Era of the Intensely English Cowboy*. New York: Free Press, 1989.

Bulgarian immigration

There were very few Bulgarian immigrants to North America prior to the 20th century, and they never constituted a major immigrant group. In the U.S. census of 2000 and the Canadian census of 2001, only 55,489 Americans identified themselves as having Bulgarian ancestry, and only 15,195 Canadians. The earlier Bulgarian ethnic neighborhoods were in Pittsburgh, Pennsylvania, and Granite City, Illinois, while later immigrants congregated in major cities, including Detroit, New York, Chicago, and Los Angeles. Toronto was the first the choice of most Bulgarian Canadians, and in 2001 more than half lived in Ontario.

Bulgaria occupies 42,600 square miles in the eastern Balkan Peninsula along the Black Sea between 41 and 44 degrees north latitude. Romania lies to the north; Greece and Turkey, to the south; and Serbia and Montenegro and Macedonia, to the west. Several major plains dominate the landscape. In 2002, the population was estimated at 7,707,495, the majority of which are ethnically Bulgarian. A minority of Turks lives in Bulgaria and practices Islam, while most of the country adheres to Bulgarian Orthodox. Slavs first settled Bulgaria in the sixth century. In the seventh century Turkic Bulgars arrived, amalgamating with the Slavs. The nation was Christianized during the ninth century. The Ottoman Turks invaded Bulgaria at the end of the 14th century and ruled for more than 400 years. Frequent revolts led to the exile and forced migration of large number of Bulgarians to Russia, the Ukraine, Moldavia, Macedonia, Hungary, Romania, and Serbia. The first immigrants who began coming to North America just after the start of the 20th century were almost all single men who planned to return to Bulgaria after earning a stake. They worked on railroads or in other forms of migrant labor, thus not establishing large ethnic communities. Bulgaria gained territory during the Aegean War but lost it again as an ally of Germany in World War I (1914–18). In 1944, following its withdrawal from an alliance with Axis powers in World War II (1939–45), Bulgaria came under Communist rule, aided by the Soviet Union. A Communist regime remained in power until 1991 when a new constitution came into effect. Despite democratization, the economy went into a sharp decline that incited national protests in 1997.

It is extremely difficult to establish accurate immigration figures for Bulgarians. Until the early 20th century, they were often listed as Turks, Serbs, Greeks, or Macedonians, depending on the particular passport they were holding. In some periods, they were grouped with Romanians. Given the estimated numbers of Bulgarian immigrants over a century, one would expect their numbers to be much larger now. This may be explained in part by the large return migration during the Balkan Wars (1912–13) and World War I, in part by the constantly shifting boundaries throughout the region, making "nationality" a problematic category.

A handful of Bulgarian converts to Protestant Christianity immigrated to the United States during the last half of the 19th century, mainly for training, though some chose to stay. A few hundred Bulgarian farmers settled in Canada before the turn of the century. The first major wave of Bulgarian immigration, however, was sparked by the failed Ilinden revolt in Turkish Macedonia in 1903. Combined with the economic distress of native Bulgarians, 50,000 had immigrated to the United States by 1913 and perhaps 10,000 to Canada. Most Bulgarians were poor, and travel was difficult from remote regions of southeastern Europe, so their numbers never approximated those of other European groups. After World War II, a repressive Communist regime made immigration virtually impossible, sealing the borders in 1949, though several thousand Bulgarians escaped and came to the United States as refugees, often after several years in other countries. Between passage of the restrictive JOHNSON-REED ACT of 1924 and the IMMIGRATION ACT of 1965, which abolished national quotas, it is estimated that only 7,660 Bulgarians legally entered the United States, though some came illegally through Mexico. The restrictive American legislation led more Bulgarians to settle in Canada, with 8,000–10,000 immigrating during the 1920s and 1930s and several thousand more between 1945 and 1989.

With the introduction of multiparty politics in 1989, travel restrictions were eased, leading to a new period of emigration from Bulgaria. Between 1992 and 2002, more than 30,000 Bulgarians immigrated to the United States, most being skilled workers and professionals. There was a similar surge of immigration in Canada. Of 9,105 Bulgarian immigrants in Canada in 2001, 7,240 (80 percent) came between 1991 and 2001, and 62 percent of these came between 1996 and 2001.

Further Reading

Altankov, Nicolay. *The Bulgarian Americans*. Palo Alto, Calif.: Ragusan Press, 1979.

Boneva, B. "Ethnic Identities in the Making: The Case of Bulgaria." *Cultural Survival Quarterly* 19, no. 2 (1995): 76–78.

Carlson, C., and D. Allen. *The Bulgarian Americans.* New York: Chelsea House, 1990.

Christowe, Stoyan. *The Eagle and the Stork: An American Memoir.* New York: Harper's Magazine Press, 1976.

Morawska, Eva. "East Europeans on the Move." In *The Cambridge Survey of World Migration.* Cambridge: Cambridge University Press, 1996.

Paprikoff, G. *Works of Bulgarian Emigrants: An Annotated Bibliography.* Chicago: G. Paprikoff, 1985.

Petroff, L. *Sojourners and Settlers: The Macedonian Community in Toronto to 1940.* Toronto: University of Toronto Press, 1995.

Puskás, Julianna, ed. *Overseas Migration from East-Central and Southeastern Europe, 1880–1940.* Budapest: Hungarian Academy of Science, 1990.

Trajkov, V. *A History of the Bulgarian Immigration to North America.* Sofia, Bulgaria: [n.a] 1991.

Bulosan, Carlos (1911–1956) *labor activist*

Carlos Bulosan, a Filipino migrant worker, emerged as one of America's most respected writers and labor activists during the 1940s. Although he was disillusioned later in life, his novels reflect the optimism of immigrant opportunity in the United States.

Bulosan emigrated from Luzon Island in the Philippines in 1930. Having had considerable contact with Americans and having heard favorable reports from relatives and friends, he traveled to Seattle, Washington, where poverty forced him to sell his services to a labor contractor, who put him to work in the Alaskan canneries. From the dangerous first season in the canneries through a variety of low-wage agricultural jobs in Washington, California, Idaho, Montana, and Oregon, Bulosan learned firsthand the deceptiveness of the "American dream." Not only were jobs hard to find during the depression, but racial prejudice was common. Riding boxcars across the West, he witnessed the plight of African Americans, Chinese, Jews, and fellow Filipinos, who along with poor whites were struggling to make ends meet with dignity. Bulosan nevertheless met with many acts of kindness by ordinary Americans and marveled at the moral complexity of the country: "America is not a land of one race or one class of men," he wrote. "We are all Americans that have toiled and suffered and known oppression and defeat, from the first Indian that offered peace in Manhattan to the last Filipino pea pickers."

Determined to give his people a voice and to help immigrants cope with their difficulties, Bulosan expressed his experience in stories and poems. In 1934, he established the radical magazine *The New Tide* and became active in labor politics. He also published in mainstream magazines such as the *New Yorker* and *Harper's Bazaar.* In 1950, he became editor of the highly politicized yearbook of the United Cannery and Packing House Workers of America. At

Filipino agricultural laborers in a lettuce field in the Imperial Valley, California, 1939. Having come to the United States as a laborer in 1930, Carlos Bulosan became an important labor leader in the 1940s. By the 1980s, Filipinos were second only to the Chinese in overall numbers of Asian immigrants. *(Photo By Dorothea Lange/Library of Congress Prints & Photographs Division [LC-USF34-019340-E])*

the time of his death from tuberculosis in 1956, he was little known, but Filipino immigrants of the 1960s and 1970s revived interest in his life and work. Bulosan is best remembered for three semiautobiographical World War II–era works dealing with the paradox of American attitudes toward Asian immigrants: *The Voice of Bataan* (1943), *The Laughter of My Father* (1944), and *America Is in the Heart* (1946). The 1973 republication of the latter novel led to its widespread use in college classrooms and a greater appreciation for Bulosan.

See also FILIPINO IMMIGRATION.

Further Reading

Bulosan, Carlos. *America Is in the Heart: A Personal History.* New York: Harcourt, Brace, 1946.

———. *On Becoming Filipino: The Selected Writings of Carlos Bulosan.* Ed. E. San Juan, Jr. Philadelphia: Temple University Press, 1995.

Evangelista, Susan. *Carlos Bulosan and His Poetry: A Biography and Anthology.* Quezon City, Philippines: Ateneo de Manila University Press, 1985.

Lasker, Bruno. *Filipino Immigration to Continental United States and to Hawaii.* Chicago: University of Chicago Press, 1931.

Morantte, P. C. *Remembering Carlos Bulosan.* Quezon City, Philippines: New Day Publishers, 1984.

Takaki, Ronald. *Strangers from a Different Shore: A History of Asian Americans.* New York: Penguin, 1990.

Burlingame Treaty

The Burlingame Treaty between the United States and China (1868) granted "free migration and immigration" to the Chinese. Although it did not permit naturalization, it did grant Chinese immigrants most-favored-nation status regarding rights and exemptions of noncitizens.

Although emigration from China was officially forbidden, within four years of the discovery of gold in California, from 1848 to 1852, 25,000 Chinese had immigrated to California in the hope of striking it rich on "Gold Mountain." The bloody Taiping Rebellion (1850–64) against the Qing Dynasty led thousands more to seek asylum abroad. The Chinese were generally well received.

With the United States embarking on a period of rapid development of mines, railroads, and a host of associated industries in the West, Secretary of State William H. Seward sought a treaty with China that would provide as much cheap labor as possible. Negotiating for China was a highly respected former U.S. ambassador to China, Anson Burlingame, whose principal goal was to moderate Western aggression in China. In the Burlingame Treaty, signed on July 28, 1868, the United States agreed to a policy of non-interference in the development of China. The treaty also recognized "the inherent and inalienable right of man to change his home and allegiance" and provided nearly unlimited immigration of male Chinese laborers until the 1882 passage of the CHINESE EXCLUSION ACT.

Further Reading

Biggerstaff, Knight. "The Official Chinese Attitude toward the Burlingame Mission." *American Historical Review* 41 (July 1936): 682–702.

Hsu, Immanuel C. Y. *China's Entrance into the Family of Nations: The Diplomatic Phase, 1858–1880.* Cambridge, Mass.: Harvard University Press, 1998.

U.S. Congress, Senate. *Report of the Joint Special Committee to Investigate Chinese Immigration.* Report 689. Washington, D.C.: G.P.O., 1877.

Williams, F. W. *Anson Burlingame and the First Chinese Mission to Foreign Powers.* New York: Scribner's, 1912.

Cabot, John (Giovanni Caboto)

(ca. 1450–ca. 1499) *explorer*

Giovanni Caboto, one of the ablest seamen of his day, spent the last years of his life searching for a northwestern route to the Indies. Sailing under the English flag, he became the first European since the Vikings (ca. 1000) to set foot on the North American mainland. He also established English claims to what would later become Canada and the thirteen colonies.

The record of both Caboto's life and voyages is obscure, as no journals or logs have survived, and the accounts of his son, Sebastian, are questionable. He was born somewhere in Italy, becoming a Venetian citizen in 1476. An experienced sailor in the Adriatic, Mediterranean, and Red Seas, he moved to Spain around 1490, seeking support for a westward voyage. Rejected by both Spain and Portugal, he successfully gained the support of Henry VII of England in 1496 and hence became known to history as John Cabot. On May 20, 1497, he and some 20 seamen set sail from Bristol in the caravel *Matthew* and on June 22 sighted the North American continent. Landing probably either on Newfoundland or Cape Breton Island, he claimed the region for England and returned with reports of rich fishing grounds. This success ensured a second voyage with the support of both the king and local merchants. Cabot departed Bristol with five ships in May 1498. Circumstances surrounding the return of one ship, while Cabot and crews on the other four perished, remains a mystery. Evidence suggests, however, that he further explored the Newfoundland fisheries and claimed territories for England along the Atlantic seaboard as far south as the Carolinas.

Further Reading

Firstbrook, Peter. *Voyage of the Matthew.* San Francisco: KQED Books and Tapes, 1997.

Harisse, Henry. *John Cabot, the Discoverer of North America, and Sebastian, His Son.* London: B. F. Stevens, 1896.

Morison, Samuel Elliot. *The European Discovery of America: The Northern Voyages, A.D. 500–1600.* New York: Oxford University Press, 1971.

Williamson, James A. *The Cabot Voyages and Bristol Discovery under Henry VII.* Cambridge, Mass.: Harvard University Press, 1962.

California gold rush

The discovery of gold at Sutter's Mill in the Sacramento Valley of California in January 1848 enticed thousands of immigrants from around the world. Between 1848 and the granting of statehood in 1850 more than 90,000 people migrated to California, most from within the United States, but large numbers also from Mexico, Chile, Australia, and others from many regions of Europe. Almost all arrived through the port of SAN FRANCISCO, turning a sleepy village into a city of 25,000 in less than two years. Between 1850 and 1852, more than 20,000 people entered California, almost all men. By 1852, the Californian population had risen to more than 250,000. Among the immigrants were large numbers of Chinese workers from the impoverished and flood-ravaged province of Guangdong (Canton), who were especially responsive to the attractions of Gam Saan (Gold Mountain), as California was called in China. In the early years, 70 percent of Chinese immigrants were miners, though they moved into railroad construction and a variety of service industries as the placer deposits (those most easily reached with simple and inexpensive equipment) played out.

Further Reading

Almaguer, Tomas. *Racial Faultlines: The Historical Origins of White Supremacy in California.* Berkeley: University of California Press, 1994.

Brands, H. W. *The Age of Gold: The California Gold Rush and the New American Dream.* New York: Doubleday, 2002.

Johnson, Susan Lee. *Roaring Camp: The Social World of the California Gold Rush.* New York: W. W. Norton, 2000.

Liu Pei-chi. *A History of the Chinese in the United States of America, 1848–1911.* Taipei, Taiwan: Commission of Overseas Affairs, 1976.

Takaki, Ronald. *Strangers from a Different Shore: A History of Asian Americans.* New York: Penguin, 1989.

Calvert, Sir George   See MARYLAND COLONY.

Cambodian immigration

There was virtually no Cambodian immigration to North America prior to 1975. As a result of the Vietnam War (1964–1975) and subsequent regional fighting, large numbers of Cambodians were granted refugee status by both the United States and Canada. In the U.S. census of 2000 and the Canadian census of 2001, 206,052 Americans and 20,430 Canadians claimed Cambodian descent, though many working with Cambodians suggest the actual number is much higher. Almost half of all Cambodians in the United States live in California, with the largest concentrations in Long Beach and Stockton. There is also a significant population in Lowell, Massachusetts. In Canada, Cambodians were widely spread following sponsorship opportunities, though more settled in Montreal than elsewhere.

Cambodia occupies 68,100 square miles of the Indochina Peninsula in Southeast Asia between 10 and 15 degrees north latitude. Laos forms part of its northern border, together with Vietnam, which is also to its east. The Gulf of Thailand lies to the west. Forests cover most of the country including the flat areas around Tonle Sap Lake in the central region and the mountains of the southeast. In 2002, the population was estimated at 12,491,501. The Khmer ethnic group makes up 90 percent of the population, which also includes 5 percent Vietnamese and 1 percent Chinese citizens. Theravada Buddhism is practiced by 95 percent of the people. The Khmer dynasty ruled Cambodia and much of the Indochina Peninsula between the 9th and 13th centuries. France established a protectorate in the country in 1863, linking the areas of modern Vietnam, Laos, and Cambodia in the colonial territory of French Indochina. France withdrew in 1954, dividing the region into North Vietnam, South Vietnam, Cambodia, and Laos. Throughout the 1960s and 1970s, Cambodia was embroiled in COLD WAR conflicts with North and South Vietnam. When the United States pulled out of Vietnam in 1975, Cambodian Maoist insurgents, organized in a guerrilla group known as Khmer Rouge, captured the capital city of Phnom Penh. Under the leader Pol Pot, most Cambodians were driven into the countryside and brutally forced to build up agricultural surpluses. It is estimated that between 1 and 2 million died as a result of execution, starvation, or disease. In 1979, Vietnam launched a full-scale invasion of the country over border disputes, toppling the Khmer

The headline of a *Harper's Weekly* in 1877 read "Chinese immigrants at the San Francisco Custom-House." A sleepy Mexican village before the gold rush of 1848, San Francisco had a population of more than 250,000 by 1852 and quickly became the center of Chinese immigration. *(Library of Congress, Prints & Photographs Division [LC-USZ62-93673])*

Rouge. Thousands fled to Thailand, and many were eventually granted asylum in third countries. Vietnam withdrew troops in 1989, paving the way for United Nations–sponsored elections under a new constitutional monarchy. Khmer Rouge rebels continued to violently protest the government until their leader broke away to support the monarchy in 1996.

In the immediate aftermath of the Vietnam War, perhaps as many as 8,000 Cambodians eventually found their way to the United States before the end of the decade. The first widespread resettlement of Cambodian refugees in the United States began, however, in 1979. Most were resettled by voluntary agencies (VOLAGs) affiliated with churches that had first been organized in 1975 in order to deal with the massive influx of Vietnamese refugees. The VOLAGs were contracted by the U.S. government to teach English and locate sponsors who would assume responsibility for up to two years. During the 1980s, about 114,000 Cambodian refugees were resettled in the United States, with almost 70 percent coming between 1980 and 1984. The majority of refugees in both the United States and Canada were poorly educated and from rural areas. As a tenuous stability returned to Cambodia during the 1990s, immigration leveled off, averaging a little less than 2,000 per year between 1992 and 2002.

It is estimated that prior to 1975 there were only 200 Cambodians in Canada. Between 1975 and 1980 some students, diplomats, and businessmen, left in limbo by the diplomatic isolation of their country under the Khmer regime, were granted permanent resident status. Most Cambodian Canadians, however, were refugees admitted during the 1980s and early 1990s, when Canada accepted more than 18,000. The largest number entered in 1980, when 3,269 were resettled. Of the 18,740 Cambodians in Canada in 2001, 11,240 came between 1981 and 1990, and only 3,315 between 1991 and 2001.

Further Reading

Adelman, Howard. *Canada and the Indochinese Refugees*. Regina, Canada: L. A. Weigl Educational Associates, 1982.

Chan, Sucheng, ed. *Not Just Victims: Conversations with Cambodian Community Leaders in the United States*. Urbana: University of Illinois Press, 2003.

Dorais, Louis-Jacques. *The Cambodians, Laotians and Vietnamese in Canada*. Ottawa: Canadian Historical Association, 2000.

Dorais, Louis-Jacques, Lise Pilon, and Huy Nguyen. *Exile in a Cold Land*. New Haven, Conn.: Yale University Press, 1987.

Ebihara, May M., Carol A. Mortland, and Judy L. Ledgerwood, eds. *Cambodian Culture since 1975: Homeland and Exile*. Ithaca, N.Y.: Cornell University Press, 1994.

Haines, David W., ed. *Refugees as Immigrants: Cambodians, Laotians, and Vietnamese in America*. Totowa, N.J.: Rowman and Littlefield, 1989.

Hein, Jeremy. *From Vietnam, Laos and Cambodia: A Refugee Experience in the United States*. New York: Simon and Schuster, 1995.

McLellan, Janet. *Cambodian Refugees in Ontario: An Evaluation of Resettlement and Adaptation*. North York, Canada: York Lanes Press, 1995.

Mortland, Carol A. "Khmer." In *Case Studies in Diversity: Refugees in America in the 1990s*. Ed. David W. Haines. Westport, Conn.: Praeger, 1997.

O'Connor, Valerie. *The Indochina Refugee Dilemma*. Baton Rouge: Louisiana State University Press, 1990.

Rumbaut, Rubén G. "A Legacy of War: Refugees from Vietnam, Laos and Cambodia." In *Origins and Destinies: Immigration, Race and Ethnicity in America*. Eds. Silvia Pedraza and Rubén G. Rumbaut. Belmont, Calif.: Wadsworth, 1996.

Smith-Hefner, Nancy J. *Khmer American: Identity and Moral Education in a Diasporic Community*. Berkeley: University of California Press, 1999.

Welaratna, Usha. *Beyond the Killing Fields: Voices of Nine Cambodian Survivors in America*. Stanford, Calif.: Stanford University Press, 1993.

Canada—immigration survey and policy overview

Canada has frequently been referred to as "a nation of immigrants," though the percentage of immigrants has always been less than the term would suggest. In its peak periods during the 1860s and the first decade of the 20th century, the percentage was less than one-quarter of the population and since 1940 has stabilized between 16 and 18 percent. In 2001, the Canadian population of just under 30 million was 18 percent immigrant. Another consistent, related theme is the persistence of outmigration, mostly to the United States. With a few exceptions, most periods of Canadian history saw more people leaving than coming, or only modest gains in net immigration. Finally, Canadian immigration policy was until the 1970s largely exclusionary, heavily favoring immigrants from Britain, the United States, and western Europe.

Canada occupies 3,851,809 square miles of the northern reaches of the North American continent, making it by area the second largest country in the world. Most of Canada lies above the 49th parallel, northward to the Arctic Ocean and extending from the Atlantic Ocean in the east to the Pacific Ocean in the west. Difficult terrain and harsh winters have kept the Canadian population relatively small throughout its history. Parts of modern Canada were visited by the Vikings, around 1000, though they left no permanent mark on the culture. JOHN CABOT (sailing for England, 1497) and JACQUES CARTIER (French, 1534) were the next Europeans to explore the Atlantic coasts. Their claims on behalf of their respective countries laid the foundation for an intense rivalry for control of Canada, one of the hallmarks of international affairs from 1604 to 1763. British victory in the SEVEN YEARS' WAR (1756–63) guaranteed the predominance of British culture patterns, but more than 150 years of French settlement left an indelible mark, particularly in the province of QUEBEC.

Settlement of St. Croix Island (1604) and Quebec (1608) by Frenchmen Samuel de Champlain and Pierre du Gua, sieur de Monts, marked the beginning of colonization of the lands claimed for France by Cartier. Within NEW FRANCE there were three areas of settlement: ACADIA, the mainland and island areas along the Atlantic coast; LOUISIANA, the lands drained by the Mississippi, Missouri, and Ohio river valleys; and Canada, the lands on either side of the St. Lawrence Seaway and just north of the Great Lakes. Among these, only Canada, with the important settlements of Quebec and Montreal, developed a significant population. A harsh climate and continual threats from the British and the Iroquois made it difficult for private companies to attract settlers to Canada; only about 9,000 came during the entire period of French control. The principal economic activity was the fur trade, which was incompatible with family emigration and therefore left New France sparsely populated and vulnerable to the more rapidly expanding British. In 1663, Louis XIV (r. 1643–1715) made New France a royal colony but was only moderately successful at bringing in more colonists.

At the end of the Seven Years' War, Canada's French population of some 70,000 was brought under control of the British Crown, which organized the most populous areas as part of the colony of Quebec. At first administering the region under British law and denying Catholics important rights, the British further alienated their new citizens. Then, in an attempt to win support of Quebec's French-speaking population, Governor Guy Carleton, in 1774, persuaded the British parliament to pass the QUEBEC ACT, which guaranteed religious freedom to Catholics, reinstated French civil law, and extended the southern border of the province to the Ohio River, incorporating lands claimed by Virginia and Massachusetts. This marked the high point of escalating tensions with the thirteen colonies to the south that would explode into the American Revolution (1775–83) and eventually result in the loss of the colonies and trans-Appalachian regions south of the Great Lakes.

With the loss of the thirteen colonies came the migration to Canada of 40,000–50,000 United Empire Loyalists, who had refused to take up arms against the British Crown and were thus resettled at government expense, most with grants of land in NOVA SCOTIA, NEW BRUNSWICK, and western Quebec. The special provisions of the Quebec Act that had preserved the culture of the French and encouraged their loyalty, angered the new English-speaking American colonists. As a result, the British government divided the region into two colonies by the Constitutional Act of 1791. Lower Canada, roughly the modern province of Quebec, included most of the French-speaking population. There, government was based on French civil law, Catholicism, and the seigneurial system of land settlement. Upper Canada, roughly the modern province of Ontario, included most of the English-speaking population and used English law and property systems. Both colonies had weak elected assemblies. After the War of 1812 (1812–15), hard times led English, Irish, and Scottish settlers to immigrate to British North America in record numbers. Fearing loss of control of the government of Lower Canada, some French Canadians revolted in 1837, which triggered a rebellion in Upper Canada. Both rebellions were quickly quashed, and the British government unified the two Canadas into the single province of Canada (1841) (see DURHAM REPORT). This form of government did not work well, however, as the main political parties had almost equal representation in the legislature and thus had trouble forming stable ministries.

From 1848, the rapidly growing provinces in British North America won self-government and virtual control over local affairs. By the 1860s, there was general agreement on the need for a stronger central government, which led to the confederation movement. In 1867, representatives of Ontario, Quebec, New Brunswick, and Nova Scotia agreed to petition the British government for a new federal government. The British North America Act (1867) provided a parliamentary government for the new dominion, with the British monarch remaining head of state and the British government continuing to be responsible for foreign affairs until 1931, when Canada gained complete independence. In the east, PRINCE EDWARD ISLAND and NEWFOUNDLAND feared domination by the larger provinces but eventually joined the Dominion of Canada, in 1873 and in 1949, respectively. The new western provinces also joined: Manitoba in 1870, British Columbia in 1871, Alberta in 1905, and Saskatchewan in 1905. The lightly populated Northwest Territories and the Yukon Territory of the far north became part of Canada in 1870 and 1898, respectively. And finally, after 23 years of negotiation, in 1999 the territory of Nunavut was carved from the Northwest Territories as a homeland for the native Inuit peoples.

For about 30 years following confederation, more people left Canada than arrived as immigrants, most lured away by economic prospects in the rapidly industrializing United States. Sir John Macdonald, the prime minister for most of the period (1867–73 and 1878—91), valued western development as a means of strengthening the nation and actively promoted policies designed to attract immigrants. The first piece of immigrant legislation was the IMMIGRATION ACT of 1869, mainly aimed at safe travel and protection from passenger abuse. With powers granted to the cabinet by the act itself, orders-in-council could be used to amend the legislation, thus avoiding passage of completely new measures. Through such orders-in-council, classes of undesirable elements such as criminals, prostitutes, and the destitute were specified in amendments, moving Canada toward an increasingly restrictive immigration policy. In 1885, the government introduced a $50 head tax on Chinese immigrants, effectively barring widespread immigration from China.

An advertisement in Swedish for Canadian land from the first decade of the 20th century. Both Canada and the United States advertised widely for agricultural immigrants to fill their empty prairies. *(Canadian Department of the Interior/National Archives of Canada/C-132141/TC-0754)*

Still, the Canadian government was interested in European laborers, especially if they were willing to farm the western prairies. The federal government, which administered western lands under the Department of Agriculture, tried to encourage immigration with a generous homestead provision. The most important single piece of legislation was the DOMINION LANDS ACT (1872), under which any male head-of-family at least 21 years of age could obtain 160 acres of public homestead land for a $10 registration fee and six months' residence during the first three years of the claim. The policy was on the whole a failure. An average of fewer than 3,000 homesteaders per year between 1874 and 1896 took advantage of the program. Lack of railway access and isolation contributed to the slow rate of development. As the government continually sought funding for the building of the Canadian Pacific Railway, it also launched plans to sell

lands to colonization companies. The plan failed between 1874 and 1877 and again between 1881 and 1885. The generous provision of sale of land to colonization companies at $2 per acre, with the promise of a rebate once settlement and transportation links to other settlements had been established, led to little more than massive land speculation. Although 26 companies had procured grants totaling nearly 3 million acres by 1883, only one company fulfilled its agreement. More successful were group settlement plans that set aside large tracts for specific immigrant groups such as the Mennonites (see MENNONITE IMMIGRATION), Scandinavians, Icelanders (see ICELANDIC IMMIGRATION), Jews (see JEWISH IMMIGRATION), Hungarians (see HUNGARIAN IMMIGRATION), and Doukhobors.

From the mid–1890s until World War I (1914–18; see WORLD WAR I AND IMMIGRATION), favorable government policies, eastern industrialization, and the opening of the western provinces to agriculture brought 300,000–400,000 immigrants each year, most from the British Isles and central and southern Europe. This relatively open policy was nevertheless opposed by virtually all francophone nationalists in Quebec, who feared that the French minority was being deliberately swamped with English speakers. The flood of immigrants led to passage of the 1906 IMMIGRATION ACT, which greatly expanded the categories of undesirable immigrants, enhanced the power of the government to make judgments regarding deportation, and set the tone for the generally arbitrary expulsion of undesirable immigrants that characterized Canadian policy throughout much of the 20th century. In the period between World War I and World War II (1939–45; see WORLD WAR II AND IMMIGRATION), economic depression and international turmoil kept immigration low, averaging less than 20,000 per year. After the war, immigration remained a significant demographic force in the country, especially during times of international crisis. The IMMIGRATION ACT of 1952 nevertheless continued to invest the minister of citizenship and immigration with almost unlimited powers regarding immigration. As late as 1957, 95 percent of all immigrants to Canada were from Europe or the United States. That changed rapidly in the 1960s, as European countries abandoned their colonial empires in Africa and Asia and the Canadian public began to support a more active policy toward refugee resettlement. A new series of IMMIGRATION REGULATIONS in 1967 introduced for the first time the principle of nondiscrimination on the basis of race or national origin, virtually ending the "white Canada" policy that had prevailed until that time. The following year, the Union Nationale government in Quebec established its own Ministry of Immigration, which was recognized by the federal government as a result of the Couture-Cullen Agreement in 1978. As a result, Quebec gained effective control of nonsponsored immigration into the province and the right to establish its own criteria. While the goal of the federal government was increasingly multicultural in character, Quebec pursued what it called "cultural convergence," receptive to non-francophone cultures but clearly valuing maintenance of francophone predominance.

Between 1965 and 2001, European immigration to Canada dropped from 73 to 10 percent of the total. Between 1852, when Statistics Canada began publishing records, and 2001, about 16 million immigrants came to Canada. Of these, almost 2 million came in the period between 1991 and 2001, and almost two-thirds of these were from Asia, mainly from China, India, Pakistan, Korea, and the Philippines.

See also ALIEN LAND ACT; CHINESE IMMIGRATION ACT; IMMIGRATION ACT (1910); IMMIGRATION ACT (1976); IMMIGRATION AND REFUGEE PROTECTION ACT; IMMIGRATION APPEAL BOARD ACT; P.C. 695.

Further Reading

Badets, Jane, and Tina Chui. *Canada's Changing Immigrant Population.* Ottawa: Statistics Canada, 1994.

Beaujot, Roderic. *Population Change in Canada.* Toronto: McClelland and Stewart, 1991.

Behiels, Michael D. *Quebec and the Question of Immigration: From Ethnocentrism to Ethnic Pluralism, 1900–1985.* Ottawa: Canadian Historical Association, 1991.

Bumsted, J. M. *Canada's Diverse Peoples: A Reference Sourcebook.* Santa Barbara, Calif.: ABC-CLIO, 2003.

Burnet, Jean R., with Harold Palmer. *"Coming Canadians": An Introduction to a History of Canada's Peoples.* Toronto: McClelland and Stewart, 1989.

Careless, J. M. S. *Canada: A Story of Challenge.* Cambridge: Cambridge University Press, 1953.

Cowan, Helen I. *British Emigration to British North America: The First Hundred Years.* Toronto: University of Toronto Press, 1961.

Dirks, Gerald E. *Controversy and Complexity: Canadian Immigration Policy during the 1980s.* Montreal and Kingston: McGill–Queen's University Press, 1995.

Eccles, William J. *France in America.* New York: Harper & Row, 1972.

Friesen, Gerald. *The Canadian Prairies: A History.* Toronto: University of Toronto Press, 1984.

Garcia y Griego, Manuel. "Canada: Flexibility and Control in Immigration and Refugee Policy." In *Controlling Immigration: A Global Perspective.* Eds. Wayne A. Cornelius, P. L. Martin, and J. F. Hollifield. Stanford, Calif.: Stanford University Press, 1994.

Granatstein, J. L., et al. *Nation: Canada since Confederation.* 3d ed. Toronto: McGraw-Hill Ryerson, 1990.

Hansen, Marcus Lee. *The Mingling of the Canadian and American Peoples.* Vol. 1, *Historical.* New Haven, Conn.: Yale University Press; Toronto: Ryerson Press; London: Humphrey Milford, Oxford University Press; 1940.

Hawkins, Freda. *Canada and Immigration: Public Policy and Public Concern.* Montreal: McGill–Queen's University Press, 1988.

Hoerder, Dirk. *Creating Societies: Immigrant Lives in Canada.* Montreal: McGill–Queen's University Press, 1999.

Iacovetta, Franca. *A Nation of Immigrants: Women, Workers and Communities in Canadian History, 1840s–1960s.* Toronto: University of Toronto Press, 1998.

Johnson, Stanley. *A History of Emigration from the United Kingdom to North America, 1763–1912.* London: Routledge and Sons, 1913.

Kelley, Ninette, and Michael Trebilcock. *The Making of the Mosaic: A History of Canadian Immigration Policy.* Toronto: University of Toronto Press, 1998.

Knowles, Valerie. *Strangers at Our Gates: Canadian Immigration and Immigration Policy, 1540–1997.* Toronto: Dundurn Press, 1997.

Laquian, Aprodicio, and Eleanor Laquian. *Silent Debate: Asian Immigration and Racism in Canada.* Vancouver: University of British Columbia Press, 1997.

Macdonald, Norman. *Canada: Immigration and Colonization, 1841–1903.* Toronto: Macmillan of Canada, 1966.

Magocsi, Paul Robert, ed. *Encyclopedia of Canada's Peoples.* Toronto: University of Toronto Press, 1999.

Simmons, Alan B. "Latin American Migration to Canada: New Linkages in the Hemispheric Migration and Refugee Flow Systems." *International Journal* 48 (Spring 1993): 282–309.

Troper, Harold. "Canada's Immigration Policy since 1945." *International Journal* 48 (Spring 1993): 255–281.

Woodsworth, James S. *Strangers within Our Gates.* Toronto: University of Toronto Press, 1972.

Canadian immigration to the United States

From the earliest period of European settlement in North America in the 17th century, France and England both found it difficult to attract settlers to the cold northern colonies that eventually became Canada. As communities and economic opportunities grew to the south, however, Canadians, most of whom spoke English, found it relatively easy to relocate to the United States. As a result, Canada has, throughout much of its history, suffered a net loss of migration, despite the immigration of more than 16 million people between 1852 and 2002. According to the 2000 U.S. census, 647,376 Americans claimed Canadian descent, though the number clearly underrepresents those whose families once inhabited Canada. Between 1820 and 2002, more than 4.5 million Canadians immigrated to the United States, though many were born in European countries and only temporarily resided in Canada before moving on to the south.

The first major migration of Canadians to the lands of the present-day United States was in 1755, when Britain captured ACADIA from France during the ongoing colonial conflict that developed into the SEVEN YEARS' WAR (1756–63). Over the next several years, most of the French-speaking Acadians were scattered throughout Britain's southern colonies, with about 4,000 eventually settling together in LOUISIANA, where they formed a distinctive "Cajun" culture. Tensions between British North America and the thirteen American colonies that eventually won their independence in the American Revolution (1775–83) were high between 1763 and 1815. Though common cultural and economic interests fostered a gradual normalization of relations between the two countries, immigration remained small prior to the 1850s. There was still a considerable amount of good farmland in Canada, and talk of federation promoted hope for economic development in the future.

Records before the second decade of the 20th century are unreliable, but it seems that Canadian immigration to the United States rose steadily from the 1850s. Around 1860, more Canadians left the country than European and U.S. immigrants arrived. As the United States rapidly industrialized after the Civil War (1861–65), Canadians frequently took advantage of the demand for labor, moving across the international border much as if they were moving internally. French Canadians in Quebec, dissatisfied with the old siegneurial system, left en masse, usually for the textile mills of New England. Farmers dissatisfied with weather and isolation in the prairie provinces frequently sought better conditions to the south. In the 1880s alone, 390,000 immigrated to the United States. Between 1891 and 1931, another 8 million followed. Three-quarters were born in Europe, but as many as 2 million were Canadian born. By 1900, Canadian immigrants comprised 8 percent of America's foreign-born population. Even with passage of the restrictionist JOHNSON-REED ACT of 1924, Canadians were exempt and continued to come in large numbers, with almost 1 million immigrating in the 1920s. Generally, French-speaking Canadians settled in New England, while English speakers often moved to New York or California.

Canadian immigration declined during the depression and World War II era but picked up significantly during the 1950s and 1960s, as Canadians took advantage of job opportunities in a booming U.S. economy. Following passage of the IMMIGRATION AND NATIONALITY ACT of 1965, however, which established hemispheric quotas, numbers declined dramatically. Between the early 1960s and the early 1980s, the Canadian share of immigrants to the United States dropped from 12 percent to 2 percent. Still, between 1931 and 1990, about 1.4 million Canadians officially entered the United States, though the actual figures were much higher. Statistics prior to the United States census of 1910 and the Canadian census of 1911 are estimates, as Canadian movements were treated as internal migration rather than international immigration, and there were almost no regulations before 1965.

Ratification of the NORTH AMERICAN FREE TRADE AGREEMENT (NAFTA), reducing trade barriers between Canada, the United States, and Mexico, further strengthened economic ties between Canada and the United States. NAFTA stipulated that business managers and other professionals should be allowed to move more freely across borders. Between 1991 and 2002, about 185,000 Canadians came to the United States, with larger numbers than ever coming as well-paid professionals.

See also CANADA—IMMIGRATION SURVEY AND POLICY OVERVIEW; FRENCH IMMIGRATION.

Further Reading

Brault, Gerard J. *The French Canadian Heritage in New England.* Hanover, N.H.: University Press of New England; Kingston: McGill–Queen's University Press, 1986.

Chiswick, Barry R., ed. *Immigration, Language, and Ethnicity: Canada and the United States.* Washington, D.C.: AEI Press, 1992.

Ducharme, Jacques. *The Shadows of the Trees: The Story of French-Canadians in New England.* New York: Harper and Row, 1943.

Hansen, Marcus Lee, and John Bartlett Brebner. *The Mingling of the Canadian and American Peoples.* New Haven, Conn.: Yale University Press, 1940.

Lines, Kenneth. *British and Canadian Immigration to the United States since 1920.* San Francisco: R. and E. Research Associates, 1978.

Long, John F., and Edward T. Pryor, et al. *Migration between the United States and Canada.* Washington, D.C.: Current Population Reports/Statistics Canada, February 1990.

Marchand, S. A. *Arcadian Exiles in the Golden Coast of Louisiana.* New Haven, Conn.: Yale University Library, 1943.

Samuel, T. J. "Migration of Canadians to the U.S.A.: The Causes." *International Migration* 7 (1969): 106–116.

St. John-Jones, L. W. "The Exchange of Population between the U.S.A. and Canada in the 1960s." *International Migration* 11 (1973): 32–51.

Truesdell, Leon E. *The Canadian-Born in the United States, 1850–1930.* New Haven, Conn.: Yale University Press, 1943.

Vedder, R. K., and L. E. Gallaway. "Settlement Patterns of Canadian Emigrants to the U.S., 1850–1960." *Canadian Journal of Economics* 3 (1970): 476–486.

Cape Verdean immigration

Although Cape Verdeans have never constituted a large immigrant group in North America, they formed an important cog in the 19th-century Atlantic whaling industry before finally settling in New England. In the U.S. census of 2000, 77,203 Americans claimed Cape Verdean descent, though the actual figure is much higher. Most settled in Massachusetts and Rhode Island. According to the Canadian census of 2001, there were only 320 Cape Verdeans in Canada, though here too the figure is likely low. Most live in Toronto or Montreal.

Cape Verde is group of Atlantic islands occupying 1,600 square miles off the west coast of Africa between 15 and 17 degrees north latitude. The nearest countries are Mauritania and Senegal to the east. Cape Verde comprises 15 stark volcanic islands populated by an estimated 405,163 citizens. Portuguese settlers began to colonize the islands in the 15th century and soon began to import African slaves. Consequently, 70 percent of the people of Cape Verde are Creole mulattos, while Africans comprise the rest. Roman Catholicism is the principal religion. Through a regular series of droughts, imposition of the slave trade until 1878, and oppressive Portuguese labor legislation well into the 20th century, many Cape Verdeans chose to seek their fortunes at sea on American whaling ships, staying in New England to harvest cranberries. The earliest Cape Verdean settlers arrived during the mid-19th century, but they did not come in significant number until the early 20th century, when Cape Verdean seaman were routinely carrying laborers from their homeland to New Bedford, Massachusetts, and Providence, Rhode Island.

Until the restrictive EMERGENCY QUOTA ACT of 1921 and JOHNSON-REED ACT of 1924, Cape Verdeans arrived freely as Portuguese subjects. Thereafter, almost none were allowed in. During the 1920s and 1930s, many of those already in the country moved to Ohio and Michigan to work in the auto and steel industries. This situation remained until 1975 when Cape Verde gained its independence. Under provisions of the IMMIGRATION AND NATIONALITY ACT of 1965, their potential allotment of visas immediately rose from 200 to 20,000.

The number of Cape Verdeans in both the United States and Canada is significantly higher than official figures suggest for a number of reasons. Until 1975, most carried Portuguese passports, reported themselves as Portuguese, and often associated with Portuguese communities in North America. Immigration agents usually grouped them with Portuguese immigrants, or in the ambiguous "Other Atlantic Islands" category, making exact counts difficult. In census questions, some claimed African-American or African-Canadian status. With the coming of independence, a newer generation asserted their Cape Verdean identity and began to speak their native Crioulo, a distinct creolized language based on Portuguese. It has been estimated that between 43,000 and 85,000 Cape Verdeans immigrated to the United States between 1820 and 1976, based on a percentage of total Portuguese immigrants.

In North America, Cape Verdeans, were both oppressed as Africans and isolated within the black community as Roman Catholics. As a result, they tended to maintain distinct communities dominated by extended families. Given their grouping with European Portuguese immigrants prior to 1975, it is impossible to say how many Americans are descended from Cape Verdeans, but generally accepted estimates place the figure at about 400,000. About 10,000 Cape Verdeans immigrated to the United States between 1992 and 2002. The total immigrant population in Canada is a little more than 300, with about one-third coming during the 1990s.

Further Reading

Busch, B. C. "Cape Verdeans in the American Whaling and Sealing Industry, 1850–1900." *American Neptune* 25, no. 2 (1985): 104–116.

Carreira, A. *The People of the Cape Verde Islands: Exploitation and Emigration.* Trans. Christopher Fyfe. Hamden, Conn.: Archon Books, 1982.

Halter, Marilyn. *Between Race and Ethnicity: Cape Verdean American Immigration, 1860–1965.* Urbana: University of Illinois Press, 1993.

Hayden, R. C. *African-Americans and Cape Verdean–Americans in New Bedford: A History of Community and Achievement.* Boston: Select Publications, 1993.

Lobban, R. A. *Cape Verde: Crioulo Colony to Independent Nation.* Boulder, Colo.: Westview Press, 1995.

Machado, D. M. "Cape Verdean Americans." In *Hidden Minorities: The Persistence of Ethnicity in American Life.* Ed. J. H. Rollins. Washington, D.C.: University Press of America, 1981.

Carpatho-Rusyn immigration   See RUSSIAN IMMIGRATION.

Carolina colonies

The Carolina colony, later divided, was the gift of Charles II (r. 1660–85) to eight loyal courtiers who had followed him into exile during the English Civil War. Led by Sir John Colleton, on March 24, 1663, the "true and absolute Lords Proprietors of Carolina" were granted proprietary control of all lands between the VIRGINIA COLONY and Florida. There, they developed a plantation society, heavily dependent on slavery, producing wood, naval stores, hides, rice, and tobacco for the international market. By the mid-18th century, slaves made up the majority of South Carolina's population. A policy of religious toleration led to a diverse European population throughout the Carolinas, including large numbers of Scots (15 percent of the European population), Irish and Scots Irish (11 percent), Germans (5 percent), and French Huguenots (3 percent).

The earliest attempt to settle in the Carolinas was the ill-fated ROANOKE COLONY venture of 1584–90. Taking up land bestowed by Queen Elizabeth, SIR WALTER RALEIGH carefully planned the first English colony in territory claimed by Spain but far north of any area of actual settlement. Located inside the Outer Banks, Roanoke was difficult to reach, requiring navigation of treacherous Cape Hatteras. Relations with the native peoples were bad from the beginning. When Sir Francis Drake visited the colony in 1586, the remaining settlers determined to return to England with him. A second attempt by Raleigh in 1587 fared worse. Diplomatic tensions and war with Spain kept any English ships from visiting Roanoke until 1590. By then, the colony had been deserted, and the settlers either killed or absorbed into the local population.

Hoping to grow rich through land sales and rents, the Lords Proprietors of Carolina subdivided their grant into the Albemarle region, bordering Virginia; the Cape Fear region, along the central coast; and Port Royal, in present-day South Carolina. With personal investment by Carolina proprietors and the vigorous leadership of Anthony Ashley Cooper (later the earl of Shaftesbury), they instituted the Fundamental Constitutions of Carolina, which provided for a local aristocracy. Those purchasing large tracts of land received a title and the right to a seat on the Council of Nobles. Smaller landowners sat in an assembly with the right to accept or reject council bills. Unsuited to the wilds of a new territory where small farmers were needed to work the land, the system attracted few settlers. As a result, the early economy of the colony was based on logging and a vigorous trade with local tribes, especially in deerskins. Europeans introduced firearms into an already volatile system of tribal conflict and encouraged the capture of Native Americans who were then taken into slavery. By 1708, there were 1,400 Indian slaves, and 2,900 African slaves in the Carolinas.

Overpopulation in the British sugar island of Barbados eventually led to the creation of a successful plantation economy along Carolina's southern coast, most notably growing indigo and rice for the cash market. Almost half the white inhabitants of the Port Royal region had emigrated from Barbados, many of them wealthy younger sons who brought experience and slaves, as well as a political independence that separated them from the early proprietors. As a result, although the economy flourished, the government was in disarray. By 1719, an increasingly representative form of local government had asserted itself, and the last proprietary governor was overthrown. Ten years later, King George I (r. 1714–27) established the royal colonies of North Carolina and South Carolina.

The revocation in 1685 of the Edict of Nantes, which had granted a degree of religious tolerance to French Protestants (Huguenots), led to the settlement of about 500 Huguenots in the Carolina colonies. After attempts to raise silkworms and grapes failed, many settled in and around Charleston, becoming merchants and businessmen. Most did well economically and by 1750 were indistinguishable, except for surnames, from their English counterparts. The Scots-Irish often came as indentured servants (see INDENTURED SERVITUDE) and tended to settle in the backcountry when their service was completed. The War of the Spanish Succession (1701–14) and the severe winter of 1708–09 drove thousands of Germans to migrate, first to England as refugees, then to the British colonies, including about 600 to the backcountry of the Carolinas. On the frontier, the clannish Scots-Irish and Germans were joined from the 1740s by others who migrated from northern colonies down the Great Philadelphia Road (also known as the Great Wagon Road), which ran from Philadelphia to Camden, South Carolina. It is estimated that by the time of the American Revolution (1775–83), the Scots-Irish may have comprised a majority of the 140,000 inhabitants of the Carolina backcountry. The religious toleration of the Carolinas also attracted a variety of migrant groups seeking religious freedom as well as land, including Baptists, Quakers, Presbyterians, Moravians, and members of the Reformed Church.

Further Reading

Hofstadter, Richard. *America at 1750: A Social Portrait.* New York: Alfred A. Knopf, 1971.

Lefler, Hugh T., and William S. Powell. *Colonial North Carolina: A History.* New York: Scribner's, 1973.

Sirmans, M. Eugene. *Colonial South Carolina: A Political History, 1663–1763.* Chapel Hill: Institute of Early American History and Culture, University of North Carolina Press, 1966.

Unser, Daniel H., Jr. *Indians, Settlers, and Slaves in a Frontier Exchange Economy.* Chapel Hill: Institute of Early American History and Culture, University of North Carolina Press, 1992.

Weir, Robert M. *Colonial South Carolina: A History.* Millwood, N.Y.: KTO, 1983.

Wood, Peter H., et al., eds. *Powhatan's Mantle: Indians in the Colonial Southeast.* Lincoln: University of Nebraska Press, 1989.

Carriage of Passengers Act (United States)
(1855)

The rapid influx of Irish, German, and Chinese immigrants into the United States after 1845 was accompanied by a series of steamship disasters and the prevalence of cholera, typhus, and smallpox among arriving immigrants. In late 1853, New York senator Hamilton Fish, a Republican, called for a select committee to "consider the causes and the extent of the sickness and mortality prevailing on board of emigrant ships" and to determine what further legislation might be necessary.

With the support of President Franklin Pierce, Congress repealed the MANIFEST OF IMMIGRANTS ACT (1819) and subsequent measures relating to transportation of immigrants, replacing them on March 3, 1855, with "an act to extend the provisions of all laws now in force relating to the carriage of passengers in merchant-vessels, and the regulation thereof." Its main provisions included

1. Limitation of passengers, with no more than one person per two tons of ship burden
2. Requirement of ample deck space—14–18 square feet per passenger, depending on the height between decks—and adequate berths
3. Requirement of ample foodstuffs, including the following per each passenger: 20 pounds of "good navy bread," 15 pounds of rice, 15 pounds of oatmeal, 10 pounds of wheat flour, 15 pounds of peas and beans, 20 pounds of potatoes, one pint of vinegar, 60 gallons of fresh water, 10 pounds of salted pork, and 10 pounds of salt beef (with substitutions allowed where specific provisions could not be secured "on reasonable terms")
4. Requirement of the captain to maintain sanitary conditions on board
5. Extension of all provisions to steamships, superseding the Steamship Act of August 13, 1852

With advances in shipbuilding technology greatly increasing the size of ships, modifications in the space and food requirements were made in a carriage of passengers act of July 22, 1882.

Further Reading

Bromwell, William J. *History of Immigration to the United States, 1819–1855.* 1855. Reprint, New York: Augustus M. Kelley, 1969.

Hutchinson, E. P. *Legislative History of American Immigration Policy, 1798–1965.* Philadelphia: University of Pennsylvania Press, 1981.

Cartier, Jacques (1491–1557) *explorer*

The French king Francis I's (r. 1515–47) search for a seasoned mariner to lead his country's challenge to Spain and Portugal in the recently discovered Americas brought to the forefront Jacques Cartier. Although Cartier found neither gold nor the Northwest Passage to Asia, his three voyages to the Americas between 1534 and 1542 firmly established French claims to Canada (see CANADA—IMMIGRATION SURVEY AND POLICY REVIEW).

Cartier was raised in the bustling seaport of Saint-Malo in northern France, and had almost certainly traveled to the Americas as a young man, perhaps in the company of Giovanni da Verrazano. Cartier first sailed from Saint-Malo with two ships and 61 men in April 1534. Exploring the coasts of northern NEWFOUNDLAND, Anticosta Island, and PRINCE EDWARD ISLAND, he claimed the region for France and returned to a hero's welcome. Freshly outfitted with three ships, in May 1535, he returned to the New World to explore the St. Lawrence River, certain that he had found the fabled western passage through the continent. Native tales of the fabulous wealth of "Saguenay" led him further inland, where he established French claims to the areas surrounding the future cities of Quebec and MONTREAL, in present-day QUEBEC province. With the kidnapped Huron chief Donnaconna personally conveying details of the mysterious land of Saguenay to Francis I, in 1541, the French king outfitted Cartier for a third journey, with five ships and 1,000 men. The settlement of Charlesbourg Royal was founded in 1542, but native opposition and infighting between Cartier and Jean-François de La Rocque de Roberval, a late royal appointment as Cartier's nominal superior, led to abandonment of the settlement in 1543. Although Francis I was disappointed to find no wealth in NEW FRANCE, Cartier's explorations led to further development 50 years later.

Further Reading

Blashfield, Jean F. *Cartier: Jacques Cartier's Search for the Northwest Passage.* Minneapolis, Minn.: Compass Point Books, 2002.

Cartier, Jacques. *The Voyages of Jacques Cartier.* Introduction by Ramsay Cook. Toronto: University of Toronto Press, 1993.

Trudel, Marcel. *The Beginnings of New France, 1524–1663.* Toronto: McClelland and Stewart, 1972.

Vachon, André. *Dreams of Empire: Canada before 1700.* Ottawa: Public Archives of Canada, 1982.

Castle Garden

Castle Garden was the first formal immigrant depot of the United States, operating from 1855 until 1892 at the southern tip of New York's Manhattan Island. Built as a fort prior to the War of 1812, it soon became an entertainment center, most famous for hosting the Swedish singer Jenny Lind in 1850. In 1855, the New York State Board of Commissioners of Immigration converted it into a processing station for immigrants arriving at the city (see NEW YORK, NEW YORK).

Prior to 1855, immigrants arrived haphazardly at a variety of New York City docks. The chaotic scenes there, as bags were sorted and directions given in many languages, reflected the disorganized state of immigration policy. Only in 1847 was a state board of immigration established, hospitals and temporary quarters established on the city's Ward's Island, and an employment office established on Canal Street. Still, in 1849, the courts judged immigrants to be a type of "foreign commerce" and hence left their care to the Treasury Department. With neither a federal immigration bureaucracy nor an official national policy, local port officials kept few records, and those they did keep were often inaccurate. As hundreds of thousands of immigrants, largely from Ireland and Germany, poured into New York City every year after the mid-1840s, the state commissioners realized that a better system was needed for tracking immigrant entry, guarding against disease, and protecting newly arrived immigrants from exploitation.

After 1855, immigrants were ferried from their ships to Castle Garden, where immigration officers counted them and obtained information regarding age, religion, occupation, and value of personal property. Immigrants were required to bathe with soap and water. And though few ever received direct financial assistance, they were able to exchange money, purchase food at reasonable rates (kitchen facilities were provided), buy railroad tickets, and receive job advice, all relatively free from the influence of predatory "providers." There was no formal housing there, but immigrants were provided with temporary shelter. During the Civil War (1861—65), Union recruiting officers met arrivals at Castle Garden, offering large bonuses and other incentives for joining the army.

As the volume of immigration increased dramatically in the 1870s, states receiving large numbers of immigrants petitioned the federal government for revision of immigration policies. State and local authorities had earlier levied a head tax on immigrants to provide services, but this had been declared unconstitutional in the Passenger Cases of

An illustration from *Harper's Weekly,* May 29, 1880, depicts immigrants landing at Castle Garden, New York City. From 1855, Castle Garden served as the main immigration depot for the United States until Ellis Island was opened in 1892. *(Library of Congress, Prints & Photographs Division [LC-USZ62-99403])*

1849. An alternate system was devised putting more of the burden on transporters, allowing shipmasters to either post bonds or pay commutation fees for healthy passengers. This, too, the courts declared unconstitutional, in 1876, on the grounds it interfered with "foreign commerce," an area reserved to congressional oversight. After years of appeals, New York State officials threatened to close Castle Garden unless the federal government agreed to fund its operations. As a result, in 1882 a head tax of 50¢ was assessed on every immigrant in order to meet the initial costs of reception. New federal guidelines in 1890 requiring more extensive physical and mental examinations, along with the massive influx of immigrants—almost 5 million coming through New York alone during the 1880s—led the federal government to establish a new immigrant depot at ELLIS ISLAND.

Further Reading

Andrews, William Loring. *The Iconography of the Battery and Castle Garden.* New York: Charles Scribner's Sons, 1901.

Hall, A. Oakey. *When Jenny Lind Sang in Castle Garden.* New York: Ladies' Home Journal, 1896.

Novatny, Ann. *Strangers at the Door: Ellis Island, Castle Garden, and the Great Migration to America.* Riverside, Conn.: Chatham Press, 1972.

Svejda, George J. *Castle Garden as an Immigrant Depot.* Washington, D.C.: Division of History, Office of Archaeology and Historic Preservation, 1968.

census and immigration

The United States and Canada each conduct a national census every 10 years for the purpose of gaining reliable statistics on their evolving populations. These statistics are used to produce a variety of official population studies and are made available to government agencies, scholars, businesses, health care officials, and others interested in better understanding population composition in order to provide governmental, social, or commercial services. The statistics are particularly relevant to the formulation of government immigration policies and to the development of social services for immigrants, who are likely to be in greater need of those services than the general population is. The most recent census taken in the United States was in March 2000,

CHAMPLAIN, SAMUEL DE 53

and in Canada, in May 2001. In both countries, it is illegal for anyone associated with census taking to reveal information about individuals.

U.S. Census

The first U.S. national census was taken in 1790, as mandated by Article 1, Section 2 of the U.S. Constitution, for the purpose of apportioning representation to the various states. As the country grew and became more complex, new categories were added to the census. In 1850, questions were first included on a wide array of social issues, including "place of birth." In 1850, the foreign-born population was 9.7 percent. During peak years of immigration (1860–1920), it fluctuated between 13 and 15 percent of the population. In 1970, due to restrictive policies, the foreign-born population reached an all-time low at 4.7 percent. The unexpected and rapid increase in the NEW IMMIGRATION from Asia and Latin America since 1970 steadily drove the percentage higher. In 2000, the 28.4 million foreign-born Americans represented 10.4 percent of the total population. Data on Americans born outside the United States are generally comparable between 1850 and 2000, though there are certain inherent weaknesses and refinements that must be taken into account. For instance, in 1890, children born in foreign countries who had an American citizen as a parent began to be counted as "native" rather than "foreign born." Also, evolving political boundaries, particularly in Europe, have made it difficult to know the exact ethnicity of many immigrants, or the modern country to which one might assign one's ancestry.

Canadian Census

The first Canadian national census, provided for under Section 8 of the Constitution Act (British North America Act) of 1867, was taken in 1871, primarily to apportion parliamentary representation. From the first census, ancestral origins were recorded. In 1881, British Columbia, Manitoba, and Prince Edward Island were added to the four original provinces of Nova Scotia, New Brunswick, Quebec, and Ontario. New questions relating to religion, birthplace, citizenship, and period of immigration were added in 1901. The census was initially the responsibility of the Ministry of Agriculture and then the Ministry of Trade and Commerce (1912) before the Dominion Bureau of Statistics was created in 1918. In order to mark economic development, the Bureau of Statistics introduced a simplified quinquennial (every five years) census in 1956. In 1971, respondents were asked to complete their own census questionnaire for the first time, and the Dominion Bureau of Statistics was renamed Statistics Canada.

See also RACIAL AND ETHNIC CATEGORIES.

Further Reading

Anderson, Margo J. *The American Census: A Social History.* New Haven, Conn.: Yale University Press, 1988.
——, ed. *Encyclopedia of the U.S. Census.* Washington, D.C.: Congressional Quarterly Press, 2000.
Bryant, Barbara Everett, and William Dunn. *Moving Power and Money: The Politics of Census Taking.* Ithaca, N.Y.: New Strategic Publications, 1995.
Edmonston, Barry, and Charles Schultze, eds. *Modernizing the U.S. Census.* Washington, D.C.: National Academy Press, 1995.
"History of the Census of Canada." Statistics Canada. Available online. URL: http://www.statcan.ca/english/census96/history. htm. Modified July 5, 2001.
Kent, Mary M., et al. "First Glimpses from the 2000 U.S. Census." *Population Bulletin* 56, no. 2 (June 2001).
Robey, Bryant. "Two Hundred Years and Counting: The 1990 Census." *Population Bulletin* 44, no. 1 (1989).
Rodriguez, Clara E. *Changing Race: Latinos, the Census, and the History of Ethnicity in the United States.* New York: New York University Press, 2000.
Skerry, Peter. *Counting on the Census? Race, Group Identity, and the Evasion of Politics.* Washington, D.C.: Brookings Institution, 2000.
U.S. Census Bureau. Available online. URL: http://www.census.gov.
U.S. Office of Management and Budget. "Revisions to the Standards for the Classification of Federal Data on Race and Ethnicity." *Federal Register* 62, no. 210 (October 30, 1997): 58,782–58,790.

Champlain, Samuel de (ca. 1567–1635) *explorer, businessman*

Samuel de Champlain was the principal founder of NEW FRANCE and the first European explorer of much of modern Quebec and Ontario.

Champlain was born in the Atlantic French seaport of Brouage. Little is known of his early life, but he became a devout Roman Catholic as French Catholics and Huguenots battled for his hometown. Champlain's skill as a cartographer, artist, and author of his first journey to the Americas with a Spanish expedition in 1599 led to his commission by Henry IV, king of France (r. 1589–1610) to establish a French colony in North America. Although JACQUES CARTIER had claimed ACADIA and the St. Lawrence Seaway in the 1530s, the bitter winters had restricted French interest to fishing along coastal waters. Champlain founded ill-fated colonies at St. Croix Island (1604) and Port Royal, NOVA SCOTIA (1606), before establishing the first permanent French settlement in North America at Quebec (1608), where only eight of the original 24 Frenchmen survived the first winter. In 1627, he became head of the COMPAGNIE DE LA NOUVELLE FRANCE, often known as the Company of One Hundred Associates, which was granted title to all French lands and a monopoly on all economic activity except fishing, in return for settling 4,000 French Catholics in Canada. Although the fur trade flourished, Frenchmen paid little attention to Champlain's calls to establish farming settlements. At the time of his death in 1635, the population of Quebec was only about 200. His own wife had returned to France after four years, disliking the hardship and isolation. For more than a quarter of a century, Champlain worked strenuously to hold Canada against British incursions, to maintain close relations with the Algonquians and Hurons, and to convert the Native Americans to Christianity.

Further Reading

Bishop, Martin. *Champlain: The Life of Fortitude.* 1948. Reprint, New York: Octagon Books, 1979.

Heidenreich, C. E. *Explorations and Mapping of Samuel de Champlain, 1603–1632.* Toronto: B. V. Gutsell, 1976.

Morison, Samuel Eliot. *Samuel de Champlain: Father of New France.* Boston: Little, Brown, 1972.

Parkman, Francis. *France and England in North America.* Vol. 1. New York: Library of America, 1983.

Trudel, Marcel. *The Beginnings of New France, 1524–1663.* Toronto: McClelland and Stewart, 1972.

Vachon, André. *Dreams of Empire: Canada before 1700.* Ottawa: Public Archives of Canada, 1982.

Chavez, Cesar (1927–1993) *labor organizer*

Cesar Chavez became the most visible public spokesman for the rights of migrant farmworkers in the United States during the 1960s and 1970s and the first national symbol of the Mexican-American labor community. His work as a labor organizer led him to oppose consistently the agribusiness industry's use of both legal and illegal labor from Mexico and thus brought him into conflict with other Hispanic leaders who criticized his lack of commitment to La Raza (the people).

Chavez's father migrated with his family to Yuma, Arizona, from Chihuahua, Mexico, in 1888. With the depression came loss of the family store in 1934 and the family homestead in 1939, leading Chavez and the other members of his family to become permanent migrant laborers. Living in the San Jose barrio of Sal Si Puedes after two years in the U.S. Navy (1944–46), Chavez became interested in community work and the political philosophies of nonviolence. He worked with the Community Service Organization (CSO) throughout the 1950s, rising to the position of executive director (1958–62). In 1958, Chavez became directly involved in labor organization, leading a campaign in Oxnard, California, to oust braceros (Mexican laborers) who had been brought in to drive down labor wages (see BRACERO PROGRAM). The campaign was initially successful, but Chavez realized that results would not be permanent without a labor union to see that agreements were kept. In 1962, he established the Farm Workers Association (FWA) but chose to maintain its independence from the AMERICAN FEDERATION OF LABOR–CONGRESS OF INDUSTRIAL ORGANIZATIONS (AFL-CIO) and its branch the Agricultural Workers Organizing Committee (AWOC), hoping to

maintain the strong sense of community activism that had been part of the CSO.

Chavez emerged as a national figure in 1965 when he led the FWA into a Delano, California, grape workers' strike that had been initiated by AWOC's local director Larry Itilong on behalf of Filipino-American workers protesting the hiring of low-wage braceros. The Delano strike captured the attention of reformers of all classes and races, and many from around the United States volunteered to help. In 1966, Chavez led a much-publicized march from Delano to Sacramento in order to present the matter to Governor Pat Brown and continued to expand consumer boycotts. With an emphasis on nonviolence, community solidarity, and religious fervor, Chavez's work resembled to many Americans the efforts of Martin Luther King, Jr., on behalf of African Americans. Later that year, under Chavez's suggestion, the FWA took the name National Farm Workers Union (later changed to United Farm Workers of America [UFW]) and joined with AWOC in order to give farmworkers greater bargaining power. In July 1970, the grape strike finally

Cesar Chavez, photographed in 1966, was the first major organizer of legal Mexican and Mexican-American migrant farm laborers. His United Farm Workers of America waged a long and bitter but ultimately successful strike against grape growers in California (1966–70). *(Library of Congress, Prints & Photographs Division [LC-USZ62-111017])*

ended, with workers earning substantial increases in pay and the union organization strengthened.

Although the Delano grape strike was his most visible piece of labor activism, Chavez continued to organize strikes and to speak out against illegal immigration and its detrimental effect on wages. As the 1970s progressed, he was increasingly attacked by members of the Hispanic community who argued that his commitment to working-class issues worked against the greater good of Hispanics generally, including illegal Mexican immigrants who hoped to better their lives by coming to the United States. He nevertheless continued to work with the governments of both the United States and Mexico in order to secure protections for the interests of legal Mexican Americans in the United States. Chavez encouraged the U.S. government to include provisions in the IMMIGRATION REFORM AND CONTROL ACT (1986) applying sanctions against employers who knowingly hired illegal immigrants. In 1990, he signed an agreement with the Mexican government stipulating that Mexican citizens who were members of the UFW could also qualify for Mexican social security benefits.

Further Reading

Etulain, Richard W., ed. *Cesar Chavez: A Brief Biography with Documents.* New York: Palgrave, 2002.

Ferris, Susan, and Ricardo Sandoval. *The Fight in the Fields: Cesar Chavez and the Farmworkers Movement.* New York: Harcourt Brace Jovanovich, 1997.

Griswold del Castillo, Richard, and Richard A. Garcia. *Cesar Chavez: A Triumph of Spirit.* Norman: University of Oklahoma Press, 1995.

Levy, Jacques E. *Cesar Chavez: Autobiography of La Causa.* New York: W. W. Norton, 1975.

Chicago, Illinois

For most of the 19th and 20th centuries, the city of Chicago was one of the most desirable destinations for immigrants. Emerging in the late 19th century as the hub of midwestern development, Chicago had good rail access from eastern ports of entry, and its slaughterhouses and industries provided jobs for unskilled workers. Large numbers of Germans, Irish, Swedes, Norwegians, Canadians, Czechs, Poles, Greeks, and Italians clustered there in the 19th and early 20th centuries. After World War II (1939–45), Bosnian Muslims, Latvians, Lithuanians, Pakistanis, Mexicans, and Hasidic Jews created significant enclaves in Chicago. According to the 2000 U.S. census, Chicago had the third largest Hispanic population in the United States (753,644, behind New York City and Los Angeles) and the seventh largest Asian population (125,974). Its foreign-born population was about 1.1 million.

Chicago began as a small military outpost established in 1816. By 1833, it was incorporated as a village with a pop-

Charles Sawer, gateman at Union Station, Chicago, Illinois, 1943. In multiethnic Chicago, a man like Sawer was useful in the train station, where he served as an interpreter in Yiddish, Polish, German, Russian, Slovak, and Spanish. *(Photo by Jack Delano/Library of Congress, Prints & Photographs Division [LC-USW3-015557-E])*

ulation of more than 150. When the government forced a land settlement on the local Indian tribes, removing them west of the Mississippi River, the European population boomed. By 1848, a canal was completed linking Chicago to the Mississippi, and by 1856, it was the hub of 10 railroads. The city continued to grow during and after the Civil War (1861–65), becoming the leading grain, livestock, and lumber market in the world. In 1870, Chicago's population of almost 300,000 was 17 percent German (52,316) and 13 percent Irish (40,000), with the percentage of foreign born rapidly rising. Unprepared for the rapid influx of inhabitants, the city was host to overcrowding, disease, and degraded living conditions.

In response to the plight of the immigrants, in 1889, JANE ADDAMS opened the Hull-House settlement to provide assistance to the urban poor. The large pool of unskilled labor fueled the city's economic development but also led to tensions. In May 1886, the deadly Haymarket bombing during a labor rally revived nativist fears of immigrant radicalism. By 1890, Chicago was second only to New York in population and a magnet for numerous immigrant groups. In 1900, Swedes comprised almost 9 percent of Chicago's population (150,000), making it second only to Stockholm in Swedish population. By 1920, it was the largest Norwegian city in the world besides Oslo, and there was already a Polish population of 400,000. Between 1910 and 1920, at the peak of early 20th-century immigration, about three-fourths of Chicago's population was either first- or second-generation immigrant.

After World War I (1914–18), most of the immigrant groups, including Czechs, Italians, Poles, and Greeks, began to disperse into new neighborhoods and eventually the suburbs, replaced by African Americans and other southerners moving north for industrial work. A Mexican community was well established by 1920, having moved north to work in steel mills and meatpacking plants. By the 1920s, the children and grandchildren of the "new immigrants" were developing a strong middle-class base (see NEW IMMIGRATION). Together with economic ascendancy came greater opportunities for leadership and financial backing, both necessary to begin to influence the political process. A milestone was reached in 1930 when Anton J. Cermak, born in a mining town northwest of Prague, was elected mayor of Chicago. From that point forward, most of the old European immigrant groups rapidly assimilated into the mainstream of Chicago social and political life. Still, Chicago was a city of immigrants. In 1927, almost 30 percent of its population was born in Europe. The Jewish population alone, composed largely of poor eastern Europeans, was 275,000.

After World War II (1939–45), Chicago continued to attract immigrants. Historically a city populated mainly by Europeans and African Americans, it became one of the most ethnically diverse cities in the world. Mexicans continued to join the "colony" established after 1910, settling mainly in South Chicago. Apart from the largely assimilated Germans and Irish, Mexican Americans formed the largest ethnic group in Chicago by far, with a population of 1,132,147 in 2001 (in the greater Chicago-Gary-Kenosha area). Vietnamese, Laotians, and Cambodians fleeing in the aftermath of the Vietnam War (1964–75) and the Khmer repression came in large numbers during the late 1970s and early 1980s, congregating in the North Side neighborhood of Uptown. By 2000, there were about 25,000 Southeast Asians living in Chicago. Asian Indians were one of the most rapidly growing populations, settling mainly in western and northwestern suburbs. Indian Americans benefited greatly from provisions of the IMMIGRATION AND NATIONALITY ACT of 1965, abolishing racial quotas and favoring skilled workers such as engineers and medical professionals. The act also gave preference to family reunification, which enabled Indians to bring their families to Chicago. Between 1980 and 2000, their numbers grew from about 32,000 to 123,000. There were also large populations of Puerto Ricans (161,655) and Chinese (78,277). In 1990–91, more than 5,000 Soviet Jews were relocated in Chicago, representing more than 9 percent of all Jewish émigrés to the United States. During the 1990s, Chicago was still the fourth most popular destination for immigrants, ranking behind New York City, Los Angeles, and Miami, Florida.

Further Reading

Allswang, John M. *A House for All Peoples: Ethic Politics in Chicago 1890–1936.* Lexington: University Press of Kentucky, 1971.

Anderson, Philip J., and Dag Blanck. *Swedish-American Life in Chicago: Cultural and Urban Aspects of an Immigrant People, 1850–1930.* Uppsala, Sweden: Uppsala University, 1991.

Beijbom, Ulf. *Swedes in Chicago: A Demographic and Social Study of the 1846–1880 Immigration.* Vaxjo, Sweden: Emigrants' House, 1971.

Cohen, Lizabeth. *Making a New Deal: Industrial Workers in Chicago, 1919–1939.* New York: Cambridge University Press, 1990.

Cutler, Irving. *The Jews of Chicago: From Shtetl to Suburb.* Champaign: University of Illinois Press, 1996.

Erdmans, Mary Patrice. *Opposite Poles: Immigrants and Ethnics in Polish Chicago, 1976–1990.* University Park: Pennsylvania State University Press, 1998.

Jones, Peter D'A., and Melvin C. Holli. *Ethnic Chicago.* Grand Rapids, Mich.: Erdmans, 1981.

Kantowicz, Edward R. *Polish-American Politics in Chicago, 1888–1940.* Chicago: University of Chicago Press, 1975.

Keil, Hartmut, and John B. Jentz, eds. *German Workers in Industrial Chicago, 1850–1910: A Comparative Perspective.* DeKalb: Northern Illinois University Press, 1983.

Kopan, A. T. *The Greeks in Chicago.* Urbana: University of Illinois Press, 1989.

Kourvetaris, G. A. *First- and Second-Generation Greeks in Chicago.* Athens: National Center for Social Research, 1971.

Lovoll, Odd S. *A Century of Urban Life: The Norwegians in Chicago before 1930.* Urbana, Ill.: Norwegian American Historical Society, 1988.

McCaffrey, L. J. *The Irish in Chicago.* Urbana: University of Illinois Press, 1987.

Nelli, Humberto S. *Italians in Chicago, 1880–1930.* New York: Oxford University Press, 1975.

Pacyga, Dominic A. *Polish Immigrants and Industrial Chicago: Workers on the South Side, 1880–1922.* Columbus: Ohio State University Press, 1991.

Parot, Joseph J. *Polish Catholics in Chicago, 1850–1920.* DeKalb: Northern Illinois University Press, 1981.

Philpott, Thomas L. *The Slum and the Ghetto: Neighborhood Deterioration and Middle-Class Reform, Chicago, 1880–1930.* New York: Oxford University Press, 1978.

Rassogianis, Alex. "The Growth of Greek Business in Chicago: 1900–1930." M.A. thesis, University of Wisconsin at Milwaukee, 1982.

Chicano

The term *Chicano* is a politicocultural indicator of one's identification as a pure-blood or mestizo (mixed race) descendant of the native peoples of the old Aztec homeland of Aztlán. Its origins are unclear, but it was first widely used by young people in the U.S. Southwest during the 1950s. As frustration set in over the lack of economic and social progress during the 1960s, many Mexican-American leaders throughout the southwestern states adopted the term as an affirmation of their Indian past and a rejection of European-American values. Going beyond the traditional political tactics of earlier Mexican-American organizations, Chicano leaders encouraged greater militancy in their activism. JOSE ANGEL GUTIERREZ established the Mexican American Youth Organization in Texas, organizing a series of consciousness-raising high school "walkouts" to protest Anglocentric textbooks and educational discrimination. In Denver, Colorado, (Rodolfo) CORKY GONZALES left the Democratic Party in 1965 to form a Chicano-rights organization, the Crusade for Justice. He was also instrumental in defining the Chicano movement by helping draft the manifesto El Plan Espiritual de Aztlán (1969) and writing its most enduring piece of literature, the epic poem *I Am Joaquín*. Both men were prominent in establishing the national LA RAZA UNIDA PARTY (LRUP), the political arm of the Chicano movement, which was most prominent in the mid-1970s. During the 1970s, the Chicano movement was closely associated with CESAR CHAVEZ's struggle to improve conditions for migrant farmworkers, the vast majority of whom were Mexicans. By the late 1970s, Chicano activism began to subside and with it, the political prevalence of the term.

See also MEXICAN IMMIGRATION; TIJERINA, REIES LÓPEZ.

Further Reading

Acuña, Rodolfo. *Occupied America: The Chicano Struggle for Liberation.* 3d ed. New York: Harper and Row, 1988.
Gómez Quiñones, Juan. *Chicano Politics: Reality and Promise, 1940–1990.* Albuquerque: University of New Mexico Press, 1990.
Gonzalez, Gilbert G., and Raul Fernandez. "Chicano History: Transcending Cultural Models." *Pacific Historical Review* 63 (November 1994): 469.

Chilean immigration

The earliest migration of Chileans to the north came during the California gold rush of 1848–49, when some 7,000 immigrated to the United States, with most settling in San Francisco and Santa Clara Counties. In 2000, 68,849 persons of Chilean origin resided in the United States, with the highest concentrations in Los Angeles; Miami, Florida; and New York City. According to the Canadian census of 2001, 34,115 Canadians claimed Chilean descent, most residing in Toronto and Montreal. Because the earliest "Chilenos" frequently intermarried, the modern Chilean American is more likely to be part of a general community than of an ethnic enclave.

Chile is a long, narrow country of 288,800 square miles along the west coast of South America between 17 and 55 degrees south latitude. With a coastline of 2,600 miles, it has a long seafaring tradition that has invited immigration from many countries, including Spain, Italy, Germany, Ireland, Greece, Yugoslavia, and Lebanon. Peru forms its border to the north, Bolivia to the northeast, Argentina to the east, and the Pacific Ocean to the west. The Andes Mountains, some of the highest in the world, stretch north to south along its eastern border against the Atacama Desert in the north, plains in the central region, and forests in the south. An archipelago makes up much of southern Chile including the largest island, Tierra del Fuego, which is shared with Argentina. In 2002, the population was estimated at 15,328,467, with more than 5 million in the urban area of the capital city of Santiago. About two-thirds of the population is of mixed European and Indian descent (mestizo), and almost all the others of European descent. Roman Catholicism is the dominant religion, claimed by 89 percent of the population. The other 11 percent are Protestant Christians.

The Inca Empire ruled over Chile until the 16th-century Spanish conquest. Chile fought for its independence between 1810 and 1818, after which it established a significant economic relationship with the United States. Chilean men often served on American whaling ships and sometimes settled in northeastern U.S. ports. More than 7,000 entered California during the gold rush of 1848–49, many of whom were experienced miners. Nevertheless, throughout the 19th and early 20th centuries there was only sporadic emigration. Chile's civil war of 1891 led thousands to immigrate to the United States, Europe, and Argentina. After 1938, when a leftist government was elected, conservative Chileans began migrating to the United States, steadily increasing the Chilean populations in New York City and Los Angeles. Middle- and upper-class Chileans frequently came to the United States for education. The election of marxist Salvador Allende in 1970 led to an even larger exodus. Allende was assassinated in 1973 by a repressive, U.S.-backed military junta under General Augusto Pinochet, thus creating a new wave of emigration of leftists who had supported Allende. Both the United States and Canada were reluctant to admit avowed marxists, fearing political complications domestically and the appearance of undermining their anticommunist allies in Chile. Continued pressure from church, humanitarian, labor, and Hispanic groups nevertheless led to minor refugee modifications. During 1973 and 1974, Canada admitted about 7,000 Chilean refugees. In 1978, the United States launched the Hemispheric 500 Program, providing parole for several thousand Chilean and Argentinean political prisoners. In the following year, Canada created a new refugee category for "Latin American Political Prisoners and Oppressed Persons." In both cases, the standards for entry were higher than those for people from Southeast Asia and Eastern Europe, where applicants were fleeing communist regimes. During the 1970s, 17,600 Chileans immigrated to the United States, coming from both sides of the political spectrum and often clashing in their new country.

After widespread international criticism for human rights abuses, in 1990, Pinochet was forced to return the country to civilian rule. Of more than 1 million Chileans who were either exiled or forced to flee the country, about 10 percent settled in the United States. Between 1992 and 2002, the United States admitted 17,887 Chilean immigrants. Angered by American COLD WAR support for Pinochet, many Chileans chose to emigrate elsewhere. Of Canada's 24,495 Chilean immigrants in 2001, almost 11,000 came between 1971 and 1980 and about 5,700 between 1991 and 2001.

Further Reading

Beilharz, E., and C. U. Lopez. *We Were Forty-Niners! Chilean Accounts of the California Gold Rush.* Pasadena, Calif.: Ward Ritchie, 1976.

Collier, Simon, with William F. Sater. *A History of Chile, 1808–1994.* Cambridge: Cambridge University Press, 1996.

Duran, Marcela. "Life in Exile: Chileans in Canada." *Multiculturalism* 3, no. 4 (1980): 13–16.

Hudson, Rex A. *Chile: A Country Study.* 3d ed. Washington, D.C.: U.S. Government Printing Office, 1995.

Kay, Diana. *Chileans in Exile: Private Struggles, Public Lives.* Wolfeboro, N.H.: Longwood Academic, 1987.

Lopez, Carlos U. *Chilenos in California: A Study of the 1850, 1852, and 1860 Censuses.* San Francisco: R. and E. Research Associates, 1973.

Moaghan, Jay. *Chile, Peru, and the California Gold Rush of 1849.* Berkeley: University of California Press, R. and E. Research Associates, 1973.

Pereira Salas, Eugenio. *Los primeros contactos entre Chile y los Estados Unidos, 1778–1809.* Santiago: Andres Bello, 1974.

Pozo, José del. *Los Chilenos del Quebec y los Estudios avanzados: Memorias y tesis sobre Chile en Canadá.* Montreal: Publicació de PRO-TACH, 1994.

Rockett, Ian R. H. "Immigration Legislation and the Flow of Specialized Human Capital from South America to the United States." *International Migration Review* 10 (1976): 47–61.

Wright, Thomas C., and Rody Oñate, eds. *Flight from Chile.* Albuquerque: University of New Mexico Press, 1998.

Chinese Exclusion Act (United States) (1882)

The Chinese Exclusion Act was the first measure to specifically exclude an ethnic group from immigrating to the United States. It formed the basis of American anti-Asian immigration policy and was not repealed until 1943, when the United States and China became allies during World War II (see WORLD WAR II AND IMMIGRATION).

When the Chinese first came to California in large numbers, in the 1850s in the wake of the gold rush, they were generally well received as among "the most worthy of our newly adopted citizens." By the 1870s, they constituted almost 10 percent of the population of California, but with the economic hard times of the 1870s, many westerners blamed the 100,000 Chinese immigrants for taking jobs and depressing wages. Increasing agitation from the early 1870s was for a time deflected by merchants, industrialists, steamship companies, missionaries, and East Coast intellectuals who argued in favor of the Chinese presence in America. By the late 1870s, politicians in the Midwest and East took an interest in placating an increasingly violent white labor force and thus were inclined to agree to limitations on Chinese immigration. In addition to organized opposition from labor groups such as the Workingmen's Party, RACISM played a large role in anti-Chinese attitudes. Growing anti-Chinese opposition led to passage of the PAGE ACT (1875) and appointment of a Senate committee to investigate the question of Chinese immigration (January 1876). In 1879, Henry George published *Progress and Poverty,* one of the most influential economic tracts of the 19th century, in which he concluded that the Chinese were economically backward and "unassimilable." In the same year, President Rutherford B. Hayes encouraged Congress to examine ways of limiting Chinese immigration. After much debate and many abortive bills, the United States and China signed the Angell Treaty (1881), which modified the BURLINGAME TREATY (1868) and gave the United States authority to regulate the immigration of Chinese laborers. A bill was quickly brought forward to exclude Chinese laborers for 20 years, but it was vetoed by President Chester A. Arthur, who argued that such a long period of exclusion would contravene the articles of the Angell Treaty. Arthur reluctantly signed a revised measure on May 6, 1882. Its major provisions included

1. exclusion of all Chinese laborers for 10 years, starting 90 days from enactment of the new law
2. denial of naturalization to Chinese aliens already in the United States
3. registration of all Chinese laborers already in the United States, who were still allowed to travel freely to and from the United States

Chinese officials and their domestic servants were exempted from the prohibition. In 1888, the SCOTT ACT imposed new restrictions on Chinese immigration. The exclusions were extended in 1892 and again, for an indefinite period of time, in 1902. As a result of the 90-day deferral period, almost 40,000 additional Chinese laborers entered the United States, raising the Chinese population to about 150,000.

Further Reading

Chan, Sucheng, ed. *Entry Denied: Exclusion and the Chinese Community in America, 1882–1943.* Philadelphia: Temple University Press, 1991.

Daniels, Roger. *Guarding the Golden Door: American Immigration Policy and Immigrants since 1882.* New York: Hill and Wang, 2004.

Gyory, Andrew. *Closing the Gate: Race, Politics, and the Chinese Exclusion Act.* Chapel Hill: University of North Carolina Press, 1998.

Miller, Stuart C. *The Unwelcome Immigrant: The American Image of the Chinese, 1785–1882.* Berkeley: University of California Press, 1969.

Rhoads, Edward J. M. "'White Labor' vs. 'Coolie Labor': The 'Chinese Question' in Pennsylvania in the 1870s." *Journal of American Ethnic History* 21 (Winter 2002): 3–33.

Takaki, Ronald. *Strangers from a Different Shore.* Boston: Little, Brown, 1989.

Chinese immigration

The Chinese were the first large Asian group to settle in both the United States and Canada and proved integral to the economic development of the North American west. As visible minorities, they were also the first to suffer from RACISM as well as NATIVISM. The CHINESE EXCLUSION ACT (1882) in the United States and the CHINESE IMMIGRATION ACT (1885) in Canada were the first pieces of

A Chinese store in the interior of the "upper country," British Columbia, ca. 1910. Between 1881 and 1884, more than 17,000 Chinese immigrants arrived in Vancouver, most to work on the Canadian Pacific Railway. Fears of a "yellow" west led to Canada's first anti-immigrant legislation based on race, the Chinese Immigration Act of 1885. *(National Archives of Canada/PA-122688)*

immigration legislation in each country to deny entry on the basis of race.

From the mid-1850s to 2002, more than 1.5 million Chinese immigrated to the United States, not including hundreds of thousands of ethnic Chinese from other countries. About 600,000 Chinese entered Canada during the same period. Over time, the Chinese in North America proved to be resilient, adaptable, and successful in moving up the economic ladder. As a result, by the 1990s they were often refused minority status in a variety of programs emphasizing racial balancing. In the U.S. census of 2000 and the Canadian census of 2001, about 2.9 million Americans and 1.1 million Canadians claimed Chinese descent. San Francisco was the early center of Chinese settlement in the United States. During the 20th century, however, significant Chinatowns were established in major cities across the United States. According to the U.S. census of 2000, New York City (536,966), San Francisco (521,645), and Los Angeles (472,637) have the largest Chinese populations in the United States. Toronto (435,685) and Vancouver (347,985) have the largest Chinese populations in Canada as recorded in the Canadian census of 2001.

China is the world's largest country in population (1.3 billion in 2002) and third largest in landmass (3,696,100 square miles). It is bordered on the north by Russia, Korea, and Mongolia; to the west by Kazakhstan, Kyrgyzstan, Afghanistan, and India; to the south by Nepal, Bhutan, India, Myanmar, Laos, and Vietnam; and to the east by the Pacific Ocean. Developing one of the world's earliest great civilizations along the Yellow River by about 1600 B.C., China exerted from thereon broad cultural influence throughout eastern and southeastern Asia, most notably in Japan, Korea, and Vietnam. Throughout its long imperial rule, China's political and cultural supremacy was seldom questioned by either rulers or neighbors. Even when enemies such as the Mongols (1279–1368) and the Manchus (1644–1911) conquered China, they largely embraced its (Han) culture, maintaining the country's long traditions. It was not until the 1830s that China's encounter with the West and its new industrial technologies led some to question China's traditional reliance upon the Confucian values of the ancient past. By the late 19th century, China had been carved into spheres of European influence. The Qing dynasty of the Manchus was so severely weakened that the country was defeated by the much smaller but rapidly modernizing Japan (Sino-Japanese War, 1894–95), and the dynasty itself was overthrown by republican forces in 1911. Throughout its history, China's dense population left it particularly vulnerable to the famines and floods that frequently ravaged the country. This, coupled with China's economic superiority in Asia, helped establish an ongoing tradition of migration that led to the establishment of large Chinese communities throughout Southeast Asia. Thus, when opportunities arose to migrate to North America,

immigrants responded within a traditional framework for migration.

The first significant period of immigration to North America came between 1849 and 1882, when some 300,000 young, impoverished, and mostly male peasants came as contract laborers during the CALIFORNIA GOLD RUSH. The young men of coastal Guangdong (Canton) Province, who suffered from increasing competition from European manufactured goods, loss of jobs, and interethnic conflicts, had both the means of learning of North American opportunities and access to the ships that would take them there. Few made money for themselves in the goldfields, but they proved to be valuable laborers for large mining corporations, and they frequently earned a living providing mining camps with food, supplies, and a variety of services. After the mines played out, the Chinese stayed to work on railroad construction, swamp reclamation, and in agriculture and fishing. They were considered ideal laborers and constituted about 80 percent of the labor force of the Central Pacific Railroad during the construction of the first transcontinental railroad, completed in 1869. Prohibited from becoming citizens, most planned to improve their financial position, then eventually return to China, an attitude reinforced by the rise of militant anti-Chinese sentiment throughout the West. By 1882, when Chinese immigration was virtually prohibited, there were about 110,000 Chinese in the United States, most in California and other western states.

The pattern of immigration and exclusion was remarkably similar in Canada, though on a smaller scale. Chinese people first came in significant numbers to British Columbia with the Fraser River gold rush of 1858. Within two years their population was 4,000. After the goldfields were exhausted, the Chinese increasingly became servants, ran low-capital businesses such as laundries and restaurants, and worked in agriculture and on the railroads. Between 1881 and 1884, it is estimated that 17,000 were brought in to work on the Canadian Pacific Railway, more than half directly from China, but a significant number from the United States as well. As a result of local Canadian opposition, in 1885, the Chinese Immigration Act was passed, imposing a $50 head tax on Chinese immigrants, thus drastically reducing their entry.

From 1882 until 1943, generally only students, merchants, and diplomats were allowed to come freely to the United States. With Canadian restrictions less severe, some laborers continued coming to Canada with the expectation of meeting relatives or of illegally entering the United States. Between 1886 and 1911, more than 55,000 paid the head tax, but many of these either returned to China or migrated to the United States. Due to the initial gender imbalance (27 men to one woman in 1890), prohibitions on interracial marriage, and immigration restrictions, the vast majority of Chinese women in North America were forced to become prostitutes, most sold into sexual slavery by impoverished Chinese families. This unusual social structure was usually hidden away in "Chinatowns," where most Chinese lived and did business and where few whites, save missionaries and public officials, ever ventured. This social exclusion was strengthened in Canada with passage of a Chinese exclusion law of 1923, based on the doctrine that the two races were wholly different and could not work toward the same goals. Though making some provision for Chinese who had entered under the head tax to travel between China and Canada, the new regulations allowed virtually no new immigrants between 1924 and 1946.

World War II (1939–45) encouraged some change in both American and Canadian attitudes toward the Chinese. With China an important ally against Imperial Japan, and thousands of Chinese Americans volunteering for military service and working in defense-related industries, in 1943, Congress repealed the Chinese Exclusion Act. Although the number of allowable immigrants remained small, Chinese aliens did gain the right to naturalization. The WAR BRIDES ACT brought some 6,000 into the country outside the quota, and various Refugee Acts associated with the COLD WAR enabled another 30,000 mostly well-educated Chinese to enter. In Canada, Chinese were granted access to more professions, and it was made easier for them to acquire citizenship. The Chinese Immigration Act of 1947 and Order in Council P.C. 2115 did not represent a major change in immigration policy, however, as it only allowed Chinese Canadians who were citizens to bring their spouses and minor children into the country. During the 1940s, only about 5 percent were Canadian or British citizens.

The IMMIGRATION AND NATIONALITY ACT OF 1965 finally removed race as a barrier to immigration to the United States, opening a new era to which the Chinese eagerly responded. In addition to large numbers coming to reunite with family members, some 250,000 highly educated scientists, engineers, and intellectuals migrated to the United States between 1965 and 2000 to take advanced degrees, with most remaining in the country. Tens of thousands emigrated from Taiwan (see TAIWANESE IMMIGRATION) and Hong Kong, principally for education and economic opportunities. Normalization of diplomatic relations with the People's Republic of China (PRC) in 1979 opened a new immigration market. Following the end of the Vietnam War in 1975, more than 1 million Vietnamese, Laotian, and Cambodian refugees entered the United States; perhaps one-third were ethnic Chinese, who tended to settle in Chinatowns. Finally, during the 1980s and 1990s, the smuggling of Chinese laborers from the PRC became a growing problem. In 2000, the Immigration and Naturalization Service estimated that there were about 115,000 unauthorized Chinese living in the United States, the largest number for any country outside the Western Hemisphere.

Between 1992 and 2002, more than 700,000 Chinese from the PRC, Hong Kong, and Taiwan immigrated to the United States. Canada's IMMIGRATION REGULATIONS of 1967 similarly eliminated racial considerations in immigrant selection, leading to an upsurge in Chinese immigration, most coming from Hong Kong. Between 1991 and 2001, more than 400,000 Chinese immigrated to Canada, making them the fastest growing visible minority in the country. Hong Kong was the number one source country for Canadian immigration throughout most of the 1990s and was only replaced by the People's Republic of China in 1997 as Hong Kong's position within the PRC was regularized. Taiwan also placed in the top six source countries during most of the 1990s.

See also ANGEL ISLAND.

Further Reading

Chan, Anthony. *Gold Mountain: The Chinese in the New World.* Vancouver, Canada: New Star Books, 1983.

Chan, Sucheng. *Entry Denied: Exclusion and the Chinese Community in America, 1882–1943.* Philadelphia: Temple University Press, 1991.

Chang, Iris. *The Chinese in America: A Narrative History.* New York: Viking Press, 2003.

Chen, Yong. *Chinese San Francisco, 1850–1943: A Trans-Pacific Community.* Stanford, Calif.: Stanford University Press, 2000.

Chin, Ko-lin. *Smuggled Chinese: Clandestine Immigration to the United States.* Philadelphia: Temple University Press, 1999.

Daniels, Roger. *Asian America: Chinese and Japanese in the United States since 1850.* Seattle: University of Washington Press, 1988.

Hing, Bill Ong. *Making and Remaking Asian America through Immigration Policy, 1850–1990.* Stanford, Calif.: Stanford University Press, 1993.

Lai, David Chuenyan. *Chinatowns: Towns within Cities in Canada.* Vancouver, Canada: University of British Columbia Press, 1988.

Lai, Him Mark. *Becoming Chinese American: A History of Communities and Institutions.* Walnut Creek, Calif.: AltaMira Press, 2004.

Lee, Erika. *At America's Gates: Chinese Immigration during the Exclusion Era, 1882–1943.* Chapel Hill: University of North Carolina Press, 2003.

Lee Tunh-hai. *A History of Chinese in Canada.* Yangmingshan, Taiwan: Zhonghua dadian bian yin hui, 1967.

Ling, Huping. *Surviving on the Gold Mountain: A History of Chinese-American Women and Their Lives.* New York: State University of New York Press, 1998.

Liu, Po-chi. *A History of the Chinese in the United States of America, 1848–1911.* Taipei: Commission of Overseas Chinese, 1976.

McClain, Charles J. *In Search of Equality: The Chinese Struggle against Discrimination in Nineteenth-Century America.* Berkeley: University of California Press, 1994.

McCunn, Ruthanne Lum. *Chinese American Portraits.* San Francisco: Chronicle Books, 1988.

Me, Dianne, Mark Lin, and Ginger Chih. *A Place Called Chinese America.* Dubuque, Iowa: Kendall/Hunt, 1985.

Miller, Stuart C. *The Unwelcome Immigrant: The American Image of the Chinese, 1785–1882.* Berkeley: University of California Press, 1969.

Pan, Lynn, ed. *The Encyclopedia of the Chinese Overseas.* Cambridge, Mass.: Harvard University Press, 1999.

———. *Sons of the Yellow Emperor: A History of the Chinese Diaspora.* Boston: Little, Brown, 1990.

Saxton, Alexander. *The Indispensable Enemy: Labor and the Anti-Chinese Movement in California.* Berkeley: University of California Press, 1995.

Skeldon, Ronald. "Migration from China." *Journal of International Affairs* 49, no. 2 (1996): 434–455.

Steiner, Stan. *Fusang: The Chinese Who Built America.* New York: Harper and Row, 1979.

Tan, Jin, and Patricia E. Roy. *The Chinese in Canada.* Ottawa: Canadian Historical Association, 1985.

Tsai, Shih-shan Henry. *China and the Overseas Chinese in the United States, 1868–1911.* Fayetteville: University of Arkansas Press, 1983.

———. *The Chinese Experience in America.* Bloomington: Indiana University Press, 1986.

Tung, William L. *The Chinese in America, 1820–1973: A Chronology and Fact Book.* Dobbs Ferry, N.Y.: Oceana Publications 1974.

Wickberg, Edgar, ed. *From China to Canada: A History of the Chinese Communities in Canada.* Toronto: McClelland and Stewart, 1982.

Zeng Yi and Zhang Qinwu. "Conditions in China Influencing Out-migration." In *The Silent Debate: Asian Immigration and Racism in Canada.* Eds. Eleanor Laquian, Aprodicio Laquian, and Terry McGee. Vancouver, Canada: Institute of Asian Research, University of British Columbia, 1998.

Chinese Immigration Act (Canada) (1885)

Incorporating recommendations from the Royal Commission on Chinese Immigration (1884–85), the Chinese Immigration Act was the first Canadian legislation to formally limit immigration based on race. While not prohibiting immigration altogether, its severe restrictions formed the basis of official Canadian policy toward the Chinese until after World War II.

Protests began almost immediately after Chinese laborers started to arrive in large numbers to work on the Canadian Pacific Railway in the early 1880s. More than 17,000 arrived in Vancouver alone between 1881 and 1884. Although white Canadians complained that the Chinese were dirty, disease ridden, and lacking morals, employers were not slow to recognize their value, as they worked for 30–50 percent less than European laborers, who were in any case in short supply. Although Prime Minister John Macdonald was, like most Canadians, opposed to permanent Chinese settlement, as he told the House of Commons, "Either you must have labour or you can't have the railway." Following the recommendations of the Royal Commission, the Chinese Immigration Act imposed a $50 head tax on Chinese laborers and limited ships to one Chinese immigrant per 50 tons of cargo. Excluded from the head tax were tourists, students, diplomats, and merchants. The measure

was amended in 1908, limiting head tax exclusions and expanding the list of prohibited immigrants. A revised act of 1923 eliminated the head tax but instituted exclusionary clauses so broad that Chinese immigration was virtually halted until repeal of the Chinese Immigration Act in 1947: During that period, only 15 Chinese were legally permitted to immigrate to Canada.

Further Reading
Kelley, Ninette, and Michael Trebilcock. *The Making of the Mosaic: A History of Canadian Immigration Policy.* Toronto: University of Toronto Press, 1998.

Roy, Patricia E. "A Choice between Evils: The Chinese and the Construction of the Canadian Pacific Railway in British Columbia." In *The CPR West: The Iron Road and the Making of a Nation.* Vancouver and Toronto: Douglas and McIntyre, 1984.

Wickberg, Edgar, ed. *From China to Canada: A History of the Chinese Communities in Canada.* Toronto: McClelland and Stewart, 1982.

CIC   See DEPARTMENT OF MANPOWER AND IMMIGRATION.

Citizenship and Immigration Canada   See DEPARTMENT OF MANPOWER AND IMMIGRATION.

Civil Liberties Act (United States) (1988)   See JAPANESE INTERNMENT, WORLD WAR II AND IMMIGRATION.

Civil Rights Act (United States) (1964)

The Civil Rights Act of 1964 made it illegal to discriminate in employment or the use of public facilities on the basis of race, color, religion, gender, or national origin. It also outlawed poll taxes and arbitrary literacy tests that had traditionally been used to exclude African Americans and other minorities from voting. The act gave the attorney general broad powers to bring legal suit against violators who continued to practice segregation. Finally, the act provided for creation of the Equal Employment Opportunity Commission (EEOC) to assist in assuring fairness in employment practices.

Though the Civil Rights Act marked the legislative high point of the Civil Rights movement led by African Americans, its provisions were equally applicable to immigrants. A changing social consciousness based on the justice of the Civil Rights movement and the imperatives of the COLD WAR helped pave the way for the nonracially based IMMIGRATION AND NATIONALITY ACT of 1965. As Attorney General Robert F. Kennedy observed to Congress in 1964, except in immigration, "Everywhere else in our national life, we have eliminated discrimination based on national origins."

Further Reading

Abraham, Henry J., and Barbara A. Perry. *Freedom and the Court.* 6th ed. New York: Oxford University Press, 1994.

Bell, Derrick A., Jr. *Race, Racism, and American Law.* 2d ed. Boston: Little, Brown, 1980.

Bullock, Charles S., III, and Charles M. Lamb. *Implementation of Civil Rights Policy.* Monterey, Calif.: Brooks-Cole, 1984.

Coast Guard, U.S.

The Coast Guard is the part of the U.S. Armed Forces responsible for enforcing maritime laws, search-and-rescue operations at sea, interdictment of drugs and illegal aliens, protection of the marine environment, and protection of maritime borders. It operates as a branch of the DEPART-MENT OF HOMELAND SECURITY in peacetime but is integrated with the U.S. Navy during time of war. Organized along similar lines, the Coast Guard and navy routinely cooperate in Greenland, Iceland, and other Arctic areas. Coast Guard vessels and personnel have provided naval support in all U.S. wars, including the war against Iraq (2003).

The Coast Guard was founded in 1790, although it did not take its present name until 1915 when the Revenue Cutter Service and the Life-saving Service merged. Responsibilities of the Light House Service were transferred to the Coast Guard in 1939, and those of the Bureau of Marine Inspection and Navigation in 1946. The largest peacetime operation of the guard was during the MARIEL BOATLIFT of 1980–81, when more than 125,000 Cuban refugees sailed from their homeland to Florida, most in crowded small craft not suited to sea voyages. Coast Guard resources were called in from bases along the East Coast, and 900 reservists were called to active duty. In the wake of the SEPTEMBER 11, 2001, attacks, supervision of the Coast Guard was transferred in 2003 from the Department of Transportation to the newly created Department of Homeland Security.

Further Reading

Canney, Donald L. *U.S. Coast Guard and Revenue Cutters, 1790–1935.* Annapolis, Md.: Naval Institute Press, 1995.

Johnson, Robert Erwin. *Guardians of the Sea: History of the United States Coast Guard, 1915 to the Present.* Annapolis, Md.: Naval Institute Press, 1987.

Colbert, Jean-Baptiste (1619–1683) *statesman*

Jean-Baptiste Colbert was a member of the Great Council of State and the French king Louis XIV's *intendant de finance* (superintendant of finance). He was responsible for implementing mercantile reforms designed to extract New World wealth for the French Crown. After the failures of the COM-PAGNIE DE LA NOUVELLE FRANCE (Company of New France), he established the Compagnie des Indes Occidentals (French West Indies Company) to govern NEW FRANCE and compete with England and Spain in the Americas. Though generally successful in managing French finances, he was never able to attract large numbers of French settlers to New France.

Born into a prosperous family from Reims, Colbert became an agent for Cardinal Mazarin in 1651. In 1661, he was appointed superintendant of finance and quickly became the most important adviser to Louis XIV, gradually taking charge of the navy, the merchant marine, commerce, the royal household, and public buildings. Colbert worked tirelessly to repair France's financial structure, wrecked by years of corruption and neglect. He made the tax system more efficient, expanded industry, and promoted the export of French luxury goods. Through strict regulation and supervision, he tightened royal control over finance and built one of the strongest navies in Europe. The American colonies had suffered particular neglect during the previous 40 years. In order to revive American self-sufficiency, Colbert appointed JEAN TALON as intendant of New France, and together they promoted immigration, economic diversification, and trade with the West Indies. In the last years of Colbert's life, expensive wars promoted by his rival, the war minister marquis de Louvois, undermined many of the benefits of his financial reorganization. Cold and unpopular with the public, Colbert was nevertheless an incredibly efficient administrator who enhanced French power in the Americas.

Further Reading

Cole, Charles Woolsey. *Colbert and a Century of French Mercantilism.* 2 vols. Hamden, Conn.: Archon Books, 1939.

Eccles, W. J. *Canada under Louis XIV, 1663–1701.* Toronto: McClelland and Stewart, 1964.

Goubert, Pierre. *Louis XIV and Twenty Million Frenchmen.* 1966. Reprint, New York: Pantheon Books, 1970.

Murat, Ines. *Colbert.* Charlottesville: University Press of Virginia, 1984.

cold war

The period of intense political and ideological struggle between democratic countries led by the United States and the Soviet Union (1945–91) and its communist satellites is often referred to as the cold war. As the Soviet Union sought to surround itself with friendly communist states in the wake of the enormous devastation of World War II (1939–45), the United States aided anticommunist, rightwing governments in all parts of the world. Ideological differences thus permeated the processes of modernization and decolonization of European empires. Millions of people were displaced in the struggle between communism and democracy and sought permanent haven in North America.

After World War II, national quotas established in the JOHNSON-REED ACT of 1924 remained the fundamental basis of U.S. immigration policy. Instead of wholesale immigration reform, exceptions to traditional policy were made to meet specific needs. In 1945, President Harry S. Truman issued a directive reserving some 42,000 quota slots for European refugees, commonly known as "Displaced Persons." The WAR BRIDES ACT (1946) made provisions for the wives and children of American soldiers. DISPLACED PERSONS ACTs were passed in 1948 and 1950 and the REFUGEE RELIEF ACT in 1953, the latter allowing visas for up to 2,000 immigrants of Chinese origin wishing to emigrate in the wake of the 1949 Communist victory over the Nationalists in the Chinese civil war.

American isolationists, fearing that special legislation would allow communist agents access to the country, passed the restrictive McCarran Internal Security Act (1950) and the MCCARRAN-WALTER IMMIGRATION AND NATURALIZATION ACT (1952), each over President Truman's veto. Although eliminating race as a barrier to naturalization, the latter measure retained the national origins formula of 1924 and strengthened the government's ability to denaturalize and deport immigrants associated with subversive groups. With the simultaneous development of decolonization around the world and the Civil Rights movement in the United States, support grew for a liberalization of immigration policy. Senator JOHN F. KENNEDY's *A Nation of Immigrants* (1958) espoused the ideological value of a racially neutral immigration policy. Fundamental reform became possible under Kennedy as president and his successor, Lyndon Baines Johnson. The IMMIGRATION AND NATIONALITY ACT (1965) allowed each country in the Eastern Hemisphere an overall quota, with a maximum total for each hemisphere and a broadening of family exemptions from the quota. Refugees from communism, Middle Eastern violence, and natural catastrophe were classed as a preference group to be allotted up to 6 percent of each country's visa quota and expected to number about 17,400 annually. The number of refugees admitted was always higher, however, as all presidents employed parole authority to exempt hundreds of thousands of refugees, principally those fleeing communist regimes. Between 1962 and 1979, almost 700,000 Cubans escaping Fidel Castro's government were paroled into the United States and more than 400,000 Vietnamese and other Southeast Asians.

With more than 2 million refugees being paroled into the United States between 1948 and 1980, it became clear that migration pressures brought on by the cold war could not be adequately met by the provisions of the Immigration and Nationality Act of 1965. The REFUGEE ACT of 1980 increased the normal refugee flow to 50,000 annually and accepted the 1968 United Nations definition of a refugee as one unwilling to return to his native land "because of persecution, or a well-founded fear of persecution." The measure also established a new category, "Asylee," which allowed 5,000 refugees already in the country illegally or as students to apply for formal entry. Almost immediately, the new policy was tested by the MARIEL BOATLIFT, which brought 125,000 Cubans to the United States within a matter of weeks in spring 1980 and demonstrated that presidential parole powers would continue to be used to exceed legislative limits. Although all asylees were potentially eligible for admission under a broader definition of "Refugee," in fact, most of those admitted were fleeing communist regimes. Thus, Cubans and Nicaraguans fared better than Haitians, Guatemalans, and Salvadorans, though all qualified.

As the cold war began to wind down after 1985, it became clear that future immigration policy would be driven by economic, rather than ideological, factors, with MEXICAN IMMIGRATION and those overstaying visas from many countries being immediate matters of concern. In October 1991, the U.S. government removed some 300,000 names from a list of "undesirable aliens" begun in 1952 in an effort to keep communist infiltrators out of the country. Between 1946 and 1994, more than 90 percent of 3 million refugees admitted to the United States had been fleeing communist regimes, principally in Poland, the Soviet Union, Romania, China, Nicaragua, Vietnam, Laos, Cambodia, Ethiopia, and Afghanistan.

In the first two years after World War II, Canada maintained the highly restrictive P.C. 695 (1931) as the basis of its immigration policy, which allowed little room for humanitarian relief. By 1947, pressure from the Canadian public, a variety of ethnic organizations, and the Canadian National Committee on Refugees led to a more liberal immigration policy. Promulgated in a series of orders in council, regulatory changes, and international agreements, increasing numbers of Asians were admitted, along with refugees from the old Commonwealth countries and Europe.

The IMMIGRATION ACT of 1952 regularized Canadian immigration policy, though it remained essentially conservative. The cabinet was given power of limiting immigration on the basis of ethnicity, nationality, or occupation. The most notable admission under the act was that of 40,000 Hungarians who had fled the Soviet invasion of their country in 1956. Ultimately, Canada accepted some 300,000 refugees from central and Eastern Europe between 1947 and 1967. Generally well educated and highly politicized, these refugees balanced what had traditionally been a left-leaning immigrant community. Canada dismantled its racial restrictions in 1962 in a series of regulation reforms.

The further liberalization of Canadian IMMIGRATION REGULATIONS in 1967 changed the character of the immigrant community, with more than half now coming from developing nations. The emergence of a federal policy of multiculturalism and tentative steps toward rapprochement with the Soviet Union under Prime Minister Pierre Trudeau by 1971 lessened cold war implications for Canadian immigration. Although most refugees were still those fleeing communist regimes in Czechoslovakia, Poland, the Soviet Union, and Vietnam, leftist refugees from Chile, South Africa, Haiti, and Central America were less feared than in the United States and were generally welcomed. This openness led to the controversial harboring of as many as 100,000 American draft evaders and deserters during the Vietnam War (1964–75). On the other hand, some 60,000 Southeast Asians were admitted in 1979–80, fleeing brutal communist regimes in Vietnam, Laos, and Cambodia.

Further Reading

Burnet, Jean R., with Howard Palmer. *"Coming Canadians": An Introduction to a History of Canada's Peoples.* Toronto: McClelland and Stewart, 1988.

Chan, Kwok B., and Doreen Marie Indra, eds. *Uprooting Loss and Adaptation: The Resettlement of Indochinese Refugees in Canada.* Ottawa: Canadian Public Health Association, 1987.

Goldsmith, Renee Kasinsky. *Refugees from Militarism: Draft-Age Americans in Canada.* Totowa, N.J.: Littlefield, Adams, 1976.

Haines, David W., ed. *Refugees as Immigrants: Cambodians, Laotians, and Vietnamese in America.* Totowa, N.J.: Rowman and Littlefield, 1989.

Hawkins, Freda. *Canada and Immigration: Public Policy and Public Concern.* Montreal: McGill–Queen's University Press, 1972.

Loescher, Gil, and John A. Scanlan. *Calculated Kindness: Refugees and America's Half-Open Door, 1945 to the Present.* New York: Free Press, 1986.

Mitchell, Christopher, ed. *Western Hemisphere Immigration and United States Foreign Policy.* University Park: Pennsylvania State University Press, 1992.

Nackerud, Larry, et al. "The End of the Cuban Contradiction in U.S. Refugee Policy." *International Migration Review* 33, no. 1 (Spring 1999): 176–92.

Tucker, Robert W., Charles B. Keely, and Linda Wrigley, eds. *Immigration and U.S. Foreign Policy.* Boulder, Colo.: Westview Press, 1990.

Vernant, J. *The Refugee in the Post-War World.* New Haven, Conn.: Yale University Press, 1953.

Whitaker, Reg. *Double Standard: The Secret Story of Canadian Immigration.* Toronto: Lester and Orpen Dennys, 1987.

Colombian immigration

The Colombian community in the United States is ethnically diverse and forms the largest immigrant group from South America. Generally, Colombians have maintained close ties to their home country and have thus been slow to assimilate. Because of Colombia's history of relations with United States, settlement in Canada has always been small. In the U.S. census of 2000 and the Canadian census of 2001, 470,684 Americans and 15,865 Canadians claimed Colombian descent. New York City; Chicago, Illinois; and Miami, Florida; have the highest concentrations of Colombian Americans. The largest Colombian communities in Canada are in Toronto and Montreal.

Colombia occupies 400,600 square miles of northwestern South America between 13 degrees north latitude and 4 degrees south latitude. Venezuela lies to the north and to the east along with Brazil. Peru and Ecuador lie to the south; the Pacific Ocean, Panama, and the Caribbean Sea are to the west. Several chains of the Andes run north to south in the western half of the country. Rich plains cover the northernmost regions, while more barren flatlands cover the east. In 2002, the population was estimated at 40,349,388, with more than 6 million in the urban area of Bogotá. The majority of the people claim Roman Catholicism as their religion. Colombians are ethnically divided among mestizos, who make up 58 percent of the population; whites, who compose another 20 percent; mulattos, 14 percent; and blacks, 4 percent. In the early 16th century, Spain conquered the native peoples who inhabited Colombia and ruled there until the area gained its independence in 1819 and the republic of Gran Colombia was founded. In 1830, the confederation collapsed when Venezuela and Ecuador withdrew to form independent nations, and small numbers of Colombians began to emigrate. From 1830 to 1886, the remaining territory of Gran Colombia went through various political transformations (and names), ending with the establishment of Colombia. After World War I, there was a significant migration of Colombian professionals, mainly to New York City. By 1930, perhaps as many as 25,000 Colombians had immigrated there. Throughout the 20th century, Colombia was ravaged by political violence in both rural and urban areas, in the last quarter century often linked to the activities of powerful drug-trafficking cartels. Political unrest between 1945 and 1955 was a powerful spur to immigration, leading a largely middle-class, white community to settle in Queens, New York. With their country in deep economic recession during the 1960s, Colombian immigration increased significantly and became more diversified, with the largest number of immigrants coming from mixed ancestry groups. According to the Immigration and Naturalization Service (INS), almost 120,000 entered the country between 1960 and 1977. In 1999, an earthquake struck Colombia, killing more than 1,100 and displacing an additional 250,000. Immigration continued to increase during the 1990s, along with nationwide protests against political violence and human rights violations. Between 1990 and 2002, about 190,000 Colombians immigrated to the United States, many joining family members already in the country. In 2000, the U.S. appropriated $1.3 billion to help Colombia fight drug trafficking, and right-wing paramilitary forces began a campaign against leftist guerrillas.

Although most Colombians entered the United States legally, it was estimated by the INS that in 2002 there were 141,000 unauthorized Colombians in the United States, making them the fourth largest unauthorized group, behind Mexico, El Salvador, and Guatemala. Unofficial estimates place the figure at more than twice that number. Canada was never a popular destination for Colombians. Most immigrants are recent. Of Canada's 15,500 Colombians, 6,480 arrived between 1996 and 2001. Many were well educated, immigrating to take advantage of economic opportunities. Most Colombians living in Canada were born in South America.

Further Reading

Chaney, Elsa M. "Colombian Migration to the United States." In *The Dynamics of Migration: International Migration.* Washington, D.C.: Interdisciplinary Communications Program, Smithsonian Institution, 1976.

Cordova, Carlos B., and Jorge del Pinal. *Hispanics-Latinos: Diverse People in a Multicultural Society.* Washington, D.C.: National Association of Hispanic Publications, U.S. Census Bureau, 1996.

Cornelius, Wayne, ed. *The Dynamics of Migration: International Migration.* Washington, D.C.: Smithsonian, 1976.

Garcia Castro, Mary. "Work Versus Life: Colombian Women in New York." In *Women and Change in Latin America.* Eds. June Nash and Helen Safa. South Hadley, Mass.: Bergin and Garvey, 1986.

Guarnizo, Luis Eduardo, and Luz Marina Díaz. "Trans-national Migration: A View from Colombia." *Ethnic And Racial Studies* 22, no. 2 (1998): 397–421.

Portes, Alejandro. "Determinants of the Brain Drain." *International Migration Review* 10, no. 4 (1976): 489–508.

Redden, C. A. *A Comparative Study of Colombian and Costa Rican Emigrants to the United States.* New York: Arno Press, 1980.

Rockett, Ian. "Immigration Legislation and the Flow of Specialized Human Capital from South America to the United States." *International Migration Review* 10, no. 1 (1976): 47–62.

Columbus, Christopher (1451–1506) *explorer*

Sailing for Spain during four voyages between 1492 and 1504, Christopher Columbus laid the foundation for an extensive Spanish empire in North, Central, and South America and eventually the Europeanization of the Western Hemisphere. As the first Europeans to reach the Americas since the 11th century, Columbus and his men unwittingly carried diseases that eventually killed perhaps half of the native populations of the Americas, leading to widespread destruction of native cultures.

Born in Genoa, Italy, Columbus became a mariner at an early age. After moving to Lisbon, Portugal, he sailed widely in the Mediterranean, the eastern Atlantic, and along the West African coast. During the 1480s, he determined that it was possible to reach China and the Indies by sailing westward, a novel idea that was rejected by Portuguese king John II. After several entreaties to the Spanish court, Columbus gained the support of Queen Isabella in 1492. On the first voyage (1492–93), he established Spanish claims to the Bahamas, Cuba, and Hispaniola (modern Haiti and the

Dominican Republic) and made the first European settlement in the New World on the northern shore of Hispaniola. On the second voyage, he made landfall on the island of Dominica and sailed up the Leeward Islands to Hispaniola, only to discover that the settlement had been destroyed. Before returning to Spain, he mapped the southern coast of Cuba, discovering Jamaica in the process, and left his brother Diego in charge of Isabella, a new settlement farther east along the northern coast of Hispaniola. On the third voyage (1496–1500), Columbus made landfall on Trinidad before finally setting foot on mainland South America (in Venezuela) for the first time in 1496. Based on the huge volume of water emanating from the Orinoco River, he rightly inferred that it represented the drainage of "a new world, hitherto unknown." Returning to Hispaniola, he found the fledgling colony in disarray. Mismanagement and quarrels with local officials led to Columbus's being returned to Spain in chains. Despite the lack of promised wealth, he nevertheless persuaded the Crown to sponsor a fourth voyage (1502–04). After landfall on Martinique and still convinced that the area he had discovered was only a short distance from China, he explored the Central American coastline in search of a strait that would led him there. Eventually abandoning the quest for a strait, Columbus also failed to discover gold, returning to Spain in disgrace.

Although unsuccessful in locating vast riches, Columbus's geographic achievement was momentous. He deciphered the North Atlantic wind system, enabling future mariners to travel to and from the New World with reasonable hope of safe passage. He also explored much of the coastal Caribbean basin and established the Greater Antilles as a base for further Spanish imperial expansion throughout the 16th century.

Further Reading

Colón, Fernando, ed. *The Life of the Admiral Christopher Columbus by His Son Ferdinand.* Rev. ed. New Brunswick, N.J.: Rutgers University Press, 1992.

Columbus, Christopher. *The Four Voyages of Christopher Columbus.* Ed. and trans. J. M. Cohen. New York: Penguin, 1992.

Fernández-Armesto, Felipe. *Columbus.* New York: Oxford University Press, 1991.

Morison, Samuel Eliot. *Admiral of the Ocean Sea: A Life of Christopher Columbus.* Boston: Little, Brown, 1942.

Sale, Kirkpatrick. *The Conquest of Paradise: Christopher Columbus and the Columbian Legacy.* New York: Plume Books, 1992.

Compagnie de la Nouvelle France (Company of New France, Company of One Hundred Associates)

The Compagnie de la Nouvelle France was a commercial company organized in 1627 by the government of France as a means of aggressively colonizing NEW FRANCE. It administered the region on behalf of the Crown until 1663, when New France was made a royal colony.

For the first two decades of French interest in North America, fishing, the fur trade, and missionary activity predominated, none requiring large-scale settlement. With the advent of mercantilistic economic theory and its focus on maintaining a favorable balance of trade, overseas colonies were viewed as important to state finances. Louis XIII's chief minister, Cardinal Richelieu, responded to the lobbying of explorer and entrepreneur SAMUEL DE CHAMPLAIN, by creating the Compagnie de la Nouvelle France, often known as the Company of One Hundred Associates. The associates provided 300,000 livres of working capital and were to settle 4,000 French Catholics between 1627 and 1643. In return, they were given title to all French lands and granted a monopoly on all economic activity except fishing. In order to maintain control of the colony, Protestants and naturalized citizens were prohibited from permanent settlement.

The company enjoyed little success. In addition to bad weather that inhibited immigration, England constantly threatened French interests, destroying expeditions in 1628 and 1629 and occupying Quebec from 1629 to 1632. The first substantial group of settlers, not sent until 1634, included merchants, landless noblemen, skilled workers, and indentured servants (see INDENTURED SERVITUDE). The company employed the seigneurial system for distributing land, giving large tracts to companies or individuals, known as seigneurs, or lords, who would undertake to establish settlements. Under the new system, settlements were established at Trois-Rivières (1634) and on the island of Montreal (1642), though they failed to attract substantial settlement. In 1645, the company relinquished its monopoly of the fur trade to a group of businessmen known as La Communauté des Habitants, along with direct responsibility for settlement, while retaining control of lands. By the early 1660s, it was clear that private settlement schemes would not work. Only 3,000 settlers populated the vast area of New France, and more than one-third of these settlers had been born in North America. Although 60 siegneuries had been granted, the settlement provisions had largely gone unfulfilled. In 1663, the government of the region was completely reorganized. The company was disbanded on February 24, 1663, and the colony brought directly under royal control. The Crown then transferred the administration of New France into the hands of the Compagnie des Indes Occidentals (French West Indies Company).

See also COLBERT, JEAN BAPTISTE.

Further Reading

Eccles, William J. *France in America*. New York: Harper and Row, 1972.

Trudel, Marcel. *The Beginnings of New France, 1524–1663*. Toronto: McClelland and Stewart, 1972.

Vachon, André. *Dreams of Empire: Canada before 1700*. Ottawa: Public Archives of Canada, 1982.

Connecticut colony

The Connecticut colony, chartered by Charles II in 1662, was an outgrowth of the great Puritan migration of the 1630s. First claimed by the Dutch in 1614, it was not effectively settled until the 1630s, when English settlers began to arrive in large numbers from MASSACHUSETTS COLONY. Determined to find greater freedom and less settled areas, Congregationalists founded the villages of Hartford, Windsor, and Wethersfield in the Connecticut River Valley by 1636. They joined to form the colony of Connecticut, led by the dynamic minister Joseph Hooker. Two years later New Haven was established as a Puritan theocracy but was absorbed by the thriving valley settlements when Connecticut was granted its charter. Under Hooker's leadership, Congregationalists of Connecticut adopted the Fundamental Orders (1639), which provided for citizen voting in selecting government officials. By 1700, Connecticut and Rhode Island were the only two English colonies with corporate charters granting full self-government. Having been settled largely before the end of the SEVEN YEARS' WAR (1756–63), Connecticut remained until the AMERICAN REVOLUTION (1776–83) heavily English in character, with almost no non-English enclaves.

Further Reading

Cressy, David. *Coming Over: Migration and Communication between England and New England in the Seventeenth Century*. Cambridge: Cambridge University Press, 1987.

Foster, Stephen. *The Long Argument: English Puritanism and the Shaping of New England Culture, 1570–1700*. Chapel Hill: Institute of Early American History and Culture, University of North Carolina Press, 1991.

Gura, Philip F. *A Glimpse of Sion's Glory: Puritan Radicalism in New England, 1620–1660*. Middletown, Conn.: Wesleyan University Press, 1984.

Taylor, Robert J. *Colonial Connecticut: A History*. Millwood, N.Y.: KTO, 1979.

Contract Labor Act   See ALIEN CONTRACT LABOR ACT.

Croatian immigration

Croatians were the earliest south Slavic group to settle in North America in significant numbers. In the U.S. census of 2000 and the Canadian census of 2001, 374,241 Americans and 97,050 Canadians claimed Croatian descent. The earliest Croatian concentrations in the United States were in San Francisco, but in the 20th century these shifted to Pittsburgh and western Pennsylvania. About two-thirds of Canadian Croatians live in Ontario, although there is also a large settlement in Vancouver.

Croatia occupies 21,800 square miles of the Balkan Peninsula between 42 and 47 degrees north latitude along the Adriatic Sea. Slovenia and Hungary lie to the north,

Bosnia and Herzegovina and Serbia and Montenegro to the east. Flat plains cover the northeast region of the country, while highlands stretch along the coast. In 2002, the population was estimated at 4,334,142. The people are ethnically divided between Croats, mostly Roman Catholics, who make up 78 percent of the population; and Serbs, mostly Orthodox Christian, who make up 12 percent. Almost 700,000 ethnic Croats also live in neighboring Bosnia and Herzegovina. The Croat language is similar to Serbian but written with the Latin alphabet. Croats briefly had an independent kingdom in the Middle Ages but were from the 12th century westernized under Hungarian influence, apart from the Serbs. They remained autonomous until conquered by the Turks during the 16th century, though northern areas of Croatia were restored to the Habsburg (Austrian) Empire in 1699. Croatia was granted crownland status along with Slavonia following the Hungarian Revolution of 1848–49, during which Croatia aided Austria. In 1867, the area was reunited with Hungary until 1918, when it joined other south Slavic nations in declaring the Kingdom of Serbs, Croats, and Slovenes, later known as Yugoslavia. At the end of World War II, in 1945, Croatia became a constituent republic of Yugoslavia. Croatia declared its independence in 1991, causing an outbreak of ethnic war between Serbs and Croats. Following several cease-fires, Serbian rebels declared the independent republic of Krajina in 1994. The Croatian government continued fighting and finally captured Krajina in 1998, restoring the republic.

Some Croatian adventurers and sailors came to the Gulf Coast region of the United States as early as the 17th century. The earliest Croatian settlement was in New Orleans and the coastal regions of Mississippi, where a community of 3,000–4,000 had been established by the time of the Civil War (1861–65). Croatians—or Dalmatians, as they were frequently called—also began to move to the American West, where they worked as fishermen, small businessowners, and eventually farmers and fruit growers. In 1857, they had established in San Francisco the first charitable society in the United States organized to help Slavic immigrants, the Slavonic Illyrian Mutual and Benevolent Society. By 1880, the Croatian community in the United States had grown to 20,000. After 1880, Croatians were part of the massive migration of eastern and southern Europeans to North America, most settling in the Great Lakes industrial belt, where they often worked in heavy industry. Because Slavic groups frequently were not distinguished from one another and immigrants were often classified according to the country of emigration, it is impossible to say how many Croatians came, but one estimate places the number in the 1930s at around a half million. Between 1899 and 1924, however, almost half of them returned to their homeland. With the disruptions of World War II and the advent of a Communist government in Yugoslavia, about 40,000 Croatians were admitted into the United States under a variety of measures,

including the DISPLACED PERSONS ACT (1948) and the REFUGEE RELIEF ACT (1953). A small but steady immigration during the 1970s and 1980s added almost 50,000 more. Between 1992 and 2002, about 18,000 Croatians immigrated to the United States, including 5,675 refugees.

Croatian adventurers known as Kolumbusari sought their economic fortunes in Canada as early as the 16th century, though they rarely brought their families with them. Most were miners, loggers, or fishermen. The first significant number of Croatian settlers in Canada arrived in British Columbia in 1890. The region continued to attract miners, lumbermen, and fishermen until World War I, many coming by way of the United States. Croatians were among the 6,000 to 10,000 "bunkhouse men" who immigrated between 1900 and 1912, helping to open western territories. As mines opened across Canada after the war, Croatians migrated, spreading throughout the country. During the 1920s, about 20,000 Croats entered Canada, many having been diverted from the United States in the wake of the JOHNSON-REED ACT of 1924, but almost one-quarter of Croatians returned to their homeland, keeping population growth relatively small in Canada. The first Croatian Peasant Society was founded in Toronto in 1930. After World War II, from 1946 to 1958, some 22,000 refugees and displaced Croatians arrived in Canada, often with advanced degrees and specialized training that had not been characteristic of earlier immigrants. Of Canada's 39,375 Croatian immigrants in 2001, more than half came in the 1960s and 1970s and more than a quarter between 1991 and 2001.

See also AUSTRO-HUNGARIAN IMMIGRATION; YUGOSLAV IMMIGRATION.

Further Reading

Colaković, Branko M. *Yugoslav Migrations and America*. San Francisco: R. and E. Research Associates, 1973.

Gorvaorchin, Gerald G. *Americans from Yugoslavia*. Gainesville: University of Florida Press, 1961.

Markotić, Vladimir, ed. *Biographical Directory of Americans and Canadians of Croatian Descent*. Calgary, Canada: Canadian Centre for Ethnic Studies, 1973.

Meler, V. *The Slavonic Pioneers of California*. San Francisco: Ragusan Press, 1972.

Prpić, George. *The Croatian Immigrants in America*. New York: Philosophical Library, 1971.

Rasporich, Anthony W. *For a Better Life: A History of the Croatians in Canada*. Toronto: McClelland and Stewart, Department of the Secretary of State, 1982.

Shapiro, Ellen. *The Croatian Americans*. New York: Chelsea House, 1989.

Cuban immigration

Cubans are usually considered to be the most successful Hispanic immigrant group, with educational and economic profiles near those of the U.S. population as a whole. They constitute the third largest Hispanic immigrant group in the United States, behind only Mexicans and Puerto Ricans (see *HISPANIC* AND RELATED TERMS). Their migration to the United States was fostered by both proximity and a unique diplomatic relationship that did not apply to Canada. In the U.S. census of 2000 and the Canadian census of 2001, 1,241,685 Americans claimed Cuban descent, but only 6,200 Canadians. Cuban settlement in the United States after 1959 overwhelmingly centered in MIAMI, FLORIDA, adding to important earlier settlements in New York City; New Orleans, Louisiana; Key West, Florida; and Ybor City, Florida. Almost two-thirds of Cuban Americans live in Florida.

Cuba is the largest Caribbean island, occupying 42,800 square miles between 19 and 24 degrees north latitude. The nearest countries include the United States and the Bahamas to the north, Haiti to the east, and Jamaica to the south. The northern coast of the island is high and rocky. Flat plains stretch along the southern coast. In 2002, the population was estimated at 11,184,023, 96 percent of which is made up of whites and mestizos. Prior to Fidel Castro's rule, the majority of the population practiced Roman Catholicism. CHRISTOPHER COLUMBUS landed at Cuba in 1492 and found native inhabitants. Spain held the island until 1898, excepting the British occupation of Havana from 1762 to 1763. Uprisings against Spanish rule began in 1868 and culminated in a full-scale revolution in 1895. Although Cuba was a Spanish colony until 1898, the island's close proximity to the United States made its economic and political stability a matter of concern to the U.S. government. In the wake of its first war for independence in 1868, thousands of Cubans sought refuge in the United States, with most settling in New York City or Tampa, Florida. The U.S. drove Spain out of Cuba in 1898, but poor economic conditions and repressive political regimes continued to drive refugees across the 90-mile channel that separated Cuba and the United States. Frequently, they would return to Cuba as political and economic conditions changed. The United States withdrew troops in 1902, but since 1903, it has leased land in Guantánamo Bay for a naval base. During the first half of the 20th century, American investors continued to be heavily involved in Cuba's sugar-based economy.

In 1952, former president Fulgencio Batista took control of the government and established himself dictator, with tacit support of the U.S. government. During his regime, about 10,000 Cubans were naturalized as U.S. citizens. Beginning in 1956, Fidel Castro led an open rebellion against the increasingly harsh and corrupt government. Batista fled in 1959 and Castro assumed leadership of the country and consolidated power under the Communist Party. Mass emigration, principally to the United States, followed. An estimated 700,000 left during the first several years. Within his first year in power, Castro nationalized the majority of the country's industries and began to accept aid from the Soviet Union and other communist nations. In 1961, the United States–supported invasion of Cuba by Cuban émigrés at the Bay of Pigs proved to be a disaster, further heightening tensions between the two countries. The United States followed with an export embargo in 1962. Later that year, the United States discovered that Cuba was harboring Soviet nuclear missiles. President JOHN FITZGERALD KENNEDY warned Cuba of impending military consequences and imposed a military blockade to prohibit Soviet warheads from reaching the island, which led to the eventual withdrawal of the missiles. Cuba's COLD WAR involvement in Central America and Africa, including sending military troops to aid a civil war faction in Angola from 1975 to 1978, further strained relations with the United States. Between 1959 and 1980, almost 1 million Cubans emigrated from their Caribbean island home to the United States, where they enjoyed preferential treatment by the U.S. government as victims of Castro's Communist regime. The MARIEL BOATLIFT of 1980 represented a turning point in U.S. policy toward Cuban immigrants. In response to a severely strained economy, in April, Castro opened the port of Mariel to allow more than 125,000 Cubans to leave for the United States, including 24,000 with criminal records. This influx of poor Cubans, having little to do with cold war politics, destroyed an already declining belief that Cuban immigrants should be treated differently than others, and their immigration was thereafter gradually normalized and brought under ordinary immigration control. Castro relaxed his strict policy in 1994, following national demonstrations and the exodus of thousands of Cubans on homemade rafts trying to float to Florida. The United States imposed economic sanctions in 1996 following the destruction of two exile planes operating against Castro. Relations improved again in 1999. In 2000, Cuba and the United States fought an international legal battle over ELIÁN GONZÁLEZ, a young boy whose mother died in an attempt to bring her son to Miami, but whose father resided in Cuba.

After Castro's revolution, most Cubans came to the United States in one of four waves of migration, adding to some 50,000 Cubans or those of Cuban descent already living in the United States. In the immediate aftermath of Castro's takeover (1959–62), more than 200,000 came to settle in southern Florida, particularly in the Miami-Dade County area. In keeping with earlier Cuban refugees, most believed that a future turn in political fortunes would allow them to return to their homeland. In order to ease their transition and establish a clear commitment to resisting communism, the administration of Dwight Eisenhower established the Cuban Refugee Emergency Center (1960). Many of these early postrevolution immigrants were part of the corrupt, toppled Batista government; most were men and women of the middle and upper classes, including government officials, industrialists, bankers, and professionals; and most were of European descent. President Kennedy built upon

Eisenhower's policies, establishing the Cuban Refugee Program (February 3, 1961), which provided a wide range of social services to Cuban immigrants, including health care and subsidized educational loans. The United States also suspended parts of its immigration policy, waiving numerical restrictions on the number of visas that could be issued to Cubans. During 1961 and 1962, 99 percent of all waivers were granted in order to provide for "refugees from communism." Castro at first allowed relatively unhindered emigration on regular commercial flights from Havana, the capital. These were not stopped even in the wake of a disastrous U.S.-backed invasion attempt by Cuban émigrés at the Bay of Pigs (April 1961). With the Cuban missile crisis of October 1962, however, Castro closed airports to commercial traffic, and the United States actively sought to isolate Cuba by seeing that commercial flights did not resume. Although visa "waivers" continued to be issued, it became almost impossible for Cubans to emigrate because of the American attempt to isolate Cuba from the world community.

The second great wave of migration began in autumn 1965, when Castro opened the port of Camarioca to anyone seeking to bring relatives out of Cuba and promised not to prosecute those who gathered for the purpose of immigration. President Lyndon Johnson responded by declaring that "those who seek refuge here in America will find it," immediately undermining the limitations established by the newly passed U.S. IMMIGRATION AND NATIONALITY ACT (1965). After heated debate, Congress passed the Cuban Adjustment of Status Act (1966), exempting refugees who had been admitted as parolees without a visa from the requirement of traveling to a third country to formalize their status. This measure established a legal distinction between Cuban and all other immigrants from the Western Hemisphere, based on America's cold war ideology. As a result of these policies, almost 300,000 Cubans entered the United States between 1965 and 1973, most on chartered "freedom flights." This wave of migration was more diverse racially than the first and included a much higher percentage of women, as Castro had forbidden skilled workers to emigrate. It also included up to half of Cuba's doctors, lawyers, professors, and other professional groups. In order to ease the burden imposed by Cuban immigrants in Florida, the Cuban Refugee Resettlement Program was established in 1961, providing transportation and financial assistance to refugees who would immediately relocate. Between 1961 and 1978, more than 300,000 Cubans were resettled, mostly in New York, New Jersey, California, and Illinois.

After seven years of hostility toward emigration (1973–80), a worsening economy pushed Castro to reverse his policy, leading to the migration of 125,000 Cubans during the Mariel Boatlift. Whereas America's ideological commitment to deter communism overrode all other considerations in the 1960s, the governmental consensus in favor of granting Cubans special immigration status began to break down in the 1970s. The resulting U.S. REFUGEE ACT (1980) required Cubans to meet the same "strict standards for asylum" as other potential refugees from the Western Hemisphere, placing them in the same category as Haitians who had been arriving illegally in large numbers throughout the 1970s (see HAITIAN IMMIGRATION). Facing a weak economy, on April 20, 1980, Cuban president Fidel Castro opened the port of Mariel to emigrants and encouraged "anti-social elements" to leave. Within five months, more than 125,000 Cubans had been transported to the United States, including 24,000 with criminal records. At first the *marielitos* were treated as refugees, but by June 20, the administration of President Jimmy Carter enacted sanctions against those transporting Cuban migrants and confirmed that Cubans would be coupled with Haitians as "entrants (status pending)" rather than as refugees. Fearing both an exodus of skilled technicians and deterioration of relations with the United States, on September 25, Castro closed the harbor at Mariel to emigration. Negotiations by the Carter administration and the following administration of Ronald Reagan in the wake of the Mariel Boatlift led to agreements in the mid-1980s that came close to normalizing immigrant relations between the two countries. Cuba agreed to accept 2,746 "excludable" Mariel Cubans, and the United States agreed to issue up to 20,000 annual "preference immigrant visas to Cuban nationals," though only about 2,000 were issued each year between 1988 and 1994.

With the ending of Soviet subsidies following the breakup of the Soviet Union (1991), the Cuban economy neared collapse, driving increasing numbers of *balseros* (emigrants on rafts) attempting to reach American shores. Between 1985 and 1990, only a few hundred *balseros* arrived each year. In 1991, the number increased to more than 2,000, and two years later, to 3,656. In 1994, Castro ended his policy of pursuing Cubans seeking to flee to the United States, leading to the departure of 37,000 Cubans during August and September. Faced with a potential repeat of the Mariel influx, the Clinton administration ordered rafters to be intercepted and sent to refugee camps at Guantánamo Naval Base or in Panama. On May 2, 1995, the U.S. government ended its policy of automatically admitting Cuban refugees, stipulating that future Cuban immigrants would be required to apply according to normal procedures. By an agreement signed on September 9, 1995, the United States agreed to a minimum annual level of Cuban immigration at 20,000, excluding relatives of U.S. citizens. In return, the Cuban government reinstated border controls in order to prevent illegal departures. Between 1992 and 2002, about 225,000 Cubans legally immigrated to the United States. Of Canada's 4,940 Cuban immigrants, more than half arrived between 1996 and 2001.

Further Reading

Ackerman, Holly, and Juan M. Clark. *The Cuban Balseros: Voyage of Uncertainty.* Miami, Fla.: Cuban American National Council, 1995.

Boswell, Thomas D. *A Demographic Profile of Cuban Americans.* Miami, Fla.: Cuban American National Council, 1994.

Boswell, Thomas D., and James R. Curtis. *The Cuban-American Experience.* Totowa, N.J.: Rowman and Allanheld, 1984.

Dominguez, Jorge I., ed. *Cuba: Internal and International Affairs.* Beverley Hills, Calif.: Sage Publications, 1982.

García, María Cristina. *Havana USA: Cuban Exiles and Cuban Americans in South Florida, 1959–1994.* Berkeley: University of California Press, 1996.

Masud-Piloto, Robert. *From Welcomed Exiles to Illegal Immigrants: Cuban Migration to the United States, 1959–1995.* Lanham, Md.: Rowman and Littlefield, 1996.

Mitchell, Christopher, ed. *Western Hemisphere Immigration and United States Foreign Policy.* University Park: Pennsylvania State University Press, 1992.

Morley, Morris H. *Imperial State and Revolution: The United States and Cuba, 1952–1986.* Cambridge: Cambridge University Press, 1987.

Olson, James S., and Judith E. Olson. *Cuban-Americans: From Trauma to Triumph.* New York: Twayne, 1995.

Pedraza-Bailey, Silvia. *Political and Economic Migrants in America.* Austin: University of Texas Press, 1985.

Portes, Alejandro, and Robert L. Bach. *Latin Journey: Cuban and Mexican Immigrants in the United States.* Berkeley: University of California Press, 1985.

Welch, Richard E., Jr. *Response to Revolution: The United States and the Cuban Revolution, 1959–1961.* Chapel Hill: University of North Carolina Press, 1985.

Customs and Border Protection, U.S. (CBP)

Customs and Border Protection is the federal agency within the Border and Transportation Security Directorate (BTS) responsible for law enforcement and inspections along U.S. borders. It operates under the jurisdiction of the DEPARTMENT OF HOMELAND SECURITY (DHS). CBP employs almost 40,000 men and women in protecting the country's borders, intercepting illegal drugs and other contraband, and enforcing trade and immigration laws at the border.

Customs and Border Protection was created as a result of the Homeland Security Act of 2002, which dissolved the IMMIGRATION AND NATURALIZATION SERVICE (Department of Justice), the U.S. Customs Service (Department of the Treasury), and the Agricultural Quarantine and Inspection program (Department of Agriculture), and transferred security-related functions to the newly created DHS. The U.S. BORDER PATROL was merged into the CBP, and all border-related functions were then coordinated. An early goal of the CBP was to create "One Face at the Border," with former customs, INS, and agricultural inspectors all working in a single agency under a unified chain of command.

Further Reading

Butikofer, Nathan R. *United States Land Border Security Policy: The National Security Implications of 9/11 on the "Nation of Immigrants" and Free Trade in North America.* Monterey, Calif.: Naval Postgraduate School, 2003.

Krauss, Erich. *On the Line: Inside the U.S. Border Patrol.* Sacramento, Calif.: Citadel Press, 2004.

Krouse, William J. *Department of Homeland Security: Proposals to Consolidate Border and Transportation Security Agencies.* Washington, D.C.: Congressional Research Service, 2002.

"Under One Roof." *Government Executive* 35, no. 5 (2003): 26.

United States Department of Homeland Security Handbook. Washington, D.C.: International Business Publications, 2003.

U.S. Customs and Border Protection Web site. Available online. URL: http://www.cbp.gov/xp/cgov/home.xml. Accessed July 5, 2004.

Czech immigration

Czechs were among the earliest eastern European peoples to immigrate to North America, first coming in large numbers to the United States in the 1850s. In the U.S. Census of 2000 and the Canadian census of 2001, 1,703,930 Americans and 274,740 Canadians claimed Czech or Czechoslovakian descent. Although Czechs were widely spread in agricultural areas of the United States, they had large enclaves in Chicago, Illinois; Cleveland, Ohio; and New York City. Czechs are dispersed throughout Canada, with significant concentrations in Toronto, Montreal, Vancouver, and Winnipeg.

The Czech Republic occupies 30,300 square miles of eastern central Europe between 48 and 51 degrees north latitude. Poland lies to the north and to the east; Slovakia to the southeast; Austria, to the south; and Germany, to the north and west. The land is hilly with a plateau surrounded by mountains in the west. In 2002, the population was estimated at 10,264,212. Ethnic Czechs comprise 94 percent of the population, and the closely related Slovaks make up 3 percent. The population is divided mainly between atheists and Roman Catholics, each group reaching about 40 percent. The Czech regions of Bohemia and Moravia were part of the Moravian Empire, the Holy Roman Empire, and the Austro-Hungarian Empire prior to the proclamation of the republic of Czechoslovakia in 1918. Heavy population pressure during the 19th century and a failed nationalist revolution in 1848 led an increasing number of Czechs to seek their fortunes outside the country. From the 14th century, the Czech city of Prague was in many ways the cultural center of eastern Europe. In 1938, Czechoslovakia was partitioned. After agreements with Britain and France, Nazi Germany under Adolf Hitler occupied the westernmost portion of Czechoslovakia, known as the Sudetenland. Russian and Czech troops began to liberate Czechoslovakia in 1944, freeing Prague in 1945. Under Soviet pressure, a Communist prime minister was chosen, and by 1948, the government was fully under Communist control. A serious move toward liberalization began in 1968 when the Stalinist ruler was deposed. A series of liberal leaders attempted democratic reforms but were ousted by troops from the Soviet Union, Poland, East Germany, Hungary, and Bulgaria. The invasion caused some 40,000 refugees to flee the country, which was returned to a more orthodox communist rule. In 1989, tens of thousands of protesters demanding free elections took to the streets of Prague, where a violent police crackdown occurred. Communist rulers stepped down, and a popular regime took control. Following peaceful negotiations in 1992, Slovakia declared its independence and separated from what was renamed the Czech Republic. The Czech Republic joined the North Atlantic Treaty Organization in 1999 and the European Union in 2004.

The westernmost of the Slavic peoples of Europe, Czechs from the Austrian Empire followed much the same pattern of settlement in North America as did southern Germans, though few immigrated during the colonial period. The first significant immigration followed the abortive REV-OLUTIONS OF 1848. By 1860, there were already more than 10,000 Czechs in the United States, many of them having migrated to Chicago; St. Louis, Missouri; and Cleveland. Others, arriving as family units, usually chose, before 1880, to farm in the Mississippi valley, Nebraska, Kansas, and Texas. After 1880, Czech immigrants increasingly found work in mines and steel mills, and most stayed to raise fam-

Czech children in front of a bandstand. More than 12,000 Czech refugees were admitted to Canada following the Soviet occupation of 1968 and a similar number to the United States. *(George Shultz Collection/Double Delta Industries, Inc./#231)*

ilies in the United States. By 1900, more than 56 percent of Czech Americans were born in the New World. By World War I (1914–18), some 350,000 Czechs had immigrated to the United States, with Illinois being the most favored state of settlement, and Chicago and Cleveland, the leading centers of Czech culture. With the restrictive JOHNSON-REED ACT of 1924, Czech immigration declined until the Nazi occupation, which brought some 20,000 additional immigrants to the United States. With Communists gaining control of the Czech government after World War II, the United States opened its doors to Czech refugees as a part of its COLD WAR commitment. Between 1946 and 1975, more than 27,000 Czechs were admitted. With increasing political opposition to the Communist Party during the 1980s, the number of refugee claims rose significantly. Between 1983 and 1989, more than 7,000 Czechoslovak refugees were admitted. The Czech Republic has recognized personal freedoms since its independence in 1989. As a result, the number of immigrants has declined dramatically to about 1,000 per year between 1992 and 2002.

Czech immigration to Canada developed more slowly. The first significant migration came after 1880, when a small number of Czech farmers from the United States and a handful of immigrants from the Austro-Hungarian Empire established several settlements in southeastern Saskatchewan and Alberta. European Czechs often settled near Slovakian and Hungarian communities. After 1910, a number of Czech Baptist communities were established in the Swan river valley of southern Manitoba. Prior to World War I, Winnipeg had the largest Czech urban population, though it remained small. According to the census of 1911, there were only 1,800 Czechs in Canada. While these early Czech immigrants came mainly for economic opportunity, most after 1918 were admitted as refugees as a result of various political crises. During the 1920s, the newly created state of Czechoslovakia had a strong economy and a relatively stable political system, thus discouraging immigration. The small number of Czechs who did come to Canada tended to be urban workers and overwhelmingly flocked to Montreal and southern Ontario. The number of immigrants declined to less than 100 annually during the 1930s and stopped almost altogether following the partition and occupation of Czechoslovakia in 1937–38. Thousands of Czechs displaced by World War II and the Communist takeover of 1948 fled to refugee camps in Germany and Austria. Between 1948 and 1952, about 10,000 Czechoslovaks immigrated to Canada; probably about half were Czechs. Immigration remained small until the Soviet Union's brutal suppression of the Prague uprising of August 1968, leading Canada to admit about 12,000 refugees, a third of whom were professionals or skilled trade workers. Of Canada's 29,310 Czech or Czechoslovakian immigrants in 2001, only 3,225 arrived between 1991 and 2001.

See also AUSTRO-HUNGARIAN IMMIGRATION.

Further Reading

Barton, Josef J. *Peasants and Strangers: Italians, Rumanians, and Slovaks in an American City, 1890–1950.* Cambridge, Mass.: Harvard University Press, 1975.

———. "Religion and Cultural Change in Czech Immigrant Communities, 1850–1920." In *Immigrants and Religion in Urban America.* Ed. R. M. Miller and T. D. Marzik. Philadelphia: Temple University Press, 1977.

Bicha, K. D. *The Czechs in Oklahoma.* Norman: University of Oklahoma Press, 1980.

Capek, T. *The Czechs (Bohemians) in America: A Study of Their National, Cultural, Political, Social, Economic, and Religious Life.* 1920. Reprint, New York: Arno Press, 1969.

Gellner, John, and John Smerek. *The Czechs and Slovaks in Canada.* Toronto: University of Toronto Press, 1968.

Habenicht, Jan. *History of Czechs in America.* 1910. Reprint, St. Paul: Geck and Slovak Genealogical Society of Minnesota, 1996.

Jerabek, E. *Czechs and Slovaks in North America: A Bibliography.* New York: Czechoslovak Society of Arts and Sciences in America, 1976.

Karytova-Magstadt, S. *To Reap a Bountiful Harvest: Czech Immigration beyond the Mississippi, 1850–1900.* Iowa City, Iowa: Rudi Publishing, 1993.

Kirschbaum, S. J. *A History of Slovakia: The Struggle for Survival.* New York: St. Martin's Press, 1995.

Kirschbaum, Joseph M. *Slovaks in Canada.* Toronto: Canadian Ethnic Press Association of Ontario, 1967.

Laska, V., ed. *The Czechs in America, 1633–1977: A Chronology and Fact Book.* Dobbs Ferry, N.Y.: Oceana Publications, 1978.

Luebke, Frederick C. *Ethnicity on the Great Plains.* Lincoln: University of Nebraska Press, 1981.

Machann, Clint, and J. W. Mendl. *Krasna Amerika: A Study of the Texas Czechs, 1851–1939.* Austin, Tex.: Eakin Press, 1983.

Rosicky, R. *A History of Czechs (Bohemians) in Nebraska.* Omaha: Czech Historical Society of Nebraska, 1929.

Stolarik, M. Mark. *Growing Up on the South Side: Three Generations of Slovaks in Bethlehem, Pennsylvania, 1880–1976.* Lewisburg, Pa.: Bucknell University Press, 1985.

———. *The Slovak Americans.* New York: Chelsea House, 1988.

Danish immigration

Though Viking Danes were probably among the first Europeans to settle North America, the first Danish settlement of lasting importance came in the 1640s, when about 500 Danes composed half the population of the Dutch New Netherlands colony. In the U.S. census of 2000 and the Canadian census of 2001, 1,430,897 Americans and 170,780 Canadians claimed Danish descent. Because of their rapid assimilation, Danes are spread fairly evenly throughout the U.S. and Canadian populations. Most Danes during the 19th century originally settled in the upper Midwest in the United States, with particular concentration in Iowa. The largest early Danish settlements in Canada, between 1903 and 1917, were in Alberta.

Denmark occupies 16,300 square miles of northern Europe between the North Sea and the Baltic Sea from 54 to 58 degrees north latitude. Sweden lies to the northeast and Germany to the south. Denmark is made up of the Jutland Peninsula and 500 islands, 100 of which are inhabited. Greenland and the Faeroe Islands govern themselves, but fall under Danish jurisdiction. The land is mostly flat and highly developed. In 2002, the population was estimated at 5,352,815. Ethnic groups include Scandinavian, Eskimo, Faeroese, and German. Evangelical Lutheranism is the religious preference of more than 90 percent of the people. From ancient times, Denmark was a center of fishing and trade. Viking raiders during the Middle Ages were mostly Danes. Denmark reached the peak of its power between 1397 and 1523, when Denmark, Norway, Sweden, and

parts of northern Germany were united under Danish control. Sweden withdrew in 1523, initiating a long period of international decline. Norway was lost in 1815, and Schleswig-Holstein in 1864. Iceland remained part of Denmark until 1944. Denmark joined the European Union in 1993.

Although a small number of Danes had immigrated to the United States annually from colonial times, it was only after the American Civil War (1861–65) that they came in large numbers. Denmark's population rose dramatically during the 19th century, from 900,000 to almost 2.5 million. This combined with Prussian expansion and a rapidly mechanizing economy threw Denmark's old agricultural system into chaos, with many Danes losing land and being forced into urban industrial jobs, when they could find them. It has been estimated that during the late 19th century, one in 10 Danes emigrated, most to the United States. In line with most other western European countries, they came in waves between 1866 and 1873, 1880 and 1893, 1900 and 1914, and 1920 and 1929. Between 1865 and 1930, about 325,000 Danes entered the country, with almost 12,000 entering in the peak year of 1882. In addition to those immigrating to the United States for economic reasons, some 17,000 Danes came between 1849 and 1904 after converting to the Church of Jesus Christ of Latter-day Saints (Mormons), most settling near Salt Lake City, Utah. Another group of some 50,000 Danes from Schleswig arrived after German occupation of their region in 1864, especially objecting to German military service and the use

74

of the German language in education. After 1930, Danish immigration averaged a few hundred per year, including 6,389 between 1992 and 2002.

The Dane Jens Munk visited Canada in 1619 searching for the Northwest Passage but established no colony. The oldest Danish settlement in Canada was established in New Brunswick in 1872, though it included only seven families and 10 single men. The number of Danes in Canada remained small until the first decade of the 20th century. In 1903, a group of Danish immigrants from Nebraska began to settle a township near Innisfail, Alberta. A number of additional colonies were established in Alberta, Manitoba, and Saskatschewan between 1903 and 1917. As these Danes were usually classified as Americans, it is difficult to determine their numbers. When the United States limited immigration with the JOHNSON-REED ACT of 1924, Danish agriculturalists increasingly looked to the Canadian West, a trend that continued through the 1950s. During the 1920s, the Canadian Pacific Railway and the Danish Department of Colonization and Development cooperated in promoting Danish settlement on the Canadian prairies. Furthermore, after spending six months in Canada in 1925, Olaf Linck recommended in *Canada, the Great Land of the Future* that young and healthy Danes consider emigration there in order to increase their opportunities and to relieve population pressures at home. Although almost 19,000 Danes immigrated to Canada between 1919 and 1931, Canada virtually halted immigration during the Great Depression. After World War II, Canada once again encouraged Danish immigration, highly regarding the training and skill of the artisans. Whereas only 10,984 Danes immigrated to the United States during the 1950s, 27,750 entered Canada. As the Danish economy improved in the 1960s, few chose to emigrate. Of 17,805 Danish immigrants in Canada in 2001, only 3,625 came after 1970.

Further Reading

Barton, H. Arnold. "Where Have the Scandinavian-Americanists Been?" *Journal of American Ethnic History* 15, no. 1 (Fall 1995): 46–55.

Bender, Henning, and Birgit Flemming Larsen, eds. *Danish Emigration to Canada*. Aalborg, Denmark: Danish Worldwide Archives and Danish Society for Emigration History, 1991.

———. *Danish Emigration to the U.S.A.* Aalborg, Denmark: Danish Worldwide Archives and Danish Society for Emigration History, 1992.

Hvidt, Kristian. *Flight to America—the Social Background to 300,000 Danish Emigrants*. New York: Academic Press, 1975.

Lovoll, O. S. *Nordics in America: The Future of Their Past*. Northfield, Minn.: Norwegian-American Historical Association, 1993.

Paulsen, Frank. *Danish Settlements on the Canadian Prairies: Folk Traditions, Immigrant Experiences, and Local History*. Ottawa: Centre for Folk Culture Studies, 1992.

Petersen, Peter L. *The Danes in America*. Minneapolis, Minn.: Lerner, 1987.

Stilling, N. P., and A. L. Olsen. *A New Life*. Aalborg, Denmark: Danish Worldwide Archives, 1994.

Delaware colony

The Delaware region was explored by Henry Hudson in 1609 as he searched for a passage to Asia. The Dutch first settled near present-day Lewes in 1631 but were driven out by the native peoples. Sweden settled the area as a commercial venture in 1638, giving it the name New Sweden and bringing in Swedish and Finnish settlers. In the 1640s, both the Netherlands and Sweden claimed the region, and in 1655 the Dutch finally incorporated New Sweden into their more northerly colony of New Netherland. As a result of a series of Anglo-Dutch wars in the 1660s and 1670s, Delaware became English territory. Originally administered as part of NEW YORK COLONY, in 1682 it became a part of the PENNSYLVANIA COLONY grant to William Penn. Known as the three lower counties, the Delaware region sought autonomy, which was granted in the Charter of Liberties (1701). Its first separate legislature met in 1704. By the time of the AMERICAN REVOLUTION (1775–83), most of the early Swedes and Finns had become indistinguishable from their more numerous English and Dutch neighbors.

Further Reading

Christensen, Gardell D., and Eugenia Burney. *Colonial Delaware*. New York: Nelson, 1975.

Horle, Craig William, ed. *Records of the Courts of Sussex County, Delaware, 1677–1710*. Philadelphia: University of Pennsylvania Press, 1992.

Munroe, John A. *Colonial Delaware: A History*. Millwood, N.Y.: KTO, 1978.

Department of Citizenship and Immigration Canada   See DEPARTMENT OF MANPOWER AND IMMIGRATION.

Department of Homeland Security (DHS)

Established by the Homeland Security Act (2002), the Department of Homeland Security (DHS) was the administrative response to the terrorist attacks of SEPTEMBER 11, 2001. The DHS coordinates most of the antiterror elements within the U.S. government in a new cabinet-level network of agencies tasked with the specific mission of preventing terrorist attacks within the United States, reducing vulnerability to terrorism, and minimizing damage from potential terrorist attacks. The DHS became fully operational on March 1, 2003.

The DHS is divided into five directorates. Border and Transportation Security (BTS), the largest, is responsible for securing the nation's borders and protecting its transportation systems. Agencies within the BTS include the Transportation Security Administration, the Animal and Plant Health Inspection Service, and the Federal Law Enforcement Training Center. The BTS performs security functions previously under the direction of the U.S. Customs Service and the IMMIGRATION AND NATURALIZATION SERVICE. The Emergency Preparedness and Response Directorate (EPR) is responsible for preparing against terrorist attack and natural disasters and for overseeing necessary recoveries. The Science and Technology Directorate (S&T) is devoted to research and development necessary for preparing against and responding to potential terrorist attacks involving weapons of mass destruction. The Information Analysis and Infrastructure Protection Directorate (IAIP) identifies and assesses intelligence information from many sources, issues warnings, and recommends preventive action. The Management Directorate is responsible for management and personnel matters related to the work of the DHS.

In addition to the five directorates, other agencies work under the umbrella of the DHS. Except in time of war or under the direct order of the president, the U.S. COAST GUARD operates under the DHS. The U.S. Secret Service is responsible for protecting government officials from harm and the U.S. currency from counterfeiting. The Bureau of Citizenship and Immigration Services, which includes the U.S. CITIZENSHIP AND IMMIGRATION SERVICES, administers immigration policy and provides services to all immigrants. The Office of State and Local Government Coordination ensures a coordinated response in case of terrorist attack, while the Office of Private Sector Liaison enables businesses, trade associations, and other nongovernmental organizations to work directly with the DHS on any security issues. The Office of Inspector General operates independently to audit and investigate any allegations of fraud, inefficiency, or mismanagement within the DHS. The relative importance and particular responsibilities of the various directorates and agencies are likely to change as the DHS develops.

Further Reading

Anikeeff, Anthony H., et al. *Homeland Security Law Handbook.* Rockville, Md.: ABS Consulting, 2003.

Butikofer, Nathan R. *United States Land Border Security Policy: The National Security Implications of 9/11 on the "Nation of Immigrants" and Free Trade in North America.* Monterey, Calif.: Naval Postgraduate School, 2003.

Gressle, Sharon S. *Homeland Security Act of 2002: Legislative History and Propagation.* Washington, D.C.: Congressional Research Service, 2002.

Haynes, Wendy. "Seeing Around Corners: Crafting the New Department of Homeland Security." *Review of Policy Research* 21, no. 3 (2004): 369–395.

Homeland Security Statutes. Rockville, Md.: Government Institutes, ABS Consulting, 2003.

United States Department of Homeland Security Handbook. Washington, D.C.: International Business Publications, 2003.

United States Department of Homeland Security Web site. Available online. URL: http://www.dhs.gov/dhspublic. Accessed July 5, 2004.

Department of Manpower and Immigration

The Department of Manpower and Immigration, created by the Government Organization Act of 1966, was the branch of the Canadian government responsible for administering immigration policies between 1966 and 1994. The measure consolidated various functions previously performed by the Department of Citizenship and Immigration and the Department of Labour and formed the basis for the structure of Canadian immigration management into the 21st century.

When Liberals were returned to office in 1963, they began systematically to analyze immigration guidelines, fearful of the substantial increase in unskilled immigrants. Determining that Canada's future immigration policy should be closely tied to the country's economic needs, the Liberals introduced a number of reforming measures, including the Government Organization Act. Most powers relating to immigrants as laborers would rest with the Manpower Division. According to the guiding theory of the reorganization, all employment services would be provided equally to all residents, both long established and new arrivals. As Freda Hawkins observed in *Canada and Immigration: Public Policy and Public Concern,* theoretically "it would make no difference whether a man arrived at a Toronto Canada Manpower Centre from Rome, Halifax, or Sudbury—he would have the same treatment." In fact, this led to what one critic called a "twilight zone in the planning and development of services for immigrants to facilitate their adjustment to Canadian life." Critics during the debate condemned the measure as a "grave error of national policy." Nevertheless, the Government Organization Act became law on June 16, 1966. It created a Department of Manpower and Immigration and a Department of Indian Affairs and Northern Development, while putting matters of citizenship under the secretary of state. The Immigration Appeal Board Act, passed on March 23, 1967, established an appeal board completely independent of the new Department of Manpower and Immigration. In 1994 a further reorganization created the Department of Citizenship and Immigration Canada (CIC), once again linking citizenship and immigration procedures in the same government department.

Further Reading

Hawkins, Freda. *Canada and Immigration: Public Policy and Public Concern.* 2d ed. Kingston and Montreal: McGill–Queen's University Press, 1988.

House of Commons Standing Committee on Citizenship and Immigration. *Canadian Citizenship: A Sense of Belonging.* Ottawa: Public Works and Government Services Canada, June 1944.

Detroit, Michigan

Located on the Detroit River, which separates the United States from Canada, Detroit became one of the great industrial cities of the United States by the end of the 19th century, attracting immigrant labor from eastern Europe and the Middle East. It became an important cultural hub for Italians, Bulgarians, Romanians, and Serbs, among others. From the 1970s, greater Detroit became increasingly recognized as the center of Arab settlement in the United States, with a population of approximately 200,000.

France's Fort Pontchartrain, established in 1701, was the first settlement founded along the north bank of the Detroit River. The opening of the Erie Canal in 1825 encouraged settlement from New York and New England, and completion of the Sault (Soo) Sainte Marie Canals along the Canadian border fostered the early development of Detroit as an industrial center. Between 1860 and 1880, the population grew from 45,600 to 116,000. A good transport system and a large supply of labor helped Detroit become the capital of the automotive industry during the early 20th century, and by 1910, the population had jumped to 465,766. Although the percentage of foreign-born immigrants declined from 44 percent in 1870 to 40 percent in 1890 and 34 percent in 1910, the dramatic increase in population meant that the majority of citizens during this period were either first- or second-generation immigrants. Prior to World War I (1914–18), Detroit plants and factories attracted large numbers of Greeks, Macedonians, Poles, Romanians, and Serbs. Syrian Druzes and Ottoman Turks created significant Muslim communities that would later serve as magnets for their coreligionists from other parts of the Middle East. Between 1880 and 1920, the largest non-Anglo ethnic groups in the city were Irish, Germans, and Poles.

With passage of the restrictive JOHNSON-REED ACT in 1924, Detroit plants and factories increasingly turned to domestic labor supplies, mainly poor southerners, both black and white. Earlier immigrants nevertheless continued to migrate to Detroit for jobs, and Canada provided a back-door for unauthorized immigration. With U.S. entry into World War II (1939–45) in 1941, the auto plants were transferred to military production, further stimulating the northward migration. Between 1910 and 1950, the population more than tripled to 1,849,568. As overcrowding became a problem and crime increased, by the late 1950s, people who could afford to were rapidly moving to the suburbs. At the same time, Arabs from a variety of religious and ethnic backgrounds were migrating westward from New York City and by 1970, had made Detroit the leading Arab

city in the United States, with a population of more than 70,000. The auto industry and the large Muslim community continued to attract immigrants from the Middle East, especially Iraqis, Yemenis, Palestinians, and Bosniaks. Despite provisions of the NORTH AMERICAN FREE TRADE AGREEMENT (NAFTA) which have encouraged the export of industrial jobs, Detroit remained the automotive capital of the country into the 21st century.

The 1990s saw a massive influx of Hispanic and Asian immigrants to Detroit, significantly altering the ethnic character of the city. Asian growth, including those from multiracial backgrounds, jumped 133 percent, and Hispanics 61 percent. In 2000, metropolitan Detroit had the seventh largest foreign-born population in the United States, though its percentage of foreign born was relatively low at 7.4 percent. It is only 14th in the nation as a magnet for immigrants, but still attracts people from around the world. The largest communities are still the older, largely assimilated German, Irish, Polish, and Italian. In 2000, however, the official Mexican and Arab populations were both over 100,000, with the actual figure much higher. Among the recent ethnic groups, the largest were Asian Indians (49,782), Lebanese (47,411), and Iraqis (10,628). As one journalist put it, Detroit "is more of a mosaic than a blend of racially mixed people."

Further Reading
Abraham, Nabeel. "The Yemeni Immigration Community of Detroit: Background, Emigration, and Community Life." In *Arabs in the New World.* Eds. Sameer Y. Abraham and Nabeel Abraham. Detroit: Wayne State University Press, 1983.
Abraham, Nabeel, and Andrew Shryock, eds. *Arab Detroit: From Margin to Mainstream.* Detroit: Wayne State University Press, 2000.
Arellano, Amber, and Kathleen Gray. "A Shifting Ethnic Mosaic." *Detroit Free Press,* March 29, 2001. Available online. URL: http://www.freep.com/news/census/crace29_20010329.htm. Accessed February 20, 2004.
Sengstock, M.C. "Iraqi Christians in Detroit: An Analysis of an Ethnic Occupation." In *Arabic-Speaking Communities in American Cities.* Ed. B. C. Aswad. New York: Center for Migration Studies and Association of Arab-American University Graduates, 1974.
Vargas, Zaragoza. *Proletarians of the North: A History of Mexican Industrial Workers in Detroit and the Midwest. 1917–1933.* Berkeley: University of California Press, 1993.
Vinyard, J. M. *The Irish on the Urban Frontier: Detroit, 1850–1880.* New York: Arno Press, 1974.
Zunz, Olivier. *The Changing Face of Inequality: Urbanization, Industrial Development, and Immigrants in Detroit, 1880–1920.* Chicago: University of Chicago Press, 1982.

Dillingham Commission

Between 1907 and 1910 the Dillingham Commission, established by the U.S. government, completed a study whose findings reflected the popular opinion of many native-born Americans that new immigrants from eastern and southern Europe were less desirable than earlier immigrants from western and northern Europe. The commission's recommendation of a literacy test was not adopted at the time, but a bill embodying the restriction was finally passed over President Woodrow Wilson's veto in 1917. The commission's findings also served as the basis of additional restrictive immigration legislation in the 1920s.

An IMMIGRATION ACT in 1907 codified and extended previous restrictive legislation and established a commission to evaluate U.S. immigration policy. Commission members from the Senate were Chairman William Paul Dillingham of Vermont (a Republican), Henry Cabot Lodge of Massachusetts (Republican), and Asbury Latimer of South Carolina (Democrat); members from the House of Representatives were Benjamin F. Howell of New Jersey (Republican), William S. Bennet of New York (Republican), and John L. Burnett of Alabama (Democrat); and presidential appointees were William R. Wheeler, Jeremiah W. Jenks, and Charles P. Neill. On December 5, 1910, a two-volume summary of the commission's findings was presented to Congress, and early in the following year, the massive 42-volume report was released. The commission's study concluded that during the 1880s a fundamental change occurred in immigration to the United States. Most who had come under the "old" immigration "mingled freely with . . . native Americans," and thus were assimilated. The NEW IMMIGRATION that had begun around 1883 was marked by an increase in transient, unskilled laborers who flocked to urban enclaves where they resisted assimilation. Recommendations of the committee included

1. new immigration legislation should "look especially to the economic well-being of our people"
2. industry should not be promoted to the detriment of wage levels and conditions of employment
3. a five-year period of deportability for immigrants accused of serious crimes, and a three-year period of deportability for those who become public charges
4. continuation of restrictions on Chinese, Japanese, and Korean immigration
5. further restrictions on unskilled immigrants
6. a literacy test as the best means of restricting immigration

Although there is much of value in the information and statistics gathered by the commission, its conclusions reflect the restrictionist bias of the committee members, who established an artificial dichotomy between "old" and "new" immigrants that obscured many variations from one ethnic group to another. The commission also failed to consider the effect of the recency of immigration, which clearly affected education, achievement, and rate of assimilation.

Further Reading

Handlin, Oscar. *Race and Nationality in American Life.* Boston: Little, Brown, 1957.
Hutchinson, E. P. *Legislative History of American Immigration Policy, 1798–1965.* Philadelphia: University of Pennsylvania Press, 1981.
Jones, Maldwyn A. *American Immigration.* Chicago: University of Chicago Press, 1960.
Report of the United States Immigration Commission. 41 vols. Washington, D.C., 1911.

Displaced Persons Act (United States) (1948)

Bills to assist central European refugees were brought before Congress in 1937 and 1939, but it was not found necessary to pass new legislation because the number of refugees could be accommodated under existing legislation. The magnitude of the refugee problem was so greatly enhanced by the destruction of World War II (1939–45), however, that new legislation became imperative. By mid-1945, there were already almost 2 million displaced persons, with thousands still fleeing from Soviet domination in eastern Europe (see WORLD WAR II AND IMMIGRATION). The main provisions of the Displaced Persons Act included approval of 220,000 visas to be issued for two years without regard to quota but charged to the appropriate quotas in future years; up to 3,000 nonquota visas for displaced orphans; and granting to the attorney general, with the approval of Congress, the right to adjust the status of up to 15,000 displaced persons who entered the country prior to April 1, 1948.

The act was amended on June 16, 1950, to add another 121,000 visas, for a total of 341,000, through June 1951, chargeable against future quotas at a maximum rate of one-fourth of quotas for three fiscal years (1951–54) and at one-half of quotas thereafter as needed. The number of visas for orphans was raised to 5,000 and taken as a part of the total authorization of 341,000. The provision for adjusting the status of previously admitted displaced persons was extended to those who had entered the United States prior to April 30, 1949. An additional section was added to the Displaced Persons Act, providing 5,000 additional nonquota visas for orphans under the age of 10 who were coming for adoption, to an agency, or to reside with close relatives.

On June 28, 1951, the Displaced Persons Act was again amended to extend the time for issuing the 341,000 visas to the end of 1951 and through the first half of 1952 for displaced orphans.

Further Reading

Daniels, Roger. *Guarding the Golden Door: American Immigration Policy and Immigrants since 1882.* New York: Hill and Wang, 2004.
Holborn, Louise W. *The International Refugee Organization, a Specialized Agency of the United Nations: Its History and Work, 1946–1952.* London: Oxford University Press, 1956.

Hutchinson, E. P. *Legislative History of American Immigration Policy, 1798–1965.* Philadelphia: University of Pennsylvania Press, 1981.
Zucker, Norman L., and Naomi Flink Zucker. *The Guarded Gate: The Reality of American Refugee Policy.* San Diego, Calif.: Harcourt Brace Jovanovich, 1987.

Dominican immigration

Between 1980 and 2000, the Dominican Republic was second only to Mexico among source nations in the Western Hemisphere for immigration to the United States. In the U.S. census of 2000 and the Canadian census of 2001, 764,945 Americans and 4,965 Canadians claimed Dominican descent. The Immigration and Naturalization Service estimated that there were also about 91,000 Dominicans in the country illegally, though many observers believe the actual figure to be two or three times that amount. Most Dominicans in the United States live in the Northeast, with by far the greatest concentration—about 550,000—in the New York metropolitan area.

The Dominican Republic occupies 18,700 square miles of the island of Hispaniola in the West Indies between 18 and 20 degrees north latitude. The Atlantic Ocean forms the northern coastline, the Caribbean, the south. Haiti occupies the western portion of Hispaniola and the island of Puerto Rico is the nearest to the east. A high mountain range rises in the center of the country forming a fertile valley in the north. In 2002, the population was estimated at 8,581,477. The people are of mixed ethnicities, including whites and blacks, and almost all are Roman Catholic. CHRISTOPHER COLUMBUS landed on Hispaniola in 1492 and found native Arawak and Carib Indians. Spain held the island until 1697 when the western third was ceded to France and named Haiti. In 1801, the eastern portion of the island was seized by Haitians and then ruled intermittently by Haiti or Spain throughout the 19th century. U.S. Marines occupied the country from 1916 to 1924, when a constitutional government was established. From 1930 to 1961, General Rafael Leonidas Trujillo Molina subjected the island to harsh rule. Following Trujillo's assassination in 1961, the country moved toward anarchy and civil war. Fear of a communist takeover led to a U.S. invasion in 1965 in support of a pro-Western regime, and a 17-month occupation. Former Trujillo aide Joaquín Balaguer was subsequently elected and remained in office almost continuously until 1996.

During the Trujillo regime, fewer than 17,000 mostly privileged Dominicans left the island. With Trujillo's assassination and the resulting political instability of the 1960s, the number of immigrants increased, leading to a substantial Dominican community even before the new provisions of the IMMIGRATION AND NATIONALITY ACT (1965) took effect. Over the next 40 years, the tide increased dramatically, with more than 93,000 coming in the 1960s, 148,000 in the 1970s, 252,000 in the 1980s, and 335,000 in the 1990s. The emigration was fueled by the dramatic shift from an isolated, agricultural country to a more diversified economy, including significant manufacturing sectors. As a result of international loans, the Dominican Republic went deeply into debt, and eventually a large percentage of the workforce was displaced. During the 1960s and 1970s, Dominicans found work in northern U.S. cities, as previous residents fled to the suburbs and the American economy evolved, requiring a greater number of unskilled laborers in a variety of service industries. During the 1980s, Dominicans sent hundreds of millions of dollars to their country. Dominican migrants tended to be young (averaging 22 years of age), 60 percent women, and often coming as sojourners who intended someday to return to their island home.

Between 1985 and 1995, it is estimated that almost one-10th of the Dominican Republic's population of 7.5 million emigrated, almost 60 percent coming to the United States. Dominicans have one of the highest rates of dependence on public assistance of any immigrant group, and the highest among nonrefugees. Immigration peaked between 1990 and 1994, when it averaged 45,000 annually. Between 1998 and 2002, the number remained steady at around 20,000 per year.

Immigrants of the 1960s and 1970s sometimes came for political reasons, though they were seldom formally classified as refugees. Most came for economic opportunity, a trend that increased as the Dominican economy imploded during the 1980s. A small but highly visible minority of Dominicans came to the United States to play professional baseball. In 2002, 1,630 of the 3,066 (53 percent) professional baseball players born outside the 50 states were from the Dominican Republic, including stars such as Sammy Sosa, Vladimir Guerrero, Pedro Martínez, Manny Ramírez, and Albert Pujols. More than 90 percent of Canadian Dominicans immigrated after 1980.

Further Reading
Aponte, Sarah. *Dominican Migration to the United States, 1970–1997: An Annotated Bibliography.* New York: CUNY Dominican Studies Institute, 1999.
Atkins, G. Pope, and Larman C. Wilson. *The Dominican Republic and the United States: From Imperialism to Transnationalism.* Athens: University of Georgia Press, 1998.
Eugenia, Georges. *The Making of a Transnational Community.* New York: Columbia University Press, 1990.
Gmelch, G. *Double Passage: The Lives of Caribbean Migrants Abroad and Back Home.* Ann Arbor: University of Michigan Press, 1992.
Grasmuck, Sherri, and Patricia Pessar. *Between Two Islands: Dominican International Migration.* Berkeley: University of California Press, 1991.
———. "Dominicans in the United States: First- and Second-Generation Settlement, 1960–1990." In *Origins and Destinies: Immigration, Race, and Ethnicity in America.* Eds. Silvia Pedraza and Ruben G. Rumbaut. Belmont, Calif: Wadsworth, 1996.

Kasinitz, Phillip. *Caribbean New York: Black Immigrants and the Politics of Race.* Ithaca, N.Y.: Cornell University Press, 1992.

Klein, Alan M. *Sugarball: The American Game, the Dominican Dream.* New Haven, Conn.: Yale University Press, 1991.

Mitchell, Christopher. "U.S. Foreign Policy and Dominican Migration to the United States." In *Western Hemisphere Immigration and United States Foreign Policy.* Ed. Christopher Mitchell. University Park: Pennsylvania State University Press, 1992.

Palmer, R. W. *Pilgrims from the Sun: West Indian Migration to America.* New York: Twayne, 1995.

Pessar, Patricia. "The Dominicans: Women in the Household and Garment Industry." In *New Immigrants in New York.* Ed. Nancy Foner. New York: Columbia University Press, 1987.

Richardson, Bonham. *Caribbean Migration.* Knoxville: University of Tennessee Press, 1983.

Torres-Saillant, Silvio, and Ramona Hernández. *The Dominican Americans.* Westport, Conn.: Greenwood Press, 1998.

Dominion Lands Act (Canada) (1872)

The Dominion Lands Act was designed to entice settlers to the western prairies of Canada by granting 160 acres of free land to anyone 21 years of age or older who paid a $10 registration fee, built a permanent residence, planted at least 30 acres of land, and lived on the land six consecutive months for three years. Women were allowed to claim lands only if they were the sole heads of families. Although not very successful in attracting foreign immigrants, the offer of free land did entice thousands of Canadians to leave Ontario and Quebec for the opportunities of the west.

After acquiring Rupert's Land and the Northwest Territories from the Hudson's Bay Company in 1869, the Canadian government was eager to attract settlers to the region. A transcontinental railway had been promised in hopes of persuading British Columbia to join the Canadian confederation in 1871, yet it was unlikely to be a successful commercial venture without customers along the way. Also, there was concern about U.S. aggression in some border regions, particularly in the Red River region of Manitoba. As a result, SIR JOHN ALEXANDER MACDONALD's government fashioned the Dominion Lands Act and based it on the United States's successful HOMESTEAD ACT (1862). Despite the generous provisions, most European immigrant farmers chose to settle in the United States. Although homestead entries averaged about 3,000 annually between 1874 and 1896, there were in many years almost as many cancellations. In 1874, the government of Alexander Mackenzie amended the act to provide for sale of land at reduced prices to colonization companies that would develop lands at no cost to the government. Although many schemes were put forward, only one of 26 major efforts was successful. Ultimately, significant group settlements of Mennonites, Hungarians, Jews, and Icelanders were attracted to the Canadian west, but most came under specially negotiated group settlement programs.

Further Reading

Johnson, Stanley C. *A History of Emigration from the United Kingdom to North America, 1763–1912.* London: G. Routledge, 1913.

Macdonald, Norman. *Canada: Immigration and Colonization, 1841–1903.* Toronto: Macmillan of Canada, 1966.

Norrie, K. H. "The Rate of Settlement of the Canadian Prairies, 1870–1911." In *Perspectives on Canadian Economic History.* Ed. Douglas McCalla. Toronto: Copp Clark Pitman, 1987.

Douglas, Thomas (fifth earl of Selkirk, Lord Selkirk) (1771–1820) *businessman, philanthropist*

Thomas Douglas, fifth earl of Selkirk, was a Whig politician and philanthropist who was deeply concerned for the welfare of Scottish crofters (tenant farmers with very small holdings) being driven from the Highlands during the clearances—the removal of former tenant farmers by legislatively "enclosing" communal lands—after 1750. He founded a prosperous settlement of 800 Highlanders on PRINCE EDWARD ISLAND in 1803 and a less successful settlement of 15 families at Baldoon, Upper Canada, in 1804. After acquiring a controlling interest in the Hudson's Bay Company between 1808 and 1812, Lord Selkirk convinced the governing committee to sell him 116,000 square miles of Rupert's Land, extending from Lake Winnipeg in the north to the headwaters of the Red River in the south. In one of the great land deals of all time, Selkirk purchased a tract of land almost as large as Britain and Ireland combined for the cost of 10 shillings, financial provisions for 200 company men, and a promise to settle 1,000 people within 10 years. The settlement of 270 Scots in the RED RIVER COLONY (1812–16) led to vigorous opposition from the North West Fur Company and eventually to bloodshed, when company troops drove colonists from Fort Douglas and Fort Daer in 1815 and 1816. Selkirk personally led an attack on the North West Fur Company's chief post of Fort William, reestablishing his settlement as Kildonan (1817). A protracted legal struggle cost much of his fortune. His projects nevertheless laid the foundations of Winnipeg and Manitoba. Selkirk wrote two major works, *Observations on the Present State of the Highlands of Scotland* (1805) and *A Sketch of the British Fur Trade in North America* (1816). He returned to Scotland in 1818.

Further Reading

Bowsfield, Hartwell. *Selkirk.* Toronto: Clarke, Irwin, 1968.

Bryce, George. *The Life of Lord Selkirk: Coloniser of Western Canada.* Toronto: Musson, 1912.

Bryce, George. *Mackenzie, Selkirk, Simpson.* London: Oxford University Press, 1926.

Gray, J. M. *Lord Selkirk of Red River.* Toronto: Macmillan of Canada, 1963.

Martin, C. *Lord Selkirk's Work in Canada.* Toronto: Oxford University Press, 1916.

Selkirk, Lord. *The Collected Writings of Lord Selkirk, 1799–1820.* 2 vols. Ed. J. M. Bumsted. Winnipeg, Canada: Manitoba Record Society, 1984, 1988.

———. *Lord Selkirk's Diary, 1803–1804: A Journal of his Travels in British North America and the Northeastern United States.* Ed. Patrick C. T. White. Toronto: Champlain Society, 1958.

Durham Report

Following a series of rebellions in Canada in 1837 John George Lambton, Lord Durham, was commissioned by the British government to temporarily govern Canada, to investigate the causes of discontent, and to make recommendations regarding British governance of the region. Durham completed his report in 1839, recommending that Upper and Lower Canada be united and that responsible government be granted.

Following the War of 1812 (1812–15), the rapid influx of English, Irish, and Scottish immigrants caused many French Canadians to fear that their cultural heritage and special political status in Lower Canada (QUEBEC) would be lost. With the French controlling the legislature and the English controlling the legislative council, it was difficult to reach a political consensus. In Upper Canada (Ontario), farmers and minority religious groups were dissatisfied with the heavy-handed political control of the landowners, merchants, and clergy of the Church of England. Loss of faith in the colonial government led to revolts in Lower Canada (November 1837, November 1838) and Upper Canada (December 1837). Though the colonial militia was able to quickly defeat the insurrectionists, it was clear to British officials that the colonial system of government in Canada needed reform.

In order to facilitate a thorough reform, Lord Durham was given unprecedented powers. He was appointed governor in chief of the Canadas, Nova Scotia, New Brunswick, and Prince Edward Island, as well as being given the new title of governor-general, which also covered Newfoundland. As high commissioner, he had responsibility "for the adjustment of certain important questions . . . respecting the form and future government" of Lower and Upper Canada. Durham arrived in Quebec at the end of May 1838, spending most of his time in Lower Canada until his departure on November 1. Durham's report, completed by the end of January 1839, acknowledged a deeply rooted hostility between British and French interests, recommending that the old policy of endeavoring "to preserve a French Canadian nationality in the midst of Anglo-American colonies and states" should be abandoned. As a result, Durham recommended that the two Canadas be combined, giving English speakers (550,000) a clear majority over the French (450,000) and one that would naturally be increased "by the influence of English emigration." Durham also recommended that provisions be made for other North American colonies to join a Canadian confederation. In the Act of Union (1840), the British government followed Durham's recommendation to unite the colonies, but they chose not to grant responsible government, fearing loss of colonial control. Although responsible government was not immediately granted, the union led to a united reform movement and an eventual grant of self-government under Durham's son-in-law, James Bruce, Lord Elgin, in 1848.

Further Reading
Craig, Gerald M. *Upper Canada: The Formative Years, 1784–1841.* Toronto: McClelland and Stewart, 1963.

Durham, Earl of. *Life and Letters of the First Earl of Durham, 1792–1840.* Ed. S. J. Reid. London: Longmans, Green, 1906.

Martin, Ged. *Britain and the Origins of Canadian Confederation, 1837–1867.* Vancouver, Canada: University of British Columbia Press, 1995.

Dutch immigration

Coming to the Hudson River Valley of New York as early as 1614, the Dutch were among the earliest European settlers in the New World and exerted considerable political and economic influence in New York well into the 19th century. Their descendants formed the first significant migration to Canada as part of the Loyalist evacuation during and after the American Revolution (1775–83, see AMERICAN REVOLUTION AND IMMIGRATION). In the U.S. census of 2000 and the Canadian census of 2001, 4,542,494 Americans and 923,310 Canadians claimed Dutch descent. As the earliest area of Dutch settlement (1621), New Amsterdam, later New York City (see NEW YORK, NEW YORK), remained their cultural center. The earliest Dutch Canadians settled in NOVA SCOTIA and NEW BRUNSWICK, though later immigrants concentrated in Toronto, Ontario, and Vancouver, British Columbia.

The Netherlands occupies 13,100 square miles of northwestern Europe along the North Sea between 51 and 54 degrees north latitude. Germany lies to the east and Belgium to the south. The land is flat and barely above sea level. An extensive network of dikes is utilized to reclaim and protect lowlying farmland. Netherland dependencies include several Caribbean islands known as the Netherlands Antilles and Aruba. The population of the Netherlands, estimated at 15,981,472 in 2002, is highly urbanized. Thirty-four percent of the people identify themselves as Roman Catholic and 25 percent as Protestant. Julius Caesar first conquered the region, which was originally inhabited by Celtic and Germanic tribes. After the collapse of Charlemagne's empire in the ninth century, northwestern Europe entered into an era of regional nobilities. During the 14th century the region fell under the control of the dukes of Burgundy and in the early 16th century became part of the Spanish Habsburg empire. In 1579, a confederation of lowland provinces was formed, leading to a declaration of Netherlander independence in 1581. During the 17th century, the Dutch republic rose to imperial,

Netherlands ambassador J. H. van Roijin and his wife greet Dutch immigrants arriving by ship in Montreal, June 1947. Thousands of Dutch agriculturalists immigrated to Canada after World War II as part of the Netherlands Farm Families Movement, a program jointly sponsored by the Canadian and Dutch governments. *(Photo by George Hunter/National Archives of Canada/PA-123476)*

economic, and cultural renown, establishing colonies in North America (New Netherland), South America (Suriname and an area of Brazil), the Caribbean, South Africa, India and Ceylon (present-day Sri Lanka), and the East Indies. Its merchant fleet was the largest in Europe. In 1795, the Netherlands became part of the French Batavian Republic. In the settlement of the Napoleonic Wars (1803–15), diplomats at the Congress of Vienna combined Belgium and the Netherlands as a brake against future French expansion. Belgium, French-speaking and Catholic, seceded in 1830. Despite neutrality during World War II (1939–45), the Netherlands was occupied by Germany from 1940 to 1945. In 1949, following years of fighting, the Netherlands granted colonial Indonesia its independence. Irian Jaya was ceded in 1963. Since World War II, immigration to the Netherlands from its former imperial colonies has reshaped the ethnic composition of the Dutch population.

Dutch immigration to North America occurred in three stages. The earliest, from 1614 to 1664, centered on the commercial venture of the New Netherland colony. Fort Nassau (later Albany) was founded in 1614, and the region was later developed by the Dutch West India Company. New Netherland was never very attractive to Dutch commercialists, however. By 1664, when England wrested control of the region from the Netherlands, the population of the colony was less than 10,000, and only 70 percent of these were Dutch. Although immigration from the Netherlands almost totally ceased, by the first U.S. census in 1790, the Dutch population was estimated at 100,000, testimony to the high rate of natural increase among all Americans.

In the pioneer, or "free," stage of immigration between 1820 and 1914, some 200,000 Dutch migrated to America, most of them peasants and artisans. Low mortality rates and high fertility fueled a rapid rise in population. Dutch citizens suffered from other problems common to most European countries of the period, including high taxes and widespread government regulations. The Holland Land Company offered land for sale in America, principally in New York State, but during the first four decades of the 19th century, only a few dozen Dutch emigrated annually. Evaluating the raw numbers is difficult because there were significant numbers of Belgian and German workers in Holland. Legal actions taken against pietistic Calvinists after their secession from the national church in 1834, and the effects of potato blight in the mid-1840s led to increased group immigration, with most representing the lower middle classes, including farmers and artisans. Between 1840 and 1940, emigration was about 250,000, considerably smaller than emigration from comparable countries like Sweden. Though the Dutch economy was often weak, emigrants frequently chose to settle in Dutch colonies in the East and West Indies. Nevertheless, by the mid-1840s, a small but steady stream of mainly Orthodox Calvinists began to concentrate in Michigan, Iowa, Wisconsin, and Illinois. The famine year of 1847 saw 8,090 Dutch migrate (from a population of just more than 3 million), a rate of migration that would never again be approached. Often congregations followed a pastor or other recognized leader.

During the 1860s, the pattern of Dutch migration shifted from smaller groups to a mass movement, facilitated by the development of railways and other systems of transportation. Throughout the 1870s, Dutch immigration to the United States averaged about 1,000 per year. As grain prices dropped worldwide from the late 1870s and industrial crops such as madder and colza (rape) became obsolete, the Dutch compensated by concentrating on labor-intensive fruits, vegetables, and flowers, and the use of artificial fertilizers in order to stave off agricultural crisis. Although emigration prior to World War I (1914–18) never reached the proportions of other countries in western Europe, a vigorous campaign by dissident religious groups, business companies, transportation companies, and governmental agencies led to increased migration that peaked in 1882 when 9,517 immigrated to the United States. Rates of migration remained relatively high between 1907 and 1913 (averaging 119 per 100,000).

Only in the 1890s were the first significant agricultural settlements established in Canada, mostly in Saskatchewan and Alberta as cheap land became more difficult to find in the United States. Although the Dutch population in Canada was about 30,000 in 1871, most were Canadian born. Numbers thereafter grew gradually, to about 56,000

in 1911. As U.S. immigration policy became more restrictive in the 1920s, Dutch agriculturalists increasingly turned to Canada, settling mainly in Ontario. The Dutch immigration was unusual in its exceptionally low rate of return migration (less than 5 percent before 1890) and its high rate of single-stage migration to an intended destination (near 70 percent).

The third stage of Dutch immigration came between 1945 and the early 1960s, when the devastation of World War II (1939–45) caused severe housing shortages and considerable economic dislocation, leading some 80,000 to immigrate to the United States. The Canadian government admitted some 5,000 Dutch refugees and 15,000 Dutch farmers under the Netherlands Farm Families Movement program, seeking to encourage settlement in rural areas. With the improvement of the Dutch economy in the 1960s, immigration decreased dramatically. Between 1991 and 2002, more than 15,000 Netherlanders immigrated to the United States.

Further Reading

Brinks, Herbert J. *Dutch American Voices: Letters from the United States, 1850–1930.* Ithaca, N.Y.: Cornell University Press, 1995.
Ganzevoort, Herman. *A Bittersweet Land: The Dutch Experience in Canada, 1890–1980.* Toronto: McClelland and Stewart, Department of the Secretary of State, 1988.
Hinte, Jacob von. *Netherlanders in America: A Study of Emigration and Settlement in the Nineteenth and Twentieth Centuries in the United States of America.* Ed. Robert P. Swierenga. Trans. Adriaan de Wit. Grand Rapids, Mich.: Baker Book House, 1985.
Ishwaran, K. *Family, Kinship, and Community: A Study of Dutch Canadians.* Toronto: University of Toronto Press, 1977.
Lucas, Henry S. *Dutch Immigrant Memoirs and Related Works.* 1955. Reprint, Grand Rapids, Mich.: Eerdmans, 1997.
———. *Netherlanders in America: Dutch Immigration to the United States and Canada, 1789–1950.* 1955. Reprint, Grand Rapids, Mich.: Eerdmans, 1989.
Petersen, William. *Planned Migration: The Social Determinants of the Dutch-Canadian Movement.* Berkeley and Los Angeles: University of California Press, 1955.
Rink, Oliver A. *Holland on the Hudson: An Economic and Social History of Dutch New York.* Cooperstown, N.Y.: Cornell University Press, New York State Historical Association, 1986.
Ritchie, Robert C. *The Duke's Province.* Chapel Hill: University of North Carolina Press, 1977.
Swierenga, Robert P. *Faith and Family: Dutch Immigration and Settlement in the United States, 1820–1920.* New York: Holmes and Meier, 2000.

E

East Indian immigration   See INDIAN IMMIGRATION.

Ecuadorean immigration

Almost all Ecuadorean immigration to North America has occurred since the 1960s. In the U.S. census of 2000 and the Canadian census of 2001, 260,559 Americans and 8,785 Canadians claimed Ecuadorean descent. Some assessments place the U.S. figures at more than twice that amount, taking into account a high rate of illegal immigration. During the mid-1990s, the Ecuadorean consulate in Manhattan estimated the total number of Ecuadoreans to be almost twice the official figure. In 2000, the Immigration and Naturalization Service estimated that 108,000 Ecuadoreans were in the United States illegally. More than half of Ecuadoreans live in New York City, with a substantial population also in Los Angeles. In Canada, more than 80 percent of Ecuadoreans live in Ontario.

Ecuador occupies 106,800 square miles of northwestern South America between 2 degrees north latitude and 5 degrees south latitude. Colombia forms the country's border to the north, Peru to the east and to the south, and the Pacific Ocean to the west. Ranges of the Andes Mountains split the country into areas of hot lowlands along the coast, cooler highlands in the central regions, and tropical lowlands to the east. Ecuador includes the Galapagos Islands lying almost 800 miles off the coast. In 2002, the population was estimated at 13,183,978. Mestizos compose the largest ethnic group, making up 55 percent of the population. Amerindians make up another 25 percent, Spanish 10 percent, and blacks 10 percent. Almost all practice Roman Catholicism. In 1533, Spain conquered the indigenous Inca Empire and ruled Ecuador until 1822, when Simón Bolívar and José de San Martín drove them out. After independence, the region of Ecuador joined with Colombia, Panama, and Venezuela to form Gran Colombia, but Ecuador and Venezuela withdrew from the union in 1830. Oil exports became the cornerstone of the Ecuadorean economy throughout the industrial age, but since 1982, the country has faced economic crisis due to declining revenues. An earthquake in 1987 destroyed a large section of the country's major oil pipeline and left 20,000 homeless. Elected officials, struggling to solve Ecuador's financial problems, finally adopted the U.S. dollar as the national currency in 2000.

There were almost no Ecuadoreans in the United States prior to World War II (1939–45). After the arrival of several thousand in the 1950s, however, a tightening of restrictions led to a significant decline. As Ecuador suffered frequent incursions from more powerful neighbors, economic and political instability worsened, leading more Ecuadoreans to seek opportunities in the United States. Two events during the mid-1960s powered a great wave of immigration. The Ecuadorean Land Reform, Idle Lands, and Settlement Act of 1964 was designed to aid the poor by redistributing land to peasant farmers. Uneducated and untrained in modern agriculture, debt frequently forced them to sell their lands, leaving them without a livelihood. The desire for economic opportunity coincided with the passage of the U.S. IMMIGRATION AND NATIONALITY ACT of 1965, which allowed more immigration from Western Hemispheric nations and led to a steady increase in numbers. Almost 37,000 Ecuadoreans came during the 1960s, 50,000 in the 1970s, and 56,000 during the 1980s. Between 1992 and 2002, an average of about 7,200 Ecuadoreans immigrated to the United States each year.

In the 1950s, a few Ecuadoreans immigrated to Canada from Azuay Province, whose main industry in the production of straw hats had declined dramatically. The first large-scale migration began, however, in the late 1960s, when many poor immigrants were attracted by Italian builders seeking cheap labor. The peak of Ecuadorean immigration came between 1970 and 1975, when about 20,000 arrived. Of 10,095 Ecuadorean immigrants in Canada in 2001, about 4,000 arrived between 1991 and 2001. Most observers place the actual number of Ecuadoreans in Canada at two or even three times the official figure of 8,785.

Further Reading

Hanratty, D., ed. *Ecuador: A Country Study.* Washington, D.C.: Federal Research Division, Library of Congress, 1991.

Hurtado, Osvaldo. *Political Power in Ecuador.* Albuquerque: University of New Mexico Press, 1980.

Kyle, David. *Transnational Peasants: Migrations, Networks and Ethnicity in Andean Ecuador.* Baltimore: Johns Hopkins University Press, 2000.

Mata, Fernando. *Immigrants from the Hispanic World in Canada: Demographic Profiles and Social Adaptation.* Toronto: [n.a] 1988.

Pooley, E. "Little Ecuador." *New York* 18 (September 16, 1985), p. 32.

Egyptian immigration

Egyptians have never emigrated in large numbers from their homeland. In the U.S. census of 2000 and the Canadian census of 2001, 142,832 Americans and 41,310 Canadians claimed Egyptian descent. The largest concentrations of Egyptians in the United States are in the New York metropolitan area (especially Jersey City and Manhattan), Los Angeles, and Chicago. Quebec was the preferred destination for most Egyptians during the early phrase of immigration, though by 2001 Toronto and Montreal had equally large communities.

Egypt occupies 383,900 square miles of the northeast corner of Africa between 23 and 32 degrees north latitude. The Mediterranean Sea forms its border to the north; Israel and the Gaza Strip, to the east; Sudan, to the south; and Libya, to the west. Egypt is mostly barren excepting the fertile Nile Valley along which most of the population lives. In 2002, the population was estimated at 69,536,644, with more than 10 million in the capital city of Cairo. More than 90 percent of Egyptians are Muslim, and about 6 percent are

Coptic Christians. Egypt is an ancient nation with archaeological records of native dynasties dating back to 3200 B.C. The Persians invaded Egypt in 341 B.C. and were followed by the Greeks, Romans, Byzantines, and Arabs. The Mamluks ruled from 1250 until 1517 when the Ottoman Turks added Egypt to their empire. Britain assumed administration of Egypt following Turkish decline and maintained power until 1952, when Egypt gained its independence following a military uprising. A republic was proclaimed in 1953 and has remained relatively stable. Between 1948 and 1979, Egypt participated in several wars against Israel. Though Egypt lost the Sinai Peninsula in 1967, it regained it by negotiation in 1982 and became the first Arab state to recognize the legitimacy of Israel. In 1991, Egypt gave political and military support to Allied forces during the Persian Gulf War of 1991. Throughout the 1990s and into the 21st century a strong element of Islamic fundamentalism was present in Egypt, though the government officially condemned it.

Egyptian society has historically migrated little. The earliest emigrants from Egypt were not Egyptian at all, but rather Armenian refugees from the Ottoman Empire who had first settled in Egypt before immigrating to the United States in the 1920s (see ARMENIAN IMMIGRATION). Following World War II (1939–45), Egyptians immigrated to North America mainly for economic and educational opportunities, though a small number of Copts began to find their way to the United States. By the 1960s, an increasing number were emigrating for political reasons. Copts and Jews often felt isolated in an increasingly nationalistic atmosphere, and they occasionally qualified as refugees. Even when they were not persecuted, they often found few opportunities in the predominantly Muslim society. After Egypt's defeat in the Arab-Israeli War of 1967, a small but steady exodus began. In the decade after 1967, about 15,000 Egyptians, mainly Copts, came to the United States, including many scientists and other professionals. As economic power in the Middle East shifted from Egypt to the Persian Gulf States in the 1970s, the Egyptian economy declined and many well-trained Egyptians found themselves without jobs. Poorer, unskilled labor tended to work in other Middle Eastern countries, while the better educated, especially if they were Christian, came to the United States or Canada. Most settled in the greater New York area, but others began to settle in Washington, D.C., southern California, Illinois, and Michigan. Between 1992 and 2002, more than 50,000 Egyptians immigrated to the United States.

A few usually well-to-do Egyptian immigrants came to Canada during the 1950s; however, most between 1956 and 1966 were non-natives. Of the 8,825 immigrants during that period, 32 percent were Armenians; 15 percent, Lebanese; 11 percent, Greeks; 6 percent, Jews; and 3 percent, Italians. Between 1967 and 1975, Egyptians were generally welcomed in Canada because of their high levels of education and training, and about three-quarters chose to settle in Quebec Province, mostly in Montreal. By the mid-1970s, however, a greater number of native Egyptians were more comfortable with English and took advantage of the jobs produced by the economic growth in Toronto. By the early 1980s, the annual number of immigrants had declined from about 900 to about 500. With the introduction of new provisions in the Canadian immigration code to encourage investors, Egyptian immigration once again picked up, with 5,455 Egyptians arriving between 1986 and 1991. Of Canada's 35,980 immigrants in 2001, 12,295 arrived between 1991 and 2001.

See also ARAB IMMIGRATION.

Further Reading

Awad, Mohammed. *Egyptian with a Million Dollars.* Cairo: n.p., n.d.

Brewer, Douglas J., and Emily Teeter. *Egypt and the Egyptians.* New York: Cambridge University Press, 1999.

Hagopian, Elaine C., and Ann Paden, eds. *The Arab Americans: Studies in Assimilation.* Wilmette, Ill.: Medina University Press International, 1969.

Metz, Helen C. *Egypt: A Country Study.* Washington, D.C.: Federal Research Divison, Library of Congress, 1991.

Orfalea, Gregory. *Before the Flames: A Quest for the History of Arab Americans.* Austin: University of Texas Press, 1988.

Patrick, T. H. *Traditional Egyptian Christianity: A History of the Coptic Orthodox Church.* St. Cloud, Minn.: North Star Press, 1996.

Sell, R. "International Migration among Egyptian Elites: Where They've Been; Where They're Going." *Journal of Arab Affairs* 92 (1990): 147–176.

Watterson, B. *Coptic Egypt.* Edinburgh: Scottish Academic Press, 1988.

Ellis Island

The Ellis Island immigration station, located in New York harbor, was the entry point for three-quarters of American immigrants between its opening in 1892 and the implementation of the restrictive JOHNSON-REED ACT of 1924. Between 1892 and its closing in 1954, it was the introduction to America for more than 12 million immigrants. It became for most European immigrants a symbol of American opportunity for a better life during an era of almost unrestricted European immigration. In 1932, the Ellis Island station stopped receiving steerage-class immigrants and finally closed in 1954. It was reopened in 1990 as the National Immigration Museum, part of the Statue of Liberty National Monument.

Beginning in 1855, immigrants were processed through the CASTLE GARDEN station at the southern tip of Manhattan Island. As the volume of immigration increased dramatically in the 1870s and 1880s, however, it became clear that it would no longer be adequate for processing hundreds of thousands of immigrants each year. Almost 5 million were processed during the 1880s alone. The problem was made worse when New York State officials threatened to close Castle Garden unless the federal government agreed to fund its operations, which was done in 1882 by levying a head tax of 50¢ on every immigrant, gradually raised to $8 by 1917. New federal guidelines in 1890 requiring more extensive physical and mental examinations, combined with the massive influx of immigrants, finally led the federal government to establish a new immigrant depot, this time on Ellis Island. While it was being constructed, between 1890 and 1892, immigrants were processed in a wholly inadequate federal barge office.

Ellis Island was named for its last private owner, Samuel Ellis, who purchased it in the 1770s. The site chosen for the facilities had formerly housed a naval arsenal, Fort Gibson. The new structure was designed to process up to 5,000 immigrants per day. The building of the facilities was accompanied by the creation of a new bureaucracy. In 1891, the office of superintendent of immigration was created, ending the uneasy and ill-defined collaboration between the federal government and state boards and commissions, and finally providing the United States—one century and 16 million immigrants later—with a formal framework for addressing immigrant concerns. In a day when immigrants were welcomed by politicians and policy makers as cheap labor for developing the economy, the process at Ellis Island was meant to help immigrants into the country. Examinations tended to be brief, unless someone displayed obvious deformities or illness. Most immigrants passed through the facilities on the day they arrived, and the rejection rate for most of its history was about 1 percent. Immigration officials were nevertheless charged with screening "any convict, lunatic, idiot" or "paupers or persons likely to become a public charge," the latter known as the LPC clause. Contract laborers were also prohibited after passage of the ALIEN LABOR ACT (Foran Act) of 1885, and about 1,000 aliens were denied entrance each year between 1892 and 1907 on these grounds.

The first structures on Ellis Island were nothing like the substantial and familiar Main Building—now housing the National Immigration Museum—that immigrants recall in their memoirs. Instead, they were all built of Georgia pine and were opened for business on January 1, 1892. On June 14, 1897, a fire destroyed virtually everything, including many immigration records dating back to 1855. Before rebuilding, the government stipulated that the new structures had to be fireproof. The permanent reception center was opened in 1900, though it soon proved to be inadequate.

During the first year of operation, in 1892, about 446,000 immigrants landed in New York, but numbers declined significantly through the 1890s, averaging about 231,000 per year between 1893 and 1899. Much to the surprise of many officials, however, immigration through New York increased dramatically after 1898. From about 179,000 arrivals in 1898, the immigrant flow peaked in 1906–07, when almost 1.9 million landed in New York. In 1913–14, another almost 1.8 million immigrants were processed. As a result, new dormitories, hospitals, kitchens, and other structures were built or expanded between 1900 and 1915.

When an immigrant ship arrived in New York harbor, first- and second-class passengers were given a cursory examination on board and were then transferred to shore. Most only saw the Ellis Island facilities from a distance or actually went there if some question had been raised on board. Steerage, or third-class, passengers were examined more carefully, for they were, in the minds of immigration officials, far more likely to become public charges. After traveling in crowded and rank conditions on the bottom decks of steamships for up to two weeks, immigrants would gather their belongings to be ferried to Ellis Island. Most immigrants were given a cursory medical examination—the "six second physical," as it came to be called—and had their papers checked against shipping manifests. They were then briefly interviewed, as immigration officials worked from the ship's manifest log that contained the answers to 29 questions previously completed by the immigrant. The whole process typically took three to five hours. Those admitted typically purchased rail or coastal steamer tickets to their final destinations and were then ferried to either Manhattan or the Jersey shore. The small number refused entry were detained pending an appeal or deportation.

With the massive influx of "new immigrants," mainly from southern and eastern Europe (see NEW IMMIGRATION), in the first decade of the 20th century, many Americans were skeptical about the policy of relatively unrestricted immigration. Nevertheless, most immigrants were treated fairly, if perfunctorily, and many officials took a genuine interest in their welfare. Long before he became mayor of New York City (1934–45), Fiorello La Guardia championed the immigrant cause, working as an interpreter at Ellis Island (1907–10).

After World War I (1914–18), American consulates were established around the world and were responsible for issuing visas and checking credentials, thus lessening the work at the

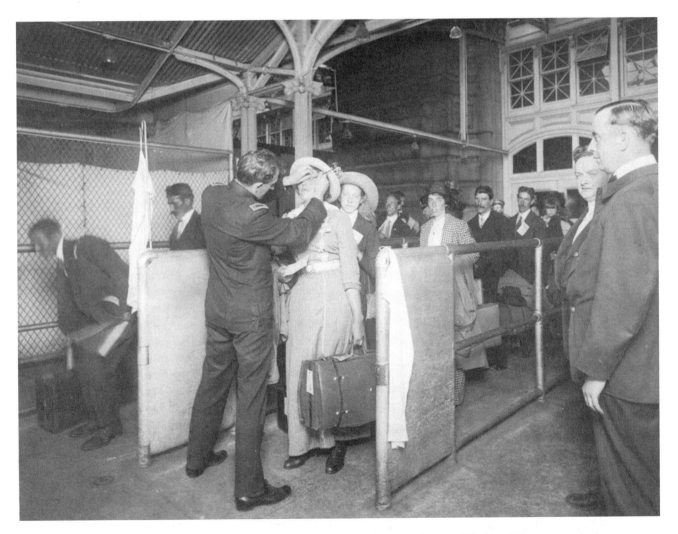

An inspector performs the required eye examination for the highly contagious trachoma at Ellis Island. Rigorous medical examinations and hygienic regimens were imposed on immigrants in both European and U.S. ports. *(National Archives #090-G-125-12)*

port of entry. Passage of the restrictive quota legislation of 1921 and 1924 (see EMERGENCY QUOTA ACT; JOHNSON-REED ACT) also significantly reduced the number of immigrants allowed into the United States and marked the beginning of Ellis Island's decline as a processing center. Whereas annual immigration averaged about 740,000 between 1903 and 1914, it dropped to about 152,000 between 1925 and 1930, and 30,000 during the Great Depression years of the 1930s. By that time, Ellis Island had become better known for detention than for entry and in 1932, finally stopped receiving steerage-class immigrants.

During World War II (1939–45), the Ellis Island facilities were used to house enemy merchant detainees and as a training ground for the U.S. COAST GUARD. They were finally closed in 1954. In 1965, the area was incorporated with the Statue of Liberty National Monument and opened to the public on a limited basis. After the largest historic restoration in U.S. history, beginning in 1984 and costing $160 million, the Main Building was opened to the public in 1990 as the Ellis Island Immigration Museum. The museum traces the role that Ellis Island played in the lives of millions of immigrants, placing it in the context of the broader patterns of immigration to the United States. A variety of exhibits, many including personal testimonies in video and interactive displays, cover more than 40,000 square feet of floor space. Included in the museum's collections are oral histories from some 2,000 immigrants, the result of the Ellis Island Oral History Program, which is housed there. There is also a research library with special collections on the Statue of Liberty, immigration, ethnic groups, and Ellis Island itself.

The list of famous Americans who passed through Ellis Island is long, and includes individuals from every area of American culture. Here is a small sample:

Country of Origin	Immigrants
Austria	Felix Frankfurter, Baron von Trapp
England	Bob Hope, Jule Styne
Hungary	Bela Lugosi
Italy	Frank Capra, Frank Costello, Rudolph Valentino
Jamaica	Marcus Garvey
Lebanon	Kahlil Gibran
Lithuania	Al Jolson, Pauline Newman
Norway	Knute Rockne
Poland	Samuel Goldwyn, Meyer Lansky, Hyman Rickover
Romania	Edward G. Robinson
Russia	Irving Berlin, Max Factor, Isaac Asimov, Mary Antin
Trinidad	C. R. L. James

Further Reading

Chermayeff, Ivan, Fred Wasserman, and Mary J. Shapiro. *Ellis Island: An Illustrated History of the Immigrant Experience.* New York: Macmillan, 1991.

Coan, Peter Morton. *Ellis Island Interviews: In Their Own Words.* New York: Checkmark Books, 1997.

Houghton, Gillian. *Ellis Island: A Primary Source History of an Immigrant's Arrival in America.* New York: Rosen Publishing, 2003.

Kraut, Alan M. *Silent Travelers: Germs, Genes, and the "Immigrant Menace."* New York: Basic Books, 1994.

La Guardia, Fiorello H. *The Making of an Insurgent: An Autobiography, 1882–1919.* Philadelphia: Lippincott, 1948.

Perec, Georges, and Robert Bober. *Ellis Island.* New York: New Press, 1995.

Pitkin, Thomas. *Keepers of the Gate: A History of Ellis Island.* New York: New York University Press, 1975.

Yans-McLaughlin, Virginia, and Marjorie Lightman. *Ellis Island and the Peopling of America.* New York: New Press, 1997.

Emergency Quota Act (United States) (1921)

Signed in May 1921, the Emergency Quota Act established the first ethnic quota system for selective admittance of immigrants to the United States. With widespread concern about the importation of communist and other radical political ideas, Americans widely supported more restrictive legislation. The measure limited immigration to 357,800 annually from the Eastern Hemisphere; more than half the quota was reserved for immigrants from northern and western Europe.

Even as the United States entered World War I in 1917, there was substantial concern over the "dumping" of dangerous and poor immigrant refugees from Europe. When the IMMIGRATION ACT of 1917 failed to halt a continuing flood of hundreds of thousands of Europeans after the war, support for an ethnic quota grew. Support for immigration restriction included, for the first time, many within the business community, who found that immigrants from Canada, Mexico, and the West Indies were dramatically lessening the need for potentially radicalized European labor. In order to ensure that Bolsheviks, anarchists, Jews, and other "undesirables" were kept to a minimum, the Emergency Quota Act set the number of immigrants from each national origin group at 3 percent of the foreign-born population of that country in 1910. During 1909 and 1910, immigration from England, Ireland, Scotland and Scandinavia had been particularly high. About 1 percent of the quota was allotted to non-Europeans.

Further Reading

Daniels, Roger. *Guarding the Golden Door: American Immigration Policy and Immigrants since 1882.* New York: Hill and Wang, 2004.

Erickson, Charlotte. "Some Thoughts on the Social and Economic Consequences of the Quota Acts." *European Contributions to American Studies* 10 (1986): 28–46.

Hutchinson, E. P. *Legislative History of American Immigration Policy, 1798–1965.* Philadelphia: University of Pennsylvania Press, 1981.

LeMay, Michael C. *From Open Door to Dutch Door: An Analysis of U.S. Immigration Policy since 1820.* New York: Praeger, 1987.

Empire Settlement Act (Canada) (1922)

With the dramatic decline of immigrant admissions and rise in alien deportations during World War I (1914–18; see WORLD WAR I AND IMMIGRATION), the Canadian government tried several means of attracting agriculturalists and domestics. Its first choice of source country was Great Britain. In 1922, the Canadian and British governments reached an agreement leading to passage of the Empire Settlement Act in the British Parliament, a measure encouraging immigration to Canada of British agriculturalists, farm laborers, domestic laborers, and children under 17. Inducements varied according to specific schemes devised under the measure but included the sale of land on credit, agricultural training, and most prominently, establishment of a special transportation rate for the targeted groups. Numerous amendments and extensions to the act during the 1920s eventually covered a number of specialized programs, including the unsuccessful plan to resettle 10,000 unemployed British miners, giving them jobs in the Canadian west harvesting wheat. Three-quarters of the 8,000 who came to Canada eventually returned. More successful was the program providing transportation assistance and guaranteeing standard wages and transition support for more than 22,000 domestic workers. Child immigrants remained in high demand in Canada, though increased scrutiny by government and humanitarian groups led to tighter restrictions in 1924. Eventually about 130,000 British immigrants were given assistance under the measure during the 1920s and 1930s, though Canadian support faded from the late 1920s on.

Further Reading

Avery, Donald. *"Dangerous Foreigners": European Immigrant Workers and Labour Radicalism in Canada, 1896–1932.* Toronto: McClelland and Stewart, 1979.

Bagnell, Kenneth. *The Little Immigrants: The Orphans Who Came to Canada.* Toronto: Macmillan, 1980.

Kelley, Ninette, and Michael Trebilcock. *The Making of the Mosaic: A History of Canadian Immigration Policy.* Toronto: University of Toronto Press, 1998.

Schnell, R. L. "The Right Class of Boy: Youth Training Schemes and Assisted Emigration to Canada under the Empire Settlement Act, 1922–39." *History of Education* 24, no. 2 (March 1995): 73–90.

enclosure movement

An economic and social process during the 17th and 18th centuries that gradually destroyed the old open-field system of agriculture in Britain. The resulting efficiency led to a surplus of farm laborers increasingly dependent on wages. As the surplus grew in the late 18th century, agricultural workers from marginalized areas looked to emigration as a means of economic relief.

As a part of a favorable economic transformation that laid the foundation for the Industrial Revolution, British landowners raised productivity by increasing specialization and by alternating use of arable and grass lands, which in turn led to greater demand for what had previously been considered marginal land. In order to improve production by draining land, hedging fields, and rotating crops, lands previously used collectively by village farmers were taken over by large landowners. During the early 18th century this was done locally by private agreement. By the 1760s, it became a matter of national legislation. Between 1760 and 1793, 1,611 enclosure acts were passed, favoring larger landowners and causing much rural distress. The Highlands of Scotland were particularly hard hit, leading to a large SCOTTISH IMMIGRATION to British North America and later, the United States.

See also BRITISH IMMIGRATION.

Further Reading

Neeson, J. M. *Commoners: Common Right, Enclosure and Social Change in England, 1700–1820.* Reprint. Cambridge: Cambridge University Press, 1996.

Thirsk, Joan, ed. *Agricultural Change: Policy and Practice 1500–1750.* Cambridge: Cambridge University Press, 1990.

English immigration   See BRITISH IMMIGRATION.

entertainment and immigration

Entertainment in early 19th century North America was centered in the home. While the upper classes might attend opera, the theater, and the symphony; the middle class, minstrel shows or plays; and the working classes, saloon variety shows, most people were entertained at home by family and friends, and the development of amateur musical or theatrical talent was considered a mark of social grace. In rural areas and among the poor, folk music and dances developed. Immigrants of high artistic achievement usually represented in their performances the European elite culture routinely copied in America and Canada, playing in productions of Shakespeare or in classical symphonies. Popular immigrant entertainment was usually associated more narrowly with immigrant folk culture—German church hymns, Irish ballads, and local Ukrainian folk troupes, for example. Prior to the 20th century, the vast majority of immigrants were either unskilled or semiskilled laborers or agriculturalists, who wished to fondly remember their homelands in their entertainments. Sometimes these nostalgic longings developed

P. Mohyla Ukrainian Institute Drama Group, Saskatoon, Saskatchewan, 1919. Ethnic drama troupes like this were common in Canada and the United States, helping to maintain ethnic identity and solidarity. *(George E. Dragan Collection/National Archives of Canada/PA-088603)*

into rich performance communities in the large cities, including an extensive repertoire of Yiddish-language adaptations of both classics of the stage and melodrama. Though most ethnic performers never joined the mainstream English stage, they nevertheless served large audiences. The first phase of immigrant entertainment then was self-consciously fashioned by performers for their own ethnic groups and had little impact on society at large. Immigrants themselves were scarcely included in the songs and plays of the mainstream culture, and when they were, it was usually as a stereotype, such as the drunken Irishman or the Jewish shylock. It usually took immigrants many years to acquire an understanding of American art forms; once they did, however, they played a powerful role in defining the cultural landscape.

Two closely related developments in the entertainment industry at the end of the 19th century opened doors for many immigrants. The rapid growth of cities during the Industrial Revolution, particularly after 1880, led to the creation of a variety of venues that were an extension of the British music hall and designed specifically for mass popular entertainment, thus marking the beginnings of American vaudeville. In the 1890s, the music publishing industry was transformed by the deliberate search for composers and lyricists to supply the new mass market. Tin Pan Alley, the collective name given to the New York music publishing

district, was constantly searching for clever lyrics and great tunes and was willing to take on anyone who could write to meet a popular style. Together, vaudeville and Tin Pan Alley ushered in a new age of mass entertainment.

Perhaps the most representative talent of the period was singing star Sophie Tucker, born to a Russian-Jewish woman in Poland in 1884. She came to the United States as an infant and grew up in Connecticut. At the age of 10, Tucker was singing in the family café. In the first decade of the new century, she was performing blackface, before joining the Ziegfeld Follies in 1909. Billed as the "Last of the Red-Hot Mamas," she starred on Broadway and on film. As vaudeville faded in the 1930s, she continued to pack nightclubs and performed on radio and television. She was one of the first recording stars, when primitive Edison cylinders were being used, and produced albums into the 1950s. An even bigger star, Al Jolson was billed during the first half of the 20th century as "The World's Greatest Entertainer." Born Asa Yoelson in Lithuanian Russia in 1886, Jolson came to America with his Jewish family in 1894. Attracted to the latest ragtime craze, he became deeply immersed in American popular culture. He sang in the circus, performed on the comedy stage, developed a comedy act, and began to perform in blackface. He debuted on Broadway in 1911. Around 1918, he began writing lyrics. With *The Jazz Singer* in 1927, he helped usher in the era of talking films; in it, he sang "Blue

Skies," the tune of another Russian immigrant, Irving Berlin. Though the vaudevillian style was waning in the 1930s, Jolson made the transition to radio, became wildly popular entertaining U.S. troops, and continued to entertain until his death in 1950.

The entertainment industry enabled immigrants both to transcend their ethnic backgrounds and to help transform the perception of immigrants. Tucker was famous for her trademark song "My Yiddishe Momme." Others, such as George M. Cohan and Chauncey Olcott, of Irish descent, did much to dispel stereotypes with songs like "Yankee Doodle Dandy," "You Can't Deny You're Irish," and "When Irish Eyes Are Smiling." America's best-loved popular composer of the first half of the 20th century, Irving Berlin, was prolific, writing more than 900 songs for Tin Pan Alley, the vaudeville stage, film, and Broadway musicals. Born Israel Baline in czarist Russia in 1888, he composed dozens of classic American songs, including "God Bless America," "White Christmas," "Easter Parade," and symbolically, "There's No Business Like Show Business."

From the early days of the film industry, immigrants found a niche for their talents and capital. Jews were among the first movie theater owners, and most of the early Hollywood studios were either started or controlled by Jewish immigrant businessmen, including Samuel Goldwyn (born in Poland), Harry Warner (born in Poland), and Carl Laemmle (born in Germany). Italian-born Frank Capra became one of America's best-loved film directors, promoting mainstream American ideals in movies such as *Mr. Smith Goes to Washington* (1939) and *It's a Wonderful Life* (1947). Charlie Chaplin, born in England, was considered by many to be America's great comic genius of the early 20th century. Elia Kazan, born Elia Kazanjoglou in Constantinople, directed some of the most culturally searching films and plays of the century, including *On the Waterfront* (1953) and *East of Eden* (1954).

In the 1950s and early 1960s, the entertainment industry was conscious of ethnicity and frequently embraced it. Cuban Desi Arnaz was integral to the success of the beloved *I Love Lucy* television program, and the music of crooners such as Frank Sinatra, Tony Bennett, and Dean Martin—the latter the son of an Italian barber—was freely laced with the sentiments of old Italy. As immigration became more global with the IMMIGRATION AND NATIONALITY ACT of 1965, improved transportation and communications opened the United States and Canada to international trends in entertainment, reinforcing areas already started by immigrants. Though Arnaz and others had helped popularize Cuban music in the 1950s, an interest in a wider world music began to develop, with explorations of the instruments and rhythms of India, Brazil, and Africa. The popular music of the British Invasion of the mid-1960s, spearheaded by the Beatles and the Rolling Stones, was deeply rooted in American folk and ethnic music, especially blues and jazz, as well as songs from the old Tin Pan Alley tradition. Ironically, the segregationist mindset of the American entertainment industry was finally changed, in part, with the help of English and Irish musicians who enthusiastically embraced the music of black America and brought it back to the land of its roots.

From the 1970s, the entertainment industry in North America was internationalized by visitors from abroad and immigrants from within. Improvements in transportation and communication enabled filmmakers, actors, comedians, musicians, and other performers to tap the richest entertainment market in the world. The flood of immigrants from non-European countries following the relaxation of immigration restrictions during the 1960s and 1970s created new audiences for all forms of international entertainment. European, Indian, Iranian, Chinese, and Japanese filmmakers worked more frequently in the United States and began to have their films more widely viewed in North America. Non-English-language films were seldom unqualified commercial successes, but they developed dedicated followings, particularly in major urban centers, and were regularly reviewed by critics. Some directors, such as Taiwan's Ang Lee, studied in the United States and stayed to do much of their work there. Lee's master's project, *Fine Line,* was full of immigrant themes, with an Italian man fleeing the Mafia and a Chinese woman hiding from immigration officials. Opportunities for classical musicians and dancers continued to attract many foreign artists to the large cultural centers of the United States, including New York, Boston, Los Angeles, and San Francisco. The 1961 defection of Rudolph Nureyev, Russia's leading dancer, on grounds of artistic freedom brought international attention to the cultural implications of the COLD WAR.

A wide variety of world music forms were brought to North America, the "music capital" of the world, for sales and exposure. British groups remained the most popular non-American acts, as Pink Floyd, Led Zeppelin, Elton John, the Bee Gees, and others regularly toured the United States and Canada. Occasionally Australian (Men at Work, Kylie Minogue), Swedish (ABBA), Irish (U-2), and other European performers would enjoy popularity, but no other country consistently produced successful rock and pop music in North America as did Great Britain. Latin music, well known to jazz musicians before World War II (1939–45), became more broadly popular in the 1950s and 1960s, as hundreds of thousands of Cuban refugees immigrated to the United States between 1957 and 1981 and Mexico emerged as the number-one source country for American immigration. With millions of North Americans whose first language was Spanish, a specialized Latino music scene developed, with various local forms. Tejano, for instance, combining country and Mexican traditions, became wildly popular among Chicanos in the Southwest, before Texas singer Selena took it into the mainstream with hits in the 1990s. Gloria Estefan, born in Havana, had previously done the same for Cuban salsa, taking her band, the Miami Sound Machine, from Spanish-language dance clubs to the top of the U.S. pop charts in the late 1980s. During the 1970s and 1980s, Spain's Julio Iglesias became the leading Latin singer in the world and hugely successful in North America. A new generation of Latino artists continued to successfully fuse Latin and pop idioms into the 21st century, including Ricky Martin (Puerto Rican), Enrique Iglesias (Spanish, Julio's son), and Shakira (Colombian-Lebanese), among others, Some immigrants, such as Carlos Santana, entered the rock mainstream directly. Santana had his own blues-rock band in the 1960s and 1970s, then reemerged in the 1990s to play with a host of new stars.

Not all world music was equally popular. The Indian sitar music of Ravi Shankar became fashionably stylish in the 1960s and 1970s without being commercially successful. The francophone musical tradition in Canada remained highly regionalized, with the exception of the phenomenal crossover appeal of Celine Dion in the 1990s. Reggae, on the other hand, brought from Jamaica and popularized by Bob Marley, was embraced by North American audiences to become part of the musical mainstream. In 2002, Sean Paul's dancehall reggae united reggae and modern hip hop, whose raps were influenced by the ska and rock-steady precursors to reggae in the 1960s. African musicians became popular in the 1990s when Paul Simon featured a South African backup band, and the Dave Matthews Band of South Africa became one of the most popular acts of the decade. Most often, however, these innovators were only temporary migrants in the United States and Canada, recording music in New York City; Chicago, Illinois; Muscle Shoals, Alabama; or Nashville, Tennessee, or touring to promote their work.

Some entertainers, however, stayed to become permanent residents or citizens, preferring to be close to their biggest market or seeking to evade political turmoil or the high tax rates common in Europe. The Russian classical composer Igor Stravinsky moved to the United States in order to teach at Harvard for one year but ended settling in West Hollywood and becoming a citizen in 1945. British-born John Lennon of Beatles fame waged a long battle with the U.S. government in order to win his green card in 1973. Many stage and film stars, including Ingrid Bergman (Sweden), Richard Burton (Wales), and Arnold Schwarzenegger (Austria) came to work in the United States, then chose to remain.

See also SPORTS AND IMMIGRATION.

Further Reading

Bona, Mary Jo, and Anthony Julian Tamburri, eds. *Through the Looking Glass: Italian and Italian-American Images in the Media.* Staten Island, N.Y.: American Italian Historical Association, 1994.

Erdman, Harley. *Staging the Jew: The Performance of American Ethnicity.* New Brunswick, N.J.: Rutgers University Press, 1962.
Friedman, Lester D., ed. *Unspeakable Images: Ethnicity and the American Cinema.* Chicago: University of Illinois Press, 1991.
Jones, Dorothy R. *The Portrayal of China and India on the American Screen, 1896–1955: The Evolution of Chinese and Indian Themes, Locales, and Characters as Portrayed on the American Screen.* Cambridge, Mass.: Center for International Studies, MIT, 1955.
Kanellos, Nicolás. *Hispanic Theater in the United States.* Houston: Arte Público Press, 1984.
———. *A History of Hispanic Theatre in the United States: Origins to 1940.* Austin: University of Texas Press, 1990.
Maloney, Paul. *Scotland and the Music Hall, 1850–1914.* Manchester, U.K.: Manchester University Press, 2003.
Marchetti, Gina. *Romance and the "Yellow Peril": Race, Sex and Discursive Strategies in Hollywood Fiction.* Berkeley: University of California Press, 1993.
Marcuson, Lewis R. *The Stage Immigrant: The Irish, Italians, and Jews in American Drama, 1920–1960.* New York: Garland, 1990.
Naficy, H. *The Making of Exile Cultures: Iranian Television in Los Angeles.* Minneapolis: University of Minnesota Press, 1993.
Parenti, Michael. "The Media Are the Mafia: Italian-American Images and the Ethnic Struggle." *National Review* 30, no. 10 (1979): 20–27.
Rogin, Michael. *Blackface, White Noise: Jewish Immigrants in the Hollywood Melting Pot.* Berkeley: University of California Press, 1996.
Seller, Maxine Schwartz, ed. *Ethnic Theatre in the United States.* Westport, Conn.: Greenwood Press, 1983.
Shaheen, J. *The TV Arab: Our Popular Press.* Bowling Green, Ohio: Bowling Green University Popular Press, 1984.
Slobin, Mark. *Tenement Songs: The Popular Music of the Jewish Immigrants.* Urbana: University of Illinois Press, 1982.
Torres, Sasha, ed. *Living Color: Race and Television in the United States.* Durham, N.C.: Duke University Press, 1988.
Whitcomb, Ian. *Irving Berlin and Ragtime America.* New York: Century, 1987.

Estonian immigration

Estonian immigration to North America has been small and closely tied to political events in Europe. In the U.S. census of 2000 and the Canadian census of 2001, 25,034 Americans and 22,085 Canadians claimed Estonian descent. Early settlement in the United States included in New York City, San Francisco, and Astoria, Oregon. In 2000, most Estonians in the United States lived in the Northeast, with a significant number also in California. Toronto was the center of Estonian settlement in Canada.

Estonia occupies 17,400 square miles of eastern Europe along the Baltic Sea and the Gulf of Finland between 57 and 59 degrees north latitude. Russia lies to the east and Latvia to the south. In 2002, the population was estimated at 1,423,316, 65 percent of which are ethnic Estonians. Russians made up another 28 percent of the population. Chief religions of the country were Evangelical Lutheranism and

An Estonian family near Jewett City, Connecticut, 1942. A failed revolution in Russia in 1905 led to the first major wave of Estonian immigration to the United States. *(Photo by John Collier/Library of Congress, Prints & Photographs Division [LC-USF34-083824-C])*

Russian Orthodox. Prior to World War I (1914–18) Estonia was a province of the Russian Empire. As such, it is impossible to determine how many Estonians immigrated prior to 1922 because they were almost universally referred to as Russians, representing the country of their birth. A few Estonians were among the Swedish party that settled the colony of New Sweden along the Delaware River during the 17th century (see DELAWARE COLONY), and small groups settled near Pierre, South Dakota; New York City; and San Francisco after 1894. It was not until the failed socialist Revolution of 1905, however, that the first large group of Estonians came to the United States, many of them committed Socialists. With the independence of Estonia in 1920 and passage of the restrictive EMERGENCY QUOTA ACT (1921) and JOHNSON-REED ACT (1924), Estonian immigration declined significantly. Estonia was conquered by the Soviet Union in 1940 and incorporated as a Soviet Socialist Republic, driving thousands of refugees into displaced persons camps in Germany after World War II (1939–45). Between 1946 and 1955 more than 15,000 were accepted in the United States as refugees. Under Soviet rule, Estonians generally were not allowed to emigrate, but upon gaining their independence in 1991, it became more common. Between 1992 and 2002, about 2,500 Estonians immigrated to the United States.

Only a handful of Estonians, mainly individuals and a few families, settled in Canada prior to World War II. The earliest Estonians were probably fishermen working out of Prince Rupert, British Columbia. Between 1899 and 1903, there were 16 Estonian farms near Sylvan Lake (modern Alberta). By 1916, there were about 1,500 Estonians in Canada. Only 700 immigrated during the 1920s and 1930s, including members of a failed settlement near St. Francis,

British Columbia. After World War II, Canada admitted about 14,000 Estonian refugees, most between 1947 and 1951, and often after they had first made stops in Sweden or Germany. Of 6,395 Estonians in Canada in 2001, almost 80 percent arrived prior to 1961; only 845 immigrated between 1991 and 2001. Most Estonians who immigrated to the United States and Canada as refugees were well educated and staunchly anticommunist and tended to assimilate quickly.

See also RUSSIAN IMMIGRATION; SOVIET IMMIGRATION.

Further Reading

Aun, Karl. *The Political Refugees: A History of the Estonians in Canada.* Toronto: McClelland and Stewart, 1985.

Kurlents, Alfred, ed. *Eestlased Kanadas (Estonians in Canada).* Vol. 2. Toronto: Kanada Eestlaste Ajaloo Komisjon, 1985.

Larr, Mart. *War in the Woods: Estonia's Struggle for Survival, 1944–1956.* Trans. Tiina Ets. New York: Compass Press, 1992.

Pennar, Jaan, et al., eds. *The Estonians in America, 1627–1975: A Chronology and Factbook.* Dobbs Ferry, N.Y.: Oceana Publications, 1975.

Raun, Toivo U. *Estonia and Estonians.* 2d ed. Stanford, Calif.: Hoover Institution Press, 2002.

Tannberg, Keresti, and Tonu Parming. *Aspects of Cultural Life: Sources for the Study of Estonians in America.* New York: Estonian Learned Society in America, 1975.

Walko, M. Ann. *Rejecting the Second Generation Hypothesis: Maintaining Estonian Ethnicity in Lakewood, New Jersey.* New York: AMS Press, 1989.

Ethiopian immigration

Ethiopians were among the first Africans to voluntarily immigrate to the United States, mainly as a result of COLD WAR conflicts. In the U.S. census of 2000 and the Canadian census of 2001, 86,918 Americans and 15,725 Canadians claimed Ethiopian descent. Main concentrations of settlement included Washington, D.C., Los Angeles, New York City, and Dallas, Texas. About half of all Ethiopian Canadians lived in Toronto.

Ethiopia occupies 431,800 square miles of East Africa between 4 and 17 degrees north latitude. It is bordered by the Red Sea and Eritrea to the north; Somalia and Djibouti, to the east; Kenya, to the south; and Sudan, to the west. A high-altitude plateau dominates the eastern portion of the land, while the mountains of the Great Rift Valley cover the west. In 2002, the population was estimated at 65,891,874 and was divided into two major ethnic groups and a number of smaller ones. The Oromo made up 40 percent of the population, and Amhara and Tigrean another 32 percent. Nearly 50 percent of Ethiopians were Muslim; 40 percent, Ethiopian Orthodox; and 12 percent, animists. Ethiopia wielded regional dominance in the medieval period. In 1880 Ethiopia was invaded by Italy but remarkably managed to maintain its independence during the colonial era of the 19th and early 20th centuries, excepting the northern coastal province of Eritrea, which became an Italian protectorate in 1889. Italy successfully conquered the country's heartland in 1935. Freed by Britain in 1941, Ethiopia was ruled by Haile Selassie I until 1974, when he was ousted by a military junta. In 1977, Ethiopia began to cooperate with Communist Russia and Cuba, countries that helped Ethiopia defeat invading Somalian troops in 1978. In 1984, a severe famine killed nearly 1 million people. Both the political unrest and famine led to widespread immigration.

There is no record of formal Ethiopian immigration to the United States prior to 1980, though some were admitted as students prior to that time. The REFUGEE ACT of that year established a formal procedure for admitting African refugees. Ethiopians formed the largest group between 1982 and 1994, about 68 percent of the African total. Between 1976 and 1994, more than 33,000 Ethiopian refugees were resettled in the United States, often after spending time in Sudanese camps. In 1993, Eritrea declared independence from Ethiopia, and a war ensued until 2000 when the province won its independence. The war cost Ethiopia nearly $3 billion and displaced approximately 350,000 Ethiopians. Multiparty elections for a federal republic were first held in 1995, following a coup by the Ethiopian People's Revolutionary Democratic Front. Between 1992 and 2002, annual Ethiopian immigration to the United States averaged about 5,000. Between 1983 and 2001, more than 31,000 Ethiopian refugees were admitted to the United States.

Prior to the political turmoil of the 1970s, only a handful of Ethiopian students resided in Canada. With the refugee crisis of the 1980s, Canada began to screen and admit a number of Ethiopians, mostly those who spoke English and came from middle- and upper-class families. Many came from countries of first asylum, including Kenya, Italy, Egypt, and Greece. Toronto was the number-one destination as it provided the greatest job opportunities. Of 13,710 Ethiopian immigrants in 2001, fewer than 600 had arrived prior to 1981, and more than 8,100, between 1991 and 2001.

Further Reading

Chichon, D., E. M. Gozdziak, and J. G. Grover, eds. *The Economic and Social Adjustment of Non-Southeast Asian Refugees.* Dover, N.H.: Research Management Corporation, 1986.

Koehn, P. H. *Refugees from Revolution: U.S. Policy and Third World Migration.* Boulder, Colo.: Westview Press, 1991.

Moussa, Helene. *Storm and Sanctuary: The Journey of Ethiopian and Eritrean Women Refugees.* Dundas, Ontario: Artemis Enterprises, 1993.

Ofcansky, Thomas P., and LaVerle Berry. *Ethiopia: A Country Study.* Washington, D.C.: Library of Congress, 1993.

Sorenson, John. "Politics of Social Identity: Ethiopians in Canada." *Journal of Ethnic Studies* 19, no. 1 (1991): 67–86.

Woldemikael, T. M. "Ethiopians and Eritreans." In *Refugees in America in the 1990s: A Reference Handbook.* Ed. D. W. Haines. Westport, Conn.: Greenwood Press, 1996.

ethnicity and race   See RACIAL AND ETHNIC CATEGORIES; RACISM.

Evian Conference

Sponsored by the United States, the Evian Conference brought 30 nations together in Evian, France, to discuss the plight of European refugees during summer 1938.

In 1937, recognizing the worsening condition of Jews in Europe, President Franklin Roosevelt relaxed screening rules for refugees. At the same time, the American public was strongly opposed to an increased Jewish presence in the country, with one poll suggesting that 82 percent were against the entry of large numbers of Jewish refugees. Roosevelt invited 32 nations to attend the largely ineffectual conference. Just as the United States public was unwilling to take the lead in relocating Jewish refugees, all other countries shrank from taking aggressive action. During the 1930s, Canada had been especially marked by international policy makers as a large country with available land for resettling overcrowded and mistreated populations, from the Japanese to the Jews. The Canadian government under WILLIAM LYON MACKENZIE KING thus attended reluctantly, fearing that Canada's appearance would suggest a readiness to accept more Jewish refugees. Canadians generally were isolationists, and Quebecois especially were opposed to both international involvements of every kind and resettlement of Jews in particular. All countries at the conference eventually agreed with the Canadian view that "governments with unwanted minorities must equally not be encouraged to think that harsh treatment at home is the key that will open the doors to immigration abroad." The conference did lead to establishment of the Intergovernmental Committee on Refugees, but lack of funds and international support hampered its work. Adolf Hitler, the Nazi leader of Germany, interpreted the results as confirmation that the Jews had little international support.

Further Reading

Abella, Irving, and Harold Troper. *None Is Too Many: Canada and the Jews of Europe, 1933–1948.* Toronto: Lester and Orpen Dennys, 1982.

Breitman, Richard, and Alan M. Kraut. *American Refugee Policy and European Jewry, 1933–1945.* Bloomington: Indiana University Press, 1987.

Feingold, Henry L. *The Politics of Rescue: The Roosevelt Administration and the Holocaust, 1938–1945.* Detroit: Wayne State University Press, 1973.

Stewart, Barbara McDonald. *United States Government Policy on Refugees from Nazism, 1933–1940.* New York: Garland Publishing, 1982.

Fairclough, Ellen Louks (1905–) *politician*
Ellen Louks Fairclough, Canada's first woman federal cabinet minister, presided over a major overhaul of the country's longstanding "white Canada" immigration policy. Regulations implemented on February 1, 1962, eliminated almost all elements of race-related exclusion and led to a significant increase in immigration from Africa, the Middle East, and Latin America, most notably from the West Indies (see WEST INDIAN IMMIGRATION).

Born in Hamilton, Ontario, Ellen Louks became a chartered accountant. During the 1930s she helped her husband, businessman D. H. Gordon Fairclough, to organize the Young Conservative Association of Hamilton. She served as a city alderman (1946–49) and deputy mayor (1950) before winning a seat in the House of Commons in 1950. When John Diefenbaker became prime minister in 1957, he named Fairclough secretary of state and in the following year appointed her to the newly created post of minister of citizenship and immigration. Upon taking up the post in May 1958, she was immediately confronted with the press of applicants for sponsored immigration and a growing backlog in applications. The Conservative government sought to limit the extent of family sponsorship, then backed down. As Fairclough explained, she rescinded the restrictive Order in Council 1959–310 because it was based on previous legislation enacted by the Liberals, and she was therefore willing to reconsider the government's position in anticipation of more extensive revisions. These revisions were finally implemented in the immigration regulations of 1962, which established skills, rather than race, as the basis for Canadian immigration. The new regulations also made the General Board of Immigration Appeals largely independent of the Department of Citizenship and Immigration. In 1962, Fairclough was made postmaster general but was defeated in the election of 1963, at which time she retired from politics.

Further Reading

Conrad, Margaret. "'Not a Feminist, but . . .': the Political Career of Ellen Louks Fairclough, Canada's First Feminine Federal Cabinet Minister." *Journal of Canadian Studies* 31, no. 2 (Summer 1996): 5–28.
Fairclough, Ellen Louks. *Saturday's Child: Memoirs of Canada's First Female Cabinet Minister.* Toronto: University of Toronto Press, 1995
Hawkins, Freda. *Canada and Immigration: Public Policy and Public Concern.* 2d ed. Kingston and Montreal: Institute of Public Administration of Canada and McGill–Queen's University Press, 1988.
Newman, Peter Charles. *Renegade in Power: The Diefenbaker Years.* Indianapolis, Ind.: Bobbs-Merrill, 1964.

Federation for American Immigration Reform   See NATIVISM.

Fiancées Act   See WAR BRIDES ACT.

Fijian immigration   See SOUTH ASIAN IMMIGRATION.

Filipino immigration

Because the United States had acquired the Philippines as a colonial territory in 1898, Filipinos were in some ways privileged immigrants during the 20th century and second in number only to Chinese among Asian immigrants to the United States. They were third in Canada, behind Chinese and East Indian immigrants. In the U.S. census of 2000 and the Canadian census of 2001, 2,364,815 Americans and 327,550 Canadians claimed Filipino descent. The largest concentrations of Filipinos in the United States are in California, Hawaii, and Chicago, Illinois, with significant areas of settlement in cities with large naval bases, including San Diego, California; Bremerton, Washington; Jacksonville, Florida; and Charleston, South Carolina. More than half of Filipino Canadians live in Ontario, with a large settlement also in Vancouver, British Columbia.

The Philippines is a country of 7,100 islands occupying 115,000 square miles in the South China and Philippine Seas between 5 and 19 degrees north latitude. Nearby countries include Taiwan to the north and Malaysia and Indonesia to the south. Most of the population, an estimated 82,841,518, resides on 11 major mountainous islands that take up the greatest part of the country's land area. About 83 percent of the population practices Roman Catholicism; 9 percent, Protestantism; and 5 percent, Islam. Malay peoples indigenously inhabited the Philippine Islands when Magellan landed there with his Spanish fleet in 1521. Spain governed the islands until 1898, when they were ceded to the United States following the Spanish-American War. A nationalist uprising broke out the following year but was successfully suppressed by U.S. forces by 1905. From 1941 to the end of World War II in 1945, the islands were occupied by Japan. In 1946, the Philippines was granted independence, and a republican government was formed. Between 1972 and 1981, President Ferdinand Marcos (first elected in 1965) ruled the country by martial law. Marcos was deposed in 1986, leading to significant political destabilizing under President Corazon Aquino. Between the 1965 election of Marcos and his 1986 overthrow, some 300,000 Filipinos immigrated to the United States. Communist and Muslim insurgents launched a coup

Prisoners taken by the United States during the Filipino insurrection, 1898–1902. By 1930, there were more than 63,000 Filipinos in Hawaii, having largely replaced Chinese, Japanese, and Korean workers banned from entry into the United States. *(National Archives #72-91212)*

in 1989 that was defeated with help from the United States. A Muslim region in the south was eventually granted autonomy in 1996, ending the ongoing rebellion.

Some of the earliest Filipino immigrants to North America were sailors who left their ships in New Orleans, Louisiana, during the 19th century. The number of immigrants remained small, however, until the first decade of the 20th century. With provisions of the CHINESE EXCLUSION ACT (1882) and the GENTLEMEN'S AGREEMENT (1907) largely excluding Chinese, Japanese, and Korean laborers, there was high demand for cheap agricultural labor in Hawaii and California. In 1906, the Hawaiian Sugar Planters' Association began to actively recruit in the Philippines, and by the mid-1920s, there was a large voluntary workforce seeking admission. By 1931, 113,000 Filipino workers had come to Hawaii. About 39,000 eventually returned to the Philippines, but more than 18,000 eventually migrated to California. In addition to these, some 27,000 Filipinos immigrated directly to the mainland, most hired under the PADRONE SYSTEM of labor supply. Most Filipino immigrants were young men, and as late as 1940, the ratio of Filipino men to women was still 3.5 to 1. With the rise in unemployment during the depression, the TYDINGS-MCDUFFIE ACT of 1934 limited Filipino immigration to 50 per year. As important, with the Philippines being made a commonwealth and destined for independence, Filipinos were reclassified from nationals to aliens.

A second period of immigration, particularly associated with military developments, occurred between 1946 and 1964. Filipino Americans had served with distinction during World War II, helping substantially in driving the Japanese from the Philippines. The WAR BRIDES ACT of 1946 enabled American soldiers to bring some 5,000 Filipina brides to the United States following World War II. The Military Bases Agreement of 1947 permitted the United States to make use of 23 sites in the Philippines and thus to maintain a formidable presence there into the 1990s. Exemptions to the Tydings-McDuffie Act enabled the United States to recruit more than 22,000 Filipinos into the navy (between 1944 and 1973), most of whom were assigned to work in mess halls or as personal servants. Exemptions also enabled some 7,000 additional Filipino agricultural workers into the country.

A new phase of immigration began with the IMMIGRATION AND NATIONALITY ACT of 1965, which both eliminated race as a factor in the selection process and classified immediate relatives of U.S. citizens as special immigrants, thus admitted outside the annual quota of 20,000. The significant family reunification numbers were augmented in 1974 when the Philippines instituted an ongoing overseas employment program. This led to an average of more than 600,000 Filipino workers migrating each year, though most of these went to the countries of the Middle East and East Asia. A large percentage of those immigrating to the United

States were highly trained professionals, especially doctors and nurses. Emigration to Canada remained small in part because Canadian immigration policy encouraged migration only of professional and skilled workers.

As in most developing countries, worker migration was seen as beneficial in both easing unemployment and increasing remittances to the Philippines. In 1995, for instance, remittances totaled $4.87 billion, or about 2.5 percent of the gross national product, and the amounts remained high into the first decade of the 21st century. Between 1991 and 2002, more than 600,000 Filipinos immigrated to the United States.

It is difficult to arrive at precise figures for Filipino immigration to Canada. Not only were Filipinos grouped under the category "Other Asians" until 1967, but they also followed a distinctive pattern of immigration with no precedents in the Chinese, Japanese, or Asian Indian communities. There were virtually no immigrants prior to World War II, and fewer than 100 by 1964. Beginning in 1965, however, a steady immigration began, which was accelerated by the new IMMIGRATION REGULATIONS of 1967, which included a points system that gave preference to skilled workers in high demand areas, such as health care. Between 1971 and 1992, total immigration from the Philippines placed them in the top 10 of source countries, and between 1994 and 2002, the country ranked from second to sixth each year, with a total of about 110,000 immigrants. Unlike other Asian groups, most Filipino immigrants were women who came for job opportunities in medical fields, especially nursing, and clerical areas. Although the gender differential gradually became more balanced, by the 1990s Filipina women still composed about 60 percent of the immigrant population.

Another difference between Filipino and other Asian immigration is that most early immigrants came first from the United States, where their relationship afforded special opportunities for access to the country. Sometimes unable to remain in the United States, they learned that visas were available for skilled technicians in Canada, particularly in Ontario. By the early 1970s, they were bringing family members and encouraging others to emigrate directly from the Philippines. As Canadian immigration policy in the 1980s gave special weight to family reunification, more Filipinos took advantage of the provisions. During the 1980s and 1990s, Filipino immigrants were less likely to choose Toronto, though it remained the foremost Filipino community in Canada with a population of 140,000 in 2001. Vancouver's was second, with more than 60,000. Of 232,670 Filipino immigrants in Canada in 2001, about 96 percent arrived after 1970.

See also BULOSAN, CARLOS.

Further Reading

Brands, H. W. *Bound to Empire: The United States and the Philippines.* New York: Oxford University Press, 1992.

Cariaga, Roman R. *The Filipinos in Hawaii: Economic and Social Conditions, 1906–1936*. San Francisco: R. and E. Research Associates, 1974.

Carino, Benjamin. "Filipino Americans: Many and Varied." In *Origins and Destinies: Immigration, Race, and Ethnicity in America*. Eds. Silvia Pedraza and Rubén G. Rumbaut. Belmont, Calif.: Wadsworth, 1996.

Cheng, Lucie, and Edna Bonacich, eds. *Labor Immigration under Capitalism: Asian Workers in the United States before World War II*. Berkeley: University of California Press, 1984.

Cusipag, Ruben J., and Maria Corazon Buenafe. *Portrait of Filipino Canadians in Ontario, 1960–1990*. Ontario, 1993.

Espina, Maria E. *Filipinos in Louisiana*. New Orleans, La.: A. F. Laborde and Sons, 1988.

Espiritu, Yen Le. *Filipino American Lives*. Philadelphia: Temple University Press, 1995.

Guyotte, Roland L. "Generation Gap: Filipinos, Filipino Americans, and Americans, Here and There, Then and Now." *Journal of American Ethnic History* 17 (Fall 1997): 64–70.

Laquian, Eleanor M. *A Study of Filipino Immigration to Canada, 1962–1972*. Ottawa: United Council of Filipino Associations in Canada, 1973.

Lasker, Bruno. *Filipino Immigration to the Continental United States and to Hawaii*. Chicago: University of Chicago Press, 1931.

Mangiafico, Luciano. *Contemporary American Immigrants: Patterns of Filipino, Korean, and Chinese Settlement in the United States*. New York: Praeger, 1988.

Melendy, H. Brett. "Filipinos in the United States." *Pacific Historical Review* 43, no. 4 (1974): 520–547.

Pido, Antonio J. A. *The Filipinos in America: Macro/Micro Dimensions of Immigration and Integration*. Staten Island, N.Y.: Center for Migration Studies, 1992.

Ramos, Rodel J. *In Search of a Future: The Struggle of Immigrants*. Scarborough, Canada: RJRAMOS Enterprises, 1994.

Root, Maria P. P., ed. *Filipino Americans: Transformation and Identity*. Newbury Park, Calif.: Sage Publications, 1997.

San Juan, Epifanio, et al. *From Exile to Diaspora: Versions of the Filipino Experience in the United States*. Boulder, Colo.: Westview Press, 1998.

Teodore, Luis V., Jr., ed. *Out of This Struggle: The Filipinos in Hawaii*. Honolulu: University Press of Hawaii, 1981.

Toff, Nancy, ed. *The Filipino Americans*. New York: Chelsea House, 1989.

Finnish immigration

Finns were among the earliest settlers in North America, forming a substantial portion of the colony of New Sweden, founded in 1638 along the Delaware River (see DELAWARE COLONY). In the U.S. census of 2000 and the Canadian census of 2001, 623,573 Americans and 114,690 Canadians claimed Finnish descent. Finns were widely dispersed throughout the northern tier of the United States, with Michigan and Minnesota having the largest numbers. More than half of Canadian Finns live in Ontario.

Finland occupies 117,800 square mile of Scandinavian Europe between 60 and 70 degrees north latitude along the Gulf of Bothnia and the Gulf of Finland. Norway borders Finland to the north, Russia to the east, and Sweden to the west. The southern and central regions of the country are relatively flat, with many lakes. Northern regions are mountainous. In 2002, the population was estimated at 5,175,783. Ethnic Finns make up 93 percent of the people, while Swedes compose another 6 percent. About 89 percent of the population claims Evangelical Lutheranism as their religion. Eurasians first settled Finland, but Sweden controlled the territory from 1154 until 1809, when it became an independent grand duchy of Russia. Throughout the 19th century, Finland was granted extraordinary freedoms of self-government and religion and exemption from Russian military service. Pan-Slavic policies during the first decade of the 20th century, however, spurred a rise in nationalism that led to a declaration of independence in 1917. Finland was first recognized as a republic in 1919, after the Bolshevik Revolution in Russia and the creation of the Soviet Union. The Soviet Union took control of large amounts of Finnish territory in 1939 and even more throughout World War II (1939–45). Following the war, however, a treaty of mutual assistance was signed (1948), enabling Finland to develop largely outside the COLD WAR conflicts so prevalent in other parts of Europe. A new treaty was signed in 1992, and in 1995 Finland became a member of the European Union.

Finns were among the colonists who established New Sweden along the Delaware River in 1638. As the colony successively changed hands, however, first going to the Dutch and then the English, by the 18th century, Finns had blended into the predominant British culture. In Alaska, Finns and Russians settled in the 1840s and 1850s, especially around Sitka. Perhaps 500 moved to British Columbia and California when Alaska was purchased by the United States in 1867, finding work in mines or on the railroads. The number of Finnish immigrants remained small until the 1860s, when widespread economic depression led to massive emigration, particularly from northern Finland. Most of the immigrants had taken part in the Laestadian religious revival of the 1860s, and their migration was characterized by families hoping to maintain a separatist lifestyle. Finland was also experiencing unprecedented population growth, tripling during the 19th century and creating a large surplus population for which there were few jobs and no land. From the 1890s, the majority of immigrants were young and from the more populated south, motivated by both economic opportunity and, after 1904, opposition to Czar Nicholas II's newly imposed nationalistic policies and forced military service. A high percentage of Finns had become politically radicalized prior to leaving Europe and often became involved with socialist or anarchist politics upon their arrival. It has been estimated that some 300,000

Finns settled permanently in the United States between 1864 and 1924. The actual number of immigrants was higher, but there was an unusually high rate of return among Finnish radicals. In the 1920s and early 1930s, 10,000 immigrated to the Soviet Union, although thousands of ordinary Finns seeking a better life still sought permission to immigrate to the United States. When passage of the restrictive JOHNSON-REED ACT in 1924 drastically cut the Finnish quota, Finns increasingly turned their attention to Canada.

While a few hundred Finns migrated to British Columbia when Alaska was purchased, others were just beginning to seek economic opportunities outside Finland and Sweden. Immigration figures prior to World War I (1914–18) are unreliable, as they were frequently classified or grouped in various combinations with Swedes, Norwegians, Russians, or, in the case of continental migration, Americans. Perhaps 5,000 Finns immigrated during the 19th century, and another 20,000 between 1900 and 1914. With the application of restrictive legislation in the United States, more than 36,000 Finns flocked to Canada between 1921 and 1930, before they, too, were shut out by Canada's depression-era policies in the 1930s. Undoubtedly many of these Finnish immigrants used Canada as a backdoor to the United States, but thousands stayed to settle. Many who did were active in socialist politics, founding radical newspapers and helping to organize the Lumber Workers Industrial Union of Canada in northern Ontario. Disheartened by slow progress and the onset of the depression, thousands left Canada during the 1930s, most for Finland, but many too for neighboring Soviet Karelia.

The Russian invasion of Finland in 1939 prompted a new wave of sympathy for the Finns and a new era of Finnish immigration. Between 1948 and 1960, more than 17,000 immigrated to Canada, many fearing renewed Soviet aggression. During the later 20th century, immigration to both the United States and Canada was small, composed mainly of students and professionals seeking educational or economic advancement. Between 1992 and 2002, an average of fewer than 600 immigrated to North America, with about five-sixths of them coming to the United States. Because Finns tended to immigrate individually, rather than communally, they became largely indistinguishable from the greater society, just as had been the case in the colonial period.

Further Reading

Dahlie, Jorgen, and Tissa Fernando, eds. *Ethnicity, Power and Politics in Canada*. Toronto: Methuen, 1981.

Engle, E. *Finns in North America*. Annapolis, Md.: Leeward, 1975.

Hammasti, P. G. *Finnish Radicals in Astoria, Oregon, 1904–1940*. New York: Arno, 1979.

Hoglund, A. W. *Finnish Immigrants in America, 1880–1920*. Madison: University of Wisconsin Press, 1960.

Jalkanen, R. J., ed. *The Finns in North America: A Social Symposium.* East Lansing: Michigan State University Press for Suomi College, 1969.

Karni, M. G., ed. *Finnish Diaspora*. 2 vols. Toronto: Multicultural History Society of Ontario, 1981.

Kerkkonen, M. "Finland and Colonial America." In *Old Friends—Strong Ties*. Eds. V. Niitemaa et al. Turku, Finland: Institute for Migration, 1976.

Kero, Reino *Migration from Finland to North America in the Years between the United States Civil War and the First World War*. Turku, Finland: Turun Yliopisto, 1974.

Kivisto, P. *Immigrant Socialists in the United States: The Case of Finns and the Left*. Rutherford, N.J.: Fairleigh Dickinson University Press, 1984.

Kolehmainen, J. I. *From Lake Erie's Shores to the Mahoning and Monogahela Valleys: A History of the Finns in Ohio, Western Pennsylvania, and West Virginia*. Painsville: Ohio Finnish-American Historical Society, 1977.

Kolehmainen, J. I., and G. W. Hill. *Haven in the Woods: The Story of the Finns in Wisconsin*. Madison: State Historical Society of Wisconsin, 1951.

Lindström-Best, Varpu. *Defiant Sisters: A Social History of Finnish Immigrant Women in Canada*. 2d ed. Toronto: Multicultural History Society of Ontario, 1992.

———. *The Finns in Canada*. Ottawa: Canadian Historical Association, 1985.

Ross, C., and K. M. Wargelin Brown, eds. *Women Who Dared: The History of Finnish American Women*. St. Paul: Immigration History Research Center, University of Minnesota, 1986.

Virtanen, Keijo. *Settlement and Return: Finnish Emigrants (1860–1930) in the International Overseas Return Migration Movement*. Helsinki, Finland: Migration Institute, 1979.

Wasatjerna, H. R., ed. *History of the Finns in Minnesota*. Trans. T. Rosvoll. Duluth, Minn.: Finnish-American Historical Society, 1957.

Foran Act   See ALIEN CONTRACT LABOR ACT.

Fourteenth Amendment (United States) (1868)

Proposed in 1865 and ratified in 1868, the Fourteenth Amendment to the Constitution of the United States defined citizenship to include former slaves and to protect them from violations of their civil rights. Aimed at state abuses against African Americans in the wake of the Civil War (1861–65), it also provided equal protection to naturalized immigrants.

Section One of the amendment stated that "all persons born or naturalized in the United States . . . are citizens of the United States" and that the government may not deprive them of "life, liberty, or property, without due process of law," or deny them "equal protection" before the law. The "due process" clause was later interpreted by the courts to extend to state as well as federal law; and the "equal protection" clause, to such categories as sex and disability, as well as race. Other sections of the amendment eliminated the three-fifths compromise, by which only 60 percent of the slave population was counted for purposes of state representation in the House of Representatives; prohibited the holding of public office by anyone who had sworn an oath to the government and then rebelled; voided debts incurred in support of rebellion; and gave Congress the authority to pass enforcing legislation.

Fourteenth Amendment protections extended specifically to immigrants in many ways, especially as courts began to interpret its clauses more broadly in the 20th century. Segregation of housing by race was, in part, invalidated on Fourteenth Amendment grounds. The Supreme Court referred to it in GRAHAM V. RICHARDSON (1971) in establishing that "alienage," like race, was inherently suspect as a category before the law. Also, when the state of Texas refused to finance the education of illegal alien children, the Supreme Court ruled in PLYLER V. DOE (1982) that the Fourteenth Amendment did not apply to citizens alone, but under the equal protection clause to all people "within the jurisdiction" of the state.

Further Reading

Abraham, Henry J., and Barbara A. Perry. *Freedom and the Court: Civil Rights and Liberties in the United States*. 8th ed. St. Lawrence: University of Kansas Press, 2003.

Benedict, Michael Les. *A Compromise of Principle: Congressional Republicans and Reconstruction, 1863–1869*. New York: W. W. Norton, 1974.

Cox, John H. *Politics, Principle, and Prejudice: Dilemma of Reconstruction America, 1865–66*. New York: Free Press, 1963.

Foner, Eric. *Reconstruction: America's Unfinished Revolution, 1863–1877*. New York: HarperCollins, 1988.

Hyman, Harold M., and William Wiecek. *Equal Justice Under Law: Constitutional Development, 1835–1875*. New York: Harper and Row, 1982.

French colonization   See NEW FRANCE.

French immigration

As one of the founding nations of colonial Canada, the French helped define the political and cultural character of the modern country. In the Canadian census of 2001, 4,710,580 Canadians—almost 16 percent of the total population—claimed French or Acadian origins (see ACADIA), second only to those claiming English descent. The true number was undoubtedly considerably higher, however, as almost 12 million respondents claimed "Canadian" descent, and almost 100,000, "Quebecois." In the U.S. census of 2000, 10,659,592 Americans claimed either French or French-Canadian descent. Although French Americans were largely assimilated, there were significant concentrations in the counties of Worcester and Middlesex, in Massachusetts, and in Providence, Rhode Island. Rural concentrations were highest in LOUISIANA parishes, among descendants of the Acadian refugees. French settlement in Canada was concentrated in the province of QUEBEC, where French culture was maintained and a large degree of autonomy preserved in the face of expanding British influence. Almost 90 percent of Canadians who mainly speak French live in Quebec.

France occupies 210,400 square mile in western Europe, between the Atlantic Ocean, and Mediterranean Sea. Spain lies to the southwest; Italy, Switzerland, and Germany to the east, Luxembourg and Belgium to the north. In 2002, the population was estimated at 59,551,227. During the Middle Ages a strong French national identity emerged from a variety of Celtic, Latin, Teutonic, and Slavic influences. As one of the great imperial powers from the 16th century, France gained control of colonial territories in North America, the Caribbean, South America, Africa, India, and Southeast Asia. Although France failed to establish any substantial settlement colonies outside of North America, in the wake of decolonization after 1945, millions of inhabitants of former colonial territories became French citizens, changing the demographic character of the nation. By 2000, 82 percent of the population was Roman Catholic, and 7 percent, Muslim, the latter mostly from the former French colonies of Algeria and Morocco. France allied itself with the fledgling United States of America during the revolution against Britain and generally maintained cordial relations with the United States throughout the 20th century, though differences over relations with the Middle East increasingly strained Franco-American relations during the later 20th and early 21st century. Although traditionally hostile to Great Britain in foreign affairs during the 18th and 19th centuries, France and Britain were allies during the two world wars and partners in both the North Atlantic Treaty Organization and the European Union.

French explorer JACQUES CARTIER claimed Acadia and the St. Lawrence Seaway in the 1530s, but the bitter winters restricted French interest to fishing along coastal waters. SAMUEL DE CHAMPLAIN established the first permanent French settlement in North America at Quebec (1608), where only eight of the original 24 French settlers survived the first winter. In 1627, Champlain became head of the COMPAGNIE DE LA NOUVELLE FRANCE, which was granted title to all French lands and a monopoly on all economic activity except fishing, in return for settling 4,000 French Catholics in Canada. Although the fur trade flourished, the French were little interested in farming settlements. Within New France, there were three areas of settlement: Acadia, the mainland and island areas along the Atlantic coast; Louisiana, the lands drained by the Mississippi, Missouri, and Ohio river valleys; and Canada, the lands on either side of the St. Lawrence Seaway and just north of the Great

Lakes. Among these, only Canada, with the important settlements of Quebec and Montreal, developed a significant population.

A harsh climate and continual threats from the British and the Iroquois, made it difficult for private companies to attract settlers to Canada. In 1663, Louis XIV (r. 1648–1713) made New France a royal colony but was only moderately successful at enticing colonists. Revocation of the Edict of Nantes (1685), which had provided freedom of worship, drove 15,000 Protestant French Huguenots to British North America, many of whom were wealthy or skilled artisans. Most settled in New York, though important settlements were also founded in Pennsylvania, Virginia, and South Carolina. During the SEVEN YEARS' WAR (1756–63), 6,000 French speakers in present-day Nova Scotia, New Brunswick, and Prince Edward Island were exiled to Britain's southern colonies and to Louisiana, then still in the hands of France. There, they became the largest French-speaking enclave in the United States, the Cajuns. Canada's remaining French population of some 70,000 was brought under control of the British Crown, which organized the most populous areas as the colony of Quebec. During the entire period of French control, only about 9,000 French settlers actually immigrated to New France.

In general, the French did not immigrate in great numbers compared with other Europeans. When they did immigrate, it tended to be to the United States and as individuals rather than as groups. During the French Revolution (1789–99) some 10,000 political refugees escaped to the United States, many by way of French colonies in the Caribbean. That number included some 3,000 African French Creoles who established themselves in Philadelphia. A record number of French immigrants came as a result of the CALIFORNIA GOLD RUSH, including about 30,000 between 1849 and 1851.

French immigration during the late 19th and early 20th centuries was sporadic and often related to political events and economic crises. One peak period was 1871–80, when more than 72,000 arrived. Some were refugees from the failed Paris commune of 1870. Many immigrated from Alsace and Lorraine in the wake of the transfer of the region to Germany after the Franco-Prussian War (1870–71). Many others came as France faced economic depression beginning in 1872. A second peak came in the first decade of the 20th century, when more than 73,000 arrived, many seeking economic opportunities. Still, given its size and population, France's contribution to the greatest decade of immigration seems small, measuring only 0.8 percent of the 8.8 million immigrants to arrive in the United States between 1901 and 1910. During the 1930s, French immigration declined dramatically, with only about 1,200 coming per year. After World War II (1939–45), rates of immigration remained low and declined significantly after the initial years of hardship immediately following the war.

Between 1941 and 1960, about 90,000 French citizens immigrated to the United States; between 1961 and 1980, about 70,000; and between 1981 and 2000 about 65,000. Between 1992 and 2002, French immigration averaged about 3,000 annually. On the whole, the French do not have a strong tradition of emigration; those who did immigrate to the United States tended to eschew ethnic identification and to assimilate relatively quickly.

Despite the fact that French immigration to Canada almost totally ceased after the Seven Years' War, as late as the first census in 1871, the French composed 32 percent of the Canadian population, and 40 years later, in 1911, 26 percent. French immigrants were still favored throughout the 20th century, along with British and Americans, although it was difficult to get French citizens to come. In some cases, French Canadians were actually leaving. During the 1860s, the difficulty in acquiring land under the old French seigneurial land system led thousands of young French Canadians to migrate to New England, where they frequently worked in industry or the building trades, usually with the intention of returning. Most, however, ended up staying in the United States.

During the early 20th century, few French immigrated to Canada—only about 35,000 between 1900 and 1944. In 1921, the French-born population was about 19,000 and continued to decline until the late 1940s.

The Canadian IMMIGRATION ACT of 1952 once again placed the French in the most-favored category for immigration, with all "citizens of France born in France or in Saint-Pierre and Miquelon Islands" eligible for admission so long as they had means of support or employment. This, coupled with two converging trends between 1945 and the mid-1970s, promoted an increase in immigration. The postwar slump during the late 1940s and early 1950s led thousands of French to apply for Canadian visas. Also, around 1960 political leaders in Quebec began to see French immigration as a means of reversing the decline of francophone citizens, as their birthrates fell and more Anglophones began to enter Quebec. As a result, a number of agreements reached with the Canadian federal government enabled them to launch initiatives to attract French immigrants. Almost 90,000 came to Canada—most to Quebec—between 1945 and 1970, but their numbers declined thereafter. Of some 70,000 French immigrants in Canada in 2001, about 44,000 came after 1970, and the French-Canadian percentage of the population continued to decline to 16 percent.

Further Reading

Allain, M., and G. Conrad, eds. *France and North America*. 3 vols. Lafayette: University of Southwestern Louisiana Press, 1973–87.

Brasseaux, Carl A. *Acadian to Cajun: Transformation of a People, 1803–1877.* Jackson: University Press of Mississippi, 1992.

———. *The "Foreign French": Nineteenth-Century French Immigration into Louisiana.* 2 vols. Lafayette: University of Southwestern Louisiana, 1990, 1992.

———. *The Founding of New Acadia: The Beginnings of Acadian Life in Louisiana, 1765–1803.* Baton Rouge: Louisiana State University Press, 1987.

Brault, Gerard J. *The French-Canadian Heritage in New England.* Hanover, N.H.: University Press of New England, 1986.

Creaghy, R. *Nos cousins d'Amérique: Histoire des Français aux Etats-Unis.* Paris: Payot, 1988.

Doty, C. Stewart. *The First Franco-Americans: New England Life Histories from the Federal Writers' Project, 1938–1939.* Orono: University of Maine at Orono Press, 1985.

Ekberg, Carl J. *French Roots in the Illinois Country: The Mississippi Frontier in Colonial Times.* Urbana: University of Illinois Press, 1998.

Houde, Jean-Louis. *French Migration to North America, 1600–1900.* Chicago: Editions Houde, 1994.

Louder, Dean, and Eric Waddell. *French America: Mobility, Identity, and Minority Experience across the Continent.* Baton Rouge: Louisiana State University Press, 1983.

Martel, Marcel. *French Canada: An Account of Its Creation and Break-Up, 1850–1967.* Ottawa: Canadian Historical Association, 1998.

———. *Le deuil d'un pays imaginé. Rêves, lutes et déroute du Canada français. Les rapports entre le Québec et la francophonie canadienne (1867–1975).* Ottawa: Presses de l'Université d'Ottawa, CRCCF, 1997.

Pula, James S. *The French in America, 1488–1974: A Chronology and Fact Book.* Dobbs Ferry, N.Y.: Oceana, 1975.

Quintal, C. *The Little Canadas of New England.* Worcester, Mass.: French Institute, Assumption College, 1983.

Ramirez, Bruno. *On the Move: French-Canadian and Italian Migrants in the North Atlantic Economy, 1860–1914.* Toronto: McClelland and Stewart, 1991.

Roby, Yves. *Les Franco Américains de la Nouvelle-Angleterre, 1776–1930.* Sillery, Quebec: Éditions du Septentrion, 1990.

Silver, Arthur. *The French-Canadian Idea of Confederation: 1864–1900.* 2d ed. Toronto, 1997.

Weil, François. "French Migration to the Americas in the Nineteenth and Twentieth Centuries as a Historical Problem." *Study Emigrazione* 33, no. 123 (1996): 443–460.

———. *Les Franco-Americains.* Paris: Belin, 1989.

Zoltvany, Y. F. *The French Tradition in America.* New York: Harper and Row, 1969.

French and Indian War   See SEVEN YEARS' WAR.

G

Gentlemen's Agreement

The Gentlemen's Agreement was an informal set of executive arrangements between the United States and Japan in 1907–08 that defused a hostile standoff over the results of Japanese labor migration to California. President Theodore Roosevelt persuaded the San Francisco school board to rescind an order segregating Chinese, Japanese, and Korean students in return for a promise to halt the flow of Japanese laborers into the United States.

Japan's emergence as an important East Asian power following the Russo-Japanese War (1904–05) heightened tensions between the United States and Japan. In the wake of the war, Japanese immigration to the United States exploded, reaching up to 1,000 a month by 1906. Japan also posed a potential threat to the Philippines, an American colony since 1898. Tensions were to some extent alleviated with the signing of the Taft-Katsura Agreement (1905), by which Japan agreed not to invade the Philippines in return for recognition of Japanese supremacy in Korea. In the same year, however, both houses of the California legislature urged their Washington, D.C., delegation to propose formal limitations on Japanese immigration. The crime and uncertainty following the San Francisco earthquake in April 1906 led to increased hostility toward Japanese immigrants. The mayor and the Asiatic Exclusion League, with almost 80,000 members, pressured the San Francisco school board to pass a measure segregating Japanese students (October 11). The resolution not only violated Japan's most-favored nation status but deeply offended the Japanese nation and led to talk of war between the two countries.

Not wishing local affairs to undermine international policy, Roosevelt sought a diplomatic solution. In his annual address, on December 4, he repudiated the school board's decision and praised Japan. Between December 1906 and January 1908, three separate but related agreements were reached that addressed both Japanese concerns over the welfare of the immigrants and California concerns over the growing numbers of Japanese laborers. In February 1907, immigration legislation was amended to halt the flow of Japanese laborers from Hawaii, Canada, or Mexico, which in turn led the San Francisco school board to rescind (March 13) its segregation resolution. In discussions of December 1907, the Japanese government agreed to restrict passports for travel to the continental United States to nonlaborers, former residents, or the family members of Japanese immigrants. This allowed for the continued migration of laborers to Hawaii and for access to the United States by travelers, merchants, students, and PICTURE BRIDES. Japanese foreign minister Tadasu Hayashi agreed to the terms of the discussions in January 1908. With the dramatic decline in the numbers of Japanese laborers, Filipinos were increasingly recruited to take their place. To demonstrate that America's East Asian policy was not made from a position of weakness, Roosevelt followed the Gentlemen's Agreement with a world tour of 16 American battleships, with a symbolic stop in Japan.

Further Reading

Esthus, Raymond A. *Theodore Roosevelt and Japan.* Seattle: University of Washington Press, 1967.

Kikumura, Akemi. *Issei Pioneers: Hawaii and the Mainland, 1885 to 1924.* Los Angeles: Japanese American National Museum, 1992.

Morris, Edmund. *Theodore Rex.* New York: Random House, 2001.

Neu, C. E. *An Uncertain Friendship: Theodore Roosevelt and Japan, 1906–1909.* Cambridge, Mass.: Harvard University Press, 1967.

U.S. Department of State. *Report of the Hon. Roland S. Morris on Japanese Immigration and Alleged Discriminatory Legislation against Japanese Residents in the United States.* 1921. Reprint, New York: Arno Press, 1978.

———. *Foreign Relations of the United States, 1924.* Washington, D.C.: GPO, 1939.

Georgia colony

The Georgia colony was unique among Britain's American colonies. It was founded in 1732 as a penal colony for the "worthy" poor in the disputed territory between the British CAROLINA COLONIES and Spanish Florida. It was the last British colony established on the Atlantic seaboard.

Fearing the possible northward expansion of Spain, the British Crown granted General James Oglethorpe and a board of trustees a charter for settling the land between the Savannah and the Altamaha Rivers. Oglethorpe believed that he could give London paupers a fresh start in the New World, while also thwarting any Spanish aggression. Immigration was encouraged, but the terms were not generous. A head of household could claim a grant of 50 acres of land and an additional 50 acres for each servant. On the other hand, one could not amass more than 500 acres of land and could pass it down only to an eldest son; otherwise, the land reverted to the trustees. Slavery was prohibited.

Because the trustees in London retained total control of the government of Georgia, the colonists complained from the beginning. They harried Oglethorpe and the trustees into making fundamental reforms. In 1738, land and inheritance laws were made more liberal, and in 1750, settlers were allowed to import slaves. In 1751, Georgia was returned to the Crown, which authorized an assembly. With the purchase of large tracts of lands from local Indian tribes in 1763, 1766, and 1773, the government was able to attract a wide variety of settlers seeking lands of "the most fertile quality," most notably several thousand Scots-Irish who arrived by way of Charleston, as well as small numbers of Austrian Lutherans and Moravians and a Jewish community in Savannah. The coastal region remained predominantly English, while the backcountry filled with what historian Bernard Bailyn called "a remarkably poly-ethnic and poly-linguistic community."

Further Reading

Bailyn, Bernard. *Voyagers to the West: A Passage in the Peopling of America on the Eve of the Revolution.* New York: Alfred A. Knopf, 1986.

Coleman, Kenneth. *Colonial Georgia: A History.* New York: Scribner's, 1976.

Davis, Harold E. *The Fledgling Province: Social and Cultural Life in Colonial Georgia, 1733–1776.* Chapel Hill: Institute of Early American History and Culture, University of North Carolina Press, 1976.

German immigration

Germans are one of the few immigrant groups to substantially define American character from the founding of the republic to the turn of the 21st century. Almost 43 million Americans claimed German ancestry in the 2000 U.S. census, making them by far the largest ancestry group. Those claiming English, Scottish, Scots-Irish, and Welsh descent number about 35 million. German immigration was less prominent in Canadian cultural development, though still the largest group among the nonfounding peoples. In the Canadian census of 2001, 2,742,765 Canadians claimed German descent. The German heritage was not monolithic, however, for Germans came at irregular intervals across four centuries from many European states, bringing with them diverse religious and political traditions. Though Anglo-Americans misunderstood their aloofness during the colonial era, Germans earned a reputation for industry, honesty, and diligence. In the colonial period, German immigration was concentrated in the PENNSYLVANIA COLONY. During the 19th century, German settlement shifted to the upper Midwest and Great Plains, including Wisconsin, Minnesota, North Dakota, South Dakota, and Nebraska, where German influence was greatest. There were also significant German concentrations in most of the major Atlantic seaports, most notably New York City. German Canadians are widely dispersed, with large numbers in Ontario, the prairie provinces, British Columbia, and Nova Scotia.

Located in central Europe, Germany has an area of 137,846 square mile. It is bordered on the north by Denmark, on the east by Poland and the Czech Republic, on the south by Austria and Switzerland, and on the west by Luxembourg, Belgium, and the Netherlands. The Germanic tribes of the region successfully resisted Roman encroachments, but the region was not organized politically until the early ninth century, when Charlemagne's Holy Roman Empire was formed. Throughout the Middle Ages, Germany was largely ruled by an Austrian emperor as a decentralized state with more than 300 separate principalities. Two of these, Austria and Prussia, were major powers, but most were small states, governed by an array of kings, dukes, counts, margraves, electors, and ecclesiastical princes. In addition to political diversity, Germans were divided in religion. From the time of the Protestant Reformation of the 16th century, most northern Germans adopted Lutheranism, while most southern Germans remained Roman Catholics, and there were dozens of smaller Protestant sects scattered throughout the region. Political and religious diversity led to a wide variety of conditions under which Germans chose to leave Europe. Some emigrated to escape the restrictions of Lutheran or Catholic state churches, while others sought personal freedoms unknown in Europe. Most were seeking better economic opportunities. Napoléon's conquest of Europe between 1796 and 1815 led to significant territorial changes, including the redrawing of German boundaries. The German Confederation took the place of the old Holy Roman Empire, and the number of independent states was reduced to 39. During the 1860s, Prussia outmaneuvered Austria politically and defeated her militarily to gain the predominant hand in the future of a united Germany. Following the Franco-Prussian War (1870–71), the first German empire was established under Prussian leadership and with Austria excluded. Widely blamed by Europeans for bringing about World War I (1914–18) and by her own people for losing the war, Germany became politically destabilized in the 1920s, leading to the rise of the National Socialist Workers' (Nazi) Party under Adolf Hitler. Again defeated in a world war (1939–45), Germany was immediately divided into what became a democratic and economically dynamic nation in the west and a Soviet-dominated, state economy in the east. During the COLD WAR, West Germany was the front line for western resistance to the potential expansion of the Soviet Union in Europe. In 1990, the two Germanies were reunited, a move culturally welcomed but economically difficult and one that placed a drag on what had been one of the world's dynamic economies during the 1980s.

Poor Germans, including many Christian sectarians—Mennonites (see MENNONITE IMMIGRATION), Baptists, Dunkers, Moravians, Brethren, and Schwenkfelders (see SCHWENKFELDER IMMIGRATION)—came to America in the 18th and early 19th century as indentured servants (see INDENTURED SERVITUDE), and many of them were also redemptioners. The redemption system enabled emigrants to travel free of charge, with the shipowner recouping his investment by selling the emigrant's labor, usually for a four-year term. German settlers were recruited by the London Company for the first voyage to Jamestown (1607), and 13 German and Dutch Mennonite families seeking religious freedom were brought by William Penn to the Pennsylvania colony in 1681. Germans did not immigrate to North America in large numbers until 1709, when bad crops and heavy taxes drove several thousand of them to western New York and Pennsylvania. In the 1750s, some 3,000 Germans migrated to Nova Scotia, where they became known for their skill in shipbuilding and fishing. Most Germans emigrated from Dutch ports on the North Sea, easily accessed

by citizens of states near the Rhine River: Pfalz, Baden, Würtemberg, Hesse, Nassau, Cologne, Osnabrück, Münster, and Mainz. Most of the 100,000 immigrants to America entered through Philadelphia, settling in the nearby countryside, where they became known as the Pennsylvania Dutch (from a corruption of the German word for their own people, the *Deutsch*). The SEVEN YEARS' WAR (1756–63) and the AMERICAN REVOLUTION (1775–83) virtually ended German immigration to the United States for 50 years and encouraged the gradual assimilation of the first wave of German Americans. By 1790, when the first U.S. census was taken, 8.6 percent of the American population was German, with the heaviest concentration in Pennsylvania (33 percent).

While 13 colonies remained the primary destination for German emigrants, two significant German groups settled in Canada prior to the American Revolution. Some 2,000 Palatines settled in Lunenburg and Halifax between 1750 and 1752. Approximately 600 Palatines and Swabians followed, settling in Nova Scotia in the 1760s. After the Revolution, German Americans who had remained loyal to the British Crown (United Empire Loyalists) were granted free land in Canada. Most were either small farmers or disbanded soldiers and were settled along the northern shores of the St. Lawrence River, Lake Ontario, and Lake Erie and in an area southeast of Montreal. Between 1778 and 1784, most of these German Loyalists traveled inland routes to their new homes in Ontario, where they formed the third most populous ethnic group (behind the English and French) throughout the 19th and 20th centuries. Finally, some 64 German families settled in York County in 1794.

After the economic and political turmoil of the French Revolution, French Revolutionary Wars, and Napoleonic Wars (1789–1815), German immigration resumed on a large scale. The southwestern German states, which had been particularly hard hit by the effects of rapid population growth, crop failures, high taxes, and an antiquated cottage industry, continued to supply most of the emigrants via the Rhine River and the port cities of Amersterdam, Rotterdam, and Antwerp. The situation was worsened by declining potato crops in 1842 and the complete failure of the crop in 1846. German rulers sometimes sponsored organizations such as the Central Society for German Emigrants (Berlin, 1844) and the National Emigration Society (Darmstadt, 1847) in order to alleviate domestic problems. With the reduction of interstate German tolls by the Zollverein (tariff union) in 1834, travel to the more desirable German ports of Bremen and Hamburg became easier, encouraging emigration from Westphalia, Oldenberg, Saxony, Prussia, and Mecklenburg. The typical German immigrant after 1830 was more likely to be skilled and with some education, choosing America or Canada as a place to maintain family status, rather than to establish it.

Emigrants gather in Hamburg, Germany, to purchase tickets from the Hamburg-Amerika Line. The company provided a village for prospective emigrants, including rooms, baths, churches, and synagogues. The sign above the clock reads "Mein Feld ist die Welt" (My Field Is the World). *(National Archives #131-SSA-7)*

Immigration to the United States peaked proportionally in the 1850s, with nearly a million German speakers emigrating to escape the effects of the abortive democratic REVOLUTIONS OF 1848, to flee social or religious persecution, or simply to take advantage of the burgeoning American economy. The economic downturn of the late 1850s and the American Civil War (1861–65) discouraged immigration for a decade, but it rebounded with the revival of the U.S. economy (1866–73). With endemic low wages in Germany and the unsettling effects of Prussian statesman Otto von Bismarck's wars of German unification (1863–71), many Germans believed that prosperity would never return to their homeland. Almost 1.5 million emigrated in the 1880s. As German industry developed in the 1890s, displaced rural workers more often migrated to German industrial centers than to America, although almost 1 million still came between 1890 and 1914.

Most of the 5 million Germans who immigrated to America in the 19th century were agriculturalists, seeking land, and thus were attracted to the Midwest—Ohio, Illinois, Michigan, Wisconsin, Minnesota, and Missouri. After the Civil War, some whose families had migrated to Russia in

the late 18th century began to immigrate to America. Like their cultural brethren from Germany, they were divided, based on location (Black Sea area, Caucasus area, Volga area, Volhynia area) and religious affiliation (Lutheran, Mennonite, Hutterite Brethren). The freeing of Russian serfs (1862), the introduction of compulsory military service (1871), and attempts to force Russian education upon their communities drove a substantial minority of the 1.5 million German-speaking Russians to the United States, where they tended to settle in the Great Plains states. By 1920, 45 percent of the more than 300,000 German-speaking Russians lived in North Dakota, South Dakota, Nebraska, and Colorado. No matter the country of origin, however, German immigrants usually resisted assimilation. German-language parochial schools were common. In rural areas, the immigrants clustered around their particular churches—Lutheran, Reform, Catholic, or one of the Pietist denominations. In cities such as Milwaukee, Wisconsin; St. Louis, Missouri; Louisville, Kentucky; and Cincinnati, Ohio, where Germans sometimes numbered more than a quarter of the population, they played a large role in shaping urban culture, establishing newspapers, educational clubs, beer gardens, and mutual-benefit societies. Whether in rural or urban centers, German clannishness had by mid-century already led to the rise of a strong nativist feeling (see NATIVISM), which increased in the years prior to World War I.

As second- and third-generation urban Germans gained success as entrepreneurs, industrialists, and managers, they began to adopt American urban culture and simultaneously to shape it. German-language school enrollments peaked between 1880 and 1900, when some 500,000 students were being instructed at least in part in German. The German family unit remained strong, especially on the farms and in the communities of the Midwest and plains states. Rural Germans, who owned more than 10 percent of American farms in 1900, often continued to speak German and to maintain their distinct culture well after World War II.

Canada continued to attract a small but steady stream of German immigrants throughout the 19th century. Between 1800 and 1830, numerous groups of New Jersey and Pennsylvania Mennonites, pressured by overpopulation, were attracted by free land grants and the promise of religious freedom. Most settled in Waterloo County, Ontario, which then became a destination for later German immigrants, most of whom were not Mennonites. By the turn of the 20th century, most of Ontario's Germans had been largely assimilated, though the more remote settlements of Waterloo County retained their German distinctiveness into the 21st century. After the mid-19th century, cheap land became scarce in eastern Canada, prompting greater streams of immigration to the western prairies. Between the 1870s and 1911, some 140,000 people of German descent settled on the Canadian plains, about one-third of them having been born in Europe. This group included 7,500 Mennonites who emigrated from Russia in the 1870s and settled in southern Manitoba. Germans throughout Canada were often praised as models of industriousness.

German cultural assimilation in both Canada and the United States was proceeding rapidly when World War I erupted in 1914. The German-language press in America, 30 percent smaller than it had been in 1894, was pro-German and almost unanimously called for national neutrality. When the United States finally entered the war in 1917, German Americans were harassed and widely mistrusted and expected to display "one-hundred percent Americanism." Within a few years, hundreds of schools removed the German language as a course offering, and communities renamed streets and banned German books and music. By 1919, German churches were reluctant to use their native language, and parochial schools were often closed. This heightened cultural pressure, along with rapid industrial development, increased economic mobility, and a generally more relaxed attitude toward entertainment, aided German assimilation into mainstream American society. Although some of the 500,000 German immigrants who entered the United States in the 1920s and 1930s were attracted to the

anti-Semitism of the Irish-Canadian-American activist priest Father Charles E. Coughlin, the German-American Bund, and the Nazi Party, few were committed followers. Many new immigrants were actually refugees from Hitler's Nazi regime, which had come to power in 1933. German ethnicity was not a major issue during World War II.

In the aftermath of World War II, the United States resettled almost 450,000 displaced persons (1948–52; see DISPLACED PERSONS ACT). Almost half were ethnic Germans, many of whom had previously lived in various countries throughout eastern Europe, including Czechoslovakia, Hungary, Latvia, Estonia, Lithuania, Poland, Romania, Russia, and Yugoslavia; about 63,000 were Jews. Thereafter, German immigration leveled off, with most coming for educational and economic opportunities. With the German economy booming during much of the postwar era, most Germans stayed at home. Between 1992 and 2002, German immigration to the United States averaged about 7,300 per year.

Canada continued to attract German religious minorities in the 20th century, including 20,000 Mennonites (1923–30) among some 90,000 Germans who emigrated from Poland, Germany, Austria, and Czechoslovakia between 1919 and 1935. Several thousand Hutterites migrated from North and South Dakota in the United States to Manitoba, Saskatchewan, and Alberta. Between 1946 and 1965, about 300,000 immigrants from West Germany entered Canada, most well educated and seeking "adventure" or economic opportunity and choosing to settle in Canada's largest cities. Of 174,075 German immigrants in Canada in 2001, almost 97,000 came before 1961, and 128,000 before 1971. About 15,000 immigrated between 1991 and 2001.

See also AUSTRIAN IMMIGRATION.

Further Reading

Arends, S. F. *The Central Dakota Germans: Their History, Language, and Culture.* Washington, D.C.: Georgetown University Press, 1989.

Bailyn, Bernard. *From Protestant Peasants to Jewish Intellectuals: The Germans in the Peopling of America.* Oxford: Berg, 1988.

Bassler, Gerhard P. *The German Canadian Mosaic Today and Yesterday: Identities, Roots, and Heritages.* Ottawa: German-Canadian Congress, 1991.

Bausenhart, Werner. *German Immigration and Assimilation in Ontario, 1783–1918.* New York, Ottawa, Toronto: Legas, 1989.

Eisenach, G. J. *Pietism and the Russian-Germans in the United States.* Berne, Ind.: Berne Publishers, 1948.

Faust, Albert B. *The German Element in the United States.* 2 vols. 1909. Reprint, New York: Arno Press, 1969.

Ferenczi, Imre, and Walter Wilcox. *International Migrations.* Geneva, Switzerland: International Labor Office, 1929.

Fogelman, Aaron Spencer. *Hopeful Journeys: German Immigration, Settlement, and Political Culture in Colonial America, 1717–1775.* Philadelphia: University of Pennsylvania Press, 1996.

Hawgood, John A. *The Tragedy of German America.* New York: Putnam, 1940.

Hoerder, Dirk, and Jorg Nagler, eds. *People in Transit: German Migrations in Comparative Perspective, 1820–1930.* Stanford, Calif.: Stanford University Press, 1993.

Johnson, H. B. "The Germans." In *They Chose Minnesota.* Ed. J. D. Holmquist. St. Paul: Minnesota Historical Society Press, 1981.

Jordan, Terry G. *German Seed in Texas Soil.* Austin: University of Texas Press, 1966.

Kalbfleisch, H. K. *The History of the Pioneer German Language Press of Ontario, 1835–1918.* Toronto: University of Toronto Press, 1968.

Kamphoefner, Walter. "German Americans: Paradoxes of a Model Minority." In *Origins and Destinies: Immigration, Race, and Ethnicity in America.* Eds. Silvia Pedraza and Rubén G. Rumbaut. Belmont, Calif.: Wadsworth, 1996.

———. *The Westfalians: From Germany to Missouri.* Princeton, N.J.: Princeton University Press, 1987.

Kloss, Heinz. *Atlas of 19th and Early 20th Century German-American Settlements.* Marburg, Germany: Elwert, 1974.

Köllmann, Wolfgang, and Peter Marschalck. "German Emigration to the United States." *Perspectives in American History* 7 (1973): 499–557.

Lehmann, Heinz. *The German Canadians, 1750–1937: Immigration, Settlement and Culture.* Trans. Gerhard P. Bassler. St. John's, Canada: Jesperson, 1986.

Levine, Bruce C. *The Migration of Ideology and the Contested Meaning of Freedom: German-Americans in the Mid-Nineteenth Century.* Washington, D.C.: German Historical Institute, 1992.

———. *The Spirit of 1848: German Immigrants, Labor Conflict, and the Coming of the Civil War.* Urbana: University of Illinois Press, 1992.

Luebke, Frederick. *Bonds of Loyalty: German Americans and World War I.* DeKalb: Northern Illinois University Press, 1974.

———. *Germans in the New World: Essays in the History of Immigration.* Champaign: University of Illinois Press, 1990.

———. *Immigrants and Politics: The Germans of Nebraska, 1880–1900.* Lincoln: University of Nebraska Press, 1969.

McLaughlin, K. M. *The Germans in Canada.* Ottawa: Canadian Historical Association, 1985.

O'Connor, Richard. *The German Americans.* Boston: Little, Brown, 1968.

Pickle, Linda S. *Contented among Strangers: Rural German-Speaking Women and Their Families in the Nineteenth-Century Midwest.* Urbana: University of Illinois Press, 1996.

Rippley, Lavern J. *The German-Americans.* Boston: Twayne, 1976.

Roeber, A. G. *Palatines, Liberty and Property: German Lutherans in Colonial America.* Baltimore: Johns Hopkins University Press, 1993.

Sallet, R. S. *Russian-German Settlements in the United States.* Trans. L. J. Rippley and A. Bauer. Fargo: North Dakota Institute for Regional Studies, 1974.

Sauer, Angelika E. "Christian Charity, Government Policy and German Immigration to Canada and Australia, 1947–1952." In *Immigration and Ethnicity in Canada.* Eds. Anne Laperrière, Varpu Lindström, and Tamara Palmer Seiler. Montreal: Association for Canadian Studies, 1996.

Struve, Walter. *Germans of Texas: Commerce, Migration and Culture in the Days of the Lone Star Republic.* Austin: University of Texas Press, 1996.

Trefousse, H. L., ed. *Germany and America: Essays on Problems of International Relations and Immigration.* Brooklyn, N.Y.: Brooklyn College Press, 1980.

Trommler, Frank, and Joseph McVeigh, eds. *America and the Germans: An Assessment of a Three-Hundred-Year History.* 2 vols. Philadelphia: University of Pennsylvania Press, 1985.

Walker, Mack. *Germany and the Emigration, 1816–1885.* Cambridge, Mass.: Harvard University Press, 1964.

Wieden, Fritz. *The Trans-Canada Alliance of German Canadians: A Study in Culture.* Windsor, Canada: Tolle Lege Enterprises, 1985.

Wittke, Carl F. *Refugees of Revolution: The German Forty-Eighters in America.* Philadelphia: University of Pennsylvania Press, 1952.

Zucker, Alfred E., ed. *The Forty-Eighters: Political Refugees of the German Revolutions of 1848.* New York: Columbia University Press, 1959.

Ghanaian immigration

Most Ghanaians came to the United States and Canada after independence in 1957, seeking education and business opportunities. In the U.S. census of 2000 and the Canadian census of 2001, 49,944 Americans and 16,935 Canadians claimed Ghanaian descent. The largest concentrations of American Ghanaians lived in Washington, D.C., New York City, Baltimore, Chicago, and Boston. About two-thirds of Canadian Ghanaians lived in Toronto.

Ghana occupies 88,700 square miles of the southern coast of West Africa between 5 and 12 degrees north latitude. Burkina Faso forms its border to the north; Togo, to the east; and the Ivory Coast, to the west. Ghana is composed mainly of plains. Lake Volta occupies much of the southeastern portion of the country. In 2002, Ghana's population was estimated at 19,894,014, with nearly 2 million in the capital of Accra. The people were divided into many ethnic groups, including the Akan (44 percent), the Moshi-Dagomba (16 percent), the Ewe (13 percent), and the Ga (8 percent). Ghana was also religiously divided, with 30 percent Muslims, 24 percent Christians, and 38 percent practicing indigenous beliefs. Named for an African empire that had flourished along the Niger River (400–1240), Ghana became linked to the triangular trade with Europe and the Americas during the 17th and 18th centuries that brought more than 10 million slaves to the New World, most to the Caribbean sugar islands and Brazil. In 1874, Britain defeated the most powerful of the local tribes, the Asante, establishing a dominant political presence in the region it called the Gold Coast. Ghana became independent in 1957, but its first 40 years of independence were marked by political instability. The first president, Kwame Nkrumah, built hospitals and schools and promoted development projects such as the Volta River hydroelectric and aluminum plants but also ran the country into debt, jailed opponents, and established a one-party socialist state. He was overthrown in 1966 by a police-army coup that expelled Chinese and East German teachers and technicians. Elections were held in 1969, but four further coups occurred in 1972, 1978, 1979, and 1981. The 1979 and 1981 coups, led by Flight Lieutenant Jerry Rawlings, were followed by suspension of the constitution and banning of political parties. A new constitution, allowing multiparty politics, was approved in April 1992. In 1993, more than 1,000 people were killed in ethnic clashes in northern Ghana. Kofi Annan, a career United Nations (UN) diplomat from Ghana, became UN secretary general on January 1, 1997.

Millions of Americans are descended from slaves who were brought from the Gold Coast between the 17th and early 19th centuries, though it is impossible to say exactly how many came from the present-day country of Ghana (see AFRICAN FORCED MIGRATION; SLAVERY). During the 20th century, a handful of Ghanaian students were educated in the United States, including Nkrumah. During the 1960s the Ghanaian government awarded scholarships for advanced study in the United States and the Soviet Union, with many of the students staying on in the United States. This formed the basis for a small program of family reunification as the political and economic turmoil of the 1970s and 1980s worsened. In 1995, remittances to Ghana were estimated at $300 million. Ghana is fourth among the sub-Saharan African countries as a source country for immigration—behind Nigeria, Ethiopia, and South Africa—averaging more than 4,000 annually between 1995 and 2002.

Ghanaian immigration to Canada was inconsequential until the 1990s. Of 16,985 immigrants residing in Canada in 2001, only 215 came before 1971. Immigration increased to about 1,500 in the 1970s and about 3,700 in the 1980s. Between 1991 and 2001, however, almost 11,000 Ghanaians entered Canada, most for educational and economic opportunities. Little study has yet been done on their community, but indicators suggest that it is likely to grow.

Further Reading

Alexander, Ken, and Avis Glaze. *The African-Canadian Experience.* Toronto: Umbrella Press, 1996.
Apraku, Kofi K. *African Emigrés in the United States: A Missing Link in Africa's Social and Economic Development.* New York: Praeger, 1991.
Attah-Poku, Agyemang. *The Social-Cultural Adjustment Question: The Role of Ghanaian Immigrant Ethnic Associations in America.* Brookfield, Vt.: Avebury, 1996.
Berry, LaVerele Benette, ed. *Ghana: A Country Study.* 3d ed. Landham, Md.: Bernan, 1996.
Kuada, J. E. , and Y. Chachah. *Ghana: The Land, the People, and Their Culture.* Copenhagen, Denmark: African Information Centre, 1989.
Makinwa-Adebusoye, P. K. "Emigration Dynamics in West Africa." *International Migration* 33, nos. 3–4 (1995): 435–467.
Winks, Robin W. *The Blacks in Canada.* Montreal: McGill–Queen's University Press, 1971.

Gompers, Samuel (1850–1924) *labor leader*

Samuel Gompers was the most influential early labor leader in the United States. The son of Jewish parents who had emigrated from Holland to England in 1844, he and his family immigrated to New York City in 1863. Gompers was apprenticed as a cigar maker and continued this work until the mid-1870s, when he became increasingly concerned with labor organization. During the depression of 1873–77, he was elected president of a local cigar makers' union in New York City and from that time devoted his life to the labor movement. He helped to organize the American Federation of Labor (AFL) and served as its president almost continuously until his death (1886–94, 1896–1924). He was appointed to the Council of National Defense (1917) and to the Commission on International Labor Legislation at the Paris Peace Conference (1919).

Gompers was an energetic and pragmatic leader who followed the British model of trade union organization. His organization's high dues, benefits, and tight organization favored skilled workers, whom he viewed as the foundation of the labor movement. Gompers opposed both extreme labor actions and labor involvement in legislation, believing that workers must provide for themselves in organizations under their own control. As a result, he was generally held in esteem by members of the political establishment. Although a Jew by birth, he did not identify with the Jewish community. He worked to limit immigration, fearing that a mass influx of unskilled workers would drive down wages and the standard of living for workers already in the United States.

See also AMERICAN FEDERATION OF LABOR AND CONGRESS OF INDUSTRIAL ORGANIZATIONS.

Further Reading

Gompers, Samuel. *Seventy Years of Life and Labor: An Autobiography.* 2 vols. New York: E. P. Dutton, 1925.
———. *The Samuel Gompers Papers.* 7 vols. Eds. Stuart Kaufman et al. Urbana: Univeristy of Illinois Press, 1986–99.
Kaufman, S. B. *Samuel Gompers and the Origins of the American Federation of Labor.* Westport, Conn.: Greenwood Press, 1973.
Livesay, Harold C. *Samuel Gompers and Organized Labor in America.* Boston: Little, Brown, 1978.
Mandel, Bernard. *Samuel Gompers: A Biography.* Yellow Springs, Ohio: Antioch Press, 1963.
Taft, Philip. *The A.F. of L. in the Time of Gompers.* New York: Harper and Row, 1957.

Gonzales, Corky (Rodolfo Gonzalez) (1928–) *social activist*

Born in Denver, Colorado, to a family of migrant farmworkers, Rodolfo "Corky" Gonzales became one of the leading activists for fair treatment of Mexican laborers in the United States. After a career as a professional boxer (1947–55) and businessman, he began to work as a local organizer for the Democratic Party. In the early 1960s, he led a variety of organizations, including the Viva Kennedy campaign, the Denver War on Poverty, and the G.I. Forum. In 1965, he left the Democratic Party and founded the Crusade for Justice organization, with its emphasis on CHICANO empowerment. It became a cultural center that included a school, the Ballet Folklórico de Aztlán, and the newspaper *El Gallo.* As the Chicano movement developed, with its assertive pride in the native and mestizo heritage of Mexico, Gonzales played a leading role both in organization and inspiration. He led a Chicano contingent in the Poor People's March on Washington, D.C. (1968), was a key participant in the Chicano Moratorium against the Vietnam War (1972), and organized the annual Chicano Youth Liberation Conference, including the 1969 Denver meeting at which El Plan Espiritual de Aztlán manifesto was drafted. His 1967 epic poem, *I Am Joaquín,* became the literary touchstone of the Chicano movement, tracing the cultural heart of the native peoples of Mexico and the American Southwest back to Aztec kings and emperors. He was a cofounder of La Raza Unida (1970), the political arm of the Chicano movement, and in 1972 led the movement to create LA RAZA UNIDA PARTY (LRUP). Although the LRUP received 7 percent of the vote in Texas, it was not successful nationally.

Further Reading

Gómez-Quiñones, Juan. *Chicano Politics: Reality and Promise, 1940–1990.* Albuquerque: University of New Mexico Press, 1990.

"Gonzales, Rodolfo." In *Dictionary of Literary Biography* 122: *Chicano Writers.* Second Series. Detroit: Gale, 1992.

Martinez, Eliud. "I Am Joaquin as Poem and Film: Two Modes of Chicano Expression." *Journal of Popular Culture* 13 (1980): 505–515.

Rosales, F. Arturo. *Chicano: The History of the Mexican American Civil Rights Movement.* Houston: Arte Público Press, 1996.

González, Elián (1993–) *Cuban immigrant*

Elián González became the focus of an intense public debate over America's Cuban immigration policy after surviving a shipwreck in which his mother died during a November 1999 escape from Cuba. After living with Miami relatives for five months, the six-year-old was forcibly removed by U.S. marshals on April 22, 2000, and on June 28 was returned to Cuba.

González was one of three Cubans rescued from the sea on November 25, 1999, after his mother and 10 others drowned following the swamping of their small boat. He lived in Miami with a great-uncle, Lázaro, who immediately began the process for securing political asylum or refugee status for his nephew. Meanwhile González's father, Juan Miguel, claimed that his son had been kidnapped and demanded that he be returned to Cuba. For the next five

months, an international diplomatic battle was waged in the world media, involving both custody rights and immigration policy. At various times, González indicated that he did, or did not, want to return. On January 5, 2000, the IMMIGRATION AND NATURALIZATION SERVICE (INS) determined that the boy's father should decide where he would live, but González's uncle refused to relinquish him and sued to retain custody. Hundreds of protesters, many of whom were Cubans who had themselves fled Fidel Castro's regime, took to the streets the following day, arguing against the boy's return to communist Cuba. Miami mayor Joseph Carollo and Miami-Dade County mayor Alex Penelas publicly supported the protests. On April 22, U.S. attorney general Janet Reno ordered federal marshals to seize González and reunite him with his father, who had flown to the United States from Cuba. In June, a three-judge panel of the United States Court of Appeals upheld the INS decision that a parent alone could act for a child in matters of immigration. After the U.S. Supreme Court refused to hear an appeal of the federal court decision supporting the INS decision, González and his father returned to Cuba on June 28.

Almost a decade after the end of the cold war, the Elián González case demonstrated the potency of anti-Castro feelings among Cuban Americans and tested the resolve of government policy makers intent on transcending cold war attitudes regarding Cuban immigration. Although Castro refrained from publicly exploiting González, the boy's father was promoted within the Communist Party and awarded the Carlos Manuel de Céspedes Medal, Cuba's highest civilian honor. The González family received special privileges but also was shadowed by Cuban agents to ensure that there was no further communication with the Miami relatives.

Further Reading

Eig, Larry M. *The Case of Elián González: Legal Basics.* Washington, D.C.: Congressional Research Service, Library of Congress, 2000.

Fighting for Freedom: Facts, Findings and Opinions on the Elián González Case. Miami: Cuban American National Foundation, 2000.

John, Michael. *Betrayal of Elián González.* Tampa, Fla.: MaxGo, 2000.

Miami Herald staff. "'Normal Life' in Cuba Keeps Child Out of Spotlight, Father in It." April 22, 2001. Herald.com. Available online. URL: www.miami.com/herald/special/news/elian/docs/010806.htm.

"Elián González." U.S. Citizenship and Immigration Services. Available online. URL: http://www.uscis.gov/graphics/publicaffairs/eliang.htm. Accessed May 6, 2004.

Gonzalez, Henry B. (1916–2000) *politician*

Henry Gonzalez was the first Mexican American to be elected to the Texas state senate in the modern era, setting an example for Hispanics in the political mainstream. He represented the best of what one of his political opponents called the "old-fashioned public servant" tradition, anxious to remedy civil inequalities by working through the established political traditions of the state and country.

Gonzalez's parents were part of the great wave of emigration out of Mexico following the revolution of 1910. After earning a law degree at St. Mary's University School of Law in 1943, Gonzalez served in military and naval intelligence. He lost his bid for the Texas state legislature in 1950 but won a seat on the San Antonio city council and in 1956 was elected to the state senate. Speaking out tirelessly against segregation measures in 1957, he won statewide prominence and eventually the support of Governor Price Daniel, Senator Ralph Yarborough, Vice President Lyndon Johnson, and President JOHN FITZGERALD KENNEDY. In 1960, he successfully ran for the U.S. House of Representatives, where he served until his retirement. In 1989, he became chairman of the House Banking, Finance, and Urban Affairs Committee and played a prominent role in crafting the new lending and accounting regulations in the wake of the savings and loan crisis.

Further Reading
"Gonzalez, Henry B." *Current Biography Yearbook 1993.* New York: H. W. Wilson, 1993.

Hitchens, Christopher. "No Fool on the Hill." *Harper's* 285 (October 1992): 84–96.

Jarboe, Jan. "The Eternal Challenger." *Texas Monthly* 20 (October 1992): 120ff.

Rodriguez, Eugene, Jr. *Henry B. Gonzalez: A Political Profile.* New York: Arno Press, 1976.

Graham v. Richardson (1971)

According to this U.S. Supreme Court decision of 1971, the classification of "alien" is suspect under the FOURTEENTH AMENDMENT. As a "discrete and insular minority," aliens require a high level of judicial protection. In order to be considered constitutional, such a classification must be related to a compelling governmental interest.

The case was originally brought by Carmen Richardson, a Mexican citizen legally admitted to the United States in 1956, against the Arizona commissioner of public welfare, who had denied her public welfare disability benefits on the basis of her not having met the 15-year residency requirement for noncitizens. In a class-action suit, she argued that the residency requirement abridged her constitutional right to "equal protection" under the Fourteenth Amendment. The state appealed her victory in the federal court to the Supreme Court, which ruled that residency requirements did violate the "equal protection" clause. According to the decision, state interest in protecting its financial resources was not sufficiently compelling to override the promised protections. Additionally, the Court ruled that, because the Constitution granted the federal government authority over the admission of aliens and the condi-

tion of their residence, state laws interfering with federal laws violate the supremacy clause. A number of exceptions were subsequently made to *Graham v. Richardson,* including lower burdens of proof for excluding aliens from certain government positions and employment as public school teachers.

Further Reading
Federal Immigration Law Report. Washington, D.C.: Washington Service Bureau, 1983–.

Wiessbrodt, David. *Immigration Law and Procedure: In a Nutshell.* 4th ed. St. Paul, Minn.: West Group, 1998.

U.S. Supreme Court. *Graham v. Richardson,* 403 U.S. 365 (1971). FindLaw. Available online. URL: http://caselaw.lp.findlaw.com/scripts/getcase.pl?navby=case&court=US&vol=403&page=365. Accessed October 6, 2003.

Greek immigration

Greeks emigrated from their homeland and from many parts of the Ottoman (Turkish) Empire beginning in the 1890s, forming one of the most homogeneous ethnic groups in North America. In the U.S. census of 2000 and the Canadian census of 2001, 1,153,307 Americans and 215,105 Canadians claimed Greek descent. The largest concentrations of Greek settlement are in New York, California, Illinois, and Massachusetts in the United States and Toronto and Montreal in Canada.

Greece occupies 50,400 square miles of the Balkan Peninsula in southeastern Europe. Albania, Macedonia, and Bulgaria lie to the north, and Turkey, to the east. In 2002, the population was estimated at 10,623,835, 98 percent of whom were Greek; 98 percent also claimed their religion as Greek Orthodox. During the second millennium B.C., Greeks developed one of the most sophisticated cultures in the world. Population growth and a lack of natural resources forced thousands to migrate during the first millennium B.C., leading to the establishment of Greek colonies throughout the Mediterranean coastal regions of Europe, including the island of Cyprus. Although the Greek city-states managed to resist Persian invasions early in the fifth century B.C., they fell under the domination of the Macedonian Alexander the Great, who nevertheless spread Greek culture from the eastern Mediterranean to the gates of India. Greece was conquered by the Romans in the second century B.C., became part of the Byzantine Empire after the fall of Rome in 476, and was transferred to the Ottoman Empire after the fall of Constantinople in 1453. The Greek war of independence (1821–29) led to the establishment of the first independent Greek state in 2,000 years. The destruction of the war also led American missionaries to sponsor several dozen Greek immigrants, mostly orphans. Between the 1820s and World War I (1914–18), Greece and Turkey were frequently at odds over territories with mixed populations, including Crete, Cyprus, and coastal regions of western mainland Turkey. Greece suffered a disastrous defeat in the Greco-Turkish War of 1921–23, leading more than 1.25 million Greeks in Turkey and more than 400,000 Turks in Greece to return to their home regions. Greece joined the North Atlantic Treaty Organization in 1952, becoming a cornerstone of the western COLD WAR effort. In 1982, Greece joined the European Community (later the European Union), the first country in eastern Europe to do so and steadily moved toward integrating its economy with Europe generally.

Exact figures for Greek immigration are difficult to determine, as immigrants were usually classified according to country of birth. A significant number of Greeks, therefore, were included in figures for Turkey, Bulgaria, Yugoslavia, and Egypt. The first significant Greek colony in North America was founded in 1768 at New Smyrna, Florida, near St. Augustine. Between 1768 and the abandonment of the colony in 1777, about 450 Greek, Italian, and Corsican settlers traveled to the region. By 1860, fewer than 400 Greeks lived in the United States. Poor economic conditions in Greece in the 1880s led to a massive wave of emigration between 1890 and 1924, when more than 500,000 immigrated to the United States, most notably from Laconia and Arcadia provinces in southern Greece. Between 1901 and 1920, tens of thousands of Greeks left the Ottoman Empire for the United States, fleeing persecution. More than 80 percent of the immigrants were men, most of whom went to work in New England mills and factories, western railroads and mines, or in northern urban factories and service industries. Most intended to return to Greece after earning a sufficient sum of money, though less than one-third actually did so. As the United States became more xenophobic after World War I, hostility toward Greeks and other eastern Europeans increased, leading to a number of restrictive immigration measures between 1917 and 1924. In 1921, the last year of relatively open immigration, 28,000 Greeks immigrated to the United States; under provisions of the JOHNSON-REED ACT of 1924, annual immigration was limited to100, though the number was increased to 307 by the end of the decade. Legal petitions, mostly for the reunification of families, led to the immigration of almost 11,000 between 1924 and 1929. Many of the 30,000 Greek immigrants between 1925 and 1945 came as PICTURE BRIDES. After World War II (1939–45), a Greek civil war (1946–49) led to widespread displacements and the admission of some 75,000 Greeks during the following two decades, many under various refugee and displaced persons acts. With passage of the nonquota IMMIGRATION AND NATIONALITY ACT in 1965, about 160,000 Greeks immigrated during the 1960s and 1970s. Since 1980, the numbers continuously declined, averaging fewer than 1,000 per year between 1998 and 2002.

Although a few Greek sailors visited Canada prior to the 19th century, the first settlements were established following the Greek war of independence. By 1900, however, there were still fewer than 300 Greeks in Canada, mostly young men who considered themselves as sojourners who eagerly hoped to return to their homeland. Though Greece's preindustrial economy and heavy taxation and Ottoman oppression in Turkey provided great impetus for emigration, Greeks were not admitted in large numbers to Canada, which preferred skilled agriculturalists. By 1931, when depression stopped almost all immigration to Canada, there were still only 9,450 Greeks in the country. More liberal regulations after World War II, however, led to a significant increase in immigration. Many of the refugees who were admitted in the late 1940s and early 1950s started an extensive chain migration of family members. Between 1946 and 1970, more than 100,000 Greeks immigrated to Canada. The immigration peaked in 1967, declining thereafter as the economy improved, political stability returned, and new labor opportunities became available in Germany and other European countries. During the mid-1970s, there was a brief surge in immigration of Greek Cypriots, when 200,000 Greeks were driven from their homes by a Turkish invasion. By the late 1990s, the Greek Cypriot community, centered in the Toronto area, numbered 25,000. Although Canadian Greeks were traditionally less inclined to marry outside their group, by the 1990s it was becoming common, leading to a loss of a distinctive Greek cultural identity. Of 75,770 Greek immigrants living in Canada in 2001, only 7,000 immigrated after 1981.

Further Reading
Fairchild, Henry. *Greek Immigration to the United States.* New Haven, Conn.: Yale University Press, 1911.
Georgakas, Dan, and Charles C. Moskos, Jr. *New Directions in Greek-American Studies.* New York: Pella, 1991.
Kopan, A. T. *The Greeks in Chicago.* Urbana: University of Illinois Press, 1989.
Kourvetaris, George A. *Studies on Greek Americans.* Boulder, Colo.: East European Monographs, 1997.
Kunkelman, Gary. *The Religion of Ethnicity: Belief and Belonging in a Greek-American Community.* New York: Garland, 1990.
Moskos, Charles C., Jr. *Greek Americans: Struggle and Success.* 2d ed. New Brunswick, N.J.: Transaction, 1989.
Moskos, Charles C., Jr., Dan Georgakas, and Alexandros Kitroff. "Greek Americans" and "Greek Americans: A Response." In *Journal of the Hellenic Diaspora* 14, nos. 1–2 (Spring–Summer 1987): 55–61.
Panagopoulos, E. P. *New Smyrna: An Eighteenth Century Greek Odyssey.* Gainesville: University of Florida Press, 1996.
Papaioannou, G. *From Mars Hill to Manhattan: The Greek Orthodox in America under Patriarch Athenagoras I.* Minneapolis, Minn.: Light and Life, 1976.
Saloutos, Theodore. *The Greeks in the United States.* Cambridge, Mass.: Harvard University Press, 1964.

———. *They Remember America: The Story of Repatriated Greek Americans.* Berkeley: University of California Press, 1952.

Scourby, Alice. *The Greek Americans.* New York: Twayne, 1984.

Zotos, S. *Hellenic Presence in America.* Wheaton, Ill.: Pilgrimage Press, 1976.

Vlassis, George. *The Greeks in Canada.* Ottawa: LeClerc Printers, 1942.

Guadalupe Hidalgo, Treaty of   See U.S.-MEXICAN WAR.

Guatemalan immigration

Guatemalan immigration to North America was largely the product of the civil unrest in Guatemala during the 1980s and 1990s. As in the case of most Central American immigrants, those from Guatemala tended to be young and possessing few job skills. In the U.S. census of 2000 and the Canadian census of 2001, 372,487 Americans and 9,550 Canadians claimed Guatemalan descent. The actual number in the United States was considerably higher, however, as the Immigration and Naturalization Service (INS) in 2000 estimated that 144,000 unauthorized Guatemalans were living in the country. The largest concentrations of Guatemalans in the United States are in Los Angeles; Houston, Texas; Chicago; and New York City. In Canada, the largest groups are in Toronto and Montreal.

Guatemala occupies 41,800 square miles in Central America and is the most populous country in Central America. In 2002, the population was estimated at 12,974,361. Guatemala is bordered by Mexico on the north and west, El Salvador on the south, and Honduras and Belize on the east. The people are 56 percent mestizo and 44 percent Amerindian. The majority of Guatemalans are Roman Catholic, though many practice a syncretic Catholicism incorporating Mayan religious rites. About 30 percent are Evangelical Pentecostal Protestants. The old Mayan Empire flourished in what is today Guatemala for more than 1,000 years before the arrival of the Spanish in 1523, and most of the native Indians today are Maya. After gaining independence from Spain in 1821, Guatemala endured political disorder for most of its history. It was briefly a part of Mexico and then of the Central American Federation before becoming a republic in 1839. After 1945, when a liberal government was elected to replace long-term dictator Jorge Ubico, the country was caught up in COLD WAR politics that led to an ongoing civil war. When the Communist Party in Guatemala was implicated in the radical agrarian reform program of Colonel Jacobo Arbenz Guzmán, he was overthrown by a U.S.-supported right-wing coup. As opposition to military leadership developed, it has been estimated that government "death squads" executed 20,000 civilians between 1966 and 1976. Dissident army officers seized power in 1982,

denouncing the presidential election as fraudulent and pledging to restore "authentic democracy" to the nation. Political violence caused large numbers of Guatemalans to seek refuge in Mexico. Another military coup occurred in October 1983 before the nation returned to civilian rule in 1986. During more than 35 years of armed conflict, some 200,000 people were killed, most the victims of right-wing governments and their paramilitary allies. U.S. president Bill Clinton, on a visit to Guatemala in 1999, apologized for aid the United States had given to forces that had "engaged in violence and widespread repression."

It is impossible to say how many Guatemalans immigrated to the United States before 1960, as statistics for separate Central American countries were not recorded, but the numbers were small, probably around 6,000. A significant number of Guatemalans came north after 1917 following a devastating earthquake of that year. Prior to 1980, most Guatemalan immigrants were white (ladino) politicians and other members of the middle class who had resisted the right-wing government. After 1980, Guatemalan immigrants to the United States were largely Amerindians (Maya) and mestizos fleeing government counterinsurgency campaigns and grinding poverty. The United States, supporting the right-wing government as a COLD WAR bulwark in Central America, recognized few Guatemalans as political refugees. As a result, many entered the country illegally, often with the aid of Christian or other humanitarian groups. Estimates place the number of illegal immigrants at more than 300,000 between 1980 and 2000. In May 1999, the INS relaxed application rules for permanent resident status for Guatemalans who had fled repressive governments during the Guatemalan civil unrest (1980–96). As a result, they were allowed to remain in the United States during their application process and were not required to prove that they would suffer extreme hardship if returned to Guatemala. Between 1992 and 2002, about 120,000 Guatemalans immigrated legally to the United States.

There was almost no Guatemalan immigration to Canada prior to 1979. Of 13,680 immigrants in the country in 2001, only about 1,100 came before 1980. As political violence spilled over from the civil war in El Salvador, thousands of peasants were driven from their lands and many insurgents fled as refugees. Between 1974 and 1994, it has been estimated that about 13,700 Guatemalans settled in Canada, about half admitted as refugees.

Further Reading
Burns, Allan F. *Maya in Exile: Guatemalans in Florida.* Philadelphia: Temple University Press, 1992.

Hagan, Jacqueline Maria. *Deciding to Be Legal: A Maya Community in Houston.* Philadelphia: Temple University Press, 1994.

Hamilton, Nora, and Norma Stoltz Chincilla. "Central American Migration: A Framework for Analysis." *Latin American Research Review* 26 (1991): 75–110.

Jonas, Susanne. *The Battle for Guatemala: Rebels, Death Squads, and U.S. Power.* Boulder, Colo.: Westview Press, 1991.

Mahler, Sars. *American Dreaming: Immigrant Life on the Margins.* Princeton, N.J.: Princeton University Press, 1995.

Manz, B. *Refugees of a Hidden War: The Aftermath of Counterinsurgency in Guatemala.* Albany: State University of New York Press, 1988.

Meredith, Dianne. "Guatemalan Refugees and Their Process of Adaptation in Toronto." M. A. thesis, York University, 1992.

Perera, Victor. *Unfinished Conquest: The Guatemalan Tragedy.* Berkeley: University of California Press, 1993.

Popkin, Eric. "Guatemalan Mayan Migration to Los Angeles: Constructing Transnational Linkages in the Context of the Settlement Process." *Ethnic and Racial Studies* 22, no. 2 (1999): 267–289.

Rodriguez, N., and J. M. Hagan. "Undocumented Central American Migration to Houston in the 1980s." *Journal of La Raza Studies* 2, no. 1 (1989): 1–4.

Vlach, Norita. *The Quetzal in Flight: Guatemalan Refugee Families in the United States.* Westport, Conn.: Praeger, 1989.

Wright, Ronald. "Escape to Canada." *Saturday Night* 102, no. 5 (1987): 44–52.

guest children

With Europe engulfed in war starting in 1939, charitable organizations petitioned the Canadian government to provide asylum for child refugees, including Jews living in Britain, France, Switzerland, Spain, and Portugal. Eventually more than 4,500 children and 1,000 mothers were allowed to immigrate, but virtually all were non-Jewish Britons.

With the outbreak of World War II, the Canadian National Committee for Refugees (CNCR) and Canadian Friends Service Committee (CFSC) encouraged the Canadian government to admit 100 continental Jewish children who had been temporarily relocated to Britain. Initial steps were taken to allow them in, with the costs being borne by the private agencies. With British entry into the war in summer 1940, however, the Canadian government reversed its decision. The ruthless Nazi German bombing of civilian populations in Britain led to widespread sympathy for the resettlement of British children, and more than 50,000 Canadians offered to host children and mothers until the end of the war, which came in 1945. Despite the fact that Canadian Jews were prepared to host the previously approved Jewish children, the government refused to include them in the evacuation plan, fearing that it would lead to immigration of their families following the war. The Canadian government approved a plan to host up to 10,000 British children, with Britain responsible for screening and transportation costs, Canadian provincial agencies and relief organizations responsible for placement, and private citizens responsible for daily care. After about 1,500 children were placed, the sinking of the SS *City of Benares* on September 14, 1940, and the resulting deaths of 73 children, led to discontinuation of the guest children program.

Further Reading

Bilson, Geoffrey. *The Guest Children: The Story of the British Child Evacuees Sent to Canada during World War II.* Saskatoon, Canada: Fifth House, 1988.

Foster, D. S. Davies, and H. Steele. "The Evacuation of British Children during World War II: A Preliminary Investigation into the Long-Term Psychological Effects." *Aging and Mental Health* 7, no. 5 (2003): 398–408.

Knowles, Valerie. *Strangers at Our Gates: Canadian Immigration and Immigration Policy, 1540–1997.* Rev. ed. Toronto: Dundurn Press, 1997.

Gutierrez, Jose Angel (1944–) *lawyer, professor, civil rights activist*

Jose Angel Gutierrez was one of the earliest leaders of the CHICANO movement, helping to elect five Chicano city council members in the face of threats and Jim Crow laws.

While attending St. Mary's University in San Antonio, Texas, in 1967, Gutierrez helped establish the Mexican American Youth Organization (MAYO). After returning to his Texan hometown of Crystal City, he organized Chicano students in walkouts to protest discrimination and misrepresentation of the Mexican heritage in the local school system. In 1970, Gutierrez helped found LA RAZA UNIDA PARTY (LRUP), the political arm of the Chicano movement; two years later, he was elected national chairman of the organization. Although LRUP enjoyed some local successes, it never found favor nationwide and declined as the 1970s wore on. In 1976, Gutierrez received a Ph.D. in political science from the University of Texas. Later, he also obtained a law degree from the University of Houston Law School. In 1996 he was fired from his position as director of the Mexican American Studies Center at the University of Texas at Arlington but was later reinstated. He resigned his position there in December 1996, citing the ongoing discrimination against which he had directed much of his life's work.

In his autobiography, Gutierrez addressed the question of self-identification, explaining "how I became a Chicano and why I never became a Hispanic." Hispanics, he argued, identified themselves with the white, European side of their culture, while Chicanos valued the native and mixed ancestry that was common to most Mexicans (see *HISPANIC* AND RELATED TERMS).

Further Reading

Compeon, Mario, and Jose Angel Gutierrez. *La Raza Unida Party in Texas: Speeches.* New York: Pathfinder Press, 1970.

DeLeon, David. *Leaders from the 1960s: A Biographical Sourcebook of American Activism.* Westport, Conn.: Greenwood Press, 1994.

Gutierrez, Jose Angel. *The Making of a Chicano Militant: Lessons from Cristal.* Madison: University of Wisconsin Press, 1998.

Meyer, Nicholas E. "Gutierrez, Jose Angel." In *Biographical Dictionary of Hispanic Americans.* New York: Facts On File, 2001.

Gypsy immigration (Roma immigration, Romany immigration)

Gypsies, because of their itinerant lifestyle both in Europe and in North America, are among the most difficult immigrants to understand or characterize. Although most of the dozen or so Gypsy groups that inhabit North America trace their ancestry back to northern India and Pakistan, across the centuries, their paths and cultures diverged, and each considers itself a distinct ethnic group. The U.S. census of 2000 did not include a specific category for ethnic origins not associated with country of origin, but estimates place the number of U.S. Gypsies at more than 100,000. According to the Canadian census of 2001, 2,590 Canadians claimed "Gypsy (Roma)" descent, though the actual number is significantly higher. Because they emigrated from many countries across a long period of time, and each group had its preferred means of livelihood, Gypsies are found in most parts of the United States and Canada in both urban and rural areas. The largest concentrations are probably in Los Angeles and Chicago in the United States and Toronto and Montreal in Canada.

Gypsies first migrated from India through Persia and the Byzantine Empire under uncertain circumstances sometime before the 10th century. They entered the Balkan Peninsula with the Ottoman expansion of the 14th century. By 1505, they had reached as far north and west as Scotland. Occasionally they were welcomed, but usually their traveling lifestyle led to suspicion and frequently to persecution wherever they were. With no centralized government or settled institutions, Gypsies as a group fragmented, becoming broadly identified with the various regions of their travels. Spanish Gypsies are often referred to as *"calos"* or *"gitanos"*; Romanian, as "Ludar"; eastern European, as "Roma"; and English, as "Romnichels." Hungarian-Slovak Gypsies are more settled and usually referred to simply as "Gypsies." These divisions were almost always maintained in the New World.

The term *Gypsy* was taken from the word *Egyptian,* as Europeans in the Middle Ages believed them to have originated there. Although many scholars and some European Gypsies prefer the designation *Rom* (plural, *Roma*) or *Romany* most American and Canadian groups still refer to themselves as "Gypsies." The terms *Gypsy* and *Rom* are outside attempts to classify all the nomadic or seminomadic groups originating in southern Asia in a single category, despite the fact that many managed to maintain their ethnic distinctiveness in Europe during the modern era. Further confusing the situation are a number of peripatetic groups—German, Scots, Irish, American, and others—who largely adopted Gypsy culture but were not related by blood to the first Gypsy immigrants. Gypsies traditionally organized themselves into extended family clans; engaged in itinerant trades including tinkering, smithing, and music performance; and frequently moved, avoiding both government service and taxation. As a result, they were oppressed in most countries, sometimes even enslaved or forced to settle, or having their children removed and put into institutions. During World War II (1939–45), Nazi Germany's leader, Adolf Hitler, murdered more than 250,000 Gypsies in an attempt to exterminate the group. Unlike most rooted ethnic groups, Gypsies embraced many religious faiths, though they practiced each within their own cultural traditions. In the first decade of the 21st century, Gypsies still routinely suffered racial prejudice, especially in eastern Europe, where their unemployment rates were routinely five to 10 times higher than the national average.

The first Gypsies came to the New World as a result of deportations from England, France, Portugal, and Spain during the 17th and 18th centuries. Significant numbers of Romnichels immigrated to the United States around 1850, where they found a steady livelihood in the horse trade prior to World War I (1914–18). Many Gypsies, including the Roma, the Ludar, the Baschalde, and the Romungre, arrived as part of the NEW IMMIGRATION after 1880, their numbers subsumed in immigration figures for the various states from which they came. The Roma came mainly from Serbia, Russia, and Austria-Hungary and have been the group most studied. Many Roma specialized in coppersmithing and therefore migrated to urban areas to repair industrial equipment. In the cities, they also developed fortune-telling as a business. The Ludar came mainly from northwestern Bosnia and worked in traveling circuses and other animal shows. The Baschalde came from Slovakia and Hungary, and the Romungre from Hungary and Transylvania (Romania). As a result of the wars in former Yugoslavia during the 1990s, Gypsies found themselves persecuted by every side and often targeted for genocide. In 1999, the United States pledged to take up to 20,000 Kosovar refugees, many of whom were Gypsies.

Most Gypsies in Canada are Roma, though they include several tribes or subgroups, including the Kalderash and the Lowara. Few records exist, but they probably began to immigrate around 1900. Clearly some Roma entered the United States from Winnipeg and Montreal as early as 1903. Gypsies migrated in Canada and found a better reception in the west, where there were large numbers of Slavic peoples who had come from eastern Europe and the Balkans. A few homesteads were established in Alberta, but they often became absentee landlords as they traveled. By the 1920s, most Gypsies were moving to the cities, where they frequently inhabited empty stores, setting up fortune-telling or other small businesses in the front and living in the back. By the 1990s, there was a growing Gypsy population of 400–500 in Vancouver, British Columbia. In 1997, television reports of a successful Roma family in Canada led several hundred Czech Gypsies to immigrate to Canada, which did not require visas from Czech citizens, and then to apply for asylum. With as many as 5,000 Gypsies considering immigration, in November 1997, the Canadian government instituted visa requirements, making it more difficult for Gypsies to enter Canada. The mayor of one Czech town agreed to help pay their airfare, in return for their apartment rights and renunciation of their permanent residence status, reinforcing accusations of Czech racism. Although most of the original immigrants were granted refugee status or otherwise allowed to remain, further Gypsy immigration was limited.

See also AUSTRO-HUNGARIAN IMMIGRATION.

Further Reading

Crowe, David M. *A History of the Gypsies of Eastern Europe and Russia.* New York: St. Martin's, 1996.

Fonseca, Isabel. *Bury Me Standing: The Gypsies and Their Journey.* New York: Knopf, 1995.

Fraser, Angus. *The Gypsies.* 2d ed. Oxford: Basil Blackwell, 1995.

Gropper, R. C. *Gypsies in the City: Culture Patterns and Survival.* Princeton, N.J.: Darwin Press, 1975.

Kenrick, Donald, and Gillian Taylor. *Historical Dictionary of the Gypsies (Romanies).* Lanham, N.J.: Scarecrow Press, 1998.

Lockwood, W. G., and S. Salo, eds. *Gypsies and Travelers in North America: An Annotated Bibliography.* Cheverly, Md.: Gypsy Lore Society, 1994.

Lucassen, Leo, et al. *Gypsies and Other Itinerant Groups: A Socio-Historical Approach.* New York: St. Martin's Press, 1998.

Puxon, Grattan, and Donald Kenrick. *The Destiny of Europe's Gypsies.* New York: Basic Books, 1973.

Salo, Matt, ed. *100 Years of Gypsy Studies.* 2d ed. Cheverly, Md.: Gypsy Lore Society, 1990.

Salo, Matt T., and Sheila Salo. "Gypsy Immigration to the United States." In *Papers from the Sixth and Seventh Annual Meetings, Gypsy Lore Society, North American Chapter.* Ed. J. Grumet. New York: Gypsy Lore Society, 1986.

———. *The Kalderas in Eastern Canada.* Ottawa: National Museums of Canada, 1977.

———, eds. *The American Kalderas: Gypsies in the New World.* Hackettstown, N.J.: Gypsy Lore Society, 1981.

Sutherland, Anne. *Gypsies: The Hidden Americans.* London: Tavistock Publications, 1975.

Sway, Marlene. *Familiar Strangers: Gypsy Life in America.* Chicago: University of Illinois Press, 1988.

Haitian immigration

Haitian immigration to North America is a relatively new phenomenon, the product of right-wing political oppression and political instability since the 1950s. According to the U.S. census of 2000 and the Canadian census of 2001, there were 548,199 Haitian Americans and 82,405 Haitian Canadians, respectively. Between 1930 and 2000, some 400,000 Haitians immigrated to the United States, with 85 percent of them arriving after 1970. About 95 percent of Haitian Americans in the 1990s lived in the New York metropolitan area (see NEW YORK, NEW YORK) or in south Florida. There are also substantial Haitian communities in BOSTON, MASSACHUSETTS; Newark, New Jersey; Bridgeport, Connecticut; Orlando, Florida; and WASHINGTON, D.C. Haitians in Canada are overwhelmingly concentrated in MONTREAL, QUEBEC, home to 85 percent of the total population. Haitians remain among the poorest of all immigrant groups.

Haiti's history is unique in the Western Hemisphere. The island of Hispaniola, of which the country of Haiti forms the western third, was discovered by CHRISTOPHER COLUMBUS in 1492. France gained control of the western part of the island in 1697, naming it Saint-Domingue and establishing a slave-based, plantation economy. A slave insurrection beginning in 1791 led to the establishment of the first black-controlled state in the Western Hemisphere in 1804. As a result, significant numbers of French colonists immigrated to the United States, especially to New Orleans, Louisiana, often bringing their slaves with them. Poor and politically weak throughout its history, Haiti was occupied by U.S. Marines (1915–34) in order to restore political and financial stability and thus to discourage other nations from intervening. The dictatorships of François "Papa Doc" Duvalier (1957–71) and his son Jean-Claude "Baby Doc" Duvalier (1971–86) led to an increasing disparity of wealth in Haiti. Fewer than 40,000 Haitians emigrated in the 1950s and 1960s, most of them professionals, the well educated, and the upper classes.

By 1972, when poor Haitians began leaving their country in large numbers, two push factors were clearly evident. First and most important, Haiti was the poorest country in the Western Hemisphere. In 1994, per capita income was still only $817, and half the population was unemployed. Second, many Haitians were seeking personal freedom and fleeing the repressive violence of Jean-Claude Duvalier's secret police. It is estimated that more than 60,000 Haitians arrived in south Florida in small sailboats between 1971 and 1981, with thousands of others dying in the attempt. With the Duvaliers as COLD WAR allies, the United States refused to grant Haitians refugee status and routinely deported them. Though the administration of President Jimmy Carter granted these "boat people" special Cuban-Haitian Entrant Status in 1980, U.S. policy throughout the 1980s and 1990s opposed an expansion of Haitian immigration.

In 1990, the first democratic election in Haitian history brought Jean-Bertrand Aristide to power, slowing the pace of immigration. A 1991 military coup ousting Aristide led some 35,000 Haitians to flee the country on rafts, seeking asylum in the United States or at the U.S. naval base at Guantánamo Bay, Cuba. By May 1992, 12,500 boat people had crowded into the refugee center at Guantánamo Bay. Arguing that most of the fleeing Haitians were simply seeking economic opportunity rather than political protection, on May 24, 1992, President George H. W. Bush issued an executive order to intercept Haitians at sea and return them to Haiti, where they could apply for asylum at the U.S. embassy in Port-au-Prince. Eventually about 10,500 boat people were granted asylum. A 1994 ruling granting political asylum interviews at sea led to a new surge of Haitian attempts to sail to the United States. In January 1995, the U.S. government returned 4,000 potential Haitian immigrants who had been housed at Guantánamo Bay, arguing that they were no longer at risk following the return to power of Aristide. Another coup against the Aristide government in February 2004 led to concerns in the United States that a new wave of boat people would seek sanctuary in Florida. Though no major movements ensued, the Haitian situation demonstrated once again the close relationship between political stability in the Caribbean and U.S. immigration policy.

The earliest Haitians in Canada were slaves brought from Saint-Dominigue during the 18th century, though their numbers were extremely small, perhaps fewer than 10. A more significant migration came during the 1950s and 1960s, as more than 200,000 Haitians left their country, most bound for the United States and other Caribbean countries, but a few settling in Canada. After 1970, individual Haitians began to immigrate in larger numbers, with significant influxes in 1976, 1980–81, and 1991. From the mid-1980s, about two-thirds of Haitians came under family reunification provisions and mainly settled in QUEBEC. By 1992, there were about 36,000 Haitians in Canada, and 10 years later, more than twice that number. Of 52,625 immigrants in 2001, 17,275 arrived between 1991 and 2001. Although Montreal was still the preferred destination for most Haitian immigrants, an increasing number chose jobs over culture, slightly increasing the number in Ontario. In 1991, 94.5 percent of Haitians in Canada lived in Quebec; 10 years later the figure had declined to 90 percent.

Further Reading

"Boatload of Haitians Swarms Ashore in Florida." October 30, 2002. CNN.com. Available online. URL: www.cnn.com/2002/US/South/10/29/haitians.ashore/index.html. Accessed July 11, 2003.

Brasseaux, Carl A., and Glenn R. Conrad, eds. *The Road to Louisiana: The Saint Domingue Refugees, 1792–1809.* Lafayette: University of Southwestern Louisiana, 1992.

Buchanan-Stafford, Susan. "The Haitians: The Cultural Meaning of Race and Ethnicity." In *New Immigrants in New York.* Ed. Nancy Foner. New York: Columbia University Press, 1987.

Chierci, R. *Demele, "Making It": Migration and Adaptation among Haitian Boat People in the United States.* New York: AMS Press, 1991.

Gmelch, G. *Double Passage: The Lives of Caribbean Migrants Abroad and Back Home.* Ann Arbor: University of Michigan Press, 1992.

Kasinitz, Phillip. *Caribbean New York: Black Immigrants and the Politics of Race.* Ithaca, N.Y.: Cornell University Press, 1992.

Labelle, Micheline, Serge Larose, and Victor Piché. "Emigration et immigration: les Haitiens au Québec." *Sociologie et Sociétés* 15, no. 2 (1983): 73–88.

Labelle, Micheline, et al. *Histoire d'immigrées: itinéraire d'ouvrières colombiennes, grecques, haitiennes et portugaises de Montréal.* Montreal: Boréal, 1987.

Laguerre, Michel. *Diasporic Citizenship: Haitian Americans in Transnational America.* New York: St. Martin's Press, 1998.

Levine, Barry B., ed. *The Caribbean Exodus.* New York: Praeger, 1987.

Miller, Jake. *The Plight of Haitian Refugees.* New York: Praeger, 1984.

Palmer, R. W. *Pilgrims from the Sun: West Indian Migration to America.* New York: Twayne, 1995.

Richardson, Bonham. *The Caribbean in the Wider World, 1492–1992.* New York: Cambridge University Press, 1992.

———. *Caribbean Migration.* Knoxville: University of Tennessee Press, 1983.

Stepnick, Alex. *Haitian Refugees in the U.S.* London: Minority Rights Group, 1982.

Woldemikael, T. *Becoming Black American: Haitians and American Institutions in Evanston, Illinois.* New York: AMS Press, 1989.

Hakluyt, Richard (ca. 1552–1616) *geographer*

Richard Hakluyt was the principal exponent of English colonization in the Americas, long before England acquired its transatlantic empire. After the failure of the ROANOKE COLONY (1585–87), Hakluyt's writings helped sustain a lagging interest in New World settlement that would only be realized with the founding of Jamestown in 1607 (see VIRGINIA COLONY).

Born in Hertfordshire, Hakluyt attended Westminster School and Christ Church, Oxford, where he later became a lecturer on geography. As a boy, his imagination was fired by a relative, a geographer sometimes known as Richard Hakluyt the Elder, who provided a library of rare travel literature and directed him to the 107th Psalm, verses 23–24: "they which go downe to the sea in ships and occupy the great waters, they see the works of the Lord, and his wonders in the deep." Hakluyt eventually took Holy Orders and began a remarkable career in geographical investigation, always with a view toward impressing upon Queen Elizabeth the value that American settlements might hold for England.

Although he never traveled to the New World, he did more than anyone else to publicize the potential benefit of a land that "bringeth fourth all things in aboundance, as in the first creations without toil or labour." In 1582, he published *Divers Voyages touching the Discovery of America*, commissioned by SIR WALTER RALEIGH in support of Sir

Humphrey Gilbert's charter, to convince Elizabeth of the viability of an American venture. While in Paris as chaplain to the English embassy, Hakluyt collected many manuscripts in French, Spanish, and Portuguese relating to discovery, which served as the basis for his *Discourse concerning Western Discoveries* (1584). In his most enduring work, the three-volume *Principal Navigations, Voyages, and Discoveries of the English Nation* (1598–1600), he demonstrated the fruits of a lifelong search for materials, bringing together a number of firsthand and widely scattered accounts written in many languages. The Hakluyt Society was established in London in 1846 to promote the publication of geographical writing.

Further Reading

Cawley, Robert Ralston. *Unpathed Waters: Studies in the Influence of the Voyagers on Elizabethan Literature.* 1940. Reprint, New York: Octagon Books, 1967.

Hakluyt, Richard. *Principal Navigations, Voyages, and Discoveries of the English Nation.* 12 vols. London: Hakluyt Society, 1903–05.

Parks, George B. *Richard Hakluyt and the English Voyages.* 2d ed. New York: F. Ungar, 1961.

Haldimand, Frederick (1718–1791) *political leader*

As governor of QUEBEC (1778–84), Sir Frederick Haldimand was most responsible for the resettlement of British Loyalists following the American Revolution (1775–83) (see CANADA—IMMIGRATION SURVEY AND POLICY OVERVIEW). The decision to settle them in the wilderness of western Canada eventually led to the separation of the colony into two provinces in 1791.

The Swiss-born Haldimand was a distinguished career soldier who rose to the position of lieutenant-general and was appointed governor of Quebec. He had the formidable task of finding homes for some 10,000 Loyalists, mostly farmers from the backcountry of the former PENNSYLVANIA COLONY and NEW YORK COLONY who had begun to congregate in Montreal and Quebec after 1775. He first looked to settle them on Cape Breton Island, though he soon determined this to be impractical since most did not have a seafaring background. Instead, he negotiated land purchases from the Missisauga and other Indian tribes in 1782 and 1783. Supplemented by additional purchases as necessary, these lands enabled Haldimand to resettle more than 6,000 Loyalists in the wilderness of western Quebec, north of the St. Lawrence River and Lake Ontario. Free land was granted according to military rank and social status, and food, tools, and other supplies were provided until after the crop of 1786. Although this resettlement largely separated the English-speaking Loyalists from the French speakers of eastern Quebec, it also led to considerable dissatisfaction from settlers who longed for British laws, customs, and institutions. By the Constitution Act of 1791, Quebec was sepa-

rated: The western area of settlement became the province of Upper Canada; the eastern part, the province of Lower Canada.

Further Reading

Craig, Gerald M. *Upper Canada: The Formative Years, 1784–1841.* Toronto: McClelland and Stewart, 1963.

McIlraith, Jean N. *Sir Frederick Haldimand.* Toronto: Morang, 1904.

Moore, Christopher. *The Loyalists: Revolution, Exile, Settlement.* Toronto: McClelland and Stewart, 1994.

Henderson v. Mayor of New York (1876)

In the wake of the Immigration Act of 1875, the U.S. Supreme Court reversed previous decisions giving states "police power" over newly arriving immigrants, arguing that it infringed federal power to regulate commerce. The Court held that the whole country should follow a "uniform system or plan" to "govern the right to land passengers in the United States," whether they arrived in New York City, Boston, New Orleans, San Francisco, or some other port of entry.

As states began to abolish their port authorities and commissions, the burden of screening and orienting arriving immigrants fell on private organizations, which were soon overwhelmed. Philanthropic bodies petitioned Congress for funding to aid in processing the several hundred thousand immigrants arriving annually. With a small bureaucracy in the 1870s, the federal government subsidized operations such as New York City's CASTLE GARDEN, paying for it with a head tax on immigrants beginning in 1882. The first federal reception center for immigrants was opened at ELLIS ISLAND in 1892.

Further Reading

Hutchinson, E. P. *Legislative History of American Immigration Policy, 1798–1965.* Philadelphia: University of Pennsylvania Press, 1981.

U.S. Immigration Commission. *Immigration Legislation.* Vol. 39. Washington, D.C.: Government Printing Office, 1911.

Hispanic and related terms

The terms *Hispanic* and *Latino* have been broadly used to collectively designate the variety of minority groups in North America associated through a common use of the Spanish language. In July 2001, Hispanics became the largest minority group in the United States (37 million, or 13 percent of the population), for the first time overtaking African Americans (36.1 million, or 12.7 percent of the population).

Hispanic is most commonly used in government and political life, as in the naming of the Congressional Hispanic Caucus. *Latino* refers in a somewhat broader sense to

Americans of Latin American descent. Though the terms are often used interchangeably, the older *Hispanic* implies association with the European aspects of Spanish culture, while *Latino* suggests a continued association with struggles for equality and justice. The Cuban community, many long-term residents of Texas, and conservatives generally prefer the term *Hispanic,* while most New Yorkers, Californians, and Chicagoans prefer *Latino,* particularly those who have arrived in the United States fairly recently. During the 1960s, the term *CHICANO* was widely embraced throughout the southwestern United States as a mark of pride in one's native Mexican or mestizo roots.

When asked by a poll, survey, or census, Hispanics most often identify themselves either as Americans or as part of the national community from which they descended, rather than as *Hispanic* or *Latino.* The U.S. government understood that its category of "Spanish/Hispanic/Latino," devised for statistical purposes could include people of any race. The Office of Management and Budget (OMB) defined *Hispanic* or *Latino* as "a person of Cuban, Mexican, Puerto Rican, South or Central American, or other Spanish culture or origin regardless of race."

A Chicano teenager in urban America. More than 90 percent of Mexican Americans lived in cities in 2002. *(National Archives #412-DA-2842)*

The terms do not have strict definitions. Filipinos, who have a Spanish heritage, are not referred to by any of these terms. At the same time, Brazilians, whose cultural heritage is Portuguese, often are considered Hispanics.

See also RACIAL AND ETHNIC CATEGORIES.

Further Reading

Bonilla, Frank, et al., eds. *Borderless Borders: U.S. Latinos, Latin Americans, and the Paradox of Interdependence.* Philadelphia: Temple University Press, 1998.

Camarillo, Albert M., and Frank Bonilla. "Hispanics in a Multicultural Society: A New American Dilemma?" In *America Becoming: Racial Trends and Their Consequences.* Eds. Neil J. Smelser, William Julius Wilson, and Faith Mitchell. Washington, D.C.: National Academy Press, 2001.

Córdova, Carlos B., and Jorge del Pinal. *Hispanics-Latinos: Diverse People in a Multicultural Society.* Washington, D.C.: National Association of Hispanic Publications, 1996.

Dean, Frank D., and Marta Tienda. *The Hispanic Population of the United States.* New York: Russell Sage Foundation, 1988.

Hamilton, Nora, and Norma Stoltz Chincilla. "Central American Migration: A Framework for Analysis." *Latin American Research Review* 26 (1991): 75–110.

Horner, Louise L., ed. *Hispanic Americans: A Statistical Sourcebook, 2003.* San Diego, Calif.: Information Publications, 2003.

Lomeli, Francisco, ed. *Handbook of Hispanic Cultures in the United States: Literature and Art.* 2 vols. Houston, Texas: Arte Público Press, 1993.

Maciel, David R., and María Herrera-Sobek, eds. *Culture across Borders: Mexican Immigration and Popular Culture.* Tucson: University of Arizona Press, 1998.

Smith, Carter, III, and David Lindroth. *Hispanic-American Experience On File.* New York: Facts On File, 1999.

Suro, Roberto. *Strangers among Us: How Latino Immigration Is Transforming America.* New York: Alfred A. Knopf, 1998.

Holocaust   See WORLD WAR II AND IMMIGRATION.

home children

Between the 1860s and the 1930s, about 100,000 British children from urban slums were sent to Canada, where they were usually apprenticed as agricultural laborers or domestic servants until they came of age. Most of them were sent by "homes" such as those run by Dr. THOMAS BARNARDO, Christian and philanthropic institutions seeking to provide hope to destitute children.

In the colonial period, almost all children immigrated to British North America as part of a family group. As the general practice of INDENTURED SERVITUDE came to an end in the early 19th century, a small number of children were being apprenticed to farms in Canada. This process underwent a dramatic change in 1868 when British philanthropists Maria Susan Rye, Annie Macpherson, and Louisa

Birt initiated an organized campaign to remove young children from urban slums to a more healthy physical and spiritual life in Canada or Australia. The perennial problem of poverty had grown worse throughout the 19th century as urban industrial centers such as London, Liverpool, and Manchester expanded without providing adequate housing or effective sanitation. In the wake of London's last great cholera outbreak, Rye, Macpherson, and Birt appealed to the public for funds and negotiated with the Canadian government for grants-in-aid and transportation subsidies. Though there was considerable criticism from both humanitarians who objected to "herding" young children abroad like cattle and Canadian Nativists (see NATIVISM), who complained that home children were taking local jobs, there was no shortage of Canadian applicants for the apprenticed labor of young British children.

Problems associated with the apprenticing of young children were highlighted in the sensational case of George Everitt Green, a young agricultural apprentice who died in 1895 under the care of his spinster employer, seven months after his arrival in Ontario. The public was shocked when they learned that he had been starved and that his body was covered in sores and his limbs gangrenous. Some safeguards were installed, but the suicides of three home children in the winter of 1923–24 led to further investigations by the British government and a ban on all immigration by children under 14 who were not accompanied by a parent. As the Canadian economy worsened in the 1930s, labor groups intensified their opposition, and by 1939, the apprenticeship of Britain's poorest children was finally halted.

Further Reading

Bagnell, Kenneth. *The Little Immigrants: The Orphans Who Came to Canada.* Toronto: Macmillan of Canada, 1980.

Bean, Philip, and Joy Melville. *Lost Children of the Empire.* London: Hyman Unwin, 1989.

Blackburn, Geoff. *The Children's Friend Society: Juvenile Immigrants to Western Australia, South Africa, and Canada, 1834–1842.* Northbridge, Australia: Access Press, 1993.

Rose, June. *For the Sake of the Children: Inside Dr. Barnardo's, 120 Years of Caring for Children.* London: Futura, 1989.

Homestead Act (United States) (1862)

The Homestead Act was the result of steady opposition of workers' groups, western settlers, and agrarians to the U.S. government's policy of using western lands as a source of revenue. Promising 160 acres of free land to any head of household who would develop the land and live on it continuously for five years, the act did more than any other piece of legislation to open the West to family farmers. The measure also enabled immigrant groups to maintain a strong sense of Old World identity in the New World, as they often took up lands in remote regions of the upper Midwest and plains territories.

U.S. land policy had originally envisioned western lands as a means of raising revenue, and the government thus sold land competitively, with high minimum prices and in large blocks. This led to widespread speculation and little development. Gradually prices were reduced, by 1841 to $1.25 per acre when first put up for sale. Westerners generally held that the land remained without value until it was developed and thus pressed for the federal government to pass legislation discouraging speculation and encouraging settlement. The offer of free or inexpensive land became the necessary enticement as the frontier pushed westward to offset the cost of imported supplies needed on the treeless prairies before homesteads could be established. The *New York Tribune* took up the cause in the 1840s, as did the Free Soil Party after 1848. Division over land reform weakened the Democratic Party and provided an issue around which the Republicans rallied after the mid-1850s. With the South having seceded from the Union by 1861, President Abraham Lincoln and the Republicans were able to push through the Homestead Act.

Many land reformers were dissatisfied, as the act was not accompanied by legislation to explicitly halt land speculation, and much land was reserved for railway grants and Indian reservations. Prospective farmers nevertheless flocked to the lands thus opened. By 1890, 957,902 homestead claims had been filed and by the 1930s, almost 3 million. German and Scandinavian immigrants were particularly attracted, as they often had modest amounts of capital to establish themselves. Wisconsin, Minnesota, the Dakotas, Kansas, and Nebraska were substantially developed by immigrant farmers. Although only a little more than half of homesteaders actually completed the terms of their filing and speculation continued, the Homestead Act had an unprecedented impact in the rapid development of the western states and territories. As the best farmlands were taken, the government increased homestead acreage in the 20th century to 320 and then 640 acres. The Taylor Grazing Act (1934) effectively ended homesteading in the lower 48 states, organizing remaining government land into districts administered by the Bureau of Land Management.

Further Reading

Ganoe, John. "The Desert Land Act in Operation, 1877–1891." *Agricultural History* 11 (April 1937): 142–157.

Gates, Paul Wallace. "Homesteading in the High Plains." *Agricultural History* 5 (January 1977): 109–133.

———. *Public Land Policies.* New York: Arno Press, 1979.

Krall, Lisi. "U.S. Land Policy and the Commodification of Arid Land (1862–1920)." *Journal of Economic Issues* 35 (September 2001): 657–675.

Potter, Lee Ann, and Wynell Schamel. "The Homestead Act of 1862." *Social Education* 61 (October 1997): 359–365.

Schlebecker, John T. *Whereby We Thrive: A History of American Farming, 1607–1972.* Ames: Iowa State University Press, 1975.

Shannon, Fred A. *The Farmer's Last Frontier: Agriculture, 1860–1897.* New York: Farrar and Rinehart, 1945.

Wilkinson, Charles F. *Crossing the Next Meridian: Land, Water, and the Future of the West.* Washington D.C.: Island Press, 1992.

Worster, Donald. *An Unsettled Country.* Albuquerque: University of New Mexico Press, 1994.

Honduran immigration

As the poorest country in Central America, Honduras has become an important source country for northward migration since the 1960s. According to the U.S. census of 2000, 217,569 Americans claimed Honduran ancestry. In the Canadian census of 2001, only 3,025 claimed Honduran descent. Main areas of settlement in the United States include NEW ORLEANS, NEW YORK CITY, LOS ANGELES, BOSTON, and HOUSTON. Almost all Hondurans in Canada live in the Vancouver area.

Honduras occupies 43,100 square miles in Central America. Guatemala lies to the west, El Salvador to the southwest and Nicaragua to the southeast, and the Caribbean Sea to the north. In 2002, the population was estimated at 6,406,052. The people are ethnically divided among mestizos (87 percent); Amerindians (5.5 percent); and blacks and black Caribs, known as Garifuna (4.3 percent); about 97 percent are Roman Catholic. The Garifuna, who developed from the mixture of native Caribs and escaped slaves on the island of St. Vincent, were exiled to Honduras following a revolt against the British in 1797 and gradually spread to other coastal territories of Central America. After immigration, they tended to identify more closely with the Garifuna from other Caribbean countries than with mestizo Hondurans.

Maya civilization flourished in Honduras in the first millennium A.D. but declined long before Christopher Columbus arrived in 1502. After three centuries of Spanish control, Honduras gained its independence in 1821 and withdrew from the Federation of Central America in 1838. A few Honduran exiles had come to the United States prior to independence but formed no permanent community. For most of the late 19th and early 20th centuries, Honduran immigration was closely tied to the monopoly of banana growing and transportation granted by the government to the United Fruit Company and Standard Fruit Company in the 1880s. During and after World War II (1939–45), Hondurans were hired as merchant marines, housekeepers, and other household service providers, giving them entrance to the United States. Many married Americans and eventually brought their families from Honduras. General Oswaldo López Arellano, president for most of the period 1963–75 by virtue of one election and two coups, was ousted by the army in 1975 over charges of pervasive bribery by the American United Brands Company. An elected civilian government took power in 1982, initiating an economic modernization program that left many poor Hondurans without work. At the same time, growing political unrest in Nicaragua and El Salvador led to internal instability. After border violations by Nicaraguan troops in 1988, the United States sent 3,200 U.S. troops to Honduras and continued to work closely with the Honduran military into the first decade of the 21st century. Already one of the poorest countries in the Western Hemisphere—in the 1990s, two-thirds of Hondurans were living in poverty—in 1998, Honduras was devastated by Hurricane Mitch, which killed more than 9,000, destroyed 160,000 homes, and left 2 million homeless. With few prospects for improvement, Hondurans began to make the dangerous journey through Guatemala and Mexico into the United States. Several thousand continued on to Canada. In response to Hurricane Mitch, U.S. president Bill Clinton granted Temporary Protected Status for 105,000 Hondurans, enabling them to work legally in the United States for at least 18 months. Most disappeared into the illegal community, where they were joined by thousands of others. Legal immigration to the United States averaged just over 6,000 annually between 1992 and 2002. The unauthorized Honduran population, however, was estimated by the Immigration and Naturalization Service to be 138,000 in 2000.

Canada's Honduran community is small, ill defined, and since the late 1990s, closely linked to the drug trade. Of the 4,340 Hondurans in Canada in 2001, only about 400 came before 1981. During the 1980s, the poor began migrating in large numbers, abandoning once-rich mining districts for the promise of economic opportunity and, frequently, government benefits. Though the 3,200-mile journey was dangerous, hundreds took the risk each year. A visa was not required to enter Canada, and unlike the United States, application for asylum could be done inside the country. While refugee cases were pending, Hondurans were granted legal work papers and became eligible for more than $500 per month in provincial benefits—about three times the assistance they could receive in the United States—and could obtain driver's licenses, enroll their children in school, and visit community health centers at no charge. Beginning in the 1990s, Honduran drug dealers dramatically expanded the small crack-cocaine market in Vancouver, hiring hundreds of boys and young men to act as drug runners under cover of asylum. Whereas the number of dropped refugee claims was low through the mid-1990s—a little more than one-third—by 1999, the figure had jumped to 65 percent, suggesting that refugee claims were simply the means of entering the Canadian economy. Other Hondurans worked in the underground construction industry in Toronto.

Further Reading

Coelho, R. "The Black Carib of Honduras: A Study in Acculturation." Ph.D. diss., Northwestern University, 1955.

Gonzalez, N. *Sojourners of the Caribbean: Ethnogenesis and Ethnohistory of the Garifuna.* Urbana: University of Illinois Press, 1988.

Hamilton, Nora, and Norma Stolz Chinchilla. "Central American Migration: A Framework for Analysis." *Latin American Research Review* 26 (1991): 75–110.

Honduras: A Country Study. 3d ed. Washington, D.C.: Government Publishing Office, 1994.

Naylor, Robert. *Penny Ante Imperialism: The Mosquito Shore and the Bay of Honduras, 1600–1914: A Study in British Informal Empire.* Rutherford, N.J.:Fairleigh Dickinson University Press, 1989.

Schulz, Deborah Sundloff. *The United States, Honduras and the Crisis in Central America.* New York: Westview Press, 1994.

Teichroeb, Ruth, and Larry Johnson. "Honduran Children Take a Risky Journey to Escape Poverty and Deal Cocaine." *Seattle Post-Intelligencer.* May 24, 2000. Available online. URL: http://seattlepi.nwsource.com/honduras/page01.shtml. Accessed February 23, 2004.

Houston, Texas

Long a sleepy backwater nestled on Galveston Bay, by the turn of the 21st century Houston had grown to more than 1.9 million (more than 4 million in the metropolitan area), making it the fourth largest city in the United States and the second busiest port. As late as 1960, the foreign-born population was only 3 percent, but passage of the IMMIGRATION AND NATIONALITY ACT (1965) and geographic proximity to Mexico, the Caribbean, and South America led to a rapid influx of Asian and Hispanic immigrants. By 2000, there were 516,105 foreign-born immigrants (26.4 percent of the population), with the largest groups coming from Mexico, Central America, China, and Vietnam. Nearly half (49.5 percent) entered during the 1990s. By 2002, Anglos made up less than 40 percent of the city's population.

Founded in 1836, Houston had a small foreign-born population until the Mexican Revolution of 1910. Political turmoil in Mexico and economic opportunity in Houston combined to lure thousands of Mexicans, who created barrios that remained distinctly Mexican. The Great Depression of the 1930s led many Mexicans to leave, and immigration remained stagnant until the mid-1960s. After the liberalization of immigration laws in 1965, COLD WAR conflicts in Central America and Southeast Asia, coupled with a remarkable run of economic prosperity during the 1970s and 1980s, led to a new era of immigrant growth in Houston. Mexicans, Salvadorans, Guatemalans, Hondurans, Vietnamese, Laotians, and Cambodians quickly found work, especially in construction and service industries. The Hispanic population more than doubled between 1980 and 1990 (212,444 to 424,903), as did the Vietnamese population (14,000 to 33,000). With the decline of the oil industry after 1982, it is estimated that 100,000 Anglos deserted the city, opening housing and business opportunities for newly arriving immigrants. During the 1990s, Houston refashioned its economy to become less dependent on petrochemicals, attracting international industry and developing shipping and transportation networks, especially with the countries of Latin America.

Further Reading

Feagin, Joe R. *Free Enterprise City: Houston in a Political and Economic Perspective.* New Brunswick, N.J.: Rutgers University Press, 1988.

Hagan, Jacqueline Maria. *Deciding to Be Legal: A Maya Community in Houston.* Philadelphia: Temple University Press, 1994.

León, Arnoldo de. *Ethnicity in the Sunbelt: A History of Mexican Americans in Houston.* Houston: Mexican American Studies, University of Houston, 1989.

Rodriguez, Nestor P. "Undocumented Central Americans in Houston: Diverse Populations." *International Migration Review* 21 (1987): 4–26.

Hudson, Henry (ca. 1550–1611) *explorer*

The English navigator Henry Hudson was known for sailing farther north than any European had previously as he searched for the fabled northern passage to Asia. He also explored the eastern coast of North America, establishing Dutch claims in the Hudson River Valley of modern New York State.

Little is known of Hudson's early life. In 1607, he was commissioned by England's Muscovy Company to search for a polar sea route to Asia. In the *Hopewell,* he and 11 men reached Spitsbergen Island and perhaps Jan Mayen Island before being driven back by ice floes. Encouraged by reports of abundant whale and walrus populations, the company outfitted a second voyage, in 1608, which reached Novaya Zemlya before once again being turned back by ice. Hudson's legacy, however, is based on discoveries during his third voyage, made in 1609 while he was in the pay of the Dutch East India Company. Sailing in the *Half Moon,* he led a crew of 20, exploring the eastern seaboard of North America between Maine and the Delaware River. The expedition also sailed up the Hudson River as far north as modern Albany, laying the foundation for the colony of New Netherland (later NEW YORK COLONY), founded as a permanent settlement in 1624. On Hudson's fourth voyage (1610–11), sponsored by English merchants, he discovered the immense, subarctic bay that today bears his name. Trapped by ice in St. James Bay, at the southeastern end of Hudson Bay, he and his crew endured enormous hardships over the winter. The crew mutinied, and on June 23, 1611, Hudson, his 12-year-old son, and seven other crewman were cast adrift in an open boat. They were never heard from again.

A romanticized view of American Indians first sighting Henry Hudson as he sails into New York Bay, September 11, 1609. After many years of fruitlessly searching for the Northwest Passage, Hudson was in the pay of the Dutch East India Company in 1609 when he established Dutch claims to the region of modern New York. *(Painting by Edward Moran, ca. 1908/Library of Congress, Prints & Photographs Division [LC-USZ62-107822])*

Further Reading

Asher, George M., ed. *Henry Hudson the Navigator.* London: Hakluyt Society, 1860.

Johnson, Donald S., and Philip Turner, eds. *Charting the Sea of Darkness: The Four Voyages of Henry Hudson.* New York: Kodansha International, 1995.

Powys, Llewelyn. *Henry Hudson.* New York: Harper and Brothers, 1928.

Thomson, George Malcolm. *The Search for the North-West Passage.* New York: Macmillan, 1975.

Hudson's Bay Company

The Hudson's Bay Company, founded in London in 1670 to develop the fur trade of British North America, established British claims to northern and western Canada (see CANADA—IMMIGRATION SURVEY AND POLICY OVERVIEW) and opened western lands to settlement. The original charter granted rights to "the Company of Adventurers from England trading into the Hudson's bay."

The company was founded by English noblemen and merchants with the help of two disgruntled French fur traders, Médard Chouart, sieur des Groseilliers, and Pierre Esprit Radisson, who agreed to work for Charles II (r. 1660–85). The original charter provided exclusive trading rights for all lands drained by rivers flowing into Hudson Bay, an area of almost 1.5 million square miles. Company traders probed deep into the Canadian interior, trading guns, knives, and other manufactured objects for furs, especially beaver pelts. Although not organized for settlement, the company required hundreds of employees, most of whom were brought from Ireland and Scotland as indentured servants (see INDENTURED SERVITUDE). They frequently married native women, and their families formed a distinct ethnic group, the Métis, by 1800. Conflict with the French, who claimed the same lands, was endemic. A series of colonial wars, culminating in the SEVEN YEARS' WAR (1756–63), led to complete British control of Canada and a free hand for the Hudson's Bay Company. With the demise of the French threat, in 1779 the North West Company was formed in Montreal to challenge the Hudson's Bay Company's dominance of the fur trade. In order to compete, each company extended its network of fortifications, trading posts, Indian contacts, and transportation routes, thus opening isolated western settlements to further European contact. After open warfare between the two companies in the wake of the establishment of the RED RIVER COLONY (1812), the rivals eventually merged and were reorganized (1821), retaining the Hudson's Bay Company name and extending the original charter to include the Pacific Northwest and the Arctic.

As western Canada enticed larger numbers of settlers, the fur trade declined as a major commercial enterprise, and the United States surfaced as a potential threat, company administration of the huge area became untenable. In 1869, the British government negotiated a settlement with the Hudson's Bay Company that transferred the company's lands to the newly formed Dominion of Canada (1867). In return, the company received £300,000, a grant of some 45,000 acres around its 120 trading posts, and continued trading privileges on the western plains. With the fur trade almost dead by 1875, the company diversified its interests, shifting greater resources into real estate and retail marketing operations and maintaining its position as one of the largest private companies in Canada. In the wake of recession, in 1986 and 1987 the company sold its fur-auction houses and petroleum interests in order to raise cash and intensify the retailing and real estate sectors that have kept the company solvent in the years since World War II.

Further Reading

Galbraith, John S. *The Hudson's Bay Company as an Imperial Factor, 1821–69.* Berkeley and Los Angeles: University of California Press, 1957.

———. "Land Policies of the Hudson's Bay Company, 1870–1913." *Canadian Historical Review* 32 (March 1951): 1–21.

MacKay, Douglas. *The Honourable Company: A History of the Hudson's Bay Company.* 2d rev. ed. Toronto: McClelland and Stewart, 1949.

Newman, Peter C. *Company of Adventurers.* 2 vols. New York: Viking, 1985, 1987.

———. *Empire of the Bay: The Company of Adventurers That Seized a Continent.* New York: Penguin, 2000.

Rich, E. E. *Hudson's Bay Company, 1670–1870.* 3 vols. Toronto: McClelland and Stewart, 1960.

Woodcock, George. *The Hudson's Bay Company.* Toronto: Collier-Macmillan Canada, 1970.

An 1890s advertisement for the Hudson's Bay Company encourages Klondike prospectors to purchase the company's stores. After the decline of the fur trade in the 1870s, the company diversified its economic interests and moved extensively into commercial marketing. *(Library of Congress, Prints & Photographs Division [LC-USZ62-104304])*

Hughes, John Joseph (1797–1864) *religious leader*

As bishop (1838–50) and archbishop of New York (1850–64), John Hughes was among the most influential figures in what Roger Daniels calls the "Hibernization of the American Roman Catholic Church." As the first Catholic archbishop of New York, he was an outspoken defender of the Catholic Church, eloquently articulating its compatibility with traditional American political principles.

Hughes emigrated from northern Ireland to the United States in 1817. After attending Mount Saint Mary's Seminary in Philadelphia, he was ordained in 1826. He favored Irish nationalism generally but opposed violent means of promoting it. During the 1830s, he waged a vigorous press debate with Protestant leaders over the question of the validity of lay control of Catholic Church property. After moving from Philadelphia to New York in 1838, Hughes campaigned vigorously against Protestant influence in the nonsectarian public schools. Once he became archbishop of New York in 1850, he was the primary spokesperson for the Catholic Church in defense of nativist attacks from the Know-Nothing Party (see NATIVISM). Increasingly, he served the needs of the Catholic hierarchy rather than the Irish themselves, though he did continue to promote such organizations as the Irish Emigrant Society, the Emigrant Savings Bank, and the Ancient Order of Hibernians. Hughes's influence grew during the Civil War (1861–65), helping to shift the balance of ethnic influence within the church from French to Irish clergy. Although Hughes was not an abolitionist, he remained a firm unionist. He undertook a mission to France on behalf of President Abraham Lincoln (1863) and helped to quell the New York draft riots (1863).

Further Reading

Billington, Ray Allen. *The Protestant Crusade, 1800–1860.* 1938. Reprint, Chicago: Quadrangle Books, 1964.

Braun, Henry A. *Most Reverend John Hughes: First Archbishop of New York.* New York: Dodd Mead, 1892.

Dolan, Jay. *The Immigrant Church.* Baltimore: Johns Hopkins University Press, 1975.

Lannie, Vincent P. *Public Money and Parochial Education: Bishop Hughes, Governor Seward, and the New York School Controversy.* Cleveland, Ohio: Press of Case Western Reserve University, 1968.

Shaw, Richard. *Dagger John: The Unquiet Life and Times of Archbishop John Hughes of New York.* New York: Paulist Press, 1977.

Further Reading

Baird, Charles. *History of the Huguenot Emigration to America.* 2 vols. 1885. Reprint, Baltimore: Genealogical Publishing, 1998.

Butler, Jon. *The Huguenots in America: A Refugee People in New World Society.* Cambridge, Mass.: Harvard University Press, 1983.

Golden, Richard M. *The Huguenot Connection.* Doordrecht, Netherlands: Martinus Nijhoff, 1988.

Tobias, Leslie. "Manakin Town: The Development and Demise of a French Protestant Refugee Community in Colonial Virginia, 1700–1750." M.A. thesis, College of William and Mary, 1982.

Hull-House   See ADDAMS, JANE.

Huguenot immigration

French citizens who embraced the Protestant teachings of the 16th-century reformation were known as Huguenots. Because they were unwelcome in Catholic France, hundreds of thousands left their native land, with several thousand eventually making their way to the British colonies in North America. Huguenots, generally prosperous and well educated, were among the immigrant groups who were rapidly assimilated into the dominant English culture of America.

Huguenots attempted to settle in Florida (near present-day St. Augustine), the Carolinas, and the Guanabara Bay (in present-day Brazil) during the late 16th century, but none of the settlements was successful. The first Huguenots to settle successfully in the Americas sailed from the Netherlands early in the 17th century, and a small number followed throughout the century. Following Louis XIV's revocation of the Edict of Nantes (1685), which had guaranteed freedom of worship, several hundred thousand Huguenots migrated to Holland, Prussia, and Britain, and several thousand of these eventually made their way to the Americas by the end of the 17th century. The exact number is greatly disputed, in part because immigration records were not routinely kept and because Huguenots often came by way of a third country. Their favored destinations were New York (New Rochelle and NEW YORK, NEW YORK), Massachusetts (Oxford and Salem), Virginia, and the Carolinas (Charleston). Huguenots maintained their French church traditions into the second generation but by the 1750s, began to rapidly integrate with English-language Protestant churches. By the time of the American Revolution (1775–83), most Huguenots had lost their distinctiveness, having married into English families, adopted the English language, and adapted to the commercial and agricultural developments of their regions. This process was made easier by their relatively high social standing before leaving France, many having been aristocrats and trained artisans. Few Huguenots settled in Canada, as the French government prohibited their permanent residence in NEW FRANCE.

Hungarian immigration

One of the largest ethnic immigrant groups of the great migration between 1880 and 1914, Hungarians built one of the most cohesive ethnic identities in the New World. According to the 2000 U.S. census and the 2001 Canadian census, 1,398,724 Americans and 267,255 Canadians claimed Hungarian ancestry. The largest Hungarian concentrations in the United States in the 19th and early 20th centuries were in Pittsburgh, Pennsylvania; Cleveland, and Youngstown, Ohio; CHICAGO; PHILADELPHIA; and NEW YORK City. As later generations aged, they frequently moved, most often to California and Florida. Canadian cities with the largest Hungarian population are TORONTO and Vancouver.

Modern Hungary occupies 35,600 square miles in east central Europe. It is bordered by Slovakia and Ukraine to the north; Austria to the west; Slovenia, Yugoslavia, and Croatia to the south; and Romania to the east. In 2002, the population was estimated at 10,106,017. The people are ethnically divided, mainly between Hungarians (90 percent), Gypsies (4 percent), and Germans (3 percent); 68 percent are Roman Catholic; 20 percent, Calvinist; 5 percent, Lutheran; and 5 percent, Jewish. The middle Danube River basin was settled in the late ninth century by Asian warriors known as Magyars, the name still used by Hungarians for their group. The Magyars converted to Christianity around 1000. Although eventually abandoning seminomadic pastoralism and establishing a settled kingdom, their history in the strategic Carpathian basin was full of conflict, principally with Slavs, whose lands they had invaded; Germans, who were in the process of expanding eastward; and the Ottoman Turks, who were pushing north from their homeland in Anatolia. By the late 16th century, most of Hungary was brought under the control of the Austrian Habsburgs. After an abortive revolution in 1848–49 led by the dynamic Lajos Kossuth, in 1867, Hungarians were finally granted equal status with Austrians under the Austrian emperor. The Dual Monarchy thereby created the Austro-Hungarian Empire. The Hungarian portion of the empire was a microcosm of the whole, made up of many ethnic groups, including Germans, Slovaks, Gypsies, Serbs, Croats, and

Romanians. After the Austro-Hungarian Empire was defeated in World War I (1914–18), independent Hungary was greatly reduced, stripped of most regions not predominantly inhabited by Magyars. The country joined forces with Nazi Germany in an attempt to regain lost territories during World War II (1939–45) and quickly fell under Soviet control in the aftermath of the war. Although pro-Soviet communists were temporarily driven from power in a 1956 revolt, the Soviet army invaded the country, savagely suppressing the rebellion, leading to the exodus of some 200,000 Hungarians who became refugees, mostly in Austria. As the most liberal of all the Soviet satellites during the COLD WAR, Hungary moved relatively smoothly into independence as the Soviet Union lessened its grip in 1989 and quickly began to attract foreign investment.

There are accounts of notable Hungarians in North America as early as the AMERICAN REVOLUTION (1775–83). At least one Hungarian was a part of Sir Humphrey Gilbert's expedition to North America in 1583. Between the 17th and mid-19th centuries, a number of prominent Hungarians came as individuals to America and generally left glowing accounts of their experiences. Agoston Haraszthy not only praised the new country in *Journey to North America* (1844) but set an example that hundreds of thousands of Hungarians later followed, bringing his family to settle permanently in California, where he established the new viticulture industry. The first significant occurrence of group migration came in 1849–50, when several thousand Hungarian nationalists—the "forty-niners"—fled the country following a failed revolution and settled in the United States. Under Austrian domination, Hungary found itself in the midst of a far-reaching social transformation as a result of the abolition of serfdom. This freed the rural worker from the land but also absolved welfare obligations of the landlord. The continued predominance of large estates throughout most of the country made owning enough land to guard against want virtually impossible for the rural proletariat. U.S. railway and steamship agents took advantage of these conditions, sending agents and propaganda into the remotest regions of the country.

As impoverished Hungarians looked to emigration, they relied on support from their extended family of aunts, uncles, cousins, and in-laws. Despite the fact that Hungarian immigration was driven by overpopulation and economic impoverishment—factors common to most European countries in the 19th century—Hungary nevertheless sent a disproportionate number of migrants to the United States and Canada prior to World War I. The first great wave came between 1880 and 1914, when more than 1.5 million Hungarians immigrated to the United States, with more than 800,000 coming between 1900 and 1910. Most came from rural areas but worked in American mines and factories, hoping one day to return to their homeland. Maintaining such close ethnic ties, they frequently were slow to assimilate.

As a result of the restrictive JOHNSON-REED ACT (1924), immigration between the world wars was greatly reduced, to a total of about 40,000. As a result of World War II, tens of thousands of Hungarians became displaced persons, and about 25,000 entered the United States between 1945 and 1956, most under provisions of the DISPLACED PERSONS ACT (1948). A further phase of Hungarian immigration was initiated with the abortive revolution against Soviet control in 1956, leading to the admission of about 36,000 "fifty-sixers" who were admitted to the United States as refugees. Between the revolt and independence in 1989, about 18,000 Hungarians immigrated to the United States, most because of dissatisfaction with communist politics and economies. Following the demise of Soviet influence in 1989, Hungary went through a difficult economic transition to market capitalism, leading to the exodus of many young and well-educated professionals. Between 1989 and 2002, the annual average immigration was about 1,000.

Large-scale Hungarian immigration to Canada began somewhat later than to the United States, in conjunction with the mass migration to Canada's southern neighbor. The first Hungarians arriving on the newly opened prairies of present-day Manitoba in 1885 came by way of the Pennsylvania coal mines, with the support of the Canadian Pacific Railway. Although many eventually left the Assiniboia district in what is now Alberta and Saskatchewan, by 1903, the railway reached the settlement bringing more settlers directly from Hungary. Canada was seen by Hungarian church and social leaders as a potentially healthy alternative to the harsh industrial landscape of the United States. By World War I there were a half-dozen Hungarian settlements in Canada, most in present-day Saskatchewan, but only about 10,000 settlers. Facing the harsh realities of life under the punitive Treaty of Trianon ending World War I, Hungarians found new reasons to immigrate. Most would have preferred the United States, but restrictive immigration policies all but halted the flow there in the 1920s. Canada therefore became the foremost destination for Hungarians coming to the New World. About 30,000 immigrated to Canada between World War I and World War II, most under a Railway Agreement by which Canadian railways and the Canadian government sought agricultural settlers for the western prairies. With few good farmsteads remaining, most Hungarian immigrants gradually settled in central Canada, specifically in Hamilton, Toronto, Welland, Windsor, Montreal, and surrounding areas, where they became active in ethnic, political, and mutual aid societies.

Canada admitted almost 12,000 Hungarian refugees between 1946 and 1956, with most settling in Ontario and other eastern cities. The revolt of 1956 led to the final mass migration of Hungarians to Canada, more than 37,000 in 1956 and 1957. In both migrations, there were large percentages of well-educated professionals, which began to alter the perception of Hungarians as poor agriculturalists and ease the process of assimilation. Of 48,715 Hungarian immigrants in Canada in 2001, fewer than 5,000 came between 1991 and 2001.

Further Reading

Dirk, Gerald. *Canada's Refugee Policy: Indifference or Opportunity.* Montreal: McGill-Queen's University Press, 1977.

Dreisziger, N. F., ed., with M. L. Kovács, Paul Bôdy, and Bennet Kovrig. *Struggle and Hope: The Hungarian-Canadian Experience.* Toronto: McClelland and Stewart, 1982.

Glatz, Ferenc, ed. *Hungarians and Their Neighbors in Modern Times, 1867–1950.* New York: Columbia University Press, 1995.

Grácza, Rezsoe, and Margaret Grácza. *The Hungarians in America.* Minneapolis, Minn.: Lerner, 1969.

Keyserlingk, Robet H., ed. *Breaking Ground: The 1956 Hungarian Refugee Movement to Canada.* Toronto: York Lanes, 1993.

Kósa, John. *Land of Choice: The Hungarians in Canada.* Toronto: University of Toronto Press, 1957.

Kovács, Martin. *Esterházy and Early Hungarian Immigration to Canada.* Regina: Canadian Plains Studies, 1974.

Lengyel, Emil. *Americans from Hungary.* Philadelphia: J. B. Lippincott, 1948.

Miska, John. *Canadian Studies on Hungarians, 1886–1986.* Regina: Canadian Plains Research Center, 1987.

Patrias, Carmela. *The Hungarians in Canada.* Ottawa: Canadian Historical Association, 1999.

———. *Patriots and Proletarians: Politicizing Hungarian Immigrants in Interwar Canada.* Montreal: McGill–Queen's University Press, 1994.

Puskás, Julianna. *From Hungary to the United States (1880–1914).* Budapest, Hungary: Akademiai Kiado, 1982.

Romanucci-Ross, L., and G. DeVos., eds. *Ethnic Identity: Creation, Conflict, and Accommodation.* 3d ed. Walnut Creek, Calif: AltaMira Press, 1995.

Széplaki, Joseph, ed. *The Hungarians in America, 1583–1974: A Chronology and Fact Book.* Dobbs Ferry, N.Y.: Oceana Publications,1975.

Tezla, Albert. *The Hazardous Quest: Hungarian Immigrants in the United States, 1895–1920.* Budapest, Hungary: Corvina, 1993.

Várdy, Steven B. *The Hungarian Americans.* Boston: Twayne, 1985.

———. *The Hungarian Experience in North America.* New York and Philadelphia: Chelsea House, 1990.

Weinstock, S. A. *Acculturation and Occupation: A Study of the 1956 Hungarian Refugees in the United States.* The Hague, Netherland: Nijhoff, 1969.

Hutterite immigration (Hutterian Brethren immigration)

The Hutterian Brethren (Hutterites) are a communal Anabaptist Protestant sect that emigrated en masse from Russia to the United States in the 1870s. Large numbers of them then moved to the southern Canadian prairies beginning in 1919. They were one of the few ethnic communi-

ties to retain most of the distinctive features of their religious and ethnic roots throughout the 20th century. In 2003, there were approximately 36,000 Hutterites living in 434 "colonies" in North America. In Canada, they were concentrated in Alberta, Saskatchewan, and Manitoba; in the United States, most of the colonies were in South Dakota and Montana.

Emerging from the Anabaptist movement of the Protestant Reformation in 1528, the Hutterite Brethren, like the Amish (see AMISH IMMIGRATION) and Mennonites (see MENNONITE IMMIGRATION), believed in adult baptism and in pacifism. They also lived communally, holding all goods in common, a practice that often put them at odds with their neighbors. Originally German-speaking Swiss, they migrated to Moravia, in the present-day Czech Republic. In 1536, their leader, Jacob Hutter, was burned at the stake, leading to an ongoing migration in search of refuge. Hutterites were hardworking and well organized and thus frequently welcomed in other lands. They were nevertheless viewed with suspicion and envy, especially during hard economic times. Their communal lifestyle and use of Tyrolean German continued to set them apart from the native inhabitants around them. As a result, they were persecuted and driven successively from Austria, Moravia, Slovakia, Transylvania (Romania), and Wallachia (Romania). During the 18th century, most Hutterites migrated to the Ukraine, where the Russian czar promised freedom of worship and freedom from military service.

When Russian guarantees were rescinded in the 1870s, the Hutterites began a mass migration to the United States and Canada. Between 1874 and 1877, virtually all Hutterites—approximately 1,300—immigrated to the Dakota Territory. Several hundred left the communal church, eventually merging with more liberal Mennonites, though most retained their traditional social organization. Persecuted and fearing conscription during World War I (1914–18), a large group of Hutterites determined to move to Canada in 1918, founding six colonies in southern Manitoba and nine in southern Alberta. Although restrictions were placed on Hutterite immigration (1919–22) and on land purchases in Alberta (1942–72), their rural, isolated colonies prospered.

Further Reading

Gross, Leonard. *The Golden Years of the Hutterites.* Scottdale, Pa.: Herald Press, 1980.

Hostetler, John A. *Hutterite Society.* Baltimore: Johns Hopkins University Press, 1974.

Janzen, William. *Limits on Liberty: The Experience of Mennonite, Hutterite, and Doukhobor Communities in Canada.* Toronto: University of Toronto Press, 1990.

Ryan, John. *The Agricultural Economy of Manitoba Hutterite Colonies.* Toronto: McClelland and Stewart, 1977.

Icelandic immigration

Sharing a common North Atlantic heritage with Canada, Iceland became one of the few source countries to send more immigrants to Canada than to the United States. It was also one of the few countries whose emigration virtually ceased by 1910. According to the U.S. census in 2000 and the Canadian census in 2001, 42,716 Americans and 75,090 Canadians claimed Icelandic origins. California and Washington State had the largest number of Icelandic settlers in the United States, while Ontario, Manitoba, and British Columbia had the largest populations in Canada.

Iceland is an island country in the North Atlantic Ocean, occupying 38,700 square miles. Its nearest neighbors are Greenland, about 200 miles to the west, and the Faeroe Islands of Denmark, about 250 miles to the east. In 2002, the population was estimated at 277,906. About 95 percent are Icelandic, mainly descended from Norwegians and Celts, and some 95 percent are Protestant, mostly Evangelical Lutheran. Iceland was an independent republic from 930 to 1262, when it joined with Norway. Denmark incorporated Norway in 1380, and with it Iceland. Direct Danish rule lasted until 1918, when Iceland was granted autonomy under the Danish king. The last ties with the Danish Crown were finally severed in 1944, when Iceland became an independent republic. The Althing (assembly), is the world's oldest surviving parliament.

A few dozen Mormon converts from Iceland immigrated to Utah after 1854, but no large-scale migration followed. The greatest period of migration for Icelanders was the 1870s. Spurred by harsh conditions, unproductive soil, and a number of volcanic eruptions, several thousand Icelanders settled in Canada, most along the western shore of Lake Winnipeg in what was then the Northwest Territories. With a delay in establishment of territorial government, the Icelanders were given permission to form their own administrative unit known as New Iceland in 1878. Self-government lasted until 1887, when the new Manitoba government took over. In 1878, about 30 families moved from New Iceland to North Dakota, joining fewer than 200 Icelandic immigrants who had settled in Wisconsin and Minnesota earlier in the decade. From their base in Winnipeg, which boasted an Icelandic population of 7,000 during the late 19th century, Icelanders began to spread throughout the wheat lands of Manitoba and Saskatchewan. It is impossible to say exactly how many Icelanders came to North America during the 19th century, as they were usually counted as Danes. It is estimated conservatively that about 10,000 immigrated to Canada and about half that number to the United States. As conditions improved in Iceland after 1900, immigration declined dramatically. In 2001, only 415 Icelander immigrants resided in Canada, and more than half of these arrived before 1970. Immigration to the United States averaged about 130 per year between 1992 and 2002.

Further Reading

Arnason, David, and Vincent Arnason, ed. *The New Icelanders: A North American Community.* Winnipeg, Canada: Turnstone Press, 1994.

Arngrímsson, Gudjón. *Nýja Ísland: Saga of the Journey to New Iceland.* Winnipeg, Canada: Turnstone Press, 1997.

Bjornson, Val. "Icelanders in the United States." In *Scandinavian Review* 64, no. 3 (September 1976): 39–41.

Kristjanson, Wilhelm. *The Icelandic People in Manitoba: A Manitoba Saga.* Winnipeg, Canada: Wallingford Press, 1965.

Palmer, H. "Escape from the Great Plains: The Icelanders in North Dakota and Alberta." *Great Plains Quarterly* 3, no. 4 (Fall 1983): 219ff.

Pennings, Margaret. "The Big Store: The Story of Icelandic Immigration in America," B.A. thesis, University of Minnesota.

Regan, A. "Icelanders." In *They Chose Minnesota: A Survey of the State's Ethnic Groups.* Ed. S. Thernstrom. St. Paul: Minnesota Historical Society Press, 1981.

Rosenblad, Esbjörn, and Rakel Sigurdardó Hir-Rosenblad. *Iceland from Past to Present.* Trans. Alan Crozier. Reykjavík: 1993.

The Settlement of New Iceland. Rev. ed. Winnipeg, Canada: Manitoba Culture, History, and Citizenship, Historic Resources Branch, 1997.

Thorson, P. V. "Icelanders." In *Plains Folk: North Dakota's Ethnic History.* Eds. W. C. Sherman and P. V. Thorson. Fargo: North Dakota Institute for Regional Studies, 1986.

Walters, Thorstina Jackson. *Modern Sagas: The Story of the Icelanders in America.* Fargo: North Dakota Institute for Regional Studies, 1953.

illegal immigration

Until the 1990s, the term most commonly used for those who entered the United States illegally was *illegal alien.* An *alien* was defined by the IMMIGRATION AND NATURALIZATION SERVICE (INS) as "any person not a citizen of the United States." Any alien who enters and resides in the country in violation of immigration law is an illegal alien. During the 1990s, the government and governmental authorities increasingly used the term *unauthorized resident* as a synonym. The term most commonly used in Canada is *undocumented migrant.* Aliens, whether legal or illegal, still enjoy most of the rights and protections afforded by both governments. Unlike citizens, however, they are subject to deportation for breaches of the law. As potential immigrants around the world began to perceive the potential for securing better jobs, education, and health care in the 1970s in the United States and Canada and increasingly found means for getting there, illegal immigration became a major policy concern. It also led to a new wave of anti-immigration activism, particularly in the American Southwest, and a public debate that had still not been resolved in the first decade of the 21st century.

Until 1917, the United States had a largely open immigration policy; the biggest immigration questions revolved around legal, rather than illegal, immigration. Between 1875 and 1917, a number of restrictive measures were passed to exclude prostitutes, convicts, "lunatics," "idiots," and the indigent (see IMMIGRATION ACT (1906); PAGE

ACT), but these affected few people. More significant were the CHINESE EXCLUSION ACT (1882) and the GENTLEMEN'S AGREEMENT (1907), which led to the exclusion of most Chinese and Japanese laborers. Although some laborers found their way into the country, mainly through colonial Hawaii, where they were still allowed as laborers, illegal immigration did not affect the country generally. The tight restrictions of the EMERGENCY QUOTA ACT of 1921 and the JOHNSON-REED ACT of 1924, however, led to a flood of illegal immigration in the 1920s. Canada offered some cooperation, but Mexico was unresponsive, and Chinese immigrants especially continued to pour across both borders. As early as 1904, Bureau of Immigration inspectors routinely patrolled almost 2,000 miles of Mexican border, but the 75 agents assigned to the task were scarcely able to prevent illegal entry. With drastically reduced quotas following the immigration reform of 1924 came establishment of the U.S. BORDER PATROL, an enforcement agency of the Department of Labor.

The dramatic increase in immigration after 1965 was in large measure a function of the provisions of the IMMIGRATION AND NATIONALITY ACT of 1965 and government perception of COLD WAR needs to exclude especially Cubans and Vietnamese from the ordinary provisions of immigration policy. At the same time, however, illegal immigration exploded, as legal migrant laborers under the Bracero Program became illegal immigrants once the program was ended (1965). With the INS understaffed and U.S. employers exempt from criminal prosecution for hiring illegal immigrants, cheap foreign labor continued to pour into the country. Between 1970 and 1997, more than 30 million illegal immigrants were apprehended, though deportations were often difficult, and millions more eluded interception and entered the labor force.

The number of unauthorized immigrants in the United States rose dramatically in the 1990s. An INS report of February 1997 showed that there were an estimated 5 million illegal immigrants in the United States as of October 1996; four years later, the number had risen to 7 million (8.7 million according to the U.S. Census Bureau), further heightening the public debate over American responsibility toward poor, illegal immigrants. Almost 70 percent of unauthorized residents in 2000 were from Mexico, and another 14 percent from El Salvador, Guatemala, Colombia, Honduras, Ecuador, and the Dominican Republic. About 40 percent entered with tourist or worker visas but failed to return to their home countries when the visas expired. After years of debate, the U.S. Congress passed the ILLEGAL IMMIGRATION REFORM AND IMMIGRANT RESPONSIBILITY ACT in 1996, which increased the Border Patrol, provided for stiffer penalties in trafficking undocumented aliens, and made deportation easier. In March 2000, Vice President Al Gore proposed to expand the 1986 Immigration Act, which granted residency to immigrants who had lived continuously in the United States since 1972, to include those who had lived in the United States since 1986. As a result, some 500,000 undocumented immigrants were granted residency.

Canadian economic opportunities were fewer than in the United States, the attitude toward non-British immigrants more hostile, and the distances greater, so the incidence of illegal immigration was less and had less national impact. With the rapid progress of decolonization around the world, however, and passage of the IMMIGRATION REGULA-TIONS of 1967, two significant waves of undocumented immigration occurred. Between 1970 and 1973, more than 200,000 people applied for landed immigrant status. Under Section 34 of the regulations, it became permissible to apply within Canada and be guaranteed the right of appeal if denied. Thousands of potential immigrants from around the world took advantage of this administrative loophole, realizing that there would be a huge backlog of cases that would permit settlement. With up to 8,700 applications a month by October 1972, the Canadian government revoked Section 34 while offering the Adjustment of Status Program, essentially an amnesty. By the end of 1973, about 52,000 previously undocumented immigrants had been granted landed immigrant status. With economic depression looming in 1980, public opposition to immigration began to increase, along with the number of undocumented immigrants. Most of the increase involved claims for refugee status, many of which were bogus and clearly designed to give undocumented immigrants an opportunity to gain a foothold in Canada (see HONDURAN IMMIGRATION). Provisions of BILL C-55 and BILL C-84, which went into effect in 1989, streamlined the refugee determination process, increased penalties for those transporting undocumented migrants, and enhanced the government's powers of deportation. By the late 1990s, some were estimating that as many as 16,000 illegal immigrants were entering Canada annually, at a cost of up to $50,000 in social benefits for each immigrant.

With many of the 19 hijackers involved in the terrorist bombings of SEPTEMBER 11, 2001, being illegal aliens, the debate over illegal immigration was renewed in both the United States and Canada, and more stringent measures were introduced for screening and tracking immigrants and for deporting illegal aliens. In the first decade of the 21st century, illegal immigration from Mexico was the top U.S. concern and led to high-level discussions between the two governments. Canada's biggest concern was human trafficking from China and the high number of refugee claims by Chinese immigrants.

See also NATIVISM.

Further Reading

Campbell, Charles M. *Betrayal and Deceit: The Politics of Canadian Immigration.* West Vancouver, Canada: Jasmine Books, 2000.

Corcoran, Mary. *Irish Illegals: Transients between Two Societies.* Westport, Conn.: Greenwood Press, 1993.

Corona, Bert. *Bert Corona Speaks on La Raza Unida Party and the "Illegal Alien" Scare.* New York: Pathfinder Press, 1972.

Espenshade, T. J. "A Short History of U.S. Policy toward Illegal Immigration." *Population Today* 18, no. 2 (February 1990): 6–9.

Haines, David W., and Karen E. Rosenblum. *Illegal Immigration in America: A Reference Handbook.* Westport, Conn.: Greenwood Press, 1999.

Kyle, David, and Rey Koslowski, ed. *Global Human Smuggling: Comparative Perspectives.* Baltimore: Johns Hopkins University Press, 2001.

Kwong, Peter. *Forbidden Workers: Illegal Chinese Immigrants and American Labor.* New York: New Press, 1998.

Malkin, Michelle. *Invasion: How America Still Welcomes Terrorists, Criminals and Other Foreign Menaces to Our Shores.* New York: Regnery, 2002.

Smith, Paul J., ed. *Human Smuggling: Chinese Migrant Trafficking and the Challenge to America's Immigration Tradition.* Washington, D.C.: Center for Strategic and International Studies, 1997.

Illegal Immigration Reform and Immigrant Responsibility Act (IIRIRA) (United States) (1996)

As part of a 1996 initiative to curb illegal immigration, the U.S. Congress passed the Illegal Immigration Reform and Immigrant Responsibility Act (IIRIRA). The measure authorized a doubling of the number of U.S. BORDER PATROL agents between 1996 and 2001 (5,000 to 10,000) and the building of additional fences along the U.S.-Mexican border south of San Diego, in California. It also provided tougher penalties for those engaged in document fraud and alien smuggling and greater controls on public welfare provided to illegal aliens. The most controversial aspects of the measure involved the streamlining of detention and deportation hearings. This enabled illegal aliens to be deported without appeal to the courts, unless they could demonstrate a realistic fear of persecution in their home country. A review of decisions was required within seven days but could be conducted by telephone or teleconference.

President Bill Clinton did not favor many of the harshest elements of the measure and sought to reverse them through vigorous promotion of the U.S.-Mexican Binational Commission and its Working Group on Immigration and Consular Affairs. Clinton also strongly supported passage of the Nicaraguan Adjustment and Central American Relief Act (NACARA), which effectively granted amnesty to many Central American refugees whose status had remained ambiguous since the 1980s civil war in Nicaragua. In 1999, the Supreme Court let stand lower court rulings allowing appeal to the courts. The harsher provisions of the IIRIRA led to introduction in Congress of a bill called the Restoration of Fairness in the Immigration Act of 2000, which sought to eliminate retroactive consideration of minor crimes and to provide for adequate judicial review of judgments. As of mid-2004, the proposed act remained in committee.

Further Reading

Espenshade, T. J., J. L. Baraka, and G. A. Huber. "Implications of the 1996 Welfare and Immigration Reform Acts for U.S. Immigration." *Population and Development Review* 23, no. 4 (December 1997): 769–801.

Reimers, David. *Unwelcome Strangers: American Identity and the Turn Against Immigration.* New York: Columbia University Press, 1998.

Immigration Act (Canada) (1869)

Seeking to encourage economic development in the new dominion, Canada's first piece of immigration legislation was designed to attract productive immigrants. With immigrant entry now under the auspices of the Ministry of Agriculture, the act was intended to ensure safe passage for immigrants, to regulate abuses commonly perpetrated against the new arrivals by unscrupulous businessmen, and to encourage settlement. The measure was nevertheless a failure, as most immigrants continued on to the United States.

The Immigration Act contained few restrictions. It prohibited entry of paupers unless the shipmaster provided temporary support. In 1872, the measure was amended to prohibit criminals. The act required those soliciting business from immigrants to obtain a license. Boardinghouses were required to clearly post their rates. The measure also provided for government agents to assist immigrants in arranging lodging and making connections to their chosen destinations. This service eventually led to the establishment of reception centers in Halifax, Nova Scotia; Montreal and Quebec, Quebec; Kingston and Toronto, Ontario; and Winnipeg, Manitoba, where temporary lodging and meals could be found, along with advice regarding local labor opportunities and transportation. The government provided discount passage rates for domestic workers, who were in high demand. Benevolent societies such as the Women's National Immigration Society ensured that the protection of women was a priority, leading to 1892 amendments prohibiting seduction by ships' crew members. Special agents also were provided to assist women in port, and special railcars were designated for transportation to other parts of Canada.

Further Reading

Johnson, Stanley C. *A History of Emigration from the United Kingdom to North America, 1763–1912.* London: G. Routledge, 1913.

Kealey, Linda, ed. *A Not Unreasonable Claim: Women and Reform in Canada, 1880s–1920s.* Toronto: Women's Press, 1979.

Kelley, Ninette, and Michael Trebilcock. *The Making of the Mosaic: A History of Canadian Immigration Policy.* Toronto: University of Toronto Press, 1998.

Parr, Joy. *Labouring Children: British Immigrant Apprentices to Canada, 1869–1924.* Montreal: McGill–Queen's University Press, 1980.

Prentice, Alison, and Susan Trofimenkoff, eds. *The Neglected Majority: Essays in Canadian Women's History.* 2 vols. Toronto: McClelland and Stewart, 1985.

Immigration Act (Canada) (1906)

The capstone of Minister of the Interior Frank Oliver's immigration policy, the Immigration Act of 1906 consolidated all Canadian immigrant legislation, thus making it easier for "the Department of Immigration to deal with undesirable immigrants." The measure greatly expanded the number of exclusion categories, gave legislative weight to the process of deportation, and set the tone for the generally arbitrary expulsion of undesirable immigrants that characterized Canadian policy throughout much of the 20th century.

Among the excluded categories of immigrants were prostitutes and others convicted of crimes of "moral turpitude"; epileptics, the mentally challenged, and the insane; the hearing, sight, and speech impaired; and those with contagious diseases. The act also made the transportation companies responsible for the costs of deportation of both illegal immigrants and those who became public burdens within two years of arrival. The minister of the interior was given the authority to deny entry to anyone not arriving directly from the land of his or her birth or citizenship, a measure implemented by P.C. 27 in 1908 and used to effectively deny entry to Japanese and Chinese citizens who had first traveled to Hawaii. Most important, the 1906 Immigration Act established an arbitrary system in which a board of inquiry named by the minister of the interior passed judgment on admissibility, while all appeals were heard by the minister. The powers of the immigration service were also greatly enhanced by enabling it to pass any regulation "necessary or expedient" for attaining the measure's "true intent." Although Liberals and industrialists generally preferred a more open policy, the prevailing mood in the country was one of caution, seeking to avoid many of the urban problems associated with the relatively open immigration policies of the United States.

Further Reading

Johnson, Stanley C. *A History of Emigration from the United Kingdom to North America, 1763–1912.* London: G. Routledge, 1913.

Kealey, Linda, ed. *A Not Unreasonable Claim: Women and Reform in Canada, 1880s–1920s.* Toronto: Women's Press, 1979.

Kelley, Ninette, and Michael Trebilcock. *The Making of the Mosaic: A History of Canadian Immigration Policy.* Toronto: University of Toronto Press, 1998.

Parr, Joy. *Labouring Children: British Immigrant Apprentices to Canada, 1869–1924.* Montreal: McGill–Queen's University Press, 1980.

Immigration Act (Canada) (1910)

A number of orders-in-council and regulations pursuant to the 1906 IMMIGRATION ACT were further codified in the Immigration Act of 1910, which granted the cabinet wide discretionary power to regulate all areas of immigration. The measure expanded the prohibited immigrant categories of 1906 to include those who would advocate the use of "force or violence" to create public disorder, the "immoral," and charity cases who had not received clearance from either the superintendent of immigration in Ottawa or the assistant superintendent of emigration in London. This act also introduced the three-year residency requirement for establishing "domicile." Until domicile was established, an immigrant was subject to deportation if judged "undesirable." The duties of the boards of inquiry were expanded, and medical examinations were conducted on those coming by land, as well as sea. While the act did not single out particular racial or ethnic groups, Section 38 did allow the cabinet to restrict "immigrants belonging to any race deemed unsuited to the climate or requirements of Canada." This remained the ethnic basis for Canadian immigration policy until 1967. Orders-in-council later in the year demonstrated the wide power of the cabinet, establishing a $200 head tax on Asian immigrants (P.C. 926) and a $25 monetary requirement for entry (P.C. 924).

Further Reading

Johnson, Stanley C. *A History of Emigration from the United Kingdom to North America, 1763–1912.* London: G. Routledge, 1913.

Kealey, Linda, ed. *A Not Unreasonable Claim: Women and Reform in Canada, 1880s–1920s.* Toronto: Women's Press, 1979.

Kelley, Ninette, and Michael Trebilcock. *The Making of the Mosaic: A History of Canadian Immigration Policy.* Toronto: University of Toronto Press, 1998.

Parr, Joy. *Labouring Children: British Immigrant Apprentices to Canada, 1869–1924.* Montreal: McGill–Queen's University Press, 1980.

Immigration Act (Canada) (1919)

In the wake of World War I (1914–18; see WORLD WAR I AND IMMIGRATION) and the 1917 Bolshevik Revolution in Russia, and in the midst of an economic depression, the Canadian government amended its IMMIGRATION ACT of 1910 to protect against subversive activities and to limit the entry of those who might become involved in them. The revisions were supported by the business community, which had previously supported a more liberal policy. According to the president of the Canadian Manufacturers' Association, while Canada had millions of "vacant acres" that needed population, "it is wiser to go slowly and secure the right sort of citizens."

Under Section 3 of the new Immigration Act, an order-in-council excluded entry of emigrants from countries that had fought against Canada during the war. The list of inadmissible immigrants was also expanded to include alcoholics, those of "psychopathic inferiority," mental "defectives," illiterates, those guilty of espionage, and those who believed in the forcible overthrow of the government or who "disbelieved" in government at all. At the same time, revisions made it easier to deport immigrants. If it could be shown that an immigrant fell into an inadmissible class upon arrival in Canada, he or she was no longer safe from deportation after five years. Furthermore, the cabinet was authorized to prohibit entry to members of any race, class, or nationality because of contemporary economic conditions or because they were not likely to be assimilable because of "peculiar habits, modes of life and methods of holding property," a provision invoked against the entry of Hutterites (see HUTTERITE IMMIGRATION), Mennonites (see MENNONITE IMMIGRATION), and Doukhobors. Additionally, in 1921, adult immigrants were required to have $250 upon landing, and children, $125. Farm laborers and domestic workers with previous job arrangements were exempted from the landing fees. In 1923, immigration was restricted to agriculturalists, farm laborers, and domestic servants only.

Further Reading

Avery, Donald. *"Dangerous Foreigners": European Immigrant Workers and Labour Radicalism in Canada, 1896–1932.* Toronto: McClelland and Stewart, 1979.

Kelley, Ninette, and Michael Trebilcock. *The Making of the Mosaic: A History of Canadian Immigration Policy.* Toronto: University of Toronto Press, 1998.

Parr, Joy. *Labouring Children: British Immigrant Apprentices to Canada, 1869–1924.* Montreal: McGill–Queen's University Press, 1980.

Immigration Act (Canada) (1952)

The Immigration Act of 1952 was the first new immigration legislation since 1910. It was officially described as an act that "clarified and simplified" immigration procedures that had evolved across four decades, but it further established the cabinet's ample discretionary powers over immigration. It defined wide-ranging powers of the minister of citizenship and immigration and clearly established the principle that the governor-in-council could prohibit or limit immigration on the basis of a wide range of suitability issues, including race, ethnicity, citizenship, customs, health, and probable success of assimilation. The doctrine of "suitability," established in 1906 and 1910, remained the foundation of Canadian immigration policy throughout the 20th century. The Immigration Act went into effect on June 1, 1953, along with Order-in-Council P.C. 1953–859 ("Immigration Regulations").

The measure defined the rights of admission for Canadian citizens and those with Canadian "domicile." At the same time, it exhaustively listed prohibited classes, including criminals, subversives, "idiots," epileptics, beggars, the insane, the "ill," the physically "defective," and prostitutes. In addition to these categories, which had been part of the 1910 measure, homosexuals, drug addicts, and drug traffickers were added. There were no specific limits. British subjects from the United Kingdom, Australia, New Zealand, and South Africa and Irish, French, and U.S. citizens were allowed to immigrate under the measure so long as they could support themselves until finding employment. Asian immigration was limited to spouses or unmarried children under the age of 21 of Canadian citizens. The measure also provided a series of administrative prerogatives for ensuring control, including right of examination and conditions for arrest and deportation of those failing to meet standards. For immigrants who did qualify for admission, the Immigration Act offered some support. It made exploitation of immigrants a criminal offense and provided interest-free travel loans to immigrants deemed necessary for Canadian economic development.

The major weaknesses of the measure revolved around the almost unlimited discretionary power granted to the minister of citizenship and immigration. According to Section 39, no court or judge was allowed to "review, quash, reverse, restrain or otherwise interfere with any proceeding, decision or order of the Minister, Deputy Minister, Director, Immigration Appeal Board, Special Inquiry Officer or immigration officer" in reference to detentions or deportations unless the person enjoyed Canadian citizenship or domicile. With every case potentially under review by the minister, the bureaucracy was overworked. And as the language of the measure was essentially negative and favored exclusion, there was a presumption that immigration officers would not offer fair hearings. The measure was especially hard on immigrants from newly independent India, Ceylon, and Pakistan. As disappointed applicants applied to members of Parliament and lawyers for assistance, the legal weaknesses in the measure became apparent.

Following the Supreme Court's decision in *Attorney General of Canada v. Brent* (1956), the government was required to pass new regulations reducing discretionary powers of admission and establishing categories of preferred status. Privy Council order 1956–785 (1956) divided admissible immigrants into four categories:

1. British subjects born or naturalized in the United Kingdom, Australia, New Zealand, or South Africa; citizens of Ireland, the United States, or those born or naturalized in France or the islands of Saint-Pierre and Miquelon, providing they could support themselves while finding employment
2. citizens of Austria, Belgium, Denmark, West Germany, Finland, Greece, Iceland, Italy, Luxembourg, the Netherlands, Norway, Portugal, Spain, Sweden, or Switzerland, who found employment under the direction of the Department of Citizenship and Immigration, or who could establish themselves in business
3. citizens of any country of Europe or the Western Hemisphere, or of Egypt, Israel, Lebanon, or Turkey, whose relatives were both legal residents and willing to sponsor the proposed immigrant
4. citizens of any other country who were spouses of Canadian citizens or unmarried children under the age of 21

By 1962, most elements of racial and ethnic discrimination had been eliminated, replaced with standards emphasizing skills, education, and training. Rather than produce a completely new measure, however, political complications led the Canadian government to amend the regulations. The amendments of 1967, creating a new Immigration Appeal Board, addressed the most glaring weakness of the measure but were considered inadequate by most critics. In 1973, the Department of Manpower and Immigration, formed in 1966, began a review of Canadian immigration policy, but an inadequate green paper led to nationwide public hearings on the matter under a special joint committee of the Senate and the House of Commons during 1975. The findings of the committee led directly to the IMMIGRATION ACT of 1976.

Further Reading

Corbett, David C. *Canada's Immigration Policy: A Critique.* Toronto: University of Toronto Press, 1957.
Hawkins, Freda. *Canada and Immigration: Public Policy and Public Concern.* 2d ed. Kingston and Montreal: McGill–Queen's University Press, 1988.
Kelley, Ninette, and Michael Trebilcock. *The Making of the Mosaic: A History of Canadian Immigration Policy.* Toronto: University of Toronto Press, 1998.

Immigration Act (Canada) (1976)

The Immigration Act of 1976 marked a significant shift in Canadian immigration policy in limiting the wide discretionary powers of the minister of manpower and immigration. One of its major provision, in Section 7, required the minister to consult with the provinces regarding demographic factors and levels of immigration. Although the act coordinated the policies established in the 1952 Immigration Act and the various regulations subsequently passed, for the first time it expressly stated the goals of Canadian immigration policy, including family reunion, humanitarian concern for refugees, and targeted economic development. The measure, along with its attending regulations, nevertheless continued to promote a "Canadians first" policy and was designed to "support the attainment of such demographic goals as may be established by the government of Canada from time to time in respect of the size, rate of growth, structure and geographic distribution of the Canadian population." The act took effect on April 10, 1978. It was amended more than 30 times, including major revisions in 1985 and 1992, before being replaced in 2002 with the IMMIGRATION AND REFUGEE PROTECTION ACT.

In 1973, the Department of Manpower and Immigration began a review of Canadian immigration policy, but an inadequate green paper led to nationwide public hearings on the matter under a special joint committee of the Senate and the House of Commons during 1975. The findings of the committee led directly to the Immigration Act of 1976. The new measure established three categories of immigrant: family class, independent class, and humanitarian class. Priority was given to family class immigrants. Independent immigrants, usually the most prosperous, applied on their own initiative and competed in a points system that suggested their ability to fill an economic need in Canada and to be successful. Within the independent class, skilled workers qualified under a nine-factor points system that assigned numerical values to education (16 points), vocational preparation (18 points), occupation demand (10 points), experience (8 points), arranged employment (10 points), demography (10 points), age (10 points), language (15 points), and personal suitability (10 points). A minimum of 70 points were required to qualify. Entrepreneurs were required to demonstrate that their ownership of a business would provide support for a minimum of six Canadians, exclusive of the entrepreneur's family, and that they had a personal net worth of at least $300,000 and managerial experience. Investors were required to have a personal net worth of at least $500,000 and agree to invest a minimum of $250,000 in a Canadian company for a minimum of five years. Family-class immigrants, on the other hand, were exempt from the points requirements. Any Canadian citizen over 18 years of age could sponsor parents, grandparents over the age of 60, spouses or fiances, and unmarried children under 21, by guaranteeing 10 years of consecutive support. A subcategory in the family class was the assisted relative, requiring five years of support and subject to certain job-related and language qualifications. Finally, refugees were provided for as a part of the humanitarian obligation of the country, as defined by the 1951 United Nations Convention. The cabinet was given considerable latitude in easing entrance requirements for refugees, including the creation of categories of "displaced and persecuted" peoples who would not be required to meet normal entrance requirements for refugees.

See also BILL C-55; CANADA—IMMIGRATION SURVEY AND POLICY OVERVIEW.

Further Reading

Dirks, Gerald E. *Controversy and Complexity: Canadian Immigration Policy during the 1980s.* Montreal: McGill–Queen's University Press, 1995.

Hawkins, Freda. *Canada and Immigration: Public Policy and Public Concern.* 2d. ed. Kingston and Montreal: McGill–Queen's University Press, 1988.

———. *Critical Years in Immigration: Canada and Australia Compared.* Montreal: McGill–Queen's University Press, 1989.

Kelley, Ninette, and Michael Trebilcock. *The Making of the Mosaic: A History of Canadian Immigration Policy.* Toronto: University of Toronto Press, 1998.

Plaut, W. G. *Refugee Status Determination in Canada: Proposals for a New System.* Hull, Canada: Canada Employment and Immigration Commission, 1985.

Immigration Act (United States) (1864)

The 1864 Immigration Act was designed to increase the flow of laborers to the United States during the disruptions of the Civil War (1861–65). In his message to Congress in December 1863, President Abraham Lincoln urged "the expediency of a system for the encouragement of immigration," noting "the great deficiency of laborers in every field of industry, especially in agriculture and our mines." After much debate, Congress enacted legislation on July 4, 1864, providing for appointment by the president of a commissioner of immigration, operating under the authority of the secretary of state, and immigrant labor contracts, up to a maximum of one year, pledging wages against the cost of transportation to America.

Further Reading

Hutchinson, E. P. *Legislative History of American Immigration Policy, 1798–1965.* Philadelphia: University of Pennsylvania Press, 1981.

LeMay, Michael C. *From Open Door to Dutch Door: An Analysis of U.S. Immigration Policy since 1820.* New York: Praeger, 1987.

Immigration Act (United States) (1875)   See PAGE ACT.

Immigration Act (United States) (1882)

Responding to dozens of petitions from states worried about the maintenance of indigent immigrants, Congress expanded the exclusion precedent set in the PAGE ACT of 1875.

With more than a dozen petitions filed from New York, the principal state of disembarkation of immigrants, New York congressmen in both houses proposed legislation for further regulating immigration. Concerned both for the care of recently arrived immigrants and the large financial burden that states were bearing, Congress enacted the Immigration Act on August 3, 1882. The measure provided for the levying of a head tax of 50¢ per immigrant to be used to create a Treasury-administered fund for the care of immigrants upon arrival, though two years later (June 16, 1884),

This *Harper's Weekly* headline reads "Horrors of the Emigrant Ship—Scene in the hold of the 'James Foster,' Jun. [1869]." In December 1863, President Abraham Lincoln encouraged Congress to pass legislation enabling potential immigrant laborers to pledge future wages against their cost of transportation to the United States. By the 1860s, sea transportation had improved considerably from the famine-ship era of the 1840s and 1850s. Few people died, but conditions were barely tolerable for those who could not afford special accommodations. *(Library of Congress, Prints Photographs Division [LC-USZ62-105130])*

immigrants "coming by vessels employed exclusively in the trade between the ports of the Dominion of Canada or the ports of Mexico" were exempted. The 1882 act also expanded on the Page Act exclusions of convicts and women "imported for the purposes of prostitution" to prohibit the immigration of any "lunatic, idiot, or any person unable to take care of himself or herself without becoming a public charge." Exclusions were further expanded by an 1884 act.

Further Reading

Hutchinson, E. P. *Legislative History of American Immigration Policy, 1798–1965.* Philadelphia: University of Pennsylvania Press, 1981.

LeMay, Michael C. *From Open Door to Dutch Door: An Analysis of U.S. Immigration Policy since 1820.* New York: Praeger, 1987.

Immigration Act (United States) (1903)

In the wake of the assassination of President William McKinley by anarchist Leon Czolgosz in 1901, Congress began a thorough review of American immigration policy.

The Immigration Act provided a codification and extension of previously enacted immigration policy and included one of the few restrictions based on political beliefs.

In his first annual message following McKinley's assassination, in December 1901, President Theodore Roosevelt called for a thorough review of America's immigration policy. "We need," he argued, "every honest and efficient immigrant fitted to become an American citizen." Roosevelt unequivocally denounced anarchists, however, and urged Congress to "exclude absolutely . . . all persons who are known to be believers in anarchist principles." Two days after Roosevelt's message, the Industrial Commission presented its findings to Congress, including a draft bill and 18 recommendations for the codification of immigrant policy. The bill was debated for 14 months, with considerable disagreement over the use of literacy tests and the proper level of the head tax. Finally enacted on March 3, 1903, the measure

1. Reaffirmed all immigration and contract labor laws made after 1875

2. Expanded excludable classes of immigrants to include anarchists, prostitutes, epileptics, those who had "been insane within five years," and those who had ever had two or more "attacks of insanity"
3. Provided for deportation within two years of arrival of "any alien who becomes a public charge by reason of lunacy, idiocy, or epilepsy," unless he or she could clearly demonstrate that the condition had begun after arrival
4. Levied a head tax of $2 per immigrant

In 1907 excludable groups were expanded to include "imbeciles, feeble-minded [persons], and persons with physical or mental defects which might affect their ability to earn a living."

Further Reading

Hutchinson, E. P. *Legislative History of American Immigration Policy, 1798–1965.* Philadelphia: University of Pennsylvania Press, 1981.
LeMay, Michael C. *From Open Door to Dutch Door: An Analysis of U.S. Immigration Policy since 1820.* New York: Praeger, 1987.

Immigration Act (United States) (1907)

Both the general increase in the number of immigrants and the assassination of President William McKinley in 1901 fueled a growing NATIVISM in the United States and in Congress during the first decade of the 20th century. The Immigration Act of February 20, 1907, consolidated earlier legislation and raised the head tax to $4 per immigrant, excepting aliens from Canada, Newfoundland, Cuba, and Mexico. Most notable was its creation of a commission (DILLINGHAM COMMISSION) consisting of three senators, three representatives, and three presidential appointees to review U.S. immigration policy.

Further Reading

Hutchinson, E. P. *Legislative History of American Immigration Policy, 1798–1965.* Philadelphia: University of Pennsylvania Press, 1981.
LeMay, Michael C. *From Open Door to Dutch Door: An Analysis of U.S. Immigration Policy since 1820.* New York: Praeger, 1987.

Immigration Act (Literacy Act) (United States) (1917)

The Immigration Act of 1917, popularly known as the Literacy Act, marked a turning point in American immigration legislation. Prohibiting entry to aliens over 16 years of age who could not read 30–40 words in their own language, it was the first legislation aimed at restricting, rather than regulating, European immigration. It further extended the tendency toward a "white" immigration policy, creating an "Asiatic barred zone" that prohibited entry of most Asians.

The CHINESE EXCLUSION ACT of 1882 was seen by most policy makers as an exceptional case, but attitudes gradually shifted with the influx of poorly educated southern and eastern Europeans who arrived in the hundreds of thousands in the 1880s. The idea of imposing a literacy test to restrict the tide of "undesirable" Europeans was first widely proposed by progressive economist Edward W. Bemis in 1887. It found relatively little political support until the cause was taken up by the IMMIGRATION RESTRICTION LEAGUE, founded and supported by members of a number of prominent Boston families. Measures incorporating a literacy test came near success in 1895, 1903, 1912, and 1915, only to be vetoed by Presidents Grover Cleveland, Howard Taft, and Woodrow Wilson. With the United States moving ever closer to joining the war in Europe, however, hostility increased toward Germany, Ireland, and Austria-Hungary, leading to increasing support for policies supporting "one hundred percent Americanism." Representative John L. Burnett of Alabama, a Democrat, revived his bill first introduced in 1913 and vetoed by Wilson in 1915. During debate, Senator William Paul Dillingham of Vermont, a Republican and chairman of the earlier DILLINGHAM COMMISSION on immigration reform, spoke in favor of the literacy test as more practical than a percentage plan as a means of limiting immigration. Wilson vetoed the bill but was overridden by both the House (287 to 106) and the Senate (62 to 19), and the Immigration Act was formally passed on February 5, 1917.

The main provisions of the act were heavily restrictive:

1. The head tax on immigrants was raised from $4 to $8
2. The list of excludable aliens was consolidated and broadened to include an Asiatic barred zone keeping out all Asians except Japanese and Filipinos
3. Exclusion of any alien 16 or older who, if physically capable of reading, was unable to read 30–40 words "in ordinary use, printed in plainly legible type in some one of the various languages or dialects" of the immigrant's choice

The measure was less restrictive than some had hoped but was clear evidence of a rising nativist (see NATIVISM) sentiment and continued to reduce the number of immigrants, which had already declined dramatically since the outbreak of World War I in 1914.

Further Reading

Daniels, Roger. *Guarding the Golden Door: American Immigration Policy and Immigrants since 1882.* New York: Hill and Wang, 2004.
Hutchinson, E. P. *Legislative History of American Immigration Policy, 1798–1965.* Philadelphia: University of Pennsylvania Press, 1981.
LeMay, Michael C. *From Open Door to Dutch Door: An Analysis of U.S. Immigration Policy since 1820.* New York: Praeger, 1987.

Immigration Act (United States) (1924)

See JOHNSON-REED ACT.

Immigration Act (United States) (1980)

See REFUGEE ACT.

Immigration Act (United States) (1990)

The Immigration Act of 1990 was the first major revision of U.S. immigration policy since the IMMIGRATION AND NATIONALITY ACT (1965), which had been passed in the midst of the COLD WAR. The act maintained the national commitment to reunifying families, enhanced opportunities for business-related immigration, and made provision for underrepresented nationalities. It also raised the annual cap on immigration from 270,000 to 675,000 (700,000 for the first three years).

The 1990 Immigration Act divided the immigration preference classes into two broad categories—family sponsorship and employment related—and provided for annual review of the number limits in each category. Those who wished to restrict immigration favored the measure because it established an annual cap on family-based immigration. Those opposed to restriction supported the measure for its guaranteed base of preference visas and for the raising of per-country visas annually from 20,000 to 25,600, which promised some relief for the backlog of applications from Mexico and the Dominican Republic, among other countries. The measure also provided for an 18-month "Temporary Protected Status" for Salvadorans who had fled political violence in their country during the 1980s. In fact, the measure's caps were easily pierced, because refugees, asylees, IMMIGRATION REFORM AND CONTROL ACT legalizations, and Amerasians fell outside its provisions. Between fiscal years 1992 and 1998, average annual immigration under the act was just over 825,000.

Family-sponsored preferences ranged between 421,000 and 675,000 annually, depending on previous admissions. The formula limited worldwide family sponsorships to "480,000 minus the number of aliens who were issued visas or adjusted to legal permanent residence in the previous fiscal year as 1) immediate relatives of U.S. citizens, 2) children born subsequent to the issuance of a visa to an accompanying parent, 3) children born abroad to lawful permanent residents on temporary trips abroad, and 4) certain categories of aliens paroled into the United States in the second preceding fiscal year, plus unused employment preferences in the previous fiscal year." The measure also established a minimum of 226,000 family visas per year. First preference for admission was given to unmarried sons and daughters of U.S. citizens and their children; second preference to spouses, children, and unmarried sons and daughters of permanent resident aliens; third preference to married sons and daughters of U.S. citizens; fourth preference to brothers and sisters of U.S. citizens (at least 21 years of age).

The employment-based preference limit was set at 140,000 plus unused family preferences from the previous year. Immigrant applications were ranked according to the following preferences: 1) priority workers; 2) professionals with advanced degrees or exceptional abilities; 3) skilled workers, professionals, or unskilled workers in high demand; 4) special immigrants; and 5) investors. Per country limits were set at 7 percent of total family and employment limits.

Finally, the Immigration Act provided for 55,000 annual "diversity immigrants," (40,000 during the first three years). Countries sending 50,000 immigrants during the previous five years were ineligible to participate in the diversity program. All eligible countries were divided into six regions, and per country limits determined by a formula including admissions during the previous five years and the total population of the region. The annual maximum for each country under the diversity program was 3,850.

Further Reading

Barkan, Elliott Robert. *And Still They Come: Immigrants and American Society, 1920 to the 1990s.* Wheeling, Ill.: Harlan Davidson, 1996.

Law, Anna O. "The Diversity Visa Lottery—a Cycle of Unintended Consequences in United States Immigration Policy." *Journal of American Ethnic History* 21 (Summer 2002): 1–29.

Legal Immigration, Fiscal Year 2000. Office of Policy and Planning Annual Report, No. 6. Washington, D.C.: U.S. Department of Justice, 2002.

Rubin, Gary E., and Judith Golub. "The Immigration Act of 1990: An American Jewish Committee Analysis." New York: American Jewish Committee Institute of Human Relations, 1990.

Immigration and Customs Enforcement (ICE)

U.S. Immigration and Customs Enforcement (ICE) is the investigative arm of the Border and Transportation Security Directorate (BTS), and it operates under the jurisdiction of the DEPARTMENT OF HOMELAND SECURITY (DHS). The main task of ICE is to secure the nation's borders and safeguard its transportation infrastructure. It employs more than 20,000 men and women to enforce laws affecting border security and investigate homeland security crimes. There are six operational divisions within ICE, including Air and Marine Operations, responsible for deterring smuggling and terrorist activity; Detention and Removal Operations, responsible for removing deportable aliens through enforcement of the nation's immigration laws, Federal Air Marshal Service, responsible deployment of air marshals to detect, deter, and defeat hostile acts that target airlines; Federal Protective Service, responsible for maintaining safety at federal government facilities; Office of Investigations, responsible for investigating violations of immigration and custom laws that might threaten national security; and the Office of Intelligence, responsible for the collection, analysis, and dissemination of data for use by ICE, BTS, and DHS.

The ICE was created as a result of the Homeland Security Act (2002), which dissolved the IMMIGRATION AND NATURALIZATION SERVICE (Department of Justice), the U.S. Customs Service (Department of the Treasury), and the Agricultural Quarantine and Inspection program (Department of Agriculture) and transferred security-related functions to the newly created DHS as of March 1, 2003.

Further Reading

Butikofer, Nathan R. *United States Land Border Security Policy: The National Security Implications of 9/11 on the "Nation of Immigrants" and Free Trade in North America.* Monterey, Calif.: Naval Postgraduate School, 2003.

Gressle, Sharon S. *Homeland Security Act of 2002: Legislative History and Propagation.* Washington, D.C.: Congressional Research Service, 2002.

Haynes, Wendy. "Seeing Around Corners: Crafting the New Department of Homeland Security." *Review of Policy Research* 21, no. 3 (2004): 369–395.

U.S. Immigration and Customs Enforcement Web site. Available online. URL: http://www.ice.gov/graphics. Accessed July 5, 2004.

Immigration and Nationality Act (United States) (1952)   See MCCARRAN-WALTER ACT.

Immigration and Nationality Act (INA) (United States) (1965)

The Immigration and Nationality Act (INA) of 1965 marked a dramatic change in American immigration policy, abandoning the concept of national quotas and establishing the basis for extensive immigration from the developing world. Technically, the various parts of the measure were amendments to the MCCARRAN-WALTER ACT of 1952.

The provisions of the McCarran-Walter Act allotted 85 percent of immigrant visas to countries from northern and Western Europe. With President John F. Kennedy's election in fall 1960, government immigration policy began to change. Kennedy believed that immigrants were valuable to the country, and members of his administration argued that both the COLD WAR and the Civil Rights movement dictated a more open policy toward nonwhite immigrants. Furthermore, the McCarran-Walter Act had not proven to be as comprehensive as it had originally been intended, for it failed to deal directly with Refugees (see REFUGEE STATUS), which had led to passage of the REFUGEE RELIEF ACT (1953), specifically granting asylum in the United States to those fleeing communist persecution. Before his assassination in 1963, Kennedy recommended that the

quota system be phased out over a five-year period, that no country receive more than 10 percent of newly authorized allotments, that family reunification remain a priority, that the Asiatic Barred Zone be eliminated, and that residents of Jamaica and Trinidad and Tobago be granted nonquota status. After the landslide victory of President Lyndon B. Johnson in 1964, his administration was in a position to remedy the "unworkability of the national origins quota system."

The major provisions of the Immigration and Nationality Act included

1. Replacing national origins quotas with hemispheric caps of 170,000 from the Eastern Hemisphere and 120,000 from the Western Hemisphere
2. Establishing a new scale of preferences, including 1) unmarried adult children of U.S. citizens (20 percent); 2) spouses and unmarried adult children of permanent resident aliens (20 percent); 3) professionals, scientists, and artists of exceptional talent (10 percent); 4) married children of U.S. citizens (10 percent); 5) U.S. citizens' siblings who were more than 21 years of age (24 percent); 6) skilled and unskilled workers in areas where labor was needed (10 percent); and 7) those who "because of persecution or fear of persecution . . . have fled from any Communist or Communist-dominated country or area, or from any country within the general area of the Middle East" (6 percent). Unlike the provisions of previous special legislation, these 10,200 visas were allotted annually to deal with refugee situations without further legislation

Although the new legislation was designed to diversify immigration, it did so in unexpected ways. Many of the Eastern Hemisphere slots expected to go to Europeans were filled by Asians, who tended to fill higher preference categories. Having become permanent residents and eventually citizens, a wide range of family members then became eligible for immigration in high-preference categories. The INA was successful in bringing highly skilled professional and medical people to the United States. Within 10 years, for instance, immigrants constituted 20 percent of the nation's total number of physicians. At the same time, the INA was not effective in limiting the overall number of immigrants. Exemptions and refugees made overall immigration numbers larger than those permitted under the act.

Further Reading

Glazer, Nathan, ed. *Clamor at the Gates: The New American Immigration.* San Francisco: ICS Press, 1985.

Hutchinson, E. P. *Legislative History of American Immigration Policy, 1798–1965.* Philadelphia: University of Pennsylvania Press, 1981.

LeMay, Michael C. *From Open Door to Dutch Door: An Analysis of U.S. Immigration Policy since 1820.* New York: Praeger, 1987.

Reimers, David. *Still the Golden Door: The Third World Comes to America.* 2d ed. New York: Columbia University Press, 1992.

Immigration and Naturalization Service (INS)

From 1933 to 2003, the Immigration and Naturalization Service (INS) was the agency of the U.S. Department of Justice responsible for enforcing immigration laws, administering immigration benefits, and, in conjunction with the Department of State, admitting and resettling refugees. The INS commissioner served under the attorney general, and in the last year of INS operation, oversaw the work of approximately 29,000 employees, who served in 33 districts and 21 BORDER PATROL sectors along 6,000 miles of border with Canada and Mexico.

The first commissioner of immigration was appointed by President Abraham Lincoln under a bill enacted by Congress (July 4, 1864) with the express purpose of "encouraging" immigration by collecting information about the United States and disseminating it throughout Europe. The measure authorized immigrants to sign labor contracts pledging up to one year of wages against transportation costs and provided for the establishment of an emigrant office in NEW YORK, NEW YORK. Four years later, the act was repealed, leaving authority over immigration matters to the states until the Immigration Act of 1891 provided clear federal control under the newly appointed Bureau of Immigration (BI). The bureau established 24 inspection stations, including one at ELLIS ISLAND. In 1903, the BI was transferred from the Department of the Treasury to the newly established Department of Commerce and Labor. The Naturalization Act (1906) briefly extended that function to the BI (1906–13). In a 1933 executive order, immigration and naturalization oversight were combined under the INS. In 1940, the INS was shifted from the Department of Labor to the Department of Justice.

During the 1990s, enforcement programs took an increasingly larger portion of the INS budget. In 2001, 1.2 million people attempting to enter the United States illegally were caught and turned back to either Mexico or Canada. Greater vigilance came at a cost, however. Between 1993 and 2001, spending on enforcement programs grew more than six times as fast as spending on other immigrant programs and services, and the total budget ballooned from $1.52 billion to more than $5 billion. The ILLEGAL IMMIGRATION REFORM AND IMMIGRANT RESPONSIBILITY ACT (1996) gave the INS enhanced powers of removal and deportation, but the agency was widely criticized the following year for lax immigrant screening procedures. An independent audit showed that 18 percent of approximately 1 million immigrants between August 1995 and September 1996 were admitted before criminal checks were completed, and 71,000 were allowed to become citizens despite having criminal records. In August 1997, a federal advisory panel recommended abolition of the INS, with duties to be delegated to other agencies, but no action was taken on the recommendation. The terrorist attacks of SEPTEMBER 11, 2001, led by several hijackers who were in the United States illegally, invited further criticism of the INS, provoking a national debate on the effectiveness of the agency. Congressional hearings on restructuring the INS were held in late 2001 as part of the larger national security debate. President George W. Bush signed the resulting Homeland Security Act on November 25, 2002. The act abolished the INS as of March 1, 2003, transferring its functions to various agencies within the newly created DEPARTMENT OF HOMELAND SECURITY. Immigration services formerly provided by the INS were transferred to the U.S. CITIZENSHIP AND IMMIGRATION SERVICES; enforcement oversight, to the Border Transportation Security Directorate; border control, to the U.S. CUSTOMS AND BORDER PROTECTION; and interior enforcement, to the U.S. IMMIGRATION AND CUSTOMS ENFORCEMENT.

Further Reading

Daniels, Roger. *Guarding the Golden Door: American Immigration Policy and Immigrants since 1882.* New York: Hill and Wang, 2004.

Hutchinson, E. P. *Legislative History of American Immigration Policy, 1798–1965.* Philadelphia: University of Pennsylvania Press, 1981.

Kurian, George T., ed. *A Historical Guide to the U.S. Government.* New York: Oxford University Press, 1998.

LeMay, Michael C. *From Open Door to Dutch Door: An Analysis of U.S. Immigration Policy since 1820.* New York: Praeger, 1987.

Immigration and Naturalization Service v. Chadha (1983)

With its decision in *Immigration and Naturalization Service v. Chadha,* the U.S. Supreme Court invalidated the legislative veto that had enabled the U.S. Congress, in negotiation with the executive branch, to veto certain executive actions. The Court ruled that such agreements violated the doctrine of separation of powers. More specifically, it determined that one house of Congress did not have the constitutional power to veto an IMMIGRATION AND NATURALIZATION SERVICE (INS) decision to allow a foreign student to remain in the United States after his or her visa had expired.

The case revolved around the fate of Jagdish Chadha, born in Kenya of Indian parents and holding a British passport, who had come to the United States as a student in 1966. In 1973, he was required to "show cause why he should not be deported," his nonimmigrant student visa having expired the previous year. At the deportation hearing that resumed in February 1974, Chadha argued that he "had resided continuously in the United States for over seven years, was of good moral character, and would suffer 'extreme hardship' if deported." Neither Kenya, which had become independent of British colonial rule in 1963, nor Great Britain was willing to allow his return. Although the INS judge ruled in Chadha's favor and approved, through the office of the U.S. Attorney General, his application for permanent residency, the House of Representatives vetoed the approval in December 1975 and the following year ordered his deportation. Department of Justice attorneys in the administrations of both Presidents Jimmy Carter (1977–81) and Ronald Reagan (1981–89) joined the INS in arguing against the constitutionality of the legislative veto. The Court held that legislative vetoes represented a subversion of the "single, finely wrought and exhaustively considered procedure" for enacting legislation. Far more than a legal case over immigrant rights and privileges, *Immigration and Naturalization Service v. Chadha* represented an important moment in defining the extent of executive and legislative power in the U.S. political system.

Further Reading

Craig, Barbara Hinkson. *Chadha: The Story of an Epic Constitutional Struggle.* New York: Oxford University Press, 1988.

Fisher, Louis. "Judicial Misjudgments about the Lawmaking Process: The Legislative Veto Case." *Public Administration Review,* Special Issue (November 1985): 705–711.

Immigration and Refugee Protection Act (IRPA) (Canada) (2002)

After many years of heated debate and the shock of the SEPTEMBER 11, 2001, terrorist attacks, in 2002 the Canadian parliament passed the Immigration and Refugee Protection Act (IRPA), replacing the IMMIGRATION ACT of 1976. The measure had two general purposes: to redefine the criteria by which immigrants would be admitted and to provide the government with specific tools for denying entry to potential terrorists or deporting them once they were discovered.

The IRPA established three basic categories (family class, economic class, refugee class) to correspond with its objectives of reuniting families, contributing to economic development, and protecting refugees. Under reunification provisions, a Canadian citizen or permanent resident can sponsor a spouse, common-law or conjugal partner; a dependent child, including a child adopted abroad; a child under 18 to be adopted in Canada; parents or grandparents; or an orphaned child under 18 who is a brother, sister, niece, nephew, or grandchild and is not a spouse or common-law partner. Two classes were established for economic immigrants: skilled workers and business immigrants. To be considered a skilled worker, potential immigrants had to qualify according to a points system evaluating language, education, and other integrative factors; must have "at least one year of

work experience within the past 10 years in a management occupation or in an occupation normally requiring university, college or technical training as described in the National Occupational Classification (NOC) developed by Human Resources Development Canada (HRDC)," and "have enough money to support themselves and their family members in Canada." Business immigrants were chosen "to support the development of a strong and prosperous Canadian economy, either through their direct investment, their entrepreneurial activity or self-employment." Investors were required to have a net worth of at least $800,000, and entrepreneurs of $300,000, along with certain levels of business experience. Self-employed applicants were required to demonstrate their ability to contribute at a "world-class level" to Canada's cultural life or athletics, or through the "purchase and management of a farm in Canada." The measure also provided guidelines for admitting 20,000–30,000 refugees or displaced persons annually.

The measure explicitly acknowledged the "shared responsibility" of the federal government and provinces in formulating immigration policy and established a mechanism for the development and publication of federal-provincial agreements regarding the number, distribution, and settlement of permanent residents. Under these provisions, the Canada Quebec Accord gave Quebec sole selective powers for skilled applicants and business-class immigrants and full responsibility for integration services, while stipulating that the federal government remained responsible for defining immigration categories, determining inadmissibility, and enforcement. As a result of frequent abuses of the 1976 system, the new act required careful monitoring of the immigrant flow; an annual report projecting the number of foreign nationals who might become permanent residents in the following year, the number of permanent residents in each class in provinces that have responsibility for selection under a federal-provincial agreement, the linguistic profile of new permanent residents, and the number of people granted permanent residence on humanitarian grounds; and a gender-based analysis of the immigration program. The act also established the Immigration and Refugee Board (IRB) as an independent, quasi-judicial administrative tribunal with a mandate "to make well-reasoned decisions on immigration and refugee matters efficiently, fairly and in accordance with the law."

The second major purpose of the Immigration and Refugee Protection Act was to protect Canada against potentially hostile immigrants. The act provided that after enactment of the measure on June 28, 2002, all new permanent residents would receive permanent resident cards, which they could apply for after October 15, 2002, and that effective January 2004, the cards would be required for reentry of permanent residents who had traveled outside Canada. The act also provided for the removal of anyone involved in "organized crime, espionage, acts of subversion, terrorism, war crimes, human or international rights violations, criminality and serious criminality." In addition, the measure made it easier for immigration officials to detain people on "reasonable suspicion" of failing to appear for possible deportation proceedings, of posing a risk to the public, or of refusing to give information to the immigration service.

Further Reading

Hillmer, Norman, and Maureen Appel Molot, eds. *Canada among Nations, 2002: A Fading Power.* New York: Oxford University Press, 2003.

"Immigration and Refugee Protection Act. The Act and Regulations: Key Reference Material." Citizenship and Immigration Canada. Available online. URL: http://www.cic.gc.ca/english/irpa/key-ref.html. Accessed January 16, 2004.

"Immigration and Refugee Protection Regulations." Part I. *Canada Gazette* 135, no. 50 (December 15, 2001): 4,476–4,800.

"Immigration and Refugee Protection Regulations." Part I. *Canada Gazette* 136, no. 10 (March 9, 2002): 558–621.

Marrocco, Frank N., and Henry M. Goslett. *2004 Annotated Immigration Act of Canada.* Toronto: Thomson Carswell, 2003.

Immigration Appeal Board Act (Canada)
(1967)

Following a broad government reorganization of the immigration bureaucracy in Canada, the Immigration Appeal Board Act was passed, creating the Immigration Appeal Board. It provided the first independent review process of all official decisions regarding deportation and family-sponsored application denials, guaranteeing immigrants due process protections.

Following the Liberal Party's return to power in 1963, a full review of immigration procedures was undertaken, leading to a massive reorganization of governmental agencies and policies, including the Government Organization Act (1966), the IMMIGRATION REGULATIONS of 1967, and the Immigration and Appeal Board Act. After another Liberal-sponsored study, in 1966, the DEPARTMENT OF MANPOWER AND IMMIGRATION issued a white paper recommending greater emphasis on economic need and less on family sponsorship. With the combination of greater selectivity, the right to apply for landed immigrant status while in the country, and guaranteed review of deportation cases, the backlog of cases before the board grew dramatically. By 1973, Minister of Manpower and Immigration Robert Andras reported that "many persons who appealed a deportation order could count on a 20-year stay in Canada while awaiting the outcome." In order to solve the problem, an amendment to the act was passed in 1973, abolishing the automatic right of appeal while providing amnesty for those who registered within 60 days. The revisions were supported across the political spectrum and led to 39,000 immigrants from more than 150 countries being granted landed immigrant status.

Further Reading

Hawkins, Freda. *Canada and Immigration.* 2d ed. Kingston and Montreal: McGill–Queen's University Press, 1989.

———. *Critical Years in Immigration: Canada and Australia Compared.* Kingston and Montreal: McGill–Queen's University Press, 1989.

Kelley, Ninette, and Michael Trebilcock. *The Making of the Mosaic: A History of Canadian Immigration Policy.* Toronto: University of Toronto Press, 2000.

Immigration Marriage Fraud Amendments
(United States) (1986, 1990)

Amending the MCCARRAN-WALTER IMMIGRATION AND NATURALIZATION ACT (1952), the Immigration Marriage Fraud Amendments of 1986 specified a two-year residency requirement for alien spouses and children before obtaining permanent resident status. By provisions of the amendment, a couple is required to apply for permanent status within 90 days of the end of the conditional two-year period. The Immigration and Naturalization Service (INS) could then interview the couple in order to satisfy themselves that 1) the marriage was not arranged "for the purpose of procuring an alien's entry as an immigrant, 2) the marriage was still legally valid, and 3) a fee was not paid for the filing of the alien's petition. Punitively, the amendment made such marriage fraud punishable by up to five years in prison and $250,000 in fines, further grounds for deportation, and a permanent bar to future applications. The amendment also required that aliens contracting marriages after the beginning of deportation proceedings live two years outside the United States before becoming eligible for permanent resident status. A related amendment of 1990 allowed for exemptions in the case of wife or child battering, or if clear evidence could be presented to show that the marriage was contracted in good faith and not for the purpose of gaining residency.

See also PICTURE BRIDES.

Further Reading

Cordasco, Francesco. *The New American Immigration.* New York: Garland, 1987.

LeMay, Michael C. *Anatomy of a Public Policy: The Reform of Contemporary American Immigration Law.* Westport, Conn.: Praeger, 1994.

Reimers, David. *Still the Golden Door: The Third World Comes to America.* 2d ed. New York: Columbia University Press, 1992.

Immigration Reform and Control Act
(IRCA) (United States) (1986)

In the wake of massive refugee crises in Southeast Asia and Cuba (see REFUGEE STATUS), in 1981, a Select Commission on Immigration and Refugee Policy recommended to the U.S. Congress that undocumented aliens be granted amnesty and that sanctions be imposed on employers who hired undocumented workers. After years of heated debate involving ethnic and religious groups, labor and agricultural organizations, business interests, and the government, a compromise measure was reached. The Immigration Reform and Control Act (IRCA) provided amnesty to undocumented aliens continuously resident in the United States, except for "brief, casual, and innocent" absences, from the beginning of 1982; provided amnesty to seasonal agricultural workers employed at least 90 days during the year preceding May 1986; required all amnesty applicants to take courses in English and American government to qualify for permanent residence; imposed sanctions on employers who knowingly hired illegal aliens, including civil fines and criminal penalties up to $3,000 and six months in jail; prohibited employers from discrimination on the basis of national origins; increased border patrol by 50 percent in 1987 and 1988; and, in a matter unrelated to illegal aliens, introduced a lottery program for 5,000 visas for countries "adversely affected" by provisions of the IMMIGRATION AND NATIONALITY ACT of 1965.

Because the measure was meant as a one-time resolution of a longstanding problem, a strict deadline for application was established: All applications for legalization were required within one year of May 5, 1987. At the insistence of state governments, newly legalized aliens were prohibited from receiving most types of federal public welfare, although Cubans (see CUBAN IMMIGRATION) and Haitians (see HAITIAN IMMIGRATION) were exempted. By the end of the filing period, about 1.7 million people had applied for general legalization, and about 1.4 million as special agricultural workers. Of the successful applicants, almost 70 percent were from Mexico and more than 90 percent from the Western Hemisphere. The measure was not highly effective in curbing employment of illegal aliens, as officials were prohibited from interfering with workers in the field without a search warrant.

Further Reading

Bean, Frank D., Georges Vernez, and Charles B. Keely. *Opening and Closing the Doors: Evaluating Immigration Reform and Control.* Washington, D.C.: Rand Corporation and the Urban Institute, 1989.
Espenshade, Thomas, et al. "Immigration Policy in the United States: Future Prospects for the Immigration Reform and Control Act of 1986." In *Population Policy: Contemporary Issues.* Ed. Godfrey Roberts. New York: Praeger, 1990.
Gonzalez-Baker, Susan. "The 'Amnesty' Aftermath: Current Policy Issues Stemming from the Legalization Programs of the 1986 Immigration Reform and Control Act." *International Migration Review* 31 (1997): 5–27.
Laham, Nicholas. *Ronald Reagan and the Politics of Immigration Reforms.* Westport, Conn.: Praeger, 2000.
LeMay, Michael C. *Anatomy of a Public Policy: The Reform of Contemporary American Immigration Law.* Westport, Conn.: Praeger, 1994.
Meissner, D., D. Papademetrious, and D. North. *Legalization of Undocumented Aliens: Lessons from Other Countries.* Washington, D.C.: Carnegie Endowment for International Peace, 1986.
Reimers, David. *Still the Golden Door: The Third World Comes to America.* 2d ed. New York: Columbia University Press, 1992.
Rivera-Batiz, Francisco, Selig L. Schzer, and Ira N. Gang, eds. *U.S. Immigration Policy Reform in the 1980s: A Preliminary Assessment.* New York: Praeger, 1991.
Vernez, Georges, ed. *Immigration and International Relations: Proceedings of a Conference on the International Effects of the 1986 Immigration Reform and Control Act (IRCA).* Washington, D.C.: Urban Institute, 1989.

Immigration Reform Act See ILLEGAL IMMIGRATION REFORM AND IMMIGRANT RESPONSIBILITY ACT.

immigration regulations (Canada) (1967)
In the wake of the White Paper on Canadian Immigration Policy of October 1966, the Canadian government announced a new series of immigration regulations in September 1967. Although designed in large measure to systematically address the almost unregulated movement of sponsored Canadian immigrants, the regulations introduced for the first time the principle of nondiscrimination on the basis of race or national origin, virtually ending the White Canada policy that had prevailed since the beginning of the 20th century.

Following the Liberal return to power in 1963, widespread concern over the massive influx of family-sponsored, often unskilled immigrants led to a full review of immigration procedures, leading to a massive reorganization of governmental agencies and policies, including the Government Organization Act (1966), the Immigration Appeal Board Act (1967), and the immigration regulations of 1967. The new regulations created three categories of immigrants: independent, sponsored, and nominated. The admission of independent applicants was determined by a new Norms of Assessment point system, applied in nine categories: education, age, suggesting long-term suitability, fluency in English or French, employment opportunities, Canadian relatives, area of destination, occupational demand, and occupational skill. Close family relatives were admitted as sponsored immigrants, but more distant "nominated" relatives were subject to a points evaluation on the basis of education, personal characteristics, job skills, job demand, and age. Section 34 of the new regulations also enabled aliens to apply for immigrant status after arriving in Canada. The new regulations were generally welcomed as a fairer method of determining eligibility. By the early 1970s, however, it became clear that immigrants were taking advantage of the new appeals policy, leading to a massive backlog of appeals and further impetus for the more broadly conceived changes that would be embodied in the IMMIGRATION ACT of 1976.

Further Reading

Hawkins, Freda. *Canada and Immigration.* 2d ed. Kingston and Montreal: McGill–Queen's University Press, 1989.

———. *Critical Years in Immigration: Canada and Australia Compared.* Kingston and Montreal: McGill–Queen's University Press, 1989.

Kelley, Ninette, and Michael Trebilcock. *The Making of the Mosaic: A History of Canadian Immigration Policy.* Toronto: University of Toronto Press, 2000.

Immigration Restriction League (IRL)

Founded by Charles Warren in Boston in 1894, the Immigration Restriction League (IRL) proposed a literacy test for the purpose of restricting immigration. With the support of prominent Boston families and a large number of academics, the IRL came near success in 1895, 1903, 1912, and 1915. Finally, with passage of the IMMIGRATION ACT of 1917, a literacy test was adopted, with both houses of Congress overriding President Woodrow Wilson's veto. This marked a turning point in American immigrant legislation, moving away from regulation toward restriction.

As more and more Americans began to question the wisdom of an open-door policy toward immigrants, the most radical proposal for keeping out immigrants generally was the literacy test, an idea first introduced by the economist Edward W. Bemis in 1887. Bemis proposed that all male adults who could not read or write their own language should be prohibited from entering the United States. The literacy test gained little support until a cholera epidemic brought by immigrant ships in 1892 and the depression of the following year led to broader support for extreme measures. The IRL adopted the test as their political goal. Leading the organization's lobbying efforts were two Harvard classmates, Prescott Farnsworth Hall and Robert De Courcy Ward. Despite antipathies toward the Irish, the organization was prepared to accept their presence in American life at the expense of eastern and southern Europeans. As Hall put it, the question was whether the United States would be "peopled by British, German and Scandinavian stock, historically free, energetic, progressive, or by Slav, Latin and Asiatic races, historically downtrodden, atavistic, and stagnant." Although literacy legislation was vetoed on four occasions, Hall and Ward were persistent, continuing to revive the issue at every favorable opportunity, appealing to business and labor leaders as well as members of Congress. Active U.S. involvement in the European war from 1917 led to a rapid increase in xenophobia and thus to conditions favorable to passage of the restrictive legislation, which outlawed "all aliens over sixteen years of age . . . who cannot read the English language, or some other language or dialect."

See also NATIVISM.

Further Reading

Curran, Thomas. *Xenophobia and Immigration, 1820–1930.* Boston: Twayne Publishers, 1975.

Higham, John. *Strangers in the Land: Patterns of American Nativism, 1860–1925.* 2d ed. New Brunswick, N.J.: Rutgers University Press, 1988.

Solomon, Barbara Miller. *Ancestors and Immigrants.* Cambridge, Mass.: Harvard University Press, 1956.

indentured servitude

Indentured servitude as a means of colonization or immigration is a labor system in which a laborer agrees to provide labor exclusively for one employer for a fixed number of years in return for his or her travel, living expenses and often some financial consideration at the end of service. The normal contract of indenture in colonial North America provided the servant with cost of passage from Europe; food, shelter, and clothing during the period of indenture; and land or other provisions when the contract was completed. Indentures in the middle and southern colonies were usually fixed at five to seven years, with seven being most common. In New England and NEW FRANCE, a period of three or four years was most common.

The indenture system worked because it met the needs of North American entrepreneurs and agriculturalists, who were short of labor; European paupers, who were short of money; and European governments, which had too many paupers and criminals with whom to deal. Private operations such as the Virginia Company, the Plymouth Company, and the Company of New France realized that the lure of land was not enough to attract potential investors; there had to be a laboring class available to do most of the menial work. Companies advertised varying combinations of free passage to the Americas, land, tools, and clothing for a servant who completed the period of servitude. Some servants were prepurchased by colonial merchants or landowners. During the first half of the 17th century, prepurchasing posed a considerable risk for the buyer, however, for the servant was more likely to die than to complete his or her term of service. To address the risk, the Virginia Company developed a headright system that rewarded purchasers with 50 acres of land for every servant brought to the colony at their own expense. In other cases, prospective settlers would indenture themselves to the company, which would then sell the contracts upon arrival in American ports. Most indentured servants were from the agricultural classes, though craftspeople and artisans were always in demand. By the 18th century, skilled workers were sometimes able to negotiate especially favorable terms of indenture.

Many servants, like settlers generally, did not survive the voyage to the New World. If they did successfully complete their indenture, there were often legal challenges to obtaining what they had been promised. Life was harsh, and laws were passed prohibiting servants from marrying, trading, or having children. Corporal punishment was common, and infractions of the law often included extension of the term of service. Men and women indentured as a couple were sometimes divided, and if one spouse died, the other was required to serve both terms. Children were indentured until the age of 21. As news of these hardships filtered back to Britain, fewer paupers willingly undertook to indenture themselves. In the second half of the 17th century, people were frequently forced into servitude through deceit, brutality, or as an alternate punishment for crime. In some years, thousands of criminals were deported to America as indentured servants.

Indentured servitude had a profound effect on the development of North America. It was most common in the middle and southern colonies, where it accounted for more than half of all colonial immigrants but was utilized widely throughout the British and French colonies. On the Canadian prairies, servants from Scotland and Ireland married Native American women, and their children were first-generation Métis. Servants came from all classes and races and from many European countries, though English paupers and convicts made up the majority. A few rose in society according to their early expectations, with some becoming landowners and legislators. Most, however, remained servants or were provided with marginal lands when their contracts were fulfilled. Often pushed into the most dangerous and least profitable areas of settlement, these poor whites became discontented and hard to govern. The first Africans transported to America came as indentured servants sold at Jamestown, in 1619. As planters realized that a seven-year term of service created an unsteady supply of labor and that freedmen and -women were often dissatisfied with their social condition, landowners increasingly turned to SLAVERY for their labor needs in the 18th century. After the 1660s, indentured servants were almost always European, and the majority survived their indenture. As late as the 1770s, more than 40 percent of immigrants to America were indentured servants. Enlightened ideals regarding liberty, the American Revolution (1775–83; see AMERICAN REVOLUTION AND IMMIGRATION), and the growth of industrial capitalism combined to undermine the system of indentured servitude, which finally faded out around 1830.

Further Reading

Coldham, Peter Wilson. *Emigrants in Chains: A Social History of Forced Emigration to the Americas of Felons, Destitute Children, Political and Religious Non-Conformists, Vagabonds, Beggars and Other Undesirables, 1607–1776*. Baltimore: Genealogical Publishing, 1994.

Emmer, P. C., and E. van den Boogaart, eds. *Colonialism and Migration: Indentured Labor before and after Slavery*. Dordrecht, Netherlands: Nijhof, 1986.

Galenson, David W. *White Servitude in Colonial America: An Economic Analysis*. Cambridge: Cambridge University Press, 1981.

Grabbe, Hans-Jurgen. "The Demise of the Redemptioner System in the United States." *American Studies* [West Germany] 29, no. 3 (1984): 277–296.

Kettner, James H. *The Development of American Citizenship, 1608–1870*. Chapel Hill: University of North Carolina Press, 1978.

Smith, A. E. *Colonists in Bondage*. Chapel Hill: University of North Carolina Press, 1947.

Vachon, André. *Dreams of Empire: Canada before 1700*. Ottawa: Public Archives of Canada, 1982.

Indian immigration (Asian Indian immigration)

According to the 2000 U.S. census, 1,899,599 Americans claimed Asian Indian descent. Although most were Hindus and Muslims, almost 150,000 were Christians from southern India. Asian Indians were spread throughout the country, though around 70 percent lived in New York, Pennsylvania, New Jersey, Texas, Michigan, Illinois, Ohio, and California. As a group, Indians were among elite immigrants, generally well educated and often arriving with capital to invest in business or industry. At the turn of the 21st century, approximately 4 percent of American medical doctors were foreign-born Indians or of Indian descent. According to the 2001 Canadian census, approximately 100,000 Canadians claimed either South Asian ancestry or descent from an Indian ethnic group, while 713,330 identified themselves as East Indian. Indians are widely spread throughout Canada. Early settlement centered in British Columbia; after 1960, TORONTO was the favored destination.

Exact numbers of immigrants are difficult to ascertain, as the term *Indian* applies to more than a dozen ethnic groups and has been used to refer to two distinct political entities. From the late 18th century until 1947, India comprised all the diverse religious and ethnic groups governed directly or indirectly as part of British imperial territory between Afghanistan and Burma (present-day Myanmar). This included large and distinct communities of Pakistanis, Punjabis, Bengalis (Bangladeshis), Sinhalese, and Tamils, among others. Although the term *Hindu* was frequently used into the 1960s in reference to migrants from the whole of British India, it was in many cases inaccurate, as Pakistanis were most often Muslims, Punjabis either Muslims or Sikhs, and Bengalis either Hindus or Muslims. The "Indian" peoples spoke a variety of languages, including Gujarati, Urdu, Hindi, Tamil, Punjabi, Bengali, and Telegu. When Britain withdrew from its Indian empire in 1947, predominantly Muslim territories of the Sind and Punjab in the west and eastern Bengal and Assam, a thousand miles to the east, were collectively granted independence as the new state of Pakistan. The predominantly Hindu island of Ceylon (Sri

Lanka) was granted independence in the following year. What remained became the modern country of India, the seventh-largest country in the world by landmass, with 1,146,600 square miles, and second only to China in population, with just over 1 billion people. It incorporates climatic and vegetative patterns ranging from the high Himalayan Mountains in the north to the deserts of Rajasthan in the northwest to the rain forests of Assam in the northeast. With mixed ethnic and religious populations, a peaceful division of land proved impossible, and more than 1 million people died in communal violence surrounding the partition. About 80 percent of Indians are Hindus, and 14 percent Muslims. Ethnic and religious tensions in India and along the border with Pakistan remain high, providing a powerful impetus for some Indians to emigrate.

There is evidence of Indian sailors and adventurers settling in the United States as early as the 1790s, but they did not begin to migrate to North America in significant numbers until around the turn of the 20th century. They then generally came as part of two groups: poor laborers or elites. With the abolition of slavery in the British Empire in 1834, Indian labor became an important commodity. It has been estimated that between 1834 and 1934, some 30 million Indians indentured themselves for terms of labor in eastern and southern Africa, the Caribbean, Southeast Asia and western Europe. Between 1904 and 1911, 6,100 Indians immigrated to the United States, living almost exclusively on the West Coast. Many were Punjabi Sikhs who had first immigrated to western Canada but found work in lumber mills and on railway gangs in California and the Pacific Northwest. The largest concentrations were in the San Joaquin, Sacramento, and Imperial Valleys of California. Provisions of the racially restrictive ALIEN LAND ACT (1913), IMMIGRATION ACT (1917) and National Origins and Quota Act (1924), along with the 1923 Supreme Court ruling that Indians were ineligible for naturalized citizenship, made it impossible for them to assimilate, and economic depression made it unattractive for further

Indian immigrants on board the *Komogata Maru* in English Bay, Vancouver, British Columbia, 1914. Indian businessman Gurdit Singh sponsored the voyage for 376 East Indian workers sailing from Shanghai, openly challenging restrictive Canadian legislation. After a two-month court battle, the *Komogata Maru* was forced to leave Canadian waters. *(National Archives of Canada/PA-34014)*

immigrants to come. As a result, Sikhs and Muslims often took Mexican wives, creating a significant "Mexidu" culture that consisted of more than 300 families. More than 6,000 Indians were either deported or chose to leave the United States so that by 1940, fewer than 2,500 "Hindus" were living the country. Although illegal immigration through Mexico may have added several thousand more, the total number of residents was never more than a few thousand. Among the elite groups, teachers (swamis), students, and merchants were most common, representing the well educated from many ethnic groups, including Bengalis. Students who came to the United States were frequently involved with the Indian nationalist movement, but their numbers were never large. The renewal of immigration of Indians under provisions of the IMMIGRATION AND NATIONALITY ACT (1965) led to increased numbers but was of a wholly different character than the earlier migration. Most were not Sikhs, few settled in California or the West, and almost none were agriculturalists. The majority of recent Indian immigrants were well-trained professionals and entrepreneurs, who were often overqualified for the jobs they held. Between 1992 and 2002, about 480,000 Indians immigrated to the United States.

Many Sikhs sought opportunities afforded them as subjects of a British Empire that stretched across the world. They often served as soldiers or employees of steamship companies, and many eventually settled in Canada. The first significant wave of Indian immigrants came between 1903 and 1918, when more than 5,000, mainly Sikhs, arrived. In the early 20th century, this led to fairly homogenous Indian communities in western Canada, where most of the men had originally settled before bringing over their families. Denied the right to participate in the national political process, Indians focused on local community organization and loudly protested their denial of rights. By World War I (1914–18), many community leaders were members of the Socialist Party and in some way affiliated with the revolutionary Ghadar Party which sought the overthrow of the British in India. As the organization was infiltrating the United States, it was crushed in Canada and many of its leaders forced out of the country. With the breakup of the old British imperial system after World War II (1939–45), newly independent countries had to negotiate treaties providing for regular immigrant status. The Canadian government made some gestures toward India but major reform was slow in coming.

In 1947, Indians in Canada finally were enfranchised. The IMMIGRATION ACT (1952) provided for reunification of immediate family members, and the subsequent order-in-council (P.C. 1956-785) allowed an annual quota of 150 Indians beyond those eligible under the category of immediate-family sponsorship. When Canada relaxed social and ethnic barriers in the early 1960s, more South Indians began to immigrate, most frequently choosing Ontario or Quebec

for settlement. By 1969, India became one of the top 10 source countries for Canadian immigration. Immigration peaked in the early 1970s, after which an economic downturn in Canada led to more restrictive policies based on desired skills. By the turn of the 21st century, the Indian community in Canada included much ethnic diversity and numerically had shifted from west to east. In 2001, 314,685 Indian immigrants were living in Canada, with more than 235,000 born in India and most of the rest in Fiji, Trinidad and Tobago, Kenya, Uganda, and Tanzania. About 92 percent arrived after 1971, 156,000 between 1996 and 2001 alone. More than three-quarters of all immigrants came under family reunification provisions. In the 1990s, however, increasing ethnic and religious tensions in India led to a greater concern for political refugees. Whereas only six of 4,115 refugee visas were granted between 1977 and 1988, the following 10 years (1989 and 1998) saw 2,621 claims granted by the Immigration and Refugee Board, 27 percent of all claims received.

See also BANGLADESHI IMMIGRATION; PAKISTANI IMMIGRATION; SOUTH ASIAN IMMIGRATION; SRI LANKAN IMMIGRATION.

Further Reading

Agarwal, Pankaj. *Passage from India: Post-1965 Indian Immigrants and Their Children—Conflicts, Concerns, and Solutions.* Palos Verdes, Calif.: Yuvati Publications, 1991.

Barrier, N. Gerald, and Verne A. Susenbery, eds. *The Sikh Diaspora: Migration and the Experience beyond Punjab.* Columbia, Mo.: South Asia Publications, 1989.

Birbalsingh, Frank, ed. *Indenture and Exile: The Indo-Caribbean Experience.* Toronto: Tsar Publications, 1989.

Buchignani, Norman, Doreen M. Indra, with Ram Srivastava. *Continuous Journey: A Social History of South Asians in Canada.* Toronto: McClelland and Stewart, 1985.

Chandrasekhar, S., ed. *From India to America: A Brief History of Immigration.* La Jolla, Calif.: Population Review, 1986.

Daniels, Roger. *History of Indian Immigration to the United States: An Interpretative Essay.* New York: Asia Society, 1989.

Gibson, M. A. *Accommodation without Assimilation: Sikh Immigrants in an American High School.* Ithaca, N.Y.: Cornell University Press, 1989.

Helweg, A. Wesley, and Usha M. Helweg. *An Immigrant Success Story: East Indians in America.* Philadelphia: University of Pennsylvania Press, 1990.

Jensen, Joan M. *Passage from India: Asian Indian Immigrants in North America.* New Haven, Conn.: Yale University Press, 1988.

Johnston, Hugh J. M. *The East Indians in Canada.* Ottawa: Canadian Historical Association, 1984.

Joy, Annamma. *Ethnicity in Canada: Social Accommodation and Cultural Persistence among the Sikhs and the Portuguese.* New York: AMS Press, 1989.

La Brack, Bruce. "South Asians." In *A Nation of Peoples: A Sourcebook on America's Multicultural Heritage.* Ed. Elliott Robert Barkan. Westport, Conn.: Greenwood Press, 1999.

Industrial Workers of the World (IWW) demonstration in New York City in 1914. The IWW was the most important radical labor union in the United States and Canada, and it attracted many immigrants who believed that their interests were not taken seriously by traditional labor unions. *(Library of Congress, Prints & Photographs Division [LC-USZ62-30519])*

Leonard, Karen Isaksen. *Making Ethnic Choices: California's Punjabi Mexican Americans.* Philadelphia: Temple University Press, 1992.

Lessinger, Johanna. *From the Ganges to the Hudson.* Needham Heights, Mass.: Allyn and Bacon, 1995.

Petivich, Carla. *The Expanding Landscape: South Asians in the Diaspora.* Chicago: Manohar, 1999.

Sara, Parmatma. *The Asian Indian Experience in the United States.* Cambridge, Mass.: Schenkman Books, 1985.

Sheth, Pravin. *Indians in America: One Stream, Two Waves, Three Generations.* Jaipur, India: Rawat Publications, 2001.

Tatla, Darshan Singh. *Sikhs in North America: Sources for the Study of Sikh Community in North America and an Annotated Bibliography.* New York: Greenwood Press, 1991.

Van der Veer, Peter, ed. *Nation and Migration: The Politics of Space in the South Asian Diaspora.* Philadelphia: University of Pennsylvania Press, 1995.

Industrial Workers of the World (IWW, Wobblies)

Founded in 1905, the Industrial Workers of the World (IWW) was the most important of the radical labor organizations that operated in the United States and Canada. Many unskilled immigrants initially joined, then left as they became better situated in the labor market. Though immigrants often rejected the IWW for fear of losing their jobs in strike actions, the organization worked directly to foster interethnic cooperation. During World War I (1914–18; see WORLD WAR I AND IMMIGRATION), membership rose dramatically, with a corresponding wave of strikes and labor militancy. Increasingly, both domestic and foreign workers who opposed the war and believed they were not being well served by traditional craft unions joined the IWW. This led to further tensions, as industrialists and politicians sought to establish links between German activity and the radical labor movement. In 1918, the Canadian government made the IWW and 13 socialist or anarchist organizations illegal. When a move to join the Communist International was narrowly defeated in 1920, the organization began to disintegrate, reflecting in part the immigrant move toward mainstream politics and assimilation.

See also LABOR ORGANIZATION AND IMMIGRATION, TERRORISM AND IMMIGRATION.

Further Reading

Dubofsky, Melvyn. *We Shall Be All: A History of the Industrial Workers of the World.* Chicago: Quadrangle Books, 1969.

Montgomery, David. *The Fall of the House of Labor: The Workplace, the State, and American Labor Activism, 1865–1925.* New York: Cambridge University Press, 1987.

Renshaw, Patrick. *The Wobblies: The Story of Syndicalism in the United States.* Garden City, N.Y.: Doubleday, 1967.

Roberts, Barbara. *Whence They Came: Deportation from Canada, 1900–1935.* Ottawa: University of Ottawa Press, 1988.

Robin, Martin. *Radical Politics and Canadian Labour, 1890–1930.* Kingston, Canada: Industrial Relations Centre, Queen's University, 1968.

Inouye, Daniel K. (1924–) *politician*

Hawaii's first U.S. congressman and the first member of Congress of Japanese descent, Daniel Inouye has represented, for more than 40 years, the patriotism of Japanese Americans. Committed to a strong national defense, he fought for compensation to Japanese Americans who had been imprisoned in internment camps during World War II (1939–45; see JAPANESE INTERNMENT, WORLD WAR II).

The son of Japanese immigrants, Inouye was born in Honolulu and graduated from the public school system there. As a freshman in college, in 1943, he enlisted in the 442nd Regimental Combat Team and fought in Italy, where he lost his right arm and earned the Distinguished Service Cross (upgraded to the Medal of Honor in 2000). Having experienced the discrimination then common against Japanese Americans, he determined to work on behalf of social change and to that end earned a law degree from George Washington University. Inouye won a Democratic seat in the Hawaiian territorial legislature in 1954. After serving in the U.S. House of Representatives following Hawaiian statehood (1959–63), he was elected seven times as U.S. senator from Hawaii (1963–2005). In the late 1970s, he supported the efforts of the Japanese American Citizens' League, which lobbied Congress to establish the Commission on Wartime Relocation and Internment of Citizens (CWRIC). As a result of the league's efforts, the Civil Liberties Act was signed by President Ronald Reagan in 1988, providing an apology for the internment and $20,000 for each survivor then alive. Speaking in favor of the measure before the Senate on April 20, 1988, Inouye observed that the CWRIC found no documented cases of espionage or sabotage by Americans of Japanese descent and reminded senators that "proportionately and percentagewise," more Japanese Americans had served during World War II than non-Japanese, despite the fact that they were restricted to ethnic units.

Further Reading

"Biography of Daniel K. Inouye." United States Senate. Available online. URL: http://inouye.senate.gov. Accessed May 13, 2004.

Inouye, Daniel K., with Lawrence Elliot. *Journey to Washington.* Englewood Cliffs, N.J.: Prentice Hall, 1967.

International Ladies' Garment Workers' Union (ILGWU)

Founded in 1900 in New York City, the International Ladies' Garment Workers' Union (ILGWU) was remarkably successful in forcing adoption of sanitary codes and safety regulations and achieving better pay during the first two decades of the 20th century. Comprising mostly women immigrants, the organization flourished in eastern cities, though there were local unions elsewhere. The majority of early members were Jewish and Italian, establishing a pattern for the garment trade to be dominated by the newest immigrants. The union's greatest early successes were the "Uprising of 1909," in which 20,000 shirtwaist makers staged a 14-week strike, and the "Great Revolt," which saw 60,000 garment workers win "The Protocol of Peace." The organization, increasingly an owners' union, continued to function under the original name, providing clear working standards and impartial arbitration of grievances. In 1911, the Triangle Shirtwaist Fire, in which 146 workers died as flames engulfed an unsafe and unaffiliated workshop, focused national attention on the plight of garment workers. In the same year, the Independent Cloakmakers Union of Toronto became the first Canadian union to affiliate with the ILGWU.

In 1914, a similar organization known as the Amalgamated Clothing Workers of America (ACWA) was formed, with an affiliated branch established in Montreal in 1917. In 1976, the ACWA merged with the Textile Workers Union of America to form the Amalgamated Clothing and Textile Workers Union, which in turn merged with the ILGWU in 1995 to form the Union of Needletrades, Industrial and Textile Employees (UNITE), representing more than 250,000 American and Canadian workers. By the 1980s, union membership was largely from the Caribbean Basin, South America, and East Asia. International visibility of the garment trade was once again heightened in 1996, with revelations of sweatshop conditions found in the manufacture of television personality Kathie Lee Gifford's clothing line. Throughout the late 20th and early 21st century, UNITE took an increasingly activist role in international politics, joining with environmental and student groups to protest international working conditions and the policies of such international economic groups as the World Trade Organization.

Further Reading

Lorwin, Lewis Levitzki. *The Women's Garment Workers: A History of the International Ladies' Garment Worker's Union.* New York: B. W. Huebsch, 1924.

Stein, Leon. *Out of the Sweatshop: The Struggle for Industrial Democracy.* New York: Quadrangle/New York Times Book Co., 1977.

Tyler, Gus. *Look for the Union Label: A History of the International Ladies' Garment Workers' Union.* New York: M. E. Sharpe, 1995.

UNITE! Web site. Available online. URL: http://www.uniteunion.org/. Accessed May 13, 2004.

Waldinger, Roger D. *Through the Eye of the Needle: Immigrants and Enterprise in New York's Garment Trades.* New York: New York University Press, 1986.

Iranian immigration

During the 1990s, Iranians formed the largest immigrant group from the Middle East in both the United States and Canada. According to the U.S. census of 2000 and the Canadian census of 2001, 338,266 Americans and 88,220 Canadians claimed Iranian ancestry. By far the greatest concentration of Iranians in the United States was in California; about half of all Canadian Iranians lived in TORONTO.

Iran, known throughout much of its history as Persia, occupies 630,900 square miles, with Turkey and Iraq on the west; Armenia, Azerbaijan, Turkmenistan, and the Caspian Sea on the north; Afghanistan and Pakistan on the east; and the Persian Gulf and Arabia Sea on the south. In 2002, the population was estimated at 66,128,965. The people are ethnically divided between Persians (51 percent), Azerbaijani (24 percent), Gilaki/Mazandarani (8 percent), Kurds (7 percent), and Arabs (3 percent). Iran is the only country in the world with a government under the control of Shia Muslims, who comprise 89 percent of the population; 10 percent are Sunni Muslims. From their homeland in Iran, the Persians created one of the world's largest empires between the 6th and 4th centuries B.C., when they were conquered by Alexander the Great. After more than 500 years under a Greek-speaking government, the native Sasanians returned to power between A.D. 226 and 640, when Arab Muslims conquered the region. Unlike other Islamic regions, Iran's population was largely of the Shiite branch of Islam, which held that only descendants of Muhammad should rule or exercise high spiritual authority. The Safavid dynasty reached a peak of political influence and cultural development in the 16th and 17th centuries but steadily declined in power with the advent of European expansion. During the latter years of the Qajar dynasty (1779–1921), Iran's economy was largely controlled by Russians in the north and British in the south. Mohammad Reza Pahlavi, who came to power as the shah of Iran in 1941 alienated religious leaders by his campaign of rapid modernization. The shah was overthrown in 1979 and replaced by the Ayatollah Ruhollah Khomeini, who established a fundamentalist Islamic republic and waged war over border territories with Iraq throughout the 1980s Muslim extremists, angered by American support for the shah and supported by the Iranian government, also seized a group of American embassy workers in November 1979, holding them for 444 days. Not only was there an anti-Iranian backlash in the United States, with the embassy closed in Tehran it became necessary for potential immigrants to travel to a third country to obtain visas. During the 1990s, the Iranian government gradually became more moderate. Fundamentalist clerics continued to exert widespread influence however. In 2004 they declared several hundred reformers ineligible to stand for parliament, thus allowing fundamentalists to regain control of the legislature.

It is impossible to say how many Iranians may have immigrated to North America prior to World War II (1939–45), but the number was extremely small. Almost everyone from the Middle East was classified as an Arab prior to 1900, and frequently as a Syrian until 1930. The first significant group of Iranian immigrants came between 1950 and 1977, when about 35,000 came to the United States. This number is misleading, however, as nearly 400,000 nonimmigrants (visitors and students) also arrived during this period, many of whom eventually stayed in the United States. The fall of the pro-Western government of the shah in 1979 gave new impetus to educated and modernized Iranians to immigrate—in 1990, half the Iranian population 25 years or older had at least a bachelor's degree. About 200,000 sought refuge in the United States between 1979 and 2000, and eventually almost 60,000 were granted refugee or asylee status. In 2000 and 2001 alone, almost 12,000 Iranian refugees were admitted. A substantial number of them were from minority groups, including Assyrians and Armenians (most of whom were Christians), Kurds, and Jews. Altogether almost 117,000 Iranians were admitted to the United States between 1992 and 2002.

Iranians first came to Canada in significant numbers after 1964 and then after 1978. Most of these several thousand immigrants were well-trained professionals or students, in some way tied to the rapid modernization plans of the shah. Many were doctors, and most blended into Canadian professional society. After the Islamic revolution in 1979, however, most immigrants were fleeing persecution. Their numbers included supporters of the old regime, but also many students, feminist groups, and other reformers who had supported the revolution in order to oust the shah but whose modernist views were not tolerated by the new fundamentalist regime. In 1986 and 1987, for instance, the government dismissed 11,000 government employees, mostly women, in a "purification" campaign. More than 90 percent of Iranian immigrants to Canada came between 1981 and 2001. Beginning in 1996, Iran broke into the top 10 source countries for Canadian immigration. Between 1996 and 2002, more than 6,400 Iranians immigrated annually, including more than 4,200 refugees between 2000 and 2002.

Further Reading

Ansari, Abdolmaboud. *Iranian Immigrants in the United States: A Case Study of Dual Marginality.* New York: Associated Faculty Press, 1988.

———. *The Making of the Iranian Community in America.* New York: Pardis Press, 1992.

Bill, James A. *The Eagle and the Lion: The Tragedy of American-Iranian Relations.* New Haven, Conn.: Yale University Press, 1988.

Bozorgmehr, Mehdi. "Diaspora in the Post-Revolutionary Period." In *Encyclopedia Iranica*, vol. 7. Costa Mesa, Calif.: Mazda Publishers, 1900.

———, ed. "Iranians in America." (special issue). *Iranian Studies* 31, no. 1 (1998): 3–95.

Bozorgmehr, Mehdi, and George Sabagh. "High Status Immigrants: A Statistical Profile of Iranians in the United States." *Iranian Studies* 21, nos. 3–4 (1988): 4–34.

Fathi, Asghar, ed. *Iranian Refugees and Exiles since Khomeini.* Costa Mesa, Calif.: Mazda Press, 1991.

Khalili, Laleh. "Mixing Memory and Desire: Iranians in the United States." May 13, 1998. *The Iranian.* Available online. http://www.iranian.com/Features/May98/Iranams/index.html. Accessed February 24, 2004.

Moallem, Minso. "Pluralité des rapports sociaux: similarité et différence. Le cas des Iraniennes et Iraniens au Québec." Ph.D. thesis, University of Montreal, 1989.

Moghaddam, Fathali M. "Individual and Collective Integral Strategies among Iranians in Canada." *International Journal of Psychology* 22 (1987): 306–314.

Nafici, Hamid. "The Poetics and Practice of Iranian Nostalgia in Exile." *Diaspora* 1, no. 3 (Winter 1991): 285–302.

Shadbash, Sharam. "Iranian Immigrants in the United States: The Adjustment Experience of the First Generation." Ph.D. thesis, Boston University, 1994.

Iraqi immigration

Unlike some other Muslim groups, Iraqis had little exposure to Western culture before immigrating to North America in the wake of the first Persian Gulf War (1991) and therefore had more difficulty assimilating. According to the U.S. census of 2000 and the Canadian census of 2001, 37,714 Americans and 26,655 Canadians claimed Iraqi ancestry. U.S. centers of settlement include the greater DETROIT area, CHICAGO, and LOS ANGELES. About half of Iraqis in Canada live in TORONTO.

Iraq is the easternmost Arab nation, occupying 167,400 square miles. It is bordered by Jordan and Syria on the west, Turkey on the north, Iran on the east, and Kuwait and Saudi Arabia on the south. In 2002, the population was estimated at 23,331,985. The people are ethnically Arabs (65 percent), Kurds (23 percent), Azerbaijani (5.6 percent), and Turkmen (1.2 percent). More than 96 percent of Iraqis are Muslims, though there are clear divisions between the 62 percent Shia and 34 percent Sunni. The region known to the Greeks as Mesopotamia, the land between the Tigris and Euphrates Rivers, is the heart of Iraq. The well-watered river banks provided abundant crops and led to the development of the world's first civilization around 3500 B.C. A succession of empires ruled by Arabs, Persians, Indo-Europeans, and Greeks controlled the region prior to its conquest by Muslim armies in the 630s. Baghdad was one of the most advanced and sophisticated cities in the world under the Abbasid caliphate in the ninth century but gradually declined in the face of Islamic divisions and eventual Mongol conquest in 1258. The Ottoman Turks ruled Iraq from the 16th century to 1917. After World War I (1914–18), Iraq was a territory mandated to British oversight and eventually gained full independence in 1932. After considerable political turmoil, including attempted Kurdish revolts (1945, 1974) and Communist control of the central government (1973), the Baathist Saddam Hussein gained office in 1979. Iraqis benefitted in the 1970s and 1980s from considerable oil revenues and resulting social improvement, but Hussein also took the country to war and brutally repressed all political opponents. In 1980, he launched an invasion of Iran, which led to a devastating eight-year war and the death of some 1 million Iraqis. In August 1990, Iraq invaded Kuwait, leading to U.S. involvement and the first Persian Gulf War (1991) in which the Iraqi army was largely destroyed. The terrorist attacks of SEPTEMBER 11, 2001, heightened U.S. suspicions regarding Iraqi support for al-Qaeda and other terrorist organizations. This combined with Iraqi evasion of required United Nations inspections regarding the development of weapons of mass destruction, resulted in a U.S.-led invasion of Iraq in 2003. Saddam Hussein was captured by American forces on December 13, 2003. In April 2004 Iraqi leaders determined to put Hussein on trial for crimes committed during his rule, though public proceedings had not begun before the end of the year. On June 28, 2004, the U.S.-led coalition returned sovereignty to an Iraqi interim government, with nationwide elections scheduled for January 2005. About 140,000 U.S. troops remained in Iraq at the end of 2004.

Prior to World War II (1939–45), only a few hundred Iraqis immigrated to North America, most from the privileged class and for economic opportunities. Many of these were minority Chaldean Christians, who began to settle in and around Detroit as early as 1910. By the end of World War II, the Chaldean population in Detroit numbered about 1,000. Although a few students came for study after the war, immigration remained small until the 1970s, when political events drove many dissidents from the country under the flag of pan-Arab unity, Hussein crushed a Kurdish revolt in 1975, and in 1979 began a systematic suppression of communists, Kurds, Shia Muslims, and Baathists who had fallen out of favor. About 300,000 Shias were driven to Iran, and many of those eventually made their way to the United States. The first extensive immigration, however, came only after the 1991 Persian Gulf War, when about 10,000 Iraqi refugees were admitted to the United States, mostly Kurds and Shiites who had assisted or sympathized with the U.S.-led war. Between 1992 and 2002, about 50,000 Iraqis immigrated to the United States, many as refugees. Between 1996 and 2001 alone, 14,000 Iraqi refugees were admitted.

On April 9, 2003, hundreds of Iraqis celebrated in the streets of Dearborn, Michigan (suburban Detroit), celebrating the coalition capture of Baghdad and the over-throw of Hussein. In 2004, many recent Iraqi immigrants waited to see if conditions in the country would stabilize following the restoration of sovereignty to a new Iraqi government in June 2004, with an eye to returning to their home country.

Iraqi immigration to Canada was largely the result of the disruptions of the Iran-Iraq War of the 1980s and the two Persian Gulf wars of 1991 and 2003. Between 1945 and 1975, there were no more than 200 Iraqi immigrants. With the rise of Hussein and the intensification of political persecution after 1979, a small but steady stream of dissidents left the country, with almost 6,500 coming to Canada by 1992. Of 25,825 Iraqis immigrants in Canada in 2001, only 2,230 (8.6 percent) came before 1981. With constant war and the brutal suppression of Kurds and Shiites by the Iraqi government, immigration increased in the 1990s. Between 1991 and 2001, almost 20,000 Iraqis immigrated to Canada.

See also ARAB IMMIGRATION; IRANIAN IMMIGRATION.

Further Reading

Abraham, N., and S. Y. Abraham. *Arabs in the New World: Studies on Arab-American Communities.* Detroit: Center for Urban Studies, Wayne State University, 1983.
Abu-Labar, Baha. *An Olive Branch on the Family Tree: The Arabs in Canada.* Toronto: McClelland and Stewart, 1980.
Elkholy, Abdo A. *The Arab Moslems in the United States: Religion and Assimilation.* New Haven, Conn.: College and University Press, 1966.
Haddad, Yvonne Yazbeck. *The Muslims of America.* New York: Oxford University Press, 1991.
Haddad, Yvonne Yazbeck, and Jane Idleman Smith, ed. *Muslim Communities in North America.* Albany: State University of New York Press, 1994.
McCarus, Ernest, ed. *The Development of Arab-American Identity.* Ann Arbor: University of Michigan Press, 1994.
Makiya, Kanan. *Republic of Fear: The Politics of Modern Iraq.* Updated ed. Berkeley: University of California Press, 1998.
Metcalf, Barbara Daly. *Making Muslim Space in North America and Europe.* Berkeley: University of California Press, 1996.
Sengstock, M. C. *Chaldean Americans: Changing Conceptions of Ethnic Identity.* New York: Center for Migration Studies, 1982.
Suleiman, Michael W. *Arabs in America: Building a New Future.* Philadelphia: Temple University Press, 2000.
Tripp, Charles. *A History of Iraq.* Cambridge: Cambridge University Press, 2000.
Waugh, Earle H., et al., eds. *Muslim Families in North America.* Edmonton, Canada: University of Alberta Press, 1991.

Irish immigration

The Irish were the first of Europe's many impoverished peoples to seek economic advantages in the New World in large numbers in the 19th century, providing one of the great immigration streams to both Canada and the United States.

According to the 2000 U.S. census and the 2001 Canadian census, 30,528,492 Americans and 3,822,660 Canadians claimed Irish descent. Most Irish immigrants originally settled in major urban centers, most prominently NEW YORK CITY, BOSTON, PHILADELPHIA, MONTREAL, and QUEBEC. Because significant Irish immigration began early in the 17th century and continued for 300 years under a wide variety of circumstances, the Irish are now spread throughout North America and have become an integral part of American and Canadian culture.

The island of Ireland covers a little more than 32,000 square miles in the North Atlantic Ocean, about 80 miles west of Great Britain. In ancient times, it was inhabited by Celtic peoples, and the land was usually divided among multiple kings. The Irish were converted to Christianity in the fifth century by St. Patrick and for hundreds of years produced outstanding Christian scholars and missionaries. By the 12th century, English kings established a foothold near modern Dublin and gradually extended their control over the eastern half of the island. During the 1640s, most of Ireland was brought under English control by Oliver Cromwell, leading to a diffuse but persistent Irish resistance. Beginning in the 15th century, large numbers of Scots and English citizens were resettled in Ireland, mostly in the six counties of the north, on lands confiscated from the rebellious Irish nobility (see ULSTER). These settlers formed the basis of the Protestant Ascendancy, a minority population that gradually came to view itself as Irish. By the late 18th century, many members of the Protestant Ascendancy were themselves calling for either self-government or complete independence from Great Britain. After the rebellion of 1798, Ireland was brought under more direct British control with the creation of the United Kingdom of Great Britain and Ireland (1801). Throughout the 19th century, resolution of the Irish problem was continually hampered by two closely related issues: the question of the traditional unity of the island of Ireland and the cultural and religious division of the land between the Protestants of the north and the Roman Catholics of the south. The Irish Civil War (1919–21) led to the division of the land into the Republic of Eire—making up 27,133 square miles, or about 85 percent, of the island, fully independent from 1937, and Northern Ireland—the six counties of the north (5,451 square miles), which remained legislatively linked to Great Britain. Eire's population of 3.8 million (2001) was 92 percent Roman Catholic; 45 percent of Northern Ireland's 1.7 million people (2001) were Roman Catholic. With Catholic population growth in the north steadily outstripping that of Protestants, it was expected that Catholics would constitute the majority population in the north within a relatively short period of time, thus enhancing the possibility that the island will be politically reunified.

Following the Protestant Reformation of the 16th century, Irish exiles, revolutionaries, and dispossessed Catholics frequently immigrated to Spain, France, and the

Low Countries. In the 17th century alone, it has been estimated that there were 35,000 Irish soldiers in the French army. These, along with Irish merchants employed by France, made their way to NEW FRANCE in significant numbers during the 17th and 18th centuries. In 1700, there were 130 families either fully Irish or of mixed Franco-Irish heritage. As political turmoil in Ireland increased, France and New France remained popular destinations for those with strong anti-British sentiments, including a few disgruntled settlers from British colonies to the south. Protestant immigrants, however, far outnumbered Catholic immigrants until the 1820s, and most Protestants settled in the British colonies south of New

France. Between 1717 and 1775, more than 100,000 Presbyterian Scots-Irish settled in America, mainly because of high rents or famine and most coming from families who had been in Ireland for several generations. In the colonial period, they were in fact usually referred to simply as Irish, making it difficult to determine exact figures. Although Scots-Irish filtered throughout the colonies, they most frequently settled along the Appalachian frontier and largely influenced the religion and culture of the frontier regions as they developed. Altogether this represented the largest movement of any group from the British Isles to British North America in the 18th century. Many came as indentured servants (see INDENTURED SERVITUDE), driven to

This illustration from *Frank Leslie's Illustrated Newspaper,* January 20, 1866, shows Irish immigrants leaving their home for America on the mail coach from Cahirciveen, County Kerry, Ireland. With poverty rampant in Ireland, emigration was an attractive alternative for many Irish well before—and long after—the great potato famine. *(Library of Congress, Prints & Photographs Division [LC-USZ62-2022])*

the American colonies by the desperate economic condition of their homeland.

During the 18th century, Ireland grew more rapidly than any European country, with the population of the island increasing from 3 million in the 1720s to more than 8 million by the early 1840s. The exploding Irish population—which grew by 1.4 million between 1821 and 1841 alone—coincided with the fall of agricultural prices and the decline of the textile industry at the end of the Napoleonic Wars (1815), throwing hundreds of thousands out of work, with little prospect for economic improvement. The situation was made worse by the Irish land system, dominated by Protestant landlords, with most of the cottiers (tenant farmers with very small holdings) and laborers being Irish. Those most hurt economically were the larger tenant farmers, both Protestant and Catholic, who were often unable to pay rents and evicted from their lands, then entered an already depressed workforce. Rather than replace evicted farmers, landlords—often absentee in England—shifted to sheep and cattle raising as a more economically viable activity for the poor land. Also, with no system of primogeniture guaranteeing the eldest son the whole land inheritance, Irish farms were quickly divided among large families, with plots soon becoming too small to support a family. A series of potato famines further heightened the distress, adding starvation to destitution as compelling factors toward immigration.

During the 18th and early 19th centuries, the poorest laborers and cottiers tended to stay in Ireland or to immigrate to Britain, where industrialization was rapidly opening job opportunities. Protestants, generally better off financially than their Catholic neighbors, found it easier to immigrate to the New World, especially to the colonies of what would later become the United States. They had the added incentive of escaping rural violence then common, as Catholic secret societies attempted to undermine the Protestant Ascendancy.

Most Irish immigrants arrived in ports along the eastern seaboard of North America, including Halifax, Nova Scotia; Montreal, Quebec; Boston; Philadelphia; and New York. Most landed first at Canadian ports, as transportation rates there were considerably cheaper. Many then migrated southward, often after a number of years. Most immigrants stayed in the cities, but a significant number ventured into the Appalachian backcountry of Pennsylvania, South Carolina, and Georgia. By 1800, the Irish population of Philadelphia was 6,000, the largest in America. Most were Presbyterians, but there were Quakers and Episcopalians as well and an increasing number of Catholics by the turn of the century. The Irish were the largest non-English immigrant group in the colonial era, numbering perhaps 400,000 by 1790 (see BRITISH IMMIGRATION). Between 1820 and 1840, the character of Irish immigration began to change, with a greater percentage of poor Irish Catholics among them. During this period, more than one-third of all immigrants to the United States were Irish, most by way of Canada. By the 1840s, however, they usually came directly to Boston or New York City.

Although fewer Irish stayed in Canada, between 1770 and 1830, they transformed the character of the maritime colonies. NEWFOUNDLAND, once thought of only as a "colony built around a fishery," was the first area of substantial Irish settlement. By the late 18th century, more and more sojourning fishermen were choosing to settle permanently on the island, despite a formal British ban. By the 1830s, when declining trade virtually ended Irish immigration, half of Newfoundland's population was Irish (38,000). As Newfoundland's transatlantic economy suffered after 1815, more Irish Catholics chose to settle in NOVA SCOTIA or NEW BRUNSWICK. Though Irish Catholics remained a small minority on Cape Breton Island, by 1837 they constituted more than one-third of the population of Halifax, and almost a third of the population of the entire colony. Between 1827 and 1835, it is estimated that 65,000 Irish immigrated to New Brunswick, attracted both by the fisheries and the rich farmland. Most were from the Irish provinces of Munster and Ulster, and perhaps 60 percent were Catholic. The Irish formed the largest immigrant group in Canada during the first half of the 19th century, more than the English, Scottish, and Welsh combined.

The Great Famine of 1845–49 dramatically accelerated an already-growing trend. The Irish peasantry had since the 18th century relied largely on the potato for their basic food supply. In the 1840s, an average male might eat 14 pounds of potatoes each day. Pigs, the primary source of meat in the Irish diet, were also fed potatoes. When potato blight destroyed a large percentage of the potato crops in 1845, 1846, and 1848, the laboring population had few choices. A million or more may have died as a result of the famine; another million chose to emigrate. In the 1820s, 54,000 Irish immigrants came to America; in the 1840s, 781,000. The immigrant wave peaked in the 1850s when 914,000 Irish immigrants arrived, most coming through New York Harbor. With friends or family already in the United States and British North America, the decision to emigrate became easier. Between 1845 and 1860, about 1.7 million Irish settled in the United States, and another 360,000, in Canada. Although the rate of immigration declined as the century progressed, the aggregate numbers remained large. Between 1860 and 1910, another 2.3 million Irish immigrated to the United States, and about 150,000, to Canada.

Whereas 18th-century Scots-Irish had often headed for the frontier, Irish immigrants after the Great Famine almost always settled in eastern cities. Many stayed in Boston and New York to work in industry or fill newly emerging public-sector jobs as police officers or firemen. Others moved on to jobs in canal and railway construction, filtering westward along with the progress of the country. Irish people were widely discriminated against in the 19th century but created an extensive culture of self-help, aided by their numbers and an almost universal commitment to the Roman Catholic Church (see NATIVISM). The Irish helped transform the Catholic Church from a struggling minor denomination at the turn of the century to a major social and cultural force. By the 1870s, Irish Catholics came to dominate the church, which had earlier been led principally by French and German priests. In Canada, Irish Catholics joined with the significant French minority to further strengthen the Catholic Church there. By the early 20th century, Irish Americans were holding key political and financial positions in Boston, New York, and other large American cities. In Canada, they played a smaller role, however, being fewer in both number and percentage than in the United States, and having come to a society with an already-established Catholic Church in the French tradition.

As late as the 1920s, an average of more than 20,000 Irish immigrants were arriving annually in the United States. During the 1930s, however, the annual rate dropped dramatically to 1,300. During the 1930s, depression and the declaration of Irish independence (1937) combined to provide more stability in Ireland and the beginnings of a gradual improvement in the Irish economy. Between 1951 and 1990, more than 120,000 Irish immigrants arrived in the United States. Between 1992 and 2002, more than 4,000 arrived annually, with numbers falling dramatically after 1995. The Irish percentage of total immigrant arrivals averaged about 38 percent between 1820 and 1860, ensuring a substantial impact on the culture of the United States. By the post–World War II period, the Irish were part of the American mainstream, and new immigration was largely by individuals seeking greater economic opportunity. Between 1950 and 2002, Irish immigrants composed only 0.7 percent of all immigrants coming to the United States.

Irish immigration to Canada after the Great Famine tended to be more heavily Protestant than in the United States. It also marked the final widespread arrival of Irish there. In the worst years of the famine, between 1846 and 1850, about 230,000 Irish arrived in the maritime colonies and the Canadas. Nativism was prevalent in Canada as well as the United States. The Irish, often arrived ill and in poor condition and were herded into overcrowded quarantine stations where infectious diseases were rife, suggesting to local residents an association with filth and disease. At the peak of the immigration in the 1830s and 1840s, almost two-thirds of all Canadian immigrants were Irish. During that period more than 624,000 Irish immigrants arrived, accounting for more than half of all Irish immigrants between 1825 and 1978. By the 1850s, higher taxes, less regular transportation between Ireland and Canada, and lower fares to the United States diverted most Irish immigrants to the south. Between 1855 and 1869, fewer than 60,000 Irish arrived. During the 1880s and 1890s, the few who came tended to be Protestants who settled in Ontario and the west, though

Irish numbers in the western provinces remained small. Irish immigration further declined in the 20th century. Of the 25,850 Irish immigrants in Canada in 2001, more than 35 percent (9,185) arrived before 1961, and only 6 percent (1,835) after 1990. Throughout most of the 19th and 20th centuries, Irish Protestants have outnumbered Irish Catholics in Canada about two to one.

See also CANADA—IMMIGRATION SURVEY AND POLICY OVERVIEW; UNITED STATES—IMMIGRATION SURVEY AND POLICY OVERVIEW.

Further Reading
Bayor, Ronald H., and Timothy J. Meagher, eds. *The New York Irish.* Baltimore: Johns Hopkins University Press, 1996.
Brown, Thomas N. *Irish American Nationalism: 1870 to 1890.* Philadelphia: Lippincott, 1966.
Brundage, David. *The Making of Western Labor Radicalism: Denver's Organized Workers.* Urbana: University of Illinois Press, 1994.
Dezell, Maureen. *Irish America: Coming into Clover.* New York: Doubleday, 2001.
Diner, Hasia. *Erin's Daughters in America: Irish Immigrant Women in the Nineteenth Century.* Baltimore: Johns Hopkins University Press, 1983.
Dolan, Jay P. *The Immigrant Church: New York's Irish and German Catholics: 1815–1865.* Baltimore: Johns Hopkins University Press, 1975.
Elliott, Bruce S. *Irish Migrants in the Canadas: A New Approach.* Montreal and Kingston: McGill–Queen's University Press, 1988.
Emmons, David. *The Butte Irish: Class and Ethnicity in an American Mining Town, 1875–1925.* Urbana: University of Illinois Press, 1989.
Erie, Stephen R. *Rainbow's End: Irish-Americans and the Dilemmas of Urban Machine Politics, 1840–1985.* Berkeley: University of California Press, 1988.
Freeman, Joshua. *In Transit: The Transport Workers Union in New York City, 1933–1966.* New York: Oxford University Press, 1989.
Houston, Cecil J., and William J. Smyth. *Irish Emigration and Canadian Settlement: Patterns, Links, and Letters.* Toronto: University of Toronto Press, 1990.
Ignatiev, Noel. *How the Irish Became White.* New York: Routledge, 1996.
Keneally, Thomas. *The Great Shame and the Triumph of the Irish in the English Speaking World.* New York: Anchor Books, 2000.
Mackay, Donald. *Flight from Famine: The Coming of the Irish to Canada.* Toronto: McClelland and Stewart, 1990.
McCaffrey, Lawrence. *The Irish Diaspora in America.* Bloomington: Indiana University Press, 1976.
Miller, Kerby A. *Emigrants and Exiles: Ireland and the Irish Exodus to North America.* New York: Oxford University Press, 1985.
Miller, Kerby A., et al. *Irish Immigrants in the Land of Canaan: Letters and Memoirs from Colonial and Revolutionary America, 1675–1815.* Oxford: Oxford University Press, 2003.
Mitchell, Brian. *The Paddy Camps: The Irish of Lowell, 1821–1861.* Urbana: University of Illinois Press, 1988.
Murphy, Terence, and Gerald Stortz, eds. *Creed and Culture: The Place of English-Speaking Catholics in Canadian Society, 1750–1930.* Montreal: McGill–Queen's University Press, 1993.

Wilson, David A. *The Irish in Canada.* Ottawa: Canadian Historical Association, 1989.

Italian immigration

Italy was second only to Germany as a source country for immigrants to the United States after 1820. Although Italian immigration to Canada was much slower to develop, only Great Britain sent more immigrants there between 1948 and 1972. According to the 2000 U.S. census and the 2001 Canadian census, 15,723,555 Americans and 1,270,370 Canadians claimed Italian descent. Early areas of Italian concentration were NEW YORK, NEW YORK; BOSTON; and Pennsylvania, though the Italian population dispersed widely throughout the country during the 20th century. During the 19th century, almost all Italian Canadians lived in MONTREAL. By 2001, Toronto had the largest concentration of Italians, and Montreal, the second largest.

Italy consists of a long peninsula, the large islands of Sicily and Sardinia, and numerous smaller islands, all situated in the central Mediterranean Sea. It is bordered by France on the west, Switzerland and Austria on the north, and Slovenia on the east. It covers 116, 324 square miles, and in 2002, it had a population of about 58 million. More than 95 percent of the population is ethnically Italian, and more than 80 percent are Roman Catholics. Though Italy was the location of the great Roman civilization, it was divided politically throughout the Middle Ages, and its affairs often revolved around the papal court in Rome. The cultural revival known as the Renaissance began in northern Italy during the 14th century, producing some of the greatest scholars, artists, and philosophers in history. Various parts of the Italian peninsula were ruled by France, the Holy Roman Empire, Spain, and Austria until the nationalistic Risorgimento movement succeeded in unifying all the Italian states during the 1860s. Though on the victorious side of World War I (1914–18), Italians were dissatisfied with the peace settlement and hit hard by the weakened international economy. This led to the rise of the Fascist dictator Benito Mussolini, who led Italy into World War II (1939–45) on the side of Nazi Germany. After being defeated, Italy was reorganized as a republic (1946). Though politically unstable throughout the 20th century, the country avoided excessive social turmoil and played a leading role in the development of the North Atlantic Treaty Organization and the European Union.

Many of the earliest European explorers of North America were Italians, including Christopher Columbus, John Cabot, Amerigo Vespucci, and Giovanni da Verrazano. Some northern Italians traveled to North America during the 17th and 18th centuries, settling in New York, Virginia, Rhode Island, Connecticut, Pennsylvania, Maryland, and Georgia. Actual Italian settlement remained small, however, until after Italian unification during the 1860s. Between 1820 and 1860, only about 14,000 Italians immigrated to the United States, most coming as individuals from northern Italy, seeking economic opportunity. Some were attracted to the West Coast with the CALIFORNIA GOLD RUSH of 1849. By the Civil War (1861–65), Italians were widely dispersed around the country, with California (2,805) and New York (1,862) having the largest populations. The first substantial migration came after the promulgation of a new Italian constitution in 1861, which tended to benefit the industrialized and advanced north, at the expense of the already impoverished, semifeudal agricultural south. As the population in Italy soared, increasing from 25 million in 1861 to 35 million in 1901, the plight of peasant laborers in the south worsened. Large estates were still often controlled by absentee landlords who did little to bring modern technology into the farming process. As a result, desperate sharecroppers and laborers left the worn-out soil for new opportunities in the United States.

Italian immigration increased dramatically during the 1880s, with the source area gradually shifting from north to south. Between 1876 and 1924, when the restrictive JOHNSON-REED ACT was passed, more than 4.5 million Italians immigrated to the United States, about three-quarters of them from the impoverished south. Typically immigrants were young men who hoped to work one or two seasons before returning to Italy to start a better life. They usually spoke no English, so they turned to labor bosses (see PADRONE SYSTEM) who established widespread networks for providing Italian labor to construction jobs throughout the East. Because the padrones sometimes cheated the vulnerable immigrants, they were carefully scrutinized by government and social workers and began to decline in influence by the first decade of the 20th century. After the turn of the century, gender rates were more balanced. By 1910, Italian women made up more than one-third of the female workforce in New York's garment industry (see INTERNATIONAL LADIES' GARMENT WORKERS' UNION) and more than 70 percent of the total workforce of the artificial flower industry.

The rate of return for Italians was high. Between 1899 and 1924, 3.8 million Italians arrived, while 2.1 million returned to Italy during the same period. Italian immigration reached its peak in the first decade of the 20th century, when more than 2 million Italians arrived. Generally poor, uneducated, and Roman Catholic, Italians suffered severely from NATIVISM. As a result, they created social enclaves— Little Italies—in most major American cities, fostering a love of the old country and traditional ways of life, though these neighborhoods were seldom inhabited solely by Italians. In part, this was because Italian immigrants frequently moved. In the first generation, they generally lived in the worst slums of New York City, Boston, Philadelphia, Chicago, and San Francisco. By the turn of the century, Italian families had often moved to more spacious working-class neighborhoods. By 1910, there were 340,765 Italian immi-

This 1912 photo shows Mrs. Guadina, a struggling Italian immigrant in New York City, trying to complete her batch of piece work in order to be paid. According to the visiting city official, there seemed to be no food in the house, the father was out of work, and a fourth child was expected soon. *(Photo by Lewis W. Hine for the Department of Commerce and Labor, Children's Bureau/National Archives #102-LH-2821)*

grants in New York City, the largest Italian population outside Italy and much larger than such famous Italian cities as Florence and Venice. New York's Italian community, like most others in the country, was dominated by southern Italians. The one major exception to this trend was San Francisco, where fewer southern Italians migrated.

By the late 1920s, Italian immigration had dropped significantly. Though Italian Americans numbered in the millions, they still had little political power to show for it. Fiorello H. La Guardia, mayor of New York City from 1934 to 1945, was a notable exception. About 116,000 came during the 1930s and 1940s, most blending smoothly into the growing middle-class Italian community. Immigration revived during the economic boom of the 1950s and 1960s, when 400,000 arrived, but tapered off again thereafter. Greater political stability and economic development in Italy after 1980 kept immigration numbers relatively low. Between 1992 and 2002, Italian immigration averaged about 2,500 per year.

Much less receptive to non-British immigrants, Canada was slow to encourage Italian immigration. A small number of nobles aided in the French and British settlement of North America. Enrico di Tonti served as a lieutenant on several of explorer René-Robert Cavelier de La Salle's expeditions between 1679 and 1682. After the end of the Napoleonic Wars (1815), several hundred Italians who had served in the Meuron and de Watteville foreign regiments of the British army settled in Canada, principally around Drummondville, Quebec, and in southern Ontario. A small number of Italians immigrated individually during the 19th century, but the numbers remained small until the turn of the century. In 1901, there were still fewer than 11,000 Italians in Canada, almost all of whom lived in Montreal. Between the 1870s and 1914, more than 13 million Italians emigrated. Before 1900, about 70 percent were bound for Argentina, Brazil, and other South American destinations, and most of the rest for the United States. After 1900, about two-thirds settled in North America. The number choosing

Canada was small, and often closely related to work opportunities originating in the United States. The Canadian Pacific Railway, for instance, imported laborers both from the United States and Italy.

The great period of Italian immigration to Canada came during the 1950s and 1960s, when more than 500,000 immigrants arrived. Though many left Italy as temporary workers, a far greater number of the post–World War II immigrants stayed to settle. As the Canadian economy expanded, Italy became an important source for construction workers and unskilled labor, taking advantage of new Canadian policies that liberalized provisions of family sponsorship. The Canadian government concluded a bilateral agreement with Italy in 1950, allowing Italian Canadians greater opportunities for bringing family members into the country. During the 1950s, about 80 percent of Italian immigrants were sponsored family members. The more restrictive IMMIGRATION REGULATIONS of 1967 made it more difficult for unskilled Italians to qualify and coincided generally with a revival in the Italian economy. As a result, Italian immigration declined sharply during the 1970s, when only 48,000 arrived. In the 1980s, still fewer Italians came, averaging less than 2,000 per year. Of the 314,455 Italian immigrants residing in Canada in 2001, fewer than 15,000 came during between 1981 and 2001.

See also CANADA—IMMIGRATION SURVEY AND POLICY OVERVIEW; UNITED STATES—IMMIGRATION SURVEY AND POLICY OVERVIEW.

Further Reading

Alba, Richard D. "Italian Americans: A Century of Ethnic Change." In *Origins and Destinies: Immigration, Race and Ethnicity in America*. Ed. Silvia Pedraza and Rubén G. Rumbaut. Belmont, Calif.: Wadsworth, 1996.

———. *Italian Americans: Into the Twilight of Ethnicity*. Englewood Cliffs, N.J.: Prentice Hall, 1985.

Briggs, John W. *An Italian Passage: Immigrants to Three American Cities, 1890–1930*. New Haven, Conn.: Yale University Press, 1978.

De Conde, Alexander. *Half Bitter, Half Sweet: An Excursion into Italian-American History*. New York: Scribner's, 1971.

Foerster, Robert F. *The Italian Emigration of Our Times*. Cambridge, Mass.: Harvard University Press, 1924.

Gallo, Patrick. *Old Bread, New Wine: A Portrait of Italian Americans*. Chicago: Nelson-Hall, 1981.

Gans, Herbert. *Villagers: Group and Class in the Life of Italian-Americans*. New York: Free Press, 1982.

Harvey, Robert F. *From the Shores of Hardship: Italians in Canada*. Welland, Canada: Soleil, 1993.

Mangione, Jerre, and Ben Morreale. *La Storia*. New York: Harper, 1993.

Morreale, Ben, and Robert Carola. *Italian Americans: The Immigrant Experience*. Southport, Conn.: Hugh Lauter Levin Associates, 2000.

Orsi, Robert A. *The Madonna of 115th Street: Faith and Community in Italian Harlem, 1880–1950*. New Haven, Conn.: Yale University Press, 1988.

Perin, Roberto, and Franc Sturino, eds. *"Arrangiarsi": The Italian Immigration Experience in Canada*. Montreal: Guernica, 1989.

Ramirez, Bruno. *The Italians in Canada*. Ottawa: Canadian Historical Association, 1989.

Smith, Judith E. *Family Connections: A History of Italian and Immigrant Lives in Providence, Rhode Island, 1900–1940*. Albany: State University of New York Press, 1985.

Spada, A. V. *The Italians in Canada*. Ottawa and Montreal: Italo-Canadian Ethnic and Historical Research Center, 1969.

Jamaican immigration

Jamaicans are the largest West Indian immigrant group in Canada and the third largest in the United States, behind Puerto Ricans and Cubans. In the U.S. census of 2000 and the Canadian census of 2001, 736,513 Americans and 211,720 Canadians claimed Jamaican descent. The majority of Jamaicans in the United States live in New York City and other urban communities of the Northeast, though a significant number also live in Florida. Toronto is by far the preferred destination of Jamaicans in Canada.

The island of Jamaica occupies 4,200 square miles in the Caribbean Sea. Its nearest neighbors are Cuba to the north and Haiti to the east. In 2002, the population was estimated at 2,665,636. The people are 90 percent black, descended from slaves brought to Jamaica by the British during the 17th and 18th centuries. About 61 percent of the population is Protestant and 4 percent Roman Catholic. More than a third of Jamaicans are members of other religious groups, many of which teach African revivalist doctrines. The best-known Afro-Caribbean religion is Rastafarianism, which venerates Haile Selassie, who before becoming emperor of Ethiopia was named Ras Tafari, as a god. It was made internationally famous by the reggae musician Bob Marley in the 1970s, who sang about its belief in the eventual redemption and return of blacks to Africa. Jamaica was inhabited by Arawak peoples until Columbus visited the island in 1494 and brought European diseases that soon wiped out the native population. The island was occupied by Britain in the 1650s, becoming its principal sugar-producing island in the Caribbean. Jamaica won its independence in 1962. Socialist governments throughout the 1970s frequently clashed with the United States and Canada over bauxite mining interests and COLD WAR ideology, leading to considerable political unrest in Jamaica. During the 1980s, Jamaican politics became more conservative, and relations with the North American mainland improved.

Prior to the 1960s, both the United States and Canada treated immigrants from Caribbean Basin dependencies and countries, in various combinations, as a single immigrant unit known as "West Indians," making it impossible to determine exactly how many Jamaicans were among them. Before 1965, however, Jamaican immigrants clearly predominated, and English-speaking immigrants generally far outstripped others. Between 1900 and 1924, about 100,000 West Indians immigrated to the United States, many of them from the middle classes. The restrictive JOHNSON-REED ACT (1924) and economic depression in the 1930s virtually halted their immigration, but some 40,000 had already established a cultural base in New York City, particularly in Harlem and Brooklyn. About 41,000 West Indians were recruited for war work after 1941, but most returned to their homes after World War II. Isolationist policies of the 1950s and relatively open access to Britain kept immigration to the United States low until passage of the Immigration Act of 1965, which shifted the basis of immigration from country of origin to family reunification. The McCARRAN-WALTER IMMIGRATION AND NATURALIZATION ACT of 1952 had established an annual quota of only 800 for all British territories in the West Indies. When

Jamaica became independent, however, the country qualified for increased immigration quotas. Between 1992 and 2002, an average of more than 16,000 Jamaicans immigrated to the United States annually.

Many Jamaicans in both the United States and Canada were well educated and enjoyed greater economic success than other Americans of African descent. Their political influence in the United States was proportionally greater than their numbers would suggest, leading to tension between West Indians generally and African Americans. Jamaican political activist Marcus Garvey, who came to the United States in 1916, and U.S. secretary of state Colin Powell, son of Jamaican immigrants, brought considerable attention to the Jamaican immigrant community during the 20th century.

West Indian immigration to Canada remained small throughout the 20th century. Following restrictive legislation enacted in 1923, it is estimated that only 250 West Indians were admitted during the entire decade of the 1920s. By the mid 1960s, only 25,000 West Indians lived there. Canadian regulations after World War II (1939–45) prohibited most black immigration, and special programs, such as the 1955 domestic workers' campaign, allowed only a few hundred well-qualified West Indians into the country each year until 1967, when the point system was introduced for determining immigrant qualifications. Jamaica nevertheless maintained the largest source of Caribbean immigrants. Of Canada's 120,000 Jamaican immigrants in 2001, more than 100,000 came after 1970.

See also WEST INDIAN IMMIGRATION.

Further Reading

Barrett, Leonard E. *The Rastafarians*. Boston: Beacon Press, 1997.

Eato, George. *Canadians of Jamaican Heritage*. Chatham, Canada: 1986.

Foner, Nancy. "The Jamaicans: Race and Ethnicity among Migrants in New York City." In *New Immigrants in New York*. Ed. Nancy Foner. New York: Columbia University Press, 1987.

Kasinitz, Philip. *Caribbean New York: Black Immigrants and the Politics of Race*. Ithaca, N.Y.: Cornell University Press, 1992.

Owens-Watkins, Irma. *Blood Relations*. Bloomington: University of Indiana Press, 1996.

Palmer, R. W. *Pilgrims from the Sun: West Indian Migration to America*. New York: Twayne, 1995.

Parrillo, Vincent. *Strangers to These Shores*. 5th ed. Boston: Allyn and Bacon, 1997.

Vickerman, Milton. *Crosscurrents: West Indian Immigrants and Race*. New York: Oxford University Press, 1998.

Walker, James W. St. G. *The West Indians in Canada*. Ottawa: Canadian Historical Association, 1984.

Westmoreland, Guy T., Jr. *West Indian Americans*. Westport, Conn.: Greenwood Press, 2001.

Jamestown, Virginia See VIRGINIA COLONY.

Japanese immigration

For most of the 20th century, Japanese Americans formed the largest Asian ethnic group in the United States. According to the 2000 U.S. census and the 2001 Canadian census, 1,148,932 Americans and 85,230 Canadians claimed Japanese descent. Although many Japanese immigrants came to the United States as laborers, by the 1960s they had largely moved out of ethnic neighborhoods and into the American mainstream. In 2000, they were still highly concentrated in California and on the West Coast, though they were increasingly dispersing throughout the country. More than 40 percent of Japanese Canadians live in British Columbia.

Japan is a 152,200-square-mile archipelago situated in the Pacific Ocean about 100 miles east of Korea and 500 miles east of China. The Russian island of Sakhalin is Japan's nearest neighbor to the north. In 2002, the population was estimated at 126,771,662, more than 99 percent of whom were ethnic Japanese. The major religions are Buddhism and Shintoism. A mountainous country with few natural resources, Japan is among the most densely populated countries in the world, a factor largely contributing to its immigration history. Japan borrowed heavily from Chinese culture between the 5th and 10th centuries but generally adapted Chinese models to its own culture patterns and transformed them into a unique Japanese culture. After a brief period of trade and contact with Portuguese, Dutch, and English merchants and missionaries, Japan largely closed itself off from the world during the Tokugawa era (1603–1868). During the 1850s, the United States forced Japan to open its ports to trade, much as Britain had done in China during the 1830s. Unlike China, however, Japan was relatively successful in modernizing without sacrificing its culture. Borrowing heavily from Western models, after 1868, Japan created a parliamentary democracy, eliminated many elements of its feudal social system, and modernized its military. After defeating China (1894–95) and Russia (1904–05), Japan became the principal regional power in East Asia. During the 1920s and 1930s, the fragile and limited Japanese democracy was heavily influenced by the Japanese army and navy, which sought military solutions to overpopulation and a lack of natural resources. Japan's occupation of Manchuria (1931) and northern China (1937) led into World War II (1939–45), which ended with the destruction of the Japanese cities of Hiroshima and Nagasaki by U.S. atomic bombs in August 1945. With the aid of U.S. reconstruction, Japan became an important COLD WAR ally and developed one of the world's strongest economies from the 1970s on.

Patterns of Japanese immigration were similar in both the United States and Canada. Significant Japanese migration to the American West began in the 1880s in the wake of the CHINESE EXCLUSION ACT (1882). Prohibited from hiring Chinese laborers, plantation owners in Hawaii brought Japanese, many of whom had been displaced by the demise of the old Tokugawa regime: Between 1885 and 1904, more than 100,000 Japanese were brought to work in Hawaii, making them the largest ethnic group in the islands. At the same time, many Japanese students and other travelers were venturing to the mainland. By 1900, they had been joined by laborers, making a Japanese population of almost 30,000 in California. Between 1890 and 1910, a similar number landed in British Columbia, though many continued on to the United States. As thousands of Japanese migrated to North America annually in the wake of U.S. annexation of Hawaii in 1898, Americans and Canadians in California and British Columbia protested strongly. Between April and June 1900, almost 8,000 Japanese laborers arrived in British Columbia (due in part to the pent-up demand), alarming local citizens. Though the Japanese government agreed to stop immigration by the end of July, the provincial legislature feared it would only be a temporary decision and thus passed "An Act to Regulate Immigration into British Columbia," requiring Japanese to complete an application for entry in a European language. Clearly in violation of the Anglo-Japanese Treaty of 1894, the measure was disallowed by the Canadian government, leading to a constitutional impasse. A Royal Commission on Chinese and Japanese Immigration recommended that anti-Japanese legislation be allowed only if the Japanese government lifted its ban on laborers. Although almost no Japanese entered British Columbia between 1901 and 1907, American prohibitions on laborers in 1907 and a rapidly growing economy in British Columbia combined to encourage a return of Japanese laborers, between 5,000 and 10,000 in 1907–08. Once again alarmed, Canada secured a Gentlemen's Agreement that the Japanese government would issue no more than 400 passports annually to laborers and domestic servants bound for Canada.

Californians were similarly afraid of the "yellow peril," especially with the economic uncertainty following the San Francisco earthquake in April 1906. The mayor and the Asiatic Exclusion League, with almost 80,000 members, pressured the San Francisco school board to pass a measure segregating Japanese students (October 11), violating Japan's most-favored-nation status and deeply offending the Japanese nation. U.S. president Theodore Roosevelt repudiated the school board's decision and praised Japan. At the same time, between December 1906 and January 1908, he negotiated three separate but related agreements that addressed both Japanese concerns over the welfare of the immigrants and California concerns over the growing numbers of Japanese laborers. In February 1907, immigration legislation was amended to halt the flow of Japanese laborers from Hawaii, Canada, or Mexico, which in turn led the San Francisco school board to rescind (March 13) their segregation resolution. In discussions of December 1907, the

Japanese government agreed to restrict passports for travel to the continental United States to nonlaborers, former residents, or the family members of Japanese immigrants. This allowed for the continued migration of laborers to Hawaii and for access to the United States by travelers, merchants, students, and PICTURE BRIDES. While the U.S. GENTLEMEN'S AGREEMENT helped the two countries move past the crisis, the whole matter left an indelible impression of the strength of American NATIVISM.

Japanese immigration to the United States was almost totally halted with passage of the JOHNSON-REED ACT of 1924. During the 1930s and 1940s, fewer than 200 Japanese immigrated to the United States annually, and less than half that number to Canada. Relations worsened following Japan's invasion of China in 1937. When the navy of imperial Japan bombed Pearl Harbor, Hawaii, on December 7, 1941, Japanese Americans and Japanese Canadians were widely suspected of sympathy with their homeland. Despite the absence of any evidence of sabotage or espionage, on February 19, 1942, President Franklin D. Roosevelt signed Executive Order 9066, which led to the forcible internment of 120,000 Japanese Americans, two-thirds of whom were born in the United States. In the same month, the Canadian government ordered the expulsion of 22,000 Japanese Canadians from a 100-mile strip along the Pacific coast (see JAPANESE INTERNMENT).

Provisions of the MCCARRAN-WALTER IMMIGRATION AND NATURALIZATION ACT of 1952, in conjunction with the rapid development of the Japanese economy, led to a steady but unspectacular immigration starting in the 1950s, averaging almost 5,000 per year between 1961 and 1990. With a healthy Japanese economy through the 1980s, most Japanese preferred to remain at home, but the economic downturn of the 1990s led to increased migration in search of economic opportunities. Between 1992 and 2002, Japanese immigration averaged about 7,500 per year. Between 1910 and 1970, Japanese were the largest Asian ethnic group in the United States but by 2001 had dropped to sixth, behind Chinese, Filipinos, Asian Indians, Koreans, and Vietnamese.

Between 1900 and 1937, between 25,000 and 30,000 Japanese entered Canada, mostly as fishermen or laborers. These numbers are misleading, however, as many immigrants of this period used Canada as a backdoor for entry to the United States as a result of the restrictions of Canada's Gentlemen's Agreement. Between 1937 and 1952, fewer than 200 Japanese entered Canada, most as a result of family reunification or for humanitarian reasons. As the Japanese economy began to boom in the 1960s, immigration rates to Canada remained low, averaging about 500 in most years, a little higher in times of economic uncertainty. Most of these immigrants were young, well-educated professionals. Of 17,630 Japanese immigrants in Canada in 2001, almost 8,000 came between

1991 and 2001, the largest decade of immigration in the post–World War II era.

Further Reading

Adachi, Ken. *The Enemy That Never Was: A History of the Japanese Canadians.* Toronto: McClelland and Stewart, 1991.

Daniels, Roger. *Asian America: Chinese and Japanese in the United States since 1850.* Seattle: University of Washington Press, 1988.

Herman, Masako. *The Japanese in America, 1843–1973.* Dobbs Ferry, N.Y.: Oceana, 1974.

Makabe, Tomoko. *The Canadian Sansei.* Toronto: University of Toronto Press, 1998.

Moriyama, Alan T. *Imingaisha: Japanese Emigration Companies and Hawaii, 1894–1908.* Honolulu: University of Hawaii Press, 1985.

Nakano, M. *Japanese American Women: Three Generations, 1890–1900.* San Francisco: Mina Press, 1990.

Niiya, B., ed. *Encyclopedia of Japanese American History: An A-to-Z Reference from 1868 to the Present.* Updated edition. New York: Facts On File, 2000.

Roy, Patricia E. *A White Man's Province: British Columbia Politicians and Japanese Immigrants, 1858–1914.* Vancouver, Canada: University of British Columbia Press, 1989.

Spickard, Paul. *Japanese Americans: The Formation and Transformation of an Ethnic Group.* New York: Twayne, 1996.

Ward, W. Peter. *The Japanese in Canada.* Ottawa: Canadian Historical Association, 1982.

Japanese internment, World War II

Following the bombing of Pearl Harbor, Hawaii, on December 7, 1941, Japanese Americans and Japanese Canadians were widely suspected as supporters of the aggressive militarism of the Japanese Empire. Despite the absence of any evidence of sabotage or espionage, on February 19, 1942, President Franklin D. Roosevelt signed Executive Order 9066, which led to the forcible internment of 120,000 Japanese Americans, two-thirds of whom had been born in the United States. In the same month, the Canadian government ordered the expulsion of 22,000 Japanese Canadians from a 100-mile strip along the Pacific coast.

With the outbreak of war in Europe in 1939, the U.S. Congress passed the Alien Registration Act (1940), requiring all non-naturalized aliens aged 14 and older to register with the government and tightening naturalization requirements. With the U.S. declaration of war against Germany, Italy, and Japan following the attack on Pearl Harbor, more than 1 million foreign-born immigrants from those countries became "enemy aliens." Italians and Germans were so deeply assimilated into American culture, however, that they were largely left alone. More visibly distinct and ethnically related to the attackers, Japanese immigrants and Americans of Japanese descent were quickly targeted in the early-war hysteria. The territory of Hawaii was put under military rule, and the 37 percent of its population of Japanese ancestry was carefully watched, though they were not interned or evacuated. On the mainland, many politicians and members of the press, along with agricultural and patriotic pressure groups, urged action against the Japanese, leading to Executive Order 9066, empowering the War Department to remove people from any area of military significance.

Japanese Americans were forced to dispose quickly of their property, usually at considerable loss. They were often allowed to take only two suitcases with them. Internment-camp life was physically rugged and emotionally challenging. Most nisei, or second-generation Japanese in the United States, thought of themselves as thoroughly American and felt betrayed by the justice system. They nevertheless remained loyal to the country, and eventually more than 33,000 served in the armed forces during World War II. Among these were some 18,000 members of the 442nd Regimental Combat Team, which became one of the most highly decorated of the war. Throughout the war, about 120,000 were interned under the War Relocation Authority in one of 10 hastily constructed camps in desert or rural areas of Utah, Arizona, Colorado, Arkansas, Idaho, California, and Wyoming. In three related cases that came before the Supreme Court—*Yasui v. United States* (1942), *Hirabayashi v. United States* (1943), and *KOREMATSU V. UNITED STATES* (1944)—the government's authority was upheld, though a dissenting judge noted that such collective guilt had been assumed "based upon the accident of race." The camps were finally ordered closed in December 1944. The Evacuation Claims Act of 1948 provided $31 million in compensation, though this was later determined to be less than one-10th the value of property and wages lost by Japanese Americans during their internment. In Canada, the government bowed to the unified pressure of representatives from British Columbia, giving the minister of justice the authority to remove Japanese Canadians from any designated areas. While their property was at first impounded for later return, an order-in-council was passed in January 1943 allowing the government to sell it without permission and then to apply the funds to the maintenance of the camps. With labor shortages by 1943, some Japanese Canadians were allowed to move eastward, especially to Ontario, though they were not permitted to buy or lease lands or businesses. Though it was acknowledged that "no person of Japanese race born in Canada" had been charged with "any act of sabotage or disloyalty during the years of war," the government provided strong incentives for them to return to Japan. After much debate and extensive challenges in the courts, more than 4,000 returned to Japan, more than half of whom were Canadian-born citizens. More than 13,000 of those who stayed left British Columbia, leaving fewer than 7,000 in the province.

In 1978, the Japanese American Citizens' League formed the National Committee for Redress, spearheading

This photo shows the front of Sutekichi Miyagawa's internment identification card issued by the Canadian government in compliance with Order-in-Council P.C. 117, Vancouver, British Columbia, March 12, 1941. During World War II, some 120,000 Japanese Americans and 22,000 Japanese Canadians were interned or relocated. *(National Archives of Canada/PA-103542)*

efforts for a formal apology and compensation for survivors. In 1980, Congress established the Commission on Wartime Relocation and Internment of Citizens (CWRIC). After 18 months of investigations, the commission issued its final report in 1983, concluding that "a grave injustice was done to American citizens and resident aliens of Japanese descent." No documented case of sabotage or disloyalty by a Japanese American was found, and it was discovered that the Justice and War Departments had altered records and thereby misled the courts. After a further five years of negotiation, in 1988, the Civil Liberties Act was signed by President Ronald Reagan, who noted that Japanese Americans had proven "utterly loyal," providing an apology and $20,000 to each camp survivor still living. The eventual payout was more than $1.6 billion. Less than two weeks later, the Canadian government publicly apologized and provided compensation, including $12,000 to each survivor, a $12 million social and educational package for the Japanese community, and a further $12 million to the Canadian Race Relations Foundation.

Further Reading

Daniels, Roger. *Prisoners without Trial: Japanese Americans in World War II.* New York: Hill and Wang, 1993.

Hatamiya, Leslie T. *Righting a Wrong: Japanese Americans and the Passage of the Civil Liberties Act of 1988.* Stanford, Calif.: Stanford University Press, 1993.

Hillmer, Norman, ed. *On Guard for Thee: War, Ethnicity, and the Canadian State, 1939–1945.* Ottawa: Canadian Committee for the History of the Second World War, 1988.

Irons, Peter. *Justice Delayed: The Record of the Japanese American Internment Cases.* Middletown, Conn.: Wesleyan University Press, 1989.

Miki, Roy, and Cassandra Kobayashi. *Justice in Our Time: The Japanese-Canadian Redress Settlement.* Vancouver, Canada: Talonbooks, 1991.

Nakano, Takeo Ujo. *Within the Barbed Wire Fence: A Japanese Man's Account of his Internment in Canada.* Toronto: University of Toronto Press, 1980.

Roy, Patricia, et al. *Mutual Hostages: Canadians and Japanese during the Second World War.* Toronto: University of Toronto Press, 1990.

Sunahara, A. G. *The Politics of Racism: The Uprooting of Japanese Canadians during the Second World War.* Toronto: Lorimer, 1981.

Jewish immigration

The Jewish immigrant experience was unique in North American history. Jews suffered the double discrimination of being both foreign and non-Christian in countries whose cultures were largely defined by Christian patterns of belief and practice. After much discrimination in the 19th and early 20th centuries, the Jewish community as a whole nevertheless prospered in the United States and Canada. In 2001, the American Jewish population was estimated at just over 6 million, or about 2.3 percent of the population. According to the Canadian census of 2001, about 350,000 Canadians claimed Jewish descent, about 1.2 percent of the total population. NEW YORK, NEW YORK is the center of American Judaism, with a population of more than 1.5 million. Jews make up almost 9 percent of the population of New York State. Toronto and Montreal have the largest Jewish Canadian populations.

Statistics on Jewish immigration are more problematic than for most groups. Before 1948, there was no Jewish homeland, as most Jews had been driven out of Palestine in the first century by the Romans. As most immigration statistics for the 19th and 20th centuries related principally to country of origin or land of birth, Jewish numbers were obscured. Closely related to the means of collecting data was the group's wide dispersion. Jews inhabited most European countries and many Middle Eastern countries, complicating estimates based on emigration records or historical circumstances. Having come in large numbers from central Europe (where they spoke German), eastern Europe (where they spoke Yiddish), and North Africa and the Balkans (where they spoke Ladino), they had no common language and quickly gave up their Old World languages in favor of English or French. Finally, there is no clear consensus on the standards for being Jewish. Although Judaism is rooted in the traditional religious beliefs and practices that originated in Palestine during the second millennium B.C. perhaps 20 percent or more of Jews are not religious. Among those who are, the Orthodox carefully observe the historical rules of the Torah, while Reform Jews look to scripture for moral principles that can be adapted to the changing circumstances of Jewish life. Reconstructionist Jews are more concerned with the preservation of Jewish culture than Jewish religion, though the former incorporates many elements of the latter. Many wholly secular Jews continue to celebrate religious holidays and observe traditionally religious ceremonies, though only for cultural reasons.

Jews migrated to Britain's American colonies in small numbers throughout the colonial period, attracted by a religious toleration unknown in Europe. By the 1780s, there were already 3,000 Jews in America. Between 1820 and 1880, a new wave of mostly German-speaking Jews came to the United States. By the 1840s, Jews numbered almost 50,000, with significant populations in most cities on the Atlantic and Gulf coasts and throughout the Midwest. By 1860, there were 150,000 Jews and some 200 congregations in the United States. Cincinnati, Ohio, and Philadelphia, Pennsylvania, emerged as Jewish cultural centers during the 1870s, as the total Jewish population rose to a quarter million. As Jews began to enter mainstream American culture, they increasingly adapted their religious and cultural patterns to their new surroundings. Out of this accommodation arose Reform Judaism.

The greatest phase of Jewish immigration to the United States came between 1880 and 1924, a period that saw the Jewish population increase from about 250,000 to 4.5 million and saw the center of Jewish life shift from Europe to

Young Jews who were freed from Buchenwald. Highly educated German and east European Jews were welcomed as refugees from Nazi aggression, but anti-Semitism generally remained strong in the United States and Canada during World War II. *(National Archives #111-SC-207907)*

the United States. With Jewish persecution on the rise during an intensely nationalistic period in European history, some 2 million Jews—known as Ashkenazim—fled Poland, Russia, Romania, Galicia (in the Austro-Hungarian Empire), and other regions of eastern Europe. Also during this period, about 35,000 Sephardic Jews arrived, mainly from Turkey and Syria. These mainly Orthodox Jews from eastern Europe and the Middle East were often an embarrassment to well-established Reform Jews, who were well on their way toward assimilation, creating some tension within the American Jewish community. After 1890, the vast majority of Jews settled in New York City and other parts of the northern seaboard. Although half of America's Jews lived in New York City by 1914, there were many thriving, independent Jewish communities spread throughout the country. National restrictions imposed by the JOHNSON-REED ACT of 1924 limited annual Jewish immigration to about 10,000, with few allowances made for extreme anti-Semitic conditions in Europe during the 1930s. Most of the 150,000 Jews who immigrated to the United States in the years leading up to World War II (1939–45) were professionals and other members of the middle classes, about 3,000 of whom were admitted under special visas aimed at rescuing prominent artists and scientists. By and large, however, few special provisions were made for Jewish immigrants. As late as 1941, a bill that would have allowed entry to 20,000 German Jewish children was defeated in Congress. In response to the horrors of the Holocaust in which 6 million Jews died at the hands of Adolf Hitler's "final solution" to exterminate them, special provisions were made for tens of thousands of Jews under the DISPLACED PERSONS ACT (1948) and related immigrant regulations. Immigration remained relatively small until the early 1980s, when economic turmoil in the Soviet Union led to a massive exodus of Russian and Ukrainian Jews, especially after the ascension of the liberalizing Communist leader Mikhail Gorbachev in 1985. More than 200,000 eventually settled in the United States between 1980 and 2000.

The first Canadian synogogue was organized in 1768 in Montreal, a city with strong promise of commercial success. It maintained close ties to the primary congregation in New York City, though these and other ties with America were soon severed by revolution. The Jewish population in Canada remained small, growing from 451 in 1851 to only 1,333 20 years later. The perception of greater economic opportunity, combined with the increasing religious intolerance in Russia (including modern Poland and Lithuania) that erupted in violent pogroms in 1881, changed the character of Jewish immigration to North America. Whereas most Jews were of German or British origin prior to 1880, the majority thereafter emigrated from Russia, Austria-Hungary, or Romania. About 10,000 arrived in Canada by the turn of the century, many of them sponsored by Jewish charitable groups such as the Citizens Committee Jewish Relief

Fund and the Jewish Emigration Aid Society. This migration led to the establishment of a significant Jewish community in Winnipeg, Manitoba, and raised the Jewish population to 16,401.

Jewish immigration to Canada peaked between 1900 and 1914, when almost 100,000 entered the country. Most of the growth occurred in Montreal, Toronto, and Winnipeg, though congregations substantially increased in Ottawa, Hamilton, and Fort William, Ontario; Vancouver, British Columbia; and Calgary, Alberta. Congregations were established for the first time in Saskatoon and Regina, Saskatchewan, and Edmonton, Alberta. The great influx changed the character of Canadian Jewry. With more arrivals from eastern Europe, cultural homogeneity declined, while economic and political diversity increased.

While there were many similarities in the experience of American and Canadian Jews, including economic background, settlement and labor patterns, cultural life, and social discrimination, there were a number of unique factors affecting Canada's Jews. For instance, in the province of Quebec, where nearly half of Canada's Jews lived, there was no legal educational provision for Jewish children. This led to a highly organized civil rights movement between 1903 and 1930, which had no counterpart in the United States. More generally, the Jewish presence in Quebec was viewed with hostility by French-Canadian nationalists, who tended to emphasize agriculture, antistatism, and ultramontane Roman Catholicism. Whereas American Jewish life tended to be dominated by the Reform Judaism of German immigrants, Canadian Judaic culture was more Orthodox and thus less easily assimilated. This was reflected in a deeper commitment on the part of the Canadian Jewish community to Zionism; in America, Jewish leaders were lukewarm or hostile, fearing that Zionism would raise questions regarding loyalty. More ardent Zionism led to a more persistent suspicion of Jews in Canada. Finally, the substantial Jewish immigration between 1900 and 1930—some 150,000—had a larger relative impact on Canadian culture than in the United States, though it was less dispersed. While most major U.S. cities had substantial Jewish populations, Canadian Jews were overwhelmingly concentrated in Montreal and Toronto prior to 1900 and significantly in Winnipeg thereafter. Canadian policy in the 1930s was rigorously anti-Jewish, and almost no allowances were made for the growing anti-Semitism throughout Germany and other parts of Europe. And although Canada admitted more than 200,000 refugees after World War II, it generally continued to screen Jews as much as possible. Jewish immigration remained small thereafter, though about 7,000 Hungarian Jews were admitted in the wake of the Hungarian revolt of 1956 and more than 8,000 Russian Jews during the 1960s and 1970s, often by way of Israel.

Jewish immigrants, as a group, were the most successful of all the new immigrants in the United States (see NEW IMMIGRATION). Though they clearly suffered from discrimination, there were no overtly anti-Semitic politics practiced in the United States, and there was a steady expansion and support for civil rights throughout the country. With more than 500,000 Jews serving in the U.S. military during World War II, their patriotism was unquestioned, and more Jews than ever before began to enter the cultural mainstream. Through organizations such as B'NAI B'RITH and the ANTI-DEFAMATION LEAGUE, they became closely associated with humanitarian and civil liberty causes. Most important, Jews valued education and used high levels of university training to enter the most productive areas of American cultural and economic life.

See also AUSTRO-HUNGARIAN IMMIGRATION; EVIAN CONFERENCE; RUSSIAN IMMIGRATION; SOVIET IMMIGRATION; WORLD WAR II AND IMMIGRATION.

Further Reading

American Jewish Yearbook. New York: American Jewish Committee, 1900– .

Angel, M. D. *La America: The Sephardic Experience in the United States.* Philadelphia: Jewish Publication Society of America, 1982.

Abella, Irving, and Harold Troper. *None Is Too Many: Canada and the Jews of Europe, 1933–1948.* Toronto: Lester and Orpen Dennys, 1982.

Bauer, Yehuda. *American Jewry and the Holocaust: The American Jewish Joint Distribution Committee, 1939–1945.* Detroit: Wayne State University Press, 1981.

Breitman, Richard, and Alan M. Kraut. *American Refugee Policy and European Jewry, 1933–1945.* Bloomington: Indiana University Press, 1987.

Cohen, Naomi Werner. *Encounter with Emancipation: The German Jews in the United States, 1830–1914.* Philadelphia: Jewish Publication Society of America, 1984.

Davis, Alan, ed. *Anti-Semitism in Canada: History and Interpretation.* Waterloo, Canada: Wilfrid Laurier University Press, 1992.

Diner, Hasia R. *In the Almost Promised Land: American Jews and Blacks, 1915–1935.* Baltimore: Johns Hopkins University Press, 1995.

Feingold, Henry L., ed. *The Jewish People in America.* 5 vols. Baltimore: Johns Hopkins University Press, 1992.

———. *Zion in America: The Jewish Experience from Colonial Times to the Present.* New York: Hippocrene, 1981.

Glazer, Nathan. *American Judaism.* 2nd rev. ed. Chicago: University of Chicago Press, 1989.

Glenn, Susan A. *Daughters of the Shtetl: Life and Labor in the Immigrant Generation.* Ithaca, N.Y.: Cornell University Press, 1990.

Gold, Stephen J. *From the Workers' State to the Golden State: Jews from the Former Soviet Union in California.* Boston: Allyn and Bacon, 1995.

Herzberg, Arthur. *The Jews in America: Four Centuries of Uneasy Encounter, a History.* New York: Simon and Schuster, 1989.

Howe, Irving. *The World of Our Fathers.* New York: Harcourt Brace Jovanovich, 1976.

Howe, Irving, and Kenneth Libo, eds. *How We Lived: A Documentary History of Immigrant Jews in America, 1880–1930.* New York: R. Mark, 1979.

Kass, D., and S. M. Lipset. "Jewish Immigration to the United States from 1967 to the Present: Israelis and Others." In *Understanding American Jewry*. Ed. Marshall Sklare. New Brunswick, N.J.: Transaction, 1982.

Orleck, Annelise. *The Soviet Jewish Americans*. Westport, Conn.: Greenwood Press, 1999.

Rader, Jacob Marcus. *The Colonial American Jew, 1492–1776*. 3 vols. Detroit, Mich.: Wayne State University Press, 1950.

Roberts, Barbara. *Whence They Came: Deportations from Canada, 1900–1935*. Ottawa: University of Ottawa Press, 1988.

Rosenberg, Stuart E. *The Jewish Community in Canada*, Vol. 1: *A History*. Toronto: McClelland and Stewart, 1970.

Roth, Cecil, and Geoffrey Wigoder. *Encyclopedia Judaica*. Reprint. 18 vols. Philadelphia: Coronet Books, 2002.

Sachar, Howard M. *A History of the Jews in America*. New York: Alfred A. Knopf, 1992.

Swierenga, Robert P. *The Forerunners: Dutch Jewry in the North American Diaspora*. Detroit: Wayne State University, 1994.

Tulchinsky, Gerald. *Taking Root: The Origins of the Canadian Jewish Community*. Toronto: Lester Publishing, 1992.

Vigod, Bernard L. *The Jews in Canada*. Ottawa: Canadian Historical Association, 1984.

Johnson-Reed Act (United States) (1924)

Making permanent the principle of national origin quotas, the Johnson-Reed Act served as the basis for U.S. immigration policy until the MCCARRAN-WALTER IMMIGRATION AND NATURALIZATION ACT (1952). The measure established an overall annual quota of 153,700, allotted according to a formula based on 2 percent of the population of each nation of origin according to the census of 1890. Countries most favored according to this formula were Great Britain (43 percent), Germany (17 percent), and Ireland (12 percent). Countries whose immigration had increased dramatically after 1890—including Italy, Poland, Russia, and Greece—had their quotas drastically slashed.

Following passage of the EMERGENCY QUOTA ACT in 1921, isolationist opinions hardened in the country. As the politics of eastern Europe remained turbulent, the Soviet experiment became more publicized, and the racialist message of eugenics became more widely accepted, American politicians determined that a permanent measure to dramatically reduce immigration was needed. The Johnson-Reed Act ensured that the vast majority of future immigrants would, in the words of Tennessee congressman William Vaile, "become assimilated to our language, customs, and institutions," and "blend thoroughly into our body politic." Immigrants born in independent countries of the Western Hemisphere were not subject to the quota. Other nonquota immigrants included wives of citizens and their unmarried children under 18 years of age; previously admitted immigrants returning to the country; ministers and professors, their wives, and their unmarried children under 18; students; and Chinese treaty merchants. The Johnson-Reed Act prohibited entry of aliens not eligible for citizenship, thereby formally excluding entry of Japanese, Chinese, and other Asian immigrants. The 2 percent formula was designed to be temporary and was replaced with an equally restrictive formula in 1927 that provided the same national origin ratio in relation to 150,000 as existed in the entire U.S. population according to the census of 1920.

Further Reading

Daniels, Roger. *Guarding the Golden Door: American Immigration Policy and Immigrants since 1882*. New York: Hill and Wang, 2004.

Hutchinson, E. P. *Legislative History of American Immigration Policy, 1798–1965*. Philadelphia: University of Pennsylvania Press, 1981.

LeMay, Michael C. *From Open Door to Dutch Door: An Analysis of U.S. Immigration Policy since 1820*. New York: Praeger, 1987.

Loescher, Gil, and John A. Scanlan. *Calculated Kindness: Refugees and America's Half-Open Door, 1945–Present*. New York: Free Press, 1986.

K

Kennedy, John Fitzgerald (1917–1963) *politician*
The election of John F. Kennedy, a Catholic of Irish descent, as president in 1960 marked both an ethnic victory—80 percent of both Catholics and Jews voted for him, but only 38 percent of Protestants—and the beginning of the end of the old age of European immigration. During his two-and-a-half years in office (1961–63), Kennedy promoted an open immigration policy, setting the stage for the dramatic policy shift embodied in the IMMIGRATION AND NATIONALITY ACT (1965).

Born in Brookline, Massachusetts, to businessman Joseph P. Kennedy and Rose Fitzgerald Kennedy, he enjoyed a life of wealth and privilege, attending Choate School and Harvard University. He joined the U.S. Navy in September 1941 and was decorated for heroism after the sinking of his patrol torpedo boat (PT 109) in the South Pacific in August 1943. Kennedy served as a U.S. representative (1947–53) and U.S. senator (1953–61). Though a staunch Democrat, he often sided with conservatives in matters of foreign policy, rejecting his father's noted isolationism. His book *A Nation of Immigrants* (1958) promoted immigration reform, suggesting that immigrants would strengthen the nation. After a dramatic series of televised presidential debates in 1960, the young and vigorous Kennedy was narrowly elected president, defeating Republican Richard Nixon by only 119,450 votes out of almost 69 million cast. Vowing to lead "without regard to outside religious pressure," Kennedy's conduct as president demonstrated that Roman Catholics, who mainstream Protestants feared would take their "orders" from Rome, could loyally integrate their faith and politics.

Kennedy's aggressive foreign policy led to an increased commitment to displaced persons and refugees. He followed President Dwight Eisenhower's policy of paroling refugees under the extending voluntary departure (EVD) provisions of the McCARRAN-WALTER IMMIGRATION AND NATURALIZATION ACT of 1952 (exempting them from immigration quotas) and established the Cuban Refugee Program (February 3, 1961), which provided a wide range of social services to Cuban immigrants, including health care and subsidized educational loans. Kennedy urged that the program be understood "as an immediate expression of the firm desire of the people of the United States to be of tangible assistance to the refugees until such time as better circumstances enable them to return." Before Cuba's Communist leader, Fidel Castro, closed the door in the wake of the Cuban missile crisis (October 1962), 62,500 Cubans were paroled into the United States under the program. In 1962, Kennedy also paroled some 15,000 Chinese in the wake of an ongoing famine in southern China. Kennedy's actions reflected both the international pressures of the COLD WAR and his commitment to humanitarianism as a tool of international diplomacy. In 1963, he sent an immigration reform proposal to Congress, recommending that the quota system be phased out, that no country receive more than 10 percent of allotted visas, and that a seven-person immigration board be established to advise the president on immigration but no action was taken on the measure before Kennedy's assassination on November 22, 1963.

Further Reading

Burner, David. *John F. Kennedy and a New Generation.* Boston: Little, Brown, 1988.

Giglio, James N. *The Presidency of John F. Kennedy.* Lawrence: University Press of Kansas, 1991.

Kennedy, John F. *A Nation of Immigrants.* Introduction by Robert F. Kennedy, with a new preface by John P. Roche. New York: Harper and Row, 1986.

Mitchell, Christopher, ed. *Western Hemisphere Immigration and United States Foreign Policy.* University Park: Pennsylvania State University Press, 1992.

Parmet, Herbert S. *Jack: The Struggles of John F. Kennedy.* New York: Dial Press, 1980.

———. *J.F.K.: The Presidency of John F. Kennedy.* New York: Dial Press, 1983.

Schlesinger, Arthur M., Jr. *A Thousand Days: John F. Kennedy in the White House.* Boston: Houghton Mifflin, 1965.

King, William Lyon Mackenzie (1874–1950)
politician

As prime minister during World War II (1939–45; see WORLD WAR II AND IMMIGRATION), King largely reflected Canadian ethnic attitudes toward immigrants. He followed public opinion in incarcerating Italians, Germans, Japanese, and communists during the war and worked steadfastly against the admission of large numbers of European refugees, especially Jews. At the same time, he enthusiastically welcomed refugees from Britain, which had always provided Canada's most favored immigrants.

Born in Berlin (later Kitchener), Ontario, King graduated from the University of Toronto in 1895. He then studied at the University of Chicago, where he took part in the work of JANE ADDAMS's Hull-House, and eventually earned a doctorate in political economy from Harvard University. While serving as deputy minister of labour in 1907, he was sent to investigate the causes of the anti-Asian VANCOUVER RIOT. After holding hearings, he determined that the Japanese government was not primarily at fault but rather unregulated immigration from Hawaii and the work of Canadian immigration companies. King awarded Japanese and Chinese riot victims $9,000 and $26,000, respectively, and made several recommendations, including prohibition of contract labor and the banning of immigration by way of Hawaii.

King entered Parliament in 1908 when he was elected as a Liberal for Waterloo North and was appointed minister of labour in the Wilfrid Laurier government. King was chosen party leader after Laurier's death in 1919, as Canada entered a period of multiparty politics. As a result, most of his career was spent in leading several disparate political groups including Liberals, conservative French Canadians, and agrarian progressives. He was a pragmatic, rather than doctrinaire politician, which enabled him to retain the prime ministership for 21 years (1921–26, 1926–30, 1935–48)—longer than any other Canadian premier. In foreign policy, he advocated complete Canadian independence, which was achieved during the 1930s, and closer relations with the United States. Courting public opinion, especially in Quebec, King was opposed to admitting large numbers of refugees during and just after World War II. His policy was brought about by numerous restrictive measures, including raising the capital required for Jewish immigrants to be able to enter from $5,000 to $20,000 (1938), prohibiting admission of immigrants from countries with which Canada was at war (1940), and refusing to enter into general agreements for admission of refugees. King's 1947 statement on immigration suggested that immigration was wanted but affirmed that "the people of Canada do not wish, as a result of mass immigration, to make a fundamental alteration in the character of our population." During 1947 and 1948, the admission of 50,000 displaced persons was approved, representing the first stage of a dramatic reversal of Canadian isolation. King and his ministers were careful to screen out Jews, communists, and Asians, however, and most of the early immigration came from the Baltic countries and the Netherlands.

Further Reading

Avery, Donald. "Canada's Response to European Refugees, 1939–1945: The Security Dimension." In *On Guard for Thee: War, Ethnicity and the Canadian State, 1939–1945.* Eds. Norman and Bohdan Kordan. Ottawa: Canadian Government Publishing, 1989.

Hillmer, Dawson, and Robert R. MacGregor. *William Lyon Mackenzie King: A Political Biography, 1874–1923.* Toronto: University of Toronto Press, 1958.

Neatby, H. Blair. *William Lyon Mackenzie King.* 3 vols. Toronto: University of Toronto Press, 1958–1976.

Pickersgill, J. W., and Donald F. Forster, eds. *The Mackenzie King Record.* 4 vols. Toronto: University of Toronto Press, 1960–69.

Stacey, C. P. *Mackenzie King and the Atlantic Triangle.* Toronto: Macmillan of Canada, 1976.

King Tiger See TIJERINA, REIES LÓPEZ.

Korean immigration

Korean immigration to North America remained relatively small until U.S. and Canadian immigration reforms in the 1960s eliminated racial limitations on entrance. According to the 2000 U.S. census and the 2001 Canadian census, 1,228,427 Americans and 101,715 Canadians claimed Korean descent. The largest concentrations of Koreans were in southern California and the New York metropolitan area in the United States. More than half of Canadian Koreans lived in Ontario, most of them in Toronto. There was also a large concentration in Vancouver.

The Korean peninsula, surrounded on three sides by the Pacific Ocean and bordered on the north by the People's Republic of China, was historically ruled as a single kingdom. It was divided in the aftermath of World War II (1939–45), and its borders fixed as a result of a truce ending the Korean War (1950–53). South Korea, democratic and closely tied to the United States throughout the COLD WAR, occupies 37,900 square miles on the southern half of the peninsula. In 2002, the population was estimated at 47,904,370, with 49 percent being Christian and 47 percent Buddhist. Lying between South Korea and China is North Korea, which occupies 46,400 square miles. In 2002, the population of North Korea was estimated at 21,968,228. After more than 50 years of Communist rule, almost 70 percent of North Koreans are atheists or nonreligious, with most of the rest practicing traditional Korean religions, Buddhism, or Chondogyo. More than 99 percent of citizens in both the north and the south are ethnic Koreans.

Korean civilization borrowed heavily from China, and from the first century B.C. Korea was governed, to a greater or lesser extent according to the fluctuating strength of China, as a Chinese satellite. As China weakened in its conflict with the West during the late 19th century, Japan became increasingly aggressive in Korea, largely controlling the country from 1905 and formally annexing the peninsula in 1910. Following World War II, the Soviet Union occupied the peninsula above latitude 38 degrees north, while the United States occupied the peninsula south of that line. After a virtual U.S. withdrawal in 1950, North Korean troops invaded the south, supported by the Soviet Union and later by Communist Chinese troops, hoping to reunify the peninsula under a communist regime. By 1953, an uneasy truce was reached, and a de facto border was established near the original line of division. Fifty years later, the conflict was not fully resolved.

The first significant group of Korean immigrants came to the United States as plantation laborers during the first decade of the 20th century. Following U.S. annexation of Hawaii in 1898, Chinese and Japanese laborers gained more rights and thus became freer to strike or to move into better jobs. As a result of the CHINESE EXCLUSION ACT (1882), it was no longer possible to import Chinese laborers, so their jobs increasingly fell to Japanese and Korean immigrants. With poor economic prospects at home and an increasingly volatile political situation in the region, about 7,000 Koreans chose to migrate to Hawaii, most of them either bachelors or without their families. As a result of the 1907 GENTLEMEN'S AGREEMENT with the U.S. government, Japanese and Korean laborers were denied visas by the Japanese government. A clause in the agreement did allow wives to join husbands already in the United States, however. Utilizing this loophole, between 1910 and 1924, more than 1,000 Korean women became PICTURE BRIDES of men they had never met. After the restrictive JOHNSON-REED

A Korean child sits alone and crying in the street following the invasion by the U.S. Marines 1st Division and South Korean marines in Inchon, Korea, September 1950. *(National Archives/DOD, War & Conflict, #1486)*

ACT of 1924, few Koreans immigrated to the United States. Korean immigration was again triggered by the Korean War. As a central conflict in the cold war commitments of the United States, Koreans were eligible for refugee status. Between 1945 and 1965, about 20,000 Koreans entered the United States, some 6,000 of them under provisions of the WAR BRIDES ACT (1946). Provisions under the IMMIGRATION AND NATIONALITY Act (1965) led to a sharp increase in applications, with an average of more than 30,000 Korean immigrants annually between 1972 and 1992. Most of them were either skilled workers or the wives of U.S. servicemen. Immigration from Korea sharply declined after the Los Angeles riots (1992), in which Korean-American businesses were often the targets of looting, to an average of less than 16,000 between 1993 and 2000. In 2001–02, the rate of immigration was higher, averaging almost 21,000.

Koreans first came to Canada as students, after 1910, usually through the sponsorship of Christian missionaries. Their numbers were small, however, and they almost always returned home after their studies. During the 1960s, official policy in South Korea encouraging emigration, combined with the new IMMIGRATION REGULATIONS of 1967, brought the first significant group of Korean immigrants. By 1975, there were almost 13,000 Koreans in Canada. Korean immigration grew steadily from the 1970s, especially after provisions for investment immigrants were instituted in the 1980s.

Of the more than 70,000 immigrants in Canada in 2001, only 70 came prior to 1961; more than 42,000 came after 1990. During the 1970s and 1980s, immigration averaged a little more than 1,200 per year, but the numbers jumped significantly in the 1990s. Between 1996 and 2001, an average of about 6,000 Koreans immigrated to Canada annually. In 2001 and 2002, Korea ranked fourth behind China, India, and the Philippines as a source country for immigrants. The dramatic increase during the 1990s was fueled by foreign students taking advantage of opportunities in Toronto, Vancouver, and Montreal. Between 2000 and 2002, Korea was the number one source country for foreign students in Canada, averaging almost 13,000 per year.

Further Reading

Choy, Bong-Youn. *Koreans in America.* Chicago: Nelson-Hall, 1979.

Hurh, Won Moo. *The Korean Americans.* Westport, Conn.: Greenwood Press, 1998.

Kim, Illsoo. "Korea and East India: Premigration Factors and U.S. Immigration Policy." In *Pacific Bridges: The New Immigration from Asia and the Pacific Islands.* Eds. James Fawcett and Benjamin Carino. Staten Island, N.Y.: Center for Migration Studies, 1987.

———. *Urban Immigrants: The Korean Community in New York.* Princeton, N.J.: Princeton University Press, 1981.

Kim, Jung-gun. *To God's Country: Canadian Missionaries in Korea and the Beginning of Korean Migration to Canada.* D.Ed. thesis, Ontario Institute for Studies in Education, 1982.

Kwak, Tae-Hwan, and Seong Hyong Lee, eds. *The Korean American Community: Present and Future.* Seoul, South Korea: Kyungnam University Press, 1991.

Light, Ivan, and E. Bonacich. *Immigrant Entrepreneurs: Koreans in Los Angeles, 1965–1982.* Berkeley: University of California Press, 1988.

Mangiafico, Luciano. *Contemporary American Immigrants: Patterns of Filipino, Korean, and Chinese Settlement in the United States.* New York: Praeger, 1988.

Min, Pyong Gap. *Caught in the Middle: Korean Communities in New York and Los Angeles.* Berkeley: University of California Press, 1996.

———. *Ethnic Business Enterprise: Korean Small Business in Atlanta.* Staten Island, N.Y.: Center for Migration Studies, 1988.

Park, I. H., et al. *Korean Immigrants and U.S. Immigration Policy: A Predeparture Perspective.* Honolulu, Hawaii: East-West Population Institute, East-West Center, 1990.

Patterson, Wayne. *The Korean Frontier in America: Immigration to Hawaii, 1896–1910.* Honolulu: University of Hawaii Press, 1988.

Patterson, Wayne, and Huyng-Chan Kim. *Koreans in America.* Minneapolis, Minn.: Lerner Publications, 1992.

Takaki, Ronald T. *From the Land of the Morning Calm: The Koreans in America.* New York: Chelsea House, 1994.

Yoon, I. J. *The Social Origins of Korean Immigration to the United States from 1965 to the Present.* Honolulu, Hawaii: East-West Population Institute, East-West Center, 1993.

Korematsu v. United States (1944)

In a controversial 6-3 decision, the United States Supreme Court ruled that Fred Korematsu, a U.S. citizen of Japanese descent, was guilty of violating a military ban on Japanese residence in various areas of California, pursuant to the provisions of Executive Order 9066. According to the majority opinion, the nation's power to defend itself took precedence over individual constitutional rights.

In early 1942, during World War II, Korematsu was hired in a defense-related job after having failed the physical exam for military service. When JAPANESE INTERNMENT began in May 1942, under Executive Order 9066, Korematsu moved to another town, changed his name, and had facial surgery in order to present himself as a Mexican American. When his secret was discovered, he was convicted, sentenced to five years in prison, paroled, then sent to a detention camp. Afterward, he appealed to the Supreme Court. Justice Hugo L. Black, writing for the majority, supported the action of the military authorities on the grounds that "we were at war with the Japanese Empire, because the properly constituted military authorities feared an invasion of our West Coast" and because military authorities believed it necessary "that all citizens of Japanese ancestry be segregated from the West Coast temporarily." While the decision constituted a "hardship," Black argued, "hardships are a part of war." Though Black did not agree that Korematsu had been singled out for racial or ethnic discrimination, in an oft-cited section of his opinion he wrote that "all legal restrictions which curtail the civil rights of a single racial group are immediately suspect" and must be given "the most rigid scrutiny." In dissent, military expertise in the matter was questioned, and it was suggested that the cases of Japanese-American loyalty should be treated individually, as they were with persons of "German and Italian ancestry."

Further Reading

Daniels, Roger. *The Decision to Relocate the Japanese-Americans.* Malabar, Fla.: R. E. Krieger, 1986.

———. *Prisoners without Trial: Japanese Americans in World War II.* New York: Hill and Wang, 1993.

Irons, Peter. *Justice at War: The Story of the Japanese American Internment Cases.* New York: Oxford University Press, 1983.

labor organization and immigration

From the colonial period, immigrants were viewed as a potential threat to the interests of workers already in North America. In the early years of the American republic, an extraordinarily high birth rate (5.5 percent) provided the majority of laborers needed for development, thus making mass immigration unnecessary. As the United States and Canada became more industrialized after the mid-19th century, foreign-born workers were considered a necessity by entrepreneurs and industrialists, who encouraged millions to emigrate from Europe and Asia. European laborers, no matter how different, were generally considered to be assimilable, while African and Asian workers were generally considered only as temporary elements of the workforce. The influx of immigrant workers kept wages low and almost always undermined attempts to form craft or labor unions. With only two exceptions (1897–1905 and 1922–29), union membership in the United States grew and shrank inversely to the number of immigrants entering the country, leading to a general union opposition to open immigration policies.

The first national labor organization, the National Labor Union (NLU), was formed in 1866. Widespread unemployment in the wake of the Civil War (1861–65) heightened concern about jobs, and the NLU almost immediately lobbied against the Immigration Act of 1864, which provided for entry of contract laborers. The NLU disappeared during the 1870s, with the Knights of Labor emerging as the premier labor organization in the United States during the 1870s and 1880s. The Knights opposed immigration, especially that of Chinese peasant workers, and worked vigorously for the repeal of the BURLINGAME TREATY. In decrying the Chinese "evil," labor leaders emphasized the fraudulent means of migrant entry, illegal immigrants often coming across the Canadian border or under false names. The Knights' pressure contributed to the CHINESE EXCLUSION ACT (1882), but the Knights were equally concerned with general labor recruitment in Europe, which was undertaken, they argued, in order to create a labor surplus. The Knights did manage to secure amendments that put some teeth into the ineffective ALIEN CONTRACT LABOR ACT (1885), but the decline of union membership after 1886 rendered the organization less important in immigrant reform than in the previous decade.

More influential than either the NLU or the Knights of Labor was the American Federation of Labor (AFL), founded in 1881. The AFL encouraged the organization of workers into craft unions, which would then cooperate in labor bargaining. Under the energetic leadership of SAMUEL GOMPERS, an English immigrant from a Jewish family, the AFL gained strength as it won the support of skilled workers, both native and foreign born. Ethnic concerns soon became entwined with the general depression of wages caused by the massive immigration of the 1880s and 1890s. Chinese immigration was condemned from the first, and the flood of unskilled workers from southern and eastern Europe after 1880 generally were not eligible for membership in craft unions. In 1896, the organization first established a committee on immigration and in the following year, passed a resolution calling on the government to require a literacy test as the best means of keeping out unskilled laborers. The AFL also continued to oppose Chinese and Japanese immigration and supported the IMMIGRATION ACT of 1917, which required a literacy test and barred virtually all Asian immigration. At the same time, most immigrants were little interested in unionization: Many preferred to work at home, where they could care for their children and protect their cultural values. Most were suspicious of labor organizers, preferring their own labor intermediaries (see PADRONE SYSTEM). Although immigrants formed some labor organizations such as the Japanese-Mexican Labor Association (JMLA, 1903), it would take time and two dramatic events to change the immigrant perspective. The Triangle Shirtwaist Factory fire (1911) and World War I (1914–18; see WORLD WAR I AND IMMIGRATION) proved to be turning points that led to greater immigrant interest in organized labor.

With the threat of wage depression removed by the tight restrictions imposed by Immigration Acts of 1921 (see EMERGENCY QUOTA ACT) and 1924 (see JOHNSON-REED

Carnegie Steel Company mills, Homestead, Pennsylvania. Pay cuts in 1892 led to a strike by the Amalgamated Association of Iron, Steel, and Tin Workers. The resulting battle led to several deaths and widespread withdrawal from the union. *(National Archives #74-G-50-1)*

ACT), immigration was removed as a major labor issue, though unions continued to oppose immigrant labor. Foreign-born workers (13.2 percent in 1920) were more readily welcomed by the labor movement as they found it advantageous to adopt traditional American lifestyles. By 1940, they constituted less than 9 percent of the U.S. population. Labor unions nevertheless faced enormous organizational, economic, and cultural obstacles to unionization, including widespread unemployment during the Great Depression that began in 1929. Between 1922 and 1936, the unionized portion of the nonagricultural labor force stabilized between 10 and 15 percent. As immigration continued to wane and World War II (1939–45) stimulated industrial demand, unionism revived. Between 1945 and 1965, about one-third of the nonagricultural labor force was unionized. By the end of that period, the foreign-born population stood at only 4.4 percent. As Vernon Briggs, Jr., has argued in *Immigration and American Unionism* (2001), "The mirror-image effect is manifestly clear: as the foreign-born population declined in percentage terms, union membership rose in both absolute and percentage terms." In 1955, shortly after merging with the Congress of Industrial Organizations (CIO), the AFL-CIO (see AMERICAN FEDERATION OF LABOR AND CONGRESS OF INDUSTRIAL ORGANIZATIONS) recommended amendment of the Immigration and Nationality Act of 1952 but did not recommend raising the overall ceiling. The organization generally supported government provisions for refugees but strongly condemned the Mexican farm labor program (see BRACERO PROGRAM) that allowed seasonal labor into the country.

Organized labor at first was generally favorable to the legislation that became the Immigration Act of 1965, which was designed to end ethnic origin as a basis for admission, while not significantly raising the overall number of immigrants admitted. In 1963, the AFL-CIO passed a resolution supporting "an intelligent and balanced immigration policy" based on "practical considerations of desired skills." Three factors led to an unexpectedly dramatic increase in immigration, however, which once again raised alarms in the labor movement. Government used its parole authority to admit refugees in excess of stipulated ceilings, particularly with regard to Cuba and Vietnam. At the same time, illegal immigration exploded, as legal migrant laborers under the Bracero Program became illegal immigrants when the program was ended (1965). Finally, the understaffing of the Immigration and Naturalization Service (INS) and the fact that U.S. employers were exempt from criminal prosecution for hiring illegal immigrants allowed cheap foreign labor to continue to pour into the country. Between 1970 and 1997, more than 30 million illegal immigrants were apprehended, though deportations were often difficult and millions more entered the labor force. Finally, the preference given to family reunification in 1965 led to an influx of new immigrants from Latin America and Asia. In 1997, these groups constituted 77 percent of the foreign-born U.S. population.

Prior to the 1980s, organized labor supported every governmental initiative to restrict immigration. Faced with steadily declining memberships after 1975, however, some leaders reconsidered, focusing their concerns on illegal immigration rather than on general immigration policy. The AFL-CIO applauded the IMMIGRATION REFORM AND CONTROL ACT of 1986, particularly for its tough sanctions on employers of illegal immigrants. By 1993, the organization moved further toward support of immigration, explicitly stating that immigrants were not the cause of labor's problems and encouraging local affiliates to pay special attention to the needs of legal immigrant workers. In February 2000, the AFL-CIO made the historic decision to reverse its position and to support future immigration. It is unclear how vigorously this policy will be pursued in the 21st century and if it will be adopted generally by organized labor, particularly in the wake of the terrorist attacks of SEPTEMBER 11, 2001, and the continued decline of union membership.

Further Reading

Avery, Donald. 'Dangerous Foreigners': European Immigrant Workers and Labour Radicalism in Canada, 1896–1932. Toronto: McClelland and Stewart, 1979.

Briggs, Vernon M., Jr. Immigration and American Unionism. Ithaca, N.Y., and London: Cornell University Press, 2001.

———. Mass Immigration and the National Interest. 2d ed. Armonk, N.Y.: M. E. Sharpe, 1996.

Brundage, David. The Making of Western Labor Radicalism: Denver's Organized Workers. Urbana: University of Illinois Press, 1994.

DeWitt, Howard A. "The Filipino Labor Union: The Salinas Lettuce Strike of 1934." Amerasia 5, no. 2 (1978): 1–21.

Dubofsky, Melvin. Industrialism and the American Worker. New York: Cromwell, 1975.

Freeman, Joshua. In Transit: The Transport Workers Union in New York City, 1933–1966. New York: Oxford University Press, 1989.

Gabaccia, Donna. Militants and Migrants: Rural Sicilians Become American Workers. New Brunswick, N.J.: Rutgers University Press, 1988.

Galenson, W. The CIO Challenge to the AFL. Cambridge, Mass.: Harvard University Press, 1960.

Gerstle, Gary. Working-Class Americanism: The Politics of Labor in a Textile City, 1914–1960. Cambridge: Cambridge University Press, 1989.

Goldfield, M. The Decline of Organized Labor in the United States. Chicago: University of Chicago, 1987.

Greene, Victor. The Slavic Community on Strike: Immigrant Labor in Pennsylvania Anthracite. Notre Dame, Ind.: University of Notre Dame Press, 1968.

Hatton, Timothy J., and Jeffrey G. Williamson. The Impact of Immigration on American Labor Markets prior to Quotas. Working Paper no. 5185. Cambridge, Mass.: National Bureau of Economic Research, 1995.

Heron, Craig. The Canadian Labour Movement. Toronto: Lorimer, 1989.

———, ed. The Workers' Revolt in Canada, 1917–1925. Toronto: University of Toronto Press, 1998.

"Immigration." AFL-CIO Executive Council Actions, (February 16, 2000). New Orleans, Louisiana. Available online. URL: http://www.aflcio.org/aboutaflcio/ecouncil/ecOZ162006.cfm.

Karni, Michael G., and D. J. Ollila, Jr., eds. For the Common Good: Finnish Immigrants and the Radical Response to Industrial America. Superior, Wis.: Tyomies Society, 1967.

Kaufmann, S. B. Samuel Gompers and the Origins of the American Federation of Labor. Westport, Conn.: Greenwood Press, 1973.

Kwong, Peter. Forbidden Workers: Illegal Chinese Immigrants and American Labor. New York: New Press, 1997.

Lebergott, Stanley. Manpower in Economic Growth: The American Record since 1800. New York: McGraw-Hill, 1964.

Livesay, Harold C. Samuel Gompers and Organized Labor in America. Boston: Little, Brown, 1978.

Logan, H. A. Trade Unions in Canada: Their Development and Functioning. Toronto: Macmillan, 1948.

Marquez, Ben. LULAC: The Evolution of a Mexican American Political Organization. Austin: University of Texas Press, 1993.

Milkman, Ruth, ed. Organizing Immigrants: The Challenge for Unions in Contemporary California. Ithaca, N.Y.: Cornell University Press, 2000.

Montgomery, David. The Fall of the House of Labor: The Workplace, the State, and American Labor Activism, 1865–1925. New York: Cambridge University Press, 1987.

Palmer, Bryan. Working-Class Experience: Rethinking the History of Canadian Labour, 1800–1991. 2d ed. Toronto: McClelland and Stewart, 1992.

Ross, C. The Finn Factor in American Labor, Culture and Society. New York Mills, Minn.: Parta Printers, 1977.

Ruiz, Vicki. Cannery Women, Cannery Lives: Mexican American Women, Unionization, and the California Food Processing Industry, 1939–1950. Albuquerque: University of New Mexico Press, 1987.

Saxton, Alexander. The Indispensable Enemy: Labor and the Anti-Chinese Movement in California. Berkeley: University of California Press, 1995.

Schneider, Dorothee. Trade Unions and Community: The German Working Class in New York City. Urbana: University of Illinois Press, 1994.

Taft, Philip. The A.F. of L. in the Time of Gompers. New York: Harper and Row, 1957.

Yu, Renqui. To Save China, to Save Ourselves: The Chinese Hand Laundry Alliance of New York. Philadelphia: Temple University Press, 1993.

Labrador   See NEWFOUNDLAND.

Laotian immigration

Laotian immigration to North America was almost totally the product of the Vietnam War (1964–75). According to the 2000 U.S. census and the 2001 Canadian census, 198,203 Americans and 16,950 Canadians claimed Laotian descent. In addition, 186,310 Americans were from the Laotian minority Hmong. Unlike earlier post-1960s immigrant groups that tended to cluster in large cities, Laotian refugees were often settled in medium-sized cities, especially in California, including Fresno, San Diego, Sacramento, and Stockton. The Hmong were widely spread but most prominent in California and Minnesota. The largest Laotian concentrations in Canada were in Toronto and Montreal. In 2001, there were fewer than 600 Hmong in Canada.

Laos is a landlocked country occupying 89,000 square miles in Southeast Asia. It is bordered by Myanmar and China on the north, Vietnam on the east, Cambodia on the south, and Thailand on the west. In 2002, the population was estimated at 5,635,967. The people are ethnically divided between Lao Lourn (68 percent), Lao Theung (22 percent), Lao Soung, including Hmong and Yao (9 percent). About 60 percent are Buddhist, and 40 percent practice animist or other religions Laos gained its independence from the Khmer Empire (modern Cambodia) during the 14th century, peaking in regional influence late in the 17th century. Laos became a French protectorate in 1893 but regained independence as a constitutional monarchy in 1949. Conflicts among neutralist, Communist, and conservative factions created a chaotic political situation. Armed conflict increased after 1960. Three factions formed a coalition government in June 1962, with neutralist Prince Souvanna Phouma as premier. With aid from North Vietnam, Communist groups stepped up attacks against the government, and Laos was gradually drawn into the COLD WAR conflict in Southeast Asia. In 1975, the Lao People's Democratic Republic was proclaimed, with thousands of Laotians fleeing to refugee camps in Thailand.

There is no official record of Laotian immigration to the United States prior to 1975, though there was a small number of professionals who had come before that time. In 1975, those who had aided the United States and South Vietnam during the Vietnam War fled to refugee camps in Thailand, which housed more than 300,000 by the mid-1980s. As the condition of Laotian refugees became more widely known, there was general support in both the United States and Canada for assisting them. The U.S. government passed a special measure, the Indochina Migration and Refugee Assistance Act (1975), that eased entry into the country. In 1978, the Canadian government designated the Indochinese one of three admissible refugee classes. Between 1976 and 1981, more than 120,000 Laotian refugees were admitted to the United States and almost 8,000 to Canada. Because most were aided in resettlement by private organizations, they tended to be spread widely throughout both the United States and Canada. Between 1992 and 2002, an average of about 3,000 immigrants from Laos arrived in the United States annually, though the numbers declined significantly after 1997. Fewer than 1,700 of Canada's 14,000 Laotian immigrants came after 1990.

Further Reading
Adelman, Howard. *Canada and the Indochinese Refugees.* Regina, Canada: L. A. Weigl Educational Associates, 1982.
Chan, S., ed. *Hmong Means Free: Life in Laos and America.* Philadelphia: Temple University Press, 1994.
De Voe, Pamela. "Lao." In *Case Studies in Diversity: Refugees in America in the 1990s.* Ed. David W. Haines. Westport, Conn.: Praeger, 1997.
Dorais, Louis-Jacques. *The Cambodians, Laotians, and Vietnamese in Canada.* Ottawa: Canadian Historical Association, 2000.
Dorais, Louis-Jacques, Kwok B. Chan, and Doreen M. Indra, eds. *Ten Years Later: Indochinese Communities in Canada.* Montreal: Canadian Asian Studies Association, 1988.
Haines, David W., ed. *Refugees as Immigrants: Cambodians, Laotians, and Vietnamese in America.* Totowa, N.J.: Rowman and Littlefield, 1989.
Hein, Jeremy. *From Vietnam, Laos and Cambodia: A Refugee Experience in the United States.* New York: Simon and Schuster, 1995.
Koltyk, Jo Ann. *New Pioneers in the Heartland: Hmong Life in Wisconsin.* Needham Heights, Mass.: Allyn and Bacon, 1997.
O'Connor, Valerie. *The Indochina Refugee Dilemma.* Baton Rouge: Louisiana State University Press, 1990.
Proudfoot, Robert. *Even the Birds Don't Sound the Same Here: The Laotian Refugees' Search for Heart in American Culture.* New York: Peter Lang, 1990.
Rumbaut, Rubén G. "A Legacy of War: Refugees from Vietnam, Laos and Cambodia." In *Origins and Destinies: Immigration, Race and Ethnicity in America.* Eds. Silvia Pedraza and Rubén G. Rumbaut. Belmont, Calif.: Wadsworth, 1996.
Van Esterik, Penny. *Taking Refuge: Lao Buddhists in North America.* Tempe: Arizona State University Press, 1992.

La Raza Unida Party (LRUP)

The La Raza Unida Party (LRUP) was the first attempt to create a national political party to represent the rights of Mexican Americans. South Texas leaders had formed La Raza Unida in 1970 in order to elect Mexican Americans to local school boards and councils. The greatest successes came in Crystal City, Texas, where LRUP gained control of the city council and school board, enabling it to hire more Mexican-American employees, institute bilingual educational programs, and add Mexican-American history to the curriculum. Organizers spread throughout the Southwest to establish branches. By 1972, other activist organizations began to join the effort. At the 1972 El Paso convention of the Crusade for Justice, Chicano leader CORKY GONZALES called for creation of a national party. Students, journalists, and activists from many groups, including REIES LÓPEZ TIJERINA's Alianza Federal de Mercedes, attended the convention, which led to the establishment of the national

LRUP. The party received 215,000 votes (almost 7 percent) in the 1972 state election, but it received little support elsewhere.

See also MEXICAN IMMIGRATION.

Further Reading

Corona, Bert. *Bert Corona Speaks on La Raza Unida Party and the "Illegal Alien" Scare.* New York: Pathfinder Press, 1972.

García, Ignacio M. "Armed with a Ballot: The Rise of La Raza Unida Party in Texas." M.A. thesis, University of Arizona, 1990.

Muñoz, Carlos. *Youth, Identity, Power: The Chicano Movement.* London: Verso, 1989.

Rosales, Francisco A. *Chicano!: A History of the Mexican American Civil Rights Movement.* Houston, Tex.: Arte Público Press, 1996.

Santillán, Richard. *The Politics of Cultural Nationalism: El Partido de la Raza Unida in Southern California, 1969–1978.* Ann Arbor, Mich.: University Microfilms International, 1983.

Shockley, John. *Chicano Revolt in a Texas Town.* Notre Dame, Ind.: University of Notre Dame Press, 1974.

Vargas, Zaragosa. *Major Problems in Mexican American History.* Boston: Houghton Mifflin, 1999.

Vento, Arnoldo Carlos. *Mestizo: The History, Culture, and politics of the Mexican and the Chicano: The Emerging Mestizo-Americans.* Lanham, Md.: University Press of America, 1997.

Latinos   See *HISPANIC* AND RELATED TERMS; TEJANOS.

Latvian immigration

According to the U.S. census of 2000 and the Canadian census of 2001, 87,564 Americans and 22,615 Canadians claimed Latvian descent. Generally, Latvians did not form strong ethnic communities and were spread throughout many larger North American cities, including New York, Boston, Philadelphia, and Toronto. About two-thirds of Canadian Latvians live in Ontario.

Latvia is a country of 24,938 square miles situated on the Baltic Sea. It is bordered by Estonia on the north, Russia on the east, and Belarus and Lithuania on the south. The region was settled by Baltic peoples in ancient times but was ruled at various times by the Vikings, Germans, Poles, Swedes, and Russians. As a result of Russian occupation in the 18th century, about 30 percent of the present-day population is Russian, while 58 percent is Latvian, 4 percent Belarusian, 2.7 percent Ukrainian, and 2.5 percent Polish. About 40 percent of the population is Christian, almost equally divided between Protestants and Roman Catholics; 60 percent are largely unreligious.

Latvian immigrants were historically divided and thus did not form the strong ethnic communities common to many immigrant groups from eastern Europe. "Old Latvians" settling in the United States prior to World War II (1939–45) were usually young and single. Most were seeking economic opportunities, though a significant number were political activists. The latter were divided among nationalists, seeking the independence of Latvia from Russia, and socialists, who were more concerned with the condition of workers under the Russian system. Latvian immigration increased following the abortive Revolution of 1905. There was little immigration between World War I (1914–18) and World War II. Because Latvian immigrants were usually included in statistics as Russians, it is difficult to know exactly how many came during this early phase of immigration. By 1940, about 35,000 people claimed Latvian descent; it is estimated that some 25,000 Latvians immigrated to the United States prior to that time. The "New Latvian" group was created when the conflict between Soviet Russia and Nazi Germany left almost a quarter million Latvians in refugee camps after World War II. About 40,000 of these immigrated to the United States as displaced persons after 1946. Unlike the Old Latvians, they tended to see themselves as only temporarily displaced, though most chose to remain in the United States after the breakup of the Soviet Union and the establishment of an independent Latvia in 1991. Between 1992 and 2002, Latvian immigration to the United States averaged about 600 per year.

Few Latvians settled in Canada before World War II. Between 1921, when Latvians were first categorized as a group distinct from Russians, and 1945, only 409 arrived in Canada. Almost all Latvian Canadians were part of or are descended from, refugees and displaced persons who arrived between 1947 and 1957. Whereas the Old Latvians, who had come prior to the war, lived principally in Alberta, Saskatchewan, and Manitoba, more than two-thirds of the New Latvians chose Ontario. In 2001, about two-thirds of all Latvian Canadians live in Ontario, and about half of them in Toronto. Though many Latvians immigrated to Canada with professional training, they often worked in construction or related trades upon arrival. By the 1970s, they were moving back into skilled positions, especially engineering for men and medicine for women. Immigration from Latvia remained small between 1960 and 1990, generally fewer than 100 arriving in a year. Following independence in 1991, immigration among Latvians increased somewhat, as they sought economic opportunities within an increasingly global economic system. Of 7,675 Latvian immigrants in Canada in 2001, 5,155 (67 percent) arrived before 1961. About 1,500 came between 1991 and 2001.

See also RUSSIAN IMMIGRATION; SOVIET IMMIGRATION.

Further Reading

Karklis, Maruta, Liga Streips, and Laimonis Streips. *The Latvians in America, 1640–1973: A Chronology and Fact Book.* Dobbs Ferry, N.Y.: Oceana Publications, 1974.

Lieven, Anatoly. *The Baltic Revolution: Estonia, Latvia, Lithuania and the Path to Independence.* New Haven, Conn.: Yale University Press, 1993.

Plakans, Andrejs. *The Latvians: A Short History*. Stanford, Calif.: Hoover Institution Press, 1995.

Tichouskis, Heronims. *Latviešu trimdas desmit gadi* (*Ten Years of Latvians in Exile*) Toronto, 1954.

Veidemanis, Juris. *Social Change: Major Value Systems of Latvians at Home, as Refugees, and as Immigrants*. Greeley: Museum of Anthropology, University of Northern Colorado, 1982.

Lebanese immigration

The Lebanese, among the earliest Middle Eastern immigrants to come to North America in significant numbers, formed the largest Arab ethnic group in both the United States and Canada. According to the U.S. census of 2000 and the Canadian census of 2001, 440,279 Americans and 143,635 Canadians claimed Lebanese descent. Lebanese have settled widely throughout the United States, with significant concentrations in New York, Massachusetts, and Connecticut. About 41 percent of Lebanese Canadians live in Ontario, though the greatest concentration is in Montreal.

Lebanon occupies 3,900 square miles in the Middle East, along the eastern littoral of the Mediterranean Sea. It is bordered by Syria on the north and east and Israel on the south. In 2002, the population was estimated at 3,627,774. The people were 93 percent Arab—divided among Lebanese (84 percent) and Palestinians (9 percent)—and 6 percent Armenian. Lebanon is the only Arab country with a significant Christian population. In 2002, about 55 percent of Lebanese were Muslims, 37 percent Christians, and 7 percent Druze. Modern Lebanon corresponds roughly with the ancient seafaring state of Phoenicia, which flourished during the first millennium B.C. Never organized as an empire, it fell under the domination of successive large states, including Assyria, Babylon, Persia, Greece, the Arab dynasties, and eventually the Ottoman Empire, which ruled the region from the 16th century to the end of World War I (1918). As France gained increasing influence over the weakening Ottoman Empire in the late 19th century, Lebanon was organized as an autonomous region within the empire to provide protection for persecuted Christians. Lebanon became a mandated territory under French control following World War I and gained full independence by 1946. With the introduction of hundreds of thousands of Palestinian refugees from Israel during the 1970s, the Christian government of Lebanon quickly lost power. The Palestine Liberation Organization, with support from Syria, moved its war effort against Israel to Lebanon. The ensuing civil war from 1975 had not yet been fully resolved as of 2004.

It is difficult to provide a precise number of Lebanese immigrants, for they were rarely designated as such. Immigrants from the Ottoman Empire were usually classified in the category "Turkey in Asia," whether Arab, Turk, or Armenian. By 1899, U.S. immigration records began to make some distinctions, and by 1920, the category "Syrian" was introduced into the census. Most Syrians were in fact Lebanese Christians, though religious distinctions still were not noticed. The majority of Arabs in North America are the largely assimilated descendants of Christians who emigrated from the Syrian and Lebanese areas of the Ottoman Empire between 1875 and 1920. Lebanese Christians were divided into several branches, including Maronites, Eastern Orthodox, and Melkites. As Christians living in an Islamic empire, they were subject to persecution, though in good times they were afforded considerable autonomy. During periods of drought or economic decline, however, they frequently chose to emigrate. Between 1900 and 1914, about 6,000 immigrated to the United States annually. Often within one or two generations, these Lebanese immigrants had moved into the middle class and largely assimilated themselves to American life. With passage of the restrictive JOHNSON-REED ACT of 1924, immigration dropped to a few hundred per year. The next major migration of Lebanese to North America came with the advent of civil war in the 1970s. Most of these immigrants were, however, Shiite Muslims, inclined to maintain their culture rather than assimilate and usually at odds with Lebanese Christians already in the United States. Between 1988 and 2002, Lebanese immigration averaged just under 5,000 per year.

Significant Lebanese immigration to Canada began in the 1880s. The immigrants were almost all Christians who feared persecution, particularly in the wake of the massacres of 1860. Immigration began shortly thereafter, though it was restricted to mostly poor, single young men. By the 1880s, more families were emigrating, laying the foundation for the Lebanese community in Canada, centered in Montreal. Lebanese emigration from the Ottoman Empire peaked between 1900 and 1914 with an average of 15,000 per year, before World War I virtually halted immigration. Though most went to the United States, Brazil, or Argentina, significant numbers came to Canada as well. When Lebanon came under the protection of the French as a result of the Treaty of Versailles, many Lebanese immigrants returned to their homeland during the 1920s and 1930s.

As in the United States, most Lebanese immigrants arrived before 1920 or after 1975. Of Canada's 67,000 Lebanese immigrants, almost 60,000 came in the wake of the political disruptions of the 1970s. In 1976, the Canadian government created a special category for Lebanese immigrants affected by the war and continued to apply relaxed standards to Lebanese requests. After the 1989 peak of 6,100 refugee arrivals, Lebanese immigration leveled off. About 7,600 immigrants living in Canada in 2001 arrived between 1996 and 2001.

See also ARAB IMMIGRATION.

A street scene at the Sabra or Shatila refugee camp in southern Lebanon, 1983. The invasion of Lebanon by Israel in 1982 further divided Christian and Muslim Lebanese communities in the United States and led to an increase in Lebanese refugees admitted to both the United States and Canada. *(Photograph by Hariri-Rifai Makhless/Library of Congress [LC-USZ62-94063])*

Further Reading

Jabbra, Nancy, and Joseph Jabbra. *Voyageurs to a Rocky Shore: The Lebanese and Syrians of Nova Scotia.* Halifax, Canada: Institute of Public Affairs, Dalhousie University, 1984.

Kayal, P. M., and J. M. Kayal. *The Syrian Lebanese in America: A Study in Religion and Assimilation.* Boston: Twayne, 1975.

Naff, Alixa. *Becoming American: The Early Arab Immigrant Experience.* Carbondale and Edwardsville: Southern Illinois University Press, 1985.

Orfalea, Gregory. *Before the Flames: A Quest for the History of Arab Americans.* Austin: University of Texas Press, 1988.

Shehadi, Nadim, and Albert H. Hourani, eds. *The Lebanese in the World: A Century of Emigration.* London and New York: I. B. Tauris, 1993.

Wakin, Edward. *The Syrians and the Lebanese in America.* Chicago: Claretian Publishers, 1974.

Walbridge, Linda S. *Without Forgetting the Imam: Lebanese Shi'ism in an American Community.* Detroit: Wayne State University Press, 1996.

Liberian immigration

Liberia traditionally was not an important source country for immigration to North America; however, political tur- moil during the 1990s and into the 21st century and the region's special relationship to the United States led to a significant increase in immigration. According to the U.S. census of 2000 and the Canadian census of 2001, 25,575 Americans and 640 Canadians claimed Liberian descent. Some Liberian American groups estimate the numbers in the United States to be much higher, mainly because of the provisional status of large numbers of temporary admissions. New York City and Washington, D.C., have the largest Liberian populations.

Liberia comprises 37,743 square miles situated on the West African Atlantic coast between Sierra Leone and Guinea to the north and Côte d'Ivoire to the east. Established as a refuge for freed American slaves in 1821, Liberia displayed an unusual amount of political stability in an otherwise unstable region. As a result, only a few thousand Liberians immigrated to the United States during the first eight decades of the 20th century. From 1980, however, divisions between ethnic and culture groups became more pronounced and political instability more common. The most numerous ethnic groups included the Kpelle (19.4 percent), Bassa (13.9 percent), Grebo (9 percent), Gio (7.8 percent), Kru (7.3 percent), and Mano (7.1 percent). About

63 percent of Liberia's 3.2 million people (2001) practice native religions; 21 percent are Christians, and 16 percent, Muslims. From its independence in 1847 until 1980, Liberia was governed by the descendants of the original African-American settlers. The last of these leaders, President William R. Tolbert, was assassinated during a 1980 coup that ushered in the violent dictatorship of Sergeant Samuel Doe. The National Patriotic Front of Liberia (NPFL) launched an invasion from the Côte d'Ivoire in December 1989, leading to a vicious civil war that saw 250,000 killed and two-thirds of the country's citizens displaced. When fighting intensified in the capital of Monrovia in April 1996, 20,000 people took refuge in the U.S. embassy compound. In July 1997, NPFL leader Charles Taylor was elected president with 72 percent of the vote.

Unique in its relationship to the United States, Liberia received more emigrants from the United States than it sent there from its founding in 1821 until the 1960s. As some Liberians began to immigrate to the United States during the 20th century, their numbers remained extremely small through World War II (1939–45)—27 between 1925 and 1929; 30 between 1930 and 1939; 28 between 1940 and 1949. Though immigration grew in the 1950s and 1960s, it still totaled only 800 for that 20-year period. The significant period of Liberian immigration came only as a result of the civil war waged between 1989 and 1997, when almost 17,000 Liberians entered the United States, many evacuated in the last days of the war. Some were admitted as refugees, but about 10,000 were granted Temporary Protected Status (TPS), which ended in 1999. When TPS expired in September of that year, President Bill Clinton protected them from removal under the Deferred Enforced Departure (DED) program, which did not qualify immigrants for permanent residency but allowed them temporary residency and permission to work until dangerous and unstable conditions at home allow a return. The DED status was then extended annually, ensured at least through October 2004. From 1999, a number of members of Congress supported measures to regularize the status of Liberians under DED. In 2004, the Liberian Immigration Bill (S656) (H.R. 919) and the Liberian Refugee Immigration Protection Act of 2003 were still in committee. Between 1998 and 2001, more than 10,000 Liberian refugees were admitted to the United States, as well as 7,000 regular immigrants.

Further Reading

Alao, Abiodun, John MacKinlay, and Funmi Olonisakin. *Peacekeepers, Politicians, and Warlords: The Liberian Peace Process.* New York: United Nations University Press, 2000.

Huband, Mark, and Stephen Smith. *The Liberian Civil War.* Portland, Ore.: Frank Cass, 1998.

Trawally, Sidiki. "Prayers Answered: Liberians Granted TPS." Liberian Mandingo Association of New York. Available online. URL: http://www.limany.org/straw.html. Accessed February 27, 2004.

Literacy Act See IMMIGRATION ACT (United States) (1917).

Lithuanian immigration

Lithuanian immigration to North America, spurred by economic opportunity and political oppression, has been the largest among the Baltic states. According to the 2000 U.S. census and the 2001 Canadian census, 659,992 Americans and 36,485 Canadians claimed Lithuanian descent. The largest concentrations of Lithuanians were in Chicago, with other significant settlements in Cleveland, Ohio; Detroit, Michigan; Pittsburgh, Pennsylvania; New York City; and Boston. Almost a third of Lithuanian Canadians live in Toronto.

Lithuania occupies 25,212 square miles in the Baltic region of northeastern Europe. In 2001, its population was about 3.7 million people, with about 82 percent being ethnic Lithuanians; 8 percent, Russians; and 7 percent, Poles. More than 72 percent of Lithuanians are Roman Catholic, 3 percent are Orthodox, and most of the rest are unreligious.

The region of modern Lithuania was settled by Baltic peoples in ancient times. As Germans expanded eastward, however, Lithuania developed a strong state and began to expand to the east and south into Belarus and Kievan territories. Joining with Poland in 1386, the two powers combined to form one of the largest states in Europe and gradually halted the eastward advance of the Germans. Lithuanian noblemen largely adopted Polish culture and developed a political system that hampered development of a strong monarchy. As a result, the Polish-Lithuanian state was partitioned by 1795, and Russian domination of the region followed until a declaration of independence in 1918. During World War II (1939–45), Lithuania was invaded first by the Soviet Union in 1940, then by Nazi Germany in 1941, and again by the Soviet Union in 1944. Thousands of Lithuanian refugees fled from the Soviets, becoming displaced persons. Many of them eventually sought refuge in the United States.

Because Lithuanian immigrants were usually included as Russians in statistics prior to World War I (1914–18), it is difficult to know exactly how many came prior to that time. A significant number of Lithuanians first immigrated to the United States after the Civil War (1861–65), in part because the abolition of serfdom in the Russian Empire (1861) gave the peasantry greater personal freedom, but also because of an aggressive policy of russification after the failed uprising of 1863. A much larger wave of migration came between 1880 and 1914, with some estimates placing the number of immigrants as high as 300,000. Although emigration was illegal, many political dissidents risked capture, and Jews were sometimes forced to emigrate. Between the 1860s and 1914, almost 400,000 Lithuanians emigrated, about 20 percent of the population and one of the highest rates of emigration in Europe. The restrictive JOHNSON-REED AACT of 1924 virtually halted Lithuanian immigration until after World War II, when 30,000 refugees were admitted, many under the DISPLACED PERSONS ACT (1948). Whereas earlier Lithuanian immigrants had been mainly laborers, the refugees frequently came from middle- and upper-class backgrounds. Although Lithuanians continued to immigrate to the United States in small numbers—averaging a little more than 1,000 per year between 1992 and 2002—those claiming Lithuanian descent are fewer as assimilation and outmarriage occur. In 1990, 811,865 Americans claimed Lithuanian descent, 23 percent higher than the 2000 figure.

Lithuanian immigration to Canada is usually divided between the "Old Lithuanians," who came up through the 1920s, and the "New Lithuanians," mostly displaced persons, who arrived after World War II. About 150 Lithuanian soldiers fought for the British army in the War of 1812 (1812–15), and many were given land grants as a result. There was no significant chain migration, however, so their numbers remained small. In the 1880s and 1890s, few Lithuanians came to settle, though many migrated between the United States and Canada doing seasonal work. The first separate listing of Lithuanians in the Canadian census was in 1921, when there were still fewer than 2,000 in Canada. Twenty years later the official number was almost 8,000, though the actual number was probably closer to 10,000. Among these, a large percentage eventually migrated to the United States, where jobs and pay were generally better. The New Lithuanians of the post–World War II era were considerably different. Whereas many of the Old Lithuanians had been miners and sojourners, the 20,000 displaced persons accepted by Canada—one-third of the Lithuanian total—were largely educated officials and professionals who feared the return of the Soviet army. Because Canada was seeking miners, laborers, servants, and farmhands, many Lithuanians hid their true professions, did manual labor for their contracted year of work, then moved to Montreal, Toronto, Vancouver, or other Canadian cities. Many eventually migrated to the United States. With the return of Lithuanian independence in 1990, immigration to Canada revived, though it remained small. Of 6,830 Lithuanian immigrants in Canada in 2001, 4,915 came before 1961, and only 900 between 1991 and 2001.

See also RUSSIAN IMMIGRATION; SOVIET IMMIGRATION.

Further Reading

Alilunas, Leo J. *Lithuanians in the United States: Selected Studies.* San Francisco: R. and E. Research Associates, 1978.

Budreckis, Algirdas. *The Lithuanians in America, 1651–1975: A Chronology and Factbook.* Dobbs Ferry, N.Y.: Oceana Publications, 1975.

Danys, Milda. *DP: Lithuanian Immigration to Canada after the Second World War.* Toronto: Multicultural History Society of Ontario, 1986.

Fainhauz, David. *Lithuanians in the U.S.A.: Aspects of Ethnic Identity.* Chicago: Lithuanian Library Press, 1991.

Gaida, Pranas. *Lithuanians in Canada.* Toronto: Lights Printing and Publishing, 1967.

Green, Victor. *For God and Country: The Rise of Polish and Lithuanian Ethnic Consciousness in America.* Madison: State Historical Society of Wisconsin, 1975.

Kucas, Antanas. *Lithuanians in America.* San Francisco: R. and E. Research Associates, 1975.

Wolkovich-Valkavicus, William. *Lithuanian Religious Life in America: A Compendium of 150 Roman Catholic Parishes and Institutions.* West Bridgewater, Mass.: Lithuanian Religious Life in America, Corporate Fulfillment Systems, 1991.

Van Reenan, A. *Lithuanian Diaspora.* Lanham, Md.: University Press of America, 1990.

Lloydminster   See BARR COLONY.

Los Angeles, California

With a population of 16,373,645 at the turn of the 21st century, the Los Angeles metropolitan area was second only to the New York metropolitan area in size. It was the primary destination in the United States for the increasingly large immigration of Latin Americans and Asians that developed under provisions of the IMMIGRATION AND NATIONALITY ACT of 1965. Of metropolitan areas with populations over 5 million in 2000, it had the highest percentage of foreign-born inhabitants at 29.6 percent.

By the time the United States acquired California following the U.S.-MEXICAN WAR (1846–48), Nuestra Señora la Reina de los Ángeles de Porciuncula had been a Mexican city for almost 30 years and a Spanish town for almost a half-century before that. Apart from the native Mexican population that stayed on, Los Angeles historically contained relatively few foreign-born citizens. Between 1850 and 1920, the percentage of Mexican Americans living in Los Angeles declined dramatically, from a vast majority to less than 20 percent. As the city's general population boomed between 1920 and 1970 (576,673 to 2.8 million), the foreign-born population remained relatively constant, around 20 percent. Unlike most eastern urban areas, population growth in Los Angeles was principally the result of internal migration, rather than foreign immigration. Most migrants were midwestern Protestant Anglos, who eventually dominated Los Angeles politics and economic development, and most identified themselves by previous state of residence rather than ethnic background. Depression-era Anglo refugees from the dust bowl (principally the lower Great Plains) were prepared to fill menial jobs, thus limiting the need for immigrant labor. By 1970, the foreign-born population dipped to 15 percent. That downward trend was rapidly reversed after implementation of the 1965 Immigration and Nationality Act, which abolished national quotas and favored family unification in selecting immigrants.

As a result of the new legislation, Los Angeles became the center of migration for many Latino (see HISPANIC AND RELATED TERMS) and Asian immigrant groups. As Los Angeles–area industry and agriculture grew, employers lobbied for increased immigration, particularly from Mexico. Wartime demands for labor during World War I (1914–18) led Congress to exempt Mexicans as temporary workers from otherwise restrictive immigrant legislation. As a result, almost 80,000 were admitted between creation of a "temporary" farmworker program in 1917 and its termination in 1922. Fewer than half of the workers returned to Mexico, and many of them stayed in southern California. Linking with networks that organized and transported Mexican laborers, workers continued to enter the United States throughout the 1920s, with 459,000 officially recorded. Although there were no official limits on immigration from the Western Hemisphere, many Mexicans chose to bypass the official process that, since 1917, had included a literacy test, making the actual number of Mexican immigrants much higher. Most worked in agriculture in either Texas or California. The BRACERO PROGRAM brought an additional 5 million Mexican laborers between 1942 and 1964. During the 1960s and 1970s, Mexican Americans made significant gains in both political representation and economic conditions; meanwhile, Los Angeles became more segregated as non-Hispanic whites fled to the suburbs. The foreign-born Los Angeles population from Mexico rose sixfold between 1970 and 1990 (283,900 to 1.7 million). By 2000, more than 5 million Mexican Americans lived in Los Angeles, making them the largest immigrant group by far. Migration from El Salvador (see SALVADORAN IMMIGRATION) and Guatemala (see GUATEMALAN IMMIGRATION) rose at even more dramatic rates: The Salvadoran population rose from 4,800 in 1970 to 231,605 in 2000, and the Guatemalan, from 3,500 to 133,136. By 2000, Latinos composed more than 40 percent of the population of the Los Angeles metropolitan area.

Asians were among the first immigrants to Los Angeles. By 1890, there were more than 4,000 Chinese living there (see CHINESE IMMIGRATION). After the CHINESE EXCLUSION ACT (1882), the largely bachelor population declined, but the Chinese population grew rapidly after 1970. In 1970, there were about 56,000 Chinese in Los Angeles; in 2000, they numbered 472,637. Throughout most of the period between 1900 and 1970, the Japanese were the largest Asian group in Los Angeles (see JAPANESE IMMIGRATION). With their own economy very strong after 1970, however, they did not come in large numbers during the late 20th century. As a result, the Japanese population grew more slowly, from about 120,000 in 1970 to 203,170 in 2000, when they were the fifth-largest Asian group,

behind the Chinese, Filipinos (438,013), Koreans (273,191), and Vietnamese (252,278). The Asians have been called the "model minorities" because of their high levels of education, work ethic, and general social and economic success. While the Chinese, Filipinos (see FILIPINO IMMIGRATION), and Japanese tended to be highly assimilated and spread throughout the city in most areas of work, Koreans are especially known for starting small businesses, with whole families often working together (see KOREAN IMMIGRATION). The Vietnamese were somewhat less successful, mainly because they were more recent arrivals, almost all coming after 1975, and, as refugees, were able to survive in less skilled areas of work with significant support from the government (see VIETNAMESE IMMIGRATION). In 2000, more than 10 percent of the Los Angeles metropolitan population was Asian.

Given its diverse ethnic background, it is not surprising that Los Angeles suffered a number of prominent ethnic clashes, including the Chinese Massacre of 1871, which saw 20 Chinese murdered by a white mob; the Zoot Suit riots of 1943, in which young Chicanos were attacked by Anglo mobs; and the Los Angeles riot of 1992 in which Korean businesses, among others, were targeted following the controversial acquittal of four white police officers in the beating of Rodney King, an African American. Growing concern about the cost of providing assistance to illegal immigrants and fear of an increased flow from Mexico as a result of the economic crisis led Californians to approve (59 percent to 41 percent) Proposition 187, which denied education, welfare benefits, and nonemergency health care to illegal immigrants. Decisions by federal judges in both 1995 and 1998, however, upheld previous decisions regarding the unconstitutionality of the proposition's provisions. The anti-immigrant mood in Los Angeles remained strong, however, into the first decade of the 21st century. This was reflected in the massive campaign to recall California governor Gray Davis in 2003. Based in part on opposition to Davis's support for providing illegal aliens with driver's licences, Los Angeles immigrant and Hollywood movie star Arnold Schwarzenegger won a convincing victory in the recall election in October.

Further Reading

Acuña, Rodolfo F. *Anything but Mexican: Chicanos in Contemporary Los Angeles.* London: Verso, 1996.

Bergesen, Albert, and Max Herman. "Immigration, Race and Riot: The 1992 Los Angeles Uprising." *American Sociological Review* 63 (1998): 39–54.

Bonacich, Edna, and Richard R. Appelbaum. *Behind the Label: Inequality in the Los Angeles Apparel Industry.* Berkeley: University of California Press, 2000.

Bonacich, Edna, and Ivan Hubert Light. *Immigrant Entrepreneurs: Koreans in Los Angeles, 1965–1982.* Berkeley: University of California Press, 1988.

Bozorgmehr, Mehdi, George Sabagh, and Ivan Light. "Los Angeles: Explosive Diversity." In *Origins and Destinies: Immigration, Race, and Ethnicity in America*. Eds. Silvia Pedraza and Rubén G. Rumbaut. Belmont, Calif.: Wadsworth, 1996.

Davis, Mike. *Ecology of Fear: Los Angeles and the Imagination of Disaster*. New York: Metropolitan Books, 1998.

Delgado, Hector. *New Immigrants, Old Unions: Organizing Undocumented Workers in Los Angeles*. Philadelphia: Temple University Press, 1994.

Fogelson, Robert. *The Fragmented Metropolis: Los Angeles, 1850–1930*. Cambridge, Mass.: Harvard University Press, 1967.

Griswold del Castillo, Richard. *The Los Angeles Barrio, 1850–1890: A Social History*. Berkeley: University of California Press, 1979.

Kelley, Ron, Jonathan Frielander, and Anita Colby, eds. *Irangeles*. Berkeley: University of California Press, 1993.

Milkman, Ruth, and Kent Wong. *Voices from the Front Lines: Organizing Immigrant Workers in Los Angeles*. Los Angeles: Center for Labor Research and Education, University of California–Los Angeles, 2000.

Min, Pyong Gap. *Caught in the Middle: Korean Communities in New York and Los Angeles*. Berkeley: University of California Press, 1996.

Modell, John. *The Economics and Politics of Racial Accommodation: The Japanese of Los Angeles, 1900–1942*. Urbana: University of Illinois Press, 1977.

Moore, Joan W. *Going Down to the Barrio: Homeboys and Homegirls in Change*. Philadelphia: Temple University Press, 1991.

Ong, Paul, Edna Bonacich, Lucie Cheng, eds. *The New Asian Immigration in Los Angeles and Global Restructuring*. Philadelphia: Temple University Press, 1994.

Romo, Ricardo. *East Los Angeles: History of a Barrio*. Austin: University of Texas Press, 1983.

Sanchez, George J. *Becoming Mexican American: Ethnicity, Culture, and Identity in Chicano Los Angeles, 1900–1945*. New York: Oxford University Press, 1993.

Waldinger, Roger, and Mehdi Bozorgmehr, eds. *Ethnic Los Angeles*. New York: Russell Sage Foundation, 1996.

Louisiana

The watershed and mouth of the Missouri-Mississippi River system became known as Louisiana and was from the earliest days of discovery considered strategically important by many European nations. As a result, it had an unusually wide array of ethnic influences during the 17th and 18th centuries. The acquisition of Louisiana by the United States in 1803 ensured control of the continental interior and provided ample land for migrant and immigrant farmers of the new republic.

The first European to explore the region was the Spanish explorer Hernando de Soto (1541–42). Finding no mineral wealth, the Spanish paid little attention to the region. In 1682, René-Robert Cavelier de La Salle claimed the Mississippi River Valley for France, naming it Louisiana in honor of King Louis XIV. Attempts by Scottish investor John Law to colonize the region failed between 1717 and 1720, with

the exception of NEW ORLEANS, founded in 1718. Disappointed with the little income generated from the region, France ceded Louisiana to Spain from 1762 to 1800, though it was done secretly and Spain did not gain firm control until 1769. During the 1790s, the sugar industry was established, and the colony began to flourish. In addition to Spanish settlers, an increasing number of Europeans from other countries began to settle in the region. About 4,000 French colonists from ACADIA migrated to Louisiana following the capitulation of Montreal in 1760; the descendants of these migrants became known as Cajuns. During the American Revolution (1775–83), a significant number of Americans also came to New Orleans, which had been granted to the Continental Congress as a base of operations during the conflict.

In 1800, Napoleon coerced Spain into ceding Louisiana back to France, though a full transfer of control was never effected. In December 1803, in a transaction known as the Louisiana Purchase, France sold the entire Mississippi valley to the United States for about $15 million. The huge region was subdivided during the 19th century, with the present-day state of Louisiana being admitted to the Union in 1812. With the advent of the steamboat, a great period of commercial expansion began after 1812, and thousands of settlers arrived between the end of the War of 1812 (1815) and the beginning of the Civil War (1860). The northern territories of Louisiana eventually became all or part of the states of Arkansas, Missouri, Iowa, Minnesota, North Dakota, South Dakota, Nebraska, Kansas, Oklahoma, Texas, New Mexico, Colorado, Wyoming, and Montana and home to thousands of European immigrants seeking land following the Civil War, which ended in 1865.

Further Reading

Brasseaux, Carl A. *Acadian to Cajun: Transformation of a People, 1803–1877*. Jackson: University Press of Mississippi, 1992.

———. *The "Foreign French": Nineteenth-Century French Immigration into Louisiana*. 3 vols. Lafayette: University of Southwestern Louisiana, 1990–93.

———. *The Founding of New Acadia: The Beginnings of Acadian Life in Louisiana, 1765–1803*. Baton Rouge: Louisiana State University Press, 1987.

———, ed. *A Refuge for All Ages: Immigration in Louisiana History*. Lafayette: University of Southwestern Louisiana, 1996.

Brasseaux, Carl A., and Glenn R. Conrad, eds. *The Road to Louisiana: The Saint Domingue Refugees, 1792–1809*. Lafayette: University of Southwestern Louisiana, 1992.

Kukla, John. *A Wilderness So Immense: The Louisiana Purchase*. New York: Alfred A. Knopf, 2003.

Stolarik, M. Mark, ed. *Forgotten Doors: The Other Ports of Entry to the United States*. Philadelphia: Balch Institute Press, 1988.

Lower Canada

See CANADA—IMMIGRATION SURVEY AND POLICY OVERVIEW; QUEBEC.

M

Macdonald, Sir John Alexander (1815–1891)
politician

John Alexander Macdonald was one of Canada's dominant political figures during the 19th century. Throughout the long period of his leadership, he presided over a relatively open immigration policy that targeted agriculturalists from Britain, the United States, and northern Europe (see CANADA—IMMIGRATION SURVEY AND POLICY OVERVIEW).

Macdonald, born in Glasgow, Scotland, believed that the immigrant Scot was, "as a rule, of the very best class." His merchant family immigrated to the Kingston area of Canada in 1820, and by 1830, Macdonald had been apprenticed to a well-connected lawyer. He first took public office in 1844 as the Conservative member for Kingston in the Assembly of the Province of Canada. Extremely able, he rose quickly in the Canada West wing of the party and by 1851 was its effective leader. As the dominant Conservative leader during the next 40 years, Macdonald championed confederation under a British model and always remained wary of U.S. influence and threats. He became the first prime minister of the Dominion of Canada, a position he held almost continuously until his death (1867–73, 1878–91), interrupted only by his resignation over the Pacific Scandal involving improper campaign contributions from a railway syndicate.

Owing to the British North America Act (Constitution Act, 1867), which provided for concurrent federal and provincial powers regarding immigration, a national policy emerged only gradually; the minister of agriculture assumed full control of immigration in 1874. Although the Macdonald government in the IMMIGRATION ACT of 1869 adopted a laissez-faire approach that did not discriminate in the selection of immigrants, Macdonald supported a number of measures that eventually prohibited members of the "vicious classes" (criminal) (1872) and the "destitute" (1879) and severely restricted entry of the Chinese (1885). After 1878, Macdonald's chief priorities were western settlement and the building of a transcontinental railroad. As a result, he took the position of minister of the interior as well as of prime minister. Treaties with the western Indian tribes during the 1870s ended their land claims, while the DOMINION LANDS ACT (1872) introduced an extensive survey of western lands and provision of virtually free homesteads on the prairies. In 1880, he negotiated an agreement with a railway syndicate that led to the building of the Canadian Pacific Railway, completed in 1885. The railway laid a foundation for future growth, opening the western prairies to settlement and linking British Columbia to the East. Actual settlement during the Macdonald years was not rapid, however, as international depression, stiff competition from the U.S. West, and land speculation kept immigrant numbers low. More than 1 million Canadians, many of them immigrants, resettled in the United States during Macdonald's final ministries, and at his death in 1891, the entire population of the prairies stood at about 250,000.

John A. Macdonald, first Canadian prime minister, 1867–73. Macdonald generally adopted a laissez-faire attitude toward immigration, though he found Scottish immigrants to be of "the very best class" and the Chinese to be valuable for their labor, "the same as a threshing machine or any other agricultural implement which we may borrow from the United States or hire and return to its owner." *(Library of Congress, Prints & Photographs Division [LC-USZ62-122757])*

Further Reading

Creighton, Donald. *John A. Macdonald.* 2 vols. Toronto: Macmillan 1952–56.

Macdonald, John A. *Correspondence of Sir John Macdonald.* Ed. Joseph Pope. Toronto: Oxford University Press, 1920.

———. *Memoirs of the Right Honourable Sir John Alexander Macdonald.* Ed. Joseph Pope. Ottawa: J. Purie, 1894.

Swainson, Donald. *Macdonald of Kingston: First Prime Minister.* Toronto: T. Nelson and Sons, 1979.

———. *Sir John A. Macdonald: The Man and the Politician.* Kingston, Canada: Quarry Press, 1989.

Macedonian immigration

According to the U.S. census of 2000 and the Canadian census of 2001, 38,051 Americans and 31,265 Canadians claimed Macedonian descent. Detroit has the largest Macedonian community in the United States, with significant concentrations in the Chicago area and throughout Ohio. Canadian Macedonians have always been highly concentrated in the Toronto metropolitan area. About 95 percent live in Ontario.

Macedonia occupies 25,100 square miles in east Europe, on the southeast coast of the Baltic Sea. It is bordered by Bulgaria on the east, Greece on the south, Albania on the west, and Serbia on the north. In 2002, the population was estimated at 2,046,109. The people are principally ethnic Macedonians (66 percent) and Albanians (23 percent); about 67 percent are Eastern Orthodox, and 30 percent, Muslim, roughly corresponding to ethnic divisions. Macedonia enjoyed its greatest political success as the core of a great empire under Alexander the Great during the fourth century B.C. but thereafter was usually ruled as part of larger, multiethnic political units. It was successively ruled by Rome, Bulgaria, the Byzantine Empire, and the Ottoman Empire. Following the unsuccessful Ilinden uprising of 1903, about 6,000 Macedonians made their way to Canada and about 50,000 to the United States. Most were single men from peasant backgrounds, working as laborers or in transient jobs. Numbers are difficult to ascertain, as Macedonians were usually classified variously as Bulgarians, Turks, Serbs, Albanians, or Greeks. Most of these Macedonians were probably from the Bulgarian minority in the region.

After more than 500 years under Muslim Ottoman rule (1389–1912), Macedonia was wrested from Turkey but was then divided among Greeks, Bulgarians, and Serbs in the Balkan Wars of 1912 and 1913. Serbia received the largest part of the territory, with the rest going to Greece and Bulgaria. In 1913, Macedonia was incorporated into Serbia, which in 1918 became part of the Kingdom of the Serbs, Croats, and Slovenes (later Yugoslavia). The restrictive JOHNSON-REED ACT of 1924 all but halted immigration to the United States from Yugoslavia, and tens of thousands returned to Europe. The Macedonian population in North America continued to grow, however, as there was a strong community in Toronto, and many Macedonians entered the United States by way of Canada in order to avoid the quotas. During the depression years of the 1930s, Macedonian business organizations were formed in Toronto that led to the establishment of bakeries, restaurants, dairies, hotels, and other business enterprises.

Following World War II (1939–45), the Yugoslav Federation was reconstituted as a communist state but one which recognized a certain degree of Macedonian autonomy. Thousands of Macedonians were displaced by the war, with about 6,000 immigrating to Canada in the late 1940s. There was little movement after the 1940s, however, as Yugoslavia strictly controlled emigration; only about 2,000 Macedonians went to the United States between 1945 and 1960. Others came through Greece, where Macedonians formed a small minority. The Yugoslav government liberalized immigration policies in the 1960s, leading as many as 40,000 Macedonians to emigrate, many to Canada and the

United States. With independence in 1991, Macedonians again sought refuge abroad.

The breakup of Yugoslavia beginning in 1991 was accompanied by much bloodshed, creating hundreds of thousands of refugees and much political instability. Macedonia itself became independent in 1991 and was admitted to the United Nations in 1993. A UN force, including several hundred U.S. troops, was deployed there to deter the warring factions in Bosnia from carrying their dispute into Macedonia. In 1994, both Russia and the United States recognized Macedonia. By 1999, however, ethnic cleansing in the Serbian province of Kosovo drove more than 250,000 Kosovars into Macedonia. More than 90 percent were eventually repatriated, though some sought refuge in the West. Ethnic Albanian guerrillas launched an offensive in 2001 in northwestern Macedonia, further destabilizing the country. Between 1994 and 2002, an average of more than 700 Macedonians immigrated to the United States. Of Canada's 7,215 Macedonian immigrants in 2001, 2,170 came between 1991 and 2001.

See also GREEK IMMIGRATION; GYPSY IMMIGRATION; YUGOSLAV IMMIGRATION.

Further Reading

Herman, Harry V. *Men in White Aprons: A Study of Ethnicity and Occupation.* Toronto: Peter Martin, 1978.
Petroff, Lillian. *Sojourners and Settlers: The Macedonian Community in Toronto to 1940.* Toronto: University of Toronto Press, 1995.
Pribichevich, Stoyan. *Macedonia: Its People and History.* University Park: Pennsylvania State University Press, 1982.
Prpić, Georg J. *South Slavic Immigration in America.* Boston: Twayne Publishers, 1978.

mafia

The mafia, a loose collection of Italian crime organizations, entered the United States from Italy during the last half of the 19th century. Though it is still hotly debated whether Italian-American groups were ever linked directly to the Mafia in Italy, they did serve as power brokers in many American cities, extorting payment for "protection" and providing goods and services often denied through legal channels.

Emerging in response to centuries of Arab and Norman domination in Sicily and southern Italy, agents of absentee landlords came to hold control over the land and thus the livelihood of local peasants. At the same time that they were extracting payment from the people, they could deliver economic opportunities and protection from foreign overlords. This system was widely imported to the United States during the 1890s with the dramatic increase in immigration from southern Italy. With the murder of the New Orleans, Louisiana, police superintendent in 1890, tales of a highly organized network of Italian criminals began to circulate, variously known as the mafia, the Black Hand, the Neapolitan

Camorra, or La Cosa Nostra. In 1891, the *New York Tribune* reported that "in large cities throughout the country, Italians of criminal antecedents and propensities are more or less closely affiliated. . . . Through their agency the most infernal crimes have been committed and have gone unpunished." Evidence suggests that while Italians, like other immigrants shut out of urban political and economic benefits, did organize as a means of economic advancement, the groups were largely local and unconnected until Prohibition in the 1920s. The idea of a tightly organized national organization remained largely submerged until the 1950s, when hearings chaired by Estes Kefauver concluded that the mafia was an international organization with "sinister" criminal goals. Investigations by Attorney General Robert F. Kennedy in the 1960s and *The Godfather* film series of the 1970s perpetuated what immigration historian Robert Daniels calls "the Mafia syndrome." According to Daniels, the Corleone family in *The Godfather* "resembles real gangsters about as much as Paul Bunyan does real lumberjacks." The consensus of scholars is that Italian association with crime always represented a tiny portion of the population and that it was consistent with patterns of most immigrant groups with limited access to the economic benefits of society and forced to live in urban slums.

Further Reading

Albini, Joseph L. *The American Mafia: Genesis of a Legend.* New York: Meredith Corporation, 1971.
Blok, Anton, and Charles Tilly. *The Mafia of a Sicilian Village, 1860–1960.* London: Blackwell, 1974.
Fox, Stephen R. *Blood and Power: Organized Crime in Twentieth-Century America.* New York: Morrow, 1989.
Sifakis, Carl. *The Mafia Encyclopedia.* New York: Facts On File, 1999.

mail-order brides   See PICTURE BRIDES.

Manifest of Immigrants Act (United States) (1819)

The Manifest of Immigrants Act was the first piece of U.S. legislation regulating the transportation of migrants to and from America and the first measure requiring that immigration statistics be kept. The United States maintained uninterrupted data on individuals coming into the country from the time this act was passed.

Concerned with the dramatic increase in immigration during 1818 and responding to several instances of high mortality on transatlantic voyages, Congress passed on March 2, 1819, "an Act regulating passenger-ships and vessels." It specified

1. a limit of two passengers per every five tons of ship burden

2. for all ships departing the United States, at least 60 gallons of water, 100 pounds of bread, 100 pounds of salted provisions, and one gallon of vinegar for every passenger
3. the requirement of ship captains or masters to report a list of all passengers taken on board abroad, including name, sex, age, and occupation. The report was also to include the number of passengers who had died on board the ship during the voyage.

Six acts and a number of amendments gradually modified the requirements of the 1819 act until it was finally repealed by the CARRIAGE OF PASSENGERS ACT (1855).

Further Reading

Bromwell, William J. *History of Immigration to the United States, 1819–1855.* 1855. Reprint, New York: Augustus M. Kelley, 1969.

Hutchinson, E. P. *Legislative History of American Immigration Policy, 1798–1965.* Philadelphia: University of Pennsylvania Press, 1981.

Mann Act (United States) (1910)

Usually characterized as a kind of purity legislation against the interstate transportation of women for prostitution or "other immoral purposes," the Mann Act was equally aimed at the increasing number of immigrants, averaging almost 900,000 per year in the first decade of the 20th century. The measure prohibiting commerce in "alien women and girls for the purpose of prostitution and debauchery" affected a small number of potential immigrants, but it did further extend the emphasis, begun by President Theodore Roosevelt at the beginning of the decade on encouraging immigration only of those with good moral character. Proposed by the Republican congressman James R. Mann of Illinois, the bill was reported out of the Committee on Interstate and Foreign Commerce in December 1909, along with the report, "White Slave Traffic." It was quickly passed by both houses of Congress and signed by President William H. Taft as the White Slave Traffic Act of June 25, 1910.

Further Reading

Hutchinson, E. P. *Legislative History of American Immigration Policy, 1798–1965.* Philadelphia: University of Pennsylvania Press, 1981.

LeMay, Michael C. *From Open Door to Dutch Door: An Analysis of U.S. Immigration Policy since 1820.* New York: Praeger, 1987.

Mariel Boatlift

The Mariel Boatlift of 1980 marked the beginning of the third great wave of CUBAN IMMIGRATION to the United States. Between April and October, thousands of seacraft of all kinds were sent to the Cuban port of Mariel to transport some 125,000 friends and relatives back to the United States. The number of immigrants immediately overwhelmed the ordinary provisions of the REFUGEE ACT (April 1, 1980), and the poverty and questionable background of many of the migrants led to a marked increase in American hostility to immigration.

Until the 1970s, Cuban immigration policy of the United States was driven by an ideological commitment to deter communism and thus was not subject to the restrictions of ordinary immigration legislation. Beginning in 1970, however, the governmental consensus in favor of Cuban exemptions began to break down. By 1980, the new Refugee Act required Cubans to meet the same "strict standards for asylum" as other potential refugees from the Western Hemisphere, placing escapees in the same category as Haitians (see HAITIAN IMMIGRATION), who had been arriving illegally in large numbers throughout the 1970s. Facing a weak economy, on April 20, Cuban president Fidel Castro opened the port of Mariel to Cuban emigrants after seven years of migratory suspension. Castro encouraged emigration by common criminals so as to rid the country of "anti-social elements." Within five months, more than 125,000 Cubans had been transported to the United States, including 24,000 with criminal records. At first the *marielitos* were treated as refugees, but by June 20, the government had enacted sanctions against those transporting Cuban migrants and had confirmed that Cubans would be coupled with Haitians as "entrants (status pending)," rather than as refugees. Occasional violence by Cuban detainees upset by their inability to gain formal immigrant status further undermined the perception of Cuban migrants in the public mind. Fearing both an exodus of skilled technicians and deterioration of relations with the United States, on September 25, Castro closed the harbor at Mariel to emigration.

Negotiations by the administrations of Jimmy Carter and Ronald Reagan in the wake of the Mariel Boatlift led to a December 1984 migration agreement that came close to normalizing immigrant relations between the two countries. Cuba agreed to accept 2,746 "excludable" Mariel Cubans, and the United States agreed to issue 20,000 annual "preference immigrant visas to Cuban nationals."

Further Reading

Bach, Robert L. *Latin Journey: Cuban and Mexican Immigrants in the United States.* Berkeley and Los Angeles: University of California Press, 1985.

Domínguez, Jorge I. "Cooperating with the Enemy? U.S. Immigration Policies toward Cuba." In *Western Hemisphere Immigration and United States Foreign Policy.* Ed. Christopher Mitchell. University Park: Pennsylvania State University Press, 1992.

Hamm, Mark S. *The Abandoned Ones: The Imprisonment and Uprising of the Mariel Boat People.* Boston: Northeastern University Press, 1995.

Larzelere, Alex. *Castro's Ploy, America's Dilemma: The 1980 Cuban Boat Lift.* Washington, D.C.: National Defense University Press, 1988.

Rivera, Mario A. "An Evaluative Analysis of the Carter Administration's Policy toward the Mariel Influx of 1980." Ph.D. diss., University of Notre Dame, 1982.

Maryland colony

Maryland was the sixth English colony established on the North American mainland (1634). Sir George Calvert, Lord Baltimore (ca. 1580–1632) was a favorite of the pro-Catholic Stuart kings James I (r. 1603–25) and Charles I (r. 1625–49). When he openly announced his Catholicism in 1625, Baltimore was forced to resign as secretary of state but retained the favor of Charles I, who supported the idea of a refuge for Catholics who were no longer free to worship openly in England. Baltimore had earlier established the colony of Avalon in Newfoundland (1621–23) but abandoned it as "intolerably cold." He visited Virginia but found that settlers there were strongly opposed to the settlement of Catholics. Baltimore then sought a charter from Charles I for a territory north of Virginia but died before arrangements could be completed. On June 30, 1632, Charles I granted a proprietary charter to Baltimore's son, Cecilius Calvert, second lord Baltimore. Taking into account the importance of also attracting Protestant settlement to ensure the economic success of the settlement, the charter mandated that Catholics "be silent upon all occasions of discourse concerning matters of Religion." On March 25, 1634, the *Ark* and the *Dove* landed about 150 settlers, the majority of whom were Protestants. Within a few days Leonard Calvert, Baltimore's brother and governor of the colony, purchased land from the Yaocomico Indians, which became the capital city of St. Marys.

Maryland was unique in that its charter made Baltimore a "palatine lord," with outright ownership of almost 6 million acres. He hoped to fund his venture by re-creating an anachronistic feudal system, with purchasers of 6,000 acres enjoying the title 'lord of the manor' and having the right to establish local courts of law. Landowners bristled at the attempts of the Calverts to restrict traditional English legislative liberties, plunging Maryland into a long period of political instability that almost destroyed the colony. English religious divisions were mirrored in Maryland, with Catholics in the upper house and Protestants in the lower house vying for control of the government, a conflict that sometimes erupted into open warfare. With the Puritan victory in the English Civil War (1642–49), Baltimore feared he might lose Maryland and thus drafted his "Act concerning Religion," extending freedom of worship to all who accepted the divinity of Christ, though the act of toleration was repealed when Puritans gained control of the local government (1654). When James II, a confessed Catholic, was driven from the English throne in 1688, Protestants forced Calvert's governor to resign and petitioned the English Crown that Maryland be made a royal colony (1691). Proprietorship was returned in 1715 to the fourth lord Baltimore, who was raised as a member of the Church of England.

Maryland remained predominantly English throughout the colonial period and by 1700 had developed a culture similar to that of neighboring Virginia, though with somewhat greater social mobility. The cultivation of tobacco defined its economic and social structure. Farms and plantations, almost always owned by English settlers, were widely dispersed along the Chesapeake, and a steady stream of indentured servants (see INDENTURED SERVITUDE)— predominantly English, Scots, and Scots-Irish—were brought over to work the fields. Around 1700, the growing number of Scots-Irish led to a temporary ban on their being transported to America. After a 1717 decision in Great Britain permitting transportation as punishment, thousands of English criminals were shipped to Maryland and Virginia. A small number of Highland Scots settled in urban areas, and a small pocket of Germans formed the bulk of the population in Frederick County, having responded to sales promotions by some of the great English landholders. In 1700, Maryland's population of about 34,000 made it the third most populous colony, behind only Virginia and Massachusetts. Altogether about 12,000 slaves were imported into Maryland, and by 1775 slaves composed one-third of the population.

See also BALTIMORE, MARYLAND.

Further Reading

Bailyn, Bernard. *Voyages to the West.* New York: Alfred A. Knopf, 1986.

Baseler, Marilyn C. *"Asylum for Mankind": America, 1607–1800.* Ithaca, N.Y.: Cornell University Press, 1998.

Breen, T. H. *Puritans and Adventurers: Change and Persistence in Early America.* New York: Oxford University Press, 1980.

———. *Tobacco Culture: The Mentality of the Great Tidewater Planters on the Eve of Revolution.* Princeton, N.J.: Princeton University Press, 1985.

Carr, Lois G., et al. *Robert Cole's World: Agriculture and Society in Early Maryland.* Chapel Hill: University of North Carolina Press, 1991.

———. eds. *Colonial Chesapeake Society.* Williamsburg, Va.: University of North Carolina Press, 1988.

Carr, Lois G., and D. W. Jordan. *Maryland's Revolution of Government.* Ithaca, N.Y.: Cornell University Press, 1974.

Fischer, David. *Albion's Seed: Four British Folkways in America.* New York: Oxford University Press, 1989.

Land, Aubrey C. *Colonial Maryland: A History.* Millwood, N.Y.: KTO, 1981.

Main, Gloria L. *Tobacco Colony: Life in Early Maryland, 1650–1720.* Princeton, N.J.: Princeton University Press, 1982.

Menard, Russell. *Economy and Society in Early Colonial Maryland.* New York: Garland, 1985.

Quinn, David B. *Early Maryland in a Wider World.* Detroit: Wayne State University Press, 1982.

Massachusetts colony

Massachusetts was first settled by English Pilgrims (see PIL-GRIMS AND PURITANS). Dissatisfied with the strictures of the Church of England, these Separatists migrated to Holland in 1608–09. Fearing loss of their English identity, in 1617 a group committed themselves to moving to America. Receiving a land patent from the London Company, 41 Pilgrims and 61 other English settlers set off for America aboard the *Mayflower* and made landfall in November 1620 at Plymouth Bay, owing to an error in navigation. Without authorization to form a civil government but too late in the season to continue voyaging, the Pilgrim leaders signed the Mayflower Compact, establishing an agreement for "the generall good of the Colonie." Through years of hardship, the Plymouth Colony was sustained by the leadership of WILLIAM BRADFORD who served as the colony's governor between 1622 and 1656 (excepting 1633–34, 1636, 1638, and 1644). Limited economic opportunities kept immigration small. After 20 years the population was still only about 2,500.

Whereas the Pilgrims of Plymouth had removed themselves from the Church of England, the Puritans who settled north of Plymouth sought to purify the church from within. The Puritan settlement of BOSTON, some 40 miles north, was more prosperous than Plymouth and was the center of the Massachusetts Bay colony. In 1629, JOHN WINTHROP and a group of wealthy Puritans who had become convinced that reform of the Church of England was impossible, secured a charter from King Charles I. Curiously omitting the standard requirement stipulating where meetings of the joint-stock company were to be held, the charter enabled the 12 associates to move to America where they could settle with little royal interference. The *Arbella* carrying Winthrop and other Puritan leaders was one of 17 ships carrying more than 1,000 settlers in March 1630. By the early 1640s, the Great Migration had brought about 20,000 settlers, less than one-third the total number of Britons coming to the New World but enough to make Massachusetts Bay the largest colony on the northern Atlantic seaboard. Although immigrants came for many reasons, religion played a larger role in New England than in other colonial regions. Population pressure and religious dissent eventually spawned three colonies from the Boston center that lasted to the American Revolution: NEW HAMPSHIRE COLONY, CONNECTICUT COLONY, and RHODE ISLAND COLONY. In 1691, the Pilgrim colony at Plymouth, with a population of only about 7,000, was absorbed into the Massachusetts Bay colony. By the time of the American Revolution, in the 1770s, the New England colonies remained the most British in ethnic character, though a small number of French Huguenots (see HUGUENOT IMMIGRATION) did rise to prominence there in the 18th century.

Massachusetts Bay was not governed as a theocracy, as is sometimes portrayed. Church members did have responsibilities for disciplining their members and choosing ministers, but church membership was voluntary. In 1631, all adult male church members were declared freemen, giving some 40 percent of the adult male population the right to vote for governor, magistrates, and local officials. The Puritans viewed their form of society as an experiment, a "city on a hill," providing an example of godly living. Immigrants were urged to go forth "with a publicke spirit, looking not on your owne things only, but also on the things of others." Town life predominated, with men and women voluntarily covenanting to follow local ordinances. A small amount of land was provided free to each family, though all were expected to pay local and colony taxes, and to contribute in support of the minister. Eventually the Puritans developed a church structure known as Congregationalism in which each village church was independent, with members agreed in "the presence of God to walk together in all his ways." Ministers were influential but were not always listened to and could not hold civil office.

Further Reading

Breen, T. H. *Puritans and Adventurers: Change and Persistence in Early America.* New York: Oxford University Press, 1980.

Cressy, David. *Coming Over.* Cambridge: Cambridge University Press, 1988.

Gill, Crispin. *Mayflower Remembered: A History of the Plymouth Pilgrims.* New York: Taplinger Publishing, 1970.

Hall, David D. *Puritanism in Seventeenth-Century Massachusetts.* New York: Holt, Rinehart and Winston, 1968.

Labaree, Benjamin W. *Colonial Massachusetts: A History.* Millwood, N.Y.: KTO, 1979.

Mayflower Compact   See PILGRIMS AND PURITANS.

McCarran-Walter Act (Immigration and Nationality Act) (United States) (1952)

The McCarran-Walter Act was an attempt to deal systematically with the concurrent COLD WAR threat of communist expansion and the worldwide movement of peoples in the wake of World War II (1939–45; see WORLD WAR II AND IMMIGRATION). It codified various legislative acts and policy decisions, continuing the highly restrictive policies of the IMMIGRATION ACT (1917), the EMERGENCY QUOTA ACT (1921), and the JOHNSON-REED ACT (1924), which relied on national quotas to determine the nature of future immigration.

The expansion of Soviet political power and the fall of China to the Communists caused many Americans to fear the effects of loosely regulated immigration. This led to passage of the McCarran Internal Security Act (September 1950), authorizing the president in time of national emergency to detain or deport anyone suspected of threatening U.S. security. Senator Patrick McCarran of New York, a Democrat, argued against a more liberal immigration policy, fearing an augmentation of the "hard-core, indigestible blocs" of immigrants who had "not become integrated into the American way of life." Together with fellow Democrat Representative Francis Walter of Pennsylvania, they drafted the McCarran-Walter Act, which preserved the national origins quotas then in place as the best means of preserving the "cultural balance" in the nation's population. The main provisions of the measure included

1. establishment of a new set of preferences for determining admittees under the national quotas
   a. nonquota: spouses and minor children of citizens; clergy; inhabitants of the Western Hemisphere
   b. first preference: needed skilled workers, up to 50 percent of quota
   c. second preference: parents of citizens, up to 30 percent of quota
   d. third preference: spouses and unmarried children of resident aliens, up to 20 percent of quota
   e. nonpreference: siblings and older children of citizens
2. provision of 2,000 visas for countries within the Asia-Pacific triangle, with quotas applied to ancestry categories (Chinese, Korean, Japanese, etc.) rather than countries of birth
3. elimination of racial restrictions on naturalization
4. granting the Attorney General's Office the authority, in times of emergency, to temporarily "parole" into the United States anyone without a visa

Allotment of visas under the McCarran-Walter Act still heavily favored northern and western European countries, which received 85 percent of the quota allotment.

Further Reading
Daniels, Roger. *Guarding the Golden Door: American Immigration Policy and Immigrants since 1882.* New York: Hill and Wang, 2004.
Dimmitt, Marius A. *The Enactment of the McCarran-Walter Act of 1952.* Lawrence: University Press of Kansas, 1971.
Hutchinson, E. P. *Legislative History of American Immigration Policy, 1798–1965.* Philadelphia: University of Pennsylvania Press, 1981.
LeMay, Michael C. *From Open Door to Dutch Door: An Analysis of U.S. Immigration Policy since 1820.* New York: Praeger, 1987.

Mennonite immigration

Old Order Mennonites were one of the few immigrant groups to maintain their distinctive identity across more than three or four generations after coming to North America. This identity was largely defined by the Anabaptist religious beliefs that led to their persecution in their Swiss and Dutch homelands and a simple, agricultural lifestyle that over the years has consistently rejected many technological innovations. By 2000, however, only about one-third of Mennonites were still engaged in agriculture. The majority had moved into the mainstream of American and Canadian life, residing in small towns and cities. According to the Mennonite churches of the United States and Canada, in 2003 there were 124,150 Mennonites in Canada and 319,768 in the United States, though these figures did not include unbaptized members of the community. The greatest concentrations of Mennonites in Canada were in Ontario and Manitoba, with smaller numbers in Saskatchewan and Alberta. The largest Mennonite communities in the United States were in Pennsylvania, Ohio, Indiana, and Kansas.

Mennonites were one of a number of independent, reforming groups known as Anabaptists (rebaptizers), who organized themselves initially in Switzerland during the 1520s. The term *Mennonite* was first used in the Netherlands to characterize the Anabaptist disciples of Menno Simons, who organized Anabaptists in the Netherlands and northern Germany during the 1530s. Unlike most Protestants of the 16th century, Mennonites rejected the idea of a state church, rejected military service, and required adult baptism at the time of confession. They also rigorously guarded the community by threat of banishment and regulation of behavior and marriage within the religious group. Mennonites divided into many groups over the years, including the Amish (see AMISH IMMIGRATION). Seeking to avoid persecution and enforced military service, Swiss Mennonites first settled in southern Germany and France before immigrating to the PENNSYLVANIA COLONY in the 1680s. They established the first permanent Mennonite settlement at Germantown. In Pennsylvania, they became part of a group of early immigrants whom the English settlers called the Pennsylvania Dutch (from *Deutsch*), linked principally by their German heritage. Both population pressure and the violence of the American Revolution (1775–83) led to a considerable exodus from Pennsylvania to Canada. Between 1785 and 1825, about 2,000 Mennonites migrated, most to Waterloo County, Ontario.

Dutch Mennonites followed a different path, migrating in successive stages to northern Germany, Prussia, and finally Russia in the 1780s. Ever seeking to avoid military service, in 1873–74 about 13,000 German Mennonites emigrated from Russia to the central prairies of the United States, settling mostly in Kansas and Nebraska. In the same migration, 8,000 migrated to Canada, most to southern Manitoba. Facing an uncertain future following the Bolshevik Revolution, some 21,000 immigrated to Canada between 1922 and 1930 with the aid of the Canadian Mennonite Board of Colonization and transportation credits extended by the Canadian

Mennonite children pray in church, Hinkletown, Pennsylvania, 1942. Persecuted throughout Europe for their clannishness and pacifism, Mennonites immigrated to the United States and Canada, seeking out isolated areas in which to settle. According to a writer in the *Manitoba Free Press* in 1876, he had "seen nothing as regards the industry equal to the Mennonites." *(Photo by John Collier/Library of Congress, Prints & Photographs Division [LC-USF34-082455-E])*

Pacific Railway. Another 4,000 settled in Mexico, Brazil, and Paraguay. After much hardship during World War II (1939–45), about 7,000 Mennonites immigrated to Canada as refugees from the Soviet Union (1947–50), with another 5,000 going to South America.

Further Reading

Driedger, Leo. *Mennonites in the Global Village.* Toronto: University of Toronto Press, 2000.

Dyck, C. J., and D. D. Martin, eds. *The Mennonite Encyclopedia: A Comprehensive Reference Work on the Anabaptist-Mennonite Movement.* 5 vols. Hillsboro, Kans., and Scottdale, Pa.: Mennonite Brethren and Herald Press, 1955–59, 1990.

Ens, Adolf. *Subjects or Citizens: The Mennonite Experience in Canada, 1870–1925.* Ottawa: University of Ottawa Press, 1994.

Epp, Frank. *Mennonites in Canada, 1786–1920: The History of a Separate People.* Toronto: Macmillan, 1974.

———. *Mennonites in Canada, 1920–1940: A People's Struggle for Survival.* Scottdale, Pa.: Herald Press, 1982.

Epp, Marlene. *Women without Men: Mennonite Refugees of the Second World War.* Toronto: University of Toronto Press, 2000.

Loewen, Harry, and Steven Nolt. *Through Fire and Water: An Overview of Mennonite History.* Scottdale, Pa.: Herald Press, 1996.

Regehr, Ted D. *Mennonites in Canada, 1939–1970: A People Transformed.* Toronto: University of Toronto Press, 1996.

Schlabach, Theron F. *Peace, Faith, Nation: Mennonites and Amish in Nineteenth-Century America.* Scottdale, Pa.: Herald Press, 1989.

Toews, Paul. *Mennonites in American Society, 1930–1970: Modernity and the Persistence of Religious Community.* Scottdale, Pa.: Herald Press, 1996.

Mexican-American War   See U.S.-MEXICAN WAR.

Mexican immigration

Mexicans hold a unique position in the cultural history of the United States. In 1848, without moving, 75,000–100,000 Mexicans became U.S. citizens when the region of modern California, Arizona, New Mexico, and Texas was transferred from Mexico to the United States following the

U.S.-MEXICAN WAR. According to the 2000 U.S. census, 20,640,711 Americans claimed Mexican descent, accounting for almost 60 percent of the Hispanic population in the country (see HISPANIC AND RELATED TERMS). Of these, more than 9 million were born in Mexico. According to IMMIGRATION AND NATURALIZATION SERVICE (INS) estimates, almost 5 million were in the United States illegally, accounting for almost 70 percent of all unauthorized residents. Mexicans were also the largest Hispanic group in Canada, with 36,575 Canadians claiming Mexican descent in 2001. Mexican Americans are spread widely throughout California, Texas, New Mexico, Arizona, Colorado, and Illinois and form the majority populations in a number of Texas and Arizona towns and cities, including El Paso, Laredo, Brownsville, and McAllen. About half of Mexican Canadians live in Ontario.

Mexico occupies 741,600 square miles in southern North America. It is bordered by the United States on the north, and Guatemala and Belize on the south. In 2002, the population was estimated at 101,879,171. Ethnic divisions include mestizos (60 percent), Amerindians (30 percent), and Mexicans of European descent (9 percent). About 89 percent are Roman Catholic and 6 percent Protestant. The Olmec civilization flourished from about 800 B.C., laying a cultural foundation for the later Maya, Toltec, and Aztec states. In 1521, the Aztecs of the central

Mexicans enter the United States at the U.S. immigration station at El Paso, Texas, 1938. The terminal point for the Mexican Central Railroad, El Paso became the national center for recruitment of Mexican labor in the 1930s. *(Photo by Dorothea Lange/Library of Congress, Prints & Photographs Division [LC-USF34-018297-E])*

valley of Mexico were brought under Spanish rule, and most of modern Mexico was brought under Spanish control by the 1530s. During 300 years of Spanish rule, Amerindian cultures were largely destroyed, replaced by the prevailing language, architecture, and learning of Spain. Mexico gained its independence in 1821 but was often ruled by political strongmen and remained relatively weak in relation to its giant neighbor to the north. Following U.S. acquisition of the Southwest in the U.S.-Mexican War, the rights of the almost 100,000 former Mexican citizens were formally guaranteed. Vestiges of their culture remained prominent in the Southwest, but the rapid influx of Anglo settlers in the wake of the gold rush of 1848 and the building of transcontinental railways from the 1860s ensured that Mexican Americans would lose almost all political influence until the latter part of the 20th century. The Mexican Revolution (1910–17) laid the foundation for political reform, though little was done to help the masses until the 1930s. Between 1940 and 1980, the Mexican economy prospered, largely on the basis of petroleum revenues. During the 1980s, however, rapid population increase and a drop in petroleum prices led to high rates of unemployment and inflation, which in turn produced a massive wave of emigration, both legal and illegal.

Mexicans first immigrated to the United States in significant numbers in the first decade of the 20th century, replacing excluded Chinese and Japanese laborers. Wartime demands for labor during World War I (1914–18), World War II (1939–45), and the Korean War (1950–53) coupled with a rapidly developing agricultural industry in the southwestern United States, led Congress to exempt Mexicans as temporary workers from otherwise restrictive immigrant legislation. As a result, almost 80,000 Mexicans were admitted between creation of a temporary farmworkers' program in 1917 and its termination in 1922. Less than half of the workers returned to Mexico. Linking with networks that organized and transported Mexican laborers, workers continued to enter the United States throughout the 1920s, with 459,000 officially recorded. Although there were no official limits on immigration from the Western Hemisphere, many Mexicans chose to bypass the official process, which since 1917 had included a literacy test, making the actual number of Mexican immigrants much higher. Most worked in agriculture in either Texas or California, but there were significant numbers in Kansas and Colorado, and migrants began to take more industrial jobs in the upper Midwest and Great Lakes region, leading to a general dispersal throughout the country. Between 1900 and the onset of the Great Depression in 1930, the number of foreign-born Mexicans in the United States rose from 100,000 to 639,000. With so many American citizens out of work, more than 500,000 Mexicans were repatriated during the 1930s.

The urgent demand for labor during World War II led to creation of the BRACERO PROGRAM in August 1942. Its main impact was to provide a large, dependent agricultural labor force, working for 30–50 cents per day under the most spartan conditions. In the long term, it led to a massive influx of Mexicans, both legal and illegal, who became magnets for further family migration under the provisions of the IMMIGRATION AND NATIONALITY ACT of 1965. Between 1942 and the ending of the Bracero Program in 1964, almost 5 million Mexican laborers legally entered the country, with several million more entering illegally to work for even lower wages. Mexican immigration rose significantly in each decade following World War II. In the 1950s, almost 300,000 came; in the 1960s, 454,000; in the 1970s, 640,000; in the 1980s, 1.6 million; and in the 1990s, 2.2 million. Between 2000 and 2002, legal immigration averaged almost 200,000 per year. The IMMIGRATION REFORM AND CONTROL ACT (1986) attempted to regularize the agricultural labor issue, granting citizenship to undocumented Mexicans who could demonstrate a 10-year period of continuous residence.

Two events in the mid-1990s had significant implications for Mexican immigration, especially to the United States. On January 1, 1994, the NORTH AMERICAN FREE TRADE AGREEMENT (NAFTA) went into effect, gradually reducing tariffs on trade between the United States, Canada, and Mexico and guaranteeing investors equal business rights in all three countries. Although thousands of jobs moved from the United States to Mexico, NAFTA did little to stem the tide of illegal immigration. Later that year, a financial crisis in Mexico led to the devaluation of the peso in December 1994–February 1995 and a potential defaulting on international obligations. International loans of more than $50 billion staved off bankruptcy, but the accompanying austerity plan in Mexico led to higher interest rates and dramatically higher consumer prices. Growing concern over the cost of providing assistance to illegal immigrants and fear of an increased flow from Mexico as a result of the economic crisis, led Californians to approve (59 percent to 41 percent) PROPOSITION 187, which denied education, welfare benefits, and nonemergency health care to illegal immigrants. Anticipating legal challenges, proponents of Proposition 187 included language to safeguard all provisions not specifically deemed invalid by the courts. Decisions by federal judges in both 1995 and 1998, however, upheld previous decisions regarding the unconstitutionality of the proposition's provisions, based on Fourteenth Amendment protections against discriminating against one class of people (in this case, immigrants). The exact status of "unauthorized immigrants" from Mexico—the euphemism for illegal aliens—continued to be hotly debated into the first decade of the 21st century.

Another response to the rapid growth of illegal Mexican immigrants was a dramatic increase in the strength and technological sophistication of the BORDER PATROL, a move reinforced in the wake of the terror attacks of SEPTEM-BER 11, 2001. In September 2003, the California legislature passed legislation allowing illegal immigrants to receive a California driver's license. With the October recall of Governor Gray Davis, new governor Arnold Schwarzenegger rescinded the measure in December, adding fuel to the debate over United States obligations to Mexicans residing in the country illegally.

On January 7, 2004, President George W. Bush proposed the Temporary Worker Program, which would "match willing foreign workers with willing American employers, when no Americans can be found to fill the jobs." More controversially, it would provide legal status to temporary workers, even if they were undocumented. Though not specifically mentioning Mexico, the announcement was clearly aimed to tackle "the Mexican problem," a point highlighted by the presence at the ceremony of the chairman of the Hispanic Alliance for Progress, the president of the Association for the Advancement of Mexican Americans, the president of the Latin Coalition, and the president of the League of United Latin American Citizens. To be granted temporary worker status, the immigrant would be required to have a job and would have to apply for renewal after the initial three-year period was up. Undocumented workers would be required to pay a one-time fee to register, whereas those abroad who applied for legal entry would not be required to pay the fee. Bush also proposed an increase in the annual number of green cards issued by the government. Mexico's president, Vicente Fox, called the proposal an "important step forward" for Mexican workers.

Mexican immigration to Canada was different from the American experience in both scale and type. Not only were numbers small—there were only 36,225 Mexican immigrants in Canada in 2001—but most Mexican immigrants were from the middle and upper-middle classes and a variety of backgrounds. One group included professionals who generally immigrated for economic improvement and often intended to stay in Canada. Another immigrant group was Mexican Mennonites who had emigrated from Canada to northern Mexico in the 1920s but returned to Canada during the 1980s economic crisis. Some Mexicans, including students, also marry Canadian citizens. Almost all Mexican immigrants are in the country legally. Although up to 5,000 contract workers were admitted each year in the 1990s, they were not formally immigrants and rarely were allowed to overstay their visas. More than half of Mexican immigrants came between 1991 and 2001. Almost one-third of them came between 1996 and 2001.

Further Reading

Acuña, Rodolfo. *Occupied America: A History of Chicanos.* 4th ed. New York: Harper and Row, 1999.
Camarillo, Albert. *Chicanos in a Changing Society: From Mexican Pueblos to American Barrios in Santa Barbara and Southern California, 1848–1930.* Cambridge, Mass.: Harvard University Press, 1979.

Cardoso, Lawrence. *Mexican Emigration to the United States, 1897–1931.* Tucson: University of Arizona Press, 1980.

Dunn, Timothy J. *The Militarization of the U.S.-Mexico Border, 1878–1992: Low Intensity Doctrine Comes Home.* Austin, Tex.: Center for Mexican American Studies, 1996.

García, Juan R. *Mexicans in the Midwest.* Tucson: University of Arizona Press, 1996.

García, Mario T. *Desert Immigrants: The Mexicans of El Paso, 1880–1920.* New Haven, Conn.: Yale University Press, 1981.

Gómez-Quiñones, Juan. *Chicano Politics: Reality and Promise, 1940–1990.* Albuquerque: University of New Mexico Press, 1990.

Griswold del Castillo, Richard, and Arnoldo de León. *North to Aztlan: A History of Mexican Americans in the United States.* New York: Twayne, 1996.

Gutiérrez, David. *Walls and Mirrors: Mexican Americans, Mexican Immigrants, and the Politics of Ethnicity.* Berkeley: University of California Press, 1995.

Martínez, Oscar J. *Border People: Life and Society in the U.S.-Mexico Borderlands.* Tucson: University of Arizona Press, 1994.

Massey, Douglas, et al. *Return to Aztlan: The Social Process of International Migration from Western Mexico.* Berkeley: University of California Press, 1987.

McWilliams, Carey. *North from Mexico.* New York: Greenwood Press, 1968.

Meier, Matt S., and Feliciano Ribera. *Mexican Americans/American Mexicans: From Conquistadors to Chicanos.* New York: Hill and Wang, 1993.

Muller, Thomas, and Thomas J. Espenshade. *The Fourth Wave: California's Newest Immigrants.* Washington, D.C.: Urban Institute, 1985.

"The New Frontier/La Nueva Frontera." *Time* (June 11, 2001), pp. 36–79.

Portes, Alejandro, and Robert L. Bach. *Latin Journey: Cuban and Mexican Immigrants in the United States.* Berkeley: University of California Press, 1985.

Rosales, Francisco A. *Chicano!: A History of the Mexican American Civil Rights Movement.* Houston, Tex.: Arte Público Press, 1996.

Samuel, T. John, Rodolfo Gutiérrez, and Gabriela Vázquez. "International Migration between Canada and Mexico: Retrospects and Prospects." *Canadian Studies in Population* 22, no. 1 (1995): 49–65.

Skerry, Peter. *Mexican Americans: The Ambivalent Minority.* Cambridge, Mass.: Harvard University Press, 1993.

Whittaker, Elvi. "The Mexican Presence in Canada: Uncertainty and Nostalgia." *Journal of Ethnics Studies* 16, no. 2 (1988): 28–46.

Zahniser, Steven S. *Mexican Migration to the United States: The Role of Migration Networks and Human Capital Accumulation.* New York: Garland, 1999.

Miami, Florida

As the southernmost metropolitan area on the eastern seaboard of the United States, Miami became one of America's principal magnets for immigrants in the 20th century. In 2000, the majority of its residents were Hispanic (see HISPANIC AND RELATED TERMS), including large numbers of Cubans, Haitians, Mexicans, and Nicaraguans. Cubans were the largest ethnic group, composing approximately 30 percent of the total population and 70 percent of the foreign-born population. Metropolitan Miami (2.2 million, 2000) was second only to the Tampa Bay area (2.3 million, 2000) in Florida Hispanic population. Miami also developed into the commercial capital of the Caribbean basin and the principal American city through which business with Latin America was conducted.

Miami was established in 1896 when Henry M. Flagler extended the Florida East Coast Railroad into what had previously been considered the rural backwater of southern Florida. In 1900, its population was only 1,700. Land speculation in the 1920s led to rapid growth (110,000 by 1930), though the Great Depression hampered development until after World War II (1939–45). Although few jobs were available, Miami provided a safe haven for political refugees from Cuba, including two deposed presidents (Gerardo Machado and Carlos Prío Socarrás).

With the advent of the COLD WAR, Miami again became a haven, this time for refugees fleeing communist regimes, particularly in Latin America. CUBAN IMMIGRATION transformed the ethnicity and economy of the city, with nearly 300,000 Cubans settling in the Miami area since 1959. During the 1960s, Miami displaced NEW ORLEANS, LOUISIANA, as the principal financial and commercial link between the United States and Latin America. With more than 100 multinational corporations and banking services, second only to NEW YORK, NEW YORK, Miami had by the 1980s emerged as one of the world's major commercial centers. Adapting to the rapid Hispanic influx, Miami-Dade County schools instituted the first public bilingual education program in the United States in 1963 and declared the area officially bilingual and bicultural in 1973. With the rapid influx of 125,000 Cubans during the MARIEL BOATLIFT (1980–81), a backlash occurred, leading to a large outflow of Anglos to northern Florida and the advent of the "English only" movement. At the same time, there was hostility in the African-American community toward Cuban immigrants, who were perceived as competitors for jobs and recipients of program benefits (such as affirmative action) set aside for minorities. These tensions, sparked by cases of police abuse led to riots in 1980, 1982, and 1989.

While many Cuban immigrants prior to 1980 were of the middle and upper classes and helped to establish a strong Hispanic economic base, the majority of Cuban, Haitian, Jamaican, Dominican, and Bahamian immigrants since that time have tended to be poor, and their settlement in Miami controversial. The first wave of Cuban immigrants nevertheless established a cohesive enclave that enabled Cubans to rapidly integrate themselves into the local political community. There have been Cuban mayors of Miami, Hialeah, West Miami, Sweetwater, and Hialeah Gardens (all within the Greater Miami area) and strong Cuban representation in the state legislature. Because of the exile ideology fostered during the 1960s, Cubans have developed a strong political presence. Unlike most immigrant groups, they overwhelmingly vote Republican, supporting active measures aimed at undermining Fidel Castro's rule in their homeland. This conservative political bent has contributed to tension between the Cuban and African-American communities.

Further Reading
Croucher, Sheila. *Imagining Miami.* Charlottesville: University Press of Virginia, 1997.

García, María Cristina. *Havana USA: Cuban Exiles and Cuban Americans in South Florida.* Los Angeles: University of California Press, 1996.

Grenier, Guillermo, and Lisandro Pérez. "Miami Spice: The Ethnic Cauldron Simmers." In *Origins and Destinies: Immigration, Race, and Ethnicity in America.* Eds. Silvia Pedraza and Rubén G. Rumbaut. Belmont, Calif.: Wadsworth, 1996.

Grenier, Guillermo J., and Alex Stepick, eds. *Miami Now: Immigration, Ethnicity and Social Change.* Miami: University of Florida Press, 1992.

Portes, Alejandro, and Alex Stepick. *City on the Edge: The Transformation of Miami.* Berkeley: University of California Press, 1993.

Mine War

A decade-long tension between management and labor erupted in two weeks of open warfare in the Illinois, Ohio, and Indiana coalfields during June 1894. The use of increasingly violent tactics divided the old (English and Irish) and new (Italian and eastern European) miners and led the public to generally withdraw support from striking miners.

The Mine War was the product of three convergent factors: poor working conditions, a rapid influx of immigrants from eastern and southern Europe after 1890, and a major depression beginning in spring 1893. While strikes in the Midwest coalfields had been commonplace since 1887, the depression heightened tensions and the presence of so many new immigrants made common labor action difficult. Many did not speak English and, having no previous understandings with management, were more prone to violence in waging strikes. Wage reductions in April 1894 led the United Mine Workers of America (UMWA) to call for a strike.

The main goal of the strike was not higher wages per se, but rather a reduction of the supply of coal nationwide to drive up coal prices and thereby wages. In this respect, the suspension of production was supported by some mine operators. Although the UMWA had a membership of only 13,000 at the time, around 170,000 bituminous coal miners throughout Illinois, Indiana, Ohio, and Pennsylvania, Maryland, Virginia, and West Virginia answered the call. Because the UMWA was not strong enough to enforce suspension of production in all fields—most notably in Maryland, Virginia, and some parts of Pennsylvania—coal

continued to reach the market. Widespread use of nonunion miners led to violent confrontations. Vandalism of mines and railroads became common, and mine owners frequently brought in Pinkerton detectives or local and federal law officers to prevent lawlessness. As conditions worsened, state militias were called out to halt the violence. The mine war was largely a failure. Wages were only slightly adjusted, and the bituminous coal market remained unstable.

By June 1894, the division between old and new miners had become prominent, with some recent immigrant groups taking control of local actions. Although miners were not strictly divided along ethnic lines, violence came to be increasingly associated with anarchism and other radical European ideas. By the mid-1890s, many old immigrants were voting for Populist candidates who were calling for immigration restrictions. Also, old-line groups such as the UMWA began to lobby Congress for an end to immigration.

Further Reading
Aurand, Harold W. *From the Molly Maguires to the United Mine Workers: The Social Ecology of an Industrial Union, 1869–1897.* Philadelphia: Temple University Press, 1971.

Bailey, Kenneth R. "'Tell the Boys to Fall into Line': United Mine Workers of America Strikes in West Virginia, January–June, 1894." *West Virginia History* 32, no. 4 (July 1971): 224–237.

Laslett, John, ed. *The United Mine Workers of America: A Model of Industrial Solidarity?* University Park: Pennsylvania State University Press, 1996.

Lens, Sidney. *The Labor Wars: From the Molly Maguires to the Sitdowns.* Garden City, N.Y.: Doubleday, 1973.

Merithew, Caroline Waldron and James R. Barrett. "'We Are All Brothers in the Face of Starvation': Forging an Interethnic Working Class Movement in the 1894 Bituminous Coal Strike." *Mid-America* 83 (Summer 2001): 121–54.

Reitman, Sharon. "Class Formation and Union Politics: The Western Federation of Miners and the United Mine Workers of America, 1880–1910." Ph.D. diss., University of Michigan 1991.

Molly Maguires

The Molly Maguires was a secret Irish Catholic society, originally bent on terrorizing English mine and landowners in the name of labor justice. At the center of labor strikes and violence from the time of the society's arrival in the United States in the 1850s, the Molly Maguires came to be associated in the minds of most Americans with lawlessness and vigilante justice.

The Mollies were an American model of the Ancient Order of Hibernians, which had revolted against English landowners in Ireland. According to legend, an Irish woman named Molly Maguire had murdered local landowners and agents in retribution for their oppression of the common people, thus attracting a passionate following among the oppressed. In the United States, the Molly Maguires used arson and murder throughout the coal mining regions of eastern Pennsylvania during the 1860s and 1870s in order to intimidate mine supervisors. They became so powerful in some places that they held official positions within municipal governments and police forces. After infiltration by an agent of the Pinkerton Detective Agency in 1875, the movement was effectively destroyed by 1877 with the arrest and execution of most of the Molly Maguire leaders.

Further Reading

Broehl, Wayne G. *The Molly Maguires.* Cambridge, Mass.: Harvard University Press, 1966.
Kenny, Kevin. *Making Sense of the Molly Maguires.* New York: Oxford University Press, 1998.
Lens, Sidney. *The Labor Wars: From the Molly Maguires to the Sitdowns.* Garden City, N.Y.: Doubleday, 1973.

Montreal, Quebec

Montreal, the second largest city in Canada and one of the largest French-speaking cities in the world, had a population of 3,380,645 in 2001. Strategically situated on the St. Lawrence River, it was the economic center of Canada from the 18th century and thus attracted large numbers of immigrants. Toronto became more important economically from the 1940s, but Montreal remained one of the great educational and cultural centers of Canada and thus continued to attract immigrants. In 2001, Italians (224,460), Jews (80,390), Haitians (69,945), Chinese (57,655), Greeks (55,865), Germans (53,850), Lebanese (43,740), and Portuguese (41,050) were the largest nonfounding groups living in the city. Between 2000 and 2002, about 31,000 immigrants settled in Montreal annually, with almost one-third coming from Africa and the Middle East and 27 percent from Asia and the Pacific. China was the largest source country, with 8,993 immigrants, but was closely followed by three francophone countries: France with 8,845; Morocco with 8,032; and Algeria with 7,061. In 2002, Montreal attracted more immigrants than Vancouver (33,000 to 30,000) for the first time since 1993.

JACQUES CARTIER explored the area of modern Montreal in 1535, but the first French settlement was not established until 1642. By the early 18th century, Montreal had become the commercial center of NEW FRANCE. The capture of the city in 1760 by British forces during the SEVEN YEARS' WAR effectively ended French political control. By the terms of the Treaty of Paris, Montreal and New France were formally transferred to Britain in 1763. Many merchants returned to France, enabling British businesses to gain gradual control as the local economy shifted from the fur trade to shipbuilding and industry. By 1850, the population reached 50,000, then doubled during the next 20 years. Completion of the Canadian Pacific Railway in 1885 further enhanced the industrial capacity of the city,

and by 1914, the population had grown to almost a half million.

In 1901, Montreal was made up almost totally of French (60.9 percent) and British stock (33.7 percent), an unusual lack of diversity for a major North American city. This changed significantly between 1900 and 1914, with a large influx of Europeans, most notably Jews, Germans, Poles, and Ukrainians. By 1911, these newcomers accounted for almost 10 percent of the population. After 1930, an increasing number of Italians, Greeks, Chinese, blacks from the United States and the Caribbean, and Lebanese arrived. Following the disruptions of World War II (1939–45), there were significant influxes from Germany, Greece, Portugal, and Italy. Relaxed immigration rules in the early 1960s led to development of the first Haitian community. Although Montreal had become considerably more diverse by the 1960s, it was still largely a European city. After 1970, immigration to Montreal was characterized by the shift in source countries from Europe to various parts of the developing world and the favoring of immigrants from former French colonies, especially Vietnam, Haiti, Morocco, and Algeria. A significant number of Central Americans and South Americans also began to arrive. With the retrocession of Hong Kong to China in 1997, Chinese immigration to Montreal was high in the 1990s.

With the majority of the population of French descent, there was considerable ethnic tension in Montreal during the 20th century. It was most evident over the question of conscription during World War I (1914–18) and World War II. During the 1960s and 1970s, Quebec Province was the center of a French-Canadian nationalist movement whose supporters were known as Quebecois; some sought full independence for the province of Quebec. By the 1960s, Montreal had become a polyglot city and was losing some of its distinctive French character, particularly as more French speakers moved to the suburbs. The debate over the value of immigration was often heated, especially as it tended to support a greater use of the English language. In the years following the terrorist attacks of September 11, 2001, there was a growing reluctance to welcome more immigrant from Islamic countries. Although Montreal was a relatively low-crime city, rising crime rates were sometimes attributed to immigrants, as in the case of Iranian refugees arriving in the early 1980s who had connections with the Southeast Asian heroin trade. By the late 1990s, more than 100 had been convicted of drug trafficking. Nevertheless, a study conducted throughout the 1990s demonstrated that most immigrants in Montreal blended well within the society and that their use of French in public life was only slightly lower than that of native Montrealers.

By summer 2002, Quebec Province was actively seeking ways to encourage immigrant settlement outside Montreal, but found the lack of specialized jobs a stumbling block. At the same time, Canadian immigration minister Denis

Coderre observed that Canada would face a shortage of up to 1 million skilled workers within five years, suggesting the likelihood that the Montreal immigrant community would continue to grow.

Further Reading

Berdugo-Cohen, Marie, and Yolande Cohen. *Juifs marocains à montreal: témoignages d'une immigration moderne.* Montreal: VLB, 1987.

Lam, Lawrence. *From Being Uprooted to Surviving: Resettlement of Vietnamese-Chinese "Boat People" in Montreal, 1980–1990.* Toronto: York Lanes Press, 1996.

Lavoie, Nathalie, and Pierre Serre. "From Bloc Voting to Social Voting: The Case of Citizenship Issues of Immigration to Montreal, 1995–1996." *Peace Research Abstracts* 39, no. 6 (2002): 763–957.

Linteau, Paul-André. *Histoire de la ville de Montréal depuis la Confédération.* Montreal: Boreal, 1992.

Marois, Claude. "Cultural Transformations in Montreal since 1970." *Journal of Cultural Geography* 8, no. 2 (1988): 29–38.

McNicoll, Claire. *Montréal, une société multiculturelle.* Paris: Belin, 1993.

Monette, Pierre. *L'immigrant Montréal.* Montreal: Triptyque, 1994.

Penisson, Bernard. "L'émigration française au Canada." In *L'émigration française: études de cas: Algérie—Canada—Etats-Unis.* Paris: Université de Paris I, Centre de recherches d'histoire nord-américaine, 1985.

Ramirez, Bruno. *The Italians of Montreal: From Sojourning to Settlement, 1900–1921.* Montreal: Editions du Courant, 1980.

———. "Workers without a Cause: Italian Immigrant Labour in Montreal, 1880–1930." In *Arrangiarsi: The Italian Immigration Experience in Canada.* Eds. Roberto Perin and Franc Sturino. Montreal: Guernica, 1989.

Robinson, Ira, Pierre Anctil, and Mervin Butovsky, eds. *An Everyday Miracle: Yiddish Culture in Montreal.* Montreal: Véhicule Press, 1990.

Robinson, Ira, and Mervin Butovsky, eds. *Renewing Our Days; Montreal Jews in the Twentieth Century.* Montreal: Véhicule Press, 1995.

Moroccan immigration

The Moroccan presence in North America was small until the 1950s. According to the U.S. census of 2000 and the Canadian census of 2001, 38,923 Americans and 21,355 Canadians claimed Moroccan descent. Most Moroccan Americans lived in large urban areas, mainly in New York and New England. Three-quarters of all Canadian Moroccans lived in MONTREAL, QUEBEC.

Morocco covers 177,117 square miles in northwestern Africa. It is bordered on the east by Algeria and on the south by Western Sahara (a contested area). Ten miles to the north, across the Mediterranean Sea, lies Spain. About three-quarters of Morocco's population of 29,237,000 (2001) is Berber, but the majority of Berbers speak Arabic and practice Islam. The country is mainly divided between Arab culture (65 percent) and Berber culture groups (33 percent), though 98 percent of the entire population is Muslim. Settled mainly by Berber tribespeople in ancient times, Morocco was an ally of Rome, forming part of its province of Mauretania. Morocco was conquered by Arab armies during the seventh century, though Berber resistance and regional independence remained prominent until the 11th century, when the Almoravid confederation conquered virtually all the country. Almost all Moroccans eventually converted to Islam. During the 14th and 15th centuries, thousands of Jews fleeing persecution in Spain and Portugal settled in Morocco. France and Spain both began to encroach on Moroccan territory during the 1840s and 1850s, and France ruled the region from 1912 to 1956, when it regained its independence. Morocco's Jews fared well under the French, but their position deteriorated when the French government installed in Vichy cooperated with Nazi Germany during World War II (1939–45). Between 1945 and 1956, most of Morocco's 270,000 Jews emigrated, with the largest number going to Israel. Some, however, came to the United States and Canada.

There were almost no Moroccans in North America prior to World War II. With tiny Muslim communities, the United States and Canada were not attractive cultural magnets for non-Jews, who made up about 98 percent of the Moroccan population. Also, until the late 1990s, France and Spain usually welcomed Moroccan workers, who found it convenient to travel back and forth between work and home. By the 1990s, however, an increasing number were turning to North America, favoring French-speaking Montreal as a destination. In 2001, more than 16,000 of Canada's 21,000 Moroccans lived in Montreal, with more than 40 percent arriving between 1991 and 2001. Most recent Moroccan immigrants to the United States tended to be somewhat better educated, though it is still early to determine the relative success of Moroccan integration. In 1990, there were about 15,000 Moroccan immigrants in the country, most residing in New York City where there was a strong activist element among Muslim leaders. The Moroccans played a large role in building New York's second mosque, the Islamic Mission of America for the Propagation of Islam and Defense of the Faith and the Faithful. Between 1992 and 2002, about 27,000 Moroccans immigrated to the United States, representing 70 percent of the entire Moroccan community in the country.

Further Reading

Abu-Laben, Baha. *An Olive Branch on the Family Tree: The Arabs in Canada.* Toronto: McClelland and Stewart, 1980.

Bibas, David. *Immigrants and the Formation of Community: A Case Study of Moroccan Jewish Immigration to America.* New York: AMS Press, 1998.

Hourani, Albert. *A History of the Arab People.* Cambridge, Mass.: Harvard University Press, 1993.

Naff, Alixa. *Becoming American: The Early Arab Experience.* Carbondale: Southern Illinois University Press, 1985.

Pennell, C. R. *Morocco since 1830: A History.* New York: New York University Press, 2001.

Waugh, Earle H., Sharon McIrvin Abu-Laban, and Regula B. Qureshi, eds. *Muslim Families in North America.* Edmonton, Canada: University of Alberta Press, 1991.

Morse, Samuel F. B. (1791–1872) *inventor, political activist*

Best remembered for developing the Morse code and the first working telegraph, Morse was also one of the leading anti-Catholic activists of his day. Because of his public prominence, his opinion carried considerable public weight, reinforcing nativist tendencies in the United States.

The son of a Calvinist minister, Morse attended Phillips Academy in Massachusetts and Yale University in Connecticut. In order to develop his craft as a professional artist, Morse traveled widely in Europe between 1829 and 1832. On his return trip to the United States, he began work on what would become his code and telegraph. Before he earned a government commission to build a telegraph line between Baltimore and Washington, D.C., in 1843, Morse was often in financial difficulty. This led him to study the new photographic techniques of Louis-Jacques-Mandé Daguerre while in France and to become one of the pioneers of photography in the United States. He was a founder and president of the National Academy of Design (1826–45, 1861–62) and was long associated with New York University (1832–71).

During a stay in Rome, Morse became intensely anti-Catholic. His native suspicion of papal authoritarianism was reenforced when a common soldier, seeing that Morse's head remained covered during a Catholic procession, used his bayonet to knock Morse's hat from his head. He carried this animosity back to the United States, making it part of his political creed. Shortly before making an unsuccessful run for mayor of New York City, he wrote letters to the *New York Observer* that were collected and published as *A Foreign Conspiracy against the Liberties of the United States* (1834). The letters were aimed at the Leopold Association of Vienna, a Catholic missionary organization whose purpose was the proselytization of the United States. In the following year, Morse published *Imminent Dangers to the Free Institutions of the United States through Foreign Immigration and Present State of the Naturalization Laws.* Morse's particular brand of NATIVISM was aimed predominantly at Catholics and especially the Irish. In *Imminent Dangers* he railed against what he termed a "naturalized *foreigner*" who professed to "become an American" but "talks (for example) of Ireland as 'his home,' as 'his beloved country,' resents anything said against the Irish as said against him, glories in being Irish, forms and cherishes an Irish interest, brings hither Irish local feuds, and forgets, in short, all his new obligations as an American, and retains both a name and a feeling and a practice in regard to his adopted country at war with propriety, with decency, with gratitude, and with true patriotism." During the Civil War (1861–65), Morse increasingly viewed immigrants as a prop to the stability of the Union, rather than a potential source of destruction.

Further Reading

Kloss, William. *Samuel F. B. Morse.* New York: Harry N. Abrams, 1988.

Mabee, Carleton. *The American Leonardo: A Life of Samuel F. B. Morse.* New York: Alfred A. Knopf, 1943.

Morse, Edward Lind, ed. *Samuel F. B. Morse: His Letters and Journals.* 2 vols. Boston: Houghton Mifflin, 1914.

Staiti, Paul J. *Samuel F. B. Morse.* Cambridge: Cambridge University Press, 1989.

National Origins Quota Act (United States)
(1924)   See JOHNSON-REED ACT.

nativism

Nativism is a strong dislike for ethnic, religious, or political minorities within one's culture. In North America it was founded principally upon the fear that immigrant attitudes will erode the distinctive features of the majority culture. Unlike ethnocentrism, a generalized, largely passive perception of the superiority of one's own culture, nativism leads to pronounced activism and sometimes hostile measures taken in order to avert a perceived danger. Nativism is common in most cultures during times of economic or political turmoil, and there have been periodic waves of nativism in both the United States and Canada throughout their histories.

In the United States, there had been from the earliest colonial days a mistrust among settlers from different countries and of different religions. These general antipathies first rose to form a nativist movement in the 1790s, when Federalists hoped to keep out what they saw as the corroding influence of radical immigrants by passing the ALIEN AND SEDITION ACTS. With the majority of settlers in British territories being Protestant Anglicans and Puritans, Quakers and Roman Catholics were seen as potential threats to the traditional English order. While these attitudes persisted in the early republic, there was no full-blown nativist frenzy until the 1830s: The influx of more than a quarter million Irish, most of them Catholic, between 1820 and 1840 led to the second great wave of nativism in the United States. As most Americans were members of Protestant denominations that fostered the ethic of American individualism, it was easy to convince people in hard times that "papal schemes" to control American society were afoot. SAMUEL F. B. MORSE's *Foreign Conspiracy against the Liberties of the United States* (1834) and Reverend Lyman Beecher's *A Plea for the West* (1835) sought to alert Americans to clandestine plots being masterminded in Rome for the cultural takeover of the country. Sensational exposés of Catholic practices were common in the press. Maria Monk's *Awful Disclosures of the Hotel Dieu Nunnery of Montreal* (1836), purporting to tell the firsthand account of the author's imprisonment in a Catholic monastery, was a best-seller and remained so long after she was discredited. In addition to vague fears of conspiracy, many Americans feared the potential power of the Roman Catholic Church to overturn the Protestant foundation of the emerging public system of education. This sometimes led to violence, as in the Philadelphia riots of 1844, when a number of Irish Catholics were killed and several churches burned. This anti-Catholic nativism led during the 1850s to the rise of the Secret Order of the Star-Spangled Banner, more commonly known as the Know-Nothing or American Party. The Know-Nothings were particularly strong in the Northeast and border regions. In the wake of their strong showing in 1854 and 1855, in which they gained control of several state governments and

This anti-Catholic cartoon from 1855, reflects the nativist perception of the threat posed by the Roman Catholic Church's influence in the United States through Irish immigration and Catholic education. The headline read: "The Propagation Society. More Free Than Welcome." The "Propagation Society" is probably the Catholic proselytizing organization the Society for the Propagation of the Faith. At right, on a shore marked "United States," Brother Jonathan, whittling, leans against a flagpole flying the stars and stripes. "Young America," a boy in a short coat and striped trousers, stands at left, holding out a Bible toward Pope Pius IX, who steps ashore from a boat at left. The latter holds aloft a sword in one hand and a cross in the other. Still in the boat are five bishops. One holds the boat to the shore with a crozier hooked around a shamrock plant. The pope says, "My friend we have concluded to take charge of your spiritual welfare, and your temporal estate, so that you need not be troubled with the care of them in future; we will say your prayer and spend your money, while you live, and bury you in the Potters Field, when you die. Kneel then! And kiss our big toe in token of submission." Brother Jonathan responds, "No you don't, Mr. Pope! You're altogether too willing; but you can't put 'the mark of the Beast' on Americans." Young America says, "You can neither coax, nor frighten our boys, Sir! We can take care of our own worldly affairs, and are determined to Know nothing but this book, to guide us in spiritual things." ("Know nothing" is a double entendre, alluding also to the nativist political party of the same name.) The first bishop reacts, "I cannot bear to see that boy, with that horrible book." Then the second bishop adds, "Only let us get a good foothold on the soil, and we'll burn up those Books and elevate this Country to the Same degree of happiness and prosperity, to which we have brought Italy, Spain, Ireland and many other lands." The third bishop notes, "Sovereign Pontiff! Say that if his friends, have any money, when he dies; they may purchase a hole for him in my cemetery, at a fair price." The fourth bishop says, "Go ahead Reverend Father; I'll hold our boat by this sprig of shamrock." *(Peter Smith [i.e. Nathaniel Currier]/Library of Congress, Prints & Photographs Division [LC-USZ62-30815])*

sent more than 100 congressmen to Washington, they attempted to restrict immigration, delay naturalization, and investigate perceived Catholic abuses. Finding little evidence to support Catholic crimes or conspiracies and with the country embroiled in the states' rights and slavery issues, Know-Nothing political influence and anti-Catholic nativism waned. Many non-Catholic Americans remained suspicious of Catholics, and occasionally anti-Catholic nativism reemerged, as in the formation of the AMERICAN PROTECTIVE ASSOCIATION (1887). Generally speaking, however, religion became less and less a primary motivation for open hostility toward immigrants.

For almost two decades following the Civil War (1861–65), immigration proceeded without strong nativist opposition. The presence of large numbers of Chinese in the West during the economic slump of the late 1870s and the rapid rise of immigration from southern and eastern Europe after 1882 laid the foundation for a renewed tide of nativism that exercised varying degrees of influence between 1885 and 1895. Rather than religion, however, most nativists of this era were fearful of either racial or political incursions. Perceiving an unacceptable level of Chinese influence, the U.S. Congress framed the CHINESE EXCLUSION ACT in 1882, although it was considered by most American politicians to be exceptional legislation and not aimed at limiting immigration generally. The Haymarket bombing in Chicago in 1886, for which several German anarchists were convicted and hanged, confirmed for many Americans the inferred link between aliens and radical politics, going back to the MOLLY MAGUIRE riots and the violent railroad strikes of the 1870s. Although the IMMIGRATION RESTRICTION LEAGUE, founded in 1894, was at first unsuccessful, it gradually chipped away at the open door for immigration, leading to rising immigrant head taxes, greater restrictions on Asian immigration, and finally, after four presidential vetoes, implementation of a literacy test in the IMMIGRATION ACT of 1917.

The theory of racial eugenics and international politics combined during World War I (1914–18) to produce an especially virulent strain of nativism. Widely read pseudoscientific works such as Madison Grant's *Passing of the Great Race* (1916) and Lothrop Stoddard's *The Rising Tide of Color* (1920) argued that Anglo-Saxon vitality and success were threatened with mongrelization if immigration continued unabated. According to Grant, interracial unions led to reversions to a "more ancient, generalized and lower" race. Blaming the Central Powers for World War I and Russians and Jews for the Bolshevik Revolution, which led to the establishment of the world's first communist state in 1917, Americans widely accepted the distinction between "old," pre-1880 immigration from western and northern Europe, and "new," post-1880 immigration from southern and eastern Europe. Throughout much of the 1920s, fear of German, Russian, and Jewish subversives was commonplace and led to a revival of the Ku Klux Klan as an antiforeign organization and to a wholesale adoption of restrictive immigrant legislation with the JOHNSON-REED ACT (1924) and the ORIENTAL EXCLUSION ACT (1924), the former practically eliminating immigration from eastern and southern Europe and the latter prohibiting virtually all Asian immigration.

Although nativism declined somewhat in the late 1920s, U.S. immigration policy remained consistently restrictionist until World War II (1939–45). Father Charles Coughlin, head of the Christian Front against communism, spoke out against the "problem" of the American Jew,

another manifestation of nativism, to an estimated 30 million listeners during the mid-1930s. Nativism undoubtedly contributed to President Franklin Roosevelt's unwillingness to support the Wagner-Rogers Bill (1939), which would have allowed annual admission beyond quotas, for two years, of 20,000 German refugees under the age of 14. Also during the depression years of the 1930s, more than 500,000 Mexican Americans were repatriated to Mexico. With the outbreak of war in Europe in 1939, restrictions on immigration were increased. Fear of undercover agents led to a drastic reduction of admissions from Nazi-occupied countries, the Alien Registration Act was passed in 1940, the IMMIGRATION AND NATURALIZATION SERVICE (INS) was moved from the Department of Labor to the Department of Justice, and a network of law enforcement agencies was authorized to compile a list of aliens for possible internment should the United States enter the war. This eventually led to the internment of some 3,500 Italians, 6,000 Germans, and, under the provisions of Executive Order 9066, 113,000 Japanese, more than 60 percent of whom were American citizens (see JAPANESE INTERNMENT, WORLD WAR II). Nativism began to ebb after World War II. The MCCARRAN-WALTER IMMIGRATION AND NATURALIZATION ACT (1952) maintained quotas but eliminated race as a barrier. U.S. COLD WAR commitments led to the admission of a variety of refugees (see REFUGEE RELIEF ACT) on an exceptional basis. Finally, the IMMIGRATION AND NATIONALITY ACT of 1965 abolished the national origins system and favored reunification of families, regardless of homeland.

The massive influx of Mexicans, especially illegal aliens, fueled a new round of nativism in the United States during the 1980s. In 1983, the Official English movement was launched in response to the growth of bilingualism, which had become common in the public schools in the 1970s to accommodate the increasing number of Spanish-speaking children. By the late 1980s, it became clear that Official English was closely linked to various restrictionist movements, including the controversial Pioneer Fund that supported eugenics research. Restrictionists redoubled their efforts when the IMMIGRATION REFORM AND CONTROL ACT (IRCA) legalized the status of nearly 3 million undocumented aliens. Although restrictionists enjoyed little success nationally, they did help organize the drive for PROPOSITION 187 in California, which denied many government services to illegal aliens, including public education. Although the measure was declared unconstitutional, it clearly reflected the views of almost 60 percent of Californians who were concerned about the growing cost of providing services and the potential difficulty in assimilating such a large Mexican population. Californians spoke again in 1998 when they passed Proposition 227, giving immigrant children only one year to learn English before entering mainstream classes. With nativist movements in the 1980s and 1990s largely localized, a general equilibrium regarding immigration appeared to take hold. But the terrorist attacks of SEPTEMBER 11, 2001, fueled fears regarding Arab and Muslim immigrants, leading to an extensive national debate on the compatibility of Islam and American political values.

Further Reading

Asher, Robert, and Charles Stephenson. *Labor Divided: Race and Ethnicity in the United States Labor Struggles, 1835–1960.* Albany: State University of New York Press, 1990.

Bennett, David. *The Party of Fear: From Nativist Movements to the New Right in American History.* 2d ed. New York: Vintage Books, 1995.

Billington, Ray Allen. *The Protestant Crusade, 1800–1860: A Study of the Origins of American Nativism.* New York: Macmillan, 1938.

Bosniak, Linda. "'Nativism' the Concept: Some Reflections." In *Immigrants Out! The New Nativism and the Anti-Immigrant Impulse in the United States.* Ed. Juan Perea. New York: New York University Press, 1997.

Grant, Madison. *The Passing of the Great Race.* 4th ed. New York: Charles Scribner's Sons, 1922.

Higham, John. *Strangers in the Land: Patterns of American Nativism, 1860–1925.* New Brunswick, N.J.: Rutgers University Press, 1988.

Knobel, Dale T. *"America for the Americans": The Nativist Movement in the United States.* New York: Twayne, 1996.

Kraut, Alan. *Silent Travelers: Germs, Genes, and the "Immigrant Menace."* New York: Basic Books, 1994.

Malkin, Michelle. *Invasion: How America Still Welcomes Terrorists, Criminals and Other Foreign Menaces to Our Shores.* New York: Regnery, 2002.

Palmer, Howard. *Patterns of Prejudice: A History of Nativism in Alberta.* Toronto: McClelland and Stewart, 1982.

Reimers, David. *Unwelcome Strangers: American Identity and the Turn against Immigration.* New York: Columbia University Press, 1998.

Robin, Marin. *Shades of Right: Nativist and Fascist Politics in Canada, 1920–1940.* Toronto: University of Toronto Press, 1992.

Sanchez, George. "Face the Nation: Race, Immigration, and the Rise of Nativism in Late-Twentieth-Century America." *International Migration Review* 31 (1997): 1,009–1,031.

Simcox, David. "Major Predictors of Immigration Restrictionism: Operationalizing 'Nativism.'" *Population and Environment* 19 (1997): 129–143.

Tenth Anniversary Oral History Project of the Federation for American Immigration Reform. Washington, D.C.: Federation for American Immigration Reform, 1989.

Naturalization Act (United States) (1802)

When Thomas Jefferson became president, there was a relaxation of the hostility toward immigrants that had prevailed during the administration of John Adams (1797–1801). The ALIEN AND SEDITION ACTS were repealed or allowed to expire, and Jefferson campaigned for a more lenient naturalization law, observing that, under the "ordinary chances of human life, a denial of citizenship, under a residence of fourteen years, is a denial to a great proportion of those who ask it." On April 14, 1802, a new naturalization measure was enacted, reducing the period of residence required for naturalization from 14 to five years. In addition, the new law required that prospective citizens give three years' notice of intent to renounce previous citizenship, swear or affirm support of the Constitution, renounce all titles of nobility, and demonstrate themselves to be of "good moral character." The Naturalization Act was supplemented on March 26, 1804, by exempting aliens who had entered the United States between 1798 and 1802 from the declaration of intention. The three-year notice was reduced to two years on May 26, 1824.

Further Reading

Bromwell, William J. *History of Immigration to the United States, 1819–1855.* 1855. Reprint, New York: Augustus M. Kelley, 1969.

Hutchinson, E. P. *Legislative History of American Immigration Policy, 1798–1965.* Philadelphia: University of Pennsylvania Press, 1981.

Morrison, Michael A., and James Brewer Stewart, eds. *Race and the Early Republic: Racial Consciousness and Nation Building in the Early Republic.* Lanham, Md.: Rowman and Littlefield, 2002.

Scott, Kenneth. *Early New York Naturalizations Abstracts of Naturalizations Records.* Baltimore: Clearfied Company, 1999.

Naturalization Acts (United States) (1790, 1795)

The Naturalization Act of 1790 was the first piece of U.S. federal legislation regarding immigration. It was designed to provide a national rule for the process of naturalization.

As a result of varying policies among the states for naturalizing citizens during the 1780s, the U.S. government passed "an act to establish an uniform rule of naturalization" on March 26, 1790. Under provisions of Article I, Section 8, of the Constitution, the measure granted citizenship to "all free white persons" after two years' residence and provided that the children of citizens born outside the borders of the United States would be "considered as natural born citizens."

A new Naturalization Act was passed on January 29, 1795, repealing the first act, raising the residency requirement to five years, and requiring three years' notice of intent to seek naturalization. This greater stringency regarding the naturalization of immigrants was continued in the ALIEN AND SEDITION ACTS (1798).

Further Reading

Hutchinson, E. P. *Legislative History of American Immigration Policy, 1798–1965.* Philadelphia: University of Pennsylvania Press, 1981.

Morrison, Michael A., and James Brewer Stewart, eds. *Race and the Early Republic: Racial Consciousness and Nation Building in the Early Republic.* Lanham, Md.: Rowman and Littlefield, 2002.
Scott, Kenneth. *Early New York Naturalizations Abstracts of Naturalizations Records.* Baltimore: Clearfield Company, 1999.

navigation acts

The navigation acts were a number of related legislative measures passed between 1651 and 1696 and designed to enhance Britain's international economic position. They reflected the mercantilistic concern for economic control of colonies and a favorable balance of trade and collectively provided a blueprint for management of Britain's first empire.

The Navigation Act of 1651, leading to the First Dutch War, required that all goods from Africa, Asia, and the Americas be imported to England in English ships and that all European goods shipped to England be carried in English ships or the ships of the country producing the goods. The First Navigation Act (1660) reinforced the previous provisions, adding that crews had to be at least 75 percent English and establishing a list of enumerated colonial goods, not produced in England, that could be supplied only to England or other British colonies. The original articles included sugar, cotton, indigo, dyewoods, ginger, and tobacco; rice, furs, molasses, resins, tars, and turpentine were later added. It also provided that only English or colonial ships could carry trade to and from the British colonies. The Staple Act of 1663 required that most foreign goods be transshipped to the American colonies through British ports. When enumerated articles passed through British ports, heavy duties were levied on them. The British government did seek to protect some American products, however, levying high tariffs on Swedish iron and Spanish tobacco and prohibiting the raising of tobacco in England. The last major piece of mercantile legislation was passed in 1696, expanding the limited British customs service and establishing vice-admiralty courts to quickly settle disputes occurring at sea. Closely related to the navigation acts were laws passed throughout the colonial period limiting the sale of American grain in England and inhibiting the development of American industries, including textiles, timber, and iron.

The navigation acts were aimed principally at the Dutch, who had controlled much of the world's middleman trade in the first half of the 17th century, and at emerging American industries poised to compete with the mother country. Among agriculturalists, small tobacco planters were especially hard hit, but on the whole the northern colonies suffered more as a result of the regulations. New England merchants routinely carried on commerce in violation of the acts throughout the 17th century. By the beginning of the 18th century, most smuggling from Europe had been stopped, and Americans had grown accustomed to purchasing English goods, which they preferred to local manufactures. After passage of the Molasses Act (1733), however, which raised prohibitive duties on molasses and sugar from the French West Indies and threatened American trade, smuggling again increased. Following the Seven Years' War (1756–63), new legislation utilized the navigation acts as a means of raising revenue for the British treasury and as a result raised the ire of American colonists.

Further Reading
Andrews, C. M. *The Colonial Period of American History,* Vol. 4. New Haven, Conn.: Yale University Press, (1938).
Beer, George L. *The Commercial Policy of England toward the American Colonies.* New York: P. Smith, 1948.
———. *The Old Colonial System, 1660–1754.* New York: P. Smith, 1933.
Dickerson, O. M. *The Navigation Acts and the American Revolution.* New York: Octagon Books, 1974.
Harper, L. A. *The English Navigation Laws: A Seventeenth-century Experiment in Social Engineering.* New York: Octagon Books, 1939.

New Brunswick

Europeans first settled the New Brunswick region of Canada in 1604, when Frenchmen SAMUEL DE CHAMPLAIN and Pierre du Gua, sieur de Monts, established a fur-trading settlement on St. Croix Island. The region surrounding the Bay of Fundy and the Gulf of St. Lawrence, known as ACADIA, became a sparsely populated part of the larger French colonial territory of NEW FRANCE. Acadia was officially transferred to Britain in 1713, though the French Acadians remained in New Brunswick until the British drove them out following the capture of the region during the French and Indian War (1754–63). Between 1763 and 1784, New Brunswick was a part the province of NOVA SCOTIA.

The population of New Brunswick changed dramatically during its first two decades in British hands. Traders from New England began arriving in the principal city of St. John in 1762 and in the following year established Maugerville, near present-day Fredericton. Many Acadians were allowed to return and were given land grants in the northern and eastern parts of the region. Most important, New Brunswick became one of the principal areas of resettlement for the United Empire Loyalists, 1775–83, who had refused to take up arms against the British Crown during the American Revolution (see AMERICAN REVOLUTION AND IMMIGRATION). Close to 14,000 landed at St. John in 1783 and were given land in the sparsely settled St. John River valley, where they founded Fredericton. In 1784, New Brunswick was made a separate province.

After 1815, hard times in Britain drove thousands of English, Scotch, and Irish settlers to New Brunswick. With increasing population came heightened tensions over the undefined border between New Brunswick and Maine and greater desire for self-government. In 1837, Britain turned over crown lands to New Brunswick and in 1842 negotiated a delimitation of the New Brunswick–Maine boundary. The province gained self-government in 1848. In 1867, New Brunswick joined Nova Scotia, Ontario, and Quebec as an original member of the Dominion of Canada.

Further Reading

Brown, Wallace. *The King's Friends: The Composition and Motives of the American Loyalist Claimants.* Providence, R.I.: Brown University Press, 1965.

Careless, J. M. S., ed. *Colonists and Canadiens, 1760–1867.* Toronto: Macmillan of Canada, 1971.

Cowan, Helen I. *British Emigration to British North America: The First Hundred Years.* Toronto: University of Toronto Press, 1961.

Ells, Margaret. "Settling the Loyalists in Nova Scotia." *Canadian Historical Association Report for 1934.* Ottawa: Canadian Historical Association, 1934.

Johnson, Stanley. *A History of Emigration from the United Kingdom to North America, 1763–1912.* London: George Routledge and Sons, 1913.

MacNutt, W. S. *The Atlantic Provinces: The Emergence of Colonial Society, 1712–1857.* Toronto: McClelland and Stewart, 1965.

———. *New Brunswick: A History, 1784–1867.* Agincourt, Canada: Gage, 1984.

Moore, Christopher. *The Loyalists: Revolution, Exile, Settlement.* Toronto: Macmillan of Canada, 1984.

Wilson, Bruce. *Colonial Identities: Canada from 1760–1815.* Ottawa: National Archives of Canada, 1988.

Wynn, Graeme. *Timber Colony: A Historical Geography of Early Nineteenth Century New Brunswick.* Toronto: University of Toronto Press, 1981.

Newfoundland

Newfoundland comprises the island of Newfoundland and the nearby coast of the mainland region of Labrador. The rocky terrain and cold and stormy weather inhibited traditional settlement, but the rich fisheries of the North Atlantic provided a livelihood for hardy fishermen from the earliest European contact. Vikings established settlements along the northern coast of Newfoundland around the year 1000 but left the region soon after. English fishermen may have reached the island in the 1480s, and John Cabot brought news of the fisheries back after his voyage of 1497. From that time forward, English, French, Portuguese, and Spanish fishermen plied the rich waters but established no permanent settlements. Although Sir Humphrey Gilbert claimed the land for England in 1583, the reality was that each country operated from temporary working camps and that the master of the first ship to arrive during a fishing season in each harbor was designated the fishing admiral and assumed ultimate authority along the local coasts. Attempts by English proprietors to establish colonial settlements failed at

Cupids on Conception Bay (1610) and Ferryland (1621, 1637–51).

France established the first heavily fortified colony at Placentia in 1662 and developed a string of trapping posts along the coast of Labrador during the first half of the 18th century. Newfoundland became a battleground during the War of the League of Augsburg (1689–98), the War of the Spanish Succession (1702–14), and the SEVEN YEARS' WAR (1756–63). By provision of the Treaty of Utrecht (1713), Britain gained the entire island of Newfoundland, though France retained use of the northern and western shore (French Shore) for drying fish. By the Treaty of Paris (1763), France gave up all claims to mainland North America but was given the small islands of Saint-Pierre and Miquelon off the southern coast of Newfoundland and retained its fishing privileges on the French Shore, which were not relinquished until 1904.

Britain never regarded Newfoundland as a settlement colony, favoring the rights of fishing interests. This policy is reflected in the appointment of naval officers as royal governors. Although most of the frontier regions of the island were settled by the 1840s, explorers of the Hudson's Bay Company were at that time just beginning to regularly probe the interior of Labrador. The majority of immigrants were from Ireland and the west of England. Largely barren, Labrador was administered by Newfoundland (1763–74, 1809–25) and QUEBEC (1774–1809) before it was divided between the two provinces in 1825. The present boundary between Quebec and Labrador was finally established in 1927. Despite a population of only some 20,000, in 1832, the British government acceded to demands for a strong local government, allowing a representative general assembly. In 1855, Newfoundland was granted responsible government, with the cabinet answerable to the assembly rather than to the governor. Newfoundland became the 10th province of the Dominion of Canada in 1949. The discovery of copper in the 1850s and iron in the 1890s led to the development of a significant mining industry in Labrador, though fishing remained Newfoundland's principal economic resource.

Further Reading

Davies, K. G., ed. *Northern Quebec and Labrador Journals and Correspondence, 1819–35.* Vol. 24. London: Hudson's Bay Record Society, 1963.

Handcock, W. Gordon. *"Soe long as there comes noe women": Origins of English Settlement in Newfoundland.* St. John, Canada: Breakwater Press, 1989.

New France

New France was the name of the French colonial empire in North America. The coastal regions, claimed in the 1530s by JACQUES CARTIER, were gradually augmented by French explorers and fur traders. In a series of wars for control of North America (1689–1763), virtually all of New France was lost to the British, the final blow coming with the SEVEN YEARS' WAR (1756–63). During the entire period of French control, only about 12,000 permanent settlers immigrated to New France, with concentrations in three regions: the fur-trading region along the St. Lawrence Seaway, known as Canada (see CANADA—IMMIGRATION SURVEY AND POLICY OVERVIEW); the Atlantic settlements, known as ACADIA; and the interior watershed, known as LOUISIANA. Despite limited settlement, French occupation led to a permanent French culture pattern in modern QUEBEC and a distinctive French influence in modern Louisiana.

During the 16th century, there was little interest in settling any part of New France. Cartier had observed of the rocky coast of Labrador, that this must have been "the land God gave to Cain." In 1541, he and the seigneur de Roberval (Jean-François de la Rocque de Roberval) attempted to establish the colony of Charlesbourg-Royal, near present-day Quebec City, but it was abandoned in the following year. Fishermen continued to ply the rich waters off Newfoundland, and merchants gradually developed a lucrative trade in furs with the Native Americans along the Atlantic and St. Lawrence coastal areas. The French government encouraged development by granting trade monopolies, but early settlements on the Magdalen Islands, Sable Island, Tadoussac, and St. Croix Island all failed.

SAMUEL DE CHAMPLAIN founded the first permanent French settlement at Quebec in 1608, a fur-trading post that linked France with the vast interior regions of North America and formed the core of the Canada settlement. Along with the commercial impulse came missionaries. In 1642, the Société de Notre-Dame de Montréal pour la conversion des Sauvages de la Nouvelle France founded Ville Marie, later known as Montreal. Administrative mismanagement, failure to secure settlers, and the constant threat from local native groups brought a complete reorganization of the government, which was brought under royal control in 1663. During the intendancy of JEAN TALON (1663–72), new energy was brought to the governance of the region. A benevolent autocracy was established in which trade was diversified, western expansion was encouraged, and planned immigration was pursued. Through an agreement with the French West Indies Company, between 1663 and 1673, several thousand settlers arrived, most from Brittany and Île-de-France, though some were recruited from Holland, Portugal, and various German states. Among this wave of immigrants, however, were few families. Most were trappers, soldiers, churchmen, prisoners, and young indentured servants (see INDENTURED SERVITUDE); by 1672, all plans for systematic immigration were stopped. After 1706, merchants from a number of European countries and their local agents were granted permission to do business in Canada, leading to a thriving trade in Quebec and Montreal. Indentured servants

occasionally came, and soldiers who were stationed in the colony as a result of the ongoing conflict with Britain sometimes stayed on. The number of slaves was always small, perhaps 4,000 Native American and African slaves for the entire duration of New France. More than a thousand convicts were forcibly transported. Remarkably, from this miscellaneous and meager collection of 9,000 immigrants, the population of Canada swelled to 70,000 at the time of the Seven Years' War.

In the 1630s, the French government had great hopes for establishing an outpost in Acadia to combat the rapidly growing population of the British colonies in New England. When a settlement plan for Nova Scotia foundered, the government offered little additional support. As a result, the small Acadian population was forced to become self-reliant, and many enjoyed closer commercial contacts with New England than with Canada. When Nova Scotia was ceded to Britain (1713) at the end of the War of the Spanish Succession, France focused Acadian development on the almost uninhabited but strategically located Île Royale (later Cape Breton), where it founded Louisbourg. During the next 45 years, Louisbourg developed into an important commercial city and fishing port and boasted one of the strongest fortified posts in North America. Although numbering several thousand inhabitants by the mid-18th century, Louisbourg fell victim to the international rivalry between Britain and France. It was captured by Britain in 1745 during the War of the Austrian Succession (1740–48) but returned at war's end. It was seized again in 1758, during the Seven Years' War. With formal capitulation to Britain in 1760, most of the French inhabitants either returned to Europe or migrated to Louisiana leaving only about a thousand settlers throughout Acadia.

French expansion into the Great Lakes and the interior waterways was spurred by the intrepid coureurs de bois (forest runners). Their restless search for new sources of furs and their native lifestyle, often taking Indian wives, greatly extended French commercial influence. Behind them came the explorers and churchmen. In 1673, Louis Jolliet and Jesuit Jacques Marquette explored the upper reaches of the Mississippi River, and in 1682, René-Robert Cavelier de La Salle followed the entire course of the river to the Gulf of Mexico, claiming for France all the lands drained by its tributaries and naming the region Louisiana, in honor of Louis XIV (r. 1648–1715). Only slowly did the French government follow. Louisiana was officially established as a colony in 1699. In order to meet the growing threat from Spain in the south and Britain on the Atlantic seaboard, France then built a string of forts from the Great Lakes along the interior waterways, including Natchitoches on the Red River (1714), the first permanent settlement, and NEW ORLEANS (1718) at the mouth of the Mississippi. Between 1712 and 1731, Louisiana was a proprietary colony, with exclusive trading rights and failed settlement schemes passing from one hand to another. It then reverted to royal control. Difficult to defend and producing disappointing revenues, Louisiana was secretly ceded to Spain in 1762. Between 1760 and 1790, about 4,000 French Acadians relocated to Louisiana.

New France suffered from several problems that made its existence as a French outpost problematic. Foremost was a lack of settlers. Despite establishment of the powerful COMPAGNIE DE LA NOUVELLE FRANCE in 1627 with royal support, it was difficult to find settlers who wished to immigrate to a cold and distant land. As late as 1663, the population was only about 3,000. By 1700, the European population of New France was still only 15,000. Also, the French government paid little attention to New France, finding it relatively easy to control according to mercantilistic principles, as virtually all trade had to come through the St. Lawrence and Quebec. These weaknesses came together during the 18th century in the developing contest with Britain for control of North America. Although France's army in Europe was superior, the king sent few troops to America. Left to defend themselves, French trading companies were at a severe disadvantage. When the Seven Years' War commenced, New France's population was only 75,000, compared to 1.2 million in Britain's various colonies. In 1763, France signed the Treaty of Paris, handing over New France east of the Mississippi River to Great Britain. In doing so, 80,000 French-speaking Canadians became British subjects.

Further Reading

Choquette, Leslie P. "Recruitment of French Emigrants to Canada, 1600–1760." In *"To Make America": European Emigration in the Early Modern Period*. Eds. Ida Altman and James Horn. Berkeley: University of California Press, 1991.

Eccles, William J. *Canada under Louis XIV, 1663–1701.* Toronto: McClelland and Stewart, 1964.

———. *France in America.* New York: Harper and Row, 1972.

Miquelon, Dale. *New France, 1701–1744: "A Supplement to Europe."* Toronto: McClelland and Stewart, 1987.

Moogk, Peter N. *La Nouvelle France: The Making of French Canada— A Cultural History.* East Lansing: Michigan State University Press, 2000.

———. "Reluctant Exiles: Emigrants from France in Canada before 1760." *William and Mary Quarterly* 46 (July 1989): 463–505.

Trigger, Bruce G. *Natives and Newcomers: Canada's "Heroic Age" Reconsidered.* Kingston, Canada: McGill–Queen's University Press, 1987.

Trudel, Marcel. *The Beginnings of New France, 1524–1663.* Toronto: McClelland and Stewart, 1972.

Vachon, André. *Dreams of Empire: Canada before 1700.* Ottawa: Public Archives of Canada, 1982.

New Hampshire colony

An early area of contention between France and England, the region of modern New Hampshire was gradually settled mainly by English immigrants and became a prime shipbuilding area for the British. By the time of the AMERICAN REVOLUTION (1775–83), almost all lands had been claimed and much of it settled, with some Scots-Irish establishing settlements in southeastern New Hampshire.

Both French and English merchants explored New Hampshire during the first two decades of the 17th century. In 1620, England's Council of New England was founded to encourage settlement in a large region including modern Maine and New Hampshire, which led to the establishment of numerous settlements during the 1620s and 1630s. John Mason was granted much of the region of New Hampshire, naming it for his native county in England. Between 1641 and 1680, it was governed as a part of the MASSACHUSETTS COLONY. It developed slowly, used mainly as a source of wood and naval stories. When it was separated from Massachusetts and established as a royal colony by Charles II in 1680, its population was less than 5,000. Although largely agricultural, New Hampshire's soil and climate were less attractive to immigrants than regions farther south, and settlers did not come in great numbers until after 1760, when they began to fill the Connecticut River Valley. Also, Indian wars in the area were common, as the French and British and their Indian allies clashed over control of the frontier. By the 1760s, New Hampshire's population was a little more than 50,000. Greatly alarmed over the effects of the NAVIGATION ACTS, New Hampshire joined the revolutionary effort against the British in 1775.

Further Reading

Daniell, Jere R. *Colonial New Hampshire: A History.* Millwood, N.Y.: KTO, 1981.

Fassett, James Hiram. *Colonial Life in New Hampshire.* Boston: Ginn and Company, 1899.

Jenness, John Scribner. *Notes on the First Planting of New Hampshire and on the Piscataqua Patents.* Portsmouth, N.H.: L. W. Brewster, 1878.

Van Deventer, David E. *The Emergence of Provincial New Hampshire, 1623–1741.* Baltimore: Johns Hopkins University Press, 1976.

new immigration

New immigration is a term principally applied to the United States, designating a shift in the most common immigrant groups. Most commonly it has been used to identify the shift in immigrant trends that occurred during the 1880s. Prior to that time, most immigrants came from Britain, Ireland, Germany, Scandinavia, and other regions of western and northern Europe. During the 1880s, the percentage of immigrants from eastern and southern Europe—the "new immigrants"—increased dramatically, with most emigrating from Italy, Austria-Hungary, and Russia. More recently the term has been applied to immigrant shifts in the wake of the IMMIGRATION AND NATIONALITY ACT OF 1965, which

A Ukrainian wedding takes place in Samburg, Saskatchewan, in 1917. The distinctive dress and customs of eastern and southern Europeans who flooded into Canada and the United States between 1880 and 1914 marked them as "new immigrants"—as opposed to the old immigrants from northern and western Europe whose ways of life were more similar to the American norm. *(George E. Dragan Collection/National Archives of Canada/PA-088459)*

abolished the national quota system and led to the dramatic increase in immigration from Mexico, Central America, and Asia. The use of the term *new immigration* in both cases suggests a group of peoples less likely to be assimilated and thus the target for various forms of NATIVISM.

Further Reading

Chiswick, Barry, and Teresa A. Sullivan. "The New Immigrants." In *State of the Union: America in the 1990s,* vol. 2d ed. Reynolds Farley. New York: Russell Sage Foundation, 1995.

Mink, Gwendolyn. *Old Labor and New Immigrants in American Political Development: Union, Party, and State, 1875–1920.* Ithaca, N.Y.: Cornell University Press, 1986.

Olson, James S. *The Ethnic Dimension in American History.* 2d ed. New York: St. Martin's Press, 1994.

Reimers, David M. *Unwelcome Strangers: American Identity and the Turn against Immigration.* New York: Columbia University Press, 1998.

New Jersey colony

Originally part of the newly conquered territory of New Netherland, in 1664, New Jersey was granted by James, Duke of York (later James II) as a proprietary colony to John, Lord Berkeley and Sir George Carteret. Promising freedom of worship and government, the two proprieters attracted a sizable population—about 14,000 by 1700, but the absence of a deep-water port kept New Jersey mainly an agricultural colony, developing in the shadow of neighboring NEW YORK COLONY.

The New Jersey coast was probably first visited by Europeans in 1524 when Giovanni da Verrazano, an Italian serving the French government, charted its coastal waters. The Dutch visited the region as early as 1609 and eventually established New Amsterdam (see NEW YORK, NEW YORK) at the mouth of the Hudson River. From there, they created a trading network that extended into the Hudson, Connecticut, and Delaware River Valleys. Outposts were founded in modern New Jersey in the 1620s, but the first permanent settlement, Bergen, was not established until 1660. Swedes, who had arrived in the 1630s, were forced out of the region in the 1650s. A growing Anglo-Dutch international rivalry led to the ouster of the Dutch West India Company from both New York and New Jersey in 1664. Shortly after Colonel Richard Nicolls was made governor of the former New Netherland, he learned that the duke of York had given New Jersey to two courtiers in reward for their services during the English Civil War. Confusion was rampant, as settlers authorized by Nicolls prior to the transfer clashed with those recruited by Berkeley and Carteret. Although Dutch settlers were allowed to keep their lands, they were sometimes drawn into the disorder. Out of the turmoil, a group of Quaker investors, including WILLIAM PENN, bought Berkeley's stake in 1674 leading to the division of the territory into East Jersey and West Jersey. West Jersey became the first Quaker colony in America. Both halves struggled and were reunited in 1702 as a royal colony. Until 1738, New Jersey was governed from New York, but riots led to the establishment of a separate government. Most of New Jersey's rural agriculturalists, including heavy concentrations of German and Scots-Irish immigrants after 1700, attempted to remain neutral during the American Revolution against Great Britain (1775–83). By 1750, about 20 percent of the population of New Jersey was Scottish or of Scots descent.

Further Reading

Griffin, Patrick. *The People with No Name: Ireland's Ulster Scots, America's Scots Irish, and the Creation of a British Atlantic World, 1689–1764.* Princeton, N.J.: Princeton University Press, 2001.

Hodges, Graham Russell. *Root and Branch: African Americans in New York and East Jersey, 1613–1863.* Chapel Hill: University of North Carolina Press, 1999.

———. *Slavery and Freedom in the Rural North: African Americans in Monmouth County, New Jersey, 1665–1865.* Madison, Wis.: Madison House, 1997.

Pomfret, John E. *Colonial New Jersey: A History.* New York: Scribner's, 1973.

Tien, Anita. "'To Enjoy Their Customs': The Cultural Adaptation of Dutch and German Families in the Middle Colonies, 1660–1832." Ph.D. diss., University of California–Berkeley, 1990.

New Orleans, Louisiana

New Orleans was one of the most important ports of entry for immigration to the United States during the 19th century, mainly because of its location at the mouth of the Mississippi River, which provided ready access to the interior of country. For the same reason, New Orleans became the premier port of shipment for southern cotton and other commodities and thus developed a large shipping trade. Between 1820 and 1860, more than 550,000 immigrants entered the United States through the port of New Orleans, making it second only to New York City (see NEW YORK, NEW YORK) in terms of numbers. By 1850, about one-quarter of Louisiana's and the majority of New Orleans's white population was foreign born. Though it declined dramatically as a port in the 20th century, its immigrant heritage—particularly French and African—remained a distinctive and appealing feature of the city's character. In 2000, the metropolitan population of New Orleans was 1,337,726. The largest immigrant groups had come early in the 19th century and were, therefore, thoroughly assimilated, most

notably French and French Canadians (211,000), Germans (139,000), and Irish and Scots-Irish (122,000).

In 1682, René-Robert Cavelier de La Salle claimed the Mississippi River Valley for France, naming it Louisiana in honor of King Louis XIV (r. 1648–1715). Attempts by Scottish investor John Law, who had been granted a commercial monopoly by the French government, to colonize the region failed between 1717 and 1720, though the founding of New Orleans in 1718 was a lasting result despite little French help in the endeavor. Although the geographic situation of the city was of the utmost importance, the land itself was swampy and ill suited to development, and the city grew slowly. From a population of 250 early in the 18th century, it grew to 4,000 by 1760 and to 8,000 by 1800. The French government was fearful of allowing Protestants and potential adversaries in, and few French citizens wished to settle in the Mississippi delta. Law brought about 2,000 Germans into the area north of the city, but the Mississippi Company he formed to promote immigration failed in 1720. About 4,000 French colonists from ACADIA migrated to Louisiana following the capitulation of MONTREAL, QUEBEC, in 1760, mainly settling outside New Orleans, but they too were intensely hostile to outsiders. Disappointed with the little income from the region, France secretly ceded Louisiana to Spain (1762–1800); Spain did not gain firm control of the region until 1769. During the 1790s, the sugar industry was established, and the colony began to flourish. In addition to a few Spanish settlers, during the American Revolution (1775–83), a significant number of Americans also came to New Orleans, which had been granted to the Continental Congress as a base of operations during the conflict. The demand for laborers, however, was never adequately met, leading to a steady increase in the importation of African slaves throughout the 18th century (see AFRICAN FORCED MIGRATION). By 1800, more than half of the region's population was African American, though the percentage was smaller in New Orleans itself.

In 1800, Napoleon coerced Spain into ceding Louisiana back to France, though a full transfer of control was never effected. Badly needing funds for his conquests in Europe, Napoleon sold the entire Mississippi Valley to the United States in December 1803 for about $15 million, a transaction known as the Louisiana Purchase. The territory was divided during the 19th century, with New Orleans and the state of Louisiana being admitted to the Union in 1812. With a potential British impediment having been thwarted at the Battle of New Orleans in 1815 and the advent of the commercial steamboat after the War of 1812, a great period of economic expansion in the region began. From the first steamboat that plied the Mississippi in 1812, the number regularly calling at the port grew to 3,000 by the 1850s. The great port and its fertile hinterland were now joined under one government and linked by a natural water highway. The population rapidly grew from about 8,000 in 1803 to 170,000 in 1860, with immigrants pouring into the region. Between 1810 and 1840, it was the fastest-growing large city in the United States, and in 1830 was the third largest city, behind New York and BALTIMORE, MARYLAND.

In 1860, about 86 percent of the population of New Orleans was white, and another 6 percent were free blacks. Overall, about 78,000 were native born, but there were large numbers of Irish (24,398), German (19,675), and French (10,564) immigrants and significant numbers of Britons, Spaniards, and Italians. New Orleans had the largest Jewish population in the South, with 8,000.

New Orleans was an attractive port of entry for a number of reasons. Because ships carrying southern cotton returned with manufactured goods that took less space, shipping companies often offered bargain fares to passengers. New Orleans was also closer to the western interior than eastern ports were, and it was readily accessible by steamboats that plied the Mississippi and Missouri Rivers. Because of Louisiana's French culture, a small number of French-speaking settlers were attracted to the city, and because of its proximity and trade connections with Central and South America, it also became the first center of Hispanic immigration to the United States.

After the Civil War (1861–65), the number of immigrants coming through the port of New Orleans dropped dramatically. Federal blockades and Union occupation had disrupted trade and passenger service during the war, and completion of the transcontinental railroad in 1869 opened the West to cheap overland transportation that competed with the traditional ocean and river routes. There were relatively few industrial jobs to attract unskilled workers. Also, as the steamships grew larger, fewer of them could pass through the sandbars at the mouth of the Mississippi. As late as 1900, however, New Orleans was among the top dozen cities in population, though it rapidly declined with the massive influx of "new immigrants" into East Coast ports (see NEW IMMIGRATION).

Tensions between whites and blacks in New Orleans ran high throughout much of the late 19th and early 20th centuries, leading to the passage of Jim Crow laws and an increasingly segregated society. This erupted in deadly riots in 1866 and 1900, as black citizens seeking to assert their constitutional rights were set upon by angry whites. Many of the city's educated black Creoles who had not been slaves were dismayed to find themselves lumped socially with the freed slaves. After the riot in 1900, African Americans fought a slow battle for civil rights. Creole activist A. P. Tureaud helped establish the local branch of the National Association for the Advancement of Colored People (NAACP) in the 1920s.

Ethnic communities remained strong in New Orleans until World War II (1939–45). Between 1950 and 1975, developers used modern technology to drain marshlands,

enabling New Orleans to double the geographic size of the metropolitan area. This led to the flight of much of the white population and the gradual dispersion of the previously confined cultural mix. The city lost much of its tax base and many jobs as whites fled to the suburbs and surrounding areas. As a result, New Orleans was not highly popular as an immigrant destination after World War II. In 2000, the largest of the new Hispanic and Asian immigrant groups that dominated after the IMMIGRATION AND NATIONALITY ACT (1967) were Vietnamese (16,000), Central Americans (16,000), about half of whom were Honduran, and Mexicans (10,000).

Further Reading

Brasseaux, Carl A. *The "Foreign French": Nineteenth-Century French Immigration into Louisiana.* 3 vols. Lafayette: University of Southwestern Louisiana, 1990–93.

———. *The Founding of New Acadia: The Beginnings of Acadian Life in Louisiana, 1765–1803.* Baton Rouge: Louisiana State University Press, 1987.

———, ed. *A Refuge for All Ages: Immigration in Louisiana History.* Lafayette: University of Southwestern Louisiana, 1996.

Brasseaux, Carl A., and Glenn R. Conrad, eds. *The Road to Louisiana: The Saint Domingue Refugees, 1792–1809.* Lafayette: University of Southwestern Louisiana, 1992.

Lewis, Peirce F. *New Orleans: The Making of an Urban Landscape.* 2d ed. Charlottesville: University of Virginia Press, 2003.

McNabb, Donald, and Louis E. Madère, Jr. "A History of New Orleans." Available online. URL: http://www.madere.com/history.html. Accessed February 28, 2004.

Stolarik, M. Mark, ed. *Forgotten Doors: The Other Ports of Entry to the United States.* Philadelphia: Balch Institute Press, 1988.

New York, New York

From its earliest days, New Amsterdam, the precursor to New York City, was one of the most heterogeneous places on earth. By 1660, the Dutch governor, William Kieft, observed that 18 languages could be heard in and around Fort Amsterdam. New York has been a multinational city of immigrants ever since. Since 1816, more than 70 percent of all immigrants arriving by sea landed first in New York. The immigrant depot of ELLIS ISLAND and the Statue of Liberty are visible testimonies to the fundamental role of immigration to New York City's history in a way that is not true of any other city in North America. In 2000, the heritage of both old and NEW IMMIGRATION was evident. Almost 23 percent of the New York metropolitan area's population of 21.2 million was foreign born, with 1.25 million coming from Asia and 1.24 million coming from the Caribbean. The largest ethnic groups in New York include the largely assimilated Italians (3.4 million), Irish (2.6 million), Germans (1.8 million), and Poles (1.1 million) and the more recently arrived Dominicans (572,915), Chinese (536,966), Asian Indians (450,142), Mexicans (331,212), and

Jamaicans (321,745). Puerto Ricans number 1.3 million, though as citizens of an American commonwealth, they are not formally immigrants.

HENRY HUDSON claimed the area for the Dutch in 1609. In 1625, settlers for the Dutch East India Company established the first permanent settlement on Manhattan Island, establishing Fort Amsterdam and purchasing the island from the native peoples. The settlement of New Amsterdam grew around the fort and, by the 1650s, was thriving, with additional settlements in the Bronx, Brooklyn, Queens, and Staten Island. As the result of three Anglo-Dutch Wars fought between 1652 and 1674, the colony of New Netherland, along with its capital city, were transferred to England. By 1700, the city, renamed New York, had a population of almost 7,000. Though initially smaller than either BOSTON or PHILADELPHIA, New York offered an excellent harbor that encouraged trade and commerce, and by 1800, the city had grown to 60,000 and become the largest city in the new republic. For the next two centuries, New York was the premier destination in

the world for immigrants. In 1898, Manhattan and most of the communities of the Bronx, Queens, Brooklyn, and Staten Island were formally united to create an unparalleled metropolis of more than 3 million people. Rapid population growth contributed to many environmental, transportation, and housing problems through the 20th century.

Although immigrants came continuously from the time of New York's founding, there were three characteristic phases of the process, each altering the nature of the immigrant community. Before 1880, the vast majority of immigrants came from western Europe. The earliest of these immigrants, prior to 1855, were processed at a variety of New York docks. As hundreds of thousands of immigrants, largely from Ireland, Germany, England, and Scandinavia, poured into the city every year after the mid-1840s, New York State commissioners realized that a better system was needed for tracking immigrant entry, guarding against disease, and protecting newly arrived immigrants from exploitation. After 1855, immigrants were ferried from their ships to CASTLE GARDEN, an old entertainment hall, where immigration officers counted them and obtained information regarding age, religion, occupation, and value of personal property. By the 1850s, more than 40 percent of New York's population was foreign born. It has been estimated that the percentage in Manhattan was more than 50 percent and that more than half of these were Irish. While German immigrants tended to use New York as a departure point for resettlement in rural areas of the Midwest and West, the Irish usually stayed in the city. The main tension in this period was between the old-line British and Dutch culture and the newly arrived, slum-dwelling Irish. Fleeing from the terrors of the Great Irish Famine (1845–51), the Irish usually arrived poor, hating the English, and committed to their Catholic faith (see IRISH IMMIGRATION). By the late 19th century, however, Irish New Yorkers were beginning to gain access to important positions of political and financial power.

After 1880, the immigrant source countries shifted from northern and western Europe to eastern and southern Europe, significantly altering the character of the city. The peoples of the NEW IMMIGRATION, drawn from dozens of ethnic groups from Italy and the Austro-Hungarian, Ottoman, and Russian Empires, were generally poor and by American standards of the day dressed oddly and practiced strange customs. As Italians, Poles, Jews, and others flooded into New York in record numbers, states receiving large numbers of immigrants petitioned the federal government for a revision of immigration policies. After years of appeals, New York State officials threatened to close Castle Garden unless the federal government agreed to fund its operations. As a result, in 1882, a head tax of 50¢ was assessed on every immigrant in order to meet the initial costs of reception. New federal guidelines in 1890 requiring more extensive physical and mental examinations, along with the

This street scene was typical of New York City's Lower East Side ca. 1910. In 1910, immigrants and their children—most from eastern and southern Europe—composed about three-quarters of the city's population. Note the varieties of dress. *(National Archives #196-GS-369)*

massive influx of immigrants—almost 5 million coming through New York alone during the 1880s—led the federal government to establish a new immigrant depot at ELLIS ISLAND in New York Harbor.

Named for its last private owner, Ellis Island had formerly housed a naval arsenal. It was designed to process up to 5,000 immigrants per day. The building of the facilities was accompanied by the creation of the office of superintendent of immigration, the first formal bureaucracy designed to deal with immigration. When an immigrant ship arrived in New York Harbor, first- and second-class passengers were given a cursory examination on board and were then transferred to shore. Most of them only saw the Ellis Island facilities from a distance, unless some question had been raised on board. "Steerage," or third-class, passengers were examined more carefully, though the rejection rate was generally only 1 percent. Most immigrants were given a cursory medical examination—the "six-second physical," as it came to be called—and had their papers checked against shipping manifests. They were then briefly interviewed by immigration officials working from the ship's manifest log, which contained the answers to 29 questions, previously completed by the immigrant. The whole process typically took three to five hours. Those admitted typically purchased tickets by rail or coastal steamer to their final destinations and were then ferried to either Manhattan or the New Jersey shore. The small number refused entry were detained pending an appeal or deportation.

In 1897, a fire destroyed the Ellis Island processing facilities, including many immigration records dating back to 1855. The permanent reception center familiar now as the National Immigration Museum was opened in 1900. During its first year of operation, about 446,000 immigrants landed in New York, but numbers declined significantly through the 1890s, averaging about 231,000 per year between 1893 and 1897. Surprising many officials, immigration increased dramatically after 1898. From about 179,000 arrivals in 1898, the immigrant flow peaked in 1906–07, when almost 1.9 million landed in New York. In 1913–14, another almost 1.8 million immigrants were processed. As a result, new dormitories, hospitals, kitchens, and other structures were built or expanded on the island between 1900 and 1915. By 1910, the foreign-born population of the city was again above 40 percent. Italians alone—more than 700,000 and mostly poor—composed 15 percent of the population. Although tens of thousands returned to Italy every year prior to World War I (1914–18), the majority stayed and more came besides. After decades of struggle and loyal service in the military in World War I and World War II (1941–45), Italians, Jews, and most other new immigrant groups moved into the mainstream of American cultural life.

After World War I, U.S. consulates were established around the world and were responsible for issuing visas and checking credentials, thus lessening the work at the port of entry in the United States. Passage of the restrictive quota legislation of 1921 (EMERGENCY QUOTA ACT) and 1924 (JOHNSON-REED ACT) also significantly reduced the number of immigrants allowed into the United States and marked the beginning of Ellis Island's decline as a processing center. Whereas annual immigration averaged about 740,000 between 1903 and 1914, it dropped to about 152,000 between 1925 and 1930, and 30,000 during the Great Depression years of the 1930s. By that time, Ellis Island had become better known for detention than for entry and in 1932, finally stopped receiving steerage-class immigrants.

The third defining phase of immigration to New York City came following the IMMIGRATION AND NATIONALITY ACT of 1965, which led to a massive and partially unexpected influx of Asian and Hispanic peoples. Italians still represented the largest ethnic group in New York City in 1980, but Dominicans and Jamaicans, ranked only 26th and 24th, respectively, in 1960, were the city's second and third largest ethnic groups 20 years later. Some European groups also grew as a result of the Immigration and Nationality Act. Italians, Greeks, and Portuguese took advantage of its provisions to reunite extended families. African Americans had migrated to New York in large numbers after World War I, but after 1965, the black population had become increasingly immigrant. By 1990, perhaps one-quarter or more black New Yorkers were foreign born, creating some tension between the various African-American communities. The post–World War II era provided many challenges for America's largest urban area, and the state and federal governments had to provide economic assistance to the city in the 1970s. City finances and conditions improved significantly during the 1980s and 1990s, though ethnic tensions were often strained. Two events during the late 1990s focused national attention on alleged civil rights abuses against blacks and immigrants. In 1997, New York police officers were accused of torturing a Haitian immigrant, Abner Louima, and one was eventually convicted. In 1999, a West African immigrant, Amadou Diallo, was killed when police officers mistook him for a rape suspect and shot him. Although four officers were indicted for murder, they were later acquitted. The terrorist attacks of SEPTEMBER 11, 2001, on the World Trade Center in Lower Manhattan dramatically affected the city's economy, with the federal government eventually pledging more than $24 billion for the reconstruction of the area of the attack. Although New York Muslims and Arabs were concerned about backlash in the wake of the attacks, the city remained peaceful as it pulled together in support of more than 320 firefighters and police officers who lost their lives, in addition to the almost 3,000 civilians who died in the attack. As if to highlight the international character of New York City, people of 80 nationalities died in the attack on the World Trade Center.

Further Reading

Baylor, Ronald, and Timothy Meagher, eds. *The New York Irish*. Baltimore: Johns Hopkins University Press, 1996.

Binder, Frederick, and David Reimers. *All the Nations under Heaven: An Ethnic and Racial History of New York City*. New York: Columbia University Press, 1995.

———. "New York as an Immigrant City." In *Origins and Destinies: Immigration, Race, and Ethnicity in America*. Eds. Silvia Pedraza and Rubén G. Rumbaut. Belmont, Calif.: Wadsworth, 1996.

Chen, Hsiang-Shui. *Chinatown No More: Taiwan Immigrants in Contemporary New York*. Ithaca, N.Y.: Cornell University Press, 1992.

Chin, Ko-lin. *Chinatown Gangs: Extortion, Enterprise, and Ethnicity*. New York: Oxford University Press, 1996.

Cohen, Miriam. *Workshop to Office: Two Generations of Italian Women in New York City, 1900–1950*. Ithaca, N.Y.: Cornell University Press, 1993.

Diner, Hasia R. *Lower East Side Memories: A Jewish Place in America*. Princeton, N.J.: Princeton University Press, 2002.

Ernst, Robert. *Immigrant Life in New York City, 1825–1863*. 1949. Reprint, New York: Octagon Books, 1979.

Ewen, Elizabeth. *Immigrant Women in the Land of Dollars: Life and Culture on the Lower East Side 1890–1925*. New York: Monthly Review Press, 1985.

Fisher, Maxine P. *The Indians of New York City*. Columbia, Mo.: South Asia Books, 1980.

Foner, Nancy. *From Ellis Island to JFK: New York's Two Great Waves of Immigration*. New Haven, Conn.: Yale University Press, 2002.

———, ed. *New Immigrants in New York*. New York: Columbia University Press, 1987.

Friedman-Kasaba, Kathie. *Memories of Migration: Gender, Ethnicity, and Work in New York, 1870–1924*. Albany: State University of New York Press, 1996.

Glazer, Nathan, and Daniel Moynihan. *Beyond the Melting Pot: The Negroes, Puerto Ricans, Jews, Italians, and Irish of New York City*. 2d ed. Cambridge, Mass.: MIT Press, 1970.

Goodfriend, Joyce D. *Before the Melting Pot: Society and Culture in Colonial New York City, 1664–1730*. Princeton, N.J.: Princeton University Press, 1992.

Hendricks, Glen. *Dominican Diaspora*. New York: Teachers College Press, 1974.

Jackson, Kenneth T., ed. *Encyclopedia of New York City*. New York: New York Historical Society, 1995.

Kasinitz, Philip. *Caribbean New York: Black Immigrants and the Politics of Race*. Ithaca, N.Y.: Cornell University Press, 1992.

Kessner, Thomas. *The Golden Door: Italian and Jewish Mobility in New York City, 1900–1915*. New York: Oxford University Press, 1977.

Kim, Illsoo. *Urban Immigrants: The Korean Community in New York*. Princeton, N.J.: Princeton University Press, 1981.

Kwong, Peter. *Chinatown, New York: Labor and Politics, 1930–1950*. New York: Monthly Review Press, 1979.

———. *The New Chinatown*. New York: Hill and Wang, 1987.

Laguerre, Michel. *American Odyssey: Haitians in New York*. Ithaca, N.Y.: Cornell University Press, 1984.

Lessinger, Johanna. *From the Ganges to the Hudson: Indian Immigrants in New York City*. Boston: Allyn and Bacon, 1995.

Lin, Jan. *Reconstructing Chinatown: Ethnic Enclave, Global Change*. Minneapolis: University of Minnesota Press, 1998.

Margolis, M. L. *Little Brazil: An Ethnography of Brazilian Immigrants in New York City*. Princeton, N.J.: Princeton University Press, 1994.

Markowitz, Fran. *A Community in Spite of Itself: Soviet Jewish Emigrés in New York*. Washington, D.C.: Smithsonian Institution Press, 1993.

Mauk, David. *The Colony That Rose from the Sea: Norwegian Maritime Migration and Community in Brooklyn, 1850–1910*. Urbana: University of Illinois Press and the Norwegian American Historical Society, 1997.

Min, Pyong Gap. *Caught in the Middle: Korean Communities in New York and Los Angeles*. Berkeley: University of California Press, 1996.

———. *Changes and Conflicts: Korean Immigrant Families in New York*. Needham Heights, Mass.: Allyn and Bacon, 1998.

Nadel, Stanley. *Little Germany: Ethnicity, Religion, and Class in New York City, 1845–80*. Urbana: University of Illinois Press, 1990.

Orsi, Robert Anthony. *The Madonna of 115th Street: Faith and Community in Italian Harlem, 1880–1950*. New Haven, Conn.: Yale University Press, 1985.

Park, Kyeyoung. *The Korean Dream: Immigrants and Small Business in New York City*. Ithaca, N.Y.: Cornell University Press, 1997.

Pencak, William, Selma Berrol, and Randall Miller, eds. *Immigration to New York*. Philadelphia: Balch Institute Press, 1991.

Rischin, Moses. *The Promised City: New York's Jews, 1870–1914*. Cambridge, Mass.: Harvard University Press, 1962.

Sánchez Korrol, Virginia E. *From Colonia to Community: The History of Puerto Ricans in New York City*. Updated ed. Berkeley: University of California Press, 1994.

Schneider, Dorothee. *Trade Unions and Community: The German Working Class in New York City*. Urbana: University of Illinois Press, 1994.

Staub, Shalom. *Yemenis in New York City*. Philadelphia: Balch Institute Press, 1989.

Sutton, Constance, and Elsa Chaney, eds. *Caribbean Life in New York City*. New York: Center for Migration Studies, 1987.

Tchen, John Kuo Wei. *New York before Chinatown: Orientalism and the Shaping of American Culture, 1776–1882*. Baltimore: Johns Hopkins University Press, 1999.

Waldinger, Roger. *Still the Promised City? African-Americans and New Immigrants in Postindustrial New York*. Cambridge, Mass.: Harvard University Press, 1996.

Watkins-Owens, Irma. *Blood Relations: Caribbean Immigrants and the Harlem Community, 1900–1930*. Bloomington: Indiana University Press, 1996.

Winnick, Louis. *New People in Old Neighborhoods: The Role of Immigrants in Rejuvenating New York's Communities*. New York: Sage Publications, 1990.

New York colony

New Amsterdam, conquered by England in 1664, was the heart of the Dutch commercial empire in North America (New Netherland). The former Dutch holdings were granted to James, Duke of York, brother of the English king Charles II and renamed. New York included present-day

Maine, much of the Massachusetts coast, Long Island, and what became the NEW JERSEY COLONY. By the time of the American Revolution (1775–83), New York was second only to the PENNSYLVANIA COLONY in its ethnic diversity.

The coastal region of the colony of New York was probably first explored by Europeans in 1524, when Giovanni da Verrazano, an Italian serving the French government, mapped the area. The Dutch visited the region as early as 1609 and eventually established Fort Orange (modern Albany) in 1624 and New Amsterdam (see NEW YORK, NEW YORK) at the mouth of the Hudson River in the following year. From these settlements, they created a trading network that extended into the Hudson, Connecticut, and Delaware River Valleys. Under the *patroon* system, members of the Dutch West India Company were granted large tracts of land in return for bringing settlers. Although the maximum number of Dutch settlers in the mid-Atlantic region was only about 10,000, they generally enjoyed good relations with the Indians and proved difficult to dislodge during the Anglo-Dutch Wars (1652–78). The Dutch government was permanently ousted in 1673.

From its establishment, the area was a polyglot mixture of Dutch, Belgians, French Huguenots, Finns, Swedes, Portuguese Jews, and English. The English government allowed the original settlers and merchants to remain in business and granted them freedom to worship in the Dutch Reformed tradition. Although intermarriage and long association diminished ethnic identities, New York, along with New Jersey, Pennsylvania, and Delaware (see DELAWARE COLONY), remained an ethnically heterogeneous region. With the devastation of the European War of the Spanish Succession (1702–14), significant numbers of German and Scots-Irish immigrants added to the ethnic mix. Many New Yorkers actively supported the American Revolution, but there were strong pockets of Loyalists, particularly in New York City and upstate. More than 30,000 eventually left the state. Although ranked only fifth in population in 1700 (19,000) behind Virginia, Massachusetts, Maryland, and Connecticut, New York grew rapidly in the 18th century. By 1800, New York City, with a population of 60,000, had overtaken both PHILADELPHIA, PENNSYLVANIA, and BOSTON, MASSACHUSETTS, as the first city of the new republic.

Further Reading

Goodfriend, Joyce D. *Beyond the Melting Pot: Society and Culture in Colonial New York City, 1664–1730.* Princeton, N.J.: Princeton University Press, 1992.

Kammen, Michael. *Colonial New York: A History.* New York: Scribner's, 1975.

Kim, Sung Bok. *Landlord and Tenant in Colonial New York: Manorial Society, 1664–1775.* Chapel Hill: University of North Carolina Press, 1978.

Merwick, Donna. *Possessing Albany, 1630-1710: The Dutch and English Experiences.* New York: Cambridge University Press, 1990.

Rink, Oliver A. *Holland on the Hudson: An Economic and Social History of Dutch New York.* Ithaca, N.Y.: Cornell University Press, 1986.

Ritchie, Robert C. *The Duke's Province: A Study of Politics and Society in Colonial New York, 1664–1691.* Chapel Hill: University of North Carolina Press, 1977.

Nicaraguan immigration

As a result of an ongoing and integral U.S. involvement with the politics of Nicaragua from the 1850s, a unique set of circumstances has brought a variety of Nicaraguan immigrants to the United States. According to the U.S. census of 2000, 177,684 Americans claimed Nicaraguan descent. There were few Nicaraguans in Canada: Only 6,190 Canadians claimed Nicaraguan descent in the 2001 census, though a number of organizations estimate the actual figure to be between 10,000 and 20,000. Miami was the center of Nicaraguan life in America, although communities could be found in most of the larger cities of California and Texas. Nicaraguans in Canada are overwhelmingly concentrated in Toronto, with a significant number living in Alberta.

Nicaragua occupies 46,400 square miles in Central America. It is bordered by Honduras on the north and Costa Rica on the south. In 2002, the population was estimated at 4,918,393. The people were ethnically divided between mestizos (69 percent), whites (17 percent), blacks (9 percent), and several Amerindian peoples (5 percent). More than 95 percent of Nicaraguans are Roman Catholic, reflecting almost 300 years of Spanish rule. The indigenous peoples of the region were conquered by Spain in 1552. Most died of disease, were killed, or intermarried with Europeans, creating the large mestizo population. After gaining independence from Spain in 1821, Nicaragua was united for a

U.S. Marines pose with children in Nicaragua during United States occupation, 1927. *(National Archives #6-523779)*

short period with other Central American countries as the United Provinces of Central America before finally becoming an independent republic in 1838. The United States became directly involved in Nicaraguan politics when in 1855, American adventurer William Walker was invited to the country to defend the ruling liberal party of General Francisco de Castellón. Walker instead seized the government for himself but was driven out of Nicaragua in 1857, ushering in a long period of conservative rule. U.S. Marines occupied the country for extensive periods between 1912 and 1933, generally in support of conservative political movements. In 1979, the marxist Sandinista National Liberation Front led a revolt that ousted dictator Anastasio Somoza. U.S. president Ronald Reagan became increasingly concerned about the threat of communism in "America's backyard" and supplied U.S. backing to the contras, forces opposing the marxist Sandinistas, once more reviving COLD WAR rivalries in the Western Hemisphere. As the Sandinistas gradually lost power in the late 1980s, thousands of Sandinistas and leftists fled to the United States and other countries of Central America.

It is difficult to document early immigration, as Nicaraguans were not counted apart from other Central Americans until 1960. Because of American involvement in Nicaragua, the United States was most often the choice of political dissidents or those fleeing political uncertainty. During the 1930s, many business and professional people also entered the country, settling in New York City, New Orleans, San Francisco, and Los Angeles. By the mid-1960s, Nicaraguans were the largest Central American national group in the United States and even more began to immigrate as a result of the 1965 IMMIGRATION AND NATIONALITY ACT. In 1970, there were almost 30,000 Nicaraguans in the United States, most of European descent. The revolution of 1979 brought 20,000 or more Somoza supporters to the United States, and most of these settled in and around Miami. As civil war and a U.S. trade embargo destroyed the economy during the 1980s, young Nicaraguan men especially began to seek refuge and opportunity in the United States, many entering the country illegally. The IMMIGRATION AND NATURALIZATION SERVICE estimated the undocumented population to be 76,000 in 1995, though some estimates suggest a figure twice as high. Under provisions of the Nicaraguan Adjustment and Central American Relief Act, in 1997, about 150,000 Nicaraguans were allowed to remain and work in the country, with many of them eventually becoming permanent residents. Between 1992 and 2002, legal immigration averaged about 10,000 annually.

There were almost no Nicaraguans in Canada until the mid-1980s, but their numbers steadily increased after 1983. In 1991 and 1992 alone, more than 3,500 were admitted. Most Nicaraguans were young and poorly educated and had often lived for some time in Honduras, Costa Rica, or the United States. In 2001, of 9,380 Nicaraguan immigrants living in Canada, only 170 came before 1981. About 88 percent (8,255) arrived between 1981 and 1995, most as refugees.

Further Reading

Fisher, Marc. "Home, Sweetwater, Home." *Mother Jones* 13, no. 10 (December 1988): 35–40.

Funkhouser, Edward. "Migration from Nicaragua: Some Recent Evidence." *World Development,* 20, no. 8 (1992): 1,209–1,218.

Immigration and Naturalization Service. *Nicaraguan Adjustment and Central American Relief Act, 1997.* Washington, D.C.: Government Printing Office, 1998.

Leslie, Leigh A. "Families Fleeing War: The Case of Central Americans." *Marriage and Family Review* 19, nos. 1–2 (1993): 193–205.

Menjívar, Cecilia. "Salvadorans and Nicaraguans: Refugees Become Workers." In *Illegal Immigration in America: A Reference Handbook.* Eds. David Haines and Karen E. Rosenblum. Westport, Conn.: Greenwood Press, 1999.

Merrill, Tim, ed. *Nicaragua: A Country Study.* 3d ed. Baton Rouge, La.: Claitors, 1995.

Simmons, Alan. "Latin American Immigration to Canada: New Linkages in the Hemispheric Migration and Refugee Flow System." *International Journal* 48, no. 2 (1993): 289–309.

Nigerian immigration

Nigeria is the number one source country for West African immigrants coming to the United States and is second to Ghana for immigration to Canada. In the U.S. census of 2000 and the Canadian census of 2001, 165,481 Americans and 9,530 Canadians claimed Nigerian descent. Nigerians live throughout the United States, but the greatest concentrations are found in Texas, California, and New York. Most Canadian Nigerians live in Ontario.

Nigeria occupies 351,200 square miles on the southern coast of West Africa. It is bordered by Benin on the west, Niger on the north, and Chad and Cameroon on the east. The population of Nigeria, estimated at 126,635,626 in 2002, is divided both ethnically and religiously. There are 10 major ethnic groups and almost 250 smaller ones, the largest being the Yoruba (17.5 percent), the Hausa (17.2 percent), the Ibo (or Igbo, 13.3 percent), and the Fulani (10.7 percent). Christians and Muslims each make up about 45 percent of the population, with the former concentrated in the south and the latter in the north. Although the Portuguese first visited Nigeria in the 15th century, the region remained under the control of hundreds of tribes until the 1860s, when Great Britain began to extend its influence inland from coastal trading ports. By 1903, British control was virtually complete, and by 1914, the approximate borders of the modern country had been established. Nigeria gained its independence in 1960. After a brief period of civilian rule, a series of coups, assassinations, and the secession of the state of Biafra in 1966 led to one of the bloodiest civil wars on the continent. By the time Biafra was subdued in 1970, some 2 million Nigerians had died. The country remained one of the most corrupt and politically unstable throughout the 20th century.

Apart from the descendants of slaves who had been brought to the Americas in the 17th and 18th centuries (see AFRICAN FORCED MIGRATION), there were almost no Nigerians in the United States prior to the 1970s. Between World War I (1914–18) and World War II (1939–45), a number of Nigerian nationalists traveled to and were sometimes educated in the United States. These included Nnamdi Azikiwe, first president of Nigeria, who studied at Lincoln University in Pennsylvania and Howard University in Washington, D.C. The numbers of Nigerians remained small, however, never totaling more than 30. The oil boom of the 1970s enabled Nigeria to send an increasing number of students abroad for education. During the late 1970s and 1980s, Nigeria was among the top six countries sending students to the United States. With the sharp decline of the Nigerian economy in the 1980s, an increasing number of Nigerians stayed in the United States and eventually brought their families to join them. As a result, between 1990 and 2000, the Nigerian-American population grew from 91,688 to 165,481. Between 1992 and 2002, immigration from Nigeria averaged almost 7,000 per year. Many Nigerians are well educated and have thus spread widely throughout the country following professional and academic careers.

It is difficult to ascertain the number of Nigerians who immigrated to Canada prior to 1973 because they were previously included in a general African category. There was, however, already a small stream of refugees from the civil war of the 1960s. Of 8,850 Nigerian immigrants in Canada in 2001, 240 came before 1971. Between 1971 and 1990, another 2,385 arrived. The rate of immigration increased significantly in the 1990s. Between 1991 and 2001, 70 percent of the Nigerian immigrant population arrived in Canada. During the 1980s, Nigeria was sometimes in the top 10 source countries sending students to Canadian universities. Many have stayed to work in the civil service, medicine, law, engineering, or other professional areas.

Further Reading

Anigbo, C. A. "The African Neo-Diaspora: Dynamics and Prospects for Afrocentrism and Counterpenetration." Ph.D. diss., Howard University, 1994.

Apraku, K. K. *African Emigres in the United States.* New York: Praeger, 1991.

Ikime, Obaro, ed. *Groundwork of Nigerian History.* Portsmouth, N.H.: Heinemann, 1999.

Makinwa-Adebusoye, P. K. "Emigration Dynamics in West Africa." *International Migration* 33, nos. 3–4 (1995): 435–467.

Offoha, Marcellina U. *Educated Nigerian Settlers in the United States: The Phenomenon of Brain Drain.* Philadelphia: Temple University Press, 1989.

Shepard, Robert B. *Nigeria, Africa, and the United States: From Kennedy to Reagan.* Bloomington: Indiana University Press, 1991.

Speer, T. "The Newest African Americans." *American Demographics* 16 (1994): 9–10.

Udofia, Paul E. *Nigerians in the United States: Potentialities and Crises.* Boston: William Monroe Trotter Institute, 1996.

North American Free Trade Agreement (NAFTA)

The North America Free Trade Agreement (NAFTA) of 1994 created a unified market of more than 370 million people with goods and services totaling $6.5 trillion annually. The elimination of tariffs was scheduled to occur over a 15-year period, though most were eliminated in the first five years. In 1994, the free-trade area was second only to the European Union in terms of value of goods and services.

After heated debate, especially in the United States and Canada, NAFTA was signed by the presidents of the United States, Mexico, and Canada on December 17, 1992. Advocates of the agreement argued that the total number of jobs would increase in all three countries and that the free movement of goods and services would result in lower costs. They also suggested that the creation of more and better jobs in Mexico would lessen the undocumented immigration into the United States. Many environmental and labor groups in the United States and Canada vigorously opposed the treaty, fearing the loss of well-paid jobs to Mexico and degradation of the environment as companies moved south. The measure was ratified by the legislatures of all three countries in 1993 and took effect on January 1, 1994.

Under NAFTA provisions, temporary admission restrictions were eased on business visitors, professionals, intracompany transferees, and traders and investors moving between countries. Cross-border truck traffic was also liberalized, although it was again tightened following the terrorist attacks of SEPTEMBER 11, 2001, and continued to be examined in light of several 2003 incidents involving the deaths of illegal Mexican immigrants being smuggled into the United States in trucks.

Further Reading

Cameron, Maxwell A., and Brian W. Thompson. *The Making of NAFTA: How the Deal Was Done.* Ithaca, N.Y.: Cornell University Press, 2000.

Caulfield, Norman. *Mexican Workers and the State: From Porfiriato to NAFTA.* Ft. Worth: Texas Christian University Press, 1998.

Martin, Philip L. *Trade and Migration: NAFTA and Agriculture.* Washington, D.C.: Institute for International Economics, 1993.

North Carolina colony   See CAROLINA COLONIES.

Northern Ireland   See ULSTER.

North Korea   See KOREAN IMMIGRATION.

North West Company

The North West Company was, according to journalist and historian Peter Newman, "the first North American business to operate on a continental scale." Between 1783 and 1821, the company created an extensive fur-trading network that stretched 3,000 miles from Montreal to the Athabasca Country of the North West and included 100 outposts along the way. The richness of the fur trade—including beaver, bear, fox, otter, muskrat, marten, mink, lynx, wolverine, fisher, and wolf, as well as deer and elk hides—yielded extensive profits for its MONTREAL, QUEBEC, investors.

In response to the loss of territories south of the Great Lakes in the American Revolution (1775–83), a number of Montreal fur-trading firms joined together during the 1780s to form the North West Company. By 1800, the company was far exceeding all rivals, including the HUDSON'S BAY COMPANY. In 1811, THOMAS DOUGLAS, fifth earl of Selkirk, who owned controlling interest in the Hudson's Bay Company, obtained from the latter a grant of 116,000 square miles of land at the fork of the Red and Assiniboine Rivers near Lake Winnipeg to establish a colony of Scottish and Irish immigrants who had been driven from their lands as a result of the ENCLOSURE MOVEMENT. In reaction, the North West Company, fearing loss of access to the valuable fur-bearing regions of the Northwest as well as to its essential supply of pemmican, joined with local Métis (Canadians of mixed white and indigenous heritage) in an attempt to drive the settlers away. This led to a frontier war, in which Lord Selkirk hired German, Swiss, French, and Polish mercenary veterans of the War of 1812 to attack the North West Company's interior headquarters at Fort William. Although the North West Company had been successful at first, sounder finance and a gradual adaptation to wilderness warfare enabled the Hudson's Bay Company to prevail. Under pressure from the British government, in 1821, the two companies merged, with North West shareholders receiving shares in the Hudson's Bay Company. In 1824, a reorganization led to an almost complete loss of influence by former shareholders of the North West Company.

Further Reading

Campbell, Marjorie Wilkins. *The North West Company.* Toronto: Macmillan of Canada, 1957.
———. *The Nor'Westers: The Fight for the Fur Trade.* Toronto: Macmillan of Canada, 1974.
Davidson, Gordon Charles. *The North West Company.* Berkeley: University of California Press, 1918.
Mitchell, Elaine Allan. "The Scot in the Fur Trade." In *The Scottish Tradition in Canada.* Ed. W. Stanford Reid. Toronto: McClelland and Stewart, 1976.
Newman, Peter C. *Caesars of the Wilderness.* Vol. 2, *Company of Adventurers.* New York: Viking, 1987.

Norwegian immigration

Norway was the number one source country for Scandinavian immigration to North America, and second only to famine-ravaged Ireland in percentage of its population to immigrate. According to the U.S. census of 2000 and the Canadian census of 2001, 4,477,725 Americans and 363,760 Canadians claimed Norwegian ancestry. Because most Norwegian immigration came before World War I (1914–18), Norwegians have become largely assimilated to North American life and live throughout most parts of the United States and Canada. The greatest concentrations are still in and around the early agricultural settlements of the upper Midwest, with the greatest urban concentrations located in New York City; Chicago, Illinois; and Minneapolis, Minnesota. Almost one-third of Canadian Norwegians live in British Columbia.

Norway occupies 118,700 square miles of the western part of the Scandinavian peninsula in northwest Europe and extends farther north than any other European country. Sweden, Finland, and Russia border Norway on the east. In 2002, the population was estimated at 4,503,440. About 96 percent of the population is Norwegian, with ethnic roots in both Germanic and Lapp cultures. About 88 percent of Norway's population is Evangelical Lutheran. During the period of Norwegian immigration to North America, religion played an important role in everyday life; by 2002, however, much of the adherence was nominal. Norway's first ruler was Harald the Fairhaired, who came to power in 872. Between 800 and 1000, Norwegian Vikings raided and occupied many coastal areas of Europe, including Russia, Ireland, England, and France. The country was united with Denmark under a common king between 1380 and 1814. Norway was ceded to Sweden in 1814 after the Napoleonic Wars but became independent in 1905. Norway remained neutral during World War I and attempted to do so during World War II (1939–45) but was occupied by Nazi Germany between 1940 and 1945. The country abandoned its neutrality after the war and joined the North Atlantic Treaty Organization (NATO). Abundant hydroelectric and petroleum resources provided a solid economic base, giving Norway one of the highest living standards in the world. In 1994, Norwegians chose not to join the European Union.

Norwegians began immigrating to the United States in significant numbers in the 1840s and continued to come until the outbreak of World War I. Although the population of Norway grew rapidly during the 19th century, so too did personal freedoms and industry. The old social distinctions remained, however, and many among Norway's peasantry—about 80 percent of the population—sought land and political equality in North America. Unlike many immigrants from eastern and southern Europe after 1880, most Norwegians came to North America with their families, intending to stay and establish a new life. By 1865, nearly 80,000 had

A Norwegian woman (with her back turned to the camera) bids her family farewell as she prepares to immigrate to America. Norway suffered more pressure from want of agricultural land than any other European nation in the 19th century, and the percentage of the Norwegian population to emigrate was second only to Ireland's. *(Library of Congress, Prints & Photographs Division [LC-USZ62-94442])*

settled in the United States, and with the end of the Civil War that same year, a great wave of Norwegian settlers arrived: 110,000 between 1866 and 1873 alone. By the 1870s, they had established a strong ethnic presence in southern Wisconsin, northern Iowa, Minnesota, and eastern parts of the Dakota territories. With a larger tide of immigration in the 1880s (176,586), 1890s (95,015), and 1900s (190,505), more Norwegians, both first and second generation, spread westward to Oregon, Washington, British Columbia, and Alaska. The Pacific coastal regions were reminiscent of western Norway, and Norwegians slipped smoothly into the fishing and trading economies. In a separate movement, the shipping boom of the late 1870s and 1880s brought 1,200 Norwegian ships to New York City annually, leading thousands of skilled seamen to jump ship and establish residence in the area, mainly Brooklyn, where they found ready employment. As a result, Brooklyn became the single largest Norwegian community in the United States. Of approximately 900,000 Norwegian immigrants to the United States, more than 85 percent came between 1865 and 1930. Between 1992 and 2002, an average of about 450 Norwegians immigrated to the United States annually.

The Canadian government encouraged Norwegian settlement, though cheaper land prices and better condition in the United States inhibited settlement in large numbers in the Canadian West until after 1900. As better lands in the United States were taken, an increasing number of Norwegians sought farmsteads on the Canadian prairies. Between 1900 and 1914, almost 20,000 Norwegians came directly from Europe and thousands more from the United States. With severe economic depression in Norway during the 1920s, 20,000 more Norwegians came before the Great Depression in the 1930s almost halted immigration. With a healthy economy at home since World War II, few Norwegians have chosen to emigrate. Average immigration in the 1980s and 1990s was only about 100 per year. Of Canada's more than 360,000 Norwegians in 2001, barely 6,000 were immigrants, three-quarters of whom immigrated before 1971.

See also RØLVAAG, OLE EDVART.

Further Reading

Bergmann, L. N. *Americans from Norway.* Westport, Conn.: Greenwood Press, 1950.

Bjork, Kenneth O. *West of the Great Divide: Norwegian Migration to the Pacific Coast, 1847–1893.* Northfield, Minn.: Norwegian-American Historical Association, 1958.

Blegen, Theodore. *Norwegian Migration to America, 1825–1860.* 1931. Reprint, Northfield, Minn.: Norwegian American Historical Association, 1940.

Gjerde, Jon. *From Peasants to Farmers: The Migration from Balestrand, Norway, to the Upper Middle West.* Cambridge: Cambridge University Press, 1985.

———. *The Minds of the West: Ethnocultural Evolution in the Rural Middle West, 1830–1917.* Chapel Hill: University of North Carolina Press, 1997.

Loken, Gulbrand. *From Fjord to Frontier: A History of the Norwegians in Canada.* Toronto: McClelland and Stewart, 1980.

Lovoll, Odd S. *The Promise Fulfilled: A Portrait of Norwegian Americans Today.* Minneapolis: University of Minnesota Press, 1998.

———. *The Promise of America: A History of the Norwegian-American People.* Rev. ed. Minneapolis: University of Minnesota Press, 1999.

Mauk, David C. *The Colony That Rose from the Sea: Norwegian Maritime Migration and Community in Brooklyn, 1850–1910.* Northfield, Minn.: Norwegian-American Historical Association, 1997.

Niemi, Einar. "Emigration from Northern Norway: A Frontier Phenomenon? Some Perspectives and Hypotheses." In *Norwegian-American Essays 1996.* Eds. Øyvind Gulliksen, Dina Tolfsby, and David Mauk. Oslo, Norway: Norwegian Emigrant Museum, 1996.

Schultz, April R. *Ethnicity on Parade: Inventing the Norwegian American through Celebration.* Amherst: University of Massachusetts Press, 1994.

Semmingsen, Ingrid. *Norway to America: A History of the Migration.* Minneapolis: University of Minnesota Press, 1978.

Nova Scotia

The peninsula of Nova Scotia was a continual source of conflict between France and Britain from the establishment of its first settlement by France at Port Royal (1605) until France was driven completely from North America in the SEVEN YEARS' WAR (1756–63). The Treaty of Utrecht (1713) had forced France from ACADIA, but the region was ill defined, and the British only substantively occupied the peninsula of Nova Scotia. The French were allowed to retain the almost uninhabited Île Royale (Cape Breton Island), where they constructed the fortress of Louisbourg. In 1749, British settlers established Halifax, which became the capital. Fleeing European persecution, French, German, and Swiss Protestants immigrated to Nova Scotia in the early 1750s. In 1755, British colonial troops began to drive out Acadians who refused to swear loyalty to the British Crown.

Following the Seven Years' War, Britain hoped to spur settlement in the Maritime Provinces—Nova Scotia, NEW BRUNSWICK, Isle St. John (PRINCE EDWARD ISLAND)—NEWFOUNDLAND, and QUEBEC, both to offset the predominant French population and to weaken the more independent colonies to the south. By issuing the Proclamation of 1763, which prohibited settlement west of the Appalachian Mountains, Britain believed that settlers would flock northward. Nova Scotia's population did grow, to 13,500 by 1767, but few of the immigrants came from the thirteen colonies. With its rugged terrain and proximity to the sea, the province became the favored destination for destitute Scottish Highlanders, who began arriving in 1773. By the early 19th century, eastern Nova Scotia had taken on a distinctly Scottish character (see SCOTTISH IMMIGRATION).

The most dramatic demographic change came with the resettling of some 35,000 United Empire Loyalists at the end of the American Revolution in 1783 (see AMERICAN REVOLUTION AND IMMIGRATION). Almost all were American-born civilians of the lower and middle classes, and most had lived in New York and Pennsylvania. In return for their loyalty, they were evacuated at government expense to Nova Scotia and given land and provisions. Fearing friction between these newcomers and native Nova Scotians, the British government hoped to resettle them along the sparsely populated St. John River valley of New Brunswick, but about 19,000 remained and founded on the rocky southeastern coast Shelburne, making it almost instantly the largest city in British North America. Within three years, however, the town was deserted. Most of the Loyalists were eventually resettled on the eastern end of the peninsula and in the valleys behind Annapolis Royal. Loyalist settlements at Sydney and Baddeck on Cape Breton led to Cape Breton's brief existence as a separate colony (1784–1820). Among the Loyalists were 3,000 free blacks, many of whom had been granted freedom under a British policy encouraging slaves to abandon their masters during the war. Most were settled around Shelburne and Birchtown. Encountering prejudice and difficult farming conditions, almost 1,200 decided to emigrate, leaving Nova Scotia for Sierra Leone in 1792.

With Canadian weaknesses exposed during the War of 1812 (1812–15), the British government once again encouraged immigration, prompting a steady stream of Scottish immigrants between 1815 and 1850. Large numbers of Irish also immigrated after the potato blight of 1845. In 1848, Nova Scotia became the first completely self-governing colony in the British Empire. The economy remained strong into the 1860s, based on the shipbuilding and timber industries, but began to decline with the advent of steamships. In 1867, Nova Scotia became a charter province of the newly confederated Canada, along with New Brunswick, Ontario, and Quebec.

Further Reading

Brown, Wallace. *The King's Friends: The Composition and Motives of the American Loyalist Claimants.* Providence, R.I.: Brown University Press, 1965.

Careless, J. M. S., ed. *Colonists and Canadiens, 1760–1867.* Toronto: Macmillan of Canada, 1971.

Cowan, Helen I. *British Emigration to British North America: The First Hundred Years.* Toronto: University of Toronto Press, 1961.

Ells, Margaret. "Settling the Loyalists in Nova Scotia." *Canadian Historical Association Report for 1934.* Ottawa: Canadian Historical Association, 1934.

Johnson, Stanley. *A History of Emigration from the United Kingdom to North America, 1763–1912.* London: George Routledge and Sons, 1913.

MacNutt, W. S. *The Atlantic Provinces: The Emergence of Colonial Society, 1712–1857.* Toronto: McClelland and Stewart, 1965.

Moore, Christopher. *The Loyalists: Revolution, Exile, Settlement.* Toronto: Macmillan of Canada, 1984.

Wilson, Bruce. *Colonial Identities: Canada from 1760–1815.* Ottawa: National Archives of Canada, 1988.

Oregon Treaty

The Oregon Country was a huge expanse of lightly inhabited territory north of Mexican California, south of Russian Alaska, and southwest of the British trapping lands of the Athabasca Country. During the first decade of the 19th century, Britain, the United States, Mexico, and Russia all claimed this vast Pacific watershed of the Rocky Mountains, roughly from the 42nd parallel northward to parallel 54 degrees 40 north, the southern boundary of Alaska. In 1818, Britain and the United States agreed to a joint occupation and in the following year, secured former Spanish claims in the south. Generally speaking, the British NORTH WEST COMPANY and HUDSON'S BAY COMPANY were most active in the northern portion of the region, and the American Pacific Fur Company, in the south. Although a few settlers, both British and American, ventured to Oregon, significant permanent settlement did not begin until the early 1840s. By 1845, 6,000 permanent American settlers inhabited the Willamette Valley, with the promise of more to follow. Oregon had become part of the bitter presidential election of 1844, in which candidate James K. Polk campaigned on the slogan, "Fifty-four forty or fight!" claiming the northernmost boundary of Oregon as his foreign-policy goal. By 1846, political considerations on both sides dictated a compromise. The United States was on the verge of war with Mexico, while Britain was on bad terms with France and dealing with the significant potential effects of the repeal of the Corn Law. As a result, a compromise was reached, dividing the Oregon Country along the 49th parallel to the Pacific but giving Britain control of the whole of Vancouver Island. The United States gained formal recognition of the primary settlement areas, as well as its first deep water port on the Pacific, while British control of the rich fur-bearing regions of the north was conceded. The Hudson's Bay Company nevertheless continued to operate trading posts in Oregon until 1871.

Further Reading

[Adopted Citizen]. *Will There Be War?* New York: W. Taylor, 1846.

Francis, Daniel. *Battle for the West: Fur Traders and the Birth of Western Canada.* Edmonton, Canada: Hurtig Publishers, 1982.

Morrison, Dorothy Nafus. *The Eagle and the Fort: the Story of John McLoughlin.* 2d ed. Portland: Press of the Oregon Historical Society, Western Imprints, 1984.

Pletcher, David M. *The Diplomacy of Annexation: Texas, Oregon, and the Mexican War.* Columbia: University of Missouri Press, 1973.

Oriental Exclusion Act (United States) (1924)

The Oriental Exclusion Act, actually a special provision of the JOHNSON-REED ACT of 1924, excluded immigrants who were ineligible for U.S. citizenship from entrance to the United States, even at the new ethnic-based, lower levels. It was the natural extension of racialist and increasingly restrictive immigration policies including the CHINESE EXCLUSION ACT of 1882, the GENTLEMEN'S AGREEMENT of 1907, and the IMMIGRATION ACT of 1917. Although the Japanese were not explicitly named, they were the clear targets of the amendment, as Chinese and Asian Indian immigration had been

For a fee, immigrants could get help in completing naturalization papers in all the major cities of the United States—unless they were Asian. Between 1870 and 1943, most Asian immigrants were prohibited from becoming naturalized citizens. *(U.S. National Archives #119-G-81-M-3)*

prohibited prior to this new legislation. Two years earlier, in *OZAWA V. UNITED STATES* (1922), the Supreme Court had ruled that Japanese were not eligible for U.S. citizenship because they were not "white." The Oriental Exclusion Act seemed to violate the Gentlemen's Agreement, which put the burden of immigration restriction on the Japanese government. There was an attempt to exempt Japanese as "entitled to enter the United States under the provision of a treaty or an agreement relating solely to immigration," but it was overwhelmingly defeated. The Japanese government protested at being singled out but to no avail.

Further Reading

Daniels, Roger. *Guarding the Golden Door: American Immigrants and Immigration Policy since 1882.* New York: Hill and Wang, 2004.
———. *The Politics of Prejudice: The Anti-Japanese Movement in California and the Struggle for Japanese Exclusion.* Berkeley: University of California Press, 1977.
Hutchinson, E. P. *Legislative History of American Immigration Policy, 1798–1965.* Philadelphia: University of Pennsylvania Press, 1981.
Murray, Francis J. "An Investigation of the Influences Responsible for Oriental Exclusion in the American Immigration Act of 1924." M.A. thesis, Niagara University, 1962.

Our Country: Its Possible Future and Its Present Crisis

Josiah Strong's influential 1885 polemic, *Our Country: Its Possible Future and Its Present Crisis,* represented both America's sense of manifest destiny and nativist fears as the NEW IMMIGRATION began to bring hundreds of thousands of eastern and southern Europeans into the country (see NATIVISM). It became a national best-seller and made Strong a celebrity.

A Congregationalist minister and missionary in the American West, Strong was a staunch expansionist, who wholeheartedly embraced the ideals of Anglo-Saxon civilization and its benefits for the uncivilized world. He believed that the English-speaking peoples were favored by God and that in "the final competition of races," they would eventually "move down upon Mexico, down upon Central and South America, out upon the islands of the sea, over upon Africa and beyond." This would be accomplished by taking trade and the Christian gospel to the world. Strong argued that Catholics could not be good U.S. citizens, as they owed their first allegiance to the Roman Catholic Church. There is, he wrote, "an irreconcilable difference between papal principles and the fundamental principles of our free institutions." Strong was also an early proponent of the Social Gospel movement, seeking to serve God by improving the condition of the poor. He helped found the League for Social Service and the Federal Council of Churches. *Our Country* was provided as an outline for a progressive and healthy America, an important part of which was immigration restriction.

Further Reading

Chai, Dong-bai. "Josiah Strong: Apostle of Anglo-Saxonism and Social Christianity." Ph.D. diss., University of Texas, 1972.

Edwards, Wendy Deichmann. "Forging an Ideology for American Missions: Josiah Strong and Manifest Destiny." Currents in World Christianity Project 59. Cambridge: Cambridge University, 1998.

Muller, Dorothea. "Josiah Strong and the Challenge of the City." Ph.D. diss., New York University, 1956.

Schulz, Richard W. "Josiah Strong: Cultural Assimilation and the Immigrant Question." Thesis, Millersville University, 1993.

Strong, Josiah. *Our Country: Its Possible Future and Its Present Crisis.* New York: Baker and Taylor for the American Home Missionary Society, 1885.

Ozawa v. United States (1922)

In this dramatic court case, the U.S. Supreme Court ruled that Japanese were not white and therefore could not be naturalized as U.S. citizens. The decision led to complete prohibition of Japanese immigration in the JOHNSON-REED ACT of 1924 in abrogation of the GENTLEMEN'S AGREEMENT of 1907.

In 1914, Takao Ozawa applied for citizenship, challenging a 1906 American law that limited naturalization to "free white persons," "aliens of African nativity," and "persons of African descent." He had arrived as a student in 1894, graduated from a California high school, and attended the University of California for three years before joining a U.S. business firm in Honolulu. After his application was denied, he appealed to the U.S. District Court for the Territory of Hawaii (1916). The district court ruled that Ozawa was "in every way eminently qualified" for citizenship except he was not white and clearly not of African ancestry. He then appealed his case to the U.S. Supreme Court, where he presented his good character, his complete loyalty to the United States, and his adoption over 20 years' residence of English and American culture in favor of his petition. He was, "at heart . . . a true American." In its decision, however, the Court held that although the term *white* was more broadly conceived than *Caucasian*—taking into account, for instance, character traits that might be linked to race ethnicity—Ozawa clearly did not qualify for citizenship.

Further Reading

Curran, Thomas J. *Xenophobia and Immigration, 1820–1930.* Boston: Twayne, 1975.

Ichioka, Yuji. "The Early Japanese Immigrant Quest for Citizenship: The Background of the 1922 Ozawa Case." *Amerasia* 4, no. 2 (1977): 12.

O'Brien, David J., and Stephen Fugita. *The Japanese American Experience.* Bloomington: Indiana University Press, 1991.

Takaki, Ronald. *Strangers from a Different Shore: A History of Asian Americans.* Boston: Little, Brown, 1989.

P

Pacific Islander immigration

The islands of the vast Pacific Ocean stretch over thousands of miles but have a small total population. Immigration to North America was therefore small in numbers but of great significance because of U.S. political involvement in the Hawaiian Islands, Samoa, Guam, and the islands of Micronesia and the British colonial connection to Fiji. In 2000, it was estimated that about 200,000 Pacific Islanders lived in the United States. About half were immigrants, and most came from Samoa, Tonga, Fiji, and the Federated States of Micronesia. In Canada in 2001, there were 31,905 immigrants from the Pacific Islands (excluding Australia), 70 percent of them from Fiji. The highest concentrations of Pacific Islanders in the United States were in Hawaii and on the West Coast, and in Canada in Vancouver and lower British Columbia.

The Pacific island region, or Oceania as it is sometimes called, covers an area almost 9,000 miles in width and 5,500 miles in length, from New Guinea in the west and New Zealand in the south to Easter Island in the southeast and Midway Island in the north. There are more than 20,000 islands in this vast area, many of which are uninhabited. The region is divided into three main culture areas: Micronesia (including Guam, the Federated States of Micronesia, the Marshall Islands, Palau, Kiribati, Nauru, and Wake Island), Melanesia (Fiji, Irian Jaya, New Caledonia, Papua New Guinea, the Solomon Islands, and Vanuatu), and Polynesia (American Samoa, the Cook Islands, Easter Island, French Polynesia, the Hawaiian Islands, Mid-

way Island, New Zealand, Niue Island, Pitcairn Islands Group, Tokelau, Tonga, Tuvalu, Wallis and Futuna Islands, and Western Samoa). Most of the islands of the Pacific fell under European or American control during the 18th and 19th centuries and became economically and technologically dependent on the great powers. Most were also conquered by Japan during World War II (1941–45), liberated by the United States, then economically supported in rebuilding their economies by the United States or former colonial powers. By 2003, Fiji, Kiribati, Nauru, New Zealand, Papua New Guinea, the Solomon Islands, Tonga, Tuvalu, Vanuatu, and Samoa had become independent. A number of the other islands or island groups were in various stages of negotiation regarding self-governance or independence. Of the thousands of islands, New Guinea and New Zealand compose more than 80 percent of the entire land mass of Oceania.

Polynesians and Melanesians immigrated to the United States in small numbers from the 1830s, when they began to form an important part of whaling crews in the South Pacific. Tens of thousands of native Hawaiians and Chinese and Japanese laborers also immigrated to the United States from Hawaii between the 1850s and 1898, when the island kingdom was annexed by the United States. That same year, Guam also was ceded to the United States as a result of a U.S. victory in the Spanish-American War. Guamanians were made U.S. citizens in 1950. There was little immigration to the United States from the non-American Pacific Islands until after World War II. In almost every island or island group, economic opportunities were severely limited, and there was growing population pressure. A significant number of Guamanians and Samoans worked for the U.S. military, and thousands eventually chose to work on bases in Hawaii or on the U.S. mainland. Second only to Samoa as an Oceania source country was Tonga, most of whose immigrants first came to study at Brigham Young University campuses in Hawaii and Utah. Between 1992 and 2002, the largest average annual migrations were from Fiji (1,200), New Zealand (800), and Tonga (360).

The largest Pacific Islander immigrant groups in Canada in 2001 were Fijian (10,035) and New Zealander (8,600). Well over 90 percent of Fijians immigrating to Canada are the descendants of indentured (Asian) Indian laborers taken to the islands between 1879 and 1920. Most Fijians immigrated for a combination of reasons, including economic opportunity and fear for the fate of the Indo-Fijian minority after independence in 1970. Immigration averaged more than 500 annually during much of the 1970s and 1980s but increased in the wake of two political coups in 1987. Of 22,335 Fijian immigrants in Canada in 2001, about half came after 1987. Almost all New Zealanders came to Canada for economic opportunities.

Further Reading

Barkan, Elliott. *Asian and Pacific Islander Migration to the United States.* Westport, Conn.: Greenwood Press, 1992.

Barringer, Herbert R., Robert W. Gardner, and Michael J. Leven. *Asians and Pacific Islanders in the United States.* New York: Russell Sage Foundation, 1993.

Buchigani, Norman. *A Social History of South Asians in Canada.* Toronto: McClelland and Stewart, 1985.

Campbell, I. C. *A History of the Pacific Islands.* Berkeley: University of California Press, 1989.

Cowling, W. E. "Motivations for Contemporary Tongan Migration." In *Tongan Culture and History.* Eds. P. Herda, J. Terrell, and N. Gunson. Canberra: Australian National University, 1990.

Franco, R. *Samoans in Hawaii: A Demographic Profile.* Honolulu, Hawaii: Population Institute, East-West Center, 1987.

McCall, G., and J. Connell, eds. *World Perspectives on Pacific Islander Migration.* Sydney, Australia: Center for South Pacific Studies, University of New South Wales, 1993.

Rogers, R. F. *Destiny's Landfall: A History of Guam.* Honolulu: University of Hawaii Press, 1995.

Souder, L. M. T. *Daughters of the Island: Contemporary Chamorro Women Organizers on Guam.* Lanham, Md.: University Press of America, 1992.

Spickard, P. R., ed. *Pacific Island Peoples in Hawaii.* Honolulu: University of Hawaii Press, 1994.

Spickard, P.R., et al. *Pacific Islander Americans: An Annotated Bibliography in the Social Sciences.* Laie, Hawaii: Institute for Polynesian Studies, Brigham Young University, 1995.

padrone system

A padrone (from the Italian *padroni* for "patrons" or "bosses") was a middleman in the labor trade, helping poor immigrants obtain transportation to North America, jobs upon arrival, and basic needs in an alien society. Though most often associated with Italian immigration during the 19th century, the labor middleman was common in many ethnic groups from colonial times, especially in arranging contracts for INDENTURED SERVITUDE. With industry largely unregulated before World War I (1914–18), it was easy for labor bosses to take advantage of poor, uneducated immigrants. In organizing labor gangs to fill contracts negotiated with railroads and other companies, padrones did provide jobs and often advanced money for transportation or other essentials, but they also charged fees for every transaction and sometimes required their clients to purchase goods from their own stores. It has been estimated that more than half the Italian labor in large U.S. cities during the late 19th and early 20th century worked under the padrone system.

As progressive legislation was passed and immigrants in the wave of NEW IMMIGRATION found more family, friends, and social contacts to assist them upon arrival, the role of the padrone changed from labor boss to economic adviser. Often well connected to economic and political leaders, the padrone was frequently able to help clients qualify for mortgages or improve their chances of moving up the business ladder. As Italians and other new immigrants became increasingly assimilated into American society after World War II (1939–45), the role of the European padrone declined. Labor brokers continued to play a significant role in the lives of poorer immigrants, especially those from Mexico, Central America, and Asia, though the modern padrone was seldom as well connected to the community as he had been early in the 20th century.

Further Reading

Harney, Robert F, and Nicholas De Maria Harney. *From the Shores of Hardship: Italians in Canada, Essays.* Welland, Canada: Soleil, 1993.

Iorizzo, Luciano J. *Italian Immigration and the Impact of the Padrone System.* New York: Arno Press, 1980.

Lopreato, Joseph. *Italian Americans.* New York: Random House, 1970.

Nelli, Humbert S. "The Italian Padrone System in the United States." *Labor History* 5 (1964): 153–167.

Peck, Gunther. *Reinventing Free Labor: Padrones and Immigrant Workers in the North American West, 1880–1930.* Cambridge: Cambridge University Press, 2000.

Pozzetta, George E., ed. *Pane e Lavoro: The Italian American Working Class, Proceedings of the Eleventh Annual Conference of the American Italian Historical Association . . . 1978.* Toronto: Multicultural History Society of Ontario, 1980.

Sheridan, F. J. "Italian, Slavic and Hungarian Unskilled Laborers in the United States." *U.S. Bureau of Labor Bulletin* 72. Washington, D.C.: U.S. Bureau of Labor, 1907.

Page Act (United States) (1875)

The Page Act was the first piece of American legislation to attempt to directly regulate immigration. It was aimed at the abuses surrounding CHINESE IMMIGRATION but in fact reflected a growing anti-Asian sentiment in the United States. It also marked a growing expansion of federal power following settlement of states' rights issues during the Civil War (1861–65).

Tens of thousands of Chinese laborers were brought to California and the American West as a result of the gold rush (1849) and the building of the transcontinental railroad (1860s). Although the Chinese were usually considered economic assets and good residents, their growing numbers alarmed many people living in the West. In December 1874, President Ulysses S. Grant called for curbs on two outgrowths of the Chinese immigration: forced labor and prostitution. California representative Horace F. Page, a Republican, sponsored the immigration legislation enacted on March 3, 1875. Its main provision included

1. prohibition of contracted labor from "China, Japan, or any Oriental country" that was not "free and voluntary"
2. prohibition of immigration of Chinese prostitutes
3. exclusion of two classes of potential immigrants from all countries: convicts and women "imported for the purposes of prostitution"

Chinese women were so rigorously screened by U.S. officials in China that most wives and other nonprostitutes were prohibited from coming as well, their numbers prior to the CHINESE EXCLUSION ACT declining more than two-thirds over the previous seven years. Among almost 40,000 Chinese who immigrated to the United States in the few months prior to enforcement of the Chinese Exclusion Act, only 136 of them were women. It is notable that in excluding convicts, an exception was made for "political offenses," thus forming the basis of American refugee policy (see REFUGEE STATUS).

Further Reading

Hutchinson, E. P. *Legislative History of American Immigration Policy, 1798–1965.* Philadelphia: University of Pennsylvania Press, 1981.

LeMay, Michael C. *From Open Door to Dutch Door: An Analysis of U.S. Immigration Policy since 1820.* New York: Praeger, 1987.

Peffer, George Anthony. "Forbidden Families: Emigration Experiences of Chinese Women under the Page Law, 1875–1882." *Journal of American Ethnic History* 6 (1986): 28–46.

Pakistani immigration

Pakistanis only began to immigrate to North America in significant numbers since the mid-1960s, when immigration policies in both the United States and Canada abandoned racial quotas. Pakistani immigrants in the 1960s and 1970s, almost all Muslims, tended to be well-educated professionals who had been exposed to Western culture in Karachi, Lahore, Rawalpindi, and other major urban areas. According to the U.S. census of 2000 and the Canadian census of 2001, 204,309 Americans and 74,015 Canadians claimed Pakistani descent. Most observer believe the actual number in Canada to be well over 100,000. The largest concentrations of Pakistani Americans were in New York City, Chicago, Philadelphia, and Los Angeles. In Canada, they have concentrated in the industrial centers of Ontario and in Montreal, with significant concentrations in Vancouver, Edmonton, Calgary, and Winnipeg.

Pakistan occupies 300,300 square miles of South Asia between 25 and 37 degrees north latitude. In 2002, the population was estimated at 144,616,639. The country is divided into four regions: Punjab, Sind, Baluchistan, and the North-West Frontier Province, each reflecting an ancient cultural tradition and dominated by distinct ethnic groups, most important among them the Punjabi, Sindhi, Baloch, and Pashtun. Pakistan is bordered by Iran and Afghanistan to the west, China to the north, and India to the east. Islam provides a unifying factor and is practiced by 97 percent of the population, though there are tensions between the majority Sunni (77 percent) and the significant Shiite minority (20 percent). The Indus River Valley, site of the ancient Harappan civilization (ca. 2500–1700 B.C.), gave its name to the South Asian region known as India. Islam reached western India during the eighth century and spread rapidly throughout the Indus valley during extended periods of Muslim rule between the 11th and 19th centuries. Between about 1750 and 1947, the entire South Asian region progressively fell under the control of Britain, which ruled without representative institutions. British India included the modern countries of India, Pakistan, and Bangladesh. From the 1880s, Britain began to permit limited and narrowly prescribed forms of local self-rule, but this tended to be dominated by the Hindu majority in the country, particularly the Bengalis in the east. When Britain finally withdrew from India in 1947, attempts were made to partition the country along religious lines. The predominantly Muslim provinces of the west joined with Muslim East Bengal, more than 1,000 miles away, to form the new state of Pakistan. In the violence that followed perhaps 1 million people were killed and 12–14 million driven from one "new" land to the other—the greatest single uprooting of people in modern times. In 1971, civil war erupted between the eastern and western portions of Pakistan. India sided with East Pakistan in the war that led to the creation of the newly independent Bangladesh. Although Pakistan made considerable progress toward democracy in the 1980s and 1990s, military disputes with India over the Kashmir region and the rise of Islamic fundamentalism have led to the maintenance of a largely military regime.

Technically, there were no Pakistanis prior to 1947, all simply being Muslim citizens of British India. Undoubtedly, by the 1920s, when South Asian immigration was virtually halted, a few hundred had already emigrated from the region to North America. Numbers prior to the 1970s are problematic because immigrants might identify themselves by place of birth, religious affiliation, or ethnic identity. In 1947, the U.S. Congress passed a measure allowing for the naturalization of South Asians, which eventually led to a small stream of immigrants. There were perhaps 2,500 Pakistanis in the United States when the IMMIGRATION AND NATIONALITY ACT was passed in 1965, repealing the limited quotas then in effect. Pakistani immigrants arriving in the 1960s and early 1970s tended to be well educated, including many engineers, scientists, and pharmacists. As a result, they generally were successful in adjusting to life in New York City, Chicago, Los Angeles, San Francisco, and other major U.S. cities. As they became naturalized citizens in the later 1970s, they sponsored parents and other relatives, who were generally less well educated. By 1980 the number had risen to more than 20,000, and five times that by 1990. Between 1992 and 2002 an average of more than 12,000 Pakistanis immigrated to the United States each year. About one-third of them lived in the Northeast.

Around the start of the 20th century, perhaps a few hundred Muslims and Sikhs from the Western Punjab migrated to British Columbia before the 1907 ban on South Asian immigration. Most of the Muslims either returned to India or migrated to the United States. After World War II (1939–45), the prohibition of all non-European immigration was amended to allow reunification of immediate family members, a provision that some of the earlier immigrants were able to take advantage of. In 1951, Canada's new quota for South Asian immigrants provided for 100 Pakistani immigrants annually, slots taken mainly by Punjabi Sikhs. With few Canadian contacts and virtually no government facilities for processing requests, Pakistanis were slow to emigrate. In the first decade under the quota system, only 901 immigrated, most of them well-trained professionals. During the 1970s and 1980s immigration quickened, with many Pakistanis coming from countries such as Uganda, Kenya, and Tanzania where they were perceived as outsiders and a threat to the traditional societies. Whereas most immigrants prior to 1980 were well educated, many who came after were less well educated, fleeing economic and communal instability in their homeland. Of the 79,315 Pakistani immigrants in Canada in 2001, 57,990 (73 percent) arrived between 1991 and 2001. Fewer than 3,000 had arrived before 1971. By 1980 the number had risen to more than 20,000, and five times that number by 1990. About one-third of them lived in the Northeast. Between 1992 and 2002, an average of more than 12,000 Pakistanis immigrated to the United States each year.

See also BANGLADESHI IMMIGRATION; INDIAN IMMIGRATION; SOUTH ASIAN IMMIGRATION; SRI LANKAN IMMIGRATION.

Further Reading

Awan, S. N. A. *People of the Indus Valley: Pakistani-Canadians.* Ottawa, S. N. A. Awan, 1989.

Buchignani, Norman, Doreen M. Indra, with Ram Srivastava. *Continuous Journey: A Social History of South Asians in Canada.* Toronto: McClelland and Stewart, 1985.

Hossain, Mokerrom. "South Asians in Southern California: A Sociological Study of Immigrants from India, Pakistan and Bangladesh." *South Asia Bulletin* 2, no. 1 (Spring 1982): 74–83.

Jensen, Joan M. *Passage from India: Asian Indian Immigrants in North America.* New Haven, Conn.: Yale University Press, 1988.

Khan, S. "A Brief History of Pakistanis in the Western United States." M.A. thesis, California State University–Sacramento, 1981.

Malik, Iftikhar Haider. *Pakistanis in Michigan: A Study of Third Culture and Acculturation.* New York: AMS Press, 1989.

Petvich, Carla. *The Expanding Landscape: South Asians in the Diaspora.* Chicago: Manohar, 1999.

Tinker, Hugh. *The Banyan Tree: Overseas Emigrants from India, Pakistan, and Bangladesh.* New York: Oxford University Press, 1977.

Van der Veer, Peter, ed. *Nation and Migration: The Politics of Space in the South Asian Diaspora.* Philadelphia: University of Pennsylvania Press, 1995.

Palestinian immigration

Palestinians are Arabs and generally were counted as part of Ottoman or ARAB IMMIGRATION figures prior to World War II (1939–45). Political events since then have made it impossible to accurately count the number of Palestinians arriving in North America. According to the U.S. census of 2000 and the Canadian census of 2001, 72,112 Americans and 14,675 Canadians claimed Palestinian descent, but the actual number of Palestinians in the United States and Canada was much higher. Palestinians have been resettled widely throughout the United States, with Detroit, Michigan; New York City; Chicago, Illinois; Houston, Texas; and Jacksonville, Florida, all having large Palestinian communities. Canadian Palestinians have favored settlement in most of the metropolitan areas of Ontario, and there is a large community in Montreal.

There is no independent Palestinian state. Most of the 6 million Palestinians live in Jordan, Syria, and Lebanon (2.5 million total); the Gaza Strip and the West Bank, the autonomous portions of Palestinian settlement within Israel (2 million); Israel itself (750,000); and the United States (200,000). Ancient Palestine was located on the eastern shore of the Mediterranean Sea at the crossroads between the great civilizations of Egypt, Mesopotamia, and Asia Minor. For a brief period, Palestine was unified as a powerful state under a series of Israelite kings, around 1000 B.C. The region was successively conquered by the Assyrians, Babylonians, Persians, Greeks, and finally Romans. During the first and second centuries A.D., most of Palestine's Jews were driven out of the region by the Romans, leading to their dispersal throughout Europe and the Mediterranean world. Most of the inhabitants of Palestine were converted to Islam during the early phases of the Muslim expansion in the seventh century, and in 638, a mosque was built on the site of the old Jewish Temple in Jerusalem, a bone of contention thereafter among Jews, Christians, and Muslims. In the 16th century, Palestine was conquered by the Ottoman Empire, divided, and ruled from Constantinople. Around 1880, some European Jews, driven by continued persecution and convinced that they would never be accepted in European societies, began to purchase land in Palestine, reestablishing a presence in the ancient homeland and marginalizing the poorer Palestinian inhabitants. In 1920, administration of the region was handed over to Great Britain as part of the post–World War I mandate system, designed by the League of Nations to lead former colonial territories to self-government. About that time, the population of Palestine was about 82 percent Muslim, 10 percent Christian, and 8 percent Jewish. By 1948, when a state of Israel was carved out of the Palestinian mandate, less than two-thirds of the total population of Palestine was Muslim. As a result, the predominantly Palestinian areas were granted Arab control, and the principally Jewish regions became the new state of Israel. Palestinian and other Arab leaders refused to accept the partition and immediately attacked Israel. During the 1948 war, 750,000 Palestinian Arabs sought what they believed would be temporary refuge in Jordan, Egypt, Lebanon, and Syria. After the Six-Day War of 1967, hundreds of thousands of refugees fled from the Jordanian West Bank and the Egyptian Gaza Strip, raising the total number of refugees to about 1.4 million. Although a concerted effort to create the conditions for peace in the Middle East began in the 1970s, centering on Israeli withdrawal from Palestinian territories in return for Arab recognition of Israel's right to exist in peace, only limited progress had been made by 2004. During the 1980s and 1990s, militant nationalists largely controlled Palestinian politics, appealing to anti-Western Arab sentiment in support of their cause.

The actual number of Palestinians in the United States and Canada is much higher than official numbers suggest. Many researchers put the number in the United States at 200,000 and in Canada at more than 30,000. Because Palestinians were technically stateless, they often held passports from Egypt, Israel, Lebanon, or Jordan. A significant number of immigrants listed in immigration documents as Lebanese and Jordanian were almost certainly Palestinian. A large number would also have entered from Kuwait, Saudi Arabia, the United Arab Emirates, Bahrain, Oman, and Qatar, where some 3 million worked prior to the 1991 Persian Gulf War.

Although most Arab immigrants prior to the JOHNSON-REED ACT of 1924 were Lebanese Christians, there was a small number of Muslim Palestinians as well. It is known that some from the West Bank town of Ramallah established small businesses in the Midwest around 1900. With passage of the MCCARRAN-WALTER ACT in 1952, relaxed quotas enabled a small number to immigrate during the 1950s and early 1960s. Most of these were well educated academics and professionals.

The greatest period of Palestinian immigration to the United States came between the Six-Day War in 1967 and 1990, after which numbers began to decline. Although official figures indicate that more than 11,000 Palestinians immigrated during the 1980s, some scholars have suggested that the number may be seven or eight times that high, driven by the rising tide of violence within Israel.

During the 1980s a small number of Palestinians entered Canada, mostly on humanitarian grounds or as refugees. With changes in immigration law in the late 1980s that allowed prospective business investors to enter Canada, a substantial number of relatively prosperous Palestinians were enticed to emigrate from Kuwait, Saudi Arabia, the United Arab Emirates, and other Middle Eastern countries where they had been living. Most Palestinian immigrants to Canada are well educated; as a group, they have the highest literacy rate in the Arab world and one of the highest rates of doctorates per capita of any nationality in the world. Of the 5,455 Palestinian immigrants officially indicated by the Canadian census of 2001, 3,610 came after 1981. Many community experts suggest that there were more than 30,000 Palestinians in Canada in the 1990s.

See also JEWISH IMMIGRATION.

Further Reading

Abraham, S. Y., and N. Abraham, eds. *The Arab World and Arab Americans: Understanding a Neglected Minority.* Detroit: Center for Urban Studies, Wayne State University, 1981.

Abu-Laban, Baha, and Faith Zeadey, eds. *Arabs in America: Myths and Realities.* Wilmette, Ill.: Association of Arab-American University Graduates, 1975.

Abu-Laban, Baha, and M. Ibrahim Alladin, eds. *Beyond the Gulf War: Muslims, Arabs, and the West.* Edmonton, Canada: MRF Publishers, 1991.

Cainkar, L. "Palestinian Women in the U.S.: Who Are They and What Kind of Lives Do They Lead?" In *Images and Reality: Palestinian Women under Occupation and in the Diaspora.* Washington D.C.: Institute for Arab Women's Studies, 1990.

Elkholy, Abdo. *The Arab Muslims in the United States.* New Haven, Conn.: College and University Press, 1966.

McCarus, Ernest, ed. *The Development of Arab-American Identity.* Ann Arbor: University of Michigan Press, 1994.

Naff, Alixa. *Becoming American: The Early Arab American Experience.* Carbondale: Southern Illinois University Press, 1985.

Orfalea, Gregory. *Before the Flames: A Quest for the History of Arab Americans.* Austin: University of Texas Press, 1988.

Pastore, John Orlando (1907–2000) *politician*

The first Italian-American governor and U.S. senator, John Pastore represented the post–World War II shift in public opinion that enabled politicians of southern and eastern European descent to play a more prominent role in statewide and national politics. He was best known for his promotion of more wholesome television programming and the concept of family viewing times.

Pastore was born in 1907 to Italian immigrants in Providence, Rhode Island, where their family of seven lived in a four-room tenement apartment. He attended public schools there and graduated from Northeastern University Law School in 1931. A gifted speaker, he rose rapidly in the Democratic Party, serving in the Rhode Island house of representatives (1935–37), as assistant attorney general of Rhode Island (1937–38, 1940–44), and as lieutenant governor (1944–45). He succeeded as governor (1945–50) when J. Howard McGrath resigned. He was twice more elected governor before winning a U.S. Senate seat (1950–76). Pastore was reelected to the Senate in 1952, 1958, 1964, and 1970. He served as cochairman of the Joint Committee on Atomic Energy and chairman of a committee on TV regulation.

Further Reading
Morgenthau, Ruth S. *Pride without Prejudice: The Life of John O. Pastore.* Providence: Rhode Island Historical Society, 1989
Pastore, John O. *The Story of Communications from Beacon Light to Telstar.* New York: Macfadden-Bartell, 1964.

P.C. 695 (Canada) (1931)

In 1931, the Canadian cabinet passed Order-in-Council P.C. 695 prohibiting almost all immigration in order to meet the growing challenges of economic depression. As a result, more than two-thirds of immigrants to Canada during the 1930s were from Britain or northern Europe. The measure remained the basis of Canadian immigration policy until 1946.

A previous measure in 1930 had limited admission to those with agricultural capital or with family already in the country. By the provisions of P.C. 695 the restrictive policy was broadened, limiting immigration to Americans and Britons from white settlement colonies, including Britain, Ireland, Newfoundland, New Zealand, Australia, and South Africa, who had a sufficient monetary reserve; agricultural capitalists; those guaranteed employment in mining or timbering; and dependents of males already residing in Canada. The policy was steadfastly maintained throughout the Great Depression, despite growing humanitarian pressures as conditions worsened in Europe. The most controversial results of the policy came after the economy began to improve in 1937, when the government rejected a special appeal on behalf of German Jews and moved slowly on the Sudeten refugee question. In 1946, the Canadian Cabinet, passed P.C. 2071 amending P.C. 695 by permitting immigration of refugees with close relative in Canada. Even with this exception, immigration was tightly controlled, excluding almost all Jews.

Further Reading
Abella, Irving, and Harold Troper. *None Is Too Many: Canada and the Jews of Europe, 1933–1948.* Toronto: Lester and Orpen Dennys, 1982
Avery, Donald. *Reluctant Host: Canada's Response to Immigrant Workers, 1896–1994.* Toronto: McClelland and Stewart, 1995.
Bothwell, Robert, Ian Drummond, and John English. *Canada, 1900–1945.* Toronto: University of Toronto Press, 1987.
Constantine, Stephen, ed. *Emigrants and Empire: British Settlement in the Dominions between the Wars.* Manchester, U.K.: Manchester University Press, 1990.
Glassford, Larry A. *Reaction and Reform: The Politics of the Conservative Party under R. B. Bennett, 1927–1938.* Toronto: University of Toronto Press, 1992.
Kelley, Ninette, and Michael Trebilcock. *The Making of the Mosaic: A History of Canadian Immigration Policy.* Toronto: University of Toronto Press, 1998.

Penn, William (1644–1718) *colonist, religious leader*

The founder of the PENNSYLVANIA COLONY, William Penn brought religious tolerance and cultural diversity to the English colonies in America. His colony became a haven for religious dissenters and open to all the peoples of Europe.

Penn was born in London into an aristocratic family with connections to the royal family. His father was an English admiral who amassed a considerable estate in Ireland. Given the best private education, Penn was nevertheless expelled from Oxford University in 1662 for holding unorthodox views. While managing the family estates in Ireland, he joined the Society of Friends (Quakers), which was a great disappointment to his family. In 1668, he published *Truth Exalted,* the first of 150 books, pamphlets, and tracts he wrote, many of which attested to his religious faith. He traveled extensively in Britain and Europe, preaching and promoting the doctrines of the Quakers and would be a significant historical figure for this alone. Penn violated numerous laws prohibiting non-Anglican preaching, meeting, and publishing and spent about two years in prison. In politics, he had friends among the supporters of Charles II (r. 1660–85) and James II (r. 1685–88) and among the Whigs who opposed the Stuart monarchy. For several years after 1691, he went into hiding, having been accused of treason.

Penn is best remembered, however, for the establishment of the Pennsylvania colony in America. In 1682, he became a proprietor of the West Jersey colony (see NEW JERSEY COLONY) but soon abandoned it in favor of territory granted to his father by Charles II perhaps in payment of a debt and perhaps to rid himself of troubling Quakers. With the charter, Penn was given the right to both land and government, and he set out to provide a refuge for Quakers who were being persecuted in Europe. As a proprietor, he advertised widely throughout Europe in pamphlets such as *A Brief Account of the Province of Pennsylvania* (1681) and *A Further Account of the Province of Pennsylvania and Its Improvements* (1685), hoping to attract settlers. Translated into many languages, these tracts enticed settlers. While the colony itself was a success and became a model of the religious toleration that Penn so deeply supported, it provided Penn as proprietor with little income. Caught in the midst of English high politics and proprietary disputes, Penn traveled to America only twice (1682, 1699),

staying about two years each time. He also proposed one of the earliest plans for the union of the American colonies, advocating a Congress with representatives from each colony. Upon returning to England in 1701, he found his finances in chaos and was briefly imprisoned. He died in 1718, enjoying little of the success of his famous colony.

Further Reading

Dunn, Mary M. *William Penn: Politics and Conscience*. Princeton, N.J.: Princeton University Press, 1987.

Dunn, Richard, and Mary Dunn, eds. *The World of William Penn*. Philadelphia: University of Pennsylvania Press, 1986.

Geiter, Mary K. *William Penn*. London: Longmans, 2000.

Peare, Catherine Owens. *William Penn: A Biography*. Philadelphia: J. P. Lippincott, 1956.

Penn, William. *The Papers of William Penn*. 5 vols. Eds. Mary Maples Dunn, Richard S. Dunn, et al. Philadelphia: University of Pennsylvania Press, 1981–87.

This engraving by John Hall, published by John Boydell in 1775, is captioned "William Penn's treaty with the Indians, when he founded the Province of Pennsylvania in North America, 1681." Penn was unique among early colonial founders in his regard for the rights of Native Americans, and he lived in general peace with the local Delaware Indians. *(Library of Congress, Prints & Photographs Division [LC-USZ62-2583])*

Soderlund, Jean R., and Richard S. Dunn, eds. *William Penn and the Founding of Pennsylvania, 1681–1684.* Reissue ed. Philadelphia: University of Pennsylvania Press, 1999.

"Symposium on William Penn." *Proceedings of the American Philosophical Society* 127 (1983): 291–338.

Pennsylvania colony

Frustrated with the proprietary politics in the NEW JERSEY COLONY, WILLIAM PENN founded Pennsylvania in 1681. Designed by Penn as a "holy experiment" in religious toleration, it became the most ethnically diverse of the thirteen colonies and a haven for persecuted Quakers and other Christian dissenters.

Penn had been a proprietor of the West Jersey colony in the 1670s and had begun to encourage Quakers to settle in the Delaware River Valley at that time. As early as 1677, he sold Pennsylvania lands to German Rhinelanders, who finally arrived in 1783. It is still unclear exactly why Charles II granted Penn the generous charter for the lands beyond the Delaware River. It may have been because of a debt to Penn's father or because he wanted to rid England of the unsettling Quaker population. In 1682, Penn published his *Frame of Government,* a document that proved unworkable but that established the principles of liberty of conscience, freedom from persecution, and due process of law. In the same year, he purchased the Three Lower Counties (future DELAWARE COLONY) from James, Duke of York, in order to guarantee access to the sea. Penn advertised widely in England, Ireland, and Germany, lauding the rich soil of Pennsylvania and the colony's high degree of personal freedom. In 1685 alone, 8,000 immigrants arrived, most from the British Isles. Within a few years, however, Penn could boast that the people of Pennsylvania were "a collection of divers nations in Europe," including "French, Dutch, Germans, Swedes, Danes, Finns, Scotch, Irish, and English." By 1760, there were 18 German communities, most in western Pennsylvania, and Germans accounted for more than one-third of the entire population of the colony. Most were Lutherans or members of Reformed churches, though there were substantial numbers of Moravians, Mennonites (see MENNONITE IMMIGRATION), Amish (see AMISH IMMIGRATION), Dunkers, and Schwenkfelders. German farmers prospered, and most kept to themselves, sparking fears among the English of a dangerous element within their community. Diversity and toleration together produced an unruly political process, with the Quaker-dominated urban areas—especially PHILADELPHIA, PENNSYLVANIA—frequently at odds with the country, especially the Three Lower Counties, which were inhabited principally by Dutch, Swede, and Finn settlers who had little connection with Penn. In 1701, Penn's Charter of Liberties granted political control to a unicameral (one-house) assembly, free from proprietary influence. By 1725, most of the 25,000 Quakers

who had migrated to the Delaware Valley lived in Pennsylvania. After 1760, German and Scots-Irish settlers rapidly filled the trans-Appalachian west, far from Quaker influence and English control. By 1790, about 65 percent of Pennsylvania's population was non-English.

Further Reading
Bronner, Edwin B. *William Penn's Holy Experiment: The Founding of Pennsylvania, 1681–1701.* New York: Columbia University Press, 1962.
Illick, Joseph E. *Colonial Pennsylvania: A History.* New York: Scribner's, 1976.
Klees, Frederic. *The Pennsylvania Dutch.* New York: Macmillan, 1950.
Myers, Albert Cook, ed. *Narratives of Early Pennsylvania.* New York: Charles Scribner's Sons, 1912.
Nash, Gary B. *Quakers and Politics: Pennsylvania, 1681–1726.* Princeton, N.J.: Princeton University Press, 1968.
Tien, Anita. "'To Enjoy Their Customs': The Cultural Adaptation of Dutch and German Families in the Middle Colonies, 1660–1832." Ph.D. diss., University of California–Berkeley, 1990.

Peruvian immigration

Significant Peruvian immigration to North America began in the 1960s and reflects the unusually diverse ethnic heritage of South America's third largest country. According to the U.S. census of 2000 and the Canadian census of 2001, 233,926 Americans and 17,945 Canadians claimed Peruvian descent. The largest Peruvian concentration in the United States is in the New York metropolitan area, particularly in Paterson, New Jersey, and Queens, New York. Ontario and Quebec both have significant Peruvian-Canadian populations.

Peru occupies 493,600 square miles on the Pacific coast of South America. Ecuador and Colombia are on Peru's northern border, Brazil and Bolivia on its eastern border, and Chile on its southern border. In 2002, the population was estimated at 27,483,864. The people are ethnically divided among Amerindians (Quechua, 47 percent; Aymara, 5 percent), mestizos (32 percent), and Europeans (12 percent). There is a small but economically and politically prominent Japanese minority (0.5 percent). Almost 90 percent of Peruvians are Roman Catholic. Peru was dominated by the Inca Empire between the 13th and 16th centuries before Francisco Pizarro conquered it for the Spanish in 1533. Spain controlled Peru, spreading Spanish learning and culture, until 1824 when Peru finally gained its independence under the leadership of Simón Bolívar. During the 19th and 20th centuries, border disputes with Bolivia, Colombia, Chile, and Ecuador led to a series of wars. Peru's export economy was devastated by the Great Depression of the 1930s, which led to the rise of the American Popular Revolutionary Alliance and an ongoing period of political instability, including a long period of military rule (1968–80). The legislature was dissolved by President Alberto Fujimori in 1992 as the government sought effective measures against two rebel movements, the Maoist Shining Path and the indigenous Tupac Amaru Revolutionary Movement. In 2000, opposition to his antidemocratic methods and political scandal rocked Fujimori's government, forcing him to flee to Japan. In the first democratic elections following the scandals, Alejandro Toledo became the first president of Quechua ancestry to be elected in Peru.

The first Peruvians may have come to the United States during the 1848 CALIFORNIA GOLD RUSH and a handful came throughout the 19th century, though no community was established. It is difficult to trace exact numbers, however, as South Americans were counted collectively until 1932. During World War II (1941–45), 1,800 Peruvian Americans of Japanese descent were interned with Japanese Americans, and some were eventually exchanged for American prisoners of war. Several hundred of these Peruvians remained in the United States and were, in 1990, partially compensated for their internment. Upper- and middle-class Peruvians were the first to flee the country's political instability after World War II. From the mid–1980s, poorer Peruvians began to immigrate. Collectively they demonstrated an unusually strong sense of national identity after migration. Many estimates suggest that the actual number of Peruvians in the United States in 2000 was well over 400,000, an increasingly large number of them students seeking political and economic stability. In 2000, the IMMIGRATION AND NATURALIZATION SERVICE estimated that 61,000 Peruvians were unauthorized residents. Between 1992 and 2002, annual average legal immigration to the United States was a little more than 10,000.

Peruvian immigration to Canada began with several small groups of mainly young men in the late 1960s. Most were Peruvians of European descent, professionally trained or skilled workers seeking economic opportunities as the Canadian economy grew. At first, their numbers were small—about 400 settled in Ontario, for instance, between 1957 and 1971. During the 1970s, however, immigration dramatically increased, with close to 10,000 Peruvians entering as landed immigrants between 1974 and 1990. Of the 17,120 Peruvian immigrants in Canada in 2001, fewer than 1,000 came before 1971; 14,020 (82 percent) arrived between 1981 and 2001.

Further Reading

Altamirano, Teófilo. *Éxodo: Peruanos en el exterior.* Lima, Peru: Pontificia Universidad Católica del Perú, 1992.

———. *Los que se fueron: Peruanos en los Estados Unidos.* Lima, Peru: Pontificia Universidad Católica de Perú, 1990.

Mata, Fernando. *Immigrants from the Hispanic World in Canada.* Ottawa: 1988.

McKee, D. L. "Some Specifics on the Brain Drain from the Andean Region." *International Migration* 21, no. 4 (1983): 488–99.

Monaghan, Jay. *Chile, Peru, and the California Gold Rush of 1849.* Berkeley: University of California Press, 1973.

Stavans, Ilan. "Two Peruvians: How a Novelist and a Terrorist Came to Represent Peru's Divided Soul." *Utne Reader* (July/August 1994), pp. 96–102.

Personal Responsibility and Work Opportunity Reconciliation Act   See WELFARE REFORM ACT.

Philadelphia, Pennsylvania

Philadelphia became in the 1680s WILLIAM PENN's "greene countrie towne," the capital city of the ethnically diverse PENNSYLVANIA COLONY. It also served as the capital of the new United States of America between 1790 and 1800. During the colonial period, more immigrants disembarked at Philadelphia than at all other British colonial ports in North America combined. Although it gradually lost prominence as a center for immigration, large numbers of European migrants eventually settled in Philadelphia. In 2000, the population of the greater metropolitan area (including Wilmington, Delaware, and Atlantic City, New Jersey) was 6,188,463, and the largest non-British immigrant groups included Irish (1,242,075), German (1,036,116), Italian (886,102), and Polish (343,465). Puerto Ricans (207,855) formed the largest Hispanic group in the city.

The site of Philadelphia was first organized into a town under the Swedes in the 1640s and, after considerable fighting, was finally taken by the English in 1674. It became a prime destination for Quaker and German immigrants seeking to take advantage of Penn's guarantees of religious liberty and bountiful land. Most of these settlers moved into the countryside in the southeastern corner of the colony. Philadelphia itself provided many economic opportunities, however. There were many Quaker merchants and businessmen who took advantage of the fine natural harbor at the confluence of the Delaware and Schuylkill Rivers. By 1710, it had become the largest city in the thirteen colonies—with a population of about 35,000 on the eve of the American Revolution (1775–83)—and remained so until the 1780s, when it was overtaken by New York City (see NEW YORK, NEW YORK). Philadelphia was at the center of the Revolution, hosting the First and Second Continental Congresses (1774–75), being occupied by the British (1777–78), and serving as the meeting place for Congress for the remainder of the war (1778–83). The Constitutional Convention was also held in Philadelphia (1787).

The rapid development of canals, railroads, and other industrial projects attracted large numbers of immigrants during the 19th century, though Philadelphia was no longer a major port of disembarkation. Irish and German immigrants predominated before the Civil War (1861–65), finding many opportunities in Philadelphia's rapidly expanding economy. By the 1840s, the Irish constituted 10 percent of the population. As in most northeastern cities, NATIVISM was strong, with considerable prejudice displayed toward the Irish in particular, who often were willing to work for considerably lower wages than their American-born counterparts. This sparked an ongoing series of anti-Irish riots between May and July of 1844.

Like most eastern seaboard cities, Philadelphia attracted thousands of Jews, Italians, Poles, and Slavs after 1880. As the port of New York became busier with the massive influx of the NEW IMMIGRATION, Philadelphia processed an increasing number of immigrants at its Washington Avenue immigration station, located on the Delaware River in the heart of the wharf district. In 1909, Congress appropriated funds for a new station. Ultimately, the project was abandoned as World War I (1914–18) and restrictive immigration legislation between 1917 and 1924 effectively stemmed the immigrant tide. The city's population grew rapidly, from 850,000 in 1880 to 1.8 million in 1920. The major source of increase after World War II (1939–45), however, was African Americans moving from the south in search of economic opportunities. By 1970, more than one-third of Philadelphia proper was black. After 1965, Philadelphia declined dramatically as a preferred location for immigrant settlement. As European immigration declined and Hispanic (see HISPANIC AND RELATED TERMS) and Asian immigration increased, Los Angeles, San Diego, and San Francisco in California; Miami, Florida; Houston, Texas; and Washington, D.C., all overtook Philadelphia. Among large metropolitan areas in 2000, Philadelphia had the lowest percentage of foreign-born population at 5.1 percent.

Further Reading
Bodnar, John. *The Transplanted: A History of Immigrants in Urban America.* Bloomington: Indiana University Press, 1985.
Clarke, D. *The Irish in Philadelphia: Ten Generations of Urban Experience.* Philadelphia: Temple University Press, 1973.
Feldberg, Michael J. *The Philadelphia Riots of 1844: A Study of Ethnic Conflict.* Westport, Conn.: Greenwood Press, 1975.
Hershberg, Theodore, et al. *Philadelphia: Work, Space, Family and Group Experience in the Nineteenth Century.* New York: Oxford University Press, 1981.
Laurie, Bruce. *Working People of Philadelphia, 1800–1850.* Philadelphia: Temple University Press, 1980.
Stolarik, M. Mark, ed. *Forgotten Doors: The Other Ports of Entry to the United States.* Philadelphia: Balch Institute Press, 1988.
Warner, Sam Bass, Jr. *The Private City: Philadelphia in Three Periods of Its Growth.* Philadelphia: University of Pennsylvania Press, 1968.

Philippine immigration See FILIPINO IMMIGRATION.

picture brides (mail-order brides)

This informal term refers to women who married single immigrant men they had never met but with whom they had exchanged photographs, usually through family intermediaries. Securing picture brides was most common among Japanese and Korean laborers in Hawaii during the early 20th century and was viewed as an extension of the traditional custom of arranged marriages. By the start of the 20th century, thousands of single laborers from Japan and Korea had become established in the United States, but with few single women from their home countries, family life was impossible. The costs of a return trip to Asia to marry was prohibitively expensive, so they used the picture-bride system instead. European immigrants sometimes sent for mail-order brides, as they were usually known in Europe, though with fewer immigration restrictions, there was less gender imbalance among Europeans. A variation of this practice developed in the 1990s, as women seeking escape from poverty and gender limitations in countries of Southeast Asia and eastern Europe advertised themselves through more than 200 matchmaking agencies for marriage to men from economically advanced, western nations.

The vast majority of Asian immigrants arriving in North America were single males, most hoping to earn enough money to return to their homeland and enjoy a better life. More often than not, they stayed, building a new life in America. With a rising tide of anti-Asian sentiment in the United States and Canada, however, and increasingly restrictive regulations in measures such as the CHINESE EXCLUSION ACT (1882), the CHINESE IMMIGRATION ACT (1885), and the GENTLEMEN'S AGREEMENT (1907), it became clear that the gender imbalance would not be redressed. Workers often turned to families or other matchmakers to help them arrange marriages in their home countries. The practice became especially prevalent after 1907, when a loophole in the Gentlemen's Agreement provided that wives of Japanese immigrants were excluded from the new restrictions. As Japan formalized its protectorate of Korea after 1907, the labor immigration of Koreans that had begun in 1903 was curtailed, though families and Japanese marriage agents did arrange for about 1,100 Korean pictures brides to enter the United States before the JOHNSON-REED ACT halted the practice in 1924. Most Japanese and Korean picture brides immigrated to Hawaii, marrying men much older than themselves. They were often shocked to see husbands who looked nothing like their pictures, though most chose to stay rather than return to their previous circumstances.

With economic malaise characteristic of many former Soviet territories, by the late 1990s it is estimated that more than 150,000 women from these regions were using mail-order bride agencies to advertise themselves in an attempt to escape their economic and social circumstances. Western men who sought out wives in this way tended to be well-educated and generally prosperous but, based on recent evidence, felt threatened by the effects of greater gender equity in western countries. The exact number of these arranged marriages is uncertain but probably averaged around 5,000 annually throughout the 1990s, less than 6 percent of the total number of spouses entering the United States and Canada each year. During the 1990s and early 2000s, the great majority of women advertising in North America as potential brides came either from Southeast Asia or the countries of the former Soviet Union.

Although the divorce rate in mail-order marriages appears to be lower than in the population generally, the system is open to abuse by both spouses. A significant number of women clearly used the policy provisions of both the United States and Canada, permitting the naturalization of wives regardless of birth country, in order to bypass ordinary immigration restrictions. Before 1986, foreign spouses in the United States generally were granted permanent residency as a matter of course. Concern over fraudulent marriages led to passage of IMMIGRATION MARRIAGE FRAUD AMENDMENTS (1986, 1990), requiring a two-year wait for conditional resident status for the alien spouse, after which both parties were required to petition the Immigration and Naturalization Service and to undergo personal interviews to determine that the marriage was legitimate. On the other hand, the rate of spousal abuse by men seeking more submissive wives seems to be higher than in the general population. In 1990, the U.S. Congress passed a bill providing for a conditional residency waiver if the spouse could demonstrate that battering or extreme cruelty had led to the dissolution of a good-faith marriage. A series of high-profile murders in Washington State involving mail-order brides led to passage of Washington State Senate Bill 6412 (2002), requiring matchmaking businesses to provide a state background check and marital history upon request to prospective brides in their native language. Senator Jeanne Kohl-Welles, a Democrat and author of the bill, led discussions with members of the U.S. Congress during 2002 about the possibility of passing a similar measure at the federal level.

Further Reading

Anderson, Michell J. "License to Abuse: The Impact of Conditional Status on Female Immigrants." *Yale Law Journal* 102, no. 6: 1,401–1,430.

Bhabha, Jacqueline, Francesca Klug, and Sue Shutter. *Worlds Apart: Women and Immigration and Nationality Law.* London: Pluto Press, 1985.

Collier, Linda, J. "Marriage Market." In *Encyclopedia of American Immigration,* Vol. 1. Ed. James Ciment. Armonk, N.Y.: Sharpe Reference, 2001.

Glodava, Mila, and Richard Onizuka. *Mail Order Brides: Women for Sale.* Fort Collins, Colo.: Alaken, 1994.

Kaprielian-Churchill, Isabel. "Armenian Refugee Women: The Picture Brides, 1920–1930." *Journal of American Ethnic History* 12, no. 3 (1981): 3–29.

Konvitz, Milton R. *The Alien and the Asiatic in American Law.* Ithaca, N.Y.: Cornell University Press, 1946.

Makabe, Tomoko. *Picture Brides: Japanese Women in Canada.* Trans. Kathleen C. Merken. Toronto: Multicultural History Society of Ontario, 1995.

Narayan, Uma. "Male-Order Brides: Immigrant Women, Domestic Violence, and Immigration Law." *Hypatia* 10, no. 1 (Winter 1995): 104–120.

Scholes, Robert J. "The 'Mail-Order Bride' Industry and Its Impact on U.S. Immigration." *Immigration and Naturalization Service Reports and Studies.* Available online. URL: http://www.ins.gov/graphics/aboutins/repsstudies/Mobappa.htm. Updated November 14, 2001.

Washington State Senate Democratic Caucus. "Locke Signs Landmark Measure Protecting Mail-Order Spouses." Available online. URL: http://www.sdc.wa.gov/Releases/Kohl-Welles/mailorder-signing.htm. Updated June 14, 2002.

Pilgrims and Puritans

The Pilgrims and the Puritans were two theologically related Christian groups that developed within the Church of England in the 16th century. Though relatively small in number, Pilgrim and Puritan settlers of the 1620s and 1630s established standards for religious conduct, morality, and hard work that came to represent the English immigrant ideal.

The Pilgrims and the Puritans were the spiritual children of the 16th-century Protestant Reformation, believers in the holiness of God, the sinfulness of humankind, and the ultimate authority of the Bible in matters of faith. King Henry VIII had rejected the authority of the pope and the Roman Catholic Church in 1535, forming the Church of England (Anglican Church) with the English monarch at its head. The Anglican Church remained a state church, with an official hierarchy and many ceremonial elements derived from the Roman church. Many English Christians sought to "purify" the Anglican Church by removing all the old elements of Romanism, including elaborate rituals, sumptuous priestly vestments, and questionable doctrinal statements. By the 1560s, these Anglicans were derisively known as Puritans. Among the Puritans, some believed that the only means of effective reform was to remove themselves from the Anglican Church. Because it was a crime to worship outside the Church of England, "separatist" congregations either had to worship secretly or leave the country. In 1608, a small congregation of Separatists moved from Scrooby, England, to Leyden, in the Netherlands, where they were granted complete freedom of worship. Fearing loss of their English identity, however, and recognizing the lack of economic opportunity in a foreign land, in 1620 a group of 102 settlers, mostly separatists and known as Pilgrims, migrated to America. Blown off course from their original destination in northern Virginia, they established a settlement, Plymouth, at their landing

This painting by Percy Moran shows Pilgrim fathers Myles Standish, William Bradford, William Brewster and John Carver signing the Mayflower Compact in a cabin aboard the Mayflower, 1620. The development of self-government in the American colonies eventually led to revolution against Great Britain, and the establishment of an independent United States of America. *(Library of Congress, Prints & Photographs Division [LC-D419-185])*

spot in southern Massachusetts, several hundred miles north of the location contracted for settlement while in England. Because they were technically outside of English jurisdiction and threatened by anarchy, family heads joined to produce the Mayflower Compact, the first written framework for a government in what is today the United States. After a disastrous first winter, which saw half their number perish, the following summer provided "all things in good plenty," thus leading to a day of giving thanks and the unofficial founding of a national holiday, Thanksgiving, that would be officially established in 1863. Founded in an area of poor soil and little economic opportunity, the colony attracted few settlers. In 1691, Plymouth joined with the more prosperous Massachusetts Bay colony (see MASSACHUSETTS COLONY), some 50 miles to the north, which had been founded by Puritans in 1629.

JOHN WINTHROP and other Puritan leaders worked vigorously to reform the Church of England from within.

By 1629, however, when it became clear that no meaningful reforms were likely, Puritan leaders obtained a royal charter for the Massachusetts Bay colony. With the curbing of religious and political freedoms in England throughout the 1630s, the colony grew rapidly to some 16,000 by the early 1640s. Having removed themselves from the Church of England in America, the Puritans developed an experimental form of church government known as Congregationalism, characterized by village church independence and voluntary association. Puritans also settled the regions of Connecticut (1636; see CONNECTICUT COLONY) and New Hampshire (1623; see NEW HAMPSHIRE COLONY), which were granted colonial charters of their own in 1662 and 1677, respectively.

Further Reading
Bradford, William. *Of Plimmoth Plantation.* Ed. Charles P. Deane. Boston: Massachusetts Historical Society, 1856.

Breen, T. H. *Puritans and Adventurers: Change and Persistence in Early America.* New York: Oxford University Press, 1980.

Gill, Crispin. *Mayflower Remembered: A History of the Plymouth Pilgrims.* New York: Taplinger Publishing, 1970.

Hall, David D. *Puritanism in Seventeenth-Century Massachusetts.* New York: Holt, Rinehart and Winston, 1968.

Kammen, Michael. *Mystic Chords of Memory: The Transformation of Tradition in American Culture.* New York: Vintage Books, 1993.

Langdon, George D. *Pilgrim Colony: A History of New Plymouth, 1620–1691.* New Haven, Conn.: Yale University Press, 1966.

Miller, Perry, and Thomas H. Johnson, eds. *The Puritans.* 2 vols. 2d ed. New York: Harper and Row, 1963.

Winthrop, John. *Winthrop's Journal: "History of New England," 1630–1649.* New York: Charles Scribner's Sons, 1908.

Plyler v. Doe (1982)

In its 1982 ruling, the U.S. Supreme Court found that the state of Texas had failed to support sufficiently its case for the legitimate right of the state to deny education to illegal immigrants. The decision stemmed from the May 1973 decision of the Texas legislature to charge public school tuition to children illegally residing in the state. The restriction of state services, patterned on a number of federal programs, was designed to "prevent undue depletion" of "limited revenues available for education," and explicitly to keep the "ever-increasing flood of illegal aliens" from undermining the "fiscal integrity of the state's school-financing system." The justices struck down the legislation by a 5-4 vote, conceding that public education was not a fundamental right, but arguing that denial of free tuition to illegal aliens violated the equal protection clause of the Fourteenth Amendment to the Constitution. Writing for the minority, Chief Justice Warren Burger argued that "by definition, illegal aliens have no right whatever to be here, and the state may reasonably, and constitutionally, elect not to provide them with governmental service at the expense of those who are lawfully within the state." The increasing tide of illegal immigration during the 1990s led some groups to attempt to have the public services issue reviewed by the more conservative Court of the 1990s. *Plyler v. Doe* was cited in an injunction against California's PROPOSITION 187 (1994), which sought to deny government services to illegal aliens.

Further Reading

Karst, Kenneth. *Belonging to America: Equal Citizenship and the Constitution.* New Haven, Conn.: Yale University Press, 1989.

Kellough, Patrick Henry, and Jean L. Kellough. *Public Education and the Children of Illegal Aliens.* Monticello, Ill.: Vance Bibliographies, 1985.

"Plyler v. Doe." In *Congressional Quarterly. Historic Documents of 1982.* Washington, D.C.: Congressional Quarterly, 1983.

Schuck, Peter H., and Robert M. Smith. *Citizenship without Consent: Illegal Aliens in the American Polity.* New Haven, Conn.: Yale University Press, 1985.

Plymouth Colony   See MASSACHUSETTS COLONY.

Polish immigration

Poles represent the largest eastern European immigrant group in the United States and the second largest in Canada, behind Ukrainians. According to the U.S. census of 2000 and the Canadian census of 2001, 8,977,444 Americans and 817,085 Canadians claimed Polish ancestry. Poles spread throughout the United States, but the majority settled in the industrial North, especially in Buffalo and New York, New York; Chicago, Illinois; Pittsburgh, Pennsylvania; Milwaukee, Wisconsin; Detroit, Michigan; and Cleveland, Ohio. Almost half of Canada's Poles live in Ontario, with large concentrations in Vancouver, British Columbia; Winnipeg, Manitoba; and Montreal, Quebec.

Poland occupies 117,400 square miles on the Baltic Sea in east-central Europe. It is bordered by Germany on the west, the Czech Republic and Slovakia on the south, Lithuania, Belarus, and the Ukraine on the east, and Russia on north. In 2002, the population was 38,633,912. About 94 percent of the people are ethnic Poles and more than 90 percent are Roman Catholic. Slavic tribes in the area were converted to the Roman Catholic Church in the 10th century. Poland was a great power from the 14th to the 17th centuries. Unable to create a strong monarchy, it gradually declined in influence and was eventually partitioned (1772–95) among Prussia, Russia, and Austria, with the core of the country falling under Russian control. During the 19th century, Polish nationalism ran high, leading to a number of failed insurrections. Overrun by the Austro-German armies in World War I (1914–18), Poland declared its independence on November 11, 1918, and was recognized by the Treaty of Versailles in 1919. Germany and the Soviet Union invaded Poland in September 1939, dividing the country. During World War II (1939–45), some 6 million Polish citizens were killed by the Nazis, half of them Jews. With Germany's defeat, a Polish government-in-exile in London was recognized by the United States, but by 1947, Poland fell under the control of its Communist Party, subservient to the Soviet Union. From the 1940s to 1990s, Poland figured largely in the COLD WAR strategies of both the United States and the Soviet Union. In 1980 and 1981, the trade union Solidarity grew to a membership of more than 10 million and began to directly confront the Communist government. By 1989, Poland secured free elections without the interference of the Soviet Union, thus becoming the first partner of the Eastern bloc to break away.

Some Poles came to the United States in the 18th and early 19th centuries, including noblemen Tadeusz Kościuszko and Casimir Pułaski, who fought against the British in the AMERICAN REVOLUTION (1775–83). It has been estimated that about 2,000 Poles immigrated to the

United States between 1800 and 1860, including many lesser nobles and members of the intelligentsia. There were also a number of agricultural communities established in Texas, Michigan, and Wisconsin. The first large settlement of Poles began around 1880 and continued into the 1920s, when the restrictive JOHNSON-REED ACT severely reduced the numbers allowed to enter. Exact figures are impossible to ascertain, as most Poles were counted as immigrants of the states from which they came—usually Prussia, Russia, or Austria. General estimates place the number of Polish immigrants between 1850 and 1914 at about 2.5 million. Until the 1890s, the largest numbers came from Prussia (Germany after 1871), where agricultural modernization and anti-Catholicism drove Poles toward North America. By 1900, perhaps half a million German Poles had immigrated. During the 1880s and 1890s, the downturn in international grain prices hit Austria and Russia particularly hard. Thereafter, Austrian and Russian Poles, generally less skilled and more destitute, became the more common immigrant. Most eventually went to work in mines, steel mills, or the meatpacking industry. By 1914, perhaps 800,000 had come from each country.

During the 1920s, more than 220,000 Poles immigrated to the United States before the Johnson-Reed Act established Poland's quota at fewer than 6,000 per year. By that time, however, Poles were well established in the United States and had already created 800 Polish Roman Catholic parishes. Between 1945 and 1953, more than 150,000 Poles were admitted to the United States, most as refugees or as former Allied combatants (see WORLD WAR II AND IMMIGRATION). By the 1970s, most had entered the American mainstream and were moving away from the inner cities.

A Polish immigrant husks corn, near Greenfield, Connecticut, in 1941. Prior to World War II, most Poles were of the working class and highly concentrated in the northern United States and on the prairies of Canada. *(Photo by John Collier/U.S. Library of Congress #LC-USF34-080865-D)*

After Poland's return to democracy in 1988, there was a resurgence of immigration, with most Polish immigrants seeking to escape from depressed economic conditions in the former communist country. Between 1981 and 2000, about 250,000 Poles came to the United States.

Polish immigration to Canada took roughly the same course as that to the United States. A handful of scattered noblemen, adventurers, and settlers arrived in Canada from the late 18th century through the 1850s. By 1885, perhaps 3,000 Poles lived in Canada, most having emigrated from Prussian territory. Between 1891 and 1921, the number of Poles rose steadily to more than 53,000. Unlike those who settled in the United States, a large percentage were agriculturalists, encouraged in western settlement by Minister of the Interior CLIFFORD SIFTON. Between the reestablishment of Polish independence in 1919 and implementation of the restrictive P.C. 695, about 40,000 Polish immigrants came to Canada, many diverted away from the United States by restrictions of the Johnson-Reed Act. From the 1920s, Toronto gradually replaced Winnipeg as the center of Polish culture in Canada. As in the United States, Canada accepted a large number of Polish refugees in the wake of World War II (1939–45) and the imposition of Soviet control. Between 1945 and 1956, about 64,000 Poles settled in Canada, and the numbers thereafter declined to an average of less than 2,000 per year until 1980. Through the political turmoil of the 1980s, about 10,000 Poles immigrated to Canada annually before numbers leveled off in the 1990s. Of Canada's 180,415 immigrants in 2001, about 70,000 came between 1981 and 1990, and 43,000 between 1991 and 2001.

Further Reading

Avery, D. H., and J. K. Fedorowicz. *The Poles in Canada.* Ottawa: Canadian Historical Association, 1982.

Brozek, Andrzej. *Polish Americans, 1854–1939.* Warsaw, Poland: Interpress, 1985.

Bukowczyk, John J. *And My Children Did Not Know Me: A History of Polish Americans.* Bloomington: Indiana University Press, 1987.

———, ed. *Polish Americans and Their History.* Pittsburgh, Pa.: University of Pittsburgh Press, 1996.

Duscak, T. "The Polish Presence in North America." *Choice* 32, no. 3 (1994): 399–419.

Gory, D. E. "Polish Immigration to America: Before and after the Fall of the Berlin Wall." *Polish Review* 40, no. 1 (1995): 73–79.

Heydenkorn, Benedykt, ed. *Memoirs of Polish Immigrants in Canada.* Toronto: Canadian-Polish Research Institute, 1979.

Kolinski, Dennis. "Polish Rural Settlement in America." *Polish American Studies* 50, no. 2 (Autumn 1995): 21–55.

Makowski, William Boleslaus. *History and Integration of Poles in Canada.* Niagara Peninsula: Canadian Polish Congress, 1967.

Poitrowski, T. *Vengeance of the Swallows: Memoir of a Polish Family's Ordeal under Soviet Aggression, Ukrainian Ethnic Cleansing and Nazi Enslavement, and Their Emigration to America.* Jefferson, N.C.: McFarland, 1995.

Pula, James. *Polish Americans: An Ethnic Community.* New York: Twayne, 1995.

Radecki, Henry, with Benedykt Heydenkorn. *A Member of a Distinguished Family: The Polish Group in Canada.* Toronto: McClelland and Stewart, 1976.

Reczynska, Anna. *For Bread and a Better Future: Emigration from Poland to Canada, 1918–1939.* North York: Multicultural History Society of Ontario, 1996.

Renkiewicz, Frank, ed. *The Polish Presence in Canada and America.* Toronto: Multicultural History Society of Ontario, 1982.

Thomas, William I., and Florian Znaniecki. *The Polish Peasant in Europe and America (1918–1920).* New York: Alfred A. Knopf, 1927.

Znaniecka-Lopata, H. *Polish Americans.* 2d rev. ed. New Brunswick, N.J.: Transaction, 1994.

Zubrzycki, J. *Soldiers and Peasants: The Sociology of Polish Immigration.* London: Orbis, 1988.

Portuguese immigration

The Portuguese have a long tradition of migration—to Brazil, to North America, and to other European countries. Yet of more than 1.5 million Portuguese emigrants between 1880 and 1960, less than 5 percent immigrated to North America. According to the U.S. census of 2000 and the Canadian census of 2001, 1,177,112 Americans and 357,690 Canadians claimed Portuguese ancestry. The largest concentrations of Portuguese Americans lived in New York City, New England, and California. The largest Portuguese communities in Canada were in Toronto and Montreal.

Portugal occupies 35,300 square miles on the Iberian Peninsula in the extreme southwest of Europe, including the Azores and Madeira Islands. Portugal faces the Atlantic on the west and south and borders Spain on the north and east. In 2002, the population was estimated at 10,066,253. About 92 percent are ethnic Portuguese, with the rest of diverse groups, mostly from Portugal's African and Brazilian empire. The chief religion is Roman Catholicism. Most of the Iberian Peninsula was conquered by the Muslim Moors in the eighth century, and local rulers spent the next 700 years driving them out. In the process, Henry of Burgundy was made count of Portucale by King Alfonso VI of Leon and Castile. By the 12th century, Portugal was recognized as an independent kingdom, though it sometimes fell under the political influence of its more powerful neighbor. The Portuguese had a rich seafaring tradition and took the lead in European exploration from the first decade of the 15th century. By the mid-16th century their empire included Brazil, Guinea, Angola, Mozambique, Ceylon, Formosa, and the East Indies. With a small population and relatively few resources, Portugal declined as an international power beginning in the 17th century. A republican revolution in 1910 drove out King Manoel II from power. For much of the 20th century, Portugal was ruled by dictators or military regimes. In 1982, the constitution was revised, however, leading to greater political stability.

Portuguese immigration to the United States was in many ways defined by Portugal's unique geographical positioning in the Atlantic Ocean. The earliest substantial immigration was from the colonial territory of Cape Verde, followed by a new wave beginning in the 1870s from the Azore Islands, then finally by a larger mainland and Madeira Island group from about 1900 on. Once in the United States, however, they tended to identify with the larger Portuguese community. The first Portuguese known in the Americas were Sephardic Jews who settled in Dutch New Amsterdam (later New York City) in the 1650s. One Aaron Lopez became a successful merchant after settling in Newport, Rhode Island, in 1752, and through him a labor connection was established that brought a small number of Portuguese immigrants in the late 18th and early 19th centuries. Most of these were whalers and seamen, including Cape Verdeans of mixed black and Portuguese parentage, who eventually settled in port towns, including New Bedford and Edgartown in Massachusetts; on Long Island, in New York; and Stonington, Connecticut (see CAPE VERDEAN IMMIGRATION). In the 1870s, significant numbers of Azorean Portuguese began to immigrate to the United States, mainly for economic opportunities. Significant numbers also immigrated to Hawaii (then the Sandwich Islands), where they worked on sugar plantations. Portuguese immigration from the mainland began around the turn of the 20th century, peaking at almost 90,000 between 1910 and 1920. Some Portuguese immigrants continued work in the fishing industry, but most settled in mill towns, such as Fall River and Taunton, Massachusetts, or worked as industrial laborers in Providence and Pawtucket, Rhode Island.

Two pieces of legislation greatly reduced Portuguese immigration in the 1920s. First, the IMMIGRATION ACT of 1917 required a literacy test, which few Portuguese could meet. Then the JOHNSON-REED ACT of 1924 established a low quota of emigrants from Portugal. Between 1931 and 1940, only 3,329 were admitted. In 1958, the United States passed the Azorean Refugee Act, admitting 4,800 immigrants from the island of Fayal in the wake of volcanic eruptions and earthquakes. With passage of the IMMIGRATION AND NATIONALITY ACT of 1965, which abolished racial quotas, there was a great resurgence of Portuguese immigration. During the following 20 years, almost 200,000 came to the United States. Between 1991 and 2002, the annual average immigration from Portugal was little more than 2,000.

Portuguese immigration to Canada was much slower in beginning, but the official numbers are generally considered to be greatly understated. Portuguese fishermen had plied Canadian waters since the 15th century but left no permanent settlements. Between 1900 and 1950, only about 500 Portuguese came to Canada, many illegally. In the 1950s, however, Canada openly sought agricultural and construction workers, and the Portuguese were eager to fill the positions. Almost 140,000 settled in Canada in the 1960s and 1970s, the peak period of immigration. The majority were single men from the Azores, and they lived in poor housing in the inner cities. Although they gradually progressed in the economy, most Portuguese remained out of the Canadian cultural mainstream at the turn of the 21st century. From the 1970s on, Portuguese immigration to Canada steadily declined. Of the 153,535 Portuguese immigrants in Canada in 2001, about 43,000 came between 1981 and 2001.

Further Reading

Anderson, Grace, and David Higgs. *"A Future to Inherit": The Portuguese Communities of Canada.* Toronto: McClelland and Stewart, 1976.

Cardoso, Manoel da Silveira. *The Portuguese in America: 590 B.C.–1974: A Chronology and Fact Book.* Dobbs Ferry, N.Y.: Oceana Publications, 1976.

Dias, E. Mayone. "Portuguese Immigration to the East Coast of the United States and California: Contrasting Patterns." In *Portugal in Development: Emigration, Industrialization, the European Community.* Eds. T. C. Brueau, V. M P. Da Rosa, and A. Macleod. Ottawa: University of Ottawa Press, 1984.

Higgs, David. *The Portuguese in Canada.* St. John: Canadian Historical Association, 1982.

———, ed. *Portuguese Migration in Global Perspective.* Toronto: University of Toronto Press, 1990.

Joy, Annamma. *Ethnicity in Canada: Social Accommodation and Cultural Persistence among the Sikhs and the Portuguese.* New York: AMS Press, 1989.

Noivo, Edite. *Inside Ethnic Families: Three Generations of Portuguese-Canadians.* Montreal: McGill–Queen's University Press, 1998.

Pap, Leo. *The Portuguese-Americans.* New York: Twayne, 1981.

———. *The Portuguese in the United States: A Bibliography.* New York: Center for Migration Studies, 1976.

Williams, J. *And Yet They Come: Portuguese Immigration from the Azores to the United States.* New York: Center for Migration Studies, 1982.

Prince Edward Island

Ile-St.-Jean (Isle St. John) was claimed for France by SAMUEL DE CHAMPLAIN in 1603. It was sparsely populated and was part of ACADIA, in NEW FRANCE. French immigrants began to settle the island in the 1720s, but numbers remained small, and France ceded it to Britain following the SEVEN YEARS' WAR (1756–63). After Britain acquired the territory, it anglicized the island's name. The number of settlers remained small, both because of its isolation and the difficulty for colonists to acquire clear title to the land. In 1767, the British government issued land grants to military officers and others, requiring that they bring in colonists in order to redeem their lands. Few attempted to fulfill this requirement, and absentee landlords often made outright purchase difficult. This drove many of the 600 United

Empire Loyalists, who had emigrated from America by way of Nova Scotia in 1783–84, to seek residence in other parts of the empire. Until 1769, the Isle St. John was governed as part of NOVA SCOTIA. In 1799, the British government changed the island's name to Prince Edward Island.

The first large-scale immigration to Prince Edward Island began in 1772 when 300 displaced Highland Scots arrived on the island, establishing a trend that would continue for more than 50 years as the Scottish Highlands were cleared for grazing. Among the philanthropists who promoted emigration, the most successful was THOMAS DOUGLAS, fifth earl of Selkirk, who assisted 800 Highlanders to emigrate in 1803 and hundreds more in succeeding years.

Prince Edward Island gained self-government in 1851. In 1867, it refused to join the Dominion of Canada, fearing that it would lose political control of the island. An economic downturn in the early 1870s, however, convinced most of the islanders that federation was a wise policy. In 1873, Prince Edward Island joined the Dominion of Canada as the seventh province.

Further Reading

Brown, Wallace. *The King's Friends: The Composition and Motives of the American Loyalist Claimants.* Providence, R.I.: Brown University Press, 1965.

Bumsted, J. M. *Land, Settlement, and Politics on Eighteenth Century Prince Edward Island.* Kingston, Canada: McGill–Queens University Press, 1987.

Careless, J. M. S., ed. *Colonists and Canadiens, 1760–1867.* Toronto: Macmillan of Canada, 1971.

Cowan, Helen I. *British Emigration to British North America: The First Hundred Years.* University of Toronto Press, 1961.

MacNutt, W. S. *The Atlantic Provinces: The Emergence of Colonial Society, 1712–1857.* Toronto: McClelland and Stewart, 1965.

Moore, Christopher. *The Loyalists: Revolution, Exile, Settlement.* Toronto: Macmillan of Canada, 1984.

Selkirk, Lord. *Lord Selkirk's Diary, 1803–1804: A Journal of His Travels in British North America and the Northeastern United States.* Ed. Patrick C. T. White. Toronto: Champlain Society, 1958.

Wilson, Bruce. *Colonial Identities: Canada from 1760–1815.* Ottawa: National Archives of Canada, 1988.

Proposition 187 (Save Our State Initiative)

Proposition 187 was a controversial California anti-immigration initiative approved by California voters on November 8, 1994. Because some of its provisions were almost certainly unconstitutional, federal injunctions prohibited its implementation; nonetheless, Proposition 187 symbolized a growing NATIVISM in the United States at the end of the 20th century.

Concern over the cost of providing social services to illegal immigrants, the increase of immigrant-related crime, and fear of a continuing flow of illegal immigrants from Mexico led Californians to approve (59 percent to 41 percent)

Proposition 187, which denied education, welfare benefits, and nonemergency health care to illegal immigrants. In 1994, it was estimated that more than 40 percent of all illegal immigrants in the United States were in California.

Anticipating legal challenges, proponents of Proposition 187 included language to safeguard all provisions not specifically deemed invalid by the courts. Decisions by federal judges in both 1995 and 1998, however, upheld previous decisions regarding the unconstitutionality of the proposition's provisions, based on Fourteenth Amendment protections against discriminating against one class of people, in this case immigrants.

See also PLYLER V. DOE.

Further Reading

Martin, Philip. "Proposition 187 in California." *International Migration Review* 29 (1995): 255–263.

Ono, Kent, and John M. Sloop. *Shifting Borders: Rhetoric, Immigration, and California's Proposition 187.* Philadelphia: Temple University Press, 2002.

Puerto Rican immigration

Puerto Rico is a Caribbean island commonwealth of the United States, located about 1,000 miles southeast of Miami. Puerto Ricans are U.S. citizens but do not pay federal taxes or vote in presidential elections while living in Puerto Rico. They are not required to have visas or passports to travel to the United States, and there are no quotas on their entry. According to the U.S. census of 2000 and the Canadian census of 2001, 3,406,178 Americans claimed Puerto Rican ancestry, while only 1,045 Canadians did so. More than 1.3 million Puerto Ricans live in the New York City area, and there are significant communities in Chicago, Miami, and most of the major cities in the East. During the 1990s, Puerto Ricans increasingly chose smaller towns and cities in Texas, California, and Florida.

Puerto Rico covers 3,515 square miles, facing the Atlantic Ocean to the north and the Caribbean Sea to the south. Puerto Rico was inhabited by Arawak Indians when CHRISTOPHER COLUMBUS first claimed the land for Spain in 1493. Within a few decades, virtually all the native peoples had died of disease, war, or forced labor. More than 95 percent of the population of 3,829,000 (2001) consider themselves Puerto Ricans. They are mainly descended from Europeans—most notably Spaniards, and some Corsicans, Irish, and Germans—with some Indian influences from the early period and a significant African component from the long period of slavery between the 16th and 19th centuries. Under the Spanish Crown, Puerto Rico remained relatively poor and enjoyed virtually no political rights. As a result, nationalistic rebellions broke out in the 1830s, 1860s, and 1890s. Through the Spanish-American War of 1898, the United States gained control of Puerto Rico (along with the

Philippines and Guam) and in 1900 passed the Organic (Foraker) Act, which established a civilian government largely under the control of a governor appointed by the U.S. president. The Jones Act of 1917 provided more autonomy and conferred U.S. citizenship on Puerto Ricans but left most of the power in the hands of the governor. The Crawford-Butler Act of 1947 enabled Puerto Ricans to elect their own governor, and in 1952, a new constitution was authorized, making Puerto Rico a commonwealth in association with the United States. Apart from matters of foreign policy and currency, Puerto Rico is largely autonomous. The debate over Puerto Rico's future course—full independence, continued autonomy as a commonwealth, or full statehood in the Union—raged throughout the 1980s and 1990s. Economically, the commonwealth has benefited from its association with the United States, though not as much as many had hoped. Puerto Rico has the highest per-capita income among Caribbean islands, but it would have the lowest among the states of the United States. In a nonbinding 1998 referendum, 46.5 percent of Puerto Ricans voted for statehood, demonstrating how deeply divided the population remains on the issue.

The first significant migration to U.S. territory involved 5,000 Puerto Rican contract laborers who were hired to work on sugar plantations in Hawaii between 1899 and 1901. Others began to migrate to the continental United States after World War I (1914–18). Between 1910 and 1930, the Puerto Rican population in the United States grew from 1,500 to more than 52,000. Ten years later, Puerto Ricans numbered 70,000, with 88 percent living in New York City. Improved transportation technologies, including low-cost commercial air travel, dramatically increased the rate of Puerto Rican migration after World War II (1939–45). Throughout the 1950s, an average of 45,000 came to the United States annually, with increasingly diversified destinations. By 1970, the percentage of Puerto Ricans living in New York City had declined to less than 60 percent. After a downturn in numbers in the 1970s, structural problems in the economy led to a renewed migration after 1980. Since World War II, there has always been a high rate of return migration. The numbers of Puerto Ricans in the United States nevertheless has risen significantly in every decade, from some 1.5 million in 1970 to 2 million by 1980, 2.7 million in 1990, and 3.4 million in 2000.

Further Reading

Ambert, Alba N., and María D. Álvarez, eds. *Puerto Rican Children on the Mainland: Interdisciplinary Perspectives.* New York: Garland, 1992.

Díaz-Briquets, Sergio, and Sidney Weintraub, eds. *Determinants of Emigration from Mexico, Central America, and the Caribbean.* Boulder, Colo.: Westview Press, 1991.

Rivera-Batiz, Francisco, and Carlos E. Santiago. *Island Paradox: Puerto Rico in the 1990s.* New York: Russell Sage Foundation, 1998.

———. *Puerto Ricans in the United States: A Changing Reality.* Washington, D.C.: National Puerto Rican Coalition, 1994.

Rodríguez, Clara. *Puerto Ricans: Born in the USA.* Boston: Unwin Hyman, 1989.

Sánchez-Korrol, Virginia. *From Colonia to Community: The History of Puerto Ricans in New York City, 1917–1948.* Westport, Conn.: Greenwood Press, 1983.

Torre, Carlos Antonio, Hugo Rodríguez Vecchini, and William Burgos, eds. *The Commuter Nation: Perspectives on Puerto Rican Migration.* Río Piedras, Puerto Rico: Editorial de la Universidad de Puerto Rico, 1994.

Torres, Andrés. *Between the Melting Pot and the Mosaic: African Americans and Puerto Ricans in the New York Political Economy.* Philadelphia: Temple University Press, 1995.

Puritans   See PILGRIMS AND PURITANS.

Quaker immigration

The Quakers, officially members of the Religious Society of Friends, were a pietistic Christian sect founded by George Fox in England in the 1640s. Quakers believed that Christ's presence in the hearts of individuals provided an inner light that would guide them in their beliefs and actions. As a result, they emphasized inward spiritual experience rather than conformity to outward creeds. At a time when all European states expected conformity to a state church, and the Church of England had the strong support of a parliament fearful of dissent, the Quakers were considered radical and were often persecuted. In practice, they were generally pacifists, egalitarians, and social reformers, emphasizing society's common humanitarian concerns. But they refused to swear oaths in court or recognize distinctions in society and as such were both annoying and potentially dangerous to the state and the aristocratic society in which they lived. Quaker missionaries first immigrated to the Massachusetts Bay colony in 1656, where they were not well received. Puritan magistrates drove them out of the colony and ordered the execution of several Friends between 1659 and 1661.

The transformation of Quakers from mistrusted religious radicals to model pioneers was largely the work of WILLIAM PENN, who was born into an aristocratic English family. Penn was expelled from Oxford University in 1662 for unorthodox religious views and eventually joined the Society of Friends. In 1668, he published *Truth Exalted,* the first of his 150 books, pamphlets, and tracts, and traveled extensively in Britain and Europe, preaching and promoting

the doctrines of the Quakers. Violating numerous laws prohibiting non-Anglican (Church of England) preaching, meeting, and publishing, he spent two years in prison. He nevertheless was well connected politically, having friends among the supporters of the Stuart kings as well as the Whigs who opposed the Stuart monarchy. When the NEW JERSEY COLONY foundered, in 1674, a group of Quaker investors, including Penn, bought a stake in it and divided it into East Jersey and West Jersey. West Jersey became the first Quaker colony in America, but it eventually went bankrupt and was rejoined to East Jersey in 1702 to form a royal colony. Dismayed by Quaker quarreling in Jersey, in the late 1670s, Penn turned his attention to the unsettled land west of Jersey as a possible refuge for persecuted European Quakers. In 1681, he was granted a royal charter guaranteeing both land and governance, thereby enabling him to establish the PENNSYLVANIA COLONY from the first according to Quaker principles.

In 1682, Penn published his *Frame of Government,* which established the principles of liberty of conscience, freedom from persecution, and due process of law. In the same year, he purchased the Three Lower Counties (later, DELAWARE COLONY) from James, Duke of York, in order to guarantee access to the sea. As a proprietor, he advertised widely throughout England, Ireland, and the German states, lauding the rich Pennsylvania soil and the high degree of personal freedoms enjoyed there. Indeed, the colony became a model of the religious toleration that Penn so deeply supported. Although Quakers held the most influential positions of leadership and governed according to Quaker principles—there was no army and only a small police force—Pennsylvania was from the first both ethnically and religiously diverse. In 1685 alone, 8,000 immigrants arrived, most of them Quakers from the British Isles. They largely settled in southeastern Pennsylvania, around the cosmopolitan city of PHILADELPHIA. Between the 1680s and the 1720s, Mennonites, Amish, Moravians, Dunkers, Schwenkfelders, and Lutherans arrived from across Europe and soon outnumbered the Quakers. Only a few years into the colony's development, Penn could boast that the people of Pennsylvania were "a collection of divers nations in Europe," including "French, Dutch, Germans, Swedes, Danes, Finns, Scotch, Irish, and English."

Diversity and toleration together produced an unruly political process in Pennsylvania, with the Quaker-dominated urban areas frequently at odds with the country, especially the Three Lower Counties, which were inhabited principally by Dutch, Swedish, and Finnish settlers who had little connection with Penn. In 1701, Penn's Charter of Liberties granted political control to a unicameral assembly, free from proprietary influence. By 1725, most of the 25,000 Quakers who had immigrated to the Delaware Valley lived in Pennsylvania. By 1760, Germans accounted for more than one-third of the entire population of the colony, and after 1760, German and Scots-Irish settlers rapidly filled the trans-Appalachian Pennsylvania west, far from Quaker influence and English control. By 1756, Quakers had lost political control in the colony.

Further Reading

Barclay, Robert. *Barclay's "Apology" in Modern English*. Ed. Dean Friday. Richmond, Ind.: Friends United, 1967.

Davies, Adrian. *The Quakers in English Society, 1655–1725*. New York: Clarendon Press of Oxford University Press, 2000.

Moore, Rosemary. *The Light in Their Consciences: Early Quakers in Britain, 1646–1666*. University Park: Pennsylvania State University Press, 2000.

Trueblood, Elton. *The People Called Quakers*. Richmond, Ind.: Friends United, 1971.

Quebec

The Canadian province of Quebec is unique in North America in maintaining a predominantly French heritage, despite being surrounded by English-speaking areas that would eventually become the Canadian provinces of Ontario, New Brunswick, and Newfoundland and the U.S. states of Maine, Vermont, New Hampshire, and New York. As a result, Quebec eventually gained a considerable measure of autonomy and an independent immigration policy.

SAMUEL DE CHAMPLAIN founded the first permanent French settlement at Quebec in 1608, a fur-trading post that linked France with the vast interior regions of North Amer-

Samuel de Champlain founded the first permanent French settlement in the New World at Quebec in 1608. *(Library of Congress, Prints & Photographs Division [LC-USZ62-97748])*

ica that formed the core of the large colonial territory known as NEW FRANCE. Along with the commercial impulse came missionaries. In 1642, the Société de Notre-Dame de Montréal pour la conversion des Sauvages de la Nouvelle France founded Ville Marie, later known as MONTREAL. Administrative mismanagement, failure to secure settlers, and the constant threat from the region's Native Americans brought a complete reorganization of the government, which was brought under royal control in 1663. During the entire period of French control, only about 12,000 permanent settlers immigrated to New France, with most concentrated along the St. Lawrence Seaway, which came to be known as Canada and is roughly coterminus with the modern province of Quebec. According to a Swedish visitor in the 18th century, the heartland of Canada was "a village beginning at Montreal and ending at Quebec," for "the farmhouses are never above five arpents [293 meters] and sometimes but three apart, a few places excepted."

Through an agreement with the French West Indies Company, between 1663 and 1673, several thousand settlers arrived, most from Brittany and Île-de-France, though some were recruited from Holland, Portugal, and various German states. Among this wave of immigrants, however, there were few families. Most were trappers, soldiers, churchmen, prisoners, and young indentured servants (see INDENTURED SERVITUDE); by 1672, all plans for systematic immigration were stopped. After 1706, merchants from a number of European countries and their local agents were granted permission to do business in Canada, leading to a thriving trade in Quebec and Montreal. Indentured servants occasionally came, and soldiers stationed in the colony as a result of the ongoing conflict with Britain sometimes stayed on. The number of slaves was always small, perhaps 4,000 Native American and African slaves for the entire duration of New France. More than a thousand convicts were forcibly transported. Remarkably, from this miscellaneous and meager collection of 9,000 immigrants, the population of Canada swelled to 70,000 by the 1750s. In a series of wars for control of North America (1689–1763), virtually all of New France was lost to the British, the final blow coming in the SEVEN YEARS' WAR (1756–63).

In 1763, France signed the Treaty of Paris, handing over New France east of the Mississippi River to Great Britain. Canada's French population of some 70,000 was brought under control of the British Crown, which organized the most populous areas as the colony of Quebec. At first administering the region under British law and denying Catholics important rights, the British further alienated their new citizens. In an attempt to win support of Quebec's French-speaking population, Governor Guy Carleton in 1774 persuaded the British parliament to pass the QUEBEC ACT (1774), which guaranteed religious freedom to Catholics, reinstated French civil law, and extended the southern border of the province to the Ohio River, incorporating lands claimed by Virginia and Massachusetts. This marked the high point of escalating tensions that led to the American Revolution (1775–83) and eventual loss of the thirteen colonies and trans-Appalachian regions south of the Great Lakes.

Loss of the thirteen colonies led to the migration of 40,000–50,000 United Empire Loyalists, who had refused to take up arms against the British Crown and who were thus resettled at government expense, most with grants of land in NOVA SCOTIA, NEW BRUNSWICK, and western Quebec. The special provisions of the Quebec Act, which aimed at preserving French culture and encouraging loyalty, angered the new English-speaking American colonists. As a result, the British government divided the region into two colonies by the Constitutional Act of 1791. Lower Canada, roughly the modern province of Quebec, included most of the French-speaking population. There, government was based on French civil law, Catholicism, and the seigneurial system of land settlement. Upper Canada, roughly the modern province of Ontario, included most of the English-speaking population and used English law and property

systems. Both colonies had weak elected assemblies. After the French Revolution, Revolutionary Wars, and Napoleonic Wars (1789–1815), hard times led English, Irish, and Scottish people to immigrate to British North America in record numbers. Fearing loss of control of the government of Lower Canada, some French Canadians revolted in 1837, which triggered a rebellion in Upper Canada. Both rebellions were quickly quashed, and the British government unified the two Canadas into the single Province of Canada (1841). This form of government did not work well, however, as the main political parties had almost equal representation in the legislature and thus had trouble forming stable ministries.

From 1848, the rapidly growing provinces in British North America won self-government and virtual control over local affairs. By the 1860s, there was general agreement on the need for a stronger central government, which led to the confederation movement. Passage of the British North America Act in 1867 created the Dominion of Canada and reestablished French-speaking Quebec as a separate province. Although citizens of Quebec were permitted to use both French and English as their official language and granted control of education and civil law, friction over a wide variety of issues heightened the province's sense of isolation. Quebec disapproved of government policies during the Boer War (1899–1902), World War I (1914–18), and World War II (1939–45). It was the most isolationist part of Canada, vigorously opposing all immigration but especially the immigration of Jews. By 1968, an independent Ministry of Immigration of Quebec was established, enabling Québecois to maintain control of the ethnic population of the province, ensuring the priority of francophone culture. Leaders also opposed vigorous industrialization, as enriching English entrepreneurs while destroying traditional French-Canadian culture. Finally, in the 1960s widespread disagreement over apportionment of taxes led to a separatist movement that continued into the 21st century under the banner of the Parti Québecois (formed in 1968). In a dramatic referendum in October 1995, with more than 94 percent of the electorate casting ballots, 50.6 percent voted against Quebec sovereignty. Parti Québecois leaders openly blamed "ethnics" for siding with the anglophones in order to thwart independence. Most observers believe that Quebec's independence will come in the relatively near future.

Montreal is the economic heart of the province of Quebec and thus attracts a large number of migrants from other parts of Canada, as well as immigrants from outside the country. The city of Quebec, on the other hand is more homogenous and more closely reflects the traditional concerns of the French founders. The largest non-European ethnic groups in Montreal in 2001 were Haitian (69,945, 2.1 percent of the population), Chinese (57,655, 1.7 percent of the population), and Greek (55,865, 1.6 percent of the population). No non-European ethnic group in the city of Quebec numbered more than 1,400, or 0.2 percent of the population (Chinese).

See also CANADA—IMMIGRATION SURVEY AND POLICY REVIEW.

Further Reading

Anctil, Pierre, and Gary Caldwell, eds. *Juifs et réalités juives au Quebec.* Quebec: Institut québecois de recherche sur la culture, 1984.

Behiels, Michael D. *Quebec and the Question of Immigration: From Ethnocentrism to Ethnic Pluralism, 1900–1985.* Ottawa: Canadian Historical Association, 1991.

Cairns, Alan C. *Charter versus Federalism: The Dilemmas of Constitutional Reform.* Montreal and Kingston: McGill–Queen's University Press, 1992.

Eccles, William J. *Canada under Louis XIV, 1663–1701.* Toronto: McClelland and Stewart, 1964.

———. *France in America.* New York: Harper and Row, 1972.

Martel, Marcel. *French Canada: An Account of Its Creation and Break-Up, 1850–1967.* Ottawa: Canadian Historical Association, 1998.

Ministère d'Immigration, *Rapport Annuel, 1980–81.* Quebec: Ministère d'Immigration, 1981.

Moogk, Peter N. *La Nouvelle France: The Making of French Canada—A Cultural History.* East Lansing: Michigan State University Press, 2000.

Pâquet, Martin. *Toward a Quebec Ministry of Immigration, 1945–1968.* Ottawa: Canadian Historical Association, 1997.

Trigger, Bruce G. *Natives and Newcomers: Canada's "Heroic Age" Reconsidered.* Kingston, Canada: McGill–Queen's University Press, 1987.

Vachon, André. *Dreams of Empire: Canada before 1700.* Ottawa: Public Archives of Canada, 1982.

Quebec Act (1774)

The Quebec Act of 1774 was passed by Great Britain on the heels of a constitutional crisis in Massachusetts and the failure of attempts to attract English-speaking immigrants to QUEBEC, the French culture region they had acquired at the end of the SEVEN YEARS' WAR (1756–63).

Following the war, Britain had ruled Canada by military authority. In the Proclamation of 1763, Britain prohibited settlement beyond the Appalachian Mountains, hoping to attract English-speaking settlers northward, both to dilute French influence and to halt the expansion of self-governing colonies. Having little success, Governor Guy Carleton determined that Canada would always have a French-speaking majority and that Britain should thus do all it could to gain the loyalty of the inhabitants in the event of rebellion in the thirteen colonies to the south. The Quebec Act acknowledged that "experience" had dictated that 65,000 French Catholics could not be governed according to English principles and that it was "inexpedient" at the moment to form an elective assembly. The king would thus appoint a provincial council that would oversee the continued application of French civil law in the colony and guarantee the right to practice Roman Catholicism. These provisions angered English settlers there, who in 1763 had been promised a representative assembly and a British system of law. More provocatively, the act enlarged Quebec to include much of what is now Quebec and Ontario, the area bounded by the Great Lakes, the Ohio River, the Appalachian Mountains, and the Mississippi River. Although not overtly directed at Massachusetts, the Quebec Act was the final in a series of coercive measures—the "Intolerable Acts" as they were dubbed in Massachusetts—that imposed greater Crown control over colonial politics and justice. These coercive measures led to the calling of the First Continental Congress in September 1774. Most French Canadians remained neutral during the AMERICAN REVOLUTION, (1775–83), which secured for the newly independent colonies the Ohio and Mississippi River Valleys.

Further Reading

Bailyn, Bernard, and Philip D. Morgan, eds. *Strangers within the Realm: Cultural Margins of the First British Empire.* Chapel Hill: University of North Carolina Press, 1991.

Lawson, Philip. *The Imperial Challenge: Quebec and Britain in the Age of the American Revolution.* Montreal and Kingston: McGill–Queen's University Press, 1990.

Neatby, Hilda. *Quebec, 1760–1791.* Toronto: McClelland and Stewart, 1966.

———, ed. *The Quebec Act: Protest and Policy.* Scarborough, Canada: Prentice-Hall, 1972.

Stanley, George. *Canada Invaded, 1775–1776.* Toronto: Hakkert, 1973.

racial and ethnic categories

Immigration in the 19th and 20th centuries transformed Canada and the United States from countries predominantly populated by west Europeans (notably English, French, Scots-Irish, and German) to countries composed of most of the world's racial and ethnic groups. Between 1950 and 1998, for instance, the minority population of the United States more than tripled, and it was estimated that by the middle of the 21st century, non-Hispanic whites would constitute only about 50 percent of the population. In an attempt to understand and plan for the results of population changes, questions regarding race and ethnicity have been part of the immigration process and census taking in North America over the years, though in a variety of forms according to the needs of the day (see CENSUS AND IMMIGRATION). These questions were introduced in Canada in 1765 and in the United States in 1790. Racial and ethnic identification became an essential part of governmental planning from the 1840s onward in the wake of the Irish famine, or Great Potato Famine (1845–51), and the wave of immigration that swept the United States and Canada between 1865 and 1914. There has never been a universally accepted definition of race, however. At various times in history it has stood for contemporary concepts of tribe, nation, or ethnic group. Since the 18th century *race* was increasingly used to distinguish a group based on skin color and other physical characteristics. The classification most commonly accepted throughout the West recognized three major races: Caucasians (white), Mongolians (yellow), and Africans

(black). Other taxonomists incorporated personality and moral traits in identifying race. As the 19th century progressed, romantic thought and Darwinism combined with racial classification to create an intellectual atmosphere in which RACISM flourished.

United States

Although the United States did not explicitly incorporate racial concepts into immigration policy until the CHINESE EXCLUSION ACT (1882), the practice of slavery in the South until 1865 implicitly recognized racial distinctions. Also, from colonial times, there were perceptions of desirable and undesirable immigrants. In the 1924 JOHNSON-REED ACT, the foundation of U.S. immigration policy until 1965, the government established permanent quotas based on 2 percent of the foreign-born population in 1890, reflecting the "racial" composition of the country prior to massive immigration from southern and eastern Europe. During the latter half of the 20th century, an understanding of genetics and the dramatic increase of mobility and hybridization led most scholars to accept the inadequacy of traditional racial classifications in explaining human biodiversity. By the start of the 21st century, ethnicity, rather than race, was seen as a more valuable tool for analysis and explanation, as it incorporated language, religion, geography, and custom in establishing group identities.

In addressing the needs of its citizens, however, the U.S. government could not altogether dispense with historical racial classifications. The close association of slavery and race and the lingering effects of racism encouraged in African Americans a strong sense of racial identity according to the older conception. On the other hand, the fastest-growing minority category of Hispanics was culturally, rather than racially, based (see HISPANIC AND RELATED TERMS). Quantification was especially important in 2000, as the census directly affected legislative redistricting and fair political representation. The 2000 census therefore asked two overlapping questions regarding race and Hispanic origin. Respondents were given a wide range of terms with which to identify themselves, including both traditional racial concepts (for example, "white"; "Black, African Am., or Negro"; "American Indian or Alaska Native") and specific ethnic groups (for example, "Asian Indian" or "Native Hawaiian"). In addition, respondents could identify themselves as "some other race," writing in their own self-designation. In 2000, the Office of Management and Budget (OMB) established the following definitions regarding racial and ethnic categorization for use in the census:

> *"White" refers to people having origins in any of the original peoples of Europe, the Middle East, or North Africa. It includes people who indicated their race or races as "White" or wrote in entries such as Irish, German, Italian, Lebanese, Near Easterner, Arab, or Polish.*
>
> *"Black or African American" refers to people having origins in any of the black racial groups of Africa. It includes people who indicated their race or races as "Black, African Am., or Negro" or wrote in entries such as African American, Afro American, Nigerian, or Haitian.*
>
> *"American Indian or Alaska Native" refers to people having origins in any of the original peoples of North, Central, and South America and who maintain tribal affiliation or community attachment. It includes people who indicated their race or races by marking this category or writing in their principal or enrolled tribe, such as Rosebud Sioux, Chippewa, or Navajo.*
>
> *"Asian" refers to people having origins in any of the original peoples of the Far East, Southeast Asia, or the Indian subcontinent. It includes people who indicated their race or races as "Asian Indian," "Chinese," "Filipino," "Korean," "Japanese," "Vietnamese," or "Other Asian," or wrote in entries such as Burmese, Hmong, Pakistani, or Thai.*
>
> *"Native Hawaiian and Other Pacific Islander" refers to people having origins in any of the original peoples of Hawaii, Guam, Samoa, or other Pacific Islands. It includes people who indicated their race or races as "Native Hawaiian," "Guamanian or Chamorro," "Samoan," or "Other Pacific Islander" or wrote in entries such as Tahitian, Mariana Islander, or Chuukese.*
>
> *"Some other race" was included in U.S. Census 2000 for respondents who were unable to identify with the five OMB race categories. Respondents who provided write-in entries such as Moroccan, South African, Belizean, or a Hispanic origin (for example, Mexican, Puerto Rican, or Cuban) are included in the Some Other Race category.*

For statistical purposes, the government understood that "Spanish/Hispanic/Latino" could refer to people of any race. The OMB defined "Hispanic or Latino" as "a person of Cuban, Mexican, Puerto Rican, South or Central American, or other Spanish culture or origin regardless of race."

Canada

Canada's unique history led to a distinct set of racial and ethnic classifications for purposes of enumeration and policy development, including those of European descent, those of "Aboriginal" (that is, indigenous) ancestry, an increasing number of immigrants who fit neither category, and those of multiple ethnic origins. Questions regarding race and ethnicity were modified on the 1996 census.

Before 1996, the 15 most frequent origins were listed after the question, "To what ethnic or cultural group(s) did this person's [the respondent's] ancestors belong?" along with two blank spaces for others answers to be included. In 1996, no prelisted categories were included after the question, although 24 examples of possible origins were listed, including, for the first time, "Canadian." In 1996, 5.3 million persons (19 percent) considered "Canadian" as their only ethnic origin, while another 3.5 million persons (12 percent) reported their origins to be "Canadian" and some other ethnic group. As a result of this change, which allows almost unlimited self-identification, it is difficult to compare ancestry figures before and after 1996. With no prelisted census categories, Statistics Canada categorized responses for compilation purposes.

Most ethnic questions were self-explanatory, though some require clear definition. Respondents who reported "French-only ancestry" include both those who listed France as the country of origin and those who listed Acadia as the basis of their ethnic origin. Both "North American Indian ancestry" and "Métis ancestry" (European and Indian) were considered in the compilation of "Aboriginal" figures. Finally, using the Employment Equity Act definition, the census defined a "visible minority" as "Persons, other than Aboriginal peoples, who are not-Caucasian in race or non-white in color," and incorporates in this category self-identified responses including Chinese, South Asians, Blacks, Arabs and West Asians, Filipinos, Southeast Asians, Latin Americans, Japanese, Koreans, and Pacific Islanders.

See also CANADA—IMMIGRATION SURVEY AND POLICY REVIEW; UNITED STATES—IMMIGRATION SURVEY AND POLICY REVIEW.

Further Reading

Baker, Lee D. *From Savage to Negro: Anthropology and the Construction of Race, 1896–1954.* Berkeley: University of California Press, 1998.

Banton, Michael, and Jonathan Harwood. *The Race Concept.* New York: Praeger, 1975.

Driedger, Leo, and Shiva S. Halli. *Race and Racism: Canada's Challenge.* Montreal: McGill–Queen's University Press, 2000.

Gossett, Thomas. *Race: The History of an Idea in America.* New York: Oxford University Press, 1997.

Grieco, Elizabeth M., and Rachel C. Cassidy. "Overview of Race and Hispanic Origin: Census 2000 Brief." Washington, D.C.: U.S. Census Bureau, C2KBR/01–1, March 2001.

Hannaford, Ivan. *Race: The History of an Idea in the West.* Baltimore: Johns Hopkins University Press, 1996.

Lee, Sharon M. *Using the New Racial Categories in the 2000 Census, A KIDS COUNT/PRB Report on Census 2000.* Washington, D.C.: Annie E. Casey Foundation and the Population Reference Bureau, March 2001.

Pollard, Kelvin M., and William P. O'Hare. "America's Racial and Ethnic Minorities." *Population Bulletin* 54, no. 3 (September 1999).

Sorensen. E., et al. *Immigrant Categories and the U.S. Job Market.* Washington, D.C.: Urban Institute Press, 1992.

Spain, Daphne. *America's Diversity: On the Edge of Two Centuries.* Washington, D.C.: Population Reference Bureau, 1999.

Statistics Canada. "1996 Census: Ethnic Origin, Visible Minorities." Statistics Canada Web site. Available online. URL: http://www.statcan.ca/Daily/English/980217/d980217.htm.

U.S. Office of Management and Budget. "Revisions to the Standards for the Classification of Federal Data on Race and Ethnicity." *Federal Register* 62, no. 210 (October 30, 1997): pp. 58,782–58,790.

racism

Racism is a belief that humans can be distinctly categorized according to external characteristics and that the various races are fixed and inherently different from one another. It has been an essential feature in defining intercultural relations in North America since the arrival of the Spanish in the early 16th century and the ideological foundation of English and French dominance. With a few exceptions, early European settlers believed in their own superiority, which justified the forced labor or enslavement of Native Americans and Africans and the establishment of cultural norms to which immigrants were expected to conform. Though racism implies a foundation of biological determinism, there is not a clear line between it and ethnocentrism, which judges the value of other peoples and cultures according to the standard of one's own culture (see NATIVISM). Racism operated in some form against most immigrant groups in North America, with the Irish, Jews, Italians, and Slavic peoples initially viewed as inherently different by members of the predominant English or French cultures and thus justifiably subject to menial service at low wages and expected to conform to the predominant cultural norms. In its most extreme form, racism led to institutionalized discrimination against African Americans. Following U.S. civil rights reforms of the 1960s and a general improvement in economic conditions for U.S. and Canadian immigrants, institutional and cultural racism declined. Varying degrees of racism are still common, however, having been most commonly exposed in high-profile law enforcement cases such as the 1997 beating of Haitian immigrant Abner Louima. Throughout the 1990s, heightened racial consciousness led to more frequent charges of racism in government, business, and the press.

Throughout the ancient and medieval world, humans were not identified by race. People naturally noticed external differences (phenotypes)—most notably skin color; hair color and type; shape of head, nose, and teeth; and general body build—that roughly corresponded to the later-defined "three races" of European/white/Caucasian; African/black/Negroid; and Asian/yellow/Mongoloid. Recognition of these differences in phenotypes alone did not constitute racism, however, as Africans, Asians, Native Americans, and Europeans were all willing to enslave and otherwise take advantage of peoples who looked much as they did. Extreme prejudice most often centered instead on cultural traits associated with the peoples of particular geographic regions, as in the case of the Roman Cicero railing against British slaves because they were "so stupid and so utterly incapable of being taught." The modern concept of races, the foundation of racism, began to emerge as Europeans from the 15th century onward began to explore and dominate remote regions of the world, encountering cultures vastly different in customs, belief systems, and levels of development.

Until the mid-17th century, however, European ethnocentrism still was not primarily motivated by race. The English military governor of Munster, Sir Humphrey Gilbert, had no qualms about brutally exterminating white Irish men, women, and children in Ireland in 1569, cutting off their heads and lining the path to his tent with them as an example to others. Indentured servants (see INDENTURED SERVITUDE) of every race, ethnicity, and nationality were harshly treated. Until the 1650s, it was still possible for Africans in English colonies to serve their indenture, become landowners, and even be masters to European servants. SLAVERY as a legal institution associated with race emerged only with the development of slave codes from 1661, which increasingly referred to racial distinctions in limiting the freedoms of Africans. At about the same time, the term *race* began to be used in a modern sense to designate peoples with common distinguishable physical characteristics. This sense of the term did not become widespread, however, until the 18th century when systematic classification of peoples seemed to give scientific credence to such divisions (see RACIAL AND ETHNIC CATEGORIES).

Charles Darwin's theory of evolution by means of natural selection, put forward in *On the Origin of Species*

(1859), ironically worked both to support and undermine racism. In the short term, it suggested that some races had not evolved as far as others and thus were intellectually or morally inferior. This pseudoscientific interpretation of Darwin was used to justify British and American imperial conquests, as well as continued discrimination against Native Americans and African Americans and the exploitation of non-European laborers such as the Chinese, Japanese, and Asian Indians. In the long term, however, natural selection's focus on adaptation suggested why people living in similar geographic regions developed similar physical characteristics, despite living thousands of miles apart. Based on the science of genetics, which was not developed until the 20th century, it has become generally accepted that differences in the genetic structure of humans (genotypes) are far more meaningful than differences in external features (phenotypes) and that all human beings are biologically part of the same species, with few consequential differences. The traditional identification of race by skin color is no more meaningful than identification on the basis of blood type, dentition, or sickle-cell traits, all of which cut across traditional racial lines.

This cartoon, published in California during the 1860s, suggests the racist assumptions of many Americans and Canadians in the 19th century. Note the distinctly simian (monkey- or apelike) features of the Irishman (left) and the characterization of the Chinese man (right). In 1883, Prime Minister John A. Macdonald informed the Canadian parliament that he was "sufficient of a physiologist" to understand that Chinese and European Canadians could not "combine and that no great middle race can arise from the mixture of the Mongolian and the Arian." *(Library of Congress, Prints & Photographs Division [LC-USZ62-22399])*

Further Reading

Aarim-Heriot, Najia. *Chinese Immigrants, African Americans, and Racial Anxiety in the United States, 1848–82.* Champaign: University of Illinois Press, 2003.

"Abercrombie Pulls 'Racist' Asian Theme T-shirts." CNN.com. April 19, 2002. Available online. URL: http://www.cnn.comm/2002/BUSINESS/asia/04/19/sanfran.abercrombie,reut/index.html. Accessed April 19, 2002.

Almaguer, Tomás. *Racial Fault Lines: The Historical Origins of White Supremacy in California.* Berkeley: University of California Press, 1994.

Banton, Michael, and Jonathan Harwood. *The Race Concept.* New York: Praeger, 1975.

Boyko, John. *Last Steps to Freedom: The Evolution of Canadian Racism.* 2d ed. Winnipeg, Canada: J. Gordon Shillingford, 1998.

Chase, Allan. *The Legacy of Malthus: The Social Costs of the New Scientific Racism.* New York: Alfred A. Knopf, 1977.

Conrad, Earl. *The Invention of the Negro.* New York: Paul S. Eriksson, 1967.

Cose, Ellis. *A Nation of Strangers: Prejudice, Politics, and the Populating of America.* New York: Morrow, 1992.

Daniels, Roger. *The Politics of Prejudice.* New York: Atheneum, 1968.

Driedger, Leo, and Shiva S. Halli. *Race and Racism: Canada's Challenge.* Montreal: McGill–Queen's University Press, 2000.

Ferguson, Ted. *A White Man's County.* Toronto: Doubleday, 1975.

Gould, Stephen J. *The Mismeasure of Man.* Rev. ed. New York: W. W. Norton, 1996.

Haas, Michael. *Institutional Racism: The Case of Hawaii.* Westport, Conn.: Praeger, 1992.

Higham, John. *Strangers in the Land: Patterns of American Nativism, 1860–1925.* New Brunswick, N.J.: Rutgers University Press, 1955.

Jordan, Winthrop D. *White over Black: American Attitudes toward the Negro, 1550–1812.* New York: W. W. Norton, 1977.

Laquian, Eleanor, Aprodicio Laquian, and Terry McGee, eds. *The Silent Debate: Asian Immigration and Racism in Canada.* Vancouver: Institute of Asian Research, University of British Columbia, 1998.

Massey, Douglas S. *American Apartheid: Segregation and the Making of the Underclass.* Cambridge, Mass.: Harvard University Press, 1993.

McClain, Charles J. *In Search of Equality: The Chinese Struggle against Discrimination in Nineteenth-Century America.* Berkeley: University of California Press, 1994.

McClellan, Robert. *The Heathen Chinese: A Study of American Attitudes toward China.* Columbus: Ohio State University Press, 1971.

Miller, Stuart. *The Unwelcome Immigrant: The American Image of the Chinese, 1785–1882.* Berkeley: University of California Press, 1969.

Olson, James. *Equality Deferred: Race, Ethnicity, and Immigration in America, since 1945.* Belmont, Calif.: Wadsworth, 2003.

railways and immigration

Railways were integral to immigration in several ways. First, they were the physical means by which the vast majority of European immigrants made their way from interior regions

This engraving shows the completion of the Pacific Railroad and the meeting of locomotives of the Union and Central Pacific lines. The completion of the first transcontinental railroad in the United States in the summer of 1869 made possible the settling of the great central prairies. *(Library of Congress, Prints & Photographs Division [LC-USZ62-116354])*

of Britain, the German states, and the Austrian and Russian Empires to port cities like Liverpool, in England, and Hamburg, in Germany. Prior to the development of the railroad, land travel to a distant port was slow, frequently dangerous, and often unrealistic. Once in North America, the railroad efficiently and inexpensively transported immigrants to places of opportunity far away from ports, including industrial areas, such as Cleveland, Ohio; Detroit, Michigan; Pittsburgh, Pennsylvania; St. Louis, Missouri; and Chicago, Illinois, and the agricultural lands of the interior. Earlier travel by horse and wagon or on foot were both expensive and impractical for most immigrants, especially as they were undertaken in a foreign land and across places where one's language was not spoken. Finally, the railroad was essential for bringing supplies to the interior and moving out wheat, cotton, cattle, gold, coal, and other commodities. For the West to be productive, it had to be connected to the Atlantic, Pacific, and Gulf coast ports.

Steam-powered railways were developed in Britain at the beginning of the 19th century. By the late 1820s, sub-stantial railway lines were established in both Britain and the eastern United States. Within the next 10 years railway lines were constructed in Canada and most of western Europe. In 1869, the first transcontinental railroad was completed in the United States; in 1885, the last spike in the Canadian Pacific Railway was driven in the Monashee Mountains of British Columbia, laying the foundation for westward expansion to the interior prairies and the Pacific.

The rapid growth of railways in the United States and Canada during the 19th century provided many employment opportunities for immigrants and a means of dispersing them throughout the country. The Central Pacific Railroad, as it pushed to complete the first transcontinental railroad in the United States, employed more than 10,000 Chinese laborers. In 1850, American railway lines stretched 8,683 miles, all east of the Mississippi River. By 1890, there were 163,597 miles of track, including 70,622 miles west of the Mississippi. Such large capital investments necessitated cheap labor and allowed national economies to maintain stability while absorbing thousands of immigrants.

Masses of Irish immigrants who could not afford to start farming, instead accepted backbreaking jobs with the railway. Beginning in 1862, Irish workers were employed by the Union Pacific to construct the eastern section of the first U.S. transcontinental railway. The western section of the line was constructed almost entirely by Chinese immigrants from California employed by the Central Pacific. Along with large numbers of Greeks, Italians, Japanese, and Russians, Irish and Chinese immigrants continued to play a major role in railway construction throughout the United States and Canada. Once completed, railways increased worker mobility across the nation. Wealthier immigrants, usually of German origin, could arrange rail passage from their arrival city to Midwestern states, such as the Dakotas, where free homesteads were available.

When large projects demanded an immediate labor force, workers could be contracted by labor brokers from immigrant population centers, then shipped by rail anywhere in the country. The ready supply of immigrant workers greatly accelerated railway and industrial growth in the 19th century. In Canada, with fewer concentrations of laborers, short-term labor contracts were issued to workers from eastern Europe as late as 1913.

Railway companies also played a direct role in promoting immigration to North America. Before construction began, most railway companies received federal land grants along their proposed route. As early as 1855, the Illinois Central began to recruit immigrants from Britain, Germany, and Scandinavia to encourage population growth on the granted land. In the 1870s and 1880s, other companies followed suit, such as the Northern Pacific, which actually established its own Bureau of Immigration. Companies sent recruiting agents to Europe with newsletters and brochures to entice settlers to move to preplanned communities, offering free passage and discount land to immigrants who would agree to relocate. In Canada, the Canadian Pacific Railroad used similar techniques in London to market its massive federal land grants to British immigrants. Consequently, railways established specific patterns of ethnic settlement along their lines.

At the turn of the 20th century, an influx of principally male Mexican workers flooded the agricultural and railway labor markets of the southwestern United States. Railway worker camps formed the foundation for many modern Mexican-American communities. With the rise of the automobile culture in the 20th century, railways waned as the primary means of internal transportation in the United States but continued to provide a frequently undetectable method of crossing America's southern border.

With the Canadian prairies filling more slowly than those in the United States, the role of the railroad remained more pivotal. With the dramatic decline of immigrant admissions and rise in alien deportations during World War I (1914–18), the Canadian government tried several means

of attracting agriculturalists and domestics, who were in high demand. Its first choice of source country was clearly Great Britain, but the EMPIRE SETTLEMENT ACT was relatively unsuccessful in attracting the agricultural immigrants desperately needed for developing the prairies. More successful was the Railway Agreement of 1925, which authorized the Canadian Pacific and Canadian Northern railways to recruit agriculturalists and farm laborers from southern and eastern Europe, whose immigration to Canada was at that time "non-preferred." Always seeking more customers, the railroads actively advertised in Europe and between 1925 and 1929 brought more than 185,000 immigrants to the agricultural west. The groups that most benefited from this last phase of direct railway settlement were Germans from both central Europe and Russia, Mennonites, Ukrainians, Poles, and Hungarians.

See also NEW ORLEANS, LOUISIANA.

Further Reading
Dempsey, Hugh A., ed. *The CPR West: The Iron Road and the Making of a Nation.* Vancouver, Canada, and Toronto: Douglas and McIntyre, 1984.
Eagle, John A. *The Canadian Pacific Railway and the Development of Western Canada, 1896–1914.* Kingston, Montreal, and London: McGill–Queen's University Press, 1989.
England, Robert. *The Colonization of Western Canada: A Study of Contemporary Land Settlement, 1896–1934.* London: P.S. King, 1936.
Gordon, Sarah. *Passage to Union: How the Railroads Transformed American Life, 1829–1929.* Chicago: Ivan Dee, 1996.
Gates, Paul Wallace. *The Illinois Central Railroad and Its Colonization Work.* Cambridge, Mass.: Harvard University Press, 1934.
Holbrook, Stewart H. *The Story of American Railroads.* New York: Crown, 1947.
O'Connor, Richard. *Iron Wheels and Broken Men.* New York: Putnam, 1973.

Raleigh, Sir Walter (ca. 1552–1618) *explorer, courtier, man of letters*
Although a man of many accomplishments, Sir Walter Raleigh is best known as an explorer and the founder of ROANOKE COLONY (1585), England's first colonial settlement in the Americas. Though the venture failed, Raleigh was able to challenge Spain's supremacy in the New World, and the settlers of Roanoke returned with valuable information that would later aid colonists in successfully establishing an English presence in Virginia.

Born in Devonshire, as a young man Raleigh attended Oriel College, Oxford, before joining the French Huguenot army in 1569. During the 1570s, he gained distinction as a poet and man of letters in London. In 1578 he joined his half brother, Sir Humphrey Gilbert, in search of the Northwest Passage but ended in attacking Spanish holdings in the Americas. After Raleigh spent two years fighting the Irish

(1580–81), Queen Elizabeth came to recognize him as an expert on Irish affairs, and he quickly rose in royal favor. Extravagant and arrogant, he was widely disliked at court but was knighted in 1584 and eventually rose to the position of captain of the queen's guard.

After Gilbert's death in 1583, Raleigh was given his charter to claim American lands in the name of the queen. She also grudgingly gave him a ship and a small sum of money. Though Raleigh remained in London to oversee the financing of the operation, his men made three unsuccessful attempts to establish Roanoke colony on the outer banks of the Carolinas. In and out of favor with Queen Elizabeth, Raleigh did gain permission to lead an expedition in 1595 to Guiana (modern Venezuela), where he believed he had found extensive deposits of gold, as he wrote in *The Discovery of the Large, Rich, and Beautiful Empire of Guiana . . .* (1596). Upon Elizabeth's death in 1603, he was convicted of treason. The new king, James I, stripped Raleigh of his titles and imprisoned him in the Tower of London for 13 years. He used the time to write his monumental *The History of the World* (1614). Raleigh finally convinced the cash-strapped king to release him in order to pursue English claims in Guiana. Raleigh's final expedition (1617) produced no wealth, however, and he was beheaded for treason the following year.

Further Reading

Quinn, David Beers. *Raleigh and the British Empire.* London: English Universities Press, 1962.

Raleigh, Walter. *The Works of Sir Walter Ralegh.* 8 vols. 1829. Reprint, New York: Burt Franklin, 1965.

Wallace, Willard M. *Sir Walter Raleigh.* Princeton, N.J.: Princeton University Press, 1959.

Red River colony

The Red River colony, established by THOMAS DOUGLAS, Lord Selkirk, in 1812, was the first farming settlement in western British North America. Though a collective failure economically and politically, it demonstrated that individuals could successfully farm the western prairies, laying the foundation for the settlement of Manitoba and Saskatchewan.

Selkirk, a philanthropist who had established smaller settlements on Prince Edward Island and at Baldoon, Ontario, acquired controlling interest of the Hudson's Bay Company between 1808 and 1812 with an eye toward settling Scottish crofters (tenant farmers with very small holdings) who had been driven from their Highland farms. In 1811, he purchased 116,000 square miles of Rupert's Land from the company, extending from Lake Winnipeg in the north to the headwaters of the Red River in the south. In return for this immense tract, almost as large as Britain and Ireland combined, Selkirk was responsible for providing 200 company men with a 200-acre pension when they retired. Crofters were required to pay 10 pounds each for trans-

portation and a year's supplies, with a grant of 100 acres of land at five shillings per acre to each head of household.

Such bounty seemed too good to be true, and it was. The transplanted Scots were under constant threat from the Sioux and the Métis (Canadians of native and mostly French parentage), who in 1817 proclaimed the region as their own "nation." The newcomers had no proper tools for farming the tough prairie sod, and when they did manage to raise crops or cattle, ferocious winters, wolves, grasshoppers, blackbirds, and floods were there to steal the fruits of their labor. The placement of 270 Scots in the Red River settlement (1812–16) also led to violent opposition from the North West Fur Company, whose trade routes were infringed. A protracted legal struggle cost Selkirk much of his fortune. In addition, the colony was poorly governed; Selkirk himself only visited once, in 1817. Not surprisingly, the Red River settlement grew slowly.

In 1821 the population was a little more than 400. More than half were Scots, but there was a significant number of Irish and smaller numbers of French Canadians and Swiss. As the population grew, the character of the colony changed dramatically. By the mid-1820s, most of the original settlers had died or departed for the United States or Upper Canada. By the 1830s, the population was composed almost entirely of Métis. When they rebelled against intrusion by the Canadian government in 1869–70, there were 5,754 of mixed Native American–French descent and 4,083 of mixed Native American–British descent. From this conflict emerged the province of Manitoba and parts of the Northwest Territories.

Further Reading

Friesen, Gerald. *The Canadian Prairies: A History.* Toronto: University of Toronto Press, 1984.

MacEwan, Grant. *Cornerstone Colony: Selkirk's Contribution to the Canadian West.* Saskatoon, Canada: Western Producer Prairie Books, 1977.

Morton, W. L. *Manitoba: A History.* Rev. ed. Toronto: University of Toronto Press, 1967.

Pritchett, J. P. *The Red River Valley, 1811–1849: A Regional Study.* New Haven, Conn.: Yale University Press, Ryerson Press, 1942.

Refugee Act (United States) (1980)

The Refugee Act of 1980 formed the basis of refugee policy in the United States until 1996. It declared that American policy was to "respond to the urgent needs of persons subject to persecution" by any of the following means "where appropriate":

> *Humanitarian assistance for their care and maintenance in asylum areas, efforts to promote opportunities for resettlement or voluntary repatriation, aid for necessary transportation and processing, admission to this country*

[United States] of refugees for special humanitarian concern to the United States, and transitional assistance to refugees in the United States. The Congress further declares that it is the policy of the United States to encourage all nations to provide assistance and resettlement opportunities to refugees to the fullest extent possible.

The Refugee Act was designed to bring U.S. law into compliance with international treaty obligations, particularly the United Nations Protocol Relating to the Status of Refugees, to which the United States had acceded in 1968. The act therefore separated refugee and immigration policy and adopted the broader UN definition of a refugee as

Any person who . . . owing to a well-founded fear of being persecuted for reasons of race, religion, nationality, membership of a particular social group or political opinion, is outside the country of his nationality and is unable or, owing to such fear, is unwilling to avail himself of the protection of that country; or who, not having a nationality and being outside the country of his former habitual residence . . . is unable or, owing to such fear, is unwilling to return to it.

Refugees were exempted from the immigrant preference system, as were immediate relatives. The act provided for quotas to be reviewed annually. In 1980, 50,000 new refugee applicants were admitted. The number rose to 110,000 by the mid-1990s.

Currently, the president, in consultation with Congress, establishes the annual refugee quota from each geographical area. The Department of State is then responsible for determining specific countries from which refugees will be accepted. In 1997, for instance, 78,000 refugees were permitted to enter the United States, with slots for Africa (7,000), East Asia (10,000), Eastern Europe and the former Soviet Union (48,000), Latin America and the Caribbean (4,000), and the Near and Middle East (4,000) and another 5,000 spots allocated as a reserve for trouble areas.

See also REFUGEE STATUS.

Further Reading

Kennedy, Edward M. "Refugee Act of 1980." *International Migration Review* 15 (1981): 141–156.
Loescher, Gil, and John A. Scanlan. *Calculated Kindness: Refugees and America's Half-Open Door, 1945–Present.* New York: Free Press, 1986.
Mitchell, Christopher, ed. *Western Hemisphere Immigration and United States Foreign Policy.* University Park: Pennsylvania State University Press, 1992.

Refugee Relief Act (United States) (1953)

Enacted on August 7, 1953, the Refugee Relief Act (RRA) authorized the granting of 205,000 special nonquota visas

apportioned to individuals in three classes, along with accompanying members of their immediate family, including refugees (those unable to return to their homes in a communist or communist-dominated country "because of persecution, fear of persecution, natural calamity or military operations"), escapees (refugees who had left a communist country fearing persecution "on account of race, religion, or political opinion"), and German expellees (ethnic Germans then living in West Germany, West Berlin, or Austria who had been forced to flee from territories dominated by communists). Visas were allotted to the following groups: German expellees (55,000); Italian refugees (45,000); German escapees (35,000); escapees residing in North Atlantic Treaty Organization (NATO) countries, Turkey, Sweden, Iran, or Trieste (25,000, including second, third, and fourth preferences); Greek refugees (17,000, including second, third, and fourth preferences); Dutch refugees (17,000, including second, third, and fourth preferences); refugees who had taken refuge in U.S. consular offices in East Asia but were not indigenous to the region (2,000); refugees who had taken refuge in U.S. consular offices in East Asia and were indigenous to the region (3,000); Chinese refugees (2,000); and those qualifying for aid from the United Nations Relief and Works Agency for Palestine Refugees in the Near East (2,000). The act also provided for 4,000 nonquota visas for eligible orphans under 10 years of age. An act of September 11, 1957 reassigned unused visas from the 1953 quota.

See also REFUGEE STATUS.

Further Reading

Divine, Robert. *American Immigration Policy, 1924–1952.* New Haven, Conn.: Yale University Press, 1957.
Hutchinson, E. P. *Legislative History of American Immigration Policy, 1798–1965.* Philadelphia: University of Pennsylvania Press, 1981.
Loescher, Gil, and John A. Scanlan. *Calculated Kindness: Refugees and America's Half-Open Door, 1945–Present.* New York: Free Press, 1986.
Proudfoot, Malcolm J. *European Refugees, 1939–1952: A Study in Forced Population Movement.* London: Faber and Faber, 1957.
Vernant, Jacques. *The Refugee in the Post-War World.* New Haven, Conn.: Yale University Press, 1953.

refugee status

A refugee is a special category of immigrant not subject to regular immigration quotas. In international law, a refugee is defined as a person fleeing natural disaster or past or future persecution on the basis of race, culture, or political or religious beliefs. Individual countries grant asylum—the right to legally resettle—according to national interests as embodied in domestic legislation. Because of international treaty obligations, both the United States and Canada provide special treatment to those deemed refugees, including economic assistance in first countries of asylum and selective resettlement in North America. Refugees have a legal status enabling them to work and receive welfare benefits, whereas asylum seekers are considered temporary guests who may at any point be declared illegal aliens. The United States has consistently resettled more refugees than any other country, though there has been considerable controversy over the terms of American policy.

Although Thomas Jefferson spoke eloquently on behalf of asylum for "unhappy fugitives from distress," the United States followed no consistent refugee policy until after World War II (1939–45). With virtually open immigration to the United States prior to World War I (1914–18), it was not in most cases necessary to specially designate refugees. Thousands of religious and revolutionary exiles who might today qualify for refugee status were admitted to the young republic after 1776 but with no special legislative provisions. The American government implicitly recognized the refugee status of men and women who had been convicted of polit-

A refugee child is adopted by a U.S. sailor in May 1918. Although the American and Canadian governments had admitted refugees since the early colonial period, neither developed an official refugee policy until the 1950s. *(National Archives #72-135418)*

ical crimes by excluding them from legislation aimed at prohibiting the immigration of criminals (1875, 1882, 1891, 1903, 1907, 1910). Shortly after World War II (see WORLD WAR II AND IMMIGRATION), a number of measures admitted refugees according to special circumstances: President Harry S. Truman's presidential directive of 1945 admitted 42,000 war refugees; the WAR BRIDES ACT (1946) qualified wives and children of U.S. servicemen to enter; and the DISPLACED PERSONS ACTS (1948, 1950) admitted more than 400,000 homeless Europeans. In 1951, the United Nations Convention Relating to the Status of Refugees established an international definition and prohibited forcible repatriation (refoulement), though it did not require any country to resettle refugees. The United States did not sign the Convention Relating to the Status of Refugees but devised similar policies through domestic legislation. The McCARRAN-WALTER IMMIGRATION AND NATURALIZATION ACT (1952) did not specifically address refugee status, leading to passage of the REFUGEE RELIEF ACT (1953), granting asylum in the United States to those fleeing communist persecution. This formed the primary basis for establishing refugee status in the United States throughout the COLD WAR (1945–91) and was embodied in the permanent amendment of the IMMIGRATION AND NATIONALITY ACT in 1965, which established a preference class for those who "because of persecution or fear of persecution . . . have fled from any Communist or Communist-dominated country or area, or from any country within the general area of the Middle East." From the mid-1950s through 1979, less than one-third of 1 percent of refugee admissions were from noncommunist countries, and as late as 1987, 85 percent of refugees were from the communist countries of Cuba, Vietnam, Laos, Cambodia, Afghanistan, Poland, Russia, and Romania.

The REFUGEE ACT (1980), designed to bring U.S. law into compliance with international treaty obligations, separated refugee and immigration policy and adopted the broader UN definition of a refugee, leading to a great influx of immigrants. Nevertheless, the disparity between treatment of 130,000 Cubans who were granted refugee status following the MARIEL BOATLIFT (1980) and the forcible return of thousands of Haitians, Guatemalans, and Salvadorans fleeing right-wing dictatorships was evident. Despite the broader provisions of the Refugee Act, the administration of President Ronald Reagan reduced refugee admissions by two-thirds and continued to favor those from communist countries. The ILLEGAL IMMIGRATION REFORM AND IMMIGRANT RESPONSIBILITY ACT (1996) further expanded the definition of a refugee to include anyone fleeing "coercive population control procedures," a phrase specifically aimed at China.

Canadian policy after World War II favored international cooperative efforts to assist refugees in the country of first asylum. The Canadian IMMIGRATION ACT of 1952 provides for Canadian resettlement of those who qualify under the United Nations Convention agreement, though candidates must pass through an extensive process handled by the Convention Refugee Determination Division of the Immigration and Refugee Board (IRB).

Further Reading

Dirks, Gerald E. *Canada's Refugee Policy: Indifference or Opportunism?* Montreal: McGill–Queen's University Press, 1977.

Hutchinson, E. P. *Legislative History of American Immigration Policy, 1798–1965.* Philadelphia: University of Pennsylvania Press, 1981.

Loescher, Gil, and John A. Scanlan. *Calculated Kindness: Refugees and America's Half-Open Door, 1945–Present.* New York: Free Press, 1986.

Simmons, Alan B. "Latin American Migration to Canada: New Linkages in the Hemispheric Migration and Refugee Flow Systems." *International Journal* 48 (Spring 1993): 282–309.

religion and immigration

The quest for religious freedom has played an important role in immigration to North America from the 17th century to the present day. In some cases, it has been the preeminent reason for leaving homelands in which religious persecution was endemic. In more cases, religious freedom was one issue among others, as people sought both personal freedoms and economic opportunities not available in their home countries.

The earliest settlers to come to North America mainly for religious reasons were the Pilgrims (see PILGRIMS AND PURITANS), who settled in Plymouth Bay, Massachusetts. Having already separated from the Church of England and migrated to Holland in 1610, it was then easier for them to choose the drastic step of leaving Europe forever in 1620. The much larger migration of Puritans in the 1630s and 1640s, led by JOHN WINTHROP, hoped to build a "city upon a hill," a model community where full citizenship was reserved for members of a reformed Church of England (later known as the Congregational Church). This ideal lasted only a few decades before secularization and democratization began to dilute the religious character of the MASSACHUSETTS COLONY. Nevertheless, the early religious principles of the Pilgrims and Puritans helped establish a cultural pattern that persisted broadly well into the 20th century. The decline of Puritan influence in state affairs by the late 17th century foreshadowed the religious tolerance that would be commonly practiced in the American colonies and later in the United States. Among the early British settlements in North America were other colonies founded principally for religious reasons. MARYLAND COLONY was established as a haven for persecuted Roman Catholics; RHODE ISLAND COLONY and PENNSYLVANIA COLONY both developed in response to the persecution of Baptists and QUAKERS, respectively, and were

established with religious freedom as a fundamental principle. Just as internal mobility had been common in England and within the British Isles, it was endemic in southwestern Germany, Switzerland, and the Low Countries (Belgium and the Netherlands). As a result, smaller religious sects saw immigration as a potential solution to ongoing political and social disorder. As historian Bernard Bailyn has observed, "a thousand local rivulets fed streams of emigrants moving through northern and central Europe in all directions." Migration began late in the 17th century and continued almost unabated until World War I (1914–18). By the mid-18th century there were already dozens of Amish (see AMISH IMMIGRATION), Mennonites (see MENNONITE IMMIGRATION), Dunker, and Schwenkfelder (see SCHWENKFELDER IMMIGRATION) settlements, mostly in Pennsylvania. Gradually, throughout the 18th century, the power of state religion receded and religious freedom became the norm throughout the colonies. This freedom, while not universally changing people's religious prejudices, was embodied in the first amendment to the new United States Constitution of 1789, stipulating that "Congress shall make no law respecting an establishment of religion, or prohibiting the free exercise thereof. . . ." Generally Britain's Canadian colonies were less officially tolerant, but by the 1780s, there was little attempt to punish Catholics or Dissenters. Unlike the new republic to the south, however, Catholics did not enjoy full rights until later in the 19th century, when they gradually gained rights to vote and sit in legislatures.

The first major movements from the German states to the United States in the 1830s and from Norway and Sweden in the 1850s were related to persecution of pietistic sects in those areas. The much larger migration that followed until the turn of the century was less generally a religious movement, though communities established by earlier religious emigrants made it easier for all immigrants who followed. As a result, the religious impulse was important in immigration beyond the numbers who came to North America for strictly religious reasons.

Sometimes religion was a characteristic of great but accidental importance. The Irish had been fleeing their overpopulated island in the tens of thousands since the 1820s simply to live, and the need was all the greater as a result of the Great Famine of the 1840s. Though religion was not the reason for their migration, by the 1850s, they established an ethnic Catholicism that was unprecedented and in Canada reinforced the Catholic presence of the French. The NATIVISM of the 19th century was significantly anti-Catholic in character, negatively reinforcing the American norm of white, Anglo-Saxon Protestantism. Italians too were almost universally Roman Catholic but feared no religious persecution in their homelands. That Greeks, Russians, and Ukrainians were members of Orthodox Christian churches was only incidental to their decisions to immigrate and their faith merely one of a dozen strange customs that clouded the sight of Americans and Canadians.

As nationalism grew as an ideological force throughout the 19th century, radical communal groups were almost always viewed hostilely and frequently were persecuted. As a result, groups of Amish, Mennonite, Doukhobor, and Hutterite settlers made their way to North America. The Amish and the Mennonites often settled with or near communities established in the 18th century, while the Hutterites and Doukhobors established themselves on the unsettled prairies of the United States and Canada between the 1870s and 1910. Their attempts to live communally and by pacifist principles tested the degree of religious tolerance afforded in both the United States and Canada. Both countries placed restrictions on communal living, and antipacifist sentiment was especially strong in the United States during World War I.

Although religion was less prominent a factor in driving the NEW IMMIGRATION after 1880, it continued to play an important role in defining legal tolerance for all religions. Because Italians, Poles, and many Germans were Roman Catholic, Catholicism came to be identified with ethnicity. For specific groups, religion was still the principal reason for migration. Jews, for instance, faced an intensification of religious persecution in Russia and Austria after 1880 and thus looked to the religious freedom of the United States

(especially between 1880 and 1900) and Canada (especially between 1900 and 1920). Many Jews who came, however, were not Orthodox, and some openly embraced socialist, rather than religious, solutions to problems. So, although old-stock Americans tended to identify people's religion with their ethnicity, there was in fact considerable diversity in the practice of most of the Old World religions once their practitioners were transplanted to North America. In the wake of World War II (1939–45) and the ending of colonial empires between 1950 and 1970, Jews continued to seek freedom of religion in the West.

Canada and the United States proved to be a religious haven throughout the 20th century. Despite persistent anti-Semitism, particularly in Quebec, Jews continued to immigrate to the United States and Canada, first as refugees from German-held territories in World War II, and then as refugees from the officially atheistic Soviet Union. By the 1960s, they had largely entered the cultural mainstream. Communal groups such as the Mennonites were also driven from the Soviet Union and found acceptance in the United States and Canada. More significant in terms of numbers was the vast influx of non-Protestant settlers coming as a result of liberalized, nonethnic immigration policies enacted in the 1960s. Roman Catholic Mexicans and Filipinos and other immigrants from Latin America; Buddhist Chinese, Vietnamese, Laotians, and Cambodians; Hindu Indians;

Doukhobors of the Thunder Hill Colony, Manitoba, move supplies from Yorkton, Saskatchewan, to their villages, 1899. Aided by Leo Tolstoy and Peter Kropotkin, more than 7,500 Doukhobors escaped czarist persecution to settle in the Canadian West after 1889. *(National Archives of Canada/PA-005209)*

and Muslim Indians, Pakistanis, Bangladeshis, Iranians, Egyptians, and Palestinians significantly changed the character of many areas, including California generally, and especially the major metropolitan areas of Los Angeles and San Francisco, California; Houston, Texas; Seattle, Washington; Toronto, Ontario; and Montreal, Quebec. The United States and Canada continually affirmed the freedom of religious practice. Despite occasional outbreaks of nativism, notably in the wake of the SEPTEMBER 11, 2001, terrorist attacks, which were broadly associated with Islamic religious extremism, there were few overt attacks on members of religious minorities, and when there were attacks, they were prosecuted criminally.

Further Reading

Abramson, Harold J. *Ethnic Diversity in Catholic America*. New York: Wiley, 1973.

Alexander, June. *The Immigrant Church and Community: Pittsburgh's Slovak Catholics and Lutherans, 1880–1915*. Pittsburgh, Pa.: University of Pittsburgh Press, 1987.

Balmer, Randall. *A Perfect Babel of Confusion: Dutch Religion and English Culture in the Middle Colonies*. New York: Oxford University Press, 1989.

Burns, Jeffrey M., et al., eds. *Keeping Faith: European and Asian Catholic Immigrants*. Maryknoll, N.Y.: Orbis Books, 2000.

Dolan, Jay P. *The Immigrant Church: New York's Irish and German Catholics: 1815–1865*. Baltimore: Johns Hopkins University Press, 1975.

Fenton, John Y. *South Asian Religions in the Americas: An Annotated Bibliography of Immigrant Religious Traditions*. Westport, Conn.: Greenwood Press, 1995.

———. *Transplanting Religious Traditions: Asian Indians in America*. New York: Praeger, 1988.

Gaustad, Edwin Scott. *A Religious History of America*. 2d ed. San Francisco: Harper and Row, 1990.

Kim, Jung Ha, and Pyong Gap Min, eds. *Religions in Asian America: Building Faith Communities*. Walnut Creek, Calif.: AltaMira Press, 2001.

Koszegi, Michael A., and J. Gordon Melton, eds. *Islam in North America: A Sourcebook*. New York: Garland, 1992.

McCaffrey, Lawrence. *The Irish Catholic Diaspora in America*. Washington, D.C.: Catholic University of America Press, 1997.

Murphy, Andrew R. *Conscience and Community: Revisiting Toleration and Religious Dissent in Early Modern England and America*. University Park: Pennsylvania State University Press, 2001.

Numrich, Paul David. *Old Wisdom in the New World: Americanization in Two Immigrant Theravada Buddhist Temples*. Knoxville: University of Tennessee Press, 1996.

Podell, Jane, ed. *Buddhists, Hindus, and Sikhs in America*. New York: Oxford University Press, 2001.

Prebish, Charles S., and Kenneth K. Tanaka, eds. *The Faces of Buddhism in America*. Berkeley: University of California Press, 1998.

Seager, Richard Hughes. *Buddhism in America*. New York: Columbia University Press, 1999.

Smith, Timothy. "Religion and Ethnicity in America." *American Historical Review* 83 (December 1978): 1,155–1,185.

Stephenson, G. M. *The Religious Aspects of Swedish Immigration*. Minneapolis: University of Minnesota Press, 1932.

Williams, Raymond. *Religions of Immigrants from India and Pakistan: New Threads in the American Tapestry*. Cambridge: Cambridge University Press, 1988.

Zakai, Avihu. *Exile and Kingdom: History and Apocalypse in the Puritan Migration to America*. Cambridge: Cambridge University Press, 1992.

revolutions of 1848

Throughout 1848, a series of liberal revolutions swept across most of western and central Europe, offering the promise of greater political and religious freedoms. The revolts began in Paris, France, in February. As word spread to liberals elsewhere, uprisings followed in Austria-Hungary, Italy, and the German states, leading to the establishment of representative assemblies. The most promising of these, the Frankfurt parliament, wrote a liberal constitution but found no solution to the *grossdeutsch* (greater Germany) versus *kleindeutsch* (smaller Germany) problem and was eventually dispersed by June 1849. By the end of 1849, virtually all the old regimes had been restored, driving thousands of revolutionaries and their associates into exile.

The fact that there were still 39 separate German states after settlement of the Napoleonic Wars in 1815 meant that there was almost continuous political debate over the fate of both individual states and the collective nation of the Germans. The handful of men and women who emigrated for purely political reasons after the Carlsbad Decrees of 1819 or the repression of the early 1830s was only a tiny fraction of the approximately 160,000 Germans who came to the United States between 1820 and 1840. Following the failed revolutions of 1848, the numbers increased. Still, of some 750,000 German immigrants between 1848 and 1854, only a few thousand were actual political refugees. Most Germans were responding to significant economic and social changes that made the old way of life more difficult. The majority of the exiled leaders stayed in Europe, with London, England, a favored destination. The most notable effect of the revolutions in the United States was to provide an already skilled and hardworking people with a solid core of professional leadership that eased German transition into the professions and ultimately into the mainstream of American life.

Further Reading

Kamphoefner, Walter. *The Westphalians: From Germany to Missouri*. Princeton, N.J.: Princeton University Press, 1987.

Moltmann, Gunter. "German Emigration to the United States in the First Half of the Nineteenth Century as a Form of Social Protest." In *Germany and America*. Ed. Hans Trefousse. New York: Brooklyn College Press, 1980.

Wittke, Karl. *Refugees of Revolution: The German Forty-eighters in America.* Philadelphia: University of Pennsylvania Press, 1952.

Zucker, Alfred E., ed. *The Forty-Eighters: Political Refugees of the German Revolutions of 1848.* New York: Columbia University Press, 1959.

Rhode Island colony

From the establishment of Providence Plantation by Roger Williams in 1636, Rhode Island was known as the refuge of dissident troublemakers. Principally made up of independent, agricultural communities, it remained small and almost totally populated by English settlers.

Europeans first explored coastal Rhode Island in the early 16th century. It was not permanently settled, however, until Williams sought personal and religious freedom after being driven from the MASSACHUSETTS COLONY in 1636. Having come to New England as a Puritan (see PILGRIMS AND PURITANS), he declared himself a Separatist, encouraging his congregation to break ties with the Church of England and denouncing the charter of the Massachusetts Bay colony. Other dissidents driven from Massachusetts, including William Coddington, John Clarke, and Anne Hutchinson, established Portsmouth and Newport in 1638. Fearing the evil effects of the absence of English law in Providence, a number of prominent citizens left to found Warwick in 1643. Four years later, Providence, Portsmouth, Newport, and Warwick joined together in order to repel encroachments from bordering colonies. A new charter of 1663 provided the legal basis for self-government that lasted into the 19th century. In 1686, Rhode Island was forced, along with Massachusetts Bay, Plymouth, CONNECTICUT COLONY, and NEW HAMPSHIRE COLONY, into the Dominion of New England, a heavy-handed autocratic experiment that failed as a result of the deposition of King James II of Britain during the Glorious Revolution of 1688–89.

The religious freedom that prevailed in early Rhode Island made it a refuge for several persecuted groups including Baptists, Quakers, Antinomians, Jews, and French Huguenots (Calvinists), groups that drew from diverse ethnic and national backgrounds. Although small, the colony prospered. Its diverse economy incorporated rich farmlands, whaling and fishing industries, and extensive transatlantic commerce. By the time of the AMERICAN REVOLUTION (1775–83), the colony regularly traded with England, the Portuguese islands, Africa, South America, the West Indies, and other British mainland colonies. The most lucrative commerce was in slaves, forming one leg of a triangular route that brought molasses from the West Indies to Rhode Island, whose distilleries made rum, which was then sent to Africa for the purchase of slaves. Rhode Island was, however, the first colony to prohibit the slave trade, in 1774.

Further Reading

Archer, Richard. *Fissures in the Rock: New England in the Seventeenth Century.* Hanover: University of New Hampshire, University Press of New England, 2001.

James, Sydney V. *Colonial Rhode Island: A History.* New York: Scribner, 1975.

McLoughlin, William G. *Rhode Island: A History.* New York: W. W. Norton, 1986.

Weeden, William B. *Early Rhode Island: A Social History of the People.* New York: Grafton Press, 1910.

Riis, Jacob (1849–1914) *journalist, author*

An immigrant himself, Jacob Riis became one of the first progressive photojournalists in the United States, drawing the public's attention to the plight of poor immigrants living in U.S. cities. Although he has sometimes been criticized for perpetuating ethnic stereotypes and favoring immigrants from northern and western Europe, his photographs and writings did much to encourage America's middle class to adopt more favorable attitudes toward immigration and

This photo by Frances Benjamin Johnston shows Jacob Riis, a Danish immigrant journalist and photographer, ca. 1900. Riis established his reputation as a reformer with the innovative *How the Other Half Lives: Studies among the Tenements of New York* (1890), which stressed the importance of the immigrant environment. *(Library of Congress, Prints & Photographs Division [LC-USZ62-47078])*

urban reform. *How the Other Half Lives: Studies among the Tenements of New York* (1890) remains the classic representation of the trials and the humanity of the urban poor during the great wave of immigration that swept the country between 1880 and 1914.

Riis was born in Ribe, Denmark, the third of 14 children. The family was poor, but his father was a respected teacher. Following Elisabeth Nielsen's rejection of his proposal of marriage at the insistence of her parents, Riis immigrated to the United States in 1870. After several years of itinerant labor, he established himself as a reporter and eventually bought the *South Brooklyn News*. This provided him with the resources to ask Nielsen to reconsider his proposal, which she did. Riis established his reputation as a police reporter for the New York *Tribune* (1877–90) and New York *Evening Sun* (1890–99). Working in the worst slums of New York City, he found his lifework depicting the horrors of the slums and especially the degrading conditions in which children were raised. In *How the Other Half Lives* (1890), he used innovative photographic techniques and a progressive prose to suggest that, however degraded immigrants might appear, they were not inherently bad. During the 1890s his friendship with Theodore Roosevelt (successively New York police commissioner, governor of New York, and president of the United States) led to a variety of progressive reforms aimed at slum clearance, the building of parks and playgrounds, and better treatment for the indigent.

Riis's numerous works, including *The Children of the Poor* (1892), *Out of Mulberry Street: Stories of Tenement Life in New York City* (1898), *A Ten Years' War: An Account of the Battle with the Slum in New York* (1900), and *Children of the Tenements* (1903) identified for his middle-class readers a host of other progressive causes, which were led by others. Although Riis became a U.S. citizen in 1895, he often visited his hometown and continued to extol the virtues of his native Denmark.

Further Reading
Alland, Alexander, Sr. *Jacob A. Riis: Photographer and Citizen.* Millerston, N.Y.: Aperture, 1974.
Lane, James B. *Jacob A. Riis and the American City.* Port Washington, N.Y.: Kennikat Press, 1974.
Riis, Jacob. *How the Other Half Lives.* Ed. David Leviatin. Boston: Bedford Books, 1997.
Riis, Jacob. *The Making of an American.* Ed. Roy Lubove. New York: Harper and Row, 1966.

Roanoke colony

The Roanoke colony, established as a business venture by SIR WALTER RALEIGH, was the first English settlement in the New World. Although three successive attempts at settlement failed (1585, 1586, 1587), the colony heralded England's entry into the competition for lands in the Americas, further heightening long-standing tensions with Spain.

Raleigh, as most explorers of his time, was looking for gold or silver, but he was also conscious of England's international position relative to Spain. He carefully planned the first English colony in territory claimed by Spain but far north of any actual settlement. An island located between the North Carolina mainland and the Outer Banks, Roanoke was difficult to reach, requiring navigation of the treacherous Cape Hatteras. Raleigh first sent Ralph Lane, a fellow veteran of the Irish wars, to build a fort on Roanoke. Most of the ships failed to reach the island, and food was scarce when they arrived. Relations with the native peoples were bad from the beginning. When Sir Francis Drake visited the colony in 1586, the remaining settlers determined to return to England with him. A second attempt in 1586 foundered in the West Indies. The third attempt in 1587 was led by John White, an experienced seaman who had sailed with Martin Frobisher in the 1570s and a survivor of the first venture. His intent was to settle on Chesapeake Bay, but a disagreement with a ship's captain left the colonists again on Roanoke Island. White was sent back to England for supplies, but diplomatic tensions and war with Spain kept him from returning until 1590. By then the colony had been deserted. The mysterious carving of the word *Croatoan* on a post suggested that the survivors had joined the nearby Indian settlement called Croatoan, but no other trace of the colonists was ever found. White's paintings of the landscape, animals, and peoples of the region left an indelible visual impression of a potential land of plenty.

Further Reading
Kupperman, Karen Ordahl. *Roanoke: The Abandoned Colony.* Reprint. New York: Rowman and Littlefield, 1991.
Miller, Lee. *Roanoke: Solving the Mystery of the Lost Colony.* New York: Penguin, 2002.
Quinn, David Beers. *England and the Discovery of America, 1481–1620.* New York: Alfred A. Knopf, 1974.
———. *Set Fair for Roanoke.* University of North Carolina Press, 1985.
———, ed. *The Roanoke Voyages, 1584–1590: Documents to Illustrate the English Voyages to North America under the Patent Granted to Walter Raleigh in 1584.* Mineola, N.Y.: Dover Publications, 1991.

Rølvaag, Ole Edvart (1876–1931) *author, educator*

Ole Rølvaag became one of the premier chroniclers of the Norwegian immigrant experience in the United States. His masterpiece *Giants in the Earth* (1927) is often considered one of the best, most powerfully written novels about pioneer life in America.

Rølvaag was born into a fishing family on the island of Dønna, Norway. He immigrated to the United States in

1896, working on his uncle's farm in Elk Point, South Dakota, to help pay for his education. After years of toil, he earned a bachelor's degree from St. Olaf College in Minnesota in 1905, and after a year of study at the University of Oslo, he returned to join the faculty of St. Olaf College. There he taught Norwegian language and literature until his death. He became a U.S. citizen in 1908 and married Jenny Berdahl the same year. The harshness of Rølvaag's own experience, from the years of hard work to the loss of two children, contributed to the tone of his novels, which emphasized the psychological uncertainty and loss experienced by Norwegian immigrants. Hoping to encourage second- and third-generation Norwegians to maintain their native culture, Rølvaag finally realized that it was an impossible dream. "Again and again," he wrote, second-generation Norwegians "have had impressed on them: all that has grown on American earth is good, but all that can be called *foreign* is at best suspect." Other important works include *Letters from America* (1912), *On Forgotten Paths* (1914), and *Pure Gold* (1930). The English translation *The Book of Longing* (1933) and Rølvaag's last book, *Their Father's God* (1931), were published posthumously.

Further Reading

Jorgenson, Theodore, and Nora O. Slocum. *Ole Edvart Rølvaag.* New York: Harper, 1939.
Moseley, Ann. *Ole Edvart Rølvaag.* Boise, Idaho: Boise State University, 1987.
Reigstad, Paul. *Rølvaag: His Life and Art.* Lincoln: University of Nebraska Press, 1972.

Roma immigration   See GYPSY IMMIGRATION.

Romanian immigration

Most ethnic Romanians from the Ottoman, Austrian, and Russian Empires and the state of Romania came as laborers and peasants and sought work wherever they could find it in North America. In the United States, they were attracted mainly to the industrial cities of the North, most prominently Cleveland, Ohio; Detroit, Michigan; and Chicago, Illinois. In Canada, peasants found opportunities to homestead on the prairies of what are now Saskatchewan and Alberta. According to the U.S. census of 2000 and the Canadian census of 2001, 367,310 Americans and 131,830 Canadians claimed Romanian ancestry. By 2000, Romanians were widely spread throughout North America. In the 1990s, New York, Los Angeles, and Ontario were replacing the older areas as most favored areas of settlement.

Romania occupies 88,800 square miles in southeast Europe on the Black Sea. It is bordered on the north and east by Ukraine, on the east by Moldova, on the west by Hungary and Serbia and Montenegro, and on the south by Bulgaria.

In 2002, the population was estimated at 22,364,022, with 89.1 percent of the population being Romanian, and 8.9 percent, Hungarian. More than two-thirds are adherents of the Romanian Orthodox Church; Roman Catholics and Protestants each make up about 6 percent of the population. Romanian tribes first created a Dacian kingdom that was occupied by the Roman Empire between 106 and 271. During that time, the people and their language were Romanized, setting them apart from the Slavs and Magyars who lived in surrounding areas. The foundation of the modern state structure was laid in the 13th century, particularly in the regions of Moldavia and Walachia, two principalities that were incorporated into the Ottoman Empire early in the 16th century. The western region of Transylvania, occupied by Romanians, Magyars, and Germans, formed a borderland between the lands of the Muslim Ottoman conquest and the Austrian and Hungarian lands of Christian Europe. Moldavia and Walachia were united to form Romania in 1863, and became fully independent in 1878. As an ally of Nazi Germany in World War II (1939–45), Romania lost considerable territory, including northern Bukovina, Bessarabia, and Trans-Dniestria. Falling under Soviet COLD WAR domination, Romania's economy deteriorated until it became one of the poorest countries in Europe. The country of Moldova, independent since the breakup of the Soviet Union in 1991, was essentially the old Romanian province of Bessarabia, and its people, mostly Romanians.

The first Romanians to immigrate to North America were Jews who came between 1870 and 1895 from Moldavia; Bessarabia, then under Russian control; or Bukovina, under Austrian control. Their numbers were small, but they did establish the basis for a permanent settlement in what would become Saskatchewan, in Canada. Between 1905 and 1908, they were joined by more than 200 additional homesteaders, brought to the area by Maurice, baron de Hirsch's Jewish Colonization Society. The first significant immigration in both the United States and Canada came between 1895 and 1920. During that period, it is estimated that more than 80,000 Romanians immigrated to the United States. Exact figures are difficult to determine, as most statistics were based on country of origin, which most often would have been Austria, Russia, or Hungary. Even after World War I (1914–18), with the creation of an expanded Romania, pre–World War I borders were frequently used to determine classification. Nevertheless, most Romanians came as single men intending to earn money and then return home, and the rate of return migration was high. Most were unskilled and found work in iron, steel, auto, and meatpacking industries of the U.S. North and Midwest. The Canadian experience in this period was very different, with most coming from peasant backgrounds in Transylvania and settling in Saskatchewan and Alberta. Exact numbers are difficult to determine, as the majority of Romanians actually emigrated from lands controlled by the

Austro-Hungarian or Ottoman Empires. As settled farmers, Canadian Romanians tended to stay in North America. By 1921, there were about 30,000 Romanians in Canada.

In the aftermath of World War II (see WORLD WAR II AND IMMIGRATION), thousands of "Forty-eighters" arrived as refugees. About 10,000 were admitted to the United States under provisions of the DISPLACED PERSONS ACT (1948). Most were relatively well educated and staunchly anticommunist, with a large percentage of professionals among them. Most settled in the industrial heartland, especially in New York, Chicago, Philadelphia, Detroit, Pittsburgh, Cleveland, and the mid-sized industrial towns of Ohio and western Pennsylvania. During the long years of communist rule, emigration was difficult, but with the fall of the communist regime in 1989, Romanians again began to immigrate to North America, mainly seeking economic opportunities. Between 1990 and 2002, average annual Romanian immigration to the United States was about 5,000. The movement was proportionately much greater to Canada. Of the 60,165 Romanian immigrants in Canada in 2001, more than 58 percent of them (35,170), came between 1991 and 2001. Many of them came from Yugoslavia's Vojvodina region, fleeing persecution and civil war.

See also AUSTRO-HUNGARIAN IMMIGRATION; RUSSIAN IMMIGRATION; YUGOSLAV IMMIGRATION.

Further Reading
Barton, J. *Peasants and Strangers: Italians, Rumanians, and Slovaks in an American City, 1890–1950.* Cambridge, Mass.: Harvard University Press, 1976.
Galitzi, Christine A. *A Study of Assimilation among the Roumanians in the United States.* 1929. Reprint, New York: AMS Press, 1968.
Patterson, G. J. "Greek and Romanian Immigrants as Hyphenated Americans: Towards a Theory of White Ethnicity." In *New Directions in Greek-American Studies.* Eds. D. Georgakas and C. C. Moskos. New York: Pella, 1991.
———. "The Persistence of White Ethnicity in Canada: The Case of the Romanians." *East European Quarterly* 19 (1986): 493–500.
———. *The Romanians of Saskatchewan: Four Generations of Adaptation.* Ottawa: National Museum of Man, 1977.
Tranu, Jean. *Présence roumaine au Canada.* Montreal: J. Tranu, 1986.

Romany immigration   See GYPSY IMMIGRATION.

Royal African Company

In 1672, the Royal African Company was granted a monopoly in the British slave trade in order to ensure an adequate labor force for the plantations of the Caribbean and the southern colonies of the Atlantic seaboard of North America. The company flourished between 1672 and 1698, when Parliament opened the slave trade to all merchants.

Africans were brought to America in small numbers beginning in 1619, when a Dutch warship landed about 20 workers at Port Comfort, Virginia (see AFRICAN FORCED MIGRATION). SLAVERY as a legal institution was not provided for in the colonies, however, until 1661, and most Africans in English colonies until the 1650s were probably servants. With the passage of the first NAVIGATION ACTS in 1650–51 and the advent of a royal policy under Charles II (r. 1660–85) discouraging the emigration of indentured servants (see INDENTURED SERVITUDE), a labor shortage ensued on southern plantations. In order to provide a more stable labor force for tobacco, rice, and indigo farmers, in 1660, the British government chartered the Company of Royal Adventurers Trading to Africa. During the second Anglo-Dutch War (1665–67), the company failed but was reorganized in 1672 as the Royal African Company. By the 1680s, it was averaging more than 25 annual voyages to Africa and transporting 5,000 slaves a year. Still, the company was unable either to turn a profit or supply the demand for slave labor. By 1713 the company was virtually bankrupt, although it maintained some forts on the West African coast until it was formally dissolved in 1821.

Further Reading
Collins, Edward Day. "Studies in the Colonial Policy of England, 1672–1680: The Plantations, the Royal African Company, and the Slave Trade." In *American Historical Association Annual Report . . . for the Year 1900.* Washington, D.C.: American Historical Association, 1901.
Davies, K. G. *The Royal African Company.* London and New York: Routledge/Thoemmes Press, 1999.
Galenson, David W. *Traders, Planters, and Slaves: Market Behavior in Early English America.* New York: Cambridge University Press, 1986.
Killinger, Charles Lintner. "The Royal African Company Slave Trade to Virginia, 1689–1713." M.A. thesis, College of William and Mary, 1969.
Law, Robin, David Ryden, and J. R. Oldfield. *The British Transatlantic Slave Trade.* 4 vols. London: Pickering and Chatto, 2003.

Russian immigration

Though Russia controlled parts of the modern United States and Canada, it left relatively little cultural mark during its early 19th-century settlement of the Pacific Northwest. Russian presence is thus largely the product of immigration between 1881 and 1914. According to the U.S. census of 2000 and the Canadian census of 2001, 2,652,214 Americans and 337,960 Canadians claimed Russian descent, though many of these were members of ethnic groups formerly part of the Russian Empire and Soviet Union. By 2000, Russians were spread widely throughout the United States and Canada, though more than 40 percent of Russian Americans lived in the Northeast and almost one-third of Russian Canadians lived in Ontario.

Russia is the largest country in the world by landmass, occupying 6,585,000 square miles, or more than 76 percent

A group of Russian emigrants from Siberia, ca. 1910, stand near a train. Beginning in the 1870s, the more conservative elements of religious communal groups, such as the Mennonites and Doukhobors, tended to choose western Canada with its greater accommodation of their religious practices, while those seeking individual freedom and economic opportunity most often chose the prairies of the United States. *(Library of Congress, Prints & Photographs Division [LC-USZ62-1782])*

of the total area of the former Union of Soviet Socialist Republics (USSR). It stretches from eastern Europe across northern Asia to the Pacific Ocean. Finland, Norway, Estonia, Latvia, Belarus, and Ukraine border Russia to the west; Georgia, Azerbaijan, Kazakhstan, China, Mongolia, and North Korea border on the south; the small Russian enclave of Kaliningrad, west of Lithuania, is bordered by Poland on the south. In 2002, the population was estimated at 145,470,197. In 1997, the ethnic composition of the country was 86.6 percent Russian and 3.2 percent Tatar. The remaining 10 percent was composed of relatively small numbers of more than a dozen ethnic minorities. The chief religions were Russian Orthodox and Muslim, although most Russians claimed no religious affiliation.

During the 18th, 19th, and 20th centuries, the transformation of Russian state boundaries significantly affected the character of its immigration. The old heartland of the Russian peoples was a region in eastern Europe between modern Kiev, Ukraine, and Moscow. The Slavic peoples who inhabited the Kiev region were driven northward by the Mongol invasion of the 13th century. By 1480, Ivan III (the Great) (r. 1462–1505) established Russian independence of the Mongols and began to forge a modern state. Ivan the Terrible (r. 1533–84), grandson of Ivan III, was the first

grand prince to be called "czar" (awe-inspiring) and began the expansion of the state to include significant numbers of non-Russian peoples. Between 1667 and 1795, Russia conquered huge tracts of eastern Europe, mainly from the kingdoms of Poland and Sweden. These lands included the peoples of modern Latvia, Lithuania, Estonia, eastern Poland, Belarus, and Ukraine. In 1815, following the Napoleonic Wars, Russia acquired most of the remainder of Poland and Moldova (Bessarabia). Throughout the 19th century, Russia continued to expand, especially into the Caucasus Mountain region and central Asia, occupying regions that would later become the modern countries of Armenia, Azerbaijan, Georgia, Kazakhstan, Kyrgyzstan, Turkmenistan, Tajikistan, and Uzbekistan, as well as into Finland in the north. As a result, during the great age of immigration from eastern Europe between 1880 and 1920, more than a dozen major ethnic groups were often classified by immigration agents as "Russian," though they were in fact part of these older nations. The Bolshevik Revolution of 1917 in Russia, which ushered in the world's first Communist government, soon spread to most of the surrounding territories acquired by Russia, leading to the establishment of a new state, the USSR, or Soviet Union. The USSR was roughly coterminous with the old Russian Empire prior to the revolution, except for the loss of Finland, Latvia, Estonia, Lithuania, and Poland, which became independent countries after World War I (1914–18). During World War II (1939–45), the Soviet Union reoccupied parts of Finland, Estonia, Latvia, Lithuania, Poland, and Moldova and exercised extensive control over the foreign and immigration policies of the nominally independent countries of Poland, Czechoslovakia, Hungary, East Germany, and Romania. Finally, burdened by the ongoing expense of COLD WAR conflict with the United States and internal rebellions throughout Eastern Europe, the Soviet Union collapsed in 1991, leaving 15 separate states, based largely on national boundaries prior to Russian occupation, each having its own annual immigration quota to the United States and Canada. The one important national difference was that each former Soviet socialist republic had a significant Russian population, descended mainly from bureaucrats and settlers deliberately placed by the Soviet government to facilitate control from the Russian capital of Moscow.

Russians who first migrated eastward through Siberia to Alaska and the Pacific coasts of the United States and Canada during the late 18th century were mostly trappers, merchants, and colonial officials. The first permanent Russian settlement in Alaska was on Kodiak Island in the 1780s, and Russia, along with Great Britain and the United States, claimed the Pacific Northwest. Numbers of Russian settlers in North America were always small, however. In 1867,

when Alaska was sold to the United States, fewer than 1,000 Russians lived in Alaska, but they had established a distinctive cultural presence in coastal regions. Prior to 1880, there was little Russian immigration to the United States.

Immigration from the Russian Empire during the late 19th and early 20th centuries, on the other hand, was massive—an estimated 3.2 million between 1881 and 1914—but included a relatively small proportion of ethnic Russians (fewer than 100,000). The czarist government practically forbade the immigration of the non-Jewish population, encouraging instead migration to the burgeoning industrial cities or to new farmlands in Siberia and the Russian Far East. About half of Russia's immigrants were therefore Jews, and most of the rest were religious dissenters, including Old Believers, Mennonites (see MENNONITE IMMIGRATION) Doukhobors, and Molokans. Slavic peoples recently incorporated in the Russian Empire, including Poles, Belarusians, and Carpatho-Rusans; and the descendants of Germans who had homesteaded the southern farmlands of Russia during the 18th century. The vast majority of immigrants from the Russian Empire landed in New York City and settled there or in other industrial cities of the American North. The pacifist Molokans formed the only large migration of Russians to the West Coast of the United States, with about 5,000 immigrating to California between 1904 and 1912. Although there were about 20,000 Russian Molokans in the United States in 1970—

Main Ethnic Populations in the Former Soviet Republics, 1991

Republics	Ethnic Groups
Armenia	Armenians, 93 percent
Azerbaijan	Azerbaijani, 78 percent; Armenians, 8 percent; Russians, 8 percent
Belarus	Belarusians, 78 percent; Russians, 13 percent
Estonia	Estonians, 61.5 percent; Russians, 30 percent
Georgia	Georgians, 69 percent; Armenians, 9 percent; Russians, 7 percent
Latvia	Latvians, 52 percent; Russians, 34 percent
Lithuania	Lithuanians, 80 percent; Russians, 9 percent; Poles, 8 percent
Kazakhstan	Kazakhs, 42 percent; Russians, 38 percent; Ukrainians, 5 percent
Kyrgyzstan	Kirghiz, 52 percent; Russians, 21.5 percent; Uzbeks, 13 percent
Moldova	Moldovans, 64 percent; Ukrainians, 14 percent; Russians, 13 percent
Russia	Russians, 83 percent
Tajikistan	Tajiks, 59 percent; Uzbeks, 23 percent; Russians, 10 percent
Turkmenistan	Turkmen, 68 percent; Russians, 13 percent; Uzbeks, 8.5 percent
Ukraine	Ukrainians, 71 percent; Russians, 20 percent; Belarusians, 8 percent
Uzbekistan	Uzbeks, 69 percent; Russians, 11 percent

As a result of ethnic mixing across several centuries, immigration figures from lands once controlled by Russia are difficult to establish. There might be a significant Russian component in immigration from any of these 15 countries, though the majority of Russians today come from Russia itself.

most in Los Angeles and California—they were rapidly becoming acculturated. Canada especially courted communal agriculturalists from Russia by promoting group colonization. This led to the establishment of colonies by Mennonites in Saskatchewan (1870s), the Doukhobors in Saskatchewan (1890s), and the Molokans in Alberta (1920s).

After the Bolshevik Revolution, emigration under the Soviet Union (1917–91) was virtually halted, both because of even more stringent Soviet controls and because of suspicion of radical ideologies by U.S. and Canadian officials (see SOVIET IMMIGRATION). With the breakup of the Soviet Union in 1991, Russians were finally allowed to immigrate freely to the West. Almost a half million Soviets or former Soviets immigrated to the United States during the 1990s, probably about 15 percent of them ethnic Russians. The number of ethnic Russians immigrating continued to grow through the late 1990s, from 11,529 in 1998 to 20,413 in 2001. Of Canada's 142,000 immigrants from the former Soviet Union (2001), 53 percent came between 1991 and 2001.

See also ESTONIAN IMMIGRATION; HUTTERITE IMMIGRATION; JEWISH IMMIGRATION; LATVIAN IMMIGRATION; LITHUANIAN IMMIGRATION; POLISH IMMIGRATION; UKRAINIAN IMMIGRATION.

Further Reading

Hardwick, S. *Russian Refuge: Religion, Migration and Settlement on the North American Pacific Rim.* Chicago: University of Chicago Press, 1993.

Jeletzky, T. F., ed. *Russian Canadians: Their Past and Present.* Ottawa: Borealis Press, 1983.

Kipel, Vitaut. *Belarusy u ZshA.* Minsk, 1993.

Koch, F. C. *The Volga Germans: In Russia and the Americas, from 1763 to the Present.* University Park: Pennsylvania State University Press, 1977.

Kuropas, Myron B. *The Ukrainian Americans: Roots and Aspirations, 1884–1954.* Toronto: University of Toronto Press, 1991.

Long, J. W. *From Privileged to Dispossessed: The Volga Germans, 1860–1917.* Lincoln: University of Nebraska Press, 1988.

Magosci, Paul R. *The Carpatho-Rusyn Americans.* New York: Chelsea House, 1989.

———. *Our People: Carpatho-Rusyns and Their Descendants in North America.* 3d rev. ed. Toronto: Multicultural History Society of Ontario, 1994.

———. *The Russian Americans.* New York: Chelsea House, 1987.

Morris, R. A. *Old Russian Ways: Cultural Variations among Three Russian Groups in Oregon.* New York: AMS Press, 1991.

Pilkington, Hilary. *Migration, Displacement and Identity in Post-Soviet Russia.* New York: Routledge, 1998.

Raeff, Marc. *Russia Abroad: A Cultural History of the Russian Emigration, 1919–1939.* New York: Oxford University Press, 1990.

Smith, B. S., and B. J. Barnett, eds. *Russian America: The Forgotten Frontier.* Tacoma: Washington State Historical Society, 1990.

Starr, S. F., ed. *Russia's American Colony.* Durham, N.C.: Duke University Press, 1987.

Stumpp, K. *The German-Russians: Two Centuries of Pioneering.* Lincoln, Neb.: American Historical Society of Germans from Russia, 1971.

Westerman, V. *The Russians in America: A Chronology and Fact Book.* Dobbs Ferry, N.Y.: Oceana, 1977.

S

Salvadoran immigration

Salvadoran immigration to the United States is a new phenomenon, the product of a long civil war that decimated the country during the 1980s. According to the U.S. census of 2000 and the Canadian census of 2001, 655,165 Americans and 26,735 Canadians claimed Salvadoran descent. The Immigration and Naturalization Service (INS) estimated in 2000 that another 189,000 Salvadorans were in the country illegally, though many groups believe that figure to be low. The number of Salvadoran Canadians is probably twice as high as the official count. Almost half of Salvadoran Americans live in the greater Los Angeles area, with significant concentrations in New York City, San Francisco, Houston, Chicago, and Washington, D.C. More than a third of Salvadoran Canadians live in Ontario, with large concentrations also in Quebec.

El Salvador covers 8,000 square miles in Central America. It is bordered by Guatemala on the west and Honduras on the north and east. In 2002, the population was estimated at 6,237,662. The people are largely mestizo (94 percent) with a small Amerindian population (5 percent). More than three-quarters of the population is Roman Catholic. El Salvador became independent of Spain in 1821 and of the Central American Federation in 1839. A fight with Honduras in 1969 over the presence of 300,000 Salvadoran workers left 2,000 dead. A military coup overthrew the government of President Carlos Humberto Romero in 1979, but the ruling military-civilian junta failed to quell a rebellion by leftist insurgents armed by Cuba and Nicaragua. Right-wing death squads organized to eliminate suspected leftists were blamed for thousands of deaths in the 1980s. The administration of U.S. president Ronald Reagan staunchly supported the government with military aid. After 15 years of conflict, the civil war ended January 16, 1992, as the government and leftist rebels signed a formal peace treaty. It has been estimated that 75,000 people died in the conflict.

Emigration from El Salvador was small prior to 1970. Fewer than 21,000 came to the United States between 1951 and 1970, many from the middle and upper classes, seeking greater economic opportunity and most frequently settling in Florida and California. There was virtually no immigration to Canada. The civil war in El Salvador, however, created the greatest refugee crisis in the Western Hemisphere, uprooting a quarter of the country's population and leading to massive immigration. More than half left the country, principally for Mexico, the United States, and Canada. The United States, heavily involved in the COLD WAR conflict, was throughout most of the period reluctant to admit Salvadorans as political asylees, though almost 430,000 Salvadorans were admitted between 1981 and 2000. These came mainly from the lower and middle classes and were generally less well educated. Canada, on the other hand, began to relax its admissions policies in response to the war. In March 1981, the Canadian government made it easier for Salvadorans to gain entry on humanitarian grounds and two years later allowed them to apply for visas while outside the country. Of 38,460 Salvadoran immigrants in Canada in 2001, only 1,215 arrived before 1981.

On May 20, 1999, the INS relaxed application rules for permanent resident status for Salvadorans who fled repressive governments during the Salvadoran civil war. As a result, they were allowed to remain in the United States during their application process, and they were not required to prove that they would suffer extreme hardship if returned to El Salvador. As a result of these changes, more Salvadorans took advantage of the legal application process. Between 2000 and 2002, annual Salvadoran immigration to the United States averaged 28,000.

Further Reading

Bonner, Raymond. *Weakness and Deceit: U.S. Policy and El Salvador.* New York: Times Books, 1984.

Leslie, Leigh A. "Families Fleeing War: The Case of Central Americans." *Marriage and Family Review* nos. 19, 1–2 (1993): 193–205.

Mahler, Sarah J. *American Dreaming: Immigrant Life on the Margins.* Princeton, N.J.: Princeton University Press, 1995.

———. *Salvadorans in Suburbia: Symbiosis and Conflict.* Boston: Allyn and Bacon, 1995.

Menjívar, Cecilia. *Fragmented Ties: Salvadoran Immigrant Networks in America.* Berkeley: University of California Press, 2000.

———. "Salvadorans and Nicaraguans: Refugees Become Workers." In *Illegal Immigration in America: A Reference Handbook.* Ed. David Haines and Karen E. Rosenblum. Westport, Conn.: Greenwood Press, 1999.

Mitchell, Christopher, ed. *Western Hemisphere Immigration and United States Foreign Policy.* University Park: Pennsylvania State University Press, 1992.

Montes Mozo, S., and J. J. García Vásquez. *Salvadoran Migration to the United States: An Exploratory Study.* Washington, D.C.: Hemispheric Migration Project, Center for Immigration Policy and Refugee Assistance, Georgetown University, 1988.

Neuwirth, Gertrude. *The Settlement of Salvadorean Refugees in Ottawa and Toronto.* Ottawa: Employment and Immigration Canada, 1989.

Samoan immigration See PACIFIC ISLANDER IMMIGRATION.

San Francisco, California

San Francisco was the first great immigrant city of the American West, receiving people from around the world during the CALIFORNIA GOLD RUSH of 1848–49. In 2000, its metropolitan population of 7,039,362 was one of the most culturally diverse in the United States. About 30 percent of its population was Asian and 14 percent Hispanic (see *HISPANIC* AND RELATED TERMS). The largest non-English ethnic groups of the greater metropolitan area (including Oakland and San Jose) were Mexican (988,841), Irish (649,758), Chinese (521,645), Italian (422,963), Filipino (382,224), Vietnamese (156,832), and Asian Indian (155,121).

Established by Spain as the Mission of Saint Francis of Assisi in 1776, the settlement remained small until Mexico gained its independence from Spain in 1821 and a number of Californians decided to settle the distant territory more than 2,300 miles from the capital of Mexico City, a village then named Yerba Buena. England, Russia, and the United States all sought control of the great natural harbor of San Francisco Bay, a goal that the United States achieved with victory in the U.S.-MEXICAN WAR (1846–48). The discovery of gold at Sutter's Mill in the Sacramento Valley of California in January 1848 transformed the newly acquired village on the bay. Between 1848 and the granting of statehood in 1850, more than 90,000 people migrated to California, most from within the United States, but large numbers also arrived from Mexico, Chile, Australia, and many regions of Europe. Almost all arrived through the port of San Francisco, turning a sleepy village into a city of 25,000 in less than two years. Among the immigrants were large numbers of Chinese workers from the impoverished and flood-ravaged province of Guangdong (Canton). San Francisco soon became known for its lawlessness and violent NATIVISM, especially directed at Chileans, Chinese, and Irish. By 1870, the city was almost evenly divided between those born in the United States (76,000) and those born outside the country (74,000), most of them being Irish, Chinese, German, and Italian. Bowing to pressure from San Francisco and California generally, in 1882 Congress passed the CHINESE EXCLUSION ACT, the first racial immigration legislation in the United States. Nativist legislation continued with the GENTLEMEN'S AGREEMENT (1907) and the ALIEN LAND ACT (1913).

With increasing government regulations following passage of the Chinese Exclusion Act and its related extensions, it became impossible to adequately examine immigrants at the two-story shed at the Pacific Mail Steamship Company Wharf, then in use as a processing facility. Following the example of the ELLIS ISLAND facility of New York, the government created a new immigration detention center on ANGEL ISLAND. Sometimes called "the Ellis Island of the West," Angel Island was located on the largest island in San Francisco Bay, about two miles east of Sausalito. During its 30-year history (1910–40), as many as 1 million immigrants passed through the facilities—both departing and arriving—including Russians, Japanese, Asian Indians, Koreans, Australians, Filipinos, New Zealanders, Mexicans, and citizens of various South American countries. Almost 60 percent of these immigrants were, however, Chinese. The immigration center on Angel Island was built to stringently enforce anti-Chinese legislation, rather than to aid potential immigrants. Whereas the rejection rate at Ellis Island was about 1 percent, it was about 18 percent on Angel Island, reflecting the clear anti-Chinese bias that led to its establishment.

Upon arrival in San Francisco, Europeans and first- and second-class travelers were usually processed on board and allowed to disembark directly to the city. All others were ferried to Angel Island, where the men and women were separated before undergoing stringent medical tests, performed with little regard for the dignity of the immigrant, looking particularly for parasitic infections. Afterward, prospective immigrants were housed in crowded barracks, sleeping in three-high bunk beds, awaiting interrogation. The grueling interviews, held before a Board of Special Inquiry, including two immigrant inspectors, a stenographer, and a translator, covered every detail of the background and lives of proposed entrants. Any deviation from details offered by family members resulted in rejection and deportation. And if a successful entrant ever left the country, the transcript of his interrogation was on record for use when he returned. The whole process could take weeks, as family members on the mainland had to be contacted for corroborating evidence. In the case of deportation proceedings and their appeals, an immigrant might spend months or more than a year on Angel Island. The unsanitary conditions on Angel Island and degrading treatment of Asian immigrants led to outrage among progressives, but little was done to alter the situation before a fire destroyed the administration building in 1940.

With completion of the Panama Canal in 1914, travel between the East and West Coast became more efficient, further contributing to the rapid growth of San Francisco. As Los Angeles and Oakland began to develop their port and commercial facilities, San Francisco gradually lost its preeminent position as the West Coast center of commerce.

World War II (1941–45) changed the character of San Francisco. Becoming increasingly industrial, it attracted large numbers of African Americans, principally from the South, altering the racial composition of the city. Japanese and Chinese citizens continued to demonstrate their loyalty during the war, though their fate was radically different. Under great suspicion while the United States was at war with imperial Japan, some 18,000 Japanese Americans from the greater San Francisco area were interned as a result of Executive Order 9066 (see JAPANESE INTERNMENT, WORLD WAR II). With China as an ally, however, Chinese San Franciscans earned greater respect and a wider number of job opportunities. By the 1960s, the Chinese were moving into the cultural mainstream, and the Japanese followed soon after. After World War II, San Francisco increasingly became a destination for Mexican and Central American immigrants who replaced the Irish and Italians steadily moving out of the inner city. In the 20th century, minority politics came to dominate San Francisco. While the majority of Californians supported anti-immigrant propositions, such as 187, 209, and 227 (see PROPOSITION 187), San Franciscans consistently opposed them and earned a reputation for generally liberal politics.

Further Reading

Berchell, Robert A. *The San Francisco Irish, 1848–1880.* Berkeley: University of California Press, 1980.

Broussard, Albert S. *Black San Francisco: The Struggle for Racial Equality in the West, 1900–1954.* Lawrence: University Press of Kansas, 1993.

Chen, Yong. *Chinese San Francisco, 1850–1943: A Trans-Pacific Community.* Stanford, Calif.: Stanford University Press, 2000.

Chinn, Thomas. *Bridging the Pacific: San Francisco Chinatown and Its People.* San Francisco: Chinese Historical Society of America, 1989.

Cinel, Dino. *From Italy to San Francisco: The Immigrant Experience.* Stanford, Calif.: Stanford University Press, 1982.

Gumina, Deanna Paoli. *The Italians of San Francisco, 1850–1930.* New York: Center for Migration Studies, 1978.

Jain, Usha R. *The Gujaratis of San Francisco.* New York: AMS Press, 1989.

La Brack, Bruce. *The Sikhs of Northern California, 1904–1975: A Socio-Historic Study.* New York: AMS Press, 1988.

Wong, B. P. *Ethnicity and Entrepreneurship: Immigrant Chinese in the San Francisco Bay Area.* Boston: Allyn and Bacon, 1996.

Yung, Judy. *Unbound Feet: A Social History of Chinese Women in San Francisco.* Berkeley: University of California Press, 1995.

Schwenkfelder immigration

The Schwenkfelders were a small, pietistic sect that emigrated from southern Germany and lower Silesia in the Austrian Empire beginning in 1731. After being persecuted for two centuries, and denied the right to Christian burial, they decided to follow like-minded German immigrants to the PENNSYLVANIA COLONY where religious freedom was guaranteed. They arrived in Philadelphia in six migrations between 1731 to 1737, with the largest group of 200 sailing from Rotterdam in 1734. They settled farmsteads around Philadelphia, especially in modern Berks and Lehigh Counties. By 2003, almost all Schwenkfelders had joined more established Christian denominations, though many still claimed to be followers of the old doctrine.

Schwenkfelders followed the teachings of Caspar Schwenckfeld von Ossig (1489–1561), a devout Catholic and member of the Silesian nobility. He was drawn to Martin Luther's reform teachings but disagreed with him over the exact nature of the Lord's Supper and the baptism of infants. Schwenckfeld believed that the Bible should not be literally interpreted or used as a "paper pope" but rather that believers should trust the Holy Spirit for insight into its meaning. Family was central to Schwenkfelder worship, with house churches the norm. As a result, the Society of Schwenkfelders was loosely organized, and its members freely associated with more established churches, where they could share their gifts of spiritual insight. In 2003, there was still an organized church, consisting of five congregations and about 2,600 members associated with the United Church of Christ, though many who claim Schwenkfelder roots are associated with the religious work of the Evangelical Lutherans, Presbyterians, American Baptists, the Christian Missionary Alliance, the Evangelical Association, and the Holiness Movement.

Further Reading

Brecht, Samuel K. *The Genealogical Record of the Schwenkfelder Families.* Pennsburg, Pa.: Board of Publication of the Schwenkfelder Church, 1923.

Erb, Peter. *The Spiritual Diary of Christopher Wiegner.* Waterloo, Canada: Wilfrid Laurier Press, 1978.

Weiser, C. Z. "Caspar Schwenckfeld and the Schwenkfelders." *Mercersburg Review* (July 1870): 362.

Scott Act (United States) (1888)

In response to growing antagonism toward immigrants generally and Chinese immigrants specifically, Pennsylvania representative William Scott, a Democrat, introduced legislation to extend restrictions embodied in the CHINESE EXCLUSION ACT (1882).

The Scott Act excluded immigration of "all persons of the Chinese race," excepting "Chinese officials, teachers, students, merchants, or travelers for pleasure or curiosity." A Chinese laborer who had come to the United States prior to 1882 was permitted to leave and return only if he had "a lawful wife, child, or parent in the United States, or property therein of the value of one thousand dollars, or debts of like amount due him and pending settlement." Further, all Chinese who qualified for entry, excepting "diplomatic or consular officers and their attendants," were required to obtain certificates of clearance in advance from U.S. representatives in China. The measure was passed on September 13, 1888 and approved by President Grover Cleveland on October 1, 1888.

Further Reading

Gyory, Andrew. *Closing the Gate: Race, Politics, and the Chinese Exclusion Act.* Chapel Hill: University of North Carolina Press, 1998.

Hutchinson, E. P. *Legislative History of American Immigration Policy, 1798–1965.* Philadelphia: University of Pennsylvania Press, 1981.

LeMay, Michael C. *From Open Door to Dutch Door: An Analysis of U.S. Immigration Policy since 1820.* New York: Praeger, 1987.

Takaki, Ronald. *Strangers from a Different Shore.* Boston: Little, Brown, 1989.

Scottish immigration

The large Scottish and Scots-Irish immigration of the 18th century helped define the cultural patterns of the United States and Canada. Scots and Scots-Irish Americans were the fifth largest ethnic group in the United States in 2000, with only German, Irish, English, and Italian Americans being more numerous. Scots and Scots-Irish were the third most numerous group in Canada, behind only English and French Canadians. In the U.S. census of 2000, more than 9.2 million Americans claimed Scots or Scots-Irish descent; while in the Canadian census of 2001, 4,157,210 Canadians claimed Scottish ancestry. Being among the earliest settlers to North America and coming in very large numbers from the 18th century, by the 20th century Scots were integral to both American and Canadian identity and were scattered widely throughout both countries. By the time Canada took its first post-confederation census in 1871, 26 percent of Canadians were of Scottish descent, 24 percent Irish, and 20 percent English. By the time other immigrant groups overtook the British in numbers immigrating to the United States, around the turn of the 20th century, the British culture pattern had been firmly established as the American model (see BRITISH IMMIGRATION; IRISH IMMIGRATION). In Canada, the early French enclave of Quebec became increasingly isolated as British customs and institutions took root throughout the remainder of Canada.

Scotland covers 30,414 square miles on the northern third of the island of Britain. England is its neighbor to the south. Scotland was an independent state on the island of Britain during the medieval period but fell under English influence from the 13th century as the two royal families became closely entwined through marriage. In 1603, with the death of Queen Elizabeth I, the Scottish king James IV also became king of England, as James I. The Scottish royal family, the Stuarts, was weakened as a result of the Glorious Revolution of 1688, and the Act of Union of 1707 made the kingdom of Scotland and the principality of Wales integral parts of a British empire under the United Kingdom of Great Britain. Gradually, Scots, especially in the southern lowlands, became more anglicized, and most converted to Presbyterianism. Many Highland Scots nevertheless retained their clan structure and Roman Catholicism and continued to support the ousted Stuart dynasty well into the 18th century.

Although Scots had been among the earliest immigrants to the Americas, the first widespread Scottish immigration to the New World came between 1717 and 1775, when more than 100,000 Presbyterian Scots-Irish settled in America, mainly because of high rents or famine and most coming from families who had been in Ireland for several generations (see ULSTER). In the colonial period, these Scots-Irish were usually referred to simply as Irish, making it difficult to determine exact figures. Additionally, large numbers of rebellious Scots were exiled to America by the British government. But there was also a significant voluntary migration of Scots directly from Scotland, especially after 1730, with some 40,000 coming between 1763 and 1775 alone. Although Scots and Scots-Irish became prominent throughout the colonies, they frequently settled along the Appalachian frontier and largely influenced the religion and culture of the frontier regions as they developed. Altogether this represented the largest movement of any group from the British Isles to British North America in the 18th century.

Though the politics of the Napoleonic Wars (1803–15) limited immigration after the American Revolution (1775–83; see AMERICAN REVOLUTION AND IMMIGRATION), between 1783 and 1812 about 100,000 people immigrated from Ulster, most of them Scots-Irish. Thereafter, the immigration of the Scots-Irish became closely tied to the story of Irish immigration. The immigration of Scots from Scotland itself was redirected to Canada after the American Revolution. By the time of the first Canadian census in 1871, Scots totaled 26 percent of the population, compared to 24 percent Irish and 20 percent English. After 1850, however, Scottish immigration to the United States picked up, and by 1870, the United States once again became the predominant destination for Scots immigrating to the New World. Between 1870 and 1920, about 53 percent of all Scottish immigrants went to the United States. During the difficult economic crisis in the 1920s, about 160,000 Scots immigrated to the United States, with a large percentage from declining industries.

Agricultural consolidations in Scotland after 1870 led to an increase of agriculturalists immigrating to Canada, and Scots gradually began to fill the western prairies. By 1911, people of Scots ancestry constituted between 14 and 19 percent of the populations of Manitoba, Saskatchewan, Alberta, and British Columbia. Scots continued to immigrate in significant numbers throughout much of the 20th century, though exact figures are difficult to determine because figures on Scots were not separated from aggregate numbers coming from the United Kingdom.

See also CANADA—IMMIGRATION SURVEY AND POLICY OVERVIEW; UNITED STATES—IMMIGRATION SURVEY AND POLICY OVERVIEW.

Further Reading

Bailyn, Bernard. *Voyagers to the West.* New York: Alfred A. Knopf, 1986.

Berthoff, Rowland Tappan. *British Immigrants in Industrial America: 1790–1950.* Cambridge, Mass.: Harvard University Press, 1953.

Bumsted, J. M. *The People's Clearance: Highland Emigration to British North America, 1770–1815.* Edinburgh, U.K.: Edinburgh University Press, 1982.

Dickson, R. J. *Ulster Immigration to the United States.* London: Routledge, 1966.

Donaldson, Gordon. *The Scots Overseas.* London: R. Hale, 1966.

Erikson, Charlotte. *The Invisible Immigrants: The Adaptation of English and Scottish Immigrants in Nineteenth-Century America.* Miami, Fla.: University of Miami Press, 1972.

Fischer, David Hackett. *Albion's Seed: Four British Folkways in America.* New York: Oxford University Press, 1989.

Graham, Ian C. C. *Colonists from Scotland: Emigration to North America, 1707–1783.* Ithaca, N.Y.: Cornell University Press, 1956.

Griffin, Patrick. *The People with No Name: Ireland's Ulster Scots, America's Scots Irish, and the Creation of a British Atlantic World, 1689–1764.* Princeton, N.J.: Princeton University Press, 2001.

Johnson, Stanley. *A History of Emigration from the United Kingdom to North America, 1763–1912.* London: Routledge and Sons, 1913.

Leyburn, James G. *The Scotch-Irish: A Social History.* Chapel Hill: University of North Carolina Press, 1962.

Lines, Kenneth. *British and Canadian Immigration to the United States since 1920.* San Francisco: R. and E. Research Associates, 1978.

Reid, W. Stanford. *The Scottish Tradition in Canada.* Toronto: McClelland and Stewart, 1976.

Van Vugt, William E. *Britain to America: The Mid-Nineteenth Century Immigrants to the United States.* Champaign: University of Illinois Press, 1999.

Wilson, David A. *United Irishmen, United States: Immigrant Radicals in the Early Republic.* Ithaca, N.Y.: Cornell University Press, 1998.

Selkirk, Lord   See DOUGLAS, THOMAS.

Selkirk settlement   See RED RIVER COLONY.

September 11, 2001

September 11, or 9/11, is used almost universally to identify collectively the 2001 terrorist attacks on the Pentagon in Washington, D.C., and the World Trade Center in New York City. Almost 3,000 people were killed in the attacks, including more than 300 firefighters. The 19 hijackers of four airplanes belonged to an Islamic terror network, al-Qaeda, headed by a wealthy Saudi, Osama bin Laden. Bin Laden's group was headquartered in Afghanistan, where the fundamentalist Taliban regime provided support and protection. As a result of the international outrage aimed at bin Laden and al-Qaeda, President George W. Bush and the U.S. government launched a "war on terror," which included the overthrow of the Taliban government in Afghanistan, close cooperation with countries around the world in locating and prosecuting terrorists, and increased regulation of immigration and surveillance of the activities of immigrants in the United States.

On the morning of September 11, the hijackers commandeered four commercial aircraft loaded with jet fuel and used them as highly explosive guided missiles. The two airliners hijacked from Boston's Logan International Airport slammed into the twin towers of New York's World Trade Center, and in less than two hours the 110-story structures collapsed, killing 2,749 people. Another aircraft was hijacked at the capital's Dulles International Airport and flown into the outer ring of the Pentagon, killing 189 people. A fourth aircraft hijacked at the Newark International Airport in New Jersey was destined for the U.S. Capitol but crashed in a Pennsylvania field when passengers fought with the hijackers. As investigators worldwide sifted through evidence and arrested conspirators, al-Qaeda was linked to a number of earlier high-profile terrorist attacks against

United States interests, including the murder of 18 army Rangers in Somalia in 1993, the bombings of U.S. embassies in Kenya and Tanzania in 1998, and the bombing of the USS *Cole* in Yemen in 2000.

Within minutes of the attacks, a national ground stop was instituted, preventing all aircraft from taking off, and all border ports of entry were put on high alert. Within hours, about 4,500 aircraft of all kinds were safely landed. Some commercial flights resumed service on September 13, though civil aviation only gradually recovered, struggling with low passenger demand and the cost of implementing new safety measures.

On September 20, President Bush announced creation of the new Office of Homeland Security, which became a U.S. department in March 2003. As a result of the September 11 attacks, the U.S. and Canadian governments were forced to confront terrorism as a domestic rather than an international issue, which led to a series of immigration and travel reforms. In the United States the USA PATRIOT ACT was quickly passed and signed into law (October 26, 2001), providing for greater surveillance of aliens and increasing the power of the attorney general to identify, arrest, and deport aliens. The monitoring of some aliens entering on nonimmigrant visas was instituted, new fraud-resistant travel documents were authorized, and more extensive background checks of all applications and petitions to the IMMIGRATION AND NATURALIZATION SERVICE (INS) were approved, the SEVIS database was created to track the location of aliens in the country on student visas, and the U.S. attorney general was given the right to immediately expel anyone suspected of terrorist links. Also, the State Department introduced a 20-day waiting period for visa applications from men 16 to 45 years of age from Afghanistan, Algeria, Bahrain, Djibouti, Egypt, Eritrea, Indonesia, Iran, Iraq, Jordan, Kuwait, Lebanon, Libya, Malaysia, Morocco, Oman, Pakistan, Qatar, Saudi Arabia, Somalia, Sudan, Syria, Tunisia, United Arab Emirates, and Yemen.

After many years of heated debate and the shock of the September 11 terrorist attacks, in 2002, the Canadian parliament passed the Immigration and Refugee Protection Act, which redefined the criteria by which immigrants would be admitted, and provided the government with specific tools for denying entry to potential terrorists or deporting them once they were discovered. The measure provided that after enactment on June 28, 2002, all new permanent residents would receive Permanent Resident Cards, that existing permanent residents could apply for the card after October 15, 2002, and that effective January 2004, the cards would be required for reentry of permanent residents who had traveled outside Canada. The act also provided for removal of anyone involved in "organized crime, espionage, acts of subversion, terrorism, war crimes, human or international rights violations, criminality and serious criminality." The

measure also allowed immigration officials to detain people more easily on "reasonable suspicion" of failing to appear for possible deportation proceedings, of posing a risk to the public, or of refusing information to the immigration service.

Perhaps the most profound result to immigration in the United States, at least in the short term, was the dissolution of the INS. After extensive investigations of INS procedures and the embarrassing revelation that two of the September 11 hijackers actually received visa renewals after the terrorist attacks, the INS was dissolved and its duties divided among the U.S. Customs and Border Protection (CBP), the U.S. Immigration and Customs Enforcement (ICE), and the bureau of the U.S. CITIZENSHIP AND IMMIGRATION SERVICES (USCIS), all under the DEPARTMENT OF HOMELAND SECURITY.

Ironically, policy trends in immigration already evident prior to September 11, 2001, seem not to have been radically altered. The growing nativist tendency that found expression in PROPOSITION 187 and the recall of California governor Gray Davis remains. President Bush's desire to partner with Mexican president Vicente Fox in finding a workable solution to the illegal immigration problem was temporarily put on hold but was surprisingly revived in January 2004 with Bush's proposal of a new and controversial Temporary Worker Program (see MEXICAN IMMIGRATION). And Canadian and U.S. policy differences regarding immigration remain unresolved. Despite the December 12, 2001, signing of the U.S.-Canadian "Smart Border" Declaration designed to enhance border security, in 2004, Canadians were still complaining about U.S. profiling tactics, and Americans still regarded Canada as a potential haven for terrorists.

See also AFGHAN IMMIGRATION; TERRORISM AND IMMIGRATION.

Further Reading

CBS News. *What We Saw: The Events of September 11, 2001—In Words, Pictures, and Video.* New York: Simon and Schuster, 2002.

Chang, Nancy, and Howard Zinn. *Silencing Political Dissent: How Post–September 11 Anti Terrorist Measures Threaten Our Civil Liberties.* New York: Seven Stories Press, 2002.

DeFede, Jim. *The Day the World Came to Town: 9/11 in Gander, Newfoundland.* New York: Regan Books, 2002.

Longman, Jere. *Among the Heroes: United Flight 93 and the Passengers and Crew Who Fought Back.* New York: HarperCollins, 2002.

Serbian immigration

Serbs represented the largest ethnic group within the former country of Yugoslavia, and as the dominant regional group, they were less likely to migrate than Croatians (see CROATIAN IMMIGRATION) or Slovenes (see SLOVENIAN IMMIGRATION). According to the U.S. census of 2000 and the Canadian census of 2001, 140,337 Americans and 55,540 Canadians claimed Serbian descent. These figures were low, as a large percentage of those who claimed Yugoslav ancestry (328,547 Americans and 65,505 Canadians) were undoubtedly of Serbian origin. Estimates by various ethnic organizations place the number of Serbian Americans at more than 350,000 and Serbian Canadians at more than 150,000. Major centers of Serb settlement in the United States included Chicago, Illinois; Pittsburgh, Pennsylvania; Milwaukee, Wisconsin; and San Francisco and Los Angeles in California. The largest Serbian concentrations in Canada were in Ontario.

Serbia is a republic within the federation of Serbia and Montenegro, which includes the two nominally autonomous regions of Kosovo and Vojvodina. It is the successor to the Federal Republic of Yugoslavia, formed in the wake of the dissolution of the state of Yugoslavia in 1991 and the breaking away of Slovenia, Macedonia, Croatia, and Bosnia and Herzegovina. Serbia and Montenegro occupies 39,400 square miles or about 40 percent of the former Yugoslavia. Serbia and Montenegro is located on the Balkan Peninsula in southeastern Europe and is bordered by Bosnia and Herzegovina and Croatia on the west; Hungary and Romania on the north; Bulgaria on the east; and Albania and Macedonia on the south.

Serbs were the dominant South Slavic ethnic group in the Balkan Peninsula and one of the earliest to develop a strong sense of national identity. Under the Ottoman Empire since the early 15th century, the Serbs gradually gained greater measures of independence during the 19th century, moving from province to tributary principality (1817) to autonomous principality (1830) to full independence (1878). During the Balkan Wars (1912–13), Serbia expanded its borders to a state approximating the size of modern-day Serbia and Montenegro. Serbia further expanded at the expense of the defeated Austrian and Ottoman Empires in 1919, forming the core of the Kingdom of Serbs, Croats, and Slovenes, which was renamed Yugoslavia in 1929. Throughout its brief existence, Yugoslavia wrestled with the attempt by Serbs to turn the nation into a Greater Serbia. Thus, in 1991, the dissolution of Yugoslavia proceeded along ethnic lines, with Slovenia, Croatia, Bosnia, and Macedonia declaring their independence. This left two states—Serbia and Montenegro—as the new Yugoslavia. Montenegro was about 90 percent Serbian and Serbia proper about 96 percent Serbian; both provinces, however, had significant minority populations. In Kosovo, Serbs only accounted for 13 percent of the population, with 83 percent being Albanians. In Vojvodina, there was a 22 percent minority Magyar (Hungarian) population, with Serbs making up about 70 percent. Serb aggression led to an ethnic cleansing campaign in Kosovo in 1998 and the eventual dislocation of hundreds of thousands of ethnic Albanians (see ALBANIAN IMMIGRATION).

Serbian refugees are shown at a Red Cross station, April 30, 1919. The disruption of the Balkan Wars (1912–13) and World War I (1914–18) heightened ethnic animosities in the Balkans. *(National Archives #99-181B[3])*

A relatively small number of Serbs immigrated to North America prior to World War II (1939–45). Exact numbers are impossible to determine, as prior to World War I (1914–18), Serbs entering the United States were categorized variously as "Bulgars, Serbs, and Montenegrins," "Croats and Slovenes," "Austrians and Hungarians," or "Dalmations, Bosnians, and Hercegovinians." They were similarly categorized in Canada, and after 1921, all ethnic groups—including Serbs—were labeled "Yugoslav." The first substantial number of Serbs began to immigrate in the late 19th century, either settling in midwestern industrial cities or in California, which had a climate similar to Croatia's Dalmatian coast. By 1900, some of these western settlers had migrated to take mining and railway jobs in British Columbia, Alberta, and Saskatchewan. Between 1920 and 1950, fewer than 60,000 Yugoslav citizens of all nationalities immigrated to the United States, more than 80 percent of them before the mid-1920s when restrictive legislation all but halted immigration by Slavs. During World War II, Croatia established its own state allied to Nazi Germany, but it was brought back into Yugoslavia by the authoritarian rule of the Communist leader Josip Broz, Marshal Tito

(1945–80), contributing to an already large refugee population in the region. Under the DISPLACED PERSONS ACT of 1948 and the REFUGEE RELIEF ACT of 1953, it is estimated that more than 50,000 Yugoslavs were admitted to the United States, though many of these would have been non-Serbs seeking to escape both communism and what was perceived as the pro-Serbian dominance of Tito. Between 1991 and 2002, almost 120,000 immigrants of all ethnic groups from the former Yugoslavia came to the United States, most fleeing the ethnic conflicts in Bosnia and Serbia. Of Canada's 145,380 immigrants from Yugoslavia in 2001, about 46 percent came after 1990, the majority from Serbia and Bosnia.

See also GYPSY IMMIGRATION; WORLD WAR II AND IMMIGRATION; YUGOSLAV IMMIGRATION.

Further Reading

Colaković, Branko M. *The South Slavic Immigration in America.* Boston: Twayne, 1978.
———. *Yugoslav Migrations to America.* San Francisco: R. and E. Research Associates, 1973.
Gakovich, R. P., and M. M. Radovich. *Serbs in the United States and Canada: A Comprehensive Bibliography.* St. Paul: Immigration History Research Center, University of Minnesota, 1992.
Goverchin, G. G. *Americans from Yugoslavia.* Gainesville: University of Florida Press, 1961.
Judah, Tim. *The Serbs: History, Myth and the Destruction of Yugoslavia.* New Haven, Conn.: Yale University Press, 1998.
Kisslinger, J. *The Serbian Americans.* New York: Chelsea House, 1990.
Lampe, John. *Yugoslavia as History: Twice There Was a Country.* 2d ed. Cambridge: Cambridge University Press, 2000.
Pavlovich, Paul. *The Serbians: The Story of a People.* Toronto: Serbian Heritage Books, 1988.

Seven Years' War

The Seven Years' War (1756–63) was the culmination of a century of European warfare that centered on the growing conflict between Prussia and Austria in Europe but also involved an escalating contest between Britain and France for imperial control beyond Europe. In North America, the war resulted in complete British victory, with France ceding ACADIA, Canada, and LOUISIANA east of the Mississippi River, and ensuring that the dominant culture pattern would be English.

Britain and France warred over control of NEW FRANCE in the War of the League of Augsburg (1689–97), the War of the Spanish Succession (1702–14), and the War of the Austrian Succession (1740–48), though the only permanent territorial change was British occupation of lightly populated NEWFOUNDLAND, Hudson Bay, and NOVA SCOTIA in 1713. British colonial expansion and control of the lucrative fur trade kept tensions high, however, and finally erupted into the French and Indian War (1754–63), which then expanded into the international Seven Years' War. At mid-century,

Britain controlled the Atlantic seaboard from the Gulf of St. Lawrence to Florida, while France occupied the St. Lawrence Seaway and Mississippi River Valley. In between lay the Ohio River Valley, still largely in the hands of the Iroquois Confederacy, which controlled the fur trade. As Iroquois power declined, both the British and the French sought to expand into the region, each seeking Native American allies. When France built a string of forts from Lake Erie to the confluence of the Allegheny and Monongahela Rivers in 1753, Virginia governor Robert Dinwiddie sent a small force under Lieutenant Colonel George Washington to order them out of the region. A French force returned the following year, driving Washington from Fort Necessity and establishing Fort Duquesne at the site of present-day Pittsburgh, Pennsylvania.

Britain suffered almost continual losses until 1757, when William Pitt became prime minister. He reorganized the war effort, promoting younger officers and convincing Parliament to make a major commitment of funds. In the next three years, Britain captured all the French strongholds, including Louisbourg (1758), Fort Duquesne (1758), Quebec (1759), and Montreal (1760). With the capitulation at Montreal, thousands of French colonists returned to France, and some 4,000 Acadians relocated to Louisiana, which briefly remained in French hands. In the Treaty of Paris formally ending the Seven Years' War in 1763, France ceded Acadia, Canada, and Louisiana east of the Mississippi River to Britain; the western Mississippi valley and NEW ORLEANS were handed over to Spain. France's once vast North American empire was thus reduced to two small islands, Saint-Pierre and Miquelon, south of Newfoundland.

As a result of the Seven Years' War, 80,000 French speakers were added to British Canada, and new French immigration became negligible. The conflict in Europe and a ban in the Holy Roman Empire (1768) halted most German immigration to America until the early 19th century. Perhaps most important, Britain's victory provided a significant shared experience for many British colonists of diverse ethnic backgrounds, important in the development of a distinct American identity.

Further Reading

Anderson, Fred. *The Crucible of War: The Seven Years' War and the Fate of Empire in British North America, 1754–1766.* New York: Alfred A. Knopf, 2000.
Corbett, Julian S. *England in the Seven Years' War.* 2 vols. London: Greenhill Books, 1992.
Leckie, Robert. *A Few Acres of Snow: The Saga of the French and Indian Wars.* New York: Wiley, 1999.
Marrin, Albert. *Struggle for a Continent: The French and Indian Wars, 1690–1760.* New York: Atheneum Press, 1987.
Peckham, Howard H. *The Colonial Wars, 1689–1762.* Chicago: University of Chicago Press, 1964.
Pocock, Tom. *Battle for Empire: The Very First World War, 1756–1763.* London: Michael O'Mara Books, 1998.

Sifton, Clifford (1861–1929) *politician*

As minister of the interior and superintendent general of Indian affairs (1896–1905), Clifford Sifton planned and presided over the most successful public campaign to attract settlers in Canadian history. As a result of his efforts, more than 2 million immigrants arrived in Canada between 1896 and 1911, transforming largely uninhabited western prairies into productive farmland.

As a teenager, Sifton moved with his family to Selkirk, Manitoba, eventually opening a law practice with his brother in Brandon, Manitoba. He was first elected to the provincial parliament as a Liberal for Brandon North in 1888, before becoming attorney general of Manitoba (1891–95). His skillful management of disagreements over the teaching of religion in schools impressed Prime Minister Wilfrid Laurier, who appointed Sifton minister of the interior in 1896. Long opposed to the monopolistic rights of the Canadian Pacific Railway, Sifton instituted a policy requiring land speculators and railway companies to either colonize their lands or forfeit them. Having already lost thousands of potential settlers to the United States, Sifton also cut through the extensive bureaucratic delays in applying for homesteads, eliminating the Dominions Land Board and simplifying regulations. Finally, he hired European and American agents, offering bonuses of $5 for every certified agriculturalist they recruited over the age of 12. His policies led to an eightfold increase in annual entries, from 17,000 when he took office to 146,000 in 1905 when he resigned. As eager as Sifton was to encourage the settlement of farmers, he was eager to keep out almost every other type of immigrant, especially the mechanics and laborers who tended to flock to the cities of the United States.

Determined to bring those who would actively cultivate the soil, Sifton was not disposed to "exclude foreigners of any nationality, who seemed likely to become successful agriculturalists." British immigrants continued to make up the largest group, however, averaging around 40 percent of total immigration. He also had great success in the United States, where land agents successfully persuaded almost 1 million settlers to come north. About one-third were newly arrived Germans, Scandinavians, Icelanders, and Hungarians, who brought considerable capital and expertise to their work. The third area of success, and one that transformed the ethnic composition of the prairies, was central and eastern Europe. Though Germans and Scandinavians were the most highly prized, they usually chose to immigrate to the United States. As a result, Sifton encouraged the settlement of Ukrainians (see UKRAINIAN IMMIGRATION), Poles (see POLISH IMMIGRATION), Doukhobors, and other oppressed minorities from Austria-Hungary, Russia, and Romania, who began to flock to the free land offered on the Canadian prairies. The policy was controversial, as most Canadians considered these immigrants degraded and barbarous. Sifton nevertheless recognized the superior value of their hard work and peaceable living, which dramatically assisted Canada in opening its western agricultural lands.

After Sifton's resignation over school policy for Alberta and Saskatchewan in 1905, he remained prominent in public life. He joined the Conservative Party in 1911 in support of economic protectionism and served as chairman of the Canadian Commission of Conservation (1909–18). He was knighted by King George V in 1915.

Further Reading

Brown, Robert Craig, and Ramsay Cook. *Canada 1896–1921: A Nation Transformed.* Toronto: McClelland and Stewart, 1974.

Dafoe, J. W. *Clifford Sifton in Relation to His Times.* Toronto: Macmillan of Canada, 1931.

Hall, David J. *Clifford Sifton.* 2 vols. Vancouver: University of British Columbia Press, 1981, 1985.

Appointed Canadian minister of the interior in 1896, Clifford Sifton believed in an almost unlimited potential for western development. "Our desire," he wrote to Prime Minister Wilfrid Laurier in 1901, "is to promote the immigration of farmers and farm labourers." *(Library of Congress, Prints & Photographs Division [LC-USZ62-109818])*

Simcoe, John Graves (1752–1806) *government official*

John Graves Simcoe was the first lieutenant governor of Upper Canada (1792–96) and was responsible for crafting a policy that encouraged extensive immigration into the newly formed province. Believing in the superiority of English culture, he determined to build a model British colony, weaned from French law and influence and attractive to Americans dissatisfied with the newly formed republic.

As commander of Loyalists of the New York and Connecticut campaigns during the American Revolution (1775–83), Simcoe developed an admiration for these men. Intrepid and ambitious, Simcoe devised a plan that established a strong British military presence on the frontier with the United States and encouraged migration to Upper Canada. In addition to building roads and settlements, Simcoe issued a proclamation (February 7, 1792), offering land grants of 200–1,000 acres, subject only to minor fees, a commitment to improve the land, and an oath of loyalty to the British Crown. Although several thousand settlers took advantage of the land grants, the offer did little to attract settlers from Britain. The majority of settlers came from New York and Pennsylvania, prominently including members of pacifist groups such as the Quakers, Mennonites (see MENNONITE IMMIGRATION), and Dunkers, enticed by the promise of exemption from military service. Most settlement soon fell into the hands of aristocrats, most notably Colonel Thomas Talbot and THOMAS DOUGLAS, Lord Selkirk, who were seen as the foundation of a new model England.

Further Reading
Craig, Gerald M. *Upper Canada: The Formative Years, 1784–1841.* Toronto: McClelland and Stewart, 1963.
Cruikshank, E. A., ed. *The Correspondence of Lieut. Governor John Graves Simcoe, with Allied Documents Relating to His Administration of the Government of Upper Canada.* 5 vols. Toronto: The Society, 1923–31.
Riddell, W. R. *The Life of John Graves Simcoe, First Lieutenant-Governor of the Province of Upper Canada, 1792–96.* Toronto: McClelland and Stewart, 1926.

Singh v. Minister of Employment and Immigration (1985)

On April 4, 1985, in *Singh v. Minister of Employment and Immigration,* the Supreme Court of Canada ruled that oral hearings were required in every case determining refugee status, leading to a radical restructuring of the immigration process. The case grew out of the enormous backlog of cases resulting from a cumbersome, multitiered refugee determination process that by the early 1980s had become a tool enabling nonqualifying immigrants to remain in Canada during the lengthy appeal process. For those who wanted the Canadian government to deal firmly with potentially fraudulent claims, the decision was an important step in establishing a policy of early determination of a refugee claimant's status. For those concerned with civil rights, it was a victory for due process.

The broad issue was one of procedural fairness toward refugee applicants. The 1978 Immigration Act had clearly established that the definition of a refugee under Canadian law was the same as that established by the United Nations Convention in 1951, as amended in a 1967 protocol:

> *any person who, by reason of a well-founded fear of persecution for reasons of race, religion, nationality, membership in a particular social group or political opinion, a) is outside the country of his nationality and unable or, by reason of such fear, unwilling to avail himself of the protection of that country, or; b) not having a country of nationality, is outside the country of his former habitual residence and is unable or, by reason of such fear, unwilling to return to that country.*

The difficulty lay in separating the genuine refugee from others who used the claim as a tool to enter the country and reside indefinitely, as an enormous backlog of cases made quick resolution of cases impossible. By the provisions of the Immigration Act, a multistage appeal process was instituted that provided for an examination before an immigrant officer, with right of counsel and the opportunity to correct the transcript, which was then forwarded to the Refugee Status Advisory Committee (RSAC), which reviewed the case and sent its recommendations to the minister of Employment and Immigration. If the minister denied the claim, the refugee claimant had right of appeal to the Immigrant Appeal Board (IAB). If even one of the three members of the board believed that the claim had a chance to be successful, a hearing was scheduled. But if the appeal was denied, it could then be appealed to the Federal Court of Canada. By 1981, there was a backlog of 1,500 cases; by the end of 1983 the number of cases reached 9,000. As the government sought advice about possible reforms, the backlog continued to grow, to 15,000 by 1984, and in the meantime the government was providing jobs and welfare benefits to those awaiting judgment.

In the midst of this crisis came the matter of six Asian Indians and one Guyanese who claimed UN Convention refugee status on the basis of their political activities. Four of the Indians were denied admission at the border; one evaded inquiry upon entry in 1971; one arrived as a temporary "visitor" in 1980; and the Guyanese came on a false passport in 1979, was later granted temporary status, then arrested in 1981 for working illegally. All had been denied refugee status by the minister and denied applications for redetermination by the Immigration Appeal Board. The Federal

Court of Appeal refused applications for judicial review. The Supreme Court then heard the appeal from the refusals. Invoking the Canadian Charter of Rights and Freedoms (1982), which provided legal equality for those facing discrimination "based on race, national or ethnic origin, colour, religion, sex, age or mental or physical disability," the court ruled that claimants could not be denied the right to an oral hearing in the final determination of refugee claims. According to the ruling, the charter's language guaranteeing protection for "everyone" included all who were "physically present" in Canada.

As a result of the decision, four previous studies recommending oral hearings at an early stage of the hearing process were affirmed. A temporary Bill C-55 was passed in 1985, increasing the number of refugee claims adjudicators, but the measure proved unable to meet the three-year backlog of cases. The second BILL C-55 (Refugee Reform Bill, introduced 1987) restructured the process for determining refugee status, replacing the IAB with the Immigration and Refugee Board (IRB) and two divisions, the Immigration Appeals Division (IAD) and the Convention Refugee Determination Division (CRDD). It also provided for a two-stage hearing process. In the first stage, which sought to eliminate patently unfounded claims, a preliminary joint inquiry by an independent adjudicator and a CRDD member would first determine a claimant's admissibility. The second stage of the process involved a full hearing before two members of the CRDD.

Further Reading

Campbell, Charles M. *Betrayal and Deceit: The Politics of Canadian Immigration.* West Vancouver, Canada: Jasmine Books, 2000.

Creese, Gillian. "The Politics of Refugees in Canada." In *Deconstructing a Nation.* Ed. Vic Satzewich. Halifax, Canada: Fernwood, 1992.

Glenn, H. Patrick. *Refugee Claims, the Canadian State and North American Regionalism in Hemispheric Integration, Migration and Human Rights.* Toronto: York University Centre for Refugee Studies, 1994.

Kelley, Ninette, and Michael Trebilcock. *The Making of the Mosaic: A History of Canadian Immigration Policy.* Toronto: University of Toronto Press, 1998.

Plaut, W. G. *Refugee Determination in Canada.* Ottawa: Minister of Supply and Services, 1985.

slave trade   See AFRICAN FORCED MIGRATION.

slavery

Slavery is the condition of a person being owned by someone else, forced to work, and without personal freedoms. It was practiced by many civilizations around the world from ancient times and usually seen as a condition into which anyone might fall as a result of war, debt, or crimes. The conditions of slavery varied widely, from the greatest cruelty to almost familial regard. Typically slaves were not allowed to marry or own property. In many cultures, it was not uncommon for slaves to be manumitted (granted freedom) as a reward for loyal service. This practice was reinforced from the seventh century onward by the teachings of Islam, which favored manumission. In the Roman Empire, as much as one-third of the population was at one time enslaved. With Rome's decline in the fifth century, the economic circumstances favoring slavery in Europe were removed, and it was little employed throughout the Middle Ages, except in southern Spain, Portugal, and Italy where warfare with the Muslim Moors provided a constant flow of war captives. Extensive slave labor systems flourished in the Byzantine Empire of modern Turkey and the Balkan Peninsula and in the Islamic world of northern and eastern Africa and the Middle East.

With the rise of European economic and military dominance between the 15th and 18th centuries, the character of slavery changed. During the medieval era (ca. 500–1500), the number of slaves sold out of Africa had remained stable at a few thousand a year, with most being carried by caravan to the Middle East. By the 17th century, the number of slaves from Africa had jumped to tens of thousands annually, with most being carried on ships across the Atlantic Ocean to the Americas (see AFRICAN FORCED MIGRATION). During the 18th century, the Atlantic slave trade peaked, in some years reaching more than 100,000. Also, for the first time, slavery became closely associated with race. Historically, in most slave-holding societies, slaves and slave owners were of the same race. In the 15th and 16th centuries, Spain and Portugal extended their rule over American, African, and Asian territories populated by different races of people. With rich mines and tropical territories well suited to the cultivation of labor-intensive cash crops such as sugarcane, cotton, and coffee, Iberian Europeans naturally looked for labor locally. Native Americans were at first enslaved, though later officially protected by being brought under a feudal system of forced labor and taxation (*encomienda*) that left them with few personal freedoms. As settled native peoples were exterminated by hard labor and disease, Spain and Portugal increasingly turned to Africa, where the Portuguese had established a permanent presence along the east coast from the 1480s. In 1516, Spanish king Charles I (Holy Roman Emperor Charles V) granted an *asiento* to bring 4,000 African slaves annually into New Spain, a number that steadily increased so that by the end of the 19th century, more than 5 million slaves had been brought from Africa to Spanish and Portuguese New World colonies.

By the 17th century Holland, Britain, and France were challenging the colonial supremacy of Spain and Portugal and developing similar slave plantation economies throughout the Caribbean Basin. By the early 19th century, more than 3 million slaves were brought into British, French, and Dutch colonies in the New World. In the early days of British and French settlement in North America, most labor was performed by indentured servants (see INDENTURED SERVITUDE), but with passage of the NAVIGATION ACTS, falling tobacco prices, and the difficulty of securing labor, the demand for new sources of labor grew. In 1662, the British government sought to meet the demand by granting a monopoly of the slave trade in its territories to the ROYAL AFRICAN COMPANY. In the same decade, slave codes based on old Roman models began to be enacted throughout the southern colonies, legally establishing the condition of slavery. The status of children followed that of mothers rather than fathers; slaves were increasingly forbidden to own firearms or other property, to travel freely, or to testify against white defendants; and the manumission of slaves was made more difficult. Thousands of Native Americans were enslaved, particularly in the wake of the devastating Carolina tribal wars between about 1680 and 1720. Given the Native American propensity for violence and escape, by 1715, New England colonies were already banning American Indian slavery, and continued warfare and disease soon ended attempts to systematically enslave them.

The legal and social conventions of slavery gradually developed into a doctrine of ethnocentric RACISM in which dark-skinned Africans—who were pagans and viewed as sexually licentious—were considered innately inferior to Europeans. The number of slaves in British North America grew dramatically in the 18th century. By 1770, slaves accounted for 40 percent of the population in Maryland, Virginia, and South Carolina. At the same time, slaves composed only about 5 percent of the population of the northern colonies and even less in Canada, where small farms predominated and economic conditions did not favor slavery. Altogether more than 600,000 Africans were brought as slaves to the United States. Through natural increase, by the mid-19th century their numbers had increased to almost 4 million.

The conditions under which slaves labored in North America varied greatly. Most worked as agricultural field hands, from sunrise to sunset and especially hard during the harvest. After harvest and before planting, animals had to be cared for and the numerous repairs of a farm or plantation attended to. Many also worked as domestic servants and in factories. A few became slave drivers, craftsmen, or skilled carpenters or blacksmiths. The attitude of slave owner toward slave varied as well. Many owners were brutal, inflicting severe beatings or mutilations for small infractions, sometimes forcing female slaves to engage in sexual acts. Others abjured violence except as a last resort and treated slaves almost as family members. Slave marriages were not legally recognized, but monogamy was encouraged. This did not stop slave holders from breaking up families when children reached young adulthood or when a high price might be commanded for a slave. The standard of living for most

slaves was somewhat above the subsistence level, in large measure because they represented a valuable economic asset. Food tended to be adequate in quantity and generally healthy, though plain. Slave houses were drafty, without much furniture and usually without floors. In every case, however, slaves were at the mercy of their owners, who collectively created a social environment that made resistance virtually impossible. Slaves were not allowed to leave plantations without permission, education was prohibited, and manumission was discouraged. The relatively small number of slave revolts in the United States reflects the isolation of slaves and the complete lack of means for successful revolt. The most famous insurrection, the Nat Turner rebellion of 1831, involved a band of 75 slaves who killed more than 50 whites and unsuccessfully attempted to reach a local armory in Virginia. Within two days, the rebellion was quelled, and eventually all the rebels were killed or captured, and Turner himself was executed. For the most part, resistance to slavery was more subtle, involving deliberate slowing of work, the breaking of tools, and encouragement of the idea that slaves were naturally childlike and prone to laziness.

Until the middle of the 18th century, the morality of slavery had seldom been questioned anywhere in the world. With the enhanced emphasis on natural rights and political liberty that were characteristic of the Enlightenment and the humanitarian and religious activism associated with the Great Awakening, a strong antislavery movement developed in Britain, France, and America. These intellectual movements coincided with the beginnings of the industrial revolution, which shifted economic predominance from the land to the factory and other economic enterprises that did not benefit from slavery. The slave trade was abolished in Britain in 1807, in the United States in 1808, and in France in 1819. Slavery itself was banned throughout the British Empire, including the Canadian colonies, in 1833 when the government agreed to compensate slaveholders for their economic losses. In the United States, where slavery was more prevalent and had become more deeply entrenched with the rising importance of short-staple cotton from the 1790s, the abolitionist reform movement became more radical and found a commanding voice in William Lloyd Garrison, who founded the *Liberator* journal and encouraged free African Americans such as Frederick Douglass to speak at antislavery meetings. Garrison's call for immediate and unconditional abolition of slavery polarized attitudes. Although most Americans were not convinced that slavery was morally wrong, many were troubled, and Garrison and other abolitionists did succeed in bringing the fate of nearly 4 million Americans of African descent to the national stage. The United States split into two political camps over slavery and eventually fought the Civil War to determine whether individual states or the federal government had the authority to regulate slavery. In 1863, President Abraham Lincoln freed all slaves under Confederate (southern) control, and in 1865, slavery was abolished with the ratification of the Thirteenth Amendment to the Constitution. African Americans were freed from slavery in 1865 but were systematically discriminated against until the Civil Rights movement of the 1950s and 1960s.

Further Reading

Anbinder, Tyler. *Nativism and Slavery: The Northern Know-Nothings and the Politics of the 1850s.* New York: Oxford University Press, 1992.

Berlin, Ira. *Many Thousands Gone: The First Two Centuries of Slavery in North America.* Cambridge, Mass.: Belknap Press, 1998.

Blassingame, John W. *The Slave Community: Plantation Life in the Antebellum South.* New York: Oxford University Press, 1972.

Boskins, Joseph. *Into Slavery: Racial Decisions in the Virginia Colony.* Philadelphia: J. B. Lippincott, 1976.

Davis, David Brion. *The Problem of Slavery in the Age of Revolution, 1770–1823.* Ithaca, N.Y.: Cornell University Press, 1975.

Eltis, David. *The Rise of African Slavery in the Americas.* New York: Cambridge University Press, 2000.

Foner, Eric. *Nothing but Freedom: Emancipation and Its Legacy.* Baton Rouge: Louisiana State University Press, 1983.

Harding, Vincent. *There Is a River: The Black Struggle for Freedom in America.* San Diego, Calif.: Harcourt Brace Jovanovich, 1981.

Higginbotham, A. Leon, Jr. *In the Matter of Color: Race and the American Legal Process, the Colonial Period.* New York: Oxford University Press, 1978.

Jordan, Winthrop D. *White over Black: American Attitudes toward the Negro, 1550–1812.* New York: W. W. Norton, 1968.

Lovejoy, Paul E. *Transformations in Slavery: A History of Slavery in Africa.* Cambridge: Cambridge University Press, 1983.

Morgan, Edmund. *American Slavery, American Freedom: The Ordeal of Colonial Virginia.* New York: W. W. Norton, 1975.

Nash, Gary B. *Red, White and Black: The Peoples of Early America.* Englewood Cliffs, N.J.: Prentice Hall, 1982.

Patterson, Orlando. *Slavery and Social Death: A Comparative Study.* Cambridge, Mass.: Harvard University Press, 1982.

Schwartz, Philip J. *Twice Condemned: Slaves and the Criminal Laws of Virginia, 1705–1865.* Baton Rouge: Louisiana State University Press, 1988.

Shaw, Robert B. *A Legal History of Slavery in the United States.* Potsdam, N.Y.: Northern Press, 1991.

Stampp, Kenneth W. *The Peculiar Institution: Slavery in the Antebellum South.* New York: Alfred A. Knopf, 1956.

Slovakian immigration

Emerging from the nationalist democratic movements of the late 1980s and early 1990s, Slovakia is one of the newest countries in the world. According to the U.S. census of 2000 and the Canadian census of 2001, 797,764 Americans and 50,860 Canadians claimed Slovak ancestry. These figures underrepresent the actual numbers, as 440,000 Americans and 33,540 Canadians claimed Czechoslovakian ancestry, and these would undoubtedly include many of Slovak descent. Slovaks spread widely throughout the industrial North and upper Midwest in the United States, with particular concentrations in Pennsylvania and Ohio. About 60 percent of Slovakian Canadians live in Ontario.

Slovakia occupies 18,800 square miles in east-central Europe. It is bordered by Poland on the north, Hungary on the south; Austria and the Czech Republic on the west, and Ukraine on the east. In 2002, the population was estimated at 5,414,937. The people were about 86 percent Slovak, 10.5 percent Hungarian, and 1.7 percent Gypsy. About 60 percent of the population is Roman Catholic, and 8 percent, Protestant; there is also a large nonreligious population. Slovakia was originally settled by Illyian, Celtic, and Germanic tribes and was incorporated into Great Moravia in the ninth century. It became part of Hungary in the 11th century, but was conquered by Czech Hussites in the 15th century, before being restored to Hungarian rule in 1526. The Slovaks disassociated themselves from Hungary after World War I (1914–18), joining the Czechs of Bohemia to form the Republic of Czechoslovakia in 1918. In 1938, after agreements with Britain and France, Germany occupied the westernmost portion of Czechoslovakia, known as the Sudetenland. Russian and Czech troops began to liberate Czechoslovakia in 1944. Following World War II (1939–45), Czechoslovakia fell under Soviet domination until the fall of the Czechoslovak socialist state in 1989 and when Slovaks pressed their autonomy. In 1993, Czechoslovakia peacefully split into two states—the Czech Republic and Slovakia. Slovakia, with its less developed economy, applied to join the European Union in 1995.

Most Slovaks entered the United States as a part of the NEW IMMIGRATION between 1880 and 1924, when mainly young men came to work in mines and factories. Most, however, eventually brought their families to settle. Exact figures are difficult to determine, as Slovaks were listed as Hungarians prior to 1899 and frequently as such thereafter (see HUNGARIAN IMMIGRATION). The best estimates suggest that between 450,000 and 500,000 Slovaks became permanent residents of the United States, with hundreds of thousands eventually returning to their homeland. Following passage of the restrictive JOHNSON-REED ACT of 1924, all Czechoslovakian immigration averaged only about 600 per year until the fall of the Communist government, when numbers slightly increased. From its independence in 1993 until 2002, Slovak immigration to the United States averaged a little more than 600 per year.

The first significant Slovak immigration to Canada came between 1900 and 1914, when about 5,000 came to work in Rocky Mountain mines or in railway construction, many of them migrating from Pennsylvania. During the 1920s and 1930s, another 40,000 came, often working as farm laborers, domestics, or in the timber industry. Finally, a relatively small number of highly educated Slovaks came to Canada just after World War II and at the time of the Soviet suppression of the Prague Revolt of 1968. Again, figures are unreliable, both because immigrants from the Austrian Empire were not differentiated before World War I, but also because Slovaks emigrating from the United States were not counted. Of the 10,450 Slovakian immigrants in Canada in 2001, about half came after the democratic revolution in 1989.

See also AUSTRO-HUNGARIAN IMMIGRATION; CZECH IMMIGRATION; GYPSY IMMIGRATION.

Further Reading

Barton, Josef J. *Peasants and Strangers: Italians, Rumanians, and Slovaks in an American City, 1890–1950*. Cambridge, Mass.: Harvard University Press, 1975.

Gellner, John, and John Smerek. *The Czechs and Slovaks in Canada*. Toronto: University of Toronto Press, 1968.

Jacesova, Elena. "Slovak Emigrants in Canada as Reflected in Diplomatic Documents." *Slovakia* 35 (1991–92): 7–35.

Jerabek, E. *Czechs and Slovaks in North America: A Bibliography*. New York: Czechoslovak Society of Arts and Sciences in America, 1976.

Kirschbaum, S. J. *A History of Slovakia: The Struggle for Survival*. New York: St. Martin's Press, 1995.

Kirschbaum, Joseph M. *Slovaks in Canada*. Toronto: Canadian Ethnic Press Association of Ontario, 1967.

Stolarik, M. Mark. *Growing Up on the South Side: Three Generations of Slovaks in Bethlehem, Pennsylvania, 1880–1976*. Lewisburg, Pa.: Bucknell University Press, 1985.

———. *The Slovak Americans*. New York: Chelsea House, 1988.

———. *Immigration and Urbanization: The Slovak Experience, 1870–1918*. New York: AMS Press, 1989.

———. *Slovaks in Canada and the United States, 1870–1990: Similarities and Differences*. Ottawa: University of Ottawa Press, 1992.

Slovenian immigration

Throughout most of its history, Slovenia was governed by the Germanic Austrians or the Serb-dominated state of Yugoslavia. In 1991, Slovenia won its independence, making it one of the newest countries in the world. According to the U.S. census of 2000 and the Canadian census of 2001, 176,691 Americans and 28,910 Canadians claimed Slovenian descent. Cleveland, Ohio, became the center for Slovenian settlement in the United States, with significant concentrations throughout the industrial Midwest. More than two-thirds of Slovenian Canadians live in Ontario.

Slovenia occupies 7,800 square miles in southeast Europe. It is bordered by Italy to the west; Austria and Hungary to the north; and Croatia to the southeast. In 2002, the population was estimated at 1,930,132. Always the most ethnically homogenous region of Yugoslavia, 91 percent of its population is Slovene and about 3 percent Croat. The chief religion is Roman Catholicism. Originally from the modern regions of Poland, Ukraine, and Russia, the Slovenes settled in their current territory between the sixth

and eighth centuries. They began to fall under German domination as early as the ninth century and for a thousand years were generally under the rule of German princes. Around 1848, Slovenes scattered among several Austrian provinces began their struggle for political and national unification (see AUSTRO-HUNGARIAN IMMIGRATION; REVOLUTIONS OF 1848). In 1918, most Slovenes became part of the Kingdom of Serbs, Croats, and Slovenes, later renamed Yugoslavia (see YUGOSLAV IMMIGRATION). Slovenia declared its independence on June 25, 1991, and joined the United Nations on May 22, 1992. With few Serbs living there, the Yugoslav army put up minimal resistance to Slovenian withdrawal from Yugoslavia, and Slovenia was largely spared the war and violence that plagued Bosnia and Kosovo throughout the 1990s. Linked by trade with the European Union, Slovenia applied for full membership in 1996.

Most Slovenes immigrated to the United States as a part of the NEW IMMIGRATION between 1880 and 1923, with a smaller group coming after World War II (1939–45) between 1949 and 1956. Numbers are unreliable, as Slovenes were often grouped by immigration officials with Croats or listed as Austrians, Yugoslavs, or Germans. A reasonable total estimate for the two migrations is about 300,000. The earliest organized Slovene immigration to the United States was composed of Roman Catholic priests who in 1831 came as missionaries to the American Indian tribes of Michigan, Minnesota, and the Dakota Territory; dozens followed. Most arrivals before and just after World War I (1914–18) were of poor peasant farmers escaping overcrowded conditions. They usually came in small groups, often as single men, who then later sent for their families. By the 1880s, they were established in mining communities of Michigan and Minnesota. In the 1890s, an increasing number were settling in Cleveland and Chicago. During the early 20th century, Cleveland became the largest Slovenian city outside Slovenia, with a population of more than 30,000 Slovenians in 1920. With a relatively stable economy and political system, there has not been great pressure for Slovenians to emigrate. Between 1992 and 2002, average annual immigration to the United States was only about 70.

Significant Slovene immigration to Canada started in the 1920s, following the United States' restrictive EMERGENCY QUOTA ACT (1921) and JOHNSON-REED ACT (1924). Groups of young, healthy Slovenes were recruited by travel agents as contract laborers under the Railway Agreement of 1925. After working on farms or railroads in Saskatchewan, Manitoba, or British Columbia, many migrated to western mining towns. About 2,500 Slovenians refugees were accepted between 1947 and 1951 and often spent a year under contract before seeking city jobs. Some 6,000 Slovenians came between 1951 and 1970, mainly joining family members who had arrived during the previous periods. Of the 9,250 Slovenian immigrants in Canada in 2001, half came before 1961. Only 545 came between 1991 and 2001.

Further Reading
Genorio, Rado. *Slovenci v Kanadi*. Ljubljana, Slovenia: Institut za geografio Univerze, 1989.
Gobetz, G. Edward. *Adjustment and Assimilation of Slovenian Refugees*. New York: Arno Press, 1980.
Lenček, R., ed. *Papers in Slovene Studies*. New York: Society for Slovene Studies, 1975.
———. *Twenty Years of Scholarship*. New York: Society for Slovene Studies, 1995.
Prisland, Marie. *From Slovenia to America: Recollections and Collections*. Chicago: Slovenian Women's Union of America, 1968.
Urbanc, Peter, and Eleanor Tourtel. *Slovenians in Canada*. Hamilton, Canada: Slovenian Heritage Festival Committee, 1984.
Van Tassel, D. D., and J. J. Grabowski, eds. *The Encyclopedia of Slovene History*. Bloomington: Indiana University Press, 1996.

Smith, Al (Alfred Emmanuel Smith)
(1873–1944) *politician*

Smith was the first U.S. politician to build a national reputation by appealing to ethnic groups and was the first Roman Catholic to run for president. Although soundly defeated in the 1928 election, he helped turn immigrant voters to the Democratic Party and helped to establish the new Democratic consensus that was consolidated by President Franklin Roosevelt during the New Deal.

Smith, an ambitious Irish-American Catholic, was raised on New York City's Lower East Side. His parents were both children of Irish immigrants. Smith began his political career in the pay of the Tammany Hall political machine, although the rampant corruption grated on his ethical sensibilities. As a reward, he was picked to run for the New York State Assembly in 1903, where he sat until he was selected sheriff of New York City in 1915 and president of the Board of Aldermen two years later. Having become especially knowledgeable about industrial affairs, he gradually developed a progressive reform program that especially appealed to immigrants. In 1918, he won the governorship of New York in a surprising victory over the Republican incumbent. While in office, he oversaw a number of social reforms, including enhanced workmen's compensation provisions, higher teachers' salaries, and state care for the mentally ill. Although defeated in the Republican landslide of 1920, he came back to regain the governor's chair in 1922. Smith was defeated in the Democratic primary for president in 1924 in a divisive intraparty contest between the largely rural, Protestant, and prohibitionist South and West and the ethnically diverse and antiprohibitionist Northeast. He nevertheless was reelected as governor of New York for third and fourth terms in 1924 and 1926. The peak of his political career came in 1928 when he was nominated as Democratic presidential candidate on the first ballot. In an age of apparent economic prosperity, Smith had little chance to defeat Republican Herbert Hoover, but he did attract large numbers of foreign-born Americans to the polls, enabling Democrats to carry most large urban areas for the first time. Ironically, in later life Smith left the Democratic Party, disdaining the New Deal vision of a planned society.

Further Reading
Eldot, Paul. *Governor Alfred E. Smith: The Politician as Reformer*. New York: Garland, 1983.
Handlin, Oscar. *Al Smith and His America*. 1958. Reprint, Boston: Northeastern University Press, 1987.
Josephson, Matthew, and Hannah Josephson. *Al Smith: Hero of the Cities*. Boston: Houghton Mifflin, 1960.
Smith, Al. *Up to Now: An Autobiography*. New York: Viking Press, 1929.

Smith, John (ca. 1580–1631) *military leader, colonist*

A veteran of many European military campaigns, Captain John Smith is best known for his presidency of the governing council of Jamestown in VIRGINIA COLONY. His strong leadership during the often-desperate early years of England's first settlement in the Americas enabled the colony of Jamestown to survive and ensured an English foothold on the eastern seaboard of North America.

Smith was born in Lincolnshire, England, around 1580, to the family of a yeoman farmer. Smith spent most of his early life in travel and combat, fighting Spanish Catholics in the Netherlands and Muslims in the Mediterranean and in Hungary. Captured and enslaved by the Turks during a campaign that began in 1600, he eventually escaped, returning to England by way of Russia, Poland, the Holy Roman Empire, Germany, France, Spain, and Morocco. As a soldier of fortune, he was naturally attracted to new ventures in the Americas, though almost nothing is known regarding the exact circumstances of his initial involvement. In 1606, Smith was appointed one of seven resident councillors of the newly formed Jamestown Colony of the Virginia Company. Elected president of the council in September 1608, at a time when disease, American Indian attacks, and ill-discipline had decimated the community, Smith set about to ensure that everyone—including the well born—worked. As an experienced soldier and traveler, Smith had a wide range of needed skills, including mapping, exploration, and organization. He negotiated favorable trade with the local native groups, ensuring a more ready supply of food. His *A True Relation of Such Occurrences and Accidents of Noate as hath Hapned in Virginia since the First Planting of that Collony* (1608), written as a long letter and published in England, is considered America's first book. When he returned to England in October 1609 as a result of a serious gunpowder burn, Virginia once again fell into near anarchy.

Smith returned to North America once, in 1614, to explore the coast of New England. He offered to assist in the settlement of the Pilgrims in 1619 and to lead a military force against the Indians of Virginia in 1622 but was rejected. His most important contributions late in life were historical works that reveal much about colonial life in the earliest days of English settlement, notably *A Description of New England: Or, Observations and Discoveries of Captain John Smith* (1616), *New Englands Trials* (1620), and *The Generall Historie of Virginia, New-England, and the Summer Isles* (1624). Arrogant and ambitious, Smith undoubtedly exaggerated his role in many events of which he wrote, but historians have generally confirmed the accuracy of his work.

Further Reading

Barbour, Philip L. *The Three Worlds of Captain John Smith.* Boston: Houghton Mifflin, 1964.
Emerson, Everett H. *Captain John Smith.* New York: Twayne, 1971.
Smith, John. *The Complete Works of Captain John Smith, 1580–1631.* 3 vols. Ed. Philip L. Barbour. Chapel Hill: Institute of Early American History and Culture, University of North Carolina Press, 1986.
Vaughan, Alden T. *American Genesis: Captain John Smith and the Founding of Virginia.* Boston: Addison-Wesley, 1997.

South Asian immigration

Most early studies of immigration to the United States and Canada treated all the peoples of South Asia as a single category, including immigrants from more than a dozen ethnic groups who inhabited British India prior to 1947. Nevertheless, most pre–World War II South Asian immigrants were Sikhs from the Punjab, who created a relatively uniform Indian presence in the farming valleys of California. Prior to 1965, there were never more than 7,000 South Asians legally in the United States, and most of them were deported or left the country during the late 1920s and 1930s. Because of the preponderance of Sikhs and the small number of other South Asian immigrants prior to the 1970s, little attention was paid to distinctions, making it now impossible to determine exactly how many South Asian immigrants came from each of the modern states that emerged with the ending of British rule in India in 1947, including India, Pakistan, Ceylon (later Sri Lanka), and Bangladesh. The term *Hindu,* which was the most common designation until the 1960s, was both inaccurate and confusing, as the majority of South Asian immigrants were not religious Hindus but rather Sikhs and Muslims. Further confusing immigrant figures is the considerable transmigration that occurred as a result of the export of South Asian labor from British India during the 19th and 20th centuries. Significant numbers of people who immigrated to the United States from Uganda, Kenya, South Africa, Tanzania,

Guyana, Trinidad, Fiji, and Mauritius were either born in India, Pakistan, or Sri Lanka or were the descendants of South Asian natives. Prior to the 1980 census, South Asian immigrants were still classified as "white/Caucasians."

When the United States reopened South Asian immigration in 1946, there were only about 1,500 South Asians in the country. The turning point came with the IMMIGRATION AND NATIONALITY ACT of 1965, which led to a massive influx of South Asians. Meanwhile, in Canada, the government had much earlier (January 1, 1951) implemented a new quota system for South Asian immigrants, effectively laying the foundation for a diverse and complex South Asian population in the Americas. Under separate quotas for India, Pakistan, and Ceylon, most early immigrants were Sikh relatives. By the late 1950s, however, an increasing number were pioneer immigrants from a variety of ethnic groups, gradually eroding the near-Sikh monopoly.

See also BANGLADESHI IMMIGRATION; INDIAN IMMIGRATION; PAKISTANI IMMIGRATION; SRI LANKAN IMMIGRATION.

Further Reading

Buchignani, Norman, and Doreen M. Indra, with Ram Srivastava. *Continuous Journey: A Social History of South Asians in Canada.* Toronto: McClelland and Stewart, 1985.
La Brack, Bruce. "South Asians." In *A Nation of Peoples: A Sourcebook on America's Multicultural Heritage.* Ed. Elliott Robert Barken. Westport, Conn.: Greenwood Press, 1999.
Leonard, Karen Isaksen. *The South Asian Americans.* Westport, Conn.: Greenwood Press, 1997.

South Carolina colony   See CAROLINA COLONIES.

South Korea   See KOREAN IMMIGRATION.

Soviet immigration

Emigration from the Union of Soviet Socialist Republics (USSR; Soviet Union) was, for most of its history (1917–91), forbidden. Those who did emigrate were often dissidents and came from many, mostly non-Russian ethnic groups, including Jews, Armenians, Estonians, Latvians, Lithuanians, and Ukrainians. There was little or no sense of Soviet identity; the history, social organization, and areas of settlement varied from group to group. As a result of the dissolution of the Soviet Union in 1991, it is usually within the context of the specific ethnic groups that immigration is most meaningfully discussed.

The USSR was the largest state the modern world had seen, occupying 8,649,500 square miles, or about 30 percent more territory than modern Russia. It stretched from eastern Europe across northern Asia to the Pacific Ocean. It was bordered on the west by Finland, Norway, Poland, Czechoslovakia, Hungary, and Romania and on the south by Turkey, Iran, Afghanistan, China, Mongolia, and North Korea. At the time of its collapse, there were 15 major ethnic groups in the Soviet Union, forming the basis for the 15 states that emerged. There were many other smaller ethnic groups, as well.

During the 18th, 19th, and 20th centuries, the transformation of Russian state boundaries significantly affected the character of RUSSIAN IMMIGRATION. Ivan the Terrible (r. 1533–84), the first czar, began the expansion of the state to include significant numbers of non-Russian peoples. Between 1667 and 1795, Russia expanded westward, conquering lands mainly from the kingdoms of Poland and Sweden that included the peoples of modern Latvia, Lithuania, Estonia, eastern Poland, Belarus, and Ukraine. Russia acquired most of the remainder of Poland and Moldova (Bessarabia) in 1815, following the Napoleonic Wars. Throughout the 19th century, Russia continued to expand, especially into the Caucasus Mountain region and central Asia, occupying regions that would later become the modern countries of Armenia, Azerbaijan, Georgia, Kazakhstan, Kyrgyzstan, Turkmenistan, Tajikistan, and Uzbekistan. During the great age of immigration from eastern Europe between 1880 and 1920, therefore, more than a dozen major ethnic groups might be classified by immigration agents as "Russian," though they were in fact part of these older nations.

The Bolshevik Revolution of 1917, which ushered in the world's first communist government, soon spread to most of the surrounding territories acquired by Russia, leading to the establishment of the USSR in 1922. The USSR consisted roughly of the old Russian Empire, except for the loss of Finland, Latvia, Estonia, Lithuania, and Poland, which became independent countries after World War I (1914–18). During World War II (1939–45), the Soviet Union reoccupied parts of Finland, Estonia, Latvia, Lithuania, Poland, and Moldova and afterward exercised extensive control over the foreign and immigration policies of the nominally independent countries of Poland, Czechoslovakia, Hungary, East Germany, and Romania. Finally, in 1991, the Soviet Union collapsed. In its place were 15 separate states, each having its own annual immigration quota to the United States and Canada.

The Soviet government tightly controlled emigration. Most who did emigrate were wartime refugees, who were not allowed to return, or were Jews, who were sporadically allowed to leave legally from 1970. Whereas an average of about 125,000 immigrants came to the United States annually from the old Russian Empire between 1901 and 1920, the figure dropped to only about 6,100 during the 1920s, with most of these being anticommunist, White Russians who fled in the immediate wake of the Russian Civil War, prior to the formal establishment of the USSR (1922). The

Soviet government then banned virtually all emigration, and those who did come to the United States and Canada were often viewed with suspicion, in part because of their radical ideas and labor union involvement: Between 1931 and 1970, only about 5,000 Soviets immigrated, many of them dissidents and not all Russians. The United States accepted about 20,000 Soviet refugees under provisions of the DISPLACED PERSONS ACT of 1948 and related executive measures after World War II. About 40 percent of Canada's 125,000 refugee immigrants between 1947 and 1953 were Ukrainians (16 percent), Jews (10 percent), Lithuanians (6 percent), Latvians (6 percent), and Russians (3 percent), most of whom came from Soviet lands.

As COLD WAR tensions eased during the 1970s, the Soviet government gradually relaxed emigration restrictions, which led to an annual average immigration to the United States of about 4,800 between 1970 and 1990, mostly Jews and Armenians. It is estimated that between 1970 and 1985, about a quarter million Jews were allowed to emigrate, often as a part of Western diplomatic efforts to secure better treatment for them. Most went to Israel, but perhaps 100,000 settled in the United States. With the final collapse of the Soviet Union in 1991, a massive exodus from the economically debilitated country ensued. Almost a half million Soviets or former Soviets immigrated to the United States during the 1990s, probably about 15 percent of them ethnic Russians. The substantial immigration continued into the following decade, with about 55,000 coming in both 2001 and 2002. Of Canada's 142,000 immigrants from the former Soviet Union (2001), 53 percent came between 1991 and 2001.

See also ARMENIAN IMMIGRATION; ESTONIAN IMMIGRATION; JEWISH IMMIGRATION; LATVIAN IMMIGRATION; LITHUANIAN IMMIGRATION; UKRAINIAN IMMIGRATION.

Further Reading

Gold, Stephen J. *From the Workers' State to the Golden State: Jews from the Former Soviet Union in California*. Boston: Allyn and Bacon, 1995.

Goldman, Minton. "United States Policy and Soviet Jewish Emigration from Nixon to Bush." In *Jews and Jewish Life in Russia and the Soviet Union*. Ed. Yaacov Ro'i. Portland, Ore: Frank Cass, 1995.

Hardwick, Susan Wiley. *Russian Refuge: Religion, Migration, and Settlement on the North American Pacific Rim*. Chicago: University of Chicago Press, 1993.

Jeletzky, F., ed. *Russian Canadians: Their Past and Present*. Ottawa: Borealis Press, 1983.

Kipel, Vitaut. *Belarusy u ZshA*. Minsk, 1993.

———. "Belorussians in the United States." *Ethnic Forum* 9, nos. 1–2 (1989): 75–90.

Kuropas, Myron B. *The Ukrainian Americans: Roots and Aspirations, 1884–1954*. Toronto: University of Toronto Press, 1991.

Lupul, Manoly R. *A Heritage in Transition: Essays in the History of Ukrainians in Canada*. Toronto: McClelland and Stewart, 1982.

Magocsi, Paul R. *The Carpatho-Rusyn Americans.* New York: Chelsea House, 1989.

———. *Our People: Carpatho-Rusyns and Their Descendants in North America.* 3d rev. ed. Toronto: Multicultural History Society of Ontario, 1994.

———. *The Russian Americans.* New York: Chelsea House, 1987.

Orleck, Annelise. *The Soviet Jewish Americans.* Westport, Conn.: Greenwood Press, 1999.

Ro'i, Yaacov. *The Struggle for Soviet Jewish Emigration, 1948–1967.* Cambridge: Cambridge University Press, 1991.

Simon, Rita J. *New Lives: The Adjustment of Soviet Jewish Immigrants in the United States and Israel.* Lexington, Ky.: Lexington Books, 1985.

Spanish immigration

Significant elements of Spanish culture represent one of the major strands of the American social fabric. Although Spanish immigration has been modest since the foundation of the United States, the descendants of the settlers of Spain's New World empire—including Mexicans, Puerto Ricans, Cubans, Dominicans, Costa Ricans, Guatemalans, Hondurans, Nicaraguans, Panamanians, Salvadorans, Argentineans, Bolivians, Chileans, Colombians, Ecuadoreans, Paraguayans, Peruvians, Uruguayans, and Venezuelans, with their own mestizo cultures that incorporate indigenous, African, and Spanish cultural traits and customs—composed 12.5 percent of the population of the United States in 2000, making it the largest single minority group in the country. Latin Americans account for less than 1 percent of Canada's population. According to the U.S. census of 2000 and the Canadian census of 2001, 861,911 Americans and 213,105 Canadians claimed Spanish descent. Spanish Americans are spread widely throughout the United States, with the greatest concentrations being in New York City and Tampa, as well as Florida generally, and the former Spanish Empire lands in the American Southwest. Spanish Canadians were heavily concentrated in both Quebec and Ontario.

Spain occupies 192,600 square miles of the Iberian Peninsula in southwest Europe. Also on the peninsula, Portugal lies to the west and France to the north on the continental mainland. In 2002, the population was estimated at 40,037,995. The people are a mixture of Mediterranean and Nordic types, and the chief religion is Roman Catholicism. Spain was among the first European states to create a strong national monarchy, late in the 15th century. As a result of the voyages of CHRISTOPHER COLUMBUS and other explorers, from 1492 through the 16th century, Spain claimed the entire Caribbean Basin, most of Central and South America (excluding Brazil), and the southwestern portion of the modern United States, including all or parts of California, Nevada, Utah, Arizona, New Mexico, and Texas. The first permanent Spanish settlement in the United States was at St. Augustine, Florida, in 1565, whereas the British, French,

and Dutch had begun to establish themselves in unsettled territories in North America early in the 16th century. In the New World, Spain created an efficient and highly bureaucratic colonial government, headed in Madrid. This stemmed in part from Spanish feudal traditions and also from the desire to control the wealthy gold and silver trade coming out of Mexico and Peru. During 300 years, Spain effectively imposed its culture on the indigenous societies through force—war, death, disease, and forced labor—and intermarriage. By the 18th century, the mestizo population was larger than either the Spanish or Indian population, though the percentages varied widely throughout the empire. By the 19th century, almost all subjects of the Spanish Crown had been Christianized, though colonial Catholicisms embraced numerous elements from native religions. Although Spanish immigration to the New World was substantial, estimated at almost a half million between 1500 and 1700, most settled in Mexico, Cuba, and South America. Settlement in the northern borderlands that would later become part of the United States was small. Between 1809 and 1825, Mexico and most of Central and South America gained their independence from Spain. Texas won its independence from Mexico in 1836 and joined the Union in 1845. Three years later, an estimated 75,000 Mexican citizens of modern California, Arizona, and New Mexico became U.S. citizens when the region was transferred to the United States following the U.S.-MEXICAN WAR, 1846–48. In Texas, Anglo-American settlers composed the majority population even before Texas gained its independence from Mexico. In California, within two years of the discovery of gold (1848), settlers completely overwhelmed the 13,000 Spanish Californians.

Spanish immigration to the New World between 1846 and 1932 ranked fifth behind Great Britain, Italy, Austria-Hungary, and Germany, but most of Spain's almost 5 million immigrants went to the remaining colonies of Cuba and Puerto Rico. Immigration to North America remained small during the 19th century, averaging less than 500 per year between 1821 and 1900. As a result of the U.S. victory in the Spanish-American War of 1898, however, substantial numbers of Cubans and Puerto Ricans, a large percentage of whom were of direct Spanish descent, immigrated to the United States over the years. The United States annexed Puerto Rico in 1898, and its people eventually gained free access to the United States as citizens. The U.S. government also became heavily involved in Cuban politics, particularly during the post–World War II COLD WAR period, and thus for decades granted Cubans special immigrant status. Direct Spanish immigration jumped dramatically between 1900 and passage of the restrictive JOHNSON-REED ACT of 1924, more than 100,000 immigrants coming during that period, but the number was small compared to that of many other European countries. Spanish immigration revived somewhat during the 1960s, with a little more than 100,000 coming between 1961 and 1990. Since then, the numbers have declined. Between 1991 and 2002, Spanish immigration to the United States averaged less than 1,900 per year.

Spanish Basques were among the first immigrants to arrive in Canada in the 16th century, plying the waters off Newfoundland for fish and whales (see BASQUE IMMIGRATION). In the late 18th century, Spain established a fort on Vancouver Island, but no permanent settlement was then made. With opportunities for New World immigration in many Spanish-speaking lands, few Spaniards chose Canada. During the first half of the 20th century, only a few thousand arrived. The first organized Spanish immigration began in 1957, when Spain and Canada signed an agreement facilitating the immigration of Spanish farmers and domestic workers. Between 1957 and 1960, about 400 Spaniards were brought into the country to provide these badly needed services. After 1960, there was a steady but small number of Spanish immigration, averaging less than 600 per year between 1961 and 1989. Of 10,275 Spanish immigrants in Canada in 2001, only 1,250 arrived between 1991 and 2001.

Further Reading

Bannon, John Francis. *Spanish Borderlands Frontier, 1513–1821.* Albuquerque: University of New Mexico Press, 1984.

Bolton, Herbert E. *The Spanish Borderlands: A Chronicle of Old Florida and the Southwest.* 1921. Reprint, Albuquerque: University of New Mexico Press, 1996.

Douglass, William A., and Jon Bilbao. *Amerikanauk: The Basques in the New World.* Reno: University of Nevada Press, 1975.

Douglass, William A., Carmelo Urza, and Linda White, eds. *The Basque Diaspora.* Reno: University of Nevada Press, 2000.

Gómez, R. A. "Spanish Immigration to the United States." *The Americas* 19 (1962): 59–77.

Hudson, Charles. *Knights of Spain, Warriors of the Sun.* Atlanta: University of Georgia Press, 1997.

Mata, Fernando. "Immigrants from the Hispanic World in Canada: Demographic Profile and Social Adaptation." Unpublished, York University, 1988.

Robinson, David J., ed. *Migration in Colonial Spanish America.* Cambridge: Cambridge University Press, 1991.

Schubert, Adrian. *The Land and People of Spain.* New York: HarperCollins, 1992.

sports and immigration

Sports have long been an arena for the display of national pride, particularly in association with the modern Olympics, held every four years since 1896. Since World War II (1939–45), however, sports have become increasingly internationalized, leading many of the world's best hockey, basketball, baseball, and track athletes to North America. Modern transportation has made it easier for players to move from country to country, while modern communications—particularly television and satellite—have dramatically enhanced sporting revenues and broadcast games featuring the highest quality of individual and team performance.

Baseball and boxing were America's two great sports prior to World War II. From the mid-19th century, both were particularly associated with immigrants. As urban sports that developed at a time when immigrants flooded into U.S. cities in order to work in mills and factories, they were accessible to newcomers. They relied heavily on physical prowess and required little in the way of equipment, thus allowing anyone with real talent the potential to become successful. In this, they were tailor made to the American meritocratic ideal.

Although most early U.S. baseball players were Anglo-Americans, by the late 19th century, an increasingly large percentage were Irish and German. As the NEW IMMIGRATION flooded the country with immigrants from southern and eastern Europe beginning in the 1890s, baseball stars came from a widening circle of ethnic groups. Between 1900 and 1940, dozens of foreign-born men played in the major leagues, including players from Germany, Ireland, Canada, Norway, Sweden, Denmark, Russia, Austria-Hungary, England, Cuba, and Hawaii. Dozens more were second-generation immigrants still closely tied to their ethnic communities. Some of the greatest players in the game were proudly followed by their ethnic communities; nevertheless, their objective successes on the field and as part of multiethnic teams helped to reinforce the idea that anyone could become an American icon. Joe DiMaggio, born to Italian immigrants; Hank Greenberg, born to Romanian-Jewish immigrants; and Jackie Robinson, the first African American allowed to play in the major leagues, all demonstrated that ability counted more than background.

After World War II (1939–45), African Americans and Caribbean players of mixed or African descent played an increasingly large role in the development of baseball. Players such as Roberto Clemente, Luis Tiant, and the Alou brothers served as visible models to young Puerto Ricans, Cubans, and Dominicans who had developed a love of the sport in their own countries. By 1990, 13 percent of major leaguers were Hispanic, and by 1997, the figure had jumped to 24 percent. In 2002, 230 of 827 players on opening day major league rosters were born outside the 50 states: 79 from the Dominican Republic; 38 from Puerto Rico; 37 from Venezuela; 17 from Mexico; 11 from Japan; 10 from both Canada and Cuba; seven from Panama; six from South Korea; three from both Australia and Colombia; two each from Aruba, the Netherlands Antilles, and Nicaragua; and one each from England, Germany, and Vietnam. According to a February 4, 2002, commissioner's report, 42 percent of all professional baseball players came from outside the United States; more than three-fourths of those were from the Dominican Republic and Venezuela. Of the 3,066 foreign-born professional players, 1,630 (53 percent) were from the Dominican Republic and 744 (24 percent) were from Venezuela; 165 (5 percent) from Puerto Rico; 114 (4 percent) from Mexico; 26 were from Cuba, with half on major league rosters.

Boxing was another sport well suited to the rough, urban life of industrial, immigrant America. The first boxing champion of the United States, Yankee Sullivan, was born in Ireland. Even more popular was John L. Sullivan, a second-generation Irishman, whose name became a household word as the sport expanded and developed. His defeat of another Irish American, Paddy Ryan, in 1882 is sometimes viewed as the first true title fight in American history. If the Irish dominated early boxing, Jewish fighters were especially prominent between 1910 and 1940, when they won 26 world titles. Two of America's greatest fighters were Jack Dempsey, born to Irish immigrant stock, and Rocky Marciano (Rocco Marchegiano), whose father emigrated from Italy during World War I.

Immigrant and ethnic players were long associated with basketball but did not become prominent in the American consciousness until the sport itself became more popular in the 1960s and 1970s. Basketball was particularly associated with the inner cities, as it did not require the large field associated with baseball or football. Prior to World War II, the early professional clubs were dominated by Irish, Jewish, and Italian players. As they increasingly moved to the suburbs, however, African Americans began to predominate and by 1995 made up 82 percent of the National Basketball Association. As a result of the game's success outside the United States and Canada, more Europeans, Africans, Australians, Asians, and Latin Americans began to play, and the 1990s saw the rise of many international stars, including Hakeem Olajuwon (Nigeria), Patrick Ewing (Jamaica), Toni Kukoč (Croatia), Vlade Divac (Serbia), Tim Duncan (St. Croix), and Dirk Nowitzki (Germany) and a host of potential future stars in Yao Ming (China), Peja Stojaković (Serbia), and Pau Gasol (Spain). By 2002, the percentage of African Americans was down to 78 percent, and the 2003 draft suggested that foreign players would take a greater number of slots in the future. Of the 58 draft picks, 21 were from foreign countries, and eight of these were taken in the first round. Many commentators speculated that the game itself—not just the players—was being fundamentally changed.

Canada's preeminent sport, hockey, has also seen an influx of international players in the 1990s. Hockey was first played in Canada in the early 19th century. It gradually spread to the United States, beginning in the 1890s, and then to Europe just after the turn of the 20th century. Until World War II, it remained largely a North American sport, but the seeds that were planted in the first Olympic competition in 1920 eventually grew into a European fascination for the sport. In 1956, the Soviet Union won a gold medal in the first Olympic ice hockey competition it entered and dominated international competition for a quarter century. Ulf Sterner became the first Swedish player in the National Hockey League (NHL) in 1965, and the better European players gradually were brought to play in the world's top hockey league. By the 1990s, they were considered essential in reviving a sport that lagged behind football, basketball, and baseball in terms of public support. At the beginning of the 2002–03 season, the international character of the NHL was never more evident. Of the 383 players on opening-day rosters, only 53.6 percent were Canadian; represented significantly were the United States (13 percent), the Czech Republic (8.2 percent), Russia (6.9 percent), Sweden (6.2 percent), Finland (5 percent), and Slovakia (2.9 percent).

Some observers feared that North American sports, as they became internationalized, were losing part of their essential national character. There were also fears that sport was becoming too closely tied to international politics and finance. Some African Americans, for instance, feared that white European players were being courted because of greater television marketability. And there was no question that New York Yankees owner George Steinbrenner's pursuit of Hideki Matsui in the 2002–03 offseason was as much about tapping into the Japanese market as gaining the services of a good ballplayer. With the decline of communism around the world from the late 1980s, top athletes from former communist countries were free to market themselves internationally in a way they could not have before. The communist countries that did remain found athletes more likely than ever to defect. In 1991, René Arocha became the first Cuban player from the island country's famed national team to defect, while on a stopover in Miami. Over the following decade, more than 50 players followed. Liván Hernández defected to Mexico in 1995 and two years later led the Florida Marlins to a world championship. This became an important post–COLD WAR victory, as Hernández's achievements overshadowed the reburial on Cuban soil of the bones of revolutionary hero Ernesto "Che" Guevera, an act heavily promoted by Cuban leader Fidel Castro.

Further Reading

Bodner, Allen. *When Boxing Was a Jewish Sport.* Westport, Conn.: Praeger, 1997.

Coleman, Jim. *Hockey Is Our Game: Canada in the World of International Hockey.* Toronto: Key Porter Books, 1987.

Fainaru, Steve, and Ray Sánchez. *The Duke of Havana: Baseball, Cuba, and the Search for the American Dream.* New York: Villard, 2001.

Gorn, Elliot J. *The Manly Art: Bare-Knuckle Prize Fighting in America.* Ithaca, N.Y.: Cornell University Press, 1986.

Klein, Alan M. *Sugarball: The American Game, the Dominican Dream.* New Haven, Conn.: Yale University Press, 1991.

Krich, John. *El Beisbol: The Pleasures and Passions of the Latin American Game.* New York: Ivan R. Dee, 2002.

Levine, Peter. *Ellis Island to Ebbets Field: Sport and the American Jewish Experience.* New York: Oxford University Press, 1992.

McGraw, Dan. "The Foreign Invasion of the American Game." *Village Voice*, May 28–June 3, 2003. Available online. URL: http://www.villagevoice.com/print/issues/0322/mcgraw.php. Accessed December 29, 2003.

Mrozek, Donald J. *Sport and American Mentality.* Knoxville: University of Tennessee Press, 1983.

Price, S. L. *Pitching around Fidel: A Journey into the Heart of Cuban Sports.* New York: Ecco, 2002.

Riess, Steven A. *City Games: The Evolution of American Urban Society and the Rise of Sports.* Chicago: University of Illinois Press, 1989.

Stark, Jayson. "Age Issues Brought on by Sept. 11." ESPN Sports. April 17, 2002. Available online. URL: http://espn.go.com/mlb/columns/stark_jayson/1339359.html. Accessed March 23, 2003.

Westerbeek, Hans, and Aaron Smith. *Sport Business in the Global Marketplace.* New York: Palgrave Macmillan, 2003.

Wheeler, Lonnie. "Our Game? Influx of Foreign Players Changing Basketball." *Cincinnati Post*, July 1, 2003. Available online. URL: http://www.journalnow.com/servlet/Satellite?pagename=WSJ%2FMGArticle%2FWSJ_BasicArticle&c=MGArticle&cid=1031769914028&path=!sports&s=1037645509200. Accessed December 29, 2003.

Sri Lankan immigration

Most Sri Lankans in the United States and Canada are professionals or come from professional backgrounds and thus have done relatively well economically. According to the U.S. census of 2000 and the Canadian census of 2001, 24,587 Americans and 61,315 Canadian claimed Sri Lankan ancestry. The majority of Sri Lankan Americans live in California and New York City, with significant communities in Chicago, Texas, and Florida. The majority of Canada's Sri Lankans live in Ontario. Montreal was an important early area of settlement, but large numbers began to move westward, especially to Alberta and British Columbia.

Sri Lanka is a 25,000-square-mile island in the Indian Ocean, at some points less than 20 miles off the southeast coast of India. In 2002, the population was estimated at 19,408,635. The people are ethnically divided between two main groups, the Sinhalese (74 percent) and the Tamil (18 percent). Roughly corresponding to the ethnic distinctions is the religious division of the population, with 69 percent being Buddhist and 15 percent Hindu, as well as eight percent Christian and eight percent Muslim. During the fifth century B.C., Sinhalese arrived from the mainland, establishing a kingdom and converting to Buddhism during the third century B.C. Invading Tamils from the Madras area of India conquered much of the Sinhalese territory starting in the 11th century. The island was divided between the two groups when the Portuguese arrived early in the 16th century. The Dutch conquered the island in the 17th century, and the English captured it in 1795, thus initiating a long period of British rule, under which the island was known as Ceylon.

Sri Lankan immigration began during the period of British colonial ascendancy, particularly after 1867, when large numbers of agricultural laborers were recruited throughout British India. From the late 18th century until 1947, British India included all the territory from modern Pakistan to Burma. The exact number of Sri Lankan immigrants is difficult to determine, as the term *Indian* was applied to more than a dozen ethnic groups, including the Sinhalese and Tamils of Ceylon (see INDIAN IMMIGRATION). Significant Sri Lankan immigration did not begin until independence in 1948, when many educated Tamils and Sinhalese began to leave as the country moved toward socialism. The immigration of doctors and engineers often exceeded the numbers being trained each year in those fields. At first, most migrated to Great Britain; during the 1970s, the United States and Australia became popular destinations.

In 1951, Canada initiated a quota system for South Asian immigrants, including a provision for 50 Sri Lankans annually. In the early 1960s, the Sri Lankan government recognized the significant drain of skilled workers from the country and launched a series of measures to severely restrict emigration. Beginning in 1977, it reversed policy, especially encouraging unskilled and semi-skilled workers to seek labor opportunities outside the country. This both alleviated problems associated with domestic poverty and led to the remittance of foreign currencies. Although Sri Lanka abolished legal discrimination against the Tamils in 1978, riots and disturbances became more common, further pushing those with skills and education to seek opportunities in the West. By the mid-1980s, there were still only about 5,000 Sri Lankans of various ethnic groups in Canada. As the civil conflict between the Sinhalese and rebel Tamils evolved into full-scale civil war in 1983, the economy was destroyed, and the island appeared to become permanently divided, thus giving impetus to significant migration. Of Canada's 87,310 Sri Lankan immigrants in 2001, almost 96 percent came between 1981 and 2001. In 2001 and 2002, Sri Lanka was second only to Afghanistan in the number of refugees admitted. The civil war continued off and on in 2003 and early 2004.

Significant Sri Lankan immigration to the United States did not begin until the 1950s and even then remained small. In 1980, the Sri Lankan–American population was less than 200. As the civil war developed, however, almost 16,000 Sri Lankans immigrated to the United States by 2000. In 2001 and 2002, about 1,500 Sri Lankans immigrated each year. Tamils and Sinhalese account for about equal percentages of immigrants.

See also BANGLADESHI IMMIGRATION; PAKISTANI IMMIGRATION; SOUTH ASIAN IMMIGRATION.

Further Reading
Buchignani, Norman, and Doreen M. Indra, with Ram Srivastava. *Continuous Journey: A Social History of South Asians in Canada.* Toronto: McClelland and Stewart, 1985.

De Silva, K. M. *Managing Ethnic Tensions in Multi-Ethnic Societies: Sri Lanka, 1880–1985*. Lanham, Md.: University Press of America, 1986.

Leonard, Karen Isaksen. *The South Asian Americans*. Westport, Conn.: Greenwood Press, 1997.

Manogaron, Chelvadurai, and Bryan Pfaffenberger, eds. *Sri Lankan Tamils: Ethnicity and Identity*. Boulder, Colo.: Westview Press, 1994.

Pinnawala, Sisira. "From Brain Drain to Guest Workers and Refugees: The Politicies and Politics of Outmigration from Sri Lanka." In *The Silent Debate: Asian Immigration and Racism in Canada*. Eds. Eleanor Laquian, Aprodicio Laquian, and Terry McGee. Vancouver, Canada: Institute of Asian Research, University of British Columbia. 1998.

Ruhanage, L. K. "Sri Lankan Labor Migration: Trends and Threats." *Economic Review* 21, no. 10 (1996): 3–7.

Samarasinghe, S. W. R. De A., and Vidyamali Samarasinghe, eds. *Historical Dictionary of Sri Lanka*. Lanham, Md.: Scarecrow Press, 1997.

Sri Lanka: A Country Study. Washington, D.C.: Government Printing Office, 1990.

Statue of Liberty

The Statue of Liberty is the most visible symbol of the personal freedoms that attracted immigrants to American shores from the 17th century to the present day. Given to the people of the United States by France in 1884 as an expression of friendship, the statue commemorated French aid in the dark days of the AMERICAN REVOLUTION (1775–83). Since then, it has greeted every immigrant entering New York Harbor, promising freedom and opportunity.

Liberty Enlightening the World, the official name of the sculpture, is more than 150 feet high, not including the pedestal or torch. The bronze statue displays liberty personified, proud and graceful, holding forth the torchlight of freedom. The seven spikes of her crown stand for the light of liberty shining on the seven seas and seven continents. A tablet bearing the date of the Declaration of Independence is cradled in her left hand, and the broken chain of tyranny lies at her feet. The statue was first proposed in 1865 by French politician Edouard-René Lefebvre de Laboulaye, who greatly admired the United States. During the 1870s, the design was entrusted to sculptor Frédéric-Auguste Bartholdi, who had visited New York City in 1871 and chosen Bedloe's Island in upper New York Bay as a fitting site. While the French-American Union raised $400,000 for its construction, the American Committee, with the help of New York publisher Joseph Pulitzer, raised $300,000 to complete the pedestal. Designed to be the largest statue in modern times, the daunting task of engineering was given to Frenchman Alexandre-Gustave Eiffel, who later designed Paris's Eiffel Tower. Bartholdi had originally hoped to present the statue on the centenary of America's independence but settled for sending the right

hand clasping the torch, which was displayed at the Centennial Exposition in Philadelphia and later in New York City. *Liberty Enlightening the World* was finally christened on October 28, 1886, with President Grover Cleveland in attendance.

The symbolism of the statue evolved across time. Between 1886 and 1920, the Statue of Liberty, as it was popularly called, came to represent not just friendship between two nations but their shared commitment to freedom. Immigrants eagerly lined the decks of ships as they entered New York Harbor to catch a glimpse of the towering bronze figure. Many cried with joy. In 1935, on his arrival from Poland, Nobel Prize–winning writer Isaac Bashevis Singer remembered hearing about the statue as a small boy in Warsaw. "They all wrote about it," he recalled, "how they came to America, how they saw the Statue Liberty." In 1903, a plaque inscribed with the final lines of "The New Colossus" was placed on the pedestal. Written by Jewish American poet Emma Lazarus, the poem embodies the ideals that drew immigrants to U.S. shores, as the "Mother of Exiles" eschews the "storied pomp" of ancient glories:

Give me your tired, your poor,
Your huddled masses yearning to breathe free,
The wretched refuse of your teeming shore.
Send these, the homeless, tempest-tost to me.
I lift my lamp beside the golden door!

During World War I (1914–18), the statue became a national symbol, used on recruiting posters and for selling Liberty Bonds. For many immigrants, American freedom meant economic freedom. One young Polish Jew remembered the thrill and emotion of seeing the statue in 1920: "It was more, not freedom from oppression, I think, but more freedom from want. That was the biggest thrill, to see that statue there." For hundreds of thousands of refugees arriving after World War II (1939–45), however, the Statue of Liberty became synonymous with the "Mother of Exiles."

In 1924, the Statue of Liberty was declared a national monument, and in 1933 its care was handed over to the National Park Service. In 1965, ELLIS ISLAND and Liberty Island were joined as the Statue of Liberty National Monument.

Some 2 million people visited the Statue of Liberty each year until the terrorist attacks of September 11, 2001, led to its closing, officials citing security and safety issues as the reason. Liberty Island was reopened three months later, but visitors were not allowed to take the famous 354-step hike to the crown. The museum in the pedestal was reopened in summer 2004. The symbolism of the Statue of Liberty remains strong. According to New York City mayor Michael Bloomberg, as long as it remains closed "in some sense the terrorists have won." Without dramatic improvements in security, however, officials still considered the statue "woe-

An ocean steamer passes the Statue of Liberty, as some steerage passengers enter New York Harbor. The hope in the eyes of the variously clad immigrants is evident. In practice, many immigrants missed the sight, nervously preparing their belongings for landing. *(Library of Congress, Prints & Photographs Division [LC-USZ62-9442])*

fully unprotected" and the terrorist threat to the symbol of liberty real.

Further Reading

Hampson, Rick. "Lady Liberty's Stairwells May Never Be Full Again." *USA Today.com.* February 3, 2004. Available online. URL: http://aolsvc.news.aol.com/news/article.adp?id=200402032307 09990037. Accessed February 4, 2004.

Moreno, Barry. The *Statue of Liberty Encyclopedia.* New York: Simon and Schuster, 2000.

Spiering, Frank. *Bearer of a Million Dreams: The Complete Story of the Statue of Liberty.* Ottawa, Ill.: Jameson Books, 1986.

stereotypes See ENTERTAINMENT AND IMMIGRATION; RACISM.

Swedish immigration

Though Swedes settled in North America as early as 1638, the great period of Swedish migration was between 1870 and 1914. According to the U.S. census of 2000 and the Canadian census of 2001, 3,998,310 Americans and 282,760 Canadians claimed Swedish descent. Although the absolute numbers are small compared to other European countries, Sweden ranked third, only behind Ireland and Norway, in percentage of population to emigrate during the 19th century. Although Chicago quickly grew to have the second largest Swedish population in the world during the 19th century, the 20th century led to rapid assimilation and considerable dispersion. The greatest concentrations of Swedes are in the American Midwest and the Canadian provinces of British Columbia and Alberta.

Sweden occupies 158,700 square miles on the Scandinavian Peninsula in northern Europe. It is bordered by Norway to the west, Denmark to the south (across the Kattegat), and Finland to the east. In 2002, the population was estimated at 8,875,053. Most people are ethnic Swedes (89 percent), with a small Finnish minority (2 percent), and a significant number of guest workers from many countries. The chief religion is Evangelical Lutheran. The Swedes have lived in the region for at least 5,000 years, about as long as any European people. Gothic tribes from Sweden played a major role in the destruction of the Roman Empire. Other Swedes, commonly known as Vikings, helped create the first Russian state in the ninth century. As its state structure grew, Sweden conquered the Finns during the 12th century and united with Norway and Denmark in the 14th. In 1523, Sweden broke away from the union and emerged by the mid-17th century as the greatest power in northern Europe. The country declined in international prominence after its defeat by Russia in the Second Northern War, early in the 18th century. Sweden and Norway were again united between 1814 and 1905 before Norway declared its full independence. During the 20th century, Sweden has had a reputation for noninvolvement in international affairs, remaining neutral in both world wars. It entered the European Union in 1995.

In 1638, Sweden established a settlement along the Delaware River Valley, christening it New Sweden. The commercial enterprise never flourished, however, and by 1655, its 400 Swedish and Finnish settlers fell under the control of the Dutch colony of New Netherland to the north (see DELAWARE COLONY; NEW YORK COLONY). Most Swedish immigrants came to the United States in three waves. Though Swedes were influenced by nationalism and

religious freedom, overpopulation and the resulting lack of economic opportunity were by far the greatest cause of the mass immigration. Beginning in 1840, most emigrants were from the university towns of Uppsala and Lund. Most were young and from good social backgrounds and often influenced by romantic ideals. Gradually this migration gave way to that of various persecuted religious groups or associations, including the Janssonists, Baptists, and Mormons. Neither of these migrations was large, but both established foundations for later, larger migrations. As railways and steamships improved in the 1860s, mass emigration became common. A severe famine in the late 1860s gave impetus to the emigration trend, leading about 100,000 Swedes to go to the United States between 1868 and 1873. In some Swedish districts, virtually every farm was represented in America, providing a social framework for prospective immigrants. Between 1870 and 1914, about 1 million Swedes immigrated to the United States, and about 100,000 more during the postwar period up to the Great Depression in the 1930s. Although Swedish immigration revived somewhat after World War II (1939–45)—more than 45,000 until 1970— it declined thereafter and remained small throughout the remainder of the 20th century. Between 1970 and 2000, Swedish immigration to the United States averaged about 1,000 per year.

The first significant migration of Swedes to Canada began after 1890. Heavy promotion by the Canadian government, completion of the transcontinental railway in 1885, and declining availability of homesteads in the United States led an increasing number of Swedes to look for agricultural opportunities on the Canadian prairies. Figures prior to World War I (1914–18) are problematic, as Swedes were often enumerated with Norwegians or Scandinavians generally, and if they migrated north directly from the United States, they would have been listed as Americans. A reasonable estimate for the Swedish immigration between 1893 and 1914 is about 40,000. About 11,000 more came directly from Sweden during the 1920s, but immigration virtually halted during the depression and war years. The earliest Swedish settlements were concentrated in Manitoba, but by the 1920s, the greatest numbers of Swedes were living in Saskatchewan. After World War II, a generally healthy economy and extensive social services kept many Swedes from emigrating. In 2001, there were only 6,810 Swedish immigrants living in Canada, and 36 percent of them had come before 1961.

Swedish emigrants bound for England and the United States board steamer at Göteborg, Sweden, ca. 1905. Most Swedes initially came to America for land, though it was increasingly difficult to find after 1900. Within a decade, more than half of all Swedes were city dwellers, with Chicago becoming second only to Stockholm in Swedish population. *(Library of Congress, Prints & Photographs Division [LC-USZ62-94340])*

Further Reading

Barr, Elinor Berglund. *The Swedish Experience in Canada: An Annotated Bibliography.* Proceedings from the Swedish Emigrant Institute, no. 4 (1991).

Barton, H. Arnold. *A Folk Divided: Homeland Swedes and Swedish Americans, 1840–1940.* Carbondale: Southern Illinois University Press, 1994.

Blanck, Dag, and Harald Runblom, eds. *Swedish Life in American Cities.* Uppsala, Sweden: Center for Multiethnic Research, 1991.

Kastrup, Allan. *The Swedish Heritage in America.* St. Paul, Minn.: Swedish Council of America, 1975.

Lindberg, John S. *The Background of Swedish Emigration to the United States.* Minneapolis, Minn.: n.p., 1930.

Lindmark, S. *Swedish America, 1914–1932: Studies in Ethnicity with an Emphasis on Illinois and Minnesota.* Chicago: Swedish Pioneer Historical Society, 1971.

Ljungmark, Lars. *Swedish Exodus.* 2d ed. Carbondale: Southern Illinois University Press, 1996.

Nelson, Helge. *The Swedes and the Swedish Settlements in North America.* 2 vols. Lund, Sweden: Gleerups Forlag, 1943.

Ostergren, Robert C. *A Community Transplanted: The Trans-Atlantic Experience of a Swedish Immigrant Settlement in the Upper Middle West, 1835–1915.* Madison: University of Wisconsin Press, 1988.

Runblom, Harald, and Hans Norman, eds. *From Sweden to America: A History of the Migration.* Minneapolis and Uppsala, Sweden: University of Minnesota and University of Uppsala, 1976.

Weslager, C. A. *New Sweden on the Delaware, 1638–1655.* Wallingford, Pa.: Middle Atlantic Press, 1990.

Swiss immigration

The Swiss were among the earliest non-British or non-French European settlers in both the United States and Canada, with a substantial immigration during the 18th century. According to the U.S. census of 2000 and the Canadian census of 2001, 911,502 Americans and 110,800 Canadians claimed Swiss descent. The Swiss were readily assimilated in North America and thus are widely dispersed. Though they do not live in ethnic enclaves, the Swiss in North America are most concentrated in California, New York, New Jersey, and Wisconsin in the United States and in Toronto, Montreal, and Vancouver in Canada.

Switzerland occupies 15,300 square miles in the Alps Mountains in central Europe. It is bordered by France on the west, Italy on the south, Austria on the east, and Germany on the north. In 2002, the population was estimated at 7,283,274. About 80 percent of the population is Swiss: The country has three official languages that are the mother tongues of a given percentage of all Swiss: German (65 percent), French (18 percent), and Italian (12 percent). The largest ethnic minorities are Yugoslav (4.7 percent), Italian (4.6 percent), and Portuguese (1.9 percent), most of whom came as laborers. The chief religions are Roman Catholic and Protestant, though much of the population is only nominally religious. Switzerland, the former Roman province of Helvetia, traces its modern history to 1291, when three cantons created a defensive league. Other cantons were subsequently admitted to the Swiss Confederation, which obtained its independence from the Holy Roman Empire through the Peace of Westphalia (1648). As a mountainous, resource-poor country, Switzerland exported its troops as mercenaries as a means of generating wealth, while at the same time maintaining national neutrality in time of war. Switzerland has not been involved in a foreign war since 1515. The cantons were joined under a federal constitution in 1848, with each retaining significant autonomous powers. A world banking and commercial center, Switzerland is also the seat of many United Nations and other international agencies. In an effort to crack down on criminal transactions, the nation's strict bank-secrecy rules have been eased since 1990. Stung by charges that assets seized by the Nazis of Germany and deposited in Swiss banks in World War II (1939–45) had not been properly returned, the government announced on March 5, 1997, a $4.7 billion fund to compensate victims of the Holocaust and other catastrophes. Swiss banks agreed on August 12, 1998, to pay $1.25 billion in reparations.

Among the earliest Swiss immigrants to North America were German Mennonites, perhaps as many as several thousand, who began settling in the PENNSYLVANIA COLONY during the late 17th century (see MENNONITE IMMIGRATION). As more Swiss came in succeeding decades from a variety of religious and linguistic traditions, they spread widely throughout the colonies, though the greatest concentrations were in NEW YORK COLONY. Between 1700 and 1776, about 25,000 Swiss immigrants settled in the United States, most coming for economic reasons, although the linguistic and cultural differences between the various cantons were a hindrance to social mobility within their own country. Swiss immigration continued in a small but steady stream throughout the 19th century. Even in the 18th century, the Swiss blended well with their neighbors, often joining Moravians or other groups of "plain people." Between 1851 and 1880, average annual immigration was almost 2,500, and families gradually moved into Indiana, Illinois, Wisconsin, and other Midwest destinations. During the 1880s, the number jumped dramatically to almost 8,200 per year before slipping back to about 3,000 per year between 1891 and 1930. As with all European countries, immigration was almost halted during the Great Depression (1930s) and World War II (1939–45). Between 1971 and 2000, Swiss immigration was steady, averaging a little less than 1,000 per year.

Almost all the earliest Swiss settlers to Canada were mercenaries, who had first been hired by either the French or the English to help protect their holdings. A handful came in this way at various times in the 17th and 18th centuries, though there were no large Swiss settlements established. The greatest Swiss contribution to Canadian settlement came in the person of FREDERICK HALDIMAND, who joined the British army in 1756 and distinguished himself during the SEVEN YEARS' WAR (1756–63), rising to the position of lieutenant general. In 1777, Haldimand was appointed governor of Quebec and given the formidable task of finding homes there for some 10,000 Loyalists, mostly farmers from the Pennsylvania and New York back-country, who had begun to congregate in Montreal and Quebec after 1775. Haldimand eventually resettled more than 6,000 Loyalists in the wilderness of western Quebec (modern Ontario), north of the St. Lawrence and Lake Ontario. Two Swiss regiments were brought to Canada during the War of 1812 (1812–14), and many of the soldiers stayed on, principally in Ontario. A significant number of Pennsylvania Mennonites of Swiss descent immigrated to Upper Canada (later Ontario) as early as the 1780s, forming the basis of a developing German-speaking community. Swiss immigration to Canada tended to be small but steady, with the immigrants easily assimilating with other cultural groups. In 1871, the census showed just under 3,000 Swiss in Canada and about 4,500 10 years later. It is estimated that between 1887 and 1974 about 35,000 Swiss immigrated to Canada, though a significant but undetermined number returned to Europe. As in the case of the United States, Swiss immigration in the post–World War II era has been small but consistent. Of 20,020 Swiss immigrants living in Canada in 2001, 3,695 came between 1961 and 1970; 3,985, between 1971 and 1980; 3,450, between 1981 and 1990; and 5,025, between 1991 and 2000.

Further Reading

Bovay, Émile-Henri. *Le Canada et les Suisses, 1604–1974.* Fribourg, Switzerland: Éditions universitaires, 1976.

Fertig, G. "Transatlantic Migration from German-Speaking Parts of Central Europe, 1600–1800: Proportions, Structures, and Explanations." In *Europeans on the Move.* Ed. N. Canny. Oxford: Clarendon Press, 1994.

Gentilli, J. *The Settlement of Swiss Ticino Immigrants.* Nedlands: Department of Geography, Western Australia University, 1988.

Grueningen, J. P. von. *The Swiss in the United States.* Madison, Wis.: Swiss-American Historical Society, 1940.

Magee, Joan. *The Swiss in Ontario.* Windsor, Canada: Electra Press, 1991.

Roth, Lorraine. "Swiss Elements of the Mennonite Mosaic in Ontario." *Mennonite Historian* 15, nos. 1–2 (1989): 1–2.

Schelbert, Leo. *Swiss in North America.* Philadelphia: Balch Institute, 1974.

Syrian immigration

Syrian Christians began to emigrate from the Muslim Ottoman Empire in large numbers after 1880. Of the 250,000 who left in the following quarter century, more than 60,000 settled in North America, many becoming peddlers, shopkeepers, or small businessowners in large urban areas. In the 2000 U.S. census and 2001 Canadian census, 142,897 Americans and 22,065 Canadians claimed Syrian descent. Most Syrian Americans are descendants of this early immigration. The largest concentrations in the United States are in New York City; Detroit, Michigan; Chicago, Illinois; and Dallas, Texas, though they are in general fairly

widespread throughout the country. About half of Syrian Canadians live in the province of Quebec.

The modern state of Syria occupies 71,000 square miles in the Middle East, at the eastern end of the Mediterranean Sea. It is bordered by Lebanon and Israel on the west, Jordan on the south, Iraq on the east, and Turkey on the north. In 2002, the population was estimated at 16,728,808. The people are 90 percent Arab. The chief religions are Sunni Islam (74 percent), other forms of Islam (14 percent), and Christianity (10 percent). Syria was the site of some of the most ancient civilizations, forming parts of the Babylonian, Assyrian, Hittite, and Persian Empires. It was the center of the Greek Seleucid Empire but later was absorbed by Rome before being conquered by Arab armies in the seventh century. The Ottoman Empire ruled Syria from 1513 through the end of World War I (1914–18), after which the territories separated from Turkey by the Treaty of Sèvres (1920) were divided into the states of Syria and Greater Lebanon, both administered under a French League of Nations mandate between 1920 and 1941. With the establishment of the state of Israel in 1948, Syria refused to accept the new state's legitimacy and played a prominent role in ongoing military attempts to destroy it, particularly in 1948, 1967, 1973, and 1982. During the 1980s, Syria came to play a prominent role in governing war-torn Lebanon, a role it had not completely relinquished by 2004. Syria's role in promoting international terrorism led to the breaking of diplomatic relations with Great Britain and to limited sanctions by the European Community in 1986, though the 1990s saw a moderation of its policies. Syria condemned the August 1990 Iraqi invasion of Kuwait and sent troops to help Allied forces in the 1991 Persian Gulf War. The same year, Syria accepted U.S. proposals for the terms of an Arab-Israeli peace conference. Syria subsequently participated in negotiations with Israel, but progress toward peace was slow.

It is impossible to completely separate the strands of early Syrian-Lebanese immigration. Lebanese and Syrian Christians both came from a common, western region of the Ottoman Empire without distinct borders (see LEBANESE IMMIGRATION). These borders would again change when the region was divided from Turkey in 1920. *Lebanon,* denoting the southern area of Syria near Mount Lebanon, was virtually unknown in North America, so immigrants frequently used the term *Syrian* to designate the larger, more familiar geographical region. Immigrants from the Ottoman Empire were usually classified in the United States as being from "Turkey in Asia," whether Arab, Turk, or Armenian (see ARAB IMMIGRATION; ARMENIAN IMMIGRATION; TURKISH IMMIGRATION). By 1899, U.S. immigration records began to make some distinctions, and by 1920, the category "Syrian" was introduced into the census, though religious distinctions still were not noticed. Throughout the 20th century, there was little consistency in designation, principally because overall numbers remained small.

Between 1911 and 1955, any immigrant from the region to Canada was listed as coming from "Ottoman Greater Syria"; afterward, they might choose either designation. Some immigrants even changed their own self-designation as political fortunes, as well as boundaries, changed.

The majority of Syrians in the United States are the largely assimilated descendants of Christians who emigrated from the Syrian and Lebanese areas of the Ottoman Empire between 1875 and 1920. As Christians living in an Islamic empire, they were subject to persecution, though in good times they were afforded considerable autonomy. During periods of drought or economic decline, however, they frequently chose to emigrate. Most were Maronite, Melkite, or Greek Orthodox Christians. A second wave of immigration after World War II (1939–45) was more diverse, with immigrants about equally divided between Christian and Muslim. Whereas the first immigrants were usually poor and often illiterate, the postwar settlers were frequently well-educated professionals. Between 1989 and 2002, average immigration was more than 2,600 per year.

The same patterns of immigration apply to Canada. Most early Syrian immigrants came between 1885 and 1908, at first hoping to return to their homeland. The immigration of both Christian and Muslim Syrians after World War II, however, substantially changed the character of the Syrian community in Canada. The political instability of the 1970s and 1980s led to a significant migration, particularly in relation to the relatively small number of early Syrian immigrants. In 2001, immigrants accounted for more than 70 percent of Syrian Canadians. Of the 15,680 Syrian immigrants, 11,630 (74 percent) came after 1980.

Further Reading
Abu-Laban, Baha. *An Olive Branch on the Family Tree: The Arabs in Canada.* Toronto: McClelland and Stewart, 1985.
Dayal, P. M., and J. M. Kayal. *The Syrian Lebanese in America: A Study in Religion and Assimilation.* Boston: Twayne, 1975.
Hitti, P. K. *Syrians in America.* New York: George Doran, 1924.
Hooglund, E., ed. *Crossing the Waters: Arabic-Speaking Immigrants to the United States before 1940.* Washington, D.C.: Smithsonian Institution, 1987.
Jabbra, Nancy, and Joseph Jabbra. *Voyageurs to a Rocky Shore: The Lebanese and Syrians of Nova Scotia.* Halifax, Canada: Institute of Public Affairs, Dalhousie University, 1984.
Naff, Alixa. *Becoming American: The Early Arab American Experience.* Carbondale: Southern Illinois University Press, 1985.
Orfalea, Gregory. *Before the Flames: A Quest for the History of Arab Americans.* Austin: University of Texas Press, 1988.
Sawaie, M., ed. *Arabic-Speaking Immigrants in the United States and Canada.* Lexington, Ky.: Mazda Press, 1985.

T

Taiwanese immigration

Taiwan did not become an independent country until 1949. As one of the West's staunchest allies in the COLD WAR after 1945, Taiwan has enjoyed a special relationship with the United States, including both diplomatic and military assistance in its conflict with the Communist People's Republic of China. According to the U.S. census of 2000 and the Canadian census of 2001, 144,795 Americans and 18,080 Canadians claimed Taiwanese descent. This figure significantly underrepresents the actual number of Taiwanese in North America. The highest concentrations of Taiwanese Americans are in Los Angeles County and New York City, while 61 percent of Taiwanese Canadians live in Vancouver, British Columbia.

Taiwan is a 12,400-square-mile island about 100 miles off the southeast coast of China between the East and South China Seas. In 2002, the population was estimated at 23,370,461. The people are ethnically divided between Taiwanese (84 percent) and mainland Chinese (14 percent). The chief religions are Buddhist, Taoist, and Confucian (93 percent) and Christian (3 percent). Large-scale Chinese immigration to Taiwan began from Fujian and Guangdong Provinces in the 17th century, when the native Malayo-Polynesian tribes were driven to the mountains and their culture virtually destroyed. After a brief period of Dutch rule (1620–62), the island came under direct control of the mainland and was held by the Manchu government until it was defeated in the Sino-Japanese War (1894–95). Taiwan was then ruled by Japan until 1945. After the Nationalist (Kuomintang) government of Chiang Kai-shek was defeated by the Communists in a savage civil war (1945–49) on the Chinese mainland, 2 million Kuomintang supporters fled to Taiwan, establishing a base from which they intended to reconquer China. The United States had been a strong supporter of the Republic of China (on Taiwan) but on December 15, 1978, finally joined most of the rest of the world in formally recognizing the Communist People's Republic of China (PRC). Though severing official ties with the United States, Taiwan maintained contact via quasi-official agencies, and the United States continued to publicly oppose any attempt by the PRC to forcibly reacquire Taiwan. In 1987, martial law was lifted after 38 years, and in 1991, the 43-year period of emergency rule imposed by Chiang ended. Taiwan held its first direct presidential election March 23, 1996. Both the Taipei, Taiwan, and the Beijing, China, governments considered Taiwan an integral part of China, though Taiwan resisted Beijing's efforts in the 1990s to expand ties to the Communist-controlled mainland. Taiwan has had one of the world's strongest economies throughout its history, even during the economic recession after 1998 and was among the 10 leading capital exporters.

For a number of reasons, it is impossible to determine how many Taiwanese there are in North America. First, the term itself is ill defined. The aboriginal Taiwanese were not Chinese and today are few in number. Second, the term can be used to designate any of several ethnic groups that originally came from mainland China in the 17th and 18th centuries. Finally, it is sometimes used to refer to all the peoples from the Republic of China located on Taiwan, including aboriginal tribespeople, the Minnan and Hakka peoples resident there for several hundred years, and the descendants of mainland Chinese (themselves from a variety of subgroups) who fled to Taiwan in 1949. When self-identification is required, as in the U.S. and Canadian censuses, many immigrants from Taiwan or their descendants choose "Chinese," as it indicates their larger identification with the modern state of China that the Nationalists ruled prior to 1949.

Most Taiwanese immigrants to North America came for education and business opportunities. Because the economy has been so consistently strong, there has not been a strong economic push factor. Between 1988 and 2002, almost 170,000 citizens of Taiwan immigrated to the United States. Immigration to Canada has been strong but less consistent. Between 1994 and 1998, almost 50,000 immigrated to Canada, and Taiwan was frequently in the top five source countries for Canadian immigration. The number declined significantly thereafter. Of 67,095 Taiwanese immigrants in Canada in 2001, 53,750 (80 percent) came between 1991 and 2001. Between 2000 and 2002, Taiwan was the seventh leading source country for students studying in Canada.

Further Reading

Chen, H.-S. *Chinatown No More: Taiwan Immigrants in Contemporary New York.* Ithaca, N.Y.: Cornell University Press, 1992.

Fawcett, James T., and Benjamin V. Carino, eds. *Pacific Bridges: The New Immigration from Asia and the Pacific Islands.* New York: Center for Migration Studies, 1987.

Fong, T. P. *The First Suburban Chinatown: The Remaking of Monterey Park, California.* Philadelphia: Temple University Press, 1994.

Hing, Bill Ong. *Making and Remaking Asian America through Immigration Policy, 1850–1990.* Stanford, Calif.: Stanford University Press, 1993.

Liu, Po-Chi. *A History of the Chinese in the United States of America, 1848–1911.* Taipei, Taiwan: Commission of Overseas Chinese, 1976.

Tan, Jin, and Patricia E. Roy. *The Chinese in Canada.* Ottawa: Canadian Historical Association, 1985.

Tsai, Shih-shan Henry. *The Chinese Experience in America.* Bloomington: Indiana University Press, 1986.

Tung, William L. *The Chinese in America, 1820–1973: A Chronology and Fact Book.* Dobbs Ferry, N.Y.: Oceana Publications, 1974.

Talon, Jean (1626–1694) *government official*

As intendant of the colonial territory of NEW FRANCE, Jean Talon vigorously implemented France's new policy of colonial mercantilism. The structure of his government, a kind of benevolent autocracy, lasted nearly 100 years until the British takeover.

After a career in the service of Louis XIV (r. 1643–1715), in 1663, Talon was appointed intendant of New France by JEAN-BAPTISTE COLBERT, thus becoming responsible for finances and civil administration of the region. Talon diversified the economy and promoted trade with the French West Indies. He also pursued westward expansion, and his government-sponsored fur-trading expeditions established a pattern for private fur traders. In 1672, he dispatched Louis Jolliet to explore the course of the Mississippi River, thus establishing French claims to the Mississippi basin. After clashes with local authorities, Talon was recalled to France in 1672. His agreement with the Company of the West Indies to bring settlers to New France was at first successful, as more than 4,000 arrived between 1666 and 1675. The immigration could not be sustained, however, as most of those coming were indentured servants, convicts, soldiers released from the military, or women from orphanages or homes of charity. An efficient administrator, Talon also amassed a fortune during his nine-year tenure as intendant.

Further Reading

Choquette, Leslie P. "Recruitment of French Emigrants to Canada, 1600–1760." In *"To Make America": European Emigration in the Early Modern Period.* Eds. Ida Altman and James Horn. Berkeley: University of California Press, 1991.

Eccles, William J. *Canada under Louis XIV, 1663–1701.* Toronto: McClelland and Stewart, 1964.

Moogk, Peter. "Reluctant Exiles: Emigrants from France in Canada before 1760." *William and Mary Quarterly* 46 (July 1989): 463–505.

Tejanos

Tejanos most often refers to Mexican-origin residents of Texas, both native and foreign born, and the unique culture they created. In most cases, it is interchangeable with *Texas Mexicans* or *Mexican Americans* living in Texas. Strictly speaking, however, *Mexican Americans* would only apply after 1845 when the Republic of Texas (see TEXAS, REPUBLIC OF) joined the United States, making all Mexicans there citizens of the United States.

Tejano culture is rooted in its Spanish and Mexican history prior to 1836 and constantly fed by new immigrants from Mexico. Between 1900 and 1929, 65 percent of all Mexican immigrants crossed the border at Texas.

See also *HISPANIC* AND RELATED TERMS.

terrorism and immigration

Modern terrorism is the use of violent, brutal force against civilians and the deliberate targeting of noncombatants for political or religious reasons. It is a tactic widely abhorred in the legal traditions of the English and French who settled North America. It is most often resorted to by groups that are otherwise too weak to bring about change through legal or traditional military means. In the 19th and early 20th centuries, terrorism was most often associated with central and east European anarchists, socialists, and communists who used bombings and assassinations to influence labor policy or change the political structure. After World War II (1939–45), it became increasingly associated with fundamentalist Islamic organizations who opposed pro-Israeli policies and feared the growing secular influence of Western culture. Bombings, hostage taking, and hijackings were among the most common methods utilized by terrorists until the 1990s, when suicide bombings became the most common form of terrorist activity. At exactly what point the use of subversive activity moves from legitimate means to terrorism is closely connected with one's cultural values. As a result, when immigrants to North America were involved in violence, their activities were frequently cast in terms of terrorism. The tensions surrounding the legitimacy of terrorism were dramatically heightened as a result of attacks carried out by Islamic fundamentalists on SEPTEMBER 11, 2001, on U.S. soil, launching an extended public debate over the place of terror within the Islamic community and the ability of Muslims to be true to the more extreme interpretations of their faith while remaining good citizens of constitutional states.

Terrorism can be home grown. The Ku Klux Klan of the late 19th and early 20th centuries, the Weathermen of the 1970s, and a variety of violent militia organizations of the 1980s and 1990s all used violence as a means of addressing what were perceived as inequities within the legal and constitutional framework of the country. Until September 11, the most deadly act of terrorism in North America was the 1995 bombing of the Alfred P. Murrah Federal Building in Oklahoma City by two members—both born and raised in the United States—of an antigovernment militia. Immigrants and outsiders have, however, been more frequently branded as terrorists. In part, this tendency toward NATIVISM relates to general social and cultural differences that are necessarily present when different ethnic groups come into contact with one another. English colonists in North America, for example, were quick to condemn the British Crown's use of "barbaric" Hessian mercenaries from a region in Germany as a deliberate infliction of foreign violence during the American Revolution (1775–83). A particularly explosive aspect of these cultural differences was more often evident in politics. Prior to World War I (1914–18; see WORLD WAR I AND IMMIGRATION), the United States and Canada shared many assumptions and experiences regarding immigrants. In both countries, individual actions based on constitutional processes and representative forms of government were upheld as the only legitimate means of political change. Both countries barred the entry of paupers, the mentally ill, and those considered mentally defective. Also, immigrants routinely crossed the border between the two countries looking for work.

In many parts of the world, however, where individual rights were not protected and political pariticipation was not permitted, people often embraced collective, extragovernmental, and even violent tactics to help bring about political change. As a result, political movements associated with socialism and anarchism were particularly associated with immigrants. When an 1886 labor demonstration at the Haymarket Square in Chicago led to a bombing in which eight policemen were killed, hundreds of socialists and anarchists were arrested. Eight anarchists, seven of them German immigrants, were convicted of conspiracy, and four were hanged. Although three of the convicted men were eventually pardoned, the fear of immigrant radicalism lingered, paving the way for the widespread fear of foreign political activities in the 20th century.

Fears were heightened by a number of isolated but dramatic cases, including the assassination of President William McKinley by the anarchist Leon Czolgosz in 1901. As immigration from eastern and southern Europe peaked in the first decade of the 20th century, labor unrest and violence increased and became most visibly represented in the militant activities of the transnational INDUSTRIAL WORKERS OF THE WORLD. Nativist fears were heightened by entry into World War I, which provided a further reason for suspecting the loyalty of Germans, Bulgarians, and Austro-Hungarians. Militant labor activity in Canada led to the detention of 8,000–9,000 enemy aliens. When the Bolshevik Revolution (1917) toppled the Russian Empire, a great Red Scare gripped both Americans and Canadians. Formation of the One Big Union (OBU) in Canada (1919) and the violence of the WINNIPEG GENERAL STRIKE (1919) heightened ethnic tensions. In the United States, European war and revolution led to increasingly restrictive immigrant legislation, culminating in the JOHNSON-REED ACT of 1924 and in a revival of a newly invigorated Ku Klux Klan that was as much antiforeign as antiblack. In Canada, organizations that professed to "bring about any governmental, political, social, industrial or economic change . . . by the use of force, violence or physical injury" were declared illegal, and entry of immigrants from former enemy states was prohibited by amendments to the IMMIGRATION ACT in 1919. The period required for naturalization in Canada was also extended by the Naturalization Act of 1920.

Although the use of violence for political purposes in the United States and Canada declined from the 1930s, there remained a silent mistrust of many, but not all, immigrant groups. The relationship between immigration and terrorism was highlighted by two high-profile cases as the new millennium began. In the September 11, 2001, attacks, most of the hijackers had entered the United States legally and engaged in pilot training while in the country. It was later discovered that a number of them were in violation of the terms of their entry but that the IMMIGRATION AND NATURALIZATION SERVICE (INS) had not taken timely action against them. In October 2002, the Beltway Snipers shot 13 people in the Washington, D.C., area, killing 10 of them. The two men convicted in the attacks were John Allen Muhammad, American-born, who was loosely associated with the Nation of Islam, and his associate Lee Boyd Malvo, an undocumented alien from Jamaica who was scheduled for a deportation hearing at the time of the killings.

As a result of the September 11 attacks, the U.S. and Canadian governments were forced to confront terrorism as a domestic, rather than international, issue, which led to a series of immigration and travel reforms. In the United States the USA PATRIOT ACT was quickly passed, providing for greater surveillance of aliens and increasing the power of the Office of the Attorney General to identify, arrest, and deport aliens. The act also defined *domestic terrorism* to include "acts dangerous to human life that are a violation of the criminal laws of the United States or of any State that appear to be intended to intimidate or coerce a civilian population; to influence the policy of a government by intimidation or coercion; or to affect the conduct of a government by mass destruction, assassination, or kidnapping." Also, monitoring of some aliens entering on nonimmigrant visas was instituted, passport photographs were digitalized, more extensive background checks of all applications and petitions to the DEPARTMENT OF HOMELAND SECURITY were authorized, the SEVIS database was created to track the location of aliens in the country on student visas, and the U.S. Attorney General's Office was given the right to immediately expel anyone suspected of terrorist links. Also, the State Department introduced a 20-day waiting period for visa applications from men 16 to 45 years of age from Afghanistan, Algeria, Bahrain, Djibouti, Egypt, Eritrea, Indonesia, Iran, Iraq, Jordan, Kuwait, Lebanon, Libya, Malaysia, Morocco, Oman, Pakistan, Qatar, Saudi Arabia, Somalia, Sudan, Syria, Tunisia, United Arab Emirates, and Yemen. Any application considered to be suspicious was forwarded to the Federal Bureau of Investigation (FBI), creating a further delay.

Further Reading

Avery, Donald. *"Dangerous Foreigners": European Immigrant Workers and Labour Radicalism in Canada, 1896–1932*. Toronto: McClelland and Stewart, 1979.

Chang, Nancy. *Silencing Political Dissent: How Post–September 11 Anti-Terrorism Measures Threaten Our Civil Liberties*. New York: Seven Stories Press, 2002.

Malkin, Michelle. *Invasion: How America Still Welcomes Terrorists, Criminals & Other Foreign Menaces to Our Shores*. New York: Regnery, 2002.

Texas, Republic of

The Republic of Texas (1836–45) was a unique experiment in creating a multiethnic state in the New World. In the end, the cultural pull and political push of the United States proved irresistible to most Texans, who sought annexation to their larger neighbor almost from the time they became independent of Mexico.

In 1821, when Mexico gained its independence from Spain, expansionistic pressure from the United States was an urgent problem. The Mexican government decided on a policy of defensive immigration, encouraging Americans to settle its sparsely populated northern province of Texas. It had become clear to Mexican liberals that the Catholic Church was already too strong and should not be given the power of populating the north. Also, Mexico simply did not have a sufficient population to effectively control Texas. Its entire population, from Central America to Texas, New Mexico, and California in the north, was only 6 million. In January 1821, Moses Austin was contracted to bring 300 Catholic families to Texas in return for a large personal grant of land. Moses died in June, and his contract was assumed by his son, Stephen F. Austin. With the fall of the short-lived imperial government of Agustín de Iturbide in Mexico in 1823, a new National Colonization Law (1824) was passed, leaving immigration policy in the hands of individual states. The former provinces of Coahuila and Texas were combined into one state, and the land between the Nueces and Sabine Rivers, designated the Department of Texas. Under the state's Colonization Law (1825), Mexicans were given priority in land acquisition and were temporarily exempted from paying certain taxes. Nevertheless, by the mid-1820s, there were more Anglos than TEJANOS in Texas. Immigrants were allowed to become Mexican citizens on condition that they abide by the federal and state constitutions and practice the Christian religion. Individuals were allowed to purchase land, but most immigrants came with *empresarios* like Austin, who worked for the state governments, and were in turn entitled to about 23,000 acres of land for each 100 families they settled. Eventually 41 *empresario* contracts were signed, most by Anglo-Americans, though few of the terms were actually completed. By the late 1820s, there were perhaps 10,000 immigrants and their slaves, but few took the conditions of settlement seriously. Following a conservative coup in 1829 and the recommendation of Manuel de Mier y Terán, who observed that the Anglo-Texans were unlikely to be assimilated, the Mexican government passed the Law of April 6, 1830, in order to bring the flood of Anglo settlement under control. The measure voided all agreements except with those *empresarios* who had brought in at least 100 families already. The measure also stipulated that Americans could not colonize territory bordering on the United States. Finally, it prohibited the importation of slaves. When the Mexican general and political opportunist Antonio López de Santa Anna and the Centralists returned to power in 1834, they not only sought to enforce the 1830 treaty but also to curtail state liberties that had been earlier guaranteed. Clashes between Mexican Centralist forces and Texans began in October

1835. In November, a "Consultation" of 58 delegates from a dozen communities met to affirm the liberal Constitution of 1824. When Texas delegates met again in March 1836, they voted unanimously to declare independence (March 2) on the basis of Santa Anna's imposition of a tyranny in place of a constitutional government. Among the 59 delegates were three Mexicans: Lorenzo de Zavala, José Antonio Navarro, and José Francisco Ruíz. Despite defeats at San Antonio de Bexar (at the Alamo) and Goliad, 900 Texans under General Sam Houston routed Santa Anna's force of 1,500 at San Jacinto (April 21), forcing him to sue for peace in the Treaties of Velasco. By their terms, Santa Anna acknowledged Texas's independence, removed his troops to Mexico, and accepted the Rio Grande as the southern boundary of the new Republic of Texas. Although the Mexican congress refused to ratify the agreement, Mexico no longer had the means of reconquering the land.

Immediately, Texas voters indicated their wish for annexation by the United States, favoring the establishment of economic, social, religious, and political institutions largely as they existed in the land from which most had come. Sam Houston, the republic's first president, was a political veteran, having served as a U.S. congressman (1823–27) and as governor of Tennessee (1827–29). Despite economic woes and the potential danger of reconquest, the population of the new country grew dramatically, from about 30,000 at independence to more than 150,000 in 1845. Much of the growth came from reestablishment of the *empresario* system to encourage settlement. As a result of this policy, Irish, French, English, Scottish, Czech, Polish, Scandinavian, Canadian, and Swiss colonies were established. The most important of these were the 2,100 French speakers settled at Castroville near the Medina River west of San Antonio and the German settlement of New Braunfels. By 1844, sentiment in the United States was turning in favor of annexation, with a strong national sense of manifest destiny. When James K. Polk was elected president on an expansionist platform in November, outgoing president John Tyler proposed annexation of Texas through a joint resolution of Congress, which he signed on March 3, 1845. The U.S. government inherited the dispute over the Texas-Mexican border, which had not been settled in 1836, and this eventually led to the U.S.-MEXICAN WAR (1846–48).

See also MEXICAN IMMIGRATION.

Further Reading

De León, Arnoldo. *The Tejano Community, 1836–1900.* Albuquerque: University of New Mexico Press, 1982.

Hardin, Stephen L. *Texan Iliad: A Military History of the Texas Revolution.* Austin: University of Texas Press, 1994.

Lack, Paul D. *The Texas Revolutionary Experience: A Social and Political History.* College Station: Texas A&M University Press, 1992.

Montejano, David. *Anglos and Mexicans in the Making of Texas.* Austin: University of Texas Press, 1987.

Pletcher, David M. *The Diplomacy of Annexation: Texas, Oregon, and the Mexican War.* Columbia: University of Missouri Press, 1973.

Tijerina, André. *Tejanos and Texas under the Mexican Flag, 1821–1836.* College Station: Texas A&M University Press, 1994.

Weber, David J. *The Mexican Frontier, 1821–1846: The American Southwest under Mexico.* Albuquerque: University of New Mexico Press, 1982.

Thai immigration

Most Thai Americans are the product of the revised regulations under the IMMIGRATION AND NATIONALITY ACT of 1965 and the U.S. presence in Vietnam. Unlike other Southeast Asians, however, they came to the United States not as refugees but as professionals and spouses of members of the U.S. military. According to the U.S. census of 2000, 150,283 Americans claimed Thai descent. Only 6,965 Canadians reported Thai ancestry in the census of 2001. The greatest concentration of Thais in the United States is in California, particularly in southern California, but they are spread widely throughout the country wherever there are large military bases associated with the former American involvement in Southeast Asia. The majority of the small Thai community in Canada lives in Toronto and Vancouver.

Thailand occupies 197,400 square miles on the Indochina and Malay Peninsulas in Southeast Asia. In 2002, the population was estimated at 61,797,751. The major ethnic groups in the country are Thais (75 percent) and Chinese (14 percent). Around 95 percent of the people are Buddhist and about 4 percent Muslim. Thais began migrating from southern China during the 11th century, conquering the native inhabitants and establishing a number of Thai kingdoms. In 1350, these were united in the Kingdom of Ayutthaya. Throughout much of its history, the Thai kingdom waged war with the kings of Burma and Cambodia for supremacy in the region. After 1851, Thailand became officially known as Siam, and its kings developed good relations with the British and French. Though Siam lost some territory to both European powers, it proved to be the only Southeast Asian country capable of resisting colonization. During the 1930s, the Thais developed a constitutional monarchy, leading the government to rename the country Thailand. After occupation by Japan during World War II (1939–45), Thailand fell largely into the hands of military leaders, who closely allied themselves to the United States in its COLD WAR conflict in Vietnam, allowing U.S. bases to be established there. Thailand also became home to hundreds of thousands of Cambodians fleeing the Pol Pot regime after 1979. A steep downturn in the economy forced Thailand to seek more than $15 billion in emergency international loans in August 1997, and a new constitution won legislative approval on September 27.

There was virtually no Thai immigration to the United States prior to the 1960s. With America's growing presence there during the Vietnam War (1964–75), however, Thai doctors, nurses, and other professionals learned that the new Immigration and Nationality Act gave preference to skilled professionals, and a significant number chose to immigrate. Many U.S. servicemen married Thai women while stationed in Vietnam and brought them back to the United States after the war ended. By the late 1970s, some 5,000 Thais were in the United States, about three-quarters of them women. Many of the others were professionals or students. Thai immigration remained steady at an average of about 6,500 per year during the 1980s and early 1990s, but declined to less than 3,000 per year between 1997 and 2002, in part because a large percentage of Thai families had already been reunited. Except for students, spouses, and a small number of professionals, there has been almost no Thai immigration to Canada. Thailand has been politically stable for many years, and Thais do not have a long tradition of migration. Of 8,130 Thai immigrants in Canada in 2001, only 50 came before 1971, and 2,930 between 1991 and 2001.

Further Reading

Kangvalert, W. "Thai Physicians in the United States: Causes and Consequences of the Brain Drain." Ph.D. diss., State University of New York at Buffalo, 1986.

Kitano, Harry H. L., and Roger Daniels. *Asian Americans: Emerging Minorities.* Englewood Cliffs, N.J.: Prentice Hall, 1995.

Larson, W. *Confessions of a Mail Order Bride: American Life through Thai Eyes.* Far Hills, N.J.: New Horizon Press, 1989.

Wyatt, David K. *Thailand: A Short History.* Reprint. New Haven, Conn.: Yale University Press, 1986.

Tibetan immigration

Tibetans form one of the smallest immigrant communities in both the United States and Canada; nevertheless, the Dalai Lama, head of Tibet's government in exile in Dharamsala, India, has focused world attention on the human rights abuses against Buddhists in the Tibetan Autonomous Region (TAR) of the People's Republic of China (PRC) and gained the support of most governments for enforcement of human rights and resettlement of Tibetan refugees. Official U.S. government policy recognizes Tibet to be a part of the PRC and so keeps no separate immigration figures. According to the Canadian census of 2001, 1,425 Canadians claimed Tibetan ancestry.

Tibet is a sparsely populated region occupying 471,700 square miles of high plateaus, massive mountains, and rocky wastelands. Its 2000 population was estimated at about 2.6 million, with all but about 300,000 being Tibetans. The religion of almost all Tibetans is a branch of Buddhism called Lamaism, which recognizes two Grand Lamas as reincarnated Buddhas. The Himalayas run along Tibet's southern border with India, Nepal, and Bhutan and the Kunlun and Tanggula Mountains her northern border with China. Dur-

ing the seventh century, Tibet developed a powerful empire, still remote from the main centers of Chinese culture. Tibet borrowed heavily from Indian culture. After occupation by the Mongols in the 13th century, the Dalai Lama became the head of the Tibetan state until the early 19th century, when it was conquered by China. After the Revolution of 1911 and its overthrow of the Qing dynasty in China, Tibet became nominally independent until China reasserted control in 1951, while promising Tibetan autonomy and religious freedom. A Communist government was installed in 1953, revising the theocratic Lamaist rule, abolishing serfdom, and collectivizing the land. A Tibetan uprising in China in 1956 spread to Tibet in 1959. The rebellion was brutally crushed, and Buddhism was almost totally suppressed. The Dalai Lama and 100,000 Tibetans fled as refugees to India. Beginning in the 1960s, the Dalai Lama became an impassioned spokesman on behalf of human rights both in Tibet and around the world. From his capital in exile, he has maintained informal diplomatic contact with world leaders and proposed a self-governing Tibet "in association with the People's Republic of China." Largely on the basis of his practical attempt to solve this humanitarian crisis, in 1989, the Dalai Lama was awarded the Nobel Peace Prize.

The Chinese government was routinely condemned by human rights organizations and most world governments, including those of the United States and Canada, for systematic human rights abuses against Tibetans, including arbitrary arrests and detentions, torture, secret trials, and religious suppression. During summer and autumn 2001, the leading center for Buddhist scholarship and practice on the Tibetan plateau was dismantled, Chinese authorities citing concerns over sanitation and hygiene. The Serthar Institute (also known as the Larung Gar Monastic Encampment) had more than 8,000 monks, nuns, and lay students, including 1,000 practitioners, before Chinese work teams forcibly expelled the students, destroyed more than 1,000 homes, and drove thousands of nuns and monks from the grounds. Finally, there was growing concern among Tibetans that the Chinese government was deliberately resettling large numbers of ethnic Chinese in Tibet for the purpose of undermining Tibetan autonomy.

From the mid-1950s, the Central Intelligence Agency (CIA) began to train Tibetan guerrillas, as the United States sought to undermine the expansion of Chinese Communist influence. In 1960, the Rockefeller Foundation established eight centers for Tibetan studies in the United States, and the following year, the first graduate program in Buddhist studies was opened at the University of Wisconsin. This growing awareness of Tibet's international plight led to the slow migration of several hundred Tibetans, mostly religious leaders and teachers. In the late 1960s, several dozen Tibetan workers also immigrated to the United States. By 1985, about 500 Tibetans lived in the United States. In 1988, with support from private agencies and the U.S. government, the Tibetan United States Resettlement Project (TUSRP) was established, with the first group of 1,000 arriving in 1992. By 2002, about 8,650 Tibetans had settled in the United States, with about 40 percent living in the Northeast and 20 percent in the Midwest. Between 2,000 and 3,000 Tibetans live in New York City, and there are significant population centers in Minneapolis, Minnesota; northern California; and Boston, Massachusetts.

There were virtually no Tibetans in Canada before 1970. During the early 1970s, the Canadian government established the Tibetan Refugee Program (TRP), assisting 228 Tibetan refugees then living in India to resettle in Canada. Tibetan communities grew slowly, to a total of more than 500 by 1985. A second influx of Tibetan immigrants came between 1998 and 2001 with the arrival of about 1,000 from the New York City area who were granted refugee asylum status in Canada. By 2001, the Tibetan Canadian population had risen to more than 1,800, according to estimates. Almost 80 percent of Tibetan Canadians live in Toronto.

Further Reading

Avedon, John. *In Exile from the Lands of Snows.* New York: Alfred A. Knopf, 1986.

Barnett, Robbie, and Shirin Akiner, eds. *Resistance and Reform in Tibet.* Bloomington: Indiana University Press, 1994.

Conservancy for Tibetan Art and Culture. "North American Tibetan Community Cultural Needs Assessment Project Report." Available online. URL: http://tibetanculture.org/about/work/survey.htm. Accessed July 3, 2004.

Goldstein, Melvyn. *A History of Modern Tibet, 1913–1951: The Demise of the Lamaist State.* Berkeley: University of California Press, 1989.

Nassar, Roberta. "Social Justice Advocacy by and for Tibetan Immigrants: A Case Example of International and Domestic Empowerment." *Journal of Immigrant and Refugee Services* (2002): 21–32.

Nowak, M. *Tibetan Refugees: Youth and the New Generation of Meaning.* New Brunswick, N.J.: Rutgers University Press, 1984.

Smith, Warren. *Tibetan Nation: A History of Tibetan Nationalism and Sino-Tibetan Relations.* Boulder, Colo.: Westview Press, 1997.

Tashi, Tsering. *The Struggle for Modern Tibet.* Armonk, N.Y.: M. E. Sharpe, 1997.

U.S. Department of State. "China: Country Reports on Human Rights Practices, 2002." Bureau of Democracy, Human Rights, and Labor. March 31, 2003. Available online. URL: http://www.state.gov/g/drl/rls/hrrpt/2002/18239.htm. Accessed December 31, 2003.

Tijerina, Reies López (King Tiger) (1926–   )
social activist

Born in Falls City, Texas, to a family of migrant workers who claimed to be heirs to an old land grant, Tijerina became one of the earliest CHICANO activists in the United States. After a brief career as a minister with the Assemblies of God (1946–50), in the early 1950s he founded the utopian community of Valle de la Paz on 160 acres of land in Pinal County, Arizona. After a hostile community burned the settlement, in 1957, Tijerina jumped bail while awaiting trial for charges stemming from the jailbreak of his brother. While a fugitive in California, he claimed to have a messianic vision that impelled him to take up the cause of land grant restoration. In the late 1950s, he began to research the question of land grants that had been made by kings of Spain and guaranteed to Mexican landholders following the U.S.-MEXICAN WAR. He was most interested in the 594,500-acre Tierra Amarilla land grant in northern New Mexico. In 1963, he founded the Alianza Federal de Mercedes (Federal Alliance of Land Grants, later known as the Federal Alliance of Free City States). After years of local campaigning and speaking to politicians with little effect, on October 1966, Tijerina led an armed takeover of a campsite in the Kit Carson National Forest. After the filing of federal charges, tensions escalated with numerous cases of arson and vandalism against Anglo ranches and federal lands. On June 5, 1967, Tijerina led the Alianza in an armed raid on Tierra Amarilla and occupied the Rio Arriba County courthouse. In 1974, Tijerina was sentenced to two years in prison. With Tijerina's imprisonment, the Alianza Federal de Mercedes dissolved. Tijerina was paroled in December 1974 and received an executive pardon in 1978. Thereafter he led a secluded life, occasionally speaking out on behalf of social causes but largely avoiding the public stage. In the early 1990s, he moved to Mexico, where he continued to work on behalf of early land-grant claimants. In 2001, he donated his archive of papers, photographs, diaries, and other materials to the University of New Mexico.

Further Reading

Busto, Rudy Val. "Like a Mighty Rushing Wind: The Religious Impulse in the Life and Writing of Reies López Tijerina." Ph.D. diss., University of California, Berkeley, 1991.

Gardner, Richard. *Grito! Reies Tijerina and the New Mexico Land Grant War of 1967.* Indianapolis, Ind.: Bobbs-Merrill, 1970.

Gutiérrez, José Angel. "Tracking King Tiger: The Political Surveillance of Reies López Tijerina by the Federal Bureau of Investigation." Chicago: National Association for Chicana and Chicano Studies, 1996.

Klein, Kevin. "¡Viva la Alianza! Thirty Years after the Tierra Amarilla Courthouse Raid." *Weekly Alibi,* June 13, 1997. Available online. URL: http://weeklywire.com/ww106-13-97/alibi_featl.html.

Nabakov, Peter. *Tijerina and the Courthouse Raid.* Albuquerque: University of New Mexico Press, 1969.

Tijerina, Reies, and José Angel Gutiérrez. *They Called Me "King Tiger": My Struggle for the Land and Our Rights.* Houston, Tex.: Arte Público Press, 2000.

Tongan immigration See PACIFIC ISLANDER IMMIGRATION.

Toronto, Ontario

Toronto, with a municipal population of 2,481,494 and a census metropolitan population of 4,647,960 (2001) is Canada's largest and most diverse city. Within a single generation during the mid-20th century, the city was dramatically transformed from one of the most homogenous urban areas in the world to one of the most ethnically diverse. Urban affairs reporter John Barber recalls growing up in "a tidy, prosperous, narrow-minded town where Catholicism was considered exotic" but in 1998 found his children "growing up in the most cosmopolitan city on Earth. The same place." According to Citizenship and Immigration Canada, Toronto is "by far Canada's premier urban center for recent immigrants [those arriving after 1981]." In 1996, 878,000 recent immigrants were living there, more than 40 percent of Canada's total; if undocumented immigrants are added, almost half the city's population is immigrant. Of the country's 706,921 immigrants received in Canada between 2000 and 2002, 49 percent (346,763) came to Toronto, further enhancing the city's diversity. The largest nonfounding ethnic groups living in Toronto according to the 2001 census were Chinese (435,685), Italian (429,380), East Indian (Asian Indian) (345,855), and German (220,135).

Although missions, camps, and forts had been established near the present site of Toronto, the first permanent settlement was made in 1793 by JOHN GRAVES SIMCOE, the first lieutenant-governor of Upper Canada (1792–96), who chose the site for the establishment of a new capital, named York, for the province (now Ontario). Simcoe encouraged settlement in the area, hoping to build a model British colony attractive to Americans dissatisfied with their newly formed republic. He developed a plan to establish a strong British military presence on the frontier with the United States. In addition to building roads and settlements, Simcoe offered land grants of 200–1,000 acres. Several thousand settlers took advantage of the land grants to build the new settlement around York. Few came from Britain, with the majority migrating from New York (see NEW YORK COLONY) and Pennsylvania (see PENNSYLVANIA COLONY), and including significant numbers of Quakers (see QUAKER IMMIGRATION), Mennonites (see MENNONITE IMMIGRATION), and Dunkers. York was renamed Toronto in 1834, at which time it had a population of about 10,000.

During the 19th century, Toronto increasingly challenged Montreal as the chief financial center of the country. As the fur trade declined in importance, Toronto's manufacturing base brought more money and workers into the city. Also, with the expansion of rail travel and the opening of the prairies, Toronto became a major transportation, marketing, and banking center for the West. The industrial requirements of the two world wars brought rapid population growth, as well as hundreds of thousands of European immigrants. In 1931, Toronto was still remarkably homoge-

nous, however, with 81 percent of the population of British ancestry. The largest ethnic group was Jews, who seemed remote from the city's public persona. By World War II (1939–45), Toronto had clearly become the commercial center of Canada. The rapid influx of workers to the region created numerous problems involving housing, transportation, and city services. As a result, the Ontario legislature created the Municipality of Metropolitan Toronto, joining the governments of Toronto and 12 surrounding suburbs (1953–54). The city continued to grow rapidly in the 1950s but mainly with European immigrants—in 1961, they still accounted for 90 percent of immigrants coming to Toronto. By the 1970s, Toronto was being hailed as "the city that works," making it one of the most desirable immigrant destinations in the world. The population of the central city peaked at just over 700,000 in 1970, then declined significantly as immigrants poured in and longtime residents flocked to the suburbs.

Canada's new IMMIGRATION REGULATIONS of 1967 had a profound effect on Toronto. Although designed to address the almost unregulated movement of sponsored immigrants into the country, it introduced for the first time the principal of nondiscrimination on the basis of race or national origin, virtually ending the "white Canada" policy that had prevailed throughout the 20th century. Toronto's massive manufacturing and financial base provided the best economic opportunities for immigrants, who began to come from all parts of the world, transforming narrow Toronto into a city whose majority population is either first- or second-generation immigrant. Between 2000 and 2002, the largest immigrant groups were from China (57,604), India (51,756), and Pakistan (32,691), with large migrations also from the Philippines, Iran, Sri Lanka, the United Arab Emirates, Korea, Ukraine, Jamaica, and Russia. This massive influx of diverse peoples led to a new round of housing, transportation, and service problems in the 1990s that tarnished Toronto's golden reputation. In November 2002, the city council approved a new city plan preparing for the growth of the metropolitan area by 1 million over the following 30 years.

Further Reading

Barber, John. "Different Colours, Changing City." *Globe & Mail,* February 20, 1998. Available online. URL: http://www.lib.unb.ca/Texts/CJRS/Spring97/20.1_2/isin.pdf. Accessed June 27, 2004.

Croucher, Sheila. "Constructing the Image of Ethnic Harmony in Toronto, Canada." *Urban Affairs Review* 32, no. 3 (January 1997): 319–347.

Giles, Wenona. *Portuguese Women in Toronto: Gender, Immigration, and Nationalism.* Toronto: University of Toronto Press, 2002.

Harney, Robert. "Ethnicities and Neighbourhoods." In *Cities and Urbanization: Canadian Historical Perspectives.* Ed. Gilbert Stelter. Toronto: Copp Clark Pitman, 1990.

———, ed. *Gathering Places: Peoples and Neighbourhoods of Toronto, 1934–1945.* Toronto: Multicultural History Society of Ontario, 1985.

Harris, Richard. *Unplanned Suburbs: Toronto's American Tragedy, 1900–1950.* Baltimore: Johns Hopkins University Press, 1999.

Henry, Frances. *The Caribbean Diaspora in Toronto: Learning to Live with Racism.* Buffalo, N.Y.: University of Toronto Press, 1995.

Lemon, James. *Toronto since 1918: An Illustrated History.* Toronto: James Lorimer, 1985.

Petroff, L. *Sojourners and Settlers: The Macedonian Community in Toronto.* Toronto: University of Toronto Press, 1994.

Siemiatycki, Myer. "Immigration & Urban Politics in Toronto." Paper presented at the Third International Metropolis Conference, Israel. Available online. URL: http://www.international.metropolis.net/events/Israel/papers/Siemiatycki.html. Accessed March 1, 2004.

Turner, Tana. *The Composition and Implications of Metropolitan Toronto's Ethnic, Racial and Linguistic Populations 1991.* Toronto: Access and Equity Centre, Municipality of Metropolitan Toronto, 1995.

Vasiliadis, Peter. *Whose Are You? Identity and Ethnicity among the Toronto Macedonians.* New York: AMS Press, 1989.

Zucchi, John E. *Italians in Toronto: Development of a National Identity.* Montreal: McGill–Queen's University Press, 1988.

Treaty of Guadalupe Hidalgo   See U.S.-MEXICAN WAR.

Trinidadian and Tobagonian immigration

Two simultaneous ethnic migrations—one black and one Asian Indian—occurred from Trinidad and Tobago beginning in the mid-1960s. According to the U.S. census of 2000 and the Canadian census of 2001, 164,778 Americans and 49,590 Canadians claimed either Trinidadian or Tobagonian ancestry. The Immigration and Naturalization Service (INS) estimated that in 2000 there were 34,000 unauthorized residents as well, though the actual number is likely much higher. Some scholars place the Canadian figure much higher, perhaps more than 150,000. In the United States, the largest concentrations are in the New York metropolitan area and in Florida; in Canada, more than 60 percent live in Toronto.

The country of Trinidad and Tobago occupies two islands in the Caribbean Sea off the east coast of Venezuela, totaling 2,000 square miles of land. In 2002, the population was estimated at 1,169,682, with about 95 percent of the population living on Trinidad. The people are ethnically diverse, including blacks (40 percent), Asian Indians (14 percent), and racially mixed populations (32 percent). Roman Catholicism, Protestantism, and Hinduism are widely practiced on the islands. The islands of Trinidad and Tobago were inhabited by Arawak and Carib Indians, respectively, when Columbus sighted Trinidad in 1498. The native peoples were soon killed by disease and forced plantation labor, leading to the widespread importation of African slaves during the 17th and 18th centuries. Great Britain, which acquired the islands during the French Revolutionary and Napoleonic Wars (1792–1815), ended slavery in the 1830s, introducing laborers from India to work the plantations. Between 1845 and 1917, about 144,000 indentured Asian Indians were brought to Trinidad. Trinidad and Tobago were formally joined in 1889 and granted limited self-government in 1925. Between 1958 and 1961, the islands were part of an abortive West Indian Federation that collapsed when Jamaica withdrew in 1961. Trinidad and Tobago gained their independence in 1962. The nation was one of the most prosperous in the Caribbean, refining Middle Eastern oil and providing its own through offshore fields. In 1990, 120 Muslim extremists captured the parliament building and TV station and took about 50 hostages including the prime minister, surrendering after six days. Basdeo Panday, the country's first prime minister of Asian Indian ancestry, was elected in 1995.

Exact immigration figures are difficult to determine. Prior to the 1960s, both the United States and Canada treated immigrants from Caribbean Basin dependencies and countries as a single immigrant unit known as "West Indians." Due to the shifting political status of territories within the region during the period of decolonization (1958–83) and special international circumstances in some areas, the concept of what it meant to be West Indian shifted across time, thus making it impossible to say with certainty how many immigrants came from each island or region, or when they came. Some Trinidadians and Tobagonians came between 1899 and 1924, when perhaps 100,000 English-speaking West Indians entered the country as industrial workers or laborers. With the opening of a U.S. naval base on Trinidad in 1940, a number of local inhabitants joined or provided services to the American military. Some served during World War II (1939–45) in Europe, the U.S. Virgin Islands, and Florida. Between 1960 and 1965, 2,598 settled in the United States. Most Trinidadians and Tobagonians in the United States immigrated after the IMMIGRATION AND NATIONALITY ACT of 1965 ended racial quotas. Immigration numbers have remained steady since that time. Between 1966 and 1985, about 100,000 settled in the United States. After a brief downturn in the mid-1980s, the numbers rebounded. Between 1989 and 2002, an average of about 6,300 immigrated each year.

Trinidadians and Tobagonians first immigrated to Canada in significant numbers in the 1920s, when several hundred came to work in the mines of Nova Scotia, the shipyards of Collingwood, Ontario, and Halifax, Nova Scotia, and as personal servants in the East. Some served in the Canadian army during World War II and were therefore allowed to stay as landed immigrants. Prior to the revised IMMIGRATION REGULATIONS of 1967, however, their numbers remained small, with only about 100 domestic servants admitted to the country each year between 1955 and 1965. Between 1905 and 1965, the entire number admitted was fewer than 3,000. Freed from racial quotas after 1967, Trinidadians and Tobagonians immigrated in record numbers, with more than 100,000 admitted by 1990. Of Canada's 64,145 immigrants from Trinidad and Tobago in 2001, around 40,000 were officially listed as having arrived prior to 1991. Part of this may be explained by return migration, but accurate figures are in any case difficult to obtain because of possible census inaccuracies and illegal immigration.

Further Reading

Anderson W. *Caribbean Immigrants: A Socio-Demographic Profile.* Toronto: Canadian Scholars' Press, 1990.

Gosine, M. *Caribbean East Indians in America: Assimilation, Adaptation, and Group Experience.* New York: Windsor Press, 1990.

Henry, Francis. *The Caribbean Diaspora in Toronto.* Toronto: University of Toronto Press, 1994.

Kasinitz, Philip. *Caribbean New York.* Ithaca, N.Y.: Cornell University Press, 1992.

MacDonald, Scott B. *Trinidad and Tobago: Democracy and Development in the Caribbean.* New York: Praeger Publishers, 1986.

Palmer, Ransford W. *Pilgrims from the Sun: West Indian Migration to America.* New York: Twayne Publishers, 1995.

Reid, Ira De Augustine. *The Negro Immigrant, His Background, Characteristics, and Social Adjustment, 1899–1937.* New York: Columbia University Press, 1939.

Yelvington, Kevin A., ed. *Trinidad Ethnicity.* Knoxville: University of Tennessee Press, 1993.

Turkish immigration

Turkish immigration to North America, apart from large numbers of students, has remained relatively small. It has been supplemented, however, by a growing number of resident refugees or asylum seekers. Surrounded by instability and war in Cyprus, Armenia, Macedonia, Syria, Iraq, Iran, and the region of Kurdistan, Turkey has been the first stop for thousands of refugees hoping to immigrate to North America. According to the U.S. census of 2000 and the Canadian census of 2001, 117,575 Americans and 24,910 Canadians claimed Turkish descent. The actual number of Turks in both countries is considerably larger, as ethnic Turks have immigrated via Bulgaria, Cyprus, and Macedonia. The largest concentration of Turkish Americans are in New York City, and Rochester, New York; Washington, D.C.; and Detroit, Michigan. About 58 percent of Turkish Canadians live in Ontario, most in Toronto, and there is a sizable Turkish community in Montreal.

Turkey occupies 297,200 square miles in Asia Minor, stretching into continental Europe. It is bordered on the south and east by the Mediterranean and Aegean Seas and on the north by the Black Sea. Bulgaria and Greece border Turkey on the west; Georgia and Armenia, on the north; Iran, on the east; and Iraq and Syria, on the south. In 2001, the population was estimated at 66,229,000. Turkey's population is diverse, including 65 percent Turks, 19 percent Kurds, 7 percent Tatars, and 2 percent Arabs. More than 97 percent are Muslims, about two-thirds of these Sunni Muslims. The historic region of Asia Minor—roughly coterminus with modern Turkey—was the center of the ancient Hittite Empire (2000–1200 B.C.) and the core of the Christian Byzantine Empire (476–1453) and Muslim Ottoman Empire (1453–1918). Various Turkish tribes migrating from central Asia between the 11th and 15th centuries were converted to Islam and progressively conquered Byzantine territories. By 1453, the last Christian stronghold, Constantinople, was conquered. During the 16th century, the new Ottoman Empire expanded rapidly, conquering the Balkan Peninsula and Hungary. As late as 1689, the empire was still threatening Vienna and central Europe. The Ottoman Empire gradually declined during the 18th and 19th centuries as European countries rapidly embraced new technologies and industrialization. The combined force of nationalistic movements and European imperialism during the 19th century led to the empire's loss of Greece, North Africa, Serbia, Egypt, Romania, Bosnia, and Bessarabia prior to World War I (1914–18), which the Turks entered on the side of the losing Central Powers. At the war's end, Turkey lost its Arab lands (see ARAB IMMIGRATION; LEBANESE IMMIGRATION; SYRIAN IMMIGRATION), but an abortive attempt by the Allied Powers to partition Asia Minor was beaten back by Turkish leader Mustafa Kemal Ataturk, who helped establish a republic in 1923. By the mid-1930s Ataturk had instituted a parliamentary governmental system, secularized the courts and education, implemented a Latin alphabetical system, officially renamed the capital Istanbul, promoted women's rights, and outlawed polygyny. Since World War II (1939–45), Turkey has been a strong Western ally, particularly during the COLD WAR. It also supported the 1991 Persian Gulf War and the 2003 Iraq War. During the later 20th century, Turkey was frequently at odds with Greece over the governance of Cyprus and with its Arab neighbors over the importation of Western secularism into the region.

Turks began to emigrate from the Ottoman Empire to North America in significant numbers around 1900, with numbers peaking between then and 1923. Most immigrants were from the Balkans and the eastern provinces, where the Armenian revolt was occurring. About 22,000 immigrated during this period, more than 93 percent of these immigrants being men, though many returned when the Republic of Turkey was established in 1923. It has been estimated that 86 percent of Turkish immigrants to the United States between 1899 and 1924 returned. During the 1920s, Turks speaking many languages, including Turkish, Kurdish, Albanian, and Arabic, settled in mostly industrial enclaves throughout the northern United States, with the largest settlement in Detroit. With the Kurdish revolt against the new secular state in the 1920s and 1930s, Turks and Kurds gradually evolved separate ethnic affiliations. From World War II until passage of the IMMIGRATION AND NATIONALITY ACT of 1965, Turkish immigration was small, mostly confined to students. A significant portion of these were sponsored by the Turkish military in order to promote advanced technical training for their officers. Immigration to the United States steadily increased after 1965, averaging about 1,300 annually during the 1970s, 2,300 in the 1980s, and 3,800 in the 1990s, though many coming in the 1990s were refugees from other countries who had first come to Turkey. Nonrefugee immigration between 2000 and 2002 averaged about 3,000 per year.

The limited Turkish immigration to Canada prior to the early 1960s consisted primarily of students and professionals, especially doctors and engineers. As in the case of the United States, many of the students were sponsored by the Turkish government in order to gain greater technical skills within the military. Significant Turkish immigration to Canada began only after 1960, though this, too, remained relatively small. During the 1960s and early 1970s, most Turks came for educational and economic opportunities, but with a variety of conflicts in the 1970s and 1980s erupting in Cyprus, eastern Turkey, and Bulgaria, many left for political reasons. Many of these immigrants were unskilled and displaced workers, and others were refugees from the Turkish-Kurdish conflict. Of the 16,405 Turkish immigrants in Canada in 2001, fewer than 700 came before 1961; 3,400 between 1981 and 1990; and 7,840 between 1991 and 2001. An undetermined number of more than 4,000 Cypriots who came between 1961 and 2001 were Turkish.

Further Reading

Ahmed, Frank. *Turks in America: The Ottoman Turk's Immigrant Experience.* Greenwich, Conn.: Columbia International, 1986.

Aijian, M. M. "Mohemmedans in the United States." *The Muslim World* 10 (1920): 30–35.

Bilge, B. "Voluntary Associations in the Old Turkish Community of Metropolitan Detroit." In *Muslim Communities of North America.* Eds. Y. Yazbeck Haddad and J. Idleman Smith. Albany: State University of New York Press, 1994.

Davison, Roderic H. *Turkey: A Short Story.* 3d ed. London: Eothen Press, 1998.

Palmer, Alan. *Decline and Fall of the Ottoman Empire.* New York: M. Evans, 1994.

Wheatcroft, Andrew. *The Ottomans.* London: Viking, 1994.

Yilmazkaya, E. "Research Report for the Multicultural History Society on the Toronto Turkish Community." *Polyphony: The Bulletin of the Multicultural History Society of Ontario* 6, no. 1 (1984): 181–184.

Tydings-McDuffie Act (United States) (1934)

The Tydings-McDuffie Act grew out of widespread opposition, particularly in California, to the rapid influx of Filipino agricultural laborers after annexation of the islands following the Spanish-American War in 1898 (see FILIPINO IMMIGRATION). The measure of 1934 granted the Philippines commonwealth status and promised independence within 10 years. As a result, Filipinos were reclassified as aliens and thus no longer enjoyed unrestricted access to the United States.

In 1910, there had been only 406 Filipinos in the mainland United States; by 1930, the number had risen to 45,208. More than 30,000 lived in California, but they numbered in the thousands in Washington, Oregon, Illinois, and New York. Most Filipinos took jobs not easily filled by whites, with 60 percent working in agriculture and 25 percent as janitors, valets, dishwashers, and other areas of personal service. During the 1920s, there was already uneasiness about the growing number of Filipinos, reviving earlier nativist fears (see NATIVISM) regarding Chinese and Japanese laborers. With the rise in unemployment during the depression and the development of Filipino labor activism in the early 1930s (see CARLOS BULOSAN), a new reason for excluding Filipinos was added. Granting commonwealth status to the Philippines was largely a legal cover for racially excluding Filipinos, who were hit especially hard by the economic downturn of the depression. The Tydings-McDuffie Act limited their immigration to only 50 per year. But for the tens of thousands already in the country, it meant that, because they were not "white" and therefore could not become naturalized citizens, they were cut off from New Deal work programs. In some respects, Filipinos were in a worse position than the previously excluded Chinese and Japanese, for at least Chinese merchants were allowed to bring wives, and Japanese wives and family members had been exempted from the restrictions of the GENTLEMEN'S AGREEMENT. Exemptions to the act did, however, allow Hawaiian employers to import Filipino farm labor when needed (though remigration to the mainland was not permitted) and enabled the United States to recruit more than 22,000 Filipinos into the navy (between 1944 and 1973), most of whom were assigned to work in mess halls or as personal servants.

Further Reading

Bogardus, Emory S. "Filipino Repatriation." *Sociology and Social Research* 21 (September–October 1936): 67–71.

Catapusan, Benicio T. "Filipino Immigrants and Public Relief in the United States." *Sociology and Social Research* 23 (July–1939): 546–554.

Goethe, C. M. "Filipino Immigration Viewed as a Peril." *Current History* (January 1934), p. 354.

Moncado, Hilario. "Philippine Independence before Filipino Exclusion." *Filipino Nation* (May 1931), p. 9.

Saniel, Josepha M., ed. *The Filipino Exclusion Movement, 1927–1935.* Quezon City: University of the Philippines, 1967.

Takaki, Ronald. *Strangers from a Different Shore: A History of Asian Americans.* New York: Penguin, 1989.

Ukrainian immigration

Ukrainian immigration to Canada represented the largest of any ethnic group from eastern Europe, and the Ukrainians in Canada are one of the few ethnic groups with a larger absolute population than their counterparts in the United States. According to the U.S. census of 2000 and the Canadian census of 2001, 892,922 Americans and 1,071,060 Canadians claim Ukrainian descent. The greatest concentrations of Ukrainians in the United States are in Pennsylvania, New York, New Jersey, California, and Michigan. Ontario, British Columbia, and Manitoba have the largest number of Ukrainian Canadians. More than 15 percent of Winnipeg's population is Ukrainian.

Ukraine occupies 232,800 square miles in Eastern Europe. It is bordered by Belarus to the north; Russia to the east and northeast; Moldova and Romania to the southwest; and Hungary, Slovakia, and Poland to the west. In 2002, the population was estimated at 48,760,474, comprising mainly Ukrainians (73 percent) and Russians (22 percent). The principal religions are Ukrainian Orthodox and Ukrainian Catholic, although a large portion of the population is not religious. The Ukraine has throughout its history been a crossroads and a battleground. In the first millennium B.C., the area was occupied by Cimmerians, Scythians, and Sarmations, and in the first millennium A.D., by Goths, Huns, Bulgars, Avars, Khazars, Magyars, and Slavs, the latter becoming the predominant ethnocultural group in the region. The first great Slavic state, Kievan Rus, was founded in the ninth century, in part by Scandinavian Varangians (Vikings). It was destroyed by the Mongols in the 13th century. From the 14th century until 1991, the Ukraine was ruled successively by Lithuania, Poland, and Russia, except for a brief period following the Cossack uprising of 1648. Austria ruled the Ukrainian region of Galicia from 1772 to 1918. Ukrainians frequently tried to gain independence from Russia, without success. After resistance to Soviet policies of agricultural collectivization and Russification, Soviet leader Joseph Stalin allowed 5 million Ukrainians to die in the famine of 1932–33. During World War II (1939–45), many Ukrainians at first welcomed the Nazi invasion of 1941, though they were treated as badly by the Germans as they had been by the Soviets. In the wake of a Ukrainian nationalist movement in the 1980s and the breakup of the Soviet Union, Ukraine gained its independence in 1991. It had a difficult time, however, making the transition to a market economy, leading to widespread dissatisfaction among the people.

The first significant Ukrainian immigration to the United States came in the 1870s. Generally poor and uneducated peasants from Galicia in the Austro-Hungarian Empire (see AUSTRO-HUNGARIAN IMMIGRATION), they usually took jobs in mines and factories in Pennsylvania, New York, and New Jersey. Between the 1870s and 1914, about 500,000 Ukrainians came to the United States. With the restrictive EMERGENCY QUOTA ACT of 1921 and JOHNSON-REED ACT of 1924, quotas severely limited the immigration of Ukrainians, and only about 15,000 came prior to World War II (1939–45). During the late 1940s and early 1950s, however, some 85,000 Ukrainians settled in the United States, admitted under provisions of the Dis-placed Persons Act (1948) and other special legislation. Many of these were well educated and made a relatively smooth transition to American culture. Immediately following the fall of the Soviet state, Ukrainians began a substantial immigration to the United States, averaging almost 17,000 per year between 1992 and 2002.

Ukrainians coming to Canada first settled in Winnipeg, Manitoba, and at Beaver Creek, Yukon Territory, in 1891, though their numbers remained relatively small until the later 1890s. Encouraged by the Canadian government, Dr. Josef Oleskow traveled from L'vov (Lemberg) to explore the western prairies in 1895 for possible Ukrainian settlement sites. Oleskow's subsequent publication of pamphlets encouraged emigration, especially from the Galicia and Bukovina regions of the Austro-Hungarian Empire. Ukrainian immigration peaked in 1913, when more than 22,000 emigrants entered Canada. Records are imprecise, as Ukrainians were characterized variously as Russians, Austrians, Poles, Hungarians, Romanians, Galicians, Bukovinians, and Ruthenians, but it is estimated that between 1891 and 1914, about 170,000 Ukrainians immigrated to Canada. Most of these early settlers were peasant farmers, encouraged by the promise of inexpensive lands, who settled a frontier area from southeastern Manitoba through Saskatchewan and into northern Alberta. They played a major role in transforming largely uninhabited western prairies into productive farmland.

Some of the more than 60,000 Ukrainians who immigrated between the world wars were better educated, having been involved in the abortive Ukrainian independence movement just after World War I (1914–18; see World War I and immigration), but the largest number came again as agriculturalists. As a nonpreferred group, they could only come as part of family reunification, as experienced farmers, or as farm laborers or domestics with sponsors. After World War II (see World War II and immigration), about 34,000 Ukrainians came to Canada as displaced persons. They were often well-educated professionals, and most were intensely anticommunist. They tended to settle in industrial areas, particularly in Ontario. By 1961, Ukrainians constituted approximately 2.6 percent of the Canadian population (473,377), ranking behind only the French (30.4 percent, or 18,238,247), English (23 percent, or 4,195,175), Scottish (10.4 percent, or 1,902,302), Irish (9.6 percent, or 1,753,351), and Germans (5.8 percent, or 1,049,599). Of the more than 51,000 Ukrainian immigrants in Canada in 2001, more than 21,000 came before 1961 and about 23,000 following the dissolution of the Soviet Union.

See also Austro-Hungarian immigration; Soviet immigration.

Further Reading

Gerus, O. W., and J. E. Rea. *The Ukrainians in Canada.* Ottawa: Canadian Historical Association, 1985.

Isajiw, Wsevolod W., ed. *Ukrainians in American and Canadian Society.* Jersey City, N.J.: M. P. Kots, 1976.

Kubijovyc, Volodymyr, and Danylo Struk, eds. *Encyclopedia of Ukraine.* 5 vols. Toronto: University of Toronto Press, 1984–93.

Kuropas, M. B. *The Ukrainian Americans: Roots and Aspirations, 1884–1954.* Toronto: University of Toronto Press, 1992.

Lehr, John C. "Peopling the Prairies with Ukrainians." In *Immigration in Canada: Historical Perspectives.* Ed. Gerald Tulchinsky. Toronto: Copp Clark Longman, 1994.

Luciuk, Lubomyr Y., and Stella Hrniuk, eds. *Canada's Ukrainians: Negotiating an Identity.* Toronto: University of Toronto Press and Ukrainian Canadian Centennial Committee, 1991.

Magocsi, Paul Robert. *A History of Ukraine.* Toronto: University of Toronto Press, 1996.

Martynowych, Orest T. *Ukrainians in Canada: The Formative Period, 1891–1924.* Edmonton: Canadian Institute of Ukrainian Studies, 1991.

Marunchak, Michael H. *The Ukrainian Canadians: A History.* Rev. ed. Winnipeg and Ottawa: Ukrainian Academy of Arts and Sciences, 1982.

Subtelny, O. *Ukrainians in North America: An Illustrated History.* Toronto: University of Toronto Press, 1991.

Swyripa, Frances. *Wedded to the Cause: Ukrainian-Canadian Women and Ethnic Identity, 1891–1991.* Toronto: University of Toronto Press, 1993.

Young, Charles H. *The Ukrainian Canadians: A Study in Assimilation.* Toronto: T. Nelson and Sons, 1931.

Yuzyk, Paul. *Ukrainian Canadians: Their Place and Role in Canadian Life.* Toronto: Ukrainian Canadian Business and Professional Federation, 1967.

Ulster

Ulster, situated in the northeastern portion of the island of Ireland, was one of the major Irish kingdoms of the medieval period. It was annexed by England in 1461, and the Irish nobility was forced to swear allegiance to the English Crown. Ongoing Irish hostility resulted in the Nine Years' War (1594–1603), in which an allied Spanish fleet sacked Kinsale, port city on the southern coast of Ireland, before England ultimately suppressed the rebellion. The leader of the rebellion, Hugh O'Neill, earl of Tyrone, was pardoned and agreed to work for the English Crown. In 1607, he and other leaders of the rebellion fled into exile, abandoning their large estates. The English government parceled their land to caretakers willing to undertake the settlement of the lands, leading to the creation of widespread English and Scottish settlements throughout the counties of Armagh, Cavan, Donegal, Derry, Fermanagh, and Tyrone, known collectively as the Ulster Plantation. There was naturally great hostility on the part of native freeholders and tenants, whose rights and traditions were frequently violated. When the systematic settlement foundered, independent and individual migrations from England and Scotland created a more fragmented settlement, mixing English, Irish, and Scottish agriculturalists. Between 1605 and 1697, it is estimated that up to 200,000 Scots and 10,000 English resettled in Ireland. Most settlers in the early stages were poverty-stricken Lowland Scots. Starting in the 1640s, however, an increasing number of Highlanders joined the migration. About 10,000 Highlanders had been sent to suppress a rebellion in 1641, and many stayed on, eventually bringing their families. The descendants of these Lowland and Highland, mostly Presbyterian Scots, are known as Scots-Irish.

More than 100,000 Scots-Irish from Ulster immigrated to America between 1717 and 1775, mainly because of high rents or famine and most coming from families who had been in Ireland for several generations. In the colonial period, these Scots-Irish were usually referred to simply as Irish and represented the largest movement of any group from the British Isles to British North America in the 18th century. Together with a large emigration from Scotland itself, this movement laid the foundation for a strong Scottish ethnic component in the cultural development of both the United States and Canada (see SCOTTISH IMMIGRATION). In the U.S. census of 2000 and the Canadian census of 2001, more than 9.2 million Americans and 4.1 million Canadians claimed either Scottish or Scots-Irish ancestry.

With the Anglo-Irish Treaty of 1921, the island of Ireland was divided, creating a state within the United Kingdom called Northern Ireland, which comprised six of the nine counties of historical Ulster: Antrim, Armagh, Down, Fermanagh, Derry, and Tyrone. The remainder of the island became the Irish Free State, a dominion under the British Crown. Though not exactly coterminus with either the old medieval kingdom or the Ulster Plantation, Northern Ireland is sometimes referred to simply as Ulster.

Further Reading
Dunaway, Wayland. *The Scotch Irish of Colonial Pennsylvania.* Baltimore: Genealogical Publishing Company, 1997.
Fischer, David Hackett. *Albion's Seed: Four British Folkways in America.* New York: Oxford University Press, 1989.
Griffin, Patrick. *The People with No Name: Ireland's Ulster Scots, America's Scots Irish, and the Creation of the British Atlantic World, 1689–1764.* Princeton, N.J.: Princeton University Press, 2001.
Leyburn, James. *Scotch-Irish: A Social History.* Reprint. Chapel Hill: University of North Carolina Press, 1989.
Robinson, Philip S. *Plantation of Ulster: British Settlement in an Irish Landscape, 1600–70.* New York: Palgrave Macmillan, 1985.

United States—immigration survey and policy overview

From the establishment of the first permanent English settlement at Jamestown, Virginia (see VIRGINIA COLONY), in 1607, the area now known as the United States has attracted more immigrants than any other country in the world. In the colonial period, Europe had few obvious sources of wealth, but the Spanish Empire in the New World transformed Europe's economy in the 16th century with its production of gold and silver, and the sugar plantations of the West Indies led to unprecedented accumulations of capital. Even the fur trade of Canada was lucrative enough to lead three countries to the brink of war in the Pacific Northwest. Although the English colonies had none of these commodities in abundance, they did have good land and an equable climate, and land was still the prime commodity for most potential immigrants during the 17th and 18th centuries. With the dramatic expansion of the new republic between 1783 and 1848, the United States added not only vast expanses of land but abundant iron and coal reserves to power the coming Industrial Revolution and precious metals not found east of the Appalachians. Europeans fled their overcrowded and tradition-bound lands, flocking to the prairies and factories of America in the greatest wave of migration the world had ever seen. Between 1815 and 1930, more than 50 million people left Europe for the New World, with almost two of every three settling in the United States. Many came to escape religious or political oppression; most came to escape poverty, almost all to improve their economic condition. The same opportunities that attracted immigrants in the 19th century continued to motivate them in the 21st century. In 2002, the United States admitted almost 1.1 million immigrants from every part of the world, including more than 340,000 from Asia; 362,000 from Mexico and Central and South America; 69,000 from the Caribbean; and 60,000 from Africa—the greatest admittance rate by far of any country in the world.

Jamestown, the first permanent English settlement in the Western Hemisphere (1607), formed the core of what would later become the royal colony of Virginia (1624). English entrepreneurs had become interested in the Chesapeake region in the 1570s but found little support from Queen Elizabeth I (r. 1558–1603). The disastrous attempt to settle Roanoke Island (1584–87; see ROANOKE COLONY) forestalled English efforts. By the early 17th century, hatred of Spain and development of the joint-stock company provided both the diplomatic motive and the financial means for launching a concerted colonial challenge. Unlike the situation in Spanish lands, English settlements were haphazard and largely uncoordinated. Plymouth and MASSACHUSETTS, MARYLAND, RHODE ISLAND, and PENNSYLVANIA, were settled first as religious havens; CONNECTICUT was the result of internal expansion; DELAWARE, NEW JERSEY, NEW HAMPSHIRE, and the CAROLINAS, along with Virginia, were settled as commercial ventures; NEW YORK was conquered from the Dutch; and GEORGIA was, somewhat incongruously, both a humanitarian venture and an exercise in international diplomacy. But for a thorough mixture of all these reasons, the English colonies along the Atlantic seaboard grew in population owing to immigration in a way that neither Canada nor Mexico ever would. By 1700, the population of Virginia was 65,000, of Massachusetts 56,000, and of Maryland 34,000. Pennsylvania, after less than two decades, had attracted 19,000 settlers.

Throughout much of the 18th century, American settlers were largely left to handle their own affairs. Government interference—beyond the too-frequent colonial conflicts with France that inevitably created economic disruptions—was limited, and taxes were light. With a rapidly modernizing economy in Great Britain, recurring famines in Ireland, and overcrowding and political instability in Germany, there was an abundance of interest in America. And even for those without means, INDENTURED SERVITUDE provided an opportunity to make a new start in life. By 1720, the population was nearly 400,000 and continued to grow at an unprecedented rate, swelled by the forced migration of 250,000 African slaves, a high natural increase, and the highest rates of immigration in the colonial world. In addition to several hundred thousand English immigrants in the colonial period, there were 250,000 Scots-Irish and 135,000 Germans, as well as smaller numbers of Swiss, Scots, Swedes, and Jews. By the time of the SEVEN YEARS' WAR (1756–63) with France, the American population was about 1.5 million (as opposed to NEW FRANCE's European population of only about 75,000). At the time of the American Revolution (1775–83; see AMERICAN REVOLUTION AND IMMIGRATION), it was nearing 2.5 million. Even with the loss of 40,000–50,000 Loyalists who left the new republic for NOVA SCOTIA, NEW BRUNSWICK, and QUEBEC, the American population was young, aggressive, and ample enough to substantially develop the resources at hand.

The early period of the republic saw a slackening of immigration. Great Britain, by far the largest source of immigrants to America, was now sending its immigrants to the Caribbean, South Africa, or elsewhere, and the two countries were frequently at odds until the 1820s. The ample agricultural lands of the transappalachian region, however, were inviting to the starving and dispossessed, especially as diplomatic relations gradually improved. As a result, between 1820 and 1860 immigration increased dramatically each decade: 128,000 in the 1820s, 538,000 in the 1830s, 1.4 million in the 1840s, and 2.8 million in the 1850s. The Irish, driven by starvation even before the Great Famine of the 1840s, sent almost 2 million during this period; Germany, more than 1.5 million; and England, Scotland, and Wales more than 800,000. With the Civil War (1861–65) halting most immigration, the United States consolidated itself. There were the old stock—mainly English and Scots-Irish—and the new immigrants—the Irish and Germans, who were by the 1870s carving respectable niches for themselves in U.S. society, despite the NATIVISM of many Americans. After the Civil War, German, British, and Irish immigration continued to predominate, but a wave of Scandinavians brought new settlers for the American Midwest and prairies. Between the Civil War and World War I (1914–18) about 1.6 million Norwegians, Swedes, and Danes came to the United States, leaving a lasting mark on American culture.

Accompanying the continuing growth in immigration between 1865 and 1880 was a NEW IMMIGRATION, a shift in the most common source countries. The term has most often been used to identify the shift in immigrant trends that occurred during the 1880s: Germany, Britain, Ireland, Scandinavia, and other regions of western and northern Europe were no longer the primary source countries; instead, during the 1880s, the percentage of immigrants from eastern and southern Europe increased dramatically. The new immigrants came mainly from Italy, Austria-Hungary, and Russia. Between 1881 and 1920, almost 24 million immigrants were admitted, with almost 1.3 million coming in the peak year of 1907 alone. Of these, 4.1 million came from Italy, 4 million from Austria-Hungary, and 3.3 million from Russia and Poland. Most of these immigrants either stayed in eastern ports or moved on to industrial northern cities like Pittsburgh, Pennsylvania; Cleveland, Ohio; Detroit, Michigan; or Chicago, Illinois. Between 1900 and 1914, perhaps 3 million immigrants landed in New York City (see NEW YORK, NEW YORK), and by 1910 the foreign-born population of that city rose to more than 40 percent. About 700,000 mostly poor Italians composed 15 percent of New York's population.

Established Americans had always feared immigrants and their potential influence. The first great wave of xenophobia in the 1850s—born of the massive Irish and German immigration of the previous decade—led to the formation of the Know-Nothing Party. Pleas for restricting immigration were ignored until the panic of 1871 threw thousands out of work, leading to 1875 legislation banning convicts and prostitutes (see PAGE ACT), and eventually, in 1882, the prohibition of an entire ethnic group in the CHINESE EXCLUSION ACT. Prior to this time the United States had an open immigration policy and was willing to take almost anyone who would contribute to the development of the country. The massive wave of new immigrants from southern and eastern Europe were valuable workers, but they also seemed very foreign to most Americans, usually speaking no English, with few skills, and most often either Roman Catholic or Orthodox in faith. As a result, with the outbreak of World War I, the growing trend toward exclusion culminated in a major revision of immigration policy.

The war had slowed immigration to a trickle (see WORLD WAR I AND IMMIGRATION). With growing bitterness toward the principal opponents—Germany and Austria-Hungary—and a rising fear of radical politics and labor movements with the success of the Bolshevik Revolution

in Russia (1917), anti-immigration sentiment finally culminated in a series of exclusionary measures—the IMMI-
GRATION ACT of 1917, the EMERGENCY QUOTA ACT of
1921, and the JOHNSON-REED ACT of 1924—that established literacy tests and quotas based on the 1890s population in the United States, prior to the largest period of
immigration from eastern Europe. During the Great
Depression of the 1930s, only 500,000 immigrants were
admitted but an even greater number returned to their
homelands. World War II (1939–45; see WORLD WAR II
AND IMMIGRATION) led to the easing of immigration
restrictions for allies such as China and the Philippines,
the initiation of the BRACERO PROGRAM with Mexico, and
several special measures, including the WAR BRIDES ACT
(1945) and DISPLACED PERSONS ACTs (1948, 1950), that
enabled more than 400,000 immigrants to be admitted
outside the quota system.

As the immediate postwar conflicts with the Soviet
Union evolved into the COLD WAR, the U.S. government
needed a new strategy for dealing with both the threat of
communism and the worldwide movement of peoples displaced by more than a decade of war and oppression. The
expansion of Soviet political power and the Communist victory in China led many Americans to fear the effects of
loosely regulated immigration. This led to passage of the
McCarran Internal Security Act (September 1950), authorizing the president in time of national emergency to detain
or deport anyone suspected of threatening U.S. security.
New York senator Patrick McCarran, a Democrat, went on
to argue against a more liberal immigration policy, fearing
an augmentation of the "hard-core, indigestible blocs" of
immigrants who had "not become integrated into the American way of life." Together with Representative Francis Walter of Pennsylvania, also a Democrat, they drafted the
MCCARRAN-WALTER IMMIGRATION AND NATURALIZA-
TION ACT (1952), which preserved the national origins
quotas then in place as the best means of preserving the "cultural balance" in the nation's population. The main provisions included establishment of a new set of immigration
preferences under the national quotas, focusing on family
reunification, immigrants from the Western Hemisphere,
and skilled workers; elimination of racial restrictions on naturalization; and provision for the U.S. attorney general to
temporarily "parole" persons into the United States without
a visa in times of emergency. Allotment of visas under the
McCarran-Walter Act still heavily favored northern and
western European countries, which received 85 percent of
the quota allotment.

The next major shift in American immigration policy
came with passage of the IMMIGRATION AND NATIONALITY
ACT of 1965. The Civil Rights movement of the 1960s led
to a rethinking of the quota system, and the new measure
replaced nationality quotas with hemispheric ceilings—
170,000 annually from the Eastern Hemisphere and

A Polish emigrant embarks for America. Acute poverty and
cultural repression drove Poles to seek opportunity in the
United States. More than 1 million immigrated to America
between 1880 and 1914. *(Library of Congress, Prints &
Photographs Division [LC-USZ62-23711])*

120,000 annually from the Western Hemisphere—with
preference for relatives of U.S. citizens and permanent resident aliens. Immediate family members of citizens could
enter without being counted against the quota. As the number of immigrants from Europe began to shrink, however,
Asian and Latin American immigration increased. In 1978,
Congress replaced the hemispheric arrangement with a single annual quota of 290,000. By the 1980s, almost 50 percent of immigrants came from Mexico, Central America,
South America, and the Caribbean, while 37 percent arrived
from Asia. Immigration from Europe and Canada declined
to only 13 percent of the total.

Two factors in the 1990s led to a growing anti-immigrant attitude in the United States. In 1992, 1.1 million
immigrants entered the country, the largest number since
1907, when immigration was virtually unrestricted. As a
result, by 1997 nearly 10 percent of the American population
was foreign born, almost double the percentage from 1970.
Also, an economic downturn in the mid-1990s caused an
increasing number of Americans both to fear for their jobs
and to become active in opposing expensive government

measures providing for the economic and social welfare of immigrants. In California, where one-third of all foreign-born Americans lived, voters ignored previous U.S. Supreme Court decisions protecting immigrants' rights as a group to pass PROPOSITION 187, denying education, welfare benefits, and nonemergency health care to illegal immigrants. Federal judges killed enactment of its provisions, but there continued to be a strong national movement to impose tighter restrictions on immigration and to enforce immigration laws more vigorously. In 1993, President Bill Clinton surprised supporters by continuing outgoing president George H.W. Bush's policy of forcibly returning Haitian refugees intercepted on the high seas, approved expedited hearings for asylum seekers, and sought an additional $172.5 million for the IMMIGRATION AND NATURALIZATION SERVICE (INS) to fight illegal immigration. This led to a series of decisions speeding the deportation process, reducing automatic admission of certain immigrant groups, and limiting the importation of foreign workers. In 1996, a presidential election year, a bill was enacted providing $12 million for construction of a 14-mile fence south of San Diego, California, a substantial increase in the number of Border Patrol and INS agents, and a mandatory three-year prison sentence for smuggling illegal aliens. The WELFARE REFORM ACT (1996) also stopped welfare benefits to hundreds of thousands of legal immigrants. One of the few exceptions to the trend toward tighter restrictions was a decision by the INS in 1995 to grant asylum to women fleeing their homelands in fear of rape or beatings, prompted by state-sponsored terror against Bosnian women by Serb troops. While the challenges afforded by 13 million new immigrants between 1990 and 2002 led some to question the wisdom of continuing to accept new residents at such a rate, the debate was largely a reprise of the issues raised in the 1850s and the 1910s in the midst of two other great waves of immigration.

At the beginning of the 21st century, the presidency of George W. Bush saw two major initiatives with large implications for immigration policy. The first of these, designed to gain greater control over the immigration process, was the result of the terrorist attacks on New York City and Washington, D.C., on SEPTEMBER 11, 2001. Almost immediately the administration proposed a series of sweeping measures designed to combat terrorism, including strengthened border controls. The Uniting and Strengthening America by Providing Appropriate Tools Required to Intercept and Obstruct Terrorism Act (better known as the USA PATRIOT ACT) was quickly passed and signed into law by Bush on October 26, 2001. The act provided for greater surveillance of aliens and increasing the power of the attorney general to identify, arrest, and deport suspected terrorists. The resulting evaluation of the nation's security measures led to an extensive overhaul of the immigration service. The Homeland Security Act on November 25, 2002, abolished the INS, transferring its functions to various agencies within the newly created Department of Homeland Security. Immigration services formerly provided by the INS were transferred to U.S. CITIZENSHIP AND IMMIGRATION SERVICES; enforcement oversight, to the Border Transportation Security Directorate; border control, to the U.S. Customs and Border Protection; and interior enforcement, to the U.S. Immigration and Customs Enforcement.

The second of these initiatives was Bush's determination to work in conjunction with Mexican president Vicente Fox to regularize the participation of Mexican laborers in the U.S. economy. Though negotiations were temporarily delayed in the wake of September 11, on January 7, 2004, Bush proposed the Temporary Worker Program, which would "match willing foreign workers with willing American employers, when no Americans can be found to fill the jobs." More controversially, it would provide temporary workers with legal status, even if they were undocumented. Critics voiced concerns that it did not provide a path to citizenship for those workers. With regard to the desirability of widespread immigration, the first decade of the 21st century proved to be as contentious as the last decade of the previous century.

Further Reading

Bailyn, Bernard. *Voyages to the West.* New York: Alfred A. Knopf, 1986.

Baseler, Marilyn C. *"Asylum for Mankind": America, 1607–1800.* Ithaca, N.Y.: Cornell University Press, 1998.

Borjas, George. *Friends or Strangers: The Impact of Immigrants on the U.S. Economy.* Reprint. New York: Basic Books, 1991.

Briggs, Vernon M., Jr. *Immigration Policy and the American Labor Force.* Baltimore: Johns Hopkins University Press, 1984.

Daniels, Roger. *Coming to America.* New York: HarperCollins, 1990.

———. *Guarding the Golden Door: American Immigration Policy and Immigrants since 1882.* New York: Hill and Wang, 2004.

Debouzy, Marianne. *In the Shadow of the Statue of Liberty: Immigrants, Workers, and Citizens in the American Republic, 1880–1920.* Urbana: University of Illinois Press, 1992.

Dimmitt, Marius A. *The Enactment of the McCarran-Walter Act of 1952.* Lawrence: University Press of Kansas, 1971.

Dinnerstein, Leonard, and David M. Reimers. *Ethnic Americans: A History of Immigration.* 4th ed. New York: Columbia University Press, 1999.

Dinnerstein, Leonard, Roger L. Nichols, and David M. Reimers. *Natives and Strangers: A Multicultural History of Americans.* New York: Oxford University Press, 1997.

Divine, Robert. *American Immigration Policy, 1924–1952.* New Haven, Conn.: Yale University Press, 1957.

Fischer, David. *Albion's Seed: Four British Folkways in America.* New York: Oxford University Press, 1989.

Gimpel, James G., and James R. Edwards, Jr. *The Congressional Politics of Immigration Reform.* Boston: Allyn and Bacon, 1999.

Grabbe, Hans-Jurgen. "European Immigration to the United States in the Early National Period, 1798–1820." *Proceedings of the American Philosophical Society* 133, no. 2 (1989): 190–214.

Hansen, Marcus Lee. *The Mingling of the Canadian and American Peoples.* Vol. 1, *Historical.* New Haven, Conn.: Yale University Press;

Toronto: Ryerson Press; London: Humphrey Milford, Oxford University Press, 1940.

Higham, John. *Strangers in the Land: Patterns of American Nativism, 1860–1925.* New Brunswick, N.J.: Rutgers University Press, 1988.

Hutchinson, E. R. *Legislative History of American Immigration Policy, 1798–1965.* Philadelphia: University of Pennsylvania Press, 1981.

Jasso, Guillermina, and Mark R. Rosenzweig. *The New Chosen People: Immigrants in the United States.* New York: Russell Sage, 1990.

LeMay, Michael C. *From Open Door to Dutch Door: An Analysis of U.S. Immigration Policy since 1820.* New York: Praeger, 1987.

Loescher, Gil, and John A. Scanlan. *Calculated Kindness: Refugees and America's Half-Open Door, 1945–the Present.* New York: Free Press, 1986.

Portes, Alejandro, and Rubén G. Rumbaut. *Immigrant America: A Portrait.* 2d ed. Berkeley: University of California Press, 1995.

Reimers, David M. *Still the Golden Door: The Third World Comes to America.* 2d ed. New York: Columbia University Press, 1992.

———. *Unwelcome Strangers: American Identity and the Turn against Immigration.* New York: Columbia University Press, 1998.

Salyer, Lucy E. *Laws Harsh as Tigers: Chinese Immigrants and the Shaping of Modern Immigration Law.* Chapel Hill: University of North Carolina Press, 1995.

Upper Canada   See CANADA—IMMIGRATION SURVEY AND POLICY OVERVIEW.

USA PATRIOT Act (Uniting and Strengthening America by Providing Appropriate Tools Required to Intercept and Obstruct Terrorism Act) (United States) (2002)

In the wake of the SEPTEMBER 11, 2001, terrorist attacks, the administration of President George W. Bush proposed a series of sweeping measures designed to combat terrorism, including strengthened border controls. The USA PATRIOT Act was quickly passed and signed into law by the president on October 26, 2001.

The Patriot Act, as it became commonly known, provided for greater surveillance of aliens and for increasing the power of the attorney general to identify, arrest, and deport aliens. It also designated "domestic terrorism" to include "acts dangerous to human life that are a violation of the criminal laws of the United States or of any State that appear to be intended to intimidate or coerce a civilian population; to influence the policy of a government by intimidation or coercion; or to affect the conduct of a government by mass destruction, assassination, or kidnapping." Also, monitoring of some aliens entering on nonimmigrant visas was instituted, passport photographs were digitalized, more extensive background checks of all applications and petitions to the IMMIGRATION and NATURALIZATION SERVICE (INS) were authorized, the SEVIS (Student and Exchange Visitor Infor-

mation System) database was created to track the location of aliens in the country on student visas, and the U.S. office of the Attorney General was given the right to immediately expel anyone suspected of terrorist links. Also, the State Department introduced a 20-day waiting period for visa applications from men aged 16 to 45 from Afghanistan, Algeria, Bahrain, Djibouti, Egypt, Eritrea, Indonesia, Iran, Iraq, Jordan, Kuwait, Lebanon, Libya, Malaysia, Morocco, Oman, Pakistan, Qatar, Saudi Arabia, Somalia, Sudan, Syria, Tunisia, United Arab Emirates, and Yemen. Any application considered to be suspicious was forwarded to the Federal Bureau of Investigation (FBI), creating a further delay.

Though widely supported by the American public, the Patriot Act remained a focal point of the evolving debate about the nature of terrorism, the means necessary to combat it, and the wisdom of sacrificing civil liberties for security. Although the act specifically affirmed the "vital role" in American life played by "Arab Americans, Muslim Americans, and Americans from South Asia" and condemned any stereotyping and all acts of violence against them, some groups believed that the Patriot Act would enable the federal government to target their activities and to suppress a variety of activist groups that disagreed with the government on a wide array of issues. In January 2003, the Department of Justice produced a draft bill, the Domestic Security Enhancement Act, commonly dubbed Patriot II, which if passed would further enhance the department's powers to deny information on possible terrorist detainees and create a national terrorist database. The proposal of such further measures alarmed groups including the American Civil Liberties Union, heightening the debate in the United States over the methods necessary for combating terrorism.

Further Reading
Ball, Howard. *The USA PATRIOT Act: A Reference Handbook.* New York: ABC-CLIO, 2004.

Chang, Nancy. *Silencing Political Dissent: How Post–September 11 Anti-Terrorism Measures Threaten Our Civil Liberties.* New York: Seven Stories Press, 2002.

Malkin, Michelle. *Invasion: How America Still Welcomes Terrorists, Criminals and Other Foreign Menaces to Our Shores.* New York: Regnery, 2002.

Reams, Bernard D., Jr., and Christopher Anglim. *USA PATRIOT Act: A Legislative History of the Uniting and Strengthening of America by Providing Appropriate Tools Required to Intercept and Obstruct Terrorism Act, Public Law no. 107-56.* New York: Fred B. Rothman, 2002.

U.S. Citizenship and Immigration Services (USCIS)

U.S. Citizenship and Immigration Services (USCIS) is the agency within the DEPARTMENT OF HOMELAND SECURITY (DHS) responsible for providing services to immigrants and nonimmigrant visitors, including immigration admission, asylum and refugee processing, naturalization proceeding, administration of special humanitarian programs, and issuance of all immigration documents. The director of the USCIS reports directly to the deputy secretary for homeland security. The agency is served by about 15,000 employees and contractors. With increased emphasis throughout the U.S. government on security issues, early initiatives of the USCIS included greater reliance on electronic biometrics, with new technology systems enabling extensive storage of fingerprints, photographs, and signature information. The agency also introduced a business model of operation in order to eliminate the backlog of approximately 3.7 million cases pending at the end of fiscal year 2003.

On November 25, 2002, the Homeland Security Act was signed by President George W. Bush, transferring functions of the IMMIGRATION AND NATURALIZATION SERVICE (INS) to the newly created DHS. The functions of the INS were then divided between the USCIS, focusing on immigration services, and the Border and Transportation Security Directorate, focusing on immigration enforcement. On March 1, 2003, the INS was formally dissolved, and the USCIS became operational.

Further Reading

Daniels, Roger. *Guarding the Golden Door: American Immigration Policy and Immigrants Since 1882.* New York: Hill and Wang, 2004.

Haynes, Wendy. "Seeing Around Corners: Crafting the New Department of Homeland Security." *Review of Policy Research* 21, no. 3 (2004): 369–395.

U.S. Immigration and Citizenship Services Web site. Available online. URL: http://uscis.gov/graphics/index.htm. Accessed July 5, 2004

U.S.-Mexican War (Mexican-American War)

By defeating Mexico in the U.S.-Mexican War (1846–48), the United States added virtually all of the present American Southwest to the Union, together with some 100,000 Mexican citizens. This annexation assured a permanent and substantial non-European population in the expanding republic and further added to the cultural diversity that marked the development of the country.

General Quitman (depicted at right) enters Mexico City with a battalion of marines, September 1847. *(National Archives/DOD, War & Conflict, #106)*

The war began as a dispute over Texas (see TEXAS, REPUBLIC OF). In 1823, after Mexico had gained its independence from Spain, it encouraged Americans to settle its sparsely populated northern province of Texas, allowing them to become Mexican citizens on condition of learning Spanish and converting to Catholicism. Many came—30,000 by the mid-1830s—but few took the conditions seriously. In 1836, the Anglo-Mexicans successfully rebelled and established the independent Republic of Texas. In 1845, the U.S. government agreed to annex the young republic but inherited a dispute over the Texas-Mexican border dating back to 1836. President James K. Polk attempted to purchase northern Mexican lands to the Pacific Ocean, including Texas but was rebuffed by Mexican authorities. Polk ordered General Zachary Taylor to occupy territory as far south as the Rio Grande, the southernmost extent of Texan claims, which precipitated a Mexican attack in May 1846. The better-armed and more professional American troops routed the Mexican army in northern Mexico, securing the region by February 1847. Polk also ordered a force under General Stephen Kearney to move against the lightly populated northwestern regions of New Mexico and California, which were secured with little loss of life. In 1847, General Winfield Scott landed an army at the Mexican port Veracruz and won a decisive victory against General Antonio López de Santa Anna at Cerro Gordo on April 18, 1847. This opened the path to Mexico City, which was subdued on September 13 with the storming of Chapultepec Castle by U.S. troops under the command of Brigadier General John Quitman.

By the Treaty of Guadalupe Hidalgo (February 2, 1848), territory making up the modern states of California, Nevada, and Utah, and parts of Arizona, New Mexico, Colorado, and Wyoming was ceded to the United States in return for $15 million. The Rio Grande was established as the southern border between the two countries. The treaty also provided that all Mexican citizens living in transferred territory could continue residence and maintain full rights of property. Within one year, they could elect to maintain Mexican citizenship; otherwise, they would automatically become U.S. citizens. Most of the inhabitants remained in the region as American citizens. Although Mexican property rights were nominally protected, a vast influx of settlers following the CALIFORNIA GOLD RUSH undermined their political power, while taxes and court costs led to the progressive selling off of land by Mexican Americans. By the 1880s, most of the large Mexican estates in the American Southwest had fallen into the hands of American landowners, and the economically diverse Mexican society that had existed there was reduced to one of largely unskilled and semi-skilled labor. New Mexico, with its majority Mexican population until the 1940s, was a partial exception to this trend. The Gadsden Purchase of 1853 completed reconciliation of the border between the two countries.

Further Reading

Bauer, Karl Jack. *The Mexican War, 1846–1848.* New York: Macmillan, 1974.

Eisenhower, John S. D. *So Far from God: The U.S. War with Mexico 1846–1848.* New York: Random House, 1989.

Griswold del Castillo, Richard. *The Treaty of Guadalupe Hidalgo: A Legacy of Conflict.* Norman: University of Oklahoma Press, 1990.

Vancouver Riot

The rising demand by industrialists for Asian labor during the first decade of the 20th century led to a dramatic increase in Japanese and Chinese immigration to British Columbia and a growing fear by residents of what was called a "yellow peril." With immigration to the province having risen from 500 in 1904 to more than 12,000 in 1908, racial tensions rapidly escalated. During 1907, with the recession and resulting unemployment, Vancouver residents were shocked to read of the decision of the Canadian Nippon Supply Company to bring over Japanese laborers for the building of the Grand Trunk Pacific Railway. Erroneous reports suggested that as many as 50,000 might become part of the latest "invasion." During a public rally organized in September 1907 by the Asiatic Exclusion League, angry and impassioned mobs marched through the city, destroying Japanese and Chinese property. This resulted in an immediate government investigation led by Deputy Minister of Labour WILLIAM MACKENZIE LYON KING, who determined that the Japanese government was not responsible for the circumstances leading to the riot, but rather Canadian immigration companies that sought laborers principally from Hawaii, rather than from Japan itself. King awarded Japanese and Chinese riot victims $9,000 and $26,000, respectively, and made several recommendations, including prohibition of contract labor and the banning of immigration by way of Hawaii. Prime Minister Wilfrid Laurier also sent Minister of Labour Rodolphe Lemieux to Japan to negotiate an agreement regarding the limitation of Japanese aliens. Despite provisions of the Anglo-Japanese Treaty of Commerce and Navigation (1894), which provided for unfettered immigration, an agreement was reached by which the Japanese government voluntarily restricted the number of passports issued to its citizens traveling directly to Canada to 400 per year. By 1908 and 1909, the number of Japanese entering the country dropped from 7,601 to 495, remaining at the latter level for the following 20 years.

Further Reading

Roy, Patricia E. *A White Man's Province: British Columbia Politicians and Japanese Immigrants, 1858–1914.* Vancouver, Canada: University of British Columbia Press, 1989.

Sugimoto, H. H. "The Vancouver Riots of 1907: A Canadian Episode." In *East across the Pacific.* Eds. F. Hilary Conroy and T. Scott Miyakawa. Santa Barbara, Calif.: CLIO, 1972.

Ward, W. Peter. *White Canada Forever.* Montreal: McGill–Queen's University Press, 1978.

Vietnamese immigration

There were virtually no Vietnamese in North America prior to the Vietnam War (1964–75). Decades of war and crises drove hundreds of thousands of them into exile, however, creating one of the largest refugee communities in North America. In the U.S. census of 2000 and the Canadian census of 2001, 1,223,736 Americans and 151,410 Canadians claimed Vietnamese descent. Vietanamese refugees were resettled widely throughout the United States; nevertheless, there are large ethnic concentrations, particularly in the greater Los Angeles area and in San Francisco, in California, and in Houston, Texas. In Canada, Toronto, Montreal, and Vancouver all have large Vietnamese populations.

Vietnam occupies 125,500 square miles in Southeast Asia on the east coast of the peninsula of Indochina. It is bordered on the north by China and on the west by Laos and Cambodia. In 2002, the population was estimated at 79,939,014. Ethnic Vietnamese compose 85–90 percent of the population and Chinese about 3 percent, though the latter figure was much higher prior to the Vietnam War. There are also small numbers of Hmong, Tai, Meo, Khmer, Man, and Cham peoples. The main religions are Buddhism, Taoism, and Roman Catholicism. Nam Viet, the first highly organized kingdom in Vietnam, emerged around 200 B.C. in the north. It was conquered by China in the first century B.C., beginning a pattern of Chinese influence in Vietnam, particularly during times of international strength. In the 10th century, Annam (northern Vietnam) regained its independence, though not without future invasions and interference from China. In 1471, Annam conquered Champa to the south, a kingdom with both Buddhist and Hindu influences. From the 11th through the 17th centuries, there was a continual struggle between the various peoples of modern Vietnam, Laos, Cambodia, Burma, and Thailand for preeminence and the definition of borders, punctuated by Chinese incursions from the north. From the 17th century on, European involvement grew. France captured Saigon in 1859 and gradually gained control of Vietnam, Laos, and Cambodia. A strong independence movement developed during the 1920s. When Vietnam was returned to French control in 1945 following World War II (1939–45), guerrilla warfare erupted, leading to French defeat and withdrawal in 1954. At the Geneva Convention of that year, the region was divided into three countries—Vietnam, Laos, and Cambodia—with Vietnam temporarily divided until elections could be held. Instead, South Vietnam declared its independence, and the Communist Democratic Republic of Vietnam was established in the north. The activities of Communist infiltrators in the south—the Viet Cong—led to U.S. intervention on behalf of an ineffective South Vietnamese government in the early 1960s as part of a COLD WAR policy to contain the spread of communism. By 1968, a half million American troops were bogged down in a war of attrition, commanding the battlefields but unable to root out the guerrillas. After prolonged negotiations, a peace accord was reached in 1973, and the United States withdrew in 1975, leading to a massive exodus on the part of those who had since the 1950s aided the French or the Americans or who feared the

Vietnamese troops in action, 1961: The protracted conflict and eventual U.S. withdrawal in 1975 left hundreds of thousands of South Vietnamese collaborators at the mercy of the new Communist government. Between 1975 and 1977, approximately 175,000 Vietnamese refugees settled in the United States. *(National Archives/DOD, War & Conflict, #403)*

imposition of a communist government. Vietnam had ongoing diplomatic and border conflicts with Cambodia and China following the Vietnam War. By the 1990s, the country's government became more liberal, allowing resumption of international travel and a gradual reintegration into the world economy. In 1995, Vietnam and the United States reestablished formal diplomatic ties.

There were virtually no Vietnamese in North America prior to the 1950s, though a few came escaping the turmoil of the French departure and civil war. The first significant migration came with the U.S. withdrawal in 1975, when about 125,000 Vietnamese were brought to the United States. These included most of the government and high-ranking military figures, and their families. It is estimated that among heads of household in this group, more than 30 percent were trained in professional or management areas, though few were prepared for the sudden transition. Six camps were established across the United States to help process and resettle the refugees. After medical examinations and interviews, each was assigned to one of nine voluntary agencies (VOLAGs) that assumed responsibility for locating sponsors who would support families for up to two years. Initially, Vietnamese families were placed throughout the United States in an attempt to distribute the financial burden across the states. The most successful resettlements, however, proved to be in southern California, where an established Asian culture base already existed, including some Southeast Asians. Gradually, the refugees migrated toward the west, creating large Vietnamese enclaves in Orange

County and Los Angeles County, California. By 1976, more than 20 percent of the refugees lived in California.

The second major wave of immigration came between 1975 and the early 1980s, when those who had not been evacuated with the help of the U.S. government took to the seas in every conceivable kind of craft, many profoundly unseaworthy. They became the "boat people." Two-thirds were attacked at sea, usually more than once, and the refugees robbed and often raped, before finally landing in Thailand, Indonesia, or Malaysia. At first, the number of fleeing refugees was small but picked up dramatically in 1979 when Vietnam went to war with both Cambodia and China. The Chinese ethnic minorities of Vietnam, about 7 percent of the population, were especially vulnerable. Of almost 250,000 boat people who arrived in the United States, about 40 percent were ethnic Chinese. Vietnamese immigration peaked in 1980 (95,200) and 1981 (86,100). Unlike the first wave, which contained many of Vietnam's best-educated people, the boat people were among the poorest and least educated of any peoples to arrive in the United States after World War II (1939–45). They were assigned to VOLAGs, but in advance of their arrival, rather than afterward. The process of concentration, clearly established by 1976, continued. By 1984, more than 40 percent of Vietnamese refugees lived in California, and by 1990, about half lived there. About 11 percent lived in Texas.

In 1979, the United Nations helped establish the Orderly Departure Program (ODP), which enabled many future Vietnamese immigrants to leave Vietnam legally. The program required potential immigrants to get approval from both the Vietnamese and U.S. governments and was designed particularly to aid former South Vietnamese soldiers and the Amerasian children, about 8,000, produced as a result of the long interaction of American troops with the native population. Eventually, about 50,000 Vietnamese came under the ODP before the program was discontinued in 1987. By the mid-1980s, the Vietnamese population in the United States was more than 650,000. Though the economy gradually improved in Vietnam, immigration to the United States remained strong, averaging about 40,000 per year between 1988 and 2002.

Roman Catholic religious students were the first Vietnamese to come to Canada. Beginning in 1950, a handful of students were given grants to study at Canadian universities. Given Vietnam's French colonial background, most preferred to attend universities in French-speaking Quebec. When France cut diplomatic ties with the government in Saigon in 1965, there was a new surge of interest in Canadian universities, leading to the development of small Vietnamese enclaves in Montreal, Quebec City, Sherbrooke, Ottawa, Moncton, and Toronto. Many stayed on as professionals after their training.

By 1974, there were about 1,500 Vietnamese in Canada, most living in Quebec. Canada played a major role in the resettlement of Vietnamese refugees, admitting more than 141,000 between 1975 and 1991. During the first Vietnamese migration after the U.S. withdrawal in 1975, Canada resettled about 5,600 refugees (1975–76). Between 1978 and 1981, about 50,000 boat people were admitted, and about 80,000 more in a continuous migration between 1982 and 1991. Almost two-thirds of the first wave, who tended to be well educated and often spoke French, settled in Quebec. After 1978, however, the refugees were more evenly distributed, with 40 percent going to Ontario, and 17 percent to Quebec. After 1991, the numbers declined somewhat. Of the 148,405 Vietnamese immigrants living in Canada in 2001, only 855 arrived before 1971 and about 41,000 between 1991 and 2001.

Further Reading

Adleman, Howard. *Canada and the Indochinese Refugees.* Regina, Canada: L. A. Weigl Educational Associates, 1982.

Dorais, Louis-Jacques. *The Cambodians, Laotians and Vietnamese in Canada.* Trans. Eileen Reardon. Ottawa: Canadian Historical Association, 2000.

Dorais, Louis-Jacques, Lise Pilon Le, and Nguyên Huy. *Exile in a Cold Land: A Vietnamese Community in Canada.* New Haven, Conn.: Yale Center for International and Area Studies, 1987.

Freeman, James A. *Hearts of Sorrow: Vietnamese-American Lives.* Stanford, Calif.: Stanford University Press, 1989.

Haines, David W., ed. *Refugees as Immigrants: Cambodians, Laotions, and Vietnamese in America.* Totowa, N.J.: Rowman and Littlefield, 1989.

Heine, Jeremy. *From Vietnam, Laos and Cambodia: A Refugee Experience in the United States.* New York: Simon and Schuster, 1995.

Hung, Nguyên Manh, and David W. Haines. "Vietnamese." In *Case Studies in Diversity: Refugees in America in the 1990s.* Eds. David W. Haines. Westport, Conn.: Praeger, 1997.

Kelly, Gail Paradise. *From Vietnam to America: A Chronicle of the Vietnamese Immigration to the United States.* Boulder, Colo.: Westview, 1977.

Liu, William T., Maryanne Lamanna, and Alice Murata. *Transition to Nowhere: Vietnamese Refugees in America.* Nashville, Tenn.: Charter House, 1979.

Nguyên, D. T., and J. S. Bandare. "Emigration Pressure and Structural Change: Vietnam." Bangkok, Thailand: UNDP Technical Support Services Report, 1996.

O'Connor, Valerie. *The Indochina Refugee Dilemma.* Baton Rouge: Louisiana State University Press, 1990.

Rumbaut, Rubén G. "A Legacy of War: Refugees from Vietnam, Laos and Cambodia." In *Origins and Destinies: Immigration, Race and Ethnicity in America.* Eds. Silvia Pedraza and Rubén G. Rumbaut. Belmont, Calif.: Wadsworth, 1996.

Rutledge, Paul James. *The Vietnamese Experience in America.* Bloomington: Indiana University Press, 1992.

Zhou, Min, and Carl Bankston. *Growing Up American: The Adaptation of Vietnamese Children to American Society.* New York: Russell Sage Foundation, 1998.

Virginia colony

Jamestown was the first permanent English settlement in the Western Hemisphere (1607) and the core of what would later become the royal colony of Virginia (1624). English entrepreneurs had become interested in the Chesapeake region in the 1570s but received little support from Queen Elizabeth I (r. 1558–1603). The failed attempts to established ROANOKE COLONY (1584–87) forestalled English efforts in the New World. By the early 17th century, an intense rivalry with Spain and development of the joint-stock company provided both the diplomatic motive and the financial means for launching a successful enterprise. On April 10, 1606, James I (r. 1603–25) granted the first Virginia charter, authorizing the London Company (soon renamed the Virginia Company) to establish settlements in the region of Chesapeake Bay. In December, the *Susan Constant,* the *Godspeed,* and the *Discovery* landed 104 men and boys whose first concern was to locate a position that could be secured from attack. Although early reports observed "faire meaddowes and goodly tall trees," Jamestown had many weaknesses as a site. Located on a marshy peninsula more than 30 miles from the mouth of the James River, it was disease-ridden, deficient in pure water, and located in territory controlled by the powerful Powhatan confederacy. Furthermore, the group consisted of many immigrants of noble birth who were searching for easy wealth: In the first year, disease, laziness, and greed nearly destroyed the colony, with only about 40 men surviving into the new year. The colony was saved only by an influx of immigrants and the discipline imposed by Captain JOHN SMITH, who gained control of the council in 1609.

A new royal charter in 1609 gave more power to the Virginia Company, which again sought colonists and investors, but military rule prevailed and conditions remained desperate until John Rolfe successfully developed a mild tobacco that appealed to Europeans. Between 1617 and 1622, settlers abandoned all other work in order to profit from the new cash crop. Sir Edwin Sandys led stock-holders in a series of reforms designed to make the colony more attractive to speculators, including establishing America's first representative assembly, the House of Burgesses (1618) and the "headright" colonizing system for distributing land, which provided 50-acre plots for those paying their own way to the New World and additional headrights if they also paid for the passage of servants.

The lure of land and tobacco worked. Between 1619 and 1622, more than 3,000 people immigrated to Virginia. Most were young, indentured Englishmen (see INDENTURED SERVITUDE), though there were significant numbers of Scots-Irish and Irish and a few Germans who had been recruited by the Virginia Company. Except for a few years of prosperity linked to high tobacco prices, however, Jamestown was a failure. By 1622, disease, contaminated water, attacks by Native Americans, and emigration had reduced the population to some 1,200, of whom only 270 were women or children, less than 8 percent of the total number of 15,000 immigrants since 1607.

In 1624, James I transformed Virginia into a royal colony, and life there gradually improved. By 1635, the population grew to 5,000. Although the Crown appointed a governor and council, settlers insisted on maintaining the House of Burgesses, which was officially recognized by Charles I (r. 1625–49) in 1639. Life in Virginia remained precarious, however, until the 1680s, with a population in flux as a result of frequent deaths, immigration, acquired freedom, and the gradual importation of slaves. Indentured servants who had gained their freedom were usually forced to the frontier and excluded from governance, grievances that led to their support of Nathaniel Bacon's rebellion in 1676. Concern over the growing number of Scots-Irish servants around 1698 led to restrictions, with only 20 allowed at any river settlement.

SLAVERY grew slowly in Virginia. The first Africans were purchased in 1619, probably as indentured servants, but by 1650, there were only 300 Africans in a population of 15,000. While slavery was practiced, it was still possible for slaves to gain freedom through manumission or conversion to Christianity. As a result, a small group of free blacks emerged in Virginia. Gradually, however, stipulations regarding lifetime service became more common in sales and court decisions. The system of perpetual slavery was strengthened with the passage of slave codes, which legalized the institution. The first codes were passed by the Virginia General Assembly in March 1661, enacted to avoid confusion over the status of children born of mixed-race relationships. Turning traditional English law on its head, the Assembly declared that the status of children should be determined by "the condition of the mother," thus ensuring that almost all biracial children would remain slaves. In 1667, the assembly determined that "the conferring of baptisme doth not alter the condition of the person as to his bondage or freedome." A 1691 law made slaveholders responsible for the costs of transporting manumitted slaves out of the colony, thus reducing the tendency to manumit. In 1705, the dozens of enactments regarding the rights and protections of slaves were combined and strengthened into a comprehensive slave code, forbidding Africans to bear arms, own property, bear witness against whites, or travel without permission. Punishment for specific crimes by maiming, whipping, branding, and execution was sanctioned. The few provisions that protected slaves were usually ignored, while those protecting planters were rigidly enforced.

Virginia was by far the most populous colony at the beginning of the 18th century. Tobacco cultivation dictated the pattern of Virginian settlement. A handful of English planters dominated politics and society from their widely dispersed plantations, with slavery as the dominant labor system. Of 80,000 Virginians in 1708, 12,000 were slaves.

According to one leading planter in 1705, Virginia still did not have any place that might "reasonably bear the Name of a Town." Colonial governors were staunchly Anglican, requiring presentation of credentials and expelling a number of Puritan ministers. In the western backcountry, a small number of Pennsylvania Germans settled alongside Scots-Irish and English freedmen. From the 1680s, lower mortality rates began to produce a stable American-born ruling class, and from this emerged the permanent patterns of 18th-century Virginian life. The College of William and Mary was established in 1693, and six years later, the capital was transferred from Jamestown to Middle Plantation, renamed Williamsburg.

Further Reading

Bailyn, Bernard. *Voyages to the West.* New York: Alfred A. Knopf, 1986.

Baseler, Marilyn C. *"Asylum for Mankind": America, 1607–1800.* Ithaca, N.Y.: Cornell University Press, 1998.

Billings, Warren M., John E. Selby, and Thad W. Tate. *Colonial Virginia: A History.* White Plains, N.Y.: Kraus International, 1986.

Breen, T. H. *Puritans and Adventurers.* New York: Oxford University Press, 1980.

———. *Tobacco Culture: The Mentality of the Great Tidewater Planters on the Eve of Revolution.* Princeton, N.J.: Princeton University Press, 1985.

Carr, Lois, et al., eds. *Colonial Chesapeake Society.* Williamsburg, Va.: North Carolina University Press, 1988.

Fischer, David. *Albion's Seed: Four British Folkways in America.* New York: Oxford University Press, 1989.

Morgan, Edmund S. *American Slavery, American Freedom: The Ordeal of Colonial Virginia.* New York: Norton, 1975.

Rutman, Darrett B., and Anita H. Rutman. *A Place in Time: Middlesex County, Virginia, 1650–1750.* New York: Norton, 1984.

Tate, Thad W., and David L. Ammerman, eds. *The Chesapeake in the Seventeenth Century: Essays on Anglo-American Society.* Chapel Hill: University of North Carolina Press, 1979.

Voting Rights Act (United States) (1965)

The Voting Rights Act, passed by the U.S. Congress and signed into law by President Lyndon B. Johnson on August 6, 1965, suspended literacy tests and nationally prohibited abridgment of the right to vote based on race or color. It also authorized the Office of the Attorney General to examine voting practices in areas where discrimination was suspected. Plans to demonstrate compliance required preclearance from the Justice Department. The act also found that poll taxes were preventing African Americans from voting, leading to a Supreme Court finding in 1966 that they were illegal. Though the measure was aimed at reversing southern discrimination against African Americans, it applied equally to all immigrants who had become naturalized citizens. As Nathan Glazer observed in *Clamor at the Gates,* the Civil Rights Act of 1964 and the Voting Rights Act of the following year went hand in hand with the nonracial IMMIGRA-TION AND NATIONALITY ACT of 1965 to represent a broadly national consensus—at least outside the South—that equality should not have a racial component (see RACISM).

Prior to World War II (1941–45), there was practically no registration of minority voters in the South. In 1940, only 3 percent of otherwise eligible black voters were registered. The federal government had been ineffectual in its haphazard attempts to undermine the disenfranchisement of blacks that was routinely being practiced in the South through the use of intimidation and various economic and literacy tests, mainly because previous Supreme Court decisions had limited congressional authority in enforcing amendments passed during the Civil War (1861–65) but also because of the strength of the southern voting bloc in the Senate. By 1957, a modest civil rights measure was passed, enabling the attorney general to seek injunctions against violation of the Fifteenth Amendment guarantee that "the right of citizens of the United States to vote shall not be denied or abridged by the United States or by any State on account of race, color, or previous condition of servitude." Beginning in the early 1960s, acts of violence, including the murder of voting-rights activists in Philadelphia, Mississippi, gained national attention. The attack by state troopers on peaceful protesters in Selma, Alabama, on March 7, 1965, convinced President Johnson that special legislation was necessary to overcome southern resistance to the implementation of equal voting rights, despite the protections already offered in the Fifteenth Amendment. According to Minnesota senator Walter Mondale, a Democrat, the "outrage" in Selma made "passage of legislation to guarantee southern Negroes the right to vote an absolute imperative for Congress."

Between 1965 and 1969, on several occasions the Supreme Court upheld the constitutionality of the preclearance requirement in Section 5, arguing that "case-by-case litigation was inadequate to combat wide-spread and persistent discrimination in voting, because of the inordinate amount of time and energy required to overcome the obstructionist tactics invariably encountered in these lawsuits."

The Voting Rights Act was amended in 1970, 1975, and 1982, further strengthening protection of voting rights. By the end of the 1960s, registration of black voters in the Deep South had increased to more than 60 percent, and an increasing number of African Americans were being elected, mainly at local and county levels.

Further Reading

Ball, Howard. "Voting Rights Act of 1965." In *The Oxford Companion to the Supreme Court of the United States.* Ed. Kermit L. Hall. New York: Oxford University Press, 1992.

Ball, Howard, Dale Krane, and Thomas P. Lauth. *Compromised Compliance: Implementation of the 1965 Voting Rights Act.* Westport, Conn.: Greenwood Press, 1982.

Garrow, David J. *Protest at Selma: Martin Luther King, Jr., and the Voting Rights Act of 1965.* New Haven, Conn.: Yale University Press, 1978.

Kousser, J. Morgan. *Colorblind Injustice: Minority Voting Rights and the Undoing of the Second Reconstruction.* Chapel Hill: University of North Carolina Press, 1999.

Lawson, Stephen. *Black Ballots: Voting Rights in the South, 1944–1969.* New York: Columbia University Press, 1976.

U.S. Department of Justice, Civil Rights Division, Voting Section. "Introduction to U.S. Voting Rights Laws." Available online. URL: http://www.usdoj.gov/crt/voting/intro/intro.htm. accessed December 30, 2003.

W

Waipahu Plantation strike

The Waipahu Plantation strike of 1906 was one of the earliest collective labor actions in the face of state intervention and sugar industry bosses. Its success demonstrated the value of collective action and laid the foundation for "blood unionism," labor unions based on ethnic identity.

Between 1850 and 1920, more than 300,000 Japanese, Chinese, Filipino, and Korean laborers were brought to Hawaii as contract laborers to raise "king sugar" for low wages on American plantations run by companies such as the Oahu Sugar Company. When the company was founded in 1897, its 943 fieldworkers earned an average of $12.50 a month. By 1900, there were more than 60,000 Japanese in the islands, the largest single ethnic group, composing about 40 percent of the population. Nevertheless, almost all supervisory positions were held by whites. In 1900, the Organic Act established Hawaii as a territory of the United States, at the same time abolishing the contract labor system, though workers sometimes had to resort to violent confrontations or strikes to win this new right. In response, in 1901, the Hawaiian Sugar Planters' Association agreed to fix wages at an artificially low level and continued to utilize loopholes to continue certain provisions of the old labor contracts. After years of heightened tensions, in 1906, 1,700 Japanese laborers struck against the Waipahu Plantation, demanding higher wages. Forty-seven armed policemen were called in to intimidate the strikers. Despite the show of force, the Japanese laborers stood firm, eventually winning concessions.

Further Reading

Coulter, John Wesley. *The Oahu Sugar Cane Plantation*. [?1933].
Moriyama, Alan T. *Imingaisha: Japanese Emigration Companies and Hawaii, 1894–1908*. Honolulu: University of Hawaii Press, 1985.
Special Review of the Main Industry of Hawaii: Sugar Industry of the Islands of Oahu, Hawaii, Maui and Kauai. Honolulu, Hawaii: Evening Bulletin, 1906.
Takaki, Ronald. *Pau Hana: Plantation Life and Labor in Hawaii, 1835–1920*. Honolulu: University of Hawaii Press, 1983.

Wakefield, Edward Gibbon (1796–1862) *author, reformer*

Edward Gibbon Wakefield was a doctrinaire and eccentric visionary, who did much to shape the British ideal of self-government in white colonies, particularly Canada, Australia, and New Zealand. Born in London, he was educated at Westminster and entered the British Foreign Service in 1814. He served three years in prison for abducting underage girls for marriage. While imprisoned, he became interested in questions of colonial development. Wakefield eventually became the most renowned proponent of systematic colonization, designed to transplant the best aspects of British society to other temperate climates around the world. In Wakefield's view, land should not be granted in large blocks or given freely to individual settlers, as these practices encouraged careless development. Instead, it should be sold to the highest bidder at a "sufficient price," and the money used to encourage the immigration of free settlers. Those who could not afford land would become laborers, who would eventually earn enough in wages to purchase their own land. Because of the concentration of capital, sound planning, and good breeding, economic growth and civilized society would grow hand in hand, making the colonies fit for "responsible government," that is, control by the local population on all purely local matters. Wakefield developed his ideas in *A Letter from Sydney* (1829) and *England and America* (1833). He accompanied John George Lambton, Lord Durham, to Canada in 1838, and significantly influenced the sections of the DURHAM REPORT (1839) relating to public lands and self-government. Though his recommendations regarding responsible government were not followed in the resulting Act of Union (1840), they were substantially implemented in 1848. Wakefield's mature program for systematic colonization was published in 1849 as *A View of the Art of Colonization in present reference to the British Empire*. Wakefield immigrated to New Zealand in 1853 and was elected to its first constitutional assembly.

Further Reading

Bloomfield, Paul. *Edward Gibbon Wakefield: Builder of the British Commonwealth*. London: Longmans, Green, 1961.

Cowan, H. I. *British Emigration to British North America: The First Hundred Years*. Toronto: University of Toronto Press, 1961.

Martin, Ged. *Edward Gibbon Wakefield: Abductor and Mystagogue*. Edinburgh, U.K.: Ann Barry, 1997.

Stuart, Peter. *Edward Gibbon Wakefield in New Zealand*. Wellington, New Zealand: Price Milburn for Victoria University, 1971.

Wald, Lillian (1867–1940) *social worker, reformer*

Lillian Wald was a pioneer in the field of public health nursing. Helping to establish the Henry Street Settlement house in New York City in 1895, she ministered to the needs of thousands of immigrants as she campaigned for progressive reforms in the United States.

Born in Cincinnati, Ohio, to German-Jewish immigrant parents who were refugees following the 1848 revolution (see REVOLUTIONS OF 1848), Wald deliberately avoided a traditional middle-class education, opting instead to enroll in the nurse training program of Manhattan's Bellevue Hospital, graduating in 1891. In 1892, she entered the Women's Medical College, where she began to teach home nursing in the tenement houses of the Lower East Side. Overwhelmed by the needs of the immigrant poor, she abandoned her formal medical career and in 1893 moved to the Lower East Side. She raised funds to purchase what became the Henry Street Settlement, which served as home to a body of nonsectarian, public health nurses who charged fees only to those who could pay. By 1914, 100 nurses were working there, and Henry Street Settlement owned nine city houses, seven vacation homes, and three stores. It also served as a community center, where Wald provided clubs, a savings bank, a health clinic, job training, and a library. She helped convince the local school board to provide school nurses, free lunches, and special assistance to the handicapped. Her opposition to World War I (1914–18) led to a decline in contributions to the Henry Street house and increasing accusations of political radicalism. Wald was a founding member of the National Association for the Advancement of Colored People, helped establish the New York State Bureau of Industries and Immigration, and served as chairman of the American Union against Militarism.

Further Reading

Carson, Mina. *Settlement Folk: The Evolution of Social Welfare Ideology in the American Settlement Movement, 1883–1930*. Chicago: University of Chicago Press, 1990.

Coss, Clare. *Lillian D. Wald: Progressive Activist*. New York: Feminist Press at the City University of New York, 1989.

Daniels, Doris Groshen. *Always a Sister: The Feminism of Lillian D. Wald*. New York: Feminist Press at the City University of New York, 1989.

Siegel, Beatrice. *Lillian Wald of Henry Street*. New York: Macmillan, 1983.

Wald, Lillian. *The House on Henry Street*. 1915. Reprint, New York: Dover, 1971.

———. *Windows on Henry Street*. Boston: Little, Brown, 1934.

War Brides Act (Act of December 28, 1945) (1945)

The War Brides Act was the first of several related measures to allow United States soldiers to bring their alien brides and families into the United States following World War II (1941–45). Originating in the U.S. House of Representatives, the Act of December 28, 1945, as the War Brides Act was officially entitled, authorized admission to the United States of alien spouses and minor children outside the ordinary quota system following World War II (see WORLD WAR II AND IMMIGRATION). In 1947, the measure was amended to include Asian spouses. The Act of June 29, 1946—commonly known as the Fiancées Act—authorized admission of fiancées for three months as nonimmigrant temporary visitors, provided they were otherwise eligible and had a bona fide intent to marry. Although provisions of the highly restrictive JOHNSON-REED ACT (1924) were still in place, these and other special postwar measures, such as the DISPLACED PERSONS ACT, played a significant role in facilitating the largest wave of immigration to the United States since the 1920s.

The War Brides Act was amended by the Act of July 22, 1947, eliminating race as a determining factor and thus allowing Chinese, Japanese, and Filipina spouses to be covered. The War Brides Act and the Fiancées Act were further amended by the Act of April 21, 1949, extending the expiration date of the original measure to September 11, 1949.

U.S. servicemen began bringing British brides home as early as 1942, but as quotas for Britain under the Johnson-Reed Act were high, these brides required no special legislation. Eventually some 115,000 British, 7,000 Chinese, 5,000 Filipina, and 800 Japanese spouses were brought to the United States, as well as about 25,000 children. About 15,000 British, 1,500 Australian, and 1,000 European fiancées were covered by the measure.

Further Reading

Hutchinson, E. P. *Legislative History of American Immigration Policy.* Philadelphia: University of Pennsylvania Press, 1981.

Lark, Regina F. "They Challenged Two Nations: Marriages between Japanese Women and American G.I.s, 1945–Present." Ph.D. dissertation, University of Southern California, 1988.

Shukert, Elfrieda, and Barbara Smith Scibetta. *War Brides of World War II.* Novato, Calif.: Presidio Press, 1988.

Virden, Jenel. *Goodbye Picadilly: British War Brides in America.* Urbana: University of Illinois Press, 1996.

Washington, D.C.

Washington, D.C., is unlike any other city in the United States. Having been established in the 1790s specifically as a new capital city for a new republic, it had no long-standing commercial base. In the 19th century, it had little of the industry that traditionally attracted immigrants. It nevertheless grew to have one of the highest immigrant populations in the country. According to the 2000 U.S. census, the Washington, D.C., metropolitan area had 832,016 foreign-born immigrants, accounting for about one of every six residents. There are particularly high concentrations of Central Americans and sub-Saharan Africans, reflecting the rapid immigrant growth of the 1990s.

The first European settlement in the district area was in Alexandria, Virginia, in 1749, but the region remained lightly populated. After the United States gained its independence from Great Britain in the American Revolution (1775–83), there was a heated political debate over the location of a new permanent capital. A compromise was reached in 1790, and the new District of Columbia founded, created from federal lands not part of any state. The complex of federal buildings, including the Capitol, was at the heart of the plan for the city laid out by the French-born American engineer Pierre Charles L'Enfant. When the government actually moved to the city in 1800, it had a population of only about 8,000. The Capitol and other government buildings were burned by the British during the War of 1812 (1812–14) but were rebuilt by the end of the decade. Early hopes that the city would become a great commercial center were never

realized, and by the time of the Civil War (1861–65), there were only about 60,000 inhabitants.

The true basis of Washington's growth proved to be war and depression, since in times of crisis the role of the federal government is greatly expanded. During the Civil War, for instance, the population doubled, to about 120,000. Another trend displayed itself then, as thousands of dispossessed migrants—freed slaves in this case—moved to the city, seeking the benefits of government and the protection of its officers. As a result, the racial and ethnic composition of the city differed greatly from other major U.S. cities. By 1900, Washington's foreign-born population was only 7 percent, compared to New York City's 37 percent and Boston and Chicago's 35 percent. At the same time, its African-American population was 31 percent, much higher than the 2 percent in New York, Boston, and Chicago.

The next great period of city growth was during World War I (1914–18), when the population rose from 350,000 to 450,000 almost wholly due to internal migration. Again, during the Great Depression of the 1930s, more jobs could be found in Washington than anywhere else, mainly because of federal projects. Between 1930 and 1940, the city's population grew from 485,000 to 665,000, with the percentage of foreign born actually shrinking to 5 percent. During World War II (1941–45), the city's population grew rapidly and peaked at more than 800,000 in 1950. During the next half century, the population declined, to 572,000 in 2000, as the suburban and metropolitan areas have grown. In 2000, the greater D.C. area, including the Virginia and Maryland suburbs, had a population of more than 3.9 million, and the larger metropolitan area, including BALTIMORE, MARYLAND, had a population of 7.6 million.

Few cities in the United States were affected more than Washington, D.C. by passage of the IMMIGRATION AND NATIONALITY ACT of 1965. The immigrant share of the population has grown dramatically since then, with most coming from Asia and Central America. In 1965, less than 5 percent of the population was foreign born; in 2000, it was more than triple that amount, the exact percentage varying according to city, county, or metropolitan basis. Between 1983 and 1996, more than 300,000 immigrants moved to the metropolitan area. Although they came from more than 100 countries, about half emigrated from El Salvador, Vietnam, South Korea, India, Pakistan, the Philippines, China, Iran, Ethiopia, and Jamaica. About 48 percent of the metro area immigrant population arrived since 1990, with El Salvador topping the list of immigrant source countries in both 1990 and 2000 (9,276 and 15,886, respectively). The District of Columbia also permanently resettled more than 3,000 refugees from all parts of the world between 1996 and 2001. The share of foreign students also continues to increase. In 1999, more than 8,000 foreign students attended the area's universities, with the largest number at George Washington (2,226), American University (1,711), Georgetown University (1,589), and Howard University (1,172).

Further Reading

"At Home in the Nation's Capital: Immigrant Trends in Metropolitan Washington." Washington, D.C.: Brookings Institution, 2003.

Bennett, L. A. *Personal Choice in Ethnic Identity: Serbs, Croats, and Slovenes in Washington, D.C.* Palo Alto, Calif.: Ragusan Press, 1978.

Cary, Francine Curro, ed. *Urban Odyssey: A Multicultural History of Washington, D.C.* Washington, D.C.: Smithsonian Institution Press, 1996.

Diner, Hasia, and Steven Diner. *Fifty Years of Jewish Self-Governance: The Jewish Community of Greater Washington, 1938–1988.* Washington, D.C.: The Council, 1989.

Keck, L. "Egyptian Americans in the Washington, D.C., Area." *Arab Studies Quarterly* 11, nos. 2–3 (1985): 103–126.

Repak, Terry A. *Waiting on Washington: Central American Workers in the Nation's Capital.* Philadelphia: Temple University Press, 1995.

Sheridan, Mary Beth. "Regions's Immigrants Faring Better than Others." *Washington Post,* June 12, 2003, p. A1.

Welfare Reform Act (Personal Responsibility and Work Opportunity Reconciliation Act)
(United States) (1996)

More formally the Personal Responsibility and Work Opportunity Reconciliation Act, the Welfare Reform Act reflected the anti-immigrant mood of the 1990s and frustration over the mounting costs of providing social services to both citizens and immigrants. U.S. president Bill Clinton angered liberal members of his own Democratic Party by signing the measure on August 22, 1996, in a move aimed at strengthening his conservative support for the November 1996 presidential election.

The major feature of the measure was to replace Aid to Families with Dependent Children (AFDC) with a new program, Temporary Assistance for Needy Families (TANF), which limited aid to two consecutive years and five years over a lifetime. More specifically, regarding immigrants, it denied cash welfare, food stamps, Medicaid, and Supplemental Security Income to legal immigrants, though it did provide reimbursement to states for emergency services rendered. In 1998, under pressure from immigrant advocacy groups, Congress restored food stamp benefits to 250,000 of 935,000 immigrants who had been declared ineligible to receive them.

Further Reading

Espenshade, T. J., J. L. Baraka, and G. A. Huber. "Implications of the 1996 Welfare and Immigration Reform Acts for U.S. Immigration." *Population and Development Review* 23, no. 4 (1997): 769–801.

West Indian immigration

West Indians are of mixed racial and ethnic background. Immigrants to North America from the region are predominantly mulattoes or blacks, the descendants of African slaves brought to work on Caribbean plantations for the English, French, Spanish, and Dutch during the 17th, 18th, and 19th centuries. Some, however, are of European descent, a significant number of Asian Indian background—particularly those from Trinidad (see TRINIDADIAN AND TOBAGONIAN IMMIGRATION) and Guyana—and a small number of Chinese descent. Prior to the 1960s, both the United States and Canada treated immigrants from Caribbean Basin dependencies and countries, in various combinations, as a single immigrant unit known as "West Indians." Due to the shifting political status of territories within the region during the period of decolonization (1958–83) and special international circumstances in some areas, the concept of what it meant to be West Indian shifted across time, thus making it impossible to say with certainty how many immigrants came from each island or region. Before 1965, however, Jamaican immigrants (see JAMAICAN IMMIGRATION) clearly predominated, and English-speaking immigrants generally far outstripped others. West Indians in both the United States and Canada tended to be well educated, often filling skilled and professional positions and enjoying greater economic success than other Americans of African descent. Their political influence, particularly in the United States, was proportionally far greater than their numbers would suggest. These factors led to considerable tension between West Indians and African Americans that eased somewhat in the 1990s.

In the narrowest sense, the term *West Indies* refers to the English-speaking territories of the western Atlantic and Caribbean Basin, including Jamaica, the Bahamas, Bermuda, the Leeward Islands (St. Kitts, Nevis, Antigua, Montserrat, British Virgin Islands), the Windward Islands, (St. Vincent, St. Lucia, Dominica, Grenada), Barbados, Trinidad, Tobago, Belize, and Guyana. While these were all still British dependencies, they could be treated more or less as a single unit. More broadly, *West Indies* sometimes includes territories settled by the Dutch (Netherlands Antilles, Aruba), French (Guadeloupe, Martinique, Haiti) and Spanish (Dominican Republic, Puerto Rico). Finally, in the broadest use of the term, *West Indies* was sometimes used to refer to all countries in the Caribbean Basin, including Cuba and the Latin American countries of Central America. Although each West Indian region is culturally distinct, shared use of the English language and Caribbean heritage led immigrants from many different English culture areas to congregate once they arrived in the United States. Frequently immigrants from French and Dutch territories settled in anglophone West Indian neighborhoods. Dominicans (see DOMINICAN IMMIGRATION), on the other hand, more closely followed the settlement patterns of Cubans (see CUBAN IMMIGRATION) and Puerto Ricans (see PUERTO

RICAN IMMIGRATION), whose immigrant status was closely tied to COLD WAR considerations.

West Indians did not begin to migrate to North America in significant numbers until the early 20th century. Between 1900 and 1924, about 100,000 West Indians immigrated to the United States, many of them from the middle classes. The restrictive JOHNSON-REED ACT (1924) and the economic depression of the 1930s virtually halted their immigration, but some 40,000 had already established a cultural base in New York City, particularly in Harlem and Brooklyn. About 41,000 West Indians were recruited for war work after 1941, but most returned to their homes after the war. Isolationist policies of the 1950s and relatively open access to Britain kept immigration to the United States low until passage of the IMMIGRATION AND NATIONALITY ACT of 1965, which shifted the basis of immigration from country of origin to family reunification. The MCCARRAN-WALTER IMMIGRATION AND NATURALIZATION ACT of 1952 had established an annual quota of only 800 for all British territories in the West Indies, but as dependencies became independent of colonial ties with European states (Trinidad and Tobago and Jamaica in 1962, Barbados and Guyana in 1966, the Bahamas in 1973, Grenada in 1974, Dominica in 1978, Saint Lucia and St. Vincent and the Grenadines in 1979, Antigua and Barbuda and Belize in 1981; and St. Kitts and Nevis in 1983), they generally qualified for increased immigration.

West Indian immigration to Canada remained small throughout the 20th century. Following the restrictive legislation of 1923, it is estimated that only 250 West Indians were admitted during the entire decade of the 1920s. By the mid-1960s, only 25,000 West Indians lived there. Canadian regulations after World War II (1939–45) prohibited most black immigration, and special programs, such as the 1955 domestic workers campaign, allowed only a few hundred well-qualified West Indians into the country each year until 1967, when the points system was introduced for determining immigrant qualifications.

See also BARBADIAN IMMIGRATION; HAITIAN IMMIGRATION.

Further Reading

Bristow, Peggy, et al., eds. *"We're Rooted Here and They Can't Pull Us Up": Essays in African Canadian Women's History.* Toronto: University of Toronto Press, 1994.

Calliste, Agnes. "Canada's Immigration Policy and Domestics from the Caribbean: The Second Domestic Scheme." In *Race, Class, Gender: Bonds and Barriers. Socialist Studies: A Canadian Annual.* Vol. 5. Ed. Jesse Vorst. Toronto: Between the Lines, 1989.

———. "Women of 'Exceptional Merit': Immigration of Caribbean Nurses to Canada." *Canadian Journal of Women and the Law* 6 (1993): 85–99.

Gmelch, G. *Double Passage: The Lives of Caribbean Migrants Abroad and Back Home.* Ann Arbor: University of Michigan Press, 1992.

Kasinitz, Philip. *Caribbean New York: Black Immigrants and the Politics of Race.* Ithaca, N.Y.: Cornell University Press, 1992.

Levine, Barry, ed. *The Caribbean Exodus.* New York: Praeger, 1987.

Owens-Watkins, Irma. *Blood Relations.* Bloomington: University of Indiana Press, 1996.

Palmer, R. W. *Pilgrims from the Sun: West Indian Migration to America.* New York: Twayne, 1995.

Richardson, Bonham. *Caribbean Migration.* Knoxville: University of Tennessee Press, 1983.

Tennyson, Brian Douglas. *Canada and the Commonwealth Caribbean.* Lanham, Md.: University Press of America, 1988.

Walker, James W. St.-G. *The West Indians in Canada.* Ottawa: Canadian Historical Association, 1984.

Westmoreland, Guy T. Jr., *West Indian Americans.* Westport, Conn.: Greenwood Press, 2001.

Winks, Robin. *Canadian–West Indian Union: A Forty-Year Minuet.* London: Athlone Press, 1968.

White Slave Traffic Act   See MANN ACT.

Winnipeg general strike

Post–World War I (1914–18) ethnic tensions, economic conditions, and the fear of bolshevism all contributed to the Winnipeg general strike of May 15 to June 28, 1919. Although the strike was primarily about labor issues and enjoyed widespread support from Anglo-Canadian workers and recently returned veterans, it was portrayed by city leaders as the first step in a wave of foreign bolshevism.

Winnipeg was clearly divided between Anglo-Saxon white-collar workers in the south and west of the city and continental laborers in the north. In March 1919, the One

This photo shows Immigration Hall, Winnipeg, Manitoba, ca. 1900. Winnipeg's population grew more than 200 percent during the first decade of the 20th century, largely as a result of immigration. The Red Scare in the wake of the Bolshevik Revolution in Russia and economic hard times led to a general strike in 1919. *(National Archives of Canada/PA-122676)*

Big Union (OBU) was formed with the goal of worker control over primary industries. Foreign mine workers were especially vocal, with most chapters of the United Mine Workers of America joining the OBU. Socialist activities were on the rise throughout western Canada and were being carefully monitored by the government. The great influenza epidemic of 1918–19 hit the immigrant community of Winnipeg particularly hard, thus further heightening tensions.

After the breakdown of labor negotiations between management and the Metal Trades Council, the Winnipeg Trades and Labor Council called a general strike for May 15. More than 30,000 workers responded. Anglo-Canadian laborers were caught in the middle of a conflict between the Anglo-Canadian business community, which was determined to preserve a "Canadian" way of life on the prairie, and the demands of those who were seeking concessions for workers. As sympathy strikes were called in other western cities, the OBU attempted to create a national movement. As rumors of a national rail strike spread, the dominion government intervened and invoked a strict interpretation of Article 41 of the Immigration Act, which enabled them to deport "anarchists and Bolsheviks" or anyone teaching "unlawful destruction of property." Eventually more than 100 deportations were authorized, though not all were carried out. Of the 10 strike leaders in Winnipeg, six were Anglo-Canadian. Following the strike, the criminal code was amended, broadening the definition of sedition, raising penalties from two to a maximum of 20 years, and outlawing any institution that advocated the use of force to bring about political or economic change.

See also LABOR ORGANIZATION AND IMMIGRATION; TERRORISM AND IMMIGRATION.

Further Reading
Avery, Donald. *"Dangerous Foreigners": European Immigrant Workers and Labor Radicalism in Canada, 1896–1932.* Toronto: McClelland and Stewart, 1979.
Bercuson, David. *Confrontation at Winnipeg: Labour, Industrial Relations, and the General Strike.* Montreal: McGill–Queen's University Press, 1947.
———. *Fools and Wise Men: The Rise and Fall of the One Big Union.* Scarborough, Canada: McGraw-Hill Ryerson, 1978.
Bumsted, J. M. "1919: The Winnipeg General Strike Reconsidered." *The Beaver* (June/July 1994): 27–44.
———. *The Winnipeg General Strike of 1919: An Illustrated History.* Winnipeg: Watson and Dwyer, 1994.
McCormack, A. Ross. *Reformers, Rebels, and Revolutionaries: The Western Canadian Radical Movement, 1899–1919.* Toronto: University of Toronto Press, 1977.

Winthrop, John (1588–1649) *political and religious leader*
As Puritan leader and first governor of Massachusetts Bay (see MASSACHUSETTS COLONY), John Winthrop played a

John Winthrop was elected governor of the Massachusetts Bay colony 12 times following its establishment in 1630. He helped establish a sense of mission in early English settlers, encouraging them to develop model communities that others might look upon favorably as a moral example. *(Library of Congress, Prints & Photographs Division [LC-USZ62-9442])*

fundamental role in establishing both the Puritan cultural ethos that characterized the leading English colonists in America and England's actual political control of the Atlantic seaboard. In less than two decades, the Great Migration that he led transformed New England from a New World wilderness to a thriving outpost of English settlement.

Born in 1588 in Suffolk, England, to a prosperous landowner, Winthrop as a young man adopted strong Puritan views. He studied law at Gray's Inn and in 1617 was appointed justice of the peace in Suffolk. During the 1620s he developed a thriving law practice in London. In 1629, Winthrop lost his lucrative position as attorney in the royal Court of Wards and Liveries, as Charles I (r. 1625–49) began to remove Puritan influence from the government. Concern over England's growing anti-Puritanism, moral laxity, and weak economy led Winthrop to join with substantial merchants and landowners of the Massachusetts Bay Company. Agreeing to organize the migration to America, he was elected governor of the colony. He set off for North America in 1630 along with 400 other Puritans. Within the first year, 70 percent of the settlers had either died or returned to England. By the following year, however, the colony was firmly established under Winthrop's leadership, and he served intermittently as governor throughout his life (1630–33, 1637–39, 1642, 1646–48). At the time of his death, there were 15,000 inhabitants of the colony.

Winthrop was stern and single-minded but not an extremist. His vision for the new colony had been laid out in a sermon on shipboard during the initial voyage from England, when he argued for creation of a model community, or "city upon a hill," a people in covenant with God, with full citizenship reserved for members of a reformed Church of England (later known as the Congregational Church). Careful to guard the colony against theological error, he led the Massachusetts Bay colony to banish Anne Hutchison, Roger Williams, and John Wheelwright, among others. His son, John, became governor of the CONNECTICUT COLONY.

Further Reading

Bremer, Francis J. *John Winthrop: America's Forgotten Founding Father.* New York: Oxford University Press, 2003.
Gomes, Peter J. "A Pilgrim's Progress." *New York Times Magazine,* (April 18, 1999), pp. 102–103.
Morgan, Edmund S. *The Puritan Dilemma: The Story of John Winthrop.* Boston: Little, Brown, 1958.
Winthrop, John. *The Journal of John Winthrop, 1630–1649.* Abridged ed. Ed. Richard S. Dunn and Laetitia Yeandle. Cambridge, Mass.: Belknap Press, 1997.

World War I and immigration

The outbreak of World War I in 1914 was seen by most Americans and many Canadians as a distinctly European problem. Canada was tied to Britain, both in governance and in broad sentiment, but the United States attempted to shield itself from the influences that had helped create the war. Most important, it hoped to keep out dangerous radicals and communists who might poison the minds of millions of Europeans already in North America who had come from lands now at war. World War I ushered in an age of xenophobia and of tighter restrictions on immigration that would last, in some measure, into the 1960s.

The Great War, as it came to be called before World War II, developed from a seemingly localized struggle between the Austro-Hungarian Empire and Serbia, both bent on expansion in the Balkan Peninsula of Europe. The assassination of Austrian archduke Francis Ferdinand by Serbian nationalists in June 1914 was the culmination of a long period of international tension that began with France's defeat at the hands of Germany in the Franco-Prussian War of 1870–71. From that event developed a growing militarization of Europe and the formation of alliance systems that made it difficult to solve problems such as Francis Ferdinand's assassination by diplomatic means. Just as important in the coming of war was the intense nationalistic impulse

that had motivated much of European politics since the REVOLUTIONS OF 1848. By the second decade of the 20th century, it was impossible for autocratic rulers of multi-ethnic states to quietly quell nationalistic movements.

Throughout eastern and southern Europe after 1880, Poles, Ukrainians, Greeks, Germans, Hungarians, Czechs, Slovaks, Slovenes, Jews, and dozens of other ethnic groups were fleeing repressive regimes in Russia, Austria-Hungary, Germany, and the Ottoman Empire, seeking both economic opportunities and personal freedoms in North America. Millions of others came from Britain, Scandinavia, Italy, and other parts of Europe. With very few restrictions on European immigration to the United States and a booming economy, immigration reached all-time highs in the decade prior to the Great War. Whereas immigration had averaged about 340,000 per year during the 1890s, between 1905 and 1914, it jumped to more than 1 million per year. Although Canadian policy was more restrictive, the trend was the same. During the 1890s, immigration to Canada averaged about 37,000 per year; between 1905 and 1914, the figure rocketed to almost 250,000 per year. Thus, when war broke out, there were millions of people in both the United States and Canada who had close personal ties with countries on both sides of the conflict. This provided a powerful impulse for politicians to stay out of the war.

Following the assassination of Francis Ferdinand, Germany backed without reservation Austria-Hungary's extreme threats against Serbia—the so-called blank check. Russia mobilized troops in support of Serbia, leading to an Austrian declaration of war. Germany, fearing a two-front war, invaded France by way of Belgium, violating neutrality agreements signed with Britain and France in the 1830s. By the end of August, Britain, France, and Russia—the Allied Powers—were arrayed against Germany, Austria-Hungary, Bulgaria, and the Ottoman Empire—the Central Powers. Italy, long an ally of Germany and Austria, joined the Allied Powers in 1915. The war that many predicted would be over by Christmas soon ground to a standstill, as defensive technologies kept millions of men on both sides in hundreds of miles of trenches throughout the war.

Although U.S. president Woodrow Wilson deeply admired the British and their parliamentary system of government, he publicly urged Americans to remain "impartial in thought as well as in action." Most Americans agreed. The United States generally had remained neutral in international diplomacy. In addition, many progressives believed that war would detract from pursuit of domestic reforms that were greatly needed. Finally, most Americans, despite their sympathies, realized that there were simply too many divided loyalties for the country to take sides over issues that seemed so remote from the country's interests. Although the clear majority of Americans were of British, Scandinavian, or Italian stock, more than 2.3 million Germans and 1.5 million Irish had immigrated since 1880, and most generally opposed siding with the Allied powers. However, when the *Lusitania* was torpedoed by a German submarine on May 7, 1915, with the loss of 1,198 lives, including 139 Americans, Wilson and the public generally turned against the Central Powers For the duration of the war, the American public was bombarded with anti-German propaganda, produced both by the British government and the U.S. government's Committee on Public Information. "One hundred percent Americanism" was promoted, German language courses were discontinued, and German Americans were frequently harassed and sometimes forced to publicly express their patriotism. Immigrants from Austria-Hungary were suspect as sympathizers or as radicals or labor activists, despite the fact that many had emigrated to flee the Austrian Crown, and most supported the right of self-determination. People were unsure of Polish, Ukrainian, and Russian loyalties and feared the importation of radical communist doctrines. There was even a heightened effort to discourage the customs and traditions of Mexican laborers in the American Southwest.

The resumption of German submarine warfare in February 1917 finally brought the United States into the war, with Woodrow Wilson promoting his Fourteen Points, emphasizing the establishment of an international peace-keeping body (the League of Nations) and a major role for the United States in reshaping the Old World. Although war was declared in April 1917, American troops did not play a large part in the fighting until January 1918. The war ended on November 11, 1918; nevertheless 115,000 U.S. soldiers died, and almost twice that many were wounded. Though these figures paled in comparison to European losses, Americans tended to blame a corrupt and outdated European system that had little in common with the democratic values of America. This view was only heightened by the success of the Bolshevik Revolution in Russia in October 1917 and Russia's subsequent withdrawal from the war in March 1918. The small Socialist Party in the United States was dominated by immigrants, who were increasingly suspected of internal subversion. Finally, the widespread labor unrest of 1919 was inextricably linked to immigrant influence, consolidating the Red Scare in America. Although the move to round up and deport suspected radicals quickly ran its course by 1920, Americans were in no mood for international ventures of any kind. Congress refused to ratify the Treaty of Versailles (1919), which would have required joining the new League of Nations.

Even as the United States was entering World War I in 1917, there had been substantial concern about the "dumping" of dangerous and poor immigrant refugees from Europe. When the IMMIGRATION ACT of 1917, which had instituted an immigrant literacy test, failed to keep hundreds of thousands of Europeans from immigrating after the war, support for an ethnic quota grew. For the first time, many within the business community supported such restrictive legislation, convinced that immigrants from Canada, Mexico, and the West Indies had significantly lessened the need for potentially radicalized European labor. In order to ensure that Bolsheviks, anarchists, Jews, and other "undesirables" were kept to a minimum, the EMERGENCY QUOTA ACT set the number of immigrants from each national origin group at 3 percent of the foreign-born population of that country in 1910, a period when immigration from England, Ireland, Scotland, and Scandinavia had been particularly high. The measure limited immigration to 357,800 annually from the Eastern Hemisphere, with more than half the number reserved for immigrants from northern and western Europe. The even more restrictive JOHNSON-REED ACT of 1924 made the quotas permanent, though at reduced levels. The measure established an overall annual quota of 153,700, allotted according to a formula based on 2 percent of the population of each nation of origin according to the census of 1890. Countries most favored according to this formula were Great Britain (43 percent), Germany (17 percent), and Ireland (12 percent). Countries whose immigration had increased dramatically after 1890—including Italy, Poland, Russia, and Greece—had their quotas drastically slashed.

English-speaking Canadians were initially more enthusiastic for the war, though the francophone population and large Irish and German populations were not. The outbreak of World War I forced Canada to devise a policy for dealing with resident enemy aliens. Among the Canadian population, more than 500,000 people were in some way linked to the Central Powers, including about 400,000 of German origin, 129,103 from the Austro-Hungarian Empire, almost 4,000 from the Ottoman Empire, and several thousand from Bulgaria. Despite the fact that only about 20,000 Germans and 60,000 Ukrainians were yet to be naturalized, most fell under suspicion. The resulting War Measures Act of August 1914 enabled the governor in council to authorize any orders or regulations deemed "necessary or advisable for the security, defence, order and welfare of Canada." Enemy aliens were prohibited from possessing weapons and were eventually required to register with the police and military. Of more than 80,000 who were registered, 8,579 were interned in 24 camps across Canada. As in the case of the United States, most East Europeans were suspect, especially Ukrainians, who were viewed as the main supporters of bolshevism in Canada. Further stressing the patriotic requirement, in 1917, the Wartime Elections Act enfranchised women whose husbands, sons, or brothers were in active service, while disenfranchising everyone from enemy countries who had becomes citizens since 1902.

As Canada slipped into depression between 1919 and 1922, it too developed more restrictive immigration legislation. Under Section 3 of the IMMIGRATION ACT of 1919, an order-in-council excluded immigrants from countries that had fought against Canada during the war. The list of inadmissible immigrants was expanded to include alcoholics, those of "psychopathic inferiority," mental defectives, illiterates, those guilty of espionage, and those who believed in the forcible overthrow of the government or who "disbelieved" in government at all. At the same time, revisions made it easier to deport immigrants. Immigrants who could be shown to have fallen into an inadmissible class when they arrived in Canada were no longer safe from deportation after five years. The cabinet was also authorized to prohibit entry to any race, class, or nationality because of contemporary economic conditions or because they were not likely to be assimilable because of "peculiar habits, modes of life and methods of holding property," a provision invoked against entry of Hutterites (see HUTTERITE IMMIGRATION), Mennonites (see MENNONITE IMMIGRATION), and Doukhobors. Additionally, in 1921, adult immigrants were required to have $250 upon landing, and children, $125. Farm laborers and domestic workers with previous job arrangements were exempted from the landing fees. In 1923, immigration was restricted to agriculturalists, farm laborers, and domestic servants. The revisions were also supported by the business community, which had previously supported a more liberal policy. According to the president of the Canadian Manufacturers' Association, while it was true that Canada had millions of "vacant acres" that needed population, "it is wiser to go slowly and secure the right sort of citizens."

The Canadian government rewarded returning soldiers with grants of land, but there was a high rate of failure. As a result, by the mid-1920s, the Canadian government was again seeking agriculturalists from Europe to develop Canada's agricultural lands. The first choice was to grant land to British families. Under the EMPIRE SETTLEMENT ACT, British farmers with 25 pounds of capital upon arrival could get loans and other forms of assistance. The program eventually brought more than 100,000 British immigrants, though many of them went into other lines of work. At the same time, almost half a million Canadians immigrated to the United States between 1925 and 1932.

With the end of depression by 1923, Canada turned its attention to refugee groups still languishing in Europe, especially if they were considered helpful to Canada's economic recovery. Mennonites, who had been excluded by the orders-in-council in 1919, were once again invited in 1923. Under the provisions of the Railway Agreement of 1924, which authorized the Canadian Pacific Railway and the Canadian National Railway to recruit agriculturalists for the development of the prairies, about 185,000 central Europeans came to Canada, about half of them German speakers. Among the earliest to arrive were German-speaking Russian Mennonites, who had been doubly branded during the war as enemy sympathizers and pacifists unwilling to share the nation's burden. Between 1923 and 1930, about 20,000 settled in Canada. About 3,100 Jews were admitted by 1924, though thousands more were excluded for fear that they were tainted by communism. About 1,300 Armenians were admitted in the early 1920s, but the government practiced an essentially exclusionary policy that refused entry to most Armenians.

Further Reading

Avery, Donald. *"Dangerous Foreigners": European Immigrant Workers and Labour Radicalism in Canada, 1896–1932.* Toronto: McClelland and Stewart, 1979.

Ellis, Mark, and Panikos Panayi. "German Minorities in World War I: A Comparative Study of Britain and the USA." *Ethnic and Racial Studies* 17 (1994): 238–259.

Fernandez, Ronald. "Getting Germans to Fight Germans: The Americanizers of World War I." *Journal of Ethnic Studies* 9 (1981): 53–68.

Hoyt, Edwin P. *The Palmer Raids, 1919–1920: An Attempt to Suppress Dissent.* New York: Seabury Press, 1969.

Hutchinson, E. P. *Legislative History of American Immigration Policy, 1798–1965.* Philadelphia: University of Pennsylvania Press, 1981.

LeMay, Michael C. *From Open Door to Dutch Door: An Analysis of U.S. Immigration Policy since 1820.* New York: Praeger, 1987.

Luebke, Frederick. *Bonds of Loyalty: German Americans and World War I.* DeKalb: Northern Illinois University Press, 1974.

McCormack, A. Ross. *Reformers, Rebels, and Revolutionaries: The Western Canadian Radical Movement, 1899–1919.* Toronto: University of Toronto Press, 1977.

Murphy, Paul. *World War I and the Origins of Civil Liberties in the United States.* New York: Norton, 1979.

Nagler, Joerg A. "Enemy Aliens and Internment in World War I: Alvo von Alvensleben in Fort Douglas, Utah, a Case Study." *Utah Historical Quarterly* 58 (1990): 388–405.

Preston, William, Jr. *Aliens and Dissenters: Federal Suppression of Radicals.* 2d ed. Urbana: University of Illinois Press, 1995.

Swyripa, Frances, and John Herd Thompson, eds. *Loyalties in Conflict: Ukrainians in Canada during the Great War.* Edmonton: Canadian Institue of Ukrainian Studies, University of Alberta, 1983.

Thompson, John Herd. *Ethnic Minorities during Two World Wars.* Ottawa: Canadian Historical Association, 1991.

———. *The Harvest of War: The Prairie West, 1914–1918.* Toronto: McClelland and Stewart, 1978.

World War II and immigration

The cataclysm of World War II (1937–45) had a profound effect on immigration to North America. With restrictive immigration policies in place by the 1920s, interwar immigration to the United States and Canada had been dramatically curtailed from the peak years just before World War I (1914–18; see WORLD WAR I AND IMMIGRATION). The exigencies of war dropped the numbers further still. The United States admitted almost 1.3 million immigrants in 1907, 50,000 in 1937 when war broke out in China, and less than 24,000 in 1943. Canada's peak year had been 1913, when almost 400,000 immigrants landed; immigration in 1937 dropped to about 12,000 and further down to 7,445 in the trough year of 1943. But war also changed people's attitudes toward immigrants and those who might become immigrants and presented enormous challenges to current policies. First raised were security questions regarding potential enemies: What should be done with the millions of Japanese, Germans, and Italians living in North America? Also, with millions of men and women serving abroad, labor needs had to be met at home, and provision had to be made for foreign families acquired while overseas. Finally, there were humanitarian questions regarding the protection of children threatened by war and the eventual resettlement of refugees and other persons displaced by the war. As a result of these challenges, a number of important exceptions were made to the various immigration restrictions in the United States and Canada. Anti-Catholicism and anti-Semitism declined in the United States, and there was a generally less hostile attitude toward nonfounding ethnic groups throughout North America. Though major new immigration legislation was not passed, changing attitudes as a result of the war did pave the way for more far-reaching legislative changes in the future.

Militarism, nationalism, and ethnocentrism or racism, including anti-semitism, had been common features of political life among the totalitarian governments of Italy, Germany, and Japan during the 1930s. The first stage of World War II began when Japan, under Emperor Hirohito, invaded China on July 7, 1937. The war expanded when Germany, under the Nazi leader Adolf Hitler, invaded Poland on September 1, 1939, bringing Britain and France into the conflict. By June 1940, Nazi Germany had conquered or neutralized all of central, northern, and western Europe. Germany failed in its attempt to invade Great Britain in 1940, but gradually fortified the entire Atlantic coastline, further consolidating its control. In June 1941, Germany invaded the Soviet Union, seeking new sources of oil and other raw materials and gaining direct control over the majority of Europe's Jews. Finally, the Japanese bombing of the U.S. naval base at Pearl Harbor in Hawaii on December 7, 1941, brought the United States into a conflict that would last another three-and-a-half years, pitting the Axis powers of Germany, Italy, and Japan against the major Allied powers of the United States, Great Britain, the Soviet Union, and China. By the end of the war in early September 1945, almost 16 million Americans and more than 1 million Canadians had served in the military in every part of the world. U.S. deaths totaled more than 400,000; Canadian deaths, 45,000. The devastation in the main theaters of combat was even greater. The military death tolls were staggering: Soviet Union, 7.5 million; Germany, 3.5 million; China, 2.2 million; Japan, 1.2 million; Great Britain, Austria, Poland, and Romania more than 300,000 each. By the end of the war, more than 20 million people had been displaced from their homes in Europe, and millions more in Asia.

With Britain at war from 1939, charitable organizations almost immediately petitioned the Canadian government to provide asylum for child refugees, including Jews living in Britain, France, Switzerland, Spain, and Portugal. The ruthless Nazi bombing of civilian populations in Britain led to widespread sympathy for the resettlement of British children, and more than 50,000 Canadians offered to host GUEST CHILDREN and mothers until the end of the war. Despite the fact that Canadian Jews were prepared to host the previously approved Jewish children, the government refused to include them in the evacuation plan, fearing that it would lead to immigration of their families following the war. The Canadian government approved a plan to host up to 10,000 British children, with Britain responsible for screening and transportation costs, Canadian provincial agencies and relief organizations responsible for placement, and private citizens responsible for daily care. After the sinking of the SS *City of Benares* on September 14, 1940, and the resulting deaths of 73 children, the program was discontinued. Altogether more than 4,500 children and 1,000 mothers were allowed to immigrate; virtually all were non-Jewish Britons.

With the bombing of Pearl Harbor in December 1941, the war was brought to the doorstep of the United States. In response to the outbreak of war in Europe in 1939, the U.S. Congress had already passed the Alien Registration Act (1940), requiring all non-naturalized aliens 14 and older to register with the government and tightening naturalization requirements. With the declaration of war against Germany, Italy, and Japan following the attack on Pearl Harbor, more than 1 million foreign-born immigrants from those countries became "enemy aliens." Although Italians and Germans were at first suspect, most were so deeply assimilated into American culture, living in local communities with long traditions, that they were largely left alone. More visibly distinct and ethnically related to the attackers, Japanese immigrants and Americans of Japanese descent were quickly targeted in the early war hysteria. Japanese Americans and Japanese Canadians were widely suspected as supporters of the aggressive militarism of the Japanese Empire. The territory of Hawaii was put under military rule, and the 37 percent of its population of Japanese ancestry was carefully watched. On the mainland, many politicians and members of the press, along with agricultural and patriotic pressure groups, urged action against the Japanese. Despite the absence of any evidence of sabotage or spying and the testimony of many that they posed no threat, on February 19, 1942, President Franklin D. Roosevelt signed Executive Order 9066, which led to the forcible internment of 120,000 Japanese Americans, two-thirds of whom were born in the United States (see JAPANESE INTERNMENT, WORLD WAR II). In the same month, the Canadian government ordered the expulsion of 22,000 Japanese Canadians from a 100-mile strip along the Pacific coast.

Japanese Americans were forced to dispose of their property quickly, usually at considerable loss. Most nisei, or second-generation Japanese, thought of themselves as thoroughly American and felt betrayed by the justice system. They nevertheless remained loyal to the country, and eventually more than 33,000 served in the armed forces during World War II. Among these were some 18,000 members of the 442nd Regimental Combat Team, which became one of the most highly decorated of the war. Throughout the war, about 120,000 Japanese Americans were interned under the War Relocation Authority in one of 10 hastily constructed camps in desert or rural areas of Utah, Arizona, Colorado, Arkansas, Idaho, California, and Wyoming. The camps were finally ordered closed in December 1944. The Evacuation Claims Act of 1948 provided $31 million in compensation, though this was later determined to be less than one-10th the value of property and wages lost by Japanese Americans during their internment.

In Canada, the government bowed to the unified pressure of representatives from British Columbia, giving the minister of justice the authority to remove Japanese Canadians from any designated areas. While their property was at first impounded for later return, an order-in-council was passed in January 1943 allowing the government to sell it without permission, and then to apply the funds realized to the maintenance of the camps. With labor shortages by 1943, some Japanese Canadians were allowed to move eastward, especially to Ontario, though they were not permitted to buy or lease lands or businesses. Though it was acknowledged that "no person of Japanese race born in Canada" had been charged with "any act of sabotage or disloyalty during the years of war," the government provided strong incentives for them to return to Japan. After much debate and extensive challenges in the courts, more than 4,000 returned to Japan, more than half of whom were Canadian-born citizens. More than 13,000 of those who stayed left British Columbia, leaving fewer than 7,000 in the province.

With more than 16 million men in arms throughout the war, the U.S. government reached an agreement with Mexico to admit mostly agricultural laborers to the United States. The Emergency Farm Labor Program, commonly known as the BRACERO PROGRAM, was to cover the period from 1942 to 1947. It enabled Mexican workers to enter the United States with certain protections in order to ensure the availability of low-cost agricultural labor. Despite wages of 20–50¢ per day and deplorable living conditions in many areas, braceros, both legal and illegal, continued to come, finding the wages sufficient to send money home to their families. The effect of this wartime measure was to be far reaching. Hundreds of thousands of poor Mexican laborers were exposed to life in the United States, and their legal experience under the program soon led to an almost equal number of illegal immigrants. The Bracero Program was extended over the years until 1964, by which time Mexico had become the number one source country for immigration to the United States.

U.S. servicemen fighting side-by-side with Chinese, Filipinos, and Asian Indians against imperial Japan led to a new respect for those who were immigrants. It also became important that the U.S. government send a signal to former colonial peoples then suffering under Japanese control. For both these reasons, the government passed a series of measures that proved to be beneficial to Asian immigrant groups. As a result of President Roosevelt's Executive Order 8802 of 1941, employers were forbidden to discriminate in hiring on the basis of "race, creed, color, or national origin." This opened a wide range of jobs, especially to Filipinos who had been suffering economically since passage of the TYDINGS-MCDUFFIE ACT of 1934. The government also lifted its ban on Chinese immigration and naturalization in 1943, enabled Filipinos who had served in the U.S. military to become naturalized citizens in 1943, extended naturalization privileges to all Filipinos in 1945, and lifted restrictions on the naturalization of Asian Indians in 1946.

With the ending of the war, two problems affecting immigration came to the fore. The first and largest was the refugee question. Some 20 million people had been displaced by the war, and by mid-1945, more than 2 million were living in European camps, mostly in Germany and Austria. These included some 9 million Germans returning to their homeland, more than 4 million war fugitives, several million people who had been forced into labor camps throughout the German Reich, millions of Russian prisoners of war and Russians and Ukrainians who had served in the Germany army, and half a million Lithuanians, Latvians, and Estonians fleeing occupation by Soviet troops. Americans and Canadians were shocked to learn of what came to be known as the Holocaust, Hitler's attempted destruction of the entire Jewish population in Europe. Six million Jews had been murdered in Nazi work camps and death camps, about 60,000 were liberated, and another 200,000 had survived in hiding. New humanitarian measures were imperative to cope with the crisis.

As a result, U.S. president Harry Truman issued a directive on December 22, 1945, stating that U.S. consulates give first preference in immigration to displaced persons. No particular ethnic group was singled out, but Truman instead insisted that "visas should be distributed fairly among persons of all faiths, creeds, and nationalities." Of the 40,000 visas issued under the program, about 28,000 went to Jews. Truman realized that such a measure could only be temporary. In the debate over a more substantial solution, it became clear that anti-Semitism remained strong both in Washington, D.C., and throughout the country. The DISPLACED PERSONS ACT of 1948 superseded Truman's 1945 directive. The original proposal of 400,000 visas to displaced persons was gutted in committee, and provisions added that gave preference to persons from areas occupied by Soviet troops—the

Baltic republics and eastern Poland—and to agriculturalists. Both these provisions worked against Jewish refugees. The main provisions of the act included approval of 202,000 visas to be issued for two years without regard to quota but charged to the appropriate quotas in future years; up to 3,000 nonquota visas for displaced orphans; and granting to the Office of the Attorney General, with the approval of Congress, the right to adjust the status of up to 15,000 displaced persons who entered the country prior to April 1, 1948. Truman disliked the changes but signed the measure believing it was the best that could be gotten. The Displaced Persons Act was amended on June 16, 1950, to add another 121,000 visas, for a total of 341,000, through June 1951. The number of visas for orphans was raised to 5,000 and taken as a part of the total authorization of 341,000. The provision for adjusting the status of previously admitted displaced persons was extended to those who had entered the United States prior to April 30, 1949. Another section was added providing 5,000 additional nonquota visas for orphans under the age of 10 who were coming for adoption through an agency or to reside with close relatives.

There was a strong proimmigration lobby in Canada, but Canadian citizens were even less eager than Americans to admit Jewish refugees. In May 1946, P.C. 2071 authorized Canadian citizens with means to sponsor relatives outside the normal quota limits. The government also eased documentation requirements for displaced persons seeking entry. Finally, in July it provided for the admission of 3,000 former soldiers from the Polish Free Army, stipulating only that they work on a farm for one year. Prime Minister WILLIAM LYON MACKENZIE KING's 1947 statement on immigration suggested that it was wanted but affirmed that "the people of Canada do not wish, as a result of mass immigration, to make a fundamental alteration in the character of our population." During 1947 and 1948, a series of orders-in-council provided for the admission of 50,000 displaced persons, representing the first stage of a significant change in Canada's isolationist immigration policy. King and his ministers were careful to screen Jews, communists, and Asians, however, and most of the early refugee immigration came from the Baltic countries and the Netherlands. As the economy improved, restrictions were relaxed. Eventually a total of about 165,000 refugees were admitted to Canada between 1947 and 1953, including large numbers of Poles (23 percent), Ukrainians (16 percent), Germans and Austrians (11 percent), Jews (10 percent), Latvians (6 percent), Lithuanians (6 percent), and Hungarians (5 percent).

Less momentous but equally pressing to those affected was the question of thousands of war brides and their hero husbands seeking legal means of bringing home their wives. The U.S. Congress passed the WAR BRIDES ACT of December 28, 1945, authorizing admission to the United States of alien spouses and minor children outside the ordinary quota

system following World War II. Amendments in 1946 and 1947 authorized admission of fiancées for three months as nonimmigrant temporary visitors, provided they were otherwise eligible and had a bona fide intent to marry, and made special provision for Asian wives. Eventually some 115,000 British, 7,000 Chinese, 5,000 Filipina, and 800 Japanese spouses were brought to the United States, as well as 25,000 children and almost 20,000 fiancées.

Further Reading

Abella, Irving, and Harold Troper. *None Is Too Many: Canada and the Jews of Europe, 1933–1948.* Rev. ed. Toronto: Lester and Orpen Dennys, 1991.

Bilson, Geoffrey. *The Guest Children: The Story of the British Child Evacuees Sent to Canada during World War II.* Saskatoon, Canada: Fifth House, 1988.

Daniels, Roger. *Prisoners without Trial: Japanese Americans in World War II.* New York: Hill and Wang, 1993.

Feingold, Henry L. *The Politics of Rescue: The Roosevelt Administration and the Holocaust, 1938–1945.* New Brunswick, N.J.: Rutgers University Press, 1970.

Fox, Stephen R. *The Unknown Internment: An Oral History of the Relocation of Italian Americans during World War II.* Boston: Twayne, 1988.

Friedman, Saul S. *No Haven for the Oppressed: United States Policy toward Jewish Refugees, 1938–1945.* Detroit: Wayne State University Press, 1973.

Gamboa, Erasmo. *Mexican Labor and World War II: Braceros in the Pacific Northwest, 1942–1947.* Austin: University of Texas Press, 1990.

Hillmer, Norman, Bohdan Kordan, and Lubomyr Luciuk, eds. *On Guard for Thee: War, Ethnicity, and the Canadian State, 1939–1945.* Ottawa: Canadian Government Publishing, 1988.

Isajiw, Wsevolod, Yury Boshyk, and Roman Senkus, eds. *The Refugee Experience: Ukrainian Displaced Persons after World War II.* Edmonton: Canadian Institute of Ukrainian Studies Press, 1993.

Keyserlingk, Robert. "The Canadian Government's Attitude toward Germans and German Canadians in World War II." *Canadian Ethnic Studies* 16, no. 1 (1984): 16–28.

Lowenstein, Sharon R. *Token Refuge: The Story of the Jewish Refugee Shelter at Oswego, 1944–1946.* Bloomington: Indiana University Press, 1986.

Myer, Dillon S. *Uprooted Americans: The Japanese Americans and the War Relocation Authority during World War II.* Tucson: University of Arizona Press, 1971.

Prymak, Thomas M. *Maple Leaf and Trident: The Ukrainian Canadians during the Second World War.* Toronto: Multicultural History Society of Ontario, 1988.

Ramos, Henry A. J. *The American GI Forum.* Houston, Tex.: Arte Público Press, 1998.

Stewart, Barbara McDonald. *United States Government Policy on Refugees from Nazism, 1933–1940.* New York: Garland, 1982.

Thompson, John Herd. *Ethnic Minorities during Two World Wars.* Ottawa: Canadian Historical Association, 1991.

Wyman, David S. *The Abandonment of the Jews: America and the Holocaust, 1941–1945.* New York: Pantheon Books, 1984.

Yugoslav immigration

The disintegration of the Yugoslav state in 1991 led to persistent ethnic violence and two major conflicts in Bosnia-Herzegovina and in Kosovo. As a result, emigration from the region rose dramatically during the 1990s, changing the character of the South Slavic communities in North America. According to the U.S. census of 2000 and the Canadian census of 2001, almost 1 million Americans and 300,000 Canadians claim descent from one of the ethnic groups of Yugoslavia: Albanians (Kosovars), Bosnian Muslims (Bosniaks), Gypsies (Roma or Romanies), Montenegrins, Croats, Serbs, Slovenians, or Macedonians (see ALBANIAN IMMIGRATION; BOSNIAN IMMIGRATION; CROATIAN IMMIGRATION; GYPSY IMMIGRATION; MACEDONIAN IMMIGRATION; SERBIAN IMMIGRATION; SLOVENIAN IMMIGRATION). Because they came from many groups and were often resettled as refugees, former Yugoslav citizens settled in a wide variety of locations throughout North America.

Yugoslavia occupied 98,766 square miles on the Balkan Peninsula in southeast Europe and was bordered by Italy, Austria, Hungary, and Romania on the north; Bulgaria on the east; and Albania and Greece on the south. Slavic peoples moved into the area from modern Poland and Russia in the sixth century, gradually developing their own kingdoms but maintaining similar languages and a distinctive cultural heritage that set them apart from the Greeks, Germans, Magyars, Albanians, and Romanians who surrounded them. By the 15th century, however, all the various South Slavic peoples had been conquered—the Slovenians by Austria, the Croats by Hungary and Venice, and the Serbs, Bosnians, Macedonians, and Montenegrins by the Ottoman Empire. These peoples were moved by the nationalist movements of the 19th century, and Serbia proved strong enough, with the support of some European powers, to gain its independence from the Ottomans in 1878. During the early 20th century, the pan-Slavic movement grew under Serbian leadership, seeking to reforge the old Slavic affinities from the past. The defeat of the Austro-Hungarian and Ottoman Empires in World War I (1914–18) required the redrawing of state boundaries and led directly to the creation of the first union of the South Slavs, the Kingdom of the Serbs, Croats, and Slovenes.

The kingdom was created in 1918 and renamed Yugoslavia in 1929. The core of the new state was Serbia, whose peoples formed the largest of the Slavic populations. Joined to Serbia were Croatia, Slovenia, Bosnia-Herzegovina, Montenegro, and Macedonia. It was hoped that the common Slavic heritage of the six main groups would be stronger than their differences. From the first, however, the Croats and Slovenes were suspicious of Serbian control over the state; their fears were confirmed by Serbian king Alexander I's assumption of dictatorial powers in 1929. There was some emigration from the new state especially as a result of the displacements of World War I (see WORLD WAR I AND IMMIGRATION), but figures remained low. Between 1920 and 1950, fewer than 60,000 Yugoslav citizens of all nationalities immigrated to the United States, more than 80 percent of them before the mid-1920s when restrictive legislation all

326

but halted immigration by Slavs. During World War II (1939–45), Croatia established its own state allied to Nazi Germany, but it was brought back into Yugoslavia under the authoritarian rule of the Communist leader Josip Broz, Marshal Tito (1945–80).

During the 1980s, a rotating presidency was established in Yugoslavia in an attempt to quell ethnic unrest. With a growing economic crisis and rising national aspirations, the country splintered in 1991. Slovenia, Croatia, Bosnia-Herzegovina, and Macedonia declared their independence during 1991 and 1992 and moved toward democratic regimes, while Serbia and Montenegro, retaining the name Yugoslavia, controlled the military and continued under Communist rule. This led to a decade of bitter ethnic fighting. Serbs attacked Croatia and Bosnia (1991–95), hoping to preserve rule for the minority Serbs in those regions and attempted to kill all ethnic Albanians or drive them from Yugoslavia's southern province of Kosovo (1998–99). More than 2.5 million refugees were created by the fighting in Bosnia and Kosovo, which led to a massive surge in North American immigration. Between 1991 and 2002, almost 120,000 immigrants of all ethnic groups came to the United States from the former Yugoslavia, most fleeing the ethnic conflicts. Of Canada's 145,380 immigrants from the former Yugoslavia in 2001, about 46 percent came after 1990, the majority from modern Serbia, Montenegro, and Bosnia and Herzegovina.

At the time of its dissolution in 1991, the population of Yugoslavia was about 24 million, divided among eight major ethnoreligious groups. Croats, Slovenes, Bosnians, Serbs, Montenegrins, and Macedonians enjoyed some local representation within the Yugoslav state; the Hungarians in the Vojvodina and Albanians in Kosovo were governed directly as part of Serbia. Gypsies formed small minorities throughout Yugoslavia and were almost universally discriminated against. In 2003, the reduced Yugoslavia was restructured into a loose federation of two republics and officially

A group of Montenegrins, ca. 1855. Closely related to the Serbs, most Montenegrins emigrated from the poverty of their mountainous country before 1911. *(Library of Congress, Prints & Photographs Division [LC-USZ62-68257])*

renamed Serbia and Montenegro. Its population was estimated at 10,677,290 in 2002, with the people still ethnically divided between Serbs (63 percent), Albanians (14 percent), and Montenegrins (6 percent). Hungarians, Muslims of various groups, and mixed ethnicities each composed between 3 and 4 percent of the population. Sixty-five percent were Orthodox; 19 percent, Muslim; and 4 percent, Roman Catholic.

See also WORLD WAR II AND IMMIGRATION.

Ethnic Groups in Yugoslavia on the Eve of War, 1991

Region	Ethnic Group
Bosnia-Herzegovina	4,365,639 (Bosniak, 44 percent; Serb, 33 percent; Croat, 17 percent; other, 6 percent)
Croatia	4,703,941 (Croat, 75 percent; Serb, 15 percent; other, 10 percent)
Macedonia	2,033,964 (Macedonian, 64 percent; Albanian, 21 percent; Serb, 5 percent; Turk, 5 percent; other, 5 percent)
Montenegro	616,327 (Serb, 90 percent; Albanian, 4 percent; other, 6 percent)
Serbia	9,721,177
Serbia proper	5,753,825 (Serb, 96 percent; Bosniak, 2 percent; other, 2 percent)
Kosovo Province	1,954,747 (Albanian, 83 percent; Serb, 13 percent; other, 4 percent)
Vojvodina Province	2,012,605 (Serb, 70 percent; Hungarian, 22 percent; Croat, 5 percent; Romanian, 3 percent)
Slovenia	1,974,839 (Slovene, 91 percent; Croat, 3 percent; Serb, 3 percent; other, 3 percent)

Source: Yugoslav Survey 32 (March 1990–91).

Further Reading

Banac, Ivo. *The National Question in Yugoslavia: Origins, History, Politics.* Ithaca, N.Y.: Cornell University Press, 1989.

Čolaković, Branko M. *The South Slavic Immigration in America.* Boston: Twayne, 1978.

———. *Yugoslav Migrations to America.* San Francisco: R. and E. Research Associates, 1973.

Djilas, Milovan. *Land without Justice.* New York: Harcourt, Brace, 1958.

Gakovich, R. P., and M. M. Radovich. *Serbs in the United States and Canada: A Comprehensive Bibliography.* St. Paul: Immigration History Research Center, University of Minnesota Press, 1992.

Glenny, Misha. *The Fall of Yugoslavia: The Third Balkan War.* Rev. ed. New York: Penguin, 1996.

Goverchin, G. G. *Americans from Yugoslavia.* Gainesville: University of Florida Press, 1961.

Judah, Tim. *The Serbs: History, Myth and the Destruction of Yugoslavia.* New Haven, Conn.: Yale University Press, 1998.

Kisslinger, J. *The Serbian Americans.* New York: Chelsea House, 1990.

Lampe, John. *Yugoslavia as History: Twice There Was a Country.* 2d ed. Cambridge: Cambridge University Press, 2000.

Lencek, R., ed. *Twenty Years of Scholarship.* New York: Society for Slovene Studies, 1995.

Malcolm, Noel. *Bosnia: A Short History.* Rev. ed. New York: New York University Press, 1996.

Petroff, L. *Sojourners and Settlers: The Macedonian Community in Toronto.* Toronto: University of Toronto Press, 1994.

Glossary

One of the difficulties in immigration research lies in the evolving nature of relevant terminology. Scholars also frequently use terms in generic, nonspecific ways. Such variations are explained where appropriate in articles throughout this work. While context is usually the best guide to the way in which a word is used, it should be remembered that terms used in government documents have precise meanings related to specific immigration legislation and regulations. Below are some of the terms and acronyms commonly encountered in immigration research. Specific definitions for some terms relative to recent legislation can be found at the Web sites of the U.S. Citizenship and Immigration Services (USCIS; http://uscis.gov/graphics/glossary.htm) and Citizenship and Immigration Canada (http://www.cic.gc.ca/english/pub/imm%2Dlaw.html#glossary; http://www.cic.gc.ca/English/monitor/glossary.html). Simplified interpretations can sometimes be found in "Learn the Language of the Immigration Bureaucracy" at the NOLO: Law for All Web site (www.nolo.com/lawcenter/ency/index.cfm).

Note: Within this glossary, cross-references are in boldface.

UNITED STATES

adjustment to immigrant status Procedure allowing certain aliens admitted to the United States as nonimmigrants to have their status changed to that of permanent resident if they are eligible to receive an immigrant visa and one is immediately available. In such cases, the alien is counted as an immigrant as of the date of adjustment.

agricultural worker An alien coming temporarily to the United States as a nonimmigrant to perform agricultural labor or services, as defined by the U.S. Department of Labor.

alien Any person who is not a citizen or national of the United States. Generally referred to as a *foreign national* in Canada.

alien registration receipt card The official name of the photo identification card given to legal permanent residents of the United States; commonly known, both inside and outside the government, as a green card (despite the fact that it is presently pink). The green card enables the holder to reenter the United States after temporary absences and to work legally in the country.

Amerasian (Vietnam) Immigrant category established in the Act of December 22, 1987, providing for the admission of aliens born in Vietnam after January 1, 1962, and before January 1, 1976, whose father was a U.S. citizen.

asylee An alien in the United States who is unable or unwilling to return to his or her homeland because of persecution or a well-founded fear of persecution based on race, religion, nationality, membership in a particular social group, or political opinion. Asylees are eligible to apply for lawful permanent resident status after one year of continuous residence in the United States.

asylum Legal status granted to an asylee.

beneficiary An alien who receives immigration benefits from U.S. Citizenship and Immigration Services.

border patrol sector One of 21 geographic areas of the United States covered by the activities of U.S. Customs and Border Protection.

329

business nonimmigrant An alien temporarily in the United States engaged in international commerce on behalf of a foreign company.

country of chargeability The country to which an immigrant is charged under the quotas of the preference system.

country of former allegiance The previous country of citizenship of a naturalized U.S. citizen.

Cuban/Haitian entrant Immigrant status leading to permanent residence accorded by the Immigration Control and Reform Act of 1986 to 1) Cubans who entered illegally or were paroled into the United States between April 15 and October 10, 1980, and 2) Haitians who entered illegally or were paroled into the country before January 1, 1981, who have continuously resided in the United States since before January 1, 1982, and who were known to the Immigration and Naturalization Service before that date.

Department of Labor The U.S. government agency responsible for approving job-related visas, it determines whether there is adequate American labor to fill positions within U.S. companies.

Department of State The U.S. government agency responsible for embassies and consulates around the world, it generally determines who is eligible for visas and green cards when applications are filed outside the country.

departure under safeguards The departure of an illegal alien from the United States that is observed by a U.S. Immigration and Customs Enforcement official.

deportable alien An alien within the United States who is subject to removal, either because of application fraud or violation of terms of his or her nonimmigrant classification, under provisions of the Immigration and Nationality Act.

deportation The formal removal of an alien from the United States when immigration laws have been violated. Now referred to as *removal,* deportation is ordered by an immigration judge without any additional punishment.

derivative citizenship Citizenship conveyed to children through the naturalization of their parents.

diversity Under provisions of the Immigration Act of 1990, a category for redistributing unused visas to aliens from underrepresented countries. Beginning in fiscal year 1995, the permanent diversity quota was established at 55,000 annually. The diversity program is sometimes referred to as the *green card lottery program.*

employer sanctions Provision of the Immigration Reform and Control Act of 1986 that prohibits employers from hiring aliens known to be in violation of immigration laws. Violators are subject to civil fines for violations, and criminal penalties when a pattern of violations is proven.

exchange visitor An alien temporarily in the United States as part of a State Department–approved program involving teaching, studying, conducting research, consulting, or use of special skills.

exclusion Denial of entry to an alien following an exclusion hearing, prior to the Illegal Immigration Reform and Immigrant Responsibility Act of 1996. After April 1, 1997, the process of adjudicating inadmissibility was combined with other functions of the deportation process.

expedited removal Under provisions of the Illegal Immigration Reform and Immigrant Responsibility Act of 1996, the quick removal of inadmissible aliens who have no entry documents or who have attempted to use fraudulent documents. Generally U.S. Immigration and Customs Enforcement can order the removal without reference to an immigration judge.

fiscal year The 12-month period beginning October 1 and ending September 30. Prior to 1831 and from 1843 to 1849, the fiscal year was the same 12-month period ending September 30 of the respective year; from 1832 to 1842 and from 1850 to 1867, it was the 12-month period ending December 31 of the respective year; and from 1868 to 1976, the 12-month period ending June 30 of the respective year. The transition quarter for 1976 covers the three-month period, July–September 1976. Many immigration statistics are based on the fiscal year.

foreign government official A nonimmigrant class of admission covering aliens residing temporarily in the United States as accredited officials of a foreign government, along with their spouses and unmarried minor or dependent children.

general naturalization provisions The basic requirements for naturalization, unless a member of a special class, include 1) being 18 years of age and a lawful permanent resident with five years of continuous residence in the United States, 2) having been physically present in the country for half that period, and 3) having established "good moral character."

geographic area of chargeability One of five regions— Africa, East Asia, Latin America and the Caribbean, Near East and South Asia, and the former Soviet Union and Eastern Europe—against which refugees to the United States are charged. Annual consultations between the executive branch and the Congress determine the ceilings for each region.

green card See **alien registration receipt card.**

hemispheric ceilings Under provisions of the Immigration and Nationality Act of 1965, the ceilings imposed on immigration from each hemisphere between 1968 and 1978. Immigration from the Eastern Hemisphere was set at 170,000; immigration from the Western Hemisphere was set at 120,000. From October 1978, hemispheric ceilings were abolished in favor of a single comprehensive ceiling.

immediate relatives Certain immigrants, including spouses of citizens, unmarried children under 21, and parents of citizens 21 and older, who are exempt from the numerical limitations imposed on immigration to the United States.

immigration judge An attorney appointed by the U.S. attorney general to conduct various immigration proceedings.

inadmissible The status of an alien seeking admission who does not meet the criteria established for admission, generally because of criminal records, health problems, an inability to provide financial support, or potential subversiveness. Previously the term was *excludable*.

I-94 card A card given to all nonimmigrants entering the United States as evidence they have entered legally.

international representative A nonimmigrant class of admission under which an alien temporarily resides in the United States as an accredited representative of a foreign government to an international organization; includes spouses and unmarried minor or dependent children.

labor certification Category established by the Department of Labor in order to enable entry of alien workers on the basis of job skills or services to U.S. employers; often a first step toward obtaining a green card.

legalized aliens Under provisions of the Immigration Reform and Control Act of 1986, certain illegal aliens were eligible to apply for temporary resident status, which then could lead to permanent residency. Eligibility required continuous residence in the United States as an illegal alien from January 1, 1982; that one not be excludable, and have entered the United States either 1) illegally before January 1, 1982, or 2) as a temporary visitor before January 1, 1982, with one's authorized stay expiring before that date or with the government's knowledge of his or her unlawful status before that date.

lottery See **diversity.**

migrant A person who seeks residence in a country other than his or her own.

national A person owing allegiance to a state.

naturalization Conferring U.S. citizenship upon a person after birth. Requirements include 1) being at least 18 years of age, 2) having been lawfully admitted to the United States for permanent residence, and 3) having resided in the country continuously for at least five years. Applicants must also demonstrate a certain level of knowledge of U.S. government and history; the ability to speak, read, and write English; and "good moral character." A prominent exception is spouses of citizens, who may be naturalized after three years of residence.

nonimmigrant An alien who seeks temporary entry to the United States. Nonimmigrant classifications include foreign government officials, business travelers, tourists, aliens in transit, students, international representatives, temporary workers, representatives of foreign media, exchange visitors, fiancés of U.S. citizens, intracompany transferees, North Atlantic Treaty Organization (NATO) officials, religious workers, and some others. Most nonimmigrants can be accompanied by spouses and unmarried minor or dependent children.

nonpreference category Nonpreference visas were available to qualified applicants not entitled to a visa under one of six preference categories until the category was eliminated by the Immigration Act of 1990. Nonpreference visas for persons not entitled to the other preferences had not been available since September 1978 because of high demand in the preference categories.

Panama Canal Act immigrants A special immigrant category created by the Act of September 27, 1979, including 1) certain former employees of the Panama Canal Company or Canal Zone Government, their spouses, and accompanying children; and 2) certain former Panamanian nationals who were employees of the U.S. government in the Panama Canal Zone, their spouses, and children. The act provided for admission of a maximum of 15,000 immigrants, at a rate of no more than 5,000 each year.

parolee An alien who appears to be inadmissible, but who is allowed into the United States for urgent humanitarian reasons or for reasons of significant public benefit. Parole confers temporary status only. Parolees include those with documents but about whom there is still some question; those coming for emergencies not permitting time for ordinary application for documentation, as in the case of firefighters or other emergency workers, or for funerals; those requiring emergency medical care; those who take part in legal proceedings on behalf of the government; and those authorized for certain long-term admissions under special legislation.

per-country limit The maximum number of preference visas that can be issued to citizens of any country in a fiscal year. The limits are calculated each fiscal year depending on the total number of family-sponsored and employment-based visas available. Each country is limited to a maximum of 7 percent of the visas, though the combined workings of the preference system and per-country limits keep most countries from reaching the maximum.

permanent resident alien An alien given permanent residence in the United States; also known as a *green-card holder*. Permanent residents are commonly referred to as immigrants, though under provisions of the Immigration and Nationality Act, some illegal aliens are officially immigrants, without being permanent resident aliens. Commonly known in Canada as a *landed immigrant*.

port of entry Any location designated by the U.S. government as a point of entry for aliens and U.S. citizens, including all district and files control offices, which become locations of entry for aliens adjusting to immigrant status.

preference system The system utilized to allocate visas to the United States. Between 1981 and 1991, the 270,000 immigrant visas were allocated in six categories: 1) unmarried sons and daughters (over 21 years of age) of U.S. citizens (20 percent), 2) spouses and unmarried sons and daughters of aliens lawfully admitted for permanent residence (26 percent), 3) professionals or persons of exceptional ability in the sciences and arts (10 percent), 4) married sons and daughters of U.S. citizens (10 percent), 5) brothers and sisters of U.S. citizens over 21 years of age (24 percent), and 6) needed skilled or unskilled workers (10 percent). A nonpreference category, historically open to immigrants not entitled to a visa number under one of the six preferences just listed, had no numbers available beginning in September 1978. This system was amended by the Immigration Act of 1990, effective fiscal year 1992 and including nine categories. Family-sponsored preferences include 1) unmarried sons and daughters of U.S. citizens; 2) spouses, children, and unmarried sons and daughters of permanent resident aliens; 3) married sons and daughters of U.S. citizens; and 4) brothers and sisters of U.S. citizens. Employment-based preferences include 1) priority workers, including outstanding professors and researchers and multinational executives and managers; 2) professionals with advanced degrees or aliens with exceptional ability; 3) skilled workers, professionals without advanced degrees, and needed unskilled workers; 4) special immigrants; and 5) investors.

principal alien   The alien who applies for immigrant status and from whom another alien derives lawful status, usually spouses and unmarried minor children.

refugee   Any person outside his or her country of nationality who is unable or unwilling to return to that country because of persecution or a well-founded fear of persecution based upon race, religion, nationality, membership in a particular social group, or political opinion. Under the Refugee Act of 1980, refugee admission ceilings are established annually by the president in consultation with Congress. Refugees are eligible to adjust to lawful permanent resident status after one year of continuous presence in the United States. Commonly known in Canada as *convention refugee*.

refugee-parolee   A qualified applicant for conditional entry paroled into the United States under the authority of the attorney general between February 1970 and April 1980 because of inadequate numbers of visas.

removal   The expulsion of an alien from the United States, based on grounds of inadmissibility or deportability; formerly known as *deportation*. Those removed are not allowed to return to the United States for at least five years.

resettlement   Permanent relocation of refugees in a host country; generally carried out by private voluntary agencies working with the Department of Health and Human Services Office of Refugee Resettlement.

seasonal agricultural workers (SAW)   Under provisions of the Immigration Reform and Control Act of 1986, aliens who perform labor in perishable agricultural commodities for a specified period of time are admitted as special agricultural workers for temporary, and then permanent, residence. Applicants are required to have worked at least 90 days in each of the three years preceding May 1, 1986, to be eligible. Adjustment to permanent resident status is "essentially automatic."

special immigrants   Certain categories of immigrants exempt from numerical limitations by special legislation, including religious workers, foreign doctors, and former employees of the U.S. government.

sponsor   Generally a petitioner to the U.S. government on behalf of a prospective immigrant. Sponsors are usually prospective employers or close relatives who are citizens or permanent residents.

temporary protected status (TPS)   Status established by the Office of the Attorney General for allowing a group of persons temporary refuge in the United States, initially for periods of six to 18 months though extensions may be granted.

temporary resident   See **nonimmigrant.**

temporary worker   An alien temporarily residing in the United States for specifically designated purposes of work, including health care workers, agricultural workers, athletes and performers, and others performing work for which U.S. citizens are not available.

treaty trader or investor   A nonimmigrant class of admission, allowing an alien manager or investor, along with spouse and unmarried minor children, to enter the United States under provisions of a treaty of commerce and navigation between the United States and another country.

underrepresented countries, natives of   Under the Immigration Amendments of 1988, 10,000 visas were reserved for natives of underrepresented countries in each of fiscal years 1990 and 1991 (those receiving less than 25 percent of the maximum allowed under the country limitations in fiscal year 1988). See **diversity.**

visa   Permission granted to aliens for entry into the United States, usually represented by a stamp placed in a passport.

visa waiver program   Program provided by the Immigration Reform and Control Act of 1986 allowing business and tourist travelers of selected countries temporary entry to the United States for a period of up to 90 days without obtaining nonimmigrant visas.

voluntary departure   The departure of an alien from the United States without an order of removal, conceding removability but allowing for reapplication of admission at a port of entry at any time.

Canada

business immigrant   Investors, entrepreneurs, and self-employed immigrants who are enabled to become permanent residents of Canada as a result of meeting financial standards; spouses and children also included.

Canadian citizen   One who is Canadian by birth or who has received a citizenship certificate from Citizenship and Immigration Canada.

conjugal partner   A person outside Canada who has maintained a conjugal relationship with the sponsor for at least one year; includes both opposite-sex and same-sex couples.

convention refugee   Any person who 1) by reason of a well-founded fear of persecution for reasons of race, religion, nationality, membership in a particular social group or political opinion, is outside his or her country of nationality and is unable or unwilling to return, or 2) not having a country of nationality, is outside the country of his or her former residence and is unable or unwilling to return to that country. Commonly known in the United States simply as a *refugee*.

departure order   An order issued to a person who has violated the Immigration and Refugee Protection Act, requiring immediate departure, though it does permit reapplication for admission. A departure order becomes a deportation order if the person does not leave Canada within 30 days or fails to obtain a certificate of departure from Citizenship and Immigration Canada.

dependent   The spouse, common-law partner or conjugal partner, and children of a landed immigrant. Children must be under the age of 22, unmarried, and not in a common-law relationship; or have been full-time students since before age 22 and still substantially dependent upon parent support; or over 22 but dependent from before age 22 for medical reasons.

deportation order   A removal order issued to someone who is inadmissible to Canada on "serious grounds" or who has committed a serious violation of Canadian law; permanently bars future admission to Canada.

economic immigrant   Someone selected for admission under the Immigration and Refugee Protection Act for his or her ability to contribute to certain predesignated needs in the Canadian economy.

entrepreneur   A foreign national who is admitted to Canada on the basis of 1) a net worth of at least 300,000 Canadian dollars or 2) management and control of a business for at least two years within a period of not more than five years.

examination   A procedure whereby an immigration officer interviews or examines persons applying for visas, seeking entry to Canada, applying to change or cancel conditions of their entry to Canada, sponsoring foreign nationals, or making refugee claims.

exclusion order   A removal order barring entry to Canada for either one or two years.

family class   The class of immigrants made up of close relatives of a sponsor in Canada, including spouses; common-law or conjugal partners; dependent children; parents and grandparents; children for whom the sponsor is a guardian; siblings, nephews, nieces, and grandchildren who are orphans under 18 years of age; and children under 18 who will be adopted while in Canada.

foreign national   A person who is not a Canadian citizen or a permanent resident. This includes a stateless person. Generally referred to as an *alien* in the United States.

foreign student   A temporary resident approved to study in Canada. Under provisions of the Immigration and Refugee Protection Act of 2002, study permits identify the level of study and length of time students are permitted to remain in the country.

foreign worker   A foreign national authorized to enter Canada temporarily after having been issued an employment authorization.

government-assisted refugees   Convention refugees selected under the Immigration and Refugee Protection Act or as members of the Persons Abroad classes who receive resettlement assistance from the Canadian federal government.

investor   A foreign national who 1) has business experience, 2) has a legally obtained net worth of at least 800,000 Canadian dollars, and 3) has invested 400,000 Canadian dollars before receiving a visa.

Joint Assistance Sponsorship (JAS)   Designed to assist in difficult refugee transitions, the JAS is generally a joint undertaking including Citizenship and Immigration Canada and a private sponsoring group on behalf of refugees whose admissibility depends on sponsor support. Under the program, CIC provides financial costs of food, shelter, clothing, and essential household goods, while the sponsoring group provides orientation, settlement assistance, and emotional support.

landed immigrant   An immigrant granted permanent residence status in Canada. Commonly known in the United States as a *permanent resident alien*.

level of skill   Categories established by the National Occupational Classification (NOC) system for classifying foreign workers: 0 (managerial); A (professional); B (skilled and technical); C (intermediate and clerical); D (elemental and labor); E (not stated; usually associated with special programs).

permanent resident   Permanent residents have the right to enter or remain in Canada. Conditions may be imposed for a certain period on some permanent residents, such as entrepreneurs. A permanent resident must live in Canada for at least 730 days (two years) within a five-year period. Permanent residents must comply with this residency requirement or risk losing their status.

permanent resident card   Received by permanent residents as proof of their status in Canada. Replacing the former Record of Landing, the card is a secure, machine-readable, and fraud-resistant document, valid for five years.

pre-removal risk assessment (PRRA)   A formal process for reviewing risk to a person before he or she is deported. The PRRA gives the opportunity to apply to remain in Canada to persons who may be exposed to compelling personal risk if removed.

protected person   A foreign national on whom refugee protection is conferred. If the individual meets the specified requirements, the protected person acquires permanent resident status and has the same rights to enter and remain in Canada as a permanent resident.

provincial nominee   An immigrant selected by provinces and territories under agreements with Citizenship and Immigration Canada to meet specific skill needs in the local economy. Nominees must still meet federal admissibility requirements.

refugee   See **convention refugee.**

removal order   An order issued by the Immigration and Refugee Board or an immigration officer that requires the person named in it to leave the country within a specified time; includes exclusion orders, departure orders, and deportation orders.

self-employed person   A foreign national who has the intention and the ability to create his or her own employment by 1) making a significant contribution to the cultural or artistic life of Canada or to athletics in Canada at the world-class level, or 2) purchasing and managing a farm in Canada.

sponsor   A group, a corporation, or an unincorporated organization or association that sponsors refugees, or a Canadian citizen or permanent resident who is at least 18 years of age, resides in Canada, and has filed a sponsorship application in respect of a member of the Family Class.

study permit   A document issued by a visa or immigration officer authorizing a foreign national to study in Canada; specifies type of study and allowable duration of stay.

temporary resident   A foreign national lawfully in Canada for a temporary purpose. Temporary residents include students, foreign workers, and visitors such as tourists.

work permit   A document that authorizes a foreign national to work in Canada.

Appendix A
DOCUMENTS

The Mayflower Compact, 1620

Dissatisfied with the strictures of the Church of England, the Pilgrims migrated to Holland in 1608–09. Fearing loss of their English identity, in 1617 a group committed themselves to moving to America. Receiving a land patent from the London Company, 41 Pilgrims and 61 other English settlers set off for America aboard the Mayflower, making landfall in November 1620. An error in navigation led them to Plymouth Bay in modern-day Massachusetts instead of to their intended destination of Virginia. Without authorization to form a civil government there but too late in the season to continue the voyage, the Pilgrim leaders signed the Mayflower Compact, agreeing to support "the generall good of the Colonie."

In the name of God Amen. We whose names are underwriten, the loyall subjects of our dread soveraigne Lord King James byth [by the] grace of God, of great Britaine, Franc, & Ireland king, defender of the faith, &c. Having undertaken, for the glorie of God, and advancements of the Christian faith and honour of our king & countrie, a voyage to plant the first colonie in the Northerne parts of Virginia, doe by these presents solemnly & mutualy in the presence of God, and one of another, covenant & combine our selves togeather into a civill body politic; for our better ordering, & preservation & furtherance of the ends aforesaid; and by vertue hearof to enact, constitute, and frame shuch just & equall lawes, ordinances, Acts, constitutions, & offices, from time to time, as shall be thought most meete & convenient for the generall good of the Colonie; unto which we promise all due submission and obedience.

Source: Daniel J. Boorstin, ed., *An American Primer,* 2 vols. (Chicago: University of Chicago Press, 1966), p. 3.

A Letter on the Difficulties of Governing New France, 1685

From the time that Samuel de Champlain founded the first permanent French settlement at Quebec in 1608, entrepreneurs found it difficult to entice French citizens to venture to the New World. Administrative mismanagement, failure to secure settlers, and the constant threat from American Indian tribes sparked a complete reorganization of the government, which was brought under royal control in 1663. Though the government had some limited success in encouraging settlement, most who came were trappers, soldiers, churchmen, prisoners, and young indentured servants. This letter from a local French official, Jacques-René Brisay de Denonville, to the Paris government demonstrated the growing concern with the nature of their settlement.

13 November 1685

It seems to me that this is the place, Monseigneur, that we have to take into account the disorders which occur not only in the woods but also in our settlements. These disorders have come to the Youth of this country only through the laziness of the children, and the great liberty which the light control of fathers and mothers and Governors have exercised over youth in allowing them to go into the woods on pretext of hunting or trading. This has reached the extremity, Monseigneur, that as soon as the children can shoulder a rifle the fathers can no longer restrain them and do not dare to make them angry. You may judge what evils may ensue from such manner of living. These disorders, Monseigneur, are greater among the families of those who are *gentilshommes* [gentlemen], or those who have set themselves up to be such, because of idleness or vanity, having no means of subsistence except the woods because not being accustomed to wield the axe or pick or guide the plow their only recourse is the rifle. They have to pass their lives in the woods, where there are neither priests to trouble them, nor fathers nor Governors to constrain them. There are, Monseigneur, among those men some who distinguish themselves above others in these disorders and against whom I have promised to employ the authority which the King has entrusted to me to punish them severely. I am persuaded, Monseigneur, that you will acknowledge and will approve that I do not amuse myself with a formality of justice which would tend only to subtlety in order to hide the vice and leave the disorders unpunished. Convincing proof not always being readily established I believe, Monseigneur, that military justice in this case is more suitable than any *arrêt* [ruling] of a judge.

Mr. De la Barre has suppressed a certain order of *chevaliers,* but he has not taken away its manners or disorders. A way of dressing up like savages, stark naked, not only on carnival days but on all days of feasting and debauchery, has been treated as a nice action and joke. These manners tend only to maintain the young people in the spirit of living like savages and to communicate with them and to be eternally profligate like them, I could not express sufficiently to you Monseigneur the attraction that this savage life of doing nothing, of being constrained by nothing, of following every whim and being beyond correction, has for the young men.

It was believed for a long time that approaching the savages to our settlements was a very considerable means of accustoming these people to live like us and to be instructed in our religion. I perceive, Monseigneur, that the very opposite has occurred because instead of training them to our laws, I assure you that they communicate very much to us everything that is meanest in them, and themselves take on only what is bad and vicious in us. I have been somewhat lengthy, Monseigneur, in giving you the details of all these matters so that you may provide the remedies by the orders you give me.

Source: J. M. Bumsted, ed. *Documentary Problems in Canadian History,* vol. 1 (Georgetown, Canada: Irwin-Dorsey Press, 1969), p. 23.

An Account of Pennsylvania, 1698

Of the thirteen colonies, Pennsylvania was the next to last to be settled (the last being Georgia). Building on the experience of others, William Penn created a tolerant and prosperous society. Gabriel Thomas, a Welsh Quaker, was among the first group of settlers that sailed for Pennsylvania in 1681. He briefly returned to London in 1697 and published his glowing account of a colony of fertile lands and low taxes.

The Air here is very delicate, pleasant, and wholesome; the Heavens serene, rarely overcast, bearing mighty resemblance to the better part of France; after Rain they have commohnly a very clear Sky, the Climate is something Colder in the depth of Winter and Hotter in the height of Summer . . . than here in England, which makes the Fruit so good, and the Earth so fertile. . . . Here is much Meadow Ground. Poor People both Men and Women, will get near three times more Wages for their Labour in this Country, than they can earn either in England or Wales. . . . There is likewise Iron-Stone or Oar [ore] (lately found) which far exceeds that in England. . . . As to Minerals, or Metals, there is very good Copper, far exceeding ours in England, being much Finer, and of a more glorious Colour. . . .

There are several sorts of wild Beasts of great Profit, and good Food; viz. Panthers, Woolves, Fither [fisher], Deer, Beaver, Otter, Hares, Musk-Rats, Minks, Wild-Cats, Foxes, Rackoons, Rabits, and that strange Creature, the Possam, she having a false Belly to swallow her Young ones, by which means she preserveth them from danger, when any thing comes to disturb them. . . . There are in the Woods abundance of Red Deer (vulgarly called Stags) for I have bought of the Indians a whole Buck (both Skin and Carcass), for two Gills of Gunpoder. Excellent Food, most delicious, far exceeding that in Europe, in the Opinion of most that are Nice and Curious People. There are vast Numbers of other Wild Creatures, as Elks, Bufalos, &c., all which as well Beasts, Fowl, and Fish, are free and common to any Person who can shoot or take them, without any lett, hinderance or Opposition whatsoever. They have commonly Two Harvests in the Year; First, of English Wheat, and next of Buck, (or French) Wheat. . . .

Corn and Flesh, and what else serves Man for Drink, Food and Rayment [raiment], is much cheaper here than in England, or elsewhere; but the chief reason why Wages of Servants of all sorts is much higher here than there, arises from the great Fertility and Produce of the Place; besides, if these large Stipends were refused them, they would quickly set up for themselves, for they can have Provision very cheap, and Land for a very small matter, or next to nothing in comparison of the Purchase of Lands in England; and the farmers ther, can better afford to give that great Wages than the Farmers in England can, for several Reasons very obvious.

At First, their Land costs them (as I said but just now) little or nothing in comparison, of which the Farmers commonly will get twice the encrease of Corn for every Bushel they sow, that the Farmers in England can from the richest Land they have. In the Second place, they have constantly good price for their Corn, by reason of the great and quick vent [market] into Barbadoes and other Islands; through which means Silver is become more plentiful than here in England, considering the Number of People, and that causes a quick Trade for both corn

and Cattle. . . . Thirdly, They pay no Tithes, and their Taxes are inconsiderable; the Place is free for all Persuasions, in a Sober and Civil way; for the Church of England and the Quakers bear equal Share in the Government. They live Friendly and Well together; there is no Persecution for Religion, nor ever like to be; 'tis this that knocks all Commerce on the Head, together with high Imposts, strict Laws, and cramping Orders. . . .

What I have deliver'd concerning this Province, is indisputably true, I was an Eye-Witness to it all, for I went in the first Ship that was bound from England for that Countrey, since it received the Name of Pensilvania, which was in the Year 1681. The Ship's Name was the John and Sarah of London, Henry Smith Commander. I have declin'd giving any Account of several things which I have only heard others speak of, because I do not see them my self, for I never held that way infallible, to make Reports from Hear-say. I saw the first Cellar when it was digging for the use of our Governour Will. Penn.

Source: Daniel J. Boorstin, ed., *An American Primer,* 2 vols. (Chicago: University of Chicago Press, 1966), pp. 33–45.

An Account of New Orleans, 1763

The vast French colonial empire of New France was always sparsely populated. There were, however, three important areas of settlement: the fur-trading region along the St. Lawrence River, known as Canada; the Atlantic settlements, known as Acadia; and the mouth of the interior Mississippi River watershed, known as Louisiana. Louisiana was officially established as a colony in 1699. In order to meet the growing threat from Spain in the south and England on the Atlantic seaboard, France built a string of forts from the Great Lakes along the interior waterways, including Natchitoches (1714), the first permanent settlement, and New Orleans (1718) at the mouth of the Mississippi. Although New Orleans proved to be difficult to defend and an economic disappointment, there was great hope for the future upon its establishment. This is an account of its founding by a pioneer planter, Le Page du Pratz.

New Orleans, the Capital of the Colony, is situated to the East, on the banks of the Mississippi, in the 30 degrees of North Latitude. At my first arrival in Louisiana, it existed only in name; for on my landing I understood, M. de Biainville, Commandant General, was only gone to mark out the spot; whence he returned three days after our arrival at Isle Dauphine.

He pitched upon this spot in preference to many others, more agreeable and commodious; but for that time this was a place proper enough: Besides, it is not every man who can see so far as some others. As the principal settlement was at Mobile, it was proper to have the Capital fixed at a place from which there could be an easy communication with this Post: And thus a better choice could not have been made, as the town being on the banks of the Mississipi, vessels, tho' of a thousand ton, may lay their sides close to the shore, even at low water; or at most, need only lay a small bridge, with two of their yards, in order to load or unload, to roll barrels and bales, &c. without fatiguing the ship's crew. This town is only a league from St. John's Creek, where passengers take water for Mobile, in going to which they pass Lake St. Louis, and from thence all along the coast; a communication was necessary at that time. . . .

The Governor's houses stands in the middle of that part of town, from which we go from the place of arms to the habitation of the Jesuits, which is near the town. The house of the Ursilin Nuns is quite at the end of the town, to the right; as its also the hospital of the sick, of which the Nuns have the inspection. What I have just described faces the river. . . .

Source: Le Page du Pratz, *The History of Louisiana,* vol. 1 (London: T. Becket and P. A. De Hondt, 1763), pp. 89–93.

Excerpts from the Quebec Act, 1774

The Quebec Act of 1774 was passed by Great Britain in response to a growing movement toward political independence in Massachusetts and the failure of attempts to attract English-speaking immigrants to the French culture region that had been acquired from France following the Seven Years' War (1756–63). The Quebec Act acknowledged what "experience" had dictated—that 65,000 French Catholics could not be governed according to English principles and that it was "inexpedient" at the moment to form an elective assembly. The king would thus appoint a provincial council that would oversee the continued application of French civil law in the colony and guarantee the right to practice Roman Catholicism. These provisions angered English settlers, who in 1763 had been promised a representative assembly and a British system of law. More provocatively, the act enlarged Quebec to include much of what is now Quebec and Ontario, and the area bounded by the Great Lakes, the Ohio River, the Appalachian Mountains and the Mississippi River. Although not overtly directed at Massachusetts, the Quebec Act was the final in a series of coercive measures—the "Intolerable Acts," as they were styled in Massachusetts—that eventually led to the calling of the First Continental Congress in 1774.

Whereas his Majesty, by his Royal Proclamation, bearing the Date the seventh Day of October in the third Year of his Reign [1763], thought fit to declare the provisions which had been made in respect to certain Countries, Territories, and Islands in America, ceded to his Majesty by the definitive Treaty of Peace, concluded at Paris. . . . And whereas, by the arrangements made by the said Royal Proclamation, a very large Extent of Country, within which there were several Colonies and Settlements of the Subjects of France, who claimed to remain therein under the Faith of the said Treaty, was left, without any Provision being made for the Administration of Civil Government therein; and certain Parts of the Territory of Canada, where sedentary Fisheries had been established and carried on by the Subjects of France, Inhabitants of the said

Province of Canada, under Grants and Concessions from the Government thereof, were annexed to the Government of Newfoundland, and thereby subjected to Regulations inconsistent with the Nature of such Fisheries: May it therefore please your most Excellent Majesty that it may be enacted . . . That all the Territories, Islands, and Countries in North America, belonging to the Crown of Great Britain, bounded on the South by a Line from the Bay of Chaleurs, along the High Lands which divide the Rivers that empty themselves into the River Saint Lawrence from those which fall into the Sea, to a Point in forty-five Degrees of Northern Latitude, on the Eastern Bank of the River Connecticut, keeping in the same Latitude directly West, through the Lake Champlain, until, in the same Latitude, it meets the River Saint Lawrence; from thence up the Eastern Bank of the said River to the Lake Ontario; thence through the Lake Ontario, and the River, commonly called Niagara; and thence along by the Eastern and Southeastern Bank of Lake Erie, following the said Bank, until the same shall be intersected; and from thence along the said Northern and Western Boundaries of the said Province, until the said Western Boundary strike the Ohio: But in case the said Bank of the said Lake shall not be found to be so intersected, then following the said Bank until it shall arrive at that Point of the said Bank which shall be nearest to the Northwestern Angle of the said Province of Pennsylvania, and thence by a right Line, to the said North-western Angle of the said Province; and thence along the Western Boundary of the said Province, until it strike the River Ohio; and along the Bank of the said River, Westward, to the Banks of the Mississippi, and Northward to the Southern Boundary of the Territory granted to the Merchants Adventurers of England, trading to Hudson's Bay; and also all such Territories, Islands, and Countries, which have, since [1763] been made Part of the Government of Newfoundland, be, and they are hereby, during his Majesty's Pleasure, annexed to, and made Part and Parcel of, the Province of Quebec. . . .

Source: Shortt, Adam, and Arthur G. Doughty, eds. *Documents Relating to the Constitutional History of Canada, 1759–1791,* 2nd rev. ed., pt. I (Ottawa: Canadian Archives, 1918), pp. 571–72.

Excerpts from the Alien Act, 1798

The Alien Act was one of the first expressions of nativist feeling in the history of the United States. It was one of four measures ostensibly directed toward France in response to depredations on the high seas, but it was mainly aimed at undermining the growing strength of Thomas Jefferson's Republican Party. With Irish, French, and other newly arrived immigrants strongly supporting the Republican Party, Federalists were intent on neutralizing the potential political value of "new" Americans. The Alien Act empowered the president to expel any foreigner "suspected" of treasonous activity, though its tenure was limited to two years.

Be it enacted by the Senate and the House of Representatives of the United States of America in Congress assembled, That it shall be lawful for the President of the United States at any time during the continuance of this act, to order all such aliens as he shall judge dangerous to the peace and safety of the United States, or shall have reasonable grounds to suspect are concerned in any treasonable or secret machinations against the government thereof, to deport out of the territory of the United States within such time as shall be expressed in such order, which order shall be served to the alien by deliverying a copy thereof, or leaving the same at his usual abode, and returned to the office of the Secretary of State, by the marshal or other person to whom the same shall be directed. . . . Sec. 2. And be it further enacted, That it shall be lawful for the President of the United States, whenever he may deem it necessary for the public safety, to order to be removed out of the territory thereof, any alien who may or shall be inprison in pursuance of this act; and to cause to be arrested and sent out of the United States such of those aliens as shall have been ordered to depart therefrom. . . . Sec. 5. And be it further enacted, That it shall be lawful for any alien who may be ordered to be removed from the United States, by virtue of this act, to take with him such part of his goods, chattels, or other property, as he may find convenient; and all property left in the United States by any alien, who may be removed, as aforesaid, shall be, and remain subject to his order and disposal, in the same manner as if this act had not been passed.

Source: Smith, James Morton. *Freedom's Fetters: The Alien and Sedition Laws and American Civil Liberties* (Ithaca, N.Y.: Cornell University Press, 1956), pp. 435–438.

Excerpts from Charles Fenno Hoffman, *A Winter in the West,* 1835

The United States was developed by migrants, both from Europe and from the eastern seaboard of the United States. Though many traveled by sea, river, and canal where they could, large numbers poured along a variety of roads that were gradually carved from the wilderness after the turn of the 19th century. The largest of these was the National Road, which began in Cumberland, Maryland, and eventually stretched to Vandalia, Illinois. This 1835 account by Charles Fenno Hoffman suggests the multiethnic nature of the American frontier.

By far the greatest portion of travelers one meets with, not to mention the ordinary stage-coach passengers, consists of teamsters and emigrants. The former generally drive six horses before their enormous wagons—stout, heavy-looking beasts, descended, it is said, from the famous draught horses of Normandy. They go about twenty miles a day. The leading horses are often ornamented with a number of bells suspended from a square raised frame-work over their collars, originally adopted to warn these lumbering machines of each other's approach,

and prevent their being brought up all standing in the narrow parts of the road.

As for the emigrants, it would astonish you to witness how they get along. A covered one-horse wagon generally contains the whole worldly substance of a family consisting not unfrequently of a dozen members. The tolls are so high along this western turnpike, and horses are so comparatively cheap in the region whither the emigrant is bound, that he rarely provides more than one miserable Rosinante to transport his whole family to the far west. The strength of the poor animal is of course half the time unequal to the demand upon it, and you will, therefore, unless it be raining very hard, rarely see anyone in the wagon except perhaps some child overtaken by sickness, or a mother nursing a young infant. The head of the family walks by the horse, cheering and encouraging him on his way. The good woman, when not engaged as hinted above, either trudges along with her husband, or, leading some weary little traveller by the hand far behind, endeavours to keep the rest chained beneath the wagon to prevent the half-starved brute from foraging too freely in a friendly country—brings up the rear. . . .

The hardship of such a tour must form no bad preparatory school for the arduous life which the new settler has afterward to enter upon. Their horses, of course, frequently give out on the road; and in companies so numerous, sickness must frequently overtake some of the members.

Source: Charles Fenno Hoffman, *A Winter in the West,* vol. 1 (New York: Harper and Brothers, 1835), pp. 42–48.

An Early Expression of Nativism by Samuel F. B. Morse, 1835

Best remembered for developing the Morse code and the first working telegraph, Samuel F. B. Morse was also one of the leading anti-Catholic activists of his day. In 1834, he wrote letters to the New York Observer *that were collected and published as* A Foreign Conspiracy against the Liberties of the United States *(1834). In the following year, he published* Imminent Dangers to the Free Institutions of the United States through Foreign Immigration and Present State of the Naturalization Laws, *railing against what he termed "naturalized foreigners," especially the Irish, who professed to, in his words, "become an American" but retained in "both a name and a feeling and a practice in regard to his adopted country at war with propriety, with decency, with gratitude, and with true patriotism." During the Civil War, Morse increasingly viewed immigrants as a prop to the stability of the Union rather than a potential source of destruction.*

Already have foreigners increased in the country to such a degree that they justly give us alarm. They feel themselves so strong, as to organize themselves even as *foreigners* into *foreign bands.* . . . [T]hey are men who having *professed* to become Americans, by accepting our terms of naturalization, do yet, in direct contradiction to their professions, clan together as a separate interest. . . . [I]s it not time, high time, that a true American spirit were roused to resist this alarming inroad of foreign influence upon our institutions.

Source: Morse, Samuel F. B. *Imminent Dangers to the Free Institutions of the United States through Foreign Immigration, and the Present State of Naturalization Laws* (1835; New York: Arno Press, 1969), pp. 14–15.

Excerpts from the Durham Report, 1839

Following a series of rebellions in Canada in 1837, John George Lambton, Lord Durham, was commissioned by the British government to govern Lower Canada (Quebec) temporarily, to investigate the causes of discontent, and to make recommendations regarding British governance of the region. Durham recommended that Upper and Lower Canada be combined, giving English speakers a clear majority over the French (550,000 to 450,000), one which would naturally be increased "by the influence of English emigration." Durham also recommended that provisions be made for other North American colonies to join a Canadian confederation.

Your Majesty, in entrusting me with the Government of the province of Lower Canada, during the critical period of the suspension of the constitution, was pleased, at the same time, to impose on me a task of equal difficulty, and of far more permanent importance, by appointing me "High Commissioner for the adjustment of certain important questions depending on the provinces of Lower and Upper Canada, respecting the form and future government of the said provinces . . .". From the peculiar circumstances in which I was placed, I was enabled to make such effectual observations as convinced me, that there had existed in the constitution of the province, in the balance of political powers, in the spirit and practice of administration in every department of the government, defects that were quite sufficient to account for a great degree of mismanagement and dissatisfaction. . . .

The same observation had also impressed on me the conviction, that, for the peculiar and disastrous dissensions of this province, there existed a far deeper and far more efficient cause—a cause which penetrated beneath its political institutions into its social state,—a cause which no reform of constitution or laws, that should leave the elements of society unaltered, could remove: but which must be removed, ere any success could be expected in any attempt to remedy the many evils of this unhappy province. I expected to find a contest between a government and a people: I found two nations warring in the bosom of a single state: I found a struggle, not of principles, but of races; and I perceived that it would be idle to attempt any amelioration of laws or institutions, until we could first succeed in terminating the deadly animosity that now separates the inhabitants of Lower Canada into the hostile divisions of French and English. . . .

It will be acknowledged by every one who has observed the progress of Anglo-Saxon colonization in America, that sooner or later the English race was sure to predominate even numerically in Lower Canada, as they predominate already by their superior knowledge, energy, enterprise, and wealth. The error, therefore, to which the present contest must be attributed, is the vain endeavour to preserve a French Canadian nationality in the midst of Anglo-American colonies and states. . . .

I believe that no permanent or efficient remedy can be devised for the disorders of Lower Canada, except a fusion of the government in that of one or more of the surrounding provinces; and as I am of opinion that the full establishment of responsible government can only be permanently secured by giving these colonies an increased importance in the politics of the Empire, I find in union the only means of remedying at once and completely the two prominent causes of their present unsatisfactory condition. . . .

If the population of Upper Canada is rightly estimated at 400,000, the English inhabitants of Lower Canada at 150,000, and the French at 450,000, the union of the two provinces would not only give a clear English majority, but one which would be increased every year by the influence of English emigration; and I have little doubt that the French, when once placed, by the legitimate course of events and the working of natural causes, in a minority, would abandon their vain hopes of nationality. I do not mean that they would immediately give up their present animosities, or instantly renounce the hope of attaining their end by violent means. But the experience of the two unions in the British Isles may teach us how effectively the strong arm of a popular legislature would compel the obedience of the refractory population; and the hopelessness of success would gradually subdue the existing animosities, and incline the French Canadians population to acquiesce in their new state of political existence.

Source: Appendix to Journal of the House of the Assembly of Upper Canada. . . being the Fourth Session of the Thirteenth Provincial Parliament (Toronto: W. L. McKenzie, 1839), pp. 1–2, 6, 22, 98–99.

Treaty of Guadalupe Hidalgo, Article 8, 1848

After United States victory in the U.S.-Mexican War (1846–48), the Treaty of Guadalupe Hidalgo (February 2, 1848) provided for the transfer of the modern states of California, Nevada, and Utah and parts of Arizona, New Mexico, Colorado, and Wyoming from Mexico to the United States in return for $15 million. Article 8 guaranteed that all Mexican citizens living in transferred territory could continue residence with full rights of property. Within one year, they could elect to maintain Mexican citizenship; otherwise, they would automatically become U.S. citizens. Although Mexican property rights were nominally protected, a vast influx of settlers following the gold rush undermined the Mexicans' political *power, while taxes and court costs led to the progressive selling off of land.*

Mexicans now established in territories previously belonging to Mexico, and which remain for the future within the limits of the United States as defined by the present treaty, shall be free to continue where they now reside, or to remove at any time to the Mexican republic, retaining the property which they possess in the said territories, or disposing thereof, and removing the proceeds wherever they please, without their being subjected on this account, to any contribution, tax, or charge whatever.

Those who shall prefer to remain in the said territories, may either retain the title and rights of Mexican citizens, or acquire those of citizens of the United States. But they shall be under the obligation to make their election within one year from the date of the exchange of ratifications of this treaty, and those who shall remain in the said territories after the expiration of that year, without having declared their intention to retain the character of Mexicans, shall be considered to have elected to become citizens of the United States.

Source: Miller, Hunter, ed. *Treaties and Other International Acts of the United States of America* (Washington, D.C.: U.S. Government Printing Office, 1937), 5: 217–218.

Proclamation of Juan Cortina, 1859

As a result of the U.S.-Mexican War (1846–48), Mexico agreed to transfer upper California and New Mexico to the United States and to accept the Rio Grande as the previously disputed boundary between Texas and Mexico. The Treaty of Guadalupe Hidalgo ending the war guaranteed former Mexican citizens now in U.S. territory full protection of property and the right to become U.S. citizens, but it was not altogether clear whether the guarantees applied to the formerly disputed territory lying between the Nueces River and the Rio Grande. Tejanos long established in the region were mistreated as Anglos pushed into the region, gradually expropriating Tejano lands and their formerly prominent role in local government. One local rancher, Juan Cortina, stood up to the encroachers, killing two Anglos in Brownsville and rallying opposition to injustices against loyal Tejanos. During the Civil War, Cortina led nearly 1,000 guerrillas against Confederate forces in the Lone Star State.

PROCLAMATION

County of Cameron,
Camp in the Rancho del Carmen,
November 23, 1859

Compatriots: A sentiment of profound indignation, the love and esteem which I profess for you, the desire which you have for that tranquillity and those guarantees which are denied you, thus violating the most sacred laws, is that which moves me to address you these words, hoping that they may prove some consolation in the midst of your adversity, which heretofore has borne the appearance of predestination.

The history of great human actions teaches us that in certain instances the principal motive which gives them impulse is the natural right to resist and conquer our enemies with a firm spirit and lively will; to persist in and to reach the consummation of this object, opening a path through the obstacles which step by step are encountered, however imposing or terrible they may be. . . .

There are, doubtless, persons so overcome by strange prejudices, men without confidence or courage to face danger in an undertaking in sisterhood with the love of liberty, who, examining the merit of acts by a false light, and preferring that of the same opinion contrary to their own, prepare no other reward than that pronounced for the "bandit," for him who, with complete abnegation of self, dedicates himself to constant labor for the happiness of those who suffering under the weight of misfortunes, eat their bread, mingled with tears, on the earth which they rated. If, my dear compatriots, I am honored with that name, I am ready for the combat.

The Mexicans who inhabit this wide region [between the Nueces River and the Rio Grande], some because they were born therein, others because since the treaty Guadalupe Hidalgo, they have been attracted to its soil by the soft influence of wise laws and the advantages of a free government, paying little attention to the reasoning of politics, are honorably and exclusively dedicated to the exercise of industry, guided by that instinct which leads the good man to comprehend, as uncontradictory truth, that only in the reign of peace can he enjoy, without inquietude, the fruit of his labor. These, under an unjust imputation of selfishness and churlishness, which do not exist, are not devoid of those sincere and expressive evidences of such friendliness and tenderness as should gain for them that confidence with which they have inspired those who have met them in social intercourse. This genial affability seems as the foundation of that proverbial prudence which, as an oracle, is consulted in all their actions and undertakings. Their humility, simplicity, and docility, directed with dignity, it may be that with excess of goodness, can, if it be desired, lead them beyond the common class of men, but causes them to excel in an irresistible inclination towards ideas of equality, a proof of their simple manners, so well adapted to that which is styled the classic land of liberty. A man, a family, and a people, possessed of qualities so eminent, with their heart in their hand and purity on their lips, encounter every day renewed reasons to know that they are surrounded by malicious and crafty monsters, who rob them in the tranquil interior of home, or with open hatred and pursuit; it necessarily follows, however great may be their pain, if not abased by humiliation and ignominy, their groans suffocated and hushed by a pain which renders them insensible, they become resigned to suffering before an abyss of misfortunes.

Mexicans! When the State of Texas began to receive the new organization which its sovereignty required as an integrate part of the Union, flocks of vampires, in the guise of men came and scattered themselves in the settlements, without any capital except the corrupt heart and the most perverse intentions. Some, brimful of laws, pledged to us their protection against the attacks of the rest; others assembled in shadowy councils, attempted and excited the robbery and burning of the houses of our relatives on the other side of the river Bravo [Rio Grande]; while others, to the abusing of our unlimited confidence, when we intrusted them with our titles, which secured the future of our families, refused to return them under false and frivolous pretexts; all, in short, with a smile on their faces, giving the lie to that which their black entrails were meditating. Many of you have been robbed of your property, incarcerated, chased, murdered, and hunted like wild beasts, because your labor was fruitful, and because your industry excited the vile avarice which led them. A voice infernal said, from the bottom of their soul, "kill them; the greater will be our gain!" Ah! This does not finish the sketch of your situation. It would appear that justice had fled from this world, leaving you to the caprice of your oppressors, who become each day more furious towards you; that, through witnesses and false charges, although the grounds may be insufficient, you may be interred in the penitentiaries, if you are not previously deprived of life by some keeper who covers himself from responsibility by the pretense of your flight. There are to be found criminals covered with frightful crimes, but they appear to have impunity until opportunity furnish them a victim; to these monsters indulgence is shown, because they are not of our race, which is unworthy, as they say, to belong to the human species. But this race, which the Anglo-American, so ostentatious of its own qualities, tries so much to blacken depreciate, and load with insults, in a spirit of blindness, which goes to the full extent of such things so common on this frontier, does not fear, placed even in the midst of its very faults, those subtle inquisitions which are so frequently made as to its manners, habits, and sentiments; nor that its deeds should be put to the test of examination in the land of reason, of justice, and of honor. This race has never humbled itself before the conqueror, though the reverse has happened, and can be established; for his is not humbled who uses among his fellow-men those courtesies which humanity prescribes; charity being the root whence springs the rule of his actions. But this race, which you see filled with gentleness and inward sweetness, gives now the cry of alarm throughout the entire extend of the land which it occupies, against all the artifice interposed by those who have become chargeable with their division and discord. This race, adorned with the most lovely disposition towards all that is good and useful in the line of progress, omits no act of diligence which might correct its many imperfections, and lift its grand edifice among the ruins of the past, respecting the ancient traditions and the maxims bequeathed by their ancestors, without being dazzled by brilliant and false appearances, nor crawling to that exaggeration of institution which, like a sublime statue, is offered for their worship and adoration.

Mexicans! Is there no remedy for you? Inviolable laws, yet useless, serve, it is true, certain judges and hypocritical authorities,

cemented in evil and injustice, to do whatever suits them, and to satisfy their vile avarice at the cot of your patience and suffering; rising in their frenzy, even to the taking of life, through the treacherous hands of their bailiffs. The wicked way in which many of you have been often-times involved in persecution, accompanied by circumstances making it the more bitter, is now well known; these crimes being hid from society under the shadow of a horrid night, those implacable people, with the haughty spirit which suggests impunity for a life of criminality, have pronounced, doubt ye not, your sentence, which is, with accustomed insensibility, as you have seen, on the point of execution.

Mexicans! My part is taken; the voice of revelation whispers to me that to me is entrusted the work of breaking the chains of your slavery, and that the Lord will enable me, with powerful arm, to fight against our enemies, in compliance with the requirements of that Sovereign Majesty, who, from this day forward, will hold us under His protection. On my part, I am ready to offer myself as a sacrifice for your happiness; and counting upon the means necessary for the discharge of my ministry, you may count upon my cooperation, should no cowardly attempt put an end to my days. This undertaking will be sustained on the following bases:

First. A society is organized in the State of Texas, which devotes itself sleeplessly until the work is crowned with success, to the improvement of the unhappy condition of those Mexicans resident therein; extermination their tyrants, to which end those which compose it are ready to shed their blood and suffer the death of martyrs.

Second. As this society contains within itself the elements necessary to accomplish the great end of its labors, the veil of impenetrable secrecy covers "The Great Book" in which the articles of its constitution are written; while so delicate are the difficulties which must be overcome that no honorable man can have cause for alarm, if imperious exigencies require them to act without reserve.

Third. The Mexicans of Texas repose their lot under the good sentiments of the governor elect of the State, General Houston, and trust that upon his elevation to power he will begin with care to give us legal protection within the limits of his powers.

Mexicans! Peace be with you! Good inhabitants of the State of Texas, look on them as brothers, and keep in mind that which the Holy Spirit saith: "Thou shalt not be the friend of the passionate man; nor join thyself to the madman, lest thou learn his mode of work and scandalize thy soul."

Juan N. Cortina

Source: U.S. Congress, House, *Difficulties on the Southwestern Frontier,* 36th Cong., 1st sess., 1860, H. Exec. Doc. 52, pp. 70–82.

Excerpts from the Homestead Act, 1862

The Homestead Act was the result of steady opposition by workingmen's groups, western settlers, and agrarians to the

American government's policy of using western lands as a source of revenue. Promising 160 acres of free land to any head of household who would develop the land and live on it continuously for five years, it did more than any other piece of legislation to open the West to family farmers. The measure also enabled immigrant groups to maintain a strong sense of Old World identity in the New World, as their lands were often taken up in remote regions of the upper Midwest and plains territories. German and Scandinavian immigrants were particularly attracted, as they often had modest amounts of capital to establish themselves.

Be it enacted by the Senate and House of Representatives of the United States of America in Congress assembled, That any person who is the head of a family, or who has arrived at the age of twenty-one years, and is a citizen of the United States, or who shall have filed his declaration of intention to become such, as required by the naturalization laws of the United States, and who has never borne arms against the United States Government or given aid and comfort to its enemies, shall, from and after the first January, eighteen hundred and sixty-three, be entitled to enter one quarter section or a less quantity of unappropriated public lands, upon which said person may have filed a preemption claim, or which may, at the time the application is made, be subject to preemption at one dollar and twenty-five cents, or less, per acre; or eighty acres or less of such unappropriated lands, at two dollars and fifty cents per acre, to be located in a body, in conformity to the legal subdivisions of the public lands, and after the same shall have been surveyed: Provided, That any person owning and residing on land may, under the provisions of this act, enter other land lying contiguous to his or her said land, which shall not, with the land so already owned and occupied, exceed in the aggregate one hundred and sixty acres. . . .

Sec. 5. And be it further enacted, That if, at any time after the filing of the affidavit, as required in the second section of this act, and before the expiration of the five years aforesaid, it shall be proven, after due notice to the settler, to the satisfaction of the register of the land office, that the person having filed such affidavit shall have actually changed his or her residence or abandoned the said land for more than six months at any time, then and in that event the land so entered shall revert to the government. . . .

Sec. 8. And be it further enacted, That nothing in this act shall be so construed as to prevent any person who has availed him or herself of the befits of the first section of this act, from paying the minimum price, or the price to which the same may have graduated, for the quantity of land so entered at any time before the expiration of the five years, and obtaining a patent therefore from the government, as in other cases provided by law, on making proof of settlement and cultivation as provided by existing laws granting preemption rights.

Source: Daniel J. Boorstin, ed., *An American Primer,* 2 vols. (Chicago: University of Chicago Press, 1966), pp. 387–390.

Letters from Iowa to Norway, 1863 and 1865

After the vast influx of Irish and German immigrants during the 1830s, 1840s, and 1850s, Norwegians represented the vanguard of a new wave of western Europeans. Although personal freedom in Norway was substantial, old social distinctions remained, and good farmland was scarce and expensive. Most Norwegians came to North America with their families, intending to stay and establish a new life. By 1865, nearly 80,000 had settled in the United States. Though life was hard, the rewards were substantial. Letters like those of Gro Svendse, who settled with her husband in northwestern Iowa, were eagerly awaited in Norway and frequently led to further emigration from the homeland.

1863

Dear Parents, Sisters, and Brothers (always in my thoughts):

I have often thought that I ought to tell you about life here in the New World. Everything is so totally different from what it was in our beloved Norway. You never will really know what it's like, although you no doubt try to imagine what it might be. Your pictures would be all wrong, just as mine were. I only wish that I could be with you to tell you all about it. Even if I were to write you countless pages, I still could not tell you everything.

I remember I used to wonder when I heard that it would be impossible to keep the milk here as we did at home. Now I have learned that it is indeed impossible because of the heat here in the summertime. One can't make cheese out of the milk because of flies, bugs, and other insects. I don't know the names of all these insects, but this I do know: If one were to make cheese here in the summertime, the cheese itself would be alive with bugs. Toward late autumn it should be possible to keep the milk. The people who have more milk than they need simply feed it to the hogs.

It's difficult, too, to preserve the butter. One must pour brine over it or salt it; otherwise it gets full of maggots. Therefore it is best, if one is not too far from town, to sell the butter at once. This summer we have been getting from eight to ten cents a pound. Not a great profit. For this reason people around here do not have many cows—just enough to supply the milk needed for the household. It's not wise to have more than enough milk, because the flies are everywhere. Even the bacon must be preserved in brine, and so there are different ways of doing everything.

I have so much to tell you. We have no twilight here in the summertime. Even in June, on the longest day of the year, the sun doesn't rise before 4:23 and sets at 7:40. The nights are as dark as they are at home in autumn. We never have rain without thunder and lightning. The thunderstorms are so violent that one might think it was the end of the world. The whole sky is aflame with lightning, and the thunder rolls and crashes as though it were right above our heads. Quite often the lightning strikes down both cattle and people, damages property, and splinters sturdy oak trees into many pieces. Even though one did not fear the thunder in Norway, one can easily become frightened here.

Then there is the prairie fire or, as they call it here, "Faieren." This is terrifying, and the fire rages in both the spring and the fall. Whatever it leaves behind in the fall, it consumes in the spring, so there is nothing left of the long grass on the prairies, sloughs, and marshes. It is a strange and terrible sight to see all the fields a sea of fire. Quite often the scorching flames sweep everything along in their path—people, cattle hay, fences. . . .

Snakes are found here in the summertime and are also a worry to us. I am horribly afraid of them, particularly the rattlesnake. The rattlesnake is the same as the *klapperslange.* I have seen many of them and thousands of ordinary snakes.

I could tell you even more, but possibly many who read this letter may think I am exaggerating. I assure you that all that I have told you I have experienced myself. If they do not believe me, they should come over and find out for themselves. Then they would tell you the same things I tell you.

By the way, no one leaving Norway should sell all his possessions as most people do. Everything that is useful in Norway is also useful here. The women can make use of all their clothes, with the exception of their headdress, bodice, jackets, and kerchiefs. All these they could sell, but all the other clothes they could make over and wear here. Everything Norwegian is of better quality than what can be bought here. So I am very grateful to you, my parents, every time I touch anything I have received from you. Bedding, too, should be brought along, as it's colder here in the winter than in Norway. Even those who criticize Norway and praise America must admit this. . . .
Estherville, Emmett Co., Iowa

December 3, 1865
Precious Parents, Sisters, and Brothers:

. . . We have had a good year, a rich harvest both from the grain that we sowed as well as from the wild fruit and grain. We have plowed and fenced in three acres of new land. On this plot we raised ninety bushels of corn, twenty-four bushels of potatoes, and a plant called sugar cane or sorghum. This sugar cane is pressed and cooked into syrup or molasses. . . . We also got some fruit from our garden. It would take too long to list all of it, but I must tell you something about a fruit called "watermelon." We have an enormous quantity of them; I can't compare them to anything I ever saw in Norway. They are as big as a child's head; some are larger. They are round, and the inside is red or yellow. The melons are sweet and juicy. They are eaten just as they are taken from the field, provided they are ripe. . . . We sometimes sell melons to wayfarers passing by. We usually get ten cents apiece for them. However, most of the melons we shared with our friends and neighbors, many of whom had walked several miles in order to get a chance to taste our watermelons and muskmelons. The latter fruit is not quite so good as the first.

Our harvest was not abundant, but since it was enough to supply our needs for the year and since it was raised on land that we call our own, I want to tell you about it. This summer we plowed up three acres of land that we plan to sow with wheat next year. Had we known that Ole would come back, we would have plowed up more land this summer. Not knowing when he would return, we let it go with just three acres. By the time he did come home, it was too late to plow any more, so we're letting it go till next summer. So you see we haven't so many acres "under the plow" as they say, but it's not so easy to get ahead if one attempts too much.

This winter we are feeding twenty-one head of cattle, two pigs (a sow and a boar), two horses (a mare and a colt), and three sheep belonging to brother Ole. We also have two bulls belonging to brother Sevat Svendsen. We are paid cash for feeding these cattle. All told we have sixteen farm animals of our own, not counting the young cattle. . . .

Our house is very small and humble, but it's a shelter from the cold winter. I shall say no more about it. However, next spring, if we are all here and all is well, we hope to build a large and comfortable house. We shall build even though it costs a great deal of money to build houses in this country.

The spring of 1864 we bought twelve and a half acres of woodland for one hundred dollars, or eight dollars an acre. We borrowed the money from old Svend at seven percent interest with five years to pay. The trees are exceptionally fine, so if we should want to sell the land again, it would not be difficult to get twice the amount that we paid for it. There is not a great deal of woodland here, and therefore that type of land is much in demand and the prices are steadily rising. . . .

We have had very little pastoral service so far, but we soon hope to get more. A certain Pastor Torgersen has taken it upon himself to visit this congregation two or three times a year. I think we have been very fortunate this fall to have had two services. Two years ago we had thirteen Norwegian families in this congregation, and now we have thirty families and more are constantly moving in. Maybe in time we may be so many that we can have our own pastor.

Source: Gro Svendsen, *Frontier Mother: The Letters of Gro Svendsen,* eds. Pauline Farseth and Theodore C. Blegen (Northfield, Minn.: Norwegian-American Historical Association, 1950), pp. 39–41, 70–73.

Documents on Chinese Exclusion, 1880–1882

In the three decades following the California gold rush of 1848–49, around 300,000 Chinese immigrated to the United States. By the 1870s, they constituted almost 10 percent of the population. At first, the hardworking Chinese were generally well received, working in mines and related service industries and in railway construction. With the economic hard times of the 1870s, many westerners blamed Chinese immigrants for taking jobs and depressing wages. By the late 1870s, politicians in the Midwest and East took an interest in placating an increasingly violent white labor force and thus were inclined to agree to limitations on Chinese immigration. In 1879, Henry George published Progress and Poverty, *one of the most influential economic tracts of the 19th century, in which he concluded that the Chinese were economically backward and "unassimilable." In the same year, President Rutherford B. Hayes encouraged Congress to examine ways of limiting Chinese immigration. The United States and China modified the labor provisions of the Burlingame Treaty (1868) by negotiating a new measure, the Angell Treaty (1881), which gave the United States authority to regulate the immigration of Chinese laborers. A bill was quickly brought forward to exclude Chinese laborers for 20 years, but it was vetoed by President Chester A. Arthur, who argued that such a long period of exclusion would contravene the articles of the Angell Treaty. Arthur reluctantly signed a revised measure, the Chinese Exclusion Act on May 6, 1882. The Chinese Exclusion Act was the first measure to exclude a specific ethnic group from immigrating to the United States.*

ANGELL TREATY, 1881

. . . Whereas the Government of the United States, because of the constantly increasing immigration of Chinese laborers to the territory of the United States, and the embarrassments consequent upon such immigration, now desires to negotiate a modification of the existing Treaties which shall not be in direct contravention of their spirit: . . .

ART. I. Whenever in the opinion of the Government of the United States, the coming of Chinese laborers to the United States, or their residence therein, affects or threatens to affect the interests of that country, or to endanger the good order of the said country or of any locality within the territory thereof, the Government of China agrees that the Government of the United States may regulate, limit, or suspend such coming or residence, but may not absolutely prohibit it. The limitation or suspension shall be reasonable and shall apply only to Chinese who may go to the United States as laborers, other classes not being included in the limitations. Legislation taken in regard to Chinese laborers will be of such a character only as is necessary to enforce the regulation, limitation or suspension of immigration, and immigrants shall not be subject to personal maltreatment or abuse.

ART. II. Chinese subjects, whether proceeding to the United States as teachers, students, merchants, or from curiosity, together with their body and household servants, and Chinese laborers who are now in the United States, shall be allowed to go and come of their own free will and accord, and shall be accorded all the rights, privileges, immunities and exemptions which are accorded to the citizens and subjects of the most favored nation.

ART. III. If Chinese laborers, or Chinese of any other class, now either permanently or temporarily residing in the territory of the United States, meet with ill treatment at the hands of any other persons, the Government of the United States will exert all its power to devise measures for their protection and to secure to them the same rights, privileges, immunities and exemptions as may be enjoyed by the citizens or subjects of the most favored nation, and to which they are entitled by treaty. . . .

Source: Malloy, William, ed. *Treaties, Conventions, International Acts, Protocols, and Agreements between the United States of America and Other Powers, 1776–1909* (Washington, D.C.: U.S. Government Printing Office, 1910), 1: 237 ff.

CHINESE EXCLUSION ACT, MAY 6, 1882

An act to execute certain treaty stipulations relating to Chinese. WHEREAS, in the opinion of the Government of the United States the coming of Chinese laborers to this country endangers the good order of certain localities within the territory thereof: Therefore,

Be it enacted, That from and after the expiration of ninety days next after the passage of this act, and until the expiration of ten years next after the passage of this act, the coming of Chinese laborers to the United States be, . . . suspended; and during such suspension it shall not be lawful for any Chinese laborer to come, or, having so come after the expiration of said ninety days, to remain within the United States.

SEC. 2. That the master of any vessel who shall knowingly bring within the United States on such vessel, and land or permit to be landed, any Chinese laborer, from any foreign port or place, shall be deemed guilty of a misdemeanor, and on conviction thereof shall be punished by a fine of not more than five hundred dollars for each and every such Chinese laborer so brought, and may be also imprisoned for a term not exceeding one year.

SEC. 3. That the two foregoing sections shall not apply to Chinese laborers who were in the United States on the seventeenth day of November, eighteen hundred and eighty, or who shall have come into the same before the expiration of ninety days next after the passage of this act, . . .

SEC. 4. That for the purpose of properly identifying Chinese laborers who were in the United States . . . or shall come into the same before the expiration of ninety days next after the passage of this act, and in order to furnish them with the proper evidence of their right to go from and to come to the United States of their own free will and accord, as provided by the treaty of the United States and China . . . the collector of customs of the district from which any such Chinese laborer shall depart from the United States shall, in person or by deputy, go on board each vessel having on board any such Chinese laborer and cleared or about to sail from his district for a foreign port, and on such vessel make a list of all such laborers, which shall be entered in registry-books to be kept for that purpose, in which shall be stated the name, age, occupation, last place of residence, physical marks or peculiarities, and all facts necessary for identification of each of such Chinese laborers, which books shall be kept in the custom-house. . . .

SEC. 6. That in order to the faithful execution of articles one and two of the treaty in this act before mentioned, every Chinese person other than a laborer who may be entitled by said treaty and this act to come within the United States, and who shall be about to come to the United States, shall be identified as so entitled by the Chinese Government in each case, such identity to be evidenced by a certificate issued under the authority of said government, which certificate shall be in the English language or (if not in the English language) accompanied by a translation into English, stating such right to come, and which certificate shall state the name, title, or official rank, if any, the age, height, and all physical peculiarities former and present occupation or profession and place of residence in China of the person to whom the certificate is issued and that such person is entitled conformably to the treaty in this act mentioned to come within the United States. . . .

SEC. 12. That no Chinese person shall be permitted to enter the United States by land without producing to the proper office of customs the certificate in this act required of Chinese persons seeking to land from a vessel. Any any Chinese person found unlawfully within the United States shall be caused to be removed therefrom to the country from whence he came, by direction of the President of the United States, and at the cost of the United States, after being brought before some justice, judge, or commissioner of a court of the United States and found to be one not lawfully entitled to be or remain in the United States.

SEC. 13. That this act shall not apply to diplomatic and other officers of the Chinese Government traveling upon the business of that government, whose credentials shall be taken as equivalent to the certificate in this act mentioned, and shall exempt them and their body and household servants from the provisions of this act as to other Chinese persons.

SEC. 14. That hereafter no State court or court of the United States shall admit Chinese to citizenship; and all laws in conflict with this act are hereby repealed.

SEC. 15. That the words "Chinese laborers," whenever used in this act, shall be construed to mean both skilled and unskilled laborers and Chinese employed in mining.

Source: U.S. Statutes at Large 22 (1882), p. 58ff.

Nativism in Print, Two Examples, 1916–1917

Fear of a Japanese so-called yellow peril on the West Coast and the record pace of immigration from southern and eastern Europe since the turn of the century, along with the profound shock of World War I, led to a growing nativism in the United States after 1900. In public discourse, it was fostered by men such as Madison Grant, a wealthy New York City naturalist and urban planner, who urged the Nordic ideal, "the white man par excellence," who was about to be made extinct by the new "melting pot" society. Grant was only one of many Ameri-

cans who feared the consequences of almost unrestricted immigration. As a result, the Immigration Act of 1917 was passed, marking a turning point in American immigration legislation. Prohibiting entry to aliens more than 16 years of age who could not read 30–40 words in their own language, it was the first legislation aimed at restricting, rather than regulating, European immigration. It further extended the tendency toward a "white" immigration policy, creating an "Asiatic barred zone" that prohibited entry of most Asians.

EXCERPT FROM MADISON GRANT, *THE PASSING OF THE GREAT RACE*, 1916

We Americans must realize that the altruistic ideals which have controlled our social development during the past century and the maudlin sentimentalism that has made America "an asylum for the oppressed," are sweeping the nation toward a racial abyss. If the Melting Pot is allowed to boil without control and we continue to follow our national motto and deliberately blind ourselves to all "distinctions of race, creed or color," the type of native American of Colonial descent will become as extinct as the Athenian of the age of Pericles, and the Viking of the days of Rollo.

Source: Madison Grant, The Passing of the Great Race, new ed. (New York: Charles Scribner's Sons, 1918), p. 263.

EXCERPT FROM THE (U.S.) IMMIGRATION ACT, 1917

Immigration Act, 1917. Section 3. That the following classes of aliens shall be excluded from admission into the United States: All idiots, imbeciles, feeble-minded persons, epileptics, insane persons . . . persons with chronic alcoholism; paupers; professional beggars; vagrants; persons afflicted with tuberculosis in any form or a loathsome or dangerous contagious disease; persons not comprehended within any of the foregoing excluded classes who are found to be and are certified by the examining surgeon as being mentally or physically defective, such physical defect being of a nature which may affect the ability of such alien to earn a living; persons who have been convicted of a felony or other crime or misdemeanor involving moral turpitude; polygamists, or persons who practice polygamy or believe in and advocate the practice of polygamy; anarchists, or persons who advocate the overthrow by force or violence of the Government of the United States, or of all forms of law . . . or who advocate the assassination of public officials, or who advocate and teach the unlawful destruction of property . . .; prostitutes, or persons coming to the United States for the purpose of prostitution or immoral purposes . . .; persons hereinafter called contract laborers . . .; persons likely to become public charges . . .; persons whose ticket or passage is paid for with the money of any corporation, association, society, municipality, or foreign government, either directly or indirectly; stowaways . . .; all children under sixteen years of age unaccompanied by or not coming to one or both of their parents . . . unless otherwise provided for by existing treaties, persons who are natives of islands not possessed by the United States adjacent to the continent of Asia, situate south of the twentieth parallel latitude north, west of the one hundred and sixtieth meridian of longitude east from Greenwich, and north of the tenth parallel of latitude south, or who are natives of any country, province, or dependency situate on the Continent of Asia west of the one hundred and tenth meridian of longitude east from Greenwich and east of the fiftieth meridian of longitude east from Greenwich and south of the fiftieth parallel of latitude north, except that portion of said territory situate between the fiftieth and sixty-fourth and thirty-eighth parallels of latitude north, and no alien now in any way excluded from, or prevented from entering the United States shall be admitted to the United States. . . .

That after three months from the passage of this Act in addition to the aliens who are by law now excluded from admission into the United States, the following persons shall also be excluded:

All aliens over sixteen years of age, physically capable of reading, who cannot read the English language, or some other language or dialect, including Hebrew or Yiddish: Provided, That any admissable alien, or any alien heretofore or hereafter legally admitted, or any citizen of the United States, may bring in or send for his father or grandfather over fifty-five years of age, his wife, his mother, his grandmother, or his unmarried or widowed daughter, if otherwise admissible, whether such relative can read or not; and such relative shall be permitted to enter. That for the purpose of ascertaining whether aliens can read the immigrant inspectors shall be furnished with slips of uniform size, prepared under the direction of the Attorney General, each containing not less than thirty nor more than forty words in ordinary use, printed in plainly legible type in some one of the various languages or dialects of immigrants. Each alien may designate the particular language or dialect in which he desires the examination to be made, and shall be required to read the words printed on the slip in such language or dialect. . . .

Source: Immigration Act, U.S. Code, 39 sec. 874.

An Autobiographical Account of the Immigration Work of a Voluntary Agency, 1920s

In 1922, reports of Russians suffering as a result of the Communist takeover in Russia led many Canadian Christian denominations to support a voluntary resettlement program. The Mennonites were most active, but there were also significant efforts made by the Roman Catholic, Lutheran, and Baptist Churches. In 1925, the Northern Conference of German Baptists formed the Baptist Immigration Society and began to work closely with the Canadian Pacific and Canadian Northern Railways to bring Baptist and other refugees to the Canadian prairies from Russia, Poland, and other eastern European countries. In 1929, with the support of the two railroads, the organization was expanded and incorporated as the German Baptist Colonization Society. Most of the east European immigrants of the 1920s were brought to Canada in small groups through the efforts of such voluntary agencies. Below, colonization secretary Reverend F. A. Bloedow describes his work in bringing German immigrants to two Manitoba settlements, at Minitonas-Swan River and Ste Rose-Ochre River.

(Translated from *Der Sendbote,* February 1936):

I was no sooner back on my legs, when the Lord had a new task for me. Brother William Kuhn came to visit us and greeted me with a hearty brother kiss, rejoicing over my recovery. At the same time he informed me that now I had to assist him and the Mission Society in matters of immigration. He based his request on my accurate knowledge of Canada and the Canadian way of life. So I had to accompany him right away to the railroad, which was to transport our immigrants in order to be presented to the proper railway authorities and so to be introduced properly to my coming task. While I was still recuperating in bed, they had already discussed the immigration matter and informed at that time of the present situation.

Soon I was in full action and met and escorted the first group from Quebec. From that time until 1939 we served approximately 2,500 immigrants. The ministry was not popular everywhere, but on the long run it proved a great blessing to our conference. Without it our conference would not be where it is. Every church received its quota of new people. Not all became a blessing. But wherever a church accepted the people properly it received advantages. Wherever this did not take place the blame was either in a non-sympathetic church leadership or the church was too weak to assimilate the new blood. One particular phase of the immigration movement has up to now been receiving sufficient attention. I refer to the new flow of real good material into the ministry through the Seminary. The immigration did bring a great number of able young students to Rochester, as a result of which today more than one half of the student body comes from the Northern Conference. And these brethren are not straw-men; they are real first-class men, who ably meet the demands in both languages.

In connection with this task I was also privileged to make a trip to Europe in the interest of immigration. But this was not a pleasure trip when we could enjoy the sights of Europe, but it was a real business trip, on which I did not even have the time to visit my own home for more than two days which I had not seen for thirty-six years. But I owe much to this journey, which brought me through almost the entire Danube mission fields, as well as to Poland, Holland and England. Everywhere, except in the two last countries, I had the privilege of proclaiming the gospel and bringing lectures. My two or three travel companions will testify to the fact that even this part of my travel activity did not remain without blessing. I shall always remember this trip with a great deal of satisfaction. I need not at this place go into details since the report appeared in this paper at that time. Suffice it to say that this journey had a fruitful effect on everything.

The immigration task was not easy. At one time I accompanied a group of 173 people from Halifax to Winnipeg. Since we had neither sleeper nor diner on the train, I had to go three days and three nights without a warm meal, and without bed, sleeping on the hard benches of the old colonist cars. During the daytime we had to watch over the passengers, lest anyone should remain behind. Frequently I arrived home dead tired, but had to arise early the next morning to look after the onward trip and housing of people. Without self-praise we can state that the work was a blessed one. As a result every church gained new members, in addition to the founding of two settlements with a church. One of these has already grown to be one of the largest if not the largest of our rural churches, which is being served by my good friend, Rev. J. Luebeck (Minitonas, Man. Ed.). The other church (St. Rose-Ochre River, Man., Ed.) has already transferred ten families to Vancouver and Kelowna.

The depression came with the years 1929 and 1930 and with this the doors for immigrants closed automatically. My co-workers on this project, the brethren E. P. Wahl, A. Kujath and R. Runtz as well as my son Wilfred and as the pastors who served as counselors and assistant, but particularly Dr. Wm. Kuhn as general manager, have deserved the thanks and acknowledgement of the entire denomination, but especially from the Northern Conference. Without immigration this conference would have become stagnant. If, however, the conference utilizes the movement properly it has the potential of becoming first among its sister conferences.

Double Service

Even after the immigration ceased, there remained much work with the collection of travel advances, loans for cows as well as the further guidance of the immigrants in many areas. This in itself could have kept a man busy fill-time, but for some time I had given my time to pastorless churches, and provided with a railroad pass looked after their needs. It was, therefore, quite natural that the mission committee asked me to attend to all pastorless churches.

Thus I came quite naturally back into travel service besides the ministry in settlement. This double service was spread over the entire conference area. Neither did it remain without visible results. I could encourage a good number of churches and advise them in the calling of a pastor. Kelowna was called into life and Vernon received its beginning. During evangelistic meetings a good number of people were converted and new churches established. After one particular beautiful revival I could baptize 41 souls; in another church there were 18, and in a third church we had over 20 souls which I could dedicate to the Lord in baptism and incorporate into the church.

Besides this service in churches I could assist in Bible schools in three Associations. This work became of great impor-

tance to the conference, but unfortunately it is still not on a proper basis. It will moreover never be properly based until a man with the necessary talent dedicate himself to this task on a conference-wide basis and establish some unity of purpose. Up to this time there has not been the clear and unified vision for this task.

Since April 1935, my service to churches is limited to two fields. For this work we have set some very definite goals and believe in the realization and assistance of our Master. We intend to add to each of these churches a preaching station. In one of the churches we have already been successful. In the other one we shall carry this out in the spring if God will give us open doors. We firmly believe in the victory of the cause of Christ even on these fields, and trust that in the not too distant future we shall see two pastors on these fields. We enjoy buildings nests for others, even if at the expense of our own assured future.

Gradually the immigration is again taking foot. With the return of better times it will under the leadership of our new government again take firm footing. We may not be able to conduct this ministry as in former times, but it will again require the full-time service of a man. God willing we should enjoy to continue directing this service for the welfare of our beloved conference. The past has given us plenty of experience and ability. God willing we shall complete 60 years of our life this year. As far as strength and joy for work I feel that our age is like unto the youth. With good health I would enjoy living 100 years, in order to partake in the completion of the Kingdom of God on this earth. If the Lord should hold me worthy to share during the coming thirty years a similar portion of work as during the past thirty years, I would with great faithfulness and dedication serve my Master and Saviour. He be praised in all eternity.

Source: William Sturhahn, *They Came from East and West: A History of Immigration to Canada* (Winnipeg, Canada: North American Baptist Immigration and Colonization Society, 1976), pp. 295–298.

A Japanese Woman's Account of Her Evacuation from British Columbia, 1942

Following the bombing of Pearl Harbor, Hawaii, on December 7, 1941, Japanese Americans and Japanese Canadians were widely suspected as supporters of the aggressive militarism of the Japanese Empire. Without evidence of any sabotage or spying, on February 19, 1942, President Franklin D. Roosevelt signed an executive order resulting in the forcible internment of 120,000 Japanese Americans, two-thirds of whom were born in the United States. In the same month, the Canadian government ordered the expulsion of 22,000 Japanese Canadians from a 100-mile strip along the Pacific coast. In the following excerpt from an interview, Maki Fukishima recalls how she lost everything in the evacuation and why she stayed in Canada.

In wartime, all kinds of rumours were circulating. Some people said that if young people were sent to the camps out east, they might have to go to war. At the time, my oldest son had a wife and a baby. I thought it would be too sad if they were separated, and we thought of a place where we could all go together. We didn't have the money to move where we wanted. So we applied for sugar beet growing in Alberta, where we could go as a family.

The people around me didn't have anything good to say about our going to the sugar beet fields. My husband's best friend said "You shouldn't go to work on beets. It's like being a traitor." Making sugar out of beets meant cooperating with the Canadian government that had a policy to produce more sugar. It would be like making bullets for rifles or a sign of loyalty to this country.

I said "We're going to the sugar beet fields, because we decided that's how we can go as a family. The last thing we'd do is aim a rifle at Japan. I've got a Rising Sun flag in my heart," and off we went. We'd never farmed, so that was a worry, but we went because we'd be together. The Japanese all had different ways of thinking, and coping with things, but we were about the only family that went from Fairview to Alberta; I didn't know what else to do.

My husband had died in January [1942] and we left Vancouver in May. My second son was working as a book-keeper in the Fraser Valley Farmers' Association. He sacrificed himself and took everybody along with him to Alberta. He was 22 or 23. At the time I wasn't naturalized, so I was an "Enemy Alien." In the late 1920s, the thinking generally was that there shouldn't be any extra Japanese around, and after it looked like a war was coming, it wasn't easy to get naturalized.

We were in Alberta four years, all during the war, and had a terrible time. When we were on the train leaving New Westminster, a telegram came. It said they didn't need any more Japanese. We'd cleared out our house, so even if we were told to go home, there wasn't any home to go to. So we went off just as we were. We got to Lethbridge in Alberta, after two whole days on the train. Nobody came to meet us, no bosses. They didn't want any Japanese coming. Then it got to be like being sold as slaves. We got taken all across Alberta from west to east, stopping at every station, and family after family got sold off.

We were just five adults and a baby, but we weren't farmers so it was very hard to find a buyer. We were leftover goods, and got sold at the very end. Nowadays, there's oil in Alberta, but then, it was nothing but poor farming villages. It was a cold place, not good for beets. Right away, we planted seeds, but they didn't grow well. July came, but now it was too hot and the beets grew and grew, it was earth that you couldn't grow daikon radish in, but it was good for leaves. We broke our backs working, but we failed.

The first year we got treated like enemies, and the people hated us. But after that year, they realized that Japanese were hard workers, and honest too, so they took a liking to us, and when you said, "All right, we're leaving the fields," now they wouldn't let us. The bosses just wouldn't sign the papers. Their beet-field labour would dry up, so they wouldn't let us leave the province. There was sugar shortage in wartime, so they had to get beets grown. There was no work at all besides beet growing, and the young people started wanting to go east. . . .

We lost everything in four years. I didn't get mad. I thought it was no use. Because we were Japanese, we had to go where they said. You can't do anything else, if this isn't the country you were born in; if you're told to get out, that's what you have to do. When we left B.C., I didn't think Japan would lose the war, and I thought it would be over soon, so we left everything behind. We left the good things, that is, and only brought the junk. My feeling was to be loyal to this country. But at that time, I hadn't been naturalized, so I was a citizen of an enemy country. I thought I'd go to Japan, because the children could get along by themselves. . . .

After the war, people had all kinds of ideas about what they should do with themselves, and I had trouble deciding, too. Some people kept saying I should go to Japan, and others said: "In Japan, they've got everything ready to welcome us." But other people said, "Even if you go back to Japan, what are you going to do after the war in a small country like that?" I was at my wits' end, I didn't know where to turn, and in the end I went and signed in to be repatriated. My second son was shocked at this, and came hurrying back from the east, and applied to the Mounties for a cancellation. He insisted we were in Canada, and he wouldn't let his mother go back to Japan alone.

He went through all the steps to change the application, and a few months later, I got news that I could stay in Canada, so my problem was solved. But I'd thought that if I was going to be a burden to my children, it would be better to live in Japan. But it isn't good for a family to get split up, no matter what.

Source: Tomoko Makabe, *Picture Brides: Japanese Women in Canada*, trans. Kathleen Chisato Merken (Toronto: Multicultural History Society of Ontario, 1995), pp. 59–62.

Anglo-American Committee of Inquiry, 1946

With the war over, the Allies met to examine a wide range of issues regarding the millions of persons who had been displaced by World War II, especially the Jews who had escaped the Holocaust. Their task, as stated in the committee report, was to "examine political, economic and social conditions in Palestine as they bear upon the problem of Jewish immigration and settlement" and "the position of the Jews in those countries in Europe where they have been the victims of Nazi and Fascist persecution." Although Palestine offered significant help to the Jews, the commission recognized that they alone could not meet Jewish needs. It was recommended that both the United States and Canada relax some immigration rules and encourage other nations to do the same.

Recommendation No. 1. We have to report that such information as we received about countries other than Palestine gave no hope of substantial assistance in finding homes for Jews wishing or impelled to leave Europe.

But Palestine alone cannot meet the emigration needs of the Jewish victims of Nazi and Fascist persecution; the whole world shares responsibility for them and indeed for the resettlement of all "displaced persons".

We therefore recommend that our Governments together, and in association with other countries, should endeavor immediately to find new homes for all such "displaced persons", irrespective of creed or nationality, whose ties with their former communities have been irreparably broken.

Though emigration will solve the problems of some victims of persecution, the overwhelming majority, including a considerable number of Jews, will continue to live in Europe. We recommend therefore that our Governments endeavor to secure that immediate effect is given to the provision of the United Nations Charter calling for "universal respect for, and observance of, human rights and fundamental freedoms for all without distinction as to race, sex, language, or religion".

Comment

In recommending that our Governments, in association with other countries, should endeavor to find new homes for "displaced persons", we do not suggest that any country should be asked to make a permanent change in its immigration policy. The conditions, which we have seen in Europe, are unprecedented, and so unlikely to arise again that we are convinced that special provision could and should be made in existing immigration laws to meet this unique and peculiarly distressing situation.

Furthermore, we believe that much could be accomplished—particularly in regard to those "displaced persons", including Jews, who have relatives in countries outside Europe—by a relaxation of administrative regulations.

Our investigations have led us to believe that a considerable number of Jews will continue to live in most European countries. In our view the mass emigration of all European Jews would be of service neither to the Jews themselves nor to Europe. Every effort should be made to enable the Jews to rebuild their shattered communities, while permitting those Jews, who wish to do so, to emigrate. In order to achieve this, restitution of Jewish property should be effected as soon as possible. Our investigations showed us that the Governments chiefly concerned had for the most part already passed legislation to this end. A real obstacle, however, to individual restitution is that the attempt to give effect to this legislation is frequently a cause of active anti-Semitism. We suggest that, for the reconstruction of the Jewish communities, restitution of their corporate property, either through reparations payments or through other means, is of the first importance.

Nazi occupation has left behind it a legacy of anti-Semitism. This cannot be combated by legislation alone. The only really effective antidotes are the enforcement by each Government of guaranteed civil liberties and equal rights, a program of education in the positive principles of democracy, [and] the sanction of a strong world public opinion combined with economic recovery and stability.

Source: Anglo-American Committee of Inquiry, Lausanne, Switzerland, April 20, 1946 (Department of State, Publication 2536, Near Eastern Series 2), found on Avalon Project, available online, URL: http://www.yale.edu/lawweb/avalon/anglo/angpre.htm, accessed March 6, 2004.

Recollections of the Refugee Years, 1946–1970

World War II displaced millions of people. Hundreds of thousands of homes were destroyed, and thousands of civilians were forced into military service and taken far from their homelands. Some had fled before advancing Soviet armies, fearful of living under Joseph Stalin's rule. At war's end, some 2 million were still living in refugee camps. Finding a home in Canada meant freedom from the camps but also new, albeit smaller, obstacles to overcome. Here are the postwar reminiscences of two refugees who settled in Canada.

Freedom and Beef Stew

To be free. To be free in a country that is free. That is why we came to Canada. No other reason at first. Just freedom.

I don't know how. I didn't read about it. I didn't know any Canadians or about Canada. I just knew it would be a free country, and when I said to my wife, "This camp is no good, we'll be here forever, so we're going to Canada," she said, "Good. It will be free, a place where we can have our children being free."

In the camp where we were interviewed, the Canadian official said Winnipeg would be a good place to go. I didn't care. I didn't know where Winnipeg was. It sounded like it might have been an Indian word. He said, "There are a lot of Jewish people and they will look after you. They have organizations and things like that and if you want, they will find you a place to stay and a place to work."

That's the way it was. We were met at the station by the hotel which is torn down, the Royal Alexandra, and there was a big bunch of refugees. We were called Displaced Persons. No home, no money. Nothing. Just ourselves and our kids, and saying we want to be free. . . .

The food. Look, mister, in the camps there was no food, and this was in October of 1946 when we left, some of the first ones to come to Canada. You got a bowl of soup. You might find a bit of meat in it. Tiny, like this. No bigger than this, my thumbnail. Bread at first was terrible, so we baked our own bread and then it got better. A few potatoes. Turnips. You know, not much vitamins, I think.

So the food. Jesus Christ! I never even saw so much food in any store in Prague, even before the Germans came. That was the Putsch. Remember? That started the world war. Not Hitler going into Poland. Nah! Nah! It was Hitler pushing around little Czechoslovakia. . . .

We went for walks when I could buy better clothing, boots, you know. Warm underwear. We went to the park, they called it City Park. Assiniboine Park. You know it? We'd go on Sundays and nobody would be there, and all this snow on the ground, and we'd run around. Even me. Laughing, saying we're free. This is a free country. We're in it. Look at the trees. Hear the train whistle way over there. There might be a rabbit we could chase. And nobody there. Eight hundred acres, maybe more. Ours. The girls would run and jump and play in the snow, and we would walk about three miles home, and I'd think, why don't Canadians go to their wonderful park? See, nobody was there.

That was Christmas of 1946. We didn't have a turkey. I don't think there was any way to cook it. We had stew and dumplings again, but it was the best in the world. Then we prayed before we ate, and I said, "Remember, children, a year ago we were in the camp and what we had to eat. Remember?" They said yes.

That Christmas was the best we ever had. I wish I could write a poem about it. I'm no good at that stuff, but I had it in my heart what I would say. I'd say, "Canada, all you people in it, excuse my bad English, but my wife and babies and me, we thank you. We thank you so much." I could cry.

Three Cheers for Miss Hudson!

When I started school, I didn't know one word of English. Not a bit of English. We were just off the boat, we'd moved to southern Ontario, and that summer we'd worked in the harvest fields and somehow, and I don't know how, my father had managed to put a down payment on a little house and he was working on a farm, as a labourer. That was the way it was in September of 1950. I was seven.

Today, you can't imagine anybody going in cold, in a way of putting it. At first there is a wall. Glass. You can see people. They're mouthing things at you, but it all makes no sense whatever. But I can remember, within a couple of weeks I was bringing home these books in English and reading them.

What happened was I had this fantastic teacher. She was just young. Her name was Miss Hudson. What she did, she kept me after school. About an hour a day. I'll go back. I could read and write before I went to my first school in Canada, but it was in Russian. So you could say I did have reading and writing experience, and that helped. All I had to do was put the English into the Russian reading and writing. Am I making sense?

She used to stay with me for an hour a day, just teaching me English, and by the end of Grade One, I skipped to Grade Three where the rest of the children my age were. They moved me up, basing it on my math and reading skills.

There was no time when I said to myself, hey, I can speak English. But by the end of Grade One I was totally fluent in English. Totally. Exactly like any other Canadian pupil. . . .

Source: Barry Broadfoot, *The Immigrant Years, From Europe to Canada, 1945–1967* (Vancouver and Toronto: Douglas and McIntyre, 1967), pp. 11–13, 105–106.

Excerpt from the McCarran-Walter Act, 1952

The McCarran-Walter Act—formally the Immigration and Nationality Act—was passed in response to both cold war fears of communist expansion and the worldwide movement of peoples in the wake of World War II. It codified previous legislative acts and policy decisions and continued restrictive policies that had been instituted during the 1920s, though it did provide some relief for Asian immigrants. In the xenophobic spirit of the times, the measure also blocked naturalization of aliens considered to be threats to national security. President Harry S. Truman vetoed the McCarran-Walter Act, arguing that the Immigration and Naturalization Service was proving itself to be an "arrogant, brazen instrument of discrimination," keeping out the "very people we want to bring in." His veto was overridden in June 1952, 57 to 26.

CHAPTER 2—NATIONALITY THROUGH NATURALIZATION

Sec. 311. The right of a person to become a naturalized citizen of the United States shall not be denied or abridged because of race or sex or because such a person is married. Notwithstanding section 405(b), this section shall apply to any person whose petition for naturalization shall hereafter be filed, or shall have been pending on the effective date of this Act.

Sec. 312. No person except as otherwise provided in this title shall hereafter be naturalized as a citizen of the United States upon his own petition who cannot demonstrate—

(1) an understanding of the English language, including the ability to read, write, and speak words in ordinary usage in the English language. . . .

(2)(2) a knowledge and understanding of the fundamentals of the history, and of the principles and form of government, of the United States.

Sec. 313. (a) Notwithstanding the provisions of section 405(b), no person shall be naturalized as a citizen of the United States—[the act lists subsections (1) through (6) which prohibit the naturalization of anarchists, communists, totalitarians, and those who believe or publish such, etc.]. . . .

Sec. 316. (a) No person, except as otherwise provided for in this title, shall be naturalized unless such petitioner, (1) immediately preceding the date of filing his petition for naturalization has resided continuously, after being lawfully admitted for permanent residence, within the United States for at least five years and during the five years . . . has been physically present therein for periods totally at least half of that time, and who has resided within the State in which petition is filed for at least six months, (2) has resided continuously within the United States from the date of the petition up to the time of admission to citizenship, and (3) during all the periods referred to in this subsection has been and still is a person of good moral character, attached to the principles of the Constitution of the

United States, and well disposed to the good order and happiness of the United States. . . .

Sec. 337. (a) A person who has petitioned for naturalization shall, in order to be and before being admitted to citizenship, take in open court an oath (1) to support the Constitution of the United States; (2) to renounce and abjure absolutely and entirely all allegiance and fidelity to any foreign prince, potentate, state, or sovereignty of whom or which the petitioner was before a subject or citizen; (3) to support and defend the Constitution and laws of the United States against all enemies, foreign and domestic; (4) to bear true faith and allegiance [to] the same; and (5)(A) to bear arms on behalf of the United States when required by law, or (B) to perform non-combatant service in the Armed Forces of the United States when required by law, or (C) to perform work of national importance under civilian direction when required by law. . . .

Source: James Ciment, ed., *Encyclopedia of American Immigration,* vol. 4 (Armonk, N.Y.: Sharpe Reference, 2001), p. 1300.

Racism in Vietnam, 1971

The Vietnam War was debilitating, both to the U.S. military and to the fabric of American society. The determined and protracted guerrilla war was unlike anything American commanders had previously faced, leading to an ever-increasing number of troops and more violent methods of securing the countryside against the incursions of the communists from the North. Despite the achievements of the Civil Rights movement, racism was still prevalent among soldiers in the military, and conscription policies led to a disproportionate number of minority soldiers, especially in high-risk positions in the field. By 1970, issues of race were joined to political concerns in the antiwar movement, leading to a special "Third World Panel" at the Winter Soldier Investigation (WSI). Beginning as the brainchild of antiwar activists, the WSI was by late 1970 taken over by the Vietnam Veterans Against the War (VVAW), who wanted to expose atrocities being committed in Vietnam, link them directly to U.S. policy, and bring American troops home from what they considered to be an unjust war. John Kerry, one of the most articulate spokesmen for the VVAW, brought this message to the Senate Foreign Relations Committee in April 1971. Ironically, the Vietnam War led to the resettlement of nearly 1 million Southeast Asian refugees in the United States and Canada, mostly from Vietnam, Laos, and Cambodia.

TESTIMONY GIVEN AT THE WINTER SOLDIER INVESTIGATION IN DETROIT, MICHIGAN, JANUARY 31, FEBRUARY 1 AND 2, 1971.

THIRD WORLD PANEL

MODERATOR. Can I have your attention? The black veterans are coming up to speak on the black experience with racism in Vietnam, and we'd like for you to give your attention, if possible. Any Third World people, you know, people of color, all of us. Do you think the minority groups could have some water, please?

Excuse me, is this the bulk of the press that's going to be covering this panel? You're not even from the press, so the press is not even covering this, right? Can somebody on the staff go see about the press?

AUDIENCE. We're here and we're important. We'll pass the word right on.

MODERATOR. Say, people, isn't this typical racism for the press? Okay, we're ready to deal. My name is Donald P. Williams. I spent eight years in the service. My unit was alerted to go to Vietnam in March of 1968. They went to Saigon, but I went to Stockholm. When I got to Stockholm, I sent my commanding officer a big picture postcard and told him good luck. I want to make an opening statement, and then we're going to have the brothers from the Third World give an opening statement. Then we'll give it to the panel.

We, the black veterans of the Vietnam war, are expressing our experience with racism in Vietnam. We intend to show by our testimony that the war in Vietnam is nothing more than an extension of the racist policies as practiced here in the United States. Racism is the motivating factor in determining America's genocidal policy against non-whites. The overwhelming majority of people killed or maimed in Vietnam are non-whites, whether they are Vietnamese, Viet Cong, or American blacks. Whites' statistics say that blacks constitute only ten percent of the total population in the United States, yet they represent at least forty percent of the fighting forces in Vietnam, and, in many cases, due to racism, blacks are the overwhelming majority in the combat areas. The statement you will hear this afternoon reflects the reality of American society's attitudes towards non-whites. This attitude emanates from years and years of oppression based on the refusal of American people to eliminate racism. At this time I'll turn you over to the brothers from the Third World and they're going to make an opening statement.

SHIMABUKURO. My name is Scott Shimabukuro and I'm representing the Asian brothers and sisters, not only in the United States and veterans, but also in Asia. Now this tribunal, or investigation, is into the treatment of Asians, and I'm relating this not only to Asians in Vietnam but to Asians all over the world. The United States has a policy of racism that in Vietnam is only an extension of this, and we feel that since this gathering is to bring these things out, we think there should have been a bigger representation from not only the Asian people in this community and in this United States, but of all Third World people, because we are the people who are receiving all these crimes against us and we feel we should be heard. We've been quiet too long.

ROMO. My name is Barry Romo. I represent, supposedly, the Chicano community, which isn't hard to do, because I'm the only one here. Chicanos constitute the largest percentage of deaths of any minorities, which is way out of proportion to their numbers. It's because of language and culture. This thing has turned into a horror show. All it has been has been the atrocities that have been committed and not the reasons why. And it boils down to one thing, and that's racism. The people dying are Third World and the people getting hurt are Third World, and that has to be brought out.

HANEY. My name is Evan Haney. I'm an Oklahoma Indian, and I would like to say that I am probably the only one here who is an Indian, and there should have been more here, but we have our own fights to do in our own communities. And, I represent the Indian community all over the United States and I would like to say that I hope to convey the feeling that you know that we are out fighting and not in a position where . . . well, I don't know what to say right now, but I represent the Indian community across the United States.

ROSE. My name is Earl Rose, and I'm a representative from the West Coast. I'd like to talk about the miseducation and how they take Third World people and through miseducation and using the word Cong as a symbol of killing, instead of using the words, "Go out and kill Vietnamese people," how the word "Cong" is used against Third World people to manipulate and to kill them. That's all. . . .

LIGHT. My name is William Light. I served in the American Division of the 1/6, E Company, Echo Recon. I was a grunt. . . .

NAKAYAMO. My name is Mike Nakayamo. I was in the First Marine Division. . . .

LIGHT. I'm going to start off with racism on a personal basis. For reasons of my own, I chose not to go over to Vietnam. Behind this, I was railroaded, and handcuffed, and taken under guard to Vietnam. They forwarded orders to my company commander of my background when I was in basic and AIT, relevant to my behavior. From the jump, he discriminated against me. I was commonly referred to as a "field nigger." I was on an operation. We were under attack by a regiment of VC. The outcome was like seven to eight guys out of about thirty-five left. The first thing my first sergeant did when he called in was to find out if I was dead or not. The majority of my company consists of white guys, but the majority of brothers are in the field. The ratio is like sixty to forty and most brothers, Puerto Ricans, and Mexicans, have to walk point to more or less prove their manhood, on an individual basis, that they are just as much man as the next guy. Consequently, there were all forms of racism. . . .

MODERATOR. I just got a message here. Michael Oliver, a Vietnam veteran, has a statement to read regarding something very important. So where's Mike?

PANELIST. Okay, ladies and gentlemen. I think I might throw a monkey wrench into the fine working machine for a second here. For the last couple of days you have been receiving testimony from the war of injustices to non-whites over in Vietnam. Now, if these injustices and these here genocides are perpetrated against the non-whites in Vietnam, the Vietnamese soldiers, and they are solely admitted since yesterday, Sunday, on television, and this morning, what do you think they've been doing to the black soldier they've been serving along with? Just think about that. . . .

AUDIENCE. Let's let our brothers speak. Our brothers from the Third World, minority groups, all of us are called underdogs, masterminds of the world; rap, brothers. . . .

NAKAYAMO. My name is Mike. I wanted to rap about racism directed against Asians in the military and in Vietnam. First of all, I felt quite a bit of racism before I joined the service, okay, that's understood. When I got into the service I experienced amplified racism. As soon as I got off the bus at my boot camp, I was referred to as Ho Chi Minh, which, you know, was . . .

AUDIENCE. A compliment!

AUDIENCE. Right on! Right on!

NAKAYAMO. Yeah! I can dig it. I was referred to as "Jap" and "gook" constantly through my training. Then I knew I was going to go overseas to fight for this country. I can rap about quite a few instances, right in boot camp, but I'll just move on to my experiences in Vietnam. While on Vietnam, I was in the infantry, but a few times they let you come back to the rear. Most Marines are allowed to go into PXs without showing an ID, and I was not allowed to go into the PX on a number of occasions with an ID because I was yellow. I was constantly referred to as "gook" in Vietnam also, and, relating this back to the United States, I know a number of my Asian brothers and sisters who are being referred to as "gooks" by returning servicemen, by American people in the Los Angeles area.

The thing that bothered me about this investigation is that it seemed as though people were trying to cover up the issue of racism, which I believe is one of the definite reasons why we are in Vietnam. We talked a lot about atrocities, but the systematic and deliberate genocide of all Asian people through the use of racism cannot be allowed any longer.

AUDIENCE. Take your time, man, you're doing good. You're telling the truth.

NAKAYAMO. I'm sure I don't have to go into detail about the racism and atrocities being committed against Asians, because you've been hearing that all week, or since Sunday. But the things that the brothers are relating have been happening in the United States since the Third World people have lived here. Now there's been a thing on relocation of Vietnamese from their homes to relocation camps. That strikes home pretty close, because my parents and grandparents, who were supposed to be American citizens, were relocated during the Second World War, and that just amplifies the racism that has been coming down in this country. And also, you know about the Indian brothers that this country belongs to. When Evan speaks, he can go into that, how they were robbed. But I want to go into the atrocities against the people here, because the people have been telling you how they treat the Asian brothers and sisters. Now they bring this home with them, and this has a great effect on the Asians here in the United States. . . .

MODERATOR. I'd like to pose some questions to the panel. Anyone can answer them. I would like to know, were those black men who were considered troublemakers forced to the front before other men more qualified.

ROMO. If I can say one word before you go on, just one word about the Chicano, the Puerto Rican, the brown. If it's all right, thank you. The brown people, the Puerto Rican, the Chicano, suffer from a problem in America, not only of racism, but of a language and a cultural difference. The ghettoizing that goes on in his early life, his economic background of relegation to farm work, etc., puts him in position that when he goes in the service, the only thing the service feels he's qualified for is the front line and infantry duty. As a consequence, when he gets to the field, he cannot relate to his officers or NCOs. He can't understand the language and he can't understand the culture behind it. As I said before, the Chicano, the brown, the Puerto Rican, suffers statistically more casualties than any other minority and the white. I think this has to be brought out and it has to be stopped.

HANEY. My name is Evan Haney, and I would like to point out that if you took the Vietnamese war, of the American war, as it is, and compared it to the Indian wars a hundred years ago, it would be the same thing. All the massacres were the same. Nowadays they use chemical warfare; back then they put smallpox in the blankets and gave them to the Indians. . . .

ROSE. I guess most of it's been said. All the brothers said real beautiful, all the Asian brothers, and my Indian brother here. I have been in the Marine Corps for ten years, ten long years in the Marine Corps. Went to Vietnam twice. When I looked around me in those ten years I found out who was really fighting this war, and all I've seen was Third World people and poor whites fighting this war. Most of the poor whites in the war were in the positions of power, more or less the sergeants and officers.

People say, how can Third World people go in the service and fight? All through the years we've been miseducated, all through high school, elementary school, and then we have one more choice left, and that's the military. To make this great big American splash, like in Hitler youth, we got to make our name in the sky. So we go into the service. My brother was there in 1965; he felt like it was his patriotic duty. I did the same thing in '65. "I'm going to wipe them all out, really do it, get my medals, really make it on the scene." Then you go out and they keep using words like Cong and slopehead and slanteyes. I said, "Hey, those are the same words they use in the States against me, against Third World people." They dehumanize these people so much that it's easy to go out and kill them or blow them away, because they are dehumanized, and it becomes in your mind, they become more dehuman to you. But as you go on, you've got to realize that this is foolish, you're killing our own brothers. So that out of ten years this is what I got out of it and it makes me very bitter. A lot I'd like to say, and I'm not going to say, because the rest is going to be practice. I have no more time to talk. . . .

LLOYD. I had a few experiences, you know. I met quite a few Vietnamese, old women and children and to me they looked up to the black man—those that had been oriented properly—looked up to the black man something like for help more or less. Most of the time we'd go in the village, we'd go in there with food or candy or clothes if we had it and the little kids were always around us and then some of them would come up and look for a tail and different things. When they run it down to you, they try to make you understand that you are part of them by being black in your blood line. We have the same blood that they have, something like, you know, it's just like about that. We related to them and why should we be fighting them and we're the same color? This is what it boils down to. . . .

Source: Congressional Record, "Extensions and Remarks," 92nd Congress, 1st Session, April 7, 1971, 2,825–2,900, 2,903–2,936; cited in Winter Soldier Investigation, available online, URL: http://lists.village.virginia.edu/sixties/HTML_docs/Resources/Primary/Winter_Soldier/ws_32_3d_W orld.html.

STATEMENT BY JOHN KERRY, VIETNAM VETERANS AGAINST THE WAR, TO THE SENATE COMMITTEE ON FOREIGN RELATIONS

April 23, 1971

I would like to talk on behalf of all those veterans and say that several months ago in Detroit we had an investigation at which over 150 honorably discharged, and many very highly decorated, veterans testified to war crimes committed in Southeast Asia. These were not isolated incidents but crimes committed on a day-to-day basis with the full awareness of officers at all levels of command. It is impossible to describe to you exactly what did happen in Detroit—the emotions in the room and the feelings of the men who were reliving their experiences in Vietnam. They relived the absolute horror of what this country, in a sense, made them do.

They told stories that at times they had personally raped, cut off ears, cut off heads, taped wires from portable telephones to human genitals and turned up the power, cut off limbs, blown up bodies, randomly shot at civilians, razed villages in fashion reminiscent of Ghengis Khan, shot cattle and dogs for fun, poisoned food stocks, and generally ravaged the countryside of South Vietnam in addition to the normal ravage of war and the normal and very particular ravaging which is done by the applied bombing power of this country. . . .

We learned the meaning of free fire zones, shooting anything that moves, and we watched while America placed a cheapness on the lives of orientals.

We watched the United States falsification of body counts, in fact the glorification of body counts. We listened while month after month we were told the back of the enemy was about to break. We fought using weapons against "oriental human beings." We fought using weapons against those people which I do not believe this country would dream of using were we fighting in the European theater. . . .

We are here in Washington to say that the problem of this war is not just a question of war and diplomacy. It is part and parcel of everything that we are trying as human beings to communicate to people in this country—the question of racism which is rampant in the military, and so many other questions such as the use of weapons; the hypocrisy in our taking umbrage at the Geneva Conventions and using that as justification for a continuation of this war when we are more guilty than any other body of violations of those Geneva Conventions; in the use of free fire zones, harassment interdiction fire, search and destroy missions, the bombings, the torture of prisoners, all accepted policy by many units in South Vietnam. That is what we are trying to say. It is part and parcel of everything. . . .

We wish that a merciful God could wipe away our own memories of that service as easily as this administration has wiped away their memories of us. But all that they have done and all that they can do by this denial is to make more clear than ever our own determination to undertake one last mission—to search out and destroy the last vestige of this barbaric war, to pacify our own hearts, to conquer the hate and fear that have driven this country these last ten years and more. And more. And so when thirty years from now our brothers go down the street without a leg, without an arm, or a face, and small boys ask why, we will be able to say "Vietnam" and not mean a desert, not a filthy obscene memory, but mean instead where America finally turned and where soldiers like us helped it in the turning.

Source: Senate Foreign Relations Committee, *Hearings on Legislative Proposals Relating to the War in Southeast Asia,* April 20–May 27, 1971, pp. 180–210.

Objectives of the Canadian Immigration Act, 1976

In 1973, the Department of Manpower and Immigration began a review of Canadian immigration policy that eventually led to nationwide public hearings under a Special Joint Committee of the Senate and the House of Commons during 1975. The Immigration Act of 1976 marked a significant shift in Canadian immigration policy in limiting the wide discretionary powers of the minister of manpower and immigration. Although it coordinated the policies established in the 1952 Immigration Act and the various regulations subsequently passed, for the first time it expressly stated the goals of Canadian immigration policy, including family reunion, humanitarian concern for refugees, and targeted economic development. The act took effect on April 10, 1978. It was amended more than 30 times, including major revisions in 1985 and 1992, before being replaced in 2002 with the Immigration and Refugee Protection Act.

OBJECTIVES

3. It is hereby declared that Canadian immigration policy and the rules and regulations made under this Act shall be designed and administered in such a manner as to promote the domestic and international interests of Canada recognizing the need

(a) to support the attainment of such demographic goals as may be established by the Government of Canada from time to time in respect of the size, rate of growth, structure, and geographic distribution of the Canadian population;

(b) to enrich and strengthen the cultural and social fabric of Canada, taking into account the federal and bilingual character of Canada;

(c) to facilitate the reunion in Canada of Canadian citizens and permanent residents with their close relatives from abroad;

(d) to encourage and facilitate the adaptation of persons who have been granted admission as permanent residents to Canadian society by promoting cooperation between the Government of Canada and other levels of government and non-governmental agencies in Canada with respect thereto;

(e) to facilitate the entry of visitors into Canada for the purpose of fostering trade and commerce, tourism, cultural and scientific activities, and international understanding;

(f) to ensure that any person who seeks admission to Canada on either a permanent or temporary basis is subject to standards of admission that do not discriminate on grounds of race, national or ethnic origin, colour, religion or sex;

(g) to fulfil Canada's international legal obligations with respect to refugees and to uphold its humanitarian tradition with respect to the displaced and the persecuted;

(h) to foster the development of a strong and viable economy and the prosperity of all regions in Canada;

(i) to maintain and protect the health, safety, and good order of Canadian society; and

(j) to promote international order and justice by denying the use of Canadian territory to persons who are likely to engage in criminal activity.

Source: Freda Hawkins, *Canada and Immigration: Public Policy and Public Concern,* 2d ed. (Kingston and Montreal: Institute of Public Administration of Canada and McGill–Queen's University Press, 1988), p. 426.

An Account of Somalis in Canada, 1990s

Muslim families were slow to come to North America, in part because immigration would separate them from the religious society that was so important in maintaining their cultures. A Somali immigrant, Faduma Abdi speaks of the challenges of living in Canada.

We are Muslims, we believe in the Islamic religion, and we practised it in our country. People from all over the world, every continent, every country maybe, come to Canada, so all the religions are here. We go to mosque on Fridays instead of Sunday like the Christians. On Saturday and Sunday, there are certain religious classes, but sometimes it is difficult to get transportation. The nearest mosque is on Dundas [Street, in Toronto], It's too far away, so sometimes it is difficult to get there. I'm Muslim, but I'm not a very religious person. We have our own clothes and our own culture. We like and are very proud to wear our traditional dresses in the summertime. Whether you are very religious or not, winter is your master because you have to wear what the other people wear. But in the summertime, we are very comfortable wearing our dresses, our style. If you are married, you have to cover your hair. That's for religious purposes. We have different *sheekh* (religious leaders). Those are in the top ranks of the religion. In some circles, if you are a woman, whether you are married or not, you have to cover your body except for maybe your eyes, your face. Our tradition is the Somali tradition. We cover our hair and our body. We are all Muslim, but some wear short dresses the way that they like. They pray five times a day, but they wear whatever they like, and others have some restrictions, but it depends, just like Catholicism.

We pray five times a day. Sometimes we pray as a family, but it is not compulsory to do it together. Amina prays on her own and the others do so as well, but on the weekend, if we are all together, we pray together in the morning (*Subah*), at noon (*Duhur*), evening (*Asar*), (*Macrib*) and the final prayers (*Isha*). That's five prayers. We pray before sunrise, after two o'clock, at six, at nine, and at ten we pray the last one before we go to bed. If it is not possible for them to pray during the day, when they come home, they have a late prayer.

My children socialize with the people at school and maybe they make conversation, but we are different from Canadian girls who want boyfriends. This is prohibited in our culture and our religion. When a girl is ready to be married, then maybe she will talk or make some conversation in order to know the boy before she gets married. But they don't have boyfriends. So my two eldest daughters go to school together, they come home together, they are friends and they walk together. When they come back from school, one of them may go to the kitchen and do her chores and one does her homework and so on, but they don't go out on dates. My son is more active than my daughters. He has some friends, but not girlfriends. I don't know whether he's hiding them from me. He goes with his Canadian friends to the school, then he comes back and usually I don't allow him to go out at night.

Source: Elizabeth McLuhan, ed., *Safe Haven: The Refugee Experience of Five Families* (Toronto, Multicultural History Society of Ontario, 1995), pp. 192–194.

Excerpts from the USA PATRIOT Act, 2001

In the immediate aftermath of the terrorist attacks in New York City and Washington, D.C., on September 11, 2001, the administration of President George W. Bush proposed a series of measures designed to combat terrorism, which included greater border controls. The Uniting and Strengthening America by Providing Appropriate Tools Required to Intercept and Obstruct Terrorism Act (USA PATRIOT Act) was signed into law on October 26, 2001. The act provided for greater surveillance of aliens and increasing the power of the attorney general to identify, arrest, and deport suspected terrorists.

TITLE I—ENHANCING DOMESTIC SECURITY AGAINST TERRORISM

Sec. 102. *Sense of Congress condemning discrimination against Arab and Muslim Americans.*

(a) FINDINGS—Congress makes the following findings:

(1) Arab Americans, Muslim Americans, and Americans from South Asia play a vital role in our Nation and are entitled to nothing less than the full rights of every American.

(2) The acts of violence that have been taken against Arab and Muslim Americans since the September 11, 2001, attacks against the United States should be and are condemned by all Americans who value freedom.

(3) The concept of individual responsibility for wrongdoing is sacrosanct in American society, and applies equally to all religious, racial, and ethnic groups.

(4) When American citizens commit acts of violence against those who are, or are perceived to be, of Arab or Muslim descent, they should be punished to the full extent of the law.

(5) Muslim Americans have become so fearful of harassment that many Muslim women are changing the way they dress to avoid becoming targets.

(6) Many Arab Americans and Muslim Americans have acted heroically during the attacks on the United States, including Mohammed Salman Hamdani, a 23-year-old New Yorker of Pakistani descent, who is believed to have gone to the World Trade Center to offer rescue assistance and is now missing.

(b) SENSE OF CONGRESS—It is the sense of Congress that—

(1) the civil rights and civil liberties of all Americans, including Arab Americans, Muslim Americans, and Americans from South Asia, must be protected, and that every effort must be taken to preserve their safety;

(2) any acts of violence or discrimination against any Americans be condemned; and

(3) the Nation is called upon to recognize the patriotism of fellow citizens from all ethnic, racial, and religious backgrounds.

TITLE IV—PROTECTING THE BORDER

Sec. 402. *Northern border personnel.*

There are authorized to be appropriated—

(1) such sums as may be necessary to triple the number of Border Patrol personnel (from the number authorized under current law), and the necessary personnel and facilities

to support such personnel, in each State along the Northern Border;

(2) such sums as may be necessary to triple the number of Customs Service personnel (from the number authorized under current law), and the necessary personnel and facilities to support such personnel, at ports of entry in each State along the Northern Border;

(3) such sums as may be necessary to triple the number of INS [Immigration and Naturalization Services] inspectors (from the number authorized on the date of the enactment of this Act), and the necessary personnel and facilities to support such personnel, at ports of entry in each State along the Northern Border; and

(4) an additional $50,000,000 each to the Immigration and Naturalization Service and the United States Customs Service for purposes of making improvements in technology for monitoring the Northern Border and acquiring additional equipment at the Northern Border.

Sec. 403. *Access by the Department of State and the INS to certain identifying information in the criminal history records of visa applicants and applicants for admission to the United States.*

(b)(1) The Attorney General and the Director of the Federal Bureau of Investigation shall provide the Department of State and the Service access to the criminal history record information contained in the National Crime Information Center's Interstate Identification Index (NCIC-III), Wanted Persons File, and to any other files maintained by the National Crime Information Center that may be mutually agreed upon by the Attorney General and the agency receiving the access, for the purpose of determining whether or not a visa applicant or applicant for admission has a criminal history record indexed in any such file.

(2) Such access shall be provided by means of extracts of the records for placement in the automated visa lookout or other appropriate database, and shall be provided without any fee or charge.

(3) The Federal Bureau of Investigation shall provide periodic updates of the extracts at intervals mutually agreed upon with the agency receiving the access. Upon receipt of such updated extracts, the receiving agency shall make corresponding updates to its database and destroy previously provided extracts.

Sec. 405. *Report on the integrated automated fingerprint identification system for ports of entry and overseas consular posts.*

(a) IN GENERAL—The Attorney General, in consultation with the appropriate heads of other Federal agencies, including the Secretary of State, Secretary of the Treasury, and the Secretary of Transportation, shall report to Congress on the feasibility of enhancing the Integrated Automated Fingerprint Identification System (IAFIS) of the Federal Bureau of Investigation and other identification systems in order to better identify a person who holds a foreign passport or a visa and may be wanted in connection with a criminal investigation in the United States or abroad, before the issuance of a visa to that person or the entry or exit from the United States by that person.

(c) RETROACTIVE APPLICATION OF AMENDMENTS—

(1) IN GENERAL—Except as otherwise provided in this subsection, the amendments made by this section shall take effect on the date of the enactment of this Act and shall apply to—

(A) actions taken by an alien before, on, or after such date; and

(B) all aliens, without regard to the date of entry or attempted entry into the United States—

(i) in removal proceedings on or after such date (except for proceedings in which there has been a final administrative decision before such date); or

(ii) seeking admission to the United States on or after such date.

Sec. 414. *Visa integrity and security.*

(a) SENSE OF CONGRESS REGARDING THE NEED TO EXPEDITE IMPLEMENTATION OF INTEGRATED ENTRY AND EXIT DATA SYSTEM—

(1) SENSE OF CONGRESS—In light of the terrorist attacks perpetrated against the United States on September 11, 2001, it is the sense of the Congress that—

(A) the Attorney General, in consultation with the Secretary of State, should fully implement the integrated entry and exit data system for airports, seaports, and land border ports of entry, as specified in section 110 of the Illegal Immigration Reform and Immigrant Responsibility Act of 1996 (8 U.S.C. 1365a), with all deliberate speed and as expeditiously as practicable; and

(B) the Attorney General, in consultation with the Secretary of State, the Secretary of Commerce, the Secretary of the Treasury, and the Office of Homeland Security, should immediately begin establishing the Integrated Entry and Exit Data System Task Force, as described in section 3 of the Immigration and Naturalization Service Data Management Improvement Act of 2000 (Public Law 106-215).

(2) AUTHORIZATION OF APPROPRIATIONS—There is authorized to be appropriated such sums as may be necessary to fully implement the system described in paragraph (1)(A).

(b) DEVELOPMENT OF THE SYSTEM—In the development of the integrated entry and exit data system under section 110 of the Illegal Immigration Reform and Immigrant Responsibility Act of 1996 (8 U.S.C. 1365a), the Attorney General and the Secretary of State shall particularly focus on—

(1) the utilization of biometric technology; and

(2) the development of tamper-resistant documents readable at ports of entry.

(c) INTERFACE WITH LAW ENFORCEMENT DATABASES—The entry and exit data system described in this section shall be able to interface with law enforcement databases for use by Federal law enforcement to identify and detain individuals who pose a threat to the national security of the United States.

(d) REPORT ON SCREENING INFORMATION—Not later than 12 months after the date of enactment of this Act, the Office of Homeland Security shall submit a report to Congress on the information that is needed from any United States agency to effectively screen visa applicants and applicants for admission to the United States to identify those affiliated with terrorist organizations or those that pose any threat to the safety or security of the United States, including the type of information currently received by United States agencies and the regularity with which such information is transmitted to the Secretary of State and the Attorney General.

Sec. 416. *Foreign student monitoring program.*

(a) FULL IMPLEMENTATION AND EXPANSION OF FOREIGN STUDENT VISA MONITORING PROGRAM REQUIRED—The Attorney General, in consultation with the Secretary of State, shall fully implement and expand the program established by section 641(a) of the Illegal Immigration Reform and Immigrant Responsibility Act of 1996 (8 U.S.C. 1372(a)).

(b) INTEGRATION WITH PORT OF ENTRY INFORMATION—For each alien with respect to whom information is collected under section 641 of the Illegal Immigration Reform and Immigrant Responsibility Act of 1996 (8 U.S.C. 1372), the Attorney General, in consultation with the Secretary of State, shall include information on the date of entry and port of entry.

(c) EXPANSION OF SYSTEM TO INCLUDE OTHER APPROVED EDUCATIONAL INSTITUTIONS—

(3) OTHER APPROVED EDUCATIONAL INSTITUTION—The term "other approved educational institution" includes any air flight school, language training school, or vocational school, approved by the Attorney General, in consultation with the Secretary of Education and the Secretary of State, under subparagraph (F), (J), or (M) of section 101(a)(15) of the Immigration and Nationality Act.

(d) AUTHORIZATION OF APPROPRIATIONS—There is authorized to be appropriated to the Department of Justice $36,800,000 for the period beginning on the date of enactment of this Act and ending on January 1, 2003, to fully implement and expand prior to January 1, 2003, the program established by section 641(a) of the Illegal Immigration Reform and Immigrant Responsibility Act of 1996 (8 U.S.C. 1372(a)).

(c) DIVERSITY IMMIGRANTS—

(1) WAIVER OF FISCAL YEAR LIMITATION—Notwithstanding section 203(e)(2) of the Immigration and Nationality Act (8 U.S.C. 1153(e)(2)), an immigrant visa number issued to an alien under section 203(c) of such Act for fiscal year 2001 may be used by the alien during the period beginning on October 1, 2001, and ending on April 1, 2002, if the alien establishes that the alien was prevented from using it during fiscal year 2001 as a direct result of a specified terrorist activity.

(2) WORLDWIDE LEVEL—In the case of an alien entering the United States as a lawful permanent resident, or adjusting to that status, under paragraph (1) or (3), the alien shall be counted as a diversity immigrant for fiscal year 2001 for purposes of section 201(e) of the Immigration and Nationality Act (8 U.S.C. 1151(e)), unless the worldwide level under such section for such year has been exceeded, in which case the alien shall be counted as a diversity immigrant for fiscal year 2002.

(3) TREATMENT OF FAMILY MEMBERS OF CERTAIN ALIENS—In the case of a principal alien issued an immigrant visa number under section 203(c) of the Immigration and Nationality Act (8 U.S.C. 1153(c)) for fiscal year 2001, if such principal alien died as a direct result of a specified terrorist activity, the aliens who were, on September 10, 2001, the spouse and children of such principal alien shall, until June 30, 2002, if not otherwise entitled to an immigrant status and the immediate issuance of a visa under subsection (a), (b), or (c) of section 203 of such Act, be entitled to the same status, and the same order of consideration, that would have been provided to such alien spouse or child under section 203(d) of such Act as if the principal alien were not deceased and as if the spouse or child's visa application had been adjudicated by September 30, 2001.

(d) EXTENSION OF EXPIRATION OF IMMIGRANT VISAS—

(1) IN GENERAL—Notwithstanding the limitations under section 221(c) of the Immigration and Nationality Act (8 U.S.C. 1201(c)), in the case of any immigrant visa issued to an alien that expires or expired before December 31, 2001, if the alien was unable to effect entry into the United States as a direct result of a specified terrorist activity, then the period of validity of the visa is extended until December 31, 2001, unless a longer period of validity is otherwise provided under this subtitle.

Source: Uniting and Strengthening America by Providing Appropriate Tools Required to Intercept and Obstruct Terrorism (USA PATRIOT) Act of 2001. Washington, D.C.: U.S. Government Printing Office, 2001.

Canada's Immigration Plan for 2002

The Canadian immigration plan for 2002 called for admission of 210,000–235,000 immigrants, with at least 10 percent refugees. Determined to bring skilled workers into Canada to aid in development, there was nevertheless a clear nod to the terrorist attacks of September 11, 2001, with greater emphasis on guarding the borders and preventing the use of fraudulent documents. The document below is the Canadian government's explanation of its goals.

THE IMMIGRATION PLAN FOR 2002

I. *Commitment to Immigration*

The government remains committed to investing in Canada's economic and social development through immigration. A planning range of 210,000 to 235,000 is confirmed for 2002. Refugees will account for more than 10 percent of newcomers to Canada in that year. Skilled workers, business people and provincial or territorial nominees, together with their families, will again make up about 60 percent of the movement in 2002, and family members of Canadian citizens and permanent residents, slightly more than one-quarter (see appendices C and D).

This is consistent with the planning range announced earlier for 2002 and reaffirms the long-term objective of moving gradually to immigration levels of approximately one percent of Canada's population, while bearing in mind Canada's absorptive capacity. The skilled workers, business immigrants, family members and refugees who enter Canada through our immigration program are increasingly important to maintaining a strong and skilled labour force. These same people also strengthen Canada's social fabric and cultural diversity.

The government remains committed to investing in Canada's economic and social development through immigration. Temporary residents are also a key element of Canada's growth. The immigration program provides for the temporary entry of skilled foreign workers and business people essential to economic development, foreign students drawn by the reputation of Canada's universities and colleges for excellence in education, research and training, and tourists eager to experience the many attractions of this country.

The commitment to immigration is inseparable from Canada's determination to deny access to those who pose criminal or security threats to Canada and other countries, and who might abuse immigrant, refugee or temporary entry programs for illicit and fraudulent ends. Investigation and interdiction abroad, screening at border and airport entry points, and removal activities in Canada are necessary adjuncts to an open immigration policy and the levels planning process.

Pursuant to immigration legislation, the Social Union Framework Agreement and federal/provincial/territorial immigration agreements, consultation is essential to immigration planning, and various federal/provincial/territorial forums exist to that end. In addition, as part of the Multi-year Planning Process, Citizenship and Immigration Canada (CIC) and the provinces and territories are working to establish a joint planning table to address common concerns and challenges related to immigration planning. Consultations with other parties who are increasingly interested in participating in immigration planning will continue.

The scope of the policies and procedures required to enhance public safety and security, and concomitant pressures on the fiscal framework, will have an important effect on future planning, as will the nature of migration flows in the coming years, and other program pressures. Given the current level of uncertainty, it would be premature to announce a planning range for 2003 at this time without further consideration and consultation to ensure that supports are in place to move to higher immigration levels.

II. *International and Domestic Contexts*
A. International

The international environment has changed significantly in the wake of the terrorist attacks in the United States. There is a heightened awareness of the sophistication and geographic reach of terrorist activities, and the need to ensure that Canada's immigration and refugee protection programs are not seen as gateways to these activities in North America.

It is difficult to predict how the current campaign against terrorism will affect the global movement of people. Other factors that influence Canada's ability to attract and process immigrants and non-immigrants in an efficient and timely manner include the following:

1. a significant increase in immigrant and non-immigrant applicants to Canada, including refugee claimants;
2. a shift in source countries; the number of people on the move worldwide; and
3. international competition to attract skilled workers. About 150 million people are on the move at any given time.

Between 1997 and 2000, the number of immigrant applications increased by 46 percent. Currently, 50 percent more applications have been received than are needed to meet program targets. The growth in non-immigrant applications during those years was unprecedented: applications for visitor visas rose by 27 percent; applications for employment authorizations (temporary work permits) rose by 43 percent; and applications for student authorizations (issued for the most part to post-secondary students) rose by 63 percent. Since 1998, there has also been a significant increase in refugee claims made in Canada, from just under 25,500 in 1998 to more than 35,000 in 2000.

Canada draws its immigrant population from a great number of countries, but over time, we have seen significant shifts in primary source countries. In 1990, the top two source countries were Hong Kong and Poland, which together accounted for some 20 percent of the movement in that year. In 2000, China and India were the two primary source countries, making up close to 30 percent of the movement.

Behind the interest in Canada as a migrant destination is the increasing worldwide mobility of people. It has been estimated that about 150 million people are on the move at any given time. Some flee persecution, civil strife, or severe political or economic upheaval; others are forced to leave as a result of natural disasters or environmental degradation; still others move primarily to seek a better way of life for themselves and their families. In short, migration as an aspect of globalization is accelerating. If it wishes to maximize the benefits of this movement, Canada cannot afford to stand still. We must proactively plan for the future.

The key to sustaining a robust immigration program hinges on striking the right balance between maximizing the benefits of immigration, such as economic growth and social development, and sustaining public confidence in the system by ensuring, through effective enforcement, that its generosity is not abused. Canada is not alone in facing increased pressures from irregular migration, including human trafficking and smuggling.

Currently, Canada, the United States, Australia and New Zealand are the only countries that encourage and plan for immigration. However, greater international economic integration and competition, ageing work forces and declining birth rates are leading countries of the European Union and Japan to reconsider their approach to the planned admission of foreign workers. It is anticipated that in the future, Canada will face serious competition in recruiting the highly skilled as most developed countries struggle with skill shortages and the effects of an ageing population.

B. Domestic

The following factors will continue to influence the composition of the immigrant movement and federal, provincial and territorial integration initiatives, as well as overall immigration targets:

1. The increasing importance of immigration to labour force and population growth.
2. The strategic advantage of immigration in a competitive global economy.
3. The continued and growing preference of immigrants for living in Canada's largest urban centres.

Like other industrialized countries, Canada faces demographic challenges. Birth rates are at a historic low, and Canada's largest age cohort—the baby boomers—is ageing. While immigration cannot significantly change the resulting age structure of the population, it is an important tool to mitigate its effects. Immigration will likely account for all net labour force growth by 2011, and projections indicate it will account for total population growth by 2031. For these reasons, ensuring that immigrants and refugees have the skills to succeed in the labour market is key to Canada's future prosperity. Equally, policies designed to attract significant numbers of highly skilled workers will give Canada economic and sociocultural advantages in the new global economy.

Programs have been in place since the mid-1990s to increase the number of economic immigrants and their families within the overall immigrant movement and to put more emphasis on education, skills and language ability in the economic selection process. Education levels are rising. In 1995, 41 percent of working-age immigrants and refugees had a post-secondary degree on landing, while 57 percent had one in 1999. By comparison, 42 percent of the total working-age Canadian population had a post-secondary degree in 1999. Nonetheless, available data point to gaps in labour market performance between immigrants, refugees and the Canadian-born. Given the growing importance of immigration to the labour force, it is especially important to help immigrants and refugees manage the transition into the labour market so that they can realize their potential as quickly as possible.

Canada benefits from the different perspectives, networks, skills and traditions that immigrants bring, as well as from their economic contributions. In addition, newcomers and Canadians share common values. As reported in the World Values Survey, most Canadian and foreign-born residents agree that children should understand other cultures, learn to respect others and take responsibility for their actions. Both groups also show strong support for the merit principle in business.

It is generally recognized that while immigration is critical to building our economy and society, it is not without challenges, specifically with regard to ensuring that adequate supports are in place to facilitate social and economic integration. Challenges include the recognition of foreign credentials, combating discrimination and finding ways to more evenly distribute the benefits of immigration across the country. In 2000, 90 percent of immigrants chose to live in Ontario, British Columbia and Quebec; nearly 75 percent settled in Toronto, Vancouver and Montréal, an increase of five percentage points in the past decade. To date, efforts to encourage immigrants to settle in smaller urban centres have met with limited success. It will be important to further explore how to attract immigrants to smaller centres and persuade them to stay there in order to reduce the pressures on Canada's largest cities.

Canada's immigration program provides a significant level of support for settlement and integration services. Its citizenship program offers newcomers the opportunity to obtain Canadian citizenship following a three-year residency period.

Settlement programs and services assist immigrants in becoming participating and contributing members of Canadian society and promote an acceptance of immigrants by Canadians. While helping newcomers adapt and learn about their rights, freedoms and responsibilities and the laws that protect them from racial discrimination, settlement programs also sensitize Canadians to different cultures and how diversity strengthens the economy and community life.

III. Other Management and Planning Considerations

The government is committed to higher levels of immigration given the importance of immigration to Canada's economy and to Canadian society as a whole. However, the appropriate infrastructure and other supports must be in place to meet the challenges that lie ahead.

The proposed Immigration and Refugee Protection Act (Bill C-11) will give CIC the tools it needs to further enhance public safety and security by introducing new inadmissibility grounds, strengthening authority to arrest criminals and people who pose security threats, and restricting access to the refugee determination system for certain categories of people, such as people who have been determined to be inadmissible on security or other serious grounds.

We must maintain appropriate balance between achieving immigration levels targets, responding to non-immigrant demands, providing timely service to all and ensuring program integrity. At the same time, to support our long-term commitment to immigration and to facilitate the entry of legitimate immigrants and refugees, Bill C-11 and its regulations will also support the following measures:

    A. The shift in selection emphasis from the worker's current occupation to an assessment of skills and experience.

    B. The strengthening of family reunification and refugee protection.

    C. The redesign of the Temporary Foreign Worker Program to introduce a simple, efficient process for skilled workers, and to allow spouses to work.

    D. Facilitation of the transition from temporary to permanent resident status by allowing qualified foreign temporary workers to be processed for landing in Canada.

In addition to this legislative initiative, a number of other initiatives are under way to improve program management and delivery. Pilot projects have been undertaken and options are being considered to allow CIC to continue to maintain an appropriate balance between achieving immigration levels targets, responding to non-immigrant demand, providing timely service to all, and ensuring program integrity. Pilot projects are testing the feasibility of centralizing some aspects of immigrant-related decision making in Canada, evaluating measures to reliably identify and process uncomplicated applications, and examining the benefits of using available standardized language tests.

Looking ahead, a number of significant challenges remain. We must continue our responsible management of the immigration program and work to ensure that appropriate supports are in place to fully realize all the potential social and economic benefits. To that end, consultations with the provinces and territories and other interested stakeholders will be essential as we move to develop our immigration plan for 2003 and beyond.

Source: Citizenship and Immigration Canada, Minister of Public Works and Government Services Canada, 2001, available online, URL: http://www.cic.gc.ca/english/pub/anrep02.html#, accessed November 12, 2004.

Highlights of the Immigration and Refugee Protection Act and Its Regulations, 2002

In an attempt to streamline immigration procedures, and, in the later stages, in response to the attacks of September 11, 2001, Canada implemented its Immigration and Refugee Protection Act (IRPA) to replace the Immigration Act of 1976. The measure was introduced to the Canadian parliament as Bill C-11 on February 21, 2001, and came into law on June 28, 2002. It focused on selecting skilled workers with the particular needs of Canada's postindustrial economy in mind. The IRPA introduced new tools for securing Canadian borders, including front-end security screening of all refugee claimants; procedures to facilitate the removal of immigrants committing serious crimes and to suspend refugee claims for people charged until legal judgments were made; and introduction of a high-tech Permanent Resident Card, to make it easier to identify illegal immigrants.

I. MANAGING THE VOLUME OF IMMIGRATION

The Act provides the government with the flexibility to link immigration to Canada's labour market needs. The government's long-term objective is to move gradually to immigration levels of approximately one percent of Canada's population, while bearing in mind Canada's absorptive capacity.

For a variety of reasons—primarily Canada's popularity as a place to live—the number of people who want to come to Canada is much greater than the number of foreign nationals Canada plans to admit in a given year. This has had an impact on the management of the immigration program, especially on how long it takes to process an application.

Section 94 of the Act requires an annual report on the number of foreign nationals projected to become permanent residents in the following year. This number is determined after consultation with the provinces and with appropriate organizations and institutions. Section 94 also requires the federal government to table an annual report to Parliament on activities under the Act, including:

    A. activities and initiatives, such as cooperation with the provinces;

    B. the number of new permanent residents during the year;

    C. the number of permanent residents in each class in provinces which have responsibility for selection under a federal-provincial agreement;

    D. the linguistic profile of new permanent residents;

    E. the number of temporary resident permits issued and the grounds of inadmissibility;

    F. the number of people granted permanent residence on humanitarian grounds; and

    G. a gender-based analysis of the immigration program.

II. CONSULTATIONS AND AGREEMENTS WITH THE PROVINCES AND TERRITORIES

Immigration accounts for a significant part of Canada's population, rate of growth and demographic structure. It can therefore have a strong impact on regional and provincial planning.

Under the Constitution, immigration is a shared responsibility between the federal government and the provinces, with federal legislation prevailing. Section 8(1) of the Act provides for federal-provincial agreements on immigration. The Minister must publish an annual list of the federal-provincial agreements that are in force. Section 10(2) of the Act provides a legal basis for the federal government to consult the provinces regarding the number, distribution and settlement of permanent residents. This provision ensures that the federal government considers regional requirements when developing or amending immigration and settlement policies.

Immigration agreements have been concluded with a number of provinces and territories. The most comprehensive of these is an agreement with the Province of Quebec. The Canada-Quebec Accord gives Quebec certain selection powers and sole responsibility for integration services. Canada maintains responsibility for defining immigration categories, determining inadmissible persons, planning levels of immigration and enforcement.

Regulations under the Act specifically describe classes of applicants destined for Quebec, such as the Quebec Skilled Worker Class. Students and temporary foreign workers intending to settle in Quebec require the province's consent. Quebec also has exclusive selection authority for all foreign nationals who are neither members of the Family Class nor persons whom the Immigration and Refugee Board has determined to be Convention refugees.

The federal government currently has agreements in place with eight provinces and one territory, covering a range of issues including settlement and integration services, language training, labour market access and the Provincial Nominee Program, which allows provinces to nominate skilled workers who settle in their jurisdiction.

III. THE IMMIGRATION AND REFUGEE BOARD

The Immigration and Refugee Board (IRB) is an independent, quasi-judicial administrative tribunal. The Board reports to Parliament through the Minister of Citizenship and Immigration. The Board's mandate is "to make well-reasoned decisions on immigration and refugee matters efficiently, fairly and in accordance with the law." The IRB consists of four divisions:

A. *The Refugee Protection Division* (RPD) is responsible for determining whether a person in Canada is a Convention refugee or a person in need of protection.

B. *The Immigration Division* (ID) conducts admissibility hearings for permanent residents and foreign nationals who are seeking admission to Canada or are already in Canada and are considered inadmissible.

C. *The Immigration Appeal Division* (IAD) is an independent tribunal with the powers of a court. It hears appeals on a variety of matters under the *Immigration and Refugee Protection Act.*

D. *The Refugee Appeal Division* (RAD) is currently not in force. When the relevant sections of the *Immigration and Refugee Protection Act* are proclaimed, the RAD will provide failed refugee claimants and the Minister with the right to a paper appeal of a decision from the IRB. Unsuccessful refugee claimants and the Minister currently have the right to apply for judicial review to the Federal Court.

All decisions made under the Act, including decisions by the divisions of the IRB, can be judicially reviewed by the Federal Court of Canada, but only after all rights of appeal under the Act have been exhausted. However, applicants must first obtain leave from a Federal Court judge to initiate such a review.

IV. IMMIGRATING TO CANADA

Since 1967, Canada's immigration program has been based on non-discriminatory principles, both in law and in practice. Citizenship and Immigration Canada (CIC) assesses foreign nationals on standards that do not discriminate on the basis of race, national or ethnic origin, colour, religion or sex. The immigration program is universal—CIC assesses applicants from around the world against universal criteria that assess their ability to adapt to Canadian life and to settle successfully.

The Act establishes three basic categories that correspond to major program objectives: reuniting families, contributing to economic development and protecting refugees. Applicants can be admitted to Canada as permanent residents under three corresponding classes: Family Class, Economic Class or Refugee Class.

A. **Family Class.** Helping families reunite in Canada is a key objective of Canada's immigration policy. Members of the Family Class are people sponsored to come to Canada by a relative, a spouse, a common-law partner or a conjugal partner who is a Canadian citizen or a permanent resident of Canada.

The Family Class applicant must be the sponsor's:

1. spouse, common-law or conjugal partner;
2. dependent child, including a child adopted abroad;
3. child under 18 to be adopted in Canada;
4. parents or grandparents; or
5. an orphaned child under 18 who is a brother, sister, niece, nephew or grandchild and is not a spouse or common-law partner.

Dependent children of a sponsored foreign national may be included in that person's application. A dependent child is either a biological child or an adopted child. Children can be dependent if they meet one of the following conditions:

1. they are under age 22 and unmarried or not in a common-law relationship;
2. they have been full-time students since before age 22, attend a post-secondary educational institution and have been substantially dependent on the financial support of a parent since before age 22 and, if married or a common-law partner, since becoming a spouse or a common-law partner; or
3. they are aged 22 or over and have been substantially dependent on the financial support of a parent since before age 22 because of a physical or mental condition.

In addition, spouses or common-law partners who are 16 years of age or older, and have legal temporary status in

Canada as visitors, students, temporary workers or temporary resident permit holders may apply under the In-Canada Class.

Applicants and their family members are subject to medical, criminal and background checks.

Successful applicants become permanent residents of Canada, giving the applicant and his or her family members the right to live, study and work in Canada for as long as they remain permanent residents.

Sponsors must support their sponsored family members or relatives after they become permanent residents of Canada.

Spouses, common-law and conjugal partners must be supported for three years.

A sponsor's dependent children under age 22 must be supported for 10 years or until they reach the age of 25, whichever comes earliest.

A sponsor's dependent children aged 22 or over must be supported for three years.

Other family members, including their own dependent children, must be supported for 10 years.

The duration of these federal undertakings applies only to sponsorship agreements outside Quebec. Sponsors who live in Quebec are governed by Quebec's laws. While a sponsorship undertaking is in effect, if the sponsored persons receive social assistance, the sponsor is in default and is required to repay the social assistance payments.

B. **Economic Class.** Permanent residents admitted to Canada under the Economic Class are selected for their skills and ability to contribute to Canada's economy. The Economic Class is comprised of two streams: skilled workers and business immigrants.

1. *Skilled workers*

Canada values skilled immigrants who can effectively compete and succeed in the country's knowledge-based economy. Foreign nationals who are skilled workers are chosen for their ability to become successfully established in Canada. The regulations under the *Immigration and Refugee Protection Act* stress education, language ability and skilled work experience rather than experience in a specific occupation.

Skilled workers are assessed according to a selection grid (point system). In order to be admitted to Canada, skilled workers must:

a. have at least one year of work experience within the past 10 years in a management occupation or in an occupation normally requiring university, college or technical training as described in the National Occupational Classification (NOC) developed by Human Resources Development Canada (HRDC);

b. have enough money to support themselves and their family members in Canada.

The *Immigration and Refugee Protection Regulations* establish a new selection grid for skilled workers. Applicants are assessed on a variety of selection criteria which evaluate their ability to adapt to the Canadian economy.

Selection Criteria	Maximum Points
Education	25
Official languages (English and/or French)	24
Employment experience	21
Age	10
Arranged employment in Canada	10
Adaptability	10
TOTAL	100

To be considered under the Federal Skilled Worker category, applicants must score a minimum of 75 out of the possible 100 points. The pass mark may be amended by the Minister to reflect changes in the Canadian labour market, economy and society as well as the changing demands of prospective newcomers to Canada.

The Provincial Nominee Program

Under the Provincial Nominee Program, most provincial and territorial governments may nominate a person for a permanent resident visa on the grounds that the individual's labour market skills are in particular demand in the province or territory. Provincial nominees are expected to live in the province that nominated them in order to contribute their particular employment skills.

Skilled workers intending to live in Quebec

The Canada-Quebec Accord gives the Province of Quebec sole responsibility for selecting skilled worker applicants and sole responsibility for integration services for newcomers who settle in Quebec. Skilled workers who intend to live in the Province of Quebec must satisfy the Quebec selection criteria and obtain a *Certificat de sélection du Québec* (Quebec certificate of selection) issued by the Government of Quebec.

2. *Business immigrants*

Business immigrants are selected to support the development of a strong and prosperous Canadian economy, either through their direct investment, their entrepreneurial activity or self-employment. Business immigration is made up of the Investor, Entrepreneur and Self-employed Person classes. To be eligible for immigration as a business immigrant, applicants who are investors and entrepreneurs require a specified net worth and business experience as set out in the Canadian immigration regulations. Self-employed applicants require specific experience.

a. *Investors.* Investor applicants must have legally obtained a net worth of at least $800,000. They must also have either controlled a portion of the equity of a qualifying business, or been responsible for the management of the equivalent of at least five full-time jobs per year in a business.

They are also required to make an investment of $400,000 through the Receiver General for Canada before a visa is issued. The investment is subsequently allocated to participating provinces and territories in Canada, which use the funds for job creation and economic development.

The investment of $400,000 is locked in for approximately five years, after which it is repaid without interest. Investments are guaranteed by participating provinces and territories. Quebec operates its own investor program.

b. *Entrepreneurs.* Entrepreneur applicants must have legally obtained a net worth of at least $300,000. They must also have controlled a portion of the equity of a qualifying business that was not operated primarily for the purpose of deriving investment income (such as interest, dividends or capital gains).

Applicants must intend and be able to own and actively manage at least one-third of a business that will contribute to the Canadian economy and create at least one full-time job, other than for the entrepreneur and family members.

Entrepreneurs and their family members are granted permanent residence under conditions that are monitored by CIC. They must report at specified intervals to an immigration officer in Canada on their progress in establishing a business which meets specified requirements and show that they have met these requirements for at least one year within three years of admission to Canada.

To be eligible for selection as a business immigrant, applicants must first meet the applicable business immigration definition of the class in which they are applying (investor, entrepreneur or self-employed). Applicants are then assessed against a selection system.

Entrepreneurs, investors and self-employed applicants are assessed against five selection criteria. Applicants must obtain a minimum of 35 points. However, the pass mark can change at the direction of the Minister.

Factors Assessed	Maximum Points
Education	25
Experience	35
Age	10
Proficiency in English and/or French	24
Adaptability	6
TOTAL	100

c. *Self-employed.* Self-employed applicants must demonstrate that they have the relevant experience and the intention and ability to become economically established in Canada by creating their own employment and contributing significantly to Canada in one of the following areas:

1. Canada's cultural life, either through performance at a world-class level or self-employment in the discipline, as in the case of dancers or experienced choreographers.
2. Canada's ability to compete in athletics, either through performance at the world-class level or self-employment in the discipline, as in the case of figure skaters and coaches.
3. Canada's economy, through the purchase and management of a farm in Canada.

Applicants are expected to establish a business and become self-supporting, but are not required to make a minimum investment, employ others or report on progress towards the establishment of the business.

Business applicants destined for Quebec

The Canada-Quebec Accord gives Quebec the right to select its business applicants using its own selection criteria.

Business applicants destined for British Columbia

A business immigration pilot project was jointly launched in British Columbia by Citizenship and Immigration Canada and the B.C. Ministry of Employment and Investment in 1999.

The program provides information to prospective entrepreneurs on business opportunities in British Columbia. Entrepreneur applicants are encouraged to visit B.C. and attend an immigration and investment seminar.

C. **Refugees and other persons in need of protection.** Canada has a long humanitarian tradition of helping people in need and lives up to its international commitments by welcoming between 20,000 and 30,000 Convention refugees and other displaced persons into Canada each year. Refugees are accepted into Canada under the following classes:

1. Convention refugees or persons needing protection selected at a visa office abroad;
2. persons in Canada accepted by the Immigration and Refugee Board as Convention refugees or persons in need of protection; and
3. persons in Canada granted protection under a Pre-Removal Risk Assessment (PRRA).

I. Refugees selected abroad

The *Immigration and Refugee Protection Act* allows foreign nationals to apply for refugee protection while outside Canada and to be selected for resettlement in Canada. To be eligible, refugees must have no lasting alternative, such as voluntary repatriation, resettlement in their country of asylum or resettlement to a third country, or there must be no possibility of such an alternative within a reasonable period of time. Three classes of people are eligible for this program.

A. *Convention Refugees Abroad Class.* Convention refugees seeking resettlement are people who are outside their country of citizenship or habitual residence and who have well-founded fears of persecution for reasons of race, religion, political opinion, nationality or membership in a particular social group.

B. *Country of Asylum Class.* The Country of Asylum Class includes people who are outside their country of citizenship or habitual residence and who have been and continue to be seriously and personally affected by civil war, armed conflict or massive violations of human rights.

C. Source Country Class. This class includes people who would meet the definition of Convention refugee but who are still in their country of citizenship or habitual residence. It also includes people who are suffering serious deprivations of the right of freedom of expression, the right of dissent or the right to engage in trade union activity, and who have been detained or imprisoned as a consequence. Only citizens or habitual residents of specific countries are eligible under this class.

The government may sponsor members of the Convention Refugees Abroad and Source Country classes. Members of any of the three classes may be privately sponsored. People selected for resettlement, regardless of their class, must demonstrate their ability to eventually re-establish in Canada and must undergo medical, security and criminality screening.

Members of these classes must be referred to a visa office by the United Nations High Commissioner for Refugees (UNHCR) or another organization with which CIC has an agreement. In exceptional circumstances, they may apply directly to the visa office. If the UNHCR refers them as in urgent need of protection, the visa office will expedite processing. When family members are separated, they may be included in the application and allowed to come to Canada within one year after the principal applicant receives a permanent resident visa.

Sponsoring refugees

Organizations, groups of Canadian citizens and permanent residents may sponsor refugees under the Private Sponsorship of Refugees Program. Sponsoring groups commit to providing assistance in the form of accommodation, clothing, food and settlement assistance for one year from the refugee's date of arrival. There are three types of sponsoring groups.

1. *Sponsorship agreement holders and their constituent groups.* A number of organizations and groups across Canada have signed sponsorship agreements to facilitate the sponsorship process. Sponsorship agreement holders are essentially pre-approved sponsors. They may sponsor refugees themselves or their constituent groups may sponsor refugees with the approval of the agreement holder.
2. *Groups of five.* A group of five Canadian citizens or permanent residents can partner to sponsor refugees living abroad. Each member of the group must be at least 18 years of age, live in the community where the refugee will live and personally provide settlement assistance and support.
3. *Community sponsors.* Other groups interested in sponsoring refugees may consider a community sponsorship. This type of sponsorship is open to organizations, associations and corporations that have the necessary finances and that can provide adequate settlement assistance to refugees. Community sponsors must be located in the community where the refugee will live.

II. In-Canada Refugee Program

A person who has arrived in Canada seeking protection may make a claim for refugee protection by notifying an immigration officer, who determines if the person is eligible to claim refugee protection.

Claiming refugee protection

Anyone may claim refugee protection at a port of entry or after entry to Canada. After completing an application form, refugee protection claimants are photographed and have their fingerprints taken. A decision on the eligibility of a refugee claim must be made within three working days or the claim is referred to the IRB. The decision may be suspended pending a decision on criminal charges or an admissibility hearing on issues of security, human rights violations, serious criminality, or organized criminality. A refugee protection claimant is issued a conditional removal order that does not come into force unless the claim is refused. If eligible, the person's claim is referred to the Refugee Protection Division for a refugee protection hearing. If an immigration officer receives new information that makes a person ineligible to make a claim, the officer may reconsider the previous eligibility decision.

Refugee protection hearings

In general, an oral hearing is held to determine refugee protection. Hearings usually take place in private to protect the safety of claimants and their families, but in some cases they are held in public. In these cases, the RPD takes necessary precautions to ensure confidentiality when the life, liberty or security of any person might be endangered. Representatives of the UNHCR may observe the hearing.

The hearing is non-adversarial and allows claimants to put forward their cases as thoroughly as possible. Claimants enjoy the protection of the *Canadian Charter of Rights and Freedoms,* have the right to participate fully in the process, be represented by counsel and, if necessary, be provided with the services of an interpreter. The hearing normally takes place before one member of the Refugee Protection Division.

If the Refugee Protection Division accepts a claim, the person applies for permanent residence within 180 days. The applicant may include family members in Canada and abroad. Permanent resident status may not be granted if there are concerns about identity or if the person is inadmissible for serious criminal or security reasons.

If the Refugee Protection Division rejects a claim, the conditional removal order comes into force, and the claimant must leave Canada immediately. The removal order is stayed if the claimant applies for leave for judicial review of the decision. People who have been issued a removal order can apply for a Pre-Removal Risk Assessment.

III. PRE-REMOVAL RISK ASSESSMENT

The *Immigration and Refugee Protection Act* provides a formal structured process for reviewing risk before a person is removed. The Pre-Removal Risk Assessment (PRRA) gives persons who may be exposed to compelling personal risk if removed the opportunity to apply to remain in Canada.

A PRRA review is conducted immediately before removal. It is done by a CIC officer who has specialized training in matters relating to personal risk and who has access to up-to-date information on conditions in other countries.

The PRRA officer assesses the risk to the individual case based on the same protection grounds as those considered by the IRB, including the criteria in the *Convention on Refugees* and the *Convention against Torture,* and risk to life or risk of cruel and unusual treatment or punishment.

IV. THE NORTH AMERICAN FREE TRADE AGREEMENT

Under Chapter 16 of the North American Free Trade Agreement (NAFTA), citizens of Canada, the United States and Mexico can gain quicker, easier temporary entry into the three countries to conduct business-related activities or investments. All provisions are equally available to citizens of the three countries. NAFTA applies to four specific categories of business persons: business visitors, professionals, intra-company transferees and persons engaged in trade or investment activities, all of whom can enter Canada without a labour market test being applied.

For more information, please refer to the booklet *Temporary Entry to Canada under the NAFTA—A Guide for American and Mexican Business Persons.*

V. WHAT HAPPENS AT THE PORT OF ENTRY

A. *Examinations.* Section 18 of the Act requires everyone seeking to enter Canada—whether visitors, newcomers, temporary residents, returning residents or citizens—to be examined by an immigration officer at the port of entry.

In the case of foreign nationals seeking permanent status or temporary residents intending to study or work temporarily in Canada, a more detailed interview may be required before entry will be granted. Individuals who want to become permanent residents must establish that they have the necessary visa or any other document required by regulations and that they have come to Canada to establish permanent residence.

Individuals who want to become temporary residents must satisfy an immigration officer that they have the necessary visa or any other document required by regulations, and that they will leave Canada by the end of the period authorized for their stay.

Individuals who want to become permanent residents and who are subject to a province's sole selection responsibility under a federal-provincial agreement must establish that they hold a document issued by the province indicating that they comply with the province's selection criteria.

Possession of a visa or a permit does not guarantee a person's admission to Canada. The examining officer at the port of entry must be satisfied that the visa or permit is valid, that the person's circumstances have not changed since the visa or permit was issued, and that the person's presence in Canada will not contravene any of the provisions of the Immigration and Refugee Protection Act and its Regulations.

B. *Security deposits.* When in doubt about the intention of a temporary resident to live up to the terms of admission, the examining officer may require payment of a deposit, or the posting of a guarantee, prior to granting entry. Cash deposits will be returned as soon as possible after all entry conditions have been met.

C. *Inadmissible classes.* Division 4 of Part I of the Act prohibits the admission of people to Canada on grounds related to security, human or international rights violations, criminality and organized criminality (sections 3437). Individuals can also be denied entry to Canada if they pose a threat to public health, if they have no visible means of support, if they misrepresent themselves or if they fail to comply with other measures in the Act (sections 3841).

Exclusions on health grounds are based solely on danger to public health or safety, or on excessive demands on health or social services in Canada. Inadmissibility on criminal grounds is determined by the sentence that could be given for equivalent offences under Canadian law.

The *Immigration and Refugee Protection Act* also protects the Canadian public by providing for the removal from Canada of persons identified as inadmissible, such as those involved in organized crime, espionage, acts of subversion, terrorism, war crimes, human or international rights violations, criminality and serious criminality.

VI. THE RIGHT TO ENTER OR REMAIN IN CANADA

A. Canadian citizens. Canadian citizens have an absolute right to come to or remain in Canada regardless of whether their citizenship was acquired through naturalization, parentage or place of birth. On entering Canada, however, they cannot merely claim that they have that status; in order to enter, they must satisfy an officer of their status.

B. Indians. People registered under Canada's Indian Act, whether or not they are Canadian citizens, also have an absolute right to come to or remain in Canada. They must also be prepared to prove their status to an immigration officer.

C. Permanent residents. Persons who have been admitted to Canada as permanent residents have the right to come to the country and remain here, provided they have not lost that status or it has not been established that they have engaged in activities, such as criminal acts, that would otherwise subject them to removal. Conditions may be imposed for a certain period on some permanent residents, such as entrepreneurs. A permanent resident must live in Canada for at least 730 days (two years) within a five-year period. In some situations, time spent outside Canada may count. All permanent residents must comply with this residency requirement or risk losing their status.

Like Canadian citizens, permanent residents also enjoy all the rights guaranteed under the *Canadian Charter of Rights and Freedoms,* such as equality rights, legal rights, mobility rights, freedom of religion, freedom of expression and freedom of association.

D. Permanent Resident Card. The Immigration and Refugee Protection Act provides for the introduction of a Permanent Resident Card to make it easier for permanent residents to re-enter Canada after travelling abroad.

As of June 28, 2002, all new permanent residents will receive Permanent Resident Cards. Existing permanent residents may apply for the card after October 15, 2002. Effective January 2004, permanent residents travelling outside Canada will need it for status identification in order to return to Canada.

The card is revoked if it is lost or stolen, if the permanent resident becomes a Canadian citizen, or if the person loses permanent resident status. If the card is lost, permanent residents may apply for a travel document in order to return to Canada, but they must satisfy an officer that they meet the residency requirements.

E. Temporary residents. Temporary residents may enter or remain in Canada temporarily as long as they comply with any conditions imposed upon them. They must leave Canada by the end of their authorized stay. Temporary residents may lose their status and privileges if they:

1. do not comply with the terms and conditions of their visit;
2. extend their stay without permission;
3. violate the conditions of their study or work permits; or
4. fail to comply with the *Immigration and Refugee Protection Act.*

F. Protected persons. A protected person is a person on whom refugee protection is conferred. If they meet the specified requirements, protected persons acquire permanent resident status and have the same rights to enter and remain in Canada as permanent residents.

G. Arrests and detention. Immigration officers can arrest foreign nationals and permanent residents who are suspected of breaching the Immigration and Refugee Protection Act. While arrests of foreign nationals can be made with or without a warrant, immigration officers must have a warrant to arrest a permanent resident or a protected person.

Immigration officers can detain people who are suspected of breaching the *Immigration and Refugee Protection Act* if they have reasonable grounds to believe that:

1. the person will not appear for immigration proceedings such as an admissibility hearing or removal from Canada;
2. the person poses a risk to the public because of past crimes, a medical condition or a history of physical violence; or
3. the person refuses to provide information to an immigration officer on his or her identity during an immigration proceeding.

Immigration officers can detain a permanent resident or a foreign national at a port of entry in order to complete an examination, or if there are reasonable grounds to believe that the person is inadmissible for reasons of security or for violating human or international rights. Children under the age of 18 are detained only as a last resort. The child's best interests are taken into account when making a decision on detention.

Whenever individuals are arrested or detained, the *Canadian Charter of Rights and Freedoms* requires that CIC officers inform them of the reasons for their arrest or detention, their right to legal representation, and their right to notify a representative of their government that they have been arrested or detained. Within 48 hours of a person's detention, immigration officers must review the reasons for the detention. A person who has been detained for 48 hours must appear as soon as possible before a member of the Immigration Division of the Immigration and Refugee Board, where a CIC officer presents information to justify the detention. The member reviews the case and decides if the individual should remain in detention or be released with or without conditions. If the person is not released, a member of the Immigration Division must review the case again in seven days and then again within every 30 days.

Detention reviews before the Immigration Division are open to the public, except those that concern refugee protection claimants. Persons who are arrested and detained under the *Immigration and Refugee Protection Act* can be released only by an immigration officer or a member of the Immigration Division of the Immigration and Refugee Board.

VII. SAFEGUARDING LAW AND ORDER

The *Immigration and Refugee Protection Act* introduces several new offences and sets severe penalties for breaches of the Act. Under Part 3 of the Act, new offences of human smuggling and trafficking in persons are introduced, with penalties of up to life in prison and fines of up to one million dollars. These provisions bring Canada into compliance with two new United Nations protocols on smuggling of migrants and on trafficking in persons, which require state parties to criminalize the act of smuggling and trafficking in humans. The Act also makes it an offence to disembark a person or a group of people at sea for the purposes of entering Canada illegally.

New offences related to possession, use, import or export, or dealing in passports, visas and other documents to contravene the Act are also introduced, with prison terms of up to five years for possession and 14 years for the use, import or export, or dealing in these documents. The Act also sets higher penalties for a number of other offences under the Act and expands the provisions of a number of offences under the previous

Immigration Act, which the *Immigration and Refugee Protection Act* replaces.

VIII. A FINAL NOTE

Under any immigration law, there are obligations on the part of both the host country and the immigrant or visitor.

Canada welcomes newcomers and visitors. At the same time, our immigration law works in the interests of Canada: to ensure the total number of permanent residents admitted to Canada and their skills and experience are linked more closely to demographic and labour market needs, and to protect the health and safety of Canadian residents.

Source: Citizenship and Immigration Canada, Minister of Public Works and Government Services Canada, 2002, available online, URL: http://www.cic.gc.ca/english/pub/imm%2Dlaw.html, accessed March 6, 2004.

Speech of President George W. Bush, Proposing New Temporary Worker Program, 2004

As governor of Texas (1994–2000), George W. Bush developed a strong record of friendship with bordering Mexico. He was determined to bring his good working relationship with Mexican president Vicente Fox to the White House in order to regularize the participation of Mexican laborers in the U.S. economy. Negotiations were temporarily delayed in the wake of September 11, 2001, but on January 7, 2004, Bush proposed a Temporary Worker Program that would "match willing foreign workers with willing American employers, when no Americans can be found to fill the jobs." More controversially, it would provide temporary workers legal status, even if they were undocumented.

Thanks for coming, thanks for the warm welcome, thanks for joining me as I make this important announcement—an announcement that I believe will make America a more compassionate and more humane and stronger country.

I appreciate members of my Cabinet who have joined me today, starting with our Secretary of State, Colin Powell. I'm honored that our Attorney General, John Ashcroft, has joined us. Secretary of Commerce, Don Evans. Secretary Tom Ridge, of the Department of Homeland Security. El Embajador of Mexico, Tony Garza. I thank all the other members of my administration who have joined us today. I appreciate the members of Congress who have taken time to come: Senator Larry Craig, Congressman Chris Cannon, and Congressman Jeff Flake. I'm honored you all have joined us, thank you for coming. I appreciate the members of citizen groups who have joined us today. Chairman of the Hispanic Alliance for Progress, Manny Lujan. Gil Moreno, the President and CEO of the Association for the Advancement of Mexican Ameri-

cans. Roberto De Posada, the President of the Latino Coalition. And Hector Flores, the President of LULAC. Thank you all for joining us.

Many of you here today are Americans by choice, and you have followed in the path of millions. And over the generations we have received energetic, ambitious, optimistic people from every part of the world. By tradition and conviction, our country is a welcoming society. America is a stronger and better nation because of the hard work and the faith and entrepreneurial spirit of immigrants. Every generation of immigrants has reaffirmed the wisdom of remaining open to the talents and dreams of the world. And every generation of immigrants has reaffirmed our ability to assimilate newcomers—which is one of the defining strengths of our country.

During one great period of immigration—between 1891 and 1920—our nation received some 18 million men, women and children from other nations. The hard work of these immigrants helped make our economy the largest in the world. The children of immigrants put on the uniform and helped to liberate the lands of their ancestors. One of the primary reasons America became a great power in the 20th century is because we welcomed the talent and the character and the patriotism of immigrant families.

The contributions of immigrants to America continue. About 14 percent of our nation's civilian workforce is foreign-born. Most begin their working lives in America by taking hard jobs and clocking long hours in important industries. Many immigrants also start businesses, taking the familiar path from hired labor to ownership.

As a Texan, I have known many immigrant families, mainly from Mexico, and I have seen what they add to our country. They bring to America the values of faith in God, love of family, hard work and self reliance—the values that made us a great nation to begin with. We've all seen those values in action, through the service and sacrifice of more than 35,000 foreign-born men and women currently on active duty in the United States military. One of them is Master Gunnery Sergeant Guadalupe Denogean, an immigrant from Mexico who has served in the Marine Corps for 25 years and counting. Last year, I was honored and proud to witness Sergeant Denogean take the oath of citizenship in a hospital where he was recovering from wounds he received in Iraq. I'm honored to be his Commander-in-Chief, I'm proud to call him a fellow American.

As a nation that values immigration, and depends on immigration, we should have immigration laws that work and make us proud. Yet today we do not. Instead, we see many employers turning to the illegal labor market. We see millions of hard-working men and women condemned to fear and insecurity in a massive, undocumented economy. Illegal entry across our borders makes more difficult the urgent task of securing the homeland. The system is not working. Our nation needs an immigration system that serves the American economy, and reflects the American Dream.

Reform must begin by confronting a basic fact of life and economics: some of the jobs being generated in America's growing economy are jobs American citizens are not filling. Yet these jobs represent a tremendous opportunity for workers from abroad who want to work and fulfill their duties as a husband or a wife, a son or a daughter.

Their search for a better life is one of the most basic desires of human beings. Many undocumented workers have walked mile after mile, through the heat of the day and the cold of the night. Some have risked their lives in dangerous desert border crossings, or entrusted their lives to the brutal rings of heartless human smugglers. Workers who seek only to earn a living end up in the shadows of American life—fearful, often abused and exploited. When they are victimized by crime, they are afraid to call the police, or seek recourse in the legal system. They are cut off from their families far away, fearing if they leave our country to visit relatives back home, they might never be able to return to their jobs.

The situation I described is wrong. It is not the American way. Out of common sense and fairness, our laws should allow willing workers to enter our country and fill jobs that Americans have are not filling. We must make our immigration laws more rational, and more humane. And I believe we can do so without jeopardizing the livelihoods of American citizens.

Our reforms should be guided by a few basic principles. First, America must control its borders. Following the attacks of September the 11th, 2001, this duty of the federal government has become even more urgent. And we're fulfilling that duty. For the first time in our history, we have consolidated all border agencies under one roof to make sure they share information and the work is more effective. We're matching all visa applicants against an expanded screening list to identify terrorists and criminals and immigration violators. This month, we have begun using advanced technology to better record and track aliens who enter our country—and to make sure they leave as scheduled. We have deployed new gamma and x-ray systems to scan cargo and containers and shipments at ports of entry to America. We have significantly expanded the Border Patrol—with more than a thousand new agents on the borders, and 40 percent greater funding over the last two years. We're working closely with the Canadian and Mexican governments to increase border security. America is acting on a basic belief: our borders should be open to legal travel and honest trade; our borders should be shut and barred tight to criminals, to drug traders, to drug traffickers and to criminals, and to terrorists.

Second, new immigration laws should serve the economic needs of our country. If an American employer is offering a job that American citizens are not willing to take, we ought to welcome into our country a person who will fill that job. Third, we should not give unfair rewards to illegal immigrants in the citizenship process or disadvantage those who came here lawfully, or hope to do so. Fourth, new laws should provide incentives for temporary, foreign workers to return permanently to their home countries after their period of work in the United States has expired.

Today, I ask the Congress to join me in passing new immigration laws that reflect these principles, that meet America's economic needs, and live up to our highest ideals. I propose a new temporary worker program that will match willing foreign workers with willing American employers, when no Americans can be found to fill the jobs. This program will offer legal status, as temporary workers, to the millions of undocumented men and women now employed in the United States, and to those in foreign countries who seek to participate in the program and have been offered employment here. This new system should be clear and efficient, so employers are able to find workers quickly and simply.

All who participate in the temporary worker program must have a job, or, if not living in the United States, a job offer. The legal status granted by this program will last three years and will be renewable—but it will have an end. Participants who do not remain employed, who do not follow the rules of the program, or who break the law will not be eligible for continued participation and will be required to return to their home.

Under my proposal, employers have key responsibilities. Employers who extend job offers must first make every reasonable effort to find an American worker for the job at hand. Our government will develop a quick and simple system for employers to search for American workers. Employers must not hire undocumented aliens or temporary workers whose legal status has expired. They must report to the government the temporary workers they hire, and who leave their employ, so that we can keep track of people in the program, and better enforce immigration laws. There must be strong workplace enforcement with tough penalties for anyone, for any employer violating these laws.

Undocumented workers now here will be required to pay a one-time fee to register for the temporary worker program. Those who seek to join the program from abroad, and have complied with our immigration laws, will not have to pay any fee. All participants will be issued a temporary worker card that will allow them to travel back and forth between their home and the United States without fear of being denied re-entry into our country.

This program expects temporary workers to return permanently to their home countries after their period of work in the United States has expired. And there should be financial incentives for them to do so. I will work with foreign governments on a plan to give temporary workers credit, when they enter their own nation's retirement system, for the time they have worked in America. I also support making it easier for temporary workers to contribute a portion of their earnings to tax-preferred savings accounts, money they can collect as they return to their native countries. After all, in many of those countries, a small nest egg is what is necessary to start their own business, or buy some land for their family.

Some temporary workers will make the decision to pursue American citizenship. Those who make this choice will be allowed to apply in the normal way. They will not be given unfair advantage over people who have followed legal procedures from the start. I oppose amnesty, placing undocumented workers on the automatic path to citizenship. Granting amnesty encourages the violation of our laws, and perpetuates illegal immigration. America is a welcoming country, but citizenship must not be the automatic reward for violating the laws of America. The citizenship line, however, is too long, and our current limits on legal immigration are too low. My administration will work with the Congress to increase the annual number of green cards that can lead to citizenship. Those willing to take the difficult path of citizenship—the path of work, and patience, and assimilation—should be welcome in America, like generations of immigrants before them.

In the process of immigration reform, we must also set high expectations for what new citizens should know. An understanding of what it means to be an American is not a formality in the naturalization process, it is essential to full participation in our democracy. My administration will examine the standard of knowledge in the current citizenship test. We must ensure that new citizens know not only the facts of our history, but the ideals that have shaped our history. Every citizen of America has an obligation to learn the values that make us one nation: liberty and civic responsibility, equality under God, and tolerance for others.

This new temporary worker program will bring more than economic benefits to America. Our homeland will be more secure when we can better account for those who enter our country, instead of the current situation in which millions of people are unknown, unknown to the law. Law enforcement will face fewer problems with undocumented workers, and will be better able to focus on the true threats to our nation from criminals and terrorists. And when temporary workers can travel legally and freely, there will be more efficient management of our borders and more effective enforcement against those who pose a danger to our country.

This new system will be more compassionate. Decent, hard-working people will now be protected by labor laws, with the right to change jobs, earn fair wages, and enjoy the same working conditions that the law requires for American workers. Temporary workers will be able to establish their identities by obtaining the legal documents we all take for granted. And they will be able to talk openly to authorities, to report crimes when they are harmed, without the fear of being deported.

The best way, in the long run, to reduce the pressures that create illegal immigration in the first place is to expand economic opportunity among the countries in our neighborhood. In a few days I will go to Mexico for the Special Summit of the Americas, where we will discuss ways to advance free trade, and to fight corruption, and encourage the reforms that lead to prosperity. Real growth and real hope in the nations of our hemisphere will lessen the flow of new immigrants to America when more citizens of other countries are able to achieve their dreams at their own home.

Yet our country has always benefited from the dreams that others have brought here. By working hard for a better life, immigrants contribute to the life of our nation. The temporary worker program I am proposing today represents the best tradition of our society, a society that honors the law, and welcomes the newcomer. This plan will help return order and fairness to our immigration system, and in so doing we will honor our values, by showing our respect for those who work hard and share in the ideals of America.

May God bless you all.

Source: "President Bush Proposes New Temporary Worker Program." White House Web site, available online, URL: http://www.whitehouse.gov/news/releases/2004/01/print/20040107-3.html, accessed March 6, 2004.

Appendix B
MAPS, GRAPHS, AND TABLES

MAPS

GRAPHS AND TABLES

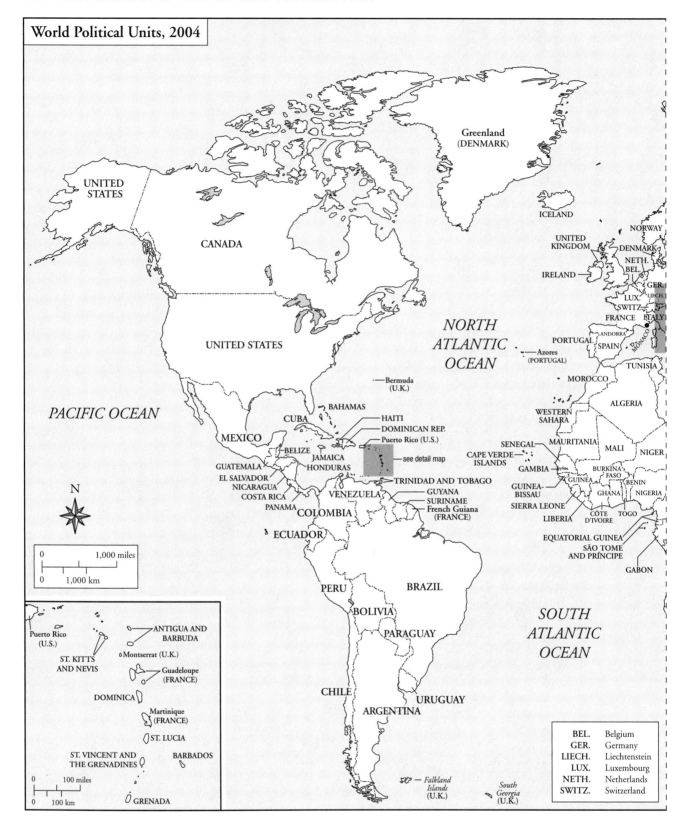

World Political Units, 2004

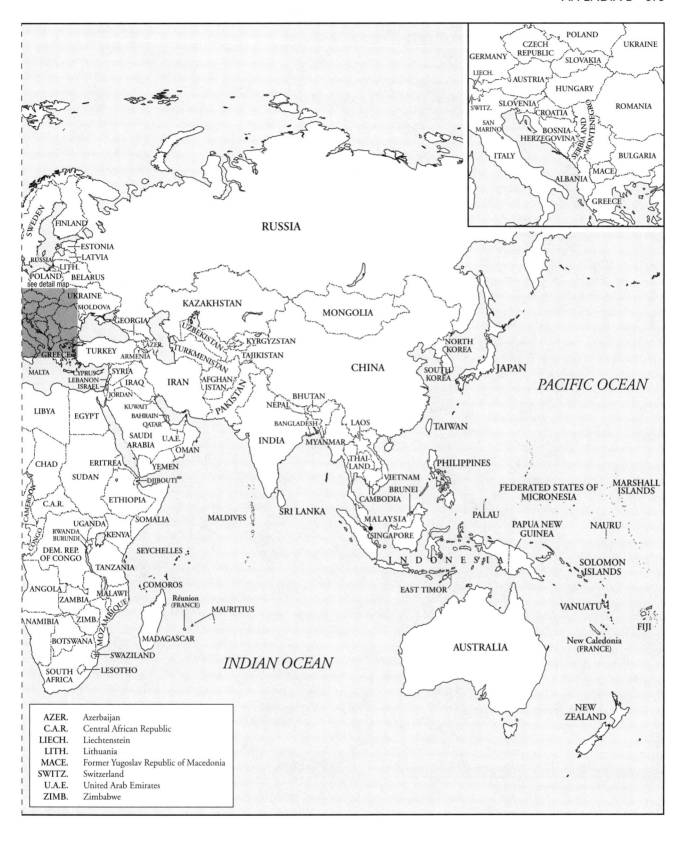

AZER.	Azerbaijan
C.A.R.	Central African Republic
LIECH.	Liechtenstein
LITH.	Lithuania
MACE.	Former Yugoslav Republic of Macedonia
SWITZ.	Switzerland
U.A.E.	United Arab Emirates
ZIMB.	Zimbabwe

North America, 2004

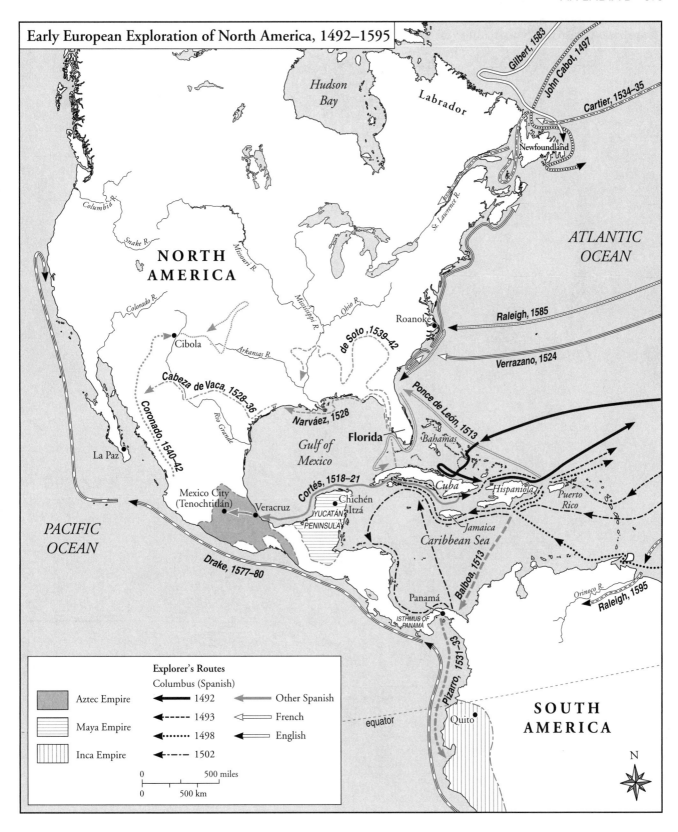

Early European Exploration of North America, 1492–1595

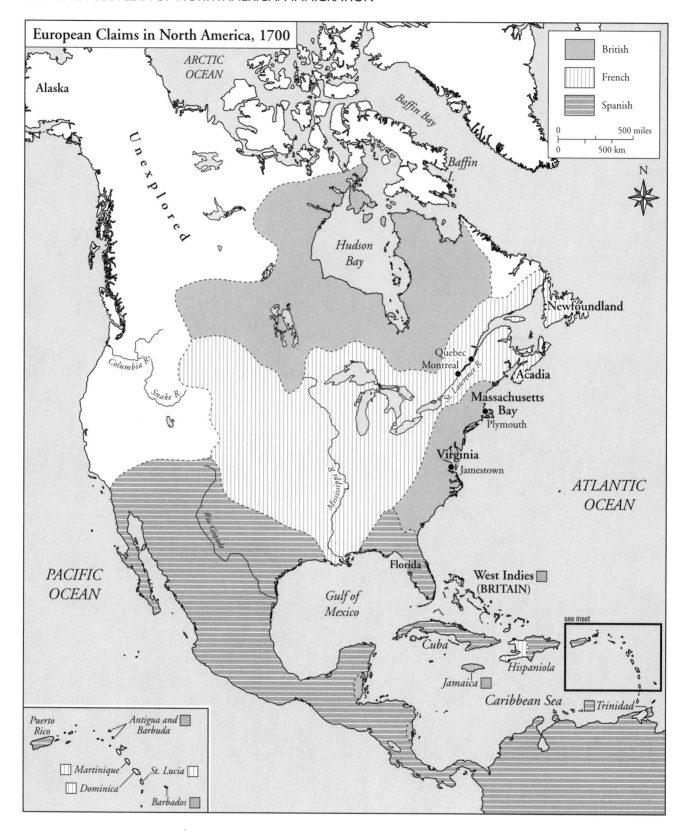

European Claims in North America, 1700

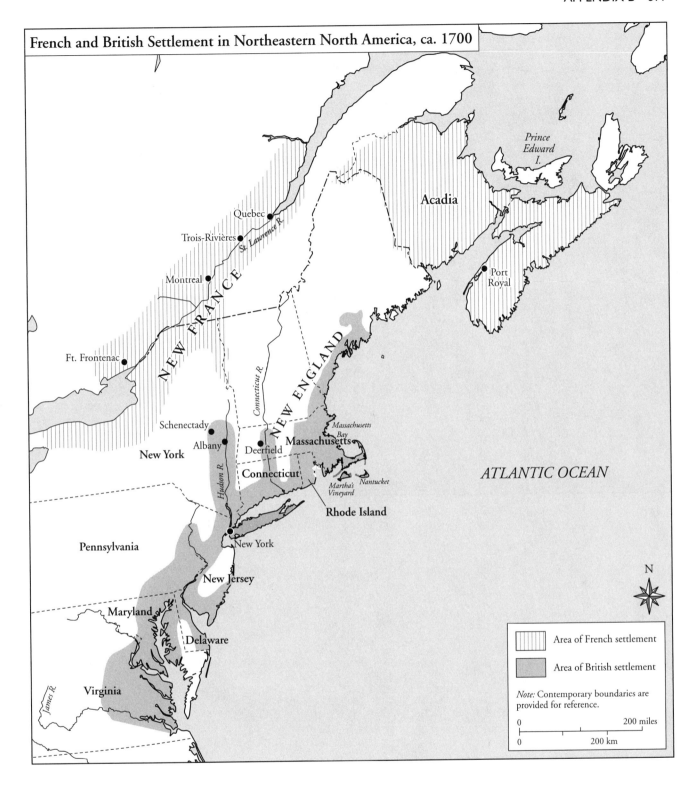

French and British Settlement in Northeastern North America, ca. 1700

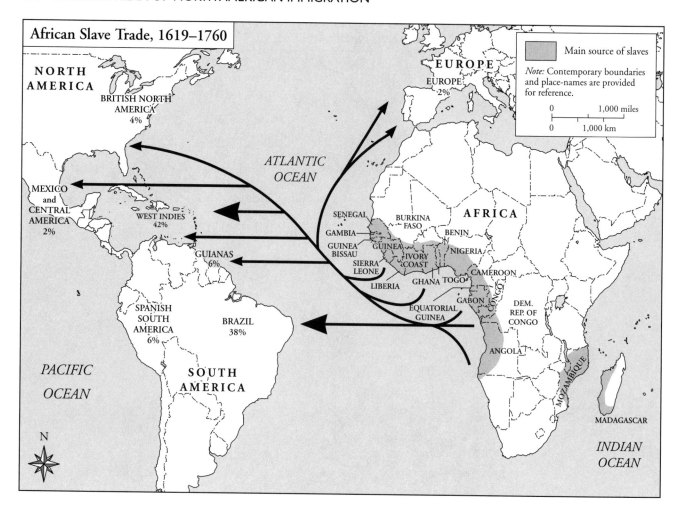

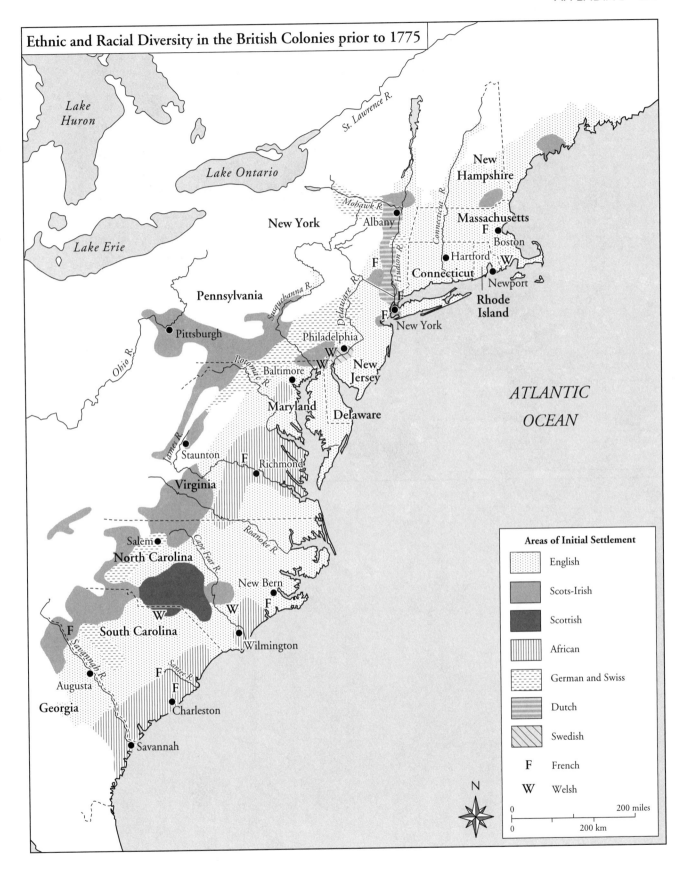

Ethnic and Racial Diversity in the British Colonies prior to 1775

Lake Huron

Lake Ontario

Lake Erie

St. Lawrence R.

New Hampshire

Mohawk R.

New York

Albany ●

Massachusetts

F

Boston ●

Hudson R.

Connecticut R.

● Hartford

Connecticut

W

Newport

Rhode Island

Pennsylvania

Susquehanna R.

F

Delaware R.

Pittsburgh ●

Ohio R.

Philadelphia ●

F

New York

F

Potomac R.

W

Baltimore ●

W

New Jersey

Maryland

Delaware

ATLANTIC OCEAN

James R.

Staunton ●

F

● Richmond

Virginia

Roanoke R.

Salem ●

North Carolina

Cape Fear R.

New Bern ●

W

F

South Carolina

W

F

Wilmington ●

F

Santee R.

Savannah R.

F

Augusta ●

F

Charleston ●

Georgia

● Savannah

N

Areas of Initial Settlement	
	English
	Scots-Irish
	Scottish
	African
	German and Swiss
	Dutch
	Swedish
F	French
W	Welsh

0   200 miles

0   200 km

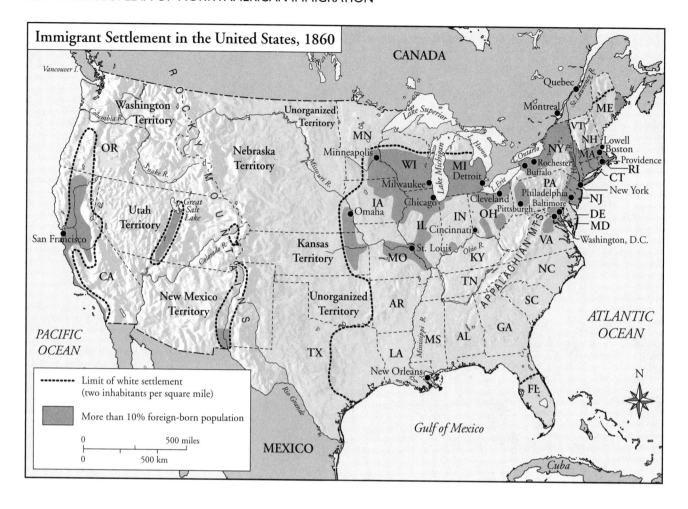

Immigrant Settlement in the United States, 1860

- - - - - Limit of white settlement
(two inhabitants per square mile)

More than 10% foreign-born population

0   500 miles

0   500 km

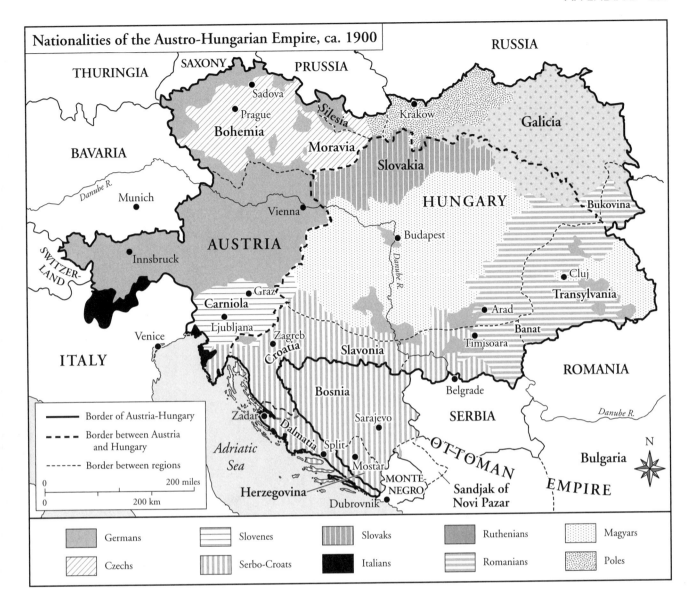

Nationalities of the Austro-Hungarian Empire, ca. 1900

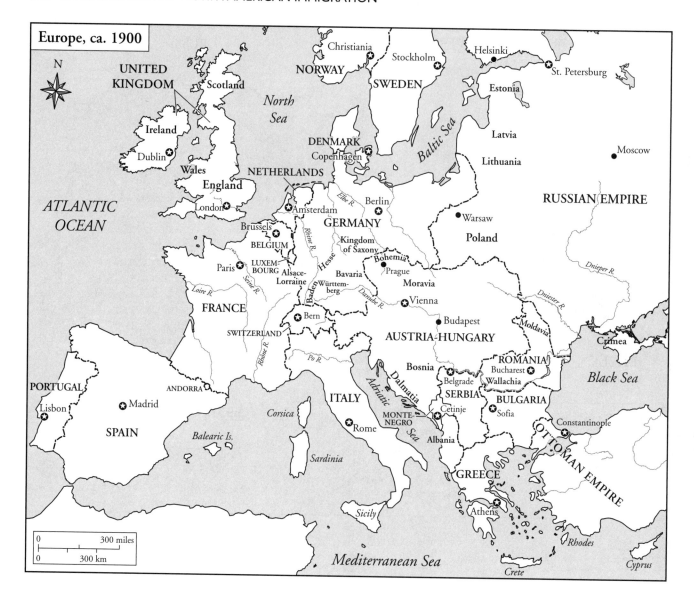

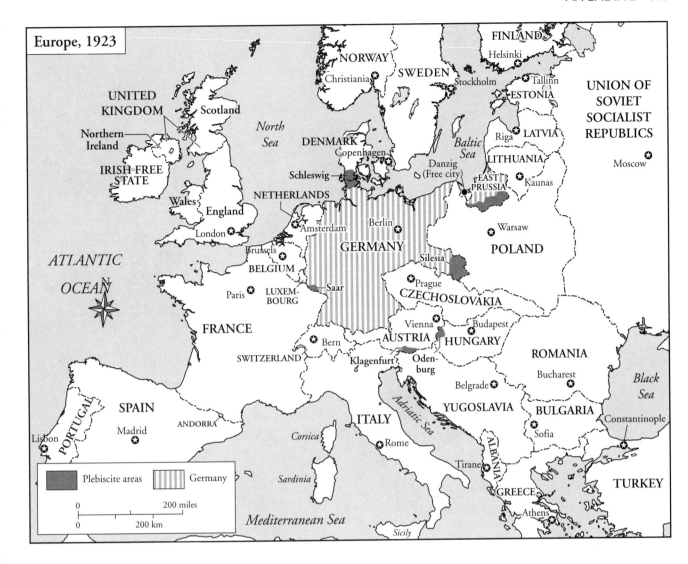

Europe, 1923

FINLAND
Helsinki
NORWAY
Christiania
SWEDEN
Stockholm
Tallinn
ESTONIA
UNION OF
SOVIET
SOCIALIST
REPUBLICS
Riga
LATVIA
Baltic
Sea
LITHUANIA
Kaunas
Moscow
UNITED
KINGDOM
Scotland
North
Sea
DENMARK
Copenhagen
Northern
Ireland
Schleswig
Danzig
(Free city)
EAST
PRUSSIA
IRISH FREE
STATE
NETHERLANDS
Berlin
Warsaw
Wales
England
Amsterdam
GERMANY
POLAND
London
Brussels
Silesia
ATLANTIC
BELGIUM
Prague
OCEAN
Paris
LUXEM-
BOURG
Saar
CZECHOSLOVAKIA
N
FRANCE
Bern
Vienna
Budapest
SWITZERLAND
AUSTRIA
HUNGARY
ROMANIA
Klagenfurt
Oden-
burg
Bucharest
Black
Sea
SPAIN
ANDORRA
ITALY
Belgrade
YUGOSLAVIA
BULGARIA
Constantinople
PORTUGAL
Corsica
Adriatic
Sea
Sofia
Lisbon
Madrid
Rome
TURKEY
Plebiscite areas   Germany
Sardinia
ALBANIA
Tirane
GREECE
0   200 miles
0   200 km
Mediterranean Sea
Athens
Sicily

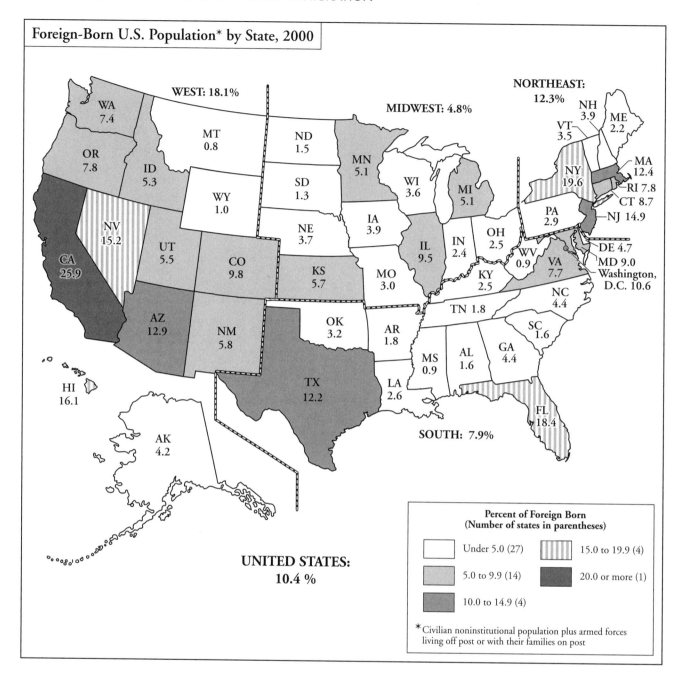

Foreign-Born U.S. Population* by State, 2000

WEST: 18.1%

MIDWEST: 4.8%

NORTHEAST: 12.3%

WA 7.4
OR 7.8
ID 5.3
MT 0.8
ND 1.5
MN 5.1
WI 3.6
MI 5.1
NY 19.6
NH 3.9
ME 2.2
VT 3.5
MA 12.4
RI 7.8
CT 8.7
NJ 14.9

NV 15.2
UT 5.5
WY 1.0
SD 1.3
IA 3.9
IL 9.5
IN 2.4
OH 2.5
PA 2.9
WV 0.9
VA 7.7
DE 4.7
MD 9.0
Washington, D.C. 10.6

CA 25.9
AZ 12.9
NM 5.8
CO 9.8
NE 3.7
KS 5.7
MO 3.0
OK 3.2
AR 1.8
TN 1.8
KY 2.5
NC 4.4
SC 1.6

HI 16.1

TX 12.2
LA 2.6
MS 0.9
AL 1.6
GA 4.4
FL 18.4

SOUTH: 7.9%

AK 4.2

UNITED STATES: 10.4 %

**Percent of Foreign Born
(Number of states in parentheses)**

Under 5.0 (27)

5.0 to 9.9 (14)

10.0 to 14.9 (4)

15.0 to 19.9 (4)

20.0 or more (1)

*Civilian noninstitutional population plus armed forces living off post or with their families on post

Old World Ethnic and Racial Groups in the British Mainland Colonies, 1700 and 1755

1700

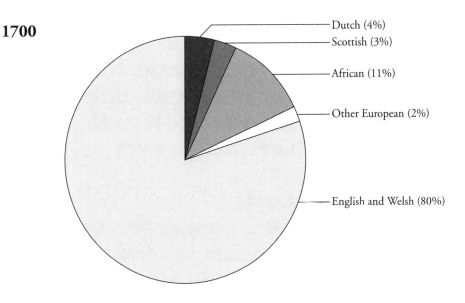

Dutch (4%)
Scottish (3%)
African (11%)
Other European (2%)
English and Welsh (80%)

1755

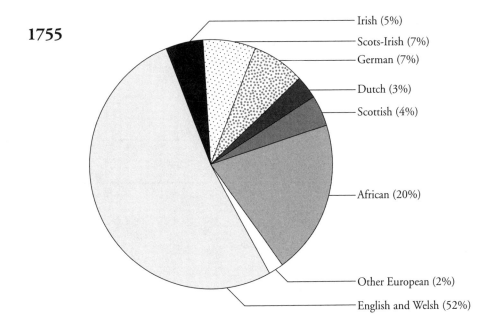

Irish (5%)
Scots-Irish (7%)
German (7%)
Dutch (3%)
Scottish (4%)
African (20%)
Other European (2%)
English and Welsh (52%)

Source: Thomas L. Purvis. "The European Ancestry of the United States Population," *William & Mary Quarterly* 61 (1984): 85–101.

Immigrants and Their Children in U.S. Cities, 1920

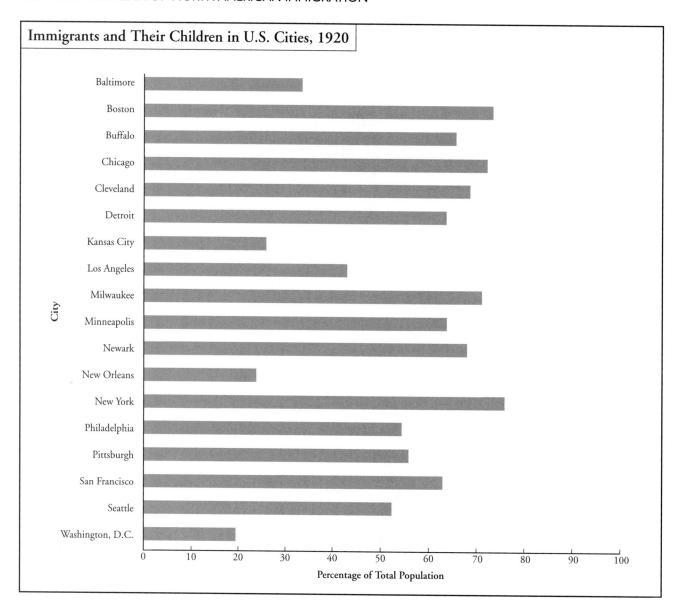

Foreign-Born Population in the United States, 1850–2000

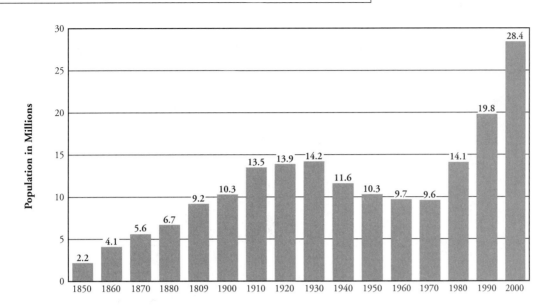

Note: Figures for 1850–1990 are based on the resident population. For 2000, figures are for the civilian noninstitutional population plus armed forces living off post or with their families on post. The Census Bureau defines foreign-born as "people residing in the United States on census day or on a survey date who were not U.S. citizens at birth."

Source: Dianne A. Schmidley, *Profile of the Foreign-Born Population in the United States: 2000.*
Washington, D.C.: U.S. Government Printing Office, 2001, p. 9.
Available online. URL: http://www.census.gov/prod/2002pubs/p23-206.pdf.

Foreign-Born Population as Percent of Total U.S. Population, 1850–2000

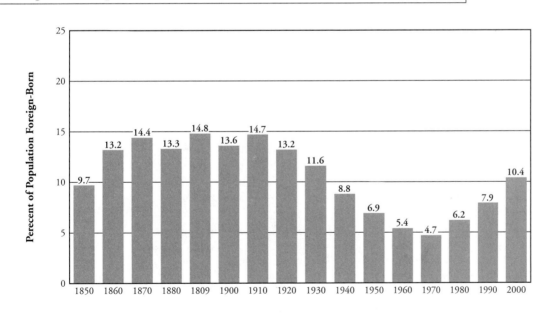

Note: Figures for 1850–1990 are based on the resident population. For 2000, figures are for the civilian noninstitutional population plus armed forces living off post or with their families on post. The Census Bureau defines foreign-born as "people residing in the United States on census day or on a survey date who were not U.S. citizens at birth."

Source: Dianne A. Schmidley, *Profile of the Foreign-Born Population in the United States: 2000.*
Washington, D.C.: U.S. Government Printing Office, 2001, p. 9.
Available online. URL: http://www.census.gov/prod/2002pubs/p23-206.pdf.

Origin of U.S. Population by Region of Birth, Selected Years, 1850–2000

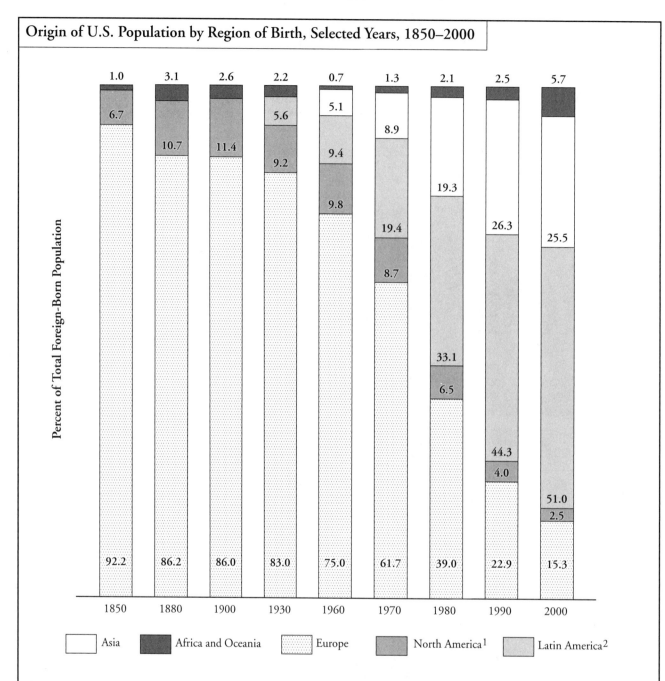

1 North America includes Canada, Bermuda, Greenland, and the islands of St. Pierre and Miquelon.
2 Latin America includes Mexico.

Note: The source from which these figures are drawn defines *foreign-born* as "people residing in the United States on census day or on a survey date who were not U.S citizens at birth." Slaves are not included in these figures. Figures for 1960–90 are based on the resident population. For 2000, figures are for the civilian noninstitutional population plus armed forces living off post or with their families on post. Figures include some but not all undocumented immigrants.

Source: Dianne A. Schmidley, *Profile of the Foreign-Born Population in the United States: 2000.* U.S. Census Bureau Current Population Reports, Series P23-206. Washington, D.C.: U.S. Government Printing Office, 2001, p. 9. Available online. URL: http://www.census.gov/prod/2002pubs/p23-206.pdf.

Foreign-Born U.S. Population by Region of Birth, 2000

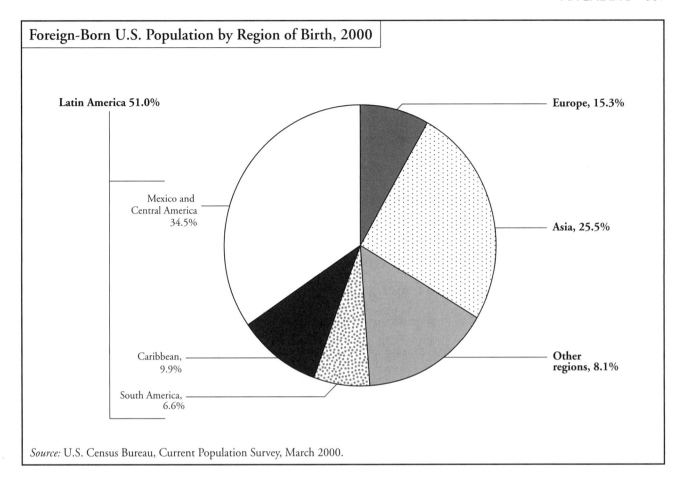

Latin America 51.0%

Mexico and
Central America
34.5%

Europe, 15.3%

Asia, 25.5%

Caribbean,
9.9%

South America,
6.6%

**Other
regions, 8.1%**

Source: U.S. Census Bureau, Current Population Survey, March 2000.

Immigration to the United States, Fiscal Years 1820–2002

Year	Number
1820–2002	68,217,481
1820	8,385
1821–30	143,439
1821	9,127
1822	6,911
1823	6,354
1824	7,912
1825	10,199
1826	10,837
1827	18,875
1828	27,382
1829	22,520
1830	23,322
1831–40	599,125
1831	22,633
1832	60,482
1833	58,640
1834	65,365
1835	45,374
1836	76,242
1837	79,340
1838	38,914
1839	68,069
1840	84,066
1841–50	1,713,251
1841	80,289
1842	104,565
1843	52,496
1844	78,615
1845	114,371
1846	154,416
1847	234,968
1848	226,527
1849	297,024
1850	369,980

Year	Number
1851–60	2,598,214
1851	379,466
1852	371,603
1853	368,645
1854	427,833
1855	200,877
1856	200,436
1857	251,306
1858	123,126
1859	121,282
1860	153,640
1861–70	2,314,824
1861	91,918
1862	91,985
1863	176,282
1864	193,418
1865	248,120
1866	318,568
1867	315,722
1868	138,840
1869	352,768
1870	387,203
1871–80	2,812,191
1871	321,350
1872	404,806
1873	459,803
1874	313,339
1875	227,498
1876	169,986
1877	141,857
1878	138,469
1879	177,826
1880	457,257

Year	Number
1881–90	5,246,613
1881	669,431
1882	788,992
1883	603,322
1884	518,592
1885	395,346
1886	334,203
1887	490,109
1888	546,889
1889	444,427
1890	455,302
1891–1900	3,687,564
1891	560,319
1892	579,663
1893	439,730
1894	285,631
1895	258,536
1896	343,267
1897	230,832
1898	229,299
1899	311,715
1900	448,572
1901–10	8,795,386
1901	487,918
1902	648,743
1903	857,046
1904	812,870
1905	1,026,499
1906	1,100,735
1907	1,285,349
1908	782,870
1909	751,786
1910	1,041,570

Year	Number
1911–20	**5,735,811**
1911	878,587
1912	838,172
1913	1,197,892
1914	1,218,480
1915	326,700
1916	298,826
1917	295,403
1918	110,618
1919	141,132
1920	430,001
1921–30	**4,107,209**
1921	805,228
1922	309,556
1923	522,919
1924	706,896
1925	294,314
1926	304,488
1927	335,175
1928	307,255
1929	279,678
1930	241,700
1931–40	**528,431**
1931	97,139
1932	35,576
1933	23,068
1934	29,470
1935	34,956
1936	36,329
1937	50,244
1938	67,895
1939	82,998
1940	70,756

Year	Number
1941–50	**1,035,039**
1941	51,776
1942	28,781
1943	23,725
1944	28,551
1945	38,119
1946	108,721
1947	147,292
1948	170,570
1949	188,317
1950	249,187
1951–60	**2,515,479**
1951	205,717
1952	265,520
1953	170,434
1954	208,177
1955	237,790
1956	321,625
1957	326,867
1958	253,265
1959	260,686
1960	265,398
1961–70	**3,321,677**
1961	271,344
1962	283,763
1963	306,260
1964	292,248
1965	296,697
1966	323,040
1967	361,972
1968	454,448
1969	358,579
1970	373,326

Year	Number
1971–80	**4,493,314**
1971	370,478
1972	384,685
1973	400,063
1974	394,861
1975	386,194
1976	398,613
1976, TQ[1]	103,676
1977	462,315
1978	601,442
1979	460,348
1980	530,639
1981–90	**7,338,062**
1981	596,600
1982	594,131
1983	559,763
1984	543,903
1985	570,009
1986	601,708
1987	601,516
1988	643,025
1989	1,090,924
1990	1,536,483
1991–2000	**9,095,417**
1991	1,827,167
1992	973,977
1993	904,292
1994	804,416
1995	720,461
1996	915,900
1997	798,378
1998	654,451
1999	646,568
2000	849,807
2001	1,064,318
2002	1,063,732

[1] Transition quarter, July 1 through September 30, 1976.

Note: The numbers shown are as follows: 1820–67, figures represent alien passengers arrived at seaports; 1868–92 and 1895–97, immigrant aliens arrived; 1892–94 and 1898–2002, immigrant aliens admitted for permanent residence. From 1892–1903, aliens entering by cabin class were not counted as immigrants. Land arrivals were not completely enumerated until 1908.

Source: U.S. Citizenship and Immigration Service, available online, URL: http://uscis.gov/graphics/shared/aboutus/statistics/IMM02yrbk/IMMExcel/table1.xls

Region and Country of Last Residence	1820	1821–1830	1831–1840	1841–1850	1851–1860	1861–1870	1871–1880	1881–1890	1891–1900
All countries	8,385	143,439	599,125	1,713,251	2,598,214	2,314,824	2,812,191	5,246,613	3,687,564
Europe	7,690	98,797	495,681	1,597,442	2,452,577	2,065,141	2,271,925	4,735,484	3,555,352
Austria-Hungary	2	2	2	2	2	7,800	72,969	353,719	592,707[23]
Austria	2	2	2	2	2	7,124[3]	63,009	226,038	234,081[3]
Hungary	2	2	2	2	2	484[3]	9,960	127,681	181,288[3]
Belgium	1	27	22	5,074	4,738	6,734	7,221	20,177	18,167
Czechoslovakia	4	4	4	4	4	4	4	4	4
Denmark	20	169	1,063	539	3,749	17,094	31,771	88,132	50,231
France	371	8,497	45,575	77,262	76,358	35,986	72,206	50,464	30,770
Germany	968	6,761	152,454	434,626	951,667	787,468	718,182	1,452,970	505,152[23]
Greece	-	20	49	16	31	72	210	2,308	15,979
Ireland[5]	3,614	50,724	207,381	780,719	914,119	435,778	436,871	655,482	388,416
Italy	30	409	2,253	1,870	9,231	11,725	55,759	307,309	651,893
Netherlands	49	1,078	1,412	8,251	10,789	9,102	16,541	53,701	26,758
Norway-Sweden	3	91	1,201	13,903	20,931	109,298	211,245	568,362	321,281
Norway	6	6	6	6	6	6	95,323	176,586	95,015
Sweden	6	6	6	6	6	6	115,922	391,776	226,266
Poland	5	16	369	105	1,164	2,027	12,970	51,806	96,720[23]
Portugal	35	145	829	550	1,055	2,658	14,082	16,978	27,508
Romania	7	7	7	7	7	7	11[7]	6,348	12,750
Soviet Union	14	75	277	551	457	2,512	39,284	213,282	505,290[23]
Spain	139	2,477	2,125	2,209	9,298	6,697	5,266	4,419	8,731
Switzerland	31	3,226	4,821	4,644	25,011	23,286	28,293	81,988	31,179
United Kingdom[5, 8]	2,410	25,079	75,810	267,044	423,974	606,896	548,043	807,357	271,538
Yugoslavia	9	9	9	9	9	9	9	9	9
Other Europe	-	3	40	79	5	8	1,001	682	282
Asia	6	30	55	141	41,538	64,759	124,160	69,942	74,862
China[10]	1	2	8	35	41,397	64,301	123,201	61,711	14,799
Hong Kong	11	11	11	11	11	11	11	11	11
India	1	8	39	36	43	69	163	269	68
Iran	12	12	12	12	12	12	12	12	12
Israel	13	13	13	13	13	13	13	13	13
Japan	14	14	14	14	14	186	149	2,270	25,942
Korea	15	15	15	15	15	15	15	15	15
Philippines	16	16	16	16	16	16	16	16	16
Turkey	1	20	7	59	83	131	404	3,782	30,425
Vietnam	11	11	11	11	11	11	11	11	11
Other Asia	3	-	1	11	15	72	243	1,910	3,628
America	387	11,564	33,424	62,469	74,720	166,607	404,044	426,967	38,972
Canada and Newfoundland[17, 18]	209	2,277	13,624	41,723	59,309	153,878	383,640	393,304	3,311
Mexico[18]	1	4,817	6,599	3,271	3,078	2,191	5,162	1,913[19]	971[19]
Caribbean	164	3,834	12,301	13,528	10,660	9,046	13,957	29,042	33,066
Cuba	12	12	12	12	12	12	12	12	12
Dominican Republic	20	20	20	20	20	20	20	20	20
Haiti	20	20	20	20	20	20	20	20	20
Jamaica	21	21	21	21	21	21	21	21	21
Other Caribbean	164	3,834	12,301	13,528	10,660	9,046	13,957	29,042	33,066
Central America	2	105	44	368	449	95	157	404	549
El Salvador	20	20	20	20	20	20	20	20	20
Other Central America	2	105	44	368	449	95	157	404	549
South America	11	531	856	3,579	1,224	1,397	1,128	2,304	1,075
Argentina	20	20	20	20	20	20	20	20	20
Colombia	20	20	20	20	20	20	20	20	20
Ecuador	20	20	20	20	20	20	20	20	20
Other South America	11	531	856	3,579	1,224	1,397	1,128	2,304	1,075
Other America	22	22	22	22	22	22	22	22	22
Africa	1	16	54	55	210	312	358	857	350
Oceania	1	2	9	29	158	214	10,914	12,574	3,965
Not Specified[22]	300	33,030	69,902	53,115	29,011	17,791	790	789	14,063

Region and Country of Last Residence	1901–1910	1911–1920	1921–1930	1931–1940	1941–1950	1951–1960	1961–1970	1971–1980	1981–1990
All countries	**8,795,386**	**5,735,811**	**4,107,209**	**528,431**	**1,035,039**	**2,515,479**	**3,321,677**	**4,493,314**	**7,338,062**
Europe	**8,056,040**	**4,321,887**	**2,463,194**	**347,566**	**621,147**	**1,325,727**	**1,123,492**	**800,368**	**761,550**
Austria-Hungary	2,145,266[23]	896,342[23]	63,548	11,424	28,329	103,743	26,022	16,028	24,885
Austria	668,209[3]	453,649	32,868	3,563[24]	24,860[24]	67,106	20,621	9,478	18,340
Hungary	808,511[3]	442,693	30,680	7,861	3,469	36,637	5,401	6,550	6,545
Belgium	41,635	33,746	15,846	4,817	12,189	18,575	9,192	5,329	7,066
Czechoslovakia	[4]	3,426[4]	102,194	14,393	8,347	918	3,273	6,023	7,227
Denmark	65,285	41,983	32,430	2,559	5,393	10,984	9,201	4,439	5,370
France	73,379	61,897	49,610	12,623	38,809	51,121	45,237	25,069	32,353
Germany	341,498[23]	143,945[23]	412,202	114,058[24]	226,578[24]	477,765	190,796	74,414	91,961
Greece	167,519	184,201	51,084	9,119	8,973	47,608	85,969	92,369	38,377
Ireland[5]	339,065	146,181	211,234	10,973	19,789	48,362	32,966	11,490	31,969
Italy	2,045,877	1,109,524	455,315	68,028	57,661	185,491	214,111	129,368	67,254
Netherlands	48,262	43,718	26,948	7,150	14,860	52,277	30,606	10,492	12,238
Norway-Sweden	440,039	161,469	165,780	8,700	20,765	44,632	32,600	10,472	15,182
Norway	190,505	66,395	68,531	4,740	10,100	22,935	15,484	3,941	4,164
Sweden	249,534	95,074	97,249	3,960	10,665	21,697	17,116	6,531	11,018
Poland	[23]	4,813[23]	227,734	17,026	7,571	9,985	53,539	37,234	83,252
Portugal	69,149	89,732	29,994	3,329	7,423	19,588	76,065	101,710	40,431
Romania	53,008	13,311	67,646	3,871	1,076	1,039	2,531	12,393	30,857
Soviet Union	1,597,306[23]	921,201[23]	61,742	1,370	571	671	2,465	38,961	57,677
Spain	27,935	68,611	28,958	3,258	2,898	7,894	44,659	39,141	20,433
Switzerland	34,922	23,091	29,676	5,512	10,547	17,675	18,453	8,235	8,849
United Kingdom[5, 8]	525,950	341,408	339,570	31,572	139,306	202,824	213,822	137,374	159,173
Yugoslavia	[9]	1,888[9]	49,064	5,835	1,576	8,225	20,381	30,540	18,762
Other Europe	39,945	31,400	42,619	11,949	8,486	16,350	11,604	9,287	8,234
Asia	**323,543**	**247,236**	**112,059**	**16,595**	**37,028**	**153,249**	**427,642**	**1,588,178**	**2,738,157**
China[10]	20,605	21,278	29,907	4,928	16,709	9,657	34,764	124,326	346,747
Hong Kong	[11]	[11]	[11]	[11]	[11]	15,541[11]	75,007	113,467	98,215
India	4,713	2,082	1,886	496	1,761	1,973	27,189	164,134	250,786
Iran	[12]	[12]	241	195	1,380	3,388	10,339	45,136	116,172
Israel	[13]	[13]	[13]	[13]	476	25,476	29,602	37,713	44,273
Japan	129,797	83,837	33,462	1,948	1,555	46,250	39,988	49,775	47,085
Korea	[15]	[15]	[15]	[15]	107	6,231	34,526	267,638	333,746
Philippines	[16]	[16]	[16]	528	4,691	19,307	98,376	354,987	548,764
Turkey	157,369	134,066	33,824	1,065	798	3,519	10,142	13,399	23,233
Vietnam	[11]	[11]	[11]	[11]	[11]	335[11]	4,340	172,820	280,782
Other Asia	11,059	5,973	12,739	7,435	9,551	21,572	63,369	244,783	648,354
America	**361,888**	**1,143,671**	**1,516,716**	**160,037**	**354,804**	**996,944**	**1,716,374**	**1,982,735**	**3,615,225**
Canada and Newfoundland[17, 18]	179,226	742,185	924,515	108,527	171,718	377,952	413,310	169,939	156,938
Mexico[18]	49,642	219,004	459,287	22,319	60,589	299,811	453,937	640,294	1,655,843
Caribbean	**107,548**	**123,424**	**74,899**	**15,502**	**49,725**	**123,091**	**470,213**	**741,126**	**872,051**
Cuba	[12]	[12]	15,901	9,571	26,313	78,948	208,536	264,863	144,578
Dominican Republic	[20]	[20]	[20]	1,150[20]	5,627	9,897	93,292	148,135	252,035
Haiti	[20]	[20]	[20]	191[20]	911	4,442	34,499	56,335	138,379
Jamaica	[21]	[21]	[21]	[21]	[21]	8,869[21]	74,906	137,577	208,148
Other Caribbean	107,548	123,424	58,998	4,590	16,874	20,935[21]	58,980	134,216	128,911
Central America	**8,192**	**17,159**	**15,769**	**5,861**	**21,665**	**44,751**	**101,330**	**134,640**	**468,088**
El Salvador	[20]	[20]	[20]	673[20]	5,132	5,895	14,992	34,436	213,539
Other Central America	8,192	17,159	15,769	5,188	16,533	38,856	86,338	100,204	254,549
South America	**17,280**	**41,899**	**42,215**	**7,803**	**21,831**	**91,628**	**257,940**	**295,741**	**461,847**
Argentina	[20]	[20]	[20]	1,349[20]	3,338	19,486	49,721	29,897	27,327
Colombia	[20]	[20]	[20]	1,223[20]	3,858	18,048	72,028	77,347	122,849
Ecuador	[20]	[20]	[20]	337[20]	2,417	9,841	36,780	50,077	56,315
Other South America	17,280	41,899	42,215	4,894	12,218	44,253	99,411	138,420	255,356
Other America	[22]	[22]	31[22]	25	29,276	59,711	19,644	995	458
Africa	**7,368**	**8,443**	**6,286**	**1,750**	**7,367**	**14,092**	**28,954**	**80,779**	**176,893**
Oceania	**13,024**	**13,427**	**8,726**	**2,483**	**14,551**	**12,976**	**25,122**	**41,242**	**45,205**
Not Specified[22]	33,523[25]	1,147	228	-	142	12,491	93	12	1,032

(continues)

Immigration by Region and Selected Country... Fiscal Years 1820–2002 (continued)

Region and Country of Last Residence	1991–1993	1991–1994	1991–1995	1994	1995	1996	1997	1998	1999
All countries	3,705,436	4,509,852	5,230,313	804,416	720,461	915,900	798,378	654,451	646,568
Europe	465,642	631,921	764,835	166,279	132,914	151,898	122,358	92,911	94,373
Austria-Hungary	11,303	13,426	15,616	2,123	2,190	2,325	1,964	1,435	1,518
Austria	8,286	9,600	10,940	1,314	1,340	1,182	1,044	610	727
Hungary	3,017	3,826	4,676	809	850	1,143	920	825	791
Belgium	2,434	3,055	3,749	621	694	802	633	557	522
Czechoslovakia	2,291	3,050	4,107	759	1,057	1,299	1,169	931	895
Denmark	2,160	2,799	3,387	639	588	795	507	447	387
France	12,429	16,021	19,199	3,592	3,178	3,896	3,007	2,961	2,664
Germany	33,727	42,667	50,563	8,940	7,896	8,365	6,941	6,923	7,442
Greece	7,557	10,096	12,500	2,539	2,404	2,394	1,483	1,183	4,061
Ireland[5]	30,039	46,564	51,415	16,525	4,851	1,611	932	907	806
Italy	46,177	48,841	51,435	2,664	2,594	2,755	2,190	1,966	1,681
Netherlands	4,532	5,891	7,175	1,359	1,284	1,553	1,197	1,036	881
Norway-Sweden	6,345	8,149	9,756	1,804	1,607	2,015	1,517	1,344	1,284
Norway	2,057	2,572	3,037	515	465	552	391	327	358
Sweden	4,288	5,577	6,719	1,289	1,142	1,463	1,126	1,017	926
Poland	68,885	96,482	110,052	27,597	13,570	15,504	11,729	8,202	8,487
Portugal	9,425	11,588	14,199	2,163	2,611	3,024	1,690	1,523	1,078
Romania	16,210	19,142	23,707	2,932	4,565	5,449	5,276	4,833	5,417
Soviet Union	128,575	193,077	247,210	64,502	54,133	61,895	48,238	28,984	32,740
Spain	6,495	8,251	9,915	1,756	1,664	1,970	1,607	1,185	1,074
Switzerland	3,569	4,752	5,871	1,183	1,119	1,344	1,302	1,090	885
United Kingdom[5, 8]	59,114	76,780	90,987	17,666	14,207	15,564	11,950	10,170	8,663
Yugoslavia	8,324	11,507	19,335	3,183	7,828	10,755	9,913	7,264	7,077
Other Europe	6,051	9,783	14,657	3,732	4,874	8,583	9,113	9,970	6,811
Asia	1,032,384	1,314,833	1,574,817	282,449	259,984	300,574	258,561	212,799	193,061
China[10]	111,324	170,191	211,303	58,867	41,112	50,981	44,356	41,034	29,579
Hong Kong	46,723	58,676	69,375	11,953	10,699	11,319	7,974	7,379	6,533
India	116,201	149,374	182,434	33,173	33,060	42,819	36,092	34,288	28,355
Iran	25,830	32,828	38,474	6,998	5,646	7,299	6,291	4,945	5,042
Israel	16,270	20,252	23,440	3,982	3,188	4,029	2,951	2,546	2,538
Japan	25,008	31,982	37,538	6,974	5,556	6,617	5,640	5,647	4,770
Korea	61,484	76,901	91,954	15,417	15,053	17,380	13,626	13,691	12,301
Philippines	195,634	248,466	298,162	52,832	49,696	54,588	47,842	33,176	29,590
Turkey	10,156	14,036	18,842	3,880	4,806	5,573	4,596	4,016	2,472
Vietnam	77,913	110,300	148,064	32,387	37,764	39,922	37,121	16,534	19,164
Other Asia	345,841	401,827	455,231	55,986	53,404	60,047	52,072	49,543	52,717
America	2,104,250	2,429,423	2,711,693	325,173	282,270	407,813	359,619	298,156	312,324
Canada and Newfoundland[17, 18]	65,370	87,613	105,730	22,243	18,117	21,751	15,788	14,295	12,948
Mexico[18]	1,288,693	1,400,108	1,490,153	111,415	90,045	163,743	146,680	130,661	146,436
Caribbean	332,721	436,471	532,492	103,750	96,021	115,991	101,095	72,948	70,386
Cuba	33,340	47,556	65,217	14,216	17,661	26,166	29,913	15,415	13,289
Dominican Republic	128,834	180,055	218,548	51,221	38,493	36,284	24,966	20,267	17,745
Haiti	67,701	80,867	94,739	13,166	13,872	18,185	14,941	13,316	16,459
Jamaica	58,018	71,927	87,988	13,909	16,061	18,732	17,585	14,819	14,449
Other Caribbean	44,828	56,066	66,000	11,238	9,934	16,624	13,690	9,131	8,444
Central America	227,335	267,591	299,611	40,256	32,020	44,336	43,451	35,368	41,441
El Salvador	99,794	117,463	129,133	17,669	11,670	17,847	17,741	14,329	14,416
Other Central America	127,541	150,128	170,478	22,587	20,350	26,489	25,710	21,039	27,025
South America	190,110	237,615	283,678	47,505	46,063	61,990	52,600	44,884	41,112
Argentina	11,286	13,760	15,999	2,474	2,239	2,878	2,055	1,649	1,578
Colombia	44,754	55,407	66,048	10,653	10,641	14,078	12,795	11,618	9,769
Ecuador	24,684	30,627	37,080	5,943	6,453	8,348	7,763	6,840	8,903
Other South America	109,386	137,821	164,551	28,435	26,730	36,686	29,987	24,777	20,862
Other America	21	25	29	4	4	2	5	-	1
Africa	83,781	108,645	148,463	24,864	39,818	49,605	44,668	37,494	33,740
Oceania	19,199	24,846	30,318	5,647	5,472	6,008	4,855	4,403	4,299
Not Specified[22]	180	184	187	4	3	2	8,317	8,688	8,771

Region and country of Last Residence[1]	1991–1999	2000	1991–2000	2001	2002	Total 179 years 1820–1998	Total 180 years 1820–1999	Total 181 years, 1820–2000	Total 182 years 1820–2001	Total 183 years 1820–2001
All countries	8,245,610	849,807	9,095,417	1,064,318	1,063,732	64,593,056	65,239,624	66,089,431	67,153,749	68,217,481
Europe	1,226,375	133,362	1,359,737	177,833	177,652	38,233,062	38,327,435	38,460,797	38,638,630	38,816,282
Austria-Hungary	22,858	2,024	24,882	2,318	4,016	4,364,122[23,24]	4,365,640[23,24]	4,367,664[23,24]	4,369,982[23,24]	4,373,998[23,24]
Austria	14,503	997	15,500	1,004	2,657	1,842,722[2,3]	1,843,449[2,3]	1,844,446[2,3]	1,845,450[2,3]	1,848,107[2,3]
Hungary	8,355	1,027	9,382	1,314	1,359	1,675,324[2,3]	1,676,115[2,3]	1,677,142[2,3]	1,678,456[2,3]	1,679,815[2,3]
Belgium	6,263	827	7,090	1,002	842	216,297	216,819	217,646	218,648	219,490
Czechoslovakia	8,401	1,415	9,816	1,921	1,862	153,307[4]	154,202[4]	155,617[4]	157,538[4]	159,400[4]
Denmark	5,523	556	6,079	741	655	375,548	375,935	376,491	377,232	377,887
France	31,727	4,093	35,820	5,431	4,596	816,650	819,314	823,407	828,838	833,434
Germany	80,234	12,372	92,606	22,093	21,058	7,156,257[23,24]	7,163,699[23,24]	7,176,071[23,24]	7,198,164[23,24]	7,219,222[23,24]
Greece	21,621	5,138	26,759	1,966	1,516	721,464	725,525	730,663	732,629	734,145
Ireland[5]	55,671	1,279	56,950	1,550	1,419	4,779,998	4,780,804	4,782,083	4,783,633	4,785,052
Italy	60,027	2,695	62,722	3,377	2,837	5,431,454	5,433,135	5,435,830	5,439,207	5,442,044
Netherlands	11,842	1,466	13,308	1,895	2,305	385,193	386,074	387,540	389,435	391,740
Norway-Sweden	15,916	1,977	17,893	2,561	2,097	2,160,586	2,161,870	2,163,847	2,166,408	2,168,505
Norway	4,665	513	5,178	588	464	758,026[6]	758,384[6]	758,897[6]	759,485[6]	759,949[6]
Sweden	11,251	1,464	12,715	1,973	1,633	1,257,133[6]	1,258,059[6]	1,259,523[6]	1,261,496[6]	1,263,129[6]
Poland	153,974	9,773	163,747	12,355	13,304	751,823[23]	760,310[23]	770,083[23]	782,438[23]	795,742[23]
Portugal	21,514	1,402	22,916	1,654	1,320	521,697	522,775	524,177	525,831	527,151
Romania	44,682	6,521	51,203	6,224	4,525	244,106[7]	249,523[7]	256,044[7]	262,268[7]	266,793[7]
Soviet Union	419,067	43,807	462,874	55,099	55,464	3,830,033[23]	3,862,773[23]	3,906,580[23]	3,961,679[23]	4,017,143[23]
Spain	15,751	1,406	17,157	1,889	1,603	299,825	300,899	302,305	304,194	305,797
Switzerland	10,492	1,349	11,841	1,796	1,503	369,046	369,931	371,280	373,076	374,579
United Kingdom[5,8]	137,334	14,532	151,866	20,258	18,057	5,247,821	5,256,484	5,271,016	5,291,274	5,309,331
Yugoslavia	54,344	12,213	66,557	21,937	28,100	183,538	190,615	202,828	224,765	252,865
Other Europe	49,134	8,517	57,651	11,766	10,573	224,297	231,108	239,625	251,391	261,964
Asia	2,539,812	255,860	2,795,672	337,566	326,871	8,365,931	8,558,992	8,814,852	9,152,418	9,479,289
China[10]	377,253	41,861	419,114	50,821	55,974	1,262,050	1,291,629	1,333,490	1,384,311	1,440,285
Hong Kong	102,580	7,199	109,779	10,307	7,952	398,277[11]	404,810[11]	412,009[11]	422,316[11]	430,268[11]
India	323,988	39,072	363,060	65,916	66,864	751,349	779,704	818,776	884,692	951,556
Iran	62,051	6,505	68,556	8,063	7,730	233,860[12]	238,902[12]	245,407[12]	253,470[12]	261,200[12]
Israel	35,504	3,893	39,397	4,925	4,938	170,506[13]	173,044[13]	176,937[13]	181,862[13]	186,800[13]
Japan	60,212	7,730	67,942	10,464	9,150	517,686[14]	522,456[14]	530,186[14]	540,650[14]	549,800[14]
Korea	148,952	15,214	164,166	19,933	20,114	778,899[15]	791,200[15]	806,414[15]	826,347[15]	846,461[15]
Philippines	463,358	40,587	503,945	50,870	48,674	1,460,421[16]	1,490,011[16]	1,530,598[16]	1,581,468[16]	1,630,142[16]
Turkey	35,499	2,713	38,212	3,477	3,934	445,354	447,826	450,539	454,016	457,950
Vietnam	260,805	25,340	286,145	34,648	32,425	699,918[11]	719,082[11]	744,422[11]	779,070[11]	811,495[11]
Other Asia	669,610	65,746	735,356	78,142	69,116	1,647,611	1,700,328	1,766,074	1,844,216	1,913,332
America	4,089,605	397,201	4,486,806	473,351	478,777	16,844,829	17,157,153	17,554,354	18,027,705	18,506,482
Canada and Newfoundland[17,18]	170,512	21,475	191,987	30,203	27,299	4,453,149	4,466,097	4,487,572	4,517,775	4,545,074
Mexico[18]	2,077,673	171,748	2,249,421	204,844	217,318	5,819,966[19]	5,966,402[19]	6,138,150[19]	6,342,494[19]	6,560,312[19]
Caribbean	892,912	85,875	978,787	96,958	94,240	3,525,703	3,596,089	3,681,964	3,778,922	3,873,162
Cuba	150,000	19,322	169,322	26,073	27,520	885,421[12]	898,710[12]	918,032[12]	944,105[12]	971,625[12]
Dominican Republic	317,810	17,441	335,251	21,256	22,474	810,201[20]	827,946[20]	845,387[20]	866,643[20]	889,117[20]
Haiti	157,640	22,004	179,644	22,535	19,189	375,938[20]	392,397[20]	414,401[20]	436,936[20]	456,125[20]
Jamaica	153,573	15,654	169,227	15,099	14,567	568,624[21]	583,073[21]	598,727[21]	613,826[21]	628,393[21]
Other Caribbean	113,889	11,454	125,343	11,995	10,490	885,519	893,963	905,417	917,412	927,902
Central America	464,207	62,708	526,915	73,063	66,520	1,242,394	1,283,835	1,346,543	1,419,606	1,486,126
El Salvador	193,466	22,332	215,798	31,054	30,539	453,717[20]	468,133[20]	490,465[20]	521,519[20]	552,058[20]
Other Central America	270,741	40,376	311,117	42,009	35,981	788,677	815,702	856,078	898,087	934,068
South America	484,264	55,392	539,656	68,279	73,400	1,693,441	1,734,553	1,789,945	1,858,224	1,931,624
Argentina	24,159	2,485	26,644	3,459	3,811	153,699[20]	155,277[20]	157,762[20]	161,221[20]	165,032[20]
Colombia	114,308	14,191	128,499	16,333	18,488	399,892[20]	409,661[20]	423,852[20]	440,185[20]	458,673[20]
Ecuador	68,934	7,658	76,592	9,694	10,564	215,798[20]	224,701[20]	232,359[20]	242,053[20]	252,617[20]
Other South America	276,863	31,058	307,921	38,793	40,537	924,052	944,914	975,972	1,014,765	1,055,302
Other America	37	3	40	4	3	110,176	110,177	110,180	110,184	110,184
Africa	313,970	40,969	354,939	50,209	56,135	614,375	648,115	689,084	739,293	795,428
Oceania	49,883	5,962	55,845	7,253	6,536	250,206	254,505	260,467	267,720	274,256
Not Specified[22]	25,965	16,453	42,418	18,106	17,761	284,653	293,424	309,877	327,983	345,744

(continues)

Immigration by Region and Selected Country... Fiscal Years 1820–2002 (continued)

[1] Data for years prior to 1906 relate to country whence alien came; data from 1906 to 1979 and 1984 to 2002 are for country of last permanent residence; and data for 1980 to 1983 refer to country of birth. Because of changes in boundaries, changes in lists of countries, and lack of data for specified countries for various periods, data for certain countries, especially for the total period 1820–2002, are not comparable throughout. Data for specified countries are included with countries to which they belonged prior to World War I.

[2] Data for Austria and Hungary not reported until 1861.

[3] Data for Austria and Hungary not reported separately for all years during the period.

[4] No data available for Czechoslovakia until 1920.

[5] Prior to 1926, data for Northern Ireland included in Ireland.

[6] Data for Norway and Sweden not reported separately until 1871.

[7] No data available for Romania until 1880.

[8] Since 1925, data for United Kingdom refer to England, Scotland, Wales, and Northern Ireland.

[9] In 1920, a separate enumeration was made for the Kingdom of Serbs, Croats, and Slovenes. Since 1922, the Serb, Croat, and Slovene Kingdom recorded as Yugoslavia.

[10] Beginning in 1957, China includes Taiwan. As of January 1, 1979, the United States has recognized the People's Republic of China.

[11] Data not reported separately until 1952.

[12] Data not reported separately until 1925.

[13] Data not reported separately until 1949.

[14] Data not available for Japan until 1861.

[15] Data not reported separately until 1948.

[16] Prior to 1934, Philippines reported as insular travel.

[17] Prior to 1920, Canada and Newfoundland recorded as British North America. From 1820 to 2001, figures include all British North America possessions.

[18] Land arrivals not completely enumerated until 1908.

[19] No data available for Mexico from 1886 to 1894.

[20] Data not reported separately until 1932.

[21] Data for Jamaica not collected until 1953. In prior years, consolidated under British West Indies, which is included in "Other Caribbean."

[22] Included in countries "Not Specified" until 1925.

[23] From 1899 to 1919, data for Poland included in Austria-Hungary, Germany, and the Soviet Union.

[24] From 1938 to 1945, data for Austria included in Germany.

[25] Includes 32,897 persons returning in 1906 to their homes in the United States.

Note: From 1820 to 1867, figures represent alien passengers arrived at seaports; 1868–91 and 1895–97, immigrant aliens arrived; 1892–94 and 1898–2002, immigrant aliens admitted for permanent residence. From 1892 to 1903, aliens entering by cabin class were not counted as immigrants. Land arrivals were not completely enumerated until 1908. Data for Czechoslovakia, Soviet Union, and Yugoslavia include independent republics.

For this table, fiscal year 1843 covers nine months ending September 1843; fiscal years 1832 and 1850 cover 15 months ending December 31 of the respective years; and fiscal year 1868 covers six months ending June 30, 1868.

- Represents zero.

Source: U.S. Citizenship and Immigration Service, available online, URL: http://uscis.gov/graphics/shared/aboutus/statistics/IMM02yrbk/IMMExcel/table2.xls

Ethnicity in Texas, 1850

Group	Number	Percent of State Total
Southern Anglo-American[1]	114,040	53.7
Northern Anglo-American	9,965	4.7
African American[2]	58,558	27.5
Spanish surname[3]	11,212	5.3
French surname[4]	1,071	0.5
German element[5]	11,534	5.4
Other foreign elements	3,900	1.8
Other[6]	2,312	1.1

[1] Includes Texas-born children of northern Anglo-Americans.

[2] Includes slave and free.

[3] Includes American-born with Spanish surname.

[4] Includes American-born with French surname.

[5] Includes foreign-born persons and their American-born offspring.

[6] Includes persons born in California, the Territories, or whose origins could not be determined.

Source: Adapted from Terry G. Jordan, "Population Origins in Texas, 1850" Geographical Review 59 (January 1969), p. 85.

Immigrant Arrivals in Canada, 1852–2002

Year	Number	Year	Number	Year	Number
1852	29,307	1894	20,829	1936	11,643
1853	29,464	1895	18,790	1937	15,101
1854	37,263	1896	16,835	1938	17,244
1855	25,296	1897	21,716	1939	16,994
1856	22,544	1898	31,900	1940	11,324
1857	33,854	1899	44,543	1941	9,329
1858	12,339	1900	41,681	1942	7,576
1859	6,300	1901	55,747	1943	8,504
1860	6,276	1902	89,102	1944	12,801
1861	13,589	1903	138,660	1945	22,722
1862	18,294	1904	131,252	1946	71,719
1863	21,000	1905	141,465	1947	64,127
1864	24,779	1906	211,653	1948	125,414
1865	18,958	1907	272,409	1949	95,217
1866	11,427	1908	143,326	1950	73,912
1867	10,666	1909	173,694	1951	194,391
1868	12,765	1910	286,839	1952	164,498
1869	18,630	1911	331,288	1953	168,868
1870	24,706	1912	375,756	1954	154,227
1871	27,773	1913	400,870	1955	109,946
1872	36,578	1914	150,484	1956	164,857
1873	50,050	1915	36,665	1957	282,164
1874	39,373	1916	55,914	1958	124,851
1875	27,382	1917	72,910	1959	106,928
1876	25,633	1918	41,845	1960	104,111
1877	27,082	1919	107,698	1961	71,689
1878	29,807	1920	138,824	1962	74,586
1879	40,492	1921	91,728	1963	93,151
1880	38,505	1922	64,224	1964	112,606
1881	47,991	1923	133,729	1965	146,758
1882	112,458	1924	124,164	1966	194,743
1883	133,624	1925	84,907	1967	222,876
1884	103,824	1926	135,982	1968	183,974
1885	79,169	1927	158,886	1969	161,531
1886	69,152	1928	166,783	1970	147,713
1887	84,526	1929	164,993	1971	121,900
1888	88,766	1930	104,806	1972	122,006
1889	91,600	1931	27,530	1973	184,200
1890	75,067	1932	20,591	1974	218,465
1891	82,165	1933	14,382	1975	187,881
1892	30,996	1934	12,476	1976	149,429
1893	29,633	1935	11,277	1977	114,914

(continues)

Immigrant Arrivals in Canada, 1852–2002 (continued)

Year	Number	Year	Number	Year	Number
1978	86,313	1987	151,999	1995	212,859
1979	112,092	1988	161,494	1996	226,039
1980	143,135	1989	191,493	1997	216,014
1981	128,639	1990	216,396	1998	174,159
1982	121,176	1991	232,744	1999	189,922
1983	89,188	1992	254,817	2000	227,346
1984	88,271	1993	256,741	2001	250,484
1985	84,334	1994	224,364	2002	229,091
1986	99,325				

Source: Statistics Canada, available online, URL: http://www.statcan.ca/english/freepub/11-516-XIE/sectiona/sectiona.htm#A350, and Citizenship and Immigration Canada, available online, URL: http://www.cic.gc.ca/english/pub/facts2002/immigration/immigration_1.html

Immigration to the United States from Austria-Hungary, 1861–1920

Year	Number
1861–1870	7,800
1871–1880	72,969
1881–1890	353,719
1891–1900	592,707
1901–1910	2,145,266
1911–1920	896,342

Source: U.S. Citizenship and Immigration Service, available online, URL: http://uscis.gov/graphics/shared/aboutus/statistics/IMM02yrbk/IMMExcel/table2.xls.

Country of Birth of Other British-born and the Foreign-born Population, Census Dates, 1871–1971

Country	Year										
	1871	1881	1891	1901	1911	1921	1931	1941	1951	1961	1971
Total All Countries[1]	594,207	602,984	643,871	699,500	1,586,961	1,955,725	2,307,525	2,017,902	2,059,911	2,844,263	3,295,535
Other British-born											
England and Wales	147,081	169,504	219,688	203,803	519,401	700,442	746,212	635,221	627,551	662,102	-
Scotland	125,450	115,062	107,594	83,631	169,391	226,481	279,765	234,824	226,343	244,052	-
Northern Ireland[2]	223,212	185,526	149,184	101,629	92,874	93,301	107,544	86,126	56,685	61,588	-
Lesser Isles	852	814	1,269	956	2,860	4,807	5,421	3,954	1,903	1,973	-
Newfoundland	3	4,596	9,336	12,432	15,469	23,103	26,410	25,837	3	3	3
Other British Commonwealth	2,358	3,113	3,502	3,771	14,526	17,226	19,478	17,807	20,567	47,887	170,105
United States	64,613	77,753	80,915	127,899	303,680	374,022	344,574	312,473	282,010	283,908	309,640
Europe Total	28,699	39,161	53,841	125,549	404,941	459,325	714,462	653,705	801,618	1,468,058	1,684,515
Republic of Ireland[2]	-	-	-	-	-	-	-	-	24,110	30,889	38,490
Scandinavia	588	2,076	7,827	18,388	61,240	64,795	90,042	72,473	64,522	74,616	60,210
France	2,908	4,389	5,381	7,944	17,619	19,247	16,756	13,795	15,650	36,103	51,655
Belgium	-	-	-	2,280	7,975	13,276	17,033	14,773	17,251	28,253	25,770
Netherland	-	-	-	385	3,808	5,827	10,736	9,923	41,457	135,033	133,525
Germany	24,162	25,328	27,752	27,300	39,577	25,266	39,163	28,479	42,693	189,131	211,060
Austria and Hungary	102	-	-	28,407	78,088	65,028	65,914	82,526	70,527	143,092	108,945
Czecho-slovakia	-	-	-	-	1,689	4,322	22,835	25,564	29,546	35,743	43,100
Switzerland	-	-	-	1,211	-	3,479	6,076	5,505	6,414	11,381	13,895
Italy	218	777	2,795	6,854	34,739	35,531	42,578	40,432	57,789	258,071	385,755
Greece	-	-	-	213	2,640	3,769	5,579	5,871	8,594	38,017	78,780
Eastern Europe											
U.S.S.R.	416	6,376	9,222	31,231	89,984	112,412	133,869	124,402	188,292	186,653	160,120
Poland	-	-	695	-	31,373	65,304	171,169	155,400	164,474	171,467	160,040
Finland	-	-	-	-	10,987	12,156	30,354	24,387	22,035	29,467	24,930
Romania	-	-	-	1,066	18,271	22,779	40,322	28,454	19,733	27,011	24,405
Yugoslavia	-	-	-	-	-	1,946	17,110	17,416	20,912	50,826	78,285
Other	305	215	169	270	6,951	4,188	4,926	4,305	7,619	22,305	85,550
Asia											
China	-	-	9,129	17,043	27,083	36,924	42,037	29,095	24,166	36,724	57,150
Japan	-	-	-	4,674	8,425	11,650	12,261	9,462	6,239	6,797	9,485
Other Asia	-	-	-	1,863	5,438	5,062	6,310	5,886	6,740	14,240	52,795
Other countries	1,942	7,455	9,413	1,421	3,165	3,294	3,051	3,512	6,089	16,934	78,800

[1] The totals for all countries in 1901, 1911, and 1921 include 14,829, 19,708 and 88, respectively, "Other British-born" whose countries of birth are unknown.

[2] Prior to 1951, the Republic of Ireland is included with Northern Ireland.

[3] Included with Canadian-born.

Source: Statistics Canada, available online, URL: http://www.statcan.ca/english/freepub/11-516-XIE/sectiona/sectiona.htm#A350

Refugees and Asylees Granted Lawful Permanent Residence Status in the United States by Region and Selected Country of Birth, Fiscal Years 1946–2002 (by decade)

Region and Country of Birth	1946–1950	1951–1960	1961–1970	1971–1980	1981–1990	1991–2000	Total 1946–2003
All countries	**213,347**	**492,371**	**212,843**	**539,447**	**1,013,620**	**1,021,266**	**3,772,411**
Europe	**211,983**	**456,146**	**55,235**	**71,858**	**155,512**	**426,565**	**1,513,325**
Albania	29	1,409	1,952	395	289	3,255	7,963
Armenia	X	X	X	X	X	2,161	2,897
Austria	4,801	11,487	233	185	424	390	17,648
Azerbaijan	X	X	X	X	X	12,072	13,320
Belarus	X	X	X	X	X	24,581	28,098
Belgium	NA	NA	NA	21	33	26	96
Bosnia-Herzegovina	X	X	X	X	X	37,591	91,774
Bulgaria	139	1,138	1,799	1,238	1,197	1,679	7,363
Croatia	X	X	X	X	X	1,807	8,273
Czech Republic	X	X	X	X	X	NA	6
Czechoslovakia[2]	8,449	10,719	5,709	3,646	8,204	1,255	38,013
Denmark	NA	NA	NA	1	5	18	29
Estonia	7,143	4,103	16	2	25	843	12,326
Finland	NA	NA	NA	2	5	10	18
France	NA	NA	NA	139	268	142	589
Georgia	X	X	X	X	X	2,593	3,015
Germany	36,633	62,860	665	143	851	1,309	106,179
Gibraltar	NA	NA	NA	1	-	-	NA
Greece	124	28,568	586	478	1,408	374	31,559
Hungary	6,086	55,740	4,044	4,358	4,942	1,285	76,508
Iceland	NA	NA	NA	2	2	-	4
Ireland	NA	NA	NA	8	6	6	22
Italy	642	60,657	1,198	346	394	412	63,717
Kazakstan	X	X	X	X	X	4,269	5,752
Kyrgystan	X	X	X	X	X	1,248	1,811
Latvia	21,422	16,783	49	16	48	2,757	41,458
Liechtenstein	NA	NA	NA	NA	-	NA	NA
Lithuania	18,694	8,569	72	23	37	1,161	28,681
Luxembourg	NA	NA	NA	-	2	-	NA
Macedonia	X	X	X	X	X	137	499
Malta	NA	NA	NA	6	5	-	14
Moldova	X	X	X	X	X	11,717	14,797
Monaco	NA	NA	NA	1	-	-	NA
Netherlands	129	14,336	3,134	8	14	36	17,735
Norway	NA	NA	NA	4	7	7	20
Poland	78,529	81,323	3,197	5,882	33,889	7,500	210,476
Portugal	12	3,650	1,361	21	21	13	5,083
Romania	4,180	12,057	7,158	6,812	29,798	15,708	76,011
Russia	X	X	X	X	X	60,404	71,989
San Marino	NA	NA	NA	1	-	-	NA
Slovak Republic	X	X	X	X	X	31	43

Region and Country of Birth	1946–1950	1951–1960	1961–1970	1971–1980	1981–1990	1991–2000	Total 1946–2003
Slovenia	X	X	X	X	X	97	242
Soviet Union[3]	14,072	30,059	871	31,309	72,306	90,533	242,889
Spain	1	246	4,114	5,317	736	443	10,946
Sweden	NA	NA	NA	3	NA	17	45
Switzerland	NA	NA	NA	12	NA	46	194
Tajikistan	X	X	X	X	X	2,546	2,728
Turkmenistan	X	X	X	X	X	410	486
Ukraine	X	X	X	X	X	109,739	134,820
United Kingdom	NA	NA	NA	58	192	120	414
Uzbekistan	X	X	X	X	X	19,539	21,994
Yugoslavia[3]	9,816	44,755	18,299	11,297	324	1,280	98,193
Unknown Europe	1,082	7,687	778	123	80	-	9,750
Asia	**1,106**	**33,422**	**19,895**	**210,683**	**712,092**	**351,347**	**1,379,836**
Afghanistan	-	1	-	542	22,946	9,725	35,231
Bahrain	NA	NA	NA	-	NA	5	5
Bangladesh	NA	NA	NA	2	NA	566	1,107
Bhutan	NA	NA	NA	NA	NA	NA	4
Burma	NA	NA	NA	70	NA	721	1,671
Cambodia	-	-	-	7,739	114,064	6,388	128,351
China[4]	319	12,008	5,308	13,760	7,928	7,608	49,244
Cyprus	NA	NA	NA	48	NA	9	67
Hong Kong	-	1,076	2,128	3,468	1,916	611	9,569
India	NA	NA	NA	41	NA	2,544	6,602
Indonesia	-	8,253	7,658	222	1,385	201	17,908
Iran	118	192	58	364	46,773	24,313	80,018
Iraq	-	130	119	6,851	7,540	22,557	44,914
Israel	NA	NA	NA	76	NA	176	294
Japan	3	3,803	554	56	110	24	4,567
Jordan	NA	NA	NA	88	NA	333	484
Korea	-	3,116	1,316	65	120	26	4,657
Kuwait	NA	NA	NA	11	NA	469	614
Laos	-	-	-	21,690	142,964	37,265	203,004
Lebanon	NA	NA	NA	595	NA	1,028	1,839
Macau	NA	NA	NA	29	NA	3	32
Malaysia	NA	NA	NA	189	NA	385	869
Maldives	NA	NA	NA	-	NA	NA	4
Mongolia	NA	NA	NA	NA	NA	31	37
Nepal	NA	NA	NA	1	NA	32	52
Oman	NA	NA	NA	1	5	NA	8
Pakistan	NA	NA	NA	20	NA	1,650	2,822
Philippines	NA	NA	NA	213	NA	968	1,368
Qatar	NA	NA	NA	NA	NA	18	19
Saudi Arabia	NA	NA	NA	10	NA	880	1,063
Singapore	NA	NA	NA	28	NA	13	57
Sri Lanka	NA	NA	NA	24	NA	354	492
Syria	4	119	383	1,336	2,145	2,125	7,008

(continues)

Refugees and Asylees Granted Lawful Permanent Residence Status in the United States by Region and Selected Country of Birth, Fiscal Years 1946–2002 (by decade) *(continued)*

Region and Country of Birth	1946–1950	1951–1960	1961–1970	1971–1980	1981–1990	1991–2000	Total 1946–2003
Thailand	-	15	13	1,241	30,259	22,759	55,662
Turkey	603	1,427	1,489	1,193	1,896	559	7,263
United Arab Emirates	NA	NA	NA	NA	NA	59	68
Vietnam	-	2	7	150,266	324,453	206,857	700,443
Yemen	NA	NA	NA	22	11	80	219
Unknown Asia	59	3,280	862	422	7,577	-	12,200
Africa	**20**	**1,768**	**5,486**	**2,991**	**22,149**	**51,649**	**112,146**
Algeria	NA	NA	NA	1	5	138	345
Angola	NA	NA	NA	4	255	91	367
Benin	NA	NA	NA	NA	NA	20	104
Botswana	NA	NA	NA	NA	85	9	99
Burkina Faso	NA	NA	NA	2	-	14	40
Burundi	NA	NA	NA	NA	8	148	390
Cameroon	NA	NA	NA	NA	9	302	519
Cape Verde	NA	NA	NA	4	13	6	25
Central African Republic	NA	NA	NA	1	1	NA	7
Chad	NA	NA	NA	7	-	43	93
Congo, Democratic Republic of[5]	NA	NA	NA	7	192	924	1,415
Congo, Republic of	NA	NA	NA	1	1	25	568
Cote d'Ivoire	NA	NA	NA	1	1	119	319
Djibouti	NA	NA	NA	NA	19	20	78
Egypt	8	1,354	5,396	1,473	426	420	9,669
Equatorial Guinea	NA	NA	NA	-	2	-	4
Eritrea	X	X	X	X	X	608	751
Ethiopia[6]	NA	61	2	1,307	18,542	17,865	41,780
Gabon	NA	NA	NA	NA	1	6	11
Gambia, The	NA	NA	NA	NA	-	54	216
Ghana	NA	NA	NA	3	135	431	837
Guinea	NA	NA	NA	NA	15	50	72
Guinea-Bissau	NA	NA	NA	NA	NA	36	124
Kenya	NA	NA	NA	4	87	1,447	2,469
Lesotho	NA	NA	NA	1	29	9	39
Liberia	NA	NA	NA	2	109	3,839	7,489
Libya	NA	NA	NA	14	363	591	997
Madagascar	NA	NA	NA	-	1	-	NA
Malawi	NA	NA	NA	8	33	23	69
Mali	NA	NA	NA	NA	NA	12	33
Mauritania	NA	NA	NA	NA	1	211	430
Mauritius	NA	NA	NA	1	NA	19	30
Morocco	NA	NA	NA	3	11	23	48
Mozambique	NA	NA	NA	3	72	31	111
Namibia	NA	NA	NA	3	71	37	117

Region and Country of Birth	1946–1950	1951–1960	1961–1970	1971–1980	1981–1990	1991–2000	Total 1946–2003
Niger	NA	NA	NA	NA	1	27	211
Nigeria	NA	NA	NA	6	14	443	1,411
Réunion	NA	NA	NA	-	1	-	NA
Rwanda	NA	NA	NA	-	3	389	772
São Tomé and Príncipe	NA	NA	NA	-	1	-	NA
Senegal	NA	NA	NA	1	NA	40	96
Seychelles	NA	NA	NA	NA	12	3	16
Sierra Leone	NA	NA	NA	2	21	272	1,772
Somalia	NA	NA	NA	6	70	16,837	25,638
South Africa	NA	NA	NA	14	285	195	516
Sudan	NA	NA	NA	4	739	5,191	9,621
Swaziland	NA	NA	NA	NA	NA	NA	7
Tanzania	NA	NA	NA	2	7	32	79
Togo	NA	NA	NA	1	NA	114	588
Tunisia	NA	NA	NA	1	NA	7	21
Uganda	NA	NA	NA	58	301	439	917
Zambia	NA	NA	NA	3	53	52	121
Zimbabwe	NA	NA	NA	3	24	32	68
Unknown Africa	12	353	88	40	130	-	623
Oceania	**7**	**75**	**21**	**37**	**22**	**291**	**523**
American Samoa	NA	NA	NA	1	-	-	NA
Australia	NA	NA	NA	21	NA	7	31
Fiji	NA	NA	NA	NA	NA	280	338
French Polynesia	NA	NA	NA	NA	NA	NA	NA
Guam	NA	NA	NA	2	-	-	NA
New Caledonia	NA	NA	NA	1	NA	NA	NA
New Zealand	NA	NA	NA	2	4	-	6
Palau	X	X	X	X	X	-	3
Papua New Guinea	NA	NA	NA	2	3	-	5
Solomon Islands	NA	NA	NA	-	-	-	4
Vanuatu	X	X	X	-	-	-	NA
Wallis and Futuna Islands	NA	NA	NA	NA	NA	NA	NA
Unknown Oceania	7	75	21	8	15	-	126
North America	**163**	**831**	**132,068**	**252,633**	**121,840**	**185,333**	**752,825**
Canada	NA	NA	NA	96	NA	80	231
Greenland	NA	NA	NA	1	1	-	NA
Mexico	NA	NA	NA	202	NA	416	870
St.-Pierre and Miquelon	NA	NA	NA	1	-	-	NA
United States	NA	NA	NA	5	NA	20	29
Caribbean	**3**	**6**	**131,557**	**251,825**	**114,213**	**154,235**	**708,540**
Anguilla	NA	NA	NA	-	5	-	5
Antigua-Barbuda	NA	NA	NA	1	-	-	NA
Bahamas, The	NA	NA	NA	1	832	14	855

(continues)

Refugees and Asylees Granted Lawful Permanent Residence Status by Region and Selected Country of Birth, Fiscal Years 1946–2002 (by decade) *(continued)*

Region and Country of Birth	1946–1950	1951–1960	1961–1970	1971–1980	1981–1990	1991–2000	Total 1946–2003
Barbados	NA	NA	NA	1	4	-	5
Bermuda	NA	NA	NA	5	-	NA	7
British Virgin Islands	NA	NA	NA	NA	NA	NA	NA
Cayman Islands	NA	NA	NA	9	NA	NA	12
Cuba	3	6	131,557	251,514	113,367	144,612	695,686
Dominica	NA	NA	NA	4	NA	6	11
Dominican Republic	NA	NA	NA	152	NA	193	399
Grenada	NA	NA	NA	1	NA	NA	3
Guadeloupe	NA	NA	NA	-	NA	-	4
Haiti	NA	NA	NA	86	NA	9,364	11,426
Jamaica	NA	NA	NA	25	NA	22	64
Martinique	NA	NA	NA	1	NA	3	4
Montserrat	NA	NA	NA	NA	NA	NA	NA
Netherlands Antilles	NA	NA	NA	3	NA	NA	9
Puerto Rico	NA	NA	NA	NA	3	NA	5
St. Kitts–Nevis	NA	NA	NA	3	1	-	4
St. Lucia	NA	NA	NA	1	1	-	3
St. Vincent and the Grenadines	NA	NA	NA	13	NA	NA	14
Trinidad and Tobago	NA	NA	NA	4	NA	5	14
Turks and Caicos Islands	NA	NA	NA	1	NA	5	6
Central America	**1**	**1**	**4**	**289**	**6,973**	**30,582**	**40,795**
Belize	NA	NA	NA	8	NA	6	19
Costa Rica	NA	NA	NA	51	NA	220	344
El Salvador	-	-	1	45	1,383	4,073	6,078
Guatemala	NA	NA	NA	47	NA	2,033	3,183
Honduras	NA	NA	NA	69	NA	1,050	1,458
Nicaragua	1	1	3	27	5,590	22,486	28,908
Panama	NA	NA	NA	42	NA	714	805
Unknown North America	159	824	507	214	653	-	2,357
South America	**32**	**74**	**123**	**1,244**	**1,986**	**5,857**	**12,992**
Argentina	NA	NA	NA	101	NA	125	423
Bolivia	NA	NA	NA	10	NA	91	158
Brazil	NA	NA	NA	16	NA	136	267
Chile	-	5	4	415	532	171	1,231
Colombia	NA	NA	NA	217	350	1,132	2,758
Ecuador	NA	NA	NA	149	NA	194	464
Guyana	NA	NA	NA	7	NA	24	56
Paraguay	NA	NA	NA	4	NA	7	17
Peru	NA	NA	NA	132	251	2,507	4,148
Suriname	NA	NA	NA	NA	NA	59	71
Uruguay	NA	NA	NA	43	NA	16	80

Region and Country of Birth	1946–1950	1951–1960	1961–1970	1971–1980	1981–1990	1991–2000	Total 1946–2003
Venezuela	NA	NA	NA	83	407	1,395	2,586
Unknown South America	32	69	119	67	446	-	733
Unknown or not reported	36	55	15	1	19	224	764

[1] Data for fiscal year 1998 have been revised due to changes in the counts for asylees. The previously reported total was 54,645.

[2] Beginning in 1993, current country not reported.

[3] Beginning in 1992, current country not reported.

[4] Includes People's Republic of China and Taiwan.

[5] Zaire prior to May 1997.

[6] Prior to 1993, data include Eritrea.

- Represents zero.   NA Not available.   X Not applicable.

Note: Total numbers for 1946–2003 include figures herein recorded for 1946–2000 plus figures (not shown) for 2001–2003.

Source: Adapted from U.S. Citizenship and Immigration Service, available online, URL: http://uscis.gov/graphics/shared/aboutus/statistics/RA2003yrbk/ra2003list.htm

Refugees and Asylees Granted Lawful Permanent Residence Status by Region and Selected Country of Birth, Fiscal Years 1991–2002

Region and Country of Birth	1991	1992	1993	1994	1995	1996	1997	1998	1999	2000	2001	2002
All countries	139,079	117,037	127,343	121,434	114,664	128,565	112,158	52,193	42,852	65,941	108,506	126,084
Europe	62,946	42,721	53,195	54,978	46,998	51,977	39,795	19,048	21,801	33,106	55,825	62,911
Albania	75	539	1,198	733	314	154	76	56	44	66	114	170
Armenia	X	479	329	342	214	182	213	158	130	114	321	265
Austria	131	90	54	25	15	15	20	6	16	18	37	71
Azerbaijan	X	1,551	2,790	2,668	1,594	1,446	1,000	196	372	455	476	497
Belarus	X	3,008	4,480	5,156	3,421	3,480	2,486	557	766	1,227	1,548	1,446
Belgium	1	1	2	2	-	3	4	2	6	5	7	7
Bosnia-Herzegovina	X	-	-	337	3,818	6,246	6,205	4,060	5,298	11,627	23,303	25,033
Bulgaria	311	562	303	138	105	100	69	33	20	38	57	34
Croatia	X	-	2	11	117	236	287	211	254	689	2,337	3,315
Czech Republic	X	X	-	-	-	-	-	-	-	3	1	2
Czechoslovakia[2]	659	319	119	41	36	21	31	9	12	8	14	15
Denmark	3	-	1	-	2	9	1	1	-	1	1	3
Estonia	9	155	125	176	83	98	89	18	33	57	93	79
Finland	2	2	3	-	2	-	-	1	-	-	-	1
France	34	13	15	10	7	24	18	3	5	13	14	15
Georgia	X	255	213	392	383	591	425	100	100	134	178	174
Germany	214	94	82	84	61	90	79	55	115	435	1,345	1,889
Gibraltar	-	-	-	-	-	-	-	-	-	-	-	-
Greece	127	28	39	65	50	33	11	8	8	5	12	5
Hungary	817	229	80	37	28	40	24	14	7	9	19	24
Iceland	-	-	-	-	-	-	-	-	-	-	-	-
Ireland	1	2	-	-	-	2	-	-	-	1	1	1
Italy	206	105	32	11	7	17	14	7	6	7	15	33
Kazakstan	X	460	544	595	600	624	612	152	210	472	659	648
Kyrgystan	X	123	114	210	155	177	200	49	46	174	305	196
Latvia	34	315	493	568	387	359	272	69	126	134	175	154
Liechtenstein	1	-	-	-	-	-	-	-	-	-	-	-
Lithuania	75	157	228	214	151	136	85	27	33	55	69	33
Luxembourg	-	-	-	-	-	-	-	-	-	-	-	-
Macedonia	X	X	X	4	20	20	19	32	8	34	114	185
Malta	-	-	-	-	-	-	-	-	-	-	2	1
Moldova	X	1,588	2,546	2,154	1,597	1,415	1,043	272	373	729	1,322	1,336
Monaco	-	-	-	-	-	-	-	-	-	-	-	-
Netherlands	5	2	7	3	-	-	3	5	8	3	8	48
Norway	1	-	-	-	1	2	1	-	1	1	1	1
Poland	4,205	1,512	731	334	245	183	143	54	36	57	71	54
Portugal	2	-	4	2	3	1	1	-	-	-	-	2
Romania	4,276	4,971	3,654	1,199	592	447	322	116	63	68	119	85
Russia	X	7,122	8,965	10,359	8,176	9,745	6,985	2,225	2,842	3,985	4,758	5,089
San Marino	-	-	-	-	-	-	-	-	-	-	-	-
Slovak Republic	X	X	-	-	2	4	9	6	5	5	5	4
Slovenia	X	-	-	-	11	17	18	16	17	18	60	70
Soviet Union[3]	51,551	3,824	6,126	5,719	5,060	3,303	2,589	5,524	4,394	2,443	1,621	1,508
Spain	96	50	37	55	33	46	29	31	25	41	39	31
Sweden	-	2	1	-	-	3	1	3	4	3	9	11

Region and Country of Birth	1991	1992	1993	1994	1995	1996	1997	1998	1999	2000	2001	2002
Switzerland	10	4	3	2	1	3	4	3	4	12	39	72
Tajikistan	X	167	301	534	654	535	239	24	45	47	100	53
Turkmenistan	X	30	40	50	71	78	66	10	25	40	28	33
Ukraine	X	13,347	16,977	19,366	14,937	16,636	12,137	3,641	4,956	7,742	11,130	10,601
United Kingdom	34	7	7	17	9	11	12	9	4	10	9	23
Uzbekistan	X	1,550	2,475	3,211	3,258	4,144	2,885	292	759	965	1,099	1,038
Yugoslavia[3]	66	58	75	154	778	1,301	1,068	993	62 5	1,156	4,190	8,556
Unknown Europe	-	-	-	-	-	-	-	-	-	-	-	-
Asia	**49,762**	**53,422**	**51,783**	**45,768**	**43,314**	**42,076**	**30,835**	**11,745**	**9,300**	**13,342**	**19,992**	**21,414**
Afghanistan	2,100	2,082	2,233	1,665	616	369	356	137	54113	257	1,044	
Bahrain	2	2	-	-	-	-	1	-	-	-	-	-
Bangladesh	15	10	7	19	36	50	91	159	84	95	204	180
Bhutan	-	-	-	-	-	-	1	-	-	1	-	1
Burma	16	19	78	114	136	101	82	79	45	51	181	372
Cambodia	2,550	1,695	808	557	268	210	163	62	39	36	75	47
China[4]	625	894	1,154	774	805	847	693	898	431	487	813	695
Cyprus	4	-	-	3	2	-	-	-	-	-	2	1
Hong Kong	75	193	90	82	48	47	19	5	16	36	247	105
India	47	34	103	133	323	485	462	373	118	466	942	1,558
Indonesia	12	13	16	41	62	30	8	4	1	14	111	58
Iran	8,515	3,093	3,875	2,186	1,245	1,212	1,447	754	1,030	956	1,364	4,806
Iraq	193	365	1,856	4,400	3,848	3,802	1,774	1,001	1,835	3,483	3,060	3,434
Israel	10	10	20	29	34	32	25	6	5	5	12	18
Japan	4	5	3	4	2	-	-	1	1	4	1	5
Jordan	15	15	42	48	64	58	46	21	14	10	11	32
Korea	1	-	1	3	5	4	3	2	1	6	3	7
Kuwait	11	13	114	94	63	74	46	29	9	16	37	61
Laos	9,127	8,026	6,547	4,482	3,364	2,155	1,363	1,110	38 3	708	520	374
Lebanon	318	140	204	88	48	77	68	39	16	30	38	101
Macau	-	1	-	-	1	-	-	1	-	-	-	-
Malaysia	93	88	37	49	44	15	16	-	13	30	210	72
Maldives	-	-	2	-	-	-	-	-	-	-	-	2
Mongolia	2	3	4	4	2	3	7	-	3	3	5	1
Nepal	-	-	3	-	5	7	12	1	3	1	2	5
Oman	-	-	-	-	-	-	-	-	-	1	1	-
Pakistan	166	129	185	181	197	194	280	130	54	134	320	467
Philippines	249	221	122	103	80	80	68	16	7	22	89	68
Qatar	-	6	2	5	3	1	-	-	1	-	1	-
Saudi Arabia	33	19	24	75	126	280	135	79	57	52	70	57
Singapore	2	2	-	1	1	1	5	1	-	-	9	5
Sri Lanka	59	22	62	33	30	42	46	27	17	16	19	52
Syria	252	96	115	34	258	208	146	707	160	149	327	261
Thailand	3,603	4,048	3,724	3,076	2,932	1,940	1,112	1,134	380	810	653	498
Turkey	109	16	79	156	58	42	35	21	15	28	32	36
United Arab Emirates	6	2	15	7	9	4	9	5	1	1	3	4
Vietnam	21,543	32,155	30,249	27,318	28,595	29,700	22,297	4,921	4,503	5,576	10,351	6,926
Yemen	5	5	9	4	4	6	19	22	4	2	22	61
Unknown Asia	-	-	-	-	-	-	-	-	-	-	-	-
Africa	**4,731**	**4,480**	**5,944**	**6,078**	**7,527**	**5,464**	**7,651**	**4,225**	**2,184**	**3,365**	**6,906**	**13,454**
Algeria	-	-	2	3	3	16	46	33	12	23	46	77
Angola	22	25	13	7	4	11	4	2	1	2	3	8

(continues)

Refugees and Asylees Granted Lawful Permanent Residence Status by Region and Selected Country of Birth, Fiscal Years 1991–2002 (continued)

Region and Country of Birth	1991	1992	1993	1994	1995	1996	1997	1998	1999	2000	2001	2002
Benin	9	1	-	-	-	1	1	1	1	6	15	50
Botswana	-	5	3	1	-	-	-	-	-	-	-	2
Burkina Faso	-	-	-	-	-	-	1	1	3	9	13	10
Burundi	4	5	4	6	4	17	41	43	6	18	64	107
Cameroon	3	-	12	14	33	68	89	55	12	16	44	77
Cape Verde	5	-	-	-	-	-	1	-	-	-	1	-
Central African Republic	1	-	1	-	-	-	1	-	-	-	-	1
Chad	1	1	3	2	3	4	2	1	12	14	18	23
Congo, Democratic Republic of[5]	57	72	109	113	130	175	146	55	21	46	77	128
Congo, Republic of	6	1	-	-	2	-	4	2	2	8	34	341
Cote d'Ivoire	2	-	3	15	19	24	19	20	3	14	52	102
Djibouti	1	2	3	6	-	-	-	7	-	1	9	22
Egypt	52	18	35	37	29	66	71	54	32	26	136	269
Equatorial Guinea	-	-	-	-	-	-	-	-	-	-	-	1
Eritrea	X	X	43	200	204	68	45	27	14	7	36	51
Ethiopia[6]	3,582	3,268	3,682	2,530	1,802	985	1,056	507	183	270	881	1,897
Gabon	-	-	-	-	-	1	3	1	1	-	-	4
Gambia, The	-	-	1	-	-	2	10	23	3	15	61	57
Ghana	64	16	35	37	54	56	67	42	14	46	81	101
Guinea	-	1	2	7	7	21	10	-	-	2	1	4
Guinea-Bissau	-	-	-	-	-	-	3	14	5	14	31	26
Kenya	32	42	42	98	165	171	291	234	131	241	332	411
Lesotho	-	9	-	-	-	-	-	-	-	-	-	-
Liberia	42	25	239	851	855	700	505	225	124	273	976	1,680
Libya	175	143	172	27	28	24	13	4	-	5	8	8
Madagascar	-	-	-	-	-	-	-	-	-	-	-	-
Malawi	9	3	-	4	2	-	2	2	1	-	4	-
Mali	-	-	1	-	-	-	4	4	2	1	8	8
Mauritania	-	1	7	4	10	10	35	64	16	64	68	62
Mauritius	-	2	1	3	1	5	4	-	2	1	7	1
Morocco	4	1	3	3	1	5	1	2	2	1	1	5
Mozambique	3	9	16	3	-	-	-	-	-	-	1	3
Namibia	6	6	17	5	-	-	-	3	-	-	1	1
Niger	-	-	-	-	-	-	27	-	-	-	70	88
Nigeria	20	9	14	21	26	40	80	112	43	78	300	442
Réunion	-	-	-	-	-	-	-	-	-	-	-	-
Rwanda	-	1	4	8	13	84	140	34	53	52	106	187
São Tomé and Príncipe	-	-	-	-	-	-	-	-	-	-	-	-
Senegal	2	2	2	-	1	7	9	3	4	10	19	16
Seychelles	3	-	-	-	-	-	-	-	-	-	-	-
Sierra Leone	4	3	2	4	25	44	78	52	18	42	215	722
Somalia	282	330	885	1,572	3,095	1,700	3,607	2,270	1,279	1,817	2,484	4,084
South Africa	77	33	37	6	23	9	7	1	1	1	11	6
Sudan	184	369	443	402	935	1,089	1,119	287	153	210	593	1,987
Swaziland	-	-	-	-	-	1	-	-	-	1	2	2

Region and Country of Birth	1991	1992	1993	1994	1995	1996	1997	1998	1999	2000	2001	2002
Tanzania	3	3	1	-	1	3	3	1	-	17	9	16
Togo	-	1	2	5	8	17	52	22	7	-	44	303
Tunisia	2	1	2	-	1	1	-	-	-	-	6	3
Uganda	54	64	87	79	36	24	46	15	22	12	35	53
Zambia	17	4	10	3	7	6	3	1	1	-	1	7
Zimbabwe	3	4	6	2	-	9	5	1	-	2	2	1
Unknown Africa	-	-	-	-	-	-	-	-	-	-	-	-
Oceania	**1**	**9**	**34**	**23**	**63**	**56**	**59**	**20**	**2**	**24**	**19**	**33**
American Samoa	-	-	-	-	-	-	-	-	-	-	-	-
Australia	1	-	2	1	-	2	-	-	1	-	2	-
Fiji	-	8	31	22	61	54	59	20	1	24	15	28
French Polynesia	-	-	-	-	1	-	-	-	-	-	-	-
Guam	-	-	-	-	-	-	-	-	-	-	-	-
New Caledonia	-	1	-	-	-	-	-	-	-	-	-	-
New Zealand	-	-	-	-	-	-	-	-	-	-	-	-
Palau	X	X	X	-	-	-	-	-	-	-	-	3
Papua New Guinea	-	-	-	-	-	-	-	-	-	-	-	-
Solomon Islands	-	-	-	-	-	-	-	-	-	-	2	1
Vanuatu	-	-	-	-	-	-	-	-	-	-	-	1
Wallis and Futuna Islands	-	-	1	-	1	-	-	-	-	-	-	-
Unknown Oceania	-	-	-	-	-	-	-	-	-	-	-	-
North America	**21,317**	**15,962**	**15,926**	**14,204**	**16,265**	**28,070**	**32,898**	**16,372**	**9,086**	**15,233**	**24,696**	**26,807**
Canada	14	5	8	10	5	3	12	6	6	11	14	26
Greenland	-	-	-	-	-	-	-	-	-	-	-	-
Mexico	74	29	29	15	37	47	60	41	33	51	67	100
St.-Pierre and Miquelon	-	-	-	-	-	-	-	-	-	-	-	-
United States	3	-	1	-	-	1	8	2	2	3	2	1
Caribbean	**8,005**	**9,969**	**11,700**	**12,672**	**14,888**	**26,597**	**31,479**	**15,480**	**8,730**	**14,715**	**23,448**	**25,706**
Anguilla	-	-	-	-	-	-	-	-	-	-	-	-
Antigua-Barbuda	-	-	-	-	-	-	-	-	-	-	-	-
Bahamas, The	3	2	4	-	1	2	1	-	1	-	3	4
Barbados	-	-	-	-	-	-	-	-	-	-	-	-
Bermuda	-	-	-	-	-	-	-	-	-	1	1	-
British Virgin Islands	1	-	-	-	-	-	-	-	-	-	-	-
Cayman Islands	-	-	-	-	-	-	-	2	-	-	-	1
Cuba	7,953	9,919	11,603	11,998	12,355	22,542	30,377	14,915	8,588	14,362	22,687	24,893
Dominica	1	-	4	-	-	-	-	1	-	-	-	-
Dominican Republic	14	27	18	8	22	19	26	18	18	23	13	25
Grenada	-	-	-	-	-	1	-	-	-	-	-	-
Guadeloupe	-	-	-	-	-	-	-	-	-	-	2	2
Haiti	31	16	68	664	2,502	4,028	1,074	537	122	322	735	769
Jamaica	2	1	3	1	4	3	-	2	1	5	4	6
Martinique	-	-	-	-	1	-	1	-	-	1	-	-
Montserrat	-	-	-	-	-	-	-	2	-	-	-	-
Netherlands Antilles	-	-	-	-	1	-	-	-	-	-	-	3
Puerto Rico	-	-	-	-	-	1	-	-	-	1	-	-
St. Kitts–Nevis	-	-	-	-	-	-	-	-	-	-	-	-
St. Lucia	-	-	-	-	-	-	-	-	-	-	1	-

(continues)

Refugees and Asylees Granted Lawful Permanent Residence Status by Region and Selected Country of Birth, Fiscal Years 1991–2002 (continued)

Region and Country of Birth	1991	1992	1993	1994	1995	1996	1997	1998	1999	2000	2001	2002
St. Vincent and the Grenadines	-	-	-	1	-	-	-	-	-	-	-	-
Trinidad and Tobago	-	-	-	-	2	1	-	2	-	-	2	3
Turks and Caicos Islands	-	4	-	-	-	-	-	1	-	-	-	-
Central America	**13,221**	**5,959**	**4,188**	**1,507**	**1,335**	**1,422**	**1,339**	**843**	**315**	**453**	**1,165**	**974**
Belize	-	-	-	1	2	2	-	-	-	1	2	1
Costa Rica	64	31	29	20	8	18	20	10	6	14	26	23
El Salvador	1,249	743	811	275	283	262	198	129	47	76	195	187
Guatemala	296	169	210	131	158	234	327	264	105	139	456	353
Honduras	133	105	165	81	119	119	109	108	48	63	124	116
Nicaragua	11,233	4,668	2,892	966	727	766	666	316	103	149	350	281
Panama	246	243	81	33	38	21	19	16	6	11	12	13
Unknown North America	-	-	-	-	-	-	-	-	-	-	-	-
South America	**320**	**442**	**461**	**383**	**497**	**922**	**890**	**712**	**417**	**813**	**936**	**1,222**
Argentina	8	15	4	9	11	13	12	13	13	27	17	58
Bolivia	6	3	6	10	9	17	10	12	5	13	15	13
Brazil	10	7	11	9	10	18	16	14	8	33	34	40
Chile	38	16	17	8	10	21	14	12	13	22	27	16
Colombia	46	74	63	70	102	116	154	171	121	215	217	380
Ecuador	14	6	25	25	11	15	10	30	28	30	40	43
Guyana	1	-	4	3	3	-	7	4	-	2	12	8
Paraguay	-	-	-	1	-	1	1	-	1	3	1	2
Peru	73	74	176	153	241	568	489	338	117	278	399	402
Suriname	2	27	16	2	4	3	1	-	1	3	2	2
Uruguay	2	-	4	2	1	-	3	-	-	4	5	5
Venezuela	120	220	135	91	95	150	173	118	110	183	167	253
Unknown South America	-	-	-	-	-	-	-	-	-	-	-	-
Unknown or not reported	2	1	-	-	-	-	30	71	62	58	132	243

[1] Data for fiscal year 1998 have been revised due to changes in the counts for asylees. The previously reported total was 54,645.
[2] Beginning in 1993, current country not reported.
[3] Beginning in 1992, current country not reported.
[4] Includes People's Republic of China and Taiwan.
[5] Zaire prior to May 1997.
[6] Prior to 1993, data include Eritrea.
- Represents zero.   NA Not available.   X Not applicable.

Source: U.S. Citizenship and Immigration Service, available online, URL: http://uscis.gov/graphics/shared/aboutus/statistics/RA2002yrblc/RAExcel/Table23.xls

West Indian Immigrants to the United States, 1956–1995

Country of Birth	1956–1965	1966–1975	1976–1985	1986–1995	Total
Antigua	1,164	3,698	12,095	1,762	18,719
Bahamas	1,646	1,203	1,132	1,609	18,959
Barbados	3,506	15,190	22,009	13,442	54,147
Dominica	651	2,949	6,112	7,198	16,910
Grenada	818	4,295	10,436	9,157	24,706
Jamaica	14,853	124,121	179,036	226,953	544,963
Montserrat	784	1,809	1,659	651	4,903
St. Kitts	1,153	5,092	11,316	3,513	21,074
St. Vincent	758	2,997	6,713	3,880	14,348
Trinidad	3,646	35,514	44,315	56,223	139,698
Guyana	2,135	20,080	69,311	86,783	178,309
Belize	1,890	5,536	17,850	16,168	41,444
Haiti	13,154	54,778	74,184	192,250	334,366
Dominican Republic	40,047	125,795	183,066	192,250	714,543
Others*	3,381	5,950	6,659	15,118	31,108

* Anguilla, Aruba, British Virgin Islands, Caymans, Guadeloupe, Leeward Islands, Martinique, Netherlands Antilles, Turks, and Windward Islands.

Source: U.S. Bureau of the Census, in *A Nation of Peoples: A Sourcebook on America's Multicultural Heritage,* ed. Elliott Robert Barkan, (Westport, Conn.: Greenwood Press, 1999), p. 521.

Immigrants Admitted by State of Intended Residence, Fiscal Years 1988–2002

State of Intended Residence	1988	1989	1990	1991	1992	1993	1994	1995	1996	1997	1998	1999	2000	2001	2002
Total	**643,025**	**1,090,924**	**1,536,483**	**1,827,167**	**973,977**	**904,292**	**804,417**	**720,461**	**915,900**	**798,378**	**654,451**	**646,568**	**849,807**	**1,064,318**	**1,063,732**
Alabama	1,402	1,792	1,775	2,706	2,109	2,298	1,837	1,900	1,782	1,613	1,608	1,275	1,904	2,257	2,570
Alaska	989	1,013	1,207	1,525	1,165	1,286	1,129	1,049	1,280	1,060	1,008	1,058	1,374	1,401	1,564
Arizona	6,697	11,238	23,737	40,642	15,792	9,778	9,141	7,700	8,900	8,632	6,211	8,667	11,980	16,362	17,719
Arkansas	808	1,074	1,245	2,559	1,039	1,312	1,031	934	1,494	1,428	914	940	1,596	2,572	2,535
California	188,696	457,417	682,979	732,735	336,663	260,090	208,498	166,482	201,529	203,305	170,126	161,247	217,753	282,957	291,216
Colorado	4,541	7,101	9,125	13,782	6,553	6,650	6,825	7,713	8,895	7,506	6,513	6,984	8,216	12,494	12,060
Connecticut	7,161	8,430	10,678	12,365	10,345	10,966	9,537	9,240	10,874	9,528	7,780	7,887	11,346	12,148	11,243
Delaware	685	708	868	1,937	1,034	1,132	984	1,051	1,377	1,148	1,063	1,026	1,570	1,850	1,862
District of Columbia	2,517	4,759	5,467	5,510	4,275	3,608	3,204	3,047	3,784	3,373	2,377	2,134	2,542	3,043	2,723
Florida	65,418	48,474	71,603	141,068	61,127	61,423	58,093	62,023	79,461	82,318	59,965	57,484	98,391	104,715	90,819
Georgia	5,677	8,093	10,431	23,556	11,243	10,213	10,032	12,381	12,608	12,623	10,445	9,404	14,778	19,431	20,555
Hawaii	6,637	7,292	8,441	8,659	8,199	8,528	7,746	7,537	8,436	6,867	5,465	4,299	6,056	6,313	5,503
Idaho	790	1,875	1,815	7,088	1,186	1,270	1,559	1,612	1,825	1,447	1,504	1,906	1,922	2,296	2,236
Illinois	27,726	69,263	83,858	73,388	43,532	46,744	42,400	33,898	42,517	38,128	33,163	36,971	36,180	48,296	47,235
Indiana	2,322	2,580	3,392	4,512	3,115	4,539	3,725	3,590	4,692	3,892	3,981	3,557	4,128	6,010	6,853
Iowa	1,697	1,760	2,252	3,331	2,228	2,626	2,163	2,260	3,037	2,766	1,655	1,780	3,052	5,029	5,591
Kansas	2,130	3,842	3,925	5,620	2,924	3,225	2,902	2,434	4,303	2,829	3,184	3,263	4,582	4,030	4,508
Kentucky	1,218	1,396	1,365	1,753	2,119	2,182	2,036	1,857	2,019	1,939	2,017	1,537	2,989	4,548	4,681
Louisiana	3,444	3,925	4,024	4,917	4,230	3,725	3,366	3,000	4,092	3,319	2,193	2,048	3,016	3,778	3,199
Maine	701	795	883	1,155	847	838	829	814	1,028	817	709	568	1,133	1,186	1,269
Maryland	11,502	14,258	17,106	17,470	15,408	16,899	15,937	15,055	20,732	19,090	15,561	15,605	17,705	22,060	23,751
Massachusetts	18,594	20,990	25,338	27,020	22,231	25,011	22,882	20,523	23,085	17,317	15,869	15,180	23,483	28,965	31,615
Michigan	9,073	9,552	10,990	16,090	14,268	14,913	12,728	14,135	17,253	14,727	13,943	13,650	16,773	21,528	21,787
Minnesota	4,665	5,704	6,627	7,461	6,851	7,438	7,098	8,111	8,977	8,233	6,981	5,956	8,671	11,166	13,522
Mississippi	760	845	931	1,254	842	906	815	757	1,073	1,118	701	698	1,083	1,340	1,155
Missouri	3,082	3,320	3,820	4,470	4,250	4,644	4,362	3,990	5,690	4,190	3,588	4,171	6,053	7,616	8,610
Montana	415	376	484	826	493	509	447	409	449	375	299	309	493	488	422
Nebraska	837	1,120	1,573	3,020	1,486	1,980	1,595	1,831	2,150	2,270	1,267	1,439	2,230	3,850	3,657
Nevada	2,726	5,242	8,270	10,470	5,086	4,045	4,051	4,306	5,874	6,541	6,106	8,305	7,827	9,618	9,499
New Hampshire	1,004	1,140	1,191	1,421	1,250	1,263	1,144	1,186	1,512	1,143	1,010	999	2,001	2,595	3,009

State of Intended Residence	1988	1989	1990	1991	1992	1993	1994	1995	1996	1997	1998	1999	2000	2001	2002
New Jersey	32,724	42,187	52,670	56,164	48,314	50,285	44,083	39,729	63,303	41,184	35,091	34,095	40,013	59,920	57,721
New Mexico	2,661	7,210	8,840	13,519	3,907	3,409	2,936	2,758	5,78 0	2,610	2,199	2,445	3,973	5,207	3,399
New York	109,259	134,766	189,589	188,104	149,399	151,209	144,354	128,406	154,095	123,716	96,559	96,979	106,061	114,116	114,827
North Carolina	3,777	4,634	5,387	16,772	6,425	6,892	6,204	5,617	7,011	5,935	6,415	5,792	9,251	13,918	12,910
North Dakota	324	323	448	565	513	601	635	483	606	535	472	314	420	558	776
Ohio	6,305	7,185	7,419	8,632	10,194	10,703	9,184	8,585	10,237	8,189	7,697	6,855	9,263	14,725	13,875
Oklahoma	2,050	4,366	5,274	6,403	3,147	2,942	2,728	2,792	3,511	3,157	2,273	2,376	4,586	3,492	4,229
Oregon	3,722	4,773	7,880	24,575	6,275	7,250	6,784	4,923	7,554	7,699	5,909	5,233	8,543	9,638	12,125
Pennsylvania	11,837	12,895	14,757	20,033	16,213	16,964	15,971	15,065	16,938	14,553	11,942	13,514	18,148	21,441	19,473
Rhode Island	2,390	3,134	3,683	3,644	2,920	3,168	2,907	2,609	3,098	2,543	1,976	2,058	2,526	2,820	3,067
South Carolina	1,360	1,787	2,130	3,836	2,118	2,195	2,110	2,165	2,151	2,446	2,125	1,773	2,267	2,882	2,966
South Dakota	254	265	287	519	522	543	570	495	519	490	356	356	465	671	902
Tennessee	2,439	2,763	2,893	3,828	2,995	4,287	3,608	3,392	4,343	4,357	2,806	2,584	4,882	6,257	5,694
Texas	43,271	112,927	174,132	212,600	75,533	67,380	56,158	49,963	83,385	57,897	44,428	49,393	63,840	86,315	88,365
Utah	2,113	2,926	3,335	5,737	2,744	3,266	2,951	2,831	4,250	2,840	3,360	3,564	3,710	5,247	4,889
Vermont	400	436	614	709	668	709	658	535	654	627	513	497	810	954	1,007
Virginia	11,908	15,690	19,005	24,942	17,739	16,451	15,342	16,319	21,375	19,277	15,686	15,144	20,087	26,876	25,411
Washington	9,890	13,630	15,129	33,826	15,861	17,147	18,180	15,862	18,833	18,656	16,920	13,046	18,486	23,085	25,704
West Virginia	482	500	552	763	723	689	663	540	583	418	375	392	573	737	636
Wisconsin	3,288	4,210	5,293	5,888	4,261	5,168	5,328	4,919	3,607	3,175	3,724	3,043	5,057	8,477	6,498
Wyoming	230	461	542	566	281	263	217	252	280	252	159	253	248	308	281

U.S. Territories and Possessions

	1988	1989	1990	1991	1992	1993	1994	1995	1996	1997	1998	1999	2000	2001	2002
Guam	1,909	1,775	1,851	2,113	2,464	3,072	2,531	2,419	2,820	2,083	1,835	1,729	1,556	1,722	1,698
Marshall Islands	-	-	-	-	-	-	1	-	-	-	-	-	-	-	-
Northern Mariana Islands	X	140	105	114	67	158	120	171	176	103	103	150	122	113	138
Puerto Rico	4,866	4,691	7,138	10,353	6,347	7,614	10,463	7,160	8,560	4,884	3,251	3,048	2,649	3,459	3,071
U.S. Virgin Islands	1,652	1,767	1,733	2,083	1,754	1,610	1,426	1,511	1,384	1,110	979	1,480	1,328	1,327	994
Armed services posts	-	-	-	-	-	-	-	-	-	-	88	105	116	96	100
Other or unknown	-	109	397	2,569	703	276	209	135	119	100	4	3	-	15	8

- Represents zero.   X Not applicable.

Source: U.S. Citizenship and Immigration Service, available online, URL: http://uscis.gov/graphics/shared/aboutus/statistics/IMM02yrbk/IMMExcel/table13.xls.

Refugee Arrivals into the United States by Country of Chargeability, Fiscal Years 1990–2002

Country of Chargeability	1990	1991	1992	1993	1994	1995	1996	1997	1998	1999	2000	2001	2002
All countries[1,2]	109,078	96,589	114,498	107,926	109,593	98,520	74,791	69,276	76,181	85,076	72,143	68,925	26,787
Europe	56,912	45,516	64,184	51,278	50,838	45,703	41,617	48,450	54,260	55,877	37,664	31,526	NA
Albania	98	1,363	1,108	458	171	51	23	9	3	8	1	3	NA
Armenia	X	X	NA	NA	NA	NA	NA	NA	NA	35	20	27	NA
Azerbaijan	X	X	NA	NA	NA	NA	NA	NA	NA	210	259	449	NA
Belarus	X	X	NA	NA	NA	NA	NA	NA	NA	1,008	1,050	971	NA
Bosnia-Herzegovina	X	X	-	1,887	7,088	9,870	12,030	21,357	30,906	22,699	19,033	14,593	NA
Bulgaria	332	585	126	34	5	3	-	-	-	-	-	-	NA
Croatia	X	X	-	-	-	-	-	-	-	1,660	2,995	1,020	NA
Czechoslovakia[3]	345	158	18	3	5	-	1	-	-	-	1-	NA	NA
Estonia	NA	NA	NA	NA	NA	NA	NA	NA	NA	71	81	57	NA
Georgia	X	X	-	-	-	-	-	-	-	50	30	49	NA
Hungary	274	7	1	-	1	-	-	-	-	-	-	-	NA
Kazakhstan	X	X	NA	NA	NA	NA	NA	NA	NA	412	284	291	NA
Kyrgyzstan	X	X	NA	NA	NA	NA	NA	NA	NA	140	147	116	NA
Latvia	NA	NA	NA	NA	NA	NA	NA	NA	NA	167	103	125	NA
Lithuania	NA	NA	NA	NA	NA	NA	NA	NA	NA	20	16	40	NA
Macedonia	X	X	X	X	NA	NA	NA	NA	NA	3	2	2	NA
Moldova	X	X	NA	NA	NA	NA	NA	NA	NA	1,035	1,056	1,168	NA
Poland	1,491	290	134	54	31	39	11	6	2	3	1	4	NA
Romania	3,650	4,452	1,499	215	67	24	16	3	-	2	4	-	NA
Russia	X	X	NA	NA	NA	NA	NA	NA	NA	4,386	3,723	4,454	NA
Slovenia	X	X	-	-	-	-	-	-	-	2	-	2	NA
Soviet Union[4]	50,716	38,661	61,298	48,627	43,470	35,716	29,536	27,072	23,349	194	282	133	NA
Tajikistan	X	X	NA	NA	NA	NA	NA	NA	NA	9	24	9	NA
Turkmenistan	X	X	NA	NA	NA	NA	NA	NA	NA	16	1	7	NA
Ukraine	X	X	NA	NA	NA	NA	NA	NA	NA	8,649	7,334	7,172	NA
Uzbekistan	X	X	NA	NA	NA	NA	NA	NA	NA	818	693	681	NA
Yugoslavia[4]	6	-	-	-	-	-	-	3	-	14,280	524	153	NA

Country of Chargeability	1990	1991	1992	1993	1994	1995	1996	1997	1998	1999	2000	2001	2002
Asia¹	43,360	42,279	41,045	45,302	46,457	40,420	22,131	11,771	13,669	14,041	13,622	15,356	NA
Afghanistan	1,594	1,480	1,452	1,233	21	4	-	-	88	365	1,709	2,930	NA
Bahrain	-	-	-	-	-	-	-	-	-	-	5	3	NA
Burma	3	14	55	94	75	36	11	182	186	295	637	54 3	NA
Cambodia	2,166	38	141	22	6	1	-	-	-	-	-	23	NA
China, People's Republic of	52	4	1	-	-	-	1	-	-	1	1	12	NA
India	-	-	-	-	-	-	4	6	-	-	-	-	NA
Indonesia	-	-	-	-	-	-	-	-	1	26	14	5	NA
Iran	3,329	2,692	1,949	1,161	851	978	1,256	1,305	1,699	1,750	5,145	6,590	NA
Iraq	67	842	3,442	4,605	4,984	3,482	2,679	2,679	1,407	1,955	3,158	2,473	NA
Jordan	-	-	-	-	-	-	-	-	-	-	5	-	NA
Kuwait	-	-	-	-	-	-	-	-	-	-	13	-	NA
Laos	8,771	9,250	7,315	6,967	6,272	3,675	2,201	939	-	19	64	22	NA
Lebanon	-	-	-	-	-	-	-	-	-	-	-	1	NA
Malaysia	-	-	-	-	-	-	-	-	-	-	-	5	NA
Maldives	-	-	-	-	-	-	-	-	-	-	1	2	NA
Pakistan	-	-	-	-	-	-	-	-	-	-	6	3	NA
Sri Lanka	-	-	-	-	-	-	-	-	-	5	4	2	NA
Syria	-	1	-	1	-	-	-	-	-	2	18	8	NA
Thailand	27,378	27,958	26,690	31,219	34,248	32,244	1 6,130	6,660	10,288	9,622	2,841	2,730	NA
Vietnam¹	-	-	-	-	-	-	-	-	-	1	-	-	NA
Yemen	-	-	-	-	-	-	-	-	-	1	1	-	NA
Africa	**3,494**	**4,768**	**5,492**	**6,969**	**5,861**	**4,779**	**7,502**	**6,069**	**6,665**	**13,048**	**17,624**	**19,070**	**NA**
Algeria	-	-	-	-	-	-	-	-	-	12	57	31	NA
Angola	59	21	4	-	6	1	2	-	-	2	2	34	NA
Benin	10	-	-	-	-	-	-	-	-	-	-	-	NA
Burkina Faso	-	-	-	-	-	-	-	1	-	1	1	-	NA
Burundi	3	-	-	3	-	8	8	33	24	223	165	109	NA
Cameroon	3	-	-	-	-	2	1	19	15	9	7	5	NA
Central African Republic	-	1	-	-	-	1	-	-	-	1	-	1	NA
Chad	1	-	-	-	-	-	-	45	41	22	2	2	NA
Congo, Democratic Republic of⁵	79	73	76	199	92	85	38	45	52	42	1,354	260	NA
Congo, Republic of⁵	-	-	-	-	-	-	-	-	-	27	11	6	NA

(continues)

Refugee Arrivals into the United States by Country of Chargeability, Fiscal Years 1990–2002 (continued)

Country of Chargeability	1990	1991	1992	1993	1994	1995	1996	1997	1998	1999	2000	2001	2002
Cote d'Ivoire	-	-	-	-	-	-	-	-	1	5	-	1	NA
Djibouti	-	-	-	-	-	-	-	16	15	8	-	12	NA
Egypt	-	-	-	-	-	-	-	-	-	-	6	8	NA
Equatorial Guinea	-	-	-	-	-	-	-	-	-	-	12	-	NA
Eritrea	X	X	X	-	6	-	14	7	9	32	94	109	NA
Ethiopia	3,228	3,948	2,972	2,765	328	239	194	197	152	1,873	1,347	1,429	NA
Gambia, The	-	-	-	-	-	-	-	16	50	13	13	5	NA
Ghana	11	-	-	2	5	9	1	4	-	5	3	2	NA
Guinea	-	-	-	-	-	-	-	-	-	6	1	4	NA
Kenya	-	1	-	-	-	-	6	-	13	2	11	13	NA
Lesotho	-	5	-	-	-	-	-	-	-	-	-	-	NA
Liberia	3	1	637	961	610	52	46	231	1,494	2,495	2,620	3,429	NA
Libya	1	344	1	-	3	-	-	-	-	-	-	5	NA
Madagascar	-	-	-	-	-	-	-	-	2	-	-	-	NA
Malawi	-	-	-	1	-	-	-	-	-	-	-	-	NA
Mauritania	-	-	-	-	-	-	-	-	-	1	-	202	NA
Mozambique	3	12	8	-	1	-	-	-	-	-	-	-	NA
Namibia	-	-	-	-	-	-	-	-	-	-	5	1	NA
Nigeria	-	-	-	-	-	-	34	7	312	625	50	85	NA
Rwanda	-	2	3	7	31	88	118	100	86	153	345	94	NA
Sierra Leone	-	-	-	-	-	48	13	57	176	675	1,128	2,004	NA
Somalia	25	192	1,570	2,753	3,555	2,506	6,436	4,974	2,951	4,320	6,026	4,951	NA
South Africa	34	19	15	8	-	-	1	1	-	-	-	-	NA
Sudan	7	24	113	244	1,220	1,705	575	277	1,252	2,393	3,833	5,959	NA
Tanzania	-	-	-	-	-	-	-	-	-	1	-	1	NA
Togo	-	-	-	-	-	25	1	30	15	93	511	280	NA
Tunisia	-	-	-	-	2	-	-	-	3	-	2	10	NA
Uganda	27	125	93	24	2	10	10	9	2	12	18	12	NA
Zambia	-	-	-	2	-	-	4	-	-	-	-	-	NA
Zimbabwe	-	-	-	-	-	-	-	-	-	-	-	6	NA

Country of Chargeability	1990	1991	1992	1993	1994	1995	1996	1997	1998	1999	2000	2001	2002
North America	**5,307**	**4,026**	**3,777**	**4,374**	**6,437**	**7,618**	**3,539**	**2,986**	**1,587**	**2,109**	**3,233**	**2,968**	**NA**
Caribbean	**4,753**	**3,933**	**3,774**	**4,372**	**6,436**	**7,618**	**3,537**	**2,986**	**1,587**	**2,109**	**3,233**	**2,968**	**NA**
Cuba	4,753	3,933	3,720	3,065	2,670	6,133	3,498	2,911	1,587	2,018	3,184	2,944	NA
Haiti	-	-	54	1,307	3,766	1,485	39	75	-	91	49	24	NA
Central America	**554**	**93**	**3**	**2**	**1**	**-**	**2**	**-**	**-**	**-**	**-**	**-**	**NA**
El Salvador	22	6	2	1	-	-	-	-	-	-	-	-	NA
Nicaragua	532	87	1	1	1	-	2	-	-	-	-	-	NA
South America	**5**	**-**	**-**	**3**	**-**	**-**	**2**	**-**	**-**	**1**	**-**	**5**	**NA**
Argentina	2	-	-	-	-	-	-	-	-	-	-	5	NA
Colombia	-	-	-	1	-	-	-	-	-	-	-	-	NA
Peru	3	-	-	-	-	-	2	-	-	1	-	-	NA
Venezuela	-	-	-	2	-	-	-	-	-	-	-	-	NA

[1] Amerasians are not included as refugee arrivals because they enter the United States on immigrant visas. In fiscal year 2002, 326 Amerasians from Vietnam arrived on immigrant visas.

[2] Country admissions data are not available for all of 2002.

[3] Data include independent and unknown republics.

[4] Prior to 1992, data include independent republics; beginning in 1992, data are for unknown republics only. For the former Soviet Union, data are not available for independent republics prior to 1999. The Department of State includes Estonia, Latvia, and Lithuania with the republics of the former Soviet Union.

[5] In May 1997, Zaire was formally recognized as the Democratic Republic of the Congo; the Congo is referred to by its conventional name, the Republic of Congo.

NOTE: Comparable arrivals data for fiscal year 2002 are not available for the region categories used by Immigration and Naturalization Service. The data for Bureau of Refugee Programs regions are Africa 2,505, East Asia 3,512, Eastern Europe 5,480, former Soviet Union 9,990, Latin America/Caribbean 1,929 and Near East/South Asia 3,697. Prior to 1996, refugee arrival data were derived from the Nonimmigrant Information System of the Immigration and Naturalization Service. Beginning in fiscal year 1996, arrival data for all years are from the Bureau of Refugee Programs Department of State. Any comparison of refugee arrival data prior to 1996 must be made with caution. Arrivals may be higher than approvals because of the arrival of persons approved in previous years.

- Represents zero.
NA Not available.
X Not applicable.

Source: U.S. Citizenship and Immigration Services, available online, URL: http://uscis.gov/graphics/shared/aboutus/statistics/RA2002yrbk/RAExcel/Table17.xls

Persons Naturalized by Region and Country of Birth, Fiscal Years 1991–2002

Region and Country of Birth	1991	1992	1993	1994	1995	1996	1997	1998	1999	2000	2001	2002
All countries	308,058	240,252	314,681	434,107	488,088	1,044,689	598,225	463,060	839,944	888,788	608,205	573,708
Europe	32,986	27,143	37,774	56,449	63,602	109,607	67,783	58,836	101,318	121,273	89,431	93,627
Albania	72	92	88	109	103	348	419	351	599	826	1,0 32	2451
Andorra	I	I	-	-	-	I	-	I	3	I	I	I
Armenia	-	12	136	641	1,215	2,957	3,037	2,530	3,190	2, 569	1,972	1,817
Austria	98	92	194	281	291	382	181	153	232	290	271	276
Azerbaijan	-	-	-	3	27	160	263	350	878	1,318	946	1,188
Belarus	-	-	I	3	89	393	727	833	1,869	3,063	2,008	2,142
Belgium	174	142	191	254	233	343	179	166	294	363	299	265
Bosnia-Herzegovina	-	-	2	18	29	44	50	33	300	1,745	2,759	4,095
Bulgaria	227	166	168	247	256	627	356	263	498	847	1,170	1,311
Croatia	-	-	3	52	168	470	212	184	358	501	519	621
Czech Republic	-	-	-	I	5	4	10	4	27	58	47	64
Czechoslovakia[1]	863	677	643	712	692	733	434	315	548	658	492	454
Denmark	177	120	155	243	230	341	165	165	239	286	227	195
Estonia	32	II	16	58	72	91	52	52	82	108	105	110
Finland	89	90	103	138	138	186	94	110	159	201	115	141
France	1,184	981	1,140	1,630	1,413	2,340	1,261	1,125	1,903	2,285	1,745	1,724
Georgia	-	-	2	4	25	70	101	76	147	407	415	444
Germany	2,296	1,938	2,591	3,763	3,658	4,664	2,946	2,517	4,169	4,522	3,212	3,431
Gibraltar	-	4	5	4	4	5	5	I	5	3	I	-
Greece	1,850	1,751	2,106	2,577	2,135	3,162	1,885	1,553	2,355	2,270	1,676	1,290
Hungary	836	616	649	855	868	1,159	568	531	884	1,074	877	829
Iceland	26	36	31	37	37	43	38	32	50	52	44	32
Ireland	749	731	1,067	1,677	1,959	3,284	1,835	1,444	3,414	5,454	4,441	3,443
Italy	1,998	1,608	3,502	5,702	4,065	5,117	2,445	2,522	4,393	4,436	2,987	2,621
Kazakhstan	-	-	2	36	21	32	46	58	226	437	429	562
Kyrgyzstan	-	-	2	-	2	I	I	18	32	87	81	128
Latvia	51	50	66	138	186	336	202	194	383	484	360	376
Liechtenstein	-	3	2	-	3	3	-	I	-	-	I	-
Lithuania	65	46	82	117	241	271	180	155	313	355	405	489
Luxembourg	9	5	7	10	8	21	9	4	15	II	9	8
Macedonia	-	-	-	-	89	298	204	137	212	310	394	560
Malta	82	57	78	102	53	123	51	39	93	116	63	86
Moldova	-	-	5	42	135	390	621	574	1,155	1,573	959	919
Monaco	2	2	I	2	5	3	I	I	8	-	4	2
Netherlands	421	320	399	613	657	976	475	397	700	813	549	515
Norway	142	110	129	171	160	265	112	92	161	192	126	109
Poland	5,568	4,699	5,592	7,062	8,092	14,047	8,037	5,911	13,127	16,405	11,661	12,823
Portugal	1,754	1,802	3,880	5,882	3,809	6,525	4,278	4,663	5,843	4,756	2,780	2,198
Romania	3,535	2,489	2,750	3,503	3,408	5,242	3,043	2,244	3,275	3,586	3,521	4,016
Russia	-	375	440	1,242	3,367	8,245	8,200	5,981	10,351	12,919	9,413	9,846
San Marino	-	2	-	2	2	-	I	I	7	6	I	2
Slovak Republic	-	-	-	2	16	20	26	35	81	200	243	301
Slovenia	-	-	I	5	20	19	13	17	36	43	42	58
Soviet Union[2]	2,889	1,338	2,168	4,865	10,338	20,137	9,286	6,987	11,300	9,195	4,576	4,305
Spain	459	461	618	817	837	2,079	756	905	1,241	1,073	724	634
Sweden	215	184	230	316	260	404	218	203	354	373	321	819
Switzerland	367	304	399	557	453	605	329	301	506	655	517	462

Region and Country of Birth	1991	1992	1993	1994	1995	1996	1997	1998	1999	2000	2001	2002
Tajikistan	-	-	1	-	8	7	15	35	167	406	369	234
Turkmenistan	-	-	-	1	1	6	5	5	27	73	60	65
Ukraine	-	9	141	583	2,715	6,959	5,971	6,952	12,190	16,849	11,828	12,110
United Kingdom	5,080	4,366	5,791	8,410	8,479	12,185	6,900	6,375	10,016	11,739	8,059	8,207
Uzbekistan	-	-	-	6	46	208	243	236	1,142	3,084	2,493	2,541
Yugoslavia[2]	1,675	1,453	2,197	2,956	2,479	3,276	1,297	1,004	1,761	2,196	2,082	2,307
Asia	**168,296**	**125,376**	**149,432**	**193,842**	**190,205**	**307,451**	**193,591**	**153,951**	**273,924**	**331,136**	**247,185**	**232,412**
Afghanistan	1,394	1,052	1,548	1,995	2,031	4,141	1,839	1,736	2,752	2,843	1,947	1,429
Bahrain	12	12	10	16	22	27	10	19	32	41	47	47
Bangladesh	900	974	961	1,190	1,323	5,407	3,577	1,211	2,280	3,323	4,419	5,628
Bhutan	2	-	-	1	1	-	3	1	3	3	4	2
Brunei	12	14	14	12	8	9	5	9	13	15	8	12
Burma	876	485	558	875	872	1,335	578	443	889	1,131	1,079	1,069
Cambodia	4,851	2,713	3,102	4,132	3,619	5,202	5,180	5,348	7,140	5,292	3,489	3,126
China, People's Republic of	16,947	13,616	16,943	22,331	21,564	34,320	20,947	16,145	38,409	54,534	34,423	32,108
Cyprus	166	171	187	196	176	250	113	129	190	205	185	150
Hong Kong	4,648	3,203	3,807	6,534	5,690	8,660	4,752	2,927	6,624	8,101	5,274	4,852
India	13,286	13,452	16,527	20,940	18,558	33,113	21,206	17,060	30,710	42,198	34,311	33,774
Indonesia	615	318	434	580	624	1,106	575	609	1,464	2,487	1,247	1,006
Iran	10,595	6,787	7,033	10,041	11,761	19,278	11,434	10,739	18,268	19,251	13,881	11,796
Iraq	1,684	1,203	1,545	1,808	1,609	2,309	1,621	2,033	3,230	5,217	3,451	3,318
Israel	2,781	2,250	2,448	3,039	2,645	3,537	2,034	1,444	2,917	3,581	2,974	2,562
Japan	951	634	1,002	1,440	1,462	2,188	1,283	1,847	3,178	3,757	2,369	1,858
Jordan	2,523	2,263	2,597	2,797	2,385	3,236	1,820	1,510	2,467	3,252	2,883	2,824
Korea	12,538	8,330	9,681	12,367	15,709	27,969	16,056	10,305	17,738	23,858	18,053	17,307
Kuwait	319	313	360	449	465	705	404	308	597	905	766	791
Laos	3,887	3,080	3,994	5,630	4,315	10,621	8,630	7,734	9,188	7,163	6,507	8,418
Lebanon	3,631	2,888	3,392	4,592	4,171	5,441	3,041	2,391	4,226	4,939	3,556	3,408
Macau	148	69	108	190	127	225	117	87	197	255	200	196
Malaysia	488	394	423	522	443	690	428	370	885	1,374	1,034	1,095
Maldives	1	1	-	1	4	-	1	-	2	1	1	-
Mongolia	1	1	1	1	1	-	-	1	7	15	9	13
Nepal	43	44	46	70	60	119	78	82	143	204	205	248
Oman	2	3	4	5	7	1	5	6	1	7	8	9
Pakistan	3,719	3,359	3,776	4,529	4,912	11,251	7,266	3,572	6,572	8,726	8,375	8,658
Philippines	34,450	28,587	33,925	40,777	37,870	51,346	30,898	24,872	38,944	46,563	35,431	30,487
Qatar	7	21	21	19	14	34	16	12	27	35	37	48
Saudi Arabia	95	105	149	158	126	193	147	80	152	310	247	309
Singapore	200	153	162	204	172	292	171	143	294	405	306	322
Sri Lanka	484	332	457	537	522	917	547	460	883	1,001	836	963
Syria	1,546	1,222	1,350	1,820	1,825	2,510	1,638	1,466	2,344	2,802	2,158	2,280
Taiwan	11,010	6,275	7,235	10,387	9,565	12,114	6,455	4,862	11,215	13,200	9,076	8,611
Thailand	1,376	946	1,129	1,634	1,707	3,912	2,287	1,986	4,046	5,225	4,104	4,026
Turkey	1,416	1,148	1,271	1,663	1,591	2,181	1,575	1,547	2,025	2,072	1,795	1,926
United Arab Emirates	2	8	14	26	17	26	45	13	44	79	84	109
Vietnam	30,078	18,422	22,520	29,555	31,728	51,910	36,178	30,185	53,316	55,934	41,596	36,835
Yemen	612	528	698	779	504	876	631	259	512	832	810	882

(continues)

Persons Naturalized by Region and Country of Birth, Fiscal Years 1991–2002 (continued)

Region and Country of Birth	1991	1992	1993	1994	1995	1996	1997	1998	1999	2000	2001	2002
Africa	**10,468**	**9,731**	**11,539**	**16,073**	**18,495**	**26,970**	**15,996**	**12,467**	**20,401**	**25,850**	**24,312**	**31,527**
Algeria	116	103	126	183	188	275	173	143	277	427	469	615
Angola	33	39	59	98	68	122	91	73	99	113	86	69
Benin	6	12	28	28	37	14	24	24	35	23	19	25
Botswana	-	1	1	4	2	8	5	-	4	8	7	4
Burkina Faso	2	1	100	290	168	8	4	3	8	16	10	7
Burundi	1	1	7	6	5	7	3	2	6	13	15	28
Cameroon	53	74	106	175	175	264	164	149	181	286	299	463
Cape Verde	184	222	215	500	529	634	573	542	849	736	581	684
Central African Republic	4	2	1	2	6	4	2	1	4	4	3	10
Chad	3	-	3	2	2	3	3	4	6	9	12	3
Comoros	1	-	-	-	-	1	1	-	3	-	1	2
Congo, Democratic Republic[3] of	46	53	75	100	91	187	81	68	127	138	115	116
Congo, Republic[3] of	2	1	5	7	5	5	3	11	42	58	90	139
Cote d'Ivoire	28	37	47	78	76	164	107	84	121	184	171	272
Djibouti	7	5	8	5	8	5	5	5	9	10	9	18
Egypt	2,689	2,115	2,065	2,620	2,671	3,877	2,238	1,498	2,687	3,492	3,786	3,701
Equatorial Guinea	6	2	2	4	5	10	2	1	5	3	-	3
Eritrea	-	-	-	54	343	518	393	443	567	824	756	812
Ethiopia	1,476	1,506	1,866	2,375	2,626	3,397	1,994	1,844	2,611	2,774	2,765	3,902
French Southern and Antarctic Lands	-	1	6	-	-	-	-	-	2	-	-	-
Gabon	3	-	-	4	3	7	3	2	5	8	5	12
Gambia, The	20	11	17	26	53	98	50	40	69	81	71	135
Ghana	680	710	735	1,145	1,578	2,905	1,588	1,073	1,548	2,035	1,832	3,328
Guinea	7	8	4	6	5	9	24	31	42	71	67	111
Guinea-Bissau	2	2	1	5	154	3	74	206	168	20	6	14
Kenya	297	258	342	419	429	695	496	399	699	933	734	865
Lesotho	3	3	3	3	5	5	4	5	1	5	3	5
Liberia	356	361	453	609	745	1,104	719	557	848	1,027	782	1,048
Libya	139	145	155	170	205	211	130	95	153	181	171	164
Madagascar	11	15	3	12	13	27	16	12	16	30	25	29
Malawi	12	16	24	40	35	40	22	35	37	50	39	44
Mali	2	6	6	11	16	30	29	19	32	48	51	72
Mauritania	2	2	3	1	8	9	3	1	12	13	19	23
Mauritius	14	14	16	29	13	37	29	23	41	60	38	37
Morocco	375	422	519	731	689	1,174	555	415	854	1,198	1,248	1,274
Mozambique	26	26	25	59	37	53	40	30	59	68	29	57
Namibia	3	4	10	7	6	8	9	5	10	13	15	13
Niger	-	-	-	3	6	489	218	321	608	556	183	110
Nigeria	1,804	1,847	2,289	3,464	4,645	6,248	3,537	1,963	3,125	4,135	4,355	6,419
Réunion	-	-	-	-	-	-	-	-	-	1	-	-
Rwanda	6	6	4	4	11	10	5	4	9	31	62	86
São Tomé and Príncipe	-	-	2	1	-	2	1	1	3	3	1	2
Senegal	33	42	67	72	87	260	223	107	188	218	251	346
Seychelles	28	20	19	17	18	12	16	7	13	27	18	12

Region and Country of Birth	1991	1992	1993	1994	1995	1996	1997	1998	1999	2000	2001	2002
Sierra Leone	198	192	297	398	578	782	492	420	487	600	518	763
Somalia	107	120	130	154	211	306	171	306	816	1,247	1,168	1,791
South Africa	906	657	833	1,192	884	1,217	661	676	1,418	1,967	1,472	1,528
St. Helena	3	1	1	-	2	2	1	2	1	1	1	1
Sudan	81	94	116	133	165	308	218	140	281	515	741	1,013
Swaziland	8	4	4	3	7	3	-	5	5	11	3	8
Tanzania	230	198	211	254	223	447	220	189	354	420	334	345
Togo	14	12	17	22	20	32	20	18	35	58	57	113
Tunisia	78	66	106	101	109	164	87	90	129	168	157	165
Uganda	151	131	157	206	277	409	264	206	348	430	297	322
Western Sahara	-	-	-	2	1	-	1	-	2	1	-	-
Zambia	115	67	124	122	120	183	105	90	168	228	158	168
Zimbabwe	97	96	126	117	132	178	99	79	174	274	207	231
Oceania	**1,374**	**1,015**	**1,276**	**1,763**	**1,817**	**3,312**	**1,812**	**1,613**	**2,385**	**2,685**	**2,594**	**2,356**
American Samoa	47	47	71	103	122	148	38	63	75	80	97	102
Australia	108	126	209	282	250	438	261	203	342	436	392	427
Christmas Island	-	2	-	2	2	1	2	-	2	-	-	-
Cocos Islands	-	-	1	-	-	-	-	-	-	-	1	-
Cook Islands	3	1	2	5	5	30	9	3	8	3	4	5
Fiji	524	399	545	711	704	1,392	711	493	775	924	1,180	1,022
French Polynesia	222	109	24	26	23	113	47	103	142	128	-	16
Guam	-	-	1	-	4	2	1	-	1	1	41	-
Kiribati	1	-	1	3	3	4	4	2	3	3	3	-
Marshall Islands	-	-	-	4	4	6	5	1	2	2	3	1
Micronesia, Federated States	-	2	3	3	5	6	1	7	2	3	4	6
Nauru	1	1	3	2	3	-	1	-	3	5	1	2
New Caledonia	3	2	2	1	2	4	2	1	4	3	4	2
New Zealand	192	104	173	238	245	342	222	196	317	421	347	356
Niue	-	1	-	-	-	8	1	-	1	1	-	-
Northern Mariana Islands	-	-	-	3	2	1	-	-	2	-	3	-
Palau	25	22	17	11	2	2	10	17	19	17	7	9
Papua New Guinea	3	2	1	3	8	13	2	-	3	8	7	7
Pitcairn Island	1	1	3	1	2	-	-	-	-	-	-	-
Samoa[4]	150	102	129	188	206	319	155	219	257	282	195	151
Solomon Islands	2	6	2	4	4	2	1	3	1	1	2	1
Tonga	90	87	86	171	220	453	336	299	423	366	301	248
Tuvalu	-	-	3	2	1	-	2	3	2	-	1	-
Vanuatu	2	1	-	-	-	1	1	-	1	1	1	1
Wallis and Futuna Islands	-	-	-	-	-	27	-	-	-	-	-	-
North America	**73,630**	**56,905**	**87,931**	**130,345**	**175,216**	**506,767**	**273,954**	**208,192**	**385,605**	**347,193**	**200,939**	**169,950**
Canada	4,514	4,025	6,505	8,684	7,597	11,663	6,639	5,545	9,353	11,365	7,551	7,591
Greenland	1	2	1	5	1	4	4	-	1	-	1	-
Mexico	22,878	12,873	23,615	46,169	81,655	254,988	142,569	112,442	207,750	189,705	103,234	76,531
St.-Pierre and Miquelon	1	1	8	5	-	-	1	2	1	-	-	-
United States	29	31	37	71	16	42	22	20	28	44	38	42

(continues)

Persons Naturalized by Region and Country of Birth, Fiscal Years 1991–2002 (continued)

Region and Country of Birth	1991	1992	1993	1994	1995	1996	1997	1998	1999	2000	2001	2002
Caribbean	**34,761**	**32,478**	**47,372**	**58,569**	**56,480**	**163,709**	**84,834**	**62,678**	**115,245**	**93,291**	**56,602**	**58,943**
Anguilla	32	24	64	88	57	41	64	86	165	67	38	30
Antigua-Barbuda	485	375	438	627	668	1,415	886	932	1,103	946	478	451
Aruba	35	26	31	80	42	107	66	38	86	85	41	50
Bahamas, The	162	165	141	238	223	671	337	265	796	591	394	401
Barbados	856	671	858	1,432	1,304	2,488	1,960	1,173	2,558	1,891	914	874
Bermuda	34	18	43	54	80	75	39	54	84	90	58	47
British Virgin Islands	56	57	86	122	62	43	102	136	205	134	48	40
Cayman Islands	20	17	37	47	55	36	288	152	137	23	15	17
Cuba	9,661	7,750	15,604	16,380	17,511	63,234	13,155	15,331	25,467	15,661	11,393	10,889
Dominica	555	288	273	405	434	1,040	621	677	977	717	372	456
Dominican Republic	6,396	8,494	12,303	11,390	9,999	29,459	21,092	11,916	23,089	25,176	15,010	15,591
Grenada	459	420	565	829	736	1,681	1,223	663	1,532	1,172	610	609
Guadeloupe	11	10	20	29	137	383	21	19	61	32	14	25
Haiti	4,455	3,988	5,190	7,989	7,884	25,012	16,477	10,416	19,550	14,428	10,408	9,280
Jamaica	6,949	6,710	7,911	12,252	11,156	25,458	20,253	15,0 40	28,604	22,567	13,978	13,973
Martinique	14	11	5	14	7	23	14	11	22	23	21	16
Montserrat	67	41	61	118	91	181	141	124	190	130	86	84
Netherlands Antilles	69	28	41	36	29	61	62	51	89	79	34	28
Puerto Rico	2	2	4	4	5	6	5	4	2	4	1	3
St. Kitts–Nevis	728	331	390	612	575	983	714	771	995	713	331	352
St. Lucia	284	195	241	393	418	824	638	531	708	610	392	418
St. Vincent and the Grenadines	329	249	334	540	492	1,112	827	475	999	832	440	462
Trinidad and Tobago	3,084	2,588	3,249	4,874	4,487	9,288	5,803	3,784	7,732	7,265	4,484	4,822
Turks and Caicos Islands	8	9	3	8	19	70	41	19	83	43	40	18
U.S. Virgin Islands	10	11	20	8	9	18	5	10	11	12	2	7
Central America	**11,446**	**7,495**	**10,393**	**16,842**	**29,467**	**73,361**	**39,885**	**27,505**	**53,227**	**52,788**	**30,513**	**26,843**
Belize	504	305	384	635	874	1,831	1,353	988	2,079	1,802	1,015	774
Costa Rica	795	547	668	1,055	1,138	2,759	1,574	1,103	2,087	1,895	1,146	1,002
El Salvador	3,691	2,061	3,038	5,643	13,702	35,478	18,273	12,267	22,991	24,073	13,663	10,716
Guatemala	1,847	1,080	1,685	3,001	5,093	13,933	7,914	5,534	11,031	11,488	6,281	5,455
Honduras	1,328	1,249	1,714	2,215	2,954	7,881	4,318	2,752	5,294	5,188	3,257	3,505
Nicaragua	1,750	1,103	1,501	2,437	3,950	11,135	4,409	3,359	6,651	5,426	3,564	3,794
Panama	1,531	1,150	1,403	1,856	1,756	3,344	2,044	1,502	3,094	2,916	1,587	1,597
South America	**21,212**	**19,969**	**26,464**	**35,014**	**38,072**	**84,520**	**42,282**	**27,550**	**54,363**	**58,009**	**42,288**	**42,888**
Argentina	1,869	1,242	1,602	2,481	2,714	5,457	2,247	1,651	3,366	3,432	2,211	2,131
Bolivia	530	417	575	803	1,186	2,367	1,093	845	1,461	1,375	908	1,100
Brazil	696	661	906	1,322	1,254	2,961	2,360	1,947	4,114	4,524	3,935	3,889
Chile	942	716	867	1,206	1,315	3,068	1,427	1,002	1,892	1,888	1,205	1,154
Colombia	5,619	6,451	9,985	12,309	12,823	27,483	11,645	7,024	13,168	14,018	10,872	10,634
Ecuador	2,231	1,855	2,701	3,965	5,381	14,547	7,463	4,674	8,411	9,487	6,571	6,402
Falkland Islands	-	1	-	-	1	-	1	-	-	1	-	-
French Guiana	5	2	1	2	1	-	1	-	2	10	1	6
Guyana	4,863	4,726	4,964	6,081	5,499	11,223	7,544	4,575	10,366	10,820	7,052	7,224
Paraguay	131	129	173	259	230	491	248	112	193	214	166	198

Region and Country of Birth	1991	1992	1993	1994	1995	1996	1997	1998	1999	2000	2001	2002
Peru	3,141	2,645	3,285	4,754	5,921	12,884	6,352	4,353	8,308	8,958	6,675	7,385
Suriname	35	46	26	87	59	134	74	45	130	163	113	120
Uruguay	400	368	581	667	679	1,372	622	397	689	693	472	486
Venezuela	750	710	798	1,078	1,009	2,533	1,205	925	2,263	2,426	2,107	2,159
Born on ship	-	-	-	-	-	1	-	-	-	-	1	-
Stateless	-	-	-	-	-	-	44	28	67	42	23	15
Unknown or not reported	92	113	265	621	681	6,061	2,763	423	1,881	2,600	1,432	933

[1] Prior to 1993, data include independent republics; beginning in 1993 data are for unknown republic only.

[2] Prior to 1992, data include independent republics; beginning in 1992 data are for unknown republic only.

[3] In May 1997, Zaire was formally recognized as the Democratic Republic of Congo; the Congo is referred to by its conventional name, the Republic of the Congo.

[4] In August 1997, Western Samoa was formally recognized as Samoa (independent state).

- Represents zero.

Source: U.S. Citizenship and Immigration Service, available online, URL: http://uscis.gov/graphics/shared/aboutus/statistics/NATZ2002yrbk/NATZExcel/Table35.xls

Canadian Immigration by Top 10 Source Countries, 1996–2000

Country	1996			1997			1998			1999			2000		
	Rank	Number	Percent	Rank	Number	Percent	Rank	Number	Percent	Rank	Number	Percent	Rank	Number	Percent
Hong Kong	1	29,871	13.33	1	22,080	10.22	4	8,083	4.64	13	3,664	1.93	17	2,857	1.26
India	2	21,166	9.45	2	19,616	9.08	2	15,327	8.80	2	17,415	9.17	2	26,064	11.47
China	3	17,479	7.8	3	18,529	8.58	1	19,749	11.34	1	29,095	15.33	1	36,718	16.16
Taiwan	4	13,165	5.88	4	13,319	6.17	6	7,164	4.11	8	5,461	2.88	14	3,511	1.55
Philippines	5	12,923	5.77	6	10,869	5.03	3	8,172	4.69	4	9,160	4.83	4	10,077	4.44
Pakistan	6	7,724	3.45	5	11,233	5.2	5	8,081	4.64	3	9,285	4.89	3	14,173	6.24
Sri Lanka	7	6,117	2.73	8	5,065	2.34	14	3,330	1.91	9	4,719	2.49	6	5,832	2.57
United States	8	5,789	2.58	9	5,029		9	4,764	2.74	7	5,514	2.90	7	5,809	2.56
Iran	9	5,770	2.58	7	7,478	3.46	7	6,772	3.89	6	5,903	3.11	8	5,606	2.47
United Kingdom	10	5,559	2.48	10	4,658	2.16	11	3,890	2.23	10	4,476	2.36	10	4,648	2.05
Korea	15	3,156	1.40	11	4,000	1.85	8	4,910	2.82	5	7,212	3.80	5	7,630	3.36
Russia	21	2,457	1.09	14	3,735	1.73	10	3,890	2.23	12	3,771	1.93	13	3,521	1.55
Yugoslavia	-	-	-	-	-	-	40	1,172	0.67	29	1,490	0.78	9	4,719	2.08
Top 10 Total	-	125,563	56.04	-	117,876	54.56	-	87,321	50.16	-	98,240	51.76	-	121,276	53.38
Other Countries	-	98,487	43.96	-	98,163	45.44	-	86,779	49.84	-	91,576	48.24	-	105,933	46.62
TOTAL	-	223,875	100	-	216,039	100	-	174,100	100	-	189,816	100	-	227,209	100

Source: Citizenship and Immigration Canada, available online; URL: http://www.cic.gc.ca/english/pub/index.html

Austrian Empire Ancestry Groups in the United States, 2000

Country of Heritage	Number
Austrian	735,128
Croatian	374,241
Czech[1]	1,703,930
Hungarian	1,398,724
Polish[2]	8,977,444
Romanian	367,310
Slovak[3]	797,764
Slovene	176,691
Ukrainian[2]	892,922

[1] Includes Czech and Czechoslovakian responses.

[2] Total, with the majority coming from the Russian Empire.

[3] Includes Slovak responses only.

Source: Census 2000, U.S. Census Bureau, available online; URL: http://factfinder.census.gov/servlet/QTTable?_ts=71159599610

Bibliography

This is a general bibliography, primarily meant to cover broad themes and topics not covered by A–Z entries in the text. It does not reproduce the several hundred bibliographies in the text. Thus, if one is interested in the Chinese, for example, one should consult the main entries—on Chinese immigration, Chinese Exclusion Act, and Chinese Immigration Act—for their bibliographies. These will be cross-referenced to related entries, such as the Burlingame Treaty, nativism, and Taiwanese immigration, which will have bibliographies of their own. For more extensive listings, including many older works, regional and local ethnic studies, and personal reflections, see the bibliographies below under General Reference Works, especially Barkan, Ciment, Magocsi, Miller, and Thernstrom. Books containing excellent, detailed bibliographic essays include Elliott Robert Barkan's *A Nation of Peoples: A Sourcebook on America's Multicultural Heritage* (Westport, Conn.: Greenwood Press, 1999), Barkan's *And Still They Come: Immigrants and American Society, 1920 to the 1990s* (Wheeling, Ill.: Harlan-Davidson, 1996), and Alan M. Kraut's *The Huddled Masses: The Immigrant in American Society, 1880–1921*, 2d ed. (Wheeling, Ill.: Harlan-Davidson, 2001). Booklets in the Canadian Historical Association's Canada's Ethnic Groups series also have good bibliographic essays. Autobiographies, letters, and oral histories are especially well covered in Barkan's *And Still They Come*, Kraut's *Huddled Masses*, and Dirk Hoerder's *Creating Societies: Immigrant Lives in Canada* (Montreal and Kingston: McGill–Queens University Press, 1999).

The field of immigration studies has flourished during the past quarter century. In addition to monographs, articles, and specialized reference works listed with each article and thematically in the bibliography, a few general reference books deserve special mention. The three-volume *Gale Encyclopedia of Multicultural America*, second edition (2000), and the two-volume *American Immigrant Cultures: Builders of a Nation* (1997) focus on immigrant groups and immigrant cultures. Coverage is uneven—reflecting the diverse nature of evidence available for the various groups—but generally extensive. The *Gale Encyclopedia* is especially useful for providing addresses, phone numbers, and Web sites for culturally based media outlets; organizations and associations; and museums and research centers. Sharpe's four-volume *Encyclopedia of American Immigration* provides a general introduction to the history, issues, groups, and documents associated with American immigration, though its focus is clearly on large immigrant groups. The preeminent one-volume reference work for the United States remains Stephen Thernstrom's *Harvard Encyclopedia of American Ethnic Groups* (1980). It is thorough and analytic, comprising more than a million words and written by the leading specialists of the day. Though published a quarter of a century ago, the articles remain of the first importance, especially for early immigrant groups and thematic topics. The *Harvard Encyclopedia* will remain a valuable tool for decades to come, but its usefulness has gradually been eroded by time and changing circumstances. Immigration from Mexico, Central and South America, and Asia, for instance, has increased dramatically since 1980, as has knowledge of the process. In 1980 it was thought sufficient to include "more than one million immigrants from Central and South America" who had settled in the United States since 1820 in a single article, mainly because separate records were not kept prior to 1960, and little work had been done on individual groups in the intervening 20 years. The economic and political circumstances of the region in the 1980s, however, coupled with new immigration policy in the United States, have completely transformed both the volume and significance of immigration from Mexico and Central America. The decline of cold war tensions, the breakup of the Soviet Union and Yugoslavia in the 1990s, and the resulting new opportunities for emigration could scarcely have been contemplated in 1980. When the *Harvard Encyclopedia* was completed, for instance, there were "approximately 2,500 Afghans" in the United States, the Soviet invasion had just begun, and there were "no published studies on Afghans living in the United States." Between 1981 and 1998, more than 41,000 Afghans immigrated to the United States and a number of valuable studies of the movement have been undertaken. Elliott Robert Barkan's *A Nation of Peoples: A Sourcebook on America's Multicultural Heritage* (1999) is the starting point for up-to-date immigration studies. In addition to offering 27 ethnic studies, Barkan provides an excellent historiographic overview and a good annotated bibliography. The strengths of *A Nation of Peoples* lie in its well-written articles and useful annotated bibliographies, containing references to leading journals and primary-source collections. However, many areas are excluded or only lightly touched upon. There is virtually no mention of sub-Saharan Africa, for instance, and many countries (for example, Guatemala, Egypt, Iraq, Jamaica) grouped under broader categories (Central and South Americans, Middle Easterners and North Africans, West Indians/Caribbeans) go largely unnoticed, both in the text and the bibliographies. Also useful is the four-volume *Encyclopedia of American Immigration,* edited by James Ciment (2001), which focuses less on immigrant groups and more on related topics such as demographics, acculturation, economics, cultural presence, and religion. It also includes more than 200 pages of related primary materials, including laws and treaties, executive orders, court cases, political platforms, government rulings, historical articles, and personal letters. Although coverage is selective, the 1,200 pages of material cover a wide variety of historical, sociological, cultural, and legal topics, including many recent developments.

There are fewer comparable reference sources for Canadian immigration. The most comprehensive by far is Paul Robert Magocsi's *Encyclopedia of Canada's Peoples* (1999), deliberately patterned after the *Harvard Encyclopedia of American Ethnic Groups.* The most current survey is J. M. Bumsted's *Canada's Diverse Peoples: A Reference Sourcebook* (2003), part of ABC-CLIO's Ethnic Diversity Within Nations Series. *Ethnicity and Culture in Canada: The Research Landscape,* edited by J. W. Berry and J. A. Laponce (1994), is also useful. For specific immigrant groups and related themes, one should consult the Canadian Historical Association's Canada's Ethnic Groups Series, published with the support of the Department of Canadian Heritage. As of 2004, there were 29 booklets in the series, each prepared by academic specialists. Finally, *The Canadian Family Tree: Canada's Peoples* (1979), produced by the Multiculturalism Directorate of the office of the secretary of state, serves as a brief ready reference. The coverage is often thin, but it includes information on some smaller immigrant groups that is difficult to find elsewhere.

GENERAL REFERENCE WORKS

Bankston, Carl L., III, ed. *Racial and Ethnic Relations in America.* 3 vols. Pasadena, Calif.: Salem Press, 2000.

Barkan, Elliott, ed. *A Nation of Peoples.* Westport, Conn.: Greenwood Press, 1999.

Boyd, Alex, ed. *Guide to Multicultural Resources, 1997/1998.* Fort Atkinson, Wisc.: Highsmith Press, 1997.

Brown, Mary Ellen. *Shapers of the Great Debate on Immigration: A Biographical Dictionary.* Westport, Conn.: Greenwood Press, 1999.

Canter, Lawrence A., and Martha S. Siegel. *U.S. Immigration Made Easy.* 8th ed. Berkeley, Calif.: Nolo Press, 2001.

Ciment, James, ed. *Encyclopedia of American Immigration.* 4 vols. Armonk, N.Y.: Sharpe Reference, 2001.

Cohen, Robin, ed. *The Cambridge Survey of World Migration.* Cambridge: Cambridge University Press, 1995.

Cordasco, Francesco. *Dictionary of American Immigration History.* Metuchen, N.J.: Scarecrow Press, 1990.

Dassanowsky, Robert von, and Jeffrey Lehman. *Gale Encyclopedia of Multicultural America.* 2d ed. 3 vols. Detroit: Gale Group, 2000.

Foner, Nancy, Rubén G. Rumbaut, Steven J. Gold, eds. *Immigration Research for a New Century: Multidisciplinary Perspectives.* New York: Russell Sage Foundation, 2000.

Green, Victor R. *American Immigrant Leaders, 1800–1910: Marginality and Identity.* Baltimore: Johns Hopkins University Press, 1987.

Haines, David W. *Refugees in America in the 1990s: A Reference Handbook.* Westport, Conn.: Greenwood Press, 1996.

Jasso, Guillermina, and Mark R. Rosenzweig. *The New Chosen People: Immigrants in the United States.* New York: Russell Sage Foundation, 1990.

Kasinitz, Philip, and Josh DeWind, eds. *The Handbook of International Migration: The American Experience.* New York: Russell Sage Foundation, 1999.

Levinson, David, and Melvin Ember, eds. *American Immigrant Cultures: Builders of a Nation.* 2 vols. New York: Macmillan Reference, 1997.

Magocsi, Paul Robert, ed. *Encyclopedia of Canada's Peoples.* Toronto: Multicultural History Society of Ontario, University of Toronto Press, 1999.

Miller, E. Willard, and Ruby M. Miller. *United States Immigration: A Reference Handbook.* Santa Barbara, Calif.: ABC-CLIO, 1996.

Noble, Allen G., ed. *To Build in a New Land: Ethnic Landscapes in North America.* Baltimore: Johns Hopkins University Press, 1992.

Pozzetta, George E. *American Immigration and Ethnicity.* 20 vols. New York: Garland Publishing, 1990–91.

Rodriguez, Junius P. *The Historical Encyclopedia of World Slavery.* Santa Barbara, Calif.: ABC-CLIO, 1997.

Thernstrom, Stephen, ed. *Harvard Encyclopedia of American Ethnic Groups.* Cambridge, Mass.: Belknap Press, Harvard University Press, 1980.

ATLASES

Allen, James Paul, and Eugene Turner. *We the People: An Atlas of America's Ethnic Diversity.* New York: Macmillan, 1988.

Asante, M., and M. Mattson. *The Historical and Cultural Atlas of African Americans.* New York: Macmillan, 1992.

Shinagawa, Larry H., and Michel Lang. *Atlas of American Diversity.* Walnut Creek, Calif.: AltaMira Press, 1998.

Tanner, Helen H., et al., eds. *The Settling of North America: The Atlas of the Great Migrations into North America from the Ice Age to the Present.* New York: Macmillan, 1995.

NORTH AMERICAN STUDIES

Canada

Abu-Laban, Yasmee. *Selling Diversity: Immigration, Multiculturalism in Canada.* Toronto: Broadview Press, 2002.

Adelman, Howard, et al., eds. *Immigration and Refugee Policy: Australia and Canada Compared.* 2 vols. Toronto: Centre for Refugee Studies, York University, 1994.

Beaujot, Roderic. *Population Change in Canada.* Toronto: McClelland and Stewart, 1991.

Behiels, Michael D. *Quebec and the Question of Immigration: From Ethnocentrism to Ethnic Pluralism, 1900–1985.* Ottawa: Canadian Historical Association, 1991.

Berry, J. W., and J. A. Laponce, eds. *Ethnicity and Culture in Canada: The Research Landscape.* Toronto: University of Toronto Press, 1994.

Bissoondath, Neil. *Selling Illusions: The Cult of Multiculturalism in Canada.* Toronto: Penguin, 1984.

Bothwell, Robert, Ian Drummond, and John English. *Canada.* 2 vols. Rev. ed. Toronto: University of Toronto Press, 1987, 1989.

Broadfoot, Barry. *The Immigrant Years: From Europe to Canada, 1945–1967.* Vancouver, Canada, and Toronto: Douglas and McIntyre, 1986.

Bumsted, J. M. *Canada's Diverse Peoples: A Reference Sourcebook.* Santa Barbara, Calif.: ABC-CLIO, 2003.

Burnet, Jean R., with Harold Palmer. *"Coming Canadians": An Introduction to a History of Canada's Peoples.* Toronto: McClelland and Stewart, 1989.

Campbell, Charles M. *Betrayal and Deceit: The Politics of Canadian Immigration.* West Vancouver, Canada: Jasmine Books, 2000.

Canadian Human Rights Foundation. *Multiculturalism and the Charter: A Legal Perspective.* Toronto: Carswell, 1987.

Constantine, Stephen, ed. *Emigrants and Empire: British Settlement in the Dominions between the Wars.* Manchester, U.K., and New York: Manchester University Press, 1990.

Corbett, David C. *Canada's Immigration Policy: A Critique.* Toronto: University of Toronto Press, 1957.

Cowan, Helen I. *British Emigration to British North America: The First Hundred Years.* Rev. ed. Toronto: University of Toronto Press, 1961.

Dirks, Gerald E. *Controversy and Complexity: Canadian Immigration Policy during the 1980s.* Montreal and Kingston: McGill–Queen's University Press, 1995.

Drieder, Leo, ed. *Multi-Ethnic Canada: Identities and Inequalities.* Toronto: Oxford University Press, 1996.

Fieras, Augie. *Engaging Diversity: Multiculturalism in Canada.* 2d ed. Scarborough, Canada: Nelson Thomson Learning, 2001.

Guillet, Edwin C. *The Great Migration: The Atlantic Crossing by Sailing-Ship, 1770–1860.* 2d ed. Toronto: University of Toronto Press, 1963.

Halli, Shiva S., and Leo Drieder, eds. *Immigrant Canada: Demographic, Economic and Social Challenges.* Toronto: University of Toronto Press, 1999.

Hawkins, Freda. *Canada and Immigration: Public Policy and Public Concern.* 2d ed. Kingston, Canada: McGill–Queen's University Press, 1988.

Hoerder, Dirk. *Creating Societies: Immigrant Lives in Canada.* Montreal and Kingston: McGill–Queen's University Press, 1999.

Iacovetta, Franca. *A Nation of Immigrants: Women, Workers and Communities in Canadian History, 1840s–1960s.* Toronto: University of Toronto Press, 1998.

———. *The Writing of English Canadian Immigrant History.* Ottawa: Canadian Historical Association, 1997.

Knowles, Valerie. *Strangers at Our Gates: Canadian Immigration and Immigration Policy, 1540–1997.* Rev. ed. Toronto: Dundurn Press, 1997.

Li, Peter S., B. Singh Bolaria, and John Boyko, eds. *Racial Minorities in Multicultural Canada.* Toronto: Garamond Press, 1983.

Macdonald, Norman. *Canada: Immigration and Colonization, 1841–1903.* Toronto: Macmillan of Canada, 1966.

Martel, Marcel. *French Canada: An Account of Its Creation and Break-up, 1850–1967.* Ottawa: Canadian Historical Association, l998.

Palmer, Howard. *Ethnicity and Politics in Canada since Confederation.* Ottawa: Canadian Historical Association, 1991.

Richmond, Anthony. *Immigration and Ethnic Conflict.* New York: St. Martin's Press, 1988.

———. *Post-War Immigrants in Canada.* Toronto: University of Toronto Press, 1967.

Timlin, Mabel F. *Does Canada Need More People?* Toronto: Oxford University Press, 1951.

Troper, Harold Martin. *Only Farmers Need Apply: Official Canadian Government Encouragement of Immigration from the United States, 1896–1911.* Toronto: Griffin House, 1972.

Whitaker, Reginald. *Canadian Immigration Policy since Confederation.* Ottawa: Canadian Historical Association, 1991.

———. *Double Standard: The Secret History of Canadian Immigration.* Toronto: Lester and Orpen Dennys, 1987.

United States

Archdeacon, Thomas J. *Becoming American: An Ethnic History.* New York: Free Press, 1983.

Barkan, Elliott R. *And Still They Come: Immigrants and American Society 1920 to the 1990s.* Wheeling, Ill.: Harlan Davidson, 1996.

Bodnar, John. *The Transplanted: A History of Urban Immigrants.* Bloomington: Indiana University Press, 1985.

Bouvier, Leon F., ed. *U.S. Immigration in the 1980s: Reappraisal and Reform.* Boulder, Colo.: Westview Press, 1988.

Cordasco, Francesco, and David Nelson Alloway. *American Ethnic Groups, the European Heritage: A Bibliography of Doctoral Dissertations Completed at American Universities.* Metuchen, N.J.: Scarecrow Press, 1981.

Daniels, Roger. *Coming to America. A History of Race and Ethnicity in American Life,* 2d ed. New York: HarperCollins, 2002.

Dinnerstein, Leonard, Roger L. Nichols, and David M. Reimers. *Natives and Strangers: A Multicultural History of Americans.* New York: Oxford University Press, 1997.

Dinnerstein, Leonard, and David M. Reimers. *Ethnic Americans: A History of Immigration.* 4th ed. New York: Columbia University Press, 1999.

Divine, Robert A. *American Immigration Policy.* New Haven, Conn.: Yale University Press, 1957.

Fuchs, Lawrence H. *The American Kaleidoscope: Race, Ethnicity and the Civic Culture.* Hanover, N.H.: Wesleyan, 1990.

Gleason, Philip. "Trouble in the Colonial Melting Pot." *Journal of American Ethnic History* 20 (Fall 2000): 3–17.

Handlin, Oscar. *The Uprooted: The Epic Story of the Great Migrations That Made the American People.* 2d ed. Philadelphia: University of Pennsylvania Press, 2002.

Jacobson, David, ed. *Immigration Reader: America in a Multidisciplinary Perspective.* Malden, Mass.: Blackwell, 1998.

Jones, Maldwyn Allen. *American Immigration.* Chicago: University of Chicago Press, 1960.

Kennedy, John F. *A Nation of Immigrants.* Rev. and enlarged ed. New York: Harpers, 1964.

Kettner, James H. *The Development of American Citizenship, 1608–1870.* Chapel Hill: University of North Carolina Press, 1978.

Kivisto, Peter. *Americans All: Race and Ethnic Relations in Historical, Structural, and Comparative Perspectives.* Belmont, Calif.: Wadsworth, 1995.

Kraut, Alan. *The Huddled Masses: The Immigrant in American Society, 1880–1921.* 2d ed. Arlington Heights, Ill.: Harlan Davidson, 2001.

Laham, Nicholas. *Ronald Reagan and the Politics of Immigration Reform.* Westport, Conn.: Praeger, 2000.

Law, Anna O. "The Diversity Visa Lottery—A Cycle of Unintended Consequences in United States Immigration Policy." *Journal of American Ethnic History* 21 (Summer 2002): 1–29.

Le May, Michael, and Elliot Robert Barkan. *U.S. Immigration and Naturalization Laws and Issues.* Westport, Conn.: Praeger, 1999.

Olson, James S. *The Ethnic Dimension in American History.* 3d ed. Naugatuck, Conn.: Brandywine Press, 1999.

Pedraza, Silvia, and Rubén G. Rumbaut, eds. *Origins and Destinies: Immigration, Race, and Ethnicity in America.* Belmont, Calif.: Wadsworth, 1996.

Portes, Alejandro, and Rubén G. Rumbaut. *Immigrant America: A Portrait.* 2d ed. Berkeley: University of California Press, 1995.

———. *Legacies: The Story of the Immigrant Second Generation.* Berkeley: University of California Press, 2001.

Potter, J. "The Growth of Population in America, 1700–1860." In *Population in History: Essays in Historical Demography.* Eds. David V. Glass and D. E. C. Eversley. Chicago: Aldine, 1972.

Pozzetta, George E., ed. *Themes in Immigration History.* New York: Garland, 1991.

Reimers, David M. *Still the Golden Door: The Third World Comes to America.* 2d ed. New York: Columbia University Press, 1992.

———. *Unwelcome Strangers: American Identity and the Turn against Immigration.* New York: Columbia University Press, 1998.

Schmidley, Dianne. *The Foreign-Born Population in the United States: March 2002.* Current Population Reports, P20-539. Washington, D.C.: U.S. Census Bureau, 2003.

Solomon, Barbara Miller. *Ancestors and Immigrants.* Cambridge, Mass.: Harvard University Press, 1956.

Sowell, Thomas. *Ethnic America: A History.* New York: Basic Books, 1981.

Stewart, Barbara McDonald. *United States Government Policy on Refugees from Nazism, 1933–1940.* New York: Garland, 1992.

Takaki, Ronald. *A Different Mirror: A History of Multicultural America.* Boston: Little, Brown, 1993.

Ueda, Reed. *Postwar Immigrant America: A Social History.* Boston: Bedford Books, 1994.

Vecoli, Rudolph. "An Inter-Ethnic Perspective on American Immigration History." In *Swedes in America: Intercultural and Interethnic Perpectives on Contemporary Research.* Ed. Ulf Beijbom. Vaxjo, Sweden: Swedish Emigrant Institute, 1993.

Waldinger, Roger. *Strangers at the Gates: New Immigrants in Urban America.* Berkeley: University of California Press, 2001.

Ward, David. *Poverty, Ethnicity, and the American City, 1840–1925.* Cambridge: Cambridge University Press, 1989.

Warren, Robert, and Ellen Percy Kraly. *The Elusive Exodus: Emigration from the United States.* Washington, D.C.: Population Reference Bureau, 1985.

Watkins, Susan Cotts, ed. *After Ellis Esland: Newcomers and Natives in the 1910 Census.* New York: Russell Sage Publications, 1994.

Wells, Robert V. *The Population of the British Colonies in America before 1776: A Survey of Census Data.* Princeton, N.J.: Princeton University Press, 1975.

Woodsworth, James S. *Strangers within Our Gates.* 1909. Reprint, Toronto: University of Toronto Press, 1972.

Ziegler, Bernard M., ed. *Immigration: An American Dilemma.* Boston: D. C. Heath, 1953.

REGIONAL STUDIES

(For specific immigrant groups, see A–Z article bibliographies.)

Africa (sub-Saharan)

Arthur, John A. *Invisible Sojourners: African Immigrant Diaspora in the United States.* Westport, Conn.: Praeger, 2000.

Carstensen, Edward. *Propositions for the Organisation of an African Emigration and Immigration.* Copenhagen, Denmark: H. H. Thiele, 1869.

Edy, Carolyn Martindale. "Recent African Immigration to the United States." M.A. thesis, University of North Carolina at Chapel Hill, 1997.

Gordon, April. "The New Diaspora—African Immigration to the United States." *Journal of Third World Studies* 15, no. 1 (1998): 79–103.

Kamya, Hugo A. "African Immigrants in the United States: The Challenge for Research and Practice." *Social Work* 42, no. 2 (March 1997): 154–165.

Makinwa-Adebusoye, P. K. "Emigraton Dynamics in West Africa." *International Migration* 33, nos. 3–4 (1995): 435–467.

Mundende, Darlington Chongo. "African Immigration to Canada since World War II." M.A. thesis, University of Alberta, 1982.

Orr, Robert J. *African Refugees and Canada's Immigration Policy.* Halifax, Canada: Centre for African Studies, Dalhousie University, 1984.

Speer, Tibbett. "The Newest African Americans Aren't Black." *American Demographics* 16, no. 1 (January 1994): 9–10.

Takougang, Joseph. "Recent African Immigrants to the United States: A Historical Perspective." *Western Journal of Black Studies* 19, no. 1 (Spring 1995): 50–57.

University of Michigan, Center for African and Afro-American Studies. *Black Immigration and Ethnicity in the United States: An Annotated Bibliography.* Westport, Conn.: Greenwood Press, 1985.

Wilson, Jill Huttar. "Africans on the Move: A Descriptive Geography of African Immigration to the United States with a Focus on Metropolitan Washington, D.C." M.A. thesis, Georgetown University, 2003.

Asia

Aguilar-San Juan, Karin, ed. *The State of Asian America: Activism and Resistance in the 1990s.* Boston: South End Press, 1994.

Barkan, Elliott R. "Whom Shall We Integrate? A Comparative Analysis of the Immigration and Naturalization Trends of Asians before and after the 1965 Immigration Act (1951–1978)." *Journal of American Ethnic History* 1, no. 3 (Fall 1983): 29–57.

Barringer, Herbert R., Robert W. Gardner, and Michael J. Leven. *Asians and Pacific Islanders in the United States.* New York: Russell Sage Foundation, 1993.

Begum, Jameela, and B. Hariharan, eds. *Canadian Diaspora: Asia-Pacific Immigration.* New Delhi, India: Creative Books, 2001.

Buchignani, Norman, and Doreen M. Indra, with Ram Srivastava. *Continuous Journey: A Social History of South Asians in Canada.* Toronto: McClelland and Stewart, 1985.

Chan, Sucheng. *Asian Americans: An Interpretative History.* Boston: Twayne, 1991.

Daniels, Roger. *Asian America: Chinese and Japanese in the United States since 1850.* Seattle: University of Washington Press, 1988.

Fawcett, James, and Benjamin Carino, eds. *Pacific Bridges, The New Immigration from Asia and the Pacific Islands.* Staten Island, N.Y.: Center for Migration Studies, 1987.

Foner, Philip, and Daniel Rosenberg. *Racism, Dissent, and Asian Americans from 1850 to the Present.* Westport, Conn.: Greenwood Press, 1993.

Fong, Timothy P. *The Contemporary Asian American Experience: Beyond the Model Minority.* Upper Saddle River, N.J.: Prentice Hall, 1998.

Gall, Susan B., and Timothy L. Gall, eds. *Statistical Record of Asian Americans.* Detroit: Gale, 1993.

Haines, David W., ed. *Refugees as Immigrants: Cambodians, Laotians, and Vietnamese in America.* Totowa, N.J.: Rowman and Littlefield, 1989.

Hamamato, Darrel Y., and Rodolfo E. Torres, eds. *New American Destinies: A Reader in Contemporary Asian Immigration.* New York: Routledge, 1997.

Hein, Jeremy. *From Vietnam, Laos, and Cambodia: A Refugee Experience in the United States.* New York: Twayne, 1995.

Hing, Bill Ong. *Making and Remaking Asian America through Immigration Policy, 1850–1990.* Stanford, Calif.: Stanford University Press, 1993.

Jackson, Carl T. *Vedanta for the West: The Ramakrishna Movement in the United States.* Bloomington: Indiana University Press, 1994.

Karnow, Stanley, and Nancy Yoshihara. *Asian Americans in Transition.* New York: Asia Society, 1992.

Kitano, Harry H. L., and Roger Daniels. *Asian Americans: Emerging Minorities.* Englewood Cliffs, N.J.: Prentice Hall, 1988.

Kitano, Harry H. L., and Sue Stanley. "The Model Minorities." *Journal of Social Issues* 29 (1973): 1–9.

Kurian, George, and Ram P. Srivastava. *Overseas Indians: A Study in Adaptation.* New Delhi, India: Vikas, 1983.

La Brack, Bruce. "South Asians." In *A Nation of Peoples: A Sourcebook on America's Multicultural Heritage.* Ed. Elliott Robert Barkan. Westport, Conn.: Greenwood Press, 1999.

Laquian, Eleanor, Aprodicio Laquian, and Terry McGee, eds. *The Silent Debate: Asian Immigration and Racism in Canada.* Vancouver, Canada: Institute of Asian Research, University of British Columbia, 1998.

Leonard, Karen Isaksen. *The South Asian Americans.* Westport, Conn.: Greenwood Press, 1997.

Melendy, H. Brett. *Asians in America: Filipinos, Koreans and East Indians.* Boston: Twayne, 1977.

Min, Pyong Gap, ed. *Asian Americans: Contemporary Trends and Issues.* Thousand Oaks, Calif.: Sage Publications, 1995.

Reimers, David M. *Still the Golden Door: The Third World Comes to America.* New York: Columbia University Press, 1985.

Rose, Peter I. "Asian Americans: From Pariahs to Paragons." *Clamor at the Gates: New American Immigration.* Ed. Nathan Glazer. San Francisco: ICS Press, 1985.

Singh, Jane, et al., eds. *South Asians in North America: An Annotated and Selected Bibliography.* Occasional Paper no. 14. Berkeley, Calif.: Center for South and Southeast Asia Studies, 1988.

Takaki, Ronald. *Strangers from a Different Shore: A History of Asian Americans.* Boston: Little, Brown, 1989.

Walker-Moffat, Wendy. *The Other Side of the Asian American Success Story.* San Francisco: Jossey-Bass, 1995.

The Caribbean

Gmelch, George. *Double Passage: The Lives of Caribbean Migrants Abroad and Back Home.* Ann Arbor: University of Michigan Press, 1992.

Kasinitz, Philip, and Milton Vickerman. "West Indians/Caribbeans." In *A Nation of Peoples: A Sourcebook on America's Multicultural Heritage.* Ed. Elliott Robert Barkan. Westport, Conn.: Greenwood Press, 1999.

Palmer, Ransford W. *In Search of a Better Life: Perspectives on Migration from the Caribbean.* New York: Praeger, 1990.

———. *Pilgrims from the Sun: West Indian Migration to America.* New York: Twayne, 1995.

Stinner, William, Klaus de Albuquerque, and Roy Bryce-Laporte, eds. *Return Migration and Remittances: Developing a Caribbean Perspective.* Washington, D.C.: Research Institute on Immigration and Ethnic Studies, Smithsonian Institution, 1982.

Vickerman, Milton. *Crosscurrents: West Indian Immigrants and Race.* New York: Oxford University Press, 1998.

Waters, Mary C. *Black Identities: West Indian Immigrant Dreams and American Realities.* Cambridge, Mass.: Harvard University Press, 1999.

Watkins-Owens, Irma. *Blood Relations: Caribbean Immigrants and the Harlem Community, 1900–1930.* Bloomington: Indiana University Press, 1996.

Europe

Bailyn, Bernard. *The Peopling of British North America: An Introduction.* New York: Alfred A. Knopf, 1986.

Baines, Dudley. *Immigration from Europe, 1815–1930.* Houndmills, U.K.: Macmillan Education, 1991.

Broadfoot, Barry. *The Immigrant Years: From Europe to Canada, 1945–1967.* Vancouver, Canada, and Toronto: Douglas and McIntyre, 1986.

Fleming, Donald, and Bernard Bailyn. *The Intellectual Migration: Europe and America, 1930–1960.* Cambridge, Mass.: Belknap Press, Harvard University Press, 1969.

Handlin, Oscar. *The Uprooted.* 2d ed. Boston: Little, Brown, 1973.

Jacobson, Matthew Frye. *Special Sorrows: The Diasporic Imagination of Irish, Polish, and Jewish Immigrants in the United States.* Cambridge, Mass.: Harvard University Press, 1995.

Luebke, Frederick C., ed. *European Immigrants in the American West: Community Histories.* Albuquerque: University of New Mexico Press, 1998.

Morawska, Ewa T. "East Europeans on the Move." In *The Cambridge Survey of World Migrations.* Ed. Robin Cohen. Cambridge: Cambridge University Press, 1996.

———. *For Bread with Butter: The Life-Worlds of East Central Europeans in Johnstown, Pennsylvania, 1890–1940.* New York: Cambridge University Press, 1985.

Mormino, Gary, and George Pozzetta. *The Immigrant World of Ybor City: Italians and Their Latin Neighbors in Tampa, 1885–1995.* Urbana: University of Illinois Press, 1987.

Nugent, Walter. *Crossings: The Great Transatlantic Migrations, 1870–1914.* Bloomington: Indiana University Press, 1992.

Portis-Winner, Irene, and R. Susel, eds. *The Dynamics of East European Ethnicity Outside of Eastern Europe with Special Emphasis on the American Case.* Cambridge, Mass.: Schenkman, 1983.

Puskas, Julianna. *Overseas Migration from East-Central and Southeastern Europe, 1880–1940.* Budapest: Hungarian Academy of Sciences, 1990.

Radzilowski, Thaddeus C., and John Radzilowski. "East Europeans." In *A Nation of Peoples: A Sourcebook on America's Multicultural Heritage.* Ed. Elliott Robert Barkan. Westport, Conn.: Greenwood Press, 1999.

Saveth, Edward N. *American Historians and European Immigrants, 1875–1925.* New York: Columbia University Press, 1948.

Taylor, Philip. *Distant Magnet: European Emigration to the U.S.A.* New York: Harper and Row, 1971.

Vecoli, Rudolph J., and Suzanne Sinke, eds. *A Century of European Migrations, 1830–1930.* Urbana: Illinois University Press, 1991.

Wyman, Mark. *DP: Europe's Displaced Persons, 1945–1951.* Philadelphia: Balch Institute, 1985.

———. *Round-Trip to America: The Immigrants Return to Europe, 1880–1930.* Ithaca, N.Y.: Cornell University Press, 1993.

Mexico, Central America, and South America

Bean, Frank D., and Marta Tienda. *The Hispanic Population of the United States.* New York: Russell Sage Foundation, 1988.

Bonilla, Frank, et al., eds. *Borderless Borders: U.S. Latinos, Latin Americans, and the Paradox of Interdependence.* Philadelphia: Temple University Press, 1998.

Camarillo, Albert. "Latin Americans: Mexican Americans and Central Americans." In *Encyclopedia of American Social History.* Vol. 2. Eds. Mary K. Cayton, et al. New York: Scribner, 1993.

Chávez, Leo. "Borders and Bridges: Undocumented Immigrants from Mexico and Central America." In *Origins and Destinies: Immigration, Race, and Ethnicity in America.* Eds. Silvia Pedraza and Rubén G. Rumbaut. Belmont, Calif.: Wadsworth, 1996.

Córdova, Carlos B., and Jorge del Pinal. *Hispanics-Latinos: Diverse People in a Multicultural Society.* Washington, D.C.: National Association of Hispanic Publications, 1996.

Davis, Mike. *Magical Urbanism: Latinos Reinvent the U.S. City.* New York: Verso, 2000.

Haas, Lisbeth. *Conquests and Historical Identities in California, 1769–1936.* Berkeley: University of California Press, 1995.

Hamilton, Nora, and Norma Stoltz Chincilla. "Central American Migration: A Framework for Analysis." In *Latin American Research Review* 26 (1991): 75–110.

Horner, Louise L., ed. *Hispanic Americans: A Statistical Sourcebook, 2000.* Palo Alto, Calif.: Information Publications, 2000.

Lomelí, Francisco, ed. *Handbook of Hispanic Cultures in the United States: Literature and Art.* 2 vols. Houston, Tex.: Arte Público Press, 1993.

Maciel, David R., and María Herrera-Sobek, eds. *Culture across Borders: Mexican Immigration and Popular Culture.* Tucson: University of Arizona Press, 1998.

Mahler, Sarah J. *America Dreaming: Immigrant Life on the Margins.* Princeton, N.J.: Princeton University Press, 1995.

Monroy, Douglas. *Thrown among Strangers: The Making of Mexican Culture in Frontier California.* Berkeley: University of California Press, 1990.

Mormino, Gary, and George Pozzetta. *The Immigrant World of Ybor City: Italians and Their Latin Neighbors in Tampa, 1885–1995.* Urbana: University of Illinois Press, 1987.

Reimers, David M. *Still the Golden Door: The Third World Comes to America.* New York: Columbia University Press, 1985.

Saltzinger, Leslie. "A Maid by Any Other Name: The Transformation of 'Dirty Work' by Central American Immigrants." In *Ethnography Unbound: Power and Resistance in the Modern Metropolis.* Ed. Michael Buroway. Berkeley: University of California Press, 1991.

Smith, Carter, III, and David Lindroth. *Hispanic-American Experience On File.* New York: Facts On File, 1999.

Weber, David J. *The Mexican Frontier, 1821–1846.* Albuquerque: University of New Mexico Press, 1982.

The Middle East

Abu-Laban, Baha. *An Olive Branch on the Family Tree: The Arabs in Canada.* Toronto: McClelland and Stewart, 1980.

Elkholy, Abdo A. *The Arab Moslems in the United States: Religion and Assimilation.* New Haven, Conn.: College and University Press, 1966.

Haddad, Yvonne Yazbeck. *The Muslims of America.* New York: Oxford University Press, 1991.

Haddad, Yvonne Yazbeck, and Jane Idleman Smith, eds. *Muslim Communities in North America.* Albany: State University of New York Press, 1994.

Hooglund, Eric J., ed. *Crossing the Waters: Arabic-Speaking Immigrants to the United States before 1940.* Washington, D.C.: Smithsonian Institution Press, 1987.

Mehdi, Beverlee Turner, ed. *The Arabs in America, 1492–1977: A Chronology and Fact Book.* Dobbs Ferry, N.Y.: Oceana, 1978.

Metcalf, Barbara Daly. *Making Muslim Space in North America and Europe.* Berkeley: University of California Press, 1996.

Naff, Alixa. *Becoming American: The Early Arab American Experience.* Carbondale: Southern Illinois University Press, 1985.

Nyang, Sulayman. *Islam in the United States of America.* Chicago: Kazi Publications, 1999.

Orfalea, Gregory. *Before the Flames: A Quest for the History of Arab Americans.* Austin: University of Texas Press, 1988.

Sawaie, Mohammed, ed. *Arabic-Speaking Immigrants in the United States and Canada: A Bibliographic Guide with Annotation.* Lexington, Ky.: Mazda Publishers, 1985.

Shain, Yossi. *Arab-Americans in the 1990's: What Next for the Diaspora?* Tel Aviv, Israel: Tel Aviv University, Tami Steinmetz Center for Peace Research, 1996.

Walbridge, Linda S. "Middle Easterners and North Africans." In *A Nation of Peoples: A Sourcebook on America's Multicultural Heritage.* Ed. Elliott Robert Barkan. Westport, Conn.: Greenwood Press, 1999.

Waugh, Earle H., et al., eds. *Muslim Families in North America.* Edmonton, Canada: University of Alberta Press, 1991.

Topical Studies

Agriculture

Barger, W. K., and Ernesto Reza. *The Farm Labor Movement in the Midwest.* Austin: University of Texas Press, 1994.

Billington, Ray Allen. *Land of Savagery, Land of Promise: The European Image of the American Frontier in the Nineteenth Century.* New York: W. W. Norton, 1981.

Cardoso, Lawrence A. "Labor Emigration to the Southwest, 1916–1920: Mexican Attitudes and Policy." *Southwestern Historical Quarterly* 79 (1979): 400–416.

Chan, Sucheng. *This Bittersweet Soil: The Chinese in California Agriculture, 1860–1910.* Berkeley: University of California Press, 1986.

Cheng, Lucy, and Edna Bonacich, eds. *Labor Immigration under Capitalism: Asian Workers in the United States before World War II.* Berkeley: University of California Press, 1984.

Chiu, Ping. *Chinese Labor in California, 1850–1880: An Economic Study.* Madison: State Historical Society of Wisconsin, 1963.

Daniel, Clete. *Bitter Harvest: A History of California Farm Workers, 1870–1941.* Berkeley: University of California Press, 1982.

Department of Labor. *U.S. Farmworkers in the Post-IRCA Period: Based on Data from the National Agricultural Workers Survey (NAWS).* Washington, D.C.: Department of Labor, 1993.

DeWitt, Howard A. *Violence in the Fields: Filipino Farm Labor Unionization during the Great Depression.* Saratoga, Calif.: Century Twenty-One Publishing, 1980.

Driscoll, Barbara A. *The Tracks North: The Railroad Bracero Program of World War II.* Austin: University of Texas Press, 1999.

Dunne, John Gregory. *Delano: The Story of the California Grape Strike.* New York: Farrar, Straus and Giroux, 1967.

Ferris, Susan, and Ricardo Sandoval. *The Fight in the Fields: Cesar Chavez and the Farmworkers Movement.* New York: Harcourt Brace Jovanovich, 1997.

Foley, Douglas. *Learning Capitalist Culture: Deep in the Heart of Tejas.* Philadelphia: University of Pennsylvania Press, 1990.

Gamboa, Erasmo. *Mexican Labor and World War II: Braceros in the Pacific Northwest, 1942–1947.* Austin: University of Texas Press, 1990.

González, Gilbert C. *Labor and Community: Mexican Citrus Worker Villages in a Southern California County, 1900–1950.* Urbana: University of Illinois Press, 1994.

Guerin-Gonzáles, Camille. *Mexican Workers and American Dreams: Immigration, Repatriation and California Farm Labor, 1900–1939.* New Brunswick, N.J.: Rutgers University Press, 1994.

Hahamovitch, Cindy. *The Fruits of Their Labor: Atlantic Coast Farmworkers and the Making of Migrant Poverty, 1870–1945.* Chapel Hill: University of North Carolina Press, 1977.

Hine, Robert V. *Community on the American Frontier: Separate but Not Alone.* Norman: University of Oklahoma Press, 1980.

Jenkins, J. Craig. *The Politics of Insurgency: The Farm Worker Movement in the 1960s.* New York: Columbia University Press, 1985.

Kiser, George C., and Martha W. Kiser. *Mexican Workers in the United States.* Albuquerque: University of New Mexico Press, 1979.

McWilliams, Carey. *Factories in the Fields: The Story of Migratory Labor in California.* 1939. Reprint, Berkeley: University of California Press, 1999.

Noble, Allen G. *To Build in a New Land: Ethnic Landscapes in North America.* Baltimore: Johns Hopkins University Press, 1992.

Pfeffer, Max. "Social Origins of Three Systems of Farm Production in the United States." *Rural Sociology* 48, no. 4 (1983): 540–562.

Pozzetta, George E., ed. *Immigrants on the Land: Agriculture, Rural Life, and Small Towns.* New York: Garland, 1991.

Rasmussen, Wayne D. *A History of the Emergency Farm Labor Supply Program, 1943–1947.* Washington, D.C.: GPO, 1951.

Sylvester, Kenneth. *The Limits of Rural Capitalism: Family, Culture, and Markets, Montcalm, Manitoba, 1870–1940.* Toronto: University of Toronto Press, 2000.

Troper, Harold Martin. *Only Farmers Need Apply: Official Canadian Government Encouragement of Immigration from the United States, 1896–1911.* Toronto: Griffin House, 1972.

Valdés, Dennis Nodin. *Al Norte: Agricultural Workers in the Great Lakes Region, 1917–1970.* Austin: University of Texas Press, 1991.

Weber, Devra. *Dark Sweat, White Gold: California Farm Workers, Cotton, and the New Deal.* Berkeley: University of California Press, 1994.

Arts and Culture

Antush, John, ed. *Recent Puerto Rican Theater: Five Plays from New York.* Houston, Tex.: Arte Público Press, 1991.

Barolini, Helen. *The Dream Book: An Anthology of Writings by Italian American Women.* New York: Schocken Books, 1985.

Cortina, Rodolfo, ed. *Cuban American Theater.* Houston, Tex.: Arte Público Press, 1991.

Ebersole, Robert. *Black Pagoda.* Gainesville: University of Florida Press, 1957.

Ellen, M. M., ed. *Across the Atlantic: An Anthology of Cape Verdean Literature.* North Dartmouth: Center for the Portuguese-Speaking World, University of Massachusetts, 1988.

Erdman, Harley. *Staging the Jew: The Performance of American Ethnicity.* New Brunswick, N.J.: Rutgers University Press, 1962.

Expressions of Islam in Buildings. Proceedings of an international seminar held in Jakarta and Yogyakarta, October 15–19, 1990. Jakarta, Indonesia: Aga Khan Trust for Cultures, 1990.

Friedman, Lester D., ed. *Unspeakable Images: Ethnicity and the American Cinema.* Chicago: University of Illinois Press, 1991.

Gardaphe, Fred. *Italian Signs, American Streets: the Evolution of the Italian American Narrative.* Durham, N.C.: Duke University Press, 1996.

Green, Rose Basile. *The Italian-American Novel.* Rutherford, N.J.: Fairleigh Dickinson University Press, 1974.

Hamamoto, Darrell Y. *Monitored Peril: Asian Americans and the Politics of TV Representation.* Minneapolis: University of Minnesota Press, 1994.

Houston, Velina, ed. *The Politics of Life: Four Plays by Asian American Women.* Philadelphia: Temple University Press, 1993.

Huerta, Jorge. *Chicano Theater: Themes and Forms.* Tempe, Ariz.: Bilingual, 1982.

Jick, Leon A. *The Americanization of the Synagogue, 1820–1870.* Hanover, N.H.: University Press of New England, 1976.

Jones, Dorothy P. *The Portrayal of China and India on the American Screen, 1896–1955: The Evolution of Chinese and Indian Themes, Locales, and Characters as Portrayed on the American Screen.* Cambridge, Mass.: Center for International Studies, MIT, 1955.

Kahera, Akel Ismail. "Image, Text and Form: Complexities of Aesthetics in an American Mosque." *Studies in Contemporary Islam* 1, no. 2 (1999): 73–85.

Kanellos, Nicolas. *Hispanic Theatre in the United States.* Houston, Tex.: Arte Público Press, 1984.

———. *A History of Hispanic Theatre in the United States: Origins to 1940.* Austin: University of Texas Press, 1990.

———. *Mexican-American Theatre: Then and Now.* Houston, Tex.: Arte Público Press, 1983.

Karanikas, A. *Hellenes and Hellions: Modern Greek Characters in American Literature.* Urbana: University of Illinois Press, 1981.

Karni, Michael G., and A. Jarvenpaa, eds. *Sampo the Magic Mill: A Collection of Finnish-American Writings.* Minneapolis, Minn.: New River, 1989.

Knippling, Alpana Sharma. *New Immigrant Literature in the United States: A Sourcebook to Our Multicultural Literary Heritage.* Westport, Conn.: Greenwood Press, 1996.

Kochar-Lindgren, Kanta. "Arts I: Literature." In *Encyclopedia of American Immigration.* Vol. 2. Ed. James Ciment. Armonk, N.Y.: Sharpe Reference, 2001.

Lester, Paul M., ed. *Images That Injure: Pictorial Stereotypes in the Media.* Westport, Conn.: Praeger, 1996.

Lomelí, Francisco, ed. *Handbook of Hispanic Cultures in the United States.* Houston, Tex.: Arte Público Press, 1993.

Lowe, Lisa. *Immigrant Acts: On Asian American Cultural Politics.* Durham, N.C.: Duke University Press, 1996.

Maciel, David R., and María Herrera-Sobek, eds. *Culture across Borders: Mexican Immigration and Popular Culture.* Tucson: University of Arizona Press, 1998.

Marchetti, Gina. *Romance and the "Yellow Peril": Race, Sex and Discursive Strategies in Hollywood Fiction.* Berkeley: University of California Press, 1993.

Marcuson, Lewis R. *The Stage Immigrant: The Irish, Italians, and Jews in American Drama, 1920–1960.* New York: Garland Publishing, 1990.

Metcaff, Barbara Daly. *Making Muslim Space in North America and Europe.* Berkeley: University of California Press, 1996.

Morreale, Don, ed. *Buddhist America: Centers, Retreats, Practices.* Santa Fe, N.M.: John Muir Publications, 1988.

Muller, Gilbert. *New Strangers in Paradise: The Immigrant Experience and Contemporary American Fiction.* Lexington: University of Kentucky Press, 1999.

Parenti, Michael. "The Media Are the Mafia: Italian-American Images and the Ethnic Struggle." *National Review* 30, no. 10 (1979): 20–27.

Pozzetta, George E., ed. *Folklore, Culture, and the Immigrant Mind.* New York: Garland, 1991.

Raz, Ram. *Essay on the Architecture of the Hindus.* Delhi, India: Indological Book House, 1972.

Rogin, Michael. *Blackface, White Noise: Jewish Immigrants in the Hollywood Melting Pot.* Berkeley: University of California Press, 1996.

Seller, Maxine Schwartz, ed. *Ethnic Theatre in the United States.* Westport, Conn.: Greenwood Press, 1983.

Simone, Roberta. *The Immigrant Experience in American Fiction: An Annotated Bibliography.* Lanham, Md.: Scarecrow Press, 1995.

Tamburi, Anthony, Fred Gardaphe, and Paul Giordana. *From the Margin: Writings in Italian Americana.* West Lafayette, Ind.: Purdue University Press, 1991.

Torres, Sasha, ed. *Living Color: Race and Television in the United States.* Durham, N.C.: Duke University Press, 1998.

Wong, Sau-ling Cynthia. *Reading Asian American Literature: From Necessity to Extravagance.* Princeton, N.J.: Princeton University Press, 1993.

Economics and Business

Aguilera, Michael. "The Labor Market Outcomes of Undocumented and Documented Immigrants: A Social and Human Capital Comparison." Ph.D. diss., State University of New York–Stony Brook, 1999.

Bean, Frank, and Stephanie Bell-Rose. *Immigration and Opportunity: Race, Ethnicity, and Employment in the United States.* New York: Russell Sage Foundation, 1999.

Bonacich, Edna, and John Modell. *The Economic Basis of Ethnic Solidarity: Small Business in the Japanese-American Community.* Berkeley: University of California Press, 1980.

Borjas, George J. *Friends or Strangers: The Impact of Immigration on the American Economy.* New York: Basic Books, 1990.

———. *Heaven's Door: Immigration Policy and the American Economy.* Princeton, N.J.: Princeton University Press, 1999.

———, ed. *Issues in the Economics of Immigration.* Chicago and London: University of Chicago Press, 2000.

Camarota, Steven A. *Importing Poverty: Immigration's Impact on the Size and Growth of the Poor Population in the United States.* Washington, D.C.: Center for Immigration Studies, 1999.

Denoon, Donald. *Settler Capitalism: The Dynamics of Dependent Development in the Southern Hemisphere.* New York: Cambridge University Press, 1983.

DeVoretz, Don J., ed. *Diminishing Returns: The Economics of Canada's Recent Immigration Policy.* Toronto: C. D. Howe Institute and the Laurier Institution, 1995.

Furio, Colomba M. "An Abstract of Immigrant Women and Industry: A Case Study—the Italian Immigrant and the Garment Industry, 1880–1950." Ph.D. diss., New York University, 1979.

Hahamovitch, Cindy. "Creating Perfect Immigrants: Guestworkers of the World in Historical Perspective." *Labor History* 44 (February 2003): 69–95.

Hammermesh, Daniel S., and Frank D. Bean. *Help or Hindrance?: The Economic Implications of Immigration for*

African Americans. New York: Russell Sage Foundation, 1998.

Kiser, George C., and Martha W. Kiser, eds. *Mexican Workers in the United States: Historical and Political Perspectives.* Albuquerque: University of New Mexico Press, 1979.

Kwong, Peter. "Impact of Chinese Human Smuggling on the American Labor Market." In *Global Human Smuggling: Comparative Perspectives.* Eds. David Kyle and Rey Koslowski. Baltimore: Johns Hopkins University Press, 2001.

Light, Ivan. *Ethnic Enterprise in America: Business and Welfare among Chinese, Japanese and Blacks.* Berkeley: University of California Press, 1972.

Light, Ivan, and Stephen J. Gold. *Ethnic Economies.* San Diego, Calif.: Academic Press, 2000.

Light, Ivan, and Carolyn Rosenstein. *Race, Ethnicity, and Entrepreneurship in Urban America.* New York: Aldine de Gruyter, 1995.

Portes, Alejandro, ed. *The Economic Sociology of Immigration: The Essays on Networks, Ethnicity and Entrepreneurship.* New York: Russell Sage Foundation, 1995.

Sassen, Saskia. *The Mobility of Labor and Capital: A Study in International Investment and Labor Flow.* Cambridge: Cambridge University Press, 1988.

Smith, James R., and Barry Edmonston. *The New Americans: Economic, Demographic, and Fiscal Effects of Immigration.* Washington, D.C.: National Academy Press, 1997.

Waldinger, Roger D., et al. *Ethnic Entrepreneurs: Immigrant Business in Industrial Societies.* Newbury Park, Calif.: Sage, 1990.

Ward, Robert, and Richard Jenkins, eds. *Ethnic Communities in Business: Strategies for Economic Survival.* New York: Cambridge University Press, 1984.

Ethnic Associations

Attah-Poku, Agyemang. *The Social-Cultural Adjustment Question: The Role of Ghanaian Immigrant Ethnic Associations in America.* Brookfield, Vt.: Avebury, 1996.

Cummings, S., ed. *Self-Help in America: Patterns of Minority Economic Development.* Port Washington, N.Y.: Kennikat Press, 1980.

Jenkins, Shirley, ed. *Ethnic Associations and the Welfare State: Services to Immigrants in Five Countries.* New York: Columbia University Press, 1988.

Pozzetta, George E., ed. *Immigrant Institutions: The Organization of Immigrant Life.* New York: Garland, 1991.

Soyer, Daniel. *Jewish Immigrant Associations and American Identity in New York, 1880–1939.* Cambridge, Mass.: Harvard University Press, 1997.

Immigration Debate, 1990s onward

Barone, Michael. *The New Americans.* New York: Regnery, 2001.

Beck, Roy Howard. *The Case against Immigration: The Moral, Economic, Social, and Environmental Reasons for Reducing U.S. Immigration Back to Traditional Levels.* New York: W. W. Norton, 1996.

Berry, J. W., and J. A. Laponce, eds. *Ethnicity and Culture in Canada: The Research Landscape.* Toronto: University of Toronto Press, 1994.

Bissoondath, Neil. *Selling Illusions: The Cult of Multiculturalism in Canada.* Toronto: Penguin Books, 1994.

Briggs, Vernon M., Jr. *Mass Immigration and the National Interest.* Armonk, N.Y.: M. E. Sharpe, 1992.

Brimelow, Peter. *Alien Nation: Common Sense about America's Immigration Disaster.* New York: Random House, 1996.

Buchanan, Patrick J. *The Death of the West: How Dying Populations and Immigrant Invasions Imperil Our Country and Civilization.* New York: Dunne Books, 2001.

Campbell, Charles M. *Betrayal and Deceit: The Politics of Canadian Immigration.* West Vancouver, Canada: Jasmine Books, 2000.

Cornelius, Wayne, P. L. Martin, and J. E. Hollifield, eds. *Controlling Immigration: A Global Perspective.* Stanford, Calif.: Stanford University Press, 1994.

Current Controversies: Illegal Immigration. Farmington Hills, Mich.: Greenhaven Press, 2001.

Daniels, Roger, and Otis L. Graham. *Debating American Immigration.* Lanham, Md.: Rowman and Littlefield, 2001.

Dittgen, Herbert. "The American Debate about Immigration in the 1990s: A New Nationalism after the Cold War?" In *The American Nation, National Identity, Nationalism.* Ed. Knud Kraakau. New Brunswick, N.J.: Transaction, 1997.

Drieder, Leo, ed. *Multi-Ethnic Canada: Identities and Inequalities.* Toronto: Oxford University Press, 1996.

Dudley, William, ed. *Illegal Immigration: Opposing Viewpoints.* Farmington, Mich.: Greenhaven Press, 2002.

———. *Examining Issues through Political Cartoons: Illegal Immigration.* Farmington Hills, Mich.: Greenhaven Press, 2003.

Fieras, Augie. *Engaging Diversity: Multiculturalism in Canada.* 2d ed. Scarborough, Canada: Nelson Thomson Learning, 2001.

Foster, Lorne. *Turnstile Immigration: Multiculturalism, Social Order, and Social Justice in Canada.* Toronto: Thompson Educational Publishing, 1998.

Glazer, Nathan. *Clamor at the Gates: The New American Immigration.* San Francisco: Institute for Contemporary Studies, 1985.

———. *We Are All Multiculturalists Now.* Cambridge, Mass.: Harvard University Press, 1997.

Gwyn, Richard. *Nationalism without Walls: The Unbearable Lightness of Being Canadian.* Toronto: McClelland and Stewart, 1995.

Heer, David. *Immigration in America's Future: Social Science Findings and the Policy Debate.* Boulder, Colo.: Westview Press, 1996.

Importing Poverty. Washington, D.C.: Center for Immigration Studies, September 1999.

Isbister, John. *The Immigration Debate: Remaking America.* Bloomfield, Conn.: Kumarian Press, 1996.

Joppke, Christian. *Immigration and the Nation-State: The United States, Germany, and Great Britain.* Oxford: Oxford University Press, 1999.

———, ed. *Challenge to the Nation-State: Immigration in Western Europe and the United States.* New York: Oxford University Press, 1998.

Kazarian, Shahe. *Diversity Issues in Law Enforcement.* 2d ed. Toronto: Edmond Montgomery, 2001.

Kleinknecht, William. *The New Ethnic Mobs: The Changing Face of Organized Crime in America.* New York: Free Press, 1996.

Lenihan, Donald. *Leveraging over Diversity: Canada as a Learning Society.* Ottawa: Centre for Collaborative Government, 2001.

Li, Peter. *Destination Canada: Immigration Debates and Issues.* Toronto: Oxford University Press, 2002.

Malkin, Michelle. *Invasion: How America Still Welcomes Terrorists, Criminals, and Other Foreign Menaces to Our Shores.* Washington, D.C.: Regnery, 2002.

Millman, Joel. *The Other Americans.* New York: Viking, 1997.

Mills, Nicholas. *Arguing Immigration: The Debate over the Changing Face of America.* New York: Touchstone Books, 1994.

Moore, Joan, and Raquel Pinderhughes, eds. *In the Barrios: Latinos and the Underclass Debate.* New York: Russell Sage Foundation, 1993.

Roleff, Tamara L., ed. *Immigration: Opposing Viewpoints in World History.* Farmington Hills, Mich.: Greenhaven Press, 2004.

Simon, Rita J., and S. H. Alexander. *The Ambivalent Welcome: Print Media, Public Opinion, and Immigration.* Westport, Conn.: Praeger, 1993.

Tichenor, Daniel J. *Dividing Lines: The Politics of Immigration Control in America.* Princeton, N.J.: Princeton University Press, 2002.

Williamson, Chilton, Jr. *The Immigration Mystique: America's False Conscience.* New York: Basic Books, 1996.

Industry and Labor

Avery, Donald. *Reluctant Host: Canada's Response to Immigrant Workers, 1896–1994.* Toronto: McClelland and Stewart, 1995.

Barrett, James R. *Work and Community in the Jungle: Chicago's Packinghouse Workers.* Urbana: University of Illinois Press, 1987.

Briggs, Vernon, Jr. *Immigration Policy and the American Labor Force.* Baltimore: Johns Hopkins University Press, 1984.

Brody, David. *Workers in Industrial America: Essays in Twentieth Century Struggle.* 2d ed. New York: Oxford University Press, 1993.

Berthoff, Rowland Tappan. *British Immigrants in Industrial America: 1790–1950.* Cambridge, Mass.: Harvard University Press, 1953.

Cheng, Lucie, and Edna Bonacich, eds. *Labor Migration under Capitalism: Asian Workers in the United States before World War II.* Berkeley: University of California Press, 1984.

Cohen, Lizabeth. *Making a New Deal: Industrial Workers in Chicago, 1919–1939.* New York: Cambridge University Press, 1990.

Collomp, Catherine. "Immigrants, Labor Markets, and the State, a Comparative Approach: France and the United States, 1880–1930." *Journal of American History* 86 (June 1999): 41–66.

Commons, John R., et al., eds. *A Documentary History of American Industrial Society.* 11 vols. Cleveland, Ohio: A. H. Clark, 1910.

———. *History of Labor in the United States.* 4 vols. New York: Augustus M. Kelley Publishers, 1918–35.

Dubofsky, Melvyn. *Industrialism and the American Worker, 1865–1920.* 3d ed. Wheeling, Ill.: Harlan-Davidson, 1996.

Emmons, David. *The Butte Irish: Class and Ethnicity in an American Mining Town, 1875–1925.* Urbana, Ill.: University of Illinois Press, 1989.

Epstein, Melech. *Jewish Labor in the United States, 1882–1952.* 2 vols. New York: Trade Union Sponsoring Committee, 1950–53.

Fenton, Edwin. *Immigrants and Unions, a Case Study: Italians and American Labor.* New York: Arno, 1975.

Gerstle, Gary. *Working-Class Americanism: The Politics of Labor in a Textile City, 1914–1960.* Princeton, N.J.: Princeton University Press, 2001.

Greene, Victor. *The Slavic Community on Strike: Immigrant Labor in Pennsylvania Anthracite.* South Bend, Ind.: University of Notre Dame, 1968.

Gutman, Herbert. *Work, Culture and Society in Industrializing America.* New York: Random House, 1977.

Kwong, Peter. *Forbidden Workers: Illegal Chinese Workers and American Labor.* New York: New Press, 1997.

Lamphere, Louise, Alex Stepick, and Guillermo Grenier. *Newcomers in the Workplace: Immigrants and the Restructuring of the U.S. Economy.* Philadelphia: Temple University Press, 1994.

Montgomery, David. *The Fall of the House of Labor: The Workplace, the State and American Labor Activism, 1865–1925.* New York: Cambridge University Press, 1987.

Parmet, Robert. *Labor and Immigration in Industrial America.* Boston: Twayne, 1981.

Peck, Gunther. "Reinventing Free Labor: Immigrant Padrones and Contract Laborers in North America, 1885–1925." *Journal of American History* 83 (December 1996): 848–871.

Piore, Michael. *Birds of Passage: Migrant Labor and Industrial Societies.* London and New York: Cambridge University Press, 1979.

Pozzetta, George E., ed. *Unions and Immigrants: Organization and Struggle.* New York: Garland, 1991.

————. *The Work Experience: Labor, Class, and Immigrant Enterprise.* New York: Garland, 1991.

Rosenblum, Gerald. *Immigrant Workers: Their Impact on American Labor Radicalism.* New York, 1973.

Waldinger, Roger D. *Still the Promised City? New Immigrants and African Americans in New York, 1940–1990.* Cambridge, Mass.: Harvard University Press, 1996.

————. *Through the Eye of the Needle: Immigrants and Enterprise in New York's Garment Trades.* New York: New York University Press, 1986.

International Migration

Brettell, Caroline B. *International Migration: The Female Experience.* Totowa, N.J.: Rowan and Littlefield, 1986.

Castles, Stephen, and Mark J. Miller. *The Age of Migration: International Population Movements in the Modern World.* 2d ed. New York: Macmillan, 1998.

Cohen, Robin, ed. *The Cambridge Survey of World Migration.* Cambridge: Cambridge University Press, 1995.

————. *The Sociology of Migration.* Cheltenham, U.K.: Elgar, 1996.

Hirschman, Charles, Josh DeWind, and Philip Kasinitz, eds. *The Handbook of International Migration: The American Experience.* New York: Russell Sage Foundation, 1999.

Hoerder, Dirk, and Leslie Page Moch, eds. *European Migrants; Global and Local Perspectives.* Boston: Northeastern University Press, 1995.

Kritz, Mary M., Charles B. Keely, and Silvano M. Tomasi, eds. *Global Trends in Migration.* Staten Island, N.Y.: Center for Migration Studies of New York, 1981.

Massey, Douglas S., et al. *Worlds in Motion: Understanding International Migration at the End of the Millennium.* Oxford: Clarendon Press, 1998.

Nugent, Walter. *Crossings: The Great Transatlantic Migrations, 1870–1914.* Bloomington: Indiana University Press, 1992.

Wang, Gugnwu, ed. *Global History and Migrations.* Boulder, Colo.: Westview Press, 1997.

Weiner, Myron. *The Global Migration Crisis.* New York: HarperCollins, 1995.

Leadership

Greene, Victor R. *American Immigrant Leaders, 1800–1910: Marginality and Identity.* Baltimore: Johns Hopkins University Press, 1987.

Higham, John. "Leadership." In *Harvard Encyclopedia of American Ethnic Groups.* Ed. Stephen Thernstrom et al. Cambridge, Mass.: Harvard University Press, 1980.

————, ed. *Ethnic Leadership in America.* Baltimore: Johns Hopkins University Press, 1977.

Politics and Citizenship

Buhle, Paul, and Dan Georgakas, ed. *The Immigrant Left in the U.S.* Albany: State University of New York Press, 1996.

De la Garza, Rudolfo O., et al. *Latino Voices: Mexican, Puerto Rican and Cuban Perspectives on American Politics.* Boulder, Colo.: Westview Press, 1992.

Erie, Stephen R. *Rainbow's End: Irish-Americans and the Dilemmas of Urban Machine Politics, 1840–1985.* Berkeley: University of California Press, 1988.

Franklin, Frank G. *The Legislative History of Naturalization in the United States from the Revolutionary War to 1861.* 1906. Reprint, New York: Arno, 1969.

Gimpel, James G., and James R. Edwards, Jr. *The Congressional Politics of Immigration Reform.* Boston: Allyn and Bacon, 1999.

Gómez-Quiñones, Juan. *Chicano Politics: Reality and Promise, 1940–1990.* Albuquerque: University of New Mexico Press, 1990.

James, Winston. *Holding Aloft the Banner of Ethiopia: Caribbean Radicalism in Early Twentieth-Century America.* London: Verso, 1998.

Jones-Correa, Michael. *Between Two Nations: The Political Life of Latin American Immigrants in New York City.* Ithaca, N.Y.: Cornell University Press, 1998.

Kettner, James H. *The Development of American Citizenship, 1608–1870.* Chapel Hill: University of North Carolina Press, 1978.

Kivisto, P. *Immigrant Socialists in the United States: The Case of Finns and the Left.* Rutherford, N.J.: Fairleigh Dickinson University Press, 1984.

Lai, Him Mark. "To Bring Forth a New China, to Build a Better America: The Chinese Marxist Left in America." *Chinese America: History & Perspectives, 1992.* San Francisco: Chinese Historical Society of America, 1992.

Mink, Gwendolyn. *Old Labor and New Immigrants in American Political Development: Union, Party and State, 1875–1920.* Ithaca, N.Y.: Cornell University Press, 1986.

Oboler, Susan. *Ethnic Labels, Latino Lives: Identity and the Politics of (Re)Presentation in the United States.* Minneapolis: University of Minnesota Press, 1995.

O'Connor, Thomas H. *The Boston Irish: A Political History.* Boston: Northeastern University Press, 1995.

Orleck, Annelise. *Common Sense and a Little Fire: Women and Working-Class Politics in the United States, 1900–1965.* Chapel Hill: University of North Carolina Press, 1995.

Poutinen, A. E. *Finnish Radicals and Religion in Midwestern Mining Towns, 1865–1914.* New York: Arno, 1979.

Pozzetta, George E., ed. *Immigrant Radicals: The View from the Left.* New York: Garland, 1991.

————. *Law, Crime, Justice: Naturalization and Citizenship.* New York: Garland, 1991.

————. *Politics and the Immigrant.* New York: Garland, 1991.

Preston, William, Jr. *Aliens and Dissenters: Federal Suppression of Radicals.* 2d ed. Urbana: University of Illinois Press, 1995.

Roche, John P. *The Early Development of United States Citizenship.* Ithaca, N.Y.: Cornell University Press, 1949.

Rosales, Francisco A. *Chicano! A History of the Mexican American Civil Rights Movement.* Houston, Tex.: Arte Público Press, 1996.

Sánchez, George J. "The 'New Nationalism,' Mexican Style: Race and Progressivism in Chicano Political Development during the 1920s." In *California Progressivism Revisited.* Ed. W. Deveerell and T. Sitton. Berkeley: University of California Press, 1994.

Sanjek, Roger. *The Future of Us All: Race and Neighborhood Politics in New York City.* Ithaca, N.Y.: Cornell University Press, 1998.

Soike, Lowell J. *Norwegian Americans and the Politics of Dissent.* Northfield, Minn.: Norwegian-American Historical Association, 1991.

Wefald, Jon. *A Voice of Protest: Norwegians in American Politics, 1890–1917.* Northfield, Minn.: Norwegian-American Historical Association, 1971.

The Press

Andersen, Arlow W. *The Immigrant Takes His Stand: The Norwegian-American Press and Public Affairs, 1847–1872.* Northfield, Minn.: Norwegian-American Historical Association, 1953.

Capps, Finis H. *From Isolationism to Involvement: The Swedish Immigrant Press in America, 1914–1945.* Chicago: Swedish Pioneer Historical Society, 1966.

Chyz, Yaroslav. *225 Years of the U.S. Foreign-Language Press in the United States.* New York: American Council for Nationalities Service, 1959.

Danky, James, and Wayne Wiegand, eds. *Print Culture in a Diverse America.* Urbana: University of Illinois Press, 1998.

Fishman, Joshua. *Language Loyalties in the United States.* London: Moulton and Co., 1966.

Hardt, Hanno. "The Foreign-Language Press in American Press History." *Journal of Communication* 39, no. 2 (Spring 1989): 114–131.

Harzig, Christiane, and Dirk Hoerder, eds. *The Press of Labor Migrants in Europe and North America, 1880s–1980.* Lexington, Ky.: Lexington Books, 1985.

Hoerder, Dirk, ed. *The Immigrant Labor Press in North America, 1840s–1970s: An Annotated Bibliography.* 3 vols. Westport, Conn.: Greenwood Press, 1987.

Hunter, Edward. *In Many Voices: Our Fabulous Foreign-Language Press.* Norman Park, Ga.: Norman College, 1960.

Hutton, Frank, and Barbara Strauss Reed, eds. *Outsiders in Nineteenth-Century Press History: Multicultural Perspectives.* Bowling Green, Ohio: Bowling Green State University Popular Press, 1995.

Ireland, Sandra L. Jones. *Ethnic Periodicals in Contemporary America: An Annotated Guide.* Westport, Conn.: Greenwood Press, 1990.

Kessler, Lauren. *The Dissident Press: Alternative Journalism in American History.* Newbury Park, Calif.: Sage, 1990.

Lester, Paul M., ed. *Images That Injure: Pictorial Stereotypes in the Media.* Westport, Conn.: Praeger, 1996.

Miller, Sally, ed. *The Ethnic Press in the United States: A Historical Analysis and Handbook.* Westport, Conn.: Greenwood Press, 1987.

———. "Immigrant and Ethnic Newspapers: An Enduring Phenomenon." *Serials Librarian* 14, nos. 1–2 (1988): 135–143.

Park, Robert. *The Immigrant Press and Its Control.* New York: Harper, 1922.

Patterson, G. J., and P. Petrescu. "The Romanian Language Press in America." *East European Quarterly* 27 (1992): 261–267.

Rodríguez, América. *Making Latino News: Race, Language, Class.* Thousand Oaks, Calif.: Sage Publications, 1999.

Ross, Robert W. *So It Was True: The American Protestant Press and the Persecution of the Jews.* Minneapolis: University of Minnesota Press, 1980.

Simon, Rita J., and Susan H. Alexander. *The Ambivalent Welcome: Print Media, Public Opinion, and Immigration.* Westport, Conn.: Praeger, 1993.

Soltes, Mordecai. *The Yiddish Press: An Americanizing Agency.* 1925. Reprint, New York: Arno Press and New York Times, 1969.

Sreenivasan, Sreenath. "As Mainstream Papers Cut Back, the Ethnic Press Expands." *New York Times,* July 22, 1996, p. D7.

Tinker, Edward Larocque. *French Newspapers and Periodicals of Louisiana.* Worcester, Mass.: American Antiquarian Society, 1933.

Wynar, Lubomyr. *Guide to the American Ethnic Press: Slavic and East European Newspaper and Periodicals.* Kent, Ohio: Center for the Study of Ethnic Publications, School of Library Science, Kent State University, 1986.

Wynar, Lubomyr, and Anna Wynar. *Encyclopedic Directory of Ethnic Newspapers and Periodicals in the United States.* Littleton, Colo.: Libraries Unlimited, 1976.

Zubrzycki, Jerzy. "The Role of the Foreign-Language Press in Migrant Integration." *Population Studies* 22 (1958): 73–82.

Refugees and Refugee Policy

Adelman, Howard, ed. *The Indochinese Refugee Movement: The Canadian Experience.* Toronto: Operation Lifeline, 1979.

Adelman, Howard, et al., eds. *Immigration and Refugee Policy: Australia and Canada Compared.* 2 vols. Toronto: Centre for Refugee Studies, York University, 1994.

Breitman, Richard, and Alan M. Kraut. *American Refugee Policy and European Jewry, 1933–1945.* Bloomington: Indiana University Press, 1987.

Carliner, David. *The Rights of Aliens and Refugees: The Basic ACLU Guide to Alien and Refugee Rights.* Carbondale: Southern Illinois University Press, 1990.

Chan, Kwok B., and Doreen Marie Indra, eds. *Uprooting, Loss and Adaptation: The Resettlement of Indochinese Refugees in Canada.* Ottawa: Canadian Public Health Association, 1987.

Draper, Paula Jean. "Muses behind Barbed Wire: Canada and the Interned Refugees." In *The Muses Flee Hitler: Cultural Transfer and Adaptation, 1940–1945.* Eds. J. C. Jackman and C. M. Borden. Washington, D.C.: Smithsonian Institution Press, 1983.

Everest, Allan S. *Moses Hazen and the Canadian Refugees in the American Revolution.* Syracuse, N.Y.: Syracuse University Press, 1976.

Goldsmith, Renee Kasinsky. *Refugees from Militarism: Draft-Age Americans in Canada.* Totowa, N.J.: Littlefield, Adams, 1976.

Goodwin-Gill, Guy S. *The Refugee in International Law.* 2d ed. Oxford, U.K.: Clarendon Press, 1996.

Gottlieb, Amy Zahl. "Refugee Immigration: The Truman Directive." *Prologue* 13 (Spring 1981): 5–18.

Haines, David W., ed. *Refugees as Immigrants: Cambodians, Laotians, and Vietnamese in America.* Totowa, N.J.: Rowman and Littlefield, 1989.

———. *Refugees in America in the 1990s: A Reference Handbook.* Westport, Conn.: Greenwood Press, 1996.

Holborn, Louise W. *The International Refugee Organization, a Specialized Agency of the United Nations: Its History and Work, 1946–1952.* London: Oxford University Press, 1956.

Koehn, P. H. *Refugees from Revolution: U.S. Policy and Third World Migration.* Boulder, Colo.: Westview Press, 1991.

Legomsky, Stephen H. *Immigration and Refugee Law and Policy.* 2d ed. Westbury, N.Y.: Foundation Press, 1997.

Long, Lynellyn D. *Ban Vinai: The Refugee Camp.* New York: Columbia University Press, 1993.

Nackerud, Larry, et al. "The End of the Cuban Contradiction in U.S. Refugee Policy," *International Migration Review* 33, no. 1 (Spring 1999): 176–192.

Plaut, W. G. *Refugee Status Determination in Canada: Proposals for a New System.* Hull: Canada Employment and Immigration Commission, 1985.

Robinson, W. Courtland. *Terms of Refuge: The Indochinese Exodus and the International Response.* New York: Zed Books, 1998.

Sutter, Valerie O'Connor. *The Indochinese Refugee Dilemma.* Baton Rouge: Louisiana State University Press, 1991.

Wittke, Carl F. *Refugees of Revolution: The German Forty-Eighters in America.* Philadelphia: University of Pennsylvania Press, 1952.

Wyman, Mark. *DP: Europe's Displaced Persons, 1945–1951.* Philadelphia: Balch Institute, 1985.

Zucker, Alfred E., ed. *The Forty-Eighters: Political Refugees of the German Revolutions of 1848.* New York: Columbia University Press, 1959.

Zucker, Norman L., and Naomi Flink Zucker. *Desperate Crossings: Seeking Refuge in America.* Armonk, N.Y.: M. E. Sharpe, 1996.

———. *The Guarded Gate: The Reality of American Refugee Policy.* New York: Harcourt Brace Jovanovich, 1987.

Religion

Abell, Aaron. *American Catholicism and Social Action: A Search for Social Justice, 1865–1900.* Garden City, N.Y.: Doubleday, 1960.

Abramson, Harold J. *Ethnic Diversity in Catholic America.* New York: Wiley, 1973.

Alexander, June. *The Immigrant Church and Community: Pittsburgh's Slovak Catholics and Lutherans, 1880–1915.* Pittsburgh, Pa.: University of Pittsburgh Press, 1987.

Balmer, Randall. *A Perfect Babel of Confusion: Dutch Religion and English Culture in the Middle Colonies.* New York: Oxford University Press, 1989.

Barry, Colman J. *The Catholic Church and German Americans.* Milwaukee, Wisc.: Bruce, 1953.

Dolan, Jay P. *The Immigrant Church: New York's Irish and German Catholics: 1815–1865.* Baltimore: Johns Hopkins University Press, 1975.

Ebaugh, Helen Rose, and Janet Saltzman Chafetz. *Religion and the New Immigrants: Continuities and Adaptations in Immigrant Congregations.* Walnut Creek, Calif.: AltaMira Press, 2000.

Fenton, John Y. *South Asian Religions in the Americas: An Annotated Bibliography of Immigrant Religious Traditions.* Westport, Conn.: Greenwood Press, 1995.

Fenton, John Y. *Transplanting Religious Traditions: Asian Indians in America.* New York: Praeger, 1988.

Gaustad, Edwin Scott. *A Religious History of America.* 2d ed. San Francisco: Harper and Row, 1990.

Gleason, Philip. *The Conservative Reformers: German American Catholics and the Social Order.* Notre Dame, Ind.: University of Notre Dame Press, 1968.

Kim, Jung Ha, and Pyong Gap Min, eds. *Religions in Asian America: Building Faith Communities.* Walnut Creek, Calif.: AltaMira Press, 2001.

Kozegi, Michael A., and J. Gordon Melton, ed. *Islam in North America: A Sourcebook.* New York: Garland, 1992.

Loewen, Royden. *Family, Church and Market: A Mennonite Community in the Old and the New Worlds.* Toronto: University of Totonto Press, 1993.

McCaffrey, Lawrence. *The Irish Catholic Diaspora in America.* Washington, D.C.: Catholic University of America Press, 1997.

Melton, J. Gordon, and Michael Koszegi, eds. *Islam in North America: A Sourcebook.* New York: Garland Publishing, 1992.

Metcalf, Barbara Daly. *Making Muslim Space in North America and Europe.* Berkeley: University of California Press, 1996.

Miller, Randall M., and Thomas D. Mazrik, eds. *Immigrants and Religion in Urban America.* Philadelphia: Temple University Press, 1977.

Morreale, Don, ed. *Buddhist America: Centers, Retreats, Practices.* Santa Fe, N.M.: John Muir Publications, 1988.

Murphy, Andrew R. *Conscience and Community: Revisiting Toleration and Religious Dissent in Early Modern England and America.* University Park: Pennsylvania State University Press, 2001.

Numrich, Paul David. *Old Wisdom in the New World: Americanization in Two Immigrant Theravada Buddhist Temples.* Knoxville: University of Tennessee Press, 1996.

Orsi, Robert. *The Madonna of One Hundred and Fifteenth Street: Faith and Community in Italian Harlem, 1880–1950.* 2d ed. New Haven, Conn.: Yale University Press, 2002.

Papaioannou, G. *From Mars Hill to Manhattan: The Greek Orthodox in America under Patriarch Athenagoras I.* Minneapolis, Minn.: Light and Life, 1976.

Perin, Roberto. *The Immigrants' Church: The Third Force in Canadian Catholicism, 1880–1920.* Ottawa: Canadian Historical Association, 1998.

Podell, Jane, ed. *Buddhists, Hindus, and Sikhs in America.* New York: Oxford University Press, 2001.

Pozzetta, George E., ed. *The Immigrant Religious Experience.* New York: Garland, 1991.

Prebish, Charles S., and Kenneth K. Tanaka, eds. *The Faces of Buddhism in America.* Berkeley: University of California Press, 1998.

Schneider, Carl E. *The German Church on the American Frontier.* St. Louis, Mo.: Eden, 1939.

Seager, Richard Hughes. *Buddhism in America.* New York: Columbia University Press, 1999.

Singh, Narindar. *Canadian Sikhs: History, Religion, and Culture of Sikhs in North America.* Ottawa: Canadian Sikhs' Studies Institute, 1994.

Smith, Timothy. "Religion and Ethnicity in America." *American Historical Review* 83 (December 1978): 1,155–1,185.

Smith-Rosenberg, Carroll. *Religion and the Rise of the American City: The New York City Mission Movement, 1812–1870.* Ithaca, N.Y.: Cornell University Press, 1971.

Stephenson, G. M. *The Religious Aspects of Swedish Immigration.* Minneapolis: University of Minnesota Press, 1932.

Thomas, Wendell. *Hinduism Invades America.* New York: Beacon Press, 1930.

Williams, Raymond. *Religions of Immigrants from India and Pakistan: New Threads in the American Tapestry.* Cambridge: Cambridge University Press, 1988.

Williams, Raymond, ed. *A Sacred Thread: Modern Transmission of Hindu Traditions in India and Abroad.* Chambersburg, Pa.: Anima Press, 1992.

Zakai, Avihu. *Exile and Kingdom: History and Apocalypse in the Puritan Migration to America.* Cambridge: Cambridge University Press, 1992.

Transportation

Bowen, Frank A. *A Century of Atlantic Travel, 1830–1930.* Boston: Little, Brown, 1930.

Dempsey, Hugh A. *The CPR West: The Iron Road and the Making of a Nation.* Vancouver and Toronto: Douglas and McIntyre, 1984.

Driscoll, Barbara A. *The Tracks North: The Railroad Bracero Program of World War II.* Austin: University of Texas Press, 1999.

Dunn, Laurence. *North Atlantic Liners, 1899–1913.* London: H. Evelyn, 1961.

Eagle, John A. *The Canadian Pacific Railway and the Development of Western Canada, 1896–1914.* Kingston and Montreal, Canada, and London: McGill–Queen's University Press, 1989.

Fishlow, Albert. *American Railroads and the Transformation of the Ante-Bellum Economy.* Cambridge, Mass.: Harvard University Press, 1965.

Guillet, Edwin C. *The Great Migration: The Atlantic Crossing by Sailing-Ship, 1770–1860.* 2d ed. Toronto: University of Toronto Press, 1963.

Hafen, LeRoy. *The Overland Trail, 1849–1869.* Cleveland, Ohio: Arthur H. Clark, 1923.

Kraus, George. "Chinese Laborers and the Construction of the Central Pacific." *Utah Historical Quarterly* 37, no. 1 (1969): 42.

Jones, Maldwyn A. *Destination America.* New York: Holt, Rinehart and Winston, 1976.

Maxtone-Graham, John. *The Only Way to Cross.* New York: Macmillan, 1972.

Sabin, E. L. *Building the Pacific Railway.* Philadelphia: J. B. Lippincott, 1919.

Taylor, George R. *The Transportation Revolution, 1815–1860.* New York: Rinehart, 1951.

Winther, Oscar O. *The Transportation Frontier: Trans-Mississippi West, 1865–1890.* New York: Holt, Rinehart and Winston, 1964.

Yen, Tzu-Kuei. "Chinese Workers and the First Transcontinental Railroad of the United States of America." Ph.D. dissertation, St. John's University, 1977.

The West

Allen, James B. *The Company Town in the American West.* Norman: University of Oklahoma Press, 1966.

Billington, Ray Allen. *Land of Savagery, Land of Promise: The European Image of the American Frontier in the Nineteenth Century.* New York: W. W. Norton, 1981.

Friesan, Gerald. *The Canadian Prairies: A History.* Toronto: University of Toronto Press, 1984.

Gjerde, Jon. *Minds of the West: Ethnocultural Evolution in the Rural Middle West, 1830–1917.* Chapel Hill: University of North Carolina Press, 1997.

Greever, William S. *The Bonanza West: The Story of Western Mining Rushes, 1848–1900.* Norman: University of Oklahoma Press, 1963.

Hine, Robert V. *Community on the American Frontier: Separate but Not Alone.* Norman: University of Oklahoma Press, 1980.

Koppel, Tom. *Kanaka: The Untold Story of Hawaiian Pioneers in BC and the Pacific Northwest.* Vancouver, Canada: Whitecap. 1995.

Loewen, Royden. *Ethnic Farm Culture in Western Canada.* Ottawa: Canadian Historical Association, 2002.

Luchetti, Cathy, and Carol Olwell. *Women of the West.* St. George, Utah: Antelope Press, 1984.

Luebke, Frederick C., ed. *European Immigrants in the American West: Community Histories.* Albuquerque: University of New Mexico Press, 1998.

Lyman, Stanford M. *The Asian in the West.* Reno: Western Studies Center, University of Nevada, 1970.

Mackintosh, W. A., and W. L. G. Joerg, eds. *Canadian Frontiers of Settlement.* Toronto: Macmillan, 1936.

Monroy, Douglas. *Thrown among Strangers: The Making of Mexican Culture in Frontier California.* Berkeley: University of California Press, 1991.

Noble, Allen G., ed. *To Build in a New Land: Ethnic Landscapes in North America.* Baltimore: Johns Hopkins University Press, 1992.

Norton, Wayne. *Help Us to a Better Land: Crofter Colonies in the Prairie West.* Regina: Canadian Plains Research Centre, 1994.

Paul, Rodman W. *Mining Frontiers of the Far West, 1848–1880.* New York: Holt, Rinehart and Winston, 1963.

Prucha, Francis P. *The Great Father: The United States Government and the American Indians.* 2 vols. Lincoln: University of Nebraska Press, 1984.

Rischin, Moses, and John Livingston, eds. *Jews of the American West.* Detroit, Mich.: Wayne State University Press, 1991.

Schneider, Carl E. *The German Church on the American Frontier.* St. Louis, Mo.: Eden, 1939.

Shepard, Bruce. *Deemed Unsuitable: Blacks from Oklahoma Move to Canadian Prairies in Search of Equality in the Early 20th Century Only to Find Racism in Their New Home.* Toronto: Umbrella, 1997.

Smith, Duane. *Rocky Mountain Mining Camps.* Bloomington: Indiana University Press, 1967.

Sylvester, Kenneth. *The Limits of Rural Capitalism: Family, Culture, and Markets, Montcalm, Manitoba, 1870–1940.* Toronto: University of Toronto Press, 2000.

Taylor, Jeffrey. *Fashioning Farmers: Ideology, Agricultural Knowledge and the Manitoba Farm Movement, 1890–1925.* Regina: Canadian Plains Research Centre, 1994.

Thompson, John Herd. *Forging the Prairie West: The Illustrated History of Canada.* Toronto: Oxford University Press, 1998.

Woods, Lawrence M. *British Gentlemen in the Wild West: The Era of the Intensely English Cowboy.* New York: Free Press, 1989.

Women and Families

Alba, Richard D., Douglas S. Massey, and Rubén G. Rumbaut. *The Immigration Experience for Families and Children.* Washington, D.C.: American Sociological Association, 1999.

Boris, Eileen. *Home to Work: Motherhood and the Politics of Industrial Homework in the United States.* New York: Cambridge University Press, 1994.

Brou, David de, and Aileen Moffatt, eds. *Other Voices: Historical Essays on Saskatchewan Women.* Regina: Canadian Plains Research Center, 1995.

Deutsch, Sarah. *No Separate Refuge: Culture, Class, and Gender on an Anglo-Hispanic Frontier in the American Southwest, 1880–1940.* New York: Oxford University Press, 1987.

Diggs, Nancy Brown. *Steel Butterflies: Japanese Women and the American Experience.* New York: State University of New York Press, 1998.

Ewen, Elizabeth. *Immigrant Women in the Land of Dollars: Life and Culture on the Lower East Side 1890–1925.* New York: Monthly Review Press, 1985.

Gabaccia, Donna R. *From the Other Side: Women, Gender and Immigrant Life in the U.S., 1820–1990.* Bloomington: Indiana University Press, 1994.

———, ed. *Seeking Common Ground: Multidisciplinary Studies of Immigrant Women in the United States.* Westport, Conn.: Greenwood Press, 1991.

Glodava, Mila, and Richard Onizuka. *Mail-Order Brides: Women for Sale.* Fort Collins, Colo.: Alaken, 1994.

Griswold, Richard del Castillo. *La Familia: Chicano Families in the Urban Southwest, 1848 to the Present.* Notre Dame, Ind.: University of Notre Dame Press, 1984.

Hareven, Tamara K. *Family Time and Industrial Time: The Relationship Between the Family and Work in a New England Community.* New York: Cambridge University Press, 1982.

Harzig, Christiane. *Peasant Maids, City Women: From the European Countryside to Urban America.* Ithaca, N.Y.: Cornell University Press, 1997.

Hondagneu-Sotelo, Pierette. *Gendered Transitions: Mexican Experiences of Immigration.* Berkeley: University of California Press, 1994.

Houstoun, Marion L., et al. "Female Predominance in Immigration to the United States since 1930: A First Look." *International Migration Review* 18, no. 4 (Winter 1989): 908–959.

Hyman, Paula E. *Gender and Assimilation in Modern Jewish History: The Roles and Representations of Women.* Seattle: University of Washington Press, 1995.

Kessler-Harris, Alice. *Out to Work: A History of Wage-Earning Women in the United States.* New York: Oxford University Press, 2003.

Kim, Bok-Lim C. "Asian Wives of U.S. Servicemen: Women in Shadows." *Amerasia Journal* 4, no. 1 (1977): 91–115.

———. *Women in Shadows: A Handbook for Service Providers Working with Asian Wives of U.S. Military Personnel.* La Jolla, Calif.: National Committee Concerned with Asian Wives of U.S. Servicemen, 1981.

Kim, Haeyun Juliana. "Voices from the Shadows: The Lives of Korean War Brides." *Amerasia Journal* 17, no. 1 (1991): 15–30.

Lark, Regina F. "They Challenged Two Nations: Marriages between Japanese Women and American G.I.s, 1945 to the Present." Ph.D. dissertation, University of Southern California, 1999.

Leach, Kristine. *Walking Common Ground: Nineteenth and Twentieth Century Immigrant Women in America.* San Francisco: Austin and Winfield, 1995.

Lemke-Santangelo, Gretchen. *Abiding Courage: African American Migrant Women and the East Bay Community.* Chapel Hill: University of North Carolina Press, 1996.

Ling, Huping. *Surviving on the Gold Mountain: A History of Chinese American Women and Their Lives.* New York: State University of New York Press, 1998.

Loewen, Royden. *Family, Church and Market: A Mennonite Community in the Old and the New Worlds.* Toronto: University of Toronto Press, 1993.

Luchetti, Cathy, and Carol Olwell. *Women of the West.* St. George, Utah: Antelope Press, 1984.

Mortimer, Delores M., and Roy S. Bryce-Laporte. *Female Immigrants to the United States: Caribbean, Latin American, and African Experiences.* Washington, D.C.: Research Institute of Immigration and Ethnic Studies, Smithsonian Institution, 1981.

Orleck, Annelise. *Common Sense and a Little Fire: Women and Working-Class Politics in the United States, 1900–1965.* Chapel Hill: University of North Carolina Press, 1995.

Peffer, George Anthony. *If They Don't Bring Their Women Here: Chinese Female Immigration before Exclusion.* Urbana: University of Illinois Press, 1999.

Pozzetta, George E., ed. *Ethnicity and Gender: The Immigrant Woman.* New York: Garland, 1991.

———. *Immigrant Family Patterns: Demography, Fertility, Housing, Kinship, and Urban Life.* New York: Garland, 1991.

Ruíz, Vicki. *From Out of the Shadows: Mexican Women in Twentieth-Century America.* New York: Oxford University Press, 1997.

Sauer, Angelika, and Matthias Zimmer, eds. *A Chorus of Different Voices: German-Canadian Identities.* New York: Peter Lang, 1998.

Shukert, Elfrieda Berthiaume, and Barbara Smith Scibetta. *War Brides of World War II.* Novato, Calif.: Presidio Press, 1988.

Simon, Rita James, ed. *Immigrant Women.* New Brunswick, N.J.: Transaction, 2001.

Swyripa, Frances. *Wedded to the Cause: Ukrainian Canadian Women and Ethnic Identity, 1891–1991.* Toronto: University of Toronto Press, 1993.

Taylor, Jeffrey. *Fashioning Farmers: Ideology, Agricultural Knowledge and the Manitoba Farm Movement, 1890–1925.* Regina: Canadian Plains Research Centre, 1994.

Tentler, Leslie Woodstock. *Wage-Earning Women: Industrial Work and Family Life in the United States, 1900–1930.* New York: Oxford University Press, 1982.

Turbin, Carole. *Working Women of Collar City: Gender, Class, and Community in Troy, New York, 1864–1886.* Urbana: University of Illinois Press, 1992.

Vernez, Georges. *Immigrant Women in the U.S. Workforce: Who Struggles? Who Succeeds?* Lanham, Md.: Lexington Books, 1999.

Weinberg, Sidney Stahl. "The Treatment of Women in Immigration History." *Journal of American Ethnic History* 11 (Summer 1992): 25–46.

———. *The World of Our Mothers: Lives of Jewish Immigrant Women.* Chapel Hill: University of North Carolina Press, 1988.

Yuh, Je-Yeon. *Beyond the Shadow of Camptown: Korean Military Brides in America.* New York: New York University Press, 2002.

WEB SITES

ACLU and Immigrant Rights. American Civil Liberties Union Freedom Network. URL: http://www.aclu.org/ImmigrantsRights/ImmigrantsRightsMain.cfm

Avalon Project. Yale Law School. URL: http://www.yale.edu/lawweb/avalon/alsedact.htm

CataLaw: Immigration Law. Center for Comparative Immigration Studies. University of California–San Diego. URL: http://www.ccis-ucsd.org

Center for Immigration Research. University of Houston. URL: http://www.uh.edu/cir/

Center for Immigration Studies. URL: http://www.cis.org

Citizenship and Immigration Canada. URL: http://www.cic.gc.ca

Federation for American Immigration Reform. URL: http://www.fairus.org

"Immigration and Migration." Latin American Network Information Center. University of Texas. URL: http://lanic.utexas.edu/la/region/immigration/

Immigration History Research Center. University of Minnesota. URL: http://www1.umn.edu/ihrc/index.htm

National Immigration Forum. URL: http://lanic.utexas.edu/la/region/immigration/

National Immigration Law Center. URL: http://www.nilc.org

Statistics Canada. URL: http://www.statcan.ca/start.html

United States Committee for Refugees. URL: http://www.uscr.org

U.S. Census Bureau. URL: http://www.census.gov

U.S. Citizenship and Immigration Services. URL: http://uscis.gov/graphics/index.htm

Entries by Subject

Homestead Act
Hudson's Bay Company
indentured servitude
International Ladies' Garment
    Workers' Union
mafia
navigation acts
North American Free Trade
    Agreement
North West Company
railways and immigration
Royal African Company
Vancouver Riot
Waipahu Plantation strike
Winnipeg general strike

EXPLORERS AND GEOGRAPHERS

Cabot, John
Cartier, Jacques
Champlain, Samuel de
Columbus, Christopher
Hakluyt, Richard
Hudson, Henry
Raleigh, Sir Walter

FRANCE

Cartier, Jacques
Champlain, Samuel de
Colbert, Jean-Baptiste
Compagnie de la Nouvelle
    France
French immigration
New France
Talon, Jean

HISPANIC ISSUES AND LEADERS

Border Patrol, U.S.
Bracero Program
Chavez, Cesar
Chicano
González, Elián
Gonzalez, Henry B.
Gonzales, Corky
Gutiérrez, José Angel
Hispanics and related terms
La Raza Unida Party
Plyler v. Doe
Proposition 187
Tejanos
Tijerina, Reies López

ILLEGAL IMMIGRATION

Border Patrol, U.S.
Coast Guard, U.S.
Customs and Border Protection,
    U.S.
illegal immigration
Immigration and Naturalization
    Service
Plyler v. Doe
USA PATRIOT Act
U.S. Citizenship and Immigration
    Services

IMMIGRANT GROUPS

Afghan immigration
African forced migration
Albanian immigration
American immigration to Canada
Amish immigration
Arab immigration
Argentinean immigration
Armenian immigration
Australian immigration
Austrian immigration
Austro-Hungarian immigration
Bangladeshi immigration
Barbadian immigration
Basque immigration
Belgian immigration
Bosnian immigration
Brazilian immigration
British immigration
Bulgarian immigration
Cambodian immigration
Canadian immigration to the
    United States
Cape Verdean immigration
Chilean immigration
Chinese immigration
Colombian immigration
Croatian immigration
Cuban immigration
Czech immigration
Danish immigration
Dominican immigration
Dutch immigration
Ecuadorean immigration
Egyptian immigration
Estonian immigration
Ethiopian immigration
Filipino immigration
Finnish immigration

French immigration
German immigration
Ghanaian immigration
Greek immigration
Guatemalan immigration
Gypsy immigration
Haitian immigration
home children
Honduran immigration
Huguenot immigration
Hungarian immigration
Hutterite immigration
Icelandic immigration
Indian immigration
Iranian immigration
Iraqi immigration
Irish immigration
Italian immigration
Jamaican immigration
Japanese immigration
Jewish immigration
Korean immigration
Laotian immigration
Latvian immigration
Lebanese immigration
Liberian immigration
Lithuanian immigration
Macedonian immigration
Mennonite immigration
Mexican immigration
Moroccan immigration
new immigration
Nicaraguan immigration
Nigerian immigration
Norwegian immigration
Pacific Islander immigration
Pakistani immigration
Palestinian immigration
Peruvian immigration
picture brides
Pilgrims and Puritans
Polish immigration
Portuguese immigration
Puerto Rican immigration
Quaker immigration
Romanian immigration
Russian immigration
Salvadoran immigration
Schwenkfelder immigration
Scottish immigration
Serbian immigration
Slovakian immigration
Slovenian immigration
South Asian immigration

RACE AND ETHNICITY

African forced migration
Chinese Immigration Act
Ozawa v. U.S.
Proposition 187
racial and ethnic categories
racism
Scott Act
slavery

REFORMERS, ACTIVISTS, AND ETHNIC LEADERS

Addams, Jane
Antin, Mary
Barnardo, Thomas John
Bulosan, Carlos
Chavez, Cesar
Gonzales, Corky
Gutiérrez, José Angel
Hughes, John Joseph
Riis, Jacob
Tijerina, Reies López
Wald, Lillian
Zangwill, Israel

REFUGEES

Displaced Persons Act
Evian Conference

González, Elián
guest children
Immigration and Refugee
    Protection Act
Mariel Boatlift
Refugee Act
Refugee Relief Act
refugee status
*Singh v. Minister of Employment
    and Immigration*

RELIGION

Aheong, Samuel P.
Amish immigration
Hughes, John Joseph
Huguenot immigration
Hutterite immigration
Mennonite immigration
Pilgrims and Puritans
Quaker immigration
religion and immigration
Schwenkfelder immigration
Tibetan immigration

TREATIES

Burlingame Treaty
Gentlemen's Agreement
Oregon Treaty

WAR AND IMMIGRATION

American Revolution and
    immigration
cold war
Japanese internment, World
    War II
Korematsu v. United States
Quebec Act
revolutions of 1848
September 11, 2001
Seven Years' War
terrorism and immigration
U.S.–Mexican War
War Brides Act
World War I and immigration
World War II and immigration

WOMEN

Addams, Jane
Antin, Mary
Immigration Marriage Fraud
    Amendment
International Ladies' Garment
    Workers' Union
picture brides
Wald, Lillian
War Brides Act

Index

Page numbers in **boldface** indicate main entries. Page numbers in *italics* indicate photographs. Page numbers followed by *g* indicate glossary entries. Page numbers followed by *m* indicate maps, graphs, and tables.